COMPLETE

Technology in Action

9th Edition

COMPLETE

Technology in Action

9th Edition

Alan Evans • Kendall Martin
Mary Anne Poatsy

PEARSON

Boston   Columbus   Indianapolis   New York   San Francisco   Upper Saddle River
Amsterdam   Cape Town   Dubai   London   Madrid   Milan   Munich   Paris   Montréal   Toronto
Delhi   Mexico City   São Paulo   Sydney   Hong Kong   Seoul   Singapore   Taipei   Tokyo

Editor in Chief: Michael Payne
AVP/Executive Acquisitions Editor: Jenifer Niles
Product Development Manager: Laura Burgess
Editorial Project Manager: Keri Rand
Editorial Assistant: Carly Prakapas
Development Editor: Toni Ackley
VP of Marketing: Patrice Lumumba Jones
Marketing Coordinator: Susan Osterlitz
Marketing Assistant: Darshika Vyas
Associate Managing Editor: Camille Trentacoste
Senior Production Project Manager: Rhonda Aversa
Senior Operation Manager/Site Lead: Nick Sklitsis
IT Procurement Lead: Natacha Moore
Operations Specialist: Maura Zaldivar-Garcia

Director of Digital Development: Zara Wanlass
Editor, Digital Learning & Assessment: Paul Gertile
Product Development Manager, Media: Cathi Profitko
Media Project Manager, Editorial: Alana Coles
Media Project Manager, Production: John Cassar
Art Director: Jonathan Boylan
Cover Design: Jonathan Boylan
Cover Art: © Robert Harding Picture Library Ltd/Alamy
Full-Service Project Management: PreMediaGlobal
Composition: PreMediaGlobal
Printer/Binder: Quad/Graphics
Cover Printer: Lehigh-Phoenix Color/Hagerstown
Text Font: 10/12 Palatino

Credits and acknowledgments borrowed from other sources and reproduced, with permission, in this textbook appear on the appropriate page within text.

Microsoft and/or its respective suppliers make no representations about the suitability of the information contained in the documents and related graphics published as part of the services for any purpose. All such documents and related graphics are provided "as is" without warranty of any kind. Microsoft and/or its respective suppliers hereby disclaim all warranties and conditions with regard to this information, including all warranties and conditions of merchantability, whether express, implied or statutory, fitness for a particular purpose, title and non-infringement. In no event shall Microsoft and/or its respective suppliers be liable for any special, indirect or consequential damages or any damages whatsoever resulting from loss of use, data or profits, whether in an action of contract, negligence or other tortious action, arising out of or in connection with the use or performance of information available from the services.

The documents and related graphics contained herein could include technical inaccuracies or typographical errors. Changes are periodically added to the information herein. Microsoft and/or its respective suppliers may make improvements and/or changes in the product(s) and/or the program(s) described herein at any time.

Microsoft® and Windows® are registered trademarks of the Microsoft Corporation in the U.S.A. and other countries. This book is not sponsored or endorsed by or affiliated with the Microsoft Corporation.

CIP Data on file

10 9 8 7 6 5 4 3 2 1

ISBN 10: 0-13-283873-7
ISBN 13: 978-0-13-283873-3

Contents at a Glance

Contents

Chapter 3

Using the Internet: Making the Most of the Web's Resources

TECHNOLOGY IN FOCUS

Chapter 4

Chapter 5

Using System Software: The Operating System, Utility Programs, and File Management 202

TECHNOLOGY IN FOCUS
Computing Alternatives 248

Chapter 6

Chapter 7

TECHNOLOGY IN FOCUS

Chapter 8

Chapter 9

TECHNOLOGY IN FOCUS
Careers in IT

Chapter 10

Behind the Scenes: Software Programming

Chapter 11

Behind the Scenes: Databases and Information Systems

Chapter 12

Behind the Scenes: Networking and Security in the Business World

Chapter 13

Behind the Scenes: How the Internet Works......................604

Dedication

For my wife Patricia, whose patience, understanding, and support continue to
make this work possible . . . especially when I stay up past midnight writing!
And to my parents, Jackie and Dean, who taught me the best way to achieve
your goals is to constantly strive to improve yourself through education.

Alan Evans

For all the teachers, mentors, and gurus who have
popped in and out of my life.

Kendall Martin

For my husband Ted, who unselfishly continues to take on more than his fair
share to support me throughout this process; and for my children, Laura,
Carolyn, and Teddy, whose encouragement and love have been inspiring.

Mary Anne Poatsy

What's New
Technology in Action, 9th Edition

The following list includes comprehensive changes for the 9th edition:

- **New Visual Table of Contents**
  All chapters have a new visual table of contents listing the chapter content and providing a visual representation of that content.

- **New and updated end-of-chapter material**
  All chapters contain revised and updated multiple choice and true-false questions, as well as new and updated end-of-chapter projects.

- QR code included for all How Cool Is This? sections

The following list includes changes specific to each chapter for the 9th edition:

Chapter 1: Using Technology to Change the World
- New How Cool Is This? topic: Wake Forest Institute for Regenerative Medicine printing human cells
- Entirely new major section: "Technology on the World Stage"
- New Ethics in IT: "Knowledge Is Power—Bridging the Digital Divide"
- Completely updated section on "Technology and Our Society"
- Updated section on boosting your productivity
- New material on technology in education and the Khan Academy

Chapter 2: Looking at Computers: Understanding the Parts
- New How Cool Is This? topic: 3D computing
- Updated information on tablet PCs
- New sections on switching your Qwerty keyboard to a Dvorak layout and testing and calibrating monitors
- New information on OLED displays
- New Dig Deeper section on how touch screens work
- New section on innovations in printing, including inkless and 3-D printing

Chapter 3: Using the Internet: Making the Most of the Web's Resources
- Updated information on properly citing Web sources
- Updated coverage of client-based e-mail and wikis
- New section on why Flash-based multimedia won't run on iPads or iPhones
- Updated material on Internet Explorer 9

Chapter 4: Application Software: Programs That Let You Work and Play
- New How Cool Is This? topic: 3D photo walkthroughs
- Updated material on Web-based software, presentation software, and note-taking software
- New sections on finding the right software and the explosion of phone apps
- New Dig Deeper section on cloud computing

- New discussion of running versus saving when downloading software

Chapter 5: Using System Software: The Operating System, Utility Programs, and File Management
- Updated information on smartphone operating systems and running multiple operating systems on a computer
- New coverage of Web-based operating systems
- New Bits and Bytes: "Power Management: Greening Your Computer" and "How to Get the Most from Windows Libraries"

Chapter 6: Understanding and Assessing Hardware: Evaluating Your System
- Revised and redesigned worksheets and checklists throughout
- Revised and updated section on "Your Ideal Computer"
- New material on solid state drives
- New Bits and Bytes: "Auto Tech"
- New Ethics in IT section on open source hardware
- New Trends in IT section on Thunderbolt

Chapter 7: Networking: Connecting Computing Devices
- New coverage of WiMAX and in-flight Internet service
- Updated information on 3G and 4G cell phone networks
- New information on wireless routers supporting wired connections, how to obtain a router for a home network, and determining which type of wireless networking a router supports
- Updated information on setting up a HomeGroup
- New Trends in IT section on cloud computing

Chapter 8: Digital Lifestyle: Managing Digital Data and Devices
- Updated information on mobile phone operating systems
- New information on tethering your PC to your cell phone and streaming music
- New section on digital publishing, etext, and ebooks
- New information on self-publishing books, publicizing bands and music online, and distributing a digital video
- New Trends in IT: "Near Field Communication"

Chapter 9: Securing Your System: Protecting Your Digital Data and Devices
- New How Cool Is This? topic: SmartGuard
- New and expanded coverage of cybercrimes, identity theft, and scareware
- New information on protecting cell phones from viruses, precautions for tablets, installing alarms on mobile devices, and keeping mobile device data secure
- Updates on the latest damage caused by hackers and identity thieves
- New Bits and Bytes: "Are Your Photographs Helping Criminals Target You?"
- New Dig Deeper on computer forensics

- New material on Apple being accused of tracking iPad and iPhone users
- New Trends in IT: "Spear Phishing: The Bane of Data Breaches"

Chapter 10: Behind the Scenes: Software Programming
- New Ethics in IT: "When Software Runs Amok"
- New chart on the most popular software languages
- New sections on Objective C and building mobile applications
- New Trends in IT: "Emerging Technologies: Unite All Your Video Game Design Tools"

Chapter 11: Behind the Scenes: Databases and Information Systems
- New information on business intelligence systems
- New Bits and Bytes: "Virtual Agents: Expert Systems Replace People on the Web"
- Updated information on data breaches and protecting data online

Chapter 12: Behind the Scenes: Networking and Security in the Business World
- New How Cool Is This? topic: OpenMeetings
- New Bits and Bytes sections on virtual doctors and SeeClickFix
- New information on cloud servers
- New Trends in IT: "Virtualization: Making Servers Work Harder"
- New Ethics in IT: "How Should Companies Handle Data Breaches?"

Chapter 13: Behind the Scenes: How It Works
- New How Cool Is This? topic: About.me
- New Bits and Bytes: "Guidelines for Choosing a Domain Name" and "Gmail Features that You Should Know About"
- Updated information about random numbers
- New Trends in IT: "Crowdsourcing: Harnessing the Power of Social Networks"

About the Authors

Alan Evans, MS, CPA

aevans@mc3.edu

Alan is currently a faculty member at Moore College of Art and Design and Montgomery County Community College teaching a variety of computer science and business courses. He holds a B.S. in accounting from Rider University and an M.S. in information systems from Drexel University, and he is a certified public accountant. After a successful career in business, Alan finally realized his true calling was education. He has been teaching at the college level since 2000. Alan enjoys giving presentations at technical conferences and meets regularly with computer science faculty and administrators from other colleges to discuss curriculum development and new methods of engaging students.

Kendall Martin, PhD

kmartin@mc3.edu

Kendall has been teaching since 1988 at a number of institutions, including Villanova University, DeSales University, Arcadia University, Ursinus College, County College of Morris, and Montgomery County Community College, at both the undergraduate and graduate level.

Kendall's education includes a B.S. in electrical engineering from the University of Rochester and an M.S. and a Ph.D. in engineering from the University of Pennsylvania. She has industrial experience in research and development environments (AT&T Bell Laboratories) as well as experience with several start-up technology firms.

As an Associate Professor at Montgomery County Community College, Kendall works with area entrepreneurs to connect them with the College community.

Mary Anne Poatsy, MBA

mpoatsy@mc3.edu

Mary Anne is a senior faculty member at Montgomery County Community College, teaching various computer application and concepts courses in face-to-face and online environments. She enjoys speaking at various professional conferences about innovative classroom strategies. She holds a B.A. in psychology and education from Mount Holyoke College and an MBA in finance from Northwestern University's Kellogg Graduate School of Management.

Mary Anne has been in teaching since 1997, ranging from elementary and secondary education to Montgomery County Community College, Gwynedd-Mercy College, Muhlenberg College, and Bucks County Community College, as well as training in the professional environment. Before teaching, she was a vice president at Shearson Lehman Hutton in the Municipal Bond Investment Banking Department.

Acknowledgments

First, we would like to thank our students. We constantly learn from them while teaching, and they are a continual source of inspiration and new ideas.

We could not have written this book without the loving support of our families. Our spouses and children made sacrifices (mostly in time not spent with us) to permit us to make this dream into a reality.

Although working with the entire team at Pearson has been a truly enjoyable experience, a few individuals deserve special mention. The constant support and encouragement we receive from Jenifer Niles, Associate Vice President/Executive Acquisitions Editor, and Michael Payne, Editor in Chief, continually makes this book grow and change. Our heartfelt thanks go to Toni Ackley, our developmental editor. Toni, new to the Technology in Action project this edition, had a positive impact on the book, and we have benefited greatly from her creative ideas and efficient time management skills. In addition, Keri Rand, our editorial project manager, has done a fantastic job of coordinating all details of the project, and was especially helpful guiding us through the murky permissions process. As Media Project Manager, Alana Coles works tirelessly to ensure that the media accompanying the text is produced professionally and is delivered in a timely fashion. Despite the inevitable problems that crop up when producing multimedia, she handles all challenges with a smile. We also would like to extend our appreciation to Rhonda Aversa, our Production Project Manager, who works tirelessly to ensure that our book is published on time and looks fabulous. The timelines are always short, the art is complex, and there are many people with whom she has to coordinate tasks.

There are many people whom we do not meet in person at Pearson and elsewhere who make significant contributions by designing the book, illustrating, composing the pages, producing multimedia, and securing permissions. We thank them all. We would also like to thank the supplement authors for this edition: Lisa Hawkins, Julie Boyles, Linda Arnold, Hilda Federico, Tonya Pierce, Abigail Miller, Stefanie Emrich, Susan Fry, Terry Holly, Kevin Cleary, Stacy Everly, Sharon Behrens, Amy Rutledge, Wanda Gibson, Barbara Edington, and Lori Damanti.

And finally, we would like to thank the reviewers and the many others who contribute their time, ideas, and talents to this project. We appreciate their time and energy, as their comments help us turn out a better product each edition.

Reviewers

Prentice Hall and the authors would like to thank the following people for their help and time in making this book what it is. We couldn't publish this book without their contributions.

Nazih Abdallah	University of Central Florida
Allen Alexander	Delaware Technical & Community College
Joan Alexander	Valencia Community College—West
Beverly Amer	Northern Arizona University
Wilma Andrews	Virginia Commonwealth University
Gregg W. Asher, Ph.D.	Minnesota State University—Mankato
LaDonna Bachand	Santa Rosa Junior College
Carolyn Barren	Macomb Community College
Wendy Barron	Lehigh Carbon Community College
LeeAnn Bates	
Elise J. Bell, MA, Educ.	City College of San Francisco
Linda Belton	Springfield Technical Community College
Bob Benavides	Collin College
David Billings	Guilford Technical Community College
Kim Binstead, Ph.D	University of Hawaii at Manoa
Susan Birtwell	Kwantlen University College
Henry Bojack	Farmingdale State University of New York
Gina Bowers-Miller	HACC Harrisburg
Julie Boyles	
Brenda K. Britt	Fayetteville Technical Community College
Cathy J. Brotherton	Riverside Community College
Gerald U. Brown Jr.	Tarrant County College
Jeff Burton	Daytona Beach Community College
Kristen Callahan	Mercer County Community College
Judy Cameron	Spokane Community College
Jill Canine	Ivy Tech Community College of Indiana
Heather Cannon	Blinn College
Judy Cestaro	California State University—San Bernardino
Deborah Chapman	University of Southern Alabama
Gerianne Chapman	Johnson & Wales University
John P. Cicero, Ph.D	Shasta College—Redding, CA
Dan Combellick	Scottsdale Community College
Joann Cook	College of DuPage
Mark Connell	SUNY Cortland
Gail Cope	Sinclair Community College
Françoise Corey	California State University, Long Beach
John Coverdale	Riverside Community College
Thad Crews	Western Kentucky University
Doug Cross	Clackamas Community College
Geoffrey Crosslin	Kalamazoo Valley Community College
Becky Cunningham	Arkansas Tech University
Becky Curtin	Harper College
John Cusaac	Fullerton College
Paul Dadosky	Ivy Tech Community College
James Bac Dang	Tarrant County College
Marvin Daugherty	Ivy Tech
Ronald G. Deardorff	Shasta Community College
Joseph DeLibero	Arizona State University

K. Kay Delk	Seminole Community College
Charles DeSassure	Tarrant County College
Gretchen V. Douglas	State University of New York at Cortland
Susan N. Dozier	Tidewater Community College
Annette Duvall	Albuquerque Technical Vocational Institute
Laurie Eakins	East Carolina University
Roland Eichelberger	Baylor University
Bernice Eng	Brookdale Community College
James Fabrey	West Chester University
Deb Fells	Mesa Community College
Catherine L. Ferguson	University of Oklahoma
Marj Feroe	Delaware County Community College
Judy Firmin	Tarrant County College
Beverly Fite	Amarillo College
Mary Fleming	Ivy Tech Community College
Howard Flomberg	The Metropolitan State College of Denver
Richard A. Flores	Citrus College
Alicen Flosi	Lamar University
Linda Foster-Turpen	Central New Mexico Community College
Susan Fry	Boise State University
Yvonne Galusha	University of Iowa
Barbara A. Garrell	Delaware County Community College
Ernest Gines	Tarrant County College
Tim Gottleber	North Lake College
Kate Le Grand	Broward College
Bob Grazinski	Central Texas College
Sherry Green	Purdue University—Calumet Campus
Debra Gross	The Ohio State University
Vivian Haddad	Nova Southeastern University
Don A. Halcomb	Bluegrass Community and Technical College
Lewis Hall	Riverside City College
Rachelle Hall	Glendale Community College
Eric Hamilton	Community College of Denver
Bill Hammerschlag	Brookhaven College
Terry Hanks	San Jacinto College—South Campus
Susan Hanson	Albuquerque Technical Vocational Institute
Marie Hartlein	Montgomery County Community College
Ronda D. Hayes	North Lake College
Susan E. Hoggard	Tulsa Community College
Jim Hendricks	Pierce College
Catherine Hines	Albuquerque Technical Vocational Institute
Norm Hollingsworth	Georgia Perimeter College
Bill Holmes	Chandler-Gilbert Community College
Mary Carole Hollingsworth	Georgia Perimeter College
Sherry Hopkins	Anne Arundel Community College
Christie Jahn Hovey	Lincoln Land Community College
Jeffrey Howard	Finger Lakes Community College
John L. Howard	East Carolina University
Judy Irvine	Seneca College
Glen Johansson	Spokane Community College
Kay Johnson	Community College of Rhode Island
Stephanie Jones	South Plains College
Steve St. John	Tulsa Community College

Kathy Johnson	DeVry Chicago
Richard B. Kalman	Atlantic Cape Community College
Dr. K. Kamel	TSU
Darrel Karbginsky	Chemkeketa Community College
Linda Kavanaugh	Robert Morris University
Robert R. Kendi	Lehigh University
Annette Kerwin	College of DuPage
David Kight	Brewton-Parker College
Kai S. Koong	University of Texas Pan American
Frank Kuehn	Pikes Peak Community College
Jackie Lamoureux	Albuquerque Technical Vocational Institute
David K. Lange	Grand Valley State University
Joanne Lazirko	University of Wisconsin—Milwaukee
Michael R. Lehrfeld	Brevard Community College
Yvonne Leonard	Coastal Carolina University
Judith Limkilde	Seneca College—King Campus
Richard Linge	Arizona Western College
Christy Lopez	East Carolina University
Mike LoSacco	College of DuPage
Joelene Mack	Golden West College
Lisa Macon	Valencia Community College
Donna Madsen	Kirkwood Community College
Daniela Marghitu	Auburn University
Norma Marler	Catawba Valley Community College
Carol Prewitt Martin	Louisiana State University at Alexandria
Toni Marucco	Lincoln Land Community College
Evelynn McCain	Boise State University
Dana McCann	Central Michigan University
Lee McClain	West Washington University
Krista McClimans	Everett Community College
Sandra M. McCormack	Monroe Community College
Sue McCrory	Missouri State University
Phil McCue	Lone Star College—Montgomery
Helen McFadyen	Mass Bay Community College—Framingham
Charles J. McNerney Ph.D.	Bergen Community College
Dr. Dori McPherson	Schoolcraft College
Laura Melella	Fullerton College
Josephine Mendoza	California State University, San Bernardino
Mike Michaelson	Palomar College
Gina Bowers Miller	Harrisburg Area Community College
Johnette Moody	Arkansas Tech University
Dona Mularkey	Southern Methodist University
Rebecca A. Mundy	University of Southern California
Linda Mushet	Golden West College
Lisa Nademlynsky	Johnson & Wales University
Maguerite Nedreberg	Youngstown State University
Brad Nicolajsen	Carteret Community College
Omar Nooraldeen	Cape Fear Community College
Judy Ogden	Johnson County Community College
Connie O'Neill	Sinclair Community College
Claudia Orr	Northern Michigan University
James R. Orr	East Carolina University
Sung Park	Pasadena City College

Brenda Parker	Middle Tennessee State University
Lucy Parker	California State University, Northridge
Patricia Partyka	Schoolcraft College
Woody Pekoske	North Carolina State University
Judy Perhamus Perry	Riverside Community College—Norco Campus
Carolyn Poe	Lone Star College—Montgomery
Mike Puopolo	Bunker Hill Community College
Paul Quan	Albuquerque Technical Vocational Institute
Ram Raghuraman	Joliet Junior College
Patricia Rahmlow	Montgomery County Community College
Shirley Reid	Indian Hills Community College
Ruth Robbins	University of Houston—Downtown
Teresa Roberts	Wilson Community College
Catherine J. Rogers	Laramie County Community College
Mary Rousseau	Broward College, South Campus
Russell Sabadosa	Manchester Community College
Peg Saragina	Santa Rosa Junior College
Judith Scheeren	Westmoreland County Community College
Samuel Scott	Pierce College
Vicky Seehusen	The Metropolitan State College of Denver
Ralph Shafer	Truckee Meadows Community College—Reno
Mirella Shannon	Columbia College
Laurie Evin Shteir	Temple University
Sheila Smart Sicilia	Onondaga Community College
Greg A. Simpson	Phoenix College—Phoenix, AZ
Robert G. Sindt	Johnson County Community College
Gary R. Smith	Paradise Valley Community College
Steven Singer	Kapi'olani Community College
Robert Smolenski	Delaware County Community College
Diane Stark	Phoenix College
James Stark	Milwaukee Area Technical College
Suzanne Mello Stark	Community College of Rhode Island
Kriss Stauber	El Camino College
Neal Stenlund	Northern Virginia Community College
Linda Stoudemayer	Lamar Institute of Technology
Catherine Stoughton	Laramie County Community College
Lynne Stuhr	Trident Technical College
Song Su	East Los Angeles College
Jim Taggart	Atlantic City Community College
John Taylor	Hillsborough Community College—Brandon Campus
Margaret Taylor	College of Southern Nevada
Dennie Templeton	Radford University
Joyce Thompson	Lehigh Carbon Community College
Lou Thompson	University of Texas at Dallas
Janine Tiffany	Reading Area Community College
Janet Towle	New Hampshire Community Technical College—Nashua
Goran Trajkovski	Towson University
Deborah Tyler	Tarrant County College
Pamella M. Uhlenkamp	Iowa Central Community College—Fort Dodge, Iowa
Erhan Uskup	Houston Community College—Northwest
Emily Vandalovsky	Bergen Community College
Bill VanderClock	Bentley Business University
Glenna Vanderhoof	Missouri State University

Letter from the Authors

Why We Wrote This Book

Our combined 46 years of teaching computer concepts have coincided with sweeping innovations in computing technology that have affected every facet of society. From iPads to Web 2.0, computers are more than ever a fixture of our daily lives—and the lives of our students. But although today's students have a greater comfort level with their digital environment than previous generations, their knowledge of the machines they use every day is still limited.

We wrote *Technology in Action* to focus on what matters most to today's student. Instead of a history lesson on the microchip, we focus on what tasks students can accomplish with their computing devices and what skills they can apply immediately in the workplace, the classroom, and at home. We strive to have the text as current as the publishing timelines will allow us, constantly looking for the next technology trend or gadget. We have augmented the text with weekly technology updates to help you keep your classroom on top of the latest breaking developments. The result is a learning system that sparks student interest by focusing on the material they want to learn (such as how to integrate computing devices into a home network) while teaching the material they need to learn (such as how networks work). The sequence of topics is carefully set up to mirror the typical student learning experience.

As they read through this text, your students will progress through stages of increasing difficulty:

1. Thinking about how technology offers them the power to change their society and their world
2. Examining why it's important to be computer fluent
3. Examining the basic components of the computer
4. Connecting to and exploring the Internet
5. Exploring software
6. Learning the operating system and personalizing the computer
7. Evaluating and upgrading computing devices
8. Exploring home networking and keeping the computer safe from hackers
9. Going mobile with smartphones, netbooks, iPads, and laptops
10. Going behind the scenes, looking at technology in more detail

We have written the book in a "spiraling" manner, intentionally introducing on a basic level in the earlier chapters those concepts that students have trouble with and then later expanding on those concepts in more detail when students have become more comfortable with them. Thus, the focus of the early chapters is on practical uses for the computer, with real-world examples to help the students place computing in a familiar context. For example, we introduce basic hardware components in Chapter 2, and then we go into increasingly greater detail on some hardware components in Chapter 6 and in the "Under the Hood" Technology in Focus feature.

The Behind the Scenes chapters venture deeper into the realm of computing through in-depth explanations of how programming, networks, the Internet, and databases work. They are specifically designed to keep more experienced students engaged and to challenge them with interesting research assignments.

We have also developed a comprehensive multimedia program to reinforce the material taught in the text and to support both classroom lectures and distance learning. The Helpdesk training content, created specifically for *Technology in Action*, enables students to take on the role of a helpdesk operator and work through common questions asked by computer users. Exciting Sound Byte multimedia—fully integrated with the text—expands student mastery of complex topics. Tech in Action Weekly delivers the latest news stories in technology to you for use in your classroom. Each is accompanied by specific discussion topics and activities to expand on what is within the textbook materials.

Now that the computer has become a ubiquitous tool in our lives, a new approach to computer concepts is warranted. This book is designed to reach the students of the twenty-first century and prepare them for the the role they can take in their country and their world.

EDITION 9 ninth

Visual Walk-Through

TOPIC SEQUENCE

Concepts are covered in a spiraling manner between chapters to mirror the typical student learning experience.

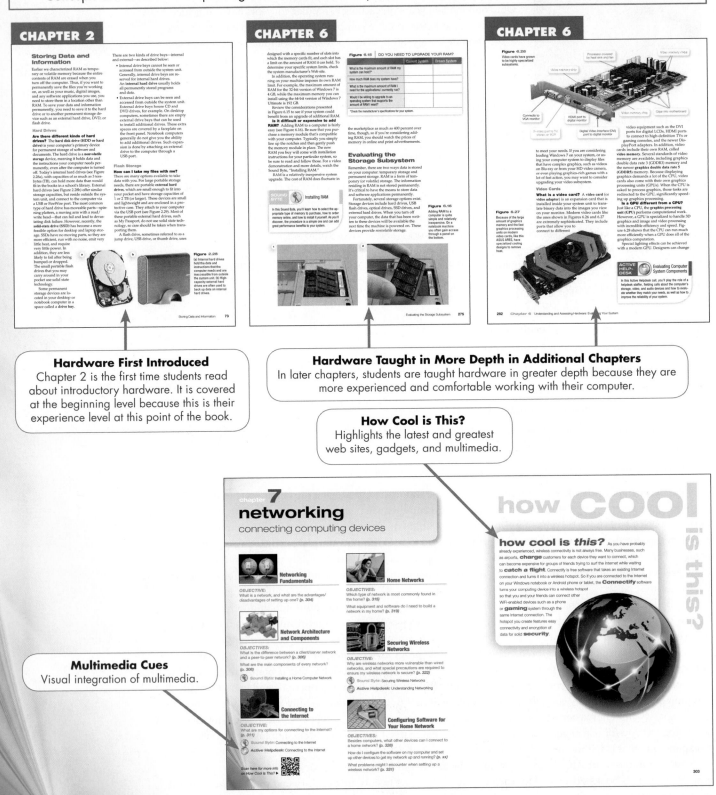

Hardware First Introduced
Chapter 2 is the first time students read about introductory hardware. It is covered at the beginning level because this is their experience level at this point of the book.

Hardware Taught in More Depth in Additional Chapters
In later chapters, students are taught hardware in greater depth because they are more experienced and comfortable working with their computer.

How Cool is This?
Highlights the latest and greatest web sites, gadgets, and multimedia.

Multimedia Cues
Visual integration of multimedia.

Student Textbook

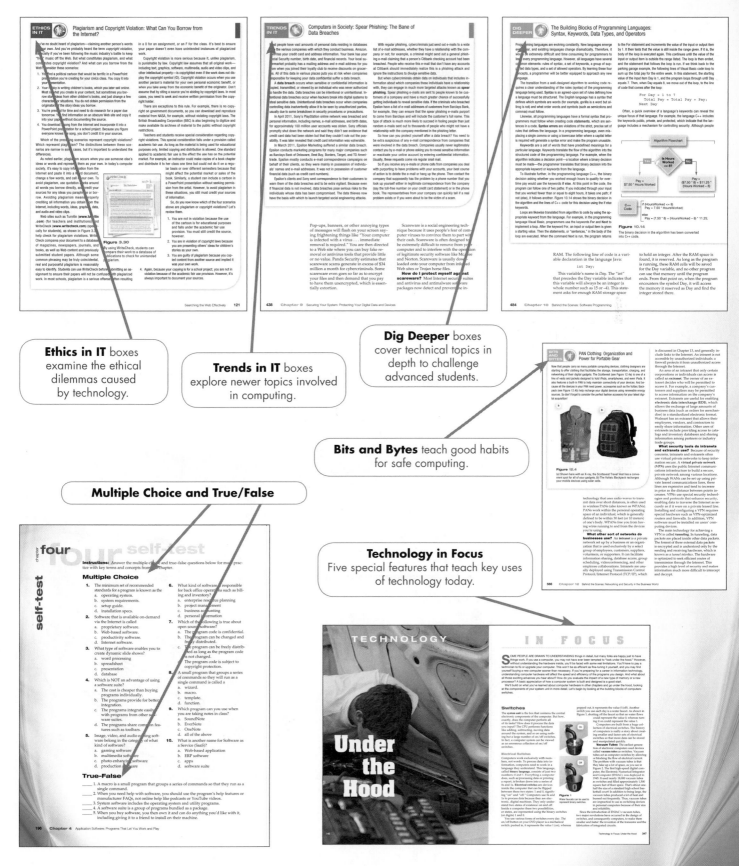

Ethics in IT boxes examine the ethical dilemmas caused by technology.

Trends in IT boxes explore newer topics involved in computing.

Dig Deeper boxes cover technical topics in depth to challenge advanced students.

Bits and Bytes teach good habits for safe computing.

Multiple Choice and True/False

Technology in Focus
Five special features that teach key uses of technology today.

The Multimedia

NINTH

Companion Website
Includes an interactive study guide, online end-of-chapter material, additional Internet exercises, and much more.

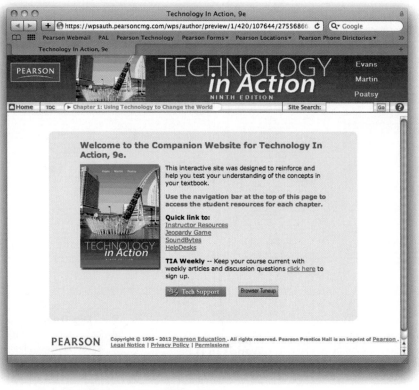

www.prenhall.com/techinaction

Active Helpdesk
Interactive training that puts the student in the role of a helpdesk staffer fielding questions from callers.

Completely Revised
Features textbook page references within each call and assessment at the end of each call.

Supervisor available to assist students.

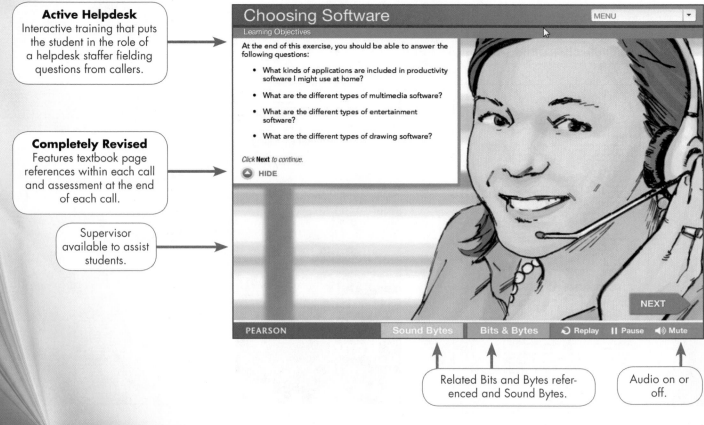

Related Bits and Bytes referenced and Sound Bytes.

Audio on or off.

Transcript button used to turn transcript on or off.

Sound Bytes
Multimedia lessons with video, audio, or animation and corresponding labs featuring multiple-choice quizzing.

Also available as podcasts.

Navigational tool.

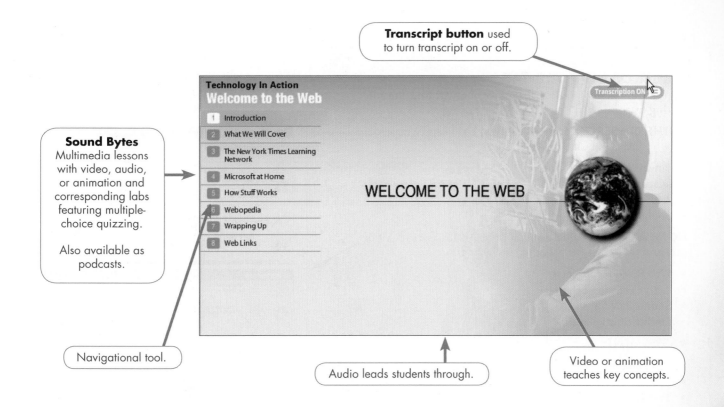

Technology In Action
Welcome to the Web

1 Introduction
2 What We Will Cover
3 The New York Times Learning Network
4 Microsoft at Home
5 How Stuff Works
6 Webopedia
7 Wrapping Up
8 Web Links

WELCOME TO THE WEB

Transcription ON

Audio leads students through.

Video or animation teaches key concepts.

Annotated Instructor Edition

Provided with each chapter are two divider pages like the ones outlined below.

FRONT OF CHAPTER TAB

On the front side of each chapter tab, you will find the following categories:

IN THE CLASSROOM: Activities you can use in a classroom or in online classes, including:

- PowerPoint Presentations
- Discussion Exercises
- Active Helpdesk Calls
- Sound Bytes

HOMEWORK: Activities used out of class for assessment or preparation for the next chapter, including:

- Web Resource Projects
- Active Helpdesk Calls
- Sound Byte Labs
- Online Study Guides

ASSESSMENT:

- Blackboard
- WebCT
- TestGen
- myitlab

The back side of each chapter tab includes the relevant Sound Bytes for that chapter.

FRONT OF ETHICS TAB

On the front of the Ethics tab, you will find the following:

OPPOSING VIEWPOINTS TABLE: Outlines debatable ethics topics that you can use in the classroom.

KEYWORDS: Provides you with additional words to search the Internet for more information related to the ethics topic.

For a list of the resources available for every chapter and where they are located, see the back of this tab.

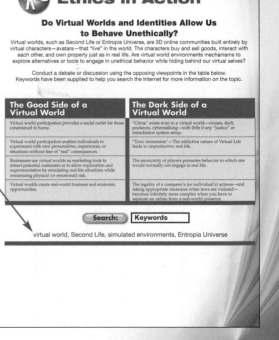

Instructor Resource CD

Instructor Resource CD

- **NEW! Interactive Course Builder** to help you integrate all the instructor resources.
- **NEW! Recommended chapter lectures** written by the authors that you can customize.
- All resources included with the *Technology in Action* Instructional System.

Contact your local Pearson sales rep to learn more about the
Technology in Action instructional system.

using technology to change the world

David Grigg / iStockphoto.com

More Than Just a Job

OBJECTIVE:

Beyond personal goals, what impact can you have on the world? *(p. 4)*

Brandon Alms / iStockphoto.com

Technology on the World Stage

OBJECTIVE:

How can becoming proficient with technology help you understand and participate in important issues in the world at large? *(p. 4)*

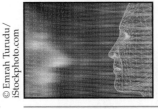

© Emrah Turudu / iStockphoto.com

Technology and Our Society

OBJECTIVE:

How can knowledge of technology help you impact the direction of our society? *(p. 9)*

Ximagination / Shutterstock.com

Technology and Your Life

OBJECTIVES:

What does it mean to be "computer literate"? *(p. 13)*

How does being computer literate make you a savvy computer user and consumer? *(p. 14)*

How can becoming computer literate help you in a career? *(p. 16)*

 Sound Byte: The History of the Personal Computer

 Sound Byte: Questions to Ask Before You Buy a Computer

Scan here for more info on How Cool Is This? ▶

how cool is *this*?
At the Wake Forest Institute for Regenerative Medicine, researcher Dr. Anthony Atala heads a group working on replacement tissue and **organ** development. One project there uses ordinary desktop **printers** to create human organs! Instead of using ink, they "bioprint" with human **cells** layer after layer. In about 40 minutes they can "print" a two-chamber heart, which starts beating on its own about five hours later. Currently these are still experimental organs, but there is great hope that complex organs with lots of blood vessels like hearts, livers, and kidneys can be reproduced this way. The gap between the need for **transplant** organs and the supply is skyrocketing as the number of patients requesting organs has doubled in the last decade, while the number of transplants has remained about the same.

More Than Just a Job

Ask yourself: Why are you in this class? It may be that this class is required for your degree. Or it may be that you thought it would be useful for you to have better computer skills when you apply for a job. Both of these are great reasons to study computers and technology, but let's step back for a moment and try to see a bigger picture.

Technology today is not just a means for career advancement or just a necessary skill set for survival in society. It has become something more—a tool that allows an individual to make an impact far beyond his or her own life. So many movies dangle the same dream in front of us— being the girl or guy who saves the world, and gets to drive a nice car while doing it! Whether it's *Transformers* or *Spider-Man*, we are drawn to heroes because we want our work and our lives to mean something and benefit others.

The material in this book can be your ticket to doing just that, to influence and to participate in projects that are changing the world. In this opening chapter, we'd like to ask you to think about what your talents and skills in technology could let you contribute on a larger scale, beyond the benefits they will bring to you.

Technology on the World Stage

Political and global issues of recent times are showing that modern technology is galvanizing groups of people in new ways. As you work this semester to develop your understanding of technology, realize that you could become the next Wael Ghonim or Ory Okolloh. You will use technology to change the world.

Political Issues

Egypt The end of 2010 saw a series of revolutions across the Arab and North African region. Protests or full-scale revolutions took place in Tunisia, Libya, Algeria, and Jordan. **Social networking** is the gathering together of groups of people using online tools to connect and exchange ideas. Social networking tools like Facebook and Twitter fueled social unrest in the face of repression and censorship in many countries. Egypt is one example that shows the impact of an individual armed with an understanding of modern technology.

The reigning government in Egypt had been in power for more than 30 years—the entire life of many young people in the country. Wael Ghonim, a Google marketing manager in Egypt, anonymously launched the Facebook page "We Are All Khaled Said" in June 2010. Khaled Said was an Egyptian businessman tortured and killed by authorities. The Facebook page became a tool that made people aware there were others who were dissatisfied with the direction of the country, even though they were not yet able to imagine other options. By January 2011, the government responded to the increasing unrest online by "turning off" the Internet for the entire country. The government told the four largest Internet providers to shut down and closed access to 93 percent of Egyptian networks. Protests against this shutdown turned violent, and Egyptian Internet providers began to restore service a few days later.

Back in the virtual world of Facebook and Twitter, thousands offered ideas on how they could protest meaningfully. Finally, a silent gathering near the sea in Alexandria was chosen. This movement from "virtual community" to physical community (see Figure 1.1) was a turning point, and by February 11, 2011, President Mubarak

AP Photo / Muhammed Abu Zaid

Figure 1.1

How big of a role did social media play in the transfer of power in Egypt in 2011?

Figure 1.2

The Ushahidi site used crisis mapping during the Kenyan election to quickly combine a torrent of reports into a useful mapping tool.

of Egypt had resigned. President Obama stated, "We had the privilege to witness history taking place. . . . Egypt will never be the same."

Social networking tools are providing a level of instant connection and instant distribution of information that is reshaping the world. For Wael Ghonim, it led to an opportunity to recast the future of his country. What can you do with social networking tools that will change the future of your community?

Kenya A single voice in Kenya combined with technology to create a tool that continues to change the world. In December 2007, angry Kenyans wielding machetes were battling the police in the streets. The closest election in Kenya's history had ended with the current president declaring victory despite suspicion and allegations of electoral fraud. Nairobi lawyer Ory Okolloh began to get messages describing acts of violence occurring all over the country. She tried to post them all on her blog site KenyanPundit, but she was quickly over-

whelmed. She put out a request for help through the blog.

Within 72 hours, two programmers, Erik Hersman and Juliana Rotich, had created Ushahidi (Swahili for "testimony"). It is a **crisis mapping tool** that collects information from e-mails, text messages, blog posts, and Twitter tweets and maps them, making the information instantly publicly available (see Figure 1.2). The developers then made Ushahidi a free platform that anyone in the world could use.To date, it has been used during the earthquakes and tsunami in Japan, to battle election violence in the Congo, to observe events in the Gaza Strip, and to monitor the 2010 snow emergency in Washington, D.C. ("Snowmageddon").

From there, the development team created a second generation product called SwiftRiver. SwiftRiver addresses a key issue in collecting eyewitness accounts in real time during a crisis: What do you read first? As thousands of tweets and posts come in, how can we pull relevant information from all this data from the crowd? SwiftRiver uses filters to rate the submitters and the quality of the information to generate a measurement of the probability the information is accurate.

In what other ways could technology prove useful in helping us face times of crisis?

Human Rights

Writer and futurist Jamais Cascio has presented ideas of how our current technological landscape might bring all citizens into a more engaged role in changing the world. In his TED talk "The Future We Will Create" (**www.ted.org**), Cascio discusses how a smartphone-carrying population can work

Figure 1.3

The Witness Project uses the power of video and a grassroots movement to advocate for human rights around the world.

to create a better world—more sustainable, more secure, and more desirable.

Having an international population armed with cameras and a means to quickly distribute their video allows the invisible to become visible in many ways (see Figure 1.3). This transparency can be used to let us see the consequences of our behavior directly, and make changes. The Witness Project, founded by Peter Gabriel, uses this strategy to stop human rights abuses throughout the world (**www .witness.org**). Their slogan is, "See it. Film it. Change it." ("See It. Film It. Change It." Copyright © 2011 by WITNESS. Reprinted by permission of WITNESS www.witness. org.) And video from the Witness Project has changed many lives; for example, it contributed to the arrest of warlords in the Democratic Republic of Congo for the recruitment of child soldiers. Using technology such as the Witness Project, what problems in your community could you shed light on and bring to the community's attention?

The Environment

Efforts similar to those just described are working to document the environmental state of the world. Environmental successes can be collected together, along with evidence to document ecological crimes. What if each of the cell phones distributed around the world was equipped with integrated atmospheric sensors? Then millions of points around the world would be constantly reporting in on air and water quality. And what if these sensors could monitor for flu viruses? Tagged with geographical information, the data could be combined with maps for easy viewing and analysis. Ideas like these are being explored by UCLA researcher Dr. Deborah Estrin, the director of the Center for Embedded Network Sensing. Can you think of other ways that your cell phone could help you improve your society?

Thanks to technology, each of us is empowered with tools and opportunities to impact the world. Your reach can go far beyond what you see around you. Learn as much as you can about using your technology to its fullest potential, to enrich the world community.

The Digital Divide

Accessible Technology If technology can provide every person with the power to change their country, even their world, what does it mean to be without access to technology? There is still a great gap between the levels of Internet access and the availability of technical tools in different regions of the world. The term coined for that gap, for the difference in ease of access to technology, is the **digital divide**. The danger of a digital divide is that it prevents us from using all of the minds on the planet to solve the problems of the planet. But that challenge also is being answered by the application of technology.

The Next Einstein Initiative (NEI) is a strategic plan to focus resources on the young talented mathematical minds of Africa (see Figure 1.4). By expanding the African Institute for Mathematical Sciences (AIMS) across the continent, the future of Africa can be profoundly changed. Cambridge professor Neil Turok founded AIMS to bring together the brightest young minds across Africa with the best lecturers in the world. He has described the power of the youthful intellect in Africa by saying, "If Africa is going to get fixed, it's by them, not by us." NEI has won funding from Google's Project 10^{100}, a push to award $10 million to a set of five projects, selected by open public voting. By capturing the enthusiasm of the world with presentations distributed through ted.com and Project 10^{100}, there is now an active push to create 15 additional AIMS centers across Africa.

There are smaller ways to address the digital divide as well. Traditional chalkboards gave way to whiteboards, which have given way to smartboards. Smartboards can display content on a computer screen, are touch interactive, and can easily record and store lecture content. But there is a price tag for all that functionality. Smartboard units can cost as much as $5,000, so they are much more common in affluent settings. A quick hack to the popular Nintendo Wii remote, however, makes it possible to create a smartboard for about $50. Researcher Johnny Lee of Google has developed, and freely distributes, software that uses the infrared camera in the tip of a Wii remote, as well as an infrared pen (which you can make for about $5) to create an inexpensive smartboard. In its first three months on Lee's Web site, the software for this was downloaded over half a million times. The final

Figure 1.4

The Next Einstein Initiative is rallying the support of the world to identify mathematical genius.

product is not as full featured as competing products, but as Lee says, "you get about 80 percent of the way there, for about 1 percent of the cost."

High Low Tech The MIT Media Lab has a research group dedicated to integrating high- and low-tech materials and processes into other cultures. Projects like Fab FM have created radio kits that can be produced and assembled at home. The Open Source Consumer Electronics project studies ways that traditional electronic circuit boards and components can be more easily shared, modified, and produced. The Junkyard Jumbotron from the MIT Center for Future Civic Media is another example of a software solution that allows low-tech parts to imitate the utility of expensive high-tech tools. The Jumbotron lets you combine a range of displays into a single virtual screen. Any kind of screen can become part of the jumbo image as long as it runs a Web browser, so laptops, smartphones, and smart televisions all can be converted on the spot to become an instant Jumbotron screen (see Figure 1.5).

There is no exaggerating the range and severity of problems facing our world, from environmental threats to dangers brought on by how we treat each other. Your understanding of technology could provide the means to change the course of our future. How will you use these powers to improve your own world?

Figure 1.5

The Junkyard Jumbotron lets users create a single screen from laptops, tablets, smartphones—anything with a Web browser.

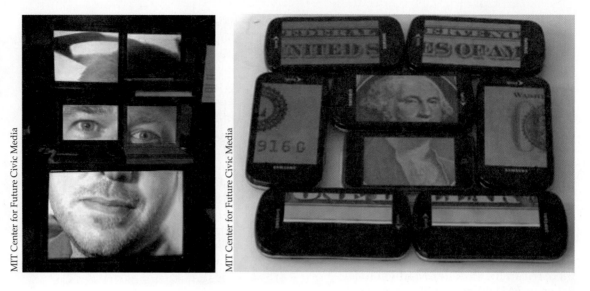

MIT Center for Future Civic Media

ETHICS IN IT

Ethics in IT: The Digital Divide and the Mobile Bridge

The digital divide, the gap between those with easy access to technology and those with little to no access (see Figure 1.6), is a social problem that leads to more complex social issues down the road. Lack of access to the Internet and computers means that people don't develop computer skills, leading to less chance of success in career and business. Less familiarity with the Internet can lead to less civic engagement and a lower level of active, engaged citizenship. So how should we attack the problem of the digital divide?

Perhaps the answer is to promote mobile devices as a means for low-income families to access the Internet. Recent studies from the University of Michigan show that without Internet access at home, teens from low-income households (family income under $30,000 a year) are more likely than their wealthier counterparts to use their cell phones to go online. So the widening penetration of cell phones might be the answer to ending the digital divide. Or is it? It depends on how you define the digital divide. If merely having access to the Internet means you have crossed the divide, the increase of mobile plan usage by lower income families is a great step.

But could it be that this "solution" just continues the problem in a new disguise? Going online using a cell phone plan is the most expensive of all options, and data transfer speeds are among the slowest. So the teens with the least money are likely paying the most to get the slowest online experience. And they are more likely to be paying for it themselves, as opposed to teens from wealthier households in which, according to the same University of Michigan study, the teens are more likely to be on family plans paid for by someone else. So by not having available free Internet access, is our society placing an unfair burden on just those groups least likely to be able to afford access?

"The willingness of poor people to pay for Internet access underscores the idea that net access is not just 'nice to have' but that it is increasingly seen as a necessity," the researchers wrote. But if your main access to the Internet is through mobile usage, does that help develop a wider range of computer skills? Often teen cell usage is limited to managing online social networks, playing games, or listening to music. Computer tasks and skills that could lead to economic advancement, like filling out job applications or running a business, are not yet handled easily on mobile devices.

Will the increasing penetration of smartphones and faster cellular Internet access eliminate the digital divide in the United States? Should our government intervene and make sure there is sufficient free access for all? Is it ethical to deprive the poorer segment of our society of a needed commodity? Answering challenging questions about technology is part of being an informed citizen.

Grant Alexander Waters

Figure 1.6

Can we bridge the digital divide through mobile devices? Should we?

Technology and Our Society

Technology is allowing us to redefine very fundamental parts of our social makeup. How we think, how we connect with each other, how we purchase and consume products—all of these areas of our society are shifting rapidly because of technology.

Technology Impacts How We Think

What We Think About What do you think about when you get home after school or work—when you are officially on your own time? In the late twentieth century, the most common trend was thinking about what to buy next. Or perhaps what to watch next, what to listen to next, what to read next—information and products were being served at an amazing rate, and a pattern of consumption became habit. As more and more Web applications began to appear that allowed each individual to become the "creator" of the Web, a new kind of Internet came into being. It was nicknamed Web 2.0, and now everyone could collaborate internationally at the click of a mouse. The twenty-first century has seen a dramatic shift—the generation of a **creative surplus**. Clay Shirky, author of *Cognitive Surplus: Creativity and Generosity in a Connected Age*, coined this term to describe the ability of the world's populace to volunteer and collaborate on large projects. The world's population has an estimated 1 trillion hours a year of free time. When that is coupled with the available media tools, and with a generosity and need to share, projects like Ushahidi and the Witness Project emerge.

Not only heart-stopping civic-minded projects appear online—there are many sites like LOLCats and video channels of backyard accidents as well. But modern theories of motivation show that what pushes people to apply their free time to projects, for no money, is the excitement of autonomy, mastery, and purpose (see Figure 1.7). **Autonomy** is the freedom to work without constant direction and control. **Mastery** is the feeling of confidence and excitement from seeing your own skills progress. So many people complete a full week of work and then play a musical instrument for hours at home, not to make money, but to feel their mastery of the instrument grow. **Purpose** is simply the understanding that you are working for something larger than yourself. Together, these three play into how we are fundamentally wired and produce incredibly motivated behavior. As we learn more about the "technology" of motivation, electronic technology offers motivated people the means to connect and to work easily with video and media. Their creative surplus becomes a powerful resource to change the world.

Figure 1.7

Our understanding of human motivation can play a role in our use of technology to impact society.

How We Think of Each Other We are trained by our society to adopt certain ideas about gender. From pink or blue booties all the way to major marketing media campaigns, specific messages and stereotypes about gender are broadcast to us constantly. Marketing often relies on identifying and exploiting specific stereotypes to sell products. If you fall into a certain demographic, say "men between the ages of 25 and 34," then your buying behavior is predicted along certain lines. Although marketing is very tuned to demographics, many groups find themselves underrepresented. For example, the highly influential Nielsen ratings of television do not even measure viewers over the age of 54. Another effect of this age bias is that certain standard storylines appear repeatedly in entertainment—movies for young men featuring fast cars, or "chick flicks" to appeal to young women.

How has the startling rise of social media networks impacted this? Online it is difficult to ascertain someone's true age—marketers only have access to your path through a particular Web site to try to determine your income or gender. But it is very easy to determine what interests you as you move around the Web. People form into groups based not on their age or income, but on their common interests. When

Joanna Blakely of the Norman Lear Center at the University of Southern California began to study the relationship between gender and online usage, she found that women outnumber men in their use of social networking. They also spend much more time on social sites. As marketers move toward relying on information from social networks, they will be increasingly driven by a female perspective and by a more complex model of what certain groups are attracted to than the classic clichés of the past.

How We Connect

Connecting Through Music In most societies, people connect intimately in gatherings, local celebrations, and festivals through shared experiences. Technology has added breadth to that aspect of our lives as well. Eric Whitacre's Virtual Choir, shown in Figure 1.8, is one example. As a wannabe rock star, Whitacre was introduced to classical choir music in college, and the experience transformed his life. He is now a professional classical composer and conductor. He began the idea of a virtual choir by posting a video of himself conducting one of his works, "Lux Aurumque," to YouTube. The idea was that listeners would follow his lead and, as they heard the piano track, each would

Figure 1.8

The Virtual Choir 2.0 performance of "Sleep" included over 2,000 singers from 58 countries.

s70/ZUMA Press/Newscom

record their part of the piece as either a soprano, alto, tenor, or bass. The submitted videos were then edited together, the audio aligned, and the first piece from the Virtual Choir was released with 50 recorded voices.

> # Tools like DYTHR represent a huge shift in how we are informed and who controls the information that governs our lives.

His next project, Virtual Choir 2.0 performing "Sleep," was released in April 2011 and was even larger in scale. It included 2,052 videos from 58 different countries. A blog connected the members of the choir and built a real sense of community and connection between members. Take a glance at the Virtual Choir Earth View (**www.ericwhiteacre.com/the-virtual-choir/earth-view**), which displays the physical location of each voice. As Whitacre remarked, ". . . human beings will go to any lengths necessary to find and connect with each other."

Connecting in New Ways Ze Frank is an artist working to explore the ways we connect now that our virtual lives are so expanded. Frank has organized numerous projects that illustrate the new ways we can connect virtually. He initiated one project named *A Childhood Walk* that invites people to go into Google Street View and record a walk that they used to take over and over as a child. People often have strong memories reappear, and Frank gathered together those memories along with photos from Google Street View to create a gallery (**www.zefrank.com/the_walk**). For the people who created these experiences, and for the audience that viewed the gallery, the results were powerful and emotional.

Another example of shifts in how we connect is demonstrated by the DYTHR project from MIT graduate students Grace Woo and Szymon Jakubczak. As people using DYTHR walk around with their mobile devices, they can broadcast a short message (see Figure 1.9). Other phones, while scanning for wireless networks, pick up and display the messages. If a message seems important, you can tap it and rebroadcast it. The more popular messages, as determined by the crowd, then begin to trickle up to the top of the list. So the crowd itself is writing the headlines, broadcasting them, and filtering them by popular demand. Tools like DYTHR represent a huge shift in how we are informed and who controls the information that governs our lives. No Internet connection or cell phone tower is required, so it is very difficult to censor. What other changes will technology bring to how we gather news and distribute it?

How We Consume

Technology is changing all aspects of how we purchase and consume goods—from strategies for convincing you to purchase a

Figure 1.9

DYTHR lets information be created, distributed, and filtered by users themselves in real time.

Figure 1.10

Best Buy uses QR tags on each product tag to direct shoppers to the Best Buy site for reviews.

Brian van der Brug/Los Angeles Times/MCT/Newscom

certain product to the mechanics of how you buy and own things.

Marketing New strategies in marketing and communications are counting on the fact that so many people have a cell phone with a camera and Internet access. A technology named **QR (quick response) codes** lets any piece of print in the real world host a live link to online information and video content. From your smartphone, simply run your QR app and hold the phone near the QR image anywhere you see it—on a product, in an advertisement, on a sign or a storefront—and your phone takes you directly to a display of information. It might be a Web site, a video, a schedule, or a social network. QR tags are being used widely in retail (see Figure 1.10), because studies show 82 percent of shoppers go to the Internet on their phone before a purchase anyway. You'll even see them on the opening page of each chapter of this book!

Marketers also have to be aware of the phenomenon of **crowdsourcing**—checking in with the voice of the crowd. Consumers are using apps like MobileVoice to check people's verdict (the "crowd") on the quality of an item. Forward-thinking companies are using this input to improve their products and services. TaxiHack, for example,

allows phone users to comment on New York City cab drivers, and AT&T has an app to let customers report locations of coverage gaps.

Recent studies show that 93 percent of adults in the United States ages 18–29 now have a cell phone. Combined with the explosion in popularity of social networking sites, consumers' experiences are changing. Shopping now begins with price comparison tools like ShopSavvy and RedLaser. These "location aware" tools begin by scanning the barcode of the item and then comparing prices with nearby stores and also with the best prices available online. Once you've selected a store, many different mobile apps let you take advantage of mobile coupons, called mobicoupons. A smartphone can simply read the barcode on the item, and then will display a barcode for a coupon. The cashier scans the mobicoupon right at the register. More and more sites are appearing that offer some type of mobile coupon, including Zavers, Yowza, MobiQpons, and Cellfire. Future trends in this area include a tighter integration with the information customer loyalty programs already store about you. Based on location and your past buying preferences, specialized coupons could be designed and delivered through the mobicoupon system.

Access Versus Ownership Even the idea of ownership is evolving under technological pressures. The shift of information to a digital form is allowing us to change our relationship to objects. Items like bicycles and cars can become "subscriptions" instead of large one-time purchases. Call a Bike is a program run in Germany. At most major street corners, there is a rack of Call a Bikes (see Figure 1.11). Place a call to the phone number printed on the bike, and it texts you a code you can use to unlock the bike lock. Ride the bike to where you're going. When you arrive, relock it. The amount of time you rode it automatically is billed (by the minute) to your phone.

Zipcar is another system using the digital communication of information to change our lifestyle habits. Many cities and most major universities now offer a Zipcar program. Residents sign up for the program and receive a key that has an RFID microchip inside. All cars are connected to a central network. You can open a Zipcar car and start the engine only when your specific key is scheduled to open and start it. GPS technology is used to track where the car is, whether it has been dropped off at the right location, and how far it has been driven. The entire process is transparent to Zipcar members. Members have 24/7 access to a vehicle—a truck, a hybrid, a convertible—when they need it, with very little advance notice, for a cost of about $7 an hour (gas and insurance included!).

These models are spreading now to smaller goods. **Swap.com** supports people so they can trade books, video games, and DVDs with one another, using the power of peer-to-peer connections to find the best set of matches for their used DVD set of *Seinfeld* in exchange for a season of *Curb Your Enthusiasm*. Rachel Botsman and Roo Rogers make the case in their book *What's Mine Is Yours: The Rise of Collaborative Consumption* that the real fuel beneath these services is a shift in our acceptance of sharing. **Collaborative consumption** implies that we are joining together as a group to use a specific product more efficiently. We are so constantly connected with each other, we have again found the power of community. Adding in the pressure of mounting environmental concerns and a global financial crisis, we are migrating toward collabora-tive consumption. There are more and more opportunities to redistribute the things we have purchased, share our lives, and share the services a product provides, instead of owning it outright. On average a car is used 1 hour a day—the other 23 hours a day it is not helping you or any of your neighbors. As Kevin Kelly, editor of *Wired* magazine, framed it, we are moving toward a time where we design around a new idea " . . . where access is better than ownership."

Technology and Your Life

Technology is creating huge changes in the world scene as well as how we behave socially, but it is also important to you on a more personal level. The more you understand technology, the greater your productivity can be and the better prepared you'll be for any career.

Boost Your Productivity

Technology now allows you to be very active in critical social and global issues. In order to take advantage of such power you need to move beyond being just a casual computer user and achieve computer literacy. Being **computer literate** means being familiar enough with computers that you

© Ernst Klinker / Alamy

Figure 1.11

Call a Bike uses digital technology to change our lifestyle from one of ownership to one of "subscription."

Figure 1.12

Do you know what all the words in a computer ad mean? Can you tell whether the ad includes all the information necessary to make a purchasing decision?

Processor:	Intel i7-965 Extreme, Factory O'Cd to 3.73 GHz
RAM:	12 GB Tri Channel Corsair DDR3 (1066 MHz)
Video:	ATI Radeon HD 5870 X2 with 1 GB DDR5
Audio:	Creative Labs X-Fi Elite Pro; HDA 7.1 surround channel sound
Network:	Native Gigabit Ethernet
Optical Drive:	Blu-ray burner
Storage Drive:	1 TB Serial ATA hard drive with support for up to 5 additional drives with RAID options
Ports:	8 USB and 2 USB 3.0 2 DVI and 1 S-Video 2 IEEE 1394 1 S/PDIF out
Physics Accelerator:	Ageia PhysX Card
Cooling:	Two-stage liquid cooling system
Portable Storage:	Bluetooth wireless 19-in-1 media hub with VoIP stereo headset
Operating System:	Windows 7 Ultimate 64-bit

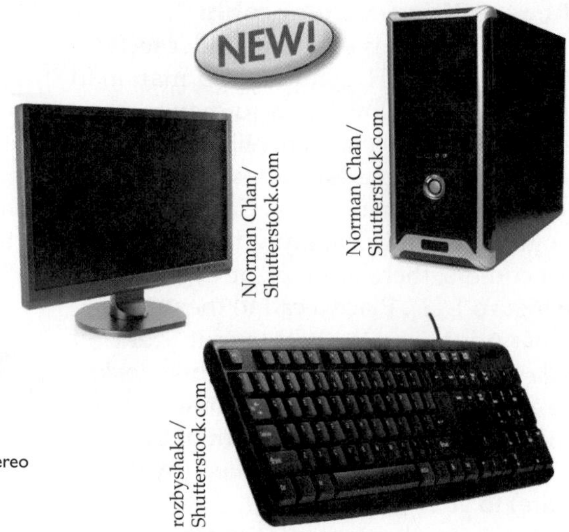

NEW!

Norman Chan/Shutterstock.com

Norman Chan/Shutterstock.com

rozbyshaka/Shutterstock.com

understand their capabilities and limitations (see Figure 1.12), and you know how to use them efficiently.

Once you can use computers in an efficient manner, you'll see changes in your own relationship with technology. You'll be a better consumer when it comes time to purchase computers, peripherals, and technology services. You'll be more sought after as a new hire and more productive as an employee. Your understanding of key concepts in technology can "future-proof" you, letting you easily and quickly react to the next round of new technologies.

Be a Savvy Computer User

Let's look at how to become a savvy computer user and consumer. What does this mean? Here are a few examples. If you are not a savvy user now, don't worry—all these topics and more are covered in the remaining chapters.

- **Avoiding hackers and viruses.** Do you know what hackers and viruses are? Both can threaten a computer's security. Being aware of how hackers and viruses operate and knowing the damage they can do to your computer can help you avoid falling prey to them.
- **Protecting your privacy.** You've probably heard of identity theft—you see and hear news stories all the time about people whose "identities" are stolen and whose credit ratings are ruined by "identity thieves." But do you know

how to protect yourself from identity theft when you're online?

- **Understanding the real risks.** Part of being computer literate means being able to separate the real privacy and security risks from things you don't have to worry about. For example, do you know what a *cookie* is? Do you know whether it poses a privacy risk for you when you're on the Internet? What about a *firewall?* Do you know what one is? Do you really need one to protect your computer?
- **Using the Internet and the Web wisely.** Anyone who has ever searched the Web can attest that finding information and finding good information are two different things. People who are computer literate make the Internet a powerful tool and know how to find the information they want effectively. How familiar with the Web are you, and how effective are your searches?
- **Avoiding online annoyances.** If you have an e-mail account, are you sure you know all the tricks you need to use e-mail appropriately (see Figure 1.13)? Chances are you've received electronic junk mail, or **spam**. How can you avoid being overwhelmed by spam? What about adware and spyware— do you know what they are? Do you know the difference between those and viruses, worms, and Trojan horses? Do you know which **software** programs, the instructions that tell the computer

Questions to Ask Before You Buy a Computer

This Sound Byte will help you consider important questions to ask before you buy a computer, such as whether you should get a laptop or a desktop, or whether you should purchase a new computer or a used or refurbished one.

Figure 1.13

Understanding how to use e-mail effectively is just one example of what it means to be computer literate.

what to do, you should install on your computer to avoid online annoyances?

- **Being able to maintain, upgrade, and troubleshoot your computer.** Learning how to care for and maintain your computer and knowing how to diagnose and fix certain problems can save you a lot of time and hassle. Do you know how to upgrade your computer if you want more memory, for example? Do you know which software and computer settings can help you keep your computer in top shape?

Everywhere you go, you see ads like the one in Figure 1.12 for computers and other devices: laptops, printers, monitors, cell phones, digital cameras, and GPS (global positioning system) devices. Do you know what all the words in the ad mean? What is *RAM*? What is a *CPU*? What are *MB*, *GB*, *GHz*, and *cache*? How fast do you need your computer to be, and how much memory should it have? Understanding computer

terminology and keeping current with technology will help you better determine which computers and devices match your needs.

Finally, becoming computer literate means knowing which technologies are on the horizon and how to integrate them into your home setup when possible (see Figure 1.14). Can you connect your laptop to a wireless network? What is Bluetooth, and does your computer have it? Can a USB 3.0 flash drive be plugged into an old USB 1.0 port? For that matter, what is a USB port? How much memory should your cell phone have? Knowing the answers to these and

Figure 1.14

Can you identify all of these devices? Do you know how to get them all to work well together?

other questions will help you make better purchasing decisions.

The benefits of being computer literate will help you in your career and in running your personal life. This book and course will make you computer literate. Chapter 9 covers how to keep your computer and your digital life secure. Chapter 6 shows you how to know if your hardware is beginning to limit your computer's performance, and how to upgrade or shop for a new system. In Chapter 3 you'll find out how to get the most from the Web, while staying free from the spam and clutter Internet surfing can leave behind.

You'll be able to save money, time, and endless frustration by having a strong background in the basics of how computers and computer systems operate.

Prepare for Your Career

Computer careers are on the rise. Regardless of which profession you pursue, if computers are not already in use in that career, they most likely will be soon. **Information technology (IT)** is a field of study focused on managing and processing information and the automatic retrieval of information. Information technology includes computers, telecommunications, and software deployment. IT careers are on the rise, and several of the fastest-growing occupations are computer related. New technology in the workplace is creating a demand for new skill levels from employees. A study from the National Research Council concludes that by the year 2030, computers will displace humans in 60 percent of the current occupations. It will be more critical than ever for employees to have advanced skills. For more information about computers and the workplace, see the Technology in Focus section, "Careers in IT." So, let's begin with a look at how computer systems are used in a wide range of careers.

We all are used to seeing computers at the checkout counter in stores, at the check-in area at an airport, and so on, but computers are being used in many ways that you probably aren't aware of. Before we begin looking at a computer's parts and how it operates, let's take a look at a whole range of industries and examine how computers are a part of getting work done. Becoming truly computer literate will undoubtedly help you perform your job more effectively. It also will make you more desirable as an employee and more likely to earn more and advance your career. Whether you plan on a career in one of these fields or will just be a user of their products and services, your life will be affected by the use of computers in areas including retail, the arts, law enforcement, the military, agriculture, and more.

Retail: Working in a Data Mine

Businesses accumulate a lot of data, but how do they manage to make sense of all of it? How do they separate the anomalies from the trends? They use a technique known as **data mining**, the process of searching huge amounts of data with the hope of finding a pattern (see Figure 1.15). For example, large retailers often study the data gathered from register terminals to determine which products are selling on a given day and in a specific location. In addition to inventory control systems, which help managers figure out how much merchandise they need to order to replace stock that is sold, the process of data mining opens the door to more detail. Managers can use mined data to determine that if a certain product is to sell

Mclek/Shutterstock.com   Richard Peterson/Shutterstock.com   Dmitriy Shironosov/Shutterstock.com

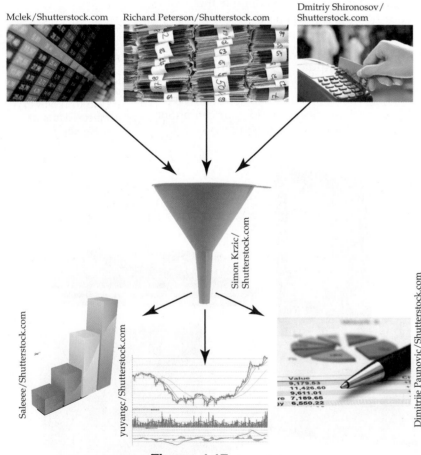

Simon Krzic/Shutterstock.com

Saleee/Shutterstock.com   yuyangc/Shutterstock.com   Dimitrije Paunovic/Shutterstock.com

Figure 1.15

Data mining is the art of combining huge volumes of raw data into views that provide insight.

well, they must lower its price—especially if they cut the price at one store and see sales increase, for example. Data mining thus allows retailers to respond to consumer buying patterns.

Did you ever wonder how Amazon or Netflix can suggest items that fit your taste? Or how such Web sites automatically display lists of items people bought after they ordered the camera you just picked out? Data mining can keep track of the purchases customers are making, along with their geographic data, past buying history, and lists of items they examined but did not purchase. This can be translated into extremely specific marketing that is immediate and customized to your shopping experience. This is the motivation behind all of the discount cards that grocery stores and drugstores offer. In exchange for tracking your personal buying habits, they offer you some kind of special pricing. How much is your private information worth?

Arts: Ink, Paints, and a Laptop? Some design students think that because they're studying art, there is no reason for them to study computers. However, unless you plan to be a "starving artist," you'll probably want to sell your work. To do so, you'll need to showcase your designs and artistic creations so that prospective employers/customers can view them. Wouldn't it be helpful if you knew how to manage a Web site like the one shown in Figure 1.16?

Using computers in the arts and entertainment fields goes far beyond using the Internet. Dance and music programs like the ones at the Atlanta Ballet and the Juilliard School of Music use computers to create new performances for audiences. A live dancer can be wired with sensors that are connected to a computer that captures

Using computers in the arts and entertainment fields goes far beyond using the Internet.

the dancer's movements. Based on the data it collects, the computer generates a virtual dancer on a screen. The computer

MADELEINEHIGHLAND

"ONLINE PORTFOLIO"

NEW FASHION ILLUSTRATION: LOOKING TO THE PAST

Often when I'm feeling creative block take hold, I'll look at fashion from the early couture masters, such as Paul Poiret, Mariano Fortuny, and Chanel. This particular garment was inspired by a 1930's Chanel evening wear ensemble.

Figure 1.16

Artists/designers such as Madeleine Highland use Web sites to showcase their creations (**http://madeleinehighland.wordpress.com**).

operator can easily manipulate this virtual dancer, as well as change the dancer's costume, with the click of a mouse. This allows artists to create new experiences for the audience.

Of course, not all artwork is created using traditional materials such as paint and canvas. Many artists today work exclusively with computers. Mastery of software programs such as Adobe Illustrator, Adobe

Photoshop, and Corel Painter is essential to creating digital art.

Other artists are pushing the envelope of creating art with computers even further. For example, MacArthur Fellow and artist Camille Utterback uses a computer to create works of art that react to the presence—and the absence—of movement of the viewers in the gallery. When no one is near the art piece, the image paints a small

Today's teachers need to be at least as computer savvy as their students.

series of dots. However, as onlookers in the gallery move closer to the work, a camera mounted on the ceiling of the art gallery captures the onlookers' movements and dimensions. A computer with specialized software then uses this captured data to create smears of color and patterns of lines that reflect their movements. Because the image itself is created from the current and past movements and sizes of the gallery patrons, the work looks different each time it is viewed. You can learn more about Utterback's digital art at **www.macfound.org**.

Video Game Design: A Long Way from Pac-Man Revenues from video game sales in the United States are now larger than the movie industry's box office. Computer games sold more than 273 million units in 2009, and rapid growth is projected to continue over the next decade. The field is competitive, and games must be creative to grab their audience. Large-scale games are

impossible to create on your own—you must be part of a team. The good news is that because computer games are best developed for a local market by people native to that market, game development will most likely stay in the United States instead of being **offshored** (sent to other countries), as many other types of programming jobs have been.

You'll need an in-depth knowledge of computers to pursue a career in game programming or as a gaming artist. Mastering software animation tools, such as Autodesk 3ds Max, will enable you to create compelling new worlds and new characters like those in the story-driven role-playing game Final Fantasy XIII (see Figure 1.17).

Education: Teaching and Learning Today's teachers need to be at least as computer savvy as their students. Computers are part of most schools, even preschools. In fact, at many colleges, students are required to have their own computers. Courses are designed around course management software such as Blackboard or Moodle, so that students can communicate outside of class, take quizzes online, and find their class materials easily. Teachers must, therefore, have a working knowledge of computers to integrate computer technology into the classroom effectively.

The Internet has obvious advantages in the classroom as a research tool for students, and effective use of the Internet allows teachers to expose students to places students otherwise could not access. There are simulations and instructional software programs on the Web that are incredible learning tools. Teachers can employ these products to give students a taste of running a global business (see Figure 1.18) or provide the experience of the Interactive Body (**bbc.co.uk/science/humanbody**).

Many museums have virtual tours on their Web sites that allow students to examine objects in the museum collections. The Art Project is one collaboration of several museums that allows online visitors to explore over a thousand pieces of art using the same technology employed in Google Street View. A custom viewer lets visitors zoom into the artwork itself at high resolution (see Figure 1.19). The information panel takes you to related videos and other related Web sites. So, even if you teach in Topeka, Kansas, you can take your students on a virtual tour of the Tate Britain in London.

Figure 1.17

Using powerful software, game developers can create complex worlds and characters to satisfy even the most demanding gamer.

Serah, come with me. Your family's waiting.

Courtesy of Square Enix

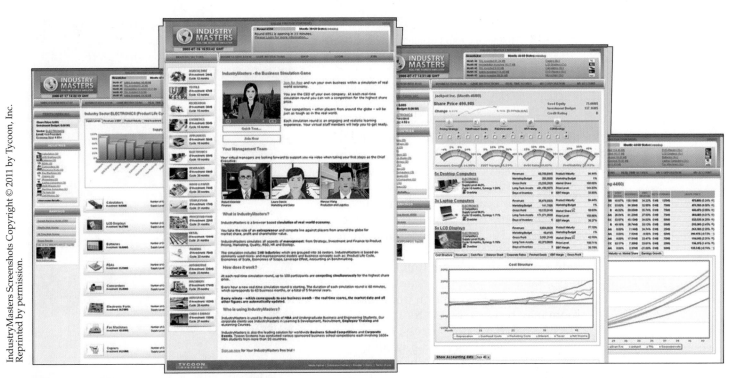

Figure 1.18

Internet applications have become sophisticated learning resources. For example, IndustryMasters (**www
.industrymasters.com**) allows students to compete online for domination of a global market while giving instructors
the chance to introduce many business concepts.

But what about when you want to take
your students to visit museums in person?
Today, technology is often used to enhance
visitors' experiences at museums. New
York's Museum of Modern Art (MoMA),
for example, offers a full range of options
for tech-savvy visitors: old-fashioned museum audio guides, podcasts you can listen

to with your smartphone, and multimedia
tours that you can download through
MoMA WiFi (**www.moma.org**) to your
own MP3 device such as a Zune or an
iTouch. These multimedia guides let you
listen to music that the artist listened to
when he or she was creating a particular
work or look at other works that reflect

Figure 1.19

The Art Project presents you with an interactive
walk through several museums. Thousands of
pieces of work are displayed in high resolution
with a pullout information panel (**www.googleart-
project.com**).

Figure 1.20

Multimedia tours using mobile devices and wireless technology are commonplace in museums and galleries.

similar techniques or themes to those of the one you're viewing (see Figure 1.20). While looking at works by more modern artists, you can watch interviews with the artist explaining his or her motivation for the work. You can even connect quickly to other members of your group and direct them to specific works you want them to see. Being literate with technology may help make your museum tour even more memorable.

Computerized education in the classroom may prove to be the tool that helps teachers reach greater success, despite increasing class sizes and tightening financial constraints. The Khan Academy (**www.khanacademy.org**) is a terrific example. Salman Khan was an investment analyst in Boston five years ago when he began to post videos to YouTube to teach algebra to his young cousins in New Orleans. Today his nonprofit Khan Academy contains over 2,200 videos, and over a million students a month use the site.

Part of the design of the Khan Academy is to use automated testing following each video series. Because the problems are automatically generated and graded, students can easily be fed similar problems until they show mastery by getting 10 in a row correct. This lets each student get repetitive drilling on just the areas they need to improve. The classroom teacher can follow what is happening in the classroom by using a dashboard (shown in Figure 1.21), a screen that shows which topics each student has mastered, which they are making progress with, and which have them spinning their wheels. Now a teacher can approach a student already knowing exactly what is frustrating them, avoiding the dreaded question, "Oh, what don't you understand?"

As an educator, being computer literate will help you integrate computer technologies like these constructively into lesson plans and interactions for your students.

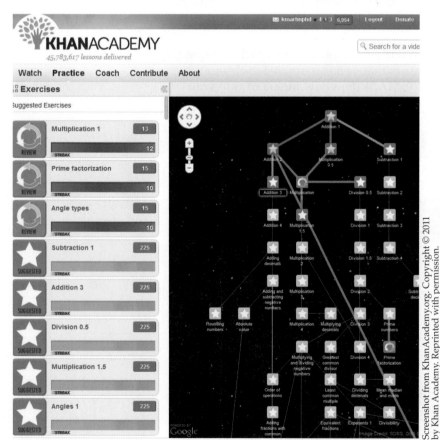

Figure 1.21

The Dashboard of the Khan Academy shows exactly which topics a student has mastered and where he or she is failing to progress.

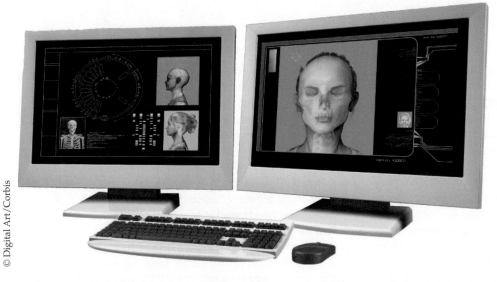

© Digital Art/Corbis

Figure 1.22
Tissue-rendering programs then add layers of muscles, fat, and skin to create faces that can be used to identify victims.

Law Enforcement: Put Down That Mouse—You're Under Arrest! Today, wearing out shoe leather to solve crimes is far from the only method available to investigators trying to catch criminals. Computers are being used in police cars and crime labs to solve an increasing number of crimes. For example, facial reconstruction systems like the one shown in Figure 1.22 can turn a skull into a finished digital image of a face, allowing investigators to proceed far more quickly with identification.

One technique used by modern detectives to solve crimes uses computers to search the vast number of databases on the Internet. Proprietary law enforcement databases such as the National Center for the Analysis of Violent Crime database enable detectives to analyze a wealth of information about similarities between crimes in an attempt to detect patterns that may reveal serial crimes. Where the law permits, detectives can also use their knowledge of wireless networking to intercept and read a criminal suspect's e-mail messages and chat sessions when he or she is online, all from the comfort of a car parked outside the suspect's home.

As detective work goes more high tech, so, too, does crime. To fight modern crime, a law enforcement specialty called computer forensics is growing. **Computer forensics** analyzes computer systems with specific techniques to gather potential legal evidence. For example, in 2009 Steven Zirko was convicted for two Chicago-area murders based on computer forensics work. FBI-trained computer forensics examiners scoured Zirko's computer and located searches for terms like "hire a hit-man" and "GHB," the date rape drug. Zirko

also had used his computer to find the daily schedule for his victim's two school-aged children and to get directions to her home. This case is one of many solved by the use of computer forensics techniques. In many cases, files, videos, and conversations conducted using a computer can be recovered by forensics specialists and used as evidence of criminal activity.

Computer forensics analyzes computer systems with specific techniques to gather potential legal evidence.

Computers are also used in training law enforcement officers to be more effective. For example, the Federal Bureau of Investigation (FBI) and the Transportation Security Administration (TSA) use computer-based training to teach officers to recognize lies and evasive behavior. Dr. Paul Ekman has spent a career studying *microexpressions*, brief (1/25th of a second) flashes of emotion. When a person is being deceptive, microexpressions, which cannot be controlled, reveal true emotions in his or her body language. The Microexpression Training Tool software system (**www.paulekman.com**), a program developed by Ekman's company, trains users to recognize emotions such as fear, disgust,

We are familiar with digital data—comfortable with carrying around music, some files, contact lists, and calendars. But where is your data when you need it? Today, your information is locked in your cell phone, your tablet computer, or your notebook computer. This mobility is revolutionary compared to the access of any prior generations, but it still requires you to take out your notebook, open it up, boot it up, and initiate a request for information. What lies ahead?

The Media Lab of MIT provides some great clues. The Fluid Interfaces group works to develop new tools to bring our data more directly into the physical world. One of the most promising of these new tools is called SixthSense (see Figure 1.23). It is a wearable device hanging around your neck consisting of a camera, a projector, and a mirror that can communicate with the Internet over wireless Bluetooth via the cell phone in your pocket. What SixthSense can do is augment your experience of reality by adding the information you need as you need it.

Say you are on your way to the airport and pull out your boarding pass. SixthSense uses pattern recognition to realize you are holding an airline ticket. It then goes out to the Internet to check if the flight is on time or if a gate change has been issued. If the flight is going to be late, the words "Delayed: 20 Minutes" would suddenly appear on the top of the boarding pass. The information is no longer trapped in your mobile device—it is part of your environment. Or say you are in a bookstore and select the title *Ambient Findability*. As you hold the book, its Amazon rating appears on the cover. You open to the inside sleeve, and the comments from readers at Amazon begin to scroll over the page. Then you can tap any one of those comments for more detail.

SixthSense is the product of work by Pranav Mistry and his advisor Patti Maes. The product can also respond to gestures, so when you make a rectangle with your fingers, it takes a photograph. When you reach your destination, any flat surface such as a wall or table can be used to "dump" your photos into a "pile." Using your hands, you can shuffle the images, or resize or rotate an image. Or draw a watch-sized circle on your wrist, and SixthSense displays an analog watch face on your arm.

Figure 1.23

SixthSense recognizes what information you need added to your environment and displays it automatically.

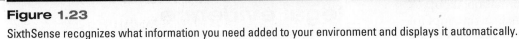

contempt, and anger in these flashes of microexpressions. You can try the online demo to see if you are a "natural," one of the rare people who can recognize and read emotion without training.

Medicine: The Chip Within When you mention implanting technology into the human body, some people conjure up images of the Terminator, a futuristic cybernetic life form from the movie *The Terminator*. But the more realistic goals of modern biomedical chip research are to provide technological solutions to physical problems and to provide a means for positively identifying individuals.

We are at a stage when biology and technology are fusing. Figure 1.26 shows a nerve cell grown on a silicon chip. The cell was cultured on the chip until it formed a network with nearby cells. The chip contains a transistor that stimulates the cell above it, which in turn passes the signal to neighboring neurons.

In fact, your hand is as good a flat surface as any to SixthSense (see Figure 1.24). Need to make a phone call? SixthSense will display a keypad on your palm. Tap out the number on the virtual keypad, and one touch of the red CALL button that appears on your palm places your call.

The shirt of the person walking toward you will also work as a projection surface. When a person walks up to us, we don't often pull out our cell phone and Google them before speaking, but as a person approaches a SixthSense wearer, it recognizes their face, heads off to their Facebook page or blog, and scans the most recent entries. It then projects the keywords that describe the person and their interests on their clothing as you watch them approach.

Currently SixthSense is small but not very stylish. The product is constructed from off-the-shelf components costing about $350. Within a few years its inventors believe it can be produced as a button-sized device, costing less than a cell phone costs now. You can monitor the progress of this device at **www.pranavmistry.com/projects/sixthsense**.

There are a number of smartphone apps available right now that use the integrated compass and camera of the phone to add information to your environment. New York Nearest Subway is a $2 app that "augments" reality. **Augmented reality** is a combination of our normal sense of the objects around us with an overlay of information displayed. The image seen through the camera's lens provides a baseline, and additional information can be displayed over the image (see Figure 1.25).

This kind of direct integration of digital information with the physical world around us is a hallmark of our digital future. Augmented reality combines the digital information we have accumulated in an immediate and spontaneous manner. So where will your new reality take you?

Figure 1.25
Augmented reality apps let you look through your phone's camera and see the world with extra information superimposed.

Figure 1.24
Any surface can become an input device using SixthSense.

One potential application of biomedical chip implants is to provide sight to the blind. Macular degeneration and retinitis pigmentosa are two diseases that account for the majority of blindness in developing nations. Both diseases result in damage to photoreceptors in the retina. (Photoreceptors convert light energy into electrical energy that is transmitted to the brain, allowing us to see.) Researchers at MIT and the Boston Retinal Implant Project are experimenting

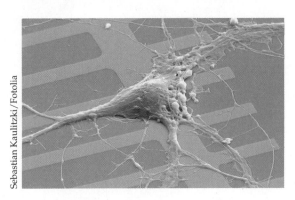

Figure 1.26
Researchers are working on creating implantable chips to repair damaged nerves and restore movement and sensation to parts of the body.

NASA Wants You . . . to Learn

As you read this chapter, hundreds of satellites are orbiting the globe and taking wonderfully detailed pictures of Earth. Until recently, these photos weren't available to the general public. However, thanks to NASA (and U.S. taxpayer dollars) and some savvy software developers, an application called World Wind is now making some 10 trillion bytes of imagery available to you. Do you need a picture of Mount Fuji for your science project or an aerial picture of your house for your PowerPoint presentation? Just download the software from learn.arc.nasa.gov, and you're ready to go. You'll find several terrific learning applications here as well. Virtual Lab lets you pretend you have your own scanning electron microscope, and Moonbase Alpha is a game built off of the Unreal engine, complete with 3D graphics, team play, and the ability to do in-play chatting. With a few clicks, you can have interactive learning resources that open the world to you.

with a microchip that would attach to the outside of the eye. The chip would take over processing from damaged photoreceptors and transmit electrical images to the brain. Biomedical chips such as these exemplify the types of medical devices you may "see" in the future.

One type of chip is already being implanted in humans as a means of verifying a person's identity. Produced by Positive ID and called *VeriMed*, this "personal ID chip" is about the size of a grain of rice and is implanted under the skin. When exposed to radio waves from a scanning device, the chip emits a signal that transmits its unique serial number to the scanner. The scanner then connects to a database that contains the name, address, and medical conditions of the person in whom the chip has been implanted.

The creators of VeriMed envision it helping keep Alzheimer's patients safe and being used with other devices (such as electronic ID cards) to provide tamperproof security measures. If someone stole your credit card, that person couldn't use it if a salesclerk had to verify your identity by scanning a chip in your arm before authorizing a transaction.

Currently, nonimplant versions of identity chips are used in hospitals. When chips are attached with bands to newborn infants, the hospital staff can monitor the location of any baby instantly. Elevators and doors are designed to allow only certain people to enter with a specific baby, even if the hospital power is interrupted. Although the use of these tags is becoming more common-

Figure 1.27

No bigger than the period at the end of this sentence, the Hitachi µ-chip can hold digital information, which can then be read when it passes a detector.

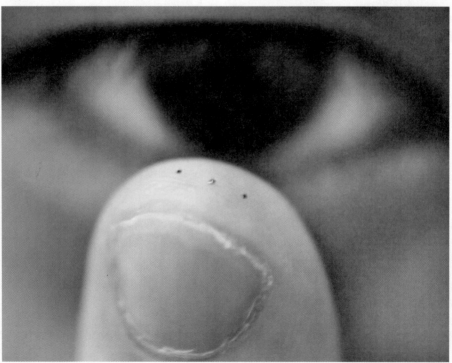

REUTERS/Eriko Sugita/Landov

...it remains to be seen whether people generally will decide that the advantages of having personal identity and medical data quickly available justifies having chips implanted into their bodies.

place, it remains to be seen whether people generally will decide that the advantages of having personal identity and medical data quickly available justifies having chips implanted into their bodies.

Hitachi has a similar device, called the μ-*chip* ("mu chip"), which is smaller than the period at the end of this sentence (see Figure 1.27). Those concerned with privacy issues worry because the μ-chip could be easily attached to, or ingested by, a person without his or her knowledge. On the other hand, researchers are excited by the possibility of using the μ-chip to monitor the safety of the food supply chain and how it might be mixed into paints to monitor heat and moisture conditions and be embedded in paper and plastics.

Science: Simulating Reality Thanks to a partnership between the National Severe Storms Lab and the National Center for Supercomputing Applications, tornado forecasting may be getting more accurate (see Figure 1.28). Scientists have been able to create a model so detailed that it takes nine days for a supercomputer to generate it, even though the computer is executing 4 trillion operations each second. Simulations also can model the structure of solar magnetic flares, which can interfere with broadcasts on Earth. By studying the data produced by these simulations, forecasters hope to improve their predictions about weather phenomena.

Other technological applications in the sciences are being used on some of the oldest sites on Earth. The ancient site of Pompeii has been under the intense scrutiny of tourists and archaeologists for decades. Sadly, decades of foot traffic and hundreds of years of exposure to the elements have eroded portions of the ruins. Today, scientists are using three-dimensional scanners and imaging software to capture a detailed record of the current condition of the ruins. The virtual re-creation of the ruins is so lifelike that archaeologists can study the ruins on screen instead of at the actual site. Using the scans as well as satellite imagery, aerial photography, and other

Figure 1.28

Software that combines radar information in new ways increases the accuracy of tornado predictions and allows for earlier warning of threatened towns.

Figure 1.29

Robots with articulated joints that mimic human limbs can balance, stand, walk, and even hug.

us to explore the nature of being human and the nature of machines.

Psychologists and computer scientists are jointly conducting research to develop computer systems that respond to human affect and emotional expression, as well as enable computer systems to develop social and emotional skills. **Affective computing** is computing that relates to emotion or deliberately tries to influence emotion. Most computers you are familiar with can perform calculations and do the tasks they are programmed for much faster than humans can, but they fail miserably in telling a good joke or modifying their behavior based on your frustration. This wide gap in the computing abilities of computers versus their emotional abilities is the target of research in affective computing.

One project to emerge is the emotional-social prosthesis (ESP) device developed by a group at the MIT Media Lab. The ESP system is targeted at helping people who have autism. Autistic individuals can have extremely high intelligence, but do not easily sense nonverbal cues such as facial expressions and tone of voice. ESP is a wearable system that isolates the movements and facial expressions of people, interprets what their mood and intention probably are, and communicates this information back to the user.

Another project at the Media Lab will help people who have difficulty maintaining focus on a specific task. This project centers on the creation of computer systems

data, scientists will eventually be able to re-create missing portions of the ruins in a virtual model. And scientists won't stop at Pompeii. This method will soon be used to make records of other decaying sites.

Psychology: You Should Smile . . . Now Science fiction shows and movies such as *Transformers* have always been populated with robots that emulate humans, seemingly effortlessly. So, when will we have Bumblebee, C-3PO, or the Terminator laughing at our jokes or bringing us our favorite snack when they recognize we're sad? It is a question that pushes

that can analyze a person's movements, watch how the person uses the mouse, and interpret the pressure patterns on the chair in which the person is seated. That data is used to determine the individual's level of attention. The computer could then interrupt an individual who is beginning to lose concentration and refocus him or her on a certain task.

While engineers work to create computers that can understand us emotionally, psychologists and computer scientists are also working to evolve systems toward a more human appearance (see Figure 1.29). A human-like robot named Robonaut 2 (R2) is a permanent resident of the Interna-

SOUND BYTE

The History of the Personal Computer

In this Sound Byte, you will explore the history of the personal computer, including the events that led to the development of today's computers and the people who made them possible.

tional Space Station (see Figure 1.30). The R2 has a torso, two arms, and two hands. Developed jointly by General Motors and NASA, it can use the same tools as station astronauts.

Figure 1.30

R2 works side by side with astronauts in space.

Image courtesy of NASA

1. **Beyond just personal goals, what impact can you have on the world?**

   Your own goals of increasing your personal knowledge and improving your career options will be met by mastering the material here. But skill and knowledge of technology can do more—it can allow you to impact the world at large.

2. **How can becoming proficient with technology help you understand and participate in important issues in the world at large?**

   Whether it is political issues, environmental issues, or questions addressing the global digital divide, it is important that you become proficient with technology to be able to participate in the discussion. Technology can be the means by which you find your voice in the world and impact others in meaningful ways, as we see happening in many examples from around the world.

3. **How can knowledge of technology help you impact the direction of our society?**

   Technology is changing how we think, how we connect with each other, and how we purchase and consume products and services. You can become a creator of new pieces of music, connect with people from around the world, and collaborate to create or consume by using current technology.

4. **What does it mean to be "computer literate"?**

   Computer literacy goes beyond knowing how to use a mouse and send e-mail. If you are computer literate, you understand the capabilities and limitations of computers and know how to use them wisely. Being computer literate also enables you to make informed purchasing decisions, use computers in your career, and understand the many ethical, legal, and societal implications of technology today. Anyone can become computer literate.

5. **How does being computer literate make you a savvy computer user and consumer?**

   By understanding how a computer is constructed and how its various parts function, you'll be able to get the most out of your computer. Among other things, you'll be able to avoid hackers, viruses, and Internet headaches; protect your privacy; and separate the real risks of privacy and security from those you don't have to worry about. You'll also be better able to maintain, upgrade, and troubleshoot your computer; make good purchasing decisions; and incorporate the latest technologies into your existing equipment.

6. **How can becoming computer literate help you in a career?**

   As computers become more a part of our daily lives, it is difficult to imagine any career that does not use computers in some fashion. Understanding how to use computers effectively will help you be a more productive and valuable employee, no matter which profession you choose.

Companion Website

The Companion Website includes a variety of additional materials to help you review and learn more about the topics in this chapter. Go to: *www.pearsonhighered.com/techinaction*

key terms

one  buzzwords

Word Bank

- affective computing
- augmented reality
- autonomy
- collaborative consumption
- computer literate

- creative surplus
- crisis mapping tools
- crowdsourcing
- data mining
- digital divide

- information technology (IT)
- mastery
- purpose
- social networking

Instructions: Fill in the blanks using the words from the Word Bank above.

Technology allows each of us to become a powerful force in changing the world. It might be that we use (1) _____ to help during a time of unexpected disaster. Perhaps we can help address the gap between those with easy access to technology and those with limited access, the (2) _____, using modern tools. We are all much more connected through the development of (3) _____ systems. Because we can share our skills and knowledge so easily, the (4) _____ available is producing even more tools and free software. There is an increasing incentive to use (5) _____ to reduce pressures on the environment and share the use of objects. Technology is also helping those with social disabilities as new tools from the area of (6) _____ help people integrate better into society. (7) _____ is growing as we are blending the information available to us directly into our environment with tools like SixthSense. Our understanding of human motivation is becoming more refined so we can capitalize on the things that engage people, to use and create solutions. (8) _____, a sense of independence; (9) _____, the ability to improve your skill level; and (10) _____, the drive to help beyond just your own immediate needs, are forces that will direct us toward solving the challenges we face locally, socially, and globally.

becoming computer literate

Using the key terms and ideas you learned in this chapter, write a one- or two-paragraph summary for your younger brother to motivate him to learn more than just how to log in to Xbox Live. Discuss the importance of being computer literate to address global and social concerns. Discuss how your brother's career will need him to become computer literate. Using the Internet, find additional examples to support your position.

Instructions: Answer the multiple-choice and true–false questions below for more practice with key terms and concepts from this chapter.

Multiple Choice

1. Which is NOT a technology that has been used to deliver assistance during times of crisis?
   a. Ushahidi   b. QR codes
   c. SwiftRiver   d. e-mail

2. Artists interface with technology often, but cannot yet
   a. use computers to generate images that respond to the environment.
   b. use computers to create a virtual storefront.
   c. use software to suggest plot endings.
   d. use software to create and enhance virtual performances.

3. People who do not read emotion easily in others hope for new progress in the field of
   a. affective computing.
   b. data mining.
   c. bioprinting.
   d. forensic science.

4. Studies reveal that human motivation is fostered by
   a. increasing levels of mastery.
   b. the ability to self-direct.
   c. directing your work toward a higher goal than just your own needs.
   d. all of the above.

5. Collaborative consumption is when people get together to
   a. find the best prices on products.
   b. exchange reviews on services and goods they have purchased.
   c. fight diseases of the respiratory tract.
   d. increase the use of a single product by sharing access to it.

6. Social networking tools
   a. played a part in revolutions in 2011.
   b. are limited to social dating.
   c. have encouraged increased censorship in the United States.
   d. include software like Microsoft Office and Adobe Illustrator.

7. Computer forensics uses computer systems and technology to
   a. simulate a person's anatomical system.
   b. train law enforcement officers to be more effective.
   c. create a crisis map.
   d. gather potential legal evidence.

8. IT is the abbreviation for
   a. information training.
   b. Internet training.
   c. Internet technology.
   d. information technology.

9. Which of the following allows retailers to respond to consumer buying patterns?
   a. RFID tags
   b. data mining
   c. smart labels
   d. Bluetooth technology

10. The crisis of a growing digital divide is being addressed by
    a. Ushahidi.
    b. the Next Einstein project.
    c. the Freecycle program.
    d. building faster computers.

True-False

_____ 1. Researchers believe that microchips may one day restore sight to the blind.

_____ 2. QR codes let companies track your past purchases and customize offers for you.

_____ 3. Supercomputers can accurately forecast tornadoes within minutes.

_____ 4. Criminal investigators may find evidence on a computer, but that evidence cannot be used in court.

_____ 5. Many modern museums offer WiFi networks and multimedia downloads to their patrons to enrich their experience.

making the transition to... next semester

1. Computer Literacy

In your college career, you'll be spending time understanding the requirements of the degree program you choose. At many schools, computer literacy requirements exist either as incoming requirements (skills students must have before they are admitted) or as outgoing requirements (skills students must prove they have before graduating). Does your program require specific computer skills? Which skills are these? Should they be required? How can students efficiently prove that they have these skills? How often does the set of skills need to be reviewed and updated?

2. The Mind of the Mob

Crowdsourcing is the gathering of data in real time, as it happens, from a growing crowd of people. Because of the large number of students who now own phones with Internet access, crowdsourcing on campus could start to be useful. In what settings would making decisions based on information from a gathering crowd on campus be valuable? How would you react to your professor using a form of crowdsourcing to determine your grade on an essay?

3. Mobile Push

A mobile application called Keyring allows you to download and store all the rewards program cards you use for the supermarket, Best Buy, the pharmacy, and so on. You can quickly scan from your phone "card" to the register at checkout and also let the companies push coupons and information to you. Would a system like this be useful on your campus? What kind of information could the college push to your mobile device that would be helpful?

4. Recycle, Repair, Redistribute

The Microsoft authorized refurbisher program and TechSoup both help provide re-sources to people in need to reduce the barrier of the digital divide. These organiza-tions recycle hardware and supply software inexpensively to needy families. How could a program be set up at your school to make people aware of these options? Could students donate materials or retrofit systems as part of their coursework? As part of a club activity? How could you make these programs work for your community?

5. Military Computing

Review the computer science programs at the U.S. Air Force Academy (**www.usafa.af.mil**), the U.S. Military Academy at West Point (**www.usma.edu**), and the U.S. Naval Academy (**www.usna.edu**). What specific courses or paths of study do these institutions have that are specific to military settings? What information do the departments' Web sites provide on why an understanding of computers matters to the military? How would this training support a transition from a military career to the civilian workplace?

1. The Productivity Paradox

In this chapter, we highlighted several careers that require computer skills. With all of the advancements in computing technology, you might expect to see a great rise in workforce productivity, yet statistics since 2004 report a decline in productivity. How is this possible? Do you think it applies in the profession you are in or plan to enter? Can you think of reasons for which the increased use of computers would decrease productivity? How has the shift toward more technology in your personal life impacted you? Are you more or less productive there? How do computers affect creativity?

2. Patients and Medical Computing

There are some major changes in the flow of medical information that impact patients every day. As more hospitals and doctor's offices begin to use electronic medical records (EMRs), the flow of information among the different doctors and care facilities a patient uses could become much more reliable. In their training and work, doctors and nurses rely on computers. What about patients? Examine Google Health at **health .google.com** for an example of an electronic medical history. How does this migration from a traditional paper records system impact the skills required for medical office workers? New ethical questions also often arise when technology changes. How would a medical facility now protect and verify its data records? What risks are there with a product like Google Health?

3. Retail: Dare to Compare

Companies often must balance both online and "bricks and mortar" environments now. What uses of QR codes would be attractive to a company selling products to 18- to 25-year-olds? How can a company best price merchandise competitively knowing that customers are using resources like PriceGrabber (**www.pricegrabber.com**)?

4. Viral Advertising

With the widespread use of video on the Web, many companies find it essential to have an online video presence to generate interest in their products. A very successful strategy is to build a series of videos, all interrelated pieces of a single story, and "leak" them one by one, building excitement by word of mouth. Heineken brewers had a very successful campaign that went "viral," ending with a short video, *The Entrance*. Find other examples of successful use of video viral marketing. What would be the required skill set for someone interested in a career in viral marketing?

5. Social Media Careers

With the explosion of users on social media sites, businesses need to establish their presence on social media sites. Just search for "Vans" or "Starbucks" on Facebook for examples of company sites. To manage their interaction with customers (and fans), companies need to hire social media managers. Using a job site such as **Monster.com**, search on "social media manager" and review the job postings. What are the educational requirements for social media managers? What technical skills do these jobs require? Given your major, what companies would you do well for as a social media manager? What steps should you take while in school to prepare yourself for a career as a social media manager?

6. Portfolio of Electronic Skills

Job seekers want to highlight their skills for prospective employers—show employers both what they can do right now to contribute and provide evidence that they can learn quickly and grow into new technologies and new responsibilities. What skills could you place in a portfolio to demonstrate your current mastery of computer concepts and computer applications? How would you document for your employer your ability to learn, quickly adapt to changes in technology, and acquire new skills?

chapter **one**one critical thinking questions

critical thinking questions

Instructions: Some ideas are best understood by experimenting with them in our own minds. The following critical thinking questions are designed to demand your full attention but require only a comfortable chair—no technology.

1. You in the World

This chapter lists many ways in which becoming computer literate is beneficial. Think of a global issue that especially calls to you. What areas of computing would be most important for you to understand in order to contribute to addressing this challenge? How would an understanding of computer hardware and software help in connecting you with the people involved and contributing your talents?

2. Interactive Art

This chapter briefly discusses the integration of computer technology and art. Pieces like *Flight Time* at the Museum of Modern Art use the vast amounts of data around us to create images and interactive exhibits that are visually exciting. What kind of design can you envision that brings the data around us into an interactive, visual experience of beauty? What computer skills would you need to acquire to make that a reality?

3. Perception of Truth

As you learned in this chapter, computer simulations are incredibly sophisticated tools. Given that the public knows that images and videos can be easily edited digitally, what role do you think simulations will play in the legal system? What impact would a simulation, a video, or an image have on a jury in deciding "truth" when the public knows that these items can be manipulated digitally?

4. . . . and Bandwidth for All

In 2010, Google announced it would select a group of communities in the United States to create an experimental fiber-optic network providing Internet connection speeds of 1 Gb/s, about 300 times the average broadband service. How would that kind of access change the way you live? How would it change the community in which you live? What new applications would be possible? Are there disadvantages you can identify? Does this program solve the digital divide or make it even more prominent?

5. Affective Computing

Affective computing is the science that attempts to produce machines that understand and can respond to human emotions and social mores. Do you think humans will ever create a machine that cannot be distinguished from a human being? In your opinion, what are the ethical and moral implications associated with that development?

6. The World Stage

How might access to (or denial of) electronic information improve the education of a country's citizens? Could that affect who the world's next technology power will be? Could it eliminate third world status? Examine the ideas behind the Next Einstein Initiative project at **www.nexteinstein.org** to explore this further. What consequence might developments in Africa have on you, your family, and your experiences?

team time

A Culture of Sharing

Problem

As more and more peer-to-peer music sharing services appeared, like BitTorrent and LimeWire, many felt a culture of theft was developing. Some argued there was a mindset among young people that property rights for intellectual works need not be respected and that people should be able to download, for free, any music, movies, or other digital content they wanted.

But there is another view of the phenomenon. Some are suggesting that the amount of constant access to each other—through texting, e-mail, blogging, and the easy exchange of digital content—has created a culture of trust and sharing. This Team Time will explore both sides of this debate in three different parts of our lives—finance, travel, and consumerism.

Task

Each of the three groups will select a different area to examine—finance, travel, or consumerism. The groups will find evidence to support or refute the idea that a culture of sharing is developing. The finance group will want to explore projects like the Grameen Bank (**www.grameenbank.com**) and Kiva (**www.kiva.org**). The travel group should examine what is happening with **www.couchsurfing.org** to start their research. The team investigating consumerism will want to take a look at goods exchange programs like Freecycle (**www.freecycle.org**).

Process

1. Divide the class into three teams.

2. Discuss the different views of a "culture of sharing." With the other members of your team, use the Internet to research up-and-coming technologies and projects that would support your position. Because people use social media tools to connect into groups to exchange ideas, does it promote trust? Does easy access to digital content promote theft, or has the value of content changed? Are there other forces like the economy and environmental state of the world that play a role in promoting a culture of sharing? What evidence can you find to support your ideas?

3. Present your group's findings to the class for debate and discussion.

4. Write a strategy paper that summarizes your position and outlines your predictions for the future. Will the pace of technology promote a change in the future from the position you are describing?

Conclusion

The future of technology is unknown, but we do know that it will impact the way our society progresses. To be part of the developments that technology will bring, no matter what area of the culture you are examining, will take good planning and attention. Begin now—learn how to stay on top of technology.

one ethics project

Should Information Be Free?

In this exercise, you will research and then role-play a complicated ethical situation. The role you play might or might not match your own personal beliefs; regardless, your research and use of logic will enable you to represent the view assigned. An arbitrator will watch and comment on both sides of the arguments, and together team members will agree on an ethical solution.

In this chapter you saw how the crisis mapping tool Ushahidi was able to collect and present information in times of political and environmental crisis. This allowed everyone to be involved in gathering the actual facts about what was happening and in helping to address very specifically the needs of people who were lost and hurt. The free exchange of information from the crowd is being used to mobilize a large number of people and provide positive action.

Problem

WikiLeaks is another example of a tool that gathers information and "frees" it by presenting it to the entire world. Whistleblowers and secret and classified media have been exposed to the world community through publication via WikiLeaks. WikiLeaks founder Julian Assange, however, is facing a range of international criminal charges.

What is the nature of information? Should it be "free"—available without censure or government controls? Is there a limit—should only certain information be free while other bits need to be kept away from the public for the greater good?

Research Areas to Consider

- WikiLeaks
- Ushahidi
- Electronic Frontier Foundation
- Government 2.0

Process

1. Divide the class into teams.

2. Research the areas cited above and devise a scenario in which information needs to be restricted.

3. Team members should write a summary that provides background information for their character—for example, a government official, an accused criminal, or an injured victim of a natural disaster—and details their character's behaviors to set the stage for the role-playing event. Then team members should create an outline to use during the role-playing event.

4. Team members should arrange a mutually convenient time to meet for the exchange, using either the chat room feature of MyITLab or the discussion board feature of Blackboard or by meeting in person.

5. Team members should present their case to the class or submit a PowerPoint presentation for review by the rest of the class, along with the summary and resolution they developed.

Conclusion

As technology becomes ever more prevalent and integrated into our lives, more and more ethical dilemmas will present themselves. Being able to understand and evaluate both sides of the argument, while responding in a personally or socially ethical manner, will be an important skill.

The History of the PC

Do you ever wonder how big the first personal computer was, or how much the first portable computer weighed? Computers are such an integral part of our lives that we don't often stop to think about how far they've come or where they got their start. In just 35 years, computers have evolved from expensive, huge machines that only corporations owned to small, powerful devices found in millions of homes. In this Technology in Focus feature, we look at the history of the computer. Along the way, we will discuss some developments that helped make the computer powerful and portable, as well as some people who contributed to its development. However, we will start with the story of the personal computer and how it grew to be as integral to our lives as the automobile is.

IN FOCUS

The First Personal Computer: The Altair

Our journey through the history of the personal computer starts in 1975. At that time, most people were unfamiliar with the mainframes and supercomputers that large corporations and the government owned. With price tags exceeding the cost of buildings, and with few if any practical home uses, these monster machines were not appealing or attainable to the vast majority of Americans. That began to change when the January 1975 cover of *Popular Electronics* announced the debut of the **Altair 8800**, touted as the first personal computer (see Figure 1). For just $395 for a do-it-yourself kit or $498 for a fully assembled unit (about $2,000 in today's dollars), the price was reasonable enough that computer fanatics could finally own their own computers.

The Altair was a very primitive computer, with just 256 bytes (not *kilo* bytes, just bytes) of memory. It didn't come with a keyboard, nor did it include a monitor or printer. Switches on the front of the machine were used to enter data in machine code (strings of 1s and 0s). Flashing lights on the front indicated the results of a program. User-friendly it was not—at least by today's standards.

Despite its limitations, computer "hackers" (as computer enthusiasts were called then) flocked to the machine. Many people who bought the Altair had been taught to program, but until that point, they had access only to big, clumsy computers. These people were often hired by corporations to program routine financial, statistical, or engineering programs in a workplace environment. The Altair offered these enthusiasts the opportunity to create their own programs. Within three months, Micro Instrumentation and Telemetry Systems (MITS), the company behind the Altair, received more than 4,000 orders for the machine.

The release of the Altair marked the start of the personal computer (PC) boom. In fact, two men who would play large roles in the development of the PC were among the first Altair owners. Recent high school graduates Bill Gates and Paul Allen were so enamored by this "minicomputer," as these personal computers were called at the time, that they

Why Was It Called the "Altair"?

For lack of a better name, the Altair's developers originally called the computer the PE-8, short for Popular Electronics 8-bit. However, Les Soloman, the *Popular Electronics* writer who introduced the Altair, wanted the machine to have a catchier name. The author's daughter, who was watching *Star Trek* at the time, suggested the name Altair. (That's where the *Star Trek* crew was traveling that week.) The first star of the PC industry was born.

AP Photo/Heinz Nixdorf Museumsforum

Figure 1

In 1975, the Altair was touted as the "world's first minicomputer" in the January issue of Popular Electronics.

wrote a compiling program (a program that translates user commands into commands that the computer can understand) for the Altair. The two friends later convinced the Altair's developer, Ed Roberts, to buy their program. This marked the start of a small company called Microsoft. We'll get to that story later. First, let's see what their future archrivals were up to.

The Apple I and II

Around the time the Altair was released, **Steve Wozniak**, an employee at Hewlett-Packard, was becoming fascinated with the burgeoning personal computer industry and was dabbling with his own computer design. He would bring his computer prototypes to meetings of the Homebrew Computing Club, a group of young computer fans in Palo Alto, California who met to discuss computer ideas. **Steve Jobs**, who was working for computer game manufacturer Atari at the time, liked Wozniak's prototypes and made a few suggestions. Together, the two built a personal computer, later known as the **Apple I**, in Wozniak's garage (see Figures 2 and 3). In that same year, on April 1, 1976, Jobs and Wozniak officially formed the **Apple Computer Company**.

No sooner had the Apple I hit the market than Wozniak began working to improve it. A year later, in 1977, the **Apple II** was born (see Figure 4). The Apple II included a color monitor, sound, and game paddles. Priced

Figure 2

(a) Steve Jobs and (b) Steve Wozniak were two computer hobbyists who worked together to form the Apple Computer Company.

Diana Walker / Getty Images

Figure 3

The first Apple computer, the Apple I, looked like a typewriter in a box. It was one of the first computers to incorporate a keyboard.

SSPL / The Image Works

around $1,300 (almost $4,700 in today's dollars), it included 4 kilobytes (KB) of random access memory (RAM) as well as an optional floppy disk drive that enabled users to run additional programs. Most of these programs were games. However, for many users, there was a special appeal to the Apple II: The program that made the computer function when the power was first turned on (the operating system) was stored in read-only memory (ROM).

Previously, the operating system had to be rewritten every time the computer was turned on. The friendly features of the operating system on the Apple II, such as automatic loading, encouraged less technically oriented computer enthusiasts to try writing their own software programs.

An instant success, the Apple II would be the most successful product in the company's early line, outshining even its successor, the **Apple III**, which was released in

SSPL / Getty Images

Figure 4

The Apple II came with a monitor and an external floppy disk drive.

1980. Eventually, the Apple II would include a spreadsheet program, a word processor, and desktop publishing software. These programs gave personal computers like the Apple functions beyond gaming and special programming, and led to their increased popularity. We will talk more about these advances later. For now, we will look at which other players were entering the market.

Enter the Competition

Around the time that Apple was experiencing success with its computers, a number of competitors entered the market. The largest among them were Commodore, RadioShack, and IBM. As Figure 5 shows, just a few years after the introduction of the Altair, the market was filled with personal computers from a variety of manufacturers.

The Commodore PET and TRS-80

Among Apple's strongest competitors were the **Commodore PET 2001**, shown in Figure 6, and Tandy RadioShack's **TRS-80**, shown in Figure 7. Commodore introduced the PET in January 1977. It was featured on the cover of *Popular Science* in October 1977 as the "new $595 home computer." Tandy RadioShack's home computer also garnered immediate popularity. Just one month after its release in 1977, the TRS-80 Model 1 had sold approximately 10,000 units. Priced at $594.95, the easy-to-use machine included a monochrome display and 4 KB of memory. Many other manufacturers followed suit over the next decade, launching new desktop computers, but none were as successful as the TRS-80 and the Commodore.

The Osborne

The Osborne Company introduced the industry's first portable computer, the **Osborne**, in April 1981 (see Figure 8). Although portable, the computer weighed 24.5 pounds, and its screen was just five inches wide. In addition to its hefty weight, it came with a hefty price tag of $1,795. Still, the Osborne included 64 KB of memory, two floppy disk drives, and preinstalled programs such as word processing and spreadsheet software. The Osborne was an overnight success, and its sales quickly reached 10,000 units per month. Despite the Osborne's popularity, the release of a successor machine, called the **Executive**, reduced sales of the Osborne significantly, and the Osborne Company eventually closed. Compaq bought the Osborne design and in 1983 produced its first portable computer.

Figure 5 | PERSONAL COMPUTER DEVELOPMENT

YEAR	APPLE	IBM	OTHER
1975			MITS Altair
1976	Apple I		
1977	Apple II		Tandy RadioShack's TRS-80 Commodore PET
1980	Apple III		
1981		IBM PC	Osborne
1983	Lisa		
1984	Macintosh	286-AT	IBM PC clones

Why Is It Called "Apple"?

Steve Jobs wanted Apple Computer to be the "perfect" computer company. Having recently worked at an apple orchard, Jobs thought of the apple as the "perfect" fruit because it was high in nutrients, came in a nice package, and was not easily damaged. Thus, he and Wozniak decided to name their new computer company Apple.

IBM PCs

By 1980, IBM recognized that it needed to get its feet wet in the personal computer market. Up until that point, the company had been a player in the computer industry, but primarily made mainframe computers, which it sold only to large corporations. It had not taken the smaller personal computer seriously. In August 1981, however, IBM released its first personal computer, appropriately named the **IBM PC**. Because many companies were already familiar with IBM mainframes, they readily adopted the IBM PC. The term *PC* soon became the term used to describe all personal computers.

Figure 6

The Commodore PET was well received because of its all-in-one design.

Jerry Mason / SPL / Photo Researchers, Inc.

Figure 7

The TRS-80 hid its circuitry under the keyboard. The computer was nicknamed "trash-80," which was more a play on its initials than a reflection of its capabilities.

Courtesy of the Computer History Museum

The IBM PC came with 64 KB of memory, expandable to 256 KB, and prices started at $1,565. IBM marketed its PC through retail outlets such as Sears and Computerland in order to reach the home market, and it quickly dominated the playing field. In January 1983, *Time* magazine, playing on its annual "person of the year" issue, named the computer "1982 machine of the year".

Other Important Advancements

It was not just the **hardware** of the personal computer that was developing during the 1970s and 1980s. At the same time, advances in programming languages and operating systems and the influx of application software were leading to more useful and powerful machines.

The Importance of BASIC

The software industry began in the 1950s with the development of programming languages such as FORTRAN, ALGOL, and COBOL. These languages were used mainly by businesses to create financial, statistical, and engineering programs for corporate enterprises. However, the 1964 introduction of **Beginners All-Purpose Symbolic Instruction Code (BASIC)** revolutionized the software industry. BASIC was a programming language that the beginning programming student could easily learn. It thus became enormously popular—and the key language

---

> In January 1983, Time magazine, playing on its annual "person of the year" issue, named the computer "1982 machine of the year."

Courtesy of the Computer History Museum

Figure 8

The Osborne was introduced as the first portable personal computer. It weighed a whopping 24.5 pounds and contained just 64 KB of memory.

of the PC. In fact, **Bill Gates** and **Paul Allen** (see Figure 9) used BASIC to write their program for the Altair. As we noted earlier, this program led to the creation of **Microsoft**, a company that produced software for the microcomputer.

The Advent of Operating Systems

Because data on the earliest personal computers was stored on audiocassettes (not floppy disks), many programs were not saved or reused. Rather, programs were rewritten as needed. Eventually Steve Wozniak designed a smaller 5.25-inchfloppy disk drive subsystem, called the **Disk II**, which was introduced in July 1978. With the introduction of the floppy drive, programs could be saved with more efficiency, and operating systems (OSs) developed.

Operating systems were (and still are) written to coordinate with the specific processor chip that controlled the computer. Apples ran exclusively on a Motorola chip, while PCs (IBMs and so on) ran exclusively on an Intel chip. **Disk Operating System (DOS)**, developed by Wozniak and introduced in December 1977, was the OS that controlled the first Apple computers. The **Control Program for Microcomputers (CP/M)**, developed by Gary Kildall, was the first OS designed for the Intel 8080 chip (the processor for PCs). Intel hired Kildall to write a compiling program for the 8080 chip, but Kildall quickly saw the need for a program that could store computer operating instructions on a floppy disk rather than on a cassette. Intel wasn't interested in buying the CP/M program, but Kildall saw a future for the program and thus founded his own company, Digital Research.

In 1980, when IBM was considering entering the personal computer market, it approached Bill Gates at Microsoft to write an OS program for the IBM PC. Although Gates had written versions of BASIC for different computer systems, he had never written an OS. He therefore recommended that IBM investigate the CP/M OS, but they could not arrange a meeting with the founder, Gary Kildall. Microsoft reconsidered the opportunity and developed **MS-DOS** for IBM computers. (This was one meeting that Digital Research certainly regretted not arranging.)

MS-DOS was based on an OS called **Quick and Dirty Operating System (QDOS)** that was developed by Seattle Computer Products. Microsoft bought the nonexclusive

Figure 9

Bill Gates and Paul Allen are the founders of Microsoft.

rights to QDOS and distributed it to IBM. Eventually, virtually all personal computers running on the Intel chip used MS-DOS as their OS. Microsoft's reign as one of the dominant players in the PC landscape had begun. Meanwhile, many other programs were being developed, taking personal computers to the next level of user acceptance.

The Software Application Explosion: VisiCalc and Beyond

Inclusion of floppy disk drives in personal computers not only facilitated the storage of operating systems, but also set off an application software explosion, because the floppy disk was a convenient way to distribute software. Around that same time, in 1978, Harvard Business School student Dan Bricklin recognized the potential for a spreadsheet program that could be used on PCs. He and his friend Bob Frankston (see Figure 10) created the program **VisiCalc**. VisiCalc not only became an instant success, but was also one of the main reasons for the rapid increase in PC sales. Finally, ordinary home users could see how owning a personal computer could benefit their lives. More than 100,000 copies of VisiCalc were sold in its first year.

After VisiCalc, other electronic spreadsheet programs entered the market. **Lotus 1-2-3** came on the market in January 1983, and **Microsoft Excel** entered the scene in 1985. These two products became so popular that they eventually put VisiCalc out of business.

Figure 10

Bob Frankston and Dan Bricklin created VisiCalc, the first business application developed for the personal computer.

Meanwhile, word processing software was gaining a foothold in the PC industry. Up to this point, there were separate, dedicated word processing machines, and the thought hadn't occurred to anyone to enable the personal computer to do word processing. Personal computers, it was believed, were for computation and data management. However, once **WordStar**, the first word processing application, came out in disk form in 1979 and became available for personal computers, word processing became another important use for the PC. In fact, word processing is now one of the most common PC applications. Competitors such as **Word for MS-DOS** (the precursor to Microsoft Word) and **WordPerfect** soon entered the market. Figure 11 lists some of the important dates in application software development.

The Graphical User Interface

Another important advancement in personal computers was the introduction of the **graphical user interface (GUI)**, which allowed users to interact with the computer more easily. Until that time, users had to use complicated command- or menu-driven interfaces to interact with the computer. Apple was the first company to take full commercial advantage of the GUI, but competitors were fast on its heels, and soon the GUI became synonymous with personal computers. Who developed the idea of the GUI? You'll probably be surprised to learn that a company known for its photocopiers was the real innovator.

Xerox

In 1972, a few years before Apple launched its first PC, photocopier manufacturer **Xerox** was hard at work in its Palo Alto Research Center (PARC) designing a personal computer of its own. Named the **Alto** (shown in Figure 12), the computer included a word processor, based on the What You See Is What You Get (WYSIWYG) principle, that incorporated a file management system with directories and folders. It also had a mouse and could connect to a network. None of the other personal computers of the time had any of these features. For a variety of reasons, Xerox never sold the Alto commercially. Several years later, it developed the Star Office System, which was based on the Alto. Despite its convenient features, the Star never became popular, because no one was willing to pay the $17,000 asking price.

The Lisa and the Macintosh

Xerox's ideas were ahead of its time, but many of the ideas of the Alto and Star would soon catch on. In 1983, Apple introduced the **Lisa**, shown in Figure 13. Named after Apple founder Steve Jobs's daughter, the Lisa was the first successful PC brought to market that used a GUI. Legend has it that Jobs had seen the Alto during a visit to PARC in 1979 and was influenced

Figure 11	APPLICATION SOFTWARE DEVELOPMENT
YEAR	**APPLICATION**
1978	**VisiCalc:** First electronic spreadsheet application. **WordStar:** First word processing application.
1980	**WordPerfect:** Thought even now to be the best word processing software for the PC, WordPerfect was eventually sold to Novell, and was later acquired by Corel.
1983	**Lotus 1-2-3:** Added integrated charting, plotting, and database capabilities to spreadsheet software. **Word for MS-DOS:** Introduced in the pages of PC World magazine on the first magazine-inserted demo disk.
1985	**Excel:** One of the first spreadsheets to use a graphical user interface. **PageMaker:** The first desktop publishing software.

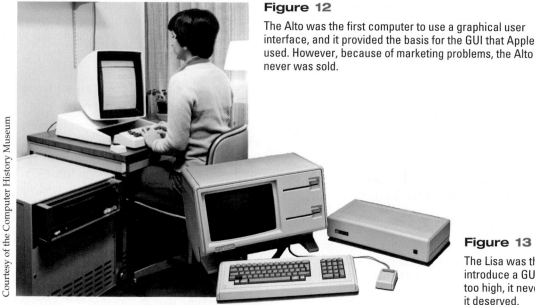

Courtesy of the Computer History Museum

SSPL / The Image Works

Figure 12

The Alto was the first computer to use a graphical user interface, and it provided the basis for the GUI that Apple used. However, because of marketing problems, the Alto never was sold.

Figure 13

The Lisa was the first computer to introduce a GUI to the market. Priced too high, it never gained the popularity it deserved.

by its GUI. He therefore incorporated a similar user interface into the Lisa, providing features such as windows, drop-down menus, icons, a hierarchical file system with folders and files, and a point-and-click device called a mouse. The only problem with the Lisa was its price. At $9,995 ($21,530 in today's dollars), few buyers were willing to take the plunge.

A year later, in 1984, Apple introduced the **Macintosh**, shown in Figure 14. The Macintosh was everything the Lisa was and then some, and at about a third of the cost. The Macintosh was also the first personal computer to utilize 3.5-inch floppy disks with a hard cover, which were smaller and sturdier than the previous 5.25-inch floppies.

The Internet Boom

The GUI made it easier for users to work on the computer. The Internet provided another reason for consumers to buy computers. Now they could conduct research and communicate with each other in a new and convenient way. In 1993, the Web browser **Mosaic** was introduced. This browser allowed users to view multimedia on the Web, causing Internet traffic to increase by nearly 350 percent.

Meanwhile, companies discovered the Internet as a means to do business, and computer sales took off.

IBM-compatible PCs became the personal computer system of choice when, in 1995, Microsoft (the predominant software provider to PCs) introduced Internet Explorer, a Web browser that integrated Web functionality into Microsoft Office applications, and **Windows 95**, the first Microsoft OS designed to be principally a GUI OS, although it still was based on DOS.

About a year earlier, in mid-1994, Jim Clark, founder of the computer company Silicon Graphics Inc., Marc Andreessen, and others from the Mosaic development

© Ed Kashi/CORBIS

Figure 14

The Macintosh became one of Apple's best-selling computers, incorporating a graphical user interface along with other innovations such as the 3.5-inch floppy disk drive.

team developed the Netscape commercial Web browser. Netscape's popularity grew quickly, and it soon became a predominant player in browser software. However, pressures from Microsoft became too strong. In the beginning of 1998, Netscape announced it was moving to the open source market, would no longer charge for the product, and would make the code available to the public.

Making the PC Possible: Early Computers

Since the first Altair was introduced in the 1970s, more than a billion personal computers have been distributed around the globe. Because of the declining prices of computers and the growth of the Internet, it's estimated that a billion more computers will be sold within the next decade. What made all of this possible? The computer is a compilation of parts, each of which is the result of individual inventions. From the earliest days of humankind, we have been looking for a

more systematic way to count and calculate. Thus, the evolution of counting machines led to the development of the computer we know today.

The Pascalene Calculator and the Jacquard Loom

The **Pascalene** was the first accurate mechanical calculator. This machine, created by the French mathematician **Blaise Pascal** in 1642, used revolutions of gears, like odometers in cars do, to count by tens. The Pascalene could be used to add, subtract, multiply, and divide. The basic design of the Pascalene was so sound that it lived on in mechanical calculators for more than 300 years.

Nearly 200 years later, **Joseph Jacquard** revolutionized the fabric industry by creating a machine that automated the weaving of complex patterns. Although not a counting or calculating machine, the **Jacquard loom** (shown in Figure 15) was significant because it relied on stiff cards with punched holes to automate the weaving process. Much later, this punch-card process would be adopted as a means for computers to record and read data.

Babbage's Engines

Decades later, in 1834, **Charles Babbage** designed the first automatic calculator, called the **Analytical Engine** (see Figure 16). The machine was actually based on another machine called the **Difference Engine**, which was a huge steam-powered mechanical calculator that Babbage designed to print astronomical tables. Babbage stopped working on the Difference Engine to build the Analytical Engine. Although it was never developed, Babbage's detailed drawings and descriptions of the Analytical Engine include components similar those found in today's computers, including the store (akin to RAM) and the mill (a central processing unit), as well as input and output devices. This invention gave Charles Babbage the title of "father of computing."

Meanwhile, Ada Lovelace, who was the daughter of poet Lord Byron and was a student of mathematics (which was unusual for women of that time), was fascinated with Babbage's Engines. She translated an Italian paper on Babbage's machine, and at the request of Babbage added her own extensive notes. Her efforts are thought to be the best description of Babbage's Engines.

Figure 15

The Jacquard loom used holes punched in stiff cards to make complex designs. This technique would later be used in punch cards that controlled the input and output of data in computers.

Courtesy of the Computer History Museum

The Hollerith Tabulating Machine

In 1890, **Herman Hollerith**, while working for the U.S. Census Bureau, was the first to take Jacquard's punch-card concept and apply it to computing. Hollerith developed a machine called the **Hollerith Tabulating Machine** that used punch cards to tabulate census data. Up until that time, census data had been tabulated manually in a long, laborious process. Hollerith's tabulating machine automatically read data that had been punched onto small punch cards, speeding up the tabulation process. Hollerith's machine became so successful that he left the Census Bureau in 1896 to start the Tabulating Machine Company. His company later changed its name to International Business Machines, or IBM.

The Z1 and the Atanasoff–Berry Computer

German inventor **Konrad Zuse** is credited with a number of computing inventions. His first, in 1936, was a mechanical calculator called the **Z1**. The Z1 is thought to be the first computer to include certain features that are integral to today's systems, such as a control unit and separate memory functions. These were important breakthroughs for future computer design.

In late 1939, John Atanasoff, a professor at Iowa State University, and his student Clifford Berry built the first electrically powered digital computer, called the **Atanasoff–Berry Computer (ABC)**, shown in Figure 17. The computer was the first to use vacuum tubes, instead of the mechanical switches used in older computers, to store data. Although revolutionary at its time, the machine weighed 700 pounds, contained a mile of wire, and took about 15 seconds for each calculation. (In comparison, today's personal computers can perform billions and billions of calculations in 15 seconds.) Most importantly, the ABC was the first computer to use the binary system. It was also the first computer to have memory that repowered itself upon booting. The design of the ABC would end up being central to that of future computers.

Figure 16

The Analytical Engine, designed by Charles Babbage, was never fully developed, but included components similar to those found in today's computers.

Courtesy of the Computer History Museum

The Harvard Mark I

From the late 1930s to the early 1950s, **Howard Aiken** and **Grace Hopper** designed the Mark series of computers at Harvard University. The U.S. Navy used these computers for ballistic and gunnery calculations. Aiken, an electrical engineer and physicist, designed the computer, while Hopper did the programming. The **Harvard Mark I**, finished in 1944, could perform all four arithmetic operations (addition, subtraction, multiplication, and division).

However, many believe Hopper's greatest contribution to computing was the invention of the **compiler**, a program that translates English-language instructions into computer language. The team was also responsible for a common computer-related expression. Hopper was the first to "debug" a computer when she removed a moth that had flown into the Harvard Mark I and

Figure 17

The Atanasoff–Berry Computer laid the design groundwork for many computers to come.

Ames Laboratory

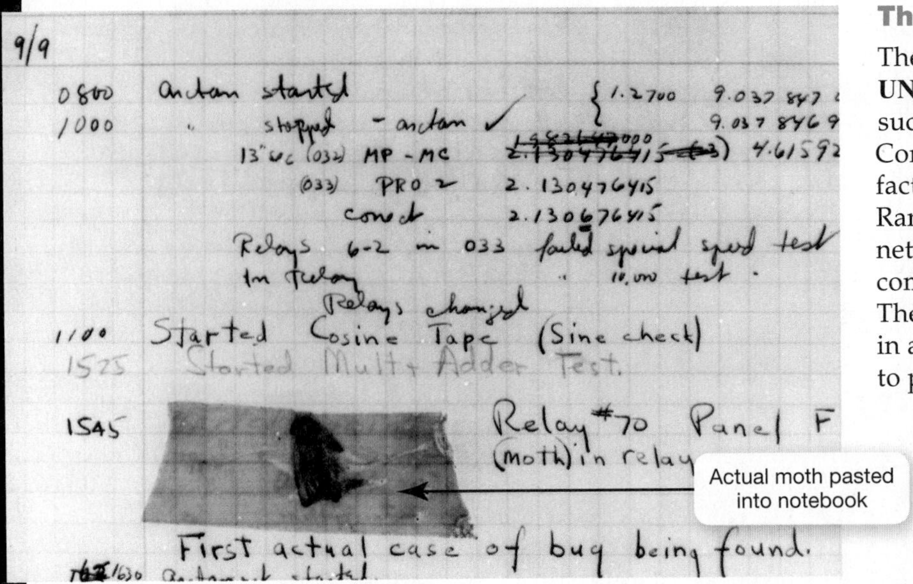

9/9

0800   anton started
1000   "   stopped – anton ✓

Actual moth pasted into notebook

First actual case of bug being found.

Figure 18
Grace Hopper coined the term computer bug when a moth flew into the Harvard Mark I, causing it to break down.

caused the computer to break down (see Figure 18). After that, problems that caused a computer not to run were called "bugs."

The Turing Machine

Meanwhile, in 1936, the British mathematician **Alan Turing** created an abstract computer model that could perform logical operations. The **Turing Machine** was not a real machine, but rather was a hypothetical model that mathematically defined a mechanical procedure (or algorithm). Additionally, Turing's concept described a process by which the machine could read, write, or erase symbols written on squares of an infinite paper tape. This concept of an infinite tape that could be read, written to, and erased was the precursor to today's RAM.

The ENIAC

The **Electronic Numerical Integrator and Computer (ENIAC)**, shown in Figure 19, was another U.S. government-sponsored machine developed to calculate the settings used for weapons. Created by **John W. Mauchly** and **J. Presper Eckert** at the University of Pennsylvania, it was placed in operation in June 1944. Although the ENIAC is generally thought of as the first successful high-speed electronic digital computer, it was big and clumsy. The ENIAC used nearly 18,000 vacuum tubes and filled approximately 1,800 square feet of floor space. Although inconvenient, the ENIAC served its purpose and remained in use until 1955.

The UNIVAC

The **Universal Automatic Computer**, or **UNIVAC**, was the first commercially successful electronic digital computer. Completed in June 1951 and manufactured by the company Remington Rand, the UNIVAC operated on magnetic tape. This set it apart from its competitors, which ran on punch cards. The UNIVAC gained notoriety when, in a 1951 publicity stunt, it was used to predict the outcome of the Stevenson–Eisenhower presidential race. After analyzing only 5 percent of the popular vote, the UNIVAC correctly identified Dwight D. Eisenhower as the victor. After that, UNIVAC soon became a household word. The UNIVAC and computers like it were considered **first-generation computers** and were the last to use vacuum tubes to store data.

Transistors and Beyond

Only a year after the ENIAC was completed, scientists at the Bell Telephone Laboratories in New Jersey invented the **transistor**, which was another means to store data. The transistor replaced the bulky vacuum tubes of earlier computers and was smaller and more powerful than tubes were. It was used in almost everything, from radios to phones. Computers that used transistors were referred to as **second-generation computers**. Still, transistors were limited as to how small they could be made.

A few years later, in 1958, **Jack Kilby**, while working at Texas Instruments, invented the world's first **integrated circuit**, a small chip capable of containing thousands of transistors. This consolidation in design enabled computers to become smaller and lighter. The computers in this early integrated-circuit generation were considered **third-generation computers**.

Other innovations in the computer industry further refined the computer's speed, accuracy, and efficiency. However, none were as significant as the 1971 introduction by the Intel Corporation of the **microprocessor chip**, a small chip containing millions of transistors. The microprocessor functions as the central processing unit (CPU), or brains, of the computer. Computers that used a microprocessor chip were called **fourth-generation computers**.

Over time, Intel and Motorola became the leading manufacturers of microprocessors. Today, the Intel Core i7 is one of Intel's most powerful processors.

As you can see, personal computers have come a long way since the Altair, and have a number of inventions and people to thank for their amazing popularity. What will the future bring? If current trends continue, computers will be smaller, lighter, and more powerful. The advancement of wireless technology will also play a big role in the development of the personal computer.

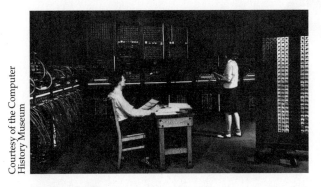

Courtesy of the Computer History Museum

Figure 19

The ENIAC took up an entire room and required several people to manipulate it.

Multiple Choice

Instructions: Answer the multiple-choice questions below for more practice with key terms and concepts from this Technology in Focus feature.

1. What was the name of the first Web browser?
   a. Mosaic
   b. Internet Explorer
   c. Netscape
   d. Firefox

2. Which programming language revolutionized the software industry?
   a. ALGOL
   b. BASIC
   c. COBOL
   d. FORTRAN

3. Why was the invention of the integrated circuit important?
   a. It enabled computers to store more data.
   b. It enabled monitors to display a better image.
   c. It enabled more processing memory.
   d. It enabled computers to become smaller and lighter.

4. Which computer is touted as the first personal computer?
   a. Altair
   b. Commodore PET
   c. Lisa
   d. Osborne

5. What was the importance of the Turing machine to today's computers?
   a. It described a system that was a precursor to today's notebook computer.
   b. It was the first electronic calculator and a precursor to the computer.
   c. It was the first computer to have a monitor.
   d. It described a process to read, write, and erase symbols on a tape and was the precursor to today's RAM.

6. Which computer first stored its operating system in ROM?
   a. Apple I
   b. Apple II
   c. Lisa
   d. Macintosh

7. What was the first word processing application?
   a. Lotus 1-2-3
   b. Word for MS-DOS
   c. WordPerfect
   d. WordStar

8. Which components are characteristic of second-generation computers?
   a. Transistors
   b. Vacuum tubes
   c. Integrated circuits
   d. Microprocessor chips

9. For what is the Atanasoff-Berry Computer best known?
   a. It was the first computer used to tabulate U.S. census data.
   b. It was the first computer to use the binary system.
   c. It was the first computer to incorporate the punch-card system.
   d. It was the first computer used as a mechanical calculator.

10. Who are the founders of Microsoft?
    a. Paul Allen and Bill Gates
    b. Bill Gates and Steve Wozniak
    c. Steve Jobs and Bill Gates
    d. Bill Gates and Gary Kildall

chapter 2

looking at computers

understanding the parts

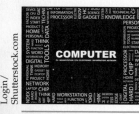
Login/Shutterstock.com

Understanding Your Computer

OBJECTIVES:

What exactly is a computer, and what are its four main functions? *(p. 52)*

What is the difference between data and information? *(p. 52)*

What are bits and bytes, and how are they measured? *(p. 52)*

 Sound Byte: Binary Numbers Interactive

 **Active Helpdesk:** Understanding Bits and Bytes

Input Devices and Output Devices

OBJECTIVES:

What devices do I use to get data into the computer? *(p. 55)*

What devices do I use to get information out of the computer? *(p. 63)*

Sound Byte: Tablet and Notebook Tour

Active Helpdesk: Using Input Devices

Active Helpdesk: Using Output Devices

© Wildcat123 | Dreamstime.com

Processing, Memory, and Storage

OBJECTIVES:

What's on the motherboard? *(p. 71)*

Where are information and programs stored? *(p. 73)*

Sound Byte: Virtual Computer Tour

© Iofoto | Dreamstime.com

Ports and Power Controls

OBJECTIVE:

How are devices connected to the computer? *(p. 75)*

 Active Helpdesk: Exploring Storage Devices and Ports

 Sound Byte: Port Tour: How Do I Hook It Up?

ImageZoo/Alamy

Setting It All Up

OBJECTIVE:

How do I set up my computer to avoid strain and injury? *(p. 79)*

Sound Byte: Healthy Computing

Scan here for more info on How Cool Is This? ▶

how cool is *this?*

The **3D experience** is pretty common at the movies, and even on some TVs, but how about on your laptop? Computer manufacturers, such as Sony, Asus, and Acer, are producing **high-end laptops** that have 3D viewing capabilities. That means that **games, photos, movies, and Web sites** can be experienced in 3D. These machines are targeted toward **gamers and 3D movie enthusiasts,** and require high-end graphics components, such as the 3D kit by NVIDIA that includes a combination of a sophisticated graphics processor unit and monitor, software, and **specialized 3D glasses** to achieve the 3D effects. If you're not thrilled with wearing those stylish glasses to enjoy the 3D special effects, then you might want to hold out for a No-Glasses 3D laptop by Toshiba, currently in the prototype stage, which uses the laptop's Web camera and eye-tracking technology to create the 3D effects.

Stockbyte/Getty Images

Understanding Your Computer

After reading Chapter 1, you can see why becoming computer literate is so important. But where do you start? You've no doubt gleaned some knowledge about computers just from being a member of society. However, although you have undoubtedly used a computer before, do you really understand how it works, what all its parts are, and what these parts do? In this section, we discuss what a computer does and how its functions make it such a useful machine.

Computers Are Data Processing Devices

Strictly defined, a **computer** is a data processing device that performs four major functions:

1. **Input:** It gathers data, or allows users to enter data.

2. **Process:** It manipulates, calculates, or organizes that data into information.

3. **Output:** It displays data and information in a form suitable for the user.

4. **Storage:** It saves data and information for later use.

What is the difference between data and information? People often use the terms *data* and *information* interchangeably. Although they may mean the same thing in a simple conversation, the actual distinction between data and information is an important one.

In computer terms, **data** is a representation of a fact, a figure, or an idea. Data can be a number, a word, a picture, or even a recording of sound. For example, the number 7135553297 and the names Zoe and Richardson are pieces of data. Alone, these pieces of data probably mean little to you.

Information is data that has been organized or presented in a meaningful fashion. When your computer provides you with a contact listing that indicates Zoe Richardson can be reached by phone at (713) 555-3297, then the previous data suddenly becomes useful—that is, it becomes information.

How do computers interact with data and information? Computers are excellent at **processing** (manipulating, calculating, or organizing) data into information. When you first arrived on campus, you probably were directed to a place where you could get an ID card. You most likely provided a clerk with personal data (such as your name and address) that was entered into a computer. The clerk then took your picture with a digital camera (collecting more data). This information was then processed appropriately so that it could be printed on your ID card (see Figure 2.1). This organized output of data on your ID card is useful information. Finally, the information was probably stored as digital data on the computer for later use.

Bits and Bytes: The Language of Computers

How do computers process data into information? Unlike humans, computers work exclusively with numbers (not words). To process data into information, computers need to work in a language they understand. This language, called **binary language**, consists of just two digits: 0 and 1. Everything a computer does, such as processing data, printing a report, or editing a photo, is broken down into a series of 0s and 1s. Each 0 and 1 is a **binary digit**, or **bit** for short. Eight binary digits (or bits) combine to create one **byte**. In computers, each letter of the alphabet, each number, and each special character (such as the @ sign) consists of a unique

Figure 2.1

Computers process data into information.

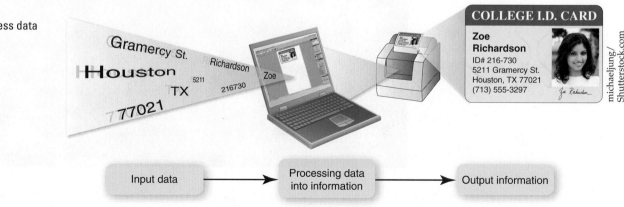

Input data → Processing data into information → Output information

COLLEGE I.D. CARD
Zoe Richardson
ID# 216-730
5211 Gramercy St.
Houston, TX 77021
(713) 555-3297

michaeljung/Shutterstock.com

combination of eight bits, or a string of eight 0s and 1s. So, for example, in binary language, the letter K is represented as 01001011. This equals eight bits, or one byte. (We discuss binary language in more detail in the Technology in Focus section "Under the Hood.")

What else can bits and bytes be used for? You've probably heard the terms *kilobyte (KB)*, *megabyte (MB)*, and *gigabyte (GB)*. Bits and bytes not only are used as the language that tells the computer what to do, but also are what the computer uses to represent the quantity of data and information that it inputs and outputs. Word processing files, digital pictures, and even software are represented inside a computer as a series of bits and bytes. These files and applications can be quite large, containing thousands or millions of bytes.

To make it easier to measure the size of these files, we need units of measure larger than a byte. Kilobytes, megabytes, and gigabytes are therefore simply amounts of bytes. As shown in Figure 2.2, a **kilobyte (KB)** is approximately 1,000 bytes, a **megabyte (MB)** is about 1 million bytes, a

gigabyte (GB) is around 1 billion bytes, and a **terabyte (TB)** is around 1 trillion bytes. As our information-processing needs have grown, so too have our storage needs. Today, personal computers are capable of storing terabytes of data, and many business computers can store up to a petabyte (one thousand terabytes) of data. The Google search engine processes more than 1 petabyte of user-generated data per *hour*—that's a lot of bytes!

How does your computer process bits and bytes? Your computer uses a combination of hardware and software to process data into information and enables you to complete tasks such as writing a letter or playing a game. An anonymous person once said that hardware is any part of a computer that you can kick when it doesn't work properly. A more formal definition of **hardware** is any part of the computer you can physically touch. However, a computer needs more than just hardware to work: It also needs some form of software (computer programs). Think of a book without words or a CD without music. Without words or music, these two common items are just shells that hold nothing.

Figure 2.2 | HOW MUCH IS A BYTE?

Name	Abbreviation	Number of Bytes	Relative Size
Byte	B	1 byte	Can hold one character of data.
Kilobyte	KB	1,024 bytes (2^{10} bytes)	Can hold 1,024 characters, or about half of a double-spaced typewritten page.
Megabyte	MB	1,048,576 bytes (2^{20} bytes)	Can hold approximately 768 pages of typed text.
Gigabyte	GB	1,073,741,824 bytes (2^{30} bytes)	This is approximately 786,432 pages of text. 500 sheets of paper is approximately 2 inches, so this represents a stack of paper 262 feet high.
Terabyte	TB	1,099,511,627,776 bytes (2^{40} bytes)	This represents a stack of typewritten pages almost 51 miles high.
Petabyte	PB	1,125,899,906,842,624 bytes (2^{50} bytes)	The stack of pages is now 52,000 miles high, or approximately one-fourth the distance from the Earth to the moon.
Exabyte	EB	1,152,921,504,606,846,976 bytes (2^{60} bytes)	The stack of pages is now 52 million miles high, or just about twice the distance between the Earth and Venus.
Zettabyte	ZB	1,180,591,620,717,411,303,424 bytes (2^{70} bytes)	The stack of pages is now 52 billion miles high. That's some 20 times the distance between the Earth and Pluto.

Similarly, a computer without software is a shell full of hardware components that can't do anything. Software is the set of computer programs that enables the hardware to perform different tasks. There are two broad categories of software: application software and system software.

When you think of software, you are most likely thinking of application software. **Application software** is the set of programs you use on a computer to help you carry out tasks such as writing a research paper. If you've ever typed a document, created a spreadsheet, or edited a digital photo, for example, then you've used a form of application software.

System software is the set of programs that enables your computer's hardware devices and application software to work together. The most common type of system software is the **operating system (OS)**—the program that controls the way in which your computer system functions. It manages the hardware of the computer system, such as the monitor and the printer. The operating system also provides a means by which users can interact with the computer. We'll cover software in greater depth in Chapters 4 and 5. For the rest of this chapter, we'll explore the basic components of computer hardware.

Types of Computers

Are all computers the same?

Considering the amount of amazing things computers can do, they are really quite simple machines. You learned in the previous section that a basic computer system is made up of software and hardware. There are two basic designs of computers: portable and stationary. A **notebook computer** (or laptop computer) is a portable computer that has a keyboard, a monitor, and other devices integrated into a single compact case. Notebooks are powered by a battery unit or an

a

b

AP Images/PRNewsFoto/Mindjet LLC

PRNewsfoto/Apple/AP Images

Figure 2.3

(a) A tablet PC has a monitor that swivels to become a touch-sensitive input device; (b) an all-in-one computer does not need a separate tower.

AC adapter. A **netbook** is a small, lightweight notebook computer that is generally 7 to 10 inches wide and has a longer battery life than a notebook computer. A **tablet PC** is similar to a notebook computer, but the monitor swivels and folds flat (see Figure 2.3a). Users then input data and commands primarily by using a special pen called a stylus across the touch screen, and input text by pressing keys on the virtual keyboard. In 2010, Apple introduced the iPad, which began a new class of mobile computers. A **tablet computer,** such as the Apple iPad or Motorola XOOM, is a mobile computer integrated into a flat multitouch-sensitive screen. It uses an onscreen virtual keyboard, but separate keyboards can be connected via Bluetooth or wires (see Figure 2.14 later in this chapter). A **desktop computer** is intended for use at a single location, and therefore is stationary. Most desktop computers consist of a separate case that houses the main components of the computer plus peripheral devices. A **peripheral device** is a component, such as a monitor or keyboard, that is connected to the computer. An **all-in-one computer,** such as the Apple iMac (Figure 2.3b) or HP TouchSmart, eliminates the need for a separate tower because these computers house the computer's processor and memory in the monitor unit. Many all-in-one models, such as the TouchSmart, also incorporate touch-screen technology.

Are there other types of computers?

Although you may never come into direct contact with the following types of computers, they are still important to our society:

- A **mainframe** is a large, expensive computer that supports hundreds of users simultaneously. Mainframes are often used in insurance companies, for example, where many people are working on similar operations, such as claims processing, all at once. Your college also may use mainframe computers to handle the multitude of processing needs throughout the campus. Mainframes excel at executing many different computer programs at the same time.

- A **supercomputer** is a specially designed computer that can perform complex calculations extremely rapidly. Supercomputers are used in situations in which complex models requiring intensive mathematical calculations are needed (such as weather forecasting or atomic energy research). The main difference between a supercomputer and a mainframe is that supercomputers are designed to execute a few programs as quickly as possible, whereas mainframes are designed to handle many programs running at the same time but at a slower pace.

- An **embedded computer** is a specially designed computer chip that resides in another device, such as your car or the electronic thermostat in your home. Embedded computers are self-contained computer devices that have their own programming and typically do not receive input from you or interact with other systems.

In the following sections, we look more closely at your computer's hardware. Each part has a specific purpose that coordinates with one of the functions of the computer—input, processing, output, or storage (see Figure 2.4). Additional devices, such as modems and routers, help a computer communicate with the Internet and other computers to facilitate the sharing of documents and other resources. We begin our exploration of hardware by looking at your computer's input devices.

Input Devices

An **input device** enables you to enter data (text, images, and sounds) and instructions (user responses and commands) into the computer. The most common input devices are the keyboard and the mouse. A **keyboard** is used to enter typed data and commands, and a **mouse** is used to enter user responses and commands.

There are other input devices as well. Microphones input sounds, and scanners and digital cameras input nondigital text and digital images, respectively. A **stylus** is an input device that looks like a skinny pen but has no ink. You use it like a mouse or pen to tap commands or draw on a screen.

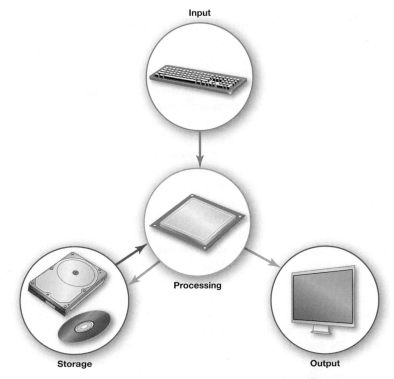

Figure 2.4

Each part of the computer serves a special function.

Keyboards

Aren't all keyboards the same? Most desktop and notebook computers come with a standard **QWERTY keyboard**. This keyboard layout gets its name from the first six letters in the top-left row of alphabetic keys on the keyboard and is the standard English-language keyboard layout. Over the years, there has been some debate over what is the best keyboard layout. The QWERTY layout was originally designed for typewriters and was meant to slow typists down and prevent typewriter keys from jamming. Although the QWERTY layout is considered inefficient because it slows typing speeds, efforts to change to more efficient layouts, such as that of the Dvorak keyboard, have not been met with much public interest. The Dvorak keyboard (see Figure 2.5) is an alternative

Figure 2.5

DVORAK keyboard layout.

Switching to a Dvorak Layout

Did you know that you can change your keyboard layout from the QWERTY format to the Dvorak format without buying a new keyboard? You can use the Windows operating system to customize the keyboard by changing the keyboard layout. The keyboard layout controls which characters appear on the screen when you press the keys on your keyboard. Computer users who suffer from a repetitive strain injury such as carpal tunnel syndrome and who would like to use the Dvorak keyboard layout may find it useful to switch layouts. You can also switch layouts to conform to different foreign languages.

To change the keyboard layout to the Dvorak layout, for example, you first must install a new language format. To do so, from the Control Panel, select Change keyboards or other input methods. Click the Keyboards and Languages tab, and then select the change keyboards button in the Region and Language dialog box. Click the Add button in the Text Services and Input Languages dialog box, scroll down to English (United States), and click the box next to United States-Dvorak. (There are also choices for left-hand and right-hand Dvorak keyboards. See Figure 2.6). Click OK. The Dvorak language has been installed. To switch to the new layout, click the keyboard icon that now appears in the taskbar and click United States-Dvorak.

You might also find it useful to cover the keys on the keyboard with stickers of the corresponding characters of the newly configured layout, so the characters on your keyboard match up to the new layout.

Figure 2.6

You can customize the layout of your keyboard using the Windows operating system.

>To change the keyboard layout, open Control Panel, click **Change keyboards or other input methods** in the Clock, Language and Region section. Click the **Change keyboards . . .** button. Click the **Add** button, scroll to find and then check the appropriate keyboard, then click **OK**.

keyboard layout that puts the most commonly used letters in the English language on "home keys," which are the keys in the middle row of the keyboard. The Dvorak keyboard's design reduces the distance your fingers travel for most keystrokes, increasing typing speed.

What's special about notebook keyboards? To save space and weight, some of the smaller notebook keyboards (14" and under) are more compact than standard desktop keyboards and, therefore, have fewer keys. To retain the same functionality as a standard keyboard, many of the notebook keys have alternate functions. For example, many notebook keyboards do not have a separate numeric keypad. Instead, some letter keys function as number keys when they are pressed in combination with another key such as the function (Fn) key. The keys you use as numeric keys on notebooks have number notations on them so you can tell which keys to use (see Figure 2.7).

Figure 2.7

On many notebooks, certain letter keys can function as number keys.

Alan Ford/Alamy

What are some alternative keyboards? The size of notebook keyboards and other portable computer devices have become quite compact. Flexible keyboards are a terrific alternative if you want a full-sized keyboard for your notebook. You can roll one up, fit it in your backpack, and plug it into the USB port when you need to use it. The virtual laser keyboard (see Figure 2.8) is about the size of a cellular phone, and is another compact keyboard alternative. It projects the image of a keyboard, and sensors detect the motion of your fingers as you "type" on a desk or other flat surface. Data is transmitted via **Bluetooth** technology, which is a wireless transmission standard that facilitates the connection of electronic computing devices such as cell phones, smartphones, and computers to peripheral devices such as keyboards and headsets. We'll discuss Bluetooth in further detail in Chapter 8.

Gamers love keyboards such as the DX1 from Ergodex. These keyboards allow placement of the keys in any position on the keyboard pad. The keys can be programmed to execute individual keystrokes or macros (a series of tasks) to perform specific tasks. This makes it easy for gamers to configure a keyboard in the most desirable way for each game they play.

How can I use my keyboard most efficiently? All keyboards have the standard set of alphabetic and numeric keys that

Figure 2.8

The virtual laser keyboard projects the image of a QWERTY keyboard on any surface. Sensors detect typing motions, and data is transmitted to a computing device via Bluetooth technology.

AP Photo/Martin Meissner

you regularly use when typing. As shown in Figure 2.9, many keyboards for notebook and desktop computers have additional keys that perform special functions.

Knowing how to use these special keys will help you improve your efficiency:

- The numeric keypad allows you to enter numbers quickly.

Figure 2.9

Keyboards have a variety of keys that help you work more efficiently.

Toggle and other keys

Internet controls

Multimedia controls

Numeric keypad

Function keys

Cursor control keys

Alt key

Windows key

Control (Ctrl) key

Artur Synenko/Shutterstock.com

- Function keys act as shortcut keys you press to perform special tasks. They are sometimes referred to as the "F" keys because they start with the letter F followed by a number. Each software application has its own set of tasks assigned to various function keys. For example, the F2 key moves text or graphics in Microsoft Word but allows editing of the active cell in Microsoft Excel. Many keys are universal: the F1 key is the Help key in most applications.

- The Control (Ctrl) key is used in combination with other keys to perform shortcuts and special tasks. For example, holding down the Ctrl key while pressing the B key adds bold formatting to selected text. The Alt key works with other keys to execute additional shortcuts and special tasks. (On Macs, the Control function is the Apple key or Command key, and the Alt function is the Option key.)

- The Insert key is a *toggle key* because its function changes between one of two options each time you press it: When toggled on, the Insert key inserts new text within a line of existing text. When toggled off, the Insert key replaces (or overwrites) existing characters with new characters as you type. Other toggle keys that switch between an on state and an off state include the Num Lock key and the Caps Lock key.

- The Windows key is specific to the Windows operating system. Used alone, it opens the Start menu, although you can use it in combination with other keys to perform shortcuts. For example, in Windows 7 and Vista, pressing the Windows key plus the M key minimizes all windows, and the Windows key plus the L key locks a computer (a good habit to get into when you leave a computer you use in a group setting such as a business office unattended).

Are all conventional keyboards connected to the computer via wires? Wireless keyboards provide additional flexibility because you are not tethered to the computer by wires. Instead, wireless keyboards are powered by batteries. They send data to the computer using a form of wireless technology that uses radio frequency (RF). A radio transmitter in the keyboard sends out radio wave signals that are received either through a small receiving device that is plugged into a USB port or a Bluetooth receiving device that is contained in the system unit. RF keyboards used on home computers can be placed as far as 6 feet to 30 feet from the computer, depending on their quality. RF keyboards that are used in business conference rooms or auditoriums can be placed as far as 100 feet away from the computer.

Mice and Other Pointing Devices

What kinds of mice are there? The mouse type you're probably most familiar with is the **optical mouse**. An optical mouse uses an internal sensor or laser to detect the mouse's movement. The sensor sends signals to the computer, telling it where to move the pointer on the screen. Optical mice do not require a mouse pad, though you can use one to enhance the movement of the mouse on an uneven surface, or to protect your work surface from being scratched.

BITS AND BYTES

Keystroke Shortcuts

Did you know that you can combine certain keystrokes to take shortcuts within an application, such as Microsoft Word, or within the operating system itself? The following are a few of the most helpful Windows shortcuts. Use them to make more efficient use of your time. For more shortcuts for Windows-based PCs, visit **www.support .microsoft.com**. For a list of shortcuts for Macs, see **www.apple.com/support**.

Text Formatting	File Management	Cut/Copy/ Paste	Windows Controls
Ctrl+B Applies (or removes) **bold** formatting to/from selected text	**Ctrl+O** Opens the Open dialog box	**Ctrl+X** Cuts (removes) selected text from document and stores in Clipboard	**Alt+F4** Closes the current window
Ctrl+I Applies (or removes) *italic* formatting to/from selected text	**Ctrl+N** Opens a new document	**Ctrl+C** Copies selected text to Clipboard	**Windows Key+Tab** Cycles through open programs using Flip 3D
Ctrl+U Applies (or removes) underlining to/from selected text	**Ctrl+S** Saves a document	**Ctrl+V** Pastes selected text (previously cut or copied) from Clipboard	**Windows Key+L** Locks the computer
	Ctrl+P Opens the Print dialog box		**Windows Key+F** Opens the Search (Find Files) dialog box

Razer

Courtesy of Mad Catz, Inc.

Figure 2.10

Customizable mice offer programmable buttons and adjustable fittings to meet most any need.

If you have special ergonomic needs, or want to be able to customize the functionality of your mouse beyond that of a standard optical mouse, there are plenty of options from which to choose. Most mice have two or three buttons that enable you to execute commands and open shortcut menus. (Mice for Macs sometimes have only one button.) As shown in (Figure 2.10), many mice, such as the Naga Epic by Razer, have additional programmable buttons and wheels that let you quickly maneuver through Web pages or games. The Cyborg R.A.T. 9 is customizable to fit any size hand and grip style, and comes with adjustable weights for optimal fit and control.

Are there wireless mice? Just as there are wireless keyboards, there are wireless mice. Wireless mice are similar to wireless keyboards in that they use batteries and send data to the computer by radio frequency or Bluetooth technologies. If you have an RF wireless keyboard, then your RF wireless mouse and keyboard usually can share the same RF receiver. Wireless mice for notebooks have their own receivers that

often clip into the bottom of the mouse for easy storage when not in use.

Apple has developed Magic Mouse, the first multi-touch wireless mouse (see Figure 2.11a). The top surface of the mouse, which is virtually the mouse itself, is the button. Use your finger to scroll in any direction, swipe your finger across the mouse to move through Web pages and photos, and tap on the mouse to click and double-click.

Small, compact devices like the MoGo Mouse (see Figure 2.11b) are designed for portability. The MoGo Mouse fits into a peripheral slot on the side of a notebook; this slot serves to store the mouse, protect it, and charge its battery all at the same time. The MoGo Mouse is wireless and uses Bluetooth technology to transmit data to the notebook.

What other tasks can be done with a mouse? Manufacturers of mice are constantly releasing new models that allow you to perform useful tasks with a few clicks of the mouse. On some mouse models, Microsoft and Logitech provide features such as the following:

- **Magnifier:** Pulls up a magnification box that you can drag around the screen to enhance viewing of hard-to-read images. This feature is often used by people with visual disabilities.
- **Web search:** Allows you to quickly highlight a word or phrase and then press the search button on the mouse to start a Web search.
- **File storage:** Includes a wireless USB receiver that contains flash memory to store or back up your files.

Figure 2.11

(a) The Magic Mouse by Apple has multi-touch technology. (b) The MoGo Mouse is a portable mouse that stores and charges in a PC Card slot.

AP Photo/Marcio Jose Sanchez

a

b

AP Photo/Damian Dovarganes

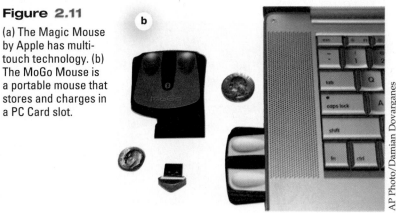

A touch screen is a display screen that responds to commands initiated by a touch with a finger or a stylus.

Do notebook computers include a mouse? Most notebooks have an integrated pointing device such as a **touch pad (or trackpad)**, a small, touch-sensitive area at the base of the keyboard (see Figure 2.12). To use the touch pad, you simply move your finger across the pad. Mac notebooks include multi-touch trackpads, which do not have buttons, but are controlled by various one-, two-, three-, and four-finger actions. For example, scrolling is controlled by brushing two fingers along the trackpad in any direction; swiping four fingers either left or right views all open applications as icons. Most touch pads are sensitive to taps, interpreting them as mouse clicks. Many notebooks also have buttons beneath the pads to record mouse clicks. Some notebooks incorporate a **trackpoint device**, a small, joystick-like nub that allows you to move the cursor with the tip of your finger.

What input devices are used with games? Game controllers such as joysticks, game pads, and steering wheels are also considered input devices because they send data to the computer. Game controllers, which are similar to the devices used on gaming consoles such as the Xbox 360 and the PlayStation, are also available for use with computers. They have buttons and miniature pointing devices that provide input to

the computer. Force-feedback joysticks and steering wheels deliver data in both directions. They translate your movements to the computer and translate its responses into forces on your hands, creating a richer simulated experience. Most game controllers, such as those for Rock Band and the Wii system, are wireless to provide extra mobility.

Touch Screens

How else can I input data and commands? You've seen and used touch-sensitive screens in fast-food restaurants, airport check-in kiosks, and ATM machines for quite some time. A **touch screen** is a display screen that responds to commands initiated by a touch with a finger or a stylus. Touch screens are becoming increasingly popular on many computing devices, especially smartphones such as the Droid and iPhone,

Figure 2.13

Virtual keyboards are found on tablets and other touch-screen devices.

and tablet computers such as the iPad and XOOM. Tablet PCs were one of the first devices with touch-screen capabilities. Although all tablet PCs have built-in keyboards that allow you to type text just as you would with a normal keyboard, the touch-screen functionality often makes it a better choice when inputting with a keyboard is impractical or unwieldy. Tablets, such as the iPad, and other touch-screen devices, use a virtual keyboard (see Figure 2.13) that displays on screen when input of text is required. These keyboards show basic keyboard configurations, and use special keys to switch to numeric, punctuation, and other special keys.

Figure 2.12

Touch pads and trackpoint devices take the place of a mouse on notebook computers.

Trackpoint device

Touch pad

SOUND BYTE

Tablet and Notebook Tour

In this Sound Byte, you'll take a tour of a tablet PC and a notebook computer, learning about the unique features and ports available on each.

All-in-one desktop PCs, as well as some other desktop and notebook computers, have touch screens, and portable media players (PMPs) such as the Apple iPod Touch have touch capability, as do some portable gaming devices such as the Nintendo DS.

AP Photo/Livescribe

Figure 2.14

The Livescribe Echo Smartpen captures writing and stores it in a flash drive for later transfer to a computer. No typing is required!

If you want to create digital notes, but cannot afford a computer, or don't want to always be lugging around a notebook, you can use a digital pen like the one shown in Figure 2.14. This pen works in conjunction with a **flash drive** (a portable electronic storage device that connects to a USB port on a computer). You can write with the pen on any conventional paper. The pen captures your writing and then wirelessly transmits and stores it in the flash drive. When the flash drive is connected to a computer, you can use software to translate your writing into digital text.

Image Input

How can I input digital images into my computer? Digital cameras, camcorders, and cell phones are common devices for capturing pictures and video, and all of them are considered input devices. Digital cameras and camcorders are usually used in remote settings (away from a computer) to capture images and video for later downloading to the computer. These devices either connect to a computer with a data cable or transmit data wirelessly. The computer automatically recognizes these devices when they are connected and makes the input of the digital data to the computer simple and easy. Scanners can also input images. They work similar to a photocopy machine, but instead of generating the image on paper, they create a digital image, which can then be printed, saved in storage, or e-mailed.

How do I capture live video from my computer or device? A **webcam** is a small camera that sits on top of a computer monitor (connected to the computer by a cable) or is built into a notebook or tablet computer. Although webcams are able to capture still images, they are used mostly for capturing and transmitting live video, and some have incorporated HD quality. Videoconferencing technology allows a person using a computer equipped with a webcam and a microphone to transmit video and audio across the Internet. Video call sites such as ooVoo (see Figure 2.15) make it easy to video conference with as many as twelve people. You can also exchange files, swap control of computers, and text

Figure 2.15

Video conferencing is simplified with software from **www.ooVoo.com**.

Oovoo Video Call Screenshot. Copyright © 2001 by Oovoo LLC. Reprinted by permission.

If you were asked to cite an example of unethical behavior while using a computer, you could easily provide an answer. You've probably heard news stories about people using computers to commit such crimes as unleashing viruses or committing identity theft. You may also have read about students who were prosecuted for illegally sharing copyrighted material such as videos. Or perhaps you heard about the case where the school district was monitoring students through notebook computer webcams without the students' knowledge. All of these are examples of unethical behavior while using a computer. However, if you were asked what constitutes ethical behavior while using a computer, could you provide an answer just as quickly?

Loosely defined, ethics is a system of moral principles, rules, and accepted standards of conduct. So what are the accepted standards of conduct when using computers (see Figure 2.16)? The Computer Ethics Institute developed the Ten Commandments of Computer Ethics, which is widely cited as a benchmark for companies that are developing computer usage and compliance policies for employees. These guidelines are applicable for schools and students as well. The ethical computing guidelines listed below are based on the Computer Ethics Institute's work.

Ethical Computing Guidelines

1. Avoid causing harm to others when using computers.
2. Do not interfere with other people's efforts at accomplishing work with computers.
3. Resist the temptation to snoop in other people's computer files.
4. Do not use computers to commit theft.
5. Agree not to use computers to promote lies.

6. Do not use software (or make illegal copies for others) without paying the creator for it.
7. Avoid using other people's computer resources without appropriate authorization or proper compensation.
8. Do not claim other people's intellectual output as your own.
9. Consider the social consequences of the products of your computer labor.
10. Only use computers in ways that show consideration and respect for others.

© Marek Uliasz/istockphoto.com

Figure 2.16

Make sure the work you claim as your intellectual output is the product of your intellect alone.

The United States has enacted laws that support some of these guidelines, such as Guideline 6, the breaking of which would violate copyright laws, and Guideline 4, which is enforceable under numerous federal and state larceny laws. Other guidelines, however, require more subtle interpretation as to what behavior is unethical because there are no laws designed to enforce them.

Consider Guideline 7, which covers unauthorized use of resources. The college you attend probably provides computer resources for you to use for coursework. But if the college gives you access to computers and the Internet, is it ethical for you to use those resources to run a business on eBay in between classes or on the weekends? Although it might not be technically illegal, you are tying up computer resources that could be used by other students for their intended purpose: learning and completing coursework. (This behavior also violates Guidelines 2 and 10.)

Throughout the chapters in this book, we touch on many topics related to these guidelines. So keep them in mind as you study, and think about how they relate to the actions you take as you use computers in your life.

---

message during the call. There is also a mobile application to make it easy to conference on the go.

Sound Input

Why would I want to input sound to my computer? In addition to letting others hear you in a video conference, equipping your computer to accept sound input opens up a variety of other possibilities. You can conduct audio conferences with work colleagues, chat with friends or family over the Internet instead of using a phone, record podcasts, and more. Inputting sound to your computer requires using a **microphone** or **mic**, a device that allows you to capture sound waves (such as your voice) and transfer them to digital format on your computer. Most notebook computers come with

built-in microphones, and some desktop computers come with inexpensive microphones.

What types of microphones are available? Unidirectional microphones pick up sound from only one direction. These are best used for recording podcasts with a single voice or making phone calls over the Internet with only one person on the sender's end of the call. Omnidirectional microphones pick up sounds from all directions at once (see Figure 2.17). These mics are best for recording more than one voice, such as during a conference call when you need to pick up the voices of multiple speakers. Bidirectional microphones receive sound equally from the front and back of the mic, and are especially good for interviews.

Clip-on microphones (also called *lavalier microphones*) are useful in environments such as presentations, where you need to keep your hands free for other activities (such as writing on a whiteboard) or move around the room. Many of these microphones are wireless.

Close-talk microphones, which are usually attached to a headset, facilitate using speech-recognition software, videoconferencing, or making telephone calls. With a microphone attached to a headset, your hands are free to perform other tasks while you speak, such as making notes or referring to paper documents, and the headset allows you to listen as well.

> **Many people who have physical challenges use computers often, but they sometimes need special input devices to access them.**

What input devices are available for people with disabilities? Many people who have physical challenges use computers often, but they sometimes need special input devices to access them. For visually impaired users, voice recognition is an obvious option. For those users whose visual limitations are less severe, keyboards with larger keys are available. Keyboards that display on a touch screen can make input easier for some individuals. These keyboards are displayed as graphics on the computer monitor. The user presses the keys with a pointing device or simply presses on the touch-screen monitor. There are also keyboards designed for individuals who can only use one hand, such as the Maltron keyboard.

People with motor control issues may have difficulty with pointing devices. To aid such users, special trackballs are available that can easily be manipulated with one finger and can be attached to almost any surface, including a wheelchair. When arm motion is severely restrained, head-mounted pointing devices can be used. Generally, these involve a camera mounted on the computer monitor and a device attached to the head (often installed in a hat). When the user moves his or her head, the camera detects the movement, which controls the cursor on the screen. In this case, mouse clicks are controlled by a switch that can be manipulated by the user's hands or feet or even by using an instrument that fits into the mouth and senses the user blowing into it.

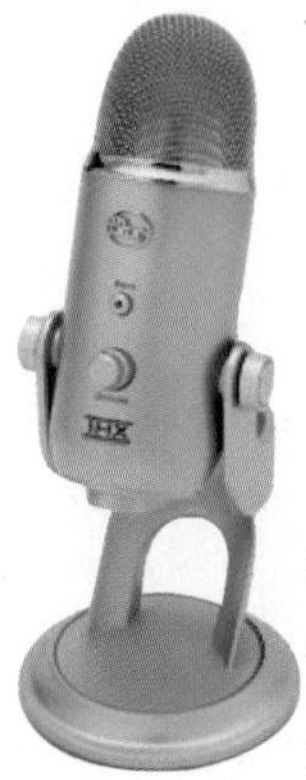

Output Devices

An **output device** enables you to send processed data out of your computer in the form of text, pictures (graphics), sounds (audio), or video. One common output device is a **monitor** (sometimes referred to as a **display screen**), which displays text,

Blue Microphones

Figure 2.17

Professional-quality microphones are essential for producing quality podcasts. The Blue Yeti can easily switch among four settings to provide the best sound recording in any situation.

graphics, and video as soft copies (copies you can see only on screen). Another common output device is the **printer**, which creates hard copies (copies you can touch) of text and graphics. Speakers and earphones (or earbuds) are the output devices for sound.

Monitors

What are the different types of monitors? The most common type of monitor is a **liquid crystal display (LCD)**. An LCD monitor, also called a flat-panel monitor, is light and energy efficient. Some newer monitors use **light-emitting diode (LED)** technology, which is more energy efficient, and may have better color accuracy and thinner panels than traditional LCD monitors. These flat panel monitors have replaced the cathode ray tube (CRT) monitor. CRT monitors are difficult to find or buy because they have become **legacy technology**, or computing devices or peripherals that use techniques, parts, and methods from an earlier time that are no longer popular. Although legacy technology may still be functional, it is quickly being replaced by newer technological advances. This doesn't mean that if you have a CRT monitor that is functioning well you should replace it with an LCD monitor. However, when your CRT monitor fails, you will most likely only be able to replace it with an LCD monitor. **Organic light-emitting diode (OLED) displays** use organic compounds that produce light when exposed to an electric current. Unlike LCDs and LEDs, OLEDs do not require a backlight to function and therefore draw less power and have a much thinner display, sometimes as thin as 3 mm (see Figure 2.18). They are also brighter and more environmentally friendly than LCDs. Because of their lower power needs, OLED displays run longer on a single battery charge than do LEDs, which is why OLED technology is currently being used in small screens of mobile devices such as cell phones, portable media players, and digital cameras.

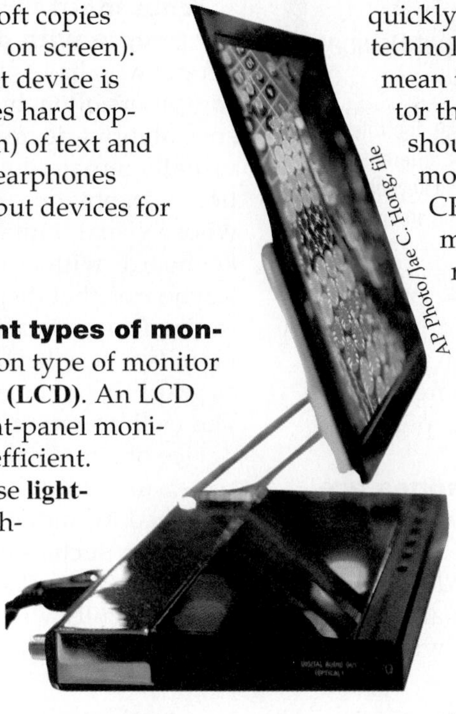

How do LCD monitors work? Monitor screens are grids made up of millions of tiny dots, each of which is called a **pixel**. Illuminated pixels create the images you see on your monitor. Each pixel is actually composed of three subpixels of red, blue, and green; some newer TVs on the market have added a fourth color: yellow. LCD monitors are made of two or more sheets of material filled with a liquid crystal solution (see Figure 2.19). A fluorescent panel at the back of the LCD monitor generates light waves. When electric current passes through the liquid crystal solution, the crystals move around and either block the fluorescent light or let the light shine through. This blocking or passing of light by the crystals causes images to form on the screen. The various combinations of red, blue, and green make up the components of color we see on our monitors.

AP Photo/Jae C. Hong, file

Figure 2.18

Because they do not need a backlight, OLED displays are much thinner, making LCD screens seem bulky.

Figure 2.19

A magnification of a single pixel in an LCD monitor.

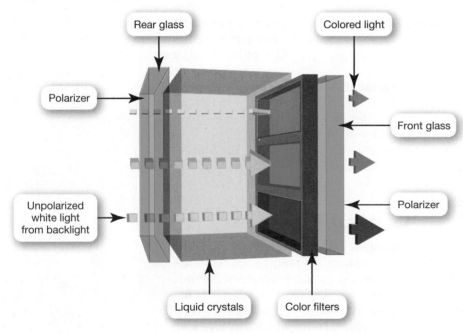

Rear glass

Colored light

Polarizer

Front glass

Unpolarized white light from backlight

Polarizer

Liquid crystals

Color filters

What factors affect the quality of an LCD monitor? When choosing an LCD monitor, there are several factors to consider, such as aspect ratio and resolution. The **aspect ratio** is the width-to-height proportion of a monitor. Traditionally, aspect ratios have been 4:3, but newer monitors are available with an aspect ratio of 16:9 or 16:10. The screen **resolution**, or the clearness or sharpness of the image, reflects the number of pixels on the screen. An LCD monitor may have a native (or maximum) resolution of 1600 × 1200 meaning it contains 1,600 vertical columns with 1,200 pixels in each column. The higher the resolution, the sharper and clearer the image will be, but generally the resolution of an LCD monitor is dictated by the screen size and aspect ratio. Although you can change the resolution of an LCD monitor beyond its native resolution, the images will become distorted. Generally, you should select a monitor with the highest resolution available for the screen size (measured in inches).

Other factors to consider when judging the quality of an LCD monitor include the following:

- **Contrast ratio:** This is a measure of the difference in light intensity between the brightest white and the darkest black that the monitor can produce. If the contrast ratio is too low, colors tend to fade when you adjust the brightness to a high or low setting. A contrast ratio between 400:1 and 1,000:1 is preferable. Some monitors may sport a dynamic contrast ratio that may be 10,000:1 or 50,000:1. This measurement is taken when the backlight is turned off completely; normal contrast ratio measurements have the backlight dimmed to its lowest setting but not completely off. Unfortunately, in normal use, the backlight is not turned off, so the dynamic contrast ratio is not a relevant measure, unless you are using an LED monitor.
- **Viewing angle:** An LCD's viewing angle, which is measured in degrees, tells how far you can move to the side of (or above or below) the monitor before the image quality degrades to unacceptable levels. For monitors that measure 17 inches or more, a viewing angle of at least 150 degrees is usually recommended.
- **Brightness:** Measured as candelas per square meter (cd/m²) or *nits*, brightness is a measure of the greatest amount of light showing when the monitor is displaying pure white. A brightness level of 300 cd/m² or greater is recommended.
- **Response time:** This is the measurement (in milliseconds) of the time it takes for a pixel to change color. A lower response time value means faster transitions; therefore, moving images will appear less jerky on the monitor.

Is a bigger screen size always better? The bigger the monitor, the more you can display, and depending on what you want to display, size may matter. In general, the larger the panel, the larger number of pixels it can display. For example, a 27-inch monitor can display 2560 × 1440 pixels, while a 21.5-inch monitor may only be able to display 1680 × 1050 pixels. However, most new monitors have at least a 1920 × 1080 resolution that is required to display Blu-ray movies. Larger screens can also allow you to view multiple documents or Web pages at the same time, creating the

Testing and Calibrating Your PC Monitor

Most new PC monitors do not need color or tint adjustments, but some can benefit from a few tweaks that will ultimately enhance your video experience. This might be especially important if you are a Web designer, digital photographer, or graphic professional. In those professions, especially, you want to make sure the colors are displayed on the monitor as accurately as possible. Before you start the calibration process, check that your monitor is set to the "native" resolution (usually the recommended setting). Some monitors have their own calibration program; otherwise, you can work through the adjustments manually or use the display utility in your operating system. If you are running Windows 7, you can use the Display Color Calibration utility found by clicking the Start button, clicking the Control Panel, and then clicking Appearance and Personalization. Click Display, and then in the Navigation Pane, click Calibrate color. The Display Color Calibration utility will check the gamma, brightness, contrast, and color balance settings. Gamma describes the relationship between the varying levels of brightness that a monitor can display. Brightness determines how dark colors appear on your display. When brightness is set too high, dark colors appear washed out. Contrast determines how white and light colors display. (Note that most notebook computers do not have controls to adjust contrast.) Color balance makes adjustments to the red, blue, and green controls.

effect of using two separate monitors side by side. Again, be mindful of cost. Buying two smaller monitors might be cheaper than buying one large monitor. For either option—a big screen or two screens—you should check that your computer has a special adapter card to support these video display devices.

What other features should I look for in an LCD monitor? Some monitors, especially those on notebook computers, come with convenient built-in features such as speakers, webcams, and microphones. A built-in multiformat card reader is convenient to display images directly on the monitor or to download pictures quickly from a camera memory card to the PC. Another nice feature to look for in a desktop LCD monitor is a built-in USB port. This will enable you to connect extra peripherals easily without reaching around the back of the PC. In addition, if you want to connect a gaming console or DVD/Blu-ray player, you should look for monitors with video ports for easy access.

How do I show output to a large group of people? Crowding large groups of people around your computer isn't practical. However, it is possible to use a **projector**, a device that can project images from your computer onto a wall or viewing screen. Projectors are commonly used in business and education settings such as conference rooms and classrooms. These projectors are small and lightweight, and some, like the 3M MPro 150 (see Figure 2.20), are small enough to fit into the palm of your hand! These portable projectors are ideal for businesspeople that have to make presentations at client locations. *Entertainment projectors,* such as the Wonderwall, include stereo speakers and an array of multimedia connectors, making them a good option for use in the home to display TV programs, DVDs, digital images, or video games in a large format. If your laptop is equipped with an HDMI port, you can connect your laptop

directly to an HDTV. Although you could connect your laptop with a DVI port, by using HDMI, you only need the one cable, eliminating the need for additional audio cables.

Printers

What are the different types of printers? There are two primary categories of printers: inkjet and laser, both of which are considered nonimpact printers. A **nonimpact printer** sprays ink or uses laser beams to transfer marks onto the paper. Today, nonimpact printers have replaced impact printers almost entirely. An **impact printer** has tiny hammerlike keys that strike the paper through an inked ribbon, making marks on the paper. The most common impact printer is the dot-matrix printer. The only place you may see a dot-matrix printer is at a company that still uses them to print multipart forms. For most users, dot-matrix printers are truly legacy technology.

What are the advantages of inkjet printers? An **inkjet printer** (see Figure 2.21) is the standard type of printer found in most homes. Inkjet printers are popular because they are affordable and produce high-quality color printouts quickly and quietly. Inkjet printers work by spraying tiny drops of ink onto paper and are great for printing black-and-white text as well as color images. In fact, when loaded with the right paper, higher-end inkjet printers can print images that look like professional-quality photos. One thing to consider when buying an inkjet

Figure 2.20

Inexpensive projectors are showing up more frequently in business and the home to provide large images for movie viewing and gaming.

Courtesy of 3M

Figure 2.21

Inkjet printers are popular among home users, especially with the rise of digital photography. Many inkjet printers are optimized for printing photos from digital cameras.

TheVectorminator/Shutterstock.com

Touch-screen technology was developed in 1971, and used primarily with ATMs and fast-food order displays. The technology for monitors and other displays was made popular by the iPod Touch, and is now in many smartphones, tablet computers, and notebook and desktop monitors. But how do touch-screen monitors know where you're touching? How do they know what you want them to do?

The basic idea behind touch screens is pretty straightforward—when you place your finger or stylus on a screen, it changes the state that the device is monitoring. The location of the touch is then translated into a command. Three basic systems are used to recognize a person's touch: resistive, capacitive, and surface acoustic wave. All of these systems require the basic components of a touch-responsive glass panel, controller, and software driver, combined with a display and computer processor.

The *resistive system* maps the exact location of the pressure point created when a user touches the screen. The *capacitive system* (see Figure 2.22) uses the change in the electrical charge on the glass panel of the monitor that is created by the user's touch, to generate a location. The third technology, *surface acoustic wave system*, uses two transducers (electrical devices that convert energy from one form to another) that are placed along the *x* and *y* axes of the monitor's glass plate. Reflectors, which are also placed on the glass, are used to reflect an electric signal sent from the sending transducer to the receiving transducer. The receiving transducer determines whether the signal has been disturbed by a touch event, and locates the touch instantly. Then, with all three systems, the display's software driver translates the touch into something the operating system can understand, similar to how a mouse driver translates a mouse's movements into a click or drag.

Because the resistive system uses pressure to register a touch, it doesn't matter if the touch is created by a finger or another device. A capacitive system must have conductive input, so generally a finger is required. The surface acoustic wave system allows touches by any object.

The iPhone introduced another complexity to the touch-screen system—a multi-touch user interface. In addition to just pressing the screen in one location, multi-touch technology can process multiple simultaneous touches on the screen. For example, pinching or spreading out the thumb and finger together enables the display to zoom out and in, respectively. The features of each touch, such as size, shape, and location, are also determined. A touch-sensitive screen, like the one used with the iPhone and iPad and with many other smartphones and tablet computers, arranges the capacitors in a coordinate system so the circuitry can sense changes at each point along the grid (see Figure 2.23). Consequently, every point when touched on the grid generates its own signal, and can do so even simultaneously as another signal is also being generated. The signals are then relayed to the device's processor. This allows the device to determine the location and movement of simultaneous touches in multiple locations.

Figure 2.23

Multi-touch screens use a coordinate-based grid to arrange the capacitors so the circuitry can detect and respond to multiple touches occurring at the same time.

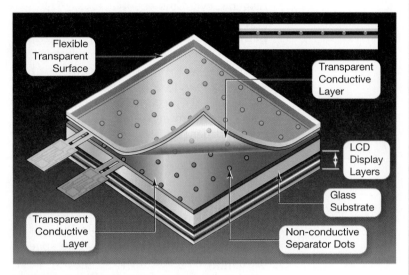

Figure 2.22

Some basic touch screens use a capacitive system to detect touches and translate them into meaningful commands that are understood by the computer's operating system.

After detecting the position and type of touch occurring on the display, the device's processor combines this information with the information it has about the application that is in use, and what was being done in the application when the touch occurred. The processor relays that information to the program in use and the command is executed. All of this happens seemingly instantaneously.

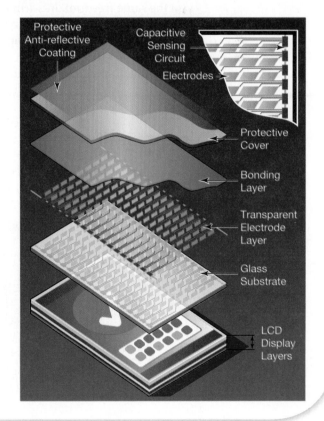

printer is the type and cost of the ink cartridges the printer needs. Some printers use two cartridges: black and color. Other printers use four or more cartridges, typically black, magenta, cyan, and yellow.

Why would I want a laser printer? Laser printers (see Figure 2.24) are most often used in office or classroom settings because they have a faster printing speed than inkjet printers and produce higher-quality printouts. A **laser printer** uses laser beams and static electricity to deliver toner (similar to ink) onto the correct areas of the page. Heat is used to fuse the toner to the page, making the image permanent. In the past, laser printers generally were not found in the home because of their high purchase price and because they did not produce great color images. Recently, however, the quality and speed have improved and the price of color laser printers has fallen dramatically, making them highly price competitive with high-end inkjet printers. If you print a high volume of pages, consider a laser printer. When you include the price of ink or toner in the overall cost, laser printers can be more economical than inkjets.

Are there wireless printers? One reason you may have bought a notebook was to be able to use a computer without the restriction of wires. Wireless printing offers you the same freedom. In addition, wireless printers allow several people to print to the same printer from different places. There are two different types of wireless printers: WiFi and Bluetooth. Both WiFi and Bluetooth printers have a range of up to approximately 300 feet. WiFi, however, sends data more quickly than Bluetooth. If your printer is not Bluetooth enabled, you can add Bluetooth by plugging a Bluetooth adapter into a USB port. This lets you take advantage of a great printing solution for photos stored on your cell phone or any other Bluetooth-enabled portable device.

Can I carry my printer with me? Although some inkjet printers are small enough to carry with you, you may want to consider a printer designed for portability for added mobility and flexibility. These compact printers can connect to your computer, camera, or smartphone via Bluetooth technology, or with a USB port. Portable printers are often compact enough to fit in a briefcase, are lightweight, and can run on battery power as well as AC power.

Are there any other types of specialty printers? An **all-in-one printer** is a device that combines the functions of a printer, scanner, copier, and fax into one machine. Popular for their space-saving convenience, all-in-one printers can use either inkjet or laser technology. A **plotter** is another type of printer. Plotters produce oversize pictures that require the drawing of precise and continuous lines, such as maps, detailed images (see Figure 2.25), and architectural plans. Plotters use a computer-controlled pen that provides a greater level of precision than the series of dots that laser or inkjet printers are capable of making.

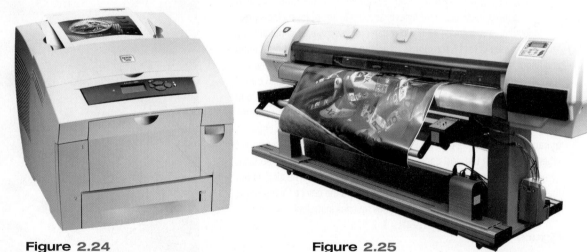

Figure 2.24

Laser printers print quickly and offer high-quality printouts.

Figure 2.25

Plotters are large printers used to print oversize images, maps, and architectural plans.

A **thermal printer**, such as the one shown in Figure 2.26, is another kind of specialty printer. These printers work either by melting wax-based ink onto ordinary paper (a process called *thermal wax transfer printing*) or by burning dots onto specially coated paper (a process called *direct thermal printing*). They are used in stores to print receipts and in airports for electronic ticketing. Many models, such as the printers that car rental agencies use to give you an instant receipt when you drop off your rental car, feature wireless infrared technology for complete portability. Thermal printers are also emerging as a popular technology for mobile and portable printing in conjunction with smartphones and similar devices.

How do I select the best printer? There is a printer for every printing need. First, you need to decide what your primary printing need is. If you will use your printer mostly to print digital images, then you will want to select a photo printer. If not, then a general-purpose printer will be a better choice. General-purpose printers have a finer, faster text output, whereas photo printers have a more distinctive color output. It's also important to determine whether you want just a printer or a device that prints and scans, copies, or faxes (an all-in-one). In addition, you should decide whether you want an inkjet or laser printer, and whether or not you want to print wirelessly. Once you have narrowed down the type of printer you want, the following criteria will help you determine the best model to meet your needs.

- **Speed:** A printer's speed determines how many pages it can print per minute. Print speed is expressed as *pages per minute* or *ppm*. The speed of inkjet printers has improved over the years, and many inkjet printers now print as fast as laser printers. Printing speeds vary by model and range from 8 ppm to 38 ppm for both laser and inkjet printers. Text documents printed in black and white print faster than documents printed in color.

- **Resolution:** A printer's resolution (printed image clarity) is measured

Zebra Technologies

Figure 2.26

Thermal printers are often used to print receipts.

ACTIVE HELP-DESK — **Using Output Devices**

In this Active Helpdesk call, you'll play the role of a helpdesk staffer, fielding calls about different output devices, including the differences between LCD and CRT monitor technologies and between inkjet and laser printers and the advantages and disadvantages of each.

in dots per inch (dpi), which is the number of dots of ink in a one-inch line. The higher the dpi, the greater the level of detail and quality of the image. You'll sometimes see dpi represented as a horizontal number multiplied by a vertical number, such as 600 × 600, but you may also see the same resolution simply stated as 600 dpi. The dpi will differ for color output than for black and white output. For general-purpose printing, 1,200 dpi is sufficient. For printing photos, 4,800 dpi is better. The dpi for professional photo-quality printers is twice that.

- **Color output:** If you're using an inkjet printer to print color images, four-color printers (cyan, magenta, yellow, and black) or six-color printers (four-color plus light cyan and light magenta) offer the highest-quality output. Although some printers come with a single ink cartridge for all colors and others have two ink cartridges (one for black and one for color), the best setup is to have an individual ink cartridge for each color so you can replace only the specific color cartridge that is empty. Color laser printers have four separate toner cartridges (black, cyan, magenta, and yellow), and the toner is blended in various quantities to produce the entire color spectrum.

- **Use and cost of the printer:** If you will be printing mostly black-and-white, text-based documents or will be sharing your printer with others, then a black-and-white laser printer is best because of its printing speed and overall economy for volume printing. If you're planning to print color photos and graphics, then an inkjet printer or color laser printer is a must, even though the cost per page will be higher. Keep in mind a printer's reported duty cycle. A duty cycle is a manufacturer's figure that refers to how long a machine can keep operating before it needs a rest, or what percentage of the time it's designed to be in use. For a printer, the duty cycle generally refers to the number of printed pages the printer can reliably produce on a monthly basis. If you buy a printer with a duty cycle of 1,000 copies per month, and you generally only print 100 copies a month, then you will have overpurchased. Alternatively, exceeding the duty cycle estimates might lead to printer malfunctions.

- **Cost of consumables:** You should carefully investigate the cost of consumables (such as printer cartridges and paper) for any printer you are considering purchasing because the cost of inkjet cartridges often can exceed the cost of the actual printer when purchased on sale. Reviews in consumer magazines such as *PC World* and *Consumer Reports* can

help you evaluate the overall cost of producing documents with a particular printer.

Sound Output

What are the output devices for sound? Most computers include inexpensive speakers. A **speaker** is an output device for sound. These speakers are sufficient to play the standard audio clips you find on the Web and usually enable you to participate in videoconferencing or phone calls made over the Internet. However, if you plan to digitally edit audio files or are particular about how your music sounds, then you may want to upgrade to a more sophisticated speaker system, such as one that includes subwoofers (special speakers that produce only low bass sounds) and surround-sound speakers. A **surround-sound speaker** is a system of speakers and audio processing that envelops the listener in a full 360-degree field of sound. Wireless speaker systems are available now to help you avoid cluttering up your rooms with speaker wire. We discuss surround sound in more detail in Chapter 6.

If you work in close proximity to other employees or travel with a notebook, then you may need to use headphones or earbuds for your sound output to avoid

---

 **Does It Matter What Paper I Print On?**

The quality of your printer is only part of what controls the quality of a printed image. The paper you use and the printer settings that control the amount of ink used are equally important. If you're printing text-only documents for personal use, then using low-cost paper is fine. You also may want to consider selecting draft mode in your printer settings to conserve ink. However, if you're printing more formal documents such as résumés, you may want to choose a higher-quality paper (determined by the paper's weight, whiteness, and brightness) and adjust your print setting to "normal" or "best."

The weight of paper is measured in pounds, with 20 pounds being standard. A heavier paper may be best for projects such as brochures, but be sure to check that your printer can handle the added thickness. The degree of paper whiteness is a matter of personal preference. Generally, the whiter the paper, the brighter the printed

color. However, for more formal documents, such as résumés, you may want to use a creamier color. The brightness of paper usually varies from 85 to 94. The higher the number, the brighter the paper, and the easier it is to read printed text. Opacity, or the "show through" of print from one side to the other, or to the next sheet, is especially important if you're printing on both sides of the paper because it determines the amount of ink that shows through from the opposite side of the paper.

If you're printing photos, then paper quality can have a big impact on the results. Photo paper is more expensive than regular paper and comes in a variety of textures ranging from matte to high gloss. For a photo-lab look, high-gloss paper is the best choice. Semigloss (often referred to as satin) is good for portraits, while a matte surface is often used for black-and-white photo printing.

---

distracting other people. Both devices will plug into the same jack on the computer that speakers connect to, so using them with a computer is easy. Studies of users of portable media players have shown that hearing might be damaged by excessive volume, especially when using earbuds, because they fit into the ear canals. Exercise caution when using these devices.

Processing and Memory on the Motherboard

We just looked at the components of your computer that you use to input and output data. But where does the processing take place, and where is the data stored? The **motherboard** is the main circuit board that contains the central electronic components of the computer, including the computer's processor (its brain), its memory, and the many circuit boards that help the computer function (see Figure 2.27). On a desktop, the motherboard is located inside the **system unit**, the metal or plastic case that also houses the power source and all the storage devices (CD/DVD drive and hard drive). With a notebook computer, the system unit is combined with the monitor and the keyboard into a single package.

What's on the motherboard? Recall that the motherboard is the main circuit board that contains the set of chips that powers the system, including the central processing unit (CPU). The motherboard also houses ROM, RAM, and cache, the chips that provide the short-term memory for the computer. The motherboard also includes slots for **expansion cards** (or **adapter cards**), which are circuit boards that provide additional functionality. Typical expansion cards found in the system unit are the sound and video cards. A **sound card** provides a connection for the speakers and microphone, whereas a **video card** provides a connection for the monitor. Many low-end

computer models have video and sound capabilities integrated into their motherboards. High-end models use expansion cards to provide video and sound capabilities. Other expansion cards provide a means for network and Internet connections. These include the **modem card**, which provides the computer with a connection to the Internet via a traditional phone line, and a **network interface card (NIC)**, which enables your computer to connect with other computers or to a cable modem to facilitate a high-speed Internet connection. Lastly, some expansion cards provide additional USB and FireWire ports.

Figure 2.27

A motherboard contains the CPU, the memory (RAM) modules, and slots for expansion cards.

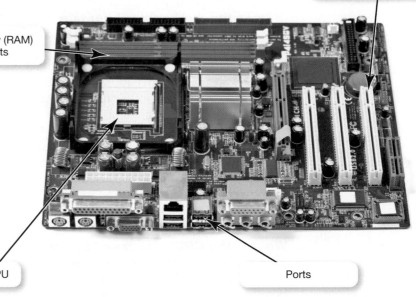

Expansion slots

Memory (RAM) slots

CPU

Ports

S.Dashkevych/Shutterstock.com

Memory

What exactly is RAM? Random access memory (RAM) is the place in a computer where the programs and data the computer is currently using are stored. RAM is much faster to read from and write to than the hard drive and other forms of storage. The processor can request the RAM's contents, which can be located, opened, and delivered to the CPU for processing in a few nanoseconds (billionths of a second). If you look at a motherboard, you'll see RAM as a series of small cards (called *memory cards* or *memory modules*) plugged into slots on the motherboard.

Because the entire contents of RAM are erased when you turn off the computer, RAM is a temporary or **volatile storage** location. To save data permanently, you need to save it to the hard drive or to another permanent storage device such as a CD or flash drive. You can think of RAM as the computer's temporary memory and the hard drive as permanent memory.

Does the motherboard contain any other kinds of memory besides RAM? In addition to RAM, the motherboard also contains a form of memory called **read-only memory (ROM)**. ROM holds all the instructions the computer needs to start up when it is powered on. Unlike data stored in RAM, which is volatile storage, the instructions stored in ROM are permanent, making ROM a nonvolatile storage location, which means the data is not erased when the power is turned off.

Processing

What is the CPU? The **central processing unit** (**CPU**, or **processor**) is sometimes referred to as the "brains" of the computer because it controls all the functions performed by the computer's other components and processes all the commands issued to it by software instructions. Modern CPUs can perform as many as tens of billions of tasks per second without error, making them extremely powerful components.

How is processor speed measured? Processor speed is measured in units of hertz (Hz). Hertz means "machine cycles per second." A machine cycle is the process of the CPU getting the data or instructions from RAM and decoding the instructions into something the computer can understand. Once the CPU has decoded the instructions, it executes them and stores the result back into system memory. Current systems run at speeds measured in **gigahertz (GHz)**, or billions of machine cycles per second. Therefore, a 3.8 GHz processor performs work at a rate of 3.8 billion machine cycles per second. It's important to realize, however, that CPU clock speed alone doesn't determine the performance of the CPU.

What else determines processor performance? Although speed is an important consideration when determining processor performance, CPU performance also is affected by other factors. One factor is the number of *cores,* or processing paths, a processor has. Initially processors could handle only one instruction at a time. Now, processors have been designed so that they can have two, four, and even eight different paths, allowing them to process more than one instruction at a time (see Figure 2.28). Applications such as virus protection software and the operating system, which are always running behind the scenes, can have their own processors, freeing up the other processor to run other applications such as a Web browser, Word, or iTunes more efficiently.

Besides the number of cores, are there other factors that determine processing power? In addition to the number of cores in a processor, you should consider other factors such as cache memory and front side bus (FSB). Front side bus determines how fast data is exchanged between the CPU and RAM. These factors will be discussed in greater detail in Chapter 6. The "best" processor will depend on your particular needs and is not always the processor with the highest GHz and the greatest number of cores. Intel, one of the leading manufacturers of computer processor chips, has created a pictorial rating system for CPU chips. Intel uses one to five stars to illustrate the relative computing power of each type of CPU within the Intel line of processors.

Figure 2.28

Two or more are faster than one! With their multi-core processors, Intel CPUs can work in parallel, processing two or more separate programs at the same time instead of switching back and forth between them.

Single path vs. dual path processors for data

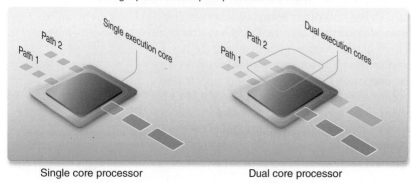

Single core processor   Dual core processor

Storing Data and Information

Earlier we characterized RAM as temporary or volatile memory because the entire contents of RAM are erased when you turn off the computer. Thus, if you want to permanently save the files you're working on, as well as your music, digital images, and any software applications you use, you need to store them in a location other than RAM. To save your data and information permanently, you need to save it to the hard drive or to another permanent storage device such as an external hard drive, DVD, or flash drive.

Hard Drives

Are there different kinds of hard drives? The **hard disk drive (HDD or hard drive)** is your computer's primary device for permanent storage of software and documents. The hard drive is a **nonvolatile storage** device, meaning it holds data and the instructions your computer needs permanently, even after the computer is turned off. Today's internal hard drives (see Figure 2.29a), with capacities of as much as 3 terabytes (TB), can hold more data than would fit in the books in a school's library. External hard drives (see Figure 2.29b) offer similar storage capacities, but reside outside the system unit, and connect to the computer via a USB or FireWire port. The most common type of hard drive has moveable parts—spinning platters, a moving arm with a read/write head—that can fail and lead to devastating disk failure. However, recently, the **solid-state drive (SSD)** has become a more feasible option for desktop and laptop storage. SSDs have no moving parts, so they are more efficient, run with no noise, emit very little heat, and require very little power. In addition, they are less likely to fail after being bumped or dropped. The small portable flash drives that you may carry around in your pocket use solid state technology.

Some permanent storage devices are located in your desktop or notebook computer in a space called a **drive bay**.

There are two kinds of drive bays—internal and external—as described below:

- Internal drive bays cannot be seen or accessed from outside the system unit. Generally, internal drive bays are reserved for internal hard drives. An **internal hard drive** usually holds all permanently stored programs and data.
- External drive bays can be seen and accessed from outside the system unit. External drive bays house CD and DVD drives, for example. On desktop computers, sometimes there are empty external drive bays that can be used to install additional drives. These extra spaces are covered by a faceplate on the front panel. Notebook computers generally do not give you the ability to add additional drives. Such expansion is done by attaching an external drive to the computer through a USB port.

Flash Storage

How can I take my files with me? There are many options available to take data with you. For large portable storage needs, there are portable **external hard drives**, which are small enough to fit into your pocket and have storage capacities of 1 or 2 TB (or larger). These devices are small and lightweight and are enclosed in a protective case. They attach to your computer via the USB port (see Figure 2.30). Most of these portable external hard drives, such as My Passport, do not use solid state technology, so care should be taken when transporting them.

A flash drive, sometimes referred to as a jump drive, USB drive, or thumb drive, uses

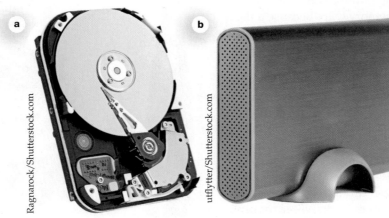

Ragnarock/Shutterstock.com

utflytter/Shutterstock.com

Figure 2.29

(a) Internal hard drives hold the data and instructions that the computer needs and are inaccessible from outside the system unit. (b) High-capacity external hard drives are often used to back up data on internal hard drives.

BITS AND BYTES

Taking Care of Flash Drives

Flash drives have become a convenient means of portable storage, primarily because of their diminutive physical size, but also because of their expansive storage capacities. Although they are fairly rugged and withstand much abuse, flash drive failures can occur. Therefore, it is important to know how to care for your flash drive to extend its useful life, and to keep your data safe.

1. Like any other mechanical device, do not submerge a flash drive in water or expose it to extreme temperatures. Take care to not leave it where it's at risk of being spilled on.

2. Keep the end covered or closed when not plugged into the computer. This prevents dust and other particles from interfering with the connections.

3. Never defrag a flash drive. It is not necessary, and can reduce the life expectancy of the drive.

4. A flash drive has a limited amount of writes in its lifetime. Depending on the device, it can be 10,000 or 100,000, which seems like a lot, but over years of extensive use, could add up. It's best to make edits to documents on the computer, and then transfer the finished document to your flash drive.

5. Remember to remove the flash drive correctly. All files and folders must be closed, with no active documents running, before the device is removed. To properly stop the device, use the "Safely remove hardware" feature in the taskbar, or select Eject from Windows Explorer. Mac users should select Eject from the Finder menu. If you find that you cannot stop the flash drive by these methods, you will need to power down the computer first before removing the drive.

as much as 256 GB. Flash drives plug into USB ports. When you plug a flash drive into your computer's USB port, it appears in the Windows or Macintosh operating system as another disk drive. You can write data to it or read data from it in the same manner as reading and writing data to and from hard drives.

Another convenient means of portable storage is a **flash memory card** such as a Memory Stick or CompactFlash card. Like the flash drive, memory cards use solid-state flash memory. Most desktops and notebooks include slots for flash memory cards, but if your computer is not equipped, there are memory card readers that can be plugged into a USB port. Flash memory cards let you transfer digital data between your computer and devices such as digital cameras, smartphones, video cameras, and printers. Although incredibly small—some are even smaller than the size of a postage stamp—these memory cards have capacities that exceed the capacity of a DVD. We discuss flash memory in more detail in Chapter 8.

Optical Storage

What other kinds of storage devices are available? Internal hard drives are used to store your data, files, and installed software programs. Hard drives store their data on magnetized platters. Also included on most desktop and notebook computers is at least one **optical drive** that can read from and maybe even write to CDs, DVDs, or

Figure 2.30

Smaller external hard drives enable you to take a significant amount of data and programs on the road with you.

Inga Nielsen/Shutterstock.com

Figure 2.31

Flash drives are a convenient means of portable storage, and come in many different shapes and sizes.

Handout/KRT/Newscom

solid-state flash memory, storing information on an internal memory chip. Because a flash drive contains no moving parts, it is quite durable. It is also tiny enough to fit into your pocket, making it a very convenient means of portable storage. Often flash drives are combined with other devices such as pens or pocketknives (see Figure 2.31) for added convenience. Despite their diminutive size, flash drives have significant storage capacity—currently

Rafael Angel Irusta Machin/Alamy

Blu-ray Discs. Data is saved to a **compact disc (CD)**, **digital video (or versatile) disc (DVD)**, or **Blu-ray Disc (BD)** as tiny pits that are burned into the disc by a high-speed laser. CDs were initially created to store audio files. DVDs are the same size and shape as CDs but can hold more data. DVDs that store data on just one side and in one layer can store about seven times more data. If you're looking for more storage capacity, a double-sided/single-layer DVD is the next step. These discs have up to 8.5 GB of storage, and a double-sided/double-layer DVD can store nearly 16 GB of data. What if you want even more storage capacity? Blu-ray is the latest incarnation of optical storage to hit the market. Blu-ray Discs, which are similar in size and shape to CDs and DVDs, can hold as much as 50 GB of data—enough to hold approximately 4.5 hours of movies in the high-definition (HD) digital format that has become so popular. Many systems are now available with BD-ROM drives and even Blu-ray burners. External BD drives are another inexpensive way to add HD storage capacity to your system.

Figure 2.32 shows the storage capacities of the various portable storage media used in your computer system.

Connecting Peripherals to the Computer

Throughout this chapter, we have discussed peripheral devices that input, store, and output data and information. A **port** is a place through which a peripheral device attaches to the computer so that data can be exchanged between it and the operating system. Many ports are located on the back of a notebook computer and the system unit of a desktop computer. However, some commonly used ports are placed on the front and sides of many desktop and notebook computers (see Figure 2.33) for easier access when connecting devices such as flash drives or digital and video cameras.

High-Speed and Data Transfer Ports

What is the most common way to connect devices to a computer?
A **universal serial bus (USB) port** is now the most common port type used to connect input and output devices to the computer. This is mainly because of a USB port's ability

Figure 2.32 | STORAGE MEDIA CAPACITIES

Medium	Image	Typical Capacity
Solid-state drive (SSD)	 Oleksiy Mark/ iStockphoto.com	5 TB or more
External portable hard drive	 joel-t/ iStockphoto .com	4 TB or more
Mechanical hard drive	 © D. Hurst / Alamy	As much as 6 TB or more
Flash drive	 Christopher Testi/ Shutterstock .com	900 GB or more
Flash memory card	 © Richard Naude/Alamy	128 GB
Blu-ray (dual layer)	 AP/Photo/ PRNewsFoto/Sony Electronics Inc.	50 GB
Blu-ray (BD)	 © Coyote- Photography .co.uk/Alamy	25 GB
DVD DL (dual layer)	 © Studio 101/ Alamy	8.5 GB
DVD	 © Niels Poulsen/ Alamy	4.7 GB
CD	 © Studio 101/ Alamy	700 MB

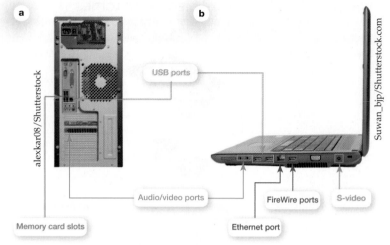

Figure 2.33

Many of the same ports appear on both (a) desktop and (b) notebook computers.

alexkar08/Shutterstock
Suwan_bjp/Shutterstock.com

Parallel ports were often used to connect printers to computers. The speed advantage offered by USB ports has made serial and parallel ports legacy technology.

What are other types of ports? You may also see other ports, such as **FireWire 400** and **FireWire 800**. The FireWire 400 interface moves data at 400 Mbps, while the FireWire 800 doubles the rate to 800 Mbps. Devices such as external hard drives, digital video cameras, portable music players, and digital media players all benefit from the speedy data transfer capabilities of FireWire. The FireWire 3200 standard, with data transfer rates of 3.2 Gbps, has been ratified but has yet to reach the market. FireWire 400 ports and connectors have two different configurations, as shown in Figure 2.35. FireWire 400 ports on computers generally have six pins, while FireWire ports on digital cameras have four pins.

To transfer data between the two devices, a special cable that has an appropriate connector at each end is needed. The faster FireWire 800 requires a nine-pin connection

Figure 2.34

(a) USB 3.0 and
(b) USB 2.0 connectors.

Courtesy of Seagate Technology, Inc.

to transfer data quickly. USB 2.0 ports (see Figure 2.34b) are the current standard and transfer data at 480 megabits per second (Mbps), approximately 40 times faster than the original USB ports. USB ports can connect a wide variety of peripherals to the computer, including keyboards, printers, mice, smartphones, external hard drives, flash drives, and digital cameras. The new USB 3.0 standard provides transfer speeds of 4.8 Gbps, which is 10 times the speed of USB 2.0. In addition, USB 3.0 charges devices faster than its predecessor. USB 3.0 (shown in Figure 2.34a) (per new note with image) should quickly become the port of choice.

A traditional serial port sends data one bit (piece of data) at a time. Serial ports were often used to connect modems (devices used to transmit data over telecommunications lines) to the computer. Sending data one bit at a time was a slow way to communicate. A parallel port could send data between devices in groups of bits at speeds of 500 Kbps and was much faster than traditional serial ports.

Figure 2.35

FireWire ports come in different configurations, two of which are illustrated here.

© Editorial Image, LLC/Alamy
Ronald Hudson/Fotolia

and is found on storage devices such as external and portable hard drives.

Connectivity and Multimedia Ports

Which ports help me connect with other computers and the Internet?
Another set of ports on your computer helps you communicate with other computers. A **connectivity port** can give you access to networks and the Internet or enable your computer to function as a fax machine. To find a connectivity port, look for a port that resembles a standard phone jack but is slightly larger. This port is called an **Ethernet port** (see Figure 2.36). Ethernet ports transfer data at speeds up to 10,000 Mbps. You can use an Ethernet port to connect your computer to a digital subscriber line (DSL) or cable modem, or a network. Many computers still feature a second connectivity port that will accept a standard phone line connector. This jack is the **modem port**. It uses a traditional telephone signal to connect to the Internet over a phone line.

How do I connect monitors and multimedia devices?
Other ports on the back and sides of the computer include the audio and video ports (see Figure 2.37). Video ports are necessary to hook up monitors. Whether you are attaching a monitor to a desktop computer, or adding a second, larger display to a notebook computer, you will use video ports. The **video graphics array (VGA)** port is the port to which CRT monitors connect. Many older LCD monitors also connect with a VGA port. The newer LCD monitors, as well as other multimedia devices such as televisions, DVD players, and projectors, connect to **digital video interface (DVI)** and **S-video (super video)** ports. Audio ports are where you connect headphones, microphones, and speakers to the computer.

How can I connect my computer to TVs and gaming consoles? The latest digital connector designed for use in high-definition home theater environments is a **high-definition multimedia interface (HDMI)**, a compact audio–video interface that carries both high-definition video and

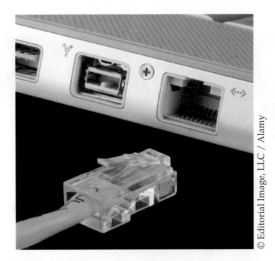

Figure 2.36

An Ethernet port and an Ethernet connector.

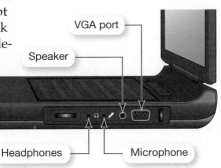

Figure 2.37

Video ports connect your monitors and multimedia devices to the computer; audio ports are used to connect speakers, headphones, and microphones.

uncompressed digital audio on one cable. (DVI can only carry video signals.) Because HDMI can transmit uncompressed audio and video, there is no need to convert the signal, which could ultimately reduce the quality of the sound or picture. Most DVD players, TVs, and game consoles have at least one HDMI port (see Figure 2.38).

Adding Ports: Expansion Cards and Hubs

What if I don't have all the ports I need? Because almost everything connects to your computer using USB ports, your desktop computer should have at least six USB ports, and a notebook computer should have at least three USB ports. Therefore, if you are looking to add the newest ports to an older computer or to expand the number of ports on your computer, you can use special expansion cards. You can install expansion cards into an open expansion slot on the motherboard in your desktop system unit to provide additional ports. If your notebook computer requires additional ports,

Figure 2.38

HDMI is the latest digital connector type for HD home theater equipment.

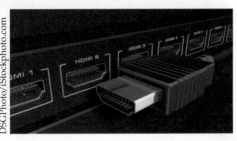

USB 3.0   USB 2.0 FireWire

© Andrew Kitching / Alamy

a

© Editorial Image, LLC / Alamy

b

Figure 2.39

Expansion cards can (a) fit on the motherboard or (b) in a card slot to provide your computer with additional ports.

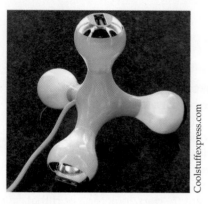

Coolstuffexpress.com

Figure 2.40

If you don't have enough USB ports to support your USB devices, consider getting an expansion hub, which can add four or more USB ports to your system.

Figure 2.41

You can use an empty drive bay to add additional ports and even a flash card reader to the front panel of the system unit.

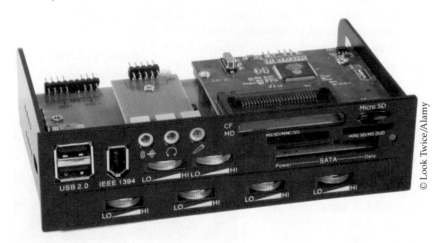

© Look Twice/Alamy

you can add them with an express card adapter. Figure 2.39 shows an example of such expansion cards.

Another alternative is adding an expansion hub (shown in Figure 2.40). An expansion hub is a device that connects to one port, such as a USB port, to provide additional new ports. It works like the multiplug extension cords used with electrical appliances.

You also can add ports to an empty drive bay, giving you easy-to-reach new ports. one The shown in Figure 2.41, fits into a regular drive bay and adds front-panel access to two USB 2.0 ports, a FireWire port audio jacks, and digital media card reader.

Power Controls

What's the best way to turn my computer on and off? The **power supply,** which is housed inside the system unit, transforms the wall voltage to the voltages required by computer chips. A desktop system typically has a power-on button on the front panel of the system unit, though you may also find power-on buttons on some keyboards. On notebooks, the power-on button is generally located near the top of the keyboard. Powering on your computer from a completely turned off state, such as when you start your computer in the morning, is called a **cold boot.** Powering off your computer properly helps to save energy, keeps your computer more secure, and ensures that your data is saved. You can turn your computer off by pressing the computer's power button or using the Shut Down button on the Start menu.

Should I turn off my computer every time I'm done using it? Some people say you should leave your computer on at all times. They argue that turning your computer on and off throughout the day subjects its components to stress because the heating and cooling process forces the components to expand and contract repeatedly. Other people say you should shut down your computer when you're not using it. They claim that it's not as environmentally friendly, and you'll end up wasting money on electricity to keep the computer running all the time. Modern operating systems include power-management settings that allow the most power-hungry components of the system (the hard drive and monitor) to shut down after a short idle period. With the power-management options of Windows 7, for example, you really need to shut down your computer completely only when you need to repair or install hardware in the system unit or move the system unit to another location. However, if you use your computer only for a little while each day, it would be best to power it off completely after each daily use.

Can I "rest" my computer without turning it off completely? As mentioned earlier, your computer has power-management settings that help it conserve energy. In Windows 7, the two main methods of power management are Sleep and Hibernate. When your computer enters **Sleep mode**, all of the documents, applications, and data you were using remain in RAM (memory), where they are quickly accessible when you restart your computer.

Hibernate is another power-saving mode (available in systems with less than 4GB of RAM) that stores your data in memory and saves it to your computer's hard drive. In either Sleep or Hibernate mode, the computer enters a state of greatly reduced power consumption, which saves energy. The big advantage to using Hibernate is that if there is a power failure while your computer is conserving power, your information is protected from loss, because it is saved on the hard drive. To put your computer into Sleep or Hibernate, open the Start menu and select the appropriate Sleep or Hibernate option. To wake up your computer, tap a key on the keyboard or move the mouse. In a few seconds, the computer will resume with exactly the same programs running and documents displayed as when you put it to sleep.

In Windows 7, you can change what happens when you click the arrow next to the Shut Down button in the Start menu. By accessing the Power Options dialog box (see Figure 2.42), you can decide if you want your computer to Sleep, Hibernate, or Shut Down when you click the power button.

What's the restart option in Windows for? If you're using Windows 7, you have the option to restart the computer when you click the right arrow button next to the Shut Down button on the Start menu (see Figure 2.43). Restarting the system while it's powered on is called a **warm boot**. You might need to perform a warm boot if the operating system or other software application stops responding or if you have installed new programs. It takes less time to perform a warm boot than to power down completely and then restart all of your hardware.

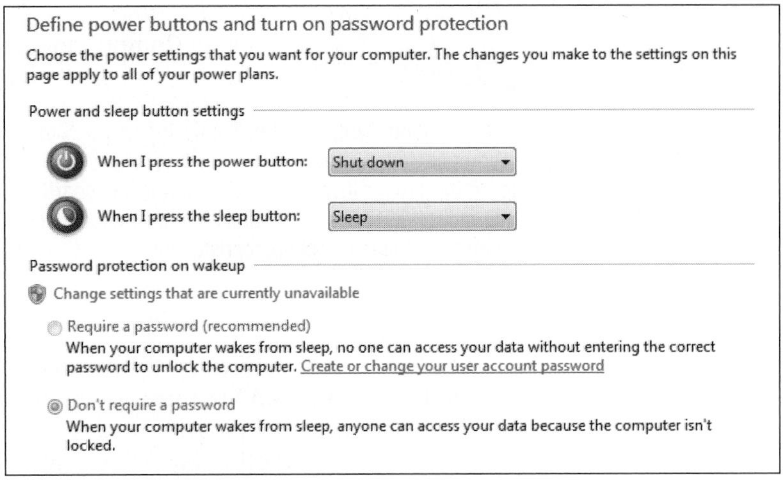

Figure 2.42

You can determine what happens when you click the power button on your computer through Power Options.

>To access Power Options, click the **Start** button, click **Control Panel**, click **Hardware and Sound,** and then select **Power Options.**

Setting It All Up

It's important that you understand not only your computer's components and how they work together but also how to set up these components safely. *Merriam-Webster's Dictionary* defines **ergonomics** as "an applied science concerned with designing and arranging things people use so that the people and things interact most efficiently and safely." ("Definition of ergonomics" from MERRIAM-WEBSTER'S COLLEGIATE® DICTIONARY, 11TH EDITION. Copyright © 2011 by Merriam-Webster,

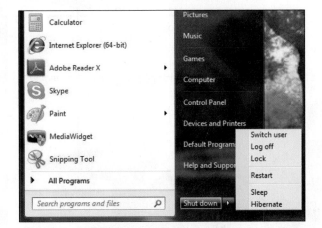

Figure 2.43

The Start menu in Windows 7 presents several power options. For a warm boot, choose Restart. To power down the computer completely, choose Shut Down. To put your computer into a lower power mode, select Sleep or Hibernate.

>To select a particular power option, click the **Start** menu button in the taskbar and then click the right arrow button.

Incorporated (www.merriam-webster.com). Reprinted by permission.) In terms of computing, ergonomics refers to how you set up your computer and other equipment to minimize your risk of injury or discomfort.

Why is ergonomics important? You don't have to have a desk job to run the risk of becoming injured by working improperly on a computer. Studies suggest that teenagers, on average, spend 31 hours online each week. When you factor in other computer uses such as typing school reports and playing video games, there is great potential for injury. The repetitive nature of long-term computer activities can place too much stress on joints and pull at the tendons and muscles, causing repetitive stress injuries such as carpal tunnel syndrome and tendonitis. These injuries can take months or years to develop to a point where they become painful, and by the time you notice the symptoms, the damage has already taken place. If you take precautionary care now, you may prevent years of unnecessary pain later on.

How can I avoid injuries when I'm working at my computer? As Figure 2.44 illustrates, it is important to arrange your monitor, chair, body, and keyboard in ways that will help you avoid injury, discomfort, and eyestrain as you work on your computer. The following additional guidelines can help keep you comfortable and productive:

- **Position your monitor correctly**. Studies suggest it's best to place your monitor at least 25 inches from your eyes. You may need to decrease the screen resolution to make text and images more readable at that distance. Experts recommend that the monitor be positioned either at eye level or so that it is at an angle 15 to 20 degrees below your line of sight.

- **Purchase an adjustable chair.** Adjust the height of your chair so that your feet touch the floor. (You may need to use a footrest to get the right position.) The back support needs to be adjustable so that you can position it to support your lumbar (lower back) region. You should also be able to move the seat or adjust the back so that you can sit without exerting pressure on your knees. If your chair doesn't adjust, placing a pillow behind your back can provide the same support.

- **Assume a proper position while typing.** A repetitive strain injury (RSI) is a painful condition caused by repetitive or awkward movements of a part of the body. Improperly positioned keyboards are one of the leading causes of RSIs in computer users. Your wrists should be flat (not bent) with respect to the keyboard, and your forearms should be parallel to the floor. Additionally, your wrists should not be resting on the keyboard while typing. You can either adjust the height of your chair or install a height-adjustable keyboard tray to ensure a proper position. Specially designed ergonomic keyboards such as the one shown in Figure 2.45 can help you achieve the proper wrist position.

Figure 2.44

Using proper equipment that is adjusted correctly helps prevent repetitive strain injuries while working at a computer.

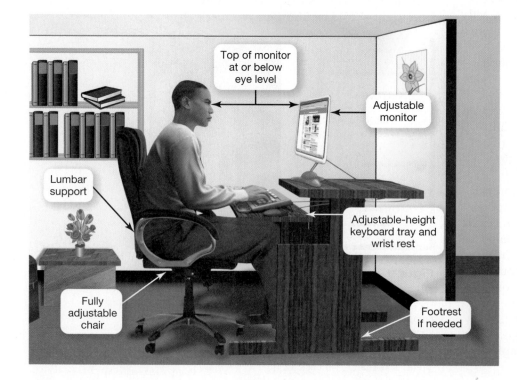

Top of monitor at or below eye level

Adjustable monitor

Lumbar support

Adjustable-height keyboard tray and wrist rest

Fully adjustable chair

Footrest if needed

- **Take breaks from computer tasks.** Remaining in the same position for long periods of time increases stress on your body. Shift your position in your chair and stretch your hands and fingers periodically.

  Likewise, staring at the screen for long periods of time can lead to eyestrain, so rest your eyes by periodically taking them off the screen and focusing them on an object at least 20 feet away.

- **Ensure the lighting is adequate.** Ensuring that you have proper lighting in your work area is a good way to minimize eyestrain. To do so, eliminate any sources of direct glare (light shining directly into your eyes) or reflected glare (light shining off the computer screen) and ensure there is enough light to read comfortably. If you still can't eliminate glare from your computer screen, you can purchase an antiglare screen to place over your monitor. Look for ones that are polarized or have a purplish optical coating. These will provide the greatest relief.

Figure 2.45

Ergonomic keyboards that curve and contain built-in wrist rests help maintain proper hand position and minimize wrist strain.

Dmitry Melnikov/Shutterstock

Is ergonomics important when using mobile devices? Working with mobile computing devices presents interesting challenges when it comes to injury prevention. For example, many users work with notebooks resting on their laps, placing the monitor outside of the optimal line of sight and thereby increasing neck strain. The table in Figure 2.46 provides guidelines on preventing injuries when computing on the go.

So whether you're computing at your desk or on the road, consider the ergonomics of your work environment. Doing so will help you avoid injury and discomfort.

Figure 2.46 | PREVENTING INJURIES WHILE ON THE GO

	PDA/Smartphone RSIs	PMP Hearing Damage	Small-Screen Vision Issues	Lap Injuries	Back, Neck, and Shoulder Injuries
Malady	Repetitive strain injuries (such as DeQuervain's tendonitis) from constant typing of instant messages.	Hearing loss from high decibel sound levels in earbuds or headphones.	Blurriness and dryness caused by squinting to view tiny screens on mobile devices.	Burns on legs from heat generated by notebook.	Pain caused from carrying notebook (messenger) bag hung over your shoulder.
Preventative measures	Restrict length and frequency of messages, take breaks often, and perform other motions with your thumbs and fingers during breaks to relieve tension.	Turn down volume (you should be able to hear external noises such as people talking), use software programs that limit sound levels (not over 60 decibels), and use external, over-ear style headphones instead of earbuds.	Blink frequently or use eye drops to maintain moisture level in eyes, after 10 minutes take a break and focus your eyes on something at least 8 feet away for 5 minutes, use an adequate amount of light, increase the size of fonts.	Place a book, magazine, or notebook cooling pad between your legs and your notebook.	Use a conventional backpack with two shoulder straps, lighten the load by only carrying essential equipment, and consider buying a lightweight notebook.

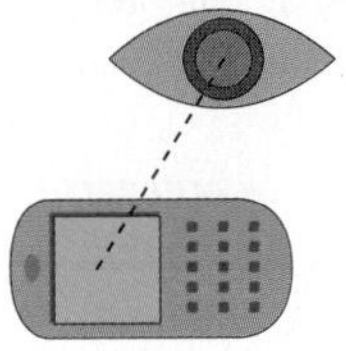

With the advent of the computer, many speculated that we would become a paperless society. Instead of saving printed documents and other output as was done prior to the PC, information would be saved in a digital state: hard drives replacing filing cabinets, online photo buckets replacing photo albums and scrapbooks, and e-books replacing our favorite novels and textbooks. Hard drive capacities do enable us to save more digital content and online storage systems enable us to save pictures and other files to "the cloud." Additionally, e-book readers have increased in popularity. But, has all of this push toward digital content begun to make the printer obsolete? Surprisingly, no. In this digital age, more than ever, people still have a deep-rooted need to see, feel, mark, share, or use their digital images or information in a physical form. New technologies that push the boundaries of printing, such as inkless printing, printing from the cloud, and 3D printing, are being developed and refined.

Inkless Printing

We've all experienced it: needing to print out an important document only to find that our print cartridge is so low that either nothing prints, or the resulting document appears in varying shades of pink and green. Inkless printing avoids this dilemma by eliminating the need for print cartridges altogether. Inkless printing systems, such as that developed by Zink, store ink in the paper itself, rather than in toner or ink cartridges. The Zink printer heats the color crystals in the paper with precise heat pulses of specific duration and temperature to produce a full color print. This technology is currently being used in small portable camera and printer devices such as Dell's Wasabi printer and PoGo by Polaroid (see Figure 2.47). The PoGo instant digital camera has an integrated printer, and the PoGo instant digital printer connects to your cellphone or digital camera via Bluetooth to print pictures on the go.

The PrePeat is an innovative office printer that uses no ink or toner because it uses rewritable plastic sheets made from PET plastic that can be erased and reprinted about 1,000 times per sheet. The heat-sensitive plastic sheets are fed into the printer and a line thermal head either prints a new document in black and white or erases an existing document and reprints another, allowing you to re-use paper again and again. This technology is ideal for documents that are only read once, such as office memos or emails. Although the technology is very expensive (the printer is about $5,500 and each sheet of special paper is $3.30), it provides another lead into helping reduce the incredible toll paper and ink printing has on our environment.

Cloud Printing

What happens if you want to print something from your smartphone or tablet? With the growing proliferation of mobile devices, the need to send a print document to a printer is increasing, but as yet unavailable. Currently, to print a document you must have a printer associated with your

AP Photo/Jae C. Hong

Figure 2.47

Using an inkless printing system, the PoGo instant digital camera and printer make printing on the go possible.

computer. Usually this is not a problem because at home, school, or in the office, there is generally one printer, and all the PCs connected to it have the right software and cables or wireless capabilities. But, to print something from your mobile device, the solution has been to transfer the document via e-mail to a Web-based storage service such as Dropbox so a printer-connected computer could access it. Not surprisingly, Google has released Google Cloud Print in beta form, a service that enables "any application (web, desktop, or mobile) on any device to print to any printer."

In Google's vision, there would be "cloud-aware" printers (see Figure 2.48). Such printers would need neither a PC connection of any kind nor a print driver. The printer is simply registered with one or more cloud print services and awaits print jobs. Cloud-aware printers don't exist yet, but Google is hoping that manufacturers will see the universal need and interest in this concept and begin to develop the appropriate software and hardware. In the meantime, Google has provided a work-around for traditional printers—those that are in our homes, schools, and offices. Installing a small piece of software gives the legacy printer a proxy that registers the printer with Google Cloud Print, and printing requests can then be sent via the cloud, directed to the traditional printer.

3D Printing

Printing a 3D model of a proposed building or new prototype is common for architects and engineers. The process builds a model one layer at a time from the bottom up. The procedure begins by spreading a layer of powder on a platform. Then, depending on technology, uses nozzles similar to those in an inkjet printer to spray tiny drops of glue at specific places to solidify the powder, or it is solidified through a melting process. The printer repeats solidifying layers of powder until the model is built to specifications. This technology has spurred the manufacturing of a variety of consumer goods, from toys to clothing. Shapeways (**www.shapeways.com**) uses

3D printing to enable anyone to turn their 3D designs into real physical models. Then, those models can be personalized, bought, or sold through Shapeways' online community.

3D printing is being used in the medical community as well. Bespoke Innovations (**www.bespokeinnovations.com**) is using 3D printing to create prosthetic limbs with more life-like form and textures, as well as giving the recipient the ability to further personalize the prosthetic to include tattoos! As mentioned in Chapter 1, researchers at Wake Forest Institute for Regenerative Medicine have developed a way to use similar inkjet technologies to build heart, bone, and blood vessel tissues in the lab, as well as to "print" restorative cells directly into a soldier's wound at the site where the injury occurred, thus significantly improving the soldier's chances of survival.

Taking traditional technologies, such as inkjet printing, and applying them to solve current human struggles is a long and tedious process, but without these pioneers experimenting with different applications, society would advance a lot more slowly.

Figure 2.48

"Cloud aware" printers will only need an Internet connection and then could be accessed from any mobile device.

1. What exactly is a computer, and what are its four main functions?

Computers are devices that process data. They help organize, sort, and categorize data to turn it into information. The computer's four major functions are: (1) input: gather data, or allow users to enter data; (2) process: manipulate, calculate, or organize that data; (3) output: display data and information in a form suitable for the user; and (4) storage: save data and information for later use.

2. What is the difference between data and information?

Data is a representation of a fact or idea. The number 3 and the words *televisions* and *Sony* are pieces of data. Information is data that has been organized or presented in a meaningful fashion. An inventory list that indicates that "three Sony televisions" are in stock is processed information. It allows a retail clerk to answer a customer query about the availability of merchandise. Information is more powerful than raw data.

3. What are bits and bytes, and how are they measured?

To process data into information, computers need to work in a language they understand. This language, called *binary language*, consists of two numbers: 0 and 1. Each 0 and each 1 is a binary digit, or bit. Eight bits create one byte. In computers, each letter of the alphabet, each number, and each special character consists of a unique combination of eight bits (one byte)—a string of eight 0s and 1s. For describing large amounts of storage capacity, the terms *megabyte* (approximately 1 million bytes), *gigabyte* (approximately 1 billion bytes), and *terabyte* (approximately 1 trillion bytes) are used.

4. What devices do I use to get data into the computer?

An input device enables you to enter data (text, images, and sounds) and instructions (user responses and commands) into a computer. You use keyboards to enter typed data and commands, whereas you use the mouse to enter user responses and commands. Keyboards and mice come in both wired and wireless versions, as well as other special layouts and designs to fit almost every need.

Touch screens are display screens that respond to commands initiated by a touch with a finger or a stylus. Images are input into the computer with scanners, digital cameras, camcorders, and cell phones. Live video is captured with webcams and digital video recorders. Microphones capture sounds. There are many different types of microphones, including desktop, headset, and clip-on models.

5. What devices do I use to get information out of the computer?

Output devices enable you to send processed data out of your computer. It can take the form of text, pictures, sounds, or video. Monitors display soft copies of text, graphics, and video, while printers create hard copies of text and graphics. LCDs are the most popular type of monitor.

There are two primary categories of printers used today: inkjet and laser. Specialty printers are also available. These include all-in-one printers, plotters, and thermal printers. When choosing a printer, you should be aware of factors such as speed, resolution, color output, and cost.

Speakers are the output devices for sound. Most computers include speakers, with more sophisticated systems including subwoofers and surround sound.

6. What's on the motherboard?

The motherboard, the main circuit board of the system, contains a computer's central processing unit (CPU), which coordinates the functions of all other devices on the computer. The performance of a CPU is affected by the speed of the processor (measured in gigahertz), the amount of cache memory, the speed of the front side bus (FSB), and the number of processing cores. RAM, the computer's volatile memory, is also located on the motherboard. RAM is where all the data and instructions are held while the computer is running. ROM, a permanent type of memory, is responsible for housing instructions to help start up a computer. The motherboard also houses a set of slots for expansion cards, which have specific functions that augment the computer's basic functions. Typical expansion cards found in the system unit are the sound and video cards.

7. Where are information and programs stored?

To save programs and information permanently, you need to save them to the hard drive or to another permanent storage device such as a CD, DVD, or flash drive. The hard drive is your computer's primary device for permanent storage of software and files. The hard drive is a nonvolatile storage device, meaning it holds the data and instructions your computer needs permanently, even after the computer is turned off. Mechanical hard drives have spinning platters on which data is saved, whereas newer solid-state hard drives (SSD) use solid-state memory, similar to that used with flash drives. External hard drives are essentially internal hard drives that have been made portable by enclosing them in a protective case and making them small and lightweight. Optical drives that can read from and write to CD, DVD, or Blu-ray Discs are another means of permanent, portable storage. Data is saved to compact discs (CDs), digital video discs (DVDs), and Blu-ray Discs (BDs) as tiny pits that are burned into the disc by a high-speed laser. Flash drives are another portable means of storing data. Flash drives plug into USB ports. Flash memory cards let you transfer digital data between your computer and devices such as digital cameras, smartphones, video cameras, and printers.

8. How are devices connected to the computer?

There are a wide variety of ports that allow you to hook up peripheral devices (such as your monitor and keyboard) to your system.

The most common type of port used to connect devices to a computer is the USB port. USB technology has replaced serial ports and parallel ports, which are now considered legacy technology. USB 2.0 is the current standard but will be quickly replaced by the newer, faster USB 3.0 standard. FireWire ports provide additional options for data transfer.

Connectivity ports, including Ethernet ports and modem ports, give you access to networks and the Internet and enable your computer to function as a fax machine. Multimedia ports include VGA, DVI, and S-video ports. They connect the computer to monitors and other multimedia devices. Audio ports are where you connect headphones, microphones, and speakers to the computer. HDMI ports are used as a connection between monitors, TVs, and gaming consoles and work with both audio and video content.

9. How do I set up my computer to avoid strain and injury?

Ergonomics refers to how you arrange your computer and equipment to minimize your risk of injury or discomfort. This includes positioning your monitor correctly, buying an adjustable chair that ensures you have good posture while using the computer, assuming a proper position while typing, making sure the lighting is adequate, and not looking at the screen for long periods of time. Other good practices include taking frequent breaks and using other specially designed equipment such as ergonomic keyboards. Ergonomics is also important to consider when using mobile devices.

 Companion Website

The Companion Website includes a variety of additional materials to help you review and learn more about the topics in this chapter. Go to: *www.pearsonhighered.com/techinaction*

key terms

Word Bank

• CPU	• LED	• RAM
• DVI	• microphone	• ROM
• ergonomics	• monitor	• speakers
• external hard drive	• mouse	• SSD
• FireWire	• notebook	• system unit
• inkjet printer	• optical mouse	• USB
• laser printer	• QWERTY	• webcam

Instructions: Fill in the blanks using the words from the Word Bank above.

Jackie had been getting a sore back and stiff arms when she sat at her desk, so she redesigned the (1) _____ of her notebook setup. She placed the notebook in a stand so the (2) _____ was elevated to eye level and was 25 inches from her eyes. She decided to improve her equipment in other ways. Her (3) _____ was old, so she replaced it with a wireless (4) _____ that didn't need a mouse pad. To plug in the wireless receiver, she used a(n) (5) _____ port on the front of her (6) _____. She considered buying a larger (7) _____ keyboard with a number pad so she could more easily input numeric data. Because she often printed papers for her classes, Jackie decided to buy a printer that could print text-based pages quickly. Although she decided to keep her (8) _____ to print photos, she decided to buy a new (9) _____ to print her papers faster. While looking at printers, Jackie also noticed widescreen (10) _____ monitors that would provide a larger display than that on her notebook, so she bought one on sale. She hooked up the monitor to the (11) _____ port on the back of the notebook. Jackie also bought a(n) (12) _____ that was attached to a headset and a(n) (13) _____ so she could talk to her friends over the Internet. Jackie also knew she had to buy a(n) (14) _____ to back up all her files. Finally, knowing her system could use more memory, Jackie checked out prices for additional (15) _____.

becoming computer literate

There is such a variety of computers on the market today. Each type of device satisfies a different need—for example, a notebook computer is good for those who do not want to be tied down to working in one spot, while netbook computers are also great mobile devices, but their diminutive size may be a limiting factor for some users.

Instructions: Create a presentation that details the differences between all-in-one, desktop, notebook, tablet PC, tablet, and netbook computers. Include the pros and cons of each device, and list what kind of users may benefit from using each device. You should also incorporate images for each device. You may use the Internet for information, device pictures, and illustrations, but remember to credit all sources.

two self-test

Instructions: Answer the multiple-choice and true–false questions below for more practice with key terms and concepts from this chapter.

Multiple Choice

1. What is a gigabyte?
a. one million bytes
b. one billion bytes
c. one billion bits
d. one trillion bits

2. The type of computer that might help run your refrigerator or car is
a. a mainframe computer.
b. a supercomputer.
c. an embedded computer.
d. none of the above.

3. What enables your computer to connect with other computers?
a. expansion card
b. adapter card
c. video card
d. network interface card

4. Which is NOT a built-in input device for a notebook?
a. trackpoint
b. touch pad
c. optical mouse
d. none of the above

5. To add ports to your computer, what do you need?
a. a digital media card reader
b. an external hard drive
c. an expansion card
d. a flash memory card

6. Which holds the instructions the computer needs to start up?
a. CPU   c. USB
b. RAM   d. ROM

7. Which is TRUE about mainframe computers?
a. They perform complex calculations rapidly.
b. They support hundreds of users simultaneously.
c. They execute many programs at a fast pace.
d. They excel at running a few programs quickly.

8. Which is NOT important to consider when buying a printer?
a. paper
b. duty cycle
c. cost of consumables
d. resolution

9. Which type of microphone is best for recording a single voice?
a. omnidirectional
b. bidirectional
c. unidirectional
d. all of the above

10. What type of storage device can you use to transfer digital data between your computer and devices such as digital cameras?
a. flash memory card
b. optical drive
c. connectivity port
d. HDMI port

True-False

_____ 1. Data and information are interchangeable terms.

_____ 2. The hard drive is an example of a nonvolatile storage device.

_____ 3. Ergonomics is important only with desktop computers, not mobile devices.

_____ 4. LED and LCD monitors are considered legacy technology.

_____ 5. The clock speed of the CPU is the only measure of a processor's expected performance.

making the
transition to...
next semester **two** chapter

making the
transition to...
next semester

1. **Study Abroad**

   You are preparing for your semester abroad in an immersion program in France. All the work you turn in will be written in French. Investigate the differences between a keyboard that you'd use in France and a traditional American English keyboard. What options do you have to incorporate an international keyboard into your notebook computer?

2. **Watching Device Demos**

   YouTube is a great resource for product demonstrations. Open your browser, navigate to the YouTube Web site (**www.youtube.com**), and search on any type of computer peripheral discussed in this chapter to see if you can find a demonstration of a cool product.

   How helpful are these demonstrations? Make a video demonstration of a computing device you have and post it to your course management system, or present it to your classmates (as specified by your instructor).

3. **Communicating with the Computer**

   You are involved in many group projects at school. Between your work, your classes, and other outside responsibilities, you are finding it difficult to always meet in person. Investigate the devices you would need to be able to have virtual group meetings.

4. **Turn Your Monitor into a TV**

   You've heard how easy it is to convert an LCD monitor into a TV. Your parents just bought a new computer and are giving you their old PC monitor. You need a new TV for your dorm room, so you decide to give it a try.

   a. What does your monitor need to retrofit it into a TV? What other devices do you need?
   b. How much will it cost? How much do new LCD TVs cost?
   c. Is this something you would consider doing? Why or why not?
   d. What would you do if your parents gave you their old LCD TV? Could you turn it into a monitor? If so, what would you need to do that?

5. **Green Computing**

   Reducing energy consumption and promoting the recycling of computer components are key aspects of many businesses' "green" (environmentally friendly) initiatives. Using the Web, research the following:

   a. What are the key attributes of the Energy Star and EPEAT Gold green PC certifications? Does your PC have these certifications?
   b. What toxic components are contained in computers and monitors? Where can you recycle computers and monitors in your area?
   c. Check out **www.goodcleantech.com** and find out which companies are currently working toward better green technology. If your school had to replace computers in a lab, which environmentally friendly company would you recommend? Why?

making the transition to... the workplace

1. Backing up Your Work

You have embarked on a position as a freelance editor. You will be using your own computer. Until now you have not worried too much about backing up your data. Now, however, it's extremely important that you back up all your work frequently.

Research the various backup options that are available including online backup, external hard drives, and portable flash storage. What are the size limitations of each? What are the initial and ongoing costs of each? How frequently do the various options allow you to perform backups? Which option would you would choose, and why?

2. What Hardware Will You Use?

When you arrive at a new position for a company, your employer will most likely provide you with a computer. Based on the career you are in now or are planning to pursue, answer the following questions:

a. What kind of computer system would the company mostly likely provide to you—desktop, notebook, tablet PC, or something else? How does that compare with the type of system you would prefer to work with?

b. If you were required to use a type of computer you had never used before (such as a Mac instead of a PC), how would you go about learning to use the new computer?

c. What other devices might your employer provide? Consider such items as smartphones or printers. How important is it for these devices to conform to the latest trends?

d. Should you be able to use employer-provided equipment, such as a smartphone, for personal benefit? Does your answer differ if you have to pay for part or all of the device?

3. Exploring Monitors

You have been asked to help edit video for a friend. You have a great notebook computer, which is powerful enough to handle this type of task, but you need to buy a separate LCD monitor to hook up to your computer and are not exactly sure what to buy. You know it should be larger than 15 inches, capable of displaying HD, and can't cost more than $200.

a. Research five different monitors that would fit your needs. Create a table that lists each monitor and its specifications, including display type, screen size, aspect ratio, native resolution, and response time. Also list the types of ports and connectors the monitor has.

b. Note whether each monitor has HDMI. Why would HDMI capability be important or not important?

c. Research two LED monitors. Would an LED monitor be a viable option? Explain.

d. Explain which of the five monitors would best suit your needs and why.

4. Communications Devices

You have been assigned to create podcasts for the department in which you work. The podcasts will involve interviews and personal reflections, as well as capturing sound from groups of people. Investigate the best microphones for these jobs. Which type of microphone would work best for each type of function? Is there a microphone that could be used for all needs? If so, which one? Would buying one microphone be more economical than buying three different mics? Why or why not?

5. Choosing the Best Laser Printer

You are looking to replace your inkjet printer with a laser printer. You haven't decided whether a color laser printer is necessary.

a. What are the cost considerations between getting a laser printer and a color laser printer (i.e., initial costs, costs of cartridges, and so on)?

b. Investigate wireless and Bluetooth options. What are the considerations involved with regard to these features?

c. Investigate all-in-one laser printers that have printer, scanner, and fax capabilities. How much more expensive are they than laser printers? Are there any drawbacks to these multipurpose machines? Do they perform each function as well as their stand-alone counterparts do? Can you print in color on these machines?

Based on your research, which printer would be your choice, and why?

critical thinking questions

Instructions: Some ideas are best understood by experimenting with them in our own minds. The following critical thinking questions are designed to demand your full attention but require only a comfortable chair—no technology.

1. Computer of the Future

Think about how mobile our computing devices have become and the convergence of different devices such as cameras, phones, and computers. What do you think the computer of the future will be like? What capabilities will it have that computers currently don't have? Do you see desktop computers becoming obsolete in the near future?

2. Table Monitors and Surface Monitors

Table monitors and surface monitors are tabletop devices that are designed to "grab" and manipulate objects on the display. Like an iPod Touch or iPhone, the display is multi-touch and can accept simultaneous input from multiple users, so the table monitor can be helpful with games or other products that require interactivity. Microsoft launched a product called Surface in 2007, and although it never really took off, you see similar devices featured on some TV crime-fighting shows as detectives manipulate crime evidence and photos. Why do you think this device never really captured the interest of the public? Would this be a useful object to have in your home, classroom, or office? Why or why not?

3. External Storage

Hard drives are great for storing data and information on your computer, but there are many reasons why you might want to have alternate storage devices. List various external and mobile storage devices that are discussed in this chapter, and describe the purposes and uses of each one. Note which of these device types you currently use, and for what purpose. Note also the device(s) you might have a need to use in the next year or so.

4. Ethics Violations

Review the Ethics piece in this chapter. Which of the Ten Commandments of Ethical Computing do you think your classmates have violated? Why do you think these violations occur, and what do you think could be done to reduce or eliminate such unethical behaviors?

5. "Smart" Cars

Cars are becoming more technically advanced every day. They are now able to parallel park by themselves, avoid collisions, alert you if you are falling asleep at the wheel, provide emergency response, and sense if you are going to back up over something inadvertently. What other technical advances do you see cars incorporating? Do you think that any of these current or potential advancements could result in unexpected negative consequences? If so, what?

6. iPad

The Apple iPad has been enthusiastically accepted because of its multi-touch screen, useful applications, and small, light frame. The iPad 2 includes two cameras, but it is without certain features that might make it even better. If Steven Jobs, the CEO of Apple, were to ask you for your advice as to what to include in the next version of the iPad, what would you suggest?

team time

Which Mobile Device Is the Best?

Problem

You have joined a small business that is beginning to evaluate its technology setup. Because of the addition of several new sales representatives and other administrative employees, many new computers need to be purchased. You are trying to decide which mobile devices would be better to purchase: notebook computers, tablet PCs, tablet computers (iPads), or a combination of these devices.

Task

Split your class into small groups, divide each group into three teams, and assign the following tasks:

Member A explores the benefits and downfalls of notebook computers.
Member B explores the benefits and downfalls of tablet PCs.
Member C explores the benefits and downfalls of tablet computers.

Process

1. Form the teams. Think about what the technology goals are for the company and what information and resources you need to tackle this project.
2. Research and then discuss the components of each system you are recommending. Are any components better suited for the particular needs of certain types of employees (sales representatives versus administrative staff)? Consider all the input, output, processing, and storage devices. Are any special devices or peripherals required?
3. Consider the different types of employees in the company. Would a combination of devices be better than a single solution? If so, what kinds of employees would get which type of computer?
4. As a team, write a summary position paper. Support your system recommendation for the company. Each team member should include why his or her type of computer will be part of the solution or not.

Conclusion

Notebooks, tablet PCs, and tablet computers have their own merits as computing systems. Being aware of the options in the marketplace, knowing how to analyze the trade-offs of different designs, and recognizing the different needs each type fulfills allows you to become a better consumer as well as a better computer user.

Green Computing

Ethical conduct is a stream of decisions you make all day long. In this exercise, you will research and then role-play a complicated ethical situation. The role you play may or may not match your own personal beliefs but your research and use of logic will enable you to represent whichever view is assigned. An arbitrator will watch and comment on both sides of the arguments, and together the team will agree on an ethical solution.

Green computing—conducting computing needs with the least possible amount of power—is on everyone's minds. Although it's hard to argue with an environmentally conscious agenda, the pinch to our pocketbooks and the loss of some comforts sometimes makes green computing difficult. Businesses, including colleges, need to consider a variety of issues and concerns before jumping into a complete green overhaul.

Research Areas to Consider

- End-of-life management: E-waste and recycling
- Energy-efficient devices
- Costs of green computing
- Government funding and incentives

Process

Divide the class into teams.

1. Research the areas cited above and devise a scenario in which your college is considering modifying its current technology setup to a more green IT strategy.
2. Team members should write a summary that provides background information for their character—for example, environmentalist, college IT administrator, or arbitrator—and details their character's behaviors to set the stage for the role-playing event. Then, team members should create an outline to use during the role-playing event.
3. Team members should arrange a mutually convenient time to meet for the exchange, using the chat room feature of MyITLab, the discussion board feature of Blackboard, or meeting in person.
4. Team members should present their case to the class or submit a PowerPoint presentation for review by the rest of the class, along with the summary and resolution they developed.

Conclusion

As technology becomes ever more prevalent and integrated into our lives, more and more ethical dilemmas will present themselves. Being able to understand and evaluate both sides of the argument, while responding in a personally or socially ethical manner, will be an important skill.

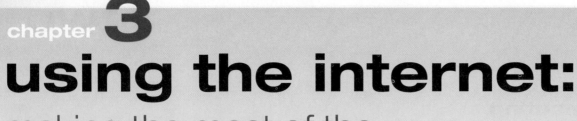

chapter 3

using the internet:
making the most of the Web's resources

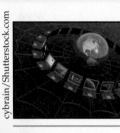

cybrain/Shutterstock.com

The Internet and How It Works

OBJECTIVES:

What is the origin of the Internet? *(p. 96)*

How does data travel on the Internet? *(p. 97)*

ra2 studio/Shutterstock.com

Communicating and Collaborating Through the Internet

OBJECTIVES:

How can I communicate and collaborate using Web 2.0 technologies? *(p. 98)*

How can I communicate with e-mail? *(p. 100)*

 Sound Byte: Creating a Web-Based E-mail Account

Sound Byte: Blogging

Angela Waye/Shutterstock.com

Web Entertainment

OBJECTIVE:

What multimedia files are found on the Web, and what software is needed? *(p. 106)*

Maxx-Studio/Shutterstock.com

Conducting Business over the Internet: E-Commerce

OBJECTIVE:

What is e-commerce, and what online safeguards are there? *(p. 110)*

 Active Helpdesk: Doing Business Online

marema/Shutterstock.com

Using the Web Effectively

OBJECTIVES:

What is a Web browser, and what is a URL and its parts? *(p. 112)*

How can I use hyperlinks and other tools to get around the Web? *(p. 113)*

How do I search the Internet effectively, and how can I evaluate Web sites? *(p. 117)*

 Sound Byte: Welcome to the Web

 Active Helpdesk: Getting Around the Web

 Sound Byte: Finding Information on the Web

Active Helpdesk: Using Subject Directories and Search Engines

Scan here for more info on How Cool Is This? ▶

how cool is *this?*

Looking for answers on the Web? Check out WolframAlpha, a **new way to search** for information on the Web!

Where do you go when you need to find something online? Google? Dogpile? Although these and other common Internet tools **help** you find information, they generally lead you to where you can find an answer, but don't always provide the answer—or an answer that you trust. Enter WolframAlpha (**www.wolframalpha.com**), a "**computational knowledge engine**" that computes the answers to a wide range of questions that have factual answers.

For example, if you ask, "What is the monthly payment for a $20,000, five-year loan at 5% interest?" you'll get not only the payment, but also the total interest paid and the effective interest rate. A search for "pear" results in average nutrition facts, taxonomy information, and the digital representation of the color "pear." WolframAlpha **understands questions** and computes answers, unlike traditional Internet search tools that simply retrieve Web files that might contain an answer.

The foundation of this unique tool is a set of models from a variety of fields of knowledge, combined with **massive** amounts of data and algorithms that represent **real-world knowledge**. It knows about technology, geography, cooking, business, travel, music, and more. The information it delivers uses more than 5,000 different **visual representations** such as tables and graphs. There are also several topic-specific mobile apps that relate to specific educational and professional areas such as statistics, calculus, and music theory.

Ask WolframAlpha a question today to see how cool it really is.

Lukiyanova Natalia / frenta/Shutterstock.com

The Origin of the Internet

It's hard to imagine life without the **Internet**, the largest computer network in the world. The Internet is actually a network of networks that connects billions of computer users globally. We use it to shop, to communicate, to research, to find places and get directions, and to entertain ourselves (see Figure 3.1). It's accessible from our computers, smartphones, portable music players (PMPs), and gaming systems, and we can get to it while at home, at work, at school—even at Starbucks or in the car. But what exactly is the Internet, and how did it begin?

Why was the Internet created? The concept of the Internet was developed while the United States was in the midst of the Cold War with the Soviet Union. At that time, the U.S. armed forces needed a computer system that would operate efficiently

computers had been networked since the early 1960s, there was no reliable way to connect computers from different manufacturers because they used different proprietary designs and methods of communication. What was lacking was a common communications method that all computers could use. The Internet was created to respond to these two concerns: establishing a secure form of military communications and creating a means by which all computers could communicate.

Who invented the Internet? The modern Internet evolved from an early U.S. government-funded "internetworking" project called the Advanced Research Projects Agency Network (ARPANET). ARPANET began as a four-node network involving UCLA, Stanford Research Institute, the University of California at Santa Barbara, and the University of Utah in Salt Lake City. The first real communication occurred in late 1969 between the computer at Stanford and the computer at UCLA. Although the system crashed after the third letter was transmitted, it was the beginning of a revolution. Many people participated in the creation of the ARPANET, but two men

Figure 3.1

From buying shoes on eBay to getting directions on your cell phone to checking messages, the Internet makes it all possible.

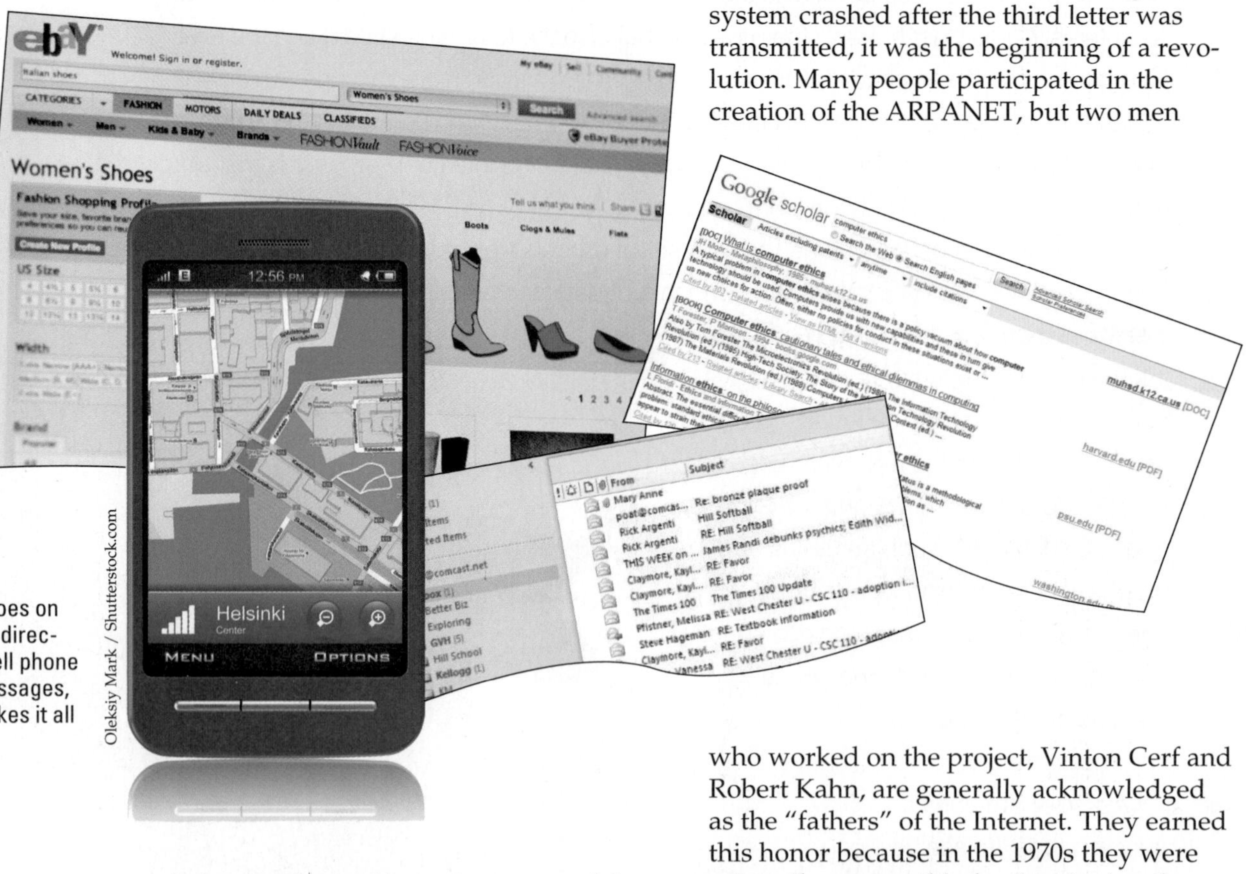

© NetPhotos / Alamy

Oleksiy Mark / Shutterstock.com

and that was located in various parts of the country so that it could not be disrupted easily in the event of an attack.

At the same time, researchers hoped the Internet would address the problems involved with getting different computers to communicate with each other. Although

who worked on the project, Vinton Cerf and Robert Kahn, are generally acknowledged as the "fathers" of the Internet. They earned this honor because in the 1970s they were primarily responsible for developing the communications protocols (standards) that are still in use on the Internet today.

So are the Web and the Internet the same thing? Because the **World Wide Web** (**WWW** or the **Web**) is what we use the most, we sometimes think of the Internet and the Web as being interchangeable. However, the Web is a subset of the Internet, dedicated to broadcasting HTML pages and the means by which we access information over the Internet. The Web is based on the Hypertext Transfer Protocol (HTTP), hence the *http://* at the beginning of Web addresses. Other components of the Internet include FTP and BitTorrent, which will be discussed later in this chapter. What distinguishes the Web from the rest of the Internet is its use of:

- Common communications protocols that enable different computers to talk to each other and display information in compatible formats
- Special links that enable users to navigate from one place to another on the Web

Did the same people who created the Internet create the Web? The Web was created many years after the original Internet. In 1989, Tim Berners-Lee, a physicist at the European Organization for Nuclear Research (CERN), wanted a method for linking his research documents so that other researchers could access them. In conjunction with Robert Cailliau, Berners-Lee developed the basic architecture of the Web and created the first **Web browser** (or **browser**), software that enables a user to display and interact with text and other media on the Web. The original browser could handle only text and was usable only on computers running the NeXT operating system, a commercially unsuccessful operating system, which limited its usage. So Berners-Lee put out a call to the Internet community to assist with development of browsers for other platforms.

In 1993, the National Center for Supercomputing Applications released its Mosaic browser for use on the Macintosh and Windows operating systems. Mosaic could display graphics as well as text. The once-popular Netscape Navigator browser evolved from Mosaic and heralded the beginning of the Web's monumental growth.

The Internet and How It Works

The Internet is an integral part of our lives, and our ability to use and interact with the Internet and the World Wide Web will only converge even more with our daily lives. Therefore, it's important to understand how the Internet works and the choices available for connecting to it.

The Internet2 program

The Internet2 is a research and development consortium of more than 350 universities (supported by government and industry partners) that seeks to expand the possibilities of the Internet by developing new Internet technologies and disseminating them as rapidly as possible to the rest of the Internet community. Many of the current technologies of the commercial Internet are possible because of the research done by the Internet2 consortium. The Internet2 backbone supports extremely high-speed communications—up to 8.8 terabits per second (TBps)—and provides an excellent testing area for new data transmission technologies.

How does the Internet work? Computers connected to the Internet communicate with (or "talk" to) each other in turns, just as we do when we ask a question and get an answer. Thus, a computer connected to the Internet acts in one of two ways: it is either a **client**, a computer that asks for data, or it is a **server**, a computer that receives the request and returns the data to the client. Because the Internet uses clients and servers, it is referred to as a **client/server network**. We'll discuss such networks in more detail in Chapter 7.

How do computers talk to each other? Suppose you want to order something from **Amazon.com**. As Figure 3.2 illustrates, the following events take place:

1. When you type the address of a collection of Web pages, called a Web site, such as **www.Amazon.com** in your Web browser, your computer acts as a client computer because you are asking for data from Amazon's Web site.

2. Your browser's request for this data travels along several pathways that

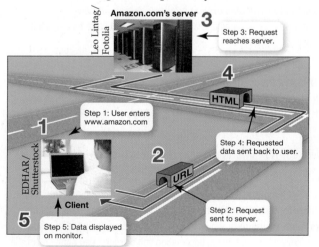

Figure 3.2

How the Internet's client/server network works.

can be likened to interstate highways. The largest and fastest pathways are the main arteries of the Internet, called **Internet backbones**. All intermediary pathways connect to these backbones.

3. Your data flows along the backbone and then on to smaller pathways until it reaches its destination, which is the server computer for Amazon's Web site.

4. The server computer returns the requested data to your computer using the most expedient pathway system (which may be different from the pathway the request took).

5. Your Web browser interprets the data and displays it on your monitor.

How does the data get sent to the correct computer? Each time you connect to the Internet, your computer is assigned a unique identification number. This number, called an **Internet Protocol address** (or **IP address**), is a set of four numbers separated by periods and commonly referred to as a *dotted quad* or *dotted decimal*

such as 123.45.245.91. IP addresses are the means by which all computers connected to the Internet identify each other. Similarly, each Web site is assigned an IP address that uniquely identifies it. However, because the long strings of numbers that make up IP addresses are difficult for people to remember, Web sites are given text versions of their IP addresses. So Amazon's Web site has an IP address of 72.21.211.176 and a text name of www.amazon.com. When you type "www.amazon.com" into your browser window, your computer (with its own unique IP address) looks for Amazon's IP address (72.21.211.176). Data is exchanged between Amazon's server computer and your computer using these unique IP addresses.

Communicating and Collaborating Through the Internet

Think of all the different ways you communicate with your friends, family, professors, and business associates over the Internet. You can use instant messaging, group communications, social networking, Web logs and video logs, wikis, podcasts, and Webcasts to communicate via the Internet. You can even talk over the phone through the Internet, which will be discussed in Chapter 8. Over time, our use of the Internet has evolved from passively using Web content created for us to actively creating, sharing, and collaborating on our own Web content. **Web 2.0** describes an evolved type of Web interaction between people, software, and data. It can be classified as the *social Web*, in which the user is also a participant. Additionally, Web 2.0 describes a trend of new applications to combine the functionality of multiple applications. Hundreds of companies now exist to help us share, recommend, collaborate, create, and socialize (see Figure 3.3). The following discussions focus more on the social, collaborative, and communicative nature of Web 2.0 applications. Other Web-based productivity applications will be discussed in Chapter 4. Like any other means of communication and collaboration, you need to know how to use these tools efficiently to get the most out of them.

Social Networking

What is social networking? **Social networking** is a means by which people use the Internet to communicate and share

BITS AND BYTES

Citing Web Site Sources

After you've evaluated a Web site and determined it to be a credible source of information that you will use in a research paper, you will need to list the source in the Works Cited section of your paper. There are formal guidelines as to how to cite Web content. Unlike those for citing books and periodicals, however, these standards are still being developed. At a minimum, the following components should be included in the citation: author, title of document or publication, date of publication or last revision, date accessed, and complete URL. Note that URL citations are no longer required by the MLA, but if a citation is still desired, it should appear in angle brackets. The following are examples of Web citations in both Modern Language Association (MLA) and American Psychological Association (APA) style for an article found in *Reuters* online:

Example of MLA style
Aspan, Maria. "ADP says investigating data breach." 15 June 2011. <u>Reuters</u>. 24 June 2011 <http://www.reuters.com/article/2011/06/15/us-adp-breach-idUSTRE75E5BB20110615>.

Example of APA style
Aspan, M. (2011, June 15). ADP says investigating data breach. Retrieved from http://www.reuters.com/article/2011/06/15/us-adp-breach-idUSTRE75E5BB20110615

The current version of Microsoft Word includes citation and bibliography formatting for most of the standard formats. If Word is not available, you can go to Son of Citation Machine (**www.citationmachine.net**), which is an interactive tool designed to output citations in proper MLA or APA format, using information you provide in an online form, as well as information from Purdue Online Writing Lab (**owl.english.purdue.edu**).

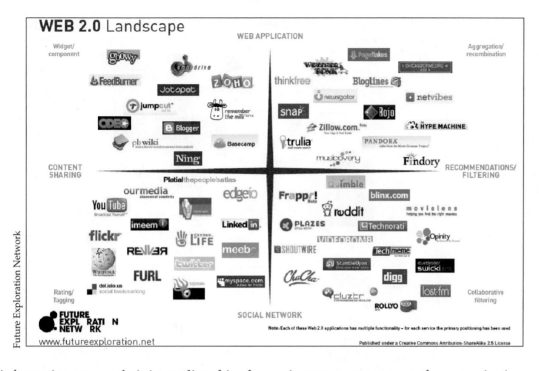

Figure 3.3

Hundreds of companies and Web sites make up the Web 2.0 landscape, which helps us share, recommend, collaborate, create, and socialize.

information among their immediate friends, and meet and connect with others through common interests, experiences, and friends. Social networking services such as Facebook (**www.facebook.com**) and Twitter (**www.twitter.com**) have become widely popular because they provide ways for members to communicate with their friends through a variety of means such as by voice, chat, instant message, and videoconference so that members don't need separate communication accounts. These services were first accepted broadly among the younger, nonprofessional population, but now many adults create their own social networking profiles. Most Facebook and Twitter users, for example, are over the age of 25. Ning (**www.ning.com**) is a social networking site that allows you to create your own network around a common topic or join a social networking group that has already been formed. Ning is not free, so if creating your own social network is of interest to you, you might also want to check out SocialGO (**www.socialgo.com**) and Mixxt (**www.mixxt.net**)—both are good free alternatives.

How is social networking used in business? Networking has long been a means of creating links between you and your friends—and their friends and acquaintances. Traditionally, networking has been helpful in the business community for the purposes of finding and filling open job positions as well as finding clients. The Internet, with its speedy connections and

instantaneous means of communicating, facilitates such business networking as well as promoting more socially based networks. Professional, business-oriented online networks such as LinkedIn (**www.linkedin.com**) are helpful for members seeking potential clients, business opportunities, jobs, or job candidates. Like a true business network, LinkedIn helps you meet other professionals through the people you know. But, social networking has taken on an entirely different role in business in recent years. Now businesses use social networking for marketing and communicating directly with their customers. Often companies post special deals and offers on their Facebook page, or solicit responses from followers that may help with product development or future marketing campaigns (see Figure 3.4).

Are there precautions I should take with my social networking content? When social networking sites first became popular, there was huge concern over privacy issues, especially for young teenagers who put personal information on their pages without considering the possibility of that information being misused by a stalker or identity thief. Although those concerns still exist, many of the most popular social networking sites have improved their privacy policies, thereby reducing, but not eliminating, such concerns. Still, users must be cautious about the type of content they post on these sites. For example, think before you add information like "your

Figure 3.4

Social networking sites are becoming useful marketing and networking tools for businesses.

mother's maiden name" or "your first pet's name" because these are often security questions that are used to verify your identity.

Social networking sites are a great way to exchange photos, but again, use caution when posting images. Although privacy settings may offer some comfort, some images may be available for view through search engines and may not require site registration to be viewed. Online images may become public property and subject to reproduction, and there might be some images that you don't want distributed. Additionally, many employers and colleges use social networks as another means of gaining information about a potential applicant before granting an interview or extending a job offer. The responsibility for your content rests with you. Make sure your profile, images, and site content project an image that accurately represents you.

E-Mail

Why do I need e-mail? Despite the popularity of social networking as a means of communication, e-mail is still the primary means of communication over the Internet. Approximately 89 percent of adult Americans who access the Internet send and receive e-mail. **E-mail** (short for **electronic mail**) is a written message that is sent and received over the Internet. The messages can be formatted and enhanced with graphics and may also include other files as attachments. E-mail is the primary method of electronic communication worldwide because it's fast and convenient. E-mail can be a means of exchanging and collaborating on documents via attachments, as well as creating documentation of

conversations. For social exchanges, e-mail often offers a more "private" conversation away from some of the very public exchanges on social networks.

Is e-mail private? Although e-mail is a more private exchange of information as compared to the very public social networking sites, e-mails really are not private. In fact, the information in e-mail is no more private than a postcard. E-mails can be easily viewed by others, by being either printed out or forwarded, so you never know who eventually could read your e-mail. Also, most e-mail is not encrypted, so you should never use e-mail to send personal or sensitive information such as bank account numbers or Social Security numbers. Doing so could lead to identity theft. Employers have access to e-mail sent from the workplace, so use caution when putting negative or controversial content in an e-mail. It could come back to haunt you. Finally, remember that even after you've deleted a message, it doesn't really vanish. Many Internet service providers and companies archive e-mail, which can then be accessed or subpoenaed in the event of a lawsuit or investigation.

How do I write a good e-mail? E-mail between friends does not have to follow any specific guidelines and can be as casual as your IM or texting exchanges. But when you send e-mail for professional reasons, like at your job, then you should be aware of proper e-mail etiquette. Following good e-mail etiquette maintains professionalism, increases efficiency, and might even help protect a company from costly lawsuits.

Common guidelines include being concise and to the point, using spell check, and avoiding texting abbreviations such as *u*, *r*, *LOL*, *BRB*, and others. Also, make sure you include a meaningful subject line. This helps recipients prioritize, organize, and categorize e-mails, and identify contents later on after the e-mail has been read. One problem with e-mail is that the meaning within the message often can be misinterpreted. Therefore, some means of conveying emotion (when necessary) can be helpful. Often emoticons—simple strings of characters that reflect facial expressions—can help reflect the writer's emotions. Use them sparingly to retain their effectiveness. Finally, include a signature line with your basic contact or corporate information.

Are there different types of e-mail accounts? Many people have more than one e-mail account. You may have a personal account, a work account, and an account you use when filling out forms on the Internet. To read, send, and organize your e-mail, you can use an **e-mail client**. E-mail clients such as Microsoft Outlook are software programs running on your computer that access your Internet service provider (ISP), which acts like an electronic post office. However, with these e-mail clients, you are able to view your e-mail only from the computer on which the e-mail client program has been installed, which can be less than convenient if you travel or want to view your e-mail when you're away from that computer.

Today, most high-speed providers and ISPs offer the services of a Web-based e-mail client so that users can look at their e-mail directly from the Web. Web-based e-mail uses the Internet as the e-mail client. Free e-mail accounts such as Yahoo! Mail, Hotmail, or Gmail are Web-based e-mail clients.

What are the advantages of a Web-based e-mail account? Unlike client-based e-mail, which is accessible only from a computer on which the e-mail client is installed, Web-based e-mail accounts make your e-mail accessible from any device that can access the Internet. No special e-mail client software is necessary to install. Even if you use a client-based account, having a secondary Web-based e-mail account, such as Yahoo! or Gmail, also provides you with a more consistent e-mail address. Your other e-mail accounts and addresses may change when you switch ISPs or change employers, so having a consistent e-mail address is important.

Why would I need a client-based e-mail program? At one point, the biggest advantage of using a client-based e-mail program was that they were more full-featured programs than Web-based e-mail systems, enabling users to easily sort and organize their e-mail, and coordinate with corresponding calendars. Current Web-based e-mail systems are becoming more full-featured every year, so the advantages of having a client-based e-mail program are not as significant. However, although many free Web-based e-mail systems such as Yahoo! feature similar organizational tools as client-based e-mail programs, they are riddled with advertisements that can be annoying and distracting (see Figure 3.5). Additionally, a benefit of using a client-based e-mail program such as Microsoft Outlook is that it makes it easy to coordinate with others who are on the same corporate network (or virtual private network [VPN]), simplifying scheduling meetings and coordinating events.

Instant Messaging

What is instant messaging? **Instant messaging (IM)** services are programs that enable you to communicate in real time with others who are online (see Figure 3.6). Although IM is most often used for casual conversations between friends, many businesses use IM as a means of quick and instant communication between coworkers. Students also use IM to communicate with their instructors as well as their classmates. Most instant messaging services provide integration with social networks, enabling you to get updates from your Facebook, Twitter, and other social network accounts without logging into each individual site. If you want to chat with more than one person, you can hold simultaneous individual conversations, or if you all want to chat together, you can create custom IM chat groups. Many IM services offer an audio chat feature so you can speak with your buddies

SOUND BYTE

Creating a Web-Based E-mail Account

In this Sound Byte, you'll see a step-by-step demonstration that explains how to create a free Yahoo! Web-based e-mail account. You'll also learn the options available with such accounts.

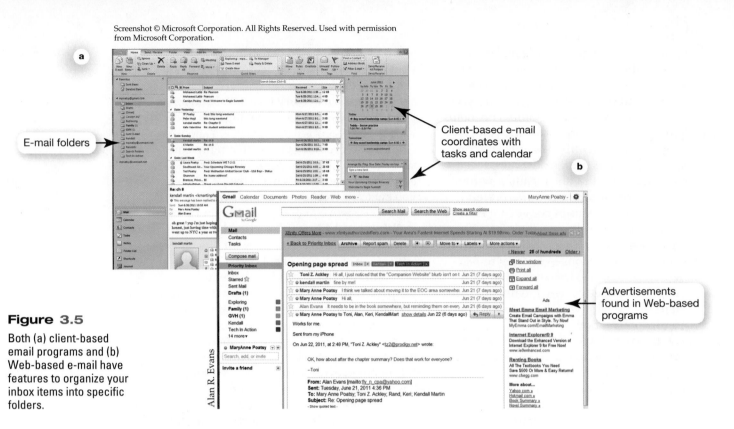

a

E-mail folders

Client-based e-mail coordinates with tasks and calendar

b

Advertisements found in Web-based programs

Alan R. Evans

Figure 3.5

Both (a) client-based email programs and (b) Web-based e-mail have features to organize your inbox items into specific folders.

if you have a microphone and speakers. A Webcam allows you to conduct video chats.

AIM, Google Chat, Windows Live Messenger, and Yahoo! Messenger have become very popular instant-messaging services. Most of these services are proprietary, meaning you can chat only with those who share the same IM service. But there are universal chat services such as Trillian and Digsby that allow users of all the popular IMs to chat with each other regardless of the service they use. Meebo is a Web-based universal chat service that lets you communicate with users

on a variety of IM services from any computer anywhere.

How do I keep track of my IM contacts? When you use IM, you set up a list of contacts, often called a *buddy list*. To communicate (or chat) with someone from your buddy list, that person must be online at the same time as you are. When someone wants to chat with you, a window pops open with his or her message. If it's not convenient to chat at that time, you can close or ignore the message. Some programs such as Yahoo! and AOL's AIM offer stealth settings so that you can appear offline to certain buddies.

Figure 3.6

Instant messaging services such as Facebook Chat enable you to have real-time online conversations.

Weblogs (Blogs) and Video Logs (Vlogs)

What is a blog? A **blog** or **Weblog**, is a personal log or journal posted on the Web. The beauty of blogs is that they are simple to create, manage, and read. Anyone can create a blog, and there are millions of blogs available to read, follow, and comment on.

Several key characteristics define a blog. Blogs are generally written by a single author and are arranged as a listing of entries on a single page, with the most recent blog (entry) appearing at the top of the list. In addition, blogs are public. Blogs have searchable

Facebook

and organized content, making them user friendly. They are accessible from anywhere using a Web browser.

The traditional form of a blog is primarily text-based but may also include images and audio. A **video log** (**vlog** or **video blog**) is a personal journal that uses video as the primary content. It can also contain text, images, and audio. Vlogs quickly are becoming a highly popular means of personal expression, and many can be found by searching the most popular video-sharing site, YouTube (**www.youtube.com**). Software such as Vlog It! makes adding video content to your blog easy, although you can also easily upload unedited video straight from your computer, video camera, or cell phone.

Why would I want to create a blog? Many people use blogs as a sort of personal scrapbook. Whenever the urge strikes, they just write a stream-of-consciousness flow of thoughts or a report of their daily activities. Many blogs, however, focus on a particular topic. For example, **www.themovieblog.com** contains reviews and opinions about movies, and **www.engadget.com** (see Figure 3.7) is a blog that devotes itself to discussing techno-gadgets. Many corporations, such as WalMart and Best Buy, have blogs written by employees. Technorati (**www.technorati.com**) and Blogcatalog (**www.blogcatalog.com**) are two of many blog directories that can help you find blogs that best fit your interests.

How do I create a blog? It is easy to write and maintain a blog, and many Web sites provide the necessary tools for you to create your own. Two sites that offer free blog hosting are Blogger (**www.blogger.com**) and WordPress (**www.wordpress.com**). You can add other features to your blog such as pictures or subpages. Another alternative is to host your blog yourself. Hosting your own blog requires that you have your own Web site and a URL so that people can access it.

SOUND BYTE Blogging

In this Sound Byte, you'll see why blogs are one of today's most popular publishing mediums. You'll also learn how to create and publish your own blog.

Are there problems with blogs? The popularity of blogs has brought about a new problem: spam blogs (splogs), which are artificially created blog sites filled with fake articles or stolen text (a tactic known as *blog scraping*). Splogs, which contain links to other sites associated with the splog's creator, have the intention of either increasing traffic to, or increasing search engine rankings for, these usually disreputable or useless Web sites. Although not terribly bad, splogs are another unwanted form of content that continues to grow like weeds on the Web.

Wikis

What are wikis? The viewer of a traditional Web site cannot change the content. In contrast, a **wiki** is a type of Web site that allows users to add, remove, or edit the content. Wikis add the extra benefit of tracking revisions so that past versions can be easily accessed at any time by any eligible reader. Like blogs, wikis can be used to express thoughts and opinions about certain topics. However, because wikis can be edited, they can present an emergent "common" opinion rather than the individual opinion of the initial writer.

What are wikis used for? Wikis provide an excellent source for collaborative writing, both in and out of the classroom. The popular collaborative online encyclopedia Wikipedia (**www.wikipedia.org**) uses wiki technology so that the content can be updated continually. Some Web-based document products, such as Google Docs (**docs.google.com**), have wiki-like features to promote online collaboration. Wikipedia is hosted by the Wikimedia Foundation, which

Figure 3.7

(a) Some blogs, like this one from Engadget, are set up as online reviews organized by category. (b) Alternatively, they can appear as personal journals that record a blogger's thoughts, viewpoints, and feelings in reverse chronological order.

Content © 2011 AOL Inc. Engadget is a trademark of AOL Inc. Used with permission.

BeckyAurora Thompson

also hosts other useful collaborative projects such as Wikibooks (textbooks), Wikiversity (learning tools), and Wikisource (document library), among others. Wiki technology is currently incorporated in course management systems such as Blackboard, to encourage collaborative learning in online courses. Wikis are also becoming popular tools for business collaboration. Rather than passing documents back and forth via e-mail and losing track of which updated version is the most recent, wikis allow all who have access to the wiki page to post their ideas and modify the content of just one document (see Figure 3.8). A history of all changes is kept so users can revert to earlier versions if desired.

These same collaborative efforts apply to a variety of other useful applications. For example, wikiHow (**www.wikihow.org**) is an online project that uses both wikis and the collaborative process to build a large, online how-to manual. Blender (**www.blender.org**), an open source software application for 3D modeling, uses MediaWiki, a more feature-rich wiki implementation product, to provide users with documentation, help with game development and 3D modeling, and tutorials for Blender software.

How accurate is Web content that anyone can change? The idea behind content that is managed and edited by many users, such as that found in Wikipedia and other large public wikis, is that the group will keep the content valid. Those challenging the validity of publicly editable wikis argue that the content cannot be trusted because wikis are easily tampered with, whereas supporters argue that the community of users can quickly catch erroneous content and correct it.

Wikipedia content has been continually measured for accuracy and has been found to be nearly as accurate as the *Encyclopedia Britannica,* but not as accurate as other reference sources. Free and easy access to edit pages can lead to improper manipulation and temporary inaccuracies, thus prompting caution when using a wiki as a source reference. Tighter access controls have been implemented to thwart malicious editing of the wiki content; users who want editing privileges are required to register. Citizendium (**www.citizendium.org**), another open wiki encyclopedia, requires contributors to provide real names and sign an ethics pledge, and all postings are monitored.

Podcasts and Webcasts

What is a podcast? A **podcast** is a clip of audio or video content that is broadcast over the Internet using compressed audio and video files such as MP3s and MP4s. This content might include radio shows, audiobooks, magazines, and even educational programs. The word *podcast* is a combination of *broadcasting* and *iPod*—not because you have to use an iPod but because iPods are the most popular form of portable media player (PMP) and because people download audio files to listen to on their iPods. However, you don't have to listen to podcasts on a portable media player. You can listen to podcasts on your computer or even on a smartphone as long as the device can play the content. To listen to a podcast on your computer, you'll need a media player such as iTunes or Windows Media Player. If you want to enjoy a video podcast on your PMP, you need to make sure your mobile device can play video as well as audio files.

So what makes podcasting different from just listening to an audio file on the computer or a PMP? The difference is that podcasts are files that come to you through syndication so you do not have to search for the current episode once you have subscribed to the series. Perhaps you are used to getting your news from a certain Web site, but the only way you can determine that new content has been added is to go to the site and look for the newly added information.

Figure 3.8

Rather than collaborating by exchanging e-mails and attachments—and potentially losing track of the most recent version of a document—different users can collaborate on a wiki page.

Elijah provides initial text
(in black)

Project Home
Week 7: *Publicity Law*
9/17/12 – 9/23/12

9/18/12
Mackenzie-Jordan Law Associates has a significant number of celebrity clients. One of the most important aspects of our legal counsel to these individuals is to help protect the use of their images and likenesses.
Sometimes this is referred to as the right of publicity. This right is a valuable asset because there are endless licensing opportunities that can be quite lucrative.
Some states have a publicity law that protects a celebrity's image and likeness for 100 years, but as yet that law has not been enacted in the state of Texas.

9/19/12
The merchandising of celebrity images has become a huge source of income for many celebrities as well as others. In recent years, legal disputes have resulted from artists and illustrators manipulating celebrity images.
In the past, courts have typically protected the First Amendment rights of artists in these cases. But recently there have been a few cases where celebrities have been allowed to sue creators of fictional works for the violation of the right of publicity.
~~The right of publicity is intended to prevent others from capitalizing on a celebrity's fame.~~ Many people in the entertainment industry are fearful that unauthorized biographies, docudramas, and celebrity spoofs and satires will no longer be protected. Many entertainment lawyers say a celebrity's right to publicity is intended solely for ads and merchandise, not for literary works.

Jordan includes additional text (shaded yellow)

Stephanie removes text
(shaded with green and shown with strikethrough)

In contrast, if you subscribe to podcasts, when the content changes, it is brought to you. Some podcasts provide opportunities for listeners to submit questions or even take listeners' calls live. What's more, if you have several favorite Web sites, rather than individually checking the content, you can collect all the site updates in one place. Podcasts are possible because of RSS technology, which makes it more efficient for you to gather updates to your favorite content.

What is RSS? **Really Simple Syndication (RSS)** is an XML-based format that facilitates the delivery of frequent content updates on Web pages. Using RSS, Web content can be formatted in such a way that aggregators can find it and download only the new content to your computer. **Aggregators** are software programs that go out and grab the latest updates of Web material according to your specifications. They are available for all major operating systems as well as some mobile devices such as smartphones.

Where can I find podcasts? Podcasts can be found all over the Web. Most newspapers, TV news organizations, and radio sites offer podcasts of their programs. Although many podcasts are news related, many podcasts offer more entertaining and informative content. The iTunes Store (**www.itunes.com**) puts thousands of free podcasts on its site. Subscribe to broadcasts from ABC or Bloomberg News, ESPN, TED Talks, or comedy from the Adam Carolla show. You can access lessons on yoga, a foreign language, or DIY tips. Many schools are beginning to recognize this format as a way to supply students with course content updates, and instructors create podcasts of their lectures.

iTunes, Podcast Alley (**www.podcastalley.com**), and Podcast Pickle (**www.podcastpickle.com**) are aggregators as well as great directories of podcasts, organized by genre, to help you easily locate podcasts of most interest to you (see Figure 3.9). If there is a particular topic for which you'd like to hear a podcast, Podscope (**www.podscope.com**) is a podcast-specific search engine that searches podcasts for specific words or phrases and then displays the results with audio clips. YouTube is also becoming a popular source of RSS feeds for video content.

Can I create my own podcast? It is simple to create audio content that can be delivered to the Web and then listened to by people all over the world. In fact, you could become a radio broadcaster overnight.

Although high-end equipment always will produce a more sophisticated output, you really need only the most basic equipment to make your own podcast.

To record the content, at the minimum you need a computer with a microphone. If you want to make a video podcast, you also need a Web camera (webcam) or video camera. Additional software may be needed to edit the digital audio and video content. After the podcast content has been recorded and edited, it needs to be exported to MP3 format. Sound-editing software, such as the freeware program Audacity (**audacity.sourceforge.net**), can be used to record and edit audio files and then export them to MP3 format. The last steps involve creating an RSS feed and then uploading the content to the Web.

Figure 3.9

Podcasts are available in a wide variety of topics and content. Web sites such as Podcast Pickle allow you to add your own podcast to their directories.

You, as well as many of your classmates, wear flip-flops year round—even in winter—and you think that flip-flops in school colors would be an extremely popular product. Your school's bookstore carries everything else with the school's colors and logo, just not flip-flops. You have asked your friends and several classmates, and most of them indicated they would buy flip-flops in the school's colors. So what do you do next? How do you move from product concept to actually selling your physical product?

Before the advent of the Internet and e-commerce, it would have been much more difficult and expensive to get your product produced and distributed. First, you would have needed to find someone with industrial design experience to design your flip-flops. Then, to make the flip-flops, you would have had to find a manufacturer, which likely required a high minimum order (maybe tens of thousands of pairs of flip-flops). You also would have needed a package design, marketing brochures, company logo (and other branding devices), a storage facility, and more. Finally, the largest hurdle would have been convincing a brick-and-mortar retailer, such as your campus bookstore, to carry your product.

Fortunately, the Internet brings the power of the global economy right to your door. For product design and manufacturing, you can visit a site like **www.Alibaba.com** (see Figure 3.10), which helps entrepreneurs locate manufacturers of all sorts of products located in many different countries. And many manufacturers are happy to work with you to custom design your product. So if you find a flip-flop style you like, you probably can get it customized with your school colors.

But what happens if the bookstore doesn't want to sell your flip-flops? You can always set up a Web site to sell them yourself. But you'll probably need help with Web site design, company logo design, and Web programming to construct the site if you don't already have these skills.

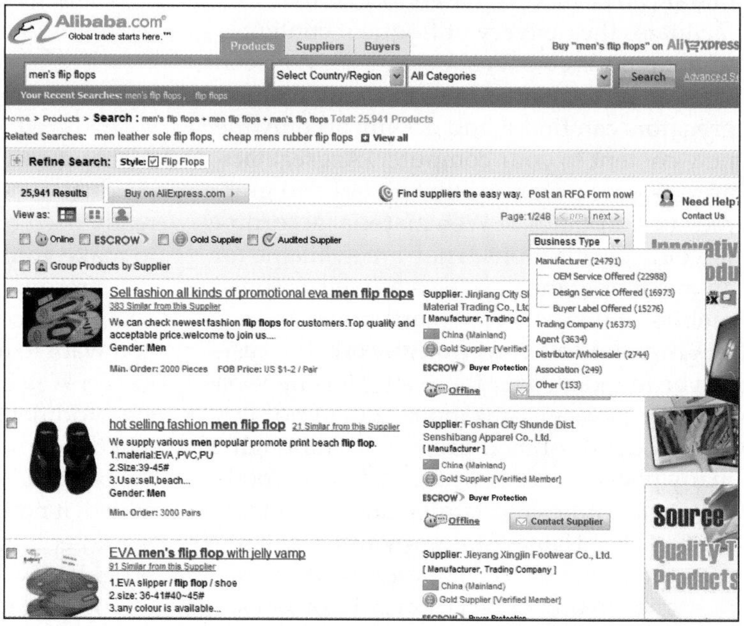

Figure 3.10

A search for men's flip-flops on Alibaba.com reveals nearly 26,000 suppliers with minimum order quantities as low as 1,000 units.

What's a Webcast? A **Webcast** is the broadcast of audio or video content over the Internet. Unlike podcasts that are prerecorded and made available for download, most Webcasts are live or one-time events. Webcasts are not updated automatically, but some, such as Microsoft's On-Demand Webcasts, are RSS feeds. Webcasts use a special kind of media technology that continuously feeds the audio and video content, which facilitates the viewing and downloading process of large audio and video files. Webcasts can include noninteractive content such as simulcasts of radio or TV broadcasts. More recent Webcasts invite interactive responses from the viewing or listening audience. For example, ORLive (**www.orlive.com**) provides surgical Webcasts that demonstrate the latest surgical innovations and techniques (see Figure 3.12). Webcasts also are used in the corporate world to broadcast annual meetings and in the educational arena to transmit seminars.

Web Entertainment

Internet radio, music files such as MP3 and advanced audio coding (AAC), streaming video, and interactive gaming are all part of the entertainment world available over the Internet. What makes the Web appealing to many people is its rich **multimedia** content. Multimedia is anything that involves one or more forms of media in addition to text.

Many types of multimedia are used on the Web. Graphics (drawings, charts, and photos) are the most basic form of multimedia. Audio files are what give sound to the Web—the clips of music you hear when you visit certain Web sites, MP3 files that you download, or live broadcasts you can listen to through Internet radio. Video files on the Web range from the simple (such as short video clips) to the complex (such as hour-long live concerts). In addition to movies,

Fortunately, you can tap the global marketplace for skilled professionals by using sites such as Guru (**www.guru.com**) or Elance (**www.elance.com**) (see Figure 3.11). These sites help you locate freelance professionals to work on projects for you. You can create a description of the job you need done (say, logo design for a flip-flop company), post it on the site, and invite freelancers to bid on your job. You can contact freelancers that look promising, review samples of their work, and decide on someone who can help you—and at a competitive price. After your Web site is designed and up and running, you can place your business on social networking sites, such as Facebook, to help potential customers discover your product and spread the word about your great flip-flops. You probably already have lots of friends on Facebook who attend your school and would be good potential customers.

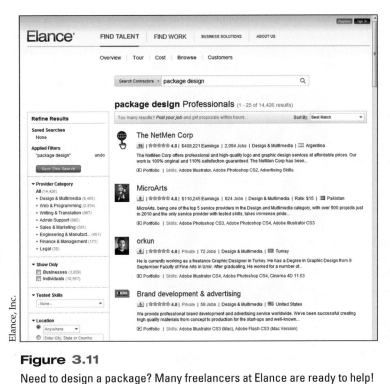

Elance, Inc.

Figure 3.11

Need to design a package? Many freelancers at Elance are ready to help!

If you aren't selling your flip-flops in a physical store, where will you store them, and who will package and ship them when customers buy them? If your parents' basement isn't large enough, you can outsource warehousing and order fulfillment to Amazon.com. Fulfillment by Amazon is a service in which Amazon (for a fee) will warehouse your inventory and then package and ship it when customer orders are received. Orders do not have to come through Amazon's site (although that is an option); you can just provide ordering information to Amazon that is collected on your site, and Amazon will take care of all the tedious work.

Although there is always a cost to starting up a business, up-front costs are much lower when you take advantage of the global marketplace and Internet tools. So take that brilliant idea you have and turn it into a business today!

ORLive.com

Figure 3.12

ORLive provides Webcasts that demonstrate the latest surgical techniques.

you can watch live or prerecorded television broadcasts, movie trailers, and sporting events. Hulu (**www.hulu.com**) is a great Web site where you can find popular TV shows and movies.

What are streaming audio and video? Because of the large file sizes of media content, watching video files such as movies or TV shows, listening to live audio broadcasting, and playing online games is possible because of streaming media. **Streaming audio** continuously feeds an audio file to your browser so you avoid having to wait for the entire file to download completely before listening to it. Likewise, **streaming video** continuously feeds a video file to your browser so that you can watch large files as they download instead of first

What's Everyone Twittering About?

Twitter (**www.twitter.com**) is a social networking and microblogging service that enables you to exchange short text messages in real time with your friends or "followers" (see Figure 3.13). It lets you specify which Twitter users you want to follow so you can read their messages in one place. All you need is a device (such as your computer or mobile device) connected to the Internet.

Twitter messages, called tweets, are limited to 140 characters, so comments exchanged in Twitter are short and simple. While Twitter works well among close-knit groups for messages such as "Joe and I are going to Murphy's Café. See you there," it can also be used to gain a sense of the "pulse" of what the general public is talking about within a broader community. Businesses are using Twitter to respond to customer queries or to broadcast new services or products. Your Twitter account tracks the number of "followers," or people who are paying attention to your tweets, and the number of "friends," or people you are following. So, "tweet" away to stay connected.

AP Photo/Charlotte Observer, Robert Lahser

Figure 3.13

Twitter is a social networking and microblogging service for staying connected to "followers" in real time.

having to download the files completely. Streaming videos make possible services such as Netflix or video on demand from your cable provider.

What kinds of games are played on the Web? Streaming audio and video helped to bring popularity to online user interactivity and online gaming. Many game Web sites, such as Addicting Games (**www.addictinggames.com**), offer thousands of free online games in arcade, puzzle, sports, shooting, word, and strategy categories. Simple multiplayer games such as backgammon, chess, and checkers became popular and offered users the chance to play the game with others from around the world.

In addition, there are many **multiplayer online games** in which play occurs among hundreds or thousands of other players over the Internet in a persistent (or always-on) game environment. In these games, you can interact with other players around the world in a meaningful context by trading, chatting, or playing cooperative or combative minigames. There are several types of **massively multiplayer online role-playing games (MMORPGs)** in which participants assume the role of a fictitious character in a virtual game world. World of Warcraft (**www.worldofwarcraft.com**), shown in Figure 3.14, and Guild Wars (**www.guildwars.com**) are among the most popular MMORPGs. Other types of multiplayer online game sites include first-person shooter games such as Battleground Europe (**www.battlegroundeurope.com**), sports games such as Football Superstars (**www.footballsuperstars.com**), and racing games such as Need for Speed (**www.needforspeed.com**). Second Life (**www.secondlife.com**) can also be considered an MMORPG, but with its own well-established, in-world virtual economy, it has transcended into a much bigger concept and function.

Do I need anything besides a browser to view or hear multimedia on the Web? Without any additional software, most graphics on the Web will appear in your browser. However, to view and hear some multimedia files—for example, podcasts, videos on YouTube, and audio files—you might need a special software program called a **plug-in** (or **player**). Figure 3.15 lists the most popular plug-ins.

If you purchased your computer within the past several years, many plug-ins probably came preinstalled on your computer. If a Web site requires a plug-in you don't have, then it usually displays a message on the screen that includes links to a site where you can download the plug-in free of charge. For example, to use streaming video, your browser might send you to the Adobe Web site, where you can download Flash Player.

Figure 3.14

World of Warcraft is a popular massive multiplayer online role-playing game.

Scripps Howard Photo Service/Newscom

Figure 3.15 | POPULAR PLUG-INS AND PLAYERS AND THEIR USES

Plug-In or Player Name	Where You Can Get It	What It Does
Adobe Reader	www.adobe.com	Views and prints portable document format (PDF) files.
Flash Player	www.adobe.com	Plays animation and movies through Web browsers.
QuickTime Player	www.apple.com	Plays MP3 animation, music, musical instrument digital interface (MIDI), audio, and video files.
Shockwave Player	www.adobe.com	Plays interactive games, multimedia, graphics, and streaming audio and video on the Web.
Silverlight	www.microsoft.com	Similar to Flash. Plays Web-based animations and videos.
Windows Media Player	www.microsoft.com	Plays MP3 and WAV files, music files, and live audio, and movies and live video broadcasts on the Web.

Do I need to update players and plug-ins? As with most technological resources, improvements and upgrades are available for players and plug-ins, and most will alert you to check for and download upgrades when they are available. It is best to keep the players and plug-ins as current as possible so that you get the full effects of the multimedia running with these players.

Are there any risks with using plug-ins? When a browser requires a plug-in to display particular Web content, it usually automatically accesses the plug-in. Depending on your settings, this access happens without asking you for consent to start the plug-in. Such automatic access can present security risks. To minimize such risks, update your plug-ins and browser software frequently so that you will have the most up-to-date remedies against identified security flaws.

Is there any way to get multimedia Web content to load faster? When you're on the Internet, your browser keeps track of the Web sites you've visited so that it can load them faster the next time you visit them. This *cache* (temporary storage place) of the text pages, images, and video files from recently visited Web sites can make your Internet surfing more efficient, but it also can congest your hard drive. Additionally, if you don't have your cache settings configured to check for updates to the Web

page, your browser may not load the most recent content. To keep your system running efficiently, delete your temporary Internet cache periodically. To ensure the most recent Web site content is displayed, click Refresh or press the F5 key if you revisit a site in the same browsing session. All popular Web browsers have an option to clear the Internet cache manually, and most have a setting to allow you to clear the cache automatically every time you exit the browser.

BITS AND BYTES

Why Can't I Run Flash-Based Multimedia on My iPad or iPhone?

Your friend showed you a great video clip on their new Blackberry PlayBook. You try to load the same movie into your iPad, but it won't run. Why not? It's not because your iPad is broken, but because Apple devices don't run Flash files. Apple's Web site gives a complete explanation of Apple's "Thoughts on Flash" (**www.apple.com/hotnews/thoughts-on-flash/**) but succinctly, Apple's main problem with Flash is that it is not "open" but rather 100% proprietary and therefore not easily controlled by Apple. Apple would rather use other open standard products such as HTML5, CSS, and JavaScript. Flash is also tough on battery consumption, has been tagged as having reliability and security issues, and doesn't work well on devices using touch commands rather than mice commands. But, what to do if you have an iPad, iPod Touch, or iPhone and want to view a Flash file? One work-around is to use the Skyfire Web browser, which turns Flash content into HTML on Skyfire's servers. The YouTube app installed on all Apple devices shows YouTube content in a different format. Unfortunately, there are no good solutions if you want to play a Flash game on an Apple device, but as Apple suggests . . . there are lots of other games to choose from.

Conducting Business over the Internet: E-Commerce

E-commerce, or **electronic commerce**, is the process of conducting business online, such as through advertising and selling products. A good example of an e-commerce business (also called an *e-business*) is Amazon.com. The company has no physical retail store presence, and its online presence offers customers a convenient way to shop for almost anything. Its success is the result of creative marketing, an expanding product line, and reliable customer service and product delivery—all hallmarks of traditional businesses as well.

Are there different types of e-commerce businesses? Traditional stores, those stores with a physical building to shop in, which also have an online presence, are referred to as *click-and-brick* businesses. These stores, such as Best Buy (**www.bestbuy.com**) and Target (**www.target.com**), provide a variety of services on their Web sites. Customers can visit their sites to check the availability of items or to get store locations and directions. Some click-and-bricks allow online purchases and in-store pickup and returns.

A significant portion of e-commerce consists of **business-to-consumer (B2C)** transactions—exchanges that take place between businesses and consumers—such as the purchases that consumers make at online stores. There is also a **business-to-business (B2B)** portion of e-commerce; this consists of businesses buying and selling goods and services to other businesses. An example is Omaha Paper Company (**www.omahapaper.com**), which distributes paper products to other companies. Finally, the **consumer-to-consumer (C2C)** portion of e-commerce consists of consumers selling to each other through online auction sites such as eBay (**www.ebay.com**) and exchange sites such as Freecycle (**www.freecycle.com**) and Craigslist (**www.craigslist.org**).

What are the most popular e-commerce activities? Approximately $200 billion each year is spent in the U.S. on goods purchased over the Internet, accounting for approximately 25 percent of all retail sales. So what is everyone buying online? Consumers buy books, music and videos, movie and event tickets, and toys and games more often online than in retail stores. Travel items such as plane tickets, hotel reservations, rental car reservations, and even automobile purchases are also frequently made online. With the advent of more lenient return policies, online retail sales of clothing and shoes also have increased. Sites such as eBay and Craigslist, together with payment exchange services such as PayPal and Google Checkout, are becoming the online equivalent of the weekend yard sale and have dramatically increased in popularity.

But e-commerce encompasses more than just shopping opportunities. Today, anything you can do inside your bank you can do online, and more than 50 percent of U.S. households do some form of online banking. Many people use online services to check their account balances, pay bills online, as well as check stock and mutual fund performance. Credit card companies allow you to view, schedule, and pay your credit card bill; brokerage houses allow you to conduct investment activities online.

E-Commerce Safeguards

Just how safe are online transactions? When you buy something online, you most likely use a credit or debit card; therefore, the exchange of money is done directly between you and a bank. Because online shopping eliminates a salesclerk or other human intermediary from the transaction, it can actually be safer than traditional retail shopping. Still, because users are told to be wary of online transactions and because the integrity of online transactions is the backbone of e-commerce, businesses must have some form of security certification to give their customers a level of comfort.

Some sites have created secure logins that you can change to before signing in, which is safer than sending your login credentials unsecured. To certify that their online transactions are secure, businesses hire security companies such as VeriSign. But just seeing the VeriSign seal is not always a guarantee that the site is secure, because the seal can be copied and pasted onto virtually any site. Therefore, be sure to check that the beginning of the URL changes from "http://" to "https://"—with the "s" standing for **secure socket layer**. Another indication that a Web site is secure is the appearance of a small icon of a closed padlock in the toolbar (in both Microsoft Internet Explorer and Mozilla Firefox). The last visual clue to help identify a safe site is a

Using PayPal for Safe Online Payments

Many people were not initially comfortable buying online from sites such as eBay because the sites required them to exchange personal financial information such as credit card numbers or banking information with complete strangers. PayPal (**www.paypal.com**) resolved that issue and is now a standard means of online payment exchanges for many online merchants. PayPal also offers buyer protection and dispute resolution services.

Here's how PayPal works (see Figure 3.16):

1. You provide your financial information to PayPal, which stores it on PayPal servers.
2. You provide only your PayPal e-mail address to the merchant.
3. The merchant receives payment from PayPal without seeing your financial information.

PayPal acts as a payment intermediary and allows anyone to pay with credit cards, bank accounts, or buyer credit without sharing financial information. PayPal is owned by eBay, the online auction site.

Google Checkout (**checkout.google.com**) offers similar services to PayPal, although there are some subtle differences. For example, you cannot pay directly from your bank account with Google Checkout, and only purchases within the U.S. can be made with Google Checkout. Google Checkout only provides customer support through forums and e-mail, whereas PayPal has increased its customer service considerably, and now you can chat live with PayPal representatives.

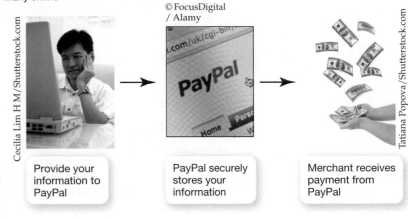

Provide your information to PayPal

PayPal securely stores your information

Merchant receives payment from PayPal

Figure 3.16

PayPal is an online payment intermediary, allowing anyone to shop without sharing financial information with the seller.

green-colored address bar as shown in Figure 3.17. Still, despite these indications, you also need to consider the validity of the site and place everything in context.

How else can I shop safely online? To ensure that your online shopping experience is a safe one, follow these guidelines:

- **Shop at well-known, reputable sites.** If you aren't familiar with a site, then investigate it with the Better Business Bureau (**www.bbb.org**) or at bizrate (**www.bizrate .com**). When you place an order, print a copy of the order and make sure you receive a confirmation number. Make sure the company has a phone number and street address in addition to a Web site.

- **Avoid making online transactions when using public computers.** Public computers might have programs that track and log your keystrokes, so you do not want to use public computers when typing sensitive information such as credit card numbers or bank account numbers. Public computers might also have other types of spyware installed to retrieve private information. Similarly, unless you have specific protection on your own notebook computer, avoid making wireless transactions in public hotspots.

- **Pay by credit card, not debit card.** Federal consumer credit laws protect credit card users, but debit card users do not have the same level of protection. If possible, reserve one credit card for Internet purchases only; even better, use a prepaid credit card that has a small credit limit. For an extra layer of security, find out if your credit card company has a service that confirms your identity with an extra password or code that only you know to use when making an online transaction or offers a one-time-use credit card number. Also, consider using a third-party payment processor such as PayPal or Google Checkout. PayPal also offers a security key that provides additional security to your PayPal account.

Doing Business Online

In this Active Helpdesk call, you'll learn about e-commerce and what e-commerce safeguards protect you when you're doing business online.

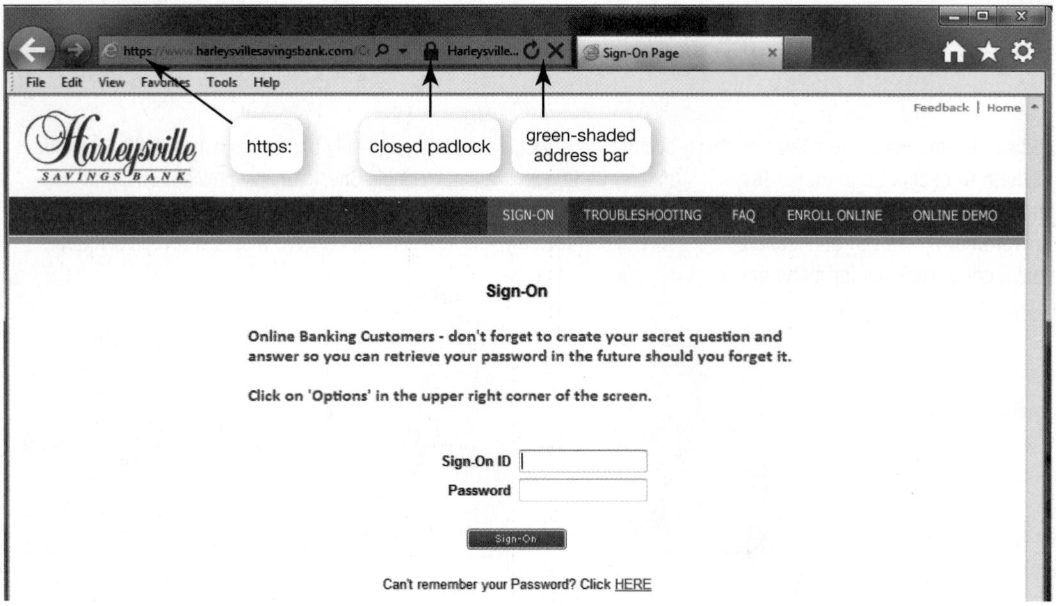

https:

closed padlock

green-shaded address bar

SIGN-ON   TROUBLESHOOTING   FAQ   ENROLL ONLINE   ONLINE DEMO

Feedback | Home

Sign-On

Online Banking Customers - don't forget to create your secret question and answer so you can retrieve your password in the future should you forget it.

Click on 'Options' in the upper right corner of the screen.

Sign-On ID _____

Password _____

Sign-On

Can't remember your Password? Click HERE

Harleysville Savings Bank

Figure 3.17

A closed padlock icon, "https" in the URL, and a green-shaded address bar are indications that the site is secure.

• **Check the return policy.** Print a copy and save it. If the site disappears overnight, this information may help you in filing a dispute or reporting a problem to a site such as the Better Business Bureau.

Whether you're doing business, playing games, or communicating with friends or colleagues, the Internet makes all of these activities more accessible. The Internet can potentially make these experiences and activities more enriched as well, although you must take precautions for the safest of experiences.

Accessing the Web: Web Browsers

None of the activities for which we use the Web could happen without an important software application: a Web browser. Recall

that a Web browser, or browser, is software installed on your computer system that allows you to locate, view, and navigate the Web. Most browsers in use today are *graphical* browsers, meaning they can display pictures (graphics) in addition to text and other forms of multimedia such as sound and video.

What are some common Web browsers? Microsoft Internet Explorer (IE) is included in the Windows operating system. It has been the most widely used browser since 1999, and still enjoys predominant market share, although its popularity has slipped over the years. Other browsers, discussed below, have become popular alternatives to Internet Explorer.

• **Firefox** is a popular open source browser from Mozilla (**www.mozilla.org**). Firefox's popularity continues to increase, capturing approximately 28 percent of the U.S. browser market. Add-ons are available to customize and increase the functionality of Firefox. Examples include Video Download Helper that converts Web videos, like those found on YouTube, to files you can save, as well as a Facebook toolbar that integrates Facebook functionality into your browser. Other handy features found in Firefox are spell checking for e-mail, blogs, and other Web postings, as well as Session Restore, which brings back all your active Web pages if the browser or system shuts down unexpectedly.

• **Safari** is a browser developed by Apple (**www.apple.com/safari**). Although it was created as the default browser for Macintosh computers and is included with the Mac OS, a Windows-based version is also available. Safari has quickly gained public acceptance.

• **Google Chrome** is the newest browser on the market, distributed by Google (**www.google.com/chrome**) (see Figure 3.18), and has enjoyed growing market share since its inception. The unique features offered by Chrome include thumbnail

BITS AND BYTES

It's Important to Keep Your Browser Software Up to Date

When new file formats are developed for the Web, browsers need new plug-ins to display content properly. Constantly downloading and installing plug-ins can be a tedious process. Although many Web sites provide links to sites that enable you to download plug-ins, not all do, resulting in frustration when you can't display the content you want. When new versions of browsers are released, they normally include the latest versions of popular plug-ins. Corrections of security breaches are typically included in these versions of browser software as well. Therefore, upgrading to the latest version of your browser software provides for safer, more convenient Web surfing. Fortunately, updates are free, and you can set most of the popular Web browsers to notify you when updates are available or to download the updates automatically.

access to your most recently visited sites from Chrome's main page and shortcuts to Google applications.

What features do browsers offer? Most of the popular Web browsers provide tabbed browsing for convenient navigation. With tabbed browsing, Web pages are loaded in "tabs" within the same browser window. Rather than having to switch among Web pages in several open windows, you can flip between the tabs in one window. You can even open several of your favorite Web sites from one folder and choose to display them as tabs. You may also save a group of tabs as a Favorites group, if there are several tabs you often open at the same time. Internet Explorer 9 offers other tab features such as "tear-off tabs" that facilitate rearranging open tabs, and "pinned tabs" that enable you to dock your most frequently accessed tabs in the task bar (see Figure 3.19). Another convenient navigation tool that most browsers share is providing thumbnail previews of all open Web pages in open tabs.

Other features shared by most of the favorite browsers include a built-in search box in which you can designate your preferred default search engine and tools for printing, page formatting, and security settings. For extra browsing privacy, most browsers also offer a privacy mode feature, such as InPrivate Browsing in Microsoft Internet Explorer, that allows users to surf without leaving a trace. Use the privacy mode when surfing the Web on public computers at college or at the public library, for example.

Getting Around the Web: URLs, Hyperlinks, and Other Tools

You gain initial access to a particular **Web site** by typing its unique address, or **Uniform Resource Locator** (**URL**, pronounced "you-are-ell"), in your browser. For example, the URL of the Web site for *Popular Science* magazine is **www.popsci .com**. By typing this URL for *Popular Science* magazine, you connect to the **home page**, or main page, of the Web site. Once you are at the home page, you can move all around the site by clicking specially formatted pieces of

text called *hyperlinks*. Let's look at these and other navigation tools in more detail.

URLs

What do all the parts of the URL mean? As noted earlier, a URL is a Web site's address. A Web site is composed of many different Web pages, each of which is a separate document with its own unique URL. Like a regular street address, a URL is composed of several parts that help identify the Web document it stands for (see Figure 3.20).

Figure 3.18

Google Chrome includes thumbnails of the most recently visited Web sites for easy access.

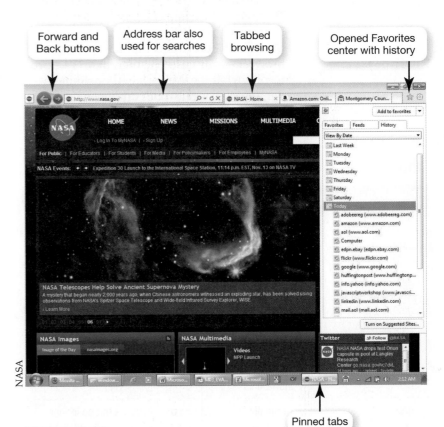

Figure 3.19

Internet Explorer (IE) includes tabbed browsing. Pinned tabs on the task bar make accessing your favorite sites even easier.

The first part of the URL indicates the *protocol* (set of rules) used to retrieve the specified document. The protocol is generally followed by a colon, two forward slashes, *www* (indicating *World Wide Web*), and the **domain name.** (Sometimes the domain name is also thought to include the *www*.) The domain name is also referred to as the *host name*. Individual pages within a Web site are further identified after the domain name, following another forward slash. These are referred to as the *path*. It should be noted that most current browsers no longer require you to enter the protocol and the www. Some, like Firefox, don't even require the domain if it's a .com. But even though these parts of the URL are not physically entered, they are still part of each Web site's URL.

What's the protocol? Most URLs begin with *http*, which is short for **Hypertext Transfer Protocol (HTTP)**. HTTP is the protocol that allows files to be transferred from a **Web server**—a computer that hosts the Web site you are requesting—so that you can see the Web site on your computer by using a browser. As discussed earlier, the HTTP protocol is what the Web is based on. Remember, the Web is only one component of the Internet. Other components, such as FTP and

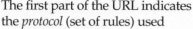

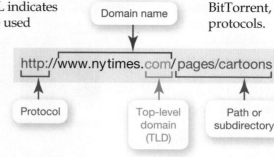

Figure 3.20

The parts of a URL.

BitTorrent, are based on different protocols.

A common protocol used to transfer files over the Internet is **File Transfer Protocol (FTP)**. It is used to upload and download files from your computer to a Web server. FTP files use an FTP file server, whereas HTTP files use a Web server. To connect to most FTP servers, you need a user ID and a password. FTP addresses, like e-mail addresses or URLs, identify one location on the Internet. To upload and download files from FTP sites, you can use a Web browser or file transfer software such as WS_FTP, Fetch, Filezilla, or WinSCP.

BitTorrent, like FTP, is a protocol used to transfer large files. To use BitTorrent, you must install a software client program. It uses a peer-to-peer networking system, so that sharing occurs between connected computers that also have the BitTorrent client installed. BitTorrent was developed in 2001 and has been gaining popularity, especially among users who want to share music, movies, and games. Use caution, however, when accessing BitTorrent content. Since it is a peer-to-peer system, there are no restrictions. It is possible for copyrighted material to be shared illegally.

What's in a domain name? The domain name identifies the site's **host**, the location that maintains the computers that store the Web site files. For example, **www.berkeley.edu** is the domain name for the University of California at Berkeley.

The suffix in the domain name after the dot (such as .com or .edu) is called the **top-level domain**. This suffix indicates the kind of organization to which the host belongs. Figure 3.21 lists the most frequently used top-level domains.

Each country has its own top-level domain. These are two-letter designations such as .za for South Africa and .us for the United States. A sampling of country codes is shown in Figure 3.22. Within a country-specific domain, further subdivisions can be made for regions or states. For instance, the .us domain contains subdomains for each state, using the two-letter abbreviation of the state. For example, the URL for Pennsylvania's Web site is **www.state.pa.us**.

Figure 3.21 | COMMON TOP-LEVEL DOMAINS AND THEIR AUTHORIZED USERS

Domain Name	Who Can Use It
.biz	Businesses
.com	Originally for commercial sites, but now can be used by anyone
.edu	Degree-granting institutions
.gov	Local, state, and federal U.S. government
.info	Information service providers
.mil	U.S. military
.name	Individuals
.net	Originally for networking organizations but no longer restricted
.org	Organizations (often not-for-profits)

Figure 3.22 | EXAMPLES OF COUNTRY CODES

Country Code	Country
.au	Australia
.ca	Canada
.jp	Japan
.uk	United Kingdom

Note: For a full listing of country codes, refer to **www.iana.org/domains/root/db/**.

What's the information after the domain name that I sometimes see? When the URL is only the domain name (such as **www.nytimes.com**), you are requesting a site's home page. However, sometimes a forward slash and additional text follow the domain name, such as in **www.nytimes.com/pages/cartoons**. The information after the slash indicates a particular file or **path** (or **subdirectory**) within the Web site. The path or subdirectory is what identifies each different page within a particular Web site; it follows the top-level domain and is preceded by a slash. In Figure 3.20, you would connect to the cartoon pages on the *New York Times* site.

Hyperlinks and Beyond

What's the best way to get around in a Web site? Unlike text in a book or a Microsoft Word document, which is linear (meaning you read it from top to bottom, left to right, one page after another), the Web is anything but linear. As its name implies, the Web is a series of connected paths, or links, that connect you to different Web sites. You can jump from one Web page (the document indicated by the path in the URL) to another Web page within the same Web site or navigate to another Web site altogether by clicking on a specially coded element called a **hyperlink**, as shown in Figure 3.23. Generally, text that operates as a hyperlink appears in a different color (often blue) and is underlined. When you pass your cursor over a hyperlinked image the cursor may change to a hand with a finger pointing upward. Sometimes images also act as hyperlinks. To access a hyperlink from an image, you simply click the image.

How do I return to a Web page I've already visited? To retrace your steps, some sites provide a **breadcrumb trail**—a list of pages within a Web site you've visited. It usually appears at the top of a page. Figure 3.23 shows an example of a breadcrumb trail. "Breadcrumbs" get their name from the fairy tale "Hansel and Gretel," in which the characters drop breadcrumbs on the trail to find their way out of a forest. By clicking on earlier links in a breadcrumb trail, you can retrace your steps back to the page on which you started.

To get back to your original location or visit a Web page you viewed previously, you use the browser's Back and Forward buttons. To back up more than one page, click the down arrow next to the Forward button to access a list of most recently visited Web sites. By selecting any one of these sites in the list, you can return directly

Figure 3.23

When you click on a hyperlink, you jump from one location on the Web to another. When you click on the links in a breadcrumb trail, you can navigate your way back through a Web site.

to that page without having to navigate through other Web sites and Web pages you've visited.

The History list on your browser's toolbar is also a handy feature. The History list shows all the Web sites and pages that you've visited over a certain period of time. These Web sites are organized according to date and can go back as far as three weeks. To access the history list in Internet Explorer, click the down arrow next to the navigation arrows.

Favorites, Live Bookmarks, and Tagging

What's the best way to mark a site so I can return to it later? If you want an easy way to return to a specific Web page without having to remember to type in the address, you can use your browser's Favorites or Bookmarks feature. Internet Explorer and Safari call this feature **Favorites**; Firefox and Google Chrome call the same feature a **Bookmark**. This feature places a marker of

the site's URL in an easily retrievable list in your browser's toolbar. To organize the sites into categories, most browsers offer tools to create folders. Most browsers also provide features to export the list of bookmarks to a file from which you can import to another computer or another browser.

Favorites and Bookmarks are great for quickly locating those sites you use the most, but they are accessible to you only when you are on your own computer. One way to access your Bookmarks and Favorites from any computer is to use MyBookmarks (**www.mybookmarks.com**), a free Internet service that stores your Bookmarks and Favorites online.

What are live bookmarks? The **live bookmark** feature of the Firefox browser adds the technology of RSS feeds to bookmarking. Because the Web is constantly changing, the site you bookmarked last week may subsequently change and add new content. Traditionally, you would notice the change only the next time you visited the site. With live bookmarks, the content comes to you. Instead of constantly checking your favorite Web pages for new content, a live bookmark delivers updates to you as soon as they become available. Live bookmarks are useful if you are interested in the most up-to-date news stories, sports scores, or stock prices.

What is social bookmarking? Social **bookmarking**, also known as **tagging**, lets you store, organize, and manage bookmarks (or tags) of Web pages. A social bookmark or tag is a **keyword** or term that is assigned to a piece of information such as a Web page, digital image, or video. A tag describes the item so that it can be found again by browsing or searching. Tags were popularized by Web 2.0 Web sites such as YouTube and Flickr.

The social bookmarking Web site Delicious (**www.delicious.com**) gives you the ability to add tags as bookmarks to your favorite Web sites (see Figure 3.24). The tag can be something meaningful to you, or you can select one from a list of suggested tags. Later, you can go back to Delicious, conduct a search using your tag, and find bookmarks tagged with the same word from

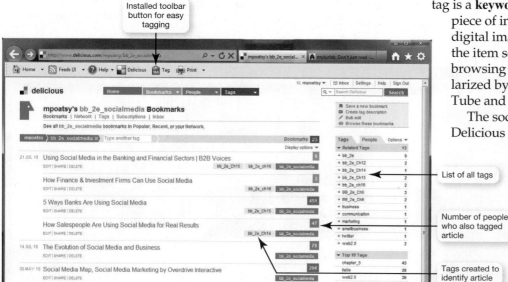

Installed toolbar button for easy tagging

List of all tags

Number of people who also tagged article

Tags created to identify article

Figure 3.24

Delicious is a social bookmarking Web site that allows you to organize and share your favorite Web sites.

everyone in your network. You can also see how many other Web users tagged the same site. Delicious offers convenient toolbars for your browsers, and many Web sites incorporate bookmarking icons for ease of use.

Figure 3.25 lists several popular social bookmarking tag tools. Diigo (**www.diigo.com**) allows you not only to tag and bookmark Web sites, but also to annotate the pages with highlights and sticky notes. Through Diigo, the Web pages can be archived, so they are always available. Digg (**www.digg.com**) and Newsvine (**www.newsvine.com**) offer similar systems for organizing news content. StumbleUpon (**www.stumbleupon.com**) is like a personalized search engine and recommends Web sites based on your personal interests and preferences, as well as the recommendations of people you know or the general surfing public.

Searching the Web Effectively

With its billions of Web pages, the Web offers visitors access to masses of information on virtually any topic. To narrow down the quantity of Web information to something more useful, use a search engine and a keyword query. A **search engine** is a set of programs that searches the Web for keywords—specific words you wish to look for (*query*)—and then returns a list of the Web sites on which those keywords are found. Popular search engines include Google, Yahoo!, Bing, and Ask.com.

For some searches, you also can search the Web using a **subject directory**, which is a structured outline of Web sites organized by topics and subtopics. Librarians' Internet Index (**www.ipl.org**) is a subject directory, and some popular search engines such as Yahoo! also feature directories. If you can't decide which search engine is best, then you may want to try a metasearch engine. **Metasearch engines**, such as Dogpile (**www.dogpile.com**), search other search engines rather than individual Web sites. Figure 3.26 lists search engines and subject directories that are alternatives to Google, Yahoo!, Bing, and Ask.com.

Search Engines

How do search engines work? Search engines have three components. The first component is a program called a spider. The **spider** constantly collects data on the Web,

© M4OS Photos / Alamy

The Canadian Press/Steve White (Canadian Press via AP Images)

Figure 3.25

Icons of some popular social bookmarking Web sites.

following links in Web sites and reading Web pages. Spiders get their name because they crawl over the Web using multiple "legs" to visit many sites simultaneously. As the spider collects data, the second component of the search engine, an indexer program, organizes the data into a large database. When you use a search engine, you interact with the third component: the search engine software. This software searches the indexed data, pulling out relevant information according to your search. The resulting list appears in your Web browser as a list of hits (sites that match your search).

Why don't I get the same results from all search engines? Each search engine uses a unique formula, or *algorithm*, to formulate the search and create the resulting index of related sites. In addition, search engines differ in how they rank the search results. Most search engines rank their results based on the frequency of the appearance of your queried keywords in Web sites as well as the location of those words in the sites. Thus, sites that include the keywords in their URL or site name most likely appear at the top of the hit list. Thus, structuring Web pages to ensure their Web site appears at the top of a Google search has become an important part of a company's marketing strategy.

In addition, search engines differ as to which sites they search. For instance, Google and Ask.com search nearly the entire Web, whereas specialty search engines search only sites that are relevant to a particular subject. Specialty search engines exist for almost every industry or interest. For example, DailyStocks (**www.dailystocks.com**) is a search engine used primarily by investors that searches for corporate information to help them make educated decisions. Search Engine Watch (**www.searchenginewatch.com**) has a list of many specialty search engines organized by industry.

Figure 3.26 | POPULAR SEARCH ENGINES AND SUBJECT DIRECTORIES

Search Tools on the Internet		
AltaVista	**www.altavista.com**	Keyword search engine.
ChaCha	**www.chacha.com**	This site lets you chat with a real live professional guide who helps you search, and it's free of charge. Also available by texting your questions to 242242.
CompletePlanet	**www.completeplanet.com**	Deep Web directory that searches databases not normally searched by typical search engines.
Dogpile	**www.dogpile.com**	Metasearch engine that searches Google, Yahoo!, and Bing.
Excite	**www.excite.com**	Portal with keyword search capabilities.
InfoMine	**www.infomine.com**	Subject directory of academic resources with keyword search engine capabilities.
Rollyo	**www.rollyo.com**	Short for "Roll Your Own Search Engine." This site lets you create your own search engine (searchroll) that searches just the sites you want it to search.
Open Directory Project	**www.dmoz.org**	Subject directory with keyword search capabilities.
Stumbleupon	**www.stumbleupon.com**	Lets you rate pages "thumbs up"or "thumbs down." As it learns your preferences, your search results improve.
Technorati	**www.technorati.com**	A great search engine for blog content.
Yippy	**www.yippy.com**	Keyword search engine that groups similar results into clouds (clusters).

Note: For a complete list of search engines, go to **www.searchengineguide.com**.

BITS AND BYTES

Searching to Do Good

There are many volunteer and charitable organizations to participate in, but for most of us it's hard to incorporate such activities into our daily lives, and it's equally difficult to contribute financially to them all. Now there is an easy way to "do good" while doing something we all do daily—use a search engine. GoodSearch (**www.goodsearch.com**) is a Yahoo!-powered search engine that donates half of its revenues to approved U.S. charities and schools that users designate. The money GoodSearch donates comes from the site's advertisers and amounts to approximately a penny per search.

If you're a big fan of the SPCA, a local hospital, or the neighborhood public elementary school, check to see if that particular organization has been approved. If so, you can add it as your designated charity and start searching. You can easily track how much GoodSearch has raised for your organization. Almost 100,000 charitable organizations are being helped by GoodSearch, but if the organization you are interested in is not on the list, as long as it is a registered U.S. not-for-profit organization, you can apply to have it added.

You can also contribute to your favorite charity by shopping online through GoodShop. Instead of going directly to your favorite Web shop, go to **www.Goodshop.com** first, find and click through to the store of your choice, and start shopping. Participating stores donate up to 30 percent of the purchased amount. So, search and shop away—and do some good!

Can I use a search engine to search just for images and videos? With the increasing popularity of multimedia, search engines such as Google, Ask.com, and Yahoo! have capabilities to search the Web for digital images and audio and video files. Use the Advanced Video Search in Google, for example, to find videos in a certain language or with subtitles, or of a specific duration or quality. Blinkx (**www.blinkx.com**) is a video search engine that helps you sift through all the video posted on the Web (see Figure 3.27).

How can I refine my searches for better results? When you conduct a Web search, you may receive a list of hits that includes thousands—even millions—of Web pages that have no relevance to the topic you're trying to search. Initially, Boolean operators were needed to help refine a search. **Boolean operators** are words such as *AND*, *NOT*, and *OR* that describe the relationships between keywords in a search.

Today, most search engines offer an advanced search page that provides the same types of strategies in a well-organized form (see Figure 3.28). Using the advanced search form can make your Internet research a lot more efficient. With the simple addition of a few words or constraints, you can narrow your search results to a more manageable and more meaningful list.

Are there other helpful search strategies? Instead of using the advanced search form, you can use other strategies to help refine your searches when entering your search phrases:

- **Search for a phrase.** To search for an exact phrase, place quotation marks around your keywords. The search engine will look for only those Web sites that contain the words in that exact order. For example, if you want information on the movie *The Green Hornet* and you type these words without quotation marks, your search results will contain pages that include either of the words *Green* and *Hornet*, although not necessarily in that order. Typing "The Green Hornet" in quotes guarantees that search results will include this exact phrase.

- **Search within a specific Web site.** To search just a specific Web site, you can use the search keyword, then *site:* followed by the Web site's URL. For example, searching with *processor site: www.wired.com* returns results about processors from the Wired.com Web site. The same method works for entire classes of sites in a given top-level domain or country code.

- **Use a wild card.** The asterisk "*" is a wild card, or placeholder, feature that is helpful when you need to search with unknown terms. Another way to think about the wild card search feature is as a "fill in the blank." For example, searching with *Congress voted * on the * bill* might bring up an article about the members of Congress who voted *no* on the *healthcare* bill or a different article about the members of Congress who voted *yes* on the *energy* bill.

How else can I customize my searches? A lot of other specialty search strategies and services are available. After

ACTIVE HELP-DESK Getting Around the Web

In this Active Helpdesk call, you'll play the role of a helpdesk staffer, fielding calls about Web browsers, URLs, and how to use hyperlinks and other tools to get around the Web.

blinkx

Over 35 million hours of video. Search it all.   Go »   Wall it! »   Safe Search is ON   Browse blinkx

World News | Entertainment | Business | Sport

Video Categories »

» Entertainment   » Health & Fitness   » Topics
» News   » Home & Living   » Travel
» Music ♪   » Family   » Video Games
» Cars   » Money   » Movies
» Environment   » Sports   » Square Eyes Blog
» Fashion   » Technology   » Summer Fun ☀
» Food   » Teen Pop

Entertainment »   Watch all » Subscribe »

» Hugh Hefner's Two New Girlfriends ⚲
The Playboy mogul has introduced his two new girlfriends, Anna Sophia Berglund and Shera Bechard, just two weeks after Crystal Harris called off the w...

inform me with today's news   entertain me with fun videos   give me my own channel

About ⁞ News ⁞ Advertisers ⁞ Investors ⁞ Partners ⁞ Products & Solutions ⁞ Contact ⁞ Facebook   © 2011 blinkx

Blinkx

Figure 3.27

Video logs use video in addition to text, images, and audio. Blinkx is a video search engine that helps you sift through the increasing number of vlogs.

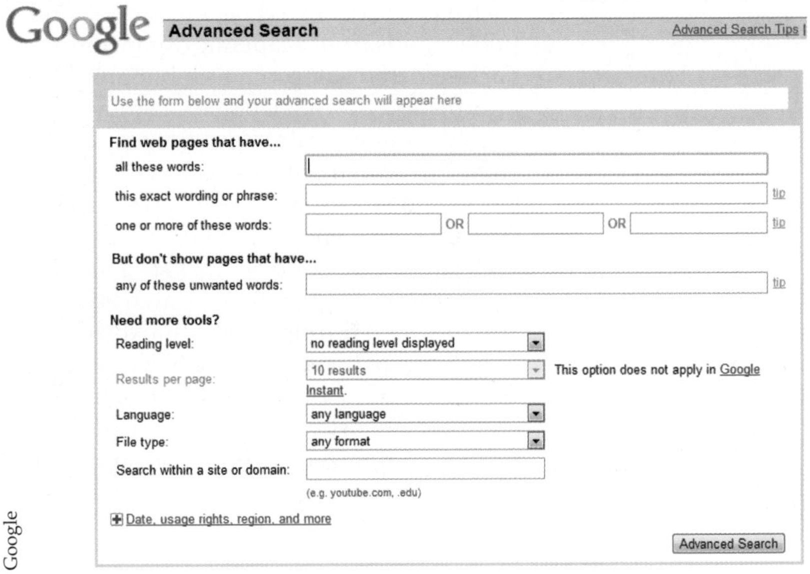

Figure 3.28

Most search engines have an advanced search form to help you refine your searches.

Google Advanced Search   Advanced Search Tips

Use the form below and your advanced search will appear here

Find web pages that have...
all these words:
this exact wording or phrase: tip
one or more of these words: OR   OR   tip

But don't show pages that have...
any of these unwanted words: tip

Need more tools?
Reading level: no reading level displayed ▾
Results per page: 10 results ▾   This option does not apply in Google Instant.
Language: any language ▾
File type: any format ▾
Search within a site or domain:
(e.g. youtube.com, .edu)

⊞ Date, usage rights, region, and more

Advanced Search

Google

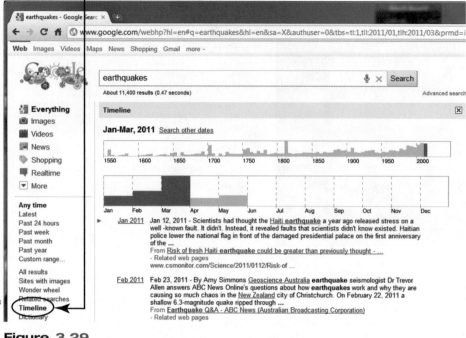

Click on Timeline

Figure 3.29

The Google Timeline enables you to zero in on search results from a specific period.

you've entered your key search words, try clicking on the Timeline feature in the search options section of the left navigation pane. The Timeline helps narrow down articles to a particular time period (see Figure 3.29). In addition to the Timeline, you can narrow your search down by reading level, related searches, or pages you have or have not visited in the past.

Try clicking on the "more" hyperlink in the Google search engine for a listing of all the various search products Google offers. Google Scholar searches scholarly literature such as peer-reviewed papers, theses, and publications from academic organizations. Each search result contains bibliographic information as well. Google Custom Search enables you to create a customized search engine to search only a selected set of sites tailored to your specific needs. This specialized search engine can be added to a Web site or blog, or designed for a specific organization. Google Book Search enables you to search through the full-text content of millions of books. Google News searches through thousands of news stories from around the world. Google News can be further customized to search stories within specific categories such as Business or Entertainment, and a News Archives Timeline

shows selected results from relevant time periods (see Figure 3.29).

Evaluating Web Sites

How can I make sure a Web site is appropriate to use for research? When you're using the Internet for research, you shouldn't assume that everything you find is accurate and appropriate to use. Before you use an Internet resource, consider the following:

1. **Authority:** Who is the author of the article or the sponsor of the site? If the author is well known or the site is published by a reputable news source (such as the *New York Times*), then you can feel more confident using it as a source than if you are unable to locate such information. *Note:* Some sites include a page with information about the author or the site's sponsor.

2. **Bias:** Is the site biased? The purpose of many Web sites is to sell products or services or to persuade rather than inform. These sites, though useful in some situations, present a biased point of view. Look for sites that offer several sets of facts, or consider opinions from several sources.

3. **Relevance:** Is the information in the site current? Material can last a long time on the Web. Some research projects (such as historical accounts) depend on older records. However, if you're writing about cutting-edge technologies, you need to look for the most recent sources. Therefore, look for a date on information to make sure it is current.

SOUND BYTE — Finding Information on the Web

In this Sound Byte, you'll learn how and when to use search engines and subject directories. Through guided tours, you'll learn effective search techniques, including how to use Boolean operators and meta-search engines.

Plagiarism and Copyright Violation: What Can You Borrow from the Internet?

You've no doubt heard of plagiarism—claiming another person's words as your own. And you've probably heard the term *copyright violation*, especially if you've been following the music industry's battle to keep "free" music off the Web. But what constitutes plagiarism, and what constitutes copyright violation? And what can you borrow from the Web? Consider these scenarios:

1. You find a political cartoon that would be terrific in a PowerPoint presentation you're creating for your civics class. You copy it into your presentation.

2. Your hobby is writing children's books, which you later sell online. Most of what you create is your content, but sometimes you borrow story ideas from other children's books, and just change a few characters or situations. You do not obtain permission from the originators of the story ideas you borrow.

3. You're pressed for time and need to do research for a paper due tomorrow. You find information on an obscure Web site and copy it into your paper without documenting the source.

4. You download a song from the Internet and incorporate it into a PowerPoint presentation for a school project. Because you assume everyone knows the song, you don't credit it in your sources.

Which of the preceding scenarios represent copyright violations? Which represent plagiarism? The distinctions between these scenarios are narrow in some cases, but it's important to understand the differences.

As noted earlier, plagiarism occurs when you use someone else's ideas or words and represent them as your own. In today's computer society, it's easy to copy information from the Internet and paste it into a Word document, change a few words, and call it your own. To avoid plagiarism, use quotation marks around all words you borrow directly, and credit your sources for any ideas you paraphrase or borrow. Avoiding plagiarism means properly crediting all information you obtain from the Internet, including words, ideas, graphics, data, and audio and video clips.

Web sites such as Turnitin (**www.turnitin.com**) (for teachers and institutions) and WriteCheck (**www.writecheck.com**) (specifically for students), as shown in Figure 3.30, help check for plagiarism violations. WriteCheck compares your document to a database of magazines, newspapers, journals, and books, as well as Web content and previously submitted student papers. Although some common phrasing may be truly coincidental, real and purposeful plagiarism is reasonably easy to identify. Students can use WriteCheck before submitting an assignment to ensure their papers will not be confused with plagiarized work. In most schools, plagiarism is a serious offense, often resulting in a 0 for an assignment, or an F for the class. It's

best to ensure your paper doesn't even have unintended instances of plagiarized work.

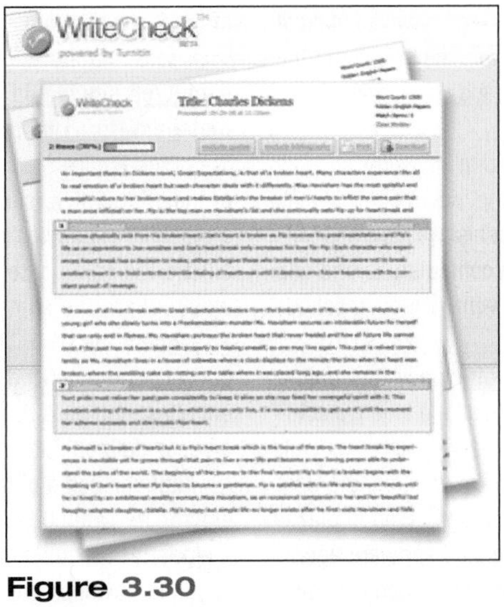

Copyright violation is more serious because it, unlike plagiarism, is punishable by law. Copyright law assumes that all original work—including text, graphics, software, multimedia, audio and video clips, and other intellectual property—is copyrighted even if the work does not display the copyright symbol (©). Copyright violation occurs when you use another person's material for your own personal economic benefit, or when you take away from the economic benefit of the originator. Don't assume that by citing a source you're abiding by copyright laws. In most cases, you need to seek and receive written permission from the copyright holder.

There are exceptions to this rule. For example, there is no copyright on government documents, so you can download and reproduce material from NASA, for example, without violating copyright laws. The British Broadcasting Corporation (BBC) is also beginning to digitize and make available its archives of material to the public without copyright restrictions.

Teachers and students receive special consideration regarding copyright violations. This special consideration falls under a provision called academic fair use. As long as the material is being used for educational purposes only, limited copying and distribution is allowed. One standard applied to academic fair use is the effect the use has on the potential market. For example, an instructor could make copies of a book chapter and distribute it to her class one time but could not do it on a regular basis or over different semesters because that might affect the potential market or sales of the book. Similarly, a student can include a cartoon in a PowerPoint presentation without seeking permission from the artist. However, to avoid plagiarism in these situations, you still must credit your sources of information.

So, do you now know which of the four scenarios above are plagiarism or copyright violations? Let's review them.

1. You are not in violation because the use of the cartoon is for educational purposes and falls under the academic fair use provision. You must still credit the source, however.

2. You are in violation of copyright laws because you are presenting others' ideas for children's stories as your own.

3. You are guilty of plagiarism because you copied content from another source and implied it was your own work.

4. Again, because your copying is for a school project, you are not in violation because of the academic fair use provision. However, it's always important to document your sources.

Figure 3.30

By using WriteCheck, students can compare their work to a database of publications to check for unintended plagiarism.

Writecheck.com

4. **Audience:** For what audience is the site intended? Ensure that the content, tone, and style of the site match your needs. You probably wouldn't want to use information from a site geared toward teens if you were writing for adults, nor would you use a site that has a casual style and tone for serious research.

5. **Links:** Are the links available and appropriate? Check out the links provided on the site to determine whether they are still working and appropriate for your needs. Don't assume that the links provided are the only additional sources of information. Investigate other sites on your topic as well. You should also be able to find the same

---

DIG DEEPER

Discovering the Semantic Web

How do we find information on the Web? Generally, we access Google or another search engine, type in the keyword or search phrase, and click the search button. As a result, millions of links to Web pages display. At best, we click on the first several links that seem reasonably relevant to our search. Rarely, if ever, do we explore all of the links that are found in the search results.

Similarly, think about all the other types of data on the Web that we access manually, such as contact information, appointment times, transportation schedules, entertainment schedules, medical treatments, and store types, locations, and hours. It would seem that computers would be helpful in plugging through all of this Web data, but oddly, that is not the case. Web pages are designed for people to read, not for computers to manipulate. Although computers can determine the parts and functionality of Web pages (headers, hyperlinks, etc.), as yet no reliable way exists for computers to process the meaning of the data so that they can use the information to see relationships or make decisions.

The **Semantic Web** (or **Web 3.0**) is an evolving extension of the World Wide Web in which information is defined in such a way to make it more easily readable by computers. Tim Berners-Lee, the inventor of the World Wide Web and the implementation of HTTP and HTML, thought up the Semantic Web.

Right now, search engines function by recognizing keywords such as appointment, dentist, and root canal, but they cannot determine in which office and on what days Dr. Smith works and what his available appointment times are. The Semantic Web would enable computers to find and manage that type of information and coordinate it with your other schedules and preferences.

Similarly, think about the convenience and efficiency that online shopping has brought to our lives. Then think about all the time we actually spend researching and comparing products, brands, stores, prices, and shipping options. Ultimately, after all that effort, we make the final buying decision and place the order. With the Semantic Web in place, you could enter your preferences into a computerized software agent, which would then search the Web for you, find the best option based on

your criteria, and place the order. Additionally, the agent would be able to record the financial transaction into your personal bookkeeping software and arrange for a technician to help install your purchase, if needed.

The Semantic Web would use software agents that roam from page to page, completing sophisticated tasks. These agents would not read words, look at pictures, and process information as humans do, but rather would search through metadata. Metadata is machine-readable data that describes other data in such a way that the agents can identify and define what they need to know. Like Web page coding, which is now done in HTML, XML, and other formats, metadata would be invisible to humans reading pages on the Web but would be clearly visible to computers, in essence turning the Web into a giant database.

The introduction of eXtensible Markup Language (XML) has helped make the user of the Web more of a participant. Web 2.0 technologies such as blogs, wikis, and social networking sites, as well as Web-based applications, are in part possible because of XML's tagging functionalities. RSS feeds also use technologies that are an underlying component of the Semantic Web.

The Semantic Web would build on this type of capability so that each Web site would have text and pictures (for people to read) and metadata (for computers to read) describing the information on the Web (see Figure 3.31). The metadata would contain all the attributes of the information, such as condition, price, or schedule availability, in a machine-readable format. Businesses, services, and software would all use the same categorization structures so that similar information would share the same attributes, ensuring consistency of metadata throughout the Web. Then, with Web data properly identified and categorized, computerized agents could read the metadata found on different sites, compare the information, and process the information based on user-defined criteria.

Although some of the Semantic Web functionalities are beginning to emerge in Web 2.0 technologies, such as Siri in the new iPhone 4S, the majority of the functionality and implementation of the Semantic Web is still in development. The World Wide Web Consortium (W3C), led by

information on at least three different Web sites to help verify the information is accurate.

The answers to these questions will help you decide whether you should consider a Web site to be a good source of information.

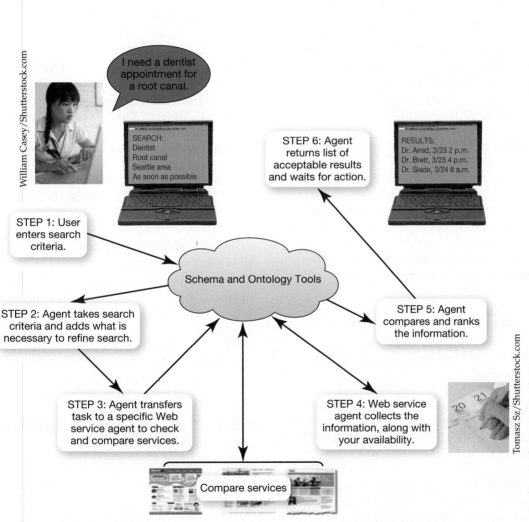

I need a dentist appointment for a root canal.

SEARCH:
Dentist
Root canal
Seattle area
As soon as possible

STEP 6: Agent returns list of acceptable results and waits for action.

RESULTS:
Dr. Amid, 3/23 2 p.m.
Dr. Brett, 3/23 4 p.m.
Dr. Slade, 3/24 8 a.m.

STEP 1: User enters search criteria.

Schema and Ontology Tools

STEP 2: Agent takes search criteria and adds what is necessary to refine search.

STEP 5: Agent compares and ranks the information.

STEP 3: Agent transfers task to a specific Web service agent to check and compare services.

STEP 4: Web service agent collects the information, along with your availability.

Compare services

William Casey/Shutterstock.com

Tomasz Sz./Shutterstock.com

Figure 3.31

Web 2.0 technologies enable us to become creators and users of Internet content. The Semantic Web enables the computer to add context to Web content, providing meaning to information from different sources.

Tim Berners-Lee, is the primary organization leading the charge. The greatest challenge is recoding all the information currently available on the Web into the type of metadata that computers could recognize. The very grandeur of that task means that we will not see a fully functional Semantic Web until sometime in the distant future. In the meantime, we can continue to benefit from each small step toward that goal.

1. What is the origin of the Internet?

The Internet is the largest computer network in the world, connecting millions of computers. Government and military officials developed the early Internet as a reliable way to communicate in the event of war. Eventually, scientists and educators used the Internet to exchange research. Today, we use the Internet and the Web (which is a part of the Internet) to shop, research, communicate, and entertain ourselves.

2. How does data travel on the Internet?

A computer connected to the Internet acts as either a client (a computer that asks for information) or a server (a computer that receives the request and returns the information to the client). Data travels between clients and servers along a system of communication lines or pathways. The largest and fastest of these pathways is the Internet backbone. To ensure that data is sent to the correct computer along the pathways, IP addresses (unique ID numbers) are assigned to all computers connected to the Internet.

3. How can I communicate and collaborate using Web 2.0 technologies?

Web 2.0 is a trend of Web interactions among people, software, and data. Examples of these technologies include blogs, wikis, and more. Blogs are journal entries posted to the Web that are generally organized by a topic or area of interest and are publicly available. Generally, one person writes the blog, and others can comment on the journal entries. Video logs are personal journals that use video as the primary content in addition to text, images, and audio. Wikis are a type of Web site that allows users to change content by adding, removing, or editing it. A wiki is designed to allow many users to collaborate on the content. Podcasts are audio or video content that is broadcast over the Internet. Users subscribe to receive updates to podcasts. Social networking sites enable users to communicate and share information with existing friends as well as to meet and connect with others through common interests, experiences, or friends.

4. How can I communicate with e-mail?

Communication was one of the reasons the Internet was developed and is one of the primary uses of the Internet today. E-mail allows users to communicate electronically without the parties involved being available at the same time, whereas instant-messaging services are programs that enable you to communicate in real time with others who are online at the same time.

5. What multimedia files are found on the Web, and what software is needed?

The Web is appealing because of its enriched multimedia content. Multimedia is anything that involves one or more forms of media in addition to text, such as graphics, audio, and video clips. Sometimes you need a special software program called a *plug-in* (or *player*) to view and hear multimedia files. Plug-ins are often installed in new computers or are offered free of charge at manufacturers' Web sites.

6. What is e-commerce, and what online safeguards are there?

E-commerce is the business of conducting business online. E-commerce includes transactions between businesses (B2B), between consumers (C2C), and between businesses and consumers (B2C). Because more business than ever before is conducted online, numerous safeguards have been put in place to ensure that transactions are protected.

7. What is a Web browser, and what is a URL and its parts?

Once you're connected to the Internet, in order to locate, navigate to, and view Web pages, you need to install special software called a Web browser on your system. The most common Web browsers are Internet Explorer, Firefox, Google Chrome, and Safari. You gain access to a Web site by typing in its address, called a Uniform Resource Locator (URL). A URL is composed of several parts, including the protocol, the domain, the top-level domain, and paths (or subdirectories).

8. How can I use hyperlinks and other tools to get around the Web?

One unique aspect of the Web is that you can jump from place to place by clicking on specially formatted pieces of text or images called *hyperlinks.* You can also use the Back and Forward buttons, History lists, breadcrumb trails, and Favorites or Bookmarks to navigate the Web. Favorites, live bookmarks, and social bookmarking help you return to specific Web pages without having to type in the URL and help you organize the Web content that is most important to you.

9. How do I search the Internet effectively, and how can I evaluate Web sites?

A search engine is a set of programs that searches the Web using specific keywords you wish to query and then returns a list of the Web sites on which those keywords are found. Search engines can be used to search for images, podcasts, and videos in addition to traditional text-based Web content. A subject directory is a structured outline of Web sites organized by topic and subtopic. Metasearch engines search other search engines.

Not all Web sites are equal, and some are better sources for research than others. To evaluate whether it is appropriate to use a Web site as a resource, determine whether the author of the site is reputable and whether the site is intended for your particular needs. In addition, make sure that the site content is not biased, the information in the site is current, and all the links on the site are available and appropriate. If multiple sites offer the same content, then it is another indication that the information is accurate.

Companion Website

The Companion Website includes a variety of additional materials to help you review and learn more about the topics in this chapter. Go to: ***www.pearsonhighered.com/techinaction***

Word Bank

- aggregator
- blogs (Weblogs)
- Bookmarks
- e-mail
- hyperlink
- instant messaging (IM)
- keyword

- metasearch engine
- podcast
- search engine
- social bookmarking
- social networking
- RSS feed
- tag

- Uniform Resource Locators (URLs)
- Web 2.0
- Web browser
- wiki

Instructions: Fill in the blanks using the words from the Word Bank above.

Knowing he has only a few minutes before class, Juan launches Internet Explorer, the (1) _____ software from Microsoft that allows him to connect to the Internet. He quickly goes to Facebook, the (2) _____ site, to catch up on the activities of his friends, and then checks his (3) _____ for any electronic mail communication he may have received from his professors. He also reads a few of the updates to the online journal **Engadget.com**, one of his favorite (4) _____.

At home, Juan types a(n) (5) _____ into Google, the (6) _____, to find Web sites he needs for a research paper. One of the first sites listed is Wikipedia, the online encyclopedia that takes advantage of the collaborative nature of (7) _____ technology. Because anyone can add, change, or edit content on Wikipedia, Juan knows that he can't rely completely on this information, but finds that it is usually a pretty good starting point for his research. Juan then checks out Dogpile.com, a(n) (8) _____ that searches the search engines Yahoo! and Bing in addition to Google. Juan clicks on a(n) (9) _____, the specially coded text in the resulting list in Dogpile, which links him to a Web site that will be useful in his research. He adds a(n) (10) _____ with a meaningful keyword in the (11) _____ site Delicious so he can see how many others find this Web page interesting, and what similar Web pages others have found that might also be helpful for Juan's research. Juan also notes the (12) _____ of the Web site so that he can add it to his bibliography. Finally, before going to bed, Juan opens up iTunes, a(n) (13) _____ that collects the latest updates of broadcasted media using a(n) (14) _____, which ensures that the latest content is available. Juan listens to the (15) _____ of one of his favorite radio shows that he subscribes to and then goes to sleep.

becoming computer literate

Using key terms from the chapter, create a presentation about all the various ways students and teachers can use social media and other communication tools to foster better communication and collaboration in the classroom, and to enrich the learning process.

self-test

Instructions: Answer the multiple-choice and true–false questions below for more practice with key terms and concepts from this chapter.

Multiple Choice

1. Which is NOT true about the Internet?
   a. It is the largest computer network in the world.
   b. It was created to establish a secure form of military communications.
   c. It was developed as an additional means of commerce.
   d. It was invented as a way for all computers to communicate.

2. What do you need to read, send, and organize e-mail from *any* computer connected to the Internet?
   a. an e-mail client program
   b. an e-mail server
   c. a social networking account
   d. a Web-based e-mail account

3. Which is NOT an example of social networking?
   a. e-mail
   b. instant messaging
   c. blogging
   d. wiki

4. Which of the following is NOT a characteristic of a blog?
   a. Blogs are used to express opinions.
   b. Blogs are generally written by a single author.
   c. Blogs are private and require password access.
   d. Blogs are arranged as a listing of entries.

5. Which of the following is true about plug-ins?
   a. Plugs-ins rarely require updating.
   b. Plug-ins track the Web sites you've visited.
   c. Plug-ins are necessary for viewing most Web graphics.
   d. Plug-ins cannot present security risks.

6. What feature is a list of links you've visited within a Web site?
   a. Favorites
   b. breadcrumb trail
   c. Bookmarks
   d. history

7. Which is NOT a component of a search engine?
   a. spider
   b. indexer program
   c. subject directory
   d. search engine software

8. When using the Internet for research, you
   a. can assume that everything you find is accurate and appropriate.
   b. should evaluate sites for bias and relevance.
   c. should always use the most current sources.
   d. can assume that the links provided on the site are the only additional sources of information.

9. Which of the following is not an Internet protocol?
   a. ARPANET   b. HTTP
   c. FTP   d. BitTorrent

10. eBay and Craigslist are examples of what kind of electronic commerce?
   a. C2C   b. B2B
   c. B2C   d. C2B

True–False

_____ 1. The information in e-mail is no more private than a postcard.

_____ 2. A search engine that searches other search engines is called a SuperSearch engine.

_____ 3. A green shaded address bar on a Web site indicates that the Web site is secure.

_____ 4. Each time you connect to the Internet, your computer is assigned the same IP address.

_____ 5. In the Web address www.facebook.com, facebook is the top-level domain.

1. Online Support Facilities

Your school most likely has many online support facilities. Do you know what they are? Go to your school's Web site and search for online support.

a. What kinds of online tutoring services are available?
b. How do you reserve a book from the library online?
c. How do you register for classes online?
d. How do you take classes online?
e. How do you buy books online?

2. Plagiarism Policies

Does your school have a plagiarism policy?

a. Search your school's Web site to find the school's plagiarism policy. What does it say?
b. How well do you paraphrase? Find some Web sites that help test or evaluate your paraphrasing skills.
c. Create an account at Turnitin. This Web site checks your written work against content on the Web and produces an originality report. Submit at least three different drafts of your work to Turnitin to check for any intended or unintended cases of plagiarism before submitting your final work for a grade. What were the results?

3. Searching Beyond Google

While Google is probably your first choice among search engines, there are many other very good search engines that are good to know about. Conduct searches for inexpensive travel deals for spring break by using the following search engines. Record your results and a summary of the differences among search engines. Would you choose to use any of these search engines again? Why or why not?

a. www.Yippy.com
b. www.Dogpile.com
c. www.Rollyo.com

4. Free Speech Online

Leila was suspended from school for several days because her posts on Facebook about her teacher and a few of her classmates were "vulgar" and "derogatory." Daniel was expelled from his school because the picture he posted of himself was in violation of his school's code of conduct. Similarly, Bill, a local employer, changed his mind about a job offer to a recent graduate after seeing questionable content on the candidate's Facebook page.

a. Should a person be penalized for his or her content on any Web site?
b. Is the issue denial of free speech or prudent reactions to improper behavior?
c. The Federal Bureau of Investigation (FBI) is working undercover in social networking sites to gather information. What are the benefits and drawbacks of this?

5. Using Web 2.0 in Education

Social networking sites, blogs, and wikis are commonly referred to as Web 2.0 technologies. Sites that use Web 2.0 offer opportunities for collaboration, creativity, and enterprise. Describe how Web 2.0 sites such as Wikipedia, YouTube, Delicious, and Digg might change how you learn and manage information.

making the transition to... the workplace

making the transition to... the workplace

1. Online Résumé Resources

Using a search engine, locate several Web resources that offer assistance in writing a résumé. For example, the University of Minnesota (**www1.umn.edu/ohr/careerdev/resources/resume**) has a résumé tutor that guides you as you write your résumé.

a. What other Web sites can you find that help you write a résumé?
b. Do these sites all offer the same services and have the same features?

2. Online Job Search

After you've created a résumé, you need to know how to get it to the right people and manage the job search process. A wealth of online job search resources is available to help you with these details. Research the following Web sites and write a brief description of each that outlines the benefits and role in a job search:

a. LinkedIn (**www.linkedin.com**)
b. JibberJobber (**www.jibberjobber.com**)
c. VisualCV (**www.visualcv.com**)
d. Monster (**www.monster.com**)

3. Evaluating Web 2.0 Content

You are aware of the guidelines you should use to evaluate the quality of content on a Web site, but you find yourself using other kinds of Web content such as blogs, wikis, social networking sites, and social bookmarks. Visit **library.albany.edu/usered/eval/evalweb** and review the new guidelines for evaluating Web content in the 2.0 environment. After reviewing the guidelines, describe the guidelines for evaluating Web content in the following:

a. Blogs and wikis
b. Google Scholar (**scholar.google.com**)
c. California Digital Library (**www.cdlib.org**)
d. Twitter (**www.twitter.com**)
e. Delicious (**www.delicious.com**)
f. Connotea (**www.connotea.org**)

4. Using Social Media for Business

You work for a local bookstore that has so far been successful at attracting a good customer base, despite the lure of the big chain stores. At their last strategic planning meeting, the owners of the bookstore decided that they wanted to have a social media presence to better interact with their loyal customer base, but also to attract new customers. Research the various ways social media is being used for businesses.

a. What are the pros and cons of using blogs, wikis, and social networking in the business community?
b. Describe the social media strategy you would recommend to the owners.

5. Facebook Privacy and Security

Your aunt contacted you last night. Your cousin, who is 14, wants a Facebook account. Your aunt has heard lots of stories of how difficult it is to protect your privacy on Facebook, and she wants your advice. Research the privacy and security settings on Facebook and create a "User's Guide" for your aunt to work through with your cousin. Make sure you include information on how to remove your cousin from Facebook search results, make contact information private, keep friendships private, adjust Wall posting visibility, set up photo album privacy, customize photo tagging, and explain what personal information should and should not be included on your cousin's profile.

Instructions: The following critical thinking questions are designed to demand your full attention but require only a comfortable chair—no technology.

1. Social Networking and Society

Social networking seems to have taken over our lives! Almost everyone is on Facebook and Twitter. But is this a good thing?

a. What advantages and disadvantages does social networking bring to your life?
b. What positive and negative effects has social networking had on society as a whole?
c. How are businesses using social networking?
d. How might you see social networking evolving in the next two or three years?

2. File Swapping Ethics

Downloading free music, movies, and other electronic media from the Internet, although illegal, still occurs on sites such as BitTorrent.

a. Do you think you should have the ability to download free music files of your choice? Do you think the musicians who oppose online music sharing have made valid points?
b. Discuss the differences you see between sharing music files online and sharing CDs with your friends.
c. The current price to buy a song online is about $1. Is this a fair price? If not, what price would you consider to be fair?

3. The Power of Google

Google is the largest and most popular search engine on the Internet today. Because of its size and popularity, some people claim that Google has enormous power to influence a Web user's search experience solely by its Web site ranking processes. What do you think about this potential power? How could it be used in negative or harmful ways?

a. Some Web sites pay search engines to list them near the top of the results pages. These sponsors therefore get priority placement. What do you think of this policy?
b. What effect (if any) do you think that Google has on Web site development? For example, do you think Web site developers intentionally include frequently searched words in their pages so that they will appear in more hits lists?
c. When you google someone, you type their name in the Google search box to see what comes up. What privacy concerns do you think such googling could present? Have you ever googled yourself or your friends?

4. Apple and Adobe Flash

Apple has made a corporate decision not to support Flash-based files on its devices. There are no good work-arounds if you want to play a Flash-based game on an Apple device, and some limited alternatives to help run other Flash-based content on an Apple device. Apple contends that working with other content written in open standard products is better for it as a company, and as a consumer, there are reasonable "alternatives" to Flash. What do you think of Apple's position? What would you recommend it to do?

Comparing Internet Search Methods

Problem

With millions of sites on the Internet, finding useful information can be a daunting—and, at times, impossible—task. However, there are methods to make searching easier, some of which have been discussed in this chapter. In this Team Time, each team will search for specific items or pieces of information on the Internet and compare search methodologies.

Process

Split your group into three or more teams, depending on class size. Each group will create a team wiki using free wiki software such as that found at **www.pbworks.com.** To appreciate the benefits of wiki collaboration fully, each team should have at least five or six members.

1. Each team should come up with a theme for its wiki. Suggestions include the following:

   • Best computer technology Web sites

   • Coolest new technology gadgets

   • All-time greatest musicians

   • All-time greatest athletes

   • Best places to visit in the United States

   • Best beaches in the United States

   • Best skiing areas around the world

2. Each student should pick one example to research and then must design a wiki page highlighting that subject. For example, if the team chose all-time greatest musicians, one student could select Bruce Springsteen and create a wiki page on Bruce Springsteen. The wiki page should contain links to other Web sites and, if possible, images and videos.

3. After the team wikis are created, teams should make their wikis available to the other teams for comments.

Conclusion

After all the team wikis have been completed and shared, discuss the following with your class. What is the benefit of using wiki technology to create team pages? How did wikis help or hinder the team process? What other conclusions can the class draw about using wiki technology?

Plagiarism

In this exercise, you will research and then role-play a complicated ethical situation. The role you play may or may not match your own personal beliefs, but your research and use of logic will enable you to represent whichever view is assigned. An arbitrator will watch and comment on both sides of the arguments, and together the team will agree on an ethical solution.

Problem

Plagiarism, or portraying another's work as your own, has been around for a long while and extends well beyond the classroom. For example, Nick Simmons, the son of Gene Simmons (KISS) and a member of A&E's *Family Jewels* reality series, created a comic book series "Incarnate." Radical Publishing picked up the series but quickly stopped publication when Internet messages accused the author of copying from other similar series. Similarly, the Australian band Men at Work was cited for copying a melody from "Kookaburra Sits in the Old Gum Tree" for its 1980s hit "Down Under" and owes the owner years of royalties.

Research Areas to Consider

- Plagiarism violations
- Comic book series "Incarnate"
- Australian band Men at Work
- Plagiarism consequences

Process

Divide the class into teams.

1. Research the areas cited above and devise a scenario in which someone has violated plagiarism rules.

2. Team members should write a summary that provides background information for their character—for example: author, publisher, or arbitrator—and details their character's behaviors to set the stage for the role-playing event. Then team members should create an outline to use during the role-playing event.

3. Team members should arrange a mutually convenient time to meet for the exchange, using the chat room feature of MyITLab, the discussion board feature of Blackboard, or meeting in person.

4. Team members should present their case to the class, or submit a PowerPoint presentation for review by the rest of the class, along with the summary and resolution they developed.

Conclusion

As technology becomes ever more prevalent and integrated into our lives, more and more ethical dilemmas will present themselves. Being able to understand and evaluate both sides of an argument, while responding in a personally or socially ethical manner, will be an important skill.

TECHNOLOGY

Security

Computer Abuse

Information Technology

ethics

In this Technology in Focus section, we explore what ethics is, how your personal ethics develop, and how your personal ethics fit into the world around you. We'll also examine how technology and ethics affect each other and how technology can be used to support ethical conduct. Finally, we'll examine several key issues in technology ethics today, including the areas of social justice, intellectual property rights, privacy, e-commerce, free speech, and computer abuse.

IN FOCUS

Intellectual Property

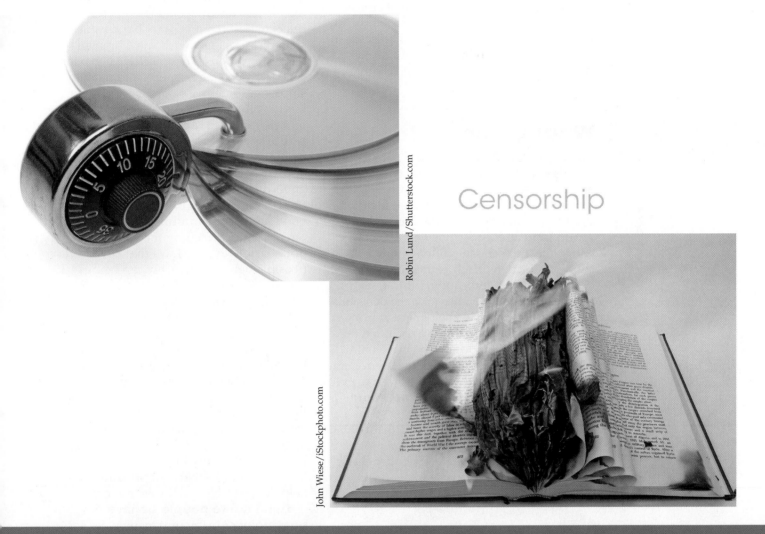

Robin Lund/Shutterstock.com

Censorship

John Wiese/iStockphoto.com

People speak of ethics—and the lack of ethics—casually all the time, but the ethical choices that individuals make are an extremely serious matter and can have a far-reaching impact. It is important to have a clear idea of what ethics are, what your personal ethics are, and how personal ethics fit into the world at large.

Ethics in Computing

You just bought a new notebook computer. You know you can go to BitTorrent to download the latest summer blockbuster movie and its soundtrack. You also probably know this is unethical. Although pirating music and videos is a valid example of unethical behavior, it has been overused as an illustration of the ethical challenges of technology. There is a vast range of ethical issues surrounding technology (as shown in Figure 1), several of which we will discuss in this section. Many other issues are discussed in the Ethics in IT sections of each chapter throughout the book.

What Is Ethics?

Ethics is the study of the general nature of morals and of the specific moral choices made by individuals. Morals involve conforming to established or accepted ideas of right and wrong (as generally dictated by society), and are usually viewed as black and white. Ethical issues often involve subtle distinctions, such as the difference between fairness and equity. Ethical values are the guidelines you use to make decisions each day. For example, the person in front of you at the coffee shop drops a dollar on the floor and doesn't notice it. Do you tell him or her about it, or do you pick up the dollar and use it to pay for your coffee?

Doesn't everyone have the same basic ethics? There are many systems of ethical conduct. Relativism is a theory that holds that there is no universal moral truth and that instead there are only beliefs, perspectives, and values. Everyone has his or her own ideas of right and wrong, and so who are we to judge anyone else? Another ethical philosophy is situational ethics, which states that decision making should be based on the circumstances of a particular situation and not on fixed laws.

Many other ethical systems have been proposed over time, some of which are defined by religious traditions. For example, the expression "Judeo-Christian ethics" refers to the common set of basic values shared across the Jewish and Christian religious traditions. These include behaviors such as respecting property and relationships, honoring one's parents, and being kind to others.

Are laws established to guide people's ethical actions? Laws are formal, written standards designed to apply to everyone. Laws are enforced by government agencies (such as the police, the Federal Bureau of Investigation, the Food and Drug Administration, and so on) and interpreted by the courts. It is not possible to pass laws that cover every possible behavior that human beings can engage in. Therefore, societal ethics provides a general set of unwritten guidelines for people to follow.

Rule utilitarianism is an ethical theory that espouses establishing moral guidelines through specific rules. The idea behind this system is that if everyone adheres to the same moral code, society as a whole will improve and people will be happier. Many societies follow this system in general terms, including the United States. For instance, laws against nudity in public places (except for a few nude beaches) in the United States help define public nudity as immoral.

Don't some people behave unethically? Although many valid systems of ethical conduct exist, sometimes people act in a manner that violates the beliefs they hold or the beliefs of the ethical system they say they follow. **Unethical behavior** can be defined as not conforming to a set of approved standards of social or professional behavior. For instance, using your phone to text message a test answer to your friend during an exam is prohibited by many colleges' rules of student conduct. This behavior is different from amoral behavior, in which a person has no sense of right and wrong and no interest in the moral consequences of his or her actions.

Figure 1

Ethics in computing covers a wide range of areas, not just privacy and security.

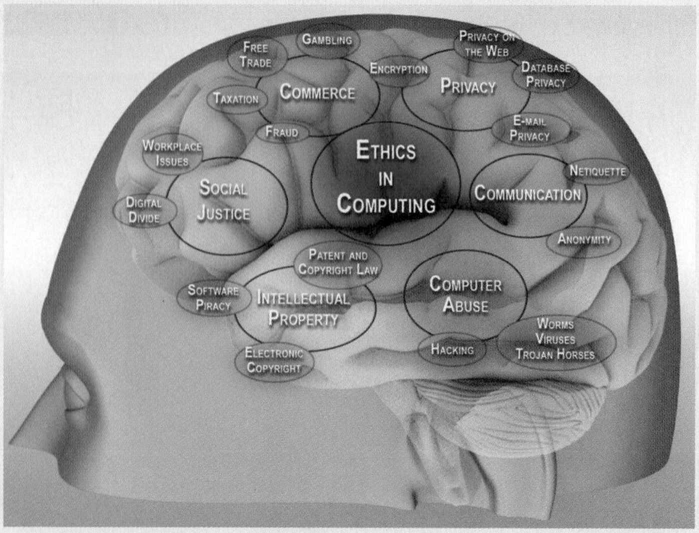

Is unethical behavior a euphemism for illegal activity? Unethical behavior does not have to be illegal. An example of an unethical but not illegal practice is supermarket slotting fees. These are fees that some supermarkets charge to produce companies and product manufacturers for the privilege of having their products placed on store shelves. This is considered unethical by many people because it puts smaller companies, which often don't have the financial resources to pay these fees, at a disadvantage.

Not all illegal behavior is unethical. Civil disobedience, which is manifested by intentionally refusing to obey certain laws, is used as a form of protest to effect change in extreme situations. Gandhi's nonviolent resistance to the British rule of India, which led to India's establishment as an independent country, is an example of civil disobedience. Although the British were ruling India, is it ever ethical for one country to control another country's people?

Which system of ethics works best? There is no universal agreement on which is the best system of ethics. Most societies use a blend of different systems. Regardless of the ethical system of the society in which you live, all ethical decisions are greatly influenced by personal ethics.

consequences of your decisions today might lead to an unhappy result for you in the short term. For instance, to get the job of your dreams, should you exaggerate a bit on your résumé and say you've already finished your college degree, even though you are still one credit short? Is this lying? Is such behavior justified in this setting? After all, you do intend to finish that last credit, and you would work really hard for this company if you were hired. If you tell the truth and state that you haven't finished college yet, then you might be passed over for the position. Making this choice is an ethical decision (see Figure 2).

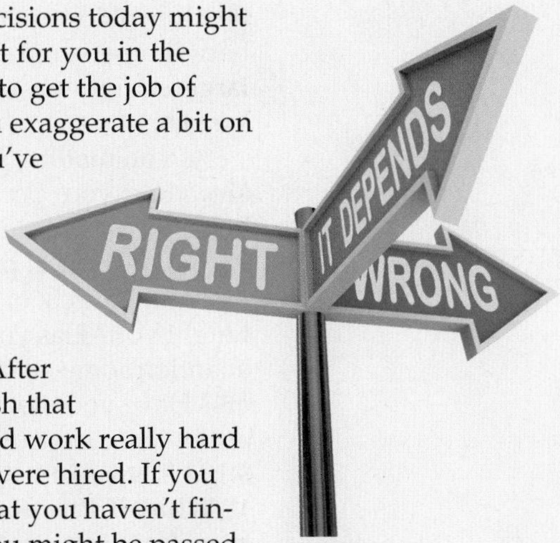

How do a person's ethics develop? Many elements contribute to your ethical development (see Figure 3). Naturally, your family has a major role in establishing the values you cherish in your own life, and these might include a cultural bias toward certain moral positions. Your religious affiliation is another major influence in your ethical life, because most religions have established specific codes of ethical conduct. How these sets of ethics interact with the values of the larger culture is often challenging. Issues such as abortion, the

iQoncept/Shutterstock.com

Figure 2

It would be nice if there were signposts to ethical conduct, but the issues are complex.

Figure 3

Many different forces shape your ethical worldview.

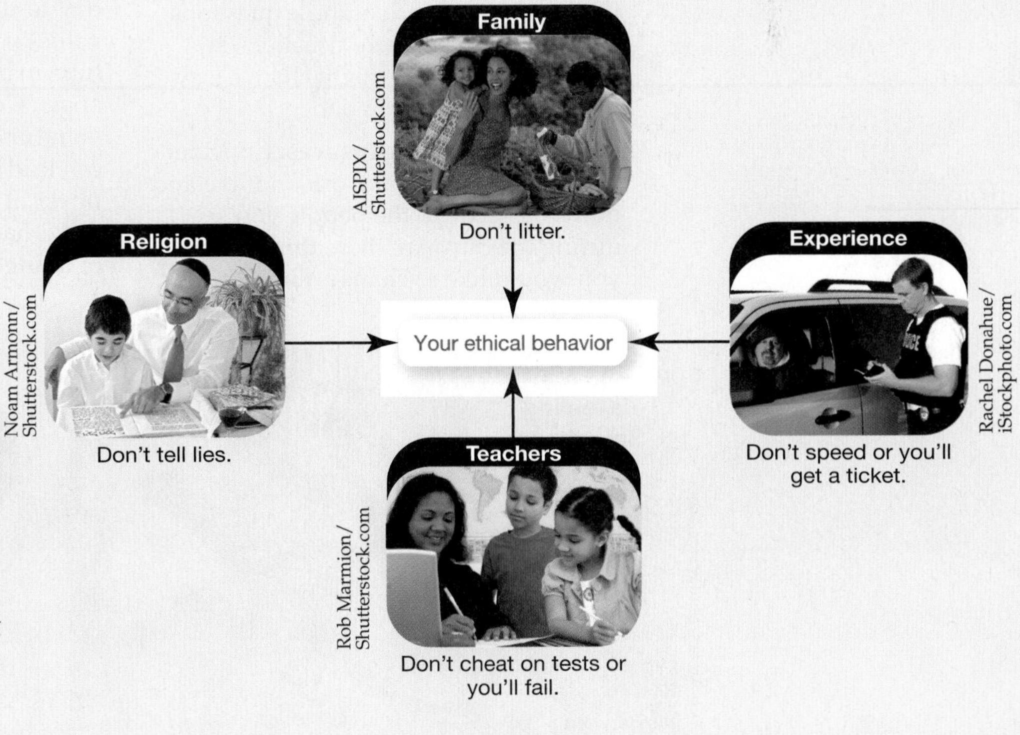

Personal Ethics

What are personal ethics?

Every day you say certain things and take specific actions, and at each point you are making decisions based on some criterion. It may be that you are trying to care for the people around you, or are trying to eliminate a source of pain or anger in your life. Your words and actions may also be driven by a combination of criteria. As you choose your words and actions, you are following a set of personal ethics—a checklist of personal decisions you have compiled to organize your life. Some people have a clear, well-defined set of principles they follow. Others' ethics are inconsistent or are applied differently in similar situations.

It can be challenging to adhere to your own ethical system if the

Family
AISPIX/Shutterstock.com
Don't litter.

Religion
Noam Armonn/Shutterstock.com
Don't tell lies.

Your ethical behavior

Experience
Rachel Donahue/iStockphoto.com
Don't speed or you'll get a ticket.

Teachers
Rob Marmion/Shutterstock.com
Don't cheat on tests or you'll fail.

death penalty, and war force confrontations between personal ethical systems and the larger society's established legal-ethical system.

As you mature, your life experiences also affect your personal ethics. Does the behavior you see around you make sense within the ethical principles that your family, your church, or your first-grade teacher taught you? Has your experience led you to abandon some ethical rules and adopt others? Have you modified how and when you apply these laws of conduct, depending on what is at stake?

What if I'm not sure what my personal ethics are? When you have a clear and firm idea of what values are most important to you, it may be easier to handle situations in your professional and your personal life that demand ethical action. Follow these steps to help define your personal ethics:

1. **Describe yourself.** Write down words that describe who you are, based on how others view you. Would a friend describe you as honest, or helpful, or kind?

2. **List your beliefs.** Make a list of all the beliefs that influence your decision making. For example, would you be comfortable working as a research assistant in a lab that infected animals with diseases and used them for medical research? How important is it to you that you never tell a lie? Consider whether your answers to each of these questions are "flexible." Are there situations in which your answers might change (say, if a friend were ill or in danger)?

3. **Identify external influences.** Consider the places where you work and live and how you relate to the people you see during the day. Are there things that you would like to change about these relationships that would merit listing them in a code of ethics?

4. **Consider "why."** After writing down your beliefs, think about why you believe them. Have you accepted them without investigation? Do they stand up in the context of your real-world experiences? For which of these values would you make short-term sacrifices in order to uphold your beliefs?

5. **Prepare a statement of values.** It can be useful to distill what you have written into a short list. By having a well-defined statement of the values you hold most important in your own life, which you can refer to in times of challenge, it will be easier for you to make ethical decisions.

Are there tangible benefits to ethical living? Society has established its own set of rules of conduct in the form of laws. Ignoring or being inconsistent in following these principles can surely have an immediate impact. Whether it is complying with a law that affects the way your business is run, or with a law that affects your personal life (don't exceed the speed limit or you'll receive a fine), decision-making principles that work with society's legal boundaries can make your life much simpler.

More and more research is showing the health benefits of ethical living. When your day-to-day decisions are in conflict with the values you consider most important as a human being, you often develop stress and anger. Constant conflict between what you value and what actions you are forced to take can lead to a variety of types of mental and physical damage.

Perhaps even happiness itself is a result of living ethically (see Figure 4).

Figure 4

The field of positive psychology shows that living and working ethically affects your happiness.

Cheating
Stealing
Selfishness
Lying

Generosity
Honesty
Trust

Yuri Arcurs/Shutterstock.com

Yuri Arcurs/Shutterstock.com

Positive psychology is a new focus in the field of psychology. Pioneered by Dr. Martin Seligman of the University of Pennsylvania, this field works to discover the causes of happiness instead of addressing the treatment of mental dysfunctions. Dr. Seligman's research has shown that, by identifying your personal strengths and values, and then aligning your life so that you can apply them every day, you can experience an increase in happiness (and a decrease in depression) equivalent to the effects of antidepressant medication and therapy. Thus, finding a way to identify and then apply your ethics and values to your daily life can have an impact on your health and happiness.

Personal Ethics and Your Worldview

How do my personal ethics fit into the world at large? All of your actions, words, and even thoughts are controlled by your personal ideas of right and wrong. But do your ethics shift when you go to work? Your employer expects you to follow the ethics and rules of conduct that the owner has established for the business. Although each person at your workplace may be trying to follow corporate ethical guidelines, each person will follow them differently based on his or her personal ethics. Person A may feel it is acceptable to tell white lies to get more funding for his project, whereas Person B might believe that telling the truth at all times is the best and only way that she can foster the teamwork and cooperation necessary to complete a project.

This doesn't mean that individuals need to blindly follow practices they feel are unethical or detrimental to society at large. Most **whistle-blowers** are people that report businesses to regulatory agencies for committing illegal acts. Other whistle-blowers expose unethical (but still legal) acts by their employers by publicizing unethical behavior through various media outlets.

In summary, when you are working in a business environment, your ethics are guided by the ethical principles that are defined by the business owner or management, but you are still ultimately guided by your personal ethics.

How do employers affect personal ethics? Should your employer have control (or even input) about your conduct outside of the office? Do behavior, integrity, and honesty off the job relate to job performance? They might. But even if they don't, your actions could reflect poorly on your employer from your employer's perspective. Consider Ellen Simonetti, who was fired by Delta Airlines for blogging. Even though Ms. Simonetti never mentioned Delta Airlines by name on her blog ("Queen of the Sky: Diary of a Dysfunctional Flight Attendant"), Delta Airlines objected to photos that she posted of herself and fellow flight attendants in their Delta uniforms. Delta Airlines felt that the photos were inappropriate and portrayed negative images of Delta Airlines employees. Another example is Jillian Tomlinson, the Australian surgeon who was suspended by her employer for discussing medical procedures, her work environment, and fellow employees, and for posting CAT scans of patients on her blog (although patient names were not revealed). Therefore, although your ethics might dictate one mode of behavior, you need to consider how your employer might view your actions (see Figure 5).

How does making ethical choices in a business setting differ from making personal ethical choices? Most personal ethical decisions involve few people, unless the decision results in a significant impact on society. When making ethical choices in the business world, give careful consideration to the stakeholders of the business. **Stakeholders** are those people or entities who are affected by the

Figure 5

Is your boss watching you? Does that make you more or less inclined to behave ethically?

"The new hidden cameras will allow us to see if anyone is violating our privacy policy by reading someone else's email."

Mike Shapiro/CartoonStock

operations of a business. Before making an ethical choice for a business, you need to consider the effect that choice will have on all of the stakeholders. Typical stakeholders for most businesses are customers, suppliers, employees, investors (shareholders), financial lenders, and society.

For instance, suppose you decide to cut costs in your restaurant by hiring undocumented workers. While this might boost profits in the short term, the long-term impact on stakeholders can be severe. Potential employees who are eligible to work in the United States will be denied jobs. If you are caught using undocumented workers, fines will be levied against the business, which will cause investors to lose money and may affect the company's ability to repay lenders. The negative publicity from being caught may cause a downturn in business, which, in turn, might force layoffs of employees or even closure of the business. Your simple decision on cutting costs isn't as simple as it may seem!

Technology and Ethics: How One Affects the Other

In both good and bad ways, technology affects our community life, family life, work environment, education, and medical research, to name only a few areas of our lives. Because technology moves faster than rules can be formulated to govern it, how technology is used is often left up to the

individual and the guidance of his or her personal ethics.

Technology constantly challenges our ethics as individuals and as a society. In the rest of this Technology in Focus feature, we will explore some issues involving the relationship between technology and ethics. Specifically, we will examine situations in which ethics and technology touch each other: social justice (whistle-blowing), intellectual property (international piracy), privacy (personal privacy and technology), e-commerce (geolocation), electronic communication issues (free speech), and computer abuse (cyberbullying).

Ethical considerations are never black and white. They are complex, and reasonable people can have different yet equally valid views. We present alternative viewpoints in each setting for you to consider and discuss. Figure 6 summarizes these issues.

Using Computers to Support Ethical Conduct

Although there are many opportunities to use computers and the Internet unethically, many more ways are available to use technology to support ethical conduct.

Many charitable organizations use the Internet and other technology tools for fundraising. When the earthquake and tsunami struck Japan in 2011, the Red Cross, the Salvation Army (see Figure 7), and other charities received many pledges via text message

Figure 6 | ETHICS IN COMPUTING

TOPIC	ETHICAL DISCUSSION	DEBATE ISSUE
Social justice	Are there limits to whistle-blowing?	Does technology provide too easy an access for whistle-blowing?
Intellectual property	Do entire countries support software piracy?	Can we impose our values and intellectual property laws on the world?
Privacy	Is personal privacy a casualty of the modern age?	Should personal privacy be protected?
E-commerce	Do geolocation devices and applications threaten privacy?	Do the benefits of geolocation devices and applications outweigh the risks?
Electronic communication	When does big business limit free speech?	Should companies allow the Chinese government to dictate when to curtail free speech?
Computer abuse	Whose responsibility is it to monitor cyberbullying?	Should parents bear all the responsibility of monitoring cyberbullying, or should it be in the hands of public officials?

from donors' phones. Many people also made donations through charities' Web sites.

And as we discussed in Chapter 1, the Internet is also a tool for organizing aid to areas in crisis. When a major earthquake struck Haiti in 2010, Ushahidi allowed organizations and individuals conducting relief efforts to collect and disseminate the latest information on victims and aid efforts. More recently, after the devastating tornado hit Joplin, Missouri, in May 2011, folks used the Red Cross Web site and Facebook to locate friends and family members. The level of personal interaction the Web supports and the speed at which information can be exchanged is allowing computer technology to support ethical conduct in powerful new ways.

When you spot unethical behavior at your company, you need a fast, secure way to report it to the appropriate members of management. The Sarbanes–Oxley Act requires companies to provide mechanisms for employees and third parties to report complaints, including ethics violations. These mechanisms are required to provide the employees with anonymity. In addition, many businesses are using their Web sites to allow whistle-blowers to report wrongdoing anonymously, replacing previous e-mail and telephone hotline systems, which did not shield employees from being identified. With an electronic system, it is easier for a company to sort and classify complaints and designate them for appropriate action.

Electronic systems such as intranets and e-mail are also excellent mechanisms for informing employees about ethics policies. Storing ethics guidelines electronically on a company intranet ensures that employees have access to information whenever they need it. By using e-mail, a company can communicate new policies, or changes to existing policies, to employees quickly and efficiently.

Figure 7

Using technology, including text messaging, helps charities facilitate donations.

Throughout your life, you will encounter many ethical challenges relating to information technology. Your personal ethics—combined with the ethical guidelines your company provides and the general ethical environment of society—will guide your decisions.

For further information on ethics, check out the following Web sites:

- **ethics.csc.ncsu.edu**
- **www.ethicscenter.net**
- **www.business-ethics.com**
- **www.businessethics.org**

Social Justice

Whistle-Blowing with Web 2.0

Summary of the Issue

In a free democracy, are there still things the public does not have a right to see? What about military secrets? What about ongoing negotiations with foreign governments? Should corporate whistle-blowers be able to distribute the documents and materials they have that allege abuses? Historically, there have been tight controls over access to the media, and exceptions have been rare. One famous case is the Pentagon Papers, a 7,000-page U.S. government report on policy and planning for the Vietnam War. State department official Daniel Ellsberg leaked the document in 1971, and it was published by *The New York Times*. A complicated series of lawsuits was then filed against *The New York Times* for making the document public.

With the tools of Web 2.0, the entire model for the distribution of information has shifted, and now everyone has the ability to create content for the Web. WikiLeaks (www.wikileaks.org) is using that ability to make private and public documents available for viewing. WikiLeaks has described itself as "a public service designed to protect whistle-blowers, journalists, and activists who have sensitive materials to communicate to the public." *Time* magazine said of WikiLeaks, "[I]t could become as important a journalistic tool as the Freedom of Information Act."

Does society have a responsibility to use technology to help achieve social justice? Where are the boundaries of that responsibility? One controversial WikiLeaks case was the leak of a video showing a U.S. Army helicopter strike from 2007 in Baghdad that claimed the lives of several civilians including two children (see Figure 8). An Army intelligence analyst delivered the classified combat video to WikiLeaks in 2010. Another video leaked showed a May 2009 air strike near the Afghanistan village of Garani that killed nearly 100 civilians, mostly children. The Pentagon had released a report on that event but refused to show video of the attack to reporters.

Questions to Think About and Research

1. Is the staff of WikiLeaks responsible for the accuracy and quality of the information it releases?

2. If information leaked through WikiLeaks leads to the death of an undercover officer, who is responsible for the consequences of the publication of information?

3. Does providing the public with official Pentagon updates of military missions mean that video of these events also must be released?

4. How does the meaning of "free speech" change as technology makes distribution of information universal and immediate? Do protections need to be modified?

POINT

Technology Provides Access to Information

The advocates of WikiLeaks argue that it allows an unprecedented means for those without power to hold those with power accountable for their actions.

1. If information can only be leaked if you happen to find an interested journalist, is society really protected?

2. Technology is not responsible for the actions or the consequences of the actions of people.

3. Technology has provided new tools that expose cover-ups, corruption, and abuses of power.

COUNTERPOINT

Technology Should Only Allow Controlled Access to Information

Critics maintain that the anonymity that WikiLeaks provides makes it difficult to check the accuracy of anything reported on the Web site.

1. The small staff of WikiLeaks cannot verify the accuracy of each document to the level of professional journalists.

2. If technology is used irresponsibly, it can cause panics because the information is available to so many people so quickly.

3. If each person in an organization can easily leak confidential information, the integrity of national security or of corporate security is at risk.

Figure 8

What boundaries should there be on the availability of sensitive information?

Intellectual Property

International Pirates

Summary of the Issue

Intellectual property (such as music, writing, and software) is protected by copyright law. But there have been challenges in enforcing these standards in other countries. What happens to "fair trade" if some countries refuse to enforce copyright laws? How should the trade partners of these countries respond?

The Business Software Alliance (BSA) estimated that in 2010, 79 percent of China's computers ran on pirated software (see Figure 9). For comparison, the BSA estimated piracy in Denmark and Sweden at levels of 25 percent. This discrepancy means that businesses in China do not have to budget for software for operating systems or for productivity software, and that gives Chinese businesses an immediate advantage in the international marketplace. Although some companies, like Microsoft, continue to do business in China despite the piracy, smaller companies cannot survive. Tom Adams, the chief executive of Rosetta Stone, pulled his company and its language training software products out of China. He describes China as a "kleptocratic society" and worries about the amount of theft of his software in that environment.

The chief executives of twelve major software companies—Microsoft, Adobe, Autodesk, Symantec, and others—have pressured the U.S. administration and lawmakers to put more pressure on China to crack down on illegal copying. With a potential market of more than 1 billion people, and an increasing number of technologically hungry purchasers, companies dread the idea of missing out on the Chinese market. But if China continues to have such disinterest in following international copyright laws, there may be a migration of foreign business to other Asian countries. Corporations like Microsoft are considering moving Asian operations to India or Indonesia because their enforcement of intellectual property laws is more stringent than in China.

It is not just China that has weakly enforced copyright laws. U.S. lawmakers recently singled out five countries that are not doing enough to prevent piracy of music, movies, and software: Canada, China, Mexico, Russia, and Spain. "We are losing billions and billions of dollars because of the lack of intellectual property protections," said Senator Orrin Hatch of Utah. "These five countries have been robbing Americans." ("China and Canada among top on US piracy watch list" by Chris Lefkow, May 19, 2010. Copyright © 2010 by AFP. Reprinted by permission.) The BSA estimated the loss at more than $51 billion per year, although there is debate around the exact value.

Most people have had the opportunity to participate in the piracy of copyrighted materials through illegal peer-to-peer sharing and the use of torrents. Now that behavior is multiplied to the level of nations, and the consequences are still being explored.

Questions to Think About and Research

1. Should a government be penalized for failing to actively enforce the laws it has within its own country? If so, what should the penalties be, and how should they be enforced?

2. Does each government have the right to make its own decision on a stand against piracy?

3. How can other countries respond to international piracy?

4. Does individual piracy have any connection to the enforcement of copyright laws on an international level?

POINT

International Copyright Protections Need to Be Vigorously Enforced

Artists and software developers depend on the integrity of the protection of intellectual property, both within the United States and internationally, to make a fair profit on their work.

1. If other countries do not fight piracy, artists and developers have a disadvantage in the marketplace.

2. By allowing massive piracy, these other countries are stealing from the United States.

3. Every country needs to have a common understanding and enforcement of intellectual property laws for trade to be fair and beneficial to everyone.

COUNTERPOINT

Global Business Demands Understanding Other Cultures

Most countries have laws on their books regarding intellectual property. It is not the job of the United States to tell a foreign government how to conduct internal affairs.

1. The existing laws on intellectual property have worked to serve the interests of these countries. If U.S. companies do not want to sell to the billion-person market of China, that is their choice.

2. Piracy exists within the United States, so it is hypocritical to be chastising foreign governments for software piracy.

3. Companies can pursue restitution for piracy through the foreign court systems.

© MARK/epa/Corbis

Figure 9

The issues of intellectual property play an important role in international trade.

Privacy

Does Social Media Erode Personal Privacy?

Summary of the Issue

Like respect and dignity, privacy is a basic human right. What, exactly, is privacy? Simply stated, privacy is the right to be left alone to do as one pleases. The idea of privacy is often associated with hiding something (a behavior, a relationship, or a secret). However, privacy really means not being required to explain your behavior to others. But social media sites such as Facebook are inherently about sharing information with others. Does this mean there is no such thing as personal privacy (see Figure 10) on social media sites?

Facebook and other social media sites earn revenue by sharing information about their users with advertisers. This helps businesses target advertisements to individuals who might be more interested in their products and services. But social media sites have recently been criticized for making their privacy policies and controls too obscure. Champions of personal privacy argue that sites that make information sharing the default option or "opt-out" (that is, users have to make a specific request or change a specific setting to stop their information from being shared) expose users to misuse of their personal details. Also, social media sites often track and store user actions and preferences (such as "liking" something on Facebook). Personal privacy advocates are suspicious of how this information is used and to whom it is sold.

Web site owners argue that the entire premise of social media is built on sharing information, which makes it easy for others to find an individual. Social media administrators feel that information sharing improves the users' experience by tailoring advertisements and offers to their specific interests. And because most social media sites do not charge users for the service, the owners of the sites need ways to generate revenue, and their most valuable asset is the information that users provide about themselves.

The large social media sites (such as Facebook) have been responding to concerns by modifying their privacy settings and making it easier for users to select which information is shared and with whom. But critics still argue that users do not have enough control over opting out of sharing information. The control and privacy of information will continue to be a fine balancing act for the foreseeable future with companies trying to make money while appeasing the concerns of privacy advocates. Leaving a trail of electronic breadcrumbs is to a certain extent inevitable. But cleaning up or hiding your "trail" is still important to many users, not because they are trying to hide something but because they just value their basic right of privacy.

Questions to Think About and Research

1. Should you be able to decide exactly what information on a social networking site you share with others? Would you be willing to pay for this privilege?

2. Do you know what your privacy settings are on the social media sites you use? Is there any information being shared publicly that you weren't aware was being shared?

3. Should social media sites be allowed to sell information collected on your surfing habits without your permission? Is this practice legal in the United States?

4. Is there any information on sites you use that you want to restrict people from seeing? Do these sites allow you to restrict the information you wish to protect?

POINT

Social Media Sites Should Protect Personal Privacy

The advocates of protecting privacy in the United States argue that the right to privacy is a basic human right that should be afforded to everyone. Personal privacy concerns should outweigh the business needs of a corporation.

1. Social media sites have an inherent duty to protect the data of their users.

2. If site owners are collecting information by recording users' surfing habits, they might misuse or lose control of the data.

3. Default privacy settings should all be opt-in, allowing users the ultimate control over who views their data.

COUNTERPOINT

Social Media Sites Are Entitled to Freely Share Information

Advocates for unrestricted sharing of information feel that business concerns outweigh privacy concerns. Social media sites offered free of charge must make money to survive, and therefore need to be able to provide information to third parties to generate revenue.

1. The "cost" of using the site is the agreement to share some of your personal information.

2. Users can make their own privacy decisions and choose not to post or share sensitive information (opt out).

3. In the digital age, loss of a certain amount of privacy is inevitable.

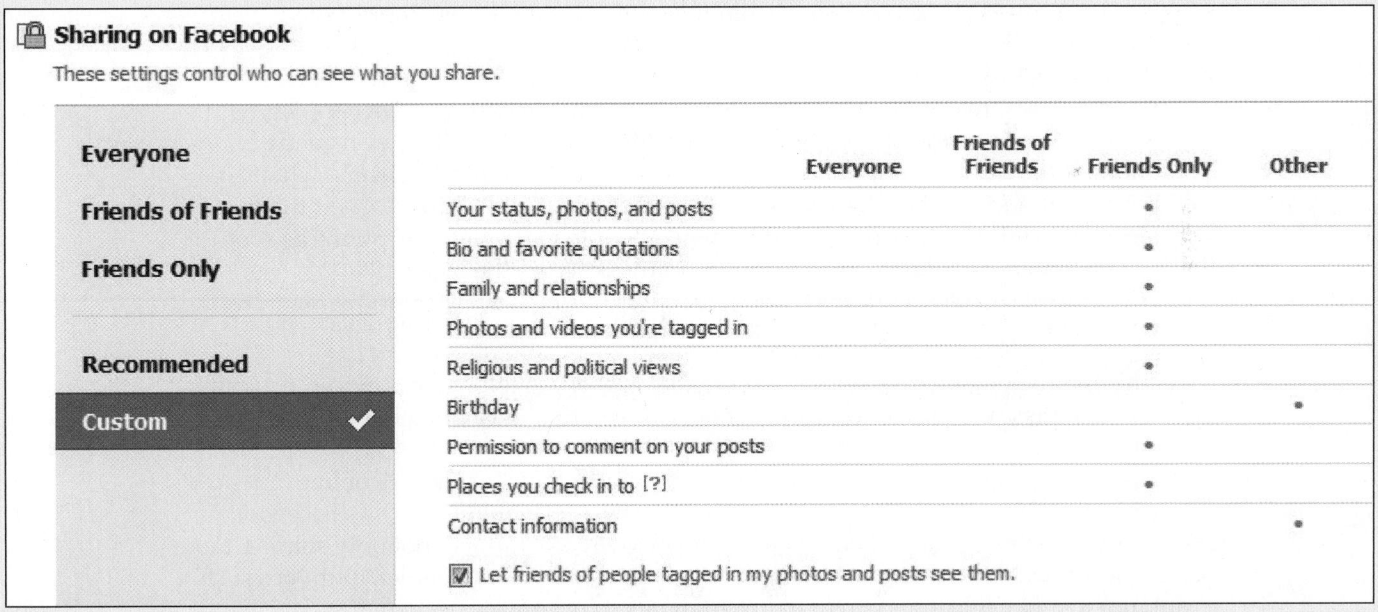

Sharing on Facebook

These settings control who can see what you share.

	Everyone	Friends of Friends	Friends Only	Other
Everyone				
Friends of Friends				
Friends Only				
Recommended				
Custom ✔				
Your status, photos, and posts			•	
Bio and favorite quotations			•	
Family and relationships			•	
Photos and videos you're tagged in			•	
Religious and political views			•	
Birthday				•
Permission to comment on your posts			•	
Places you check in to [?]			•	
Contact information				•
☑ Let friends of people tagged in my photos and posts see them.				

Figure 10

What information are you sharing on Facebook?

E-Commerce

Geolocation: Marketing Tool or Invasion of Privacy?

Summary of the Issue

"Where are you?" is the burning social-networking question these days, and your smartphone probably has the answer. The technology is called geolocation (see Figure 11), and most smartphones have a GPS (global positioning system) chip that uses satellite data or cell towers to calculate your exact position. Services such as Foursquare, Gowalla, Brightkite, and Loopt are all hoping that you will use them in the process, so you can use geolocation to find your friends or let your friends find you. Through the apps, you can receive recommendations of places to visit or things to do nearby. Some apps, such as Loopt and Gowalla, have created partnerships with local establishments that generate freebies, special offers, and travel tips. Businesses are using geolocation apps to promote their products and offer rewards for "check-ins" to help drive customers to their location.

But the question remains, when you leave your home and announce your constant whereabouts through tweets and check-ins, do you lose some of your privacy in exchange for "fun" and "convenience"? Although you can set certain levels of privacy in the apps, there is still the potential for someone with bad intentions (stalkers, robbers) to follow your updates. For example, the Web site Please Rob Me (**www.PleaseRobMe.com**) was set up to illustrate how telling the world where you are at all times may not be such a great idea. After generating much discussion and awareness, the Web site exists, but no new content is being added. Regardless, the message from the authors of the PleaseRobMe site is clear:

> The danger is publicly telling people where you are. This is because it leaves one place you're definitely not . . . home. So . . . on one end we're leaving lights on when we're going on a holiday, and on the other we're telling everybody on the Internet we're not home. It gets even worse if you have 'friends' who . . . enter your address, to tell everyone where they are. Your address . . . on the Internet . . . Now you know what to do when people reach for their phone as soon as they enter your home. That's right, slap them across the face.
>
> –Excerpt from "PleaseRobMe" by Barry Borsboom, Boy van Amstel, Frank Groeneveld from www.pleaserobme. com. Copyright © 2010 Barry Borsboom, Boy van Amstel, Frank Groeneveld. Reprinted with permission.

In addition to opening yourself up to potential robbery, geolocation devices also can track the activities you might not want publicized, and that once documented can later be used against you.

It wasn't long ago that we were concerned about using our real names online, but now we are comfortable with sharing our exact location in a very public way. As Facebook CEO Mark Zuckerberg said, "People have really gotten comfortable not only sharing more information and different kinds, but more openly and with more people." But does such acceptance justify neglecting to maintain certain levels of privacy? Again, it seems that technology has moved more quickly than society can address the potential risks and dangers.

Questions to Think About and Research

1. Do the benefits of geolocation outweigh the risks?
2. What other devices besides cell phones track and record our movements/locations as digital records?
3. How have social networks increased the risks of geolocation privacy?
4. What risks do geolocation pose for college students? How can users mitigate those risks?

POINT

Geolocation Devices Do Not Threaten Privacy

The advocates of using geolocation devices with minimal concern for threatened privacy are those who believe the social norm has shifted, and people have become comfortable with sharing more information.

1. Businesses are adopting geolocation apps as a part of their social media strategy in order to drive customers to their business. They would lose revenue if such activities ceased.

2. As the devices and apps become better and more precise, they may become useful as public safety and news-gathering devices.

3. Society may need to reevaluate its views about how much privacy is needed in people's digital lives, as well as assume greater responsibility for making sensible decisions about sharing information through the Internet.

COUNTERPOINT

Geolocation Devices Are a Threat to Privacy

The advocates for tighter privacy controls and awareness campaigns about the potential risks of using geolocation devices suggest that the threats are too big to ignore. Society has become too complacent with privacy issues.

1. Privacy settings on apps and GPS devices should be more restrictive to avoid broadcasting one's location and risking personal assault.

2. Laws and regulations will need to be created as to the use and distribution of digital location information.

3. Consumers need to be educated about geolocation and the ways it can impact them so that they are able to make informed choices.

Figure 11

Geolocation applications help you find cool places and businesses. But who do you want to find you with geolocation?

Michael D. Brown/Shutterstock.com

Does Free Speech Have a Price?

Summary of the Issue

In early 2006 when Google launched its search engine services in China, it conceded to Beijing's demands that it self-censor its search engine, restricting search results for sensitive information such as the details of the Tiananmen Square protests and of human rights groups. This decision prompted much discussion, with some condemning Google's decision for putting business profits over basic human rights. Google justified its actions by stating that a company must operate within the rules of the market in which it operates and that the benefits of increased access to information for people in China "outweighed our discomfort in agreeing to censor some results." And, compared to search results from Baidu, the leading Chinese search engine, Google was not censoring all information. However, in 2010, Google announced that it was no longer willing to censor search results and moved the site to Hong Kong where it hopes there will be less censorship. The departure was a reaction to a sophisticated targeted cyberattack that Google believes was done to gather information on Chinese human rights activists. Google had about a 35 percent market share.

Microsoft, also in the Chinese market with its new search engine, Bing, announced in response to Google's departure that it had no plans to leave. Microsoft has only a 1 percent share of the market, so the decision to stay has huge upside potential. The question remains as to how Microsoft will manage search information. When Microsoft started in China, searches on controversial topics weren't just blocked in China, they were blocked from everyone around the world (see Figure 12). Microsoft corrected that, but some current searches show that although they are not censoring as much as Baidu, they are still censoring less than Google was. Microsoft says it is trying to do the right thing. Before honoring any censor requests, Microsoft insists that Chinese authorities make legally binding requests in writing. Microsoft, along with Google and Yahoo!, joined Global Network Initiative (**www.globalnetworkinitiative.org**), a group that has established a code of conduct for free expression and privacy. The goal of GNI is to help companies do the right thing under difficult circumstances. However, it's too early to tell whether Microsoft will indeed follow Google's path or remain and abide by China's censorship requirements.

Questions to Think About and Research

1. Will Google's move from Mainland China to Hong Kong have a major impact on China's censorship laws?

2. Will Microsoft's compliance with censorship laws further Beijing's cooperation on combating software piracy in China? Are Microsoft's financial incentives even deeper than just Internet market share?

3. Can the U.S. government compel technology companies to take a firmer stance on free speech in China and elsewhere by instituting criminal charges if U.S. companies do not take reasonable steps to protect human rights?

POINT

U.S. Companies Should Comply with Local Laws

Those in favor of Microsoft's actions to remain in China feel that if a company chooses to operate in a foreign country, it knows the local laws and should be prepared to work within those laws as it does business. It is not the place of a company to try to change laws of foreign countries.

1. Microsoft conducts businesses in other countries that have censorship laws, so why not participate in China?

2. Working in China does not mean a company supports all of China's policies.

3. Microsoft's presence, as muted as it is, continues to advance the slow progress the Chinese government is making toward democracy. U.S. companies can ethically stay in China if they make an effort to improve human rights there. U.S. companies operating in China should agree on guidelines that respect human rights.

4. A U.S. company's presence has no impact on reform—reform must come from within.

COUNTERPOINT

U.S. Companies Should Put What Is Right Ahead of What Is Financially Expedient

Those who are in favor of Google's actions are believers that international corporations should begin to take a firm stance against governments that do not promote basic human rights.

1. China will never change unless there are financial and political incentives to do so. Google's departure helps pressure the Chinese government

2. Google's withdrawal from China threatens the viability of many advertising resellers in China. Will this added pressure help or hinder human rights efforts?

3. Google's decision to leave helps put pressure on China's government to play by global standards. It cannot expect to compete in the global marketplace while refusing to have a global exchange of ideas.

CENSORSHIP

kentoh/Shutterstock.com

Figure 12

Is free speech possible in countries (such as China) where information availability is restricted by law?

Computer Abuse

Cyberbullying—Who Should Protect Children from Each Other?

Summary of the Issue

Cyberbullying is just like normal bullying, but it involves the use of digital technologies such as the Internet, cell phones, or video (see Figure 13). Instead of a bully chasing someone on the playground at recess, cyberbullying involves minors (children) harassing, threatening, humiliating, embarrassing, or tormenting other minors by means of technology. Cyberbullying is a child-on-child process that might result in criminal charges depending upon the type of incident.

There are many types of cyberbullying. The main types are as follows:

- Bombarding a victim with harassing instant messages or text messages
- Stealing a password and then using the victim's account to embarrass the victim by sending harassing, threatening, or lewd messages while pretending to be the victim
- Spreading rumors or lies on social networking sites
- Posting embarrassing photos or videos on the Web (such as candid nude shots taken in a locker room)
- Infecting the victim's computer with malware, usually to spy on the victim

The effects of cyberbullying can be devastating. For children, their standing in peer groups is a critical component of their self-worth. Adults have freedom in their lives to change bad situations, such as changing jobs, when they feel their esteem is under attack. Children often feel powerless because they have such limited options. Children don't usually have the option of changing schools without uprooting the entire family. Aside from developing severe feelings of depression, rage, frustration, and powerlessness, suicide can often be the unfortunate result, as in the case of student and soccer player Alexis Pilkington, who at 17 committed suicide in 2010 after being repeatedly taunted on social networking sites.

Unfortunately, cyberbullying is often difficult for adults to detect because the bullying often takes place online and anonymously. Signs that a child is a victim of cyberbullying are often the same signs related to various types of depression. A child may suddenly lose interest in normal activities, be reluctant to go to school, lose his or her appetite, have trouble sleeping, appear upset after using the Internet, or experience unusual mood swings (such as bursting into tears for no apparent reason). Signs that a child might be perpetrating cyberbullying include excessive Internet use, sending large volumes of text messages, clearing the computer screen when others enter a room, or conducting clandestine Internet activities (refusal to say what they are doing). Vigilance over children's online activities is obviously key to spotting both victims and perpetrators of cyberbullying.

But who is responsible for monitoring children? Parents obviously need to protect their children, but bullying usually doesn't happen until children are repeatedly exposed to other groups of children such as in daycare or school. So then, should teachers and caregivers shoulder the major responsibility for detecting, reporting, and mitigating cyberbullying? Children often spend more time in school during the day than they spend under the supervision of their parents. But cyberbullying activities don't just take place in school. Most children have access to the Internet at home and can carry on campaigns of terror from the privacy of their own bedroom (see Figure 14).

Children themselves could also be made part of the solution. Research shows that one of the best ways to prevent bullying is to make children aware of what behaviors constitute bullying and the consequences of their actions.

Although there is currently no federal law prohibiting cyberbullying, many state laws have been passed that address this issue. Anti-cyberbullying laws tend to place the burden of detection on the schools. For instance, the Massachusetts law requires school employees to report bullying when they become aware of it to the school administration. But unlike many other states, the law also requires training for school employees in the detection and prevention of bullying. Most legislatures are reluctant to pass laws that instruct parents on how to raise their children because this tends to raise issues about personal freedom. Therefore, the focus so far has been primarily on teachers and caregivers detecting cyberbullying. But a coordinated effort between parents and teachers may be a better approach.

Questions to Think About and Research

1. What should parents do to protect their children from cyberbullying? How can parents protect their children when the children are not under their direct supervision?

2. What level of responsibility should school employees have for protecting children from cyberbullying?

3. Should there be federal laws that make cyberbullying a crime? If so, how would these laws be enforced?

4. What types of education for children would be beneficial in preventing cyberbullying? When should these programs begin, and how often should children be required to participate?

© Rawdon Wyatt / Alamy

Figure 13
Cyberbullying involves the use of digital technologies both to bully and to disseminate acts of bullying.

Computer Abuse

POINT

Parents Must Protect Their Children from Cyberbullying

Proponents of parental responsibility for detecting and preventing cyberbullying feel that it is a personal behavior issue. Individuals are responsible for their own behavior as long as it doesn't harm others. Parents should be allowed to educate their children according to their own standards of behavior and preferences in terms of moral behavior (such as religion).

1. Parents are ultimately responsible for protecting their children.
2. Bullying is a personal behavior issue, and all decisions regarding personal freedom and behavior should be made by parents.
3. Because educating children about bullying is key to preventing it, decisions about the content of such training needs to be controlled by parents.

COUNTERPOINT

Schools Must Bear the Major Responsibility for Protecting Students from Cyberbullying

Cyberbullying affects society because it can severely damage an individual's self-esteem. Cyberbullying is similar to other hate crimes and should enlist public officials (such as educators) in enforcement of the laws.

1. Parents do not supervise their children 24/7 and therefore require help from other responsible adults to protect their children.
2. Parents need to be assured that publicly funded institutions such as schools and libraries are "safe havens" where their children will not be exposed to malicious activities.
3. Educators have better resources than most parents for teaching children about the serious effects of cyberbullying.

Chris Whitehead/Getty Images

Figure 14
Cyberbullying should be stopped, but by whom?

Multiple Choice

Instructions: Answer the multiple-choice questions below for more practice with key terms and concepts from this Technology in Focus feature.

1. Which theory states that there is no universal moral truth?
   a. Relativism
   b. Ethical behavior
   c. Amoral behavior
   d. Personal ethics

2. The ethical theory that states that society as a whole will improve if everyone adheres to the same moral code is known as
   a. rule utilitarianism.
   b. societal ethics.
   c. moral prescription.
   d. personal ethics.

3. Which ethical philosophy states that decision making should be based on the circumstances surrounding a given situation, not fixed laws?
   a. Societal ethics
   b. Judeo-Christian ethics
   c. Relativism
   d. Situational ethics

4. Which of the following statements is *false*?
   a. Individuals who apply ethics inconsistently exhibit amoral behavior.
   b. All ethical decisions are greatly influenced by personal ethics.
   c. Unethical behavior is not always illegal.
   d. Life experience affects an individual's personal ethics.

5. Not conforming to a set of approved ethical standards is known as
   a. societal behavior.
   b. unethical behavior.
   c. amoral behavior.
   d. unprofessional behavior.

6. The field of psychology that theorizes that happiness results from ethical living is known as
   a. principled psychology.
   b. positive psychology.
   c. moral psychology.
   d. affirmative psychology.

7. Which system of ethics is most widely agreed upon to be the best system?
   a. Rule utilitarianism
   b. Relativism
   c. Situational ethics
   d. There is no universally agreed-upon best system.

8. Which is *not* a tangible benefit of ethical living?
   a. Improved health
   b. A simpler lifestyle
   c. Happiness
   d. Increased motivation

9. Which of the following actions would *not* help to identify your personal ethics?
   a. Describe yourself.
   b. Identify the influences of your work environment.
   c. Conduct a genealogic study of your extended family.
   d. Prepare a list of values that are most important to you.

10. Ethical decisions in business affect which of the following?
    a. The employees
    b. The business's clients and customers
    c. The suppliers and financial lenders
    d. The stakeholders

application software:
programs that let you work and play

Norebbo/Shutterstock.com

The Nuts and Bolts of Software

OBJECTIVE:

What's the difference between application software and system software? *(p. 158)*

ra2 studio/Shutterstock.com

Web-Based Applications

OBJECTIVE:

What are Web-based applications, and how do they differ from traditional modes of software distribution? *(p. 158)*

mmaxer/Shutterstock.com

Productivity and Business Software

OBJECTIVES:

What kinds of applications are included in productivity software? *(p. 160)*

What kinds of software do small and large businesses use? *(p. 170)*

 Sound Byte: Creating Web Queries in Excel 2010

IKO/Shutterstock.com

Media and Entertainment Software

OBJECTIVES:

What are the different types of media and entertainment software? *(p. 174)*

What are the different types of drawing software? *(p. 181)*

Sound Byte: Enhancing Photos with Image Editing Software

Active Helpdesk: Choosing Software

Timo Darco/Fotolia

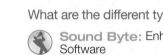

Buying, Installing, and Uninstalling Software

OBJECTIVES:

How can I purchase software or get it for free? *(p. 182)*

How do I install, uninstall, and start software? *(p. 189)*

 Active Helpdesk: Buying and Installing Software

Antonprado | Dreamstime.com

Getting Help with Software

OBJECTIVE:

Where can I go for help when I have a problem with my software? *(p. 191)*

Scan here for more info on How Cool Is This? ▶

how cool is *this?*

You've just returned from a great **vacation** and want to relive your wonderful experience. Looking at traditional digital images is nice, but wouldn't it be better if you could create a **3D walkthrough** of your favorite places? Upload your pictures to the 20 GB of free storage space of Microsoft's **Photosynth** and relive your experience in 3D. Photosynth takes a selection of photos, examines them for similarities to estimate the shape of the subject, and determines the vantage point from which each photo was taken. Using this information, Photosynth then **stitches** the images together to create a 3D effect. Check out some that others have done at **www.photosynth.net**, and then go make one from your own photos!

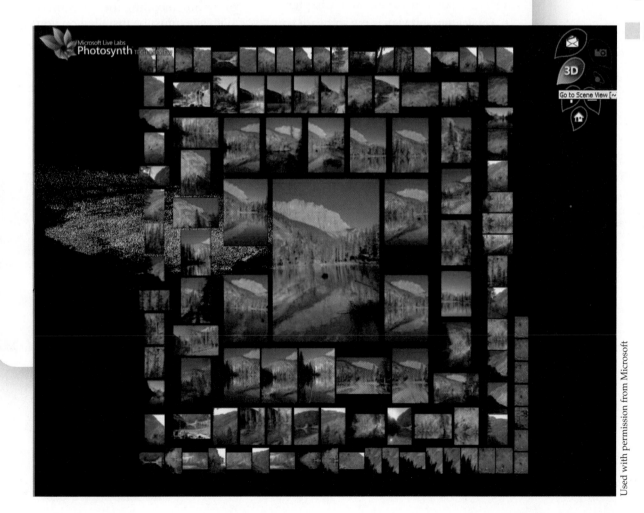

The Nuts and Bolts of Software

A computer without software is like a sandwich without filling. Although a computer's hardware is critical, a computer system does nothing without software.

What is software? Technically speaking, the term **software** refers to a set of instructions that tells the computer what to do. An instruction set, also called a **program**, provides a means for us to interact with and use the computer, even if we lack specialized programming skills. Your computer has two basic types of software: system software and application software.

- **System software** includes software such as Windows and Mac OS X, which help run the computer and coordinate instructions between application software and the computer's hardware devices. System software includes the operating system and utility programs (programs in the operating system that help manage system resources). We discuss system software in detail in Chapter 5.
- **Application software** is the software you use to do tasks at home, school, and work. You can do a multitude of things with application software, such as writing letters, sending e-mail, paying taxes, creating presentations, editing photos, and taking an online course, to name a few.

Figure 4.1 shows the various types of application software that you can use to be productive—at home and at work. In addition, applications are available to produce and edit media as well as for entertainment. Lastly, there are applications that are more applicable to business uses, whether it's for a home office, big business, specialty business, or not-for-profit organization. In this chapter, we look at each of these types in detail, starting with productivity software. By no means does this exhaust all the types of software that are in use. Other types of software, such as Web browsers, virus protection, backup and recovery, and utility software are in use every day. These types of software are discussed elsewhere in this book.

Web-Based Applications

Does all application software require installation on my computer? Most application software you acquire, whether by purchasing a CD or DVD at a retail store or by downloading the software from a Web site, must be installed on your computer before use.

There is a relatively new trend toward a distribution model of on-demand software deployment, referred to as **Software as a Service (SaaS)** that many software developers are taking advantage of. With the SaaS

Figure 4.1

Application software enables computer users to do a variety of tasks.

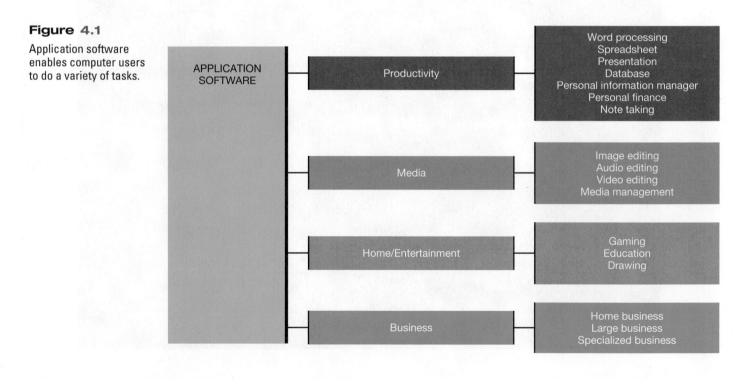

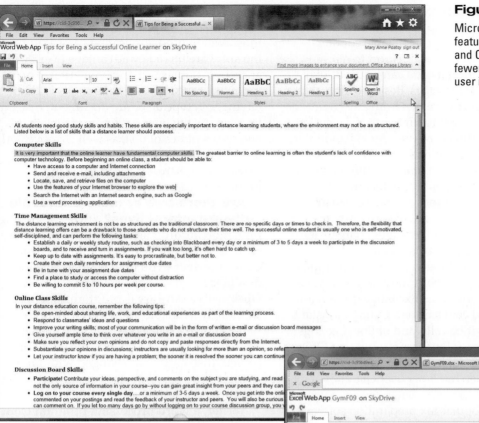

Figure 4.2
Microsoft Web Apps are similar to the full-featured versions of Word, Excel, PowerPoint, and OneNote, but the Web applications have fewer options available. The functionality and user interface are the same.

delivery model, the application is hosted online by the vendor and made available to the customer over the Internet. These applications are also referred to as **Web-based applications**. Web-based applications are run from software stored completely on a Web server instead of the traditional model that requires software to be purchased and installed on individual machines or network servers.

What kinds of Web-based applications are available? Along with its release of Office 2010, Microsoft made available Microsoft Office Web Apps. Office Web Apps are online versions of Word, Excel, PowerPoint, and OneNote, but with fewer tabs than the installed versions (see Figure 4.2).

Google Docs (**www.docs.google.com**) is a Web-based suite of productivity software with word processing, spreadsheet, and presentation capabilities. Sites such as Zoho (**www.zoho.com**) and ThinkFree (**www.thinkfree.com**) offer Web-based applications that cover not only word processing, presentation, and spreadsheet needs, but also a wealth of other business applications such as project management, three-

dimensional (3D) drawing, and customer relationship management software. Some other examples of Web-based applications include Intuit's QuickBooks online, Salesforce.com, and Citrix Online.

What advantages do Web-based applications have? As long as you have a Web browser, you can access your files, which are stored securely online. Although many of these free applications are not as fully featured as their installable counterparts, most can read and export to many different file formats and can be used with other software packages. Besides being able to access your documents from any computer or smartphone that has Internet access, Web-based applications are great for collaboration. You can invite people to share your files and work together in real time, watching as others make changes to the document.

Is all Web-based software free? Although most Web-based software programs are free, some Web sites charge a fee for their online products. Microsoft Office 365 is a subscription-based service that includes Microsoft Office Web Apps plus other Web-based services such as Exchange (for e-mail, calendar, and contacts) and Lync (for instant messaging, video calls, and online meetings). Google Apps for Business is similar to Office 365 and is free for businesses with up to 10 users, and then has a per user charge. TurboTax Online (**www.turbotax.com**) is a version of the popular tax preparation software that you can access online to prepare your tax returns. Although the standard version is free, you're charged for the more full-featured product. In addition to saving you the hassle of software installation, TurboTax Online stores your information in a secure location so you can retrieve it anytime.

Productivity Software for Home and Office

One reason to have a computer is to make it easier to tackle the tasks you have in your daily life. Productivity software is all about helping you do that, making it easier to keep your budget, send letters, or keep track of the kids' school events. It's safe to say you regularly use some form of productivity software already. **Productivity software** includes programs that enable you to perform various tasks required at home, school, and business. This category includes word processing, spreadsheet, presentation, database, and personal information manager (PIM) programs.

Word Processing Software

What is the best software to use to create general documents? Most students use **word processing software** to create and edit documents such as research papers,

letters, and résumés. Because of its general usefulness, word processing software is the most widely used application. Word processing software has a key advantage over its ancestral counterpart, the typewriter: You can make revisions and corrections without having to retype an entire document. Instead, you can quickly and easily insert, delete, and move pieces of text, as well as move and insert text from one document into another seamlessly. Microsoft Word is the most popular word processing program.

Are there free or more affordable software alternatives? If you're looking for a more affordable alternative to software such as Microsoft Word or other Microsoft Office products, you may want to consider downloading free open source software. **Open source software** is program code that is publicly available and has few restrictions. Unlike **proprietary software**, which is neither free nor open source, the code can be copied, distributed, or changed without the stringent copyright protections of software products you purchase.

Writer, a word processing program from the OpenOffice.org suite (**www.openoffice.org**), and AbiWord (**www.abiword.com**) are gaining in popularity because they are available as free downloads from the Internet. Both AbiWord and Writer have many of the same features as the higher-priced Word, making either a great choice for cost-conscious consumers (see Figure 4.3). Keep one thing in mind when you choose an open source software product: support. Unlike Microsoft Office and other proprietary applications, these applications offer little or no formal support. Instead, open source applications are supported from their community of users across Web sites and newsgroups. For more information on

BITS AND BYTES — Finding the Right Software

There are millions of applications, and new ones are developed and released every day. How can you find the right application to meet your needs? What are the cool new applications, or the ones that just don't work? The editors and analysts at *PC Magazine* have put together AppScout (**www.appscout.com**), which provides reviews of the best software, Web sites, and Web applications. AppScout might be a good place to check first when you are in need of a new application.

open source software, see the Technology in Focus feature "Computing Alternatives" on page 248.

How do I control the way my documents look? An advantage of word processing software is that you can easily create professional-looking documents. With the extensive formatting options available, you can change fonts, font styles, and sizes; add colors to text; adjust margins; add borders to portions of text or entire pages; insert bulleted and numbered lists; and organize your text into columns. You also can insert pictures from your own files or from a gallery of images and graphics, such as clip art and SmartArt, which are included with the software. You also can enhance the look of your document by creating an interesting background or by adding a "theme" of coordinated colors and styles throughout your document. Figure 4.4 shows what a document can look like when formatting options found in many word processing applications are incorporated. Although many of the open source and Web-based applications have great formatting capabilities, most are not as fully featured as Microsoft Word.

What special tools do word processing programs have? You're probably familiar with the basic tools of word processing software. Most applications come with some form of spelling and grammar

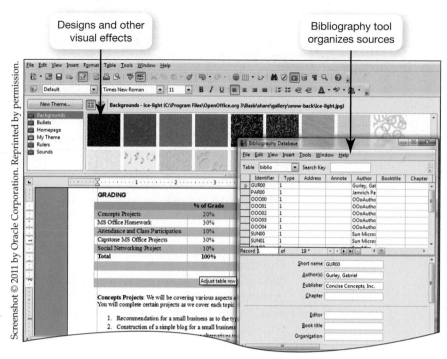

Figure 4.3

Writer, the word processing program in the OpenOffice .org suite, has many of the same features as Word.

checker and a thesaurus, for example. Another popular tool is the find-and-replace tool that allows you to search for text in your document and automatically replace it with other text.

Figure 4.4

Nearly every word processing application has formatting features to give your document a professional look.

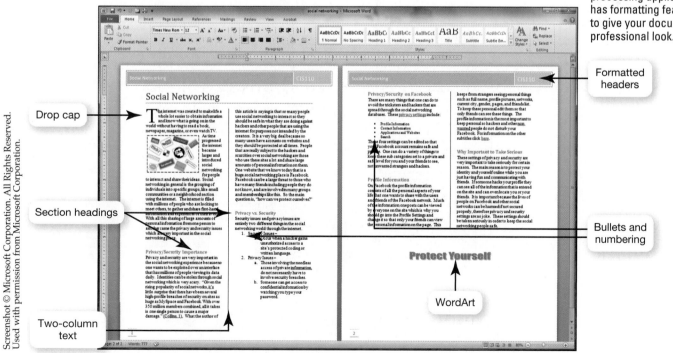

The average user is unaware of many interesting word processing software tools. For example, did you know that you could translate words or phrases into another language or automatically correct your spelling as you type? You also can automatically summarize key points in a text document, add bibliographical references, and include illustrations with different picture styles.

Spreadsheet Software

Why would I need to use spreadsheet software? Spreadsheet software—such as Microsoft Excel and OpenOffice.org Calc—enables you to do calculations and numerical analyses easily. You can use spreadsheet software to track your expenses and create a simple budget. You also can use it to determine how much you should be paying on your student loans, car loan, or credit card bills each month. You know you should pay more than the minimum payment to spend less on interest, but how much more can you afford to pay, and for which loan? Spreadsheet software can help you evaluate different scenarios, such as planning the best payment strategy.

How do I use spreadsheet software? The basic element in a spreadsheet program is the worksheet, which is a grid consisting of columns and rows. As shown in Figure 4.5, the columns and rows form individual boxes called *cells.* Each cell can be identified according to its column and row position. For example, a cell in column A, row 1 is referred to as "cell A1." You can enter several types of data into a cell:

- **Text:** Any combination of letters, numbers, symbols, and spaces. Text is often used as labels to identify the contents of a worksheet or chart.

- **Values:** Numerical data that represent a quantity or an amount and are often the basis for calculations.

- **Formulas:** Equations that you build yourself using addition, subtraction, multiplication, and division, as well as values and cell references. For example, in Figure 4.5, you would type the formula "=B8-B22" (without quotation marks) to calculate net income for September.

- **Functions:** Formulas that are preprogrammed into the spreadsheet software. Functions help you with calculations

Figure 4.5

Spreadsheet software enables you to calculate and manipulate numerical data easily with the use of built-in formulas.

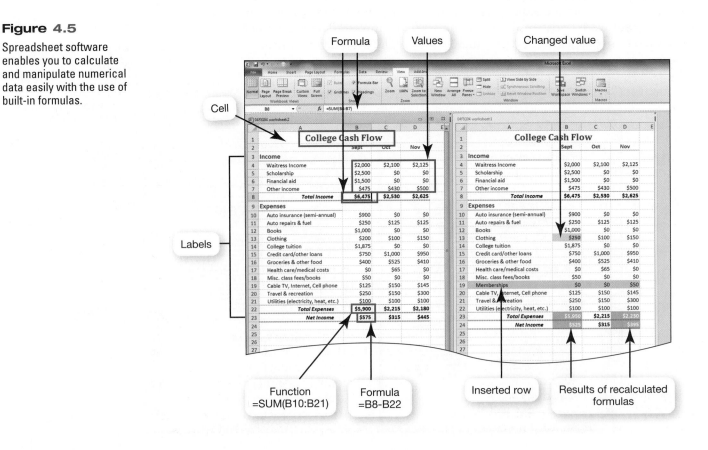

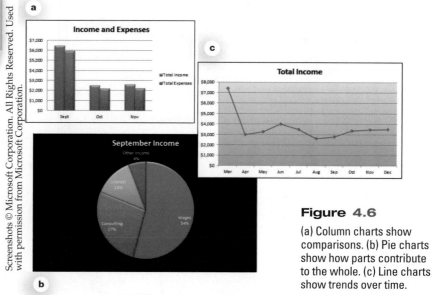

Figure 4.6

(a) Column charts show
comparisons. (b) Pie charts
show how parts contribute
to the whole. (c) Line charts
show trends over time.

ranging from the simple (such as adding
groups of numbers) to the complex (such
as determining monthly loan payments),
without you needing to know the exact
formula. Therefore, in Figure 4.5, to calculate the total of all income sources for
the month of September you could use
the built-in SUM function, which would
look like this: =SUM(B4:B7).

The primary benefit of spreadsheet software is its ability to recalculate all functions
and formulas in the spreadsheet automatically when values for some of the inputs
change. For example, as shown on the
spreadsheet on the right side of Figure 4.5,
you can insert an additional row (Member-
ships), change a value (September clothing
expense), and then recalculate the results
for Total Expenses and Net Income without
having to redo the worksheet from scratch.

Because automatic recalculation enables
you to see immediately the effects that different options have on your spreadsheet,
you can quickly test different assumptions
in the same analysis. This is called a *what-if
analysis.* Look again at Figure 4.5 and ask,
"What if I add $50 to my clothing expense?
What impact will such an increase have on
my total budget?"

**What kinds of graphs and charts
can I create with spreadsheet
software?** Sometimes it's easier to see the
meaning of numerical information when it is
shown in a graphical format such as a chart.
As shown in Figure 4.6, most spreadsheet
applications allow you to create a variety
of charts, including basic column charts,
pie charts, and line charts, with or without
three-dimensional (3D) effects. In addition to these basic charts, you can use stock
charts (for investment analysis) and scat-
ter charts (for statistical analysis), or create
custom charts. New in Excel 2010 are sparklines, which are small charts that fit into a
single cell. Sparklines (see Figure 4.7) make
it easy to show data trends.

**Are spreadsheets used for
anything besides financial analysis?**
There are so many powerful mathematical

functions built into spreadsheet programs
that they can be used for serious numerical
analyses or simulations. For example, an
Excel spreadsheet can be designed to compute the output voltage at a point in an
electrical circuit or to simulate customer
arrival and wait times. In these settings,
spreadsheet programs can often solve problems that formerly required custom programming. Many spreadsheet applications
also have limited database capabilities and
can sort, filter, and group data.

| | Current | 1 Year History | | |
		Trend	High	Low
Microsoft	$ 25.79		30.54	20.26
Apple	$ 255.96		261.09	125.83
Intel	$ 20.95		22.84	15.72
Hewlett Packard	$ 46.05		53.15	34.35
Dell	$ 13.24		16.2	11.57

Sparklines

Figure 4.7

Sparklines, a new feature for
Excel 2010, are tiny graphs
that fit into a single cell.

Presentation Software

**What software do I use to create
presentations?** You've probably sat
through presentations during which the
speaker's topic was displayed in slides projected on a screen. These presentations can
be the most basic of outlines, containing only
a few words and simple graphics, or elaborate multimedia presentations with animated
text, graphic objects, and colorful backgrounds. You use **presentation software** such
as Microsoft PowerPoint, OpenOffice.org

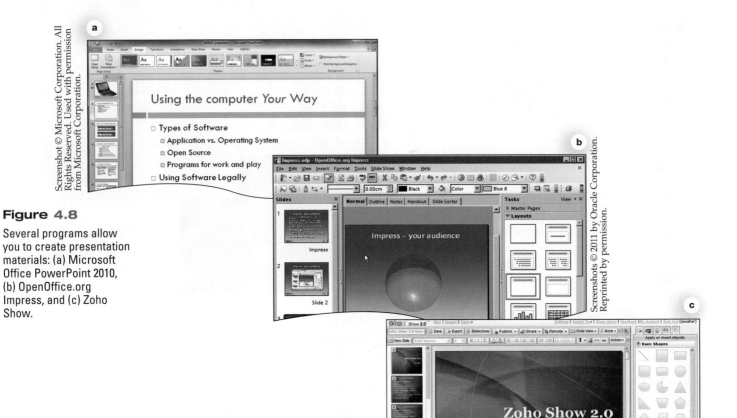

Figure 4.8

Several programs allow you to create presentation materials: (a) Microsoft Office PowerPoint 2010, (b) OpenOffice.org Impress, and (c) Zoho Show.

Impress, or Zoho Show (shown in Figure 4.8) to create these types of dynamic slide shows. Because these applications are simple to use, you can produce high-quality presentations without a lot of training. With some of the new capabilities in PowerPoint 2010, you can embed online videos, as well as change the color, add effects, and even trim video

rate videos, as well. Prezi is free for basic services, or you can pay an annual fee for greater online storage space, and the ability to work offline and to make your presentations private.

Because these applications are simple to use, you can produce high-quality presentations without a lot of training.

---

clips without the need for a separate video editing program. Prezi (**www.prezi.com**) is an online program that has an innovative way to produce presentations. Rather than being restricted to static slides, Prezi uses a larger canvas, which enables you to relate ideas better by zooming in to view the finer details and zooming out to see the bigger concept. You can also rotate the canvas for added visual interest. Prezi can incorpo-

How do I create a presentation?
Using the basic features included in presentation software, creating a slide show is simple. To arrange text and graphics on your slides, you can choose from a variety of slide layouts. These layouts give you the option of using a single or double column of bulleted text, various combinations of bulleted text, and other content such as clip art, graphs, photos, and even video clips.

You also can lend a theme to your presentation by choosing from different design templates. You can use animation effects to control how and when text and other objects enter and exit each slide. Slide transitions add different effects as you move from one slide to the next during the presentation.

Database Software

How can I use database software?
Database software such as Oracle, MySQL, and Microsoft Access are powerful applications that allow you to store and organize data. FileMaker Pro, Bento, and FileMaker Go are database alternatives for Windows, Mac OS X, and iOS. As mentioned earlier, spreadsheet applications include limited database features and are easy to use for simple database tasks such as sorting, filtering, and organizing data. However, you need to use a more robust, fully featured database application to manage larger and more complicated groups of data that contain more than one table; to group, sort, and retrieve data; and to generate reports.

Traditional databases are organized into fields, records, and tables, as shown in Figure 4.9. A field is a data category such as "First Name," "Last Name," or "Street Address." A record is a collection of related fields such as "Douglas, Seaver, Printing Solutions, 7700 First Avenue, Topeka, KS, 66603, (888) 968-2678." A table groups related records such as "Sales Contacts."

Make a Winning Presentation

Undoubtedly, you have sat through bad presentations. Don't make your audience sit through another one! Here are some tips for designing good presentations:

- **Color:** Avoid using clashing text and background colors. Instead, choose dark text on a light background or light text on a dark background.
- **Bullets:** Use bullets for key points. Limit the number to four to six bulleted points per slide.
- **Text:** Limit the amount of text on a slide to about six words per bullet point. Avoid full sentences and paragraphs.
- **Images:** Images can convey a thought or illustrate a point. Make sure any text over an image can be read easily. In Microsoft PowerPoint, consider using SmartArt diagrams for interesting visual text arrangements.
- **Font size and style:** Keep the font size large enough to read from the back of the room. Avoid script or fancy font styles. Use only one or two font styles per presentation.
- **Animation and background audio:** Keep to a minimum. They can be distracting.

How do you benefit when businesses use database software?
FedEx, UPS, and other shipping companies let customers search their online databases for tracking numbers, allowing customers to get instant information on the status of their packages. Other businesses use databases to keep track of clients, invoices, and personnel information. Often that information is available to a home computer user. For example, at Amazon.com you can use the company's Web site to access the entire history of all the

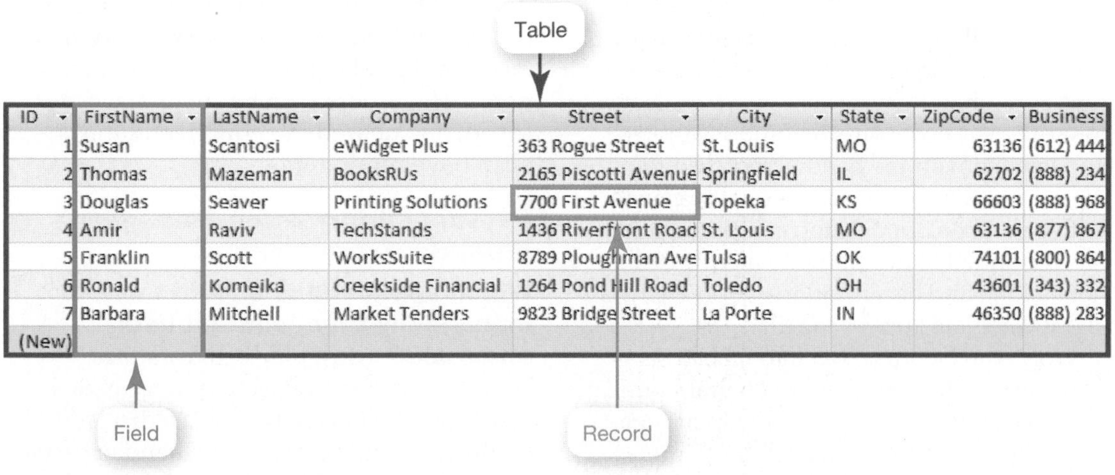

Table							

ID	FirstName	LastName	Company	Street	City	State	ZipCode	Business
1	Susan	Scantosi	eWidget Plus	363 Rogue Street	St. Louis	MO	63136	(612) 444
2	Thomas	Mazeman	BooksRUs	2165 Piscotti Avenue	Springfield	IL	62702	(888) 234
3	Douglas	Seaver	Printing Solutions	7700 First Avenue	Topeka	KS	66603	(888) 968
4	Amir	Raviv	TechStands	1436 Riverfront Road	St. Louis	MO	63136	(877) 867
5	Franklin	Scott	WorksSuite	8789 Ploughman Ave	Tulsa	OK	74101	(800) 864
6	Ronald	Komeika	Creekside Financial	1264 Pond Hill Road	Toledo	OH	43601	(343) 332
7	Barbara	Mitchell	Market Tenders	9823 Bridge Street	La Porte	IN	46350	(888) 283
(New)								

Field

Record

Figure 4.9
In databases, information is organized into tables, fields, and records.

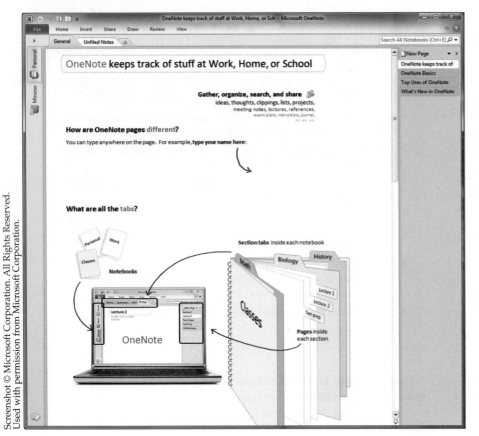

Figure 4.10

OneNote is a great way to collect and organize notes and other information. The files are readily searchable, and easy to share.

purchases you have made. Amazon, iTunes, Craigslist, and Pandora all rely on databases to organize their information.

Note Taking Software

Is there software to help with note taking? Programs are available to help students take notes during lectures and organize and maintain their lecture notes and the recordings they create from lectures. Microsoft OneNote first became popular with those who had tablet PCs, because it allows users to write their notes directly onto the tablet and later convert the handwritten text to digital text. OneNote works equally as well with a notebook or desktop computer, and has continued to develop into a powerful note taking and organizational tool. There is also a OneNote app for the iPad.

Notes can be organized into tabbed sections, similar to a multi-subject spiral-bound notebook, that provide further help in organizing and reorganizing pages (see Figure 4.10). By activating LinkedNotes from another Office application, your notes are tied directly to the specific point in the presentation or document you are reviewing, so you can jump to that exact point when you review your notes. With one click, Web links can be quickly integrated and audio or video recordings of lectures can be added. Students can search for a term across the full set of digital notebooks they have created during the semester, helping them to find connecting ideas among their courses. You can also have a stripped-down version of OneNote running so you can jot down notes or refer to your notes as you work in other applications.

Because OneNote has co-authoring and version tracking capabilities, it's also perfect for organizing team and other collaborative projects. Omnioutliner is another great note and outlining tool for Mac computers and the iPad that allows you to easily do many tasks such as take notes, manage to-do lists, and plan events.

Are there free or portable note taking applications? There are several free and online note taking options available to help you take full-blown notes or just jot down a quick reminder. Some are even available for your smartphone. Evernote (**www.evernote.com**), for example, allows you to take notes via the Web, your phone, or your computer and then sync your notes between the Web, your phone, and any computer. You can save text, audio, and images, as well as screen captures, Web pages, and photos. The beauty of Evernote is that everything is searchable. SoundNote (**www.soundnote.com**), an iPad app, is similar to Evernote, but also has a drawing feature and the ability to handle longer audio recordings. Sticky Notes (**www.sticky-notes.net**) are digital equivalents to paper sticky notes. These notes can be customized, saved, and shared via e-mail, and they even have reminders.

Personal Information Manager (PIM) Software

Which applications should I use to manage my time, contact lists, and tasks? Most productivity suites contain some form of **personal information manager (PIM) software** such as Microsoft Outlook or Lotus Organizer. Chandler (**www.chandlerproject.org**) is another PIM program that is open source and, therefore, free. These programs strive to replace the management tools found on a traditional desk—a calendar, address book, notepad, and to-do list, for example. Some PIMs contain e-mail management features so that you not only can receive and send e-mail messages, but also organize them into various folders, prioritize them, and coordinate them with other activities in your calendar (see Figure 4.11).

If you share a network at home or at work and are using the same PIM software as others on the network, you can use a PIM program to check people's availability before scheduling meeting times. Whether coordinating a team project or a family event, you can create and electronically assign tasks to group members by using a PIM. You can even track each person's progress to ensure that the tasks are finished on time.

Outlook also coordinates with OneNote, so you can create appointments, meeting

with any smartphone that runs on the Android operating system. Toodledo (**www.toodledo.com**) is an effective to-do manager that syncs with your smartphone and your desktop so you can always have all your tasks at hand wherever you are.

Productivity Software Features

What tools can help me work more efficiently with productivity software?

Whether you are working on a word processing document, spreadsheet, database, or slide presentation, you can make use of several tools to increase your efficiency:

- A **wizard** is a systematic guide that walks you through the steps necessary to complete a complicated task. At each

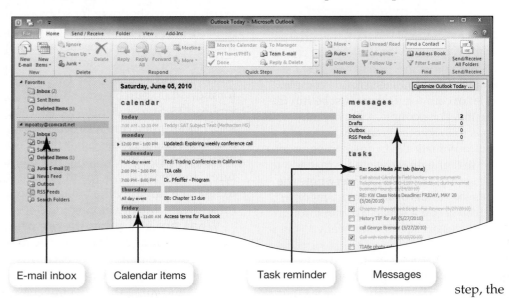

E-mail inbox   Calendar items   Task reminder   Messages

Figure 4.11

The Outlook Today feature in Microsoft Outlook includes common PIM features such as a summary of appointments, a list of tasks, and the number of new e-mail messages.

requests, and tasks directly in OneNote. If you're taking notes in a lecture or meeting, and the need to create a follow-up appointment comes up, you can do so without leaving the OneNote application.

Are there Web-based PIM programs?

Many Web-based e-mail clients, such as Yahoo! and Google, have developed coordinating calendar and contacts programs similar to Microsoft Outlook. Yahoo! includes Notepad for jotting down notes and tasks. Google's calendar and contacts sync with Outlook so you can access your Outlook calendar information by logging into Google, giving you access to your schedule anywhere you have access to a computer and an Internet connection. It also syncs

step, the wizard asks you questions. Based on your responses, the wizard helps you complete that portion of the task. When you install software, you are often guided by a wizard.

- A **template** is a predesigned form. Templates are included in many productivity applications. They provide the basic structure for a particular kind of document, spreadsheet, or presentation. Templates can include specific page layout designs, formatting and styles relevant to that particular document, and automated tasks (macros). Typical templates allow you to lay out a professional-looking résumé, structure a home budget, or communicate the results of a project in a presentation.

- A **macro** is a small program that groups a series of commands so they will run as a single command. Macros are best used to automate a routine task or a complex series of commands that must be run frequently. For example, a teacher may write a macro to sort the grades in her grade book automatically in descending order and to highlight those grades that add up to less than a C average. Every time she adds the results of an assignment or test, she can set up the macro to run through that series of steps automatically.

Software Suites

What's a software suite? A **software suite** is a group of software programs that have been bundled as a package. You can buy software suites for many different

Figure 4.12

Software suites provide users with a cheaper method of obtaining all of the software they want to buy in one bundle.

categories of software, including productivity, graphics, and virus protection (see Figure 4.12). Microsoft Office 2010 is the standard for proprietary software suites, and is available for both Windows-based and Apple computers. Apple offers productivity software for Macs in its iWork suite.

Which applications do productivity software suites contain? Most productivity software suites contain similar basic components, such as word processing, spreadsheet, presentation, and PIM software. However, depending on the version and manufacturer, they may also include other types of applications, such as database, note taking, or desktop publishing software. When you are shopping for software, it is important to figure out which bundle is the right one for your needs. For example, Microsoft Office 2010 is bundled in different ways; the three bundles that are available for individual purchase are described in Figure 4.13. Starter 2010, also from Microsoft, has stripped down versions of Word and Excel and includes advertising. Starter 2010 is installed by the computer manufacturer, and replaces Microsoft Works. Be sure to research carefully the bundling options for software you are buying.

What are the advantages of software suites? It is cheaper to buy a software suite than to buy each program individually. Another benefit of software suites is the compatibility between programs. Because the programs bundled in a software suite come from the same company, they work well together (that is, they provide for better integration) and share common features, toolbars, and menus. For example, when using applications in the Microsoft Office suite, you can seamlessly create a spreadsheet in Excel, import it into Access, and then link a query created in Access to a Word document. It would be much harder to do the same thing using different applications from a variety of software developers. Another example of a productivity suite is Apple iWork, which includes word processing (Pages), presentation (Keynote), and spreadsheet (Numbers) applications. Each program in the iWork suite can access and share certain common elements such as photographs.

Application	Function	Home and Student 2010	Home and Business 2010	Professional 2010
Word	Word processing	x	x	x
Excel	Spreadsheet	x	x	x
PowerPoint	Presentation	x	x	x
Access	Database			x
Outlook	PIM		x	x
Publisher	Desktop publishing			x
OneNote	Note taking	x	x	x

Figure 4.13

Microsoft Office 2010 suites that are best for home, work, or school.

Personal Financial Software

What software can I use to prepare my taxes? Everyone has to deal with taxes, and having the right computer software can make this burden much simpler and keep it completely under your control. **Tax preparation software** such as Intuit TurboTax and H&R Block At Home enable you to prepare your state and federal taxes on your own instead of hiring a professional. Both programs offer a complete set of tax forms and instructions, as well as videos that contain expert advice on how to complete each form. Each company also offers free Web-based versions for federal forms and instructions. In addition, error-checking features are built into the programs to catch mistakes. TurboTax also can run a check for audit alerts, file your return electronically, and offer financial planning guidance to help you effectively plan and manage your financial resources in the following year (see Figure 4.14). Remember, however, that the tax code changes annually, so you must obtain an updated version of the software each year.

Which software can I use to help keep track of my personal finances? Financial planning software helps you manage your daily finances. Intuit Quicken, AceMoney, and YNAB are popular examples. Financial planning programs include electronic checkbook registers and automatic bill payment tools. With these features, you can print checks from your computer or pay recurring monthly

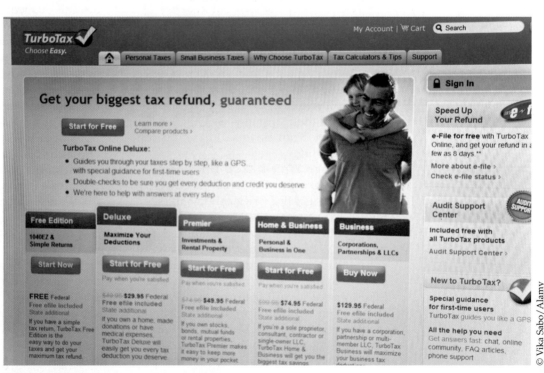

Figure 4.14

Tax preparation software such as Intuit TurboTax enables you to prepare and file your taxes using a guided, systematic process.

© Vika Sabo / Alamy

payments, such as rent or student loans, with automatically scheduled online payments. The software records all transactions, including online payments, in your checkbook register. In addition, you can assign categories to each transaction and then use these categories to create budgets and analyze your spending patterns.

Some financial planning applications also coordinate with tax preparation software. Quicken, for example, integrates seamlessly with TurboTax, so you never have to go through your checkbook and bills to find tax deductions, tax-related income, or expenses. Many banks and credit card companies also offer online services

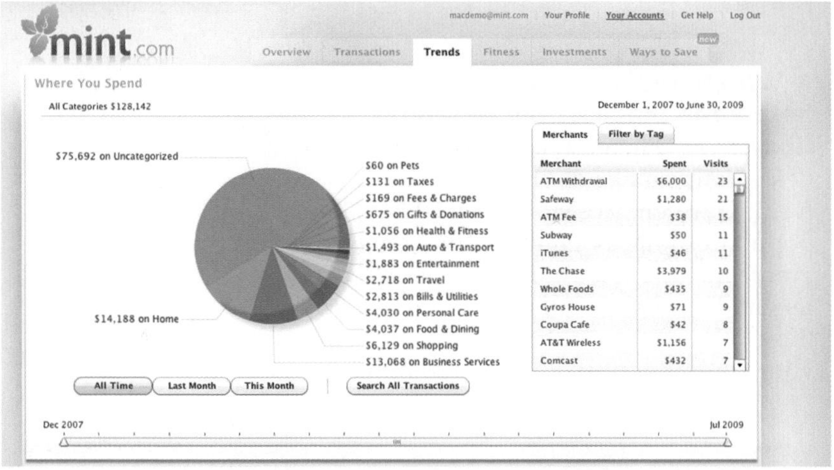

Figure 4.15

Mint.com is an online financial management tool. An extensive online community provides helpful tips and discussions with other people in similar situations.

that download a detailed monthly statement into Quicken. Quicken even offers a credit card. All of your purchases are organized into categories and are downloaded automatically to your Quicken file to streamline your financial planning and record keeping.

Are there Web-based financial planning programs? Web-based programs such as Mint (**www.mint.com**) (see Figure 4.15) and Yodlee MoneyCenter (**www.yodlee.com**) are rapidly gaining in popularity. Both are great at analyzing your spending habits and offering advice on how to manage your spending better. Like some other full-featured applications such as Quicken, you can track your investment portfolio as well. Because they are Web-based, you can monitor and update your finances from any computer in a private and secure setting. Each product also has versions of its applications to load on smartphones, so your information is con-

veniently accessible. Users also have access to a network of other users with whom to exchange tips and advice.

Business Software for Home and Office

With the amount of power available in a typical home computer, you have more opportunities than ever to run a business from your home. No matter what service or product you provide, there are common types of software that will be helpful in your business. Accounting software will help manage the flow of money, and desktop publishing and Web page creation tools will help you market and develop your new enterprise. A number of software packages are designed to organize and help with the daily operations of a typical business. If you ever plan to run a business from your own home, or even if you are just a user of large business products and services, it is helpful to know what functions business software can perform.

Home Business Software

Which programs are good for small-business owners? If you have a small business or a hobby that produces income, then you know the importance of keeping good records and tracking your expenses and income. **Accounting software** helps small-business owners manage their finances more efficiently by providing tools for tracking accounts receivable and accounts payable. In addition, these applications offer inventory management, payroll, and billing tools. Examples of accounting applications are Intuit QuickBooks and Peachtree by Sage. Both programs include templates for invoices, statements, and financial reports so that small-business owners can create common forms and reports.

What software can I use to lay out and design newsletters and other publications? **Desktop publishing (DTP) software** allows you to incorporate and arrange graphics and text in your documents in creative ways. Although many word processing applications allow you to use some of the features that are hallmarks of desktop publishing, specialized desktop publishing software such as Microsoft

Publisher, QuarkXPress, and Adobe InDesign allows professionals to design books and other publications that require complex layouts (see Figure 4.16).

What tools do desktop publishing programs include? Desktop publishing programs offer a variety of tools with which you can format text and graphics. With text formatting tools, you easily can change the font, size, and style of your text and arrange text on the page in different columns, shapes, and patterns. You also can import files into your documents from other sources, including elements from other software programs (such as a chart from Excel or text from Word) and image files. You can readily manipulate graphics with tools that crop, flip, or rotate images or modify the image's color, shape, and size. Desktop publishing programs also include features that allow you to publish to the Web.

What software do I use to create a Web page? Web page authoring software allows even the novice to design interesting and interactive Web pages, without knowing any HyperText Markup Language (HTML) code. Web page authoring applications often include wizards, templates, and reference materials to help you easily complete most Web page authoring tasks. More experienced users can take advantage of these applications' advanced features, such as features that enable you to add headlines and weather information, stock tickers, and maps to make your Web content current, interactive, and interesting. Microsoft Expression Web and Adobe Dreamweaver are two of the programs to which both professionals and casual page designers turn.

Are there other ways to create Web pages? If you need to produce only the occasional Web page and do not need a separate Web page authoring program, you'll find that many applications include features that enable you to convert your document into a Web page. For example, in some Microsoft Office applications, if you choose to save a file as a Web page, the application will automatically convert the file to a Web-compatible format.

Large Business Software

There is an application for almost every aspect of business. There are specialized programs for marketing and sales, finance, point of sale, general productivity, project management, security, networking, data management, e-commerce, and human resources, to name just a few. In the following sections, we discuss some of these specialized programs from this seemingly endless list.

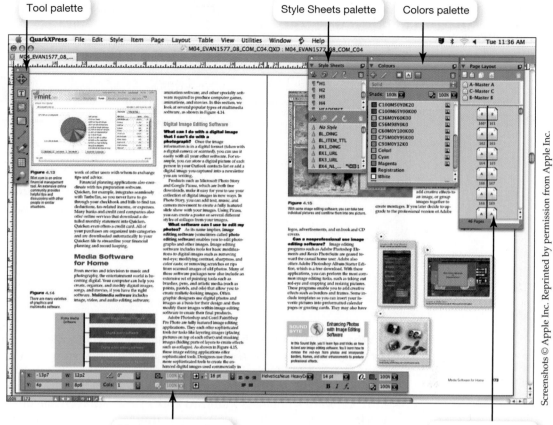

Tool palette · Style Sheets palette · Colors palette · Measurements palette · Page Layout palette

Figure 4.16

Major publishing houses use professional publishing programs such as QuarkXPress to lay out the pages of textbooks.

Figure 4.17

A Gantt chart in Microsoft Project gives project managers a visual tool for assigning personnel and scheduling and managing tasks.

What software do businesses use for planning and management? Planning is a big part of running a successful business. Software programs such as Palo Alto Software's Business Plan Pro and Marketing Plan Pro help users write strategic and development plans for general business and marketing needs. Another category of business planning software is **project management software**, such as Microsoft Project. This type of software helps project managers create and modify scheduling charts like the one shown in Figure 4.17, which help them plan and track specific tasks and coordinate personnel resources.

Customer relationship management (CRM) software stores sales and client contact information in one central database. Sales professionals use CRM programs to get in touch with and follow up with their clients. These programs also include tools that enable businesses to assign quotas and create reports and charts that document and analyze actual and projected sales data. CRM programs coordinate well with PIM software such as Outlook and can be set up to work with smartphones. GoldMine from FrontRange Solutions is one example of a CRM program.

An **enterprise resource planning (ERP) system** lets a business consolidate multiple systems into one and improve coordination of these business areas across multiple departments. ERP systems are used to control many "back office" operations and processing functions such as billing, production, inventory management, and human resources management. These systems are implemented by third-party vendors and matched directly to the specific needs of a company. Oracle and SAP are well-known companies that sell ERP software.

What software helps business travelers? **Mapping programs** are useful for nonprofessionals traveling to unfamiliar locations. More users now turn to an **online mapping service** such as Google Maps, MapQuest, Yahoo! Maps, or Google Earth than to a more traditional mapping software program because the online services are easily accessible with any Internet connection and are updated more frequently than offline ones. Mapping programs, which can

BITS AND BYTES

Need a Way to Share Files? Try PDF

Say you've created a file in Microsoft Excel, but the person to whom you want to send it doesn't have Excel, or any spreadsheet software, installed on his computer. Further, you do not want the contents of the original file to be changed. What do you do in these situations? One solution is to create a PDF file. Portable Document Format (PDF) is a file format you can create with Adobe Acrobat or CutePDF Writer, a free program available from **www.cutepdf.com.** These programs transform any file, regardless of its application or platform, into a document that can be shared, viewed, and printed by anyone who has Adobe Reader. If you are using Microsoft Office 2010 or OpenOffice.org, you can create PDF files easily with a built-in feature. Adobe Reader (available from **www.adobe.com**), the program you need to read all PDF files, is a free download.

work in conjunction with a global positioning system (GPS), are available in versions for smartphones and for cars.

Is mapping software just used to assist with travel? Travel is only one of several applications that use mapping technologies to assist businesses in making complex decisions and managing complex systems. Many companies use a geographic information system (GIS) to assist with managing, analyzing, and displaying data, most often in spatial or map form (see Figure 4.18). These maps are used by power companies to manage electric grids, by water distribution companies to manage water distribution, by shipping and transportation companies to determine the most efficient routes, and even by school districts to manage the flow of students to the appropriate schools. Many of these systems are complex, proprietary ones such as those produced by ESRI. Google Earth and interactive maps like Google Maps are simple and free examples of basic forms of a GIS.

What software is used with e-commerce? It seems that every business has an online presence to display company information or products, handle online sales, or offer customer service and support. Depending on the size of the company and its specific needs, it may use products such as IBM's WebSphere, Go-Emerchant, and ProStores Business from ProStores (an eBay company). These products offer bundled Web site creation and hosting services, shopping cart setup, and credit card processing services. For larger businesses, specialized software to handle each aspect of e-commerce is available; alternatively, a large business might develop proprietary software tailored to its specific needs.

Specialized Business Software

Some applications are tailored to the needs of a particular company or industry. Software designed for a specific industry is called **vertical market software**. For example, the construction industry uses software such as Sage Master Builder, which features estimating tools to help construction companies bid on jobs. It also integrates project management functions and accounting systems that are unique to the construction industry.

Other examples of vertical market software include property management

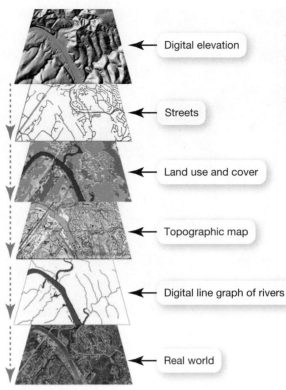

Figure 4.18

A geographic information system (GIS) applies geographic data to provide solutions to complex business situations.

Digital elevation

Streets

Land use and cover

Topographic map

Digital line graph of rivers

Real world

software for real estate professionals; ambulance scheduling and dispatching software for emergency assistance organizations; and library automation software that combines cataloging, circulation, inventory, online catalog searching, and custom report printing.

In addition to these specific business applications, which companies can buy off the shelf, programs often are custom developed to address a company's specific needs.

What software is used to make 3D models? Engineers use **computer-aided design (CAD)** programs to create automated designs, technical drawings, and 3D model visualizations. Specialized CAD software such as Autodesk's AutoCAD is used in areas such as architecture, the automotive industry, aerospace, and medical engineering.

With CAD software, architects can build virtual models of their plans and readily visualize all aspects of design before actual construction. Engineers use CAD software to design everything from factory components to bridges. The 3D nature of these programs allows engineers to rotate their models and make adjustments to their designs where necessary, thus eliminating costly building errors.

are complex and rich programs. A slightly simpler package is the open source program Blender (**www .blender.org**), which is available free of charge. A simple, Web-based, and fairly full-featured free 3D modeling application is Google's SketchUp (**sketchup.google.com**) (see Figure 4.19). SketchUp designs coordinate well with other Google applications so, for example, you could easily import a 3D image of a deck you created in SketchUp into a Google Earth image of your home.

Figure 4.19

Google's SketchUp is a free 3D modeling application.

CAD software also is being used in conjunction with GPS devices for accurate placement of fiber-optic networks around the country. The medical engineering community uses CAD to create anatomically accurate solid models of the human anatomy, allowing them to develop medical implants quickly and accurately. The list of CAD applications keeps growing as more and more

Media Software for Home

From movies and television to music and photography, the entertainment world is becoming digital. Your computer can help you create, organize, and modify digital images, songs, and movies, if you have the right software. **Multimedia software** includes image, video, and audio editing software; animation software; and other specialty software required to produce computer games, animations, and movies. In this section, we look at several popular types of multimedia software, as shown in Figure 4.20.

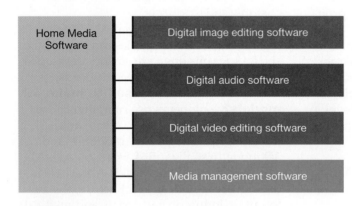

Figure 4.20

There are many varieties of graphics and multimedia software.

industries realize the benefits CAD can bring to their product development and manufacturing processes.

Many graphics, animation, video, and gaming systems use applications from Autodesk called Autodesk 3ds Max and Autodesk Maya to create 3D models with complex textures and lighting models. Autodesk 3ds Max and Autodesk Maya

Digital Image Editing Software

What can I do with a digital image that I can't do with a photograph? Once the image information is in a digital format (taken with a digital camera or scanned), you can use it easily with all your other software. For example, you can store a digital picture of each person in your Outlook contacts list or add a digital image you captured into a newsletter you are writing.

Products such as Microsoft Photo Story and Google Picasa, which are both free downloads, make it easy for you to use your collection of digital images in new ways. In Photo Story, you can add text, music, and camera movement to create a fully featured slide show with your images. Using Picasa, you can create a poster or several different styles of collages from your images.

Figure 4.21

You can create collages of your favorite images using Google's Picasa.

What software can I use to edit my photos? As its name implies, **image editing software** (sometimes called **photo editing software**) enables you to edit photographs and other images. Image editing software includes tools for basic modifications to digital images such as removing red-eye; modifying contrast, sharpness, and color casts; or removing scratches or rips from scanned images of old photos. Many of these software packages include painting tools such as brushes, pens, and artistic media (such as paints, pastels, and oils) that allow you to create realistic-looking images. Some include templates so you can insert your favorite pictures into preformatted pages for digital scrapbooks or greeting cards. Image editing programs such as Adobe Photoshop Elements and Roxio PhotoSuite are geared toward the casual home user. Google

Picasa (**picasa.google.com**) is another popular application in the online photo editing, storing, and sharing field (see Figure 4.21). Picasa, which is a free download, not only lets you organize and edit your photos, but also stores your photos on the Web. This makes it very easy to share photos by creating Web albums. Picasa helps you send images to your friends, your mobile devices, or your blog by automatically resizing a huge 12-megapixel image to a more manageable size for electronic transmission. With Picasa, you can then attach the image to an outgoing e-mail message, or transfer the image directly to your blog or to a mobile device such as an iPad or smartphone.

What image editing programs might a professional use? Often graphic designers use digital photos and images as a basis for their designs and then modify these images within image editing software to create their final products.

Adobe Photoshop and Corel PaintShop Photo Pro are fully featured image editing applications. GIMPshop (**www.gimpshop .com**) is a free download that has most of the features offered by the more expensive applications. They each offer sophisticated tools for tasks like layering images (placing pictures on top of each other) and masking images (hiding parts of layers to create effects such as collages). Designers use

SOUND BYTE

Enhancing Photos with Image Editing Software

In this Sound Byte, you'll learn tips and tricks on how to best use image editing software. You'll learn how to remove the red-eye from photos and incorporate borders, frames, and other enhancements to produce professional effects.

Most likely you have a Facebook account as well as a Web-based e-mail account such as Gmail or Hotmail that you access every day. You put your pictures on Facebook and you can see them from anywhere you can access the Internet—from home, school, or work—and you can view them on your PC, your smartphone, or your friend's notebook. Similarly, you can always check your e-mail from any computing device. You might also use Dropbox to store your files instead of carrying around a flash drive, and you might have purchased your textbooks from Amazon rather than going to your local bookstore. For your last group project, you and your teammates might have used Google Docs because it was easiest for all of you to access and collaborate on at any time. By doing any of these activities, you have participated in cloud computing.

So what is cloud computing? From the term, you might think it is something magical—and that somehow your pictures and files are floating around in space. But, in reality, your pictures, e-mail, and any other files that are stored on the Web, as well as the software that you access from the Web, are housed in data centers or server farms. These data centers and server farms are basically warehouses full of computers and servers, and they are being created all over the world, providing us with "cloud storage." Being able to work from the cloud eliminates the need to have everything stored on your own computer's disk drives, which can be restricting if you are away from your computer. Instead, cloud computing gives you access to your favorite pictures, music, files, and programs anytime you like, anywhere you like, as long as you have access to the Internet. In addition, cloud computing facilitates collaboration and communication among multiple users, and can cut down on administrative tasks for organizations maintaining large amounts of computer hardware and software.

Technically, there are two sides to cloud computing: the front end and the back end. The front end is the side we see as users, and includes our computer and the application required to access the cloud computing system—generally a Web browser like Internet Explorer or Google Chrome. Some systems have unique applications that provide network access to clients. The back end consists of the various computers and servers that house the files and programs you access "on the cloud" (see Figure 4.22). A central server that uses a special kind of software called middleware (that allows networked computers to communicate with each other), monitors the demands on the system to ensure everything runs smoothly. The computers in the data centers or server farms are designed to work together, adjusting to the varying degrees of demand placed on them at any point in time. Companies like Facebook have had to increase the amount of servers dedicated to their users as the popularity and functionality of Facebook has increased, for example.

Google is one of the first true explorers in the cloud, building applications such as Google Docs, Gmail, and Chrome in an effort to eventually create a completely virtual operating environment. A fully functioning operating environment would enable users to sign in and have "their" computer setup (desktop configurations and images, programs, files, and other personalized settings) pop up on whatever computer they are using. Additionally, cloud computing would reduce the need for all of us to have the fastest computers with the most memory and storage capabilities. Instead, we could all have simple front-end terminals with basic input and output devices because the computers on the back end will be providing all the computing muscle. We are not quite there yet, but those days are inevitably coming.

these more sophisticated tools to create the enhanced digital images used commercially in logos, advertisements, and on book and CD covers.

Are there Web-based programs available to edit, share, and store my photos? One great advantage of taking digital images is that you can easily share the images via the Internet. Initially, we had to send images as e-mail attachments—and our exuberance in sending several images at the same time often clogged someone's inbox. Several online photo sharing and photo storing sites, such as Snapfish (**www.snapfish.com**), Kodak (**www.kodak.com**), and Shutterfly (**www.shutterfly.com**), enable you to upload your digital images from your computer, create photo albums, and share them with friends and family. These sites offer printing and card-making services as well.

Flickr (**www.flickr.com**) is probably one of the best of these online photo management and photo sharing applications. It lets you organize your images and then share them publicly with millions of users, or just with your closest friends and family. Discussion boards are available so that groups can exchange comments about the images, just as you would if you were passing them around the dinner table. In addition, taking advantage of online mapping technologies, Flickr enables you to link your images to a map so that you can show exactly where you took the images or see where others took theirs.

Digital Audio Software

Why would I have digital audio files on my computer? Best-selling novels, newspapers, and radio shows all can be purchased as audio files from sellers such as Audible, Inc. (**www.audible.com**). Huge numbers of

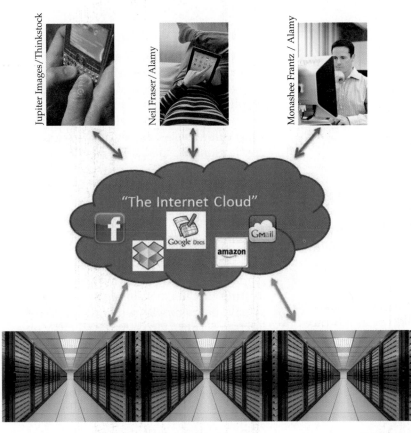

"The Internet Cloud"

Figure 4.22

There are two sides to cloud computing: the side we see as users, and the banks of computers and servers that house the files and programs we access.

Sure, there are some problems with cloud computing that users need to be aware of, such as what happens when the Internet goes down. Security and privacy are also very big concerns for cloud computing. Right now, the security of information stored on the Web is built on trusting that the passwords we set and the security systems that the data centers put in place are able to keep our information away from unauthorized users. Because even the devices in these large data centers and server farms inevitably will break down, the cloud computing systems have redundant systems to provide backup. However, for critical files that you must have, it might be a good idea to not completely rely on the cloud, and to have your own backup files. Like losing electricity, if the Internet goes down, you would have to go without, but having a backup system in place for the critical files and programs will help to reduce the inconvenience and loss of productivity while access to the Internet is being restored. But, you can't mitigate all the risks if you store all the files on your own personal computers, so you have to weigh these disadvantages against the strong advantages of the convenience of having your information when and where you want it, and the ability to have better collaboration.

free audio files are also available through the phenomenon of *podcasting*, the distribution of audio files such as radio shows and music videos over the Internet. Offered by subscription, these audio files are delivered to your computer free with the release of each episode. You may also choose to extract (*rip*) your CD collection to store on your computer. In addition, with programs such as MAGIX Music Maker or Apple GarageBand, you can compose your own songs or soundtracks with virtual instruments, voice recorders, synthesizers, and special audio effects. You may quickly have several gigabytes of audio files on your hard drive before you even know it!

Why are MP3 files so popular? MP3, short for MPEG-1 Audio Layer 3, is a type of audio compression format that reduces the file size of traditional digital audio files so that they will take up less storage capacity. It is also a standard of digital audio compression, which has made it possible to transfer and play back music on personal media players. For example, a typical CD stores between 10 and 15 songs in uncompressed format, but with files in MP3 format, the same CD can store between 100 and 180 songs. The smaller file size not only lets you store and play music in less space, but also allows quick and easy distribution over the Internet. Ogg Vorbis (or just Ogg) is a free, open source audio compression format alternative.

What can digital audio software programs do? You can find hundreds of digital audio applications that allow you to copy, play, and organize MP3 files. Most digital audio software programs, such as Apple iTunes, Windows Media Player, and Musicmatch Jukebox, enable you to do the following:

- *MP3 recording* allows you to record directly from streaming audio and other software or microphone sources to MP3 format.

- *CD ripping* allows you to copy or extract CDs and encode to the MP3 format.
- *CD burning* allows you to create your own CDs from your MP3 collection.
- *Encoding and decoding* is done by *encoders*, programs that convert files to MP3 format at varying levels of quality. Most ripping software has encoders built in to convert the files directly into MP3 format.
- *Format conversion* programs allow you to convert MP3 files to other digital audio formats such as WAV (Waveform Audio File Format), WMA (Windows Media Audio), and AIFF (Audio Interchange File Format).

Can I edit audio files? **Audio editing software** includes tools that make editing your audio files as easy as editing your text files. Software such as the open source Audacity (**http://audacity.sourceforge .net**) and Sony Sound Forge Pro 10 (**www .sonycreativesoftware.com**) enable you to perform such basic editing tasks as cutting dead air space from the beginning or end of the song or clipping a portion from the middle. Audio Acrobat (**http://marketersmojo.audioacrobat .com**), a Web-based program, makes it easy to record and stream audio and video, and hosts your audio files, as well. You also can add special sound effects, such as echo or bass boost, and remove static or hiss from your MP3 files. These applications support recording sound files from a microphone or any source you can connect through the input line of a sound card.

Digital Video Editing Software

What kind of software do I need to edit my digital videos? With the boom of digital camcorders and the improved graphics capabilities on home computers, many people are experimenting with **digital video editing software**. Several video editing applications are available at a wide range of prices and capabilities. Although the most expensive products (such as Adobe Premiere Pro and Apple's Final Cut Pro) offer the widest range of special effects and tools, some moderately priced video editing programs have enough features to keep the casual user happy. Windows Live Movie Maker and Apple iMovie have intuitive drag-and-drop features that make it simple to create professional-quality movies with little or no training (see Figure 4.23). Windows Live Movie Maker (**http://download.live.com/moviemaker**) is a free download from Microsoft. Other software developers offer free trial versions so that you can decide whether their product meets your needs before purchasing it.

Does video editing software support all kinds of video files? Video files come in a number of formats such as flash video (FLV for YouTube), MPEG-1, MPEG-2, MPEG-4, VCD, SVCD, DVD, AVI, WMV, MOV, and even AVCHD, a format for high-definition video. Many of the affordable video editing software packages support most types of video files.

Figure 4.23

Video editing programs such as Apple iMovie make it easy to create and edit movies.

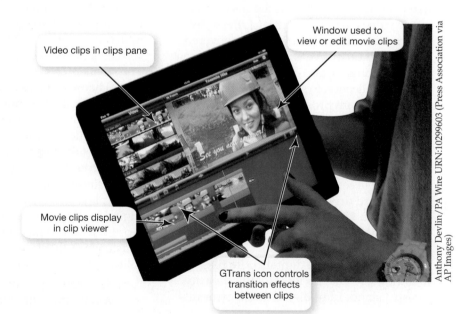

Video clips in clips pane

Window used to view or edit movie clips

Movie clips display in clip viewer

GTrans icon controls transition effects between clips

Anthony Devlin/PA Wire URN:10299603 (Press Association via AP Images)

Album covers flow in smooth display

iTunes social network

Genius recommendations based on song composition

Smart playlists select song lists based on your criteria

Figure 4.24

Software programs such as iTunes help you manage all the music files on your computer. You can sort, filter, and search your collection by artist, album, or category, and you can create playlists.

For more information on video editing software, see the section "Digital Video" on page 383 of Chapter 8.

In what format are the videos I watch on my portable media player? Videos that can be watched on portable media players, such as Apple's iPods, are in the MP4 (MPEG-4) video format. This format stores digital audio and digital video streams, as well as other items, such as text for subtitles and still images. Similar to the MP3 format, MP4 compresses the audio and video content into a more manageable file size. Most MP4 files have the file extension .mp4. However, Apple has created other MPEG-4 extensions to identify specific content such as .m4b, which is often used to identify audio book and podcast files, and .m4r, which is used to identify ringtone files for the iPhone.

Media Management Software

How do I manage the audio, video, and image files on my system? Many people add hundreds or even thousands of files to their systems by purchasing music and downloading images and video. Your hard drive is a convenient place to store all your music and images, but only if you can find what you're looking for!

Software such as Windows Media Player, Winamp, and Apple iTunes allows you to organize audio and video files so that you can sort, filter, and search your music collection by artist, album, or category (see Figure 4.24). Using these programs, you can manage individual tracks, generate playlists, and even export the files to a database or spreadsheet application for further manipulation. When you burn the songs to a CD, the programs can print liner notes that you can place inside the CD case.

Entertainment Software for Home

As the term implies, **entertainment software** is designed to provide users with thrills, chills, and all-out fun! Computer games make up the vast majority of entertainment software. These digital games began with Pong, Pac-Man, and Donkey Kong, and have evolved to include many different categories, including action, driving, puzzles, role-playing, card-playing, sports, strategy, and simulation games. Entertainment software also includes other types of computer applications, such as drawing software.

Gaming Software

Do I need special equipment to run entertainment software? As with any software, you need to make sure your system has enough processing power, memory (RAM), and hard drive capacity to run the

Figure 4.25

Computer controllers can be specialized. Rock Band controllers include a guitar, a drum set, and a microphone.

program. Because games often push the limit of sound and video quality, be sure your system has the appropriate sound cards, video cards, speakers, monitor, and DVD drives.

Some gaming software may require a special controller. Some games, such as Steel Battalion, Rock Band, and many games in the Nintendo Wii system, are sold with their own specialized controllers (see Figure 4.25). These controllers also can be adapted to your computer. Complex programs can benefit from configurable wireless controllers such as the Cyborg Evo.

Can I make video games? Now that video games represent an industry with revenue of more than $20 billion each year, designing and creating video games is emerging as a desirable career opportunity. Professionally created video games involve artistic storytelling and design, as well as sophisticated programming. Major production houses such as Electronic Arts use applications that are not easily available to the casual home enthusiast. However, you can use the editors and game engines available for games such as EverQuest, Oblivion, and Unreal Tournament to create custom levels and characters to extend the game.

If you want to try your hand at creating your own video games, multimedia applications such as Unity, Adobe Flash, and RPG Maker VX provide the tools you need to explore game design and creation. The program GameMaker (**www.yoyogames.com**) is a free product that allows you to build a game without any programming; key elements of the new game creation are dragged and dropped into place. Alice (**www.alice.org**) is another free environment to check out. It lets you easily create 3D animations and simple games. See the Sound Byte on 3D Programming the Easy Way in Chapter 10.

Educational Software

What kinds of educational applications are there? Although a multitude of educational software products are geared toward the younger set, software developers have by no means ignored adult markets. In addition to all the products relating to the younger audience, there are software products that teach users new skills such as typing, languages, cooking, and playing the guitar. Preparation software for

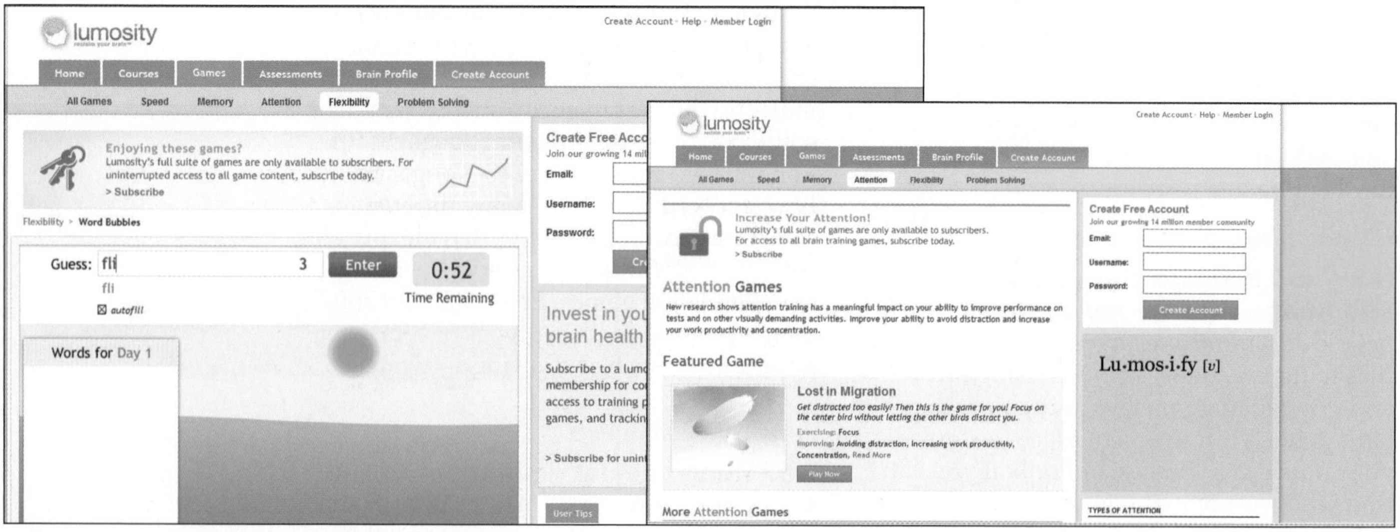

Figure 4.26

Lumosity features games to exercise your brain to improve memory, processing speed, attention, and multitasking capabilities.

students who will be taking the SAT, GMAT, LSAT, and MCAT exams is also popular. In addition, there are many computer and online brain training games and programs designed to improve the health and function of our brains. Lumosity (**www. lumosity.com**) is one such site that has a specific "workout" program (see Figure 4.26), and can be played on the PC and on your smartphone. Brain Age[2] (**www.brainage.com**) has software for the Nintendo DS and is designed for players of all ages.

What types of programs are available to train you to use software or special machines? Many programs provide tutorials for popular computer applications. These programs use illustrated systematic instructions to guide users through unfamiliar skills. Some training programs, known as **simulation programs**, allow users to experience or control the software as if it were the actual software or an actual event. Such simulation programs include commercial and military flight training, surgical instrument training, and machine operation training. Often these simulators can be delivered on CD or DVD or over the Internet.

One benefit of these simulated training programs is that they safely allow users to experience potentially dangerous situations such as flying a helicopter during high winds. Consequently, users of these training programs are more likely to take risks and learn from their mistakes—something they could not afford to do in real life. Simulated training programs also help prevent costly errors. Should something go awry, the only cost of the error is restarting the simulation program.

Choosing Software

In this Active Helpdesk call, you'll play the role of a helpdesk staffer, fielding calls about the different kinds of multimedia software, educational and reference software, and entertainment software.

Do I need special software to take courses online? As long as you have a compatible Web browser, online classes will be accessible to you. Depending on the content and course materials, however, you may need a password or special plug-ins to view certain videos or demos.

How to Open Unknown File Types

Normally, when you double-click a file to open it, the program that is associated with the selected file runs automatically. For example, when you double-click a file with a .doc or .docx extension, the file will open in Microsoft Word. However, if the file has no extension or Windows has no application currently associated with that file type, an "Open with" dialog box appears and asks what program you want to use to open the file. In other cases, a document may open with a program other than the one you wanted to use. This is because many applications can open several file types, and the program you expected the file to open in is not currently the program associated with that file type. To assign a program to a file type or to change the program to open a particular file type, follow these instructions:

1. Click the Windows Explorer icon, which is pinned to the Windows 7 taskbar by default.
2. Use the search and navigation tools in Windows Explorer to locate the file you want to change. (For example, you can search for all Word files by searching for *.doc or *.docx.) Right-click on the file, and then point to Open With.
3. A list of programs installed on your computer will appear. Click the program that you want to use to open this type of file. If you are sure the selected file type is the one that should always be used, then also check "Always use the selected program to open this kind of file" check box, and then click OK.

When you double-click that file in the future, the file will open in the program you selected.

Taking classes over the Internet is rapidly becoming a popular method of learning because it offers greater schedule flexibility for busy students. Although some courses are run from an individually developed Web site, many online courses are run using **course management software** such as Blackboard, Moodle, and Angel. These programs provide traditional classroom tools such as calendars and grade books over the Internet. Special areas are available for students and professors to exchange ideas and information through the use of chat rooms, discussion forums, and e-mail. Other areas are available for posting assignments, lectures, and other pertinent class information.

Drawing Software

What kind of software should I use for simple illustrations? Drawing software (or **illustration software**) lets you create or edit two-dimensional, line-based drawings. You can use drawing software to create technical diagrams or original nonphotographic drawings, animations, and illustrations using standard drawing and painting tools such as pens, pencils, and paintbrushes.

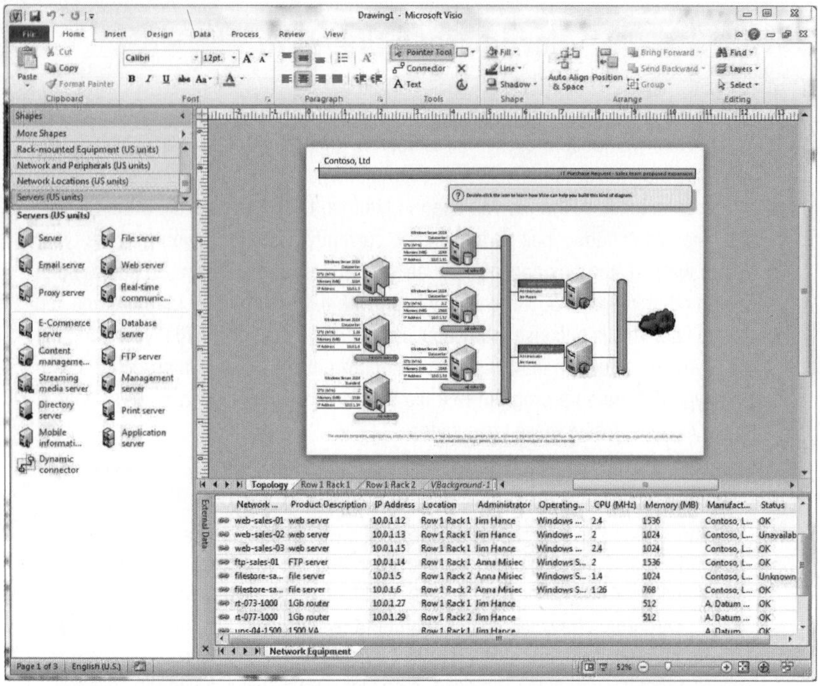

Figure 4.27

The drawing program Visio lets you create different types of diagrams easily with drag-and-drop options.

You also can drag geometric objects from a toolbar onto the canvas area to create images and use paint bucket, eyedropper, and spray can tools to add color and special effects to the drawings.

Are there different types of drawing software? Drawing software is used in both creative and technical drawings. Applications such as Adobe Illustrator include tools that let you create professional-quality creative and technical illustrations. Illustrator's tools help you create complex designs, such as muscle structures in the human body, and use special effects, such as charcoal sketches. Its warping tool allows you to bend, stretch, and twist portions of your image or text. Because of its many tools and features, Illustrator is one of the preferred drawing software programs of most graphic artists.

There are many software packages to help plan the layout of rooms, homes, and landscapes, such as those offered by Broderbund. Microsoft Visio is a program used to create technical drawings, maps, basic block diagrams, networking and engineering flowcharts, and project schedules, but it can also be used by the more casual designer. Visio uses project-related templates with special objects that you drag onto a canvas. For example, Visio allows you to quickly drag and drop objects to create diagrams like the one shown in Figure 4.27.

Visio also provides brainstorming templates to help you organize your thoughts and ideas.

Buying Software

These days, you no longer need to go to a computer supply store to buy software. You can find software in almost any retail environment. In addition, you can purchase software online, through catalogs, and at auctions.

Where can I buy software directly from the Internet? As with many other retail products, you can buy and download software directly from many companies and retail Web sites such as Microsoft (**www.microsoft.com**) and Amazon (**www.amazon.com**). You also can use the Internet to buy software that is custom developed for your specific needs. Companies such as Ascentix Corporation (**www.ascentix.com**) act as intermediaries between you (the software user) and a software developer, who tweaks open source software code to meet your particular needs.

When buying software from the Internet, you should also request that the software be sent to you on CD or DVD, if this is available. Without a physical copy of the software, it is much more difficult to reinstall the software if you change computers or if your hard drive crashes. If a physical copy is not available, make sure you create a backup and keep it in a safe place.

The Microsoft .NET program (**www.microsoft.com/net**) offers software over the Internet for all devices—not just computers—that have a connection to the Internet. Therefore, you can download software specifically for your smartphone by using .NET. In addition, the Mac OS X operating system integrates online software purchases through the App Store feature.

Software Licenses

Don't I own the software I buy? Most people don't understand that, unlike other items they purchase, the software they buy doesn't belong to them. The only thing they're actually purchasing is a license that gives them the right to use the software for their own purposes as the *only* user of that copy. The application is not theirs to lend.

"There's an App for That!"

How many of us have said or heard that phrase, indicating that we are seemingly always within access of a program that can be easily downloaded onto our mobile device that will keep us ever connected, entertained, informed, organized, and productive, no matter where we are or what we are doing?

The Apple iPhone started the trend toward mobile applications when the App Store was launched in mid-2008 along with the release of the iPhone. The app craze has been strong from the beginning, and the growth is staggering: 1 billion apps were downloaded in nine months from the Apple App Store (compared to the three years it took to download 1 billion music tracks from iTunes), and 10 billion apps were downloaded by January 2011, only two and a half years after the App Store was opened. Now there are hundreds of thousands of mobile applications created for not just the Apple iPhone, but also for the Android, Blackberry, and other smartphones. In addition, the iPad and other similar tablet devices have their own sets of apps.

Nearly 82 percent of adults have cell phones, and about one-quarter of adults do not have a home landline phone. In addition, cell phones have become "smarter," with the capability of accessing the Internet and multitasking. Combine that with a society that is becoming increasingly dependent on access to instant information, and having access to mobile apps is the perfect solution to the perfect storm—an apps culture has emerged (see Figure 4.28).

According to a recent study conducted by the Pew Research Center's Internet and American Life Project, most of the apps downloaded are entertainment related (games, music, food, travel, and sports) and information based (maps, banking, weather, and news). And according to a separate study conducted by the Nielsen Company, most apps are used in our downtime while watching television, waiting for something, or shopping and running errands. They were least used in a classroom or a meeting.

Similar to the Mac versus PC battle where most software is developed for one or the other platform, not both, mobile apps are also platform specific. If you have a smartphone powered by the Android operating system, you can only use apps from the Android Market. If you

© Arrow | Dreamstime.com

Figure 4.28

Apps that run on small mobile devices such as smartphones and tablets have created an apps culture.

have an iPhone, you can only use apps from Apple's App Store. But, if you were to compare the two leading app marketplaces, is there a significant difference between the two? The answer is yes . . . and no.

Apple has the clear advantage by being the first in the market—and therefore has nearly twice as many apps as what is in Android Market. Of the apps that have been developed, Apple has tightly controlled the types of applications that can appear in the App Store; Google, on the other hand, has let developers basically put up anything they want in the Android Market without asking permission. Therefore, many apps on the Android Market can be considered "junk," but others are quite useful even though they would not pass Apple's strict requirements.

Both stores provide simple means to navigate through the hundreds of thousands of apps. Each store has arranged apps into categories, and differentiates between the free, most popular, and newly released. However, Apple has begun to group apps together in kits such as apps for "Students," "Movie Lovers," and "Working Out." And the Genius tab is very helpful by recommending apps based on your existing library.

All in all, the trend toward delivery and use of mobile apps has taken off at full speed and is quickly becoming a way of life for many smartphone users.

What is a software license?

A **software license**, also known as an **End Users License Agreement (EULA)**, is an agreement between you, the user, and the software company (see Figure 4.29). You accept this agreement before installing the software on your machine. It is a legal contract that outlines the acceptable uses of the program and any actions that violate the agreement. Generally, the agreement will state who the ultimate owner of the

Figure 4.29

You must accept the terms of the software license before using the product.

Used with permission from Microsoft

> **Microsoft Software License Terms**
>
> MICROSOFT SOFTWARE LICENSE TERMS
> MICROSOFT OFFICE 2010 DESKTOP APPLICATION SOFTWARE
> Below are three separate sets of license terms. Only one set applies to you. To determine which license terms apply to you check the license designation printed either on your product key, near the product name on your Certificate of Authenticity, or on the download page if you obtained your product key online. If your designation is FPP, then the Retail License Terms below apply to you. If your designation is OEM, then the OEM License Terms below apply to you. If your designation is Product Key Card or PKC, then the Product Key Card License Terms below apply to you. If you need assistance finding your license type, please go to: www.microsoft.com/office/eula to determine which license you have.
>
> 1. RETAIL LICENSE TERMS.
> These license terms are an agreement between Microsoft Corporation (or based on where you live, one of its affiliates) and you. Please read them. They apply to the software named above, which includes the media on which you received it, if any. Printed-paper license terms, which may come with the software, may replace or modify an on-screen license terms. These terms also apply to any Microsoft
>
> Print   OK

Can I Borrow Software That I Don't Own?

A computer user who copies an application onto more than one computer is participating in **software piracy**, unless his or her license specifically provides for multiple distributions. When software users purchase software, they are purchasing a license to use it, rather than purchasing the actual software. That license tells you how many times you can install the software, so it is important to read it. If you make more copies of the software than the license permits, you are pirating (see Figure 4.30). Historically, the most common way software has been pirated among computer users has been by supplementing each other's software library by borrowing installation CDs and installing the software on their own computers. Larger-scale illegal duplication and distribution by counterfeiters are quite common as well. In addition, the Internet provides various ways to copy and distribute pirated software illegally.

Is it really a big deal to copy a program or two? As reported by the Business Software Alliance, over 40 percent of all software is

Figure 4.30

Making more copies than the permitted number is pirating software, and is illegal.

© Lepro/iStockphoto.com

pirated. Not only is pirating software unethical and illegal, but the practice has financial impacts on all software consumers. The financial loss to the software industry is estimated to be valued at over $50 billion. This loss decreases the amount of money available for further software research and development, while increasing the up-front costs to legitimate consumers.

To determine whether you have a pirated copy of software installed on your computer at work or at home, you should conduct a software audit. The Business Software Alliance Web site (**www.bsa.org/usa**) has several free third-party software audit tools that help you identify and track licensed and unlicensed software installed on your computer and networks. These programs check the serial numbers of the software installed on your computer against software manufacturer databases of official licensed copies and known fraudulent copies. Any suspicious software installations are flagged for your attention.

As of yet, there's no such thing as an official software police force, but if you're caught with pirated software, severe penalties do exist. A company or individual can pay up to $150,000 for each software title copied. In addition, you can be criminally prosecuted for copyright infringement, which carries a fine of up to $250,000 or a five-year jail sentence or both.

Efforts to stop groups that reproduce, modify, and distribute counterfeit software over the Internet are in full force. Software manufacturers also are becoming more aggressive in programming mechanisms into software to prevent repeated installations. For instance, with many Microsoft products, installation requires you to activate the serial number of your software with a database maintained at Microsoft. This is different from the traditional "registration" that enrolled you voluntarily and allowed you to be notified of product updates. Activation is required, and failure to activate your serial number or attempting to activate a serial number that has been used previously results in the software going into a "reduced functionality mode" after the fiftieth time you use it. Therefore, without activation, you would not be able to save documents in Office.

software is, under what circumstances copies of the software can be made, and whether the software can be installed on any other machine. Finally, the license agreement will state what, if any, warranty comes with the software.

Do you always buy just one license? Some software is purchased with a single license to cover one person's specific use. These licenses cannot be shared, and you cannot "extend" the license to install the software on more than one of your computers. However, Apple offers a Family Pack Software License Agreement that permits a user to install some of its software legally on as many as five computers that are in the same household, and some versions of Microsoft Office come with the ability to install the software on up to three computers in the same household. Businesses and educational institutions often buy multiuser licenses that allow more than one person to use the software. Some multiuser licenses are per-seat and limit the number of users overall, while others, called *concurrent licenses*, limit the number of users accessing the software at any given time.

Does open source software require a license? As you learned earlier, anyone using open source software has access to the program's code. Therefore, open source software programs can be tweaked by another user and redistributed. A free software license, the GNU General Public License, is required and grants the recipients the right to modify and redistribute the software. Without such license, the recipient would be in violation of copyright laws. This concept of redistributing modified open source software under the same terms as the original software is known as **copyleft**. Thus, all enhancements, additions, and other changes to copyleft software must also be distributed as free software.

Pre-Installed Software

What application software comes with my computer? Virtually every new computer comes with an operating system as well as some form of application software, although the particular applications depend on the hardware manufacturer and computer model. You usually can count on your computer having some form of productivity software preinstalled, such as Windows Live Essentials, which includes Photo Gallery, Movie Maker, Mail, and Messenger, as well as Microsoft Office Starter. Multimedia-enriched computers also may offer graphics software or a productivity suite that includes Web page authoring software.

Some manufacturers can include applications on your new computer that they hope you will try, so as to build interest in their product. Some of these applications, especially virus protection software, are trial versions for which a user gets a short-term temporary software license. When the license expires, the software disables (but is still installed), and a permanent license must be purchased to reinstate the software.

Are there any problems associated with pre-installed software? There is such generous space on system hard drives these days that leaving pre-installed applications on a system isn't problematic from a storage perspective. However, having so many pre-installed programs on your system can degrade the system performance by allocating memory away from active applications. For notebook computers, such software can also reduce battery life. If you

BITS AND BYTES — Getting Rid of the Bloat

You have a new computer and expect blazing fast speeds. Unfortunately, the manufacturer included lots of software that you don't want or need, and you know it degrades performance and slows down startup and shutdown times. To get rid of bloatware, you can install an application such as PC Decrapifier (**www.pcdecrapifier.com**), or if you prefer to do this yourself, consider some of these tips:

1. **Trial Antivirus Software:** Although it's absolutely necessary to have antivirus software on your new machine, often, you can transfer the unexpired portion of your license from your old machine to your new one. If that is the case, uninstall the trial version immediately, because you will be bombarded with registration prompts once the trial version expires.

2. **Toolbars:** Although toolbars can be useful, you want to select those that are most useful to you, and having too many can be repetitive. Many computers come with Google or Yahoo! toolbars installed, and possibly others. You can go through Programs and Features in the Control Panel to uninstall any unwanted toolbars.

3. **Manufacturer-Specific Software:** Some computer manufacturers also install their own software. Some of these programs can be useful, while others are help features and update reminders, which are also found in your operating system. You can remove any or all of these support applications, and instead just check the manufacturer's Web site periodically for any updates or new information.

don't use the software or don't renew the license, then the software just clogs up your system unnecessarily. For this reason, this pre-installed software is referred to as **bloatware**. The best thing to do is to delete the programs.

Can I get the manufacturer to uninstall or install software before shipping? Several years ago, Dell began to allow buyers of certain computers to decline unwanted bloatware. Dell also included an extra uninstall utility program on certain computers to make it easier to remove unwanted software. On the other hand, if you know you'll need a particular type of software not offered as standard on your new computer, you may want to see if the computer manufacturer has a special offer that will allow you to add that particular software at a reduced price. Sometimes, initially buying software through the hardware manufacturer is less expensive than buying software on the retail market. This is not always the case, so do some comparative pricing before you buy.

If my computer crashes, can I get the pre-installed software back? Although some pre-installed software, such as bloatware, is not necessary to replace if your computer crashes, other software such as the operating system is critical to reinstall. Most manufacturers use a separate partition on the hard drive that holds an image, or copy, of the pre-installed software. However, it's not always possible to reboot from the partitioned hard drive, especially when your computer crashes, so one of the first things you should do after you purchase a new computer is create a restore disc. Generally the manufacturer will have placed a utility on your system, or you can use the utility included in Windows 7, to create a restore disc. To create a restore disc with Windows 7, click the Start menu, select Control Panel, and then select System and Security. From there, select Backup and Restore, and then click Create a system repair disc from the Navigation Pane. Next, insert a blank DVD in your DVD drive and select the drive. Click Create disc. Once the copy has been made, label the disc and put it away in a safe place.

Discounted Software

Is there discounted software for students? Software manufacturers understand that students and educators often need to use software for short periods of time because of specific classes or projects. In addition, they want to encourage you to learn with their product, hoping you'll become a long-term user of their software. Therefore, if you're a student or an educator, you can purchase software that is no different from regularly priced software at prices that are sometimes substantially less than general consumer prices.

Campus computer stores and college bookstores sometimes offer discounted prices to students and faculty who possess a valid ID. Online software suppliers such as Journey Education Marketing (**www.journeyed.com**), CampusTech, Inc. (**www.campustech.com**), and Academic Superstore (**www.academicsuperstore.com**) also offer popular software to students at reduced prices.

Can I buy used software? Often you can buy software through online auction sites such as eBay. If you do so, be sure that you are buying licensed (legal) copies. Computer shows that display state-of-the-art computer equipment are generally good sources for software. However, here, too, you must exert a bit of caution to make sure you are buying licensed copies and not pirated versions.

Freeware and Shareware

Can I get software for free legally? **Freeware** is any copyrighted software that you can use for free. Plenty of freeware exists on the Web, ranging from games and screen savers to business, educational, graphics, home and hobby, and system utility software

---

Campus computer stores and college bookstores sometimes offer discounted prices to students and faculty who possess a valid ID.

---

programs. To find free software, type "freeware" in your search engine. Good sources of a large variety of freeware programs are Butterscotch (**www.butterscotch.com**), and Freeware Home (**www.freewarehome.com**).

Although they do not charge a fee, some developers release free software and request that you send them an e-mail message to thank them for their time in developing the software and to give them your opinion of it. Such programs are called *e-mailware*.

Another option is to search for an open source program to fit your needs. Open source programs are free to use on the condition that any changes you make to improve the source code also must be distributed for free. SourceForge (**www.sourceforge.net**) is an excellent site to begin your hunt for a group that may already have built a solution that will work for you.

While much legitimate freeware exists, some unscrupulous people use freeware to distribute viruses and malware. Be cautious when installing such programs, especially if you are unsure of the provider's legitimacy.

Can I try new software before it is really released? Some software developers offer beta versions of their software free

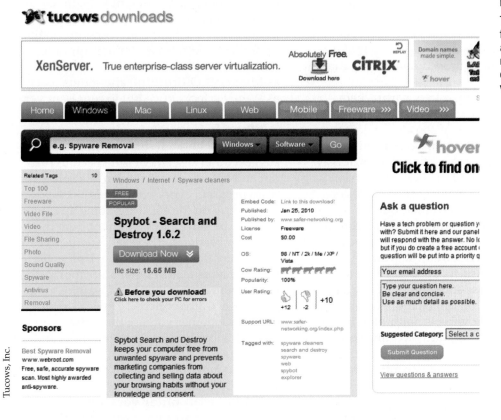

Figure 4.31

Tucows downloads is a useful site for finding shareware and freeware applications. The site provides product reviews, hardware requirements, and details about the limitations of free versions of software.

of charge. A **beta version** is an application that is still under development. By distributing free beta versions, developers hope users will report errors, or bugs, they find in their programs. Many beta versions are available for a limited trial period, and are used to help the developers correct any errors before they launch the software on the market.

Is it still freeware if I'm asked to pay for the program after using it for a while? One model for distributing software is to run a version free of charge for only a limited time. These are fully functional packages, but they expire if not purchased within a certain timeframe. This is referred to as **shareware**. Shareware is not freeware. Shareware software is distributed free, but with certain conditions. Sometimes the software is released on a trial basis only and must be registered after a certain period of time. For example, Tech-Smith Corporation (**www.techsmith.com**) offers Snagit Screen Capture and Camtasia Studio for free for a 30-day period, after which time you must purchase the software to continue using it. If you use the software after the initial trial period is over,

then you are breaking the software license agreement.

Software developers put out shareware programs to get their products into users' hands without the added expense and hassle of marketing and advertising. Therefore, quite a few great programs are available as shareware, and they can compete handily with programs on retail shelves. For a listing of other shareware programs, visit the CNET site Tucows (**www.tucows.com/downloads**), shown in Figure 4.31.

Can shareware programmers make me pay for their shareware once I have it? The whole concept of shareware assumes that users will behave ethically and abide by the license agreement. However, to protect themselves, many developers have incorporated code into the program to stop it from working completely or to alter the output slightly after the trial period expires.

Are there risks associated with installing beta versions, freeware, and shareware or downloading them from the Internet? Not all files available as shareware and freeware will work on your computer. You easily can crash your system, and may even need to reinstall your operating system as a result of loading a freeware or shareware program that was not written for your computer's operating system.

Of course, by their very nature, beta products are unlikely to be bug free, so you always run the risk of something going awry with your system. Unless you're willing to deal with potential problems, it may be best to wait until the last beta version is released. By that time, most of the serious bugs will have been worked out.

As a precaution, you should be comfortable with the reliability of the source before downloading a freeware, shareware, or beta version of software. If it's a reliable developer whose software you are already familiar with, you can be more certain that a serious bug or virus is not hiding in the software. However, downloading software from an unknown source could potentially put your system at risk of contracting a virus. (We discuss viruses in detail in Chapter 9.)

A good practice to establish before installing any software on your system is to use the Windows 7 operating system's Restore feature and create a *restore point*. That way, if anything goes wrong during installation, you can restore your system to the way it was before you started. (We discuss the System Restore utility in Chapter 5.) Also, make sure that your virus protection software is up-to-date.

Buying and Installing Software

In this Active Helpdesk call, you'll play the role of a helpdesk staffer, fielding calls about how to best purchase software or get it for free, how to install and uninstall software, and where you can go for help when you have a problem with your software.

Software Versions and System Requirements

What do the numbers after software names indicate? Software companies change their programs to repair problems (or bugs) or add new or upgraded features. Generally, they keep the software program's name but add a number to it to indicate that it is a different version. Originally, developers used numbers only to indicate different software versions (major upgrades) and releases (minor upgrades). Today, however, they also use years (such as Microsoft Office 2010) and letters (such as WordPerfect Office X5) to represent version upgrades.

When is it worth buying a newer version? Although software developers suggest otherwise, there is no need to rush out and buy the latest version of a software program every time one is available. Depending on the software, some upgrades may not be sufficiently different from the previous version to make it cost-effective for you to buy the newest version. Unless the upgrade adds features that are important to you, you may be better off waiting to upgrade every other release. You also should consider whether you use the software frequently enough to justify an upgrade and whether your current system can handle the new system requirements of the upgraded version.

If I have an older version of software and someone sends me files from a newer version, can I still open them? Software vendors recognize that people work on different versions of the same software. Vendors, therefore, make new versions backward compatible, meaning that they can recognize (open) files created with older versions. However, some software programs are not forward compatible, so older versions cannot recognize files created on newer versions of the same software.

How do I know whether the software I buy will work on my computer? Every software program has a set of **system requirements** that specify the minimum recommended standards for the operating system, processor, primary memory (RAM), and hard drive capacity. Sometimes there are other specifications for the video card, monitor, CD drive, and other peripherals. These requirements generally are printed on the software packaging or are available at the manufacturer's Web site. Before installing software on your computer, ensure that your system setup meets the minimum requirements by having sufficient storage, memory capacity, and processing capabilities.

When you download software from the Web, you can run a download or you can save it (see Figure 4.32). What's the difference? When you select Run, the program is downloaded to your machine, and generally stored in Temporary Internet Files. Then the file is "run," meaning that it is loaded into memory and the operating system runs it. Use the Run option when you need to use the downloaded file on a limited basis, such as a song or video that you only plan to watch once or twice. Some installation programs actually install the software on your machine in a permanent location when Run is selected.

When you select Save (or sometimes Save As) on a download, the file will be copied to your hard disk. There may be an AutoRun program associated with the file that starts the installation automatically. Otherwise, you may need to navigate to the stored location and execute (or run) the file independently. The big difference is that the saved file is not downloaded into a temporary location. Use Save when you want to keep the file for a longer period of time, or when you want to control where the file or program is saved.

Figure 4.32
When downloading software you have the choice of Run or Save.

Installing, Uninstalling, and Starting Software

Before you use most software, you must permanently place it, or install it, on your system. The installation process will differ slightly depending on whether you've purchased the software from a retail outlet and have an installation CD or have downloaded it from the Internet. Deleting or uninstalling software from your system requires that you take certain precautions to ensure you remove all associated programs as well.

How do I install software? When you purchase software, the program files may come on a CD or a DVD, or they may be available as a download from the Web. When installing programs from a CD or DVD, an installation wizard automatically opens when you insert the disc. By following the steps indicated by the wizard, you can install the application on your system. If the wizard doesn't open automatically for some reason, the best way to install the software is to go to the Start menu, select the Control Panel, click Programs, and then click on the Programs and Features icon. This launches the installation wizard.

How is the installation process different for software I download from the Web? When you download software from the Web, you typically do not get an installation disc. Instead, everything you need to install and run the downloaded program is contained in one file that has been compressed (or zipped) to make the downloading process quicker. For the most part, these downloaded files unzip or decompress themselves and automatically start or launch the setup program. During the installation and setup process, these programs select or create the folder on your computer's hard drive in which most of the program files will be saved. Usually, you can select a different location if you desire. Either way, note the name and location of the files, because you may need to access them later.

What do I do if the downloaded program doesn't install by itself? Some programs you download do not automatically install and run on your computer. Although the compressed files may unzip automatically as part of the download process, the setup program may not run without some help from you. In this case, you need to locate the files on the hard drive (this is why you must remember the location of the files) and find the program that is controlling the installation (usually named *setup.exe* or sometimes *install.exe*). Files ending with the .exe extension are executable files or applications. All the other files in the folder are support, help, and data files. Once the setup program begins, you will be prompted to take the actions necessary to complete the installation.

What's the difference between a custom installation and a full installation? One of the first steps in the installation wizard asks you to decide between a full installation and a custom installation. A **full installation** will copy all the files and programs from the distribution disc to the computer's hard drive. By selecting **custom installation**, you can decide which features you want installed on the hard drive. Installing only the features you know you want allows you to save space on your hard drive.

Can I just delete a program to uninstall it? An application contains many different files—library files, help files, and other text files—in addition to the main file you use to run the program. By deleting only the main file, or only the icon on your desktop, you are not ridding your system of all the pieces of the program. In addition, some applications make changes to a variety of settings, and none of these will be restored if you just delete the desktop icon or remove the main file from your programs list.

Some programs place an Uninstall Program icon in the main program folder on the Start menu. Using this icon runs

Figure 4.33

For quick access to an application you use often, you can create shortcuts on the Start Menu or taskbar.

the proper cleanup routine to clear out all of the files associated with the application, and also restores any settings that have been changed. If you can't locate the uninstall program for a particular application, click the Start menu, and then click Control Panel. Under Programs, click Uninstall a program. This will give you a list of applications installed on your system; from this list, you can choose which application you would like to uninstall.

Is there a best way to start an application? The simplest way to start an application is by clicking its icon in the All Programs list found on the Start menu. Every program that you install on your system is listed in All Programs on the Start menu. However, in Windows 7, if you find you use only a few programs often, you can place a shortcut to those programs on the taskbar or pin it to the Start menu. To place a program on the taskbar or pin it to the Start menu, right-click the program icon on your desktop or right-click the program name on the Start menu. From the shortcut menu that is displayed, select Pin to Taskbar or Pin to Start Menu. Windows then places an icon for this program on the taskbar or Start menu (see Figure 4.33). To uninstall a pinned icon from the Start Menu or a taskbar icon, right-click the icon and select "Remove from this list" or "Unpin this program from taskbar," respectively.

There is virtually an application for almost anything you want or need to do on your computer, whether it is school or work related or just for entertainment purposes. And there are a variety of types of almost every application, such as proprietary, open source, Web-based, freeware, and shareware. Have fun exploring all the various possibilities!

Figure 4.34

Microsoft Office gives you tips on tasks you're working on and answers specific questions you have about using online and offline resources.

Getting Help with Software

If you need help while you are working with software, you can access several different resources to find answers to your questions. For general help or information about a product, many manufacturers' Web sites offer answers to frequently asked questions (FAQs).

Where can I find help while I'm working in an application? Some programs offer online help and support. Online help may consist of documentation comparable to a user's manual. However, many applications' online help allows you to chat over the Internet with an online support team member. Some applications are context sensitive and offer task-specific help or screen tips to explain where your cursor is resting.

In Microsoft Office applications, you will see a question mark icon on the far top right of the program screen. This icon takes you to the main Help interface. **Integrated help** means that the documentation for the product is built directly into the software so you

don't need to keep track of bulky manuals. You can type your question, search for a term, or browse the Help topics (see Figure 4.34). Like many software packages, Microsoft Office offers help documentation, which is installed locally on your machine, and online help resources, which are updated continually.

Finally, the Help menu, found in the File tab of most Microsoft applications, lets you choose to search an index or content outline to find out the nature of almost any Microsoft application feature.

Where do I go for tutorials and training on an application? If you need help learning how to use a product, the product's developer may offer online tutorials or program tours that show you how to use the software features. Often, you can find good tutorials by searching the Internet. MalekTips (**www.malektips.com**), for example, includes a vast array of multimedia help files; you can find podcasts for applications such as Excel and Photoshop in iTunes; and even YouTube has some helpful videos.

1. What's the difference between application software and system software?

Application software is the software you use to do everyday tasks at home, school, and work. Application software includes productivity software, such as word processing and finance programs; media software, such as applications used for image and video editing; home and entertainment software, such as games or educational programs; and business software for small and large businesses. System software is the software that helps run the computer and coordinates instructions between application software and the computer's hardware devices. System software includes the operating system and utility programs.

2. What are Web-based applications, and how do they differ from traditional modes of software distribution?

Web-based applications are those that are hosted online by the vendor and made available to the customer over the Internet. This distribution model of on-demand software deployment is also referred to as Software as a Service (SaaS). Unlike traditional software that needs to be installed on individual machines or network servers, Web-based applications are accessed via an Internet connection to the host server. The appeal of Web-based applications is that they can be accessed from any machine that has an Internet connection and they can facilitate collaboration because many people can access the same file and work together in real time.

3. What kinds of applications are included in productivity software?

Productivity software programs include word processing, spreadsheet, presentation, note taking, personal information manager (PIM), and database programs. You use word processing software to create and edit written documents. Spreadsheet software enables you to do calculations and numerical and what-if analyses easily. Presentation software enables you to create slide presentations. Note taking software provides a convenient means to take extensive notes or to just jot down a few thoughts. You can easily organize and search your notes. PIM software helps keep you organized by putting a calendar, address book, notepad, and to-do lists within your computer. Database programs are powerful applications that allow you to store and organize data. Individuals can also use software to help with business-like tasks such as preparing taxes and managing personal finances.

4. What kinds of software do small and large businesses use?

Businesses, including home businesses, use software to help them with finance, accounting, strategic planning, marketing, and Web-based tasks common to most businesses. In addition, businesses may use specialized business software (or vertical market software) that is designed for their specific industry.

5. What are the different types of media and entertainment software?

Multimedia software includes digital image, video, and audio editing software; animation software; and other specialty software required to produce computer games. Many software programs are available for playing, copying, recording, editing, and organizing multimedia files. Because modern users have so many audio, video, and image files, many software solutions are available for organizing and distributing these types of files.

6. What are the different types of drawing software?

Drawing software includes a wide range of software programs that help you create and edit simple line-based drawings or create more complex designs for both imaginative and technical illustrations. Floor plans, animations, and mind maps are some of the types of images that can be created.

7. How can I purchase software or get it for free?

Almost every new computer system comes with some form of software to help you accomplish basic tasks. You must purchase all other software unless it is freeware or open source code, which you can download from the Web for free. You can also find special software called shareware you can run free of charge for a test period. Although you can find software in many stores, as a student you can purchase the same software at a reduced price with an academic discount. When you purchase software, you are actually purchasing the license to use it, and therefore must abide by the terms of the licensing agreement you accept when installing the program.

8. How do I install, uninstall, and start software?

When installing and uninstalling software, it's best to use the uninstall feature provided in the software, or if not included to use the uninstall feature that comes with the operating system. Most programs are installed using an installation wizard that walks you

through the installation. Other software programs may require you to activate the setup program, which then will begin the installation wizard. Using the uninstall feature of the operating system when uninstalling a program will help you ensure that all additional program files are removed from your computer.

9. Where can I go for help when I have a problem with my software?

Most software programs have a Help feature built into the program with which you can search through an index or subject directory to find answers. Some programs group the most commonly asked questions into a single frequently asked questions (FAQ) document. In addition, many free and fee-based help and training resources are available on the Internet and through booksellers.

 ## Companion Website

The Companion Website includes a variety of additional materials to help you review and learn more about the topics in this chapter. Go to: **www.pearsonhighered.com/techinaction**

key terms

Word Bank

- application software
- beta version
- financial planning software
- freeware
- illustration software
- image editing software
- integrated help

- presentation
- productivity software
- shareware
- software piracy
- software suite
- spreadsheet
- system requirements

- system software
- templates
- Web-based applications
- wizards
- word processing

Instructions: Fill in the blanks using the words from the Word Bank above.

Roxanne has just enrolled in college and is deciding which software she must have. She knows she's going to need some (1) _____ applications for all the different tasks she'll have to do at school and at home. She has been told it's better to buy these applications as a(n) (2) _____ instead of individually since it's usually less expensive. In picking out which bundle of software to purchase, she looks for the one that has a(n) (3) _____ software to help her create slide shows, and a(n) (4) _____ program to help her write papers, and a(n) (5) _____ program for her finance classes. Roxanne is also aware of many interesting (6) _____ such as Google Docs and Dropbox that are available on the Internet and that she can access anywhere she has an Internet connection. Lastly, to keep track of her finances, Roxanne knows she'll need some type of (7) _____.

As a graduation present, Roxanne received a new digital camera. She needs to install the (8) _____ that came with her camera to edit and manage her digital pictures. Although she's used the software a couple of times on her parents' computer, she is still glad for the (9) _____ feature to assist her with specific feature-related questions and the (10) _____ that provide systematic guides to help her do things.

Roxanne especially likes the decorative preformatted (11) _____ she can use to insert pictures and make them seem professional. She also knows of some (12) _____ games she can download without cost from the Internet and other (13) _____ programs that she could try but eventually pay for. It's tempting for her to borrow software from her friends, but she knows that it's considered (14) _____. She also knows that before installing any of the programs she must check the (15) _____ to determine if the software is compatible with her system as well as whether the system has enough resources to support the software.

becoming computer literate

Using key terms from this chapter, write a letter to a new business owner advising them of the types of software they should get to help them run their company. Make sure you identify the type of business in the letter, and think of all possible software that would fit that specific type of business in addition to general business software that most businesses would require.

Instructions: Answer the multiple-choice and true–false questions below for more practice with key terms and concepts from this chapter.

Multiple Choice

1. The minimum set of recommended standards for a program is known as the
   a. operating system.
   b. system requirements.
   c. setup guide.
   d. installation specs.

2. Software that is available on-demand via the Internet is called
   a. proprietary software.
   b. Web-based software.
   c. productivity software.
   d. Internet software.

3. What type of software enables you to create dynamic slide shows?
   a. word processing
   b. spreadsheet
   c. presentation
   d. database

4. Which is NOT an advantage of using a software suite?
   a. The cost is cheaper than buying programs individually.
   b. The programs provide for better integration.
   c. The programs integrate easily with programs from other software suites.
   d. The programs share common features such as toolbars.

5. Image, video, and audio editing software belong in the category of what kind of software?
   a. gaming software
   b. multimedia software
   c. photo enhancing software
   d. production software

6. What kind of software is responsible for back office operations such as billing and inventory?
   a. enterprise resource planning
   b. project management
   c. business accounting
   d. personal information

7. Which of the following is true about open source software?
   a. The program code is confidential.
   b. The program can be changed and freely distributed.
   c. The program can be freely distributed as long as the program code is not changed.
   d. The program code is subject to copyright protection.

8. A small program that groups a series of commands so they will run as a single command is called a
   a. wizard.
   b. macro.
   c. template.
   d. function.

9. Which program can you use when you are taking notes in class?
   a. SoundNote
   b. EverNote
   c. OneNote
   d. all of the above

10. What is another name for Software as a Service (SaaS)?
    a. Web-based application
    b. ERP software
    c. apps
    d. software suite

True–False

_____ 1. A macro is a small program that groups a series of commands so that they run as a single command.

_____ 2. When you need help with software, you should use the program's help features or manufacturer FAQs, not online help like podcasts or YouTube videos.

_____ 3. System software includes the operating system and utility programs.

_____ 4. A software suite is a group of programs bundled as a package.

_____ 5. When you buy software, you then own it and can do anything you'd like with it, including giving it to a friend to install on their machine.

1. **Picture Perfect**

   You just spent the summer volunteering in a remote village in Africa, and you have tons of pictures you want to share with friends and family. For your friends, it's easy to upload them into Facebook, but you don't want to give your family access to your Facebook account. Research different Web sites that you would consider using to upload your pictures to show your family. Create a table that lists the different services along with the pros and cons of each site. Discuss which services you would use and explain your reasoning.

2. **Software Help**

   Because your friends know you like technology, they always are coming to you for advice and help with their software. While you don't mind helping out your friends, there are some great Web sites that they also can go to. Create a presentation that explains the various ways they can get free help about all their software questions. Begin the presentation with a list of FAQs and hyperlink each question to the slide that contains the answer.

3. **Collaborating with Software**

   You have been assigned the dreaded group project. For once you have a great group of students to work with, but none of your schedules line up so you can meet in person. You decide to use Web-based applications because you have heard they are great for collaborating online. Research the differences between Google Docs and Microsoft Web Apps. Are there differences between the two products, such as getting accounts, working simultaneously, or reviewing the history of changes made to documents? Which would you recommend to your group to use for this project, and why?

4. **Choices, Choices**

   There are many word processing software options. Describe the decision process you would use to choose among a free Web-based word processing application, an open source word processing application, and a standard packaged application if you are:

   a. Traveling abroad for a semester, visiting 15 different cities, and not carrying a notebook with you
   b. Staying at home for the term and compiling a capstone report using several hundred researched sources of information
   c. Working with three people from other colleges on a joint paper that will be presented at a conference at the end of the term

5. **Using OneNote**

   You have been assigned a research paper, which will be very extensive. You are required to collect information for the paper throughout the semester, so you need a good system to keep your notes, readings, and data organized. You've heard OneNote is a great tool for just this type of project, but since you have never used the software, you do not know where to start. Go to Microsoft Online and search on "Templates for OneNote." Find several good templates that will help you get started. What are the features of the templates you chose? Discuss which template you would most likely use, and why.

1. Required Software for the Job

Almost every profession requires some use of technology and software. Identify the field you would like to enter upon graduation, and then after doing some research, compile a list of applications you expect to use in your job. If possible, list a proprietary application, as well as open source and Web-based alternatives. Note those applications for which you will need training. If your chosen field currently does not require software, discuss why that may be the case. Do you foresee a time when software may be helpful? If so, what kind of software might that be?

2. Read and Understand the EULA

Before anyone installs or downloads software they have to accept the end user license agreement (EULA). Most of us rarely take the time to read a license agreement, but often there is important information stored in the EULA that a user should know about. Find an end user license agreement for a software product that you use frequently (such as Facebook or iTunes) and read it. Look particularly at the privacy policies and the sharing features. Write a brief summary about the types of information contained in the EULA.

3. Tracking Your Personal Finances

You are finally out on your own—graduated from college and working your first job. It's time to track how much you spend versus what you are earning. You really don't want to live from paycheck to paycheck, and want to begin a savings plan to build a rainy-day fund. Investigate online financial planning sites such as Mint (**www.mint .com**) and Yodlee (**www.yodlee.com**) and then choose the one that seems best to you. If you can, download a version of the software for your smartphone. Track your expenses for a few weeks, and identify areas in which you can cut back on your spending. What are the features of the software that you like? Discuss how this may or may not help you in your goal of achieving financial independence.

4. Going Beyond PowerPoint

Your boss is tired of looking at presentations with the same designs and features and has asked you to research different presentation software packages. In particular, she has suggested you look into Prezi (**www.prezi.com**) and SlideRocket (**www .sliderocket.com**). Using one of these software applications (both have free trials), create a presentation that compares these two products to Microsoft PowerPoint, Apple Keynote, and OpenOffice.org Impress.

Instructions: Some ideas are best understood by experimenting with them in our own minds. The following critical thinking questions are designed to demand your full attention but require only a comfortable chair—no technology.

1. Can You Reuse Software?

Several years ago you purchased Adobe Acrobat so you could make PDFs and edit and mark up PDFs. You have since changed computers, and your version of Acrobat is not compatible with the operating system on your new computer. You are required to purchase an upgrade of Adobe Acrobat to run on the new machine. Your sister wants to install the old version of Adobe Acrobat on her computer since you're not using it anymore. Do you think this will be legal to do? Why or why not?

2. What's Your App?

Small applications are being developed every day for smartphones. If you have a smartphone, what applications are the most useful to you? If you do not, what kind of app do you think would be the most useful? Describe an app that is currently not available that would be your "killer app."

3. Media Management

Less than a decade ago, most home users had few media files on their computer systems. Today, many users have a library of music, a collection of digitized movies, personal photo collections, and even a large set of recorded television shows. Examine three different software packages on the market today for managing these materials. What features do they need to make the PC the primary entertainment device for a home? What would make users move their PC from the office into the living room?

4. Living on the Cloud

Cloud computing is becoming more popular, and many users are working from the cloud and not even realizing it. What kinds of software applications are you using that are completely Web-based? Why do you use them instead of installed software applications? Envision a time when all software is Web-based and describe how being totally on the cloud would be an advantage. Also list some of the disadvantages a cloud-based environment might present.

5. Software Myths and Misconceptions

There are several myths and misconceptions about software, such as the 24-hour rule, the 80/20 rule, and the Abandonment rule. The 24-hour rule claims a person can download software for 24-hours, and then have the choice of deleting it or buying it. The 80/20 rule implies that for single-use licenses, a person can install software on both a work and home computer as long as work use is not more than 80 percent, and home use is not greater than 20 percent. The Abandonment rule claims that one can use software if it is no longer supported or created by a company that is no longer in business. Explain how you think each of these is a violation of copyright law.

four team time

team time

Software for Startups

Problem

You and your friends have decided to start Recycle Technology, a not-for-profit organization that would recycle and donate used computer equipment. In the first planning session, the group recognizes the need for certain software to help them with various parts of the business such as tracking inventory, designing notices, mapping addresses for pickup and delivery, and soliciting residents by phone or e-mail about recycling events, to name a few.

Task

Split your class into as many groups of four or five as possible. Make some groups responsible for just locating free or Web-based software solutions, and other groups responsible for finding proprietary solutions. Another group could be responsible for finding mobile app solutions. The groups will present and compare results with each other at the end of the project.

Process

1. Identify a team leader who will coordinate the project and record and present results.
2. Each team is to identify the various kinds of software that Recycle Technology needs. Consider software that will be needed for all the various tasks needed to run the organization such as communication, marketing, tracking, inventory management, and finance.
3. Create a detailed and organized list of required software applications. Depending on your team, you will specify either proprietary software or open source software.

Conclusion

Most organizations require a variety of software to accomplish different tasks. Compare your results with those of other team members. Were there applications that you didn't think about, but that other members did? How expensive is it to ensure that even the smallest company has all the software required to carry out daily activities, or can the needs be met with free, open source products?

Open Source Software

Ethical conduct is a stream of decisions you make all day long. In this exercise, you will research and then role-play a complicated ethical situation. The role you play might or might not match your own personal beliefs; in either case, your research and use of logic will enable you to represent the view assigned. An arbitrator will watch and comment on both sides of the arguments, and together the team will agree on an ethical solution.

Problem

Proprietary software has set restrictions on use and can be very expensive; while open source software is freely available for users to use as is, or change, improve, and redistribute. Open source software has become acceptable as a cost-effective alternative to proprietary software, so much so that it is reported that the increased adoption of open source software has caused a drop in revenue to the proprietary software industry. But determining which software to use involves more than just reducing the IT budget.

Research Areas to Consider

- Open source software (Linux, OpenOffice.org suite, and Mozilla.org)
- Proprietary software (Microsoft Windows and Office, Apple Mac OS X and iWork)
- Copyright licensing
- Open source development

Process

1. Divide the class into teams.
2. Research the areas cited above and devise a scenario in which someone is a proponent for open source software but is being rebuffed by someone who feels "you get what you pay for" and is a big proponent of using proprietary software.
3. Team members should write a summary that provides background information for their character—for example: open source proponent, proprietary developer, or arbitrator—and details their character's behaviors to set the stage for the role-playing event. Then, team members should create an outline to use during the role-playing event.
4. Team members should arrange a mutually convenient time to meet for the exchange, either using the collaboration features of MyITLab, the discussion board feature of Blackboard, or meeting in person.
5. Team members should present their case to the class, or submit a PowerPoint presentation for review by the rest of the class, along with the summary and resolution they developed.

Conclusion

As technology becomes ever more prevalent and integrated into our lives, more and more ethical dilemmas will present themselves. Being able to understand and evaluate both sides of the argument, while responding in a personally or socially ethical manner, will be an important skill.

using system **software**

the operating system, utility programs, and file management

Operating System Fundamentals

OBJECTIVES:

What software is included in system software? *(p. 204)*

What are the different kinds of operating systems? *(p. 205)*

What are the most common operating systems? *(p. 205)*

Ferenc Szelepcsenyi / Shutterstock.com

What the Operating System Does

OBJECTIVES:

How does the operating system provide a means for users to interact with the computer? *(p. 210)*

How does the operating system help manage resources such as the processor, memory, storage, hardware, and peripheral devices? *(p. 212)*

How does the operating system interact with application software? *(p. 216)*

 Active Helpdesk: Managing Hardware and Peripheral Devices: The OS

Ivancovlad / Shutterstock.com

The Boot Process: Starting Your Computer

OBJECTIVE:

How does the operating system help the computer start up? *(p. 217)*

 Active Helpdesk: Starting the Computer: The Boot Process

The Desktop and Window Features

OBJECTIVE:

What are the main desktop and window features? *(p. 220)*

 Sound Byte: Customizing Windows

Stanislav Popov / Shutterstock.com

Organizing Your Computer: File Management

OBJECTIVES:

How does the operating system help me keep my computer organized? *(p. 222)*

 Active Helpdesk: Organizing Your Computer: File Management

 Sound Byte: File Management

Infoimages / Shutterstock.com; Tuomas Kujansuu / iStockphoto.com

Utility Programs

OBJECTIVE:

What utility programs are included in system software, and what do they do? *(p. 229)*

 Active Helpdesk: Using Utility Programs

 **Sound Byte:** File Compression
Sound Byte: Hard Disk Anatomy Interactive
Sound Byte: Letting Your Computer Clean Up After Itself

Scan here for more info on How Cool Is This? ▶

how cool is *this?*

Have you ever wanted to capture what appears on your **monitor screen**? You can use the PrtScn (print screen) key on your keyboard, but that captures only the active window, and only onto the clipboard. You then need to crop and save the file for that **screen capture** to be useful. There are also screen capture software programs that you can purchase. However, Windows 7 includes the **Snipping Tool**, and Mac OS has **Grab** to capture an entire screen image or to "grab" a free-form or rectangular "snip" of any window or object on the screen. Once captured, you can use the Snipping Tool or Grab to **annotate**, save, or **share** the object. In Windows 7, you can find the Snipping Tool by clicking the Start button, selecting All Programs, and then opening the Accessories folder. In Mac OS, Grab is found in Utilities. For more features, try **Jing** (**www .techsmith.com/jing**), a freeware tool from Tech-Smith. Jing not only captures still screen shots, but also records video of on-screen action. You can share Jing files over the Web, via instant messaging, or by e-mail.

siloto/Shutterstock.com

System Software Basics

As you learned in the previous chapter, there are two basic types of software on your computer: application software and system software. **Application software** is the software you use to do everyday tasks at home and at work. **System software** is the set of programs that helps run the computer and coordinates instructions between application software and the computer's hardware devices. From the moment you turn on your computer to the time you shut it down, you are interacting with system software. System software consists of two primary types of programs: the operating system and utility programs.

What does system software do? System software manages the computer's resources. The **operating system (OS)** component of system software is a group of programs that controls how your computer system functions. The OS manages the computer's hardware, including the processor (also called the *central processing unit*, or *CPU*), memory, and storage devices, as well as peripheral devices such as the monitor and printer. The OS also provides a consistent means for software applications to work with the CPU, and it is responsible for the management, scheduling, and coordination of tasks as well as system maintenance. Your first interaction with the OS is the **user interface**—the features of the program such as the desktop, icons, and menus that allow the user to communicate with the computer system.

System software also includes utility programs. A **utility program** is a small program that performs many of the general housekeeping tasks for the computer, such as system maintenance and file compression.

Do all computers have operating systems? Every computer, from the smallest notebook to the largest supercomputer, has an operating system. Even cell phones, game consoles, automobiles, and some appliances have operating systems. The role of the OS is critical; the computer cannot operate without it. As explained more fully in the section of this chapter titled "What the Operating System Does," the operating system coordinates the flow of data and information through the computer system by coordinating the hardware, software, user interface, processor, and system memory.

Are all operating systems alike? Although most computer users can name only a few operating systems, many types exist. Some operating systems, such as those found in household appliances and car engines, are embedded in the device and don't require any user intervention at all. Some are proprietary systems developed specifically for the devices they manage. Some operating systems are available for personal and business use to run on personal computers or mobile devices (see Figure 5.1), and other operating systems coordinate resources for many users on a network. These operating systems were traditionally classified into categories, depending on the number of users they served (single user or multiple users) and the tasks they performed (single task or multitasks). However, as devices begin to converge in their functionalities, and the operating systems continue to become more powerful, the distinction in the traditional categorization of operating systems begins to blur.

For example, personal computers were at one time run by single-task, single-user operating systems such as the **Microsoft Disk Operating System (MS-DOS)**. MS-DOS (or DOS) was

Figure 5.1

Different operating systems are found on personal computers and mobile devices.

BERTRAND BECHARD/MAXPPP/Newscom

© Helen Sessions/Alamy; AP Photo/Paul Sakuma, File; Steve Parsons/PA Wire URN:11924820 (Press Association via AP Images); © Oso Media/Alamy; © Cliff Hide/Alamy

the first widely installed operating system in personal computers. Compared to the operating systems we are familiar with today, DOS was a highly user-unfriendly OS. To use it, you needed to type specific commands, and didn't have the option to click on **icons** (pictures that represent an object such as a software application or a file or folder) or choose from a **menu** or list of commands.

Eventually, operating systems such as Apple's Mac OS and Microsoft's Windows replaced DOS because these systems allowed a single user to **multitask**, that is, to perform more than one process at a time. (The Mac and Windows operating systems are discussed in more detail later in this chapter.)

Then, networking capabilities were added to these personal computer operating systems to facilitate sharing peripheral devices and Internet access among multiple computers at home. These systems, although still traditionally used as single-user, multitask operating systems, technically became multiuser, multitask operating systems because of their networking capabilities. Similar transitions are happening with mobile devices, as cell phones and PDAs (personal digital assistants) converge to smartphones and incorporate the functionalities of cameras and personal media players. Although smartphones were initially single-task devices, with combined functionalities, the newer devices are beginning to add multitasking capabilities.

In the next section, we will look at different types of operating systems that work with a variety of computers.

Types of Operating Systems

Operating systems can be categorized by the type of device in which they are installed, such as robots and specialized equipment with built-in computers, mainframes and network computers, mobile devices, and personal computers.

Real-Time Operating Systems

Why do machines with built-in computers need an operating system? Machinery that is required to perform a repetitive series of specific tasks in an exact amount of time requires a **real-time operating system (RTOS)**. Real-time operating systems, also referred to as *embedded systems*, require minimal user interaction. This type of operating system is a program with a specific purpose, and it must guarantee certain response times for particular computing tasks; otherwise, the machine is useless. The programs are written specifically for the needs of the devices and their functions. Therefore, there are no commercially available standard RTOS software programs. Devices that must perform regimented tasks or record precise results—such as measurement instruments found in the scientific, defense, and aerospace industries—require real-time operating systems. Examples include digital storage oscilloscopes and the Mars Reconnaissance Orbiter.

Where else are RTOSs in use today? You also encounter real-time operating systems in everyday life. They are in devices such as fuel-injection systems in car engines, automobile "infotainment" systems, inkjet printers, VoIP phones, and some medical devices, as well as some common appliances. Real-time operating systems are also found in many types of robotic equipment. Television stations use robotic cameras with real-time operating systems that glide across a suspended cable system to record sports events from many angles (see Figure 5.2).

What kind of operating system controls a simple cell phone? Unlike smartphones, simple cell phones are single-function devices; they only require operating systems that perform one task at a time. These devices generally have **firmware**, instructions permanently installed onto computer chips. Some firmware can be updated by connecting the device to the computer and downloading an upgrade from the manufacturer's Web site. Other devices, such as portable audio players, digital cameras, and gaming consoles, also use firmware.

Operating Systems for Networks, Servers, and Mainframes

What kind of operating system do networks use? A **multiuser operating system** (also known as a **network operating system**) enables more than one user to access the computer system at one time by efficiently handling and prioritizing requests from multiple users. Networks (groups of computers connected to each other for the purposes of communicating and sharing resources) require a multiuser operating

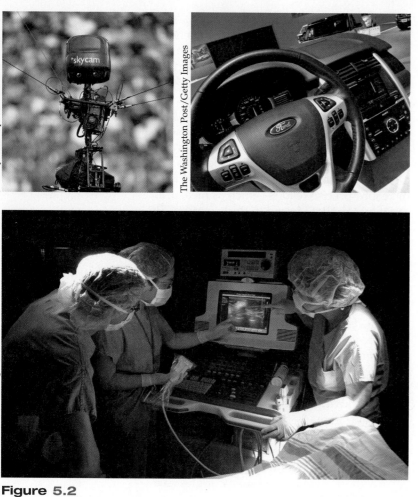

Figure 5.2

Devices such as TV sky cameras, cars, and medical equipment use real-time operating systems.

What is UNIX? UNIX is a multiuser, multitask operating system used as a network operating system, primarily with mainframes, although it is also often found on PCs. Developed in 1969 by Ken Thompson and Dennis Ritchie of AT&T's Bell Labs, the UNIX code was initially not proprietary—in other words, no company owned it. Rather, any programmer was allowed to use the code and modify it to meet his or her needs. Later, AT&T licensed the UNIX program code to the Santa Cruz Operation Group. UNIX is a brand that belongs to the company The Open Group, but any vendor that meets testing requirements and pays a fee can use the UNIX name. Individual vendors then modify the UNIX code to run specifically on their hardware. HP/UX from Hewlett-Packard, Oracle Solaris from Oracle Corporation, and AIX from IBM are some of the UNIX systems currently available in the marketplace.

What other kinds of computers require a multiuser operating system? Large corporations with hundreds or thousands of employees often use powerful computers known as *mainframes*. A **mainframe** is responsible for storing, managing, and simultaneously processing data from all users. Mainframe operating systems fall into the multiuser category. Examples include UNIX and IBM's IBM i and z/OS.

Supercomputers also use multiuser operating systems. Scientists and engineers use supercomputers to solve complex problems or to perform massive computations. Some supercomputers are single computers with multiple processors, whereas others consist of multiple computers that work together.

Operating Systems for Mobile Devices

What kind of operating system does a smartphone use? A **smartphone** does more than let the user make and answer phone calls. It also has productivity, media player, and camera features, as well as Web connectivity. Examples of smartphones include BlackBerry devices, Apple iPhone, HTC Thunderbolt, and Palm Pre. The most common operating systems that can be found on smartphones include Symbian by Nokia, BlackBerry by RIM, Windows Mobile by Microsoft, iPhone iOS by Apple, Android by Google, and webOS by Palm.

system because many users simultaneously access the **server**, which is the computer on a network that manages network resources such as printers.

The latest versions of Microsoft Windows and Mac OS X can be considered network operating systems; they enable users to set up basic networks for use in homes and small businesses. (A more complete discussion of Microsoft Windows and Mac OS can be found in the "Operating Systems for Personal Computers" section.) In larger networks, a more robust network operating system is installed on the server and manages all user requests, ensuring they do not interfere with each other. For example, on a network where users share a printer, the network would ensure the printer produces only one document at a time in the order in which the requests are made. The OS is therefore responsible for managing all the printer requests and making sure they are processed one at a time. Examples of network operating systems include Windows Server, Linux, and UNIX.

Initially, although multifunctional, smartphones were only capable of doing one task at a time. Now most modern smartphones have modest multitasking capabilities such as checking e-mail while on a phone call. Some, such as the iPhones on the AT&T network, provide greater multitasking and allow a user to talk while surfing the Web or using apps at the same time.

Do gaming consoles and personal media players require an operating system? Gaming systems, like Microsoft's Xbox 360, the Nintendo Wii, and the Sony PlayStation (see Figure 5.3), as well as personal media players like Microsoft's Zune and Apple's iPod, all require some form of customized system software that is developed specifically for the particular device. The system software includes system programs that control the device, as well as other programs that come with the personal media player or the gaming device. For example, the programs included with most portable media players allow users to manage music files on the player and to rip audio CDs. The operating systems on gaming consoles support Web browsing and file storage of media and photos as well as playing DVDs and games.

Florea Marius Catalin/iStockphoto.com

Lee Pettet/iStockphoto.com

Figure 5.3

Gaming devices such as the Nintendo Wii and PlayStation 3 have their own system software.

Operating Systems for Personal Computers

What is the Microsoft Windows operating system? Microsoft **Windows** began as an operating environment that worked with MS-DOS and incorporated a user-friendly interface like the one that was first introduced with Apple's operating system. In 1995, Microsoft released Windows 95, a comprehensive update that made changes to the user interface and incorporated multi-tasking capabilities. Windows XP was another major update; it provided networking capabilities in its consumer editions. The newest release of Microsoft's operating system, **Windows 7**, follows Windows Vista, and builds on the security and user interface upgrades that the Windows Vista release provided. It also

gives users with touch-screen monitors the ability to use touch commands to scroll, resize windows, pan, and zoom. What was once an operating system on which only one user could perform one task at a time is now a more robust operating system that can support home networking tasks. Over time, Windows improvements have concentrated on increasing user functionality and friendliness, improving Internet capabilities, and enhancing file privacy and security.

What is the difference between the various editions of Windows 7 operating systems? With each new version of its operating system, Microsoft continues to make improvements. However, it's still not a one-size-fits-all operating system. Windows 7 comes in several editions to accommodate different users. Those that are available for home users are Starter and Home Premium. Windows 7 Professional can be used by the home user, but is targeted toward small-business users. Windows 7 Ultimate is a full-featured operating system intended for businesses, but is available to home users as well. In addition, there are 32-bit and 64-bit versions of Windows. The 32-bit version is built for computers that have up to 4 GB of RAM. For those systems with more than 4 GB of RAM, a 64-bit version is required. Figure 5.4 outlines the features and benefits of each edition of Windows 7.

What is the Mac Operating System? In 1984, **Mac OS** became the first commercially available operating system to incorporate a graphical user interface (GUI) with user-friendly point-and-click technology. For more information on Mac OS, see the Technology in Focus feature "Computing Alternatives" on page 248.

Does it matter what operating system is on my computer? The type of processor in the computer determines which operating system a particular personal computer uses. The combination of operating system and processor is referred to as a computer's **platform**. For example, Microsoft Windows operating systems

Figure 5.4 | WINDOWS 7 EDITIONS

Edition	Description
Windows 7 Starter	This edition is designed to run on small netbooks and is for those users who have basic computing requirements. There is no Aero interface, and only 32-bit versions are available.
Windows 7 Home Premium	This edition incorporates multimedia functions as core components. No extra software is needed to run DVDs and other audio and video files. Networking as well as file and peripheral sharing across PCs are included.
Windows 7 Professional	As its name implies, this edition is aimed at the business market but is also appropriate for the advanced home user. This edition builds on Windows 7 Home Premium and features advanced networking capabilities.
Windows 7 Ultimate	This is the "ultimate" operating system for high-end PC users, gamers, multimedia professionals, and PC enthusiasts.

are designed to coordinate with a series of processors from Intel Corporation and Advanced Micro Devices (AMD), which share the same or similar sets of instructions. Originally, the Macintosh operating systems worked primarily with PowerPC processors from the Motorola Corporation and IBM, which were designed specifically for Apple computers. However, in 2006, Apple discontinued the use of PowerPC processors, and now uses Intel processors.

Most application software is also operating system dependent. For example, there are special Mac versions of Microsoft Office, Adobe Photoshop Elements, Intuit Quicken, and other "traditional" PC software applications.

Can I have more than one operating system on my computer? Some Mac users may want to have both Mac OS X and Windows on their machines. Or, you might want to test drive the newest operating system on your computer without uninstalling the previous version before you commit to an upgrade. Or perhaps you would like to have a Linux distribution to work with, in addition to your Windows operating system. The generous size of today's hard drives, as well as some additional software capabilities, enables users to run multiple operating systems on a single machine. A standard utility included in Mac OS X called Boot Camp allows you to boot into either Windows or OS X. But, if you want to run both Mac OS X and Windows operating systems at the same time, you could create virtual drives using virtualization software such as Parallels or VMware Fusion.

What are Web-based operating systems? Now that broadband Internet access and providing computer resources via the Internet (cloud computing) are becoming more commonplace, prototypes for Web-based operating systems are being developed. Actually, the terms *Web-based operating environment* and *portable or Web desktop* might be more accurate, because one still needs a computer, operating system, and Web browser to access a Web-based OS. The concept behind this movement is to enable complete portability of a user's computer experience.

Currently, most applications and files we use have been installed and saved on a specific computer and can be used only on that computer. A Web-based operating environment would allow users to access applications and content via the Web, regardless of the machine they are using. This means you would not need to lug your notebook computer everywhere you go. Instead, you would only need to find a computer that had Internet access to be able to have all of your applications and documents ready for you to resume work. Currently you could cobble together a similar experience by accessing Google Docs, Yahoo! Mail, and Dropbox, but with far less efficiency because that requires managing several different accounts and logins. A Web-based OS would enable you to have access to all of your settings and preferences, even a customized desktop image, as well as working documents, stored in an individual Web-based account for you to access anywhere and on any machine at any time.

Google is taking steps toward developing a complete Web-based system. Its Google Docs application and Chrome browser are the initial components of a completely Web-based operating environment. Another innovator in the Web desktop field is the open source product eyeOS (**www.eyeos.org**).

SOUND BYTE Customizing Windows

In this Sound Byte, you'll find out how to customize your desktop. You'll learn how to configure the desktop, set up a screen saver, change pointer options, customize the Start menu, and manage user accounts.

Upgrading Your Operating System

If you have had your computer for a year or two, you may be faced with the decision of whether to upgrade to the newest release version of your operating system (such as going from Windows Vista to Windows 7). Here are a few key things to consider before taking the plunge:

- **Is your current operating system still supported?** When it deploys new versions of operating systems, the company may stop supporting older versions. If your current version will no longer be supported, it's best to upgrade to a newer version.

- **Are there significant features in the new version that you want?** Operating systems are often upgraded to provide extra security, better performance, and additional features that are intended to make your computer experience more efficient, and perhaps even more fun. But, if the only features the new version offers are ones you don't need or can live without, you should reconsider upgrading.

- **Will your hardware work with the new OS?** Check the minimum operating requirements (required RAM, processor speed, hard drive space, etc.) of the new version to ensure that your computer can handle the workload of the new software. You will also need to

make sure drivers for the new OS are available for all your hardware devices and peripherals to ensure they will work properly with the new OS. Microsoft has made this easy with Windows Upgrade Advisor, which you can download from Microsoft's Web site. The Upgrade Advisor scans your hardware, devices, and installed programs for compatibility, advises you on how to resolve any issues found, and recommends what you should do before upgrading.

- **Is your application software compatible with the new version of the OS?** Usually, application software works fine with a new version of an OS. Sometimes it doesn't. Check with the software vendors regarding compatibility, especially if you're upgrading to a 64-bit system. Although Windows 7 has a compatibility feature that allows you to run some software in an earlier version of the operating system if it is not compatible with Windows 7, it doesn't work with all older file formats.

Before starting the upgrade, you should back up all your data files so you won't lose anything accidentally during the upgrading process. Backup and Restore in Windows makes this job less of a hassle.

What is Linux? Linux is an open source operating system designed for use on personal computers and as a network operating system. Open source software is freely available for anyone to use or modify as they wish. The Linux operating system is based on the central programming code of an operating system, and the rest of the code is from the GNU (pronounced "g-noo") Project and other sources. Linux began in 1991 as a part-time project of Finnish university student Linus Torvalds, who wanted to create a free OS to run on his home computer. He posted his OS code to the Web for others to use and modify. It has since been tweaked by scores of programmers as part of the Free Software Foundation GNU Project (**www.gnu.org**).

Linux has a reputation as a stable OS that is not subject to crashes or failures. Because the code is open and available to anyone, Linux can be modified or updated quickly by hundreds of other programmers around the world to meet virtually any new operating system need. For example, only a few weeks were necessary

to get the Linux OS ready for the Intel Xeon processor, a feat unheard of in proprietary OS development. Some Linux-based operating systems have been modified to run on iPods and gaming systems. Linux is also gaining popularity among computer manufacturers, which have begun to ship it with some of their latest PCs.

Where else is Linux used? Android, the new operating system developed by Google, is Linux-based. Because the overall size of Android is much smaller than that of Windows, many netbook users choose to use it in place of the factory-installed Windows operating system (see Figure 5.5). It is also popular on smartphones. Another Linux-based newcomer to the OS market is MeeGo, a joint project between Nokia and Intel, which is designed for smartphones, netbooks, and entry-level personal computers.

Where can I get Linux? You can download open source versions of Linux for free from Linux distributors such as Mandriva, Ubuntu, Fedora, Suse, Debian GNU/Linux, and Gentoo Linux. However,

© Oleksiy Maksymenko Photography/Alamy

Figure 5.5

Developed by Google, the Android operating system is based on Linux and runs easily on netbooks.

Proprietary software such as Microsoft Windows and Mac OS is developed by corporations and sold for profit. This means that the **source code**, the actual lines of instructional code that make the program work, is not accessible to the general public. Without being able to access the source code, it's difficult for a user to modify the software or see exactly how the program author constructed various parts of the system.

Restricting access to the source code protects companies from having their programming ideas stolen, and it prevents customers from using modified versions of the software. However, in the late 1980s, computer specialists became concerned that large software companies (such as Microsoft) were controlling a large portion of market share and driving out competitors. They also felt that proprietary software was too expensive and contained too many bugs (errors).

These people felt that software should be developed without a profit motive and distributed with its source code free for all to see. The theory was that if many computer specialists examined, improved, and changed the source code, a more full-featured, bug-free product would result. Hence, the open source movement was born.

So, if an operating system such as Linux is free and relatively bug-free, why does Windows, which users must pay for, have such a huge market share, and why does Linux have less than 1 percent of the desktop market? One reason is that corporations and individuals have grown accustomed to one thing that proprietary software makers can provide: technical support. It is almost impossible to provide technical support for open source software because anyone can freely modify it; thus, there is no specific developer to take responsibility for technical support. Similarly, corporations have been reluctant to install open source software extensively because of the cost of the internal staff of programmers that must support it.

Companies such as Red Hat, Ubuntu, and Xandros have been combating this problem. Red Hat offers a free, open source operating system called Fedora (see Figure 5.6). In addition, Red Hat has modified the original Linux source code and markets a version, Red Hat Enterprise Linux, as a proprietary program. Fedora is the testing ground for what eventually goes into this proprietary program. Red Hat Enterprise Linux 6 is the current system on the market, and comes in versions for servers and desktops. Purchasers of Red Hat Enterprise Linux receive a warranty and technical support. Packaging open source software in this manner has made its use much more attractive to businesses. As a result, many Web servers are hosted on computers running Linux.

AP Photo/Paul Sakuma

Figure 5.6

Companies like Red Hat provide free or low-cost Linux software, such as Fedora, but technical support is not often available.

several versions of Linux are more proprietary in nature and must be purchased. These versions come with support and other features that are not generally associated with the open source Linux. Red Hat has been packaging and selling versions of Linux since 1994 and is probably the best-known Linux distributor. For a full listing and explanation of all Linux distributors, visit DistroWatch (**www.distrowatch.com**). For more information on Linux, see the Technology in Focus feature "Computing Alternatives" on page 248.

What the Operating System Does

As shown in Figure 5.7, the operating system is like an orchestra's conductor. It coordinates and directs the flow of data and information through the computer system. In doing so, the OS performs several specific functions:

- It provides a way for the user to interact with the computer.
- It manages the processor, or CPU.
- It manages the memory and storage.
- It manages the computer system's hardware and peripheral devices.
- It provides a consistent means for software applications to work with the CPU.

In this section, we look at each of these functions in detail.

The User Interface

How does the operating system control how I interact with my computer? The operating system provides a user interface that enables you to interact with the computer. As noted earlier, the first personal computers had a DOS operating system with a command-driven interface, as shown in Figure 5.8a. A **command-driven interface** is one in which you enter commands to communicate with the computer system. The DOS commands were not always easy to understand; as a result, the interface proved to be too complicated for the average user. Therefore, PCs were used primarily in business and by professional computer operators.

Manages computer hardware and peripherals

Figure 5.7

The operating system is the orchestra conductor of your computer, coordinating its many activities and devices.

Provides a consistent interaction between applications and CPU

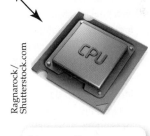

The Operating System

Provides a user interface

The command-driven interface was later improved by incorporating a menu-driven interface, as shown in Figure 5.8b. A **menu-driven interface** is one in which you choose commands from menus displayed on the screen. Menu-driven interfaces eliminated the need for users to know every command because they could select most of the commonly used commands from a menu. However, they were still not easy enough for most people to use.

Manages memory and storage

Manages the processor

What kind of interface do operating systems use today?
Current personal computer operating systems such as Microsoft Windows and Mac OS use a **graphical user interface**, or **GUI** (pronounced "gooey"). Unlike command- and menu-driven interfaces, GUIs display graphics and use the point-and-click technology of the mouse and cursor, making them much more user-friendly.

Linux-based operating systems do not have a single default GUI interface. Instead, users are free to choose among many commercially available and free interfaces, such as GNOME and KDE, each of which provides a different look and feel. For example, GNOME (pronounced "gah-NOHM") actually allows you to select which interface (Windows or Mac) you'd like your system to have. This means that if you're using Linux for the first time, you don't have to learn a new interface; you just use the one you're most comfortable with.

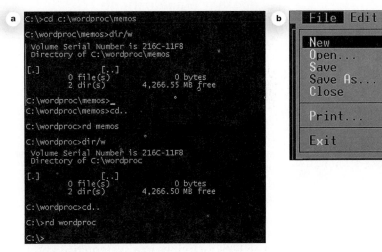

Figure 5.8

(a) A command-driven interface. (b) A menu-driven interface.

The Internet is a fantastic tool, but only if you can access it. In an effort to give children in developing countries a better opportunity to "learn, share, and create," the One Laptop per Child (OLPC) initiative was founded by Nicholas Negroponte and other faculty from MIT Media Lab, in conjunction with partners such as Google, AMD, and News Corporation. The mission of OLPC (**www.laptop.org**) is to ensure that all school-aged children in lesser-developed communities receive their own personal computers so that they are no longer excluded from the educational, economic, and entertainment benefits that computers can provide. Laptops have been distributed to over 2 million children worldwide. Most of the users are in Latin America and Africa, in countries such as Uruguay, Peru, Mongolia, Nigeria, Ethiopia, and Rwanda. Uruguay, for example, is the first major country in the world that is using the OLPC program to provide laptops to every elementary school child.

This ambitious project to develop and distribute a low-cost notebook computer (currently, the cost is $199) would provide access to electronic textbooks and other learning aids—and eventually the Internet. The main thrust of the project is to overcome the so-called digital divide (the gap between people who have access to computers and those who don't) and provide computing resources to everyone regardless of their financial means.

Figure 5.9

The XO can be easily converted from a traditional notebook to an e-book reader. A new tablet-like device, the XO-3, is currently being developed, and is scheduled for release in 2012.

The notebook itself is revolutionary in design (see Figure 5.9). Called the XO (the latest version is XO-1.5), the notebook is small and has a comfortable, child-sized, built-in handle. It also has a tablet-like monitor that can twist to turn the notebook into an electronic book (e-book) reader, which is critical in areas where books are hard to come by. The outside of the notebook is rugged and child-friendly. In addition, it is power efficient, running on less than one-tenth the power a standard notebook requires. Because access to electricity is minimal in many of the project's target areas, the notebook is self-powered by an easy-to-use pull string.

At the core of the XO laptop is Sugar, the operating system. It is based on open source code components from Red Hat's Fedora version of the Linux operating system, but has a user interface that is completely different from Windows, Mac OS, or Linux. The developers really thought about how the users of the notebook would interact with the device. The OLPC notebooks will most likely be the first computer that many of these children use, and so the user interface was designed to be as intuitive as possible.

The operating system focuses on activities rather than on applications. When the machine powers up, the first image is that of the XO man (an O on top of an X) in the middle of a circle. It is surrounded by icons that represent home, friends, and neighborhood. The computer

Processor Management

Why does the operating system need to manage the processor? When you use your computer, you are usually asking the CPU to perform several tasks at once. For example, you might be printing a Word document, chatting with your friends on Facebook, watching a movie using the Blu-ray drive, and working on an Excel spreadsheet—all at the same time, or at least what appears to be at the same time. Although the processor is the powerful brain of the computer, processing all of its instructions and performing all of its calculations, it needs the OS to arrange for the execution of all these activities in a systematic way, creating the appearance that everything is happening simultaneously.

To do so, the operating system assigns a slice of its time to each activity that requires the processor's attention. The OS must then switch among different processes millions of times a second to make it appear that everything is happening seamlessly. Otherwise, you wouldn't be able to watch a movie and print at the same time without experiencing delays in the process.

How exactly does the operating system coordinate all the activities? When you create and print a document in Word while also watching a Blu-ray movie, for example, many different devices in the computer system are involved, including your keyboard, mouse, Blu-ray drive, and printer. Every keystroke, every mouse click, and each signal to the printer and from the

Courtesy of One Laptop Per Child

includes a built-in microphone and webcam for children to create their own multimedia. For example, the multimedia tool allows children to add music to their drawings. Other activities include browsing the Internet, chatting, text editing, and playing games. At the core of each activity is the ability to collaborate, which facilitates the community learning experience. To enhance collaboration, the notebooks are all interconnected in a wireless mesh network, providing the potential for every activity to be a networked activity. Browsing, for example, would no longer be an isolated, individual activity; it could also be a collaborative group experience (see Figure 5.10a). Wireless capabilities also help extend the community beyond its physical borders. These computers make it possible for a child in Africa, for example, to connect with another child in Latin America.

In addition, the operating system uses a journaling technique for arranging and organizing files (see Figure 5.10b). The file system records what the child has done (rather than just what the student has saved), working as a scrapbook of the student's interactions with the computer as well as with peers. The journal can be tagged, searched, and sorted in a variety of ways.

Another general concept behind the operating system is that children learn through doing, so the software puts an emphasis on tools for exploration and expression, as well as encouraging students to learn by helping each other. Because Sugar is built on an open source platform, it also encourages students to explore how it works and to modify the code to meet their individual preferences.

The OLPC is not the only organization interested in increasing the reach of technology to those in less-developed nations. Intel has gone forward with its own program and produced the Classmate PC. Although the Classmate PC is more closely aligned with the traditional Windows-based PC model—it runs on either Windows or the open source OS Mandriva Discovery 2007 (a version of Linux)—it offers some of the

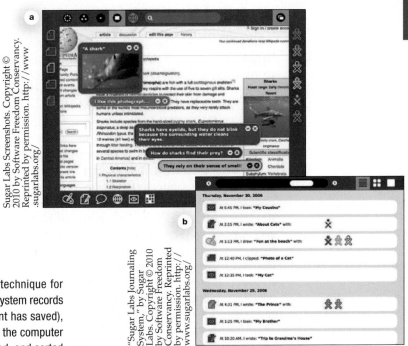

Figure 5.10

(a) One student shares a browsing experience with several others.
(b) The journaling system chronicles what the student saves as well as the student's interaction with the machine and with others.

same user-friendly hardware features as the XO machine does, such as the swivel monitor that converts to a tablet PC. Some reviewers and followers of both projects have offered the opinion that the Classmate PC is better suited for the older student user, whereas the XO laptop is geared toward a younger, less sophisticated user. With so many children waiting to be exposed to technology and to a more fun and intuitive learning process, there is most likely room in the market for both machines.

Blu-ray drive creates an action, or **event**, in the respective device (keyboard, mouse, Blu-ray drive, or printer) to which the operating system responds.

Sometimes these events occur sequentially (such as when you type characters one at a time), but other events involve two or more devices working concurrently (such as the printer printing while you continue to type and watch a movie). Although it looks as though all the devices are working at the same time, in fact, the OS switches back and forth among processes, controlling the timing of events the processor works on.

For example, assume you are typing and want to print a document. When you tell your computer to print your document, the printer generates a unique signal

called an **interrupt** that tells the operating system that it is in need of immediate attention. Every device has its own type of interrupt, which is associated with an **interrupt handler**, a special numerical code that prioritizes the requests. These requests are placed in the interrupt table in the computer's primary memory (random access memory, or RAM). The operating system processes the task assigned a higher priority before processing a task that has been assigned a lower priority. This is called **preemptive multitasking**.

In our example, when it receives the interrupt from the printer, the operating system suspends the CPU's typing activity and Blu-ray activity, and puts a "memo" in a special location in RAM called a *stack*.

The memo is a reminder of what the CPU was doing before it started to work on the printer request. The CPU then retrieves the printer request from the interrupt table and begins to process it. On completion of the printer request, the CPU goes back to the stack, retrieves the memo it placed about the keystroke or Blu-ray activity, and returns to that task until it is interrupted again, in a very quick and seamless fashion.

What happens if there is more than one document waiting to be printed? The operating system also co-ordinates multiple activities for peripheral devices such as printers. When the processor receives a request to send information to the printer, it first checks with the operating system to ensure that the printer is not already in use. If it is, the OS puts the request in an-other temporary storage area in RAM, called the *buffer*. The request then waits in the buf-fer until the **spooler**, a program that helps coordinate all print jobs currently being sent to the printer, indicates the printer is avail-able. If more than one print job is waiting, a line (or *queue*) is formed so that the printer can process the requests in order.

Memory and Storage Management

Why does the operating system have to manage the computer's memory? As the operating system coordinates the activities of the processor, it uses RAM as a temporary storage area for instructions and data the processor needs. The processor then accesses these instructions and data from RAM when it is ready to process them. The OS is therefore responsible for coordinating the space allocations in RAM to ensure that there is enough space for all of the pending instructions and data. It then clears the items from RAM when the processor no longer needs them.

Does the amount of RAM on a system control the type of OS I get? Until recently, the maximum amount of RAM found on most personal computers was 4 GB. That was considered a lot! Now, many personal computer systems that are reasonably priced provide for 8 GB or more of RAM. Systems that offer more than 4 GB of RAM require a 64-bit version of Win-dows. Although there are other factors involved in determining what operating system you get, determining the bit-version is important. At the moment, not all ap-plications and devices are compatible with 64-bit systems. If you purchase a 64-bit system, you will need to make sure that all your hardware and software programs are updated to work well with the 64-bit ver-sion of your operating system. To assist you in this process, Micro-soft has created the Windows 7 Upgrade Advisor. This down-loadable free program checks to determine whether your computer is compatible in all respects with Windows 7, including the 64-bit compatibility. If there is incompat-ibility, Windows 7 allows you the option of running in a compatibility mode to emulate a 32-bit system.

Can my system ever run out of RAM? RAM has limited capacity. Like most users, over time you will expand how you use your computer by adding new software and new peripherals. Most com-puters sold for home use have between 2 and 12 GB of RAM. If you have an older system with 1 or 2 GB of RAM, it might be sufficient if you're running a few programs at the same time. But, if you start installing and using software with greater RAM re-quirements, your system might not respond well. For example, if you want to upgrade to Windows 7, the minimum requirement for the operating system using minimal capabilities is 1 GB of RAM. Such limited RAM requirements are fine if you are using a netbook that is running Windows 7 Starter edition. However, most other systems that run more robust editions of Windows 7 may be challenged if they have only 1 GB of RAM, especially if you run graphic-inten-sive programs such as Adobe Photoshop, many gaming applications, or even the lat-est version of Microsoft Office. If you want to incorporate the translucent Aero user interface themes that are available in some versions of Windows 7, your system should have at least 2 GB of RAM and a video card with at least 256 MB of RAM. As you add and upgrade software and increase your us-age of the computer system, you will likely find that the amount of RAM you once found to be sufficient is no longer enough.

What happens if my computer runs out of RAM? When there isn't enough RAM for the operating system to store the required data and instructions, the operat-ing system borrows from the more spacious hard drive. This process of optimizing RAM storage by borrowing hard drive space is called **virtual memory**. As shown in Figure 5.11, when more RAM is needed, the operating system swaps out from RAM the data or instructions that have not been recently used and moves them to a temporary storage area on the hard drive called the **swap file** (or **page file**). If the data or instructions in the swap file are needed later, the operating system swaps them back into active RAM and replaces them in the hard drive's swap file with less active data or instructions. This process of swapping is known as **paging**.

Can I ever run out of virtual memory? Only a portion of the hard drive is allocated to virtual memory. You can manually change this setting to increase the amount of hard drive space allocated, but eventually your computer system will become sluggish as it is forced to page more and more often. This condition of excessive paging is called **thrashing**. The solution to this problem is to increase the amount of RAM in your system so that it will not be necessary for it to send data and instructions to virtual memory.

How does the operating system manage storage? If it weren't for the operating system, the files and applications you save to the hard drive and other storage locations would be anunorganized mess. Fortunately, the OS has a file-management system that keeps track of the name and location of each file you save and the programs you install. We will talk more about file management later in this chapter.

Hardware and Peripheral Device Management

How does the operating system manage the hardware and peripheral devices? Each device attached to your computer comes with a special program called a **device driver** that facilitates communication between the hardware device and the operating system. Because the OS must be able to communicate with every device in the computer system, the device driver translates the device's specialized commands into commands that the operating system can understand, and vice versa. Devices would not function without the proper device drivers because the OS would not know how to communicate with them.

Do I always need to install drivers? Today, most devices, such as flash drives, mice, keyboards, and many digital cameras, come with the driver already installed in Windows. The devices whose drivers are included in Windows are called Plug and Play devices. **Plug and Play (PnP)** is a software and hardware standard designed to facilitate the installation of new hardware in PCs by including in the OS the drivers these devices need in order to run. Because the OS includes this software, incorporating a new device into your computer system seems automatic. Plug and Play enables users to plug a new device into a port on the system unit, turn on the computer, and immediately play (use) the device. The OS automatically recognizes the device and its driver without any further user manipulations of the system.

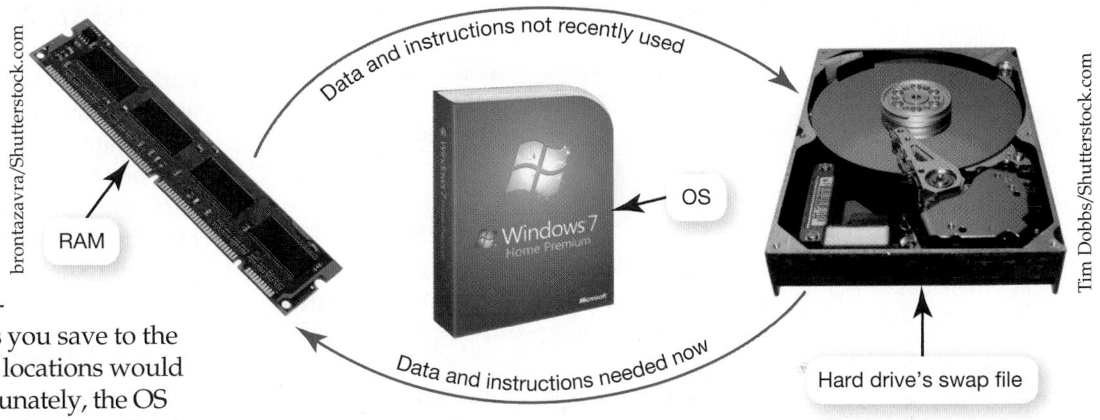

Data and instructions not recently used

OS

Windows 7 Home Premium

brontazavra/Shutterstock.com

RAM

Data and instructions needed now

Hard drive's swap file

Tim Dobbs/Shutterstock.com

What happens if the device is not Plug and Play? Some current devices, such as many types of printers and many older devices, are not Plug and Play. When you install a non–PnP device, you will be prompted to insert the driver that was provided with the device. If you obtain a non-PnP device secondhand and do not receive the device driver, or if you are required to update the device driver, you can often download the necessary driver from the manufacturer's Web site. You can also go to Web sites such as DriverZone.com (**www.driverzone.com**) or DriverGuide (**www.driverguide.com**) to locate drivers.

Can I damage my system by installing a device driver? Occasionally, when you install a driver, your system may become unstable (that is, programs may stop responding, certain

Figure 5.11

Virtual memory borrows excess storage capacity from the hard drive when there is not enough capacity in RAM.

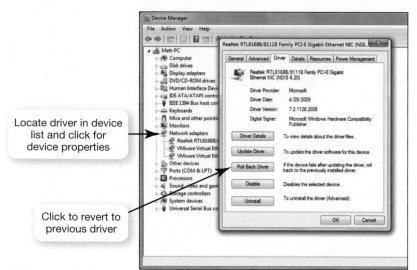

Locate driver in device list and click for device properties

Click to revert to previous driver

Figure 5.12

The Roll Back Driver feature in Windows removes a newly installed driver and replaces it with the last one that worked.

>To access the Device Manager window, click the **Start** button, **Control Panel**, **Hardware and Sound group**; then in the **Devices and Printers** group, click the **Device Manager** link. To display the Properties dialog box, double click on a device, then select **Properties**. Click the **Driver** tab.

actions may cause a crash, or the device or the entire system may stop working). Although this is uncommon, it can happen. Fortunately, to remedy the problem, Windows has a Roll Back Driver feature that removes a newly installed driver, and replaces it with the last one that worked (see Figure 5.12).

Software Application Coordination

How does the operating system help application software run on the computer? Application software feeds the CPU the instructions it needs to process data. These instructions take the form of computer code. Every computer program, no matter what its type or manufacturer, needs to interact with the CPU. For programs to work with the CPU, they must contain code that the CPU recognizes. Rather than having the same blocks of code for similar procedures in each program, the operating system includes the blocks of code—each called an **application programming interface (API)**—that application software needs in order to interact with the OS. Microsoft DirectX, for example, is a group of multimedia APIs built into the

ACTIVE HELP-DESK

Managing Hardware and Peripheral Devices: The OS

In this Active Helpdesk call, you'll play the role of a helpdesk staffer, fielding calls about how the operating system manages memory, storage, hardware, and peripheral devices.

Windows operating system that improves graphics and sounds when you're playing games or watching video on your PC.

What are the advantages of using APIs? To create applications that can communicate with the operating system, software programmers need only refer to the API code blocks when they write an application. They don't need to include the entire code sequence in the application. APIs not only prevent redundancies in software code, but also make it easier for software developers to respond to changes in the operating system.

Large software developers such as Microsoft have many applications under their corporate umbrella and use the same APIs in all or most of their applications. Because APIs coordinate with the operating system, all applications that have incorporated these APIs have similar interface features, such as toolbars and menus. Therefore, many features of the applications have the same look. An added benefit to this system is that applications sharing these formats can easily exchange data with each other. As such, it's easy to create a chart in Microsoft Excel from data in Microsoft Access and incorporate the finished chart into a Microsoft Word document.

The Boot Process: Starting Your Computer

Many things happen quickly between the time you turn on the computer and the time when it is ready for you to start using it. As you learned earlier, all data and instructions (including the operating system) are stored in RAM while your computer is on. When you turn off your computer, RAM is wiped clean of all its data (including the OS). How does the computer know what to do when you turn it on if there is nothing in RAM? It runs through a special boot process (or start-up process) to load the operating system into RAM. The term *boot*, from *bootstrap loader* (a small program used to start a larger program), alludes to the straps of leather, called *bootstraps*, that men used to use to help them pull on their boots. This is the source of the expression "pull yourself up by your bootstraps."

Power Management: Greening Your Notebook

More so than ever, we are concerned about sustainability and using products that will have little to no long-term impact on the planet. Since the majority of users leave PCs on at night or for long periods of time for various reasons, a lot of energy is wasted.

Fortunately, the newest operating systems have better power management control features. In Windows 7, notebook users can adjust their power management settings with just one click by hovering over the battery in the task pane.

You can make some easy changes to help extend the life of your notebook battery and waste less power, including:

- Lowering the brightness and dimming the display while the system is idle. By default, Windows 7 dims the display if the system is idle for 2 minutes on battery power, or 5 minutes when plugged in.
- Set the timer to turn off the display or put the computer to sleep more quickly (see Figure 5.13).

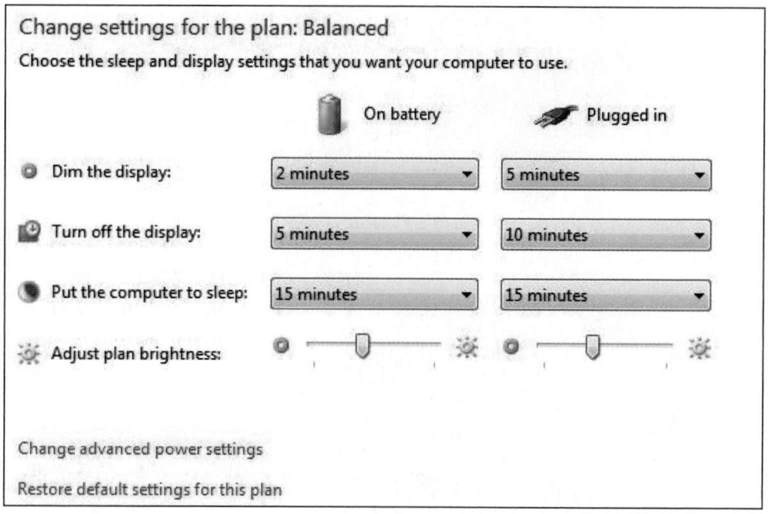

Change settings for the plan: Balanced
Choose the sleep and display settings that you want your computer to use.

	On battery	Plugged in
Dim the display:	2 minutes	5 minutes
Turn off the display:	5 minutes	10 minutes
Put the computer to sleep:	15 minutes	15 minutes
Adjust plan brightness:		

Change advanced power settings

Restore default settings for this plan

Figure 5.13

Adjusting the power management setting in Windows can help to extend the life of your battery and waste less power.

What are the steps involved in the boot process? As illustrated in Figure 5.14, the **boot process** consists of four basic steps:

1. The basic input/output system (BIOS) is activated by powering on the CPU.
2. The BIOS checks that all attached devices are in place (called a **power-on self-test** or **POST**).
3. The operating system is loaded into RAM.
4. Configuration and customization settings are checked.

How can I tell if my computer is entering the boot process? When you boot up on a PC with Windows or on a Mac, you will see the Windows or Mac OS logo display on the monitor, indicating the progress of the start-up process. Once the boot process has completed, the computer is ready to accept commands and data. Let's look at each of these steps in more detail.

Step 1: Activating BIOS

What's the first thing that happens after I turn on my computer? In the first step of the boot process, the CPU activates the **basic input/output system (BIOS)**. BIOS (pronounced "BAHY-ohs") is a program that manages the exchange of data between the operating system and all the input and output devices attached to the system, hence its name. BIOS is also responsible for loading the OS into RAM from its permanent location on the hard drive.

BIOS itself is stored on a special read-only memory (ROM) chip on the motherboard. Unlike data stored in RAM, data stored in ROM is permanent and is not erased when the power is turned off.

Step 2: Performing the Power-On Self-Test

How does the computer determine whether the hardware is working properly? The first job BIOS performs is to ensure that essential peripheral devices are attached and operational. As mentioned already, this process is called the power-on self-test, or POST. The POST consists of a test on the video card and video memory, a BIOS identification process, and a memory test to ensure that memory chips are working properly.

The BIOS compares the results of the POST with the various hardware configurations that are permanently stored in CMOS (pronounced "see-moss"). CMOS, which stands for *complementary metal-oxide semiconductor*, is a special kind of memory that uses almost no power. A little battery provides

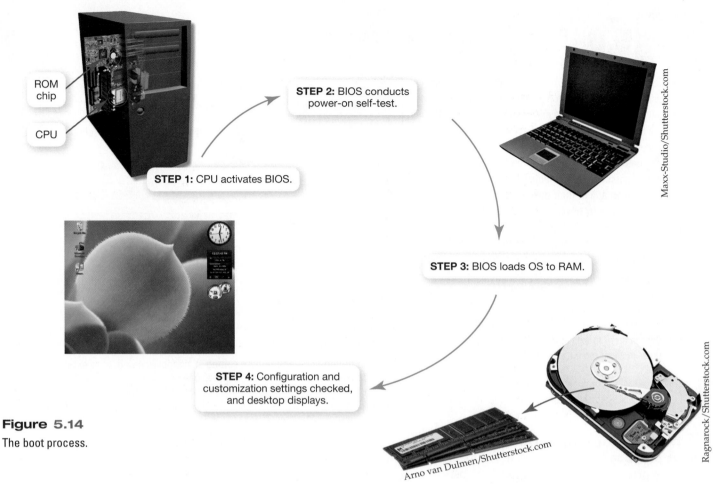

STEP 1: CPU activates BIOS.

STEP 2: BIOS conducts power-on self-test.

STEP 3: BIOS loads OS to RAM.

STEP 4: Configuration and customization settings checked, and desktop displays.

Maxx-Studio/Shutterstock.com

Ragnarock/Shutterstock.com

Arno van Dulmen/Shutterstock.com

ROM chip

CPU

Figure 5.14
The boot process.

enough power so that the CMOS contents will not be lost after the computer is turned off. CMOS contains information about the system's memory, types of disk drives, and other essential input and output hardware components. If the results of the POST compare favorably to the hardware configurations stored in CMOS, the boot process continues. If new hardware has been installed, this will cause the POST to disagree with the hardware configurations in CMOS, and you will be alerted that new hardware has been detected.

Step 3: Loading the Operating System

How does the operating system get loaded into RAM? When the first two steps are successfully completed, BIOS goes through a preconfigured list of devices in its search for the drive that contains the **system files**, which are the main files of the operating system. When it is located, the operating system loads into RAM from its permanent storage location on the hard drive.

Once the system files are loaded into RAM, the **kernel** (or **supervisor program**) is

loaded. The kernel is the essential component of the operating system. It is responsible for managing the processor and all other components of the computer system. Because it stays in RAM the entire time your computer is powered on, the kernel is said to be *memory resident*. Other parts of the OS that are less critical stay on the hard drive and are copied over to RAM on an as-needed basis so that RAM is managed more efficiently. These programs are referred to as *nonresident*. Once the kernel is loaded, the operating system takes over control of the computer's functions.

Step 4: Checking Further Configurations and Customizations

When are the other components and configurations of the system checked? CMOS checks the configuration of memory and essential peripherals in the beginning of the boot process. In this last phase of the boot process, the operating system checks the registry for the configuration of other system components. The **registry** contains all of the different configurations (settings) used by the OS and by other applications. It contains the customized settings you put into place, such as mouse speed and the display settings, as well as instructions as to which programs should be loaded first.

Why do I sometimes need to enter a login name and password at the end of the boot process? In a networked environment, such as that found at most colleges, the operating system serves many users. To determine whether a user is authorized to use the system (for example, whether a user is a valid student or college employee), authorized users are given a login name and password. The verification of your login name and password is called **authentication**. The authentication process blocks unauthorized users from entering the system.

On your home computer, you also may need to input a password to log in to your user account on your computer after your computer has completely booted up. Even in a home environment, all users with access to a Windows computer can have their own user accounts. Users can set up a password to protect their account from being accessed by another user without permission. For more information on selecting a good password, see Chapter 9.

How do I know if the boot process is successful? The entire boot process takes only a few minutes to complete. If the entire system is checked out and loaded properly, the process completes by displaying a desktop screen image. The computer system is now ready to accept your first command.

Handling Errors in the Boot Process

What should I do if my computer doesn't boot properly? Sometimes problems occur during the boot process. Fortunately, you have several options for correcting the situation. If you have recently installed new software or hardware, try uninstalling it. (Make sure you use the Uninstall a program feature in the Control Panel to remove the software.) If the problem no longer occurs when rebooting, you have determined the cause of the problem and can reinstall the device or software. If the problem does not go away, the first option is to restart your computer in Safe mode.

What is Safe mode? Sometimes Windows does not boot properly, and you end up with a screen that says "Safe Mode" in the corners, as shown in Figure 5.15. Alternatively, you can boot directly into

Starting the Computer: The Boot Process

In this Active Helpdesk call, you'll play the role of a helpdesk staffer, fielding calls about how the operating system helps the computer start up.

Safe mode by pressing the F8 key during the boot process before the Windows logo appears. **Safe mode** is a special diagnostic mode designed for troubleshooting errors. When the system is in Safe mode, only essential devices—such as the mouse, keyboard, and monitor—function. Even the regular graphics device driver will not be activated in Safe mode. Instead, the system runs in the most basic graphics mode, eliminating any screen images and nonessential icons and resulting in a neutral screen. While in Safe mode, you can use the **Device Manager**, a feature in the operating system that lets you view and change the properties of all devices attached to your computer. Safe mode boots Windows with only the original Microsoft Windows drivers that are required to boot the computer.

If Windows detects a problem in the boot process, it will add **Last Known Good Configuration** to the Windows Advanced Options Menu (also accessible by pressing the F8 key during the boot process). Every

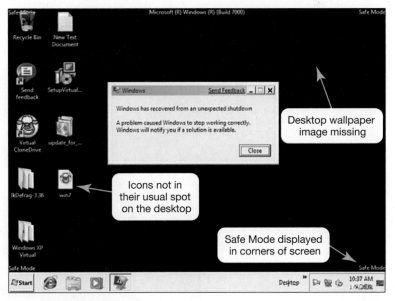

Figure 5.15

If there is an error in the boot process, your system might boot into Safe mode. Safe mode offers functionality that is limited but sufficient to allow you to perform diagnostic testing.

time your computer boots successfully, a configuration of the boot process is saved. When you choose to boot with the Last Known Good Configuration, the operating system starts your computer by using the registry information that was saved during the last shutdown. Safe mode and Last Known Good Configuration are the two most widely used methods of booting into Windows when a user cannot do so with the current configuration. Finally, if all other attempts to reboot fail, try a System Restore to roll back to a past configuration. System Restore is covered in more detail later in this chapter.

What should I do if my keyboard or another device doesn't work after I boot my computer? Sometimes during the boot process, BIOS skips a device (such as a keyboard) or improperly identifies it. Your only indication that this sort of problem has occurred is that the device won't respond after the system has been booted. When that happens, you can generally resolve the problem by rebooting. If the problem persists, you may want to check the operating system's Web site for any patches (or software fixes) that may resolve the issue. If there are no patches or the problem persists, then you may want to get technical assistance.

The Desktop and Window Features

The **desktop** is the first interaction you have with the operating system and the first image you see on your monitor. As its name implies, your computer's desktop puts at your fingertips all of the elements necessary for a productive work session. They are items that are typically found on or near the top of a traditional desk, such as files and folders.

What are the main features of the Windows desktop and Start menu? The very nature of a desktop is that it lets you customize it to meet your individual needs. As such, the desktop on your computer may be different from the desktop on your friend's computer, or even from the desktop of another account user on the same computer. In recent versions of Windows, many features that were once only found on the desktop have moved to the Start menu and the taskbar, including access to documents, programs, and computer drives and devices (see Figure 5.16). You can always create shortcuts on your desktop to these features if you find that's more convenient.

On the desktop you'll find:

- **Recycle Bin:** Location for deleted files and folders from the C drive only. Deleted files in the Recycle Bin can be recovered easily before the Recycle Bin is emptied.

- **Gadgets:** An easy-to-use miniprogram that gives you information at a glance or quick access to frequently used tools including weather information, calendar items, calculators, games, photo albums, and system tools.

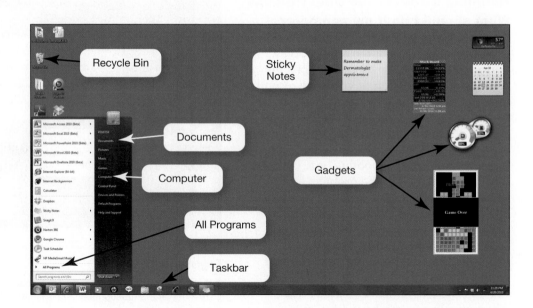

Figure 5.16

The Windows 7 desktop puts the most commonly used features of the operating system at your fingertips.

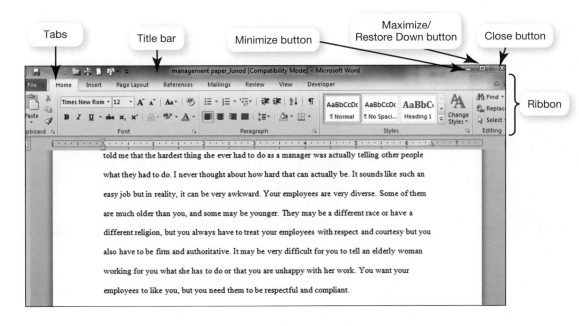

Figure 5.17

Most windows in a graphical user interface have the same common elements.

- **Taskbar:** Displays open and favorite applications for easy access. You can point to an icon to preview windows of open files or programs, or move your mouse over a thumbnail to preview a full-screen image. Or right-click an icon to view a Jump List—the most recently or commonly used files or commands for that application.

In the Windows 7 Start menu, you'll find:

- **Documents:** A convenient organizational tool that enables you to keep all your documents in one place. You can further organize your Documents folder with subfolders, similar to the way a traditional filing system is organized.

- **Computer:** Provides easy access to disk drives and system and network devices.

- **All Programs:** In the Start menu, this provides access to all programs available in the system. To prevent taking up valuable screen space, a limited number of programs displays. Use the scrollbar to gain access to programs not immediately visible. Instant Search can facilitate locating a program.

What are common features of a window? One feature introduced in the graphical user interface is **windows** (with a lowercase *w*), the rectangular panes on your computer screen that display applications running on your system. Most programs have windows that include **toolbars**, which have **icons** (shortcuts to frequently used

tasks) and **scrollbars** (bars that appear at the side or bottom of the screen that control which part of the information is displayed on the screen). As shown in Figure 5.17, the newer versions of Microsoft Office have begun to organize toolbars into a **ribbon** interface. The ribbon is further organized into task-specific tabs with relevant commands. Using the Minimize, Maximize/Restore Down, and Close buttons, you can open, close, and resize windows.

How does the Mac desktop compare with Windows? Although the Mac OS X and the Windows operating systems are not compatible, they are extremely similar in terms of functionality.

As illustrated in Figure 5.18, both Windows and Mac operating systems use windows, menus, and icons. They both also have streamlined mechanisms to access commonly used applications. Macs feature a Dock and a Dashboard with widgets. A **widget** is a mini-application that enables quick access to frequently used tools and activities (such as stock prices, to-do lists, and games). The latest version of Windows has a **taskbar** with Dock-like capabilities and **gadgets** that provide functionality similar to that of the Mac widgets.

How can I see more than one window on my desktop at a time? You can easily arrange the windows on a desktop so that they sit next to each other either horizontally or vertically. You also can arrange windows by cascading them so that they overlap one another, or you

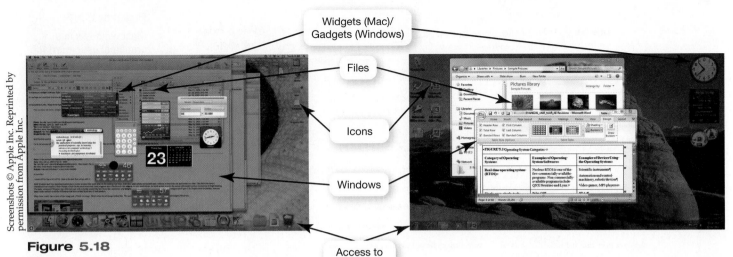

Figure 5.18

Although not compatible with each other, the Windows OS and the Mac OS have many similar features.

can simply resize two open windows so that they appear on the screen at the same time.

Showing windows side by side or stacked on top of each other makes accessing two or more active windows more convenient. To do so, right-click the taskbar and select "Show Windows Stacked" or "Show Windows Side by Side." When you want to undo the arrangement, right-click the taskbar again and select "Undo Show Stacked" (or "Undo Show Side by Side"). To bring a window back to its full size, click the Restore button in the top right corner of the window. Windows 7 introduces the "snap" feature, which is another new way to view windows side by side. Simply drag a window to either the left or right so the pointer touches the side of the desktop, and Windows will automatically resize and snap that window in place.

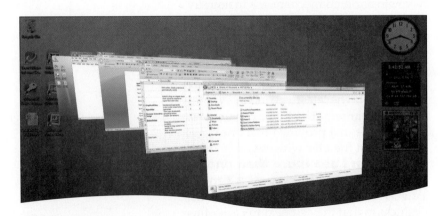

Figure 5.19

The Windows Flip 3D feature gives you the ability to move through live images of open windows.

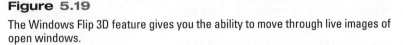
>To access Windows Flip, hold down the Windows key and then press Tab.

Windows Vista and 7 offer two more ways to navigate through open windows. To see live thumbnail images of open windows, press Alt + Tab to access Windows Flip. Pressing the Windows key + Tab initiates the Windows Flip 3D feature. You can then "flip" through open windows in a stack by pressing Tab multiple times, or by using the scroll wheel on your mouse or the arrow keys on your keyboard. The open windows appear in a three-dimensional configuration, as shown in Figure 5.19.

Can I move or resize the windows once they are tiled? Regardless of whether the windows are tiled, you can resize them and move them around the desktop. You can reposition windows on the desktop by using the mouse to point to the title bar at the top of the window and, while holding down the left mouse button, drag the window to a different location. To resize a window, place your mouse pointer over any side or corner of a window until it changes to a double-headed arrow [↕]. You can then left-click and drag the window to the new desired size. Aero Shake is a feature that allows you to grab a window by its title bar and "shake" it (hold the cursor on the title bar and quickly move the window back and forth) to minimize all other windows.

Organizing Your Computer: File Management

So far you have learned that the operating system is responsible for managing the processor, memory, storage, and devices, and that it provides a mechanism whereby applications and users can interact with the computer system. An additional function of an operating system is to enable **file management**, which provides an organizational structure to the computer's contents. The OS provides a hierarchical **directory** structure that includes folders, libraries, and drives. In this section, we discuss how you can use this hierarchical structure to make your computer more organized and efficient.

Organizing Your Files

What exactly are a file, folder, and library? Technically, a **file** is a collection of related pieces of information stored together for easy reference. A file in an operating system is a collection of program instructions or data that is stored and treated as a single unit. Files can be generated from an application such as a Word document or an Excel workbook. In addition, files can represent an entire application, a Web page, a set of sounds, or an image. Files are stored on the hard drive, a flash drive, or another permanent storage medium. As the number of files you save increases, it becomes more important to keep them organized in folders and libraries. A **folder** is a collection of files. Windows 7 introduces the concept of libraries. A **library** gathers files from different locations and displays them as if they were all saved in a single folder, regardless of where they are actually physically stored. Libraries don't store files and folders; rather, they provide easy access to a category of files no matter where they are stored. For example, you might have pictures stored all over your computer, including your external hard drive. Rather than looking through each separate location to view your pictures, you can access all of them more easily by looking in the Pictures library.

How does the operating system organize files? Windows organizes the contents of your computer in a hierarchical structure composed of drives, libraries, folders, subfolders, and files. The hard drive, represented as the C drive, is where you permanently store most of your files. Other storage devices on your computer are also represented by letters. The A drive has traditionally been reserved for a floppy drive, which you may or may not have installed on your computer. Any additional drives (such as flash or DVD drives) found on your

computer are represented by other letters (D, E, F, and so on).

How is the hard drive organized? The C drive, or hard drive, is like a large filing cabinet in which all files are stored. As such, the C drive is the top of the filing structure of the computer system and is referred to as the **root directory**. All other libraries, folders, and files are organized within the root directory. There are areas in the root directory that the operating system has filled with files and folders holding special OS files. The programs within these files help run the computer and generally shouldn't be accessed. The Windows operating system also creates libraries called Documents, Pictures, Music, and Videos that store and organize your text, image, audio, and video files, respectively. Or you can create your own libraries, folders, or subfolders to modify the default filing system to better meet your needs.

How can I easily locate and see the contents of my computer? If you use a Windows PC, **Windows Explorer** is the main tool for finding, viewing, and managing the contents of your computer. It shows the location and contents of every drive, folder, and file. As illustrated in Figure 5.20, Windows Explorer is divided into two panes, or sections.

BITS AND BYTES

How to Get the Most from Windows Libraries

Windows 7 introduced libraries, a new organizing feature that aggregates multiple folders into a single accessible location. To get the most out of using libraries, consider the following tips.

- **Add a new library:** There are four default libraries: Documents, Music, Pictures, and Videos. You can add a new library to collect other content, such as games. To do so, open Windows Explorer. In the Navigation Pane, right-click on Libraries, and click New. Type in a name for the new library. To add new locations to the library, open the new library and click on Include a Folder.
- **Share or collaborate with libraries:** Perhaps you have pictures saved on your laptop, your dad's desktop, and your mom's laptop. As long as all three computers are on the same Homegroup network, you can share each other's libraries by right-clicking the library name, clicking Share With, and then clicking either Homegroup option, depending on whether you want to allow editing privileges to those with whom you are sharing the library.
- **Create a backup library:** Do you store important data in a variety of folders on your computer? Even though it's best to back up your entire system, you might only need to back up specific folders. In that case, create a new library, and call it Backup. Add the folders you want to ensure are backed up, then point your backup software to that library.

Figure 5.20

Windows Explorer lets you see the contents of your computer.

>**Click the Start** button, and then select **Computer**.

The navigation pane on the left shows the contents of your computer. It displays commonly accessed areas organized by Favorites and libraries (Documents, Music, Pictures, and Videos) as well as all the drives of the system (under Computer) and available networks. When you select a Favorite, library, drive, or network, the files and folders of that particular area are displayed in the right pane.

How should I organize my files? Creating folders is the key to organizing your files because folders keep related documents together. Again, think of your computer as a big filing cabinet that is filled with many folders. Those folders have the capacity to hold individual files, or even other folders that contain individual files. For example, you might create one folder called Classes to hold all of your class work. Inside the Classes folder, you could create folders for each of your classes (such as CIS110, MGT111, and HIS112). Inside each of those folders, you could create subfolders for each class's assignments, completed homework, research, notes, and so on.

Grouping related files into folders makes it easier for you to identify and find files. Which would be easier—going to the CIS110 folder to find a file or searching through the hundreds of individual files in Documents hoping to find the right one? Grouping files in a folder also allows you to move them more efficiently, so you can quickly transfer critical files needing frequent backup, for instance.

Sometimes it's not possible to put all similar files into one folder. For example, you might have PowerPoint files stored in separate folders that correspond to each particular class. If you want to always have quick access to your PowerPoint files, you could create a PowerPoint Library and specify the folders where the PowerPoint files are located. The PowerPoint Library would then gather the PowerPoint files from the different locations and display them as if they were all saved in a single folder.

Viewing and Sorting Files and Folders

Are there different ways I can view and sort my files and folders? When you open any folder in Windows, the toolbar at the top displays a Views button. Clicking on the Views button offers you different ways to view the folders and files, which are discussed in more detail below. In some views, the folders are displayed as Live Icons, which is a feature that began in Windows Vista. Live Icons allows you to preview the actual contents of a specific file or folder without actually opening the file. Live Icons can be displayed in a variety of views.

- **Tiles view:** This view displays files and folders as icons in list form. Each icon represents the application associated with the file, and also includes the name and the size of the file, though the display information is customizable to include other data. The Tiles view also displays picture dimensions, a handy feature for Web page developers.

- **Details view:** This is the most interactive view. Files and folders are displayed in list form, and the additional file information is displayed in columns alongside the name of the file. You can sort and display the contents of the folder by any of the column headings, so you can sort the contents alphabetically by name or type, or hierarchically by date last modified or file size (see Figure 5.21). Right-click the column heading area to modify the display of columns.

- **List view:** This is another display of icons and names that are even smaller than in Tiles view. This is a good view if you have a lot of content in the folder and need to see most or all of it at once.

- **Small and Medium Icons views:** These views also display files and folders as icons in list form, but the icons are either small- or medium-sized, respectively. Additional file information displays in a ScreenTip (the text that appears when you place your cursor over the file icon).

- **Large and Extra Large Icons views:** Large Icons view (see Figure 5.22) shows the contents of folders as small images. There is also Extra Large Icons view, which shows folder contents and other icons as even larger images. Large Icons and Extra Large Icons views are the best to use if your folder contains picture files,

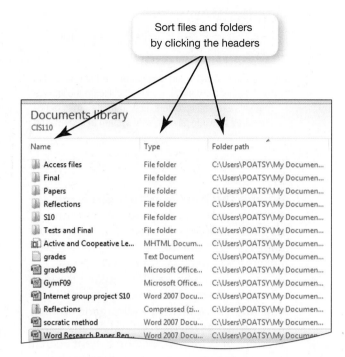

Sort files and folders by clicking the headers

or for PowerPoint presentations, because the title slide of the presentation will display, making it easier for you to distinguish among presentations. You may use the scale feature to adjust the size of the icons further. Additionally, a preview pane is available in this view. It allows you to view the first page of the selected document without having to open it completely (see Figure 5.22). For those folders that contain collections of MP3 files, you can download the cover of the CD or an image of the artist to display on any folder to identify that collection further.

Figure 5.21

Details view enables you to sort and list your files in a variety of ways to enable quick access to the correct file.

>To access Details view, right click anywhere in the Windows Explorer window, select View, and then select Details.

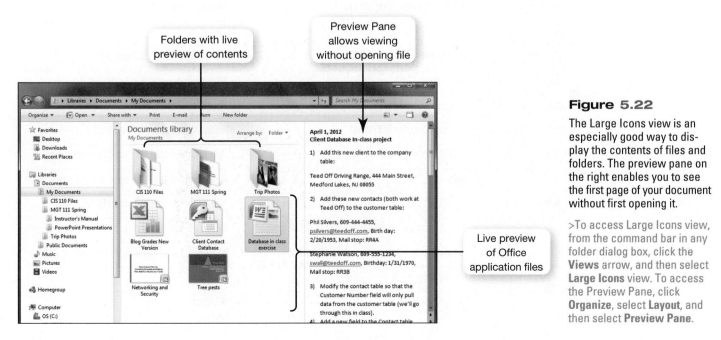

Folders with live preview of contents

Preview Pane allows viewing without opening file

Live preview of Office application files

Figure 5.22

The Large Icons view is an especially good way to display the contents of files and folders. The preview pane on the right enables you to see the first page of your document without first opening it.

>To access Large Icons view, from the command bar in any folder dialog box, click the **Views** arrow, and then select **Large Icons** view. To access the Preview Pane, click **Organize**, select **Layout**, and then select **Preview Pane**.

SOUND BYTE · File Management

In this Sound Byte, you'll examine the features of file management and maintenance. You'll learn the various methods of creating folders, how to turn a group of unorganized files into an organized system of folders, and how to maintain your file system.

What's the best way to search for a file? You've no doubt saved a file and forgotten where you saved it, or have downloaded a file from the Internet and then were not sure where it was saved. What's the quickest way to find a file? Looking through every file stored on your computer could take hours, even with a well-organized file management system. Fortunately, the newer versions of Windows include Instant Search, a search feature found on the Start menu, which searches through your hard drive or other storage device (DVD or flash drive) to locate files that match criteria you provide. Your search can be based on a part of the name of the file or just a word or phrase in the file. You can also narrow your search by providing information about the type of file, which application was used to create the

file, or even how long ago the file was saved. Instant Search can also find e-mails based on your criteria. Instant Search is found in Windows Explorer, too, and is used to search the contents of current folders. Mac OS X has a similar feature called Spotlight.

Naming Files

Are there special rules I have to follow when I name files? Files have names just like people. The first part of a file, or the **file name**, is similar to your first name, and is generally the name you assign to the file when you save it. For example, "bioreport" may be the name you assign a report you have completed for a biology class.

In a Windows application, an **extension**, or **file type**, follows the file name and a period or dot (.). Like a last name, this extension identifies what kind of family of files the file belongs to, or which application should be used to read the file. For example, if "bioreport" is a spreadsheet created in Microsoft Excel 2010, it has a .xlsx extension and its name is "bioreport.xlsx." If the bioreport file is a Word 2010 document, then it has a .docx extension and its name is "bioreport.docx." Figure 5.23 lists some common file extensions and the types of documents they indicate.

Figure 5.23 | COMMON FILE NAME EXTENSIONS

Extension	Type of Document	Application
.doc	Word processing document	Microsoft Word 2003
.docx	Word processing document	Microsoft Word 2007 and 2010
.sdw	Text	OpenOffice.org
.xlsx	Worksheet	Microsoft Excel 2007 and 2010
.accdb	Database	Microsoft Access 2007 and 2010
.pptx	Presentation	Microsoft PowerPoint 2007 and 2010
.pdf	Portable Document Format	Adobe Acrobat or Adobe Reader
.rtf	Text (Rich Text Format)	Any program that can read text documents
.txt	Text	Any program that can read text documents
.htm or .html	HyperText Markup Language for a Web page	Any program that can read HTML
.jpg	Joint Photographic Experts Group (JPEG) image	Most programs capable of displaying images
.gif	Graphics Interchange Format (GIF) image	Most programs capable of displaying images
.bmp	Bitmap image	Windows
.zip	Compressed file	WinZip

A File Type for Everyone

Imagine you are sending an e-mail to a diverse group of individuals. You are not sure what word processing software each of them uses, but you assume that there will be a mix of people who use Microsoft Word, iWorks, and Writer. How can you be sure that all users will be able to open the attachment regardless of the program installed on their computers? Save the file in Rich Text Format (.rtf), Portable Document Format (.pdf), or Plain Text (.txt) format. Rich Text Format and Plain Text files can be read by any modern word processing program, although some formatting may be lost when a document is saved in Plain Text format. Anyone can read a PDF file by downloading the free Adobe Reader from the Adobe Web site (**www.adobe .com**). To save files as RTF, PDF, or TXT files, simply change the file type when saving your file. In Microsoft Word, for example, you can select the file type in the Save as Type list shown in Figure 5.24.

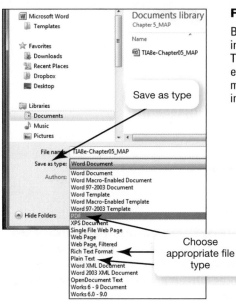

Figure 5.24

By changing a word processing file's type to PDF, RTF, or TXT, you can ensure that everyone can read your file, no matter which word processing program they use.

Why is it important to know the file extension? As shown in Figure 5.25, when you save a file created in most applications running under the Windows operating system, you do not need to add the extension to the file name; by default, it is added automatically for you. Mac and Linux operating systems do not require file extensions. This is because the information as to the type of application the computer should use to open the file is stored inside the file itself. However, if you're using the Mac or Linux operating system and will be sending files to Windows users, you should add an extension to your file name so that Windows can more easily open your files. You may also need to know the extension of files created in any of the Office 2007 or 2010 applications because they have a different file format than the earlier versions. The new versions of Office have an *x* at the end of the extension to represent the XML file format. For example, files saved in Word 2010 have a .docx file extension, whereas files save in Word 2003 have a .doc file extension. A file created in Office 2007 or 2010 cannot be read with an earlier version of Office unless it is converted or saved in the earlier format. Finally, sometimes you are sent a file by e-mail, and cannot open it. Most likely, that's because your computer does not have the program needed to open the file. Sometimes, similar programs that you already have installed can be used to open the file, so it's helpful to know what the file extension is. Sites such as **www.filext.com** can help you identify the source program.

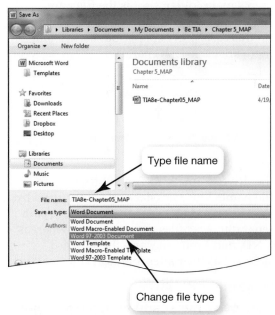

Figure 5.25

When you save a file in Microsoft Word 2010, you can select in what format you would like the file to be saved, such as a format compatible with Word 97–2003.

>The Save As features are displayed by selecting the File tab and then selecting Save As.

Figure 5.26 | FILE NAMING CONVENTIONS

	Mac OS X	Windows
File and folder name length	As many as 255 characters*	As many as 255 characters
Case sensitive?	Yes	No
Forbidden characters	Colon (:)	" / \ * ? <>	:
File extensions needed?	No	Yes
Path separator	Colon (:)	\

Note: Although Mac OS X supports file names with as many as 255 characters, many applications running on OS X still support only file names with a maximum of 31 characters.

ACTIVE HELP-DESK

Organizing Your Computer: File Management

In this Active Helpdesk call, you'll play the role of a helpdesk staffer, fielding calls about the desktop, window features (such as scrollbars and the Minimize Down and Maximize buttons), and how the operating system helps keep the computer organized.

Are there things I shouldn't do when naming my files? Each operating system has its own naming conventions, or rules, which are listed in Figure 5.26. Beyond those conventions, it's important that you name your files so that you can easily identify them. A file name such as "research.docx" may be descriptive to you if you're only working on one research paper. However, if you create other research reports later and need to identify the contents of these files quickly, you'll soon wish you had been more descriptive. Giving your files names that are more descriptive, such as bioresearch.docx or, better yet, bio101research.docx, is a good idea.

Keep in mind, however, that all files must be uniquely identified, unless they are saved

are Documents for files, Music for audio files, Pictures for graphic files, and Videos for video files. Although you can create your own libraries, these default libraries are the beginning of a well-organized system.

You can determine the location of a file by its **file path**. The file path starts with the drive in which the file is located and includes all folders, subfolders (if any), the file name, and the extension. For example, if you were saving a picture of Andrew Carnegie for a term paper for a U.S. History course, the file path might be C:\Documents\HIS182\Term Paper\Illustrations\ACarnegie.jpg.

As shown in Figure 5.27, C is the drive on which the file is stored (in this case, the hard drive), and Documents is the file's primary folder. HIS182, Term Paper, and Illustrations are successive subfolders within the Documents main folder. Last is the file name, ACarnegie, separated from the file extension (in this case, jpg) by a period. Notice that there are backslash characters (\) in between

Figure 5.27

Understanding file paths.

C:\Documents\HIS182\Term Paper\Illustrations\ACarnegie.jpg

Drive   Primary Folder   Subfolders   File Name   Extension

in different folders or in different locations. Therefore, although files may share the same file name (such as "bioreport.docx" or "bioreport.xlsx") or share the same extension ("bioreport.xlsx" or "budget.xlsx"), no two files stored on the same device and folder can share *both* the same file name and the same extension.

How can I tell where my files are saved? When you save a file for the first time, you give the file a name and designate where you want to save it. For easy reference, the operating system includes libraries where files are saved unless you specify otherwise. In Windows, the default libraries

the drive, primary folder, subfolders, and file name. This backslash character, used by Windows and DOS, is referred to as a **path separator**. Mac files use a colon (:), whereas UNIX and Linux files use the forward slash (/) as the path separator.

Working with Files

How can I move and copy files? Once you've located your file with Windows Explorer, you can perform many other file-management actions such as opening, copying, moving, renaming, and deleting files. You open a file by double-clicking the file from its storage location. Based on the file extension, the operating system then determines which application needs to be started to open the requested file and opens the file within the correct application automatically. You can copy a file to another location using the Copy command. When you copy a file, a duplicate file is created and the original file remains in its initial location. To move a file from one location to another, use the Move command. When you move a file, the original file is deleted from its former location and saved in the new location.

Where do deleted files go? The **Recycle Bin** is a folder on the desktop where files deleted from the hard drive reside until you permanently purge them from your system. Unfortunately, files deleted from other drives (such as a DVD drive, flash drive, external hard drive, or network drive) do not go to the Recycle Bin but are deleted from the system immediately. (Mac systems have something similar to the Recycle Bin, called Trash, which is represented by a wastebasket icon. To delete files on a Mac, drag the files to the Trash on the Dock.)

How do I permanently delete files from my system? Files placed in the Recycle Bin or the Trash remain in the system until they are permanently deleted. To delete files from the Recycle Bin permanently, select Empty the Recycle Bin after right-clicking the desktop icon. On Macs, select Empty Trash from the Finder menu in OS X.

Utility Programs

The main component of system software is the operating system. You have learned that the operating system is the single most essential piece of software in your computer system because it coordinates all the system's activities and provides a means by which other software applications and users can interact with the system. However, there is another set of programs included in system software, which are very important. Utility programs are small applications that perform special functions.

Some of these utility programs are incorporated into the operating system. For example, Windows has its own firewall and file-compression utilities. Other utility programs, such as antivirus and security programs, are sophisticated and require such frequent updating that they are offered as stand-alone programs or as Web-based services. Sometimes utility programs, such as Norton SystemWorks, are offered as

BITS AND BYTES   Need to Recover a Deleted File?

Should you move a file to the Recycle Bin in error, you can restore the deleted file by clicking the Recycle Bin icon on the desktop, right-clicking the erroneously deleted file, and then selecting restore. Once you empty the Recycle Bin, getting the file back is difficult, but perhaps not impossible.

Because you don't see the file name anymore, it looks as if the file has been erased from the hard drive. However, only the reference to the deleted file is deleted permanently, so the operating system has no easy way to find the file. The file data actually remains on the hard drive until it is written over. For those files that have been deleted for a while, you can use a program such as FarStone's RestoreIT! or Norton Ghost. However, the longer you wait to recover a deleted file, the smaller your chances of a full recovery, because the probability increases that your file has been overwritten by other data.

software suites, bundled with other useful maintenance and performance-boosting utilities. Still other utilities, like Lavasoft's Ad-Aware, are offered as freeware or shareware programs and are available as downloads from the Web.

Figure 5.28 illustrates some of the various types of utility programs available within the Windows operating system as well as some alternatives available as stand-alone programs. In general, the basic utilities designed to manage and tune the computer hardware are incorporated into the operating system. The stand-alone utility programs typically offer more features or an easier user interface for backup, security, diagnostic, or recovery functions. For some Windows programs, like Task Manager and Task Scheduler, no good stand-alone alternative exists.

In this section, we explore many of the utility programs you'll find installed on a Windows 7 operating system. Unless otherwise noted, you can find Windows utilities in the Control Panel or on the Start menu by selecting All Programs, Accessories, and then System Tools. We will discuss antivirus and personal firewall utility programs in Chapter 9.

Display Utilities

How can I change the appearance of my desktop? Personalization, found in Appearance and Personalization on the Control Panel or by right-clicking any empty area on the desktop and selecting Personalize, has all the features you need to change the appearance of your desktop. It provides different options for the desktop background, screen savers, and window colors. Although Windows comes with many different background themes and screen saver options

Figure 5.28 | UTILITY PROGRAMS AVAILABLE WITHIN WINDOWS AND AS STAND-ALONE PROGRAMS

Windows Utility Program	Type of Document	Application
Windows Explorer File Compression	WinZip, StuffIt	Reduces file size
Backup and Disk Imaging	Acronis True Image, Norton Ghost, SkyDrive	Backs up important files, makes a complete mirror image of current computer setup
Disk Cleanup	McAfee Total Protection	Removes unnecessary files from hard drive
Disk Defragmenter	Norton Utilities, iDefrag	Arranges files on hard drive in sequential order
Error-checking (previously ScanDisk)	SeaTools (free download from www.seagate.com)	Checks hard drive for unnecessary or damaged files
System Restore	FarStone Snapshot, Acronis Backup and Security, Norton Ghost	Restores system to previous, stable state
Task Manager and Resource Monitor		Displays performance measures for processes; provides information on programs and processes running on computer
Task Scheduler		Schedules programs to run automatically at prescribed times.

preinstalled, a vast array of downloadable options are available on the Web. Just search for "backgrounds" or "screen savers" on your favorite search engine to customize your desktop. Make sure you select one from a reputable source, though, because sometimes viruses and other unwanted or annoying files can also be downloaded with a desktop image or screensaver.

The Programs and Features Utility

What is the correct way to add new programs to the system? When you install a new program, usually the program automatically runs a wizard (a step-by-step guide) that walks you through the installation process. If a wizard does not start automatically, you should open the Control Panel, click Programs, and then click Programs and Features. This prompts the operating system to look for the setup program of the new software and starts the installation wizard.

What is the correct way to remove unwanted programs from my system? Some people think that deleting a program from the Program Files folder on the C drive is the best way to remove a program from the system. However, most programs include support files such as a help file, dictionaries, and graphics files that are not located in the main program folder found in Program Files. Depending on the supporting file's function, support files can be scattered throughout various folders within the system. You would normally miss these files by deleting only the main program file or folder from the system. By selecting the individual program's own uninstall option, or the Windows uninstaller utility found in Programs in the Control Panel, you delete not only the main program file, but also all supporting files and most registry entries.

File Compression Utilities

What is file compression? File compression makes a large file more compact, making it easier and faster to send over the Internet, upload to a Web page, or save onto a disc. As shown in Figure 5.29, Windows has a built-in **file compression utility** that takes out redundancies in a file (zips it) to reduce the file size. There are also several stand-alone freeware and shareware programs, such as WinZip (for Windows) and StuffIt (for Windows or Mac), that you can obtain to compress your files.

How does file compression work? Most compression programs look for repeated patterns of letters and replace these patterns with a shorter placeholder. The repeated patterns and the associated placeholder are cataloged and stored temporarily in a separate file called the *dictionary*. For example, in the following sentence, you can easily see the repeated patterns of letters.

The rain in Spain falls mainly on the plain.

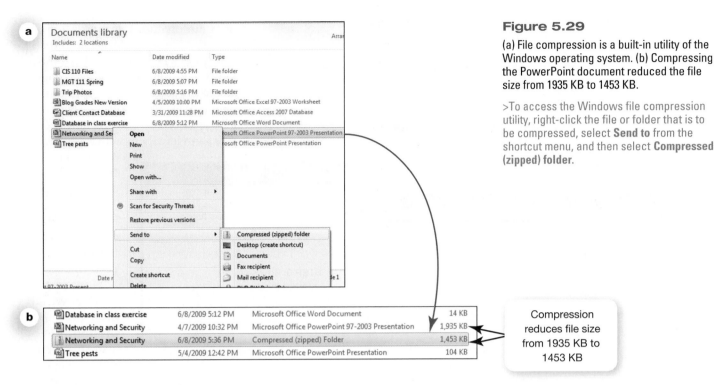

Figure 5.29

(a) File compression is a built-in utility of the Windows operating system. (b) Compressing the PowerPoint document reduced the file size from 1935 KB to 1453 KB.

>To access the Windows file compression utility, right-click the file or folder that is to be compressed, select **Send to** from the shortcut menu, and then select **Compressed (zipped) folder**.

Although this example contains obvious repeated patterns (**ain** and **the**), in a large document the repeated patterns may be more complex. The compression program's algorithm (a set of instructions designed to complete a solution in a step-by-step manner) therefore runs through the file several times to determine the optimal repeated patterns to use to obtain the greatest compression.

How effective are file compression programs? The effectiveness of file compression—that is, how much a file's size is reduced—depends on several factors, including the type and size of the individual file and the compression method used. Current compression programs can reduce text files by 50 percent or more, depending on the file. However, some files, such as PDF files, already contain a form of compression, so they do not need to be compressed further. Other file types, especially some graphics and audio formats, have gone through a compression process that reduces file size by permanently discarding data.

SOUND BYTE — File Compression

In this Sound Byte, you'll learn about the advantages of file compression and how to use Windows to compress and decompress files. This Sound Byte also teaches you how to find and install file compression shareware programs.

For example, image files such as Joint Photographic Experts Group (JPEG), Graphics Interchange Format (GIF), and Portable Network Graphics (PNG) files discard small variations in color that the human eye may not pick up. Likewise, MP3 files permanently discard sounds that the human ear cannot hear. These graphic and audio files do not need further compression.

How do I decompress a file I've compressed? When you want to restore the file to its original state, you need to decompress the file so that the pieces of file that the compression process temporarily removed are restored to the document. Generally, the program you used to compress the file has the capability to decompress the file as well (see Figure 5.30).

System Maintenance Utilities

Are there any utilities that make my system work faster? Disk Cleanup is a Windows utility that cleans, or removes, unnecessary files from your hard drive. These include files that have accumulated in the Recycle Bin as well as temporary files, which are files created by Windows to store data temporarily while a program is running. Windows usually deletes these temporary files when you exit the program, but sometimes it forgets to do this, or doesn't have time because your system freezes up or incurs a problem that prevents you from properly exiting a program. Disk Cleanup, found by clicking the

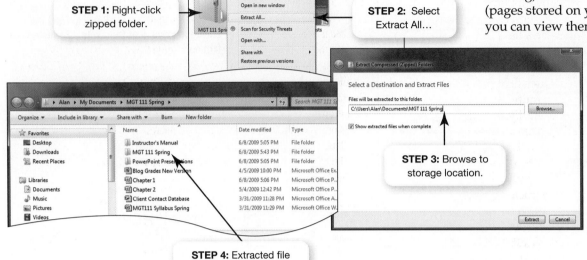

STEP 1: Right-click zipped folder.

STEP 2: Select Extract All...

STEP 3: Browse to storage location.

STEP 4: Extracted file displays in selected location.

Figure 5.30

The Extraction Wizard in Windows makes unzipping compressed folders and files easy.

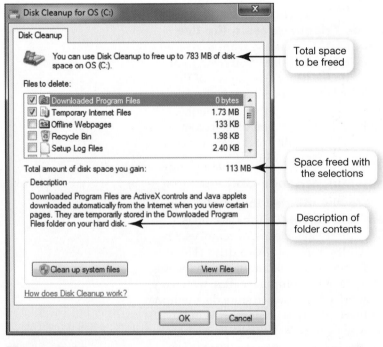

Figure 5.31

Using Disk Cleanup will help free space on your hard drive.

>Disk Cleanup is accessed by clicking **Start**, **All Programs**, **Accessories**, and then **System Tools**.

Start button, then selecting All Programs, Accessories folder, and then the System Tools folder, also removes temporary Internet files (Web pages stored on your hard drive for quick viewing) as well as offline Web pages (pages stored on your computer so you can view them without being connected to the Internet). If not deleted periodically, these unnecessary files can hinder efficient operating performance.

How can I control which files Disk Cleanup deletes? When you run Disk Cleanup, the program scans your hard drive to determine which folders have files that can be deleted and calculates the amount of hard drive space that would be freed by doing so. You check off which type of files you would like to delete, as shown in Figure 5.31.

What else can I do if my system runs slowly? Over time, as you add and delete information in a file or download updates to your software, the file pieces are saved in scattered locations on the hard drive. When the file is opened, locating all the pieces of the file takes extra time, making the operating system less efficient. Windows **Disk Defragmenter** regroups related pieces of files on the hard drive, thereby allowing the OS to work more efficiently. The process of collecting file fragments and putting them back together in a contiguous manner is known as optimization. You can find the Windows Disk Defragmenter utility by clicking the Start menu, then All Programs, Accessories, and then System Tools. Using the Windows Disk Defragmenter Analyzer feature, you should check several times a year to determine whether your drive needs to be defragmented. Macs do not have a defrag utility built into the system. Those users who feel the need to defrag their Mac can use iDefrag, an external program that can be purchased from Coriolis Systems.

How do I diagnose potential errors or damage on my storage devices? **Error-checking**, once known as ScanDisk, is a Windows utility that checks for lost files and fragments as well as physical errors on your hard drive. Lost files and fragments of files occur as you save, resave, move, delete, and copy files on your hard drive. Sometimes the system becomes confused, leaving references on the **file allocation table** or **FAT** (an index of all sector numbers in a table) to files that no longer exist or have been moved. Physical errors on the hard drive occur when the mechanism that reads the hard drive's data (which is stored as 1s or 0s) can no longer determine whether the area holds a 1 or a 0. These areas are called *bad sectors*. Sometimes Error-checking can recover the lost data, but more often, it deletes the files that are unnecessarily taking up space. Error-checking also makes a note of any bad sectors so that the system will not use them again to store data. To locate Error-checking, from the Start menu click Computer, right-click the disk you want to diagnose, select Properties, and select Tools. On Macs, you can use the Disk Utility to test and repair disks. You will find Disk Utility in the Utilities subfolder in the Applications folder on your hard drive.

How can I check on a program that has stopped running? If a program has stopped working, you can use the Windows **Task Manager** utility to check on the program or to exit the nonresponsive program. Although you can access Task Manager from the Control Panel, it is more easily accessible by pressing Ctrl + Alt and then the Delete key or by right-clicking an empty space on the taskbar at the bottom of your screen. The Applications tab of Task Manager lists all programs that you are using and indicates whether they are working properly (running) or have stopped improperly (not responding). You can terminate programs that are not responding by clicking the End Task button in the dialog box.

If you need further assistance because of a program error, it may be helpful to run an application debugger. Problem Steps Recorder (see Figure 5.32), a tool in Windows Vista and Windows 7, gathers information about the computer when there is a program error. When an error occurs, this tool automatically creates and saves a log. The log can then be viewed, printed, or delivered electronically to any technical support professional, who can then use this information to help diagnose the problem.

System Restore and Backup Utilities

Is there an undo command for the system? Suppose you have just installed a new software program and your

Problem Steps Recorder: Making Tech Support Easier

Have you ever been frustrated trying to clearly and accurately describe your problem or an error message you have received to a technical support person? Have you had trouble remembering the steps you took to encounter a problem? Or, are you on the other side, trying to help via the phone a friend or family member with their problems? If so, Windows 7 has a cool new feature called Problem Steps Recorder that you can use to capture all your mouse clicks and keystrokes (see Figure 5.32). In addition to capturing the clicks and keystrokes you make to reproduce the problem or error, the Problem Steps Recorder provides screen shots of your actions. The captured data is stored in a zipped file. You can then send the zipped file to your technical support person.

To start Problem Steps Recorder, click Start, type "psr.exe" in the search box, and press Enter. When Problem Steps Recorder displays, click the Start Record button and continue the steps to reproduce the problem or error. You can add comments as you go. The end result is a slideshow of all your actions, along with descriptions (in regular English—not code) of what you did.

Figure 5.32

The Problem Steps Recorder captures the clicks and keystrokes you make to reproduce a problem or error.

computer freezes. After rebooting the computer, when you try to start the application, the system freezes once again. You uninstall the new program, but your computer continues to freeze after rebooting. What can you do now?

The most recent versions of Windows have a utility called **System Restore** that lets you roll your system settings back to a specific date when everything was working properly. A **system restore point**, which is a snapshot of your entire system's settings, is made every week and prior to certain events, such as installing or updating software. You also can create a custom restore point manually. Should problems occur, if the computer was running just fine before you installed new software or a hardware

Using Utility Programs

In this Active Helpdesk call, you'll play the role of a helpdesk staffer, fielding calls about the utility programs included in system software and what these programs do.

To understand how disk defragmenter utilities work, you must first understand the basics of how a hard disk drive stores files. A hard disk drive is composed of several platters, or round, thin plates of metal, that are covered with a special magnetic coating that records the data. The platters are about 3.5 inches in diameter and are stacked onto a spindle. There are usually two or three platters in any hard disk drive, with data stored on one or both sides. Data is recorded on hard disks in concentric circles called tracks. Each **track** is further broken down into pie-shaped wedges, each called a **sector** (see Figure 5.33). The data is further identified by clusters, which are the smallest segments within the sectors.

When you want to save (or write) a file, the bits that make up your file are recorded onto one or more clusters of the drive. To keep track of which clusters hold which files, the drive also stores an index of all sector numbers in a table. To save a file, the computer will look in the table for clusters that are not already being used. It will then record the file information on those clusters. When you open (or read) a file, the computer searches through the table for the clusters that hold the desired file and reads that file. Similarly, when you delete a file, you are actually not deleting the file itself, but rather the reference in the table to the file.

How does a disk become fragmented? When only part of an older file is deleted, the deleted section of the file creates a gap in the sector of the disk where the data was originally stored. In the same way, when new information is added to an older file, there may not be space to save the new information sequentially near where the file was originally saved. In that case, the system writes the added part of the file to the next available location on the disk, and a reference is made in the table as to the location of this file fragment. Over time, as files are saved, deleted, and modified, the bits of information for various files fall out of sequential order and the disk becomes fragmented.

Disk fragmentation is a problem because the operating system is not as efficient when a disk is fragmented. It takes longer to locate a whole file because more of the disk must be searched for the various pieces, greatly slowing down the performance of your computer.

How can you make the files line up more efficiently on the disk? At this stage, the disk defragmenter utility enters the picture. The defragmenter tool takes the hard drive through a defragmentation process in which pieces of files that are scattered over the disk are placed together and arranged sequentially on the hard disk. Also, any unused portions of clusters that were too small to save data in before are grouped, increasing the available storage space on the disk. Figure 5.34 shows before and after shots of a fragmented disk that has gone through the defragmentation process.

For more about hard disks and defragmenting, be sure to check out the Sound Byte "Hard Disk Anatomy Interactive."

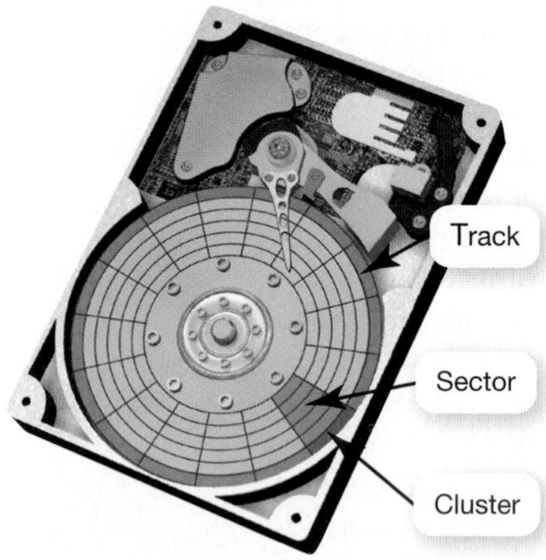

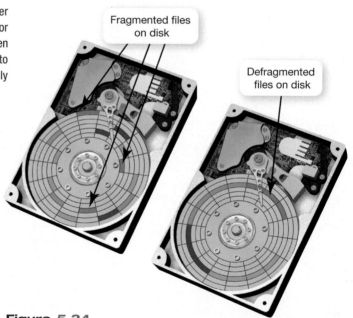

Fragmented files on disk

Defragmented files on disk

Figure 5.33

On a hard disk platter, data is recorded onto tracks, which are further broken down into sectors and clusters.

Track

Sector

Cluster

Figure 5.34

Defragmenting the hard drive arranges file fragments so that they are located next to each other. This makes the hard drive run more efficiently.

device, you could restore your computer to the settings that were in effect before the software or hardware installation. System Restore does not affect your personal data files (such as Microsoft Word documents, browsing history, or e-mail), so you won't lose changes made to these files when you use System Restore.

How does the computer remember its previous settings? Every time you start your computer or install a new application or driver, Windows automatically

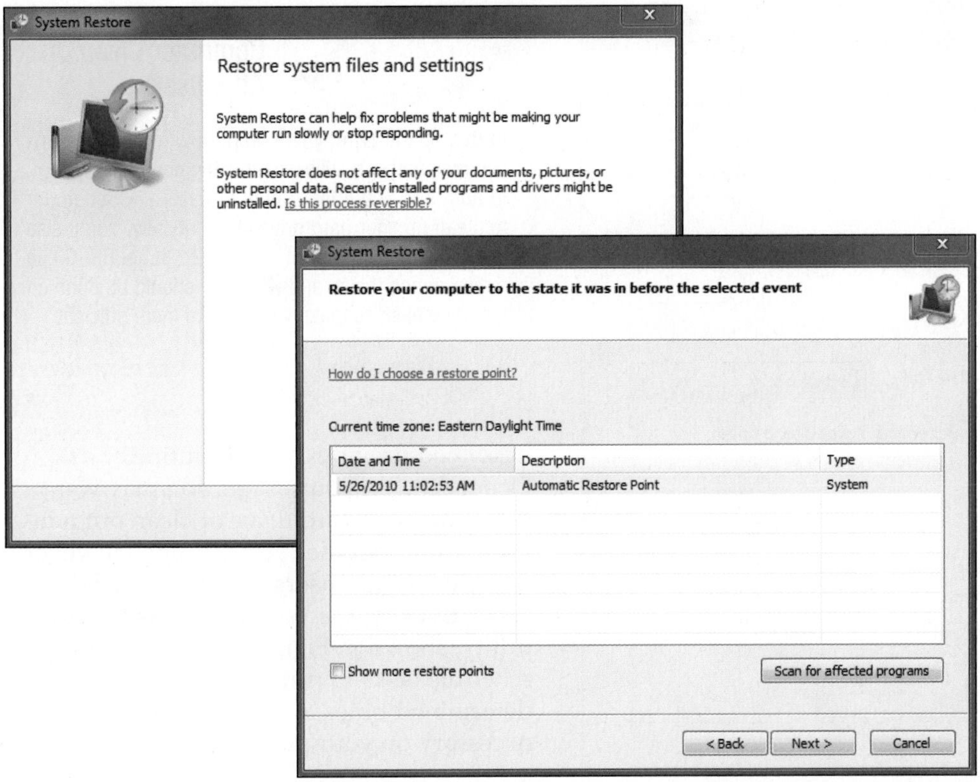

Figure 5.35

Setting a restore point is good practice before installing any hardware or software.

>The System Restore Wizard is found by clicking **Start**, **All Programs**, **Accessories**, **System Tools**. In the **System Tools** folder, click **System Restore**. The System Restore Wizard appears, with Restore Point shown on the second page of the Wizard.

creates a system restore point. You also can create and name your own restore points at any time. Creating a restore point is a good idea before making changes to your computer such as installing hardware or software. If something goes wrong with the installation process, Windows can reset your system to the restore point. As shown in Figure 5.35, Windows includes a System Restore Wizard that walks you through the process of setting restore points.

How can I protect my data in the event something malfunctions in my system? When you use the Windows **Backup and Restore** utility (found in the Control Panel), you can create a duplicate copy of all the data on your hard drive (or just the folders and files you specify) and copy it to another storage device, such as a Blu-ray Disc or external hard drive. A backup copy protects your data in the event your hard drive fails or files are accidentally erased. Although you may not need to back up every file on your computer, you should back up the files that are most important to you and keep the backup copy in a safe location. Mac OS X includes a backup utility called Time Machine that will automatically back up your files to a specified location. Apple also offers backup hardware called Time Capsules, which are wireless devices designed to work with Time Machine and record your backup data. Because Time Machine makes a complete image copy of your system, it can also be used to recover your system in the case of a fatal error. (For more information on backing up your files, see Chapter 9.)

If you encounter a non-recoverable error on a Windows machine that System Restore cannot repair, you can recover Windows from a system repair disc. A system repair disc is designed to fix problems with Windows 7. It will let you boot up Windows, and then give you options for repairing your system. It won't reinstall Windows 7 and it won't reformat your computer; it's

SOUND BYTE

Hard Disk Anatomy Interactive

In this Sound Byte, you'll watch a series of animations that show various aspects of a hard drive, including the anatomy of a hard drive, how a computer reads and writes data to a hard drive, and the fragmenting and defragmenting of a hard drive.

Task Scheduler Summary (Last refreshed: 9/16/2011 9:41:23 AM)

Overview of Task Scheduler

You can use Task Scheduler to create and manage common tasks that your computer will carry out automatically at the times you specify. To begin, click a command in the Action menu.

Tasks are stored in folders in the Task Scheduler Library. To view or perform an operation on an individual task, select

Task Status

Status of tasks that have started in the foll... | Last 24 hours ▼

Summary: 33 total - 5 running, 21 succeeded, 7 stopped, 0 failed

Task Name	Run Result	Run Start
⊞ Consolidator (last run succeede...		
⊞ GoogleUpdateTaskMachineCor...		
⊞ GoogleUpdateTaskMachineUA ...		
⊞ GoogleUpdateTaskUserS-1-5-2...		
⊞ HotStart (last run succeeded at		

Active Tasks

Active tasks are tasks that are currently enabled and have not expired.

Last refreshed at 9/16/2011 9:41:23 AM   [Refresh]

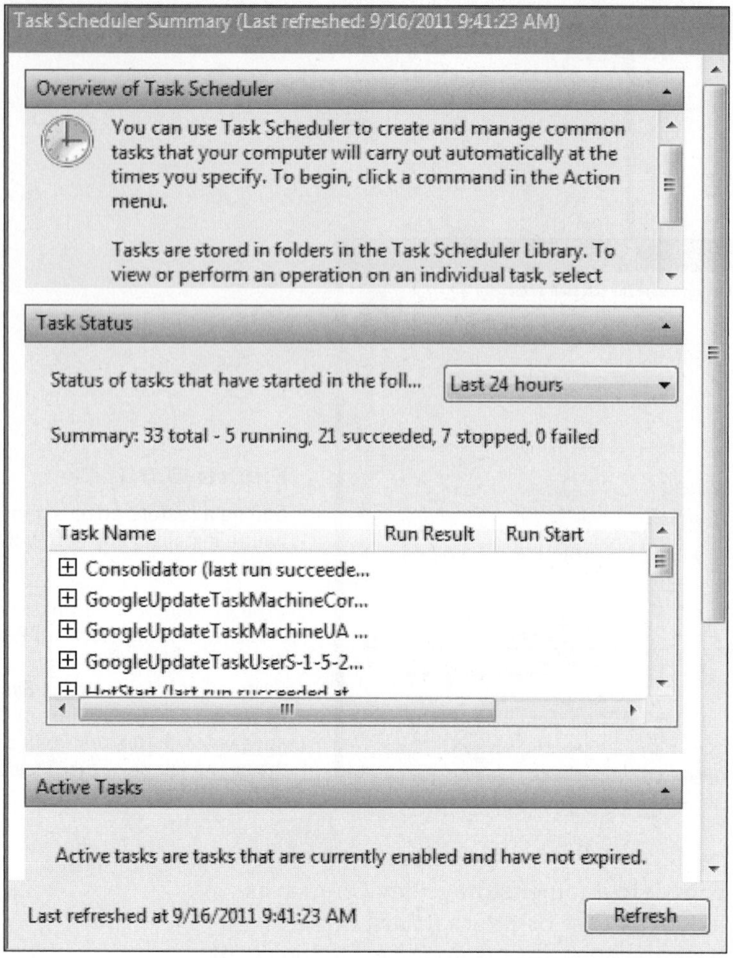

Figure 5.36

To keep your machine running in top shape, use Task Scheduler to schedule maintenance programs to run automatically at selected times and days.

>Task Scheduler is found by clicking **Start, All Programs, Accessories**, and then **System Tools**.

just a means to get to the recovery tools that are incorporated into Windows. Sometimes your computer comes with these repair discs, but often they do not. If you do not have a system repair disc, you should create one before problems arise. With Windows 7, it is easy to create a system repair disc. Insert a blank disc into the DVD drive, click Start, and type "System Repair" in the Search box. Then, click Create a System Repair Disc, make sure the appropriate drive is showing, and click Create disc.

The Task Scheduler Utility

How can I remember to perform all these maintenance procedures? To keep your computer system in top shape, it is important to run some of the utilities

described previously on a routine basis. Depending on your usage, you may want to defrag your hard drive or clean out temporary Internet files periodically. However, many computer users forget to initiate these tasks. Luckily, the Windows **Task Scheduler** utility, shown in Figure 5.36, allows you to schedule tasks to run automatically at predetermined times, with no additional action necessary on your part.

Accessibility Utilities

Are there utilities designed for users with special needs? Microsoft Windows includes an Ease of Access Center, which is a centralized location for assistive technology and tools to adjust accessibility settings. In the Ease of Access Center (see Figure 5.37), you can find tools to help you adjust the screen contrast, magnify the screen image, have screen contents read to you, and display an on-screen keyboard, as more fully explained in the following list. If you're not sure where to start or what settings might help, a questionnaire asks you about routine tasks and provides a personalized recommendation for settings that will help you use your computer. Some of these features are described below.

- **High Contrast:** Allows you to select a color scheme setting in which you can control the contrast between text and background. Because some visually impaired individuals find it easier to see white text on a dark background, there are color schemes that invert screen colors.
- **Magnifier:** A utility that creates a separate window that displays a magnified portion of the screen. This feature makes the screen more readable for users who have impaired vision.

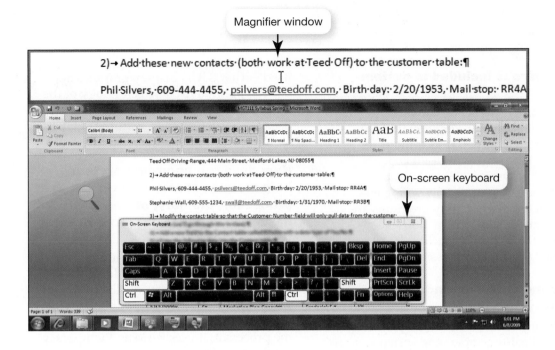

Figure 5.37

Microsoft Windows includes an Ease of Access Center to help users with disabilities. It has handy accessibility features such as a magnifier and an on-screen keyboard.

>The Ease of Access Center is found by clicking **Start, All Programs, Accessories, Ease of Access**.

- **Narrator:** A very basic speech program that reads what is on screen, whether it's the contents of a window, menu options, or text you have typed. The Narrator coordinates with text utilities such as Notepad and WordPad as well as with Internet Explorer, but it may not work correctly with other programs. For this reason, Narrator is not meant for individuals who must rely solely on a text-to-speech utility to operate the computer.

- **On-Screen Keyboard:** Displays a keyboard on the screen. You type by clicking on or hovering over the keys with a pointing device (mouse or trackball) or joystick. This utility, which is similar to the Narrator, is not meant for everyday use for individuals with severe disabilities. A separate program with more functionality is better in those circumstances.

- **Windows Speech Recognition:** An effective tool that allows you to dictate text and control your computer by voice. The Speech Recognition utility is in the Ease of Access section of the Control Panel.

Whether you use Windows, OS X, Linux, or another operating system, a fully featured operating system is available to meet your needs. As long as you keep the operating system updated and regularly use the available utilities to fine-tune your system, you should experience little trouble from your OS.

summary

1. What software is included in system software?

System software is the set of software programs that helps run the computer and coordinates instructions between application software and hardware devices. It consists of the operating system (OS) and utility programs. The OS controls how your computer system functions. Utility programs are programs that perform general housekeeping tasks for the computer, such as system maintenance and file compression.

2. What are the different kinds of operating systems?

There are many different kinds of operating systems. Real-time operating systems (RTOSs) require no user intervention. They are designed for systems with a specific purpose and response time (such as robotic machinery). Smartphones have their own specific operating systems, the latest of which allow the user to multitask. Current operating systems for desktops, notebooks, and netbooks have multitasking capabilities, as well as networking capabilities.

3. What are the most common operating systems?

Microsoft Windows is the most popular OS. It has evolved into a powerful multiuser operating system. The most recent release is Windows 7. Another popular OS is the Mac OS, which is designed to work on Apple computers. Apple's most recent release, Mac OS X, is based on the UNIX operating system. There are various versions of UNIX on the market, although UNIX is most often used on networks. Linux is an open source OS based on UNIX and designed primarily for use on personal computers, although it is often found as the operating system on servers.

4. How does the operating system provide a means for users to interact with the computer?

The operating system provides a user interface that enables users to interact with the computer. Most OSs today use a graphical user interface (GUI). Unlike the command- and menu-driven interfaces used earlier, GUIs display graphics and use the point-and-click technology of the mouse and cursor, making the OS more user-friendly. Common features of GUIs include windows, menus, and icons.

5. How does the operating system help manage resources such as the processor, memory, storage, hardware, and peripheral devices?

When the OS allows you to perform more than one task at a time, it is multitasking. To provide for seamless multitasking, the OS controls the timing of events the processor works on.

As the OS coordinates the activities of the processor, it uses RAM as a temporary storage area for instructions and data the processor needs. The OS is therefore responsible for coordinating the space allocations in RAM to ensure that there is enough space for the waiting instructions and data. If there isn't sufficient space in RAM for all the data and instructions, then the OS allocates the least necessary files to temporary storage on the hard drive, called *virtual memory*.

The OS manages storage by providing a file-management system that keeps track of the names and locations of files and programs. Programs called *device drivers* facilitate communication between devices attached to the computer and the OS. Device drivers translate the specialized commands of devices to commands that the OS can understand and vice versa, enabling the OS to communicate with every device in the computer system. Device drivers for common devices are included in the OS software, whereas other devices come with a device driver that you must install or download off the Web.

6. How does the operating system interact with application software?

All software applications need to interact with the CPU. For programs to work with the CPU, they must contain code that the CPU recognizes. Rather than having the same blocks of code appear in each application, the OS includes the blocks of code to which software applications refer. These blocks of code are called *application programming interfaces* (APIs).

7. How does the operating system help the computer start up?

When you start your computer, it runs through a special process called the *boot process*. The boot process consists of four basic steps: (1) The basic input/output system (BIOS) is activated when the user powers on the CPU. (2) In the POST check, the BIOS verifies that all attached devices are in place. (3) The operating system is loaded into RAM. (4) Configuration and customization settings are checked.

8. What are the main desktop and window features?

The desktop provides your first interaction with the OS and is the first image you see on your monitor once the system has booted up. It provides you with access to your computer's files, folders, and commonly used tools and applications. Windows are the rectangular panes on your screen that display applications running on your system. Common features of windows include toolbars, scrollbars, and Minimize, Maximize/Restore Down, and Close buttons.

9. How does the operating system help me keep my computer organized?

The OS allows you to organize the contents of your computer in a hierarchical structure of directories that includes files, folders, libraries, and drives. Windows Explorer helps you manage your files and folders by showing the location and contents of every drive, folder, and file on your computer. Creating folders is the key to organizing files because folders keep related documents together. Following naming conventions and using proper file extensions are also important aspects of file management.

10. What utility programs are included in system software, and what do they do?

Some utility programs are incorporated into the OS; others are sold as stand-alone off-the-shelf programs. Common Windows utilities include those that enable you to adjust your display, add or remove programs, compress files, defragment your hard drive, clean unnecessary files off your system, check for lost files and errors, restore your system to an earlier setting, back up your files, schedule automatic tasks, and check on programs that have stopped running.

 Companion Website

The Companion Website includes a variety of additional materials to help you review and learn more about the topics in this chapter. Go to: *www.pearsonhighered.com/techinaction*

Word Bank

- Backup and Restore
- Disk Cleanup
- Disk Defragmenter
- Error-checking
- file management
- files
- folders
- gadgets
- libraries
- Linux
- Mac OS
- operating system
- platform
- Safe mode
- Task Manager
- Task Scheduler
- utility programs
- virtual memory
- Windows Explorer

Instructions: Fill in the blanks using the words from the Word Bank above.

Vincent used (1) _____ to automatically schedule and run several (2) _____, those special-function programs that help with routine computer maintenance and repairs. Despite regularly running (3) _____ to help realign scattered file fragments on the hard drive, and (4) _____ to remove any unnecessary files, Vincent knew his computer was becoming progressively more sluggish. Vincent found he had to use the (5) _____ more frequently to check on programs that had stopped running, or to boot his system into (6) _____ so that he could perform further diagnostics while the computer was running in a limited state. Furthermore, Vincent knew with only 1 GB of RAM, his system was using (7) _____ and optimizing RAM storage by borrowing hard drive space. Vincent knew a hard drive error could happen at any time, so he had made a complete copy of his hard drive using the Windows (8) _____ utility. He relied on the (9) _____ tools to create an organized file system. He regularly created (10) _____ to better organize his files. He had been hearing lots of good reviews of Windows 7, Microsoft's new (11) _____ software, and in particular its additional file management feature, (12) _____, where he could access files, such as his pictures, from multiple locations in his computer system, without having to save them in a single folder. But many of his friends liked working with (13) _____, the Apple operating system. Both the PC and Mac operating systems included desktop features that Vincent found helpful, especially (14) _____ or widgets, the mini-programs that enable quick access to tools and activities such as calendars, stock prices, or weather indicators. Vincent wasn't sure which (15) _____ he would buy—a PC or a Mac—but he knew he needed to make a decision soon.

becoming computer literate

Using key terms from the chapter, write a letter to your 14-year-old cousin who just received her first computer, explaining the benefits of simple computer maintenance. First, explain any symptoms her computer may be experiencing, and then include a set of steps she can follow in setting up a regimen to remedy each problem. Make sure you explain some of the system maintenance utilities described in this chapter. Instruct your cousin on how to create a system repair disc and how to back up her files. Include any other utilities she might need, and explain why she should have them.

Instructions: Answer the multiple-choice and true–false questions below for more practice with key terms and concepts from this chapter.

Multiple Choice

1. Which is an example of a smartphone operating system?
a. Symbian
b. Windows 7
c. Mac OS
d. webOS

2. Which OS does not have a user interface that incorporates point-and-click technology?
a. Windows 7
b. MS-DOS
c. Linux
d. Mac OS X

3. Which is the correct order of the boot process?
a. check settings, load BIOS into RAM, activate BIOS, conduct POST
b. load OS into RAM, check settings, conduct POST, activate BIOS
c. activate BIOS, conduct POST, load OS into RAM, check settings
d. conduct POST, load OS into RAM, activate BIOS, check settings

4. Which of the following is not a file management tool?
a. folders
b. Windows Explorer
c. libraries
d. groups

5. Which best describes Plug and Play (PnP)?
a. a means for the user to interact with the computer
b. enables the processor to handle multiple operations, seemingly at the same time
c. programming code in the OS that coordinates with software
d. a feature that facilitates the installation of peripheral devices with the inclusion of drivers in the OS

6. The term that defines excessive swapping of files between RAM and virtual memory is
a. thrashing.
b. multitasking.
c. caching.
d. paging.

7. Which term describes the pictures that represent an object such as a software application or a folder?
a. icons
b. gadgets
c. taskbars
d. widgets

8. Which statement about using APIs is *not* true?
a. APIs prevent redundancies in software code.
b. APIs make it easier for developers to respond to OS changes.
c. APIs allow application software to interact with the OS.
d. APIs make it possible to close non-responding software and restart the computer.

9. Which utility eliminates the inefficiencies of the computer hard drive?
a. System Restore
b. Disk Defragmenter
c. File Compression
d. Disk Cleanup

10. Which of the following would be considered an accessibility utility?
a. System Restore
b. Narrator
c. Screen Saver
d. Safe Mode

True–False

_____ 1. All smartphones use the same operating system software.

_____ 2. The Android operating system is based on Microsoft Windows.

_____ 3. The amount of system RAM helps to determine which OS a computer uses.

_____ 4. Paging is the process of optimizing RAM storage by borrowing hard drive space.

_____ 5. Machines with built-in computers use real-time operating systems.

making the
transition to...
next semester

five five chapter

making the
transition to...
next semester

1. Organizing Your Files

Despite all the good advice, you may not have taken the time to organize your files on your computer. Click the Start button, and select Documents. Then, use the Snipping Tool to show your current file organization. If your system is well organized, explain how you set up your file management system. If you have not used file management features to organize your documents, develop a plan that outlines how you'll set up libraries, folders, and subfolders for your files.

2. Deciding On a New Computer

Your parents are getting you a new computer. Decide whether you want a desktop, notebook, or netbook and then describe how the choice may impact the operating system you get.

a. Discuss the advantages and disadvantages of Windows, Mac, and Linux operating systems.
b. Research whether you can use multiple operating systems on a single machine. Why might this be an important feature for you to consider?
c. Research how your smartphone and personal music player might sync with your computer's operating system.
d. Explain which system would be most useful to you.

3. Creating a Backup Plan

Your computer just shut down unexpectedly but, fortunately, you were able to get it back up and running without any loss of data. However, this was too close of a call, so you decide to back up your precious files once and for all. Research the specific steps you will need to take to initially create a backup and then maintain a current backup as your files change. Include in your research what stand-alone programs or operating system tools you will need to use, as well as any hardware devices or accessories you'll require. Then research the process of creating a disk image. What's the difference between creating a system backup and a disk image?

4. Portable Operating Systems

Traditionally, operating system files are stored permanently on your computer's hard drive. The operating system controls the user experience, so every computer you interact with (at home, at school, at your friend's house) may have different settings and features. Explore the concept of portable operating systems. What is a portable operating system? Why might it be useful to use one? Investigate a portable operating system, such as Slax or Ubuntu, and explain its features.

5. Smartphone OS

Your cell phone contract is up in a few weeks, and it's time to upgrade to a smartphone. Which smartphone would you buy, and why? What kind of OS does it have? What are the benefits and disadvantages of this OS compared to that of other smartphones? Is the smartphone OS compatible with the OS on your computer?

making the transition to... the workplace

1. Using a Web-Based OS

Your new job requires you to collaborate and visit with sales and management teams within the United States as well as globally. Discuss the benefits and disadvantages of using a Web-based operating system as a means to help you perform your job better.

2. Top Five Utility Programs

Create a list of the top five utilities you feel every computer should have. For each utility, discuss whether it is included in the operating system and/or if there are alternatives that can be downloaded for free or that can be purchased as stand-alone programs. Then, for each recommendation, include a review of the utility that has been written in the past year—make sure you document your sources.

3. Accessibility Features

Windows offers a lot of great accessibility tools for those needing extra assistance. The vice president for human resources at the company you work for has asked you to research some stand-alone accessibility programs to determine what else, if anything, is available. List software that is available to help those who have special computing needs.

4. Working with More Than One OS

The company you work for, which uses all Windows computers, has just acquired two other smaller companies, one that uses Macs and the other that uses Linux. Your boss, the CIO of the company, needs to decide what to do with all the various computer systems. You have been asked to provide information to your boss so that he can make an informed decision.

a. What are the advantages and disadvantages of letting the acquired companies continue using their current systems?
b. What are the advantages and disadvantages of converting all systems to one common system?

As you research, consider factors such as technical support, training for a new system, compatibility of files and calendars among all employees in the company, cost of new hardware, stability of operating systems, needed frequency of upgrades, and software compatibility.

critical thinking questions

Instructions: Some ideas are best understood by experimenting with them in our own minds. The following critical thinking questions are designed to demand your full attention but require only a comfortable chair—no technology.

1. Market Dominance

Microsoft and Apple are large corporations and have control of most of the operating system markets. While there have been some innovative changes to each of their proprietary operating systems, does their size and market dominance prevent more innovation? Why or why not? Linux, as an open source environment, is poised for greater innovation. Why do you think the Linux operating system doesn't have a greater market share?

2. A Web-Based OS

Operating system interfaces have evolved from a text-based console format to the current graphical user interface. Many believe the OS of the future will be on the cloud (the Internet) and Web-based. Discuss the implications of this type of operating system. What are the potential security issues of a Web-based operating system?

3. To Hackintosh or Not: That Is the Question

Using Mac's Boot Camp, or virtualization software such as VMware, it's possible to install Windows on a Mac. It isn't quite as easy to install Mac OS X on a PC, but it can be done. Those PCs that have been modified so that Mac OS X can be run on them are given the name *Hackintosh*. What are the benefits of tweaking a PC to run Mac OS X? Is it okay to violate Apple's End User Licensing Agreement (EULA)? If Apple changed its EULA to allow the installation of its software onto PCs, would that ultimately hurt Apple-branded computers?

4. Your Own Gadget/Widget?

There are plenty of interesting Windows gadgets and Mac OS widgets available—some for fun, some to aid in productivity, some with specific utilitarian roles. Design or describe what the best gadget or widget for you would be. What features must it have? Why would you need it?

Choosing the Best OS

Problem

You are the owner of a technology consulting firm. Your current assignments include advising several start-up clients on their technology requirements. The companies include a fashion design company, a small financial planning company, and an IT networking firm. The companies are holding off on buying anything until they hear from you as to the platform on which their computers should run. Obviously, one of the critical decisions for each company is the choice of operating system.

Task

Recommend the appropriate operating system for each company.

Process

1. Break up into teams that represent the three primary operating systems: Windows, Mac, or Linux. (Additional teams could be assigned to consider smartphone operating systems).

2. As a team, research the pros and cons of your operating system. What features does it have that would benefit each company? What features does it not have that each company would need? Why would your operating system be the appropriate (or inappropriate) choice for each company? Why is your OS better (or worse) than either of the other options?

3. Develop a presentation that states your position with regard to your operating system. Your presentation should have a recommendation and include facts to back it up.

4. As a class, decide which operating system would be the best choice for each company.

Conclusion

Because the operating system is the most critical piece of software in the computer system, the selection should not be taken lightly. The OS that is best for a fashion design agency may not be best for a financial planning firm. An IT networking firm may have different needs altogether. It is important to make sure you consider all aspects of the work environment and the type of work that is being done to ensure a good fit.

Software Piracy

In this exercise, you will research and then role-play a complicated ethical situation. The role you play may or may not match your own personal beliefs, but your research and use of logic will enable you to represent whichever view is assigned. An arbitrator will watch and comment on both sides of the arguments, and together the team will agree on an ethical solution.

Problem

Software publishers spend millions of dollars developing new products. Illegal copies of software, including operating system software, rob the developers and their shareholders of their rightful profits. In addition, some say that pervasive software piracy, especially in China, could potentially threaten job loss for U.S. software companies. However, some people believe that when they buy the software, they have the right to distribute their copy as they like, thus violating the software license agreement they accepted when installing the software.

Research Areas to Consider

- Software piracy

- Software licensing agreements

- CD piracy

- China antipiracy

Process

1. Divide the class into teams.

2. Research the areas cited above and devise a scenario in which an individual has been accused of software piracy.

3. Team members should write a summary that provides background information for their character—for example, representative of a software developer, public consumer of the software, or arbitrator—and detail their character's behaviors to set the stage for the role-playing event. Then team members should create an outline to use during the role-playing event.

4. Team members should arrange a mutually convenient time to meet for the exchange, using the collaboration feature of MyITLab, the discussion board feature of Blackboard, or meeting in person.

5. Team members should present their case to the class or submit a PowerPoint presentation for review by the rest of the class, along with the summary and resolution they developed.

Conclusion

As technology becomes ever more prevalent and integrated into our lives, more and more ethical dilemmas will present themselves. Being able to understand and evaluate both sides of the argument, while responding in a personally or socially ethical manner, will be an important skill.

TECHNOLOGY IN FOCUS

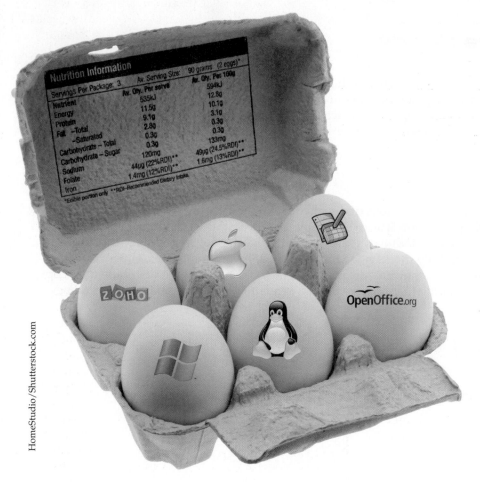

HomeStudio/Shutterstock.com

Computing | Alternatives

In this Technology in Focus feature, we explore software and hardware alternatives to working with a PC loaded up with Microsoft products. The world of computing is much broader than that, and many of the options we discuss are less expensive and more flexible. Let's get started by looking at alternatives to Microsoft Office products.

Application Software Alternatives

Corporations such as Microsoft and Apple develop proprietary software to be sold for a profit. The source code of proprietary software, the actual lines of instructional code that make the program work, is regulated and kept private within the confines of the developing company. Opponents of proprietary software contend that software should be developed without the profit motive and that the source code should be made available outside the boundaries of the developing company so that others may modify or improve the software.

Open source software is freely distributed (no royalties accrue to the creators), contains the source code, and can in turn be distributed to others. Therefore, you can download open source software for free from various Web sites, install it on as many computers as you wish, make changes to the source code if you know how to do this, and redistribute it to anyone you wish (as long as you don't charge for distributing it). In this section, we look at some open source software that you can download and use on your computer. For a list of open source resources available on the Web, visit **www .sourceforge.net**.

Productivity Software Alternative: OpenOffice.org

As mentioned in Chapter 4, the OpenOffice. org suite (which we'll refer to as Open-Office) is a free suite of productivity software programs that provides functionality similar to that of Microsoft Office. Versions of OpenOffice are available for a variety of operating systems, including Windows, Linux, and Mac. Support is offered in nearly 100 languages besides English, with more being added all the time by the development community. You can download the installation file you'll need to run OpenOffice at **www.openoffice.org**. The minimum system requirements for installing OpenOffice 3 in a Windows environment are less than those required for Microsoft Office.

The main components of OpenOffice are Writer (word processing), Calc (spreadsheet), Impress (presentation), and Base (database). These provide functionality similar to that of the Word, Excel, PowerPoint, and Access applications you might be familiar with in Microsoft Office. The OpenOffice 3 suite also includes additional programs. Draw provides the most common tools needed to communicate using graphics and diagrams, and Math creates equations and formulas for your documents.

You won't lose any compatibility with other software by using OpenOffice; it is compatible with most programs. This means that if your friend uses Microsoft Office and you send her an OpenOffice file, she can still read it, and you can read all of her Microsoft Office files, too. OpenOffice 3 is able to open Microsoft Office 2007 or 2010 files without the need for a conversion program. Although the individual applications in OpenOffice are not as fully featured as those in Microsoft Office, and do not have the ribbon interface found in the newest versions of the Office applications, OpenOffice is still a powerful productivity software suite, and the price is right.

One of the biggest advantages of an open source package like OpenOffice is that an incredible number of people continue to develop for it all the time. This means you have a huge library of extensions to select from. Extensions are small programs that install themselves into OpenOffice to provide additional functions. For example, one extension allows you to import and edit PDF files; another allows Draw to easily create barcodes. The library of extensions includes many hundreds of items, with more being added all the time.

When you launch OpenOffice (see Figure 1), you can choose a file type from the list displayed. Once you select the appropriate file type (such as spreadsheet, presentation, or text) and click Open, the appropriate application and a new, blank document will open so that you can begin working.

Writer Writer, the OpenOffice word processing application, is extremely similar in look and feel to Microsoft Word 2003 (see Figure 2). As is the case in Word, you can easily change text appearance in Writer by altering font type, style, alignment, and color. You can also easily insert graphics (pictures or clip art), tables, and hyperlinks into documents. Writer's wizards provide you with several templates you can use to create standard documents such as faxes, agendas, and letters. Special tools in Writer also allow you to create bibliographic references, indexes, and tables of contents.

Figure 1

Starting OpenOffice.org displays a list of file types from which you can choose to begin working on your project.

When saving a document in Writer, the default file format has an OpenDocument file (.odt) extension. By using the Save As command, you can save files in other formats, such as various versions of Word (.doc and .docx), Pocket Word (.psw) for mobile devices, Rich Text Format (.rtf), Text (.txt), and HTML Document (.htm). The handy Export Directly as PDF icon in Writer allows you to save documents as PDF files.

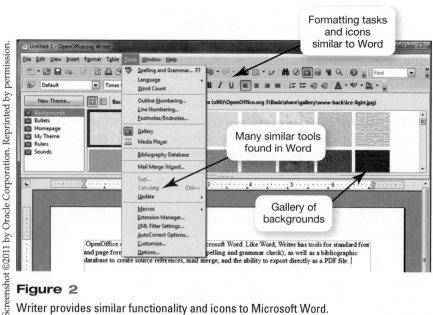

Figure 2

Writer provides similar functionality and icons to Microsoft Word.

Calc Once you open a Calc spreadsheet, you enter text, numbers, and formulas into the appropriate cells, just as you would in Microsoft Excel. You also can apply a full range of formatting options (font size, color, style, and so on) to the cells, making it easy to create files such as the monthly budget spreadsheet shown in Figure 3. Built-in formulas and functions simplify the job of creating spreadsheets. Similar to the newest versions of Excel, Calc has toolbars that change in response to the tasks at hand, so for example, when a chart is the active element in the spreadsheet, the toolbars change to reflect only those tools needed to work on charts (see Figure 3).

When saving a document in Calc, the default file format has an .ods extension. You can also save files in other formats, such as Excel (.xls and .xlsx) and Pocket Excel (.pxl) for use on mobile devices. The Export Directly as PDF icon is also available in Calc.

Impress When you select Presentation from the OpenOffice start-up interface, a wizard is displayed that offers you the option of creating a blank Impress presentation or building one from one of two supplied templates. The templates provide suggestions regarding building a presentation to introduce a new product or recommend a strategy. The number of templates included with Impress is smaller than those supplied with Microsoft PowerPoint. If you are interested in more templates, be sure to install some of the extensions available. In addition, you can also search using Google with the keywords "OpenOffice.org Impress Templates." You'll find a wide variety of templates for Impress that others have created and that you can download free of charge. The functionality of Impress is similar to that of PowerPoint, so you should not notice any major differences as you build your presentation.

Base If you want to create or just manipulate databases, Base enables you to create and modify tables, forms, queries, and reports by using wizards, design views, and SQL views. Base works seamlessly with files created in most database applications, although you will need a separate converter to work with Microsoft Access 2007 and 2010. Although Base may not be as intuitive to work with as Microsoft Access, once you understand the basic structure of the program, you will recognize that it is comparable to the functionality of Microsoft Access and SQL Server.

Database Software Alternative: MySQL

While Base, the OpenOffice database program just described, is perfectly functional, if you're interested in getting your hands on a free high-end SQL database application, the most popular open source option is MySQL (**www.mysql.com**). Sporting many of the features contained in SQL Server and Oracle Database 11g, MySQL is a powerful database program you can use to develop serious database applications. The two main components you should download and install with MySQL are the Database Server and the Query Browser. You use the Database Server to create tables for your database and enter your data. The Query Browser provides a visual interface for the database to display the results of queries you create.

Productivity Software: Web-Based Alternatives

Open source alternatives to Microsoft Office applications are attractive because they are free, and they are also convenient because of their availability. Like most other applications, though, you use these programs on the computer where you installed them. For the ultimate in accessibility and transferability, consider using Web-based Office software alternatives. You can be productive almost anywhere because you access these programs from the Internet without having to install the software on your computer. So if you are at friend's house, you can still get to your files and use the program. Moreover, with Web-based applications you can collaborate on a document online with others, thus avoiding the coordination mess that generally occurs when transferring documents among colleagues or classmates via e-mail. While Microsoft has its own set of Office Web apps that offer collaboration and anytime accessibility of Web-based software, there are some non-Microsoft alternatives. All these applications are fully compatible with Microsoft Office—including the latest formats—and run on Mac, Windows, and Linux platforms.

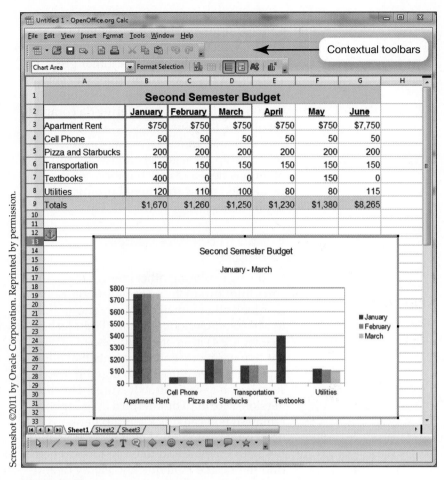

Screenshot ©2011 by Oracle Corporation. Reprinted by permission.

Figure 3

Calc offers many of the same features as Microsoft Excel, including contextual toolbars that change in response to the tasks at hand.

Google Docs (**docs.google.com**) is the leader in Web-based productivity applications. The site includes word processing, spreadsheet, and presentation functionality, as well as forms and drawing applications. If you are looking for basic productivity software that you can access from any computer, Google Docs is sufficient. But, if you're looking to produce a sophisticated spreadsheet or publication-quality report, you might need to use a more full-featured product. Keep in mind as well that when uploading files to work in Google Docs, the file cannot be larger than 1 MB.

ThinkFree Online Office (**www.thinkfree.com**) is an online productivity suite composed of word processing (Write), spreadsheet (Calc), and presentation (Show) software. ThinkFree also offers ThinkFree Mobile for Windows, Android, and iPhone smartphones so that you're covered on all your mobile devices. The My Office feature provides users with 1 GB of free Internet storage.

Zoho (www.zoho.com) is another great Web-based resource for productivity software. The site differentiates itself from other Web-based products by offering "a complete set of tools for your business" including project management software, customer relationship management software, and other business and collaboration solutions in addition to the traditional productivity applications.

E-Mail Client Alternative: Thunderbird

If you are exploring other choices for Microsoft Office productivity applications, don't overlook other e-mail clients as alternatives to Microsoft Outlook. Mozilla Thunderbird (see Figure 4) is an open source e-mail client that has many enhancements that allow you to organize e-mail with tagging, folders, search, and saved search features. The latest version, Mozilla Thunderbird 3, has tabbed e-mail so you can quickly jump between open e-mails, and improved search capabilities with timeline and filtering tools to help find the exact e-mail quickly. Plenty of add-ons, including a blog editor, calendar, calculator, and multimedia tools, are available from the Mozilla Web site (**www.mozilla .org**). Thunderbird is not Web-based (unlike

If you are exploring other choices for Microsoft Office productivity applications, don't overlook other e-mail clients as alternatives to Microsoft Outlook.

Gmail, Yahoo! Mail, and Hotmail), but can run on Windows, Mac, and Linux platforms.

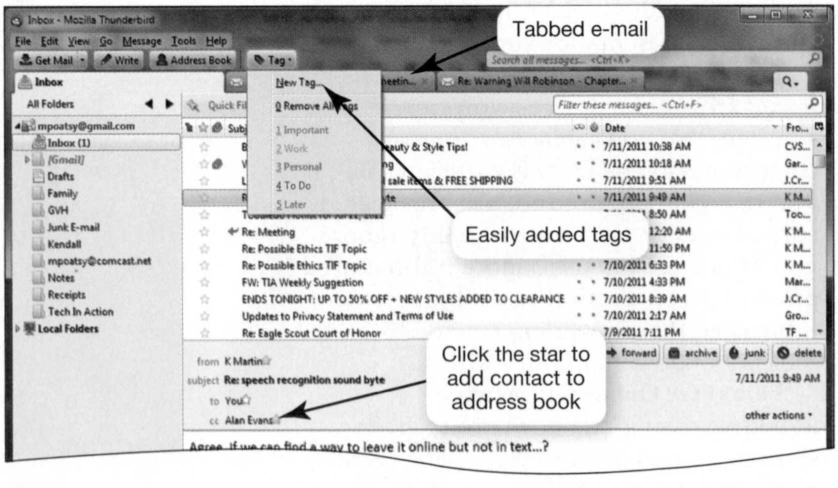

Drawing Software Alternatives: Draw, Dia, and Sketch-up

Draw: Microsoft Visio is a popular program for creating flowcharts and diagrams. However, Visio can be costly. As mentioned previously, OpenOffice includes a program called Draw that allows you to create simple graphs, charts, and diagrams.

Dia: Another option is Dia, a free program that allows you to create Visio-like diagrams and charts. You can download a Windows-compatible version of Dia from **live.gnome.org/Dia**. The Web site also offers a tutorial to get you up and running.

SketchUp: Google offers another charting option. SketchUp (**sketchup.google.com**) is a full-featured 3D modeling software application. SketchUp comes in two versions. SketchUp 7 is a free program that you can use to create, modify, and share 3D models. SketchUp Pro 7 is more fully featured and is available for about $500. SketchUp coordinates with other Google apps, such as Google Earth, so you can design a building and place it right on a Google Earth image to see how it would fit in the lot.

Web Page Authoring Software Alternative: SeaMonkey

Although Microsoft Word and OpenOffice Writer can save documents as HTML files, sometimes you need a more versatile tool

Figure 4
Thunderbird is an open source alternative to Microsoft Outlook with convenient features such as tabbed e-mail, quick tags, and improved search capabilities.

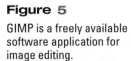

Change pixel height and width

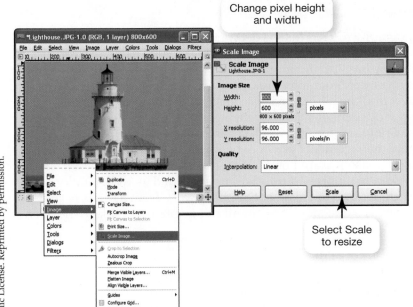

Select Scale to resize

Figure 5

GIMP is a freely available software application for image editing.

for creating Web pages, especially for larger sites with many linked pages. Adobe Dreamweaver is a popular commercial package for building Web sites, and Expression Web is a Web authoring application that is complementary to the Microsoft Office 2010 suite. Both of those solutions are proprietary applications that you must purchase. If you are looking for an open source alternative, SeaMonkey Composer, part of the SeaMonkey all-in-one Internet application suite (**www.seamonkey-project.org**), is a free, open source WYSIWYG ("what you see is what you get") Web authoring application that is compatible with the Windows, Mac, and Linux platforms. SeaMonkey Composer supports cascading style sheets, positioned layers, and dynamic image and table resizing. The SeaMonkey suite also includes a Web browser, e-mail and newsgroup client, and IRC chat.

Image Editing Software Alternative: GIMP

Do you need to create or edit some digital art but can't afford a high-end package such as Adobe Photoshop, or even a consumer package such as Adobe Photoshop Elements? Download a free copy of GIMP (short for GNU Image Manipulation Program) from **www.gimp.org** and you'll find a set of tools almost as powerful as Photoshop. GIMP is available for systems running Windows, Mac, Linux, and UNIX. Many good tutorials, available at **www.gimp.org/tutorials**, can turn you into an accomplished user in no time.

Here are some handy things you can do with GIMP in five minutes or less:

- Crop or change the size of an image (see Figure 5)

- Reduce the file size of an image by decreasing its quality

- Fix perspective distortion

GIMP also enables you to use advanced techniques such as applying image filters, creating textures and gradients, drawing digital art, creating animated images through layer manipulation, and changing a photo into a painting or sketch.

SeaMonkey Composer supports cascading style sheets, positioned layers, and dynamic image and table resizing.

Operating System Alternatives

Because Windows is the most widely used OS, with more than 90 percent of the market share, it's a prime target for viruses and other annoyances. From a virus creator or hacker's perspective, nuisances that spread via Windows have the greatest chance of causing the most aggravation. A lot of spyware, computer viruses, and other hacker nuisances are designed to take advantage of security flaws in Windows. Working with an open source alternative such as Linux or on an Apple computer with Mac OS X—neither of which is as widely used as Windows—makes your computer less of a target for these annoyances.

Linux

Installing open source application software such as OpenOffice on a Windows machine is simple. Changing your OS from Windows to an open source OS such as Linux is a bit more complex. Why would you want to install Linux if you already are running Windows?

One reason to install an open source operating system is portability. Depending on which version of Linux you use (see some options listed in Figure 6), you may be able to take it with you on a flash drive and use it on almost any computer. This portability feature appeals to people who use many different computers, such as using a computer in a remote office location or in a hotel's business center. Instead of getting used to a new configuration every time you're away from your home computer, wouldn't it be nice to have the same environment you're used to everywhere you go? Such portability also offers an additional level of protection for users of public computers. As explained in Chapter 9, using an open source OS that's installed on a portable flash drive helps reduce your risk of picking up viruses and malware from public computers. In addition, it enhances privacy, because temporary Internet files are stored on the portable device on which the OS is installed, rather than on the hard drive of the public computer you are using. Lastly, many users of netbooks, the lightest, smallest category of notebook computers, have opted to install Linux because it takes up less space on the hard drive and runs faster than the proprietary software that was installed originally by the manufacturer. In the next section, we explore the different varieties of Linux and explain how to install them.

Which Linux to Use Linux is available for download in various packages known as **distributions**, or **distros**. Think of distros as being like different makes and models of cars. Distros include the underlying Linux kernel (the code that provides Linux's basic functionality) and special modifications to the OS, and may also include additional open source software (such as OpenOffice). Which distro is right for you?

A good place to start researching distros is **www.distrowatch.com**. This site tracks Linux distros and provides helpful tips for beginners on choosing one. Figure 6 lists some popular Linux distros and their home pages.

Figure 6 | LINUX DISTRIBUTIONS

Distro	Home Page
Debian GNU/Linux	www.debian.org
Fedora Core (Red Hat)	www.fedoraproject.org
Gentoo Linux	www.gentoo.org
Mandriva Linux	www.mandriva.com
PCLinuxOS	www.pclinuxos.com
Slackware Linux	www.slackware.com
Ubuntu	www.ubuntu.com

Before you can decide which distro is right for you, there are a few things to consider. The overall requirements to run Linux are relatively modest:

- A 1.2 GHz processor
- 256 MB RAM (light on graphics edition) up to 1 GB RAM (standard desktop edition)
- 8 GB of hard drive space
- VGA graphics card capable of 640 × 480 resolution

Just like any other software program, however, Linux performs better with a faster processor and more memory. Depending on how much additional software is deployed in the distro you choose to use, your system requirements may be higher, and you may need more hard drive space. Check the specific recommendations for the distro you're considering on that distro's Web site.

Experimenting with Linux Some Linux distros (such as Ubuntu and PC-LinuxOS) are designed to run from a CD/DVD or flash drive. This eliminates the need to install files on the computer's hard drive. Therefore, you can boot up from a flash drive on an existing Windows PC and run Linux without disturbing the existing Windows installation.

Booting your existing computer from a CD/DVD or flash drive-based version of Linux is a low-risk way to experiment with Linux and see how well you like it. Ubuntu, for example, uses an extremely familiar-looking, Windows-like desktop. When you access Ubuntu, you get GIMP, OpenOffice, and many other software packages, including utilities and games.

Figure 7 shows Ubuntu in action. The computer boots from the Ubuntu disc when it detects it in the optical disc drive. As part of the installation sequence, Ubuntu automatically detects components of the computer (such as the network card) and cons Linux to recognize them. You will have no trouble browsing the Internet because Firefox, a Web browser, is included with the Ubuntu distro. You can also save any files you create with the included Open-Office suite to a flash drive.

Mandriva Linux offers several versions of its OS. Mandriva Linux 2010 is the company's most recent and most basic product. It is free, remains true to the original open source principles, and is installable. Alternatively, you can try Mandriva in the "live" mode, which doesn't require installation. Other versions with more features are available for a fee, including PowerPack 2010, which offers a more complete package that includes added multimedia and gaming software. In addition, for a small fee, you can get Mandriva Flash. Flash is Mandriva's portable OS option, and is installed on a convenient 8 GB flash drive. This portable version does not make changes on the host computer, so you can bring your computer environment anywhere you go. Mandriva Flash takes up one-quarter of the flash drive, leaving the remaining 6 GB free so you can conveniently store and take with you all your office work and Internet and multimedia files.

When you install the Mandriva OS, you also get other open source applications, such as OpenOffice, the Firefox browser, and the KMail e-mail manager, as well as several multimedia programs including applications for managing photo albums and digital music collections.

Figure 7

The Ubuntu user interface resembles the Windows desktop.

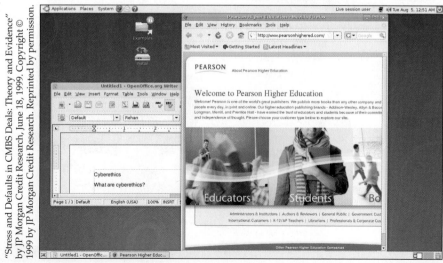

In addition to all this, Mandriva includes security features. The OS divides security levels into five rankings that range from "Poor" to "Paranoid." Your choice depends on how you're using the system. (Select "Paranoid" if you're running business transactions through your computer.) You also can set up a simple-to-con firewall called Shorewall to prevent unauthorized Internet users from accessing your personal network.

If you don't like Mandriva Linux or Ubuntu, head out to **www.distrowatch.com** and find another free Linux distro to install. With hundreds of distros available, you're sure to find one that fits your needs.

Mac OS X Lion

Many Mac users have switched from Windows because of the "coolness" of the operating system, Mac OS X. The latest version, Lion, has many slick and innovative features that are tempting to even the most loyal Windows users. If you've been using Windows for a while, you shouldn't have any problem making the transition to Mac OS X. You'll notice immediately that Mac OS X uses the same desktop metaphors as Windows, including icons for folders and a Trash Can (similar to a Recycle Bin) to delete documents. It also includes a window-based interface comparable to the one you're already accustomed to using in Windows.

Mac OS X is based on the UNIX operating system, which is exceptionally stable and reliable. Aside from stability, security and safety are great reasons to switch to Mac OS X. As mentioned above, the Mac operating system does not seem as vulnerable as Windows is to the exploitation of security flaws by hackers. This doesn't necessarily mean that Mac OS X is better constructed than Windows; it could just be that because Windows has a lead in market share, it is a more attractive target for hackers. Regardless of the reason, you're probably somewhat less likely to be inconvenienced by viruses, hacking, and spyware if you're running Mac OS X. Of course, you won't have any better protection from spam, phishing, or other Internet scams than you would with Internet Explorer, so you still need to stay alert.

Lion Features When you boot up a Mac, a program called the Finder automatically starts. This program is like Windows Explorer and controls the desktop and the windows with which you interact. It's always running when the Mac is on. With the Quick Look feature, it is possible for you to view the contents of a file without ever opening it. This allows you to flip through multipage documents, watch videos, and view an entire presentation with just a single click of the mouse. At the top of the desktop is the menu bar. The options on the menu bar change according to which program is "active" (that is, foremost on your screen) at the moment. When you click the Apple icon in the upper left corner, a drop-down menu displays, from which you can select several options. The Dock is similar to the Taskbar in Windows and includes a strip of icons that displays across the bottom of the desktop.

The newest version, Lion, introduces several features that are already available on the iPhone and iPad, such as multi-touch gestures. Instead of just tapping the trackpad, you can swipe your fingers in different ways to initiate different commands. For example, swiping three fingers left and right switches between open applications, and swiping with two fingers navigates through web pages or documents. The desktop, now called the Launchpad, looks like that of the iPhone and iPad, where all applications are visible on the screen (see Figure 8).

Lion has improved other features from previous versions. Mission Control, a new feature, combines familiar navigation tools such as Exposé (which helps you see clearly the open applica-

Figure 8

Mission Control is the command center of Lion, the newest version of Mac OS X. The desktop manager brings together familiar features such as Exposé, Dashboard, and Spaces to help you see and navigate everything running on your Mac.

© NetPhotos / Alamy

tions on your desktop all at once), Dashboard (which displays installed Widgets), and Spaces (which allows you to group applications on your desktop) into one place. Each Finder window has an area on the left known as the Sidebar, which holds any folders you specify (even though the icons don't look like folders). This makes navigation easier and faster. You can choose to view the contents of files and folders in three different views: icon view, list view, and column view. Navigating around a Finder window and copying and moving files works similarly to how it does in Windows.

If you do have some Windows software you need to run, no worries—Mac OS X lets you install Windows Vista or 7 and run them using the built-in utility Boot Camp. With Boot Camp installed, you can fire up your computer in either Windows or Mac OS X. Other software tools like VMware and Parallels let you switch between Mac OS X and Windows without rebooting at all.

Configuring a Mac In Windows, you make changes to settings and preferences through the Control Panel. In Mac OS X Lion, you use System Preferences, which is an option on the Apple menu. Selecting System Preferences from the Apple menu displays the window shown in Figure 9.

Protecting Your Mac Although Macs tend to be attacked less frequently by viruses and other hacker nuisances than are PCs running Windows, you can still be vulnerable if you don't take precautions. Mac OS X comes with a firewall, but you should take the necessary steps to configure it properly before connecting to the Internet for the first time, because the firewall is set, by default, to allow all incoming connections. As shown in Figure 10, to block all connections except those that are critical to your computer's operation, select "Allow only essential services." If you'd rather set up your firewall on a per-application basis, select the "Set access for specific services and applications" option.

In addition, hackers may be creating viruses and other nuisances to exploit security holes in the Mac OS. Mac users, like Windows users, should keep their software up to date with the latest fixes and software patches by setting their system to check automatically for software updates on a periodic basis. On Macs, this feature is available through the System Preferences window.

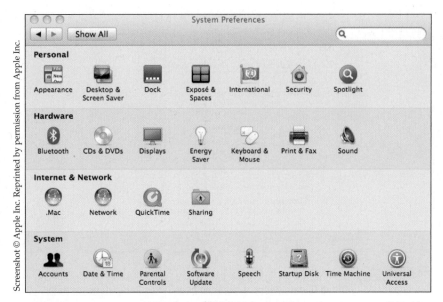

Figure 9

Much like the Control Panel in Windows, the System Preferences window allows you to customize and configure Mac OS X.

>To get to System Preferences, click the Apple menu icon in the top left corner of the screen and choose System Preferences.

Figure 11 shows the options you should choose to keep the Mac OS up to date. The Check Now button enables you to check for immediate updates, which is a great thing to do when you first set up your computer. Then you can choose to have your computer check for updates regularly by scheduling software updates to run automatically at a time convenient to you. Make sure you choose to have the updates downloaded automatically. This feature alerts you when updates are ready to be installed. In addition to these precautions, antivirus software such as Norton is available for Mac OS X.

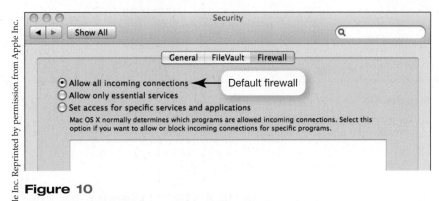

Figure 10

Macs have a firewall, but be sure to configure the firewall before you connect to the Internet.

>Click on the Security icon under the Personal section of the System Preferences window. When the Security window opens, click on the Firewall button to display the Firewall configuration screen.

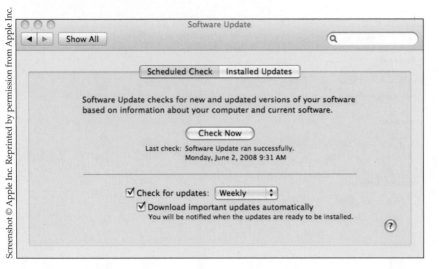

Figure 11

Keeping the Mac OS up to date with the latest software fixes and patches greatly decreases your chances of being inconvenienced by hackers.

>From the Apple menu, choose System Preferences, and then click Software Update.

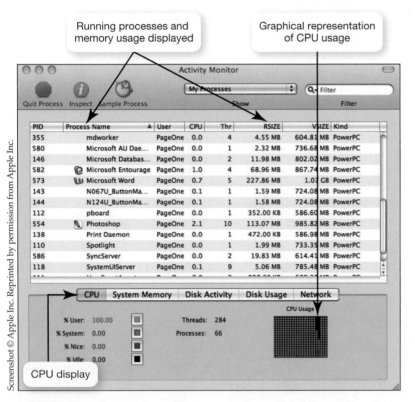

Figure 12

Similar to the Task Manager in Windows, the Activity Monitor analyzes the performance of a Mac.

>Go to the Utilities folder found in the Applications folder on your hard drive and double-click Activity Monitor to open the utility.

Mac OS X Utility Programs Just like Windows, the Mac OS contains a wide variety of utility programs to help users maintain and evaluate their computers. In Macs, utility programs are located in a folder named Utilities within the Applications folder on the hard drive.

If you're a Windows user, you know that the Windows Task Manager utility can help you determine how your system is performing. In Macs, a similar utility, shown in Figure 12, is called the Activity Monitor. It shows what programs (processes) are currently running and how much memory they're using. The CPU, System Memory, Disk Activity, Disk Usage, and Network buttons indicate the activity in each of these crucial areas.

Like the Systems Properties box in Windows, the Mac OS System Profiler shown in Figure 13 displays all the hardware (and software) installed in a Mac, including the type of processor, the amount of RAM installed, and the amount of VRAM on the video card.

As you can see, operating a Mac is fairly simple and is similar to working in the Windows environment. If you need more help beyond what we provide in this Technology in Focus feature, there are many books that will help you make a smooth transition to using an Apple computer.

Hardware Alternatives

Tired of your Windows-based PC? Is your old computer too slow for your current needs and not worth upgrading? If so, you may be in the market for some new hardware. Before you head off to Best Buy for yet another Windows-based computer, why not consider two alternatives: (1) moving to an Apple platform or (2) building your own computer.

Apple Computers

One way to decide whether a Mac is right for you, and is worth the extra money you'll pay for a Mac over a comparable Windows-based PC, is to get your hands on one and take it for a test drive. Chances are that someone you know has a Mac. Alternatively, your school might have a Mac lab or have Macs in the library. If not, then Apple has retail stores chock full of employees who are very happy to let you test out the equipment. You also can test Macs at Best Buy. Be sure to check out the full lineup of Macs (see Figure 14). The MacBook Air is Apple's thinnest notebook. It weighs three pounds, and includes a

13-inch screen and a full-sized keyboard. The MacBook weighs in at under five pounds and features the Intel Core 2 Duo processor and a 13-inch screen. The iMac line features sleek, space-saving desktop units sporting fast quad-core Intel Core i5.

Some people are switching to Macs because they love their iPhones so much. Many Apple fans think Macs are more user-friendly and stylish than their PC competitors. Professionals such as digital artists and graphic designers who create or edit computer images change to Macs because the applications these users rely on deliver superior features on the Apple platform.

Do It Yourself!

There is definitely satisfaction in doing a job yourself, and building a computer is no different. Of course, building a computer isn't for everyone, but for those who enjoy working with their hands and don't mind doing some up-front research, it can be a rewarding experience.

Many Web sites can provide guidance for building your own Windows-based computer. Tom's Hardware (**www.tomshardware .com/reviews/build-your-own-pc,2601.html**) is a good place to start. Just search on "How to build your own computer" and you'll find plenty of online help and advice. To start, you need a list of parts. Here's what you'll typically need:

1. **Case:** Make sure the case you buy is an ATX-style case, which accommodates the newest motherboards. You also want a case with adequate cooling fans. You'll want to decide between a full tower (about 24 inches tall) or a mid- or mini-tower. Also, be sure there are enough drive bays in the case to handle the hard drive and any other peripheral drives (CD/DVD, Blu-ray, and so on) you'll be installing.

2. **Motherboard:** Make sure that the motherboard you buy can accommodate the CPU you have chosen. Many motherboards come with sound, video, and network capabilities integrated into the motherboard. These may work fine for you, but be sure to check that they meet your needs. You may want to buy a motherboard without these components and install separate higher-end graphics and sound cards, instead. In that case,

	Macintosh-3
Page One Editing's PowerBook5,9	

Contents
▼ Hardware
　ATA
　Audio (Built In)
　Bluetooth
　Diagnostics
　Disc Burning
　Fibre Channel
　FireWire
　Graphics/Displays
　Hardware RAID
　Memory

Hardware Overview:

Model Name:	PowerBook G4 17"
Model Identifier:	PowerBook5,9
Processor Name:	PowerPC G4 (1.5)
Processor Speed:	1.67 GHz
Number Of CPUs:	1
L2 Cache (per CPU):	512 KB
Memory:	1 GB
Bus Speed:	167 MHz
Boot ROM Version:	4.9.6f0
Serial Number:	W86050LKSX0
Sudden Motion Sensor:	
State:	Enabled

Figure 13

The System Profiler is similar to the Systems Properties dialog box in Windows and reveals a wealth of information about the hardware and software in the computer.

>To launch System Profiler, from the Apple menu, click About this Mac, and then click the More Info button.

ensure that the motherboard has enough PCI expansion slots for the video and sound cards as well as other additional components you want to install. Also make sure that your motherboard has at least six USB ports. Some motherboards now have USB 3.0 ports as well as the older USB 2.0. It is also good to include an eSATA port to connect an external hard drive for extra storage.

3. **Processor (CPU):** Get the fastest one you can afford, because it will help to extend the life of your computer. Review the CPU section in Chapter 6 to determine all the components of a processor you should consider. Many processors come with a fan installed to cool the unit; if not, you'll need to purchase a processor cooling fan.

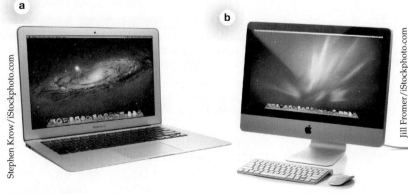

Figure 14

(a) The MacBook Air. (b) The iMac.

4. **RAM:** Check your motherboard specifications before buying RAM to ensure you buy the correct type and amount that will fit into the available slots. In addition, make sure that the amount of RAM you choose is supported by your operating system (32 bit vs. 64 bit).

5. **Hard drive:** Some cases now support up to six drives, so you may be able to make a few choices here. SSD drives are more expensive, but they are incredibly fast. In fact, many home system builders are using SSD drives as the boot drives so that the system boots in as little as 10 seconds. The price per gigabyte on mechanical drives has been rapidly coming down in recent years, so consider a large-volume drive. For optimal performance, choose a hard drive spinning at 7,200 rpm or 10,000 rpm.

6. **Power supply:** Make sure to get a power supply with adequate wattage to handle the load generated by all of the computer's components. Don't forget that as time passes you'll probably be adding more peripherals and drives to your system. Be sure to select a power supply wattage that can support that growth.

7. **Video card:** Low-end cards with 512 MB of video memory are fine for normal computer use, but for gaming or displaying high-end graphics or videos, get a card with 1 GB or more, depending on your budget. If you will be using a digital LCD monitor or hooking your gaming system to your computer, make sure that the video card has a DVI connection or an HDMI port.

8. **Sound card:** Make sure to get a PCI Express card that is compatible with Sound Blaster (the standard for sound cards).

9. **Optical drives (CD/DVD and Blu-ray):** A CD/DVD drive is necessary for software installation. You may want to install a Blu-ray drive to view your favorite movies using high-definition technology, or a Blu-ray burner to archive large volumes of data.

In addition to these components, you'll need a keyboard, a mouse or other pointing device, a monitor, and OS software.

You can buy these components at reputable Web sites such as Tiger Direct (**www.tigerdirect.com**) or NewEgg (**www.newegg.com**). Once you have the components, it is almost as simple as screwing them into the case and connecting them properly. Make sure you read all the installation instructions that come with your components before beginning installation. Don't forget to check YouTube or the Web sites of component manufacturers for handy how-to videos and step-by-step installation guides. Then read a complete installation tutorial such as the one found at the Tech Report Web site (**www.techreport.com**), which provides an excellent visual guide to assembling a computer. Now, grab your screwdriver and get started. You'll be up and running in no time. The advantages and disadvantages of building your own Windows-based computer are shown in Figure 15.

As you can see, there are many computing options other than a Windows-based computer running commercial software applications. We hope you spread your wings and try a few of them.

Figure 15 | CONSIDERATIONS WHEN BUILDING YOUR OWN COMPUTER

Advantages	Disadvantages
You get exactly the configuration and features you want.	There is no technical support when things go wrong.
You have the option of using components other than those that are used in mass-produced computers.	You'll need to examine more complex technical specifications (such as which CPU works with the motherboard you want), which may overwhelm the average computer user.
If you succeed, you will get a feeling of satisfaction from a job well done.	You will not necessarily save money.

Multiple Choice

Instructions: Answer the multiple-choice questions below for more practice with key terms and concepts from this Technology in Focus feature.

1. OpenOffice Impress is a
   a. contacts program.
   b. database program.
   c. presentation program.
   d. spreadsheet program.

2. A free alternative to Adobe Photoshop that can be used to edit images is
   a. GIMP.
   b. Thunderbird.
   c. SeaMonkey.
   d. Draw.

3. What kind of software can be installed on as many computers as you wish?
   a. proprietary software
   b. commercial software
   c. Apple software
   d. open source software

4. Which is a popular open source program for creating diagrams and charts?
   a. Visio
   b. Dia
   c. SketchUp
   d. Impress

5. What new feature of Mac OS X Lion acts as a command center for the desktop?
   a. Launchpad
   b. Mission Control
   c. Dashboard
   d. Spotlight

6. By default, files saved in Write use which extension?
   a. .txt
   b. .docx
   c. .odt
   d. .pdf

7. Which statement about Linux is *false*?
   a. Because so many developers contribute to the OS, Linux is a prime target for hackers.
   b. Linux is used on a lot of netbooks because it takes up less hard drive space than proprietary software.
   c. When stored on a flash drive, Linux provides greater privacy when surfing the Internet on public computers.
   d. Some versions of Linux can be stored on a CD and used on many different computers.

8. What is *not* necessarily an advantage of building your own computer?
   a. having outside support if something goes wrong
   b. getting the exact configuration you want
   c. using components that aren't mass produced
   d. potentially saving money

9. One popular Linux distro is
   a. Leopard.
   b. Base.
   c. OpenOffice.
   d. Ubuntu.

10. When building your own computer, which of these should not be included with the motherboard?
    a. PCI expansion slots
    b. processor cooling fan
    c. eSATA port
    d. drive bay

understanding and assessing hardware:

evaluating your system

Your Ideal Computer

OBJECTIVE:
How can I determine whether I should upgrade my existing computer or buy a new one? *(p. 264)*

Evaluating the CPU Subsystem

OBJECTIVE:
What does the CPU do, and how can I evaluate its performance? *(p. 268)*

Evaluating the Memory Subsystem: RAM

OBJECTIVE:
How does memory work in my computer, and how can I evaluate how much memory I need? *(p. 272)*

 Sound Byte: Using Windows 7 to Evaluate CPU Performance

 Active Helpdesk: Evaluating Your CPU and RAM

 Sound Byte: Memory Hierarchy Interactive

 Sound Byte: Installing RAM

Evaluating the Storage Subsystem

OBJECTIVE:
What are the computer's storage devices, and how can I evaluate whether they match my needs? *(p. 275)*

 Sound Byte: Optical Media Reading and Writing Interactive
 Sound Byte: Installing a Blu-ray Drive

Evaluating the Video and Audio Subsystems

OBJECTIVES:
What components affect the quality of video on my computer, and how do I know if I need better video performance? *(p. 281)*

What components affect my computer's sound quality? *(p. 285)*

 Active Helpdesk: Evaluating Computer System Components

Evaluating System Reliability and Making the Final Decision

OBJECTIVE:
How can I improve the reliability of my system? *(p. 287)*

how cool is *this?*

It used to be that the case for a desktop computer was just a boring rectangular box—but no longer! Consider some of the new designs on the market. On the **Phobos** computer system by BFG Technologies, the front of the case features a **touch-panel LCD** that reports system performance parameters, controls music content, and presents a summary of storage and memory usage. There is also an integrated iPod/iPhone **docking station** on the top of the case. Or consider Falcon Northwest, which delivers **custom paint** jobs on its system cases—images from its library, your own image, or even a screen from your favorite game.

The Thermaltake Level 10 wins for pure **artistry**. It isolates all the major subsections—motherboard, power supply, hard drives, optical drives—in a separate physical space. Each section is hinged and can swing open for easy access. Made of aluminum, the entire case helps disperse heat . . . and looks cool doing it!

Scan here for more info on How Cool Is This? ▶

© Hugh Threlfall/Alamy

Your Ideal Computer

It can be hard to know if your computer is the best match for your needs. New technologies emerge so quickly, and it might be hard to decide if these are expensive extras or tools you would use. Do you need to be able to burn a Blu-ray Disc? Is a webcam really going to improve how you use your computer? Doesn't it always seem like your friend's computer is faster than yours anyway?

Maybe you could get more out of newer technologies, but should you upgrade the system you have or buy a new machine? In this chapter we'll begin by helping you design the optimal system for your needs. Then we'll examine all the subsystems of a computer and learn how to evaluate their performance and what upgrades are easily available to help you end up with a system you just love.

What if I always struggle to get things done on my computer? Do you ever wonder whether your computer is fine and you just need more training to get it to work smoothly? Or do you need a more sophisticated computer system? In this chapter we'll start by determining whether your current computer is meeting your needs. We'll begin by figuring out what you want your ideal computer to be able to do. You'll then learn more about important components of your computer—its CPU, memory, storage devices, and audio and video devices—and how these components

affect system performance. Along the way, you'll find worksheets to help you conduct a system evaluation, and multimedia Sound Bytes that will show you how to upgrade various components in your system. You'll also learn about the many utilities available to help speed up and clean up your system. If it's time for you to buy a new computer, this chapter will provide you with important information you will need about computer hardware to make an informed purchasing decision.

When is the best time to buy a new computer? There never seems to be a perfect time to buy. It seems that if you can just wait a year, computers will inevitably be faster and cost less. Is this actually true?

As it turns out, it is true. In fact, a rule of thumb often cited in the computer industry, called **Moore's Law**, describes the pace at which CPUs (central processing units)—the small chips that can be thought of as the "brains" of the computer—improve. Named for Gordon Moore, the cofounder of the CPU chip manufacturer Intel, this rule predicts that the number of transistors inside a CPU will increase so fast that CPU capacity will double every 18 months. (The number of transistors on a CPU chip helps determine how fast it can process data.)

As you can see in Figure 6.1, this rule of thumb has held true for over 45 years. Imagine finding a bank that would agree to treat your money in this way. If you put 10 cents in that kind of savings account in 1965, you would have a balance of more than $800 million today! Moore himself, however, has predicted that around the year 2020 CPU chips will be manufactured in a different way, thus changing or eliminating the effects of Moore's Law altogether.

In addition to the CPU becoming faster, other system components also continue to improve dramatically. For example, the capacity of memory chips such as dynamic random access memory (DRAM)—the most common form of memory found in personal computers—increases about 60 percent every year. Meanwhile, hard drives have been growing in storage capacity by some 50 percent each year.

So should I be buying a new computer every year? No one wants to spend money every year just to keep up with technology. Even if money weren't a consideration, the time it would take to

Figure 6.1

Moore's Law predicts that CPUs will continue to get faster.

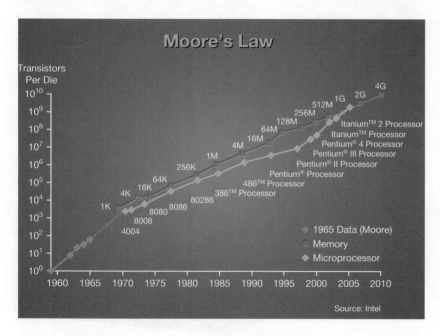

transfer all of your files and reinstall and reconfigure your software would make buying a new computer every year terribly inefficient. Landfills would be overflowing with tossed aside older equipment. Extending the life of a computer reduces the environmental and security concerns involved in the disposal of computers.

No one wants to keep doing costly upgrades that won't significantly extend the life of a system, either. How can you determine if your system is suitable or if it needs to be upgraded? Moreover, how can you know which is the better option—upgrading or buying a new computer? The first step is figuring out what you want your computer to do for you.

But what if I'm just buying my first computer? Even if you're a new computer user, you will still need to evaluate what you want your system to do for you before you buy. Being able to understand and evaluate computer systems will make you a more informed buyer. You will be comfortable answering questions like "What kinds of CPUs are there?" "How does the CPU affect system performance?" and "How much RAM do I need?"

OK, how do I know what my ideal system is? Consider what you want to be able to do with your computer. For example, do you need to bring your computer to school or work with you? Do you want to be able to edit digital photos and video? Do you want to watch and record Blu-ray Discs? Or do you mainly use your computer for word processing and Internet access? The worksheet in Figure 6.2 lists a number of ways in which you may want to use your computer. In the second column, place a check next to those computer uses that apply to you. Also, set a priority of high (1), medium (2), or low (3) in the rightmost column so that you can determine which features are most important to you.

Next, look at the list of desired uses for your computer and determine whether your current system can perform these activities. If there are things it can't do, you may need to purchase additional hardware or a new computer. For example, if you plan to edit digital video files or play games that require high video frame rates for smooth in-game motion, you may need to add more memory and upgrade your video card. Depending on the costs of the individual upgrade components, you may be better off buying a new system.

Should that system come as a notebook or a desktop? In this discussion, we'll only be considering full-size desktops and notebooks. If your main need is light weight and great portibility, a netbook or a tablet may be a workable option. Netbooks and tablets are discussed in detail in Chapter 8.

To make the best decision, it's important to evaluate where you will use the computer. The main distinction between desktops and notebooks is portability. If you indicated in Figure 6.2 that you need to take your computer with you to work or school, or even want the flexibility to move from room to room in your house, a notebook is the best choice. If portability is not an absolute requirement, you should consider a desktop.

How does a notebook compare to a desktop for value? Desktop systems are invariably a better value than notebooks in terms of computing power gained for your dollar. Because of the notebook's small footprint (the amount of space it takes up), you pay more for each component. Each piece has had extra engineering time invested to make sure it fits in the smallest space. In addition, a desktop system offers more expandability options. It's easier to add new ports and devices because of the amount of room available in the desktop computer's design.

If a large monitor is important, desktops have an edge. Although 18-inch screens are now available on some notebooks, the weight of these systems (often more than 10 pounds) makes them really more of a "desktop replacement" than a portable computing solution. Light notebooks typically have 17-inch screens or smaller, while inexpensive 24-inch monitors are readily available for desktop solutions. If you need a large screen and portability, you may end up buying a notebook and a fixed desk monitor to connect to when you are at home, an extra cost.

Desktop systems also are more reliable. Because of the amount of vibration that a notebook experiences and the added exposure to dust, water, and temperature fluctuations that portability brings, notebooks often have a shorter lifespan than desktop computers. Manufacturers offer extended warranty plans that cover accidental damage and unexpected drops; however, such plans may be costly.

Figure 6.2 | WHAT SHOULD YOUR IDEAL COMPUTER SYSTEM BE ABLE TO DO?

Computer Uses	Have It	Want It!	Priority (High, Medium, Low)
Portability Uses			
Be light enough to carry easily			
Access the Internet wirelessly			
Print wirelessly			
Long battery life			
Entertainment Uses			
Play and record CDs and DVDs			
Play and record Blu-ray Discs			
Record and edit digital videos			
Record and edit digital music			
Capture and edit digital photos			
Play graphics-intensive games			
Show video across multiple monitors			
Transfer files wirelessly to mobile devices and other computers			
Transfer files using flash memory cards			
Upload media to social networking sites			
Have your peripheral devices work easily and speedily with your computer			
Purchase/rent music and videos from the Internet			
Talk with friends and family with live video and audio			
Stream television and movies			
Other			
Educational Uses			
Perform word processing tasks			
Use educational software			
Access library archives and subscribe to e-zines			
Create multimedia presentations			
Create backups of all your files			
Record notes with synchronized audio recordings			
Other			
Business Uses			
Create spreadsheets and databases			
Work on multiple software applications quickly and simultaneously			
Conduct online banking, pay bills online, or prepare your taxes			
Conduct online job searches or post résumés			
Synchronize your mobile device (phone/media player) with your computer			
Conduct online meetings with video and audio			
Organize business contacts and manage scheduling			
Other			

How long will a notebook be useful to me? The answer to that question depends on how easy it is to upgrade your system. Take note of the maximum amount of memory you can install in your notebook because that cannot be changed a few years down the road. Internal hard drives are not easy for novices to install in a notebook, but by using a fast transfer port on your notebook, you can easily add an external hard drive for more storage space.

Notebooks are often equipped with an **ExpressCard** slot. ExpressCards (shown in Figure 6.3) can add a solid-state drive (SSD), eSATA and FireWire ports, and other capabilities to your system. You can add an ExpressCard that allows you to read flash memory cards such as Compact-Flash, Memory Sticks, and Secure Digital cards. As new types of ports and devices are introduced, like those for the USB 3.0 standard, they are manufactured in Ex-pressCard formats so you can make sure your notebook does not become obsolete before its time. Figure 6.4 summarizes the advantages and disadvantages of each style of computer.

How am I going to learn to use my new system? Of course, college courses like this one are a great idea! Colleges offer a number of other training options including online modules and weekend workshops. In addition, many online tutorials are available for software products. For specific questions or skills, be sure to check YouTube, iTunes U, and other podcast directories. Valuable series exist that answer your questions in step-by-step video demonstrations, such as MrExcel or Photoshop Quicktips. Some manufacturers, like Apple, offer classes at their stores for a yearly fee. Training shouldn't be an afterthought. Consider the time and effort involved in learning about what you want your computer to do before you buy hardware or software.

How can I turn my list into the exact system specifications? Now that you have a better idea of your ideal computer system, you can make a more informed assessment of your current computer. To determine whether your computer system has the right hardware components to do what you ultimately want it to do, you need to conduct a **system evaluation**. To do this, you look at your computer's subsystems, see what they do, and check how they perform.

The following sections will examine each subsystem. At the end of each section, you'll find a small worksheet you can use

Figure 6.3

ExpressCards add functionality to your notebook.

BITS AND BYTES

Moving to a New Computer Doesn't Have to Be Painful

Are you ready to buy a new computer but dread the prospect of transferring all your files and redoing all of your Windows settings? You could transfer all those files and settings manually, but Windows stores much information in the registry files, which can be tricky to update. So what do you do? Windows 7 incorporates Windows Easy Transfer, which lets you migrate files and settings from a Windows Vista system to a Windows 7 system via a network connection by using a flash drive or external hard drive or using optical media.

Alternatively, other PC migration software is available, such as Laplink's PC-mover, which is designed to make the transition to a new computer easier. For the latest information on such utilities, search for migration software online. You'll be ready to upgrade painlessly in no time. If you prefer to avoid the do-it-yourself option, support technicians at retail stores (such as the Geek Squad at Best Buy) will often perform the migration for a small charge.

Figure 6.4 | DESKTOP VERSUS NOTEBOOK COMPUTERS—WHICH FITS YOU?

Notebooks	Desktops
Portable: lightweight, thin	Best value: more processing power, memory, and storage capacity for lower price
Take up less physical space	More difficult to steal, less susceptible to damage from dropping or mishandling
Easier to ship or transport if the system needs repair	Easier to expand and upgrade
Smaller video display (18 inches or smaller)	Large monitors available (24 inches or larger)

to evaluate each subsystem on your computer. *Note:* This chapter discusses tools you can use to assess a Windows-based PC. For information on how to assess a Mac, refer to the Technology in Focus feature "Computing Alternatives" on page 248.

Evaluating the CPU Subsystem

Let's start by considering the type of processor in your system. As mentioned in Chapter 2, your computer's central processing unit (CPU or processor) is critically important because it processes instructions, performs calculations, and manages the flow of information through a computer system. The CPU is responsible for turning raw data into valuable information through processing operations. The CPU is located on the motherboard, the primary circuit board of the computer system. There are several types of processors on the market including Intel processors (such as the Core family with the i7, i5,

© 4kodiak/istockphoto.com — Core™ i7 (intel)

Sony Electronics Inc. — CELL/BE.

Figure 6.5

(a) The Intel i7 is the most advanced desktop CPU ever made by Intel.
(b) The PlayStation 3 gaming console uses the Cell Broadband Engine to compute 230 billion floating point calculations per second (gigaflops).

i3, and the Centrino line) and AMD processors (such as the Athlon II and Phenom X4). The Intel Core i7 is the most advanced desktop CPU made by Intel. Figure 6.5 shows the i7 as well as the Cell Broadband Engine used in the PlayStation 3.

How does the CPU work? The CPU is composed of two units: the control unit and the arithmetic logic unit (ALU). The control unit coordinates the activities of all the other computer components. The ALU is responsible for performing all the arithmetic calculations (addition, subtraction, multiplication, and division). It also makes logic and comparison decisions such as comparing items to determine if one is greater than, less than, equal to, or not equal to another.

Every time the CPU performs a program instruction, it goes through the same series of steps. First, it *fetches* the required piece of data or instruction from RAM, the temporary storage location for all the data and instructions the computer needs while it is running. Next, it *decodes* the instruction into something the computer can understand. Once the CPU has decoded the instruction, it *executes* the instruction and *stores* the result to RAM before fetching the next instruction. This process is called a machine cycle. (We discuss the machine cycle in more detail in the Technology in Focus feature "Under the Hood" on page 346.) **What makes one CPU different from another?** The primary distinction between CPUs is processing power, which is determined by a number of factors:

- Number of cores
- Clock speed
- Amount of cache memory
- Front side bus performance

A **core** is a complete processing section from a CPU embedded into one physical chip. The **clock speed** of the CPU dictates how many instructions the CPU can finish in one second. The CPU's **cache memory** is a form of random access memory that can be reached much more quickly than regular RAM. The **front side bus (FSB)** is the main path for data movement within the system, carrying data from the CPU to memory, the video card, and other components on the motherboard.

How does a multi-core CPU help me? If you had a clone of yourself sitting next to you working, you could get twice as much done, and that is the idea of multi-core processing. CPUs began to execute more than one instruction at a time quite a while ago, when hyperthreading was introduced. **Hyperthreading** provides quicker processing of information by enabling a new set of instructions to start executing before the previous set has finished. The most recent design innovation for PC processors, an improvement upon hyperthreading, is the use of *multiple cores* on one CPU chip. With multiple core technology, two or more processors reside on the same chip, enabling the execution of two sets of instructions at the same time. Applications that are always running behind the scenes, such as virus protection software and your operating system, can have their own processor, freeing the other processor to run other applications such as a Web browser, Word, or iTunes more efficiently.

In Figure 6.6c, hyperthreading allows two different programs to be processed at one time, but they are sharing the computing resources of the chip. With multiple cores, each program has the full attention of its own processing core (see Figures 6.6a and 6.6b). This results in faster processing and smoother multitasking. It is possible to design a CPU to have multiple cores *and* hyperthreading. The Intel i7-990X has six cores, each one using hyperthreading, so it simulates having twelve processors!

How does a CPU with a faster processor speed help me? Each CPU is designed to run at a specific processing speed. The faster the clock speed, the more quickly the next instruction is processed. CPUs currently have clock speeds running between 2.1 GHz and 4 GHz (billions of steps per second). Some users even push their hardware to perform faster, overclocking their processor. Overclocking means that you run the CPU at a faster speed than

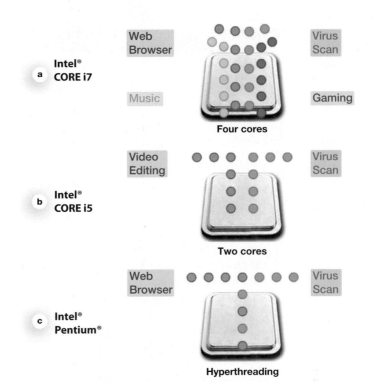

the manufacturer recommends. It produces more heat, meaning a shorter lifetime for the CPU, and usually voids any warranty.

How does more cache memory help me? Although clock speed is an important consideration when determining processor performance, CPU performance also is affected by the amount of cache memory. Because of its ready access to the CPU, cache memory gets data to the CPU for processing much faster than bringing the data in from RAM.

There are several levels of cache memory. These levels are defined by a chip's proximity to the CPU. Level 1 cache is a block of memory that is built onto the CPU chip itself for the storage of data or commands that have just been used. Level 2 cache is located on the CPU chip but is slightly farther away from the CPU, or it's on a separate chip next to the CPU and therefore takes somewhat longer to access. Level 2 cache contains more storage area than does level 1 cache. In the same way, some chips continue on to have a third cache, Level 3. Again, this level of cache is slower for the CPU to reach but larger in size.

How does the front side bus impact performance? The front side bus connects the processor (CPU) in your

Figure 6.6

(a) Some Intel processors have four cores able to run four programs simultaneously. (b) Some Intel processors have two cores. (c) The Intel Pentium 4 Hyperthreading operates with only one core, but it hyperthreads (working on two processes at once).

Figure 6.7 | PROCESSOR SPECIFICATIONS

	Model	Number of Cores	Max Clock Speed	Max FSB	Max L3 Cache
Desktop Processors	i3-2100T	2	2.50 GHz	1333 MHz	3 MB
	i5-2500	4	3.30 GHz	1333 MHz	6 MB
	i7-990X	6	3.46 GHz	1600 MHz	12 MB
Notebook Processors	i3-380UM	2	1.33 GHz	800 MHz	3 MB
	i5 Mobile 2410M	2	2.30 GHz	1333 MHz	3 MB
	i7 Mobile 2920XM	4	2.50 GHz	1600 MHz	8 MB

computer to the system memory. Think of the front side bus as the highway on which data travels between the CPU and RAM. The total number of cars that whiz by in one minute would depend on the number of lanes of highway and the speed of the cars. Similarly, the throughput of the FSB depends on how much data it transfers per cycle (bytes) and its clock frequency (Hz). The faster the FSB is, the faster you can get data to your processor. The faster you get data to the processor, the faster your processor can work on it.

How do I shop for a CPU? Modern processors are defined by the combination of the number of cores, the processor speed, the front side bus performance, and the amount of cache memory. For example, Intel has several processor families, in a range of clock speeds, cache memory sizes, and FSB speeds, as shown in Figure 6.7. Even within the same processor family, though, there is a variety of choices. For example, the i7-990X

Figure 6.8

The System Properties window identifies which CPU you have, as well as its speed.

>Click the **Start** button and then click **Computer** on the right panel of the Start menu. On the top toolbar, click **System Properties**.

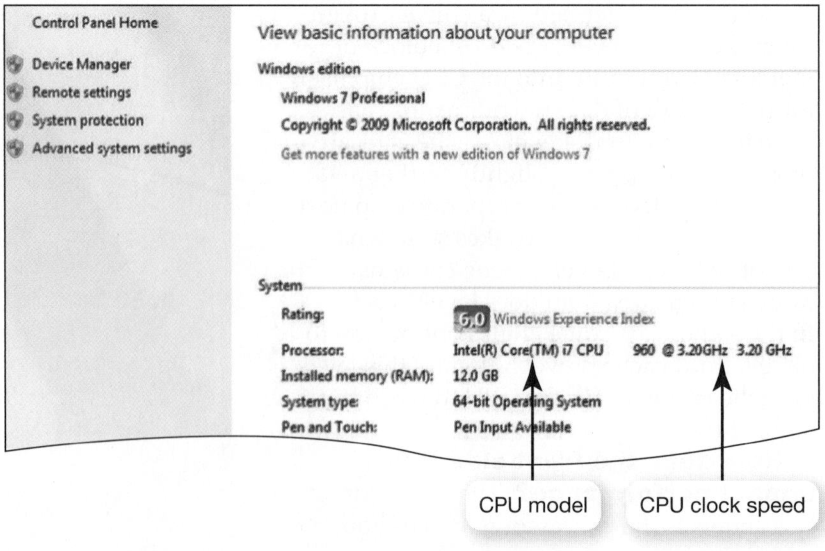

Control Panel Home

Device Manager
Remote settings
System protection
Advanced system settings

View basic information about your computer

Windows edition

Windows 7 Professional

Copyright © 2009 Microsoft Corporation. All rights reserved.

Get more features with a new edition of Windows 7

System

Rating: 6.0 Windows Experience Index
Processor: Intel(R) Core(TM) i7 CPU   960 @ 3.20GHz 3.20 GHz
Installed memory (RAM):   12.0 GB
System type: 64-bit Operating System
Pen and Touch: Pen Input Available

CPU model   CPU clock speed

processor has six cores and a 12 MB cache, whereas the i7-860S processor has four cores and an 8 MB L3 cache.

Because so many factors influence CPU design, picking the fastest CPU for the kind of work you do involves researching performance benchmarks. **CPU benchmarks** are measurements used to compare performance between processors. Benchmarks are generated by running software programs specifically designed to push the limits of CPU performance. Articles are often published comparing a number of chips, or complete systems, based on their benchmark performance. Investigate a few, using sites like **www.cpubenchmark.net**, before you select the chip that is best for you.

Why are there different CPU choices for notebooks and desktops? Both Intel and AMD make processors that are specifically designed for notebook computers. Notebook processors not only need to perform quickly and efficiently, like their desktop counterparts, but also need better power savings to improve battery life. Processors used in notebooks work to combine low power consumption, to support long battery life, and more flexible wireless connectivity options. AMD features notebook processors like the Turion X2 Mobile and the AMD Mobile Sempron, while Intel has mobile versions of the i5 and i7 series.

What CPU does my current computer have? You can easily identify the type of CPU in your current system by accessing the System Properties. As shown in Figure 6.8, you can view basic information about your computer, including which CPU is installed in your system and its speed. More detailed information, like the FSB speed and the amount of cache memory, is not shown in this screen. You can find those values by checking the manufacturer's Web site for the specific model number of CPU shown. For example, the CPU illustrated here is the Intel i7, version 960.

How can I tell whether my CPU is meeting my needs? You can tell if your CPU speed is limiting your system performance by watching how busy the CPU is as you work. Even if your CPU meets the minimum requirements specified for a particular software application, if you're running other software at the same time, you need to check how well the CPU is handling the entire load. Keep in mind that the workload your CPU experiences will vary considerably during your work day. Even though it might run Word just fine, it may not be able to handle running Word, Photoshop, iTunes, and Movie Maker at the same time. The percentage of time that your CPU is working is referred to as **CPU usage**.

Figure 6.9 helps you evaluate the factors that determine whether your CPU is meeting your needs.

A utility that measures information such as CPU usage and RAM usage is incredibly useful, both for considering whether you should upgrade and for investigating if your computer's performance suddenly seems to drop off for no apparent reason. On Windows systems, the program Task Manager gives you easy access to all this data. Mac OS X has a similar utility named Activity Monitor, which is located in your Applications folder in the Utilities folder.

SOUND BYTE

Using Windows 7 to Evaluate CPU Performance

In this Sound Byte, you'll learn how to use the utilities provided by Windows 7 to evaluate your CPU's performance. You'll also learn about shareware utilities (software that you can install and try before you purchase it) that expand on the capabilities the Task Manager utility provides.

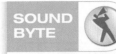

To use Task Manager to view information on CPU usage, right-click an empty area of the taskbar, select Start Task Manager, and click the Performance tab, as shown in Figure 6.10a. The **CPU usage graph** records your CPU usage for the past several seconds. (Note: If you have multiple cores and hyperthreading, you will see several CPU usage curves listed.) Of course, there will be periodic peaks of high CPU usage, but if you see that your CPU usage levels are greater than 90 percent during most of your work session, a faster CPU will contribute a great deal to your system's performance. If you use the Windows gadgets, you can add a CPU Meter gadget to track both CPU and RAM usage (see Figure 6.10b). To see exactly how to use the Task Manager and the CPU Meter gadgets, watch the Sound Byte "Using Windows 7 to Evaluate CPU Performance."

Will improving the performance of the CPU be enough to improve my computer's performance? You may think that if you have the best processor,

Figure 6.9 HOW IS YOUR CPU PERFORMING?

	Current System	Dream System
What is my computer's CPU speed?		
How much cache memory is on the CPU*?		
What is the FSB speed*?		
What is the benchmark score for your CPU? (try **www.cpubenchmark.net**)		
What kind of multilevel processing does the CPU have—multiple cores, hyperthreaded, etc.?		
Is the CPU usage value below 90% during most of my daily tasks?		

*You can find these numbers by checking the manufacturer's specifications for your model of CPU.

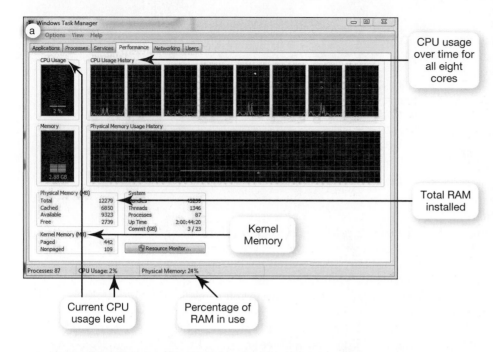

CPU usage over time for all eight cores

Total RAM installed

Kernel Memory

Current CPU usage level

Percentage of RAM in use

Figure 6.10

(a) The Performance tab of the Windows Task Manager utility shows you how busy your CPU actually is. (b) Windows gadgets let you follow CPU performance easily.

>In an empty area of the taskbar, right-click, select **Start Task Manager**, and click the **Performance** tab.

you will have the best system. However, upgrading your CPU will affect only the processing portion of the system performance, not how quickly data can move to or from the CPU. Your system's overall performance depends on many factors, including the amount of RAM installed as well as hard drive speed. Your selection of CPU may not offer significant improvements to your system's performance if there is a bottleneck in processing because of insufficient RAM or hard drive performance.

Evaluating the Memory Subsystem: RAM

Random access memory (RAM) is your computer's temporary storage space. Although we refer to RAM as a form of storage, it really is the computer's short-term memory. It remembers everything that the computer needs to process the data into information, such as data that has been entered and software instructions, but only when the computer is on. RAM is an example of **volatile storage**. When the power is off, the data stored in RAM is cleared out. This is why, in addition to RAM, systems always include **nonvolatile storage** devices for permanent storage of instructions and data when the computer is powered off. ROM memory, for example, holds the critical startup instructions. Hard drives provide the largest nonvolatile storage capacity in the computer system.

Why not use a hard drive to store the data and instructions?
It's about one million times faster for the CPU to retrieve a piece of data from RAM than from a mechanical hard drive. The time it takes the CPU to grab data from RAM is measured in nanoseconds (billionths of seconds), whereas pulling data from a fast mechanical hard drive takes an average of 10 milliseconds (ms), or thousandths of seconds. Figure 6.11 shows the various types of memory and storage that are distributed throughout your system: CPU registers, cache, RAM, and hard drives. Each of these has its own tradeoff of speed versus price. Because the fastest memory is so much more expensive, systems are designed with much less of it. This principle is influential in the design of a balanced computer system and can have a tremendous impact on system performance.

Are there different types of RAM?
Like most computer components, RAM has gone through a series of evolutions. In current systems, the RAM used most often comes in the form of double data rate 3 (DDR3) memory modules, available in several different speeds (1066 MHz, 1333 MHz, 1600 MHz). The higher the speed

the better the performance. Double data rate 5 memory (DDR5), which has an even faster data transfer rate, is seen in high-performance video graphics cards. In older systems, other types of RAM may have been used, including dynamic RAM (DRAM), static RAM (SRAM), and synchronous DRAM (SDRAM).

RAM appears in the system on **memory modules** (or **memory cards**), small circuit boards that hold a series of RAM chips and fit into special slots on the motherboard (see Figure 6.12). Most memory modules in today's systems are packaged as *dual inline memory modules* (DIMMs).

On high-end systems, manufacturers may offer an option to purchase Corsair Dominator DDR3 modules. These are tested to high levels to guarantee optimum performance. A special heat exchanger is designed into the RAM module to help it operate at a lower temperature, making it more stable and more reliable. All of these factors boost the performance of the memory and make it popular with demanding video gamers.

If you're adding RAM to any system, you must determine what type your system needs. Consult your user's manual or the system manufacturer's Web site. In addition, many online RAM resellers, such as Crucial (**www.crucial.com**), can help you determine the type of RAM that is compatible with your system by running an automated system scan program on your computer.

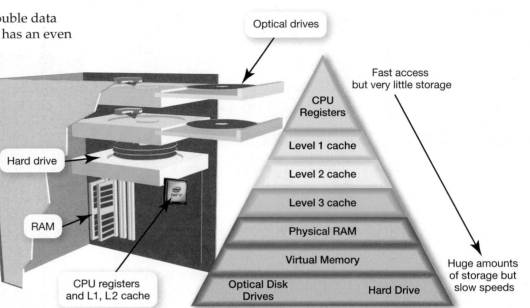

Figure 6.11

A computer system's memory has many different levels, ranging from the small amounts in the CPU to the much slower but more plentiful storage of a mechanical hard drive.

How can I tell how much RAM is installed in my computer and how it's being used? The amount of RAM that is actually sitting on memory modules in your computer is your computer's **physical memory**. The easiest way to see how much RAM you have is to look in the System Properties window. (On the Mac, choose the Apple menu and then About This Mac.) This is the same tab you looked in to determine your system's CPU type and speed, and is shown in Figure 6.8. RAM capacity is measured in gigabytes (GB), and most machines sold today, especially those running Windows, have at least 4 GB of RAM. The computer in Figure 6.13 has 12 GB of RAM installed.

Windows 7 uses a memory-management technique known as **SuperFetch**. SuperFetch monitors which applications you use the most and preloads them into your system memory so that they'll be ready to go. For example, if you have Word running, Windows 7 stores as much of the information related to Word in RAM as it can, which speeds up how fast your application

Hugh Threlfall/Alamy

Figure 6.12

A single memory module holds a series of RAM chips.

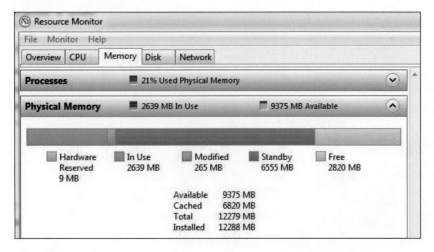

Figure 6.13

The Resource Monitor's Memory tab shows a detailed breakdown of how the computer is using memory.

>In the Task Manager, click the **Performance** tab, click **Resource Monitor;** and then click the **Memory** tab.

Application	RAM Recommended
Windows 7 (64 bit)	2 GB
Microsoft Office Professional 2010	512 MB
Internet Explorer 9	512 MB
iTunes 10	1 GB
Adobe Photoshop Elements 9	2 GB
Total RAM required to run all programs simultaneously	6 GB

responds, because pulling information from RAM is so much faster than pulling it from the hard drive. This idea of caching the data you need in RAM, having it ready to use quickly when it is asked for, is different from how memory was used in earlier operating systems. You can watch this process work using the Resource Monitor, which shows in Figure 6.13 how the 12 GB of installed RAM is being used: 3 GB is running programs, 6 GB is holding cached data and files ready for quick access, and 3 GB is currently unused.

How much RAM do I need? Because RAM is the temporary holding space for all the data and instructions that the computer uses while it's on, most computer users need quite a bit of RAM. As you learned in Chapter 5, the operating system is the main software application that runs the computer. Without it, the computer does not work. At a minimum, the system needs enough RAM to run the operating system.

The memory that your operating system uses is referred to as **kernel memory**. This memory is listed in a separate Kernel Memory table in the Performance tab. In Figure 6.10, the Kernel Memory table tells you that approximately 0.55 GB (total kernel memory) of the total 12 GB of RAM is being used to run the operating system. In fact, systems running all the new features

of Windows 7 should have a minimum of 1 GB of RAM, but for peak performance, at least 2 GB of RAM is recommended. However, because you run more applications than just the operating system, you will want to have more RAM than the just enough for the OS. New systems ship with at least 4 GB and high-end systems can come with 24 GB.

To determine how much RAM you need, list all the software applications you might be running at one time. Figure 6.14 shows an example of RAM requirements. In this example, if you are running your operating system, word processing and spreadsheet programs, a Web browser, a music player, and photo editing software simultaneously, then you will need a minimum of 6 GB of RAM. It's always best to check the system requirements of any software program before you buy it to make sure your system can handle it. System requirements can be found on the software packaging or on the manufacturer's Web site.

It's a good idea to have more than the minimum amount of RAM you need now, so you can use more programs in the future. Remember, too, that "required" means these are the minimum values recommended by the manufacturers, and having more RAM often helps programs run more efficiently. When upgrading RAM, the rule of thumb is to buy as much as you can afford but certainly no more than your system will handle.

Adding RAM

Is there a limit to how much RAM I can add to my computer? Every computer has a maximum limit on the amount of RAM it can support. A motherboard is

SOUND BYTE — Memory Hierarchy Interactive

In this Sound Byte, you'll learn about the different types of memory used in a computer system.

designed with a specific number of slots into which the memory cards fit, and each slot has a limit on the amount of RAM it can hold. To determine your specific system limits, check the system manufacturer's Web site.

In addition, the operating system running on your machine imposes its own RAM limit. For example, the maximum amount of RAM for the 32-bit version of Windows 7 is 4 GB, while the maximum memory you can install using the 64-bit version of Windows 7 Ultimate is 192 GB.

Review the considerations presented in Figure 6.15 to see if your system could benefit from an upgrade of additional RAM.

Is it difficult or expensive to add RAM? Adding RAM to a computer is fairly easy (see Figure 6.16). Be sure that you purchase a memory module that's compatible with your computer. Typically you simply line up the notches and then gently push the memory module in place. The new RAM you buy will come with installation instructions for your particular system, so be sure to read and follow those.

RAM is a relatively inexpensive system upgrade. The cost of RAM does fluctuate in the marketplace as much as 400 percent over

SOUND BYTE — Installing RAM

In this Sound Byte, you'll learn how to select the appropriate type of memory to purchase, how to order memory online, and how to install it yourself. As you'll discover, the procedure is a simple one and can add great performance benefits to your system.

Figure 6.15 | DO YOU NEED TO UPGRADE YOUR RAM?

	Current System	Dream System
What is the maximum amount of RAM my system can hold?*		
How much RAM does my system have?		
What is the maximum amount of RAM I need for the applications I currently run?		
Would I be willing to upgrade to an operating system that supports the amount of RAM I want?		

*Check the manufacturer's specifications for your system.

time, though, so if you're considering adding RAM, you should watch the prices of memory in online and print advertisements.

Evaluating the Storage Subsystem

Remember, there are two ways data is stored on your computer: temporary storage and permanent storage. RAM is a form of temporary (or volatile) storage. The information residing in RAM is not stored permanently. It's critical to have the means to store data and software applications permanently.

Fortunately, several storage options exist. Storage devices include hard drives, USB flash drives, optical drives, SSD drives, and external hard drives. When you turn off your computer, the data that has been written to these devices will be available the next time the machine is powered on. These devices provide *nonvolatile* storage.

Figure 6.16

Adding RAM to a computer is quite simple and relatively inexpensive. On a notebook machine you often gain access through a panel on the bottom.

> **When the operating system is installed on an SSD drive, the wakeup time of the system drops to just a few seconds because of the fast access.**

Hard Drive

What makes the hard drive the most popular storage device? With storage capacities exceeding 4 terabytes (TB), a **hard drive** has the largest capacity of any storage device. The hard drive is also a much more economical device than other options, because it offers the most gigabytes of storage per dollar. Most system units are designed to support more than one internal hard drive. The Apple Mac Pro has room for four hard drives, and the Thermaltake Level 10 (shown in the opening How Cool Is This?) can support six hard drives. Each one simply slides into place when you want to upgrade.

How is data stored on a hard drive? A hard drive is composed of several coated round, thin plates of metal stacked on a spindle. Each plate is called a **platter**. When data is saved to a hard drive platter, a pattern of magnetized spots is created on the iron oxide coating of each platter. When the spots are aligned in one direction, they represent a 1; when aligned in the other direction, the represent a 0.

These 0s and 1s are bits (or binary digits) and are the smallest pieces of data that computers can understand. When data stored on the hard drive platter is retrieved (or read), your computer translates these patterns of magnetized spots into the data you have saved.

How quickly does a hard drive find information? The hard drive's **access time**, the time it takes a storage device to locate its stored data and make it available for processing, is faster than that of other permanent storage devices, like optical drives. Mechanical hard drive access times are measured in milliseconds (ms), meaning thousandths of seconds. For large capacity drives, access times of approximately 12–13 milliseconds are typical. That's less than one-hundredth of a second. A DVD drive can take over 150 milliseconds to access data.

Do mechanical hard drives have the fastest access times? Not all hard drives have mechanical motors and moving parts. A **solid-state drive (SSD)** uses the same kind of memory that flash drives use. Because no spinning platters or motors are needed, SSDs run with no noise and very little heat, and require very little power. SSDs are very popular in laptops because of their lower power consumption and quiet, cool operation. Having no mechanical motors also allows solid state drives to offer incredibly fast access times, reaching data in only a tenth of a millisecond (0.1 ms). That is about 1,000 times faster than mechanical drives!

Storage capacities for SSD drives now range up to 2 TB, but that size SSD drive is very expensive. Smaller SSDs, around 256 GB, are increasingly being used as the boot (or startup) drive. When the operating system is installed on an SSD drive, the wakeup time of the system drops to just a few seconds because of its fast access. Systems designed like this often have a mechanical hard drive, or two, to provide large amounts of inexpensive storage space.

Figure 6.17 provides a listing of the various storage options and compares their access times.

Figure 6.17

Access times for nonvolatile storage options.

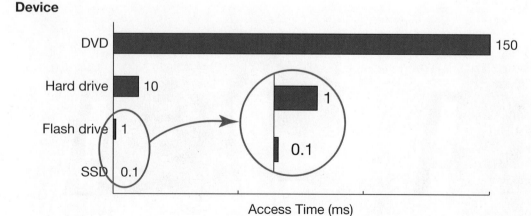

Device

Access Time (ms)

How do I know how much storage capacity I have? Typically, hard drive capacity is measured in gigabytes (GB), although hard drives with capacity in the terabytes (1 TB = 1,000 GB) are now available. Windows displays the hard drives, their capacity, and usage information, as seen in Figure 6.18. To get a slightly more detailed view, select a drive, and then right-click and choose Properties.

How much storage do I need? You need enough space to store the software applications you use, such as Microsoft Office, music players, and games. Then add space for all of the data files you own. If you have a large digital music library, that alone could require 30 to 50 GB. Do you keep all of your photographs on your hard drive? You may need another 40 GB or more for them. If you store digital video of television shows and movies, that could easily be 100 to 200 GB more, even higher if the videos are all high definition. Of course, the operating system also requires storage space. The demands on system requirements have grown with new versions of operating systems. Windows 7, the latest Microsoft operating system, can require up to 20 GB of available hard drive capacity, depending on the configuration. Figure 6.19 shows an example of storage calculation. If you plan to have a system backup on the same drive, be sure to budget for that room as well.

How do hard drives connect to my system? Internal hard drives connect using **Serial Advanced Technology Attachment (SATA)**. SATA hard drives use thin cables, and can transfer data quickly. (An older technology, Integrated Drive Electronics [IDE] was much slower.) Over 90 percent of new systems are using SATA drives now. There are currently two flavors of SATA—the original, which tranfers data at a rate of 3 gigabits per second (Gb/s) and the newer revision, which updates to a 6 Gb/s standard. If your motherboard supports the 6 Gb/s SATA, look for a hard drive that matches that data transfer rate to have the best performance. You can compare the actual data transfer rates of hard drives at sites that do performance benchmarking, like Tom's Hardware (**www.tomshardware.com**).

If you are adding an external hard drive to your system, there are two popular ports

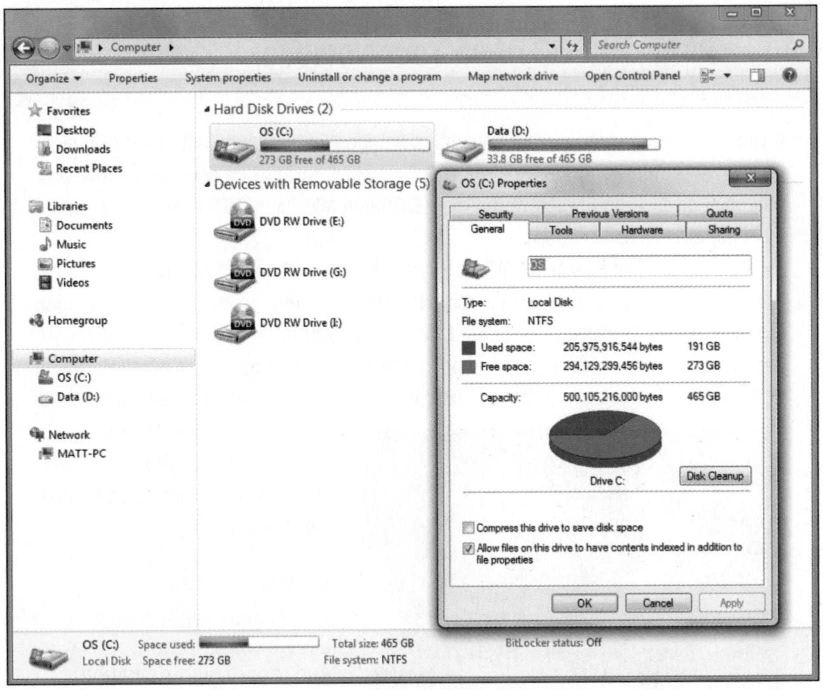

Figure 6.18

In Windows, the free and used capacity of each device in the computer system are shown in the Computer window. The General tab of the Properties dialog box gives you more detailed information.

>To view the Computer window, click **Start**, and then click **Computer**. To view the pie chart, right-click the **C drive**, and select **Properties**.

to use. Many hard drives use a USB port to connect. The USB 3.0 standard is about 10 times faster than USB 2.0, so if your system supports USB 3.0 that is the better choice. Some computer systems offer an eSATA

Figure 6.19 | SAMPLE HARD DRIVE SPACE REQUIREMENTS

Application/Data	Hard Drive Space Required
Windows 7 (64 bit)	20 GB
Microsoft Office 2010 Professional	3.5 GB
Adobe Photoshop Elements 9	2 GB
Roxio Creator 2011	3 GB installation space + 30 GB for working space = 33 GB
Video library of movies	40 GB (about 20 HD movies)
Music library	50 GB (about 7,000 songs)
Total storage in use	148.5 GB
Full backup	150 GB
Total required	298.5 GB

HDTV on Your Notebook

If you are moving through your day with a notebook in tow, why not use it to pull up your favorite television shows? There are now several USB devices that allow your notebook or desktop to receive the high-definition television (HDTV) signals whizzing by in the airwaves.

Devices like the Pinnacle HDTV stick (see Figure 6.20) are USB digital TV tuners. One end plugs into any available USB port. The other end connects to the provided digital antenna. Software is included that allows you to schedule shows to record onto your hard drive, so your notebook essentially becomes a time-shifting digital video recorder. If you are at home, you can remove the antenna and connect to your home cable television signal. It's enough to make you think about buying a larger hard drive on your next computer!

AP Photo/Paul Sakuma

Figure 6.20

The Pinnacle HDTV stick allows you to watch and record high-definition television shows on your computer.

port, shown in Figure 6.21. This is an **external SATA** port that will connect to some external hard drive models. It allows a data transfer rate of up to 3 Gb/s. The theoretical limit of USB 3.0 is 5 Gb/s, so as that technology matures expect USB 3.0 to become the fastest way to connect an external drive. **Do I want one huge drive or several smaller drives?** It depends on what is important to you: speed or security. If you purchase two smaller

Figure 6.21

An eSATA port allows you to connect an external hard drive that can transfer data at speeds faster than USB 2.0.

SOUND BYTE

Optical Media Reading and Writing Interactive

In this Sound Byte, you'll learn about the process of storing and retrieving data from CD-RW, DVD, and Blu-ray Discs. You'll be amazed to see how much precision engineering is required to burn MP3 files onto a disc.

drives, you can combine them using RAID technology. **RAID (redundant array of independent disks)** is a set of strategies for using more than one drive in a system. RAID 0 and RAID 1 are the most popular for consumer machines.

In a RAID 0 configuration, every time data is written to a hard drive, it is actually spread across two physical drives (see Figure 6.22a). The write begins on the first drive, and while the system is waiting for that write to be completed, the system jumps ahead and begins to write the next block of data to the second drive. This makes writing information to disk almost twice as fast as using just one hard drive. The downside is that if either of these disks fail, you lose all your data, because part of each file is on each drive. So RAID 0 is for those most concerned with performance.

In a RAID 1 configuration, all the data written to one drive is perfectly mirrored and written to a second drive (see Figure 6.22b). This provides you a perfect, instant by instant backup of all your work. It also means that if you buy two 1 TB drives, you only have room to store 1TB of data because the second 1 TB drive is being used as the "mirror." RAID 0 and RAID 1 configurations are available on many consumer systems and are even beginning to appear on notebook computers.

Optical Storage

Optical drives are disc drives that use a laser to store and read data. Data is saved to a compact disc (CD), digital video disc (DVD), or Blu-ray Disc (BD) within established tracks and sectors, just like on a hard drive. However, unlike hard drives, which store their data on magnetized platters, optical discs store data as tiny pits that are burned into the disc by a high-speed laser. These pits are extremely small. For CDs and DVDs, they are less than 1 micron in diameter, so nearly 1,500 pits fit across the top of a pinhead. The pits on a Blu-ray Disc are only 0.15 microns in diameter, more than twice as small as the

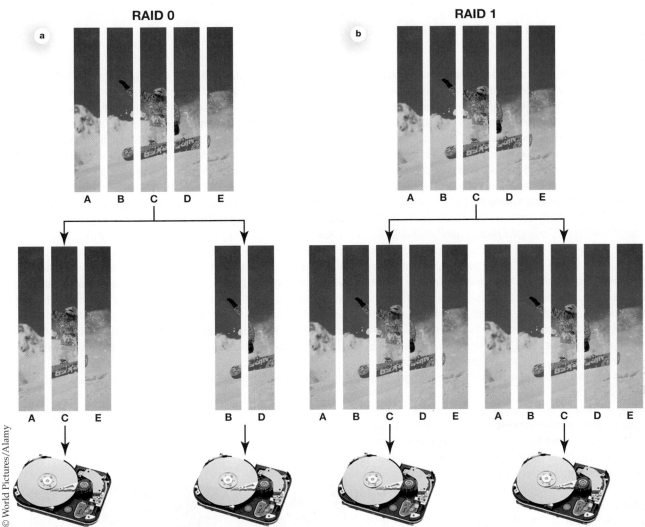

Figure 6.22

(a) RAID 0 speeds up file read/write time. (b) RAID 1 gives you an instant backup.

pits on a DVD. As you can see in Figure 6.23, data is read from a disc by a laser beam, with the pits and nonpits (called *lands*) translating into the 1s and 0s of the binary code computers understand. CDs and DVDs use a red laser to read and write data. Blu-ray Discs get their name because they are read with a blue laser light. All of them collectively are referred to as **optical media**.

Why can I store data on some discs but not others? All forms of optical media come in prerecorded, recordable, and rewritable formats. The prerecorded discs—known as CD-ROM, DVD-ROM, and BD-ROM discs—are read-only

Figure 6.23

Blu-ray lasers have a shorter wavelength, so they can focus more tightly than earlier optical media.

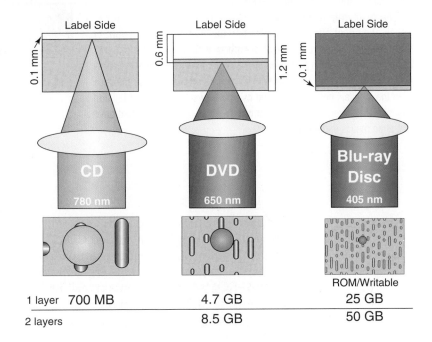

	CD 780 nm	DVD 650 nm	Blu-ray Disc 405 nm
1 layer	700 MB	4.7 GB	25 GB
2 layers		8.5 GB	50 GB

The thin metal platters that make up a hard drive are covered with a special magnetic coating that enables the data to be recorded onto one or both sides of the platter. Hard drive manufacturers prepare the disks to hold data through a process called low-level formatting. In this process, concentric circles, each called a **track**, and pie-shaped wedges, each called a **sector**, are created in the magnetized surface of each platter, setting up a gridlike pattern that identifies file locations on the hard drive. A separate process called high-level formatting establishes the catalog that the computer uses to keep track of where each file is located on the hard drive. More detail on this is presented in the Dig Deeper feature "How Disk Defragmenter Utilities Work" in Chapter 5.

Hard drive platters spin at a high rate of speed, some as fast as 15,000 revolutions per minute (rpm). Sitting between the platters are special "arms" that contain read/write heads (see Figure 6.24). A **read/write head** moves from the outer edge of the spinning platter to the center, as frequently as 50 times per second, to retrieve (read) and record (write) the magnetic data to and from the hard drive platter. As noted earlier, the average total time it takes for the read/write head to locate the data on the platter and return it to the CPU for processing is called its access time. A new hard drive should have an average access time of approximately 12 ms.

Access time is mostly the sum of two factors: seek time and latency. The time it takes for the read/write heads to move over the surface of the disk, moving to the correct track, is called the **seek time**. (Sometimes people incorrectly refer to this as access time.) Once the read/write head locates the correct track, it may need to wait for the correct sector to spin to the read/write head. This waiting time is called **latency** (or **rotational delay**). The faster the platters spin (or the faster the rpm), the less time you'll have to wait for your data to be accessed. Currently, most hard drives for home systems spin at 7,200 rpm. Some people design their systems to have a faster hard drive run the operating system, such as the Western Digital Velociraptor, which spins at 10,000 rpm. They then add a slower drive with greater capacity for storage.

The read/write heads do not touch the platters of the hard drive; rather, they float above them on a thin cushion of air at a height of 0.5 microinches. As a matter of comparison, a human hair is 2,000 microinches thick and a particle of dust is larger than a human hair. Therefore, it's critical to keep your hard drive free from all dust and dirt, because even the smallest particle could find its way between the read/write head and the disk platter, causing a **head crash**—a stoppage of the hard drive that often results in data loss.

SSDs (solid-state drives) free you from worry about head crashes at all. The flash memory of SSDs means there are no platters, no motors, and no read/write arms in this style of hard drive. Instead, a series of cells are constructed in the silicon wafers. If high voltage is applied, electrons move in and you have one state. Reverse the voltage and the electrons flow in another direction, marking the cell as storing a different value. The limiting factor for SSDs' lifespan is how many times data can be written to a cell. But the current generation of SSDs are proving to have very strong performance over time. Intel, one manufacturer of SSDs, says its drives will last five years when being written to heavily (20 GB per day).

Capacities for hard drives in personal computers can exceed 4,000 GB (4 TB). Increasing the amount of data stored in a hard drive is achieved either by adding more platters or by increasing the amount of data stored on each platter. How tightly the tracks are placed next to each other, how tightly spaced the sectors are, and how closely the bits of data are placed affect the measurement of the amount of data that can be stored in a specific area of a hard drive platter. Modern technology continues to increase the standards on all three levels, enabling massive quantities of data to be stored in small places.

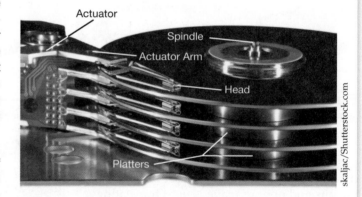

Figure 6.24

The hard drive is a stack of platters enclosed in a sealed case. Special arms fit in between each platter. The read/write heads at the end of each arm read from and save data to the platters.

optical discs, meaning you can't save any data onto them. Prerecorded CDs usually contain audio content, software programs, or games, whereas DVD-ROMs and BD-ROMs typically contain movies or prerecorded TV shows in regular or high definition, respectively. Recordable formats such as CD-R, DVD-R, and BD-R allow data to be written (saved or burned) to them. If you want to be able to use a form of optical media repetitively, writing and rewriting data to it many times, read/writeable formats such as CD-RW, DVD-RW, and BD-RE are available.

Figure 6.25 | DO YOU WANT TO UPGRADE YOUR STORAGE?

	Have It	Want It!
What is my current hard drive capacity?		
Do I want to have a very fast startup time (i.e., use an SSD drive for my operating system)?		
Do I want to implement multiple drives in RAID 0 for performance?		
Do I want to implement multiple drives in RAID 1 for instant backup?		
Do I have a DVD-ROM drive?		
Can I burn DVDs (i.e., do I have a DVD-RW drive)?		
Can I play Blu-ray Discs (i.e., do I have a Blu-ray drive)?		
Can I burn my own Blu-ray Discs (i.e., do I have a Blu-ray burner installed)?		
Do I have a working data backup solution such as external backup drives or remote data storage?		
Do I use any portable storage devices such as external hard drives?		

Do I need separate players and burners for CD, DVD, and BD formats? Although CDs and DVDs are based on the same optical technology, CD drives cannot read DVDs. Although Blu-ray discs are read with a different type of laser than CDs and DVDs, most Blu-ray players are backward compatible and can play DVDs and CDs. If you want to both play and record optical discs, you need to make sure your drive is a "burner" not just a player. Because recording drives are also backward compatible, you do not need separate burners for each form of media. A DVD burner will also record CDs, and a Blu-ray burner will most likely record both CDs and DVDs (although there may be some compatibility issues).

Are some optical drives faster than others? When you buy an optical drive, knowing the drive speed is important. Speeds are listed on the device's packaging. Record (write) speed is always listed first, rewrite speed is listed second, and playback speed is listed last. For example, a DVD-RW drive may have speeds of 24X8X12X, meaning that the device can record data at 24X speed, rewrite data at 8X speed, and play back data at 12X speed. For DVDs, the X after each number represents the transfer of 1.3 MB of data per second. So a DVD-RW drive with a 24X8X12X rating records data at 24 times 1.3 MB per second, or 31.2 MB per second. If you're

SOUND BYTE Installing a Blu-ray Drive

In this Sound Byte, you'll learn how to install a Blu-ray drive in your computer.

in the market for a new DVD burner, then you'll want to investigate the drive speeds on the market and make sure you get the fastest one you can afford.

Blu-ray drives are the fastest optical devices on the market. Blu-ray technology defines 1X speed as 36 MB per second. Because BD movies require data transfer rates of at least 54 MB per second, most Blu-ray disc players have a minimum of 2X speeds (72 MB per second). Many units are available with 12X speeds.

So how do my storage devices measure up? The table in Figure 6.25 will help you determine if your computer's storage subsystem needs upgrading.

Evaluating the Video Subsystem

How video is displayed depends on two components: your video card and your monitor. It's important that your system have the correct monitor and video card

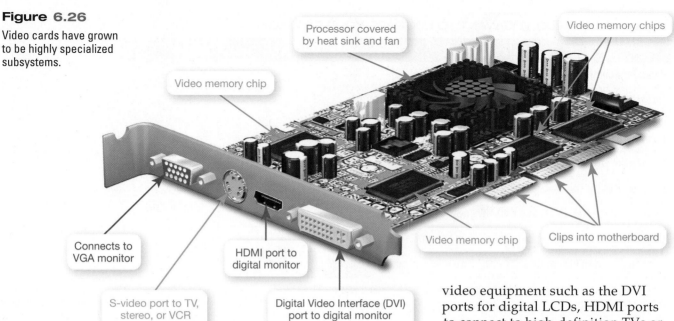

Figure 6.26
Video cards have grown to be highly specialized subsystems.

Processor covered by heat sink and fan

Video memory chip

Video memory chips

Connects to VGA monitor

HDMI port to digital monitor

Video memory chip

Clips into motherboard

S-video port to TV, stereo, or VCR

Digital Video Interface (DVI) port to digital monitor

to meet your needs. If you are considering loading Windows 7 on your system, or using your computer system to display files that have complex graphics, such as videos on Blu-ray or from your HD video camera, or even playing graphics-rich games with a lot of fast action, you may want to consider upgrading your video subsystem.

Video Cards

What is a video card? A **video card** (or **video adapter**) is an expansion card that is installed inside your system unit to translate binary data into the images you view on your monitor. Modern video cards like the ones shown in Figures 6.26 and 6.27 are extremely sophisticated. They include ports that allow you to connect to different

Figure 6.27
Modern graphics cards, like this ASUS ARES, need massive fans for heat removal.

ASUSTek Computer, Inc.

video equipment such as the DVI ports for digital LCDs, HDMI ports to connect to high-definition TVs or gaming consoles, and the newer DisplayPort adapters. In addition, video cards include their own RAM, called **video memory**. Several standards of video memory are available, including graphics double data rate 3 (GDDR3) memory and the newer **graphics double data rate 5 (GDDR5)** memory. Because displaying graphics demands a lot of the CPU, video cards also come with their own graphics processing units (GPUs). When the CPU is asked to process graphics, those tasks are redirected to the GPU, significantly speeding up graphics processing.

Is a GPU different from a CPU? Just like a CPU, the **graphics processing unit (GPU)** performs computational work. However, a GPU is specialized to handle 3D graphics and image and video processing with incredible efficiency and speed. Figure 6.28 shows that the CPU can run much more efficiently when a GPU does all of the graphics computation.

Special lighting effects can be achieved with a modern GPU. Designers can change

ACTIVE HELP-DESK

Evaluating Computer System Components

In this Active Helpdesk call, you'll play the role of a helpdesk staffer, fielding calls about the computer's storage, video, and audio devices and how to evaluate whether they match your needs, as well as how to improve the reliability of your system.

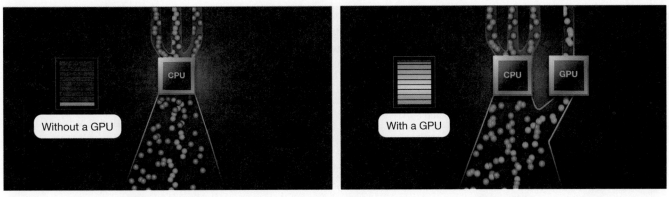

Without a GPU   **With a GPU**

Figure 6.28

The graphics processing unit (GPU) is specialized to handle processing of photos, videos, and video game images. It frees the CPU to work on other system demands.

the type of light, the texture, and the color of objects based on complex interactions. Some GPU designs incorporate dedicated hardware to allow high-definition movies to be decoded or special physics engines to model water, gravity, and rigid body movements.

Where is the GPU—on the motherboard or on the video card? Basic video processing is sometimes integrated into the motherboard. However, high-end video cards that have their own GPUs are separate from the motherboard. These sophisticated video cards connect through the ultrafast PCI Express bus. The ASUS ARES actually uses two Radeon HD 5870 GPUs that work together to add even more processing punch. Cards like this one carry their own processing RAM space, which can range between 512 MB and 4 GB, depending on the model. Together they provide an unprecedented level of realism and detail in gaming environments.

How can I tell how much memory my video card has? Information about your system's video card can be found in the Advanced Settings of the Screen Resolution dialog box. To get to the Screen Resolution dialog box, right-click on your desktop and select Screen resolution. In the Screen Resolution dialog box, click the Advanced settings link. A window will appear that shows you the type of graphics card installed in your system, as well as memory information including total available graphics memory, dedicated video memory, system video memory, and shared system memory. The documentation that came with your computer should also contain specifications for the video card, including the amount of video memory it has installed.

How much memory does my video card need? The amount of memory your video card needs depends on what you want to display on your monitor. If you work primarily in Microsoft Word and conduct general Web searches, 256 MB is a realistic minimum. For the serious gamer, a 512 MB or greater video card is essential, although cards with as much as 2 or 3 GB are available in the market and are preferred. These high-end video cards, which have greater amounts of memory, allow games to generate smoother animations and more sophisticated shading and texture. Before purchasing new software, check the specifications to ensure your video card has enough video memory to handle the load.

How many video cards can I add to a system? For users who are primarily doing text processing or spreadsheet work, one video card is certainly enough. However, computer gamers and users of high-end visualization software often take advantage of the ability to install more than one video card at a time. Two or even three video cards can be used in one system. The two major video chipset manufacturers, Nvidia and ATI, have each developed their own standards supporting the combining of multiple video cards. For Nvidia this standard is named SLI and for ATI it is called CrossFire. When the system is running at very high video resolutions, such as 1920 × 1200 or higher, multiple video cards working together provide the ultimate in performance. If you are buying a new system and might be interested in employing multiple video cards, be sure to check whether the motherboard supports SLI or CrossFire.

Figure 6.29 | BIT DEPTH AND COLOR QUALITY

Bit Depth	Color Quality Description	Number of Colors Displayed
4-bit	Standard VGA	16
8-bit	256-color mode	256
16-bit	High color	65,536
24-bit	True color	16,777,216
32-bit	True color	16,777,216 plus 8 bits to help with transparency

What else does the video card do?

The video card also controls the number of colors your monitor can display. The number of bits the video card uses to represent each pixel (or dot) on the monitor, referred to as **bit depth**, defines the color quality of the image displayed. The more bits, the better an image's color detail. A 4-bit video card

Auto Tech

The automotive industry is pushing its own hardware technology advances. The OnStar system combines software running in the OnStar mirror with a full set of sensors distributed around the car to enable your car to call for help if it detects a crash and you are not responsive. OnStar reports the direction and number of impacts, rollover status, and the maximum velocity on impact so medical workers can come better prepared. If the vehicle is stolen, OnStar can find the location and report it to authorities, can send a signal to the vehicle forcing it to gradually slow down, and can lock out the ignition so it is impossible to restart the car. And once a month your car e-mails you with a report telling you how soon you need an oil change, what the air pressure is in all four tires, and if you need to make an appointment with the garage.

displays 16 colors, the minimum number of colors your system works with (referred to as Standard VGA). Most video cards today are 24-bit cards, displaying more than 16 million colors. This mode is called *true color mode* (see Figure 6.29).

When is it time to get a new video card? If your monitor takes a while to refresh when you are editing photos, surfing the Web, or playing a graphics-rich game, then the video card could be short on memory or the GPU is being taxed beyond its capacity. You can evaluate this precisely using the software that came with your card. For example, AMD Overdrive software monitors the GPU usage level, the current temperature, and the fan speed.

You also may want to upgrade if added features such as importing analog video are important to you. If you want to use multiple monitors at the same time, you also may need to upgrade your video card. Working with multiple monitors is a great advantage if you often have more than one application running at a time (see Figure 6.30). There are video cards that can support up to six monitors from a single card. "Surround Sight" allows you to merge all six monitors to work as one screen or to combine them into any subset—for example, displaying a movie on two combined screens, Excel on one monitor, Word on another, and a browser spread across the final two.

Review the considerations listed in Figure 6.31 to see if it might be time for you to upgrade your video card. On a desktop computer, replacing a video card is fairly simple: just insert the new video card in the correct expansion slot on the motherboard.

Figure 6.30

Solutions like (a) AMD Eyefinity technology support (b) six monitors, which can be combined in any way.

Figure 6.31 | DO YOU NEED TO UPGRADE YOUR VIDEO CARD?

	Have It	Want It!
What is the total amount of video memory on my video card?		
How many monitors can my video card support?		
Does my video card support the kind of ports I need: DVI? HDMI? DisplayPort?		
Is my video card able to refresh the screen fast enough for the videos and games I play?		
Can I import video through my video card?		
Is my video card running at a high temperature?		

Evaluating the Audio Subsystem

Computers output sound by means of speakers (or headphones) and a sound card. For many users, a computer's preinstalled speakers and sound card are adequate for the sounds produced by the computer itself—the beeps and so on that the computer makes. However, if you're listening to music, viewing HD movies, hooking into a household stereo system, or playing games with sophisticated soundtracks, you may want to upgrade your speakers or your sound card.

Sound Card

What does the sound card do? Like a video card, a **sound card** is an expansion card that attaches to the motherboard inside your system unit. A sound card enables the computer to drive the speaker system. Most systems have a separate sound card, although low-end computers often have integrated the job of managing sound onto the motherboard itself.

What does a basic sound card do for me? Many computers ship with a **3D sound card**. The 3D sound technology advances sound reproduction beyond traditional stereo sound (where the human ear perceives sounds as coming from the left or the right of the performance area) and 3D sound is better at convincing the human ear that sound is omnidirectional, meaning that you can't tell from which direction the sound is coming. This tends to produce a fuller, richer sound than stereo sound. However, 3D sound is not surround sound.

What is surround sound then? **Surround sound** is a type of audio processing that makes the listener experience sound as if it were coming from all directions by using multiple speakers. The current surround sound standard is from Dolby. There are many formats available, including Dolby Digital EX and Dolby Digital Plus for high-definition audio. Dolby TrueHD is the newest standard. It features high-definition and lossless technology, which means no information is lost in the compression process. To create surround sound, Dolby takes digital sound from a medium (such as a Blu-ray Disc) and reproduces it in eight channels. Seven channels cover the listening field with placement to the left front, right front, and center of the audio stage, as well as the left rear and right rear, and then two extra side speakers are added, as shown in Figure 6.32. The eighth channel holds extremely low-frequency sound data and is sent to a subwoofer, which can be placed anywhere in the room. The name 7.1 surround indicates that there are seven speakers reproducing the full audio spectrum and one speaker handling just lower frequency bass sounds. There is also a 5.1 surround sound standard, which has a total of six speakers—one subwoofer, a center speaker, and four speakers for right/left in the front and the back. If you have a larger space or want precise location of sounds, use the newer 7.1 system.

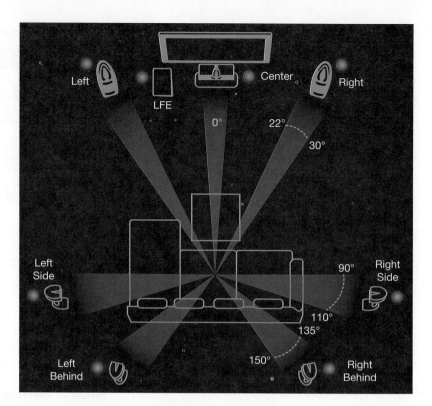

Figure 6.32

Dolby Digital 7.1 surround sound gives you better quality audio output.

To set up surround sound on your computer, you need two things: a set of surround-sound speakers and, for the greatest surround-sound experience, a sound card that is Dolby Digital–compatible. **I don't need surround sound. Why else might I need to upgrade my sound card?** Most basic sound cards contain the following input and output jacks (or ports): microphone in, speaker out, and line in. This allows you to hook up a set of stereo speakers and a microphone. But what if you want to hook up a right and left speaker individually, or attach other audio devices to your computer?

To do so, you need more ports, which are provided on upgraded sound cards like the one shown in Figure 6.33.

With an upgraded sound card, you can connect portable media players, MIDI instruments, and recording equipment to your computer. Musicians often record music

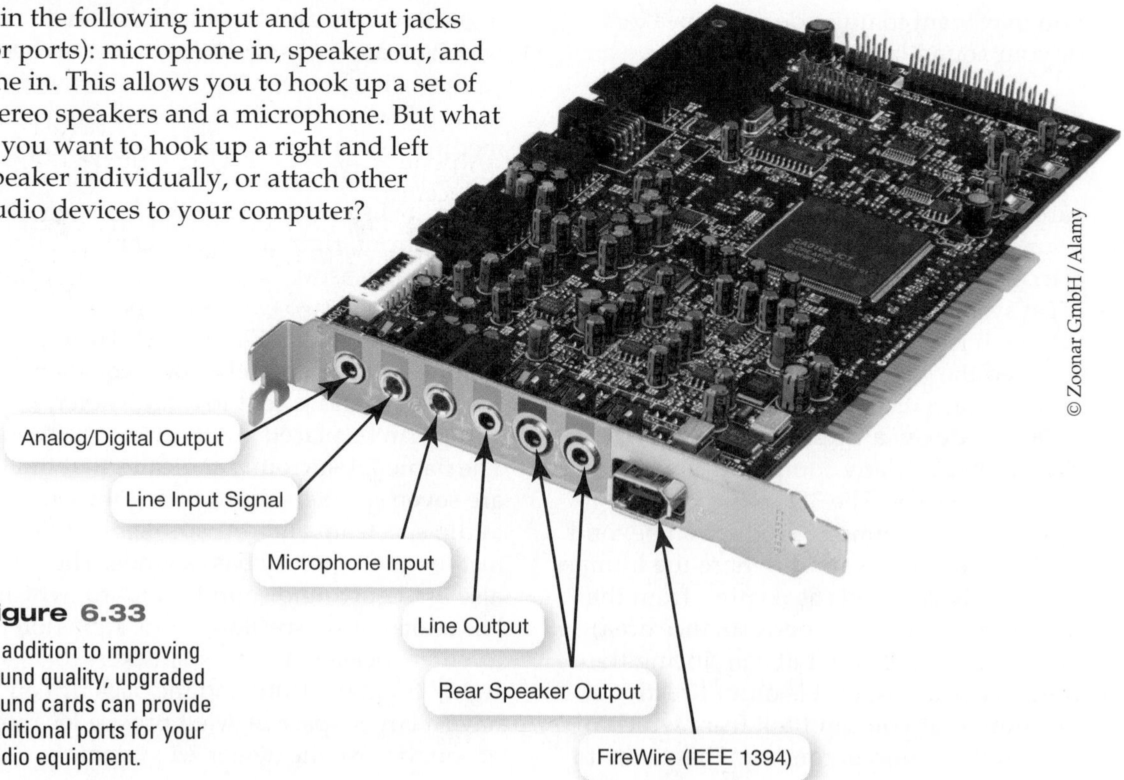

© Zoonar GmbH / Alamy

Analog/Digital Output

Line Input Signal

Microphone Input

Line Output

Rear Speaker Output

FireWire (IEEE 1394)

Figure 6.33

In addition to improving sound quality, upgraded sound cards can provide additional ports for your audio equipment.

onto their computers by connecting guitars, keyboards, digital drums, or microphones directly to sound card ports. There are also external devices that will add RCA jacks for connecting guitars and the microphone ports you need for USB or XLR cables that come from recording mikes. For example, the E-MU Audio/MIDI Interface connects to your computer using USB and is a way to add connectivity for microphones and other instruments. To determine whether your audio subsystem is meeting your needs, review the table in Figure 6.34.

Evaluating System Reliability

Many computer users decide to buy a new system not necessarily because they need a faster CPU, more RAM, or a bigger hard drive, but because they are experiencing problems such as slow performance, freezes, and crashes. Over time, even normal use can cause your computer to build up excess files and to become internally disorganized. This excess, clutter, and disorganization can lead to deteriorating performance or, far worse, system failure. If you think your system is unreliable, see if the problem is one you can fix before you buy a new machine.

| Figure 6.34 | DO YOU NEED TO UPGRADE YOUR AUDIO SUBSYSTEM? |

	Have It	Want It!
Is the speaker quality high enough for the way I am using my computer?		
Is my sound card capable of 3D sound?		
Does my sound card support Dolby Digital surround sound?		
Do I have 5.1-channel surround sound or 7.1-channel surround sound?		
Do I have an HDMI port on the audio card?		

Proper upkeep and maintenance also may postpone an expensive system upgrade or replacement.

What can I do to ensure my system performs reliably? Here are several procedures you can follow to ensure your system performs reliably:

1. Clean out your Startup folder. Some programs install themselves into your Startup folder and run automatically each time the computer starts up, whether you are using them or not.

Over time, even normal use can cause your computer to build up excess files and to become internally disorganized.

This unnecessary load uses up RAM, leaving less for other programs. To minimize this problem, check your Startup folder by clicking Start > All Programs. Then click on the Startup folder and make sure all the programs listed are important to you. Right-click on any unnecessary program and select Delete to remove it from the Startup folder. Make sure you delete *only* programs you are absolutely sure are unnecessary. Another way programs sneak their way in is to load themselves into your system tray. Keep an eye on how many icons are in the system tray and uninstall any that you do not use frequently.

2. Clear out unnecessary files. Temporary Internet files can accumulate quickly on your hard drive, taking up unnecessary space. Running the Disk Cleanup utility is a quick and easy way to ensure your temporary Internet files don't take up precious hard drive space. Likewise, you should delete any unnecessary files from your hard drive regularly, because they can make your hard drive run more slowly.

3. Run spyware and adware removal programs. These often detect and remove different pests and should be used in addition to your regular antivirus package. You can find more details on how to keep your system safe from spyware, adware, and viruses in Chapter 9.

4. Run the Disk Defragmenter utility on your hard drive. When your hard drive becomes fragmented, its storage capacity is negatively affected. When you defragment (defrag) your hard drive, files are reorganized, making the hard drive work more efficiently. But remember that this only makes sense for mechanical drives. With no motors, there is no need to defrag an SSD drive. For a more complete discussion of the Disk Defragmenter, refer to Chapter 5.

The utilities that need to be run more than once, like Disk Cleanup, Disk Defragmenter, and the antivirus, adware, and spyware programs, can be configured to run automatically at any time interval you want. You can use Windows Task Scheduler or third-party programs like Norton Security Suite to set up a sequence of programs to run one after the other every evening while you sleep, and wake up each day to a reliable, secure system.

My system crashes often during the day. What can I do? Computer systems are complex. It's not unusual to have your system stop responding occasionally. If rebooting the computer doesn't help, you'll need to begin troubleshooting:

1. Check that you have enough RAM, which you learned how to do in the section "Evaluating the Memory Subsystem: RAM" earlier in this chapter. Systems with insufficient amounts of RAM often crash.

2. Make sure you have properly installed any new software or hardware. If you're using a Windows system, use the System Restore utility to "roll back" the system to a time when it worked more reliably. (To find System Restore, just type "restore" into the Start menu search box.) For Mac systems, Mac OS X Time Machine, shown in Figure 6.35, provides automatic backup and enables you to look through and restore (if necessary) files, folders, libraries, or the entire system.

3. If you see an error code in Windows, visit the Microsoft Knowledge Base (**support .microsoft.com**), an online resource for resolving problems with Microsoft products. This may help you determine what the error code indicates and how you may be able to solve the problem. If you don't find a satisfactory answer in the Knowledge Base, try copying the entire error message into Google and searching the larger community for solutions.

Figure 6.35

Mac's Time Machine restores files, folders, libraries, and, if necessary, the entire system.

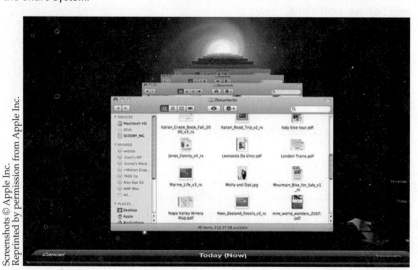

Can my software affect system reliability? Having the latest version of software products makes your system much more reliable. You should upgrade or update your operating system, browser software, and application software as often as new patches (or updates) are reported for resolving errors. Sometimes these errors are performance-related; sometimes they are potential system security breaches.

If you are having a problem that can be replicated, use the Problem Steps Recorder to capture the exact steps that lead to it. In Windows 7, go to the Start menu and search for "psr." Run the Problem Steps Recorder and go through the exact actions that create the problem you are having. At any particular step, you can click the Annotate button and add a comment about any part of the screen. PSR then produces a documented report, complete with images of your screen and descriptions of each mouse movement you made. You can then e-mail this report, which is compressed in the WinZip format, to customer support to help technicians resolve the problem.

How do I know whether updates are available for my software? You can configure Windows so that it automatically checks for, downloads, and installs any available updates for itself, Internet Explorer, and other Microsoft applications such as Microsoft Office. From the Windows Control Panel, open System and Security and then Windows Update. Click Change Settings.

Many other applications now also include the ability to check for updates. Check under the Help menu of the product, and often you will find a Check for Updates command.

What if none of this helps? Is buying a new system my only option? If your system is still unreliable after these changes, then you have two options:

1. Upgrade your operating system to the latest version. There are substantial increases in reliability with each major release of a new operating system. However, upgrading the operating system may require hardware upgrades such as additional RAM, an updated graphics processor, and an even larger hard drive. The Microsoft Windows 7 Upgrade Advisor (a free download from **www.microsoft.com**) will scan

your system to determine what upgrades might be required before you convert to Windows 7. Be sure to examine the *recommended* (not required) specifications of the new operating system.

2. Reinstall the operating system. As a last resort, you might need to reinstall the operating system. To do so, you'll want to back up all of your data files before the installation and be prepared to reinstall all your software after the installation. Make sure you have all of the original discs for the software installed on your system, along with the product keys, serial numbers, and any other activation codes so that you can reinstall them.

Making the Final Decision

Now that you have evaluated your computer system, you need to shift to questions of *value*. How closely does your system come to meeting your needs? How much would it cost to upgrade the system you have to match what you'd ideally like your computer to do, not only today but also a few years from now? How much would it cost to purchase a new system that meets these specifications?

To decide whether upgrading or buying a new system has better value for you, you need to price both scenarios. Figure 6.36 provides an upgrade worksheet you can use to evaluate both the upgrade path and the new purchase path. Purchasing a new system is an important investment of your resources, and you want to make a well-reasoned, well-supported decision.

What happens to my old computer? Be sure to consider what benefit you might obtain by having two systems. Would you have a use for the older system? Would you be able to give it to a family member? If you decide to throw it away, consider the environmental impact. Mercury in LCD screens, cadmium in batteries and circuit boards, and flame retardant in plastic housings all are toxic. An alarming, emerging trend is that discarded machines are beginning to create an e-waste crisis.

How could I recycle my old computer? Instead of throwing your computer away, you may be able to donate

Figure 6.36 | UPGRADE/NEW PURCHASE COMPARISON WORKSHEET

Needs	Hardware Upgrade Cost	Included on New System?	Additional Expense If Not Included on New System
CPU and RAM			
CPU upgrade			
RAM upgrade			
Storage			
Hard drive upgrade			
SSD drive			
DVD-RW burner			
Blu-ray burner			
Video and Audio			
Video card upgrade			
Sound card upgrade			

it to a nonprofit organization. Many manufacturers, such as Dell, offer recycling programs and have formed alliances with nonprofit organizations to help distribute your old technology to those who need it. Sites like Computers with Causes (**www.computerswithcauses.org**) organize donations of both working and nonworking

Eduardo Contreras/San Diego Union-Tribune/ZUMA Press

Figure 6.37

An electronics scrap recycler "demanufactures" printers, computers, and other electronics and then resells the usable parts.

computers, printers, and mice. You can also take your computer to an authorized computer recycling center in your area. The Telecommunications Industry Association provides an e-cycling information site you can use to find a local e-cycling center (**www.eiae.org**).

For companies that need to retire large quantities of computers, the risk of creating an environmental hazard is serious. Firms like GigaBiter (**www.gigabiter.com**) offer a solution. GigaBiter eliminates security and environmental risks associated with electronic destruction by first delaminating the hard drive and then breaking down the computer e-waste into recyclable products (Figure 6.37). The result of the final step is a sandlike substance that is 100 percent recyclable.

Can I donate a computer safely, without worrying about my personal data? Before donating or recycling a computer, make sure you carefully remove all data from your hard drive, or you could become the victim of identity theft. Credit card numbers, bank information, Social Security numbers, tax records, passwords, and personal identification numbers (PINs) are just some of the types of sensitive information that we casually record to our computers' hard drives. Just deleting files that contain proprietary personal information is not protection enough. Likewise, reformatting or erasing your hard drive does not totally remove data, as was proved by two MIT graduate students. They bought more than 150 used hard drives from various sources. Although some of the hard drives had been reformatted or damaged so the data was supposedly irrecoverable, the two students were able to retrieve medical records, financial information, pornography, personal e-mails, and more than 5,000 credit card numbers!

The U.S. Department of Defense suggests a seven-layer overwrite for a "secure erase." This means that you fill your hard drive seven times over with a random series of 1s and 0s. Fortunately, several programs exist for doing this. For PCs running Windows, look for Active@ Kill Disk, Eraser, or Cyber-Scrub. Wipe is available for Linux, and ShredIt X can be used for OS X. These programs provide secure hard drive erasures, either of specific files on your hard drive or of the entire hard drive.

Look at the back of your system and you no doubt see a messy collection of cables of every color, thickness, and design. USB cables to your printer, networking cables to the router, video cables to monitors, along with the requisite power cables, speaker cables, and maybe even a keyboard cable. Don't we all dream of a better day?

Well, that day may be near at hand. Intel has used fiber optics, the transmission of digital data through pure glass cable as thin as human hair, to develop a new input/output technology named Thunderbolt (developed under the codename Light Peak). Thunderbolt supports blazing fast transfer rates of 10 Gb/s, zooming past even the theoretical limit of the new USB 3.0 which is 4.8 Gb/s. How fast is that? Intel says that Thunderbolt could transfer a full length HD movie in under 30 seconds or copy over a library of music that would take a solid year to play through in just 10 minutes. And Thunderbolt can supply much more power to devices than the USB standard allows. It also has a very slim connector design, allowing laptop designers to make their systems even thinner (see Figure 6.38).

But one of the greatest hopes that comes with Thunderbolt is that the technology will be able to replace a number of different ports, cleaning up the cluttered design we see now on the sides of laptops and the backs of desktop units. The first devices using this technology appeared in May 2011 when Apple announced Thunderbolt ports on the MacBook Pro series. It looks like a single thin port that supports both the video standard DisplayPort and the bus standard PCI Express (see Figure 6.39). So Thunderbolt can connect monitors to computers using VGA, DisplayPort, DVI, or HDMI and can connect systems to external hard drives that use USB, FireWire, or eSATA. One Thunderbolt port can support several devices because the cables can be daisy-chained (connected one after another in a serial fashion), so having just one Thunderbolt port on a laptop allows you to connect up to six different peripherals to your system.

Thunderbolt technology also gives you two for one, because each connector can support two separate channels to send and receive data, each one still operating at the full 10 Gb/s bandwidth.

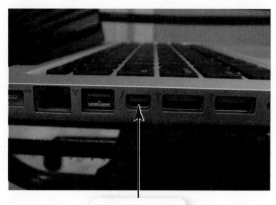

Thunderbolt port

Figure 6.38

Thunderbolt ports are very thin, allowing new design options.

What will this mean to laptop designers? Some speculate we'll see the heavy, heat-producing video cards that are integrated into gaming laptops become external graphics boxes. An incredibly thin, light laptop design would let you be wonderfully mobile all day, then when you come home you'd attach one cable. It would run from your Thunderbolt port to your 60" HDTV, then continue on to a separate graphics processor box. That same laptop is now running a huge HD monitor with a high-resolution graphics and physics engine.

Apple is not the only company that will be using the Intel technology. Hard drive companies like LaCie and Western Digital as well as audio/video processing companies like Avid and Apogee have announced Thunderbolt products. And the USB community may need to put up a bit of a fight to keep their standard around. But the allure of incredible speed, great versatility, and small, thin packaging is going to make the Thunderbolt technology a trend to watch.

Could Thunderbolt make USB a thing of the past?

Figure 6.39

Thunderbolt can carry two channels of information on the same connector.

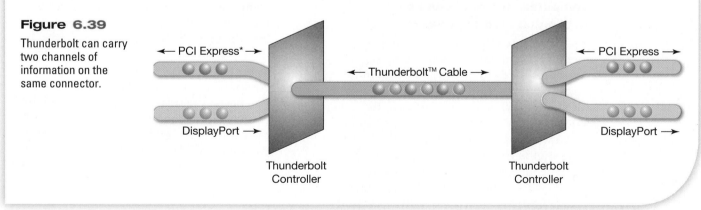

PCI Express*

DisplayPort

Thunderbolt™ Cable

Thunderbolt Controller

PCI Express

DisplayPort

Thunderbolt Controller

1. How can I determine whether I should upgrade my existing computer or buy a new one?

To determine whether you need to upgrade your system or purchase a new one, you need to define your ideal system and what you want it to do. Then you need to perform a system evaluation to assess the subsystems in your computer, including the CPU, memory, storage, video, and audio. Finally, you need to determine if it's economical to upgrade, or whether buying a new computer would be better.

2. What does the CPU do, and how can I evaluate its performance?

Your computer's CPU processes instructions, performs calculations, manages the flow of information through the computer system, and is responsible for processing the data you input into information. CPU speed is measured in gigahertz (billions of machine cycles per second). You can tell whether your CPU is limiting your system performance by watching how busy it is as you work on your computer. The percentage of time that your CPU is working is referred to as CPU usage, which you can determine by checking the Task Manager. Benchmarking software offers direct performance comparisons of different CPUs.

3. How does memory work in my computer, and how can I evaluate how much memory I need?

RAM is your computer's temporary memory. It remembers everything that the computer needs to process data into information. However, it is an example of volatile storage. When the power is off, the data stored in RAM is cleared out. The amount of RAM sitting on memory modules in your computer is your computer's physical memory. The memory your OS uses is kernel memory. At a minimum, you need enough RAM to run the OS plus the software applications you're using, plus a bit more to hold the data you will input.

4. What are the computer's storage devices, and how can I evaluate whether they match my needs?

Storage devices for a typical computer system may include a hard drive, an SSD drive, a flash drive, and CD and DVD drives. Blu-ray drives are gaining in popularity for viewing and burning high-density media. When you turn off your computer, the data stored in these devices remains. These devices are referred to as *nonvolatile* storage devices. Hard drives have the largest storage capacity of any storage device and are the most economical. Newer SSD drives have the fastest access time and data transfer rate of all nonvolatile storage options. CDs and DVDs have capacities from 700 MB to 17 GB, while Blu-ray discs can hold up to 50 GB. Portable flash drives allow easy transfer of 64 GB or more of data from machine to machine. To determine the storage capacity your system needs, calculate the amount of storage your software needs to reside on your computer. To add more storage or to provide more functionality for your system, you can install additional drives, either internally or externally.

5. What components affect the quality of video on my computer, and how do I know if I need better video performance?

How video is displayed depends on two components: your video card and your monitor. A video card translates binary data into the images you see. These cards include their own RAM (video memory) as well as ports that allow you to connect to video equipment. The amount of video memory you need depends on what you want to display on the monitor. A more powerful card will allow you to play graphics-intense games and multimedia.

6. What components affect my computer's sound quality?

Your computer's sound depends on your speakers and sound card. A sound card enables the computer to produce sounds. Users upgrade their sound cards to provide surround sound, and additional ports for audio equipment.

7. How can I improve the reliability of my system?

Many computer users decide to buy a new system because they are experiencing problems with their computer. However, before you buy a new system because you think yours may be unreliable, make sure the problem is not one you can fix. Run a full scan with antispyware and -adware software. Make sure you have installed any new software or hardware properly, check that you have enough RAM, run system utilities such as Disk Defragmenter and Disk Cleanup, clean out your Startup folder, remove unnecessary files from your system, and keep your software updated with patches. If you continue to have troubles with your system, reinstall or upgrade your OS, and, of course, seek technical assistance.

 Companion Website

The Companion Website includes a variety of additional materials to help you review and learn more about the topics in this chapter. Go to: *www.pearsonhighered.com/techinaction*

buzzwords

Word Bank

- access time
- cache memory
- cores
- CPU usage graph
- data transfer rate
- eSATA
- ExpressCards
- front side bus
- GDDR5
- GPU
- hard drive
- HDMI
- memory modules
- Moore's Law
- RAID 1
- RAM
- sound card
- SSD
- surround sound

Instructions: Fill in the blanks using the words from the Word Bank above.

Luis already has a desktop PC but just heard about a great deal on a new one. He decides to perform a system evaluation on his computer to see whether he should keep it or buy the new one. First, he watches the load on the processor using the (1)_____ in Windows. Because he has a multiple (2) _____ in his processor, there are multiple graphs to follow. Because he is often having system crashes, he begins to suspect his system is suffering from too little (3) _____. He has room for an additional two (4) _____ on his motherboard. Adding memory is something he learned how to do this semester, but would that be enough to make this machine fit his needs?

He visits the Intel Web site to check two other important factors on his model of CPU: the amount of (5) _____ and the speed of the (6) _____. It looks like the newer i7 processor would be much faster overall. It seems each generation of processors is so much faster than the last. That rule, (7) _____, is still holding true!

Luis continues to evaluate his system by checking out which components he has and which ones he'll need. He notes the storage capacity of his mechanical (8) _____ and decides he needs more room. Recently, he has been wishing his system had a(n) (9) _____ port. As it is, he is running out of space to store files. But the (10) _____, or the amount of time it takes to retrieve data from the disk drive, on any mechanical drive is slow compared to the (11) _____ in the new computer he's eyeing, which has no moving parts at all. Luis is really concerned about having a backup of his work so he's going to use two cheaper mechanical drives, connected in (12) _____ to guarantee immediate backup of every change. The new video card includes a specialized (13) _____ that can process 3D data with great speed. It would be great if he could take advantage of the 7.1 (14) _____ that is on the gaming software he runs.

It's tough to play the games he wants though since his current system doesn't meet the minimum video requirements for the newer games. The current video cards have blindingly fast (15) _____ memory, and some people even use multiple cards. Overall, with prices dropping, it seems like time to go buy that new system!

becoming computer literate

Rebecca has already built five or six PCs and tells you she can make a killer desktop system for you for under $1,300. But you do love the idea of having a light, compact notebook computer that could travel with you around campus and back and forth to work.

Instructions: Using the preceding scenario, write an e-mail to Rebecca describing to her what you need in your new system. Examine the specifications for both notebook and desktop systems in this price range and decide which one is best suited to you. Use key terms from the chapter and be sure your sentences are grammatically correct and technically meaningful.

self-test

Instructions: Answer the multiple-choice and true–false questions below for more practice with key terms and concepts from this chapter.

Multiple Choice

1. Which statement about notebook computers is FALSE?
   a. Notebooks typically have a longer lifespan than desktop computers.
   b. Notebooks are typically less reliable than desktop computers.
   c. Notebooks can be docked to larger monitors.
   d. Notebooks are more difficult to expand or upgrade.

2. SSD is classified as what type of storage?
   a. volatile   b. nonvolatile
   c. video   d. cache

3. To document a problem you are having, you can use
   a. Disk Cleanup.
   b. Problem Steps Recorder.
   c. PC Decrapifier.
   d. Resource Monitor.

4. If you want your system to run reliably, you should
   a. add all programs to the Startup folder.
   b. save all of your temporary Internet files.
   c. install programs in the system tray.
   d. defragment the hard drive.

5. Which best describes RAID 0 technology?
   a. Saved data is spread across two hard drives.
   b. Data is written to one drive and mirrored to a second drive.
   c. RAID 0 allows you to store twice the data.
   d. RAID 0 provides an instant backup of your work.

6. CPUs have several internal components, including
   a. L2 cache.
   b. ALU.
   c. level 1 cache memory.
   d. all of the above.

7. Which is *not* a type of video port?
   a. HDMI
   b. DVI
   c. USB 3.0
   d. DisplayPort

8. A sound card that supports 7.1 surround sound will drive
   a. seven speakers.
   b. one speaker.
   c. eight speakers.
   d. Dolby headphones.

9. SuperFetch is a memory-management technique that
   a. determines the type of RAM your system requires.
   b. makes the boot-up time for the system very quick.
   c. preloads the applications you use most into system memory.
   d. defragments the hard drive to increase performance.

10. What is the name for the time it takes a storage device to locate its stored data and make it available for processing?
    a. rotational latency
    b. access time
    c. data transfer rate
    d. seek time

True–False

_____ 1. A quad core CPU with hyperthreading has eight virtual CPUs.

_____ 2. The memory that your operating system uses is referred to as kernel memory.

_____ 3. SSD hard drives need to be defragged but mechanical hard drives do not.

_____ 4. Cache memory is a form of read-only memory that can be accessed more quickly by the CPU.

_____ 5. GDDR5 memory is often used in eSATA drives.

1. Personalize Your System

Likely, you spend many hours each day working on your computer using it for school, work, communication, research, and entertainment. Your computer should be a device that fits you, fits your needs, and expresses who you are.

a. Begin with the computer's form. Would you select a notebook or a desktop? What features determine that decision?

b. Next consider performance. Which type of CPU do you need? How much RAM should be installed? What kind of hard drive storage would you select? Give specific price-to-value arguments for each decision.

c. Now consider expandability. If you need this system to last for four years, what kind of ports and expansion capabilities are necessary?

2. Convertibles

The line between the capabilities of a laptop and a portable tablet have become more and more blurred with the arrival of "convertible tablets." These systems can be detached from a base unit with a full size keyboard and then function as a lightweight touch screen tablet. What kind of user would find this an ideal solution? Do you anticipate this category of computer becoming more popular?

3. Go Small or Stay Home

Manufacturers are releasing a number of systems that are trying to capitalize on size—or the lack of size! Explore some of the small form factor (SFF) computers appearing on the market.

a. Research the Falcon Northwest FragBox (**www.falcon-nw.com**).

b. Examine the Apple Mac mini (**www.apple.com**).

c. Compare those systems with the Dell Zino HD (**www.dell.com**).

Why are these SFF computers appearing? What role do you see these systems fulfilling? What kind of performance and hardware would you recommend for such a system?

4. Do-It-Yourself Computer Design

Visit Newegg (**www.newegg.com**) and do a search on "do it yourself." You will find that Newegg has created a number of bundles, which are a set of components that cover the categories outlined in this chapter: the computer case, processor, RAM, storage, video, and audio.

a. Which system looks like the best match for your needs for school next semester? Why?

b. What is the price difference between building the system and purchasing a similar unit from a major manufacturer?

c. What skills would you need before you could assemble the computer yourself?

d. What additional components (hardware and software) would you need to complete the system?

5. How Does Your System Measure Up?

A number of tools are available to measure your system's performance. Explore the following tools and use one to gather data on your current system's performance.

a. Windows 7 Gadgets: Visit the Windows 7 Personalization Gallery (**windows.microsoft .com/en-US/windows/downloads/personalize**) and find gadgets to help you monitor system performance.

b. Windows 7 Resource Monitor: Use the Resource Monitor to collect data on CPU utilization and memory usage over a typical school day.

c. Benchmarking suites: Examine a sample of consumer benchmarking programs like PassMark's PerformanceTest, Primate Lab's Geekbench, and Maxon's Cinebench. Which subsystems do each of these products evaluate?

making the transition to... the workplace

1. Judging System Performance

As you learned in this chapter, the Resource Monitor provides a detailed breakdown of how the computer is using memory at any given time.

a. Open the Resource Monitor, display the CPU tab, and open the Processes frame. What is your total CPU Usage? How many "virtual" CPUs does your machine have? Clicking on any of the column titles sorts that column, so clicking the Average CPU column shows you the applications currently using most of the CPU resources. What are the top two most intensive applications?

b. Display the Memory tab. How much memory is in use? How much is available? Of the memory available, how much has been preloaded with data and files that Windows "thinks" you will need soon?

c. Display the Disk tab. Click on the Processes with Disk Activity panel. Which programs are making the greatest total demand to read and write to the disk?

2. More and More Monitors

Video cards that support three or even more monitors are very affordable and could be of great use in a number of businesses. Investigate a set of video cards that support three, six, or eight monitors. Research multi-monitor mounting systems. How would the following jobs best arrange multiple monitors to make their workday more efficient?

a. Stockbroker   b. Software developer

c. Airport traffic control   d. Author

3. Room to Move

You are responsible for specifying the storage solution for an accounting customer's computer system. Your customer needs to always have redundancy—that is, multiple copies of the work they are doing—because of the secure nature of the records they keep and the length of time they are required to keep records. Prepare a report that describes the type of hard drive and optical storage you would recommend. Be sure to include performance specifications and price. Devise a list of questions you would need to ask your customer to be sure they have a system that meets their expectations.

4. Video Connections

You have a position in a pharmaceutical research firm. Your group does simulations of protein folding to predict if a new drug will be effective. You collaborate daily with a team in India using video conferencing. Now you have found out you also have the responsibility of creating a series of training videos to teach the Indian team how to use the newest release of software. What video and processing hardware would your workstation need to tackle this? Specify the video card performance and the CPU and memory requirements you would have for this project.

5. Let Me Tell You My Problem

You may be responsible for helping others solve various computer problems. Test out the Problem Steps Recorder in Windows 7 to see how the program can help you help them. Click the Start button and search for "psr." Run the program and click Start Record. Then just click between different applications, visit the Control Panel, and add an annotation. Save the file to your desktop and close the Problem Steps Recorder. View the annotated report. How could you use the Problem Steps Recorder to describe a problem or to gather information?

Instructions: Some ideas are best understood by experimenting with them in our own minds. The following critical thinking questions are designed to demand your full attention but require only a comfortable chair—no technology.

1. More and More

The amount of storage we have available on hard disk drives has increased again and again. What has changed that we suddenly need such huge amounts of storage? How have our storage habits changed? What is the limit—what is the largest amount of storage you can imagine using? How will cloud networking impact our future need for storage?

2. Emerging Technologies

Touch screens are now available in a range of sizes, from smartphones to iPads to larger products like the Microsoft Surface. Windows 7 has integrated support for touch screens. "Surround Sight" and 3D monitors are available in increasing numbers. What new technologies will last and become part of our collective experience? How will these technologies and devices change entertainment and how people interact with information? What future technologies would be on your wish list?

3. The Early Adopter

We are all aware of the technology price curve: when first introduced, products have the highest prices and the most instability. As these products settle into the market, they become more reliable and the prices fall, sometimes very quickly. People who make those first release purchases are called *early adopters*. What are the advantages to being an early adopter? What are the disadvantages? How do you decide at what point you should step into the technology price curve for any given product?

4. A Green Machine

Review the impacts of your computer during its entire lifecycle. How do the production, transportation, and use of the computer impact the increase of greenhouse gas emissions? How does the selection of materials and packaging impact the environment? What restricted substances (like lead, mercury, cadmium, and PVC) are found in your machine? Could substitute materials be used? How would the ultimate "green machine" be designed?

5. System Longevity

If you purchase a computer system for business purposes, the Internal Revenue Service (IRS) allows you to depreciate its cost over five years. The IRS considers this a reasonable estimate of the useful lifetime of a computer system. What do you think most home users expect in terms of how long their computer systems should last? How does the purchase of a computer system compare with other major household appliances in terms of cost, value, benefit, life span, and upgrade potential?

Many Different Computers for Many Different Needs

Problem

Even within one discipline, there are needs for a variety of types of computing solutions. Consider the Communications department in a large university. Because it is such an interdisciplinary area, there are some groups involved in video production, some groups producing digital music, and some groups responsible for creating scripts and screenplays. The department as a whole needs to decide on a complete computing strategy.

Process

Split your class into teams.

1. Select one segment of the Communications department that your team will represent: video production, digital music, or scripting. The video production team requires their labs to be able to support the recording, editing, and final production and distribution of digital video. The digital music group wants to establish a collegiate recording studio (in the model of the Drexel University recording label, Mad Dragon Records). The scripting group needs to support a collaborative community of writers and voice-over actors.

2. Analyze the computing needs of that division, with particular focus on how they need to outfit their computer labs.

3. Price the systems you would recommend and explain how they will be used. What decisions have you made to guarantee they will still be useful in three years?

4. Write a report that summarizes your findings. Document the resources you used and generate as much enthusiasm as you can for your recommendations.

Conclusion

The range of available computing solutions has never been so broad. It can be a cause of confusion for those not educated in technology. But with a firm understanding of the basic subsystems of computers, it is precisely the pace of change that is exciting. Being able to evaluate a computer system and match it to the current needs of its users is an important skill.

Benchmarking

In this exercise, you will research and then role-play a complicated ethical situation. The role you play might or might not match your own personal beliefs; in either case, your research and use of logic will enable you to represent the view assigned. An arbitrator will watch and comment on both sides of the arguments, and together the team will agree on an ethical solution.

Problem

We have seen that for complex systems like computers, performance often is determined not by comparing the specifications of individual parts but by using benchmarks, software suites that test a full area of performance. There are benchmarks for battery life, for CPU performance, and for video performance. The results of these tests become a major force in marketing and selling the product.

There have been a number of claims of unethical conduct in the area of benchmarking. Companies have been accused of using out-of-date testing software to skew their results. Some companies have manipulated the settings on the machine to artificially raise their score (for example, turning off the display and wireless network before testing for battery life). Some companies have even accused their competition of colluding with the creator of the benchmark so that it is written to favor one product over another.

Where is the line between having a competitive edge and lying when it comes to hardware assessment?

Research Areas to Consider

- SysMark 2002
- BAPCo
- MobileMark
- 2009 Nobel Prize for Physics

Process

Divide the class into teams.

1. Research the areas cited above from the perspective of either an Intel engineer working on a new CPU, an AMD engineer working on a competing CPU, or a benchmark designer.
2. Team members should write a summary that provides factual documentation for the positions and views their character takes around the issue of equitable testing of hardware. Then, team members should create an outline to use during the role-playing event.
3. Team members should arrange a mutually convenient time to meet for the exchange, either using the chat room feature of MyITLab, the discussion board feature of Blackboard, or meeting in person.
4. Team members should present their case to the class, or submit a PowerPoint presentation for review by the rest of the class, along with the summary and resolution they developed.

Conclusion

As technology becomes ever more prevalent and integrated into our lives, more and more ethical dilemmas will present themselves. Being able to understand and evaluate both sides of the argument, while responding in a personally or socially ethical manner, will be an important skill.

chapter 7

networking
connecting computing devices

Networking Fundamentals

OBJECTIVE:

What is a network, and what are the advantages/disadvantages of setting up one? *(p. 304)*

Network Architecture and Components

OBJECTIVES:

What is the difference between a client/server network and a peer-to-peer network? *(p. 306)*

What are the main components of every network? *(p. 308)*

 Sound Byte: Installing a Home Computer Network

Connecting to the Internet

OBJECTIVE:

What are my options for connecting to the Internet? *(p. 311)*

 Sound Byte: Connecting to the Internet

Active Helpdesk: Connecting to the Internet

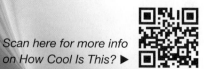

Scan here for more info on How Cool Is This? ▶

Home Networks

OBJECTIVES:

Which type of network is most commonly found in the home? *(p. 315)*

What equipment and software do I need to build a network in my home? *(p. 319)*

Securing Wireless Networks

OBJECTIVE:

Why are wireless networks more vulnerable than wired networks, and what special precautions are required to ensure my wireless network is secure? *(p. 322)*

 Sound Byte: Securing Wireless Networks

 Active Helpdesk: Understanding Networking

Configuring Software for Your Home Network

OBJECTIVES:

Besides computers, what other devices can I connect to a home network? *(p. 328)*

How do I configure the software on my computer and set up other devices to get my network up and running? *(p. 329)*

What problems might I encounter when setting up a wireless network? *(p. 331)*

how cool is *this?*

As you have probably already experienced, wireless connectivity is not always free. Many businesses, such as airports, **charge** customers for each device they want to connect, which can become expensive for groups of friends trying to surf the Internet while waiting to **catch a flight**. Connectify is free software that takes an existing Internet connection and turns it into a wireless hotspot. So if you are connected to the Internet on your Windows notebook or Android phone or tablet, the **Connectify** software turns your computing device into a wireless hotspot so that you and your friends can connect other WiFi-enabled devices such as a phone or **gaming** system through the same Internet connection. The hotspot you create features easy connectivity and encryption of data for solid **security**.

© Beboy / Fotolia

Networking Fundamentals

Now that we are into the second decade of the 21st century, many homes have more than one computing device that is capable of connecting to the Internet. A typical family, like the Jones family (see Figure 7.1), might be engaged in the following: Robert (the father) is watching a movie, which he downloaded yesterday on the large-screen HDTV in the living room while checking his Gmail on his phone. Jennifer (the mother) is in the kitchen fixing lunch while checking the

Figure 7.1

By setting up a home network, everyone in the family can connect their computing devices whenever and wherever they desire.

weather forecast and watching YouTube videos. Andy, their nine-year-old son, is in his bedroom playing an online game with his friends (via his PlayStation) and is uploading a video he made for a class project to a Web site at school. Adriana, Andy's older sister, is in the den using her notebook computer to finish a report for school. She's also watching a Blu-ray Disc of *Avatar*, which is one of her all-time favorite movies. Grandma Rita is in the family room using her iPad to view pictures from the family's last vacation and is uploading to Facebook the pictures that she took of her grandchildren during their trip to the amusement park last week. And Andrea, the youngest daughter, is playing with Rojo in the backyard and uploading video that she took of him with her phone so that everyone can see it in the family room while they eat lunch. And because both Robert and Jennifer work outside the home, they use webcams to monitor activities in the house, like ensuring their kids arrive home safely from school while they are at work. What makes all this technology transfer and sharing possible? A home network!

What is a computer network? A computer **network** is simply two or more computers that are connected via software and hardware so that they can communicate with each other. You access networks all the time whether you realize it or not. When you use an ATM, get gasoline, or use the Internet (the world's largest network), you are interacting with a network. Each device connected to a network is referred to as a **node**. A node can be a computer, a peripheral (such as an all-in-one printer), a game console, a digital video recorder, or a communications device like a modem.

The main function for most home networks is to facilitate information sharing, but networks provide other benefits.

What are the benefits of networks? There are several benefits to having computers networked. Most home users want a network to facilitate resource sharing. For example, a network allows you to share the high-speed Internet connection coming into your home. Networks also allow you to share peripheral devices, such as printers. Figure 7.2a shows two computers that are not networked. The desktop computer is connected to the printer, but the notebook is not. To print files from the notebook, users have to transfer them using a flash drive or another storage medium to the desktop, or they have to disconnect the printer from the desktop and connect it to the notebook. Using a network, a notebook computer and an iPad, as shown in Figure 7.2b, can both print from the printer without transferring files or attaching the printer to

Figure 7.2

(a) Computers are not networked, and the notebook cannot access the printer. (b) Networking allows sharing of the printer.

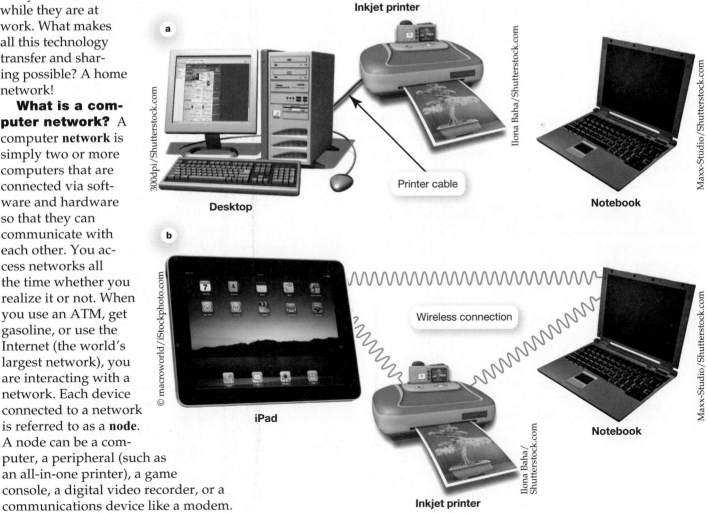

Inkjet printer

Printer cable

Desktop

Notebook

iPad

Wireless connection

Inkjet printer

Notebook

a particular device. Using a wired or wireless network to share a printer saves the cost of buying one printer for each computing device.

Besides peripheral and Internet connections, does networking facilitate any other types of resource sharing? You can also easily share files between networked computers without having to use portable storage devices such as flash drives to transfer the files. In addition, you can set sharing options in Windows or OS X that allow the user of each computer on the network to access files (such as music or videos) stored on any other computer on the network, as shown in Figure 7.3.

This Windows network has five computers attached to it. ALAN-DESKTOP, ALAN-NOTEBOOK, and PAT-NOTEBOOK are running the Windows operating system. The two MACBOOKs are running OS X. The Public folders enable file sharing because the user of any computer on the network can access the Public folder's contents. And note the final advantage of networking: computers running different operating systems can communicate on the same network.

Are there disadvantages to setting up a network? Networks involve the purchase of additional equipment to set them up, so cost is one disadvantage. Also, networks need to be administered, at least to some degree. **Network administration** involves tasks such as: (1) installing new

computers and devices, (2) monitoring the network to ensure it is performing efficiently, (3) updating and installing new software on the network, and (4) configuring, or setting up, proper security for a network. Fortunately, most home networks do not require a great deal of administration after their initial configuration, and the benefits of using a network usually outweigh the disadvantages.

Now that you know the advantages of setting up a network, in the next two sections we'll explore the basic design and components of simple networks.

Network Architectures

The term **network architecture** refers to the design of a network. Network architectures are classified according to the way in which they are controlled and the distance between their nodes.

Describing Networks Based on Network Administration

What different types of control do I have over my network? A network can be administered, or managed, in either of two main ways: locally or centrally. Local administration means that the configuration and maintenance of the network must be performed on each individual computer attached to the network. A peer-to-peer network is the most common example of a locally administered network. Central administration means that tasks can be performed from one computer and affect the other computers on the network. The most common type of centrally administered network is a client/server network.

What is a peer-to-peer network? In a **peer-to-peer (P2P) network**, each node connected to the network can communicate directly with every other node on the network. Thus, all nodes on this type of network are peers (equals). When printing, for example, a computer on a P2P network doesn't have to go through the computer that's connected to the printer. Instead, it can communicate directly with the printer. Figure 7.2b, shown earlier, shows a very small peer-to-peer network. Because they are simple to set up, P2P networks are the most common type of

Figure 7.3

Windows Explorer showing five networked computers set up for sharing.

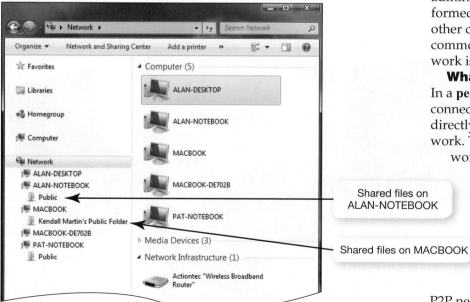

Shared files on ALAN-NOTEBOOK

Shared files on MACBOOK

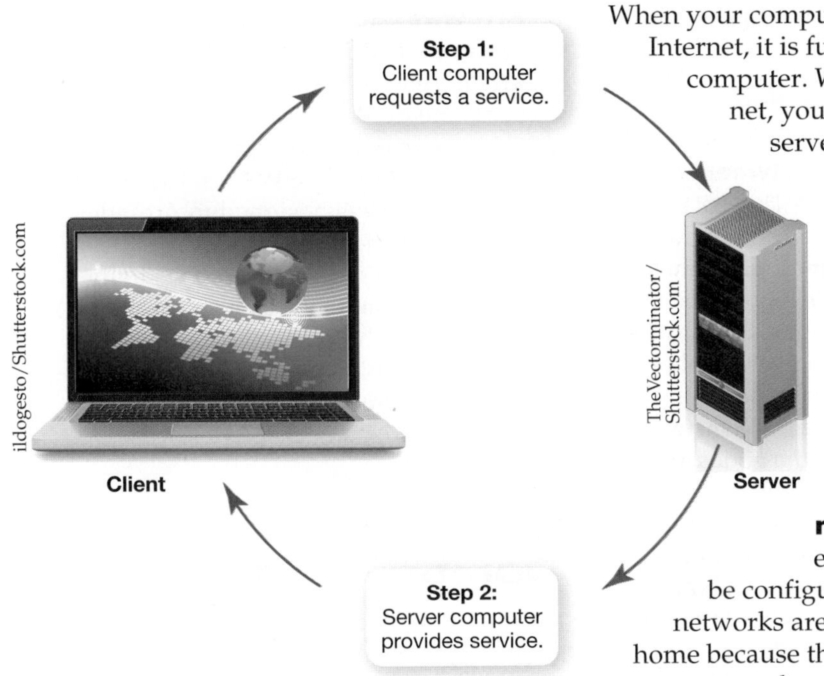

Step 1:
Client computer requests a service.

Client

Server

Step 2:
Server computer provides service.

Figure 7.4

In a client/server network, a computer acts either as a client making requests for resources or as a server providing resources.

home network. Very small schools and offices may also use P2P networks. However, most networks that have 10 or more nodes are client/server networks.

What are client/server networks?

A **client/server network** contains two different types of computers: clients and servers. A **client** is a computer on which users accomplish specific tasks (such as construct spreadsheets) and make specific requests (such as printing a file). The **server** is the computer that provides information or resources to the client computers on the network. The server on a client/server network also provides central administration for network functions such as printing. Figure 7.4 illustrates a client/server network in action.

As you learned in Chapter 3, the Internet is an example of a client/server network.

Figure 7.5

At only 8 inches high, the Acer Aspire easyStore server can perform a variety of tasks to simplify media management on a home network.

When your computer is connected to the Internet, it is functioning as a client computer. When it accesses the Internet, your computer connects to a server computer maintained by your Internet service provider (the company that sells you Internet access). The server "serves up" resources to your computer so that you can interact with the Internet.

Are client/server networks ever used as home networks? Although client/server networks can be configured for home use, P2P networks are more often used in the home because they cost less than client/server networks and are easier to configure and maintain. However, specialized types of servers, such as servers for sharing files, are now appearing on P2P networks in the home.

Nowadays, people are accumulating vast numbers of media files from digital cameras, video downloads, and music downloads. Because users often want to share this media, specialized home network servers such as the Acer Aspire easyStore server featuring Windows Home Server are now available for home networks (see Figure 7.5). A **home network server** is designed to store media, share media across the network, and back up files on computers connected to the network. All computers connected to the network can access the server.

Even though a server may now be attached to a home network, that does not change the architecture of a home network from a P2P network to a client/server network. Except for the specialized functions of the home network server, all network administration tasks (such as installation of software and changing of configuration settings) must still be performed locally, and all the nodes on the network are still peers to each other.

Describing Networks Based on Distance

How does the distance between nodes define a network? The distance between nodes on a network is another way to describe a network. A **home area network (HAN)** is a network located in a home. HANs are used to connect all of a home's digital devices, such as computers, peripherals, phones, gaming devices, digital video recorders (DVRs), and televisions. A **local area network (LAN)** is a network in which the nodes are located within a small geographic area. Examples include a network in a computer lab at school or at a fast-food restaurant.

Is it possible to connect LANs? A **wide area network (WAN)** is made up of LANs connected over long distances. Say a school has two campuses (east and west) located in different towns. Connecting the LAN at the east campus to the LAN at the west campus by telecommunications lines would allow the users on the two LANs to communicate. The two LANs would be described as a single WAN.

Are wireless networks that cover large areas like cities considered WANs? Technically, wireless networks like the one deployed in Minneapolis, which provides Internet access to city residents and visitors, are WANs. However, when a network is designed to provide access to a specific geographic area, such as an entire city, the network is usually called a **metropolitan area network (MAN)**. Many cities in the United States are now deploying MANs to provide Internet access to residents and provide convenience for tourists.

Network Components

To function, all networks must include (1) a means of connecting the nodes on the network (cables or wireless technology), (2) special devices that allow the nodes to communicate with each other and to send data, and (3) software that allows the network to run. We discuss each of these components in this section (see Figure 7.6).

Figure 7.6

Network components.

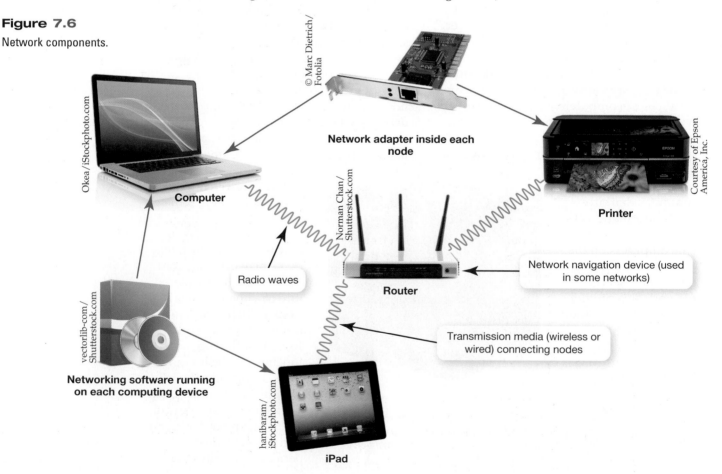

Network adapter inside each node

Computer

Printer

Radio waves

Router

Network navigation device (used in some networks)

Networking software running on each computing device

Transmission media (wireless or wired) connecting nodes

iPad

Figure 7.7

(a) Coaxial cable uses a copper core, whereas (b) fiber optic cable uses plastic or glass fibers.

Transmission Media

How are nodes on a network connected? All network nodes are connected to each other and to the network by transmission media. **Transmission media** establish a communications channel between the nodes on a network and can be either wireless or wired.

Wireless networks use radio waves to connect nodes. With the proliferation of portable devices being connected to home networks, a network with wireless connectivity is required in most homes.

Wired networks use various types of cable (wire) to connect nodes. **Twisted-pair cable** is made up of copper wires that are twisted around each other and surrounded by a plastic jacket. Normal telephone cable is a type of twisted-pair cable, although phone cable won't work for connecting a home network; a slightly different type of twisted-pair cable is used. **Coaxial cable** (Figure 7.7a) consists of a single copper wire surrounded by layers of plastic. If you have cable TV, the cable running into your TV or cable box is most likely coaxial cable. **Fiber-optic cable** (Figure 7.7b) is made up of plastic or glass fibers that transmit data at extremely fast speeds.

Does it matter what type of media you use to transfer data? The media you choose depend on the requirements of a network's users. Using wireless media is critical when portable computing devices need to be connected to a network. However, higher speed connections than can be achieved by wireless connectivity are required for certain types of network activities, such as downloading large movie files. Different types of transmission media transmit data at different speeds.

Data transfer rate (also called **bandwidth**) is the maximum speed at which data can be transmitted between two nodes on a network. **Throughput** is the actual speed of data transfer that is achieved. Throughput is always less than or equal to the data transfer rate. Data transfer rate and throughput are usually measured in megabits per second (Mbps). A megabit is 1 million bits. Twisted-pair cable, coaxial cable, and wireless media usually provide enough bandwidth for most home networks.

Network Adapters

How do the different nodes on the network communicate? Network adapters are devices installed in network nodes that enable the nodes to communicate with each other and to access the network. All desktop and notebook computers (and many peripherals) sold today contain network adapters installed *inside* the device. This type of adapter is referred to as a **network interface card (NIC)**. Different NICs are designed to use different types of transmission media. Most NICs included in computing devices today are built to use wireless media, but many can use wired media as well. Your notebook computer most likely has a wireless NIC in it that allows you to connect to wireless networks at home, school, or the coffee shop. But most notebooks also have a port that accommodates cable for a wired connection to a network.

Why would I ever consider using a wired connection with my notebook computer? Wired connections can sometimes provide greater throughput than current high-speed wireless networks.

Sharing Your Internet Connection with Your Neighbors: Legal? Ethical? Safe?

With the advances in wireless equipment, signals can travel well beyond the walls of your home. This makes it possible in an apartment or single family home (where homes are close together) for a group of neighbors to share a wireless signal and potentially save money by splitting the cost of one Internet connection among them. However, before jumping into this venture, you need to weigh a few issues carefully.

You probably aren't legally prohibited from sharing an Internet connection, but you should check on the state and local laws. Most laws are designed to prohibit piggybacking, which is using a network without the network owner's consent. However, if you are giving neighbors permission to share your connection, you probably don't violate any piggybacking laws.

Of course, your ISP might not permit you to share your Internet access with anyone. You probably have a personal account that is designed for one household. The terms of your agreement with the Internet service provider might prohibit you from sharing your connection with people outside your household. If you aren't allowed to share the type of account you have now, your ISP probably offers a type of account (such as a small business account) that will allow you to share a connection, but it will most likely be more expensive. The ISPs know that the more people that share an account, the more likely that account is to use bandwidth; so they price their accounts accordingly. You might be able to share a personal account without being detected by your ISP, but that certainly would be unethical because you should be paying for a higher level of access. Therefore, make sure to check with your ISP to determine that you have the right type of account.

The next thing you need to consider is whether the shared access should be open to all neighbors, or just to the neighbors that are contributing to the cost of the Internet connection. You could leave the connection open, like the connections at your local coffee shop, and let anyone who finds it log on and surf. You might consider this a very ethical action, because you are providing free Internet access for anyone who needs it. You could register your free hotspot with a service like JiWire (**www.jiwire .com**), and then people would be able to find it (see Figure 7.8). However, your neighbors who are helping pay the cost might have a different viewpoint and not want to fund free surfing for everyone. Make sure you work this out before proceeding.

If you are going to host a free and open hotspot, you still need to make sure that you set it up safely. You want to maintain a secure network for you and your neighbors while still allowing the occasional visiting surfer to use the connection. There are WiFi sharing services such as Fon (**www.fon.com**) or Chillifire (**www.chillifire.net**) that can provide you with special hardware or software that allows you to configure your hotspot so your network remains secure.

While offering free access to anyone will earn you lots of good karma, additional risks exist because you don't know what mischief or criminal activities someone might engage in while connected to the Internet through your account. Think very carefully before you proceed down the sharing path, and make sure you set your hotspot up to protect your internal network.

Figure 7.8

At JiWire, you can search and find free hotspots.

Some common reasons why wireless signals may have decreased throughput include:

- Wireless signals are more susceptible to interference from magnetic and electrical sources.
- Other wireless networks (such as your neighbor's network) can interfere with the signals on your network.
- Certain building materials (such as concrete and cinderblock) and metal (a refrigerator) can decrease throughput.
- Throughput varies depending on the distance from your networking equipment.

Wireless networks usually use specially coded signals to protect their data whereas wired connections don't protect their signals. This process of coding signals can slightly decrease throughput, although once coded, data travels at usual speeds.

Therefore, in situations where you want to achieve the highest possible throughput (transferring a large video), you may want to connect your notebook or other portable device to your home network using a wire temporarily. We'll discuss this type of connection in more depth when we talk about home Ethernet networks later in this chapter.

Network Navigation Devices

How is data sent through a network? **Network navigation devices** facilitate and control the flow of data through a network. Data is sent over transmission media in bundles. Each bundle is called a **packet**. For computers to communicate, these packets of data must be able to flow between network nodes. Network navigation devices, which are themselves nodes on a network, enable the transmission of data between other nodes on the network that contain NICs.

What network navigation devices will I use on my home network? The two most common navigation devices are routers and switches. A **router** transfers packets of data between two or more networks. For example, if a home network is connected to the Internet, a router is required to send data between the two networks: the home network and the Internet. A **switch** is a "traffic cop" on a network. Switches receive data packets and send them to their intended nodes on the same network (not between different networks). All routers sold for home use have switches integrated into them.

SOUND BYTE — **Installing a Home Computer Network**

Installing a network is relatively easy if you've seen someone else do it. In this Sound Byte, you'll learn how to install the hardware and configure Windows for a wired or wireless home network.

We discuss routers for home networks in more detail later in the chapter.

Networking Software

What software do home networks require? Home networks need operating system (OS) software that supports P2P networking. The Windows, OS X, and Linux operating systems all support P2P networking. You can connect computers running any of these OSs to the same home network. We also cover configuring software for home networks later in the chapter.

Is the same software used in client/server networks? Client/server networks are controlled by centralized servers that have specialized **network operating system (NOS)** software installed on them. This software handles requests for information, Internet access, and the use of peripherals for the rest of the network nodes. As opposed to P2P networks, the nodes on a client/server network do not communicate directly with each other but communicate through a server. Communicating through a server is more efficient in a network with a large number of nodes, but requires more complex NOS software than is necessary for P2P networks. Examples of NOS software include Windows Server and SUSE Linux Enterprise Server.

Before considering the components you need to create a home network, you should consider your method of Internet access.

Connecting to the Internet

One of the main reasons for setting up a home network is to share an Internet connection. You need to purchase Internet access from companies that specialize in providing this service known as **Internet service providers (or ISPs)**. ISPs may be specialized providers, like Juno, or companies that provide other services, such as phone and cable television, in addition to Internet access. You have two main choices for connections to the Internet: broadband or dial-up. Broadband uses high-speed data access whereas dial-up uses conventional phone lines and technology. Because of the higher speeds offered by broadband, over two-thirds of U.S. Internet users have broadband connections in their home. Although not completely obsolete, dial-up is fast becoming a legacy technology.

Broadband Connections

What is broadband? **Broadband**, often referred to as "high-speed Internet," refers to a type of connection that offers a faster means to connect to the Internet. Broadband usually has a data transmission rate of 5 Mbps (megabits per second) or greater. This high rate of access is in contrast to dial-up Internet access, which has a maximum transmission speed of 56 Kbps (kilobits per second).

What types of broadband are available? The standard broadband technologies in most areas are **digital subscriber line (DSL)**, which uses the same types of wiring used in standard phone lines to connect your computer to the Internet, and cable, which uses cable from your television's cable service provider to connect to the Internet. **Fiber-optic service**, which uses plastic or glass cables to transfer data at the speed of light, has in the past few years become widely available as a broadband service to the home. Satellite broadband is mostly used in rural or mountain areas that cannot get DSL, cable, or fiber-optic service.

How does cable Internet access work? A cable Internet connection uses the same coaxial cable used by cable TV; however, cable TV and cable Internet are separate services. Cable TV is a one-way service in which the cable company feeds programming signals to your television. To bring two-way Internet connections to homes, cable companies had to upgrade

SOUND BYTE

Connecting to the Internet

In this Sound Byte, you'll learn the basics of connecting to the Internet from home, including useful information on the various types of Internet connections and selecting the right ISP.

ACTIVE HELP-DESK

Connecting to the Internet

In this Active Helpdesk call, you'll play the role of a helpdesk staffer. You will field calls about various options for connecting to the Internet and how to choose an Internet service provider.

their networks with two-way data transmission capabilities.

How does DSL work? Similar to a dial-up connection, DSL uses telephone lines to connect to the Internet. However, unlike dial-up, DSL allows phone and data transmission to share the same line, thus eliminating the need for an additional phone line. Phone lines are made of pairs of twisted copper wires known as twisted-pair wiring. The bandwidth of the copper wires is split into three sections, similar to a three-lane highway on which only one lane is used to carry voice data. DSL uses the remaining two lanes to send and receive data separately at much higher frequencies. Thus, although it uses a standard phone line, a DSL connection is much faster than a dial-up connection.

Can anyone with a phone line have DSL? Having a traditional phone line in your house doesn't mean that you have access to DSL service. Your local phone company must have special DSL technology to offer you the service. Although many phone companies offer DSL technology, many rural areas in the United States still do not have DSL service available.

What are the limitations of DSL and cable? Although cable and DSL speeds are about the same, each has its own particular limitations. DSL signals are sensitive to distance. There is a maximum distance of about 3 miles between where the signal originates, called the central office, and the customer's location. The further the connection is from the central office, the weaker the signal is. Although cable is not limited by distance like DSL, cable services are shared between users, so in peak usage times, cable connection speeds can slow down.

How does fiber-optic service work? Fiber-optic service uses fiber-optic lines, which are strands of optically pure glass or plastic that are as thin as a human hair. They are arranged in bundles called optical cables and transmit data via light signals over long distances. Because light travels so quickly, this technology can bring an enormous amount of data to your home at superfast speeds. When the data reaches your house, it's converted to electrical pulses that transmit digital signals your computer can "read." Fiber-optic service uses fiber-optic cable to run very fast data connections directly to your home, although fiber-optic cable is not usually run inside the home. On a fiber-optic network, twisted-pair or coaxial cable is still used inside the home to transport the network signals.

What special equipment do I need to hook up to broadband? A broadband Internet connection requires a modem. Depending on the type of broadband service you have, you will have either a cable modem or DSL modem. The modem works to translate the broadband signal into digital data and back again. With both cable and DSL services, the modem allows the data to travel on the unused capacity of the transmission medium. Often the ISP will rent the appropriate modem to the customer or specify what type of modem the customer must buy to work properly with the ISP's technology.

For example, a DSL modem separates voice signals from data signals so that they can travel in the right "lane" on the twisted-pair wiring. Voice data travels at a slower speed than digital data, which can travel at rates ranging from 500 Kbps to 6,000 Kbps [6 megabits per second (Mbps)].

As mentioned earlier, sharing your Internet connection with more than one computer requires a router. Your modem is usually located very near the router because the router must be plugged into the modem. Some ISPs provide combination modems and routers so you may only have one device in your home that serves both functions.

What options exist when cable and DSL are not available? Satellite Internet is another way to connect to the Internet. Most people choose satellite Internet when other high-speed options are unavailable. To take advantage of satellite Internet, you need a satellite dish (see Figure 7.9), which is placed outside your home and connected to your computer with coaxial cable, the same type of cable used for cable TV. Data from your computer is transmitted between your

personal satellite dish and the satellite company's receiving satellite dish by a satellite that sits in a geosynchronous orbit thousands of miles above the Earth.

How does one access the Internet wirelessly? To access the Internet wirelessly, you need to be in a **wireless fidelity (WiFi)** hotspot and have the right equipment on your mobile device. WiFi is a standard for wireless transmissions using radio waves that is used to connect computing devices to wireless networks and the Internet. Virtually all notebooks, smartphones, game systems, and personal media players sold today come with wireless capability built in. For your own personal WiFi, it's simple to set up wireless capability on your home network by using a router that features wireless capabilities. When you are away from home, you have two main choices for connecting to the Internet: use a WiFi hotspot or sign up for 3G or 4G Internet access with a cell phone provider.

How can I access the Internet via a WiFi hotspot? Many businesses and schools, as well as public places such as airports, libraries, bookstores, and restaurants, offer WiFi connections known as hotspots. Some public places offer free WiFi access, but others require you to buy wireless access through a wireless access service plan.

Figure 7.9

ISPs that offer satellite Internet provide service even in remote areas.

To access pay WiFi services, you can pay for a single session or a monthly membership, or you can sign up for a longer-term subscription in which you receive monthly bills. Wi-Fi-FreeSpot (**www.wififreespot.com**) and WiFi HotSpot List (**www.wifihotspotlist.com**) will help you locate a free hotspot wherever you are planning to go.

In some cities and towns, local governments are installing municipal WiFi networks. The newest wireless access technology to be deployed for mobile and stationary broadband access is WiMAX. WiMAX is designed to extend local WiFi networks across greater distances, such as across a large college campus. Mobile WiMAX is an alternative to cellular transmission of voice and high-speed data. Even wireless in-flight Internet service is available! Gogo (**www.gogoinflight.com**) is a wireless broadband network that provides coverage on participating airlines across the continental United States, so when you are cleared to use your portable electronic devices, you can comfortably access wireless Internet from 35,000 feet.

What is 3G and 4G access and how does it work? 3G and 4G refer to the third and fourth generations, respectively, of cellular telephone networks. 4G is the latest service standard and offers the fastest data access speeds over cellular telephone networks. However, 3G and 4G data access is not just for phones any longer. Many devices such as iPads, Chromebooks, and notebook computers now are available with 3G or 4G capabilities built in. To utilize the 3G or 4G capabilities of a mobile device, you need to sign up for an access plan with a mobile data provider such as Verizon or AT&T.

If your computer does not have built-in 3G or 4G equipment, you can purchase a wireless data card, such as the ones shown in Figure 7.10. Wireless data cards, sometimes referred to as cellular modems, are devices that fit into either a USB port or a special slot on the side of a notebook called an Express card slot (also known as a PC card slot). The wireless data card enables users to access 3G or 4G networks. They also require a service plan.

Dial-Up Connections

Why would I ever want to consider a dial-up connection to the Internet? About seventy percent of Internet users in the United States use high-speed Internet connections such as DSL, cable, or fiber-optic. But many people still use dial-up connections through conventional phone lines. The two main reasons people choose dial-up are the unavailability of high-speed service in their area (usually rural areas) or to save money. A dial-up connection is the least costly way to connect to the Internet.

How does a dial-up connection work? A dial-up connection needs only a standard phone line and a modem. The word modem is short for modulator/demodulator. A dial-up modem is a device that converts (modulates) the digital signals the computer understands into analog signals that can travel over phone lines. The computer on the other end also must have a modem to translate (demodulate) the received analog signal back to a digital signal that the receiving computer can understand. Many computers still come with internal modems built into the system unit, although some manufacturers have ceased including them as standard equipment.

What are the disadvantages of dial-up? The major downside to dial-up is speed. Dial-up modems transfer data at a much slower rate than that of a basic broadband connection. Also, when you're on the Internet using a dial-up connection, you

Sierra Wireless for the AirCard images.

Figure 7.10

Wireless data cards add 3G or 4G functionality to computing devices that don't have the capability built in.

Figure 7.11 | COMPARING DSL, CABLE, AND FIBER-OPTIC INTERNET CONNECTION OPTIONS.

Network	DSL	Cable	Fiber-Optic
Maximum download speeds	Average speeds of 3.5 Mbps, with a maximum of 12 Mbps	Average speeds of 10 Mbps, with a maximum of 30 Mbps	Average speeds of 20 Mbps, with a maximum of 50 Mbps.
Pros	Lets you surf the Net and talk on the same phone line simultaneously.	Speeds are not dependent on distance from central office.	Increased speeds. Service is not shared or dependent on distance from central office.
Cons	Speed drops as you get farther from phone company's central office. Not every phone line will work.	Line is shared with others in neighborhood; speeds may vary due to peak and nonpeak usage. May require professional installation if cable not already present.	Cost. Although this is a diminishing concern as the technology continues to be deployed and accepted. Not available in all areas.

Note: The data transfer rates listed in this table are approximations. As technologies improve, so do data transfer rates.

tie up your phone line if you don't have a separate line.

Choosing the Right Internet Connection Option

How do I choose which Internet connection option is best for me? According to Internet World Stats, more than 77 percent of U.S. residents use the Internet. However, in 2011, the Federal Communications Commission reported that almost 100 million Americans either lack Internet access or only have access to dial-up services. Depending on the area in which you live, you might not have a choice as to the type of broadband connection that is available. Check with your local cable TV provider, phone company, and satellite TV provider(s) to determine what broadband options are available where you live and what the transfer rates are in your area.

Often the most difficult decision in choosing Internet service is choosing between high-speed plans offered by the same company. For instance, at the time of printing, Verizon offered three different fiber-optic plans that featured download speeds of either 15, 25, or 50 Mbps. While 15 Mbps is fine for streaming video, it may not be quite fast enough for streaming HD movies, especially if there are two people in the household streaming movies at the same time. Families with multiple users, especially serious gamers and children who are downloading streaming media at the same time, might very well need the 50 Mbps service. Consulting with friends and neighbors about the plan they have and whether it is meeting their needs can help you decide on the right plan for your household.

Finally, you may also need to consider which other services you want bundled into your payment, such as phone or TV. The table in Figure 7.11 compares several features of DSL, cable, and fiber-optic service to help you with your decision.

Home Networks

Now that you understand the basic components of a home network and have selected an Internet service provider, you are probably wondering where to start on installing your home network. In the following sections, we'll discuss the most common types of networks found in the home and how to get the fastest data transfer rates from your home network. We'll also explore the various types of cabling used in wired networks.

Ethernet Home Networks

What type of peer-to-peer network should I install in my home? The vast majority of home networks are Ethernet networks. An **Ethernet network** is so named because it uses the Ethernet protocol as the means (or standard) by which the nodes on the network communicate. The Ethernet protocol was developed by the Institute of Electrical and Electronics Engineers (IEEE). This nonprofit group develops many standard specifications for electronic data transmission that are adopted throughout the world. Each standard the IEEE develops is numbered, with 802.11 (wireless) and 802.3 (wired) being the standards for Ethernet networks. The Ethernet protocol makes Ethernet networks extremely efficient at moving data.

What is the current wireless standard for Ethernet networks?

The current standard that governs wireless networking for Ethernet networks is the 802.11n standard, which was ratified in 2009. Establishing standards for networking is important so that devices from different manufacturers will work well together. The 802.11 standard is also known as WiFi. Four standards are currently defined under the 802.11 WiFi standard: 802.11a, 802.11b, 802.11g, and 802.11n. Since 802.11n features the fastest data transfer rates, it is now the most desirable choice for home networks. Devices using older standards, such as 802.11g, will still work with 802.11n networks, but they will operate with slower data transfer rates. This accommodation of current devices being able to use previously issued standards in addition to the current standards is known as **backward compatibility.**

How do 802.11n wireless devices work? Wireless routers and network adapters contain transceivers. A **transceiver** is a device that translates the electronic data that needs to be sent along the network into radio waves and then broadcasts these radio waves to other network nodes. Transceivers serve a dual function because they also receive the signals from other network nodes. Devices that use the 802.11n standard achieve higher throughput by using a technology known as Multiple Input Multiple Output (MIMO).

Devices using wireless standards developed prior to the 802.11n standard only utilized one antenna for transmitting and receiving data. Devices that use **Multiple Input Multiple Output (MIMO)** technology are designed to use multiple antennas for transmitting and receiving data. The multiple antennas break the data into multiple data streams and allow for faster transmission of the data. Thus, 802.11n devices can achieve throughput of 300 Mbps or higher under ideal conditions. But as mentioned previously, many factors can reduce the throughput of a wireless connection.

How can I tell how fast the wireless connection to my network is on my computer? You can install various utilities, such as Net Meter (available at **www.download.com**), on your computer that will measure your throughput. Net Meter (see Figure 7.13) shows you the throughput you are achieving on your computer's wireless connection to your network over a period of time. Hopefully, you'll achieve throughput in the range of 50 to 200 Mbps on your wireless network, which should be sufficient for most applications (even watching video). However, if you don't achieve acceptable throughput, you might want to consider a wired Ethernet connection.

Is there any advantage to a wired connection? Up to one gigabit per second (1,000 Mbps) of throughput is possible using the **gigabit Ethernet** standard, which is the most commonly used wired Ethernet standard deployed in devices designed for home networks. Computers generally ship with gigabit Ethernet cards installed in them. For even faster data transfer speeds, 10 gigabit

---

BITS AND BYTES

Wake Up Your Computer Remotely

Having your computer on a home network with a shared Internet connection makes it possible to access your computer and its files even when you aren't at home. But if your computer is asleep, you need some way to "wake it up." Otherwise, you can't access it through the Internet. Fortunately for Mac users, there is an application called iNet WOL (Wake on LAN) designed to do this (see Figure 7.12). iNet WOL is compatible with the iPhone, iPod Touch, and iPad. The application allows you to use your portable device to wake up your computer via the Internet. Once your computer is awake, you can then use your remote access software to access it. Think of iNet WOL as an alarm clock for your computer.

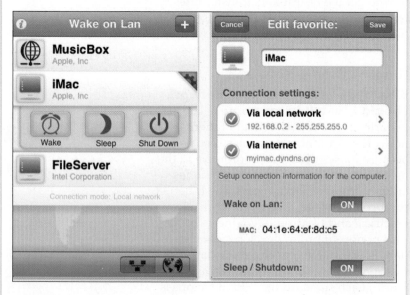

Figure 7.12

The application iNet WOL (Wake on LAN) lets you use your iPhone, iPod Touch, or iPad to wake up your computer from a remote location.

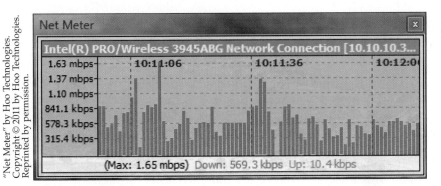

Figure 7.13

Net Meter shows this computer is achieving a rather slow maximum connection of 1.65 Mbps on a shared wireless network at a hotel.

Ethernet is available, which provides a maximum throughput of 10 gigabits per second (Gbps). But 10 gigabit networks are primarily used in businesses with large data throughput needs. For gaming and streaming HD movies, gigabit Ethernet meets the needs of most home network users.

Home Network Cabling

What type of cable do I need to connect to a wired Ethernet network? The most popular transmission media option for wired Ethernet networks is **unshielded twisted-pair (UTP) cable**. UTP cable is composed of four pairs of wires that are twisted around each other to reduce electrical interference. You can buy UTP cable in varying lengths with RJ-45 connectors (Ethernet connectors) already attached. RJ-45 connectors resemble standard phone connectors (called RJ-11 connectors) but are slightly larger and have contacts for eight wires (four pairs) instead of four wires (see Figure 7.14). You must use UTP cable with RJ-45 connectors on an Ethernet network because a phone cable will not work.

Do all wired Ethernet networks use the same kind of UTP cable? Figure 7.15 lists the three main types of UTP cable you would consider using in home-wired Ethernet networks—Cat 5E, Cat 6, and Cat 6a—and their data transfer rates. Although Cat 5E cable is the cheapest and is sufficient for many home networking tasks, it was designed for 100 Mbps wired Ethernet networks that were popular before gigabit Ethernet networks became the standard for home networking. Therefore,

you should probably not install Cat 5E cable even though it is still available in stores. Since **Cat 6 cable** is designed to achieve data transfer rates that support a gigabit Ethernet network, it is probably the best choice for home networking cable. Cat 6a cable is designed for Ultra-Fast Ethernet networks that run at speeds as fast as 10 Gbps. Installing a 10 gigabit Ethernet network in the home is probably unnecessary because today's home applications (even gaming and streaming media) don't require this rate of data transfer.

BITS AND BYTES

Blazingly Fast Wireless Connections on the Horizon

Although most people want wireless connectivity throughout their home, wired connections still provide the best throughput. But the next generation of wireless standards, called WiGig and WirelessHD, are currently under development. These standards will be designed to provide between 7 and 25 Gbps of throughput. This speed will blow away current WiFi standards (which have a current theoretical maximum transfer rate of 600 Mbps) and wired gigabit connectivity. Whereas WiFi currently operates in the 5 GHz and 2.4 GHz bands, WiGig and WirelessHD will operate in the 60 GHz band, which is currently unlicensed by the FCC. This should prevent many of the interference issues that WiFi users currently experience. But don't start looking in the stores for this equipment just yet; we are still a few years away from devices using these standards.

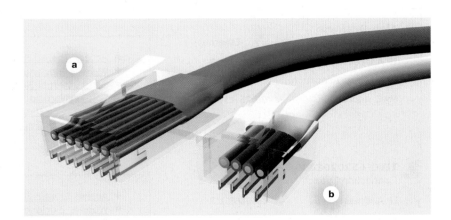

Figure 7.14

(a) An RJ-45 (Ethernet) connector, which is used on UTP cables; and (b) a typical RJ-11 connector, which is used on standard phone cords.

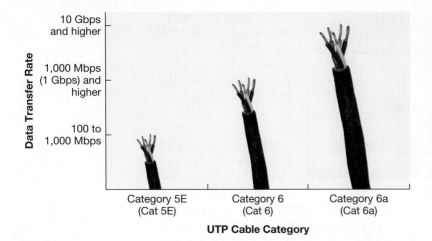

UTP Cable Category

Figure 7.15

Data transfer rates for popular home network cable types.

Fortunately, you don't have to choose between a wired or a wireless network. Ethernet networks can handle your wired and wireless needs on the same network. This gives you the best of both worlds: portability and high throughput.

Wired and Wireless on One Network

Can I have wired and wireless nodes on one Ethernet network? Yes, one Ethernet network can support nodes with

Figure 7.16

Wired and wireless connections using the same router.

both wireless and wired connections. Most people will want to connect portable devices that are constantly being moved around the home wirelessly to their network. However, many of the devices that are connected to a network, such as televisions, DVRs, and game consoles, usually stay in one location. Although these devices probably feature wireless connectivity also, it may be desirable to hook them up to wired connections to take advantage of faster throughput achieved by wired connectivity. Routers sold for home networks facilitate wired and wireless connections. Figure 7.16 shows a router network listing with wired (desktop computer) and wireless devices (TiVo DVR and notebook) connected in a home network.

Are there other types of P2P networks that can be installed in the home? Non-Ethernet networks in the home are extremely rare. Because Ethernet networks (1) are based on a well-established standard, (2) feature easy setup, (3) provide good throughput for home networking needs, and (4) are cost effective, manufacturers of home networking equipment have overwhelmingly embraced Ethernet networks.

My Network   **Connected Devices**

Alan-Notebook:

Connection Type:	(((•))) Wireless
IP Address:	192.168.1.2
IP Address Allocation:	DHCP
MAC Address:	00:19:d2:28:21:ad

- Access Shared Files
- Website Blocking
- Block Internet Services
- Port Forwarding
- View Device Details
- Rename this Device

Ethernet: 1 device(s)

Coax: 0 device(s)

Wireless: 2 device(s)

Alan-Desktop:

Connection Type:	Ethernet
IP Address:	192.168.1.3
IP Address Allocation:	DHCP
MAC Address:	00:25:11:09:99:cd

- Access Shared Files
- Website Blocking
- Block Internet Services
- Port Forwarding
- View Device Details
- Rename this Device

TIVO-6520201806A6969:

Connection Type:	(((•))) Wireless
IP Address:	192.168.1.7
IP Address Allocation:	DHCP
MAC Address:	00:11:d9:00:f6:dd

- Access Shared Files
- Website Blocking
- Block Internet Services
- Port Forwarding
- View Device Details

Does the type of operating system I'm using affect my choice of a home networking standard? Windows, OS X, and Linux all have built-in P2P networking software that will support connection to an Ethernet network. Therefore, an Ethernet network is appropriate for all computers using these three operating systems.

Configuring Home Network Equipment

By now you should have enough information to decide what nodes on your network need to be connected wirelessly and which devices would benefit from wired connections. In this section, we'll explore the various types of equipment that you need to obtain to configure your home network. And we'll explore what devices your nodes need to contain to enable them to connect to your network.

Routers and Switches: Moving Data Around Your Network

What equipment do I need for a home Ethernet network? Ethernet networks need network navigation devices to make them work; therefore, the first piece of equipment to consider is a router. Recall that routers are designed to transfer packets of data between two (or more) networks—in this case, your home network and the Internet. A router is essential on a home network to allow sharing of an Internet connection. For an Ethernet network to function properly, data must also be transmitted efficiently around the network. As you know, a switch is the device that is used on

Ethernet networks to route the data between nodes on the same network.

Because both a router and a switch are needed on home Ethernet networks, the manufacturers of home networking equipment make devices that are a combination of routers and switches. In most instances, these devices are called routers or broadband routers. But despite the name, these devices do include integrated switches. Although manufacturers do make routers with only wired capabilities, for the vast majority of home networks, people buy routers with wireless capabilities. When you examine a Windows 7 network with a router that includes an integrated switch, it can appear as two different devices (see Figure 7.17) even though there is only one device. On this home network, named GMVO5, the desktop computer is connected to the router with a cable. The two notebook computers are attached wirelessly to the router. The switch is contained within the router, even though the Windows network map shows them as two separate devices.

What do switches do on an Ethernet network? Data is transmitted through the transmission medium of an Ethernet network in packets. Imagine the data packets on an Ethernet network as cars on a road. If there were no traffic signals or rules of the road (such as stopping at a red light and proceeding on a green light), we'd see a lot more collisions between vehicles, and people wouldn't get where they were going as readily. Data packets can also suffer collisions. If data packets collide, the data in them is damaged or lost. In either case, the network doesn't function efficiently.

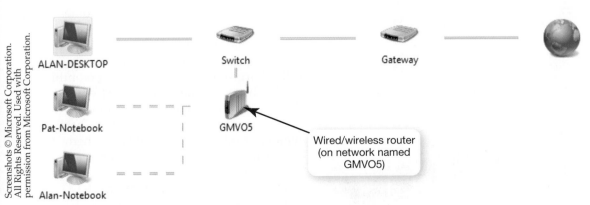

Figure 7.17

Windows network map showing three computers connected to an integrated router/switch.

As shown in Figure 7.18, a switch in an Ethernet network acts like a traffic signal (or a traffic cop) by enforcing the rules of the data road on the transmission media. The switch keeps track of the data packets and, in conjunction with network interface cards, helps the data packets find their destinations without running into each other. The switch also keeps track of all the nodes on the network and sends the data packets directly to the node for which they are headed. This keeps the network running efficiently.

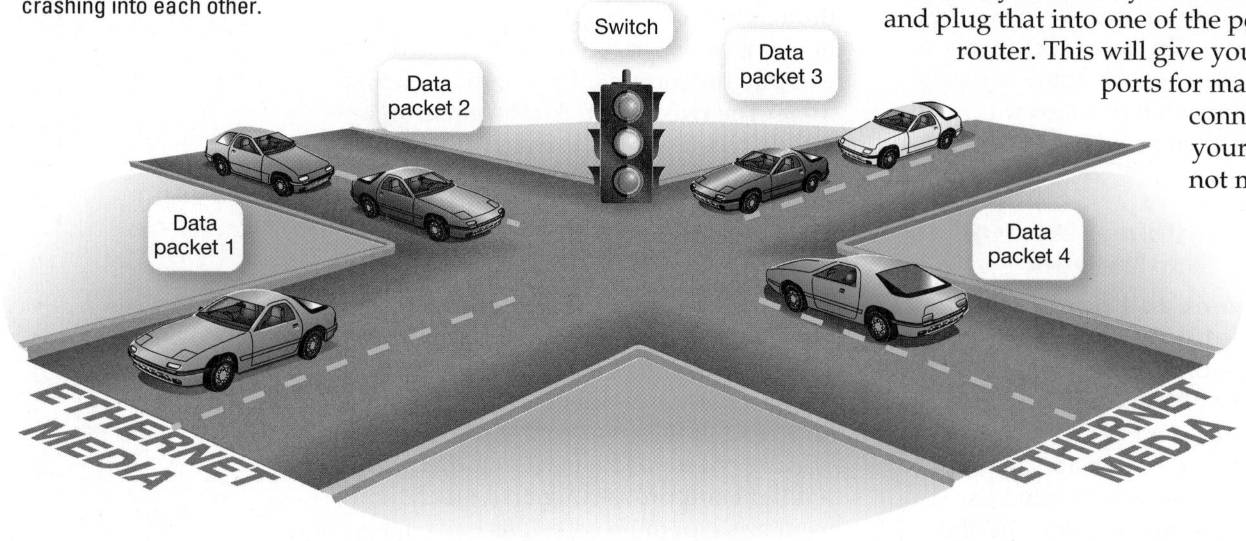

Figure 7.18

A simplified explanation is that switches (working in conjunction with NICs) act like traffic signals or traffic cops. They enforce the rules of the data road on an Ethernet network and help prevent data packets from crashing into each other.

Does my wireless router support wired connections? Most home wireless routers have three or four Ethernet ports on the back of the router to support wired connections via twisted-pair cable (see Figure 7.19). If you have a lot of devices (such as a game console, HDTV, and a notebook) in your home that may be used simultaneously, you might want to consider connecting some of them via a wired connection to increase allocated bandwidth to each wireless device. This will help increase the throughput to each wireless device.

If you find that you need additional ports for plugging in wired connections to your network, you can buy a standalone switch and plug that into one of the ports on your router. This will give you additional ports for making wired connections to your network. Do not mistakenly buy another router with an embedded switch and try adding that to your network, because the two routers will cause conflicts as they fight for control over network navigation.

Where do I obtain a router for my home network? You can purchase a router at any electronics store (such as Best Buy) or online stores (such as **www .tigerdirect.com** or **www.newegg.com**) that carry home networking equipment. Also, since networks are so common in homes now, many ISPs offer home subscribers a device that combines a broadband modem and a wireless router. ISPs typically charge either a one-time or a monthly fee for this combination device. If you already have broadband access in your home, you at least have a modem. Check with your ISP if you are not sure whether you also already have a device that contains a router.

How do I know which type of wireless networking my router supports? If you do have a router provided by your ISP, make sure to ask what

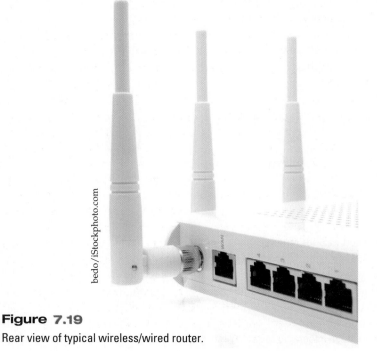

Switch

Data packet 1

Data packet 2

Data packet 3

Data packet 4

ETHERNET MEDIA

ETHERNET MEDIA

bedo/iStockphoto.com

Figure 7.19

Rear view of typical wireless/wired router.

wireless networking standard the router supports. If it supports a standard older than 802.11n, you should consider having your ISP provide you with a new router. You want to have a router that supports the fastest wireless networking standard (802.11n) so that you can achieve the highest possible throughput on your wireless nodes. If all of your wireless devices have 802.11n network adapters, but your router only supports 802.11g, you will not achieve the best throughput available to you because 802.11g devices feature much slower transfer rates than 802.11n devices (about four to six times slower).

Connecting Devices to Routers

How many computers and other devices can be connected to a router in a home network? Most home wireless routers can support up to 253 wireless connections at the same time. This number is a theoretical maximum, however—most home networks probably have fewer than ten wireless devices connected to the network. But regardless of how few or how many devices your home network has, those wireless devices share bandwidth when they are connected to a router. Therefore, the more devices actively transmitting data that you connect to a single router, the smaller the portion of the router's bandwidth each device receives.

To look at this another way, consider you have a pizza that represents your router's bandwidth. You can cut the pizza into six or eight pieces (that is, you can connect either six or eight devices to the network). If you cut the pizza into eight pieces, each person who gets a slice receives a smaller portion of pizza than they would if you had cut the pizza into six pieces. Similarly, when you connect eight devices to the network, each device has less bandwidth than it would have if only six devices were connected to the network.

Where do I place the router on my network? Your router should be connected directly to your broadband modem (see Figure 7.20). The connection is an Ethernet cable (Cat 6 cable) running from an Ethernet port on your modem to the modem port on your router.

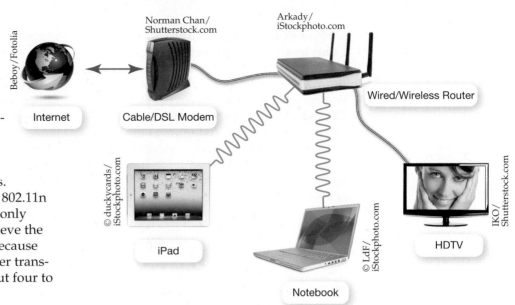

A small network with a wireless router attached.

Are wireless routers for Windows and OS X networks different? All routers that support the 802.11n standard should work with computers running Windows or OS X. However, Apple has designed routers that are optimized for working with Apple computers. So if you are connecting Apple computers to your network, you may wish to consider using an Apple AirPort router. (Windows machines can also connect to the AirPort routers.) The Apple AirPort Extreme (Figure 7.21) is a good choice for a home network. It supports up to 50 simultaneous wireless connections and has three gigabit Ethernet ports for wired connections.

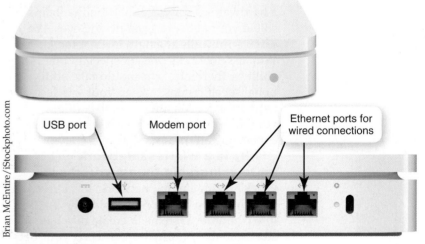

Figure 7.21

The AirPort Extreme router is often used for home networks with Apple computers.

How do I set up my router so that I can use it to connect to the Internet? If your ISP provided the router, it should already be configured properly. If you bought your own router, contact your ISP and find out about any special settings that you may need to configure your router to work with your ISP. Next, access your router from Internet Explorer (or another Web browser) by entering the router's IP address or default URL. You'll also need a username and password to log on to the router. You can usually find this information in the documentation that came with the router.

Many routers feature their own wizard (different from the Windows Networking wizards) that takes you through special configuration screens. Sometimes the wizards will ask questions such as whether IP addresses are assigned dynamically (meaning you are assigned a new IP address each time you connect to the Internet). If you're unsure of any information that needs to be entered to configure the router, contact your ISP and ask for guidance.

After ensuring that your router is set up properly, you need to consider the security of your wireless network before you begin attaching devices to it. Protecting your sensitive information is a high priority task.

Securing Wireless Networks

All computers that connect to the Internet (whether or not they are on a network) need to be secured from intruders. This is usually accomplished by using a firewall, which is a hardware or software solution that helps shield your network from prying eyes. We discuss firewalls at length in Chapter 9. Wireless networks present special vulnerabilities; therefore, you should take additional specific steps to keep your wireless network safe. It is important to configure your network security before setting up and connecting all the nodes on your network.

Why is a wireless network more vulnerable than a wired network? With a wired network, it is fairly easy to tell if a **hacker**, someone who breaks into computer systems to create mischief or steal valuable information, is using your network. However, wireless 802.11n networks have wide ranges that may extend outside

of your house. This makes it possible for a hacker to access your network without your knowledge.

Why should I be worried about someone logging onto my wireless network without my permission? Some use of other people's wireless networks is unintentional. Houses are built close together. Apartments are clustered even closer together. Wireless signals can easily reach a neighbor's residence. Most wireless network adapters are set up to access the strongest wireless network signal detected. If your router is on the east side of your house and you and your notebook are on the west side, then you may get a stronger signal from your neighbor's wireless network than from your own. **Piggybacking** is connecting to a wireless network (other than your own) without the permission of the owner. This practice is illegal in many jurisdictions, but often happens inadvertently between neighbors.

Your neighbor probably isn't a hacker, but he might be using a lot of bandwidth—your bandwidth! If he's downloading a massive movie file while you're trying to do research for a term paper, he's probably slowing you down. In addition, when some less-than-honest neighbors discover they can log onto your wireless network, they may cancel their own Internet service to save money by using yours. Some neighbors might even be computer savvy enough to penetrate your unprotected wireless network and steal personal information, just as any other hackers would.

In addition, because computer criminal activities are traceable, hackers love to work their mischief from public computers (such as those in a library or college) so they can't be identified. If a hacker is sitting in her car outside your house and logging on to your wireless network, any cyberattacks she launches might be traced back to your IP address, and you might find law enforcement officials knocking on your door. This happened to a man in Buffalo, New York, in 2011 when the FBI showed up to arrest him for downloading child pornography. It was subsequently determined that a hacker used his unprotected wireless network to commit the crime.

How is my wireless network vulnerable? Packets of information on a wireless network are broadcast through the airwaves. Savvy hackers can intercept and decode information from your transmissions that may allow them to bypass any standard protections, such as a firewall, that you have set up on your network. Therefore, to secure a wireless network, you should take the additional precautions described in the Sound Byte "Securing Wireless Networks" and as summarized below:

1. **Change your network name (SSID).** Each wireless network has its own name to identify it, which is known as the **service set identifier (SSID)**. Unless you change this name when you set up your router, the router uses a default network name that all routers from that manufacturer use (such as "Wireless" or "Netgear"). Hackers know the default names and access codes for routers. If you haven't changed the SSID, it's advertising the fact that you probably haven't changed any of the other default settings for your router, either.

2. **Disable SSID broadcast.** Most routers are set up to broadcast their SSIDs so that other wireless devices can find them. If your router supports disabling SSID broadcasting, turn it off. This makes it more difficult for a hacker to detect your network and nearly impossible for a neighbor to inadvertently connect to your network.

3. **Change the default password on your router.** Hackers know the default passwords of most routers, and if they can access your router, they can probably break into your network. Change the password on your router to something hard to guess. Use at least eight characters that are a combination of letters, symbols, and numbers.

4. **Turn on security protocols.** Most routers ship with security protocols such as Wired Equivalent Privacy (WEP) or WiFi Protected Access (WPA). Both use encryption (a method of translating your data into code) to protect data in your wireless transmissions. WPA is a much stronger protocol than WEP, so enable WPA if you have it; enable WEP if you don't. When you enable these protocols, you are forced to create a security encryption key (passphrase). When you attempt to connect a node to a security-enabled network for the

first time, you'll be required to enter the security key. The security key or passphrase (see Figure 7.22) is the code that computers on your network need to decrypt (decode) data transmissions. Without this key, it is extremely difficult, if not impossible, to decrypt the data transmissions from your network. This prevents unauthorized access to your network because hackers won't know the correct key to use. The Windows 7 Connect to a Network dialog box shows all wireless networks within range (see Figure 7.23a). Moving your cursor over the network name will reveal details about the network such as whether or not it is a secured network. Clicking on a network name allows you to connect to it, or prompts you for more information such as the SSID name and security key (see Figure 7.23b).

5. **Implement media access control.** Each network adapter on your network has a unique number (like a serial number) assigned to it by the manufacturer. This

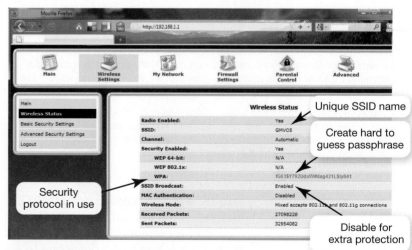

Figure 7.22

By accessing your router, you can configure the security protocols available on your router and change the SSID.

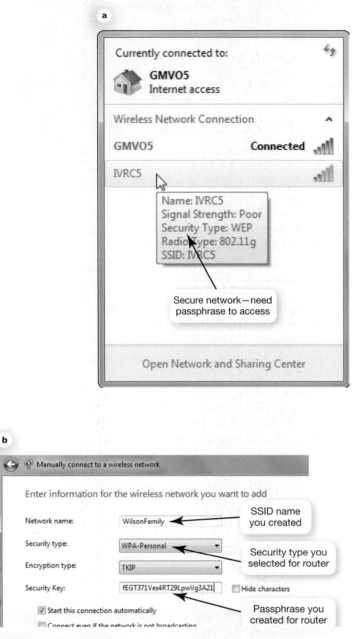

Figure 7.23

(a) The Windows 7 Connect to a network dialog box. (b) Manually connecting to a wireless network allows you to establish a connection if you know the network security key, encryption type, and SSID name.

>You can access the Network and Sharing Center by right-clicking the Network Connection icon on the taskbar and selecting **Open Network and Sharing Center** from the shortcut menu. Choose the **Set up a new connection or network** option, and then clicking on **Manually connect to a wireless network**.

authorized devices can connect to your network.

6. **Limit your signal range.** Many routers allow you to adjust the transmitting power to low, medium, or high. Cutting down the power to low or medium could prevent your signal from reaching too far away from your home, making it tougher for interlopers to poach your signal.

7. **Apply firmware upgrades**. Your router has read-only memory that has software written to it. This software is known as **firmware**. As bugs are found in the firmware (which hackers might exploit), manufacturers issue patches, just as the makers of operating system software do. Periodically check the manufacturer's Web site and apply any necessary upgrades to your firmware.

If you follow these steps, you will greatly improve the security of your wireless network. In Chapter 9, we'll explore many other ways to keep your computer safe from malicious individuals on the Internet and ensure that your digital information is secure.

After securing your router, you are ready to begin connecting your computing devices to your network. You now need to ensure that all your nodes have the proper equipment to enable them to connect to your network.

Connecting Devices to Networks

Aside from connecting computers to your home network, you probably have many other devices that would benefit from being attached to your network. Many peripheral devices, such as printers and graphics tablets, now come with built-in Ethernet adapters. Also, many home entertainment devices, portable devices, and power monitoring devices to reduce energy consumption in the home are also designed to attach to home networks. Such devices are usually described as being "network-ready."

Connecting Computers

How can I tell what network adapters are installed in my computer?
A network adapter is necessary to connect your computing device to your network. To see which network adapter(s) are installed

is called a media access control (MAC) address, and it is a number printed right on the network adapter. Many routers allow you to restrict access to the network to only certain MAC addresses. This helps ensure that only

in your Windows computer and to check whether the adapter is working, you should use the Device Manager utility program (see Figure 7.24). The installed adapters will be shown and then you can search for information on the Internet to determine the adapter's capability if you aren't sure which wireless standard it supports.

Network-Ready Devices

What is a network-ready device?
A **network-ready device** (or Internet-ready device) can be connected directly to a router instead of to a computer on the network. Network-ready devices include Blu-ray players, televisions, game consoles, and even refrigerators. These devices contain wireless and/or wired network adapters inside them. The eventual goal may be to have all electronic devices in your home be nodes on your network.

Why should I connect my printer to my home network? With a network-ready printer, only the printer needs to be powered on for any computer on the network to print to it. If a printer were connected directly to another computer (via a cable) on the network instead of being a node on the network, that computer would need to be switched on so other computers could access the printer.

What can I attach to my network to facilitate file sharing and backup of data? **Network-attached storage (NAS) devices** are specialized computing devices designed to store and manage your data. People are generating tremendous quantities of data today with digital cameras and video cameras, as well as buying music files, and these files need to be stored and shared. Although data can always be stored on individual hard drives in computers on a network, NAS devices provide for centralized data storage and access.

Popular for years on business networks, NAS devices are now being widely marketed for home networks. You can think of them as specialized external hard drives. NAS devices, like the LinkStation series from Buffalo Technology (see Figure 7.25a), connect directly to the network through a router or switch. Specialized software can then be installed on computers attached to the network to ensure that all data saved to an individual computer is also stored on the NAS as a backup. We'll discuss backing up your data in more detail in Chapter 9.

For Apple computers, the Time Capsule is a wireless router combined with a hard drive for facilitating backups of all computers connected to the network. The Time Capsule looks very similar to the AirPort router, and it works in conjunction with the Time Machine backup feature of OS X (see Figure 7.25b). If you buy a Time Capsule, you won't need to buy an AirPort router (or other router) because the Time Capsule also fulfills this function on your network. When the Time Capsule is installed on your network, Macs connected to the network will ask the user if they want to use the Time Capsule as their source for Time Machine backups. The Time Capsule is another type of NAS device.

Besides external hard drives, are there other NAS devices I could use on my network? A more sophisticated type of NAS device is a home network server. Home network servers are specialized devices that are designed to provide a specific set of services to computers on a home network. Home servers do not convert a home peer-to-peer network into a client/server network because these servers perform only a limited set of functions instead of all the functions performed on client/server networks.

Home network servers, like the Acer Aspire easyStore server (shown earlier in Figure 7.5), are often configured with Windows Home Server and connect directly as a node on your network. Home servers

Figure 7.24
This Windows Device Manager window shows a wireless and a wired network adapter installed in a notebook.

>To access Device Manager: Click the Start Button, select **Control Panel**, click on the **Hardware and Sound** group, then click on **Device Manager**.

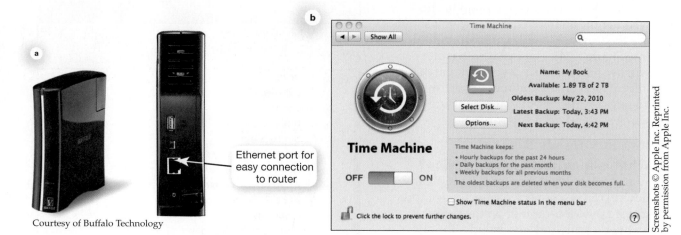

Courtesy of Buffalo Technology

Screenshots © Apple Inc. Reprinted by permission from Apple Inc.

Figure 7.25

(a) The LinkStation series from Buffalo Technology features NAS devices that can store 2 TB of data. (b) Time Machine, in conjunction with an external hard drive, provides easy backups of Macs on a network.

have the functionality of NAS devices and often handle the following tasks:

- Automatically back up all computers connected to the network
- Act as a repository for files to be shared across the network (such as music and video files)
- Function as an access gateway to allow any computer on the network to be accessed from a remote location via the Internet (see Figure 7.26)

You can access the media stored on your Windows Home Server through your Xbox 360 as long as the Xbox is also connected to your home network.

Digital Entertainment Devices on a Network

Why should I connect my digital entertainment devices to my network? The main reason for connecting entertainment devices to your network is to access and share digital content. When you attach devices to the Internet, you can access more content, such as movies, videos, or music files. You can also use gaming devices to play multiplayer games with players all over the world. The content you access is either downloaded or streamed to your entertainment devices. Viewing Netflix movies delivered over the Internet on your computer or HDTV is an example of streaming media.

When media is streamed, it is sent directly to a device (such as a computer or HDTV) without being saved to a hard drive. This requires a lot of bandwidth, so a broadband connection is required to effectively view streaming media. Media can also be downloaded (saved) to a hard drive for viewing at a later time. Although services like Amazon Instant Video now offer streaming movies, they still offer the ability to download content to your computer, Blu-ray player, HDTV, DVR, or Xbox 360 so you can view it later.

What types of digital entertainment devices can I use to view streaming or downloaded media? Network-ready televisions and home theater systems allow for direct connection to your home network (wireless or wired). These devices are configured to receive streaming media directly from the Internet. Video on demand services such as HBO GO and Netflix can stream media directly to your Internet-ready devices (including smartphones and tablets).

Figure 7.26

Windows Home Server remote access interface.

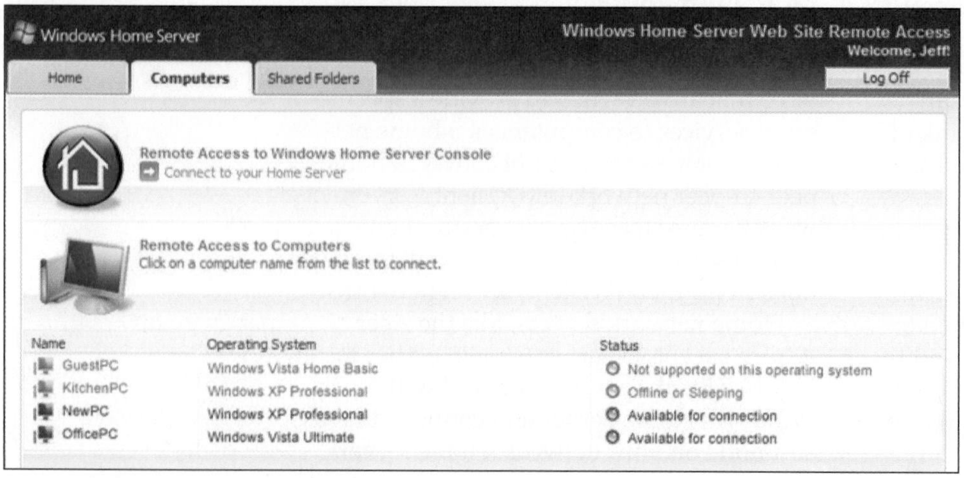

However, many people prefer to own media and buy it on permanent formats such as Blu-ray Discs. Blu-ray Disc players, such as the Sony 3D Blu-ray Disc players, offer not only high-definition resolution, but also the capability to display 3D video. These Blu-ray players feature integrated wireless connectivity for connection to your network as well as the ability to receive streaming media from various Internet service providers. You can even view videos from YouTube and listen to Pandora Internet Radio right through your Blu-ray player.

In terms of controlling your devices such as televisions and Blu-ray players, more companies are developing applications that enable your portable devices, such as PlayStation Portables or iPhones, to act as remote controls. The Media Remote app by Sony (see Figure 7.27a) for the iPhone, iPod Touch, or iPad allows you to control Sony Blu-ray players and TVs. And the Remote app from Apple lets you use your iPhone or iPad to control your iTunes or Apple TV from your handheld device over your WiFi network instead of having to directly access your computer (see Figure 7.27b).

Digital video recorders (DVRs), like the TiVo Premiere, are often used in the home to record high-definition television programs. Connecting your TiVo to your network makes it possible to receive downloads of movies directly to your TiVo from services such as Amazon Instant Video. And some home network servers, like the Hewlett Packard MediaSmart servers, now work in conjunction with TiVo devices to provide additional storage for your TiVo devices. The TiVo Desktop software (see Figure 7.28), which you download from **www.tivo.com**, allows you to transfer shows recorded on your TiVo to your computer or to portable devices such as an iPod, iPhone, iPad, BlackBerry, or PSP.

Can I connect my gaming consoles to my home network? Current gaming

Figure 7.27

New software apps make it easy to just use your phone or iPad to control (a) Blu-ray players or (b) Apple TV.

systems, like the PlayStation 3 (PS3), offer much more than just games—they can function as a total entertainment platform when connected to your network and the Internet. The PS3 has a built-in Blu-ray drive and can play Blu-ray Discs as well as DVDs and music files. You can download movies, games, and videos directly to the PlayStation. It can also be used to share media across your network and import photos or video from cameras and phones. And if you have a

Figure 7.28

The TiVo® Desktop and TiVo® Desktop Plus software facilitate transfer of recorded shows from your PC to portable devices so you can enjoy your content on the go.

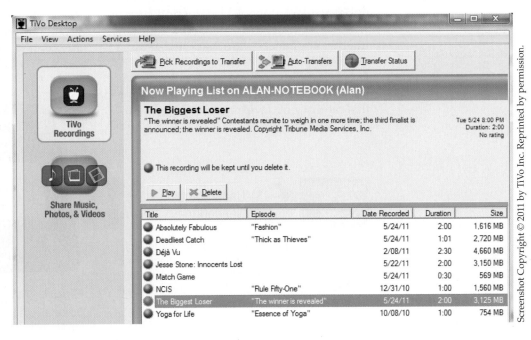

PS Vita, you can use an application called Remote Play (see Figure 7.29) to access features of your PlayStation from your Vita. You can use the Vita to turn your PlayStation on and off, access music and video files, access photos stored on your PlayStation, play games, and browse the Internet. Media is transmitted from your PlayStation and displayed on the Vita screen.

Specialized Home Networking Devices

What if I don't need the full functionality of a PC, but I still want to access Internet content? The launch of the Apple iPad signaled a resurgence of Internet appliances. The main function of an **Internet appliance** is easy access to the Internet, social networking sites, e-mail, video, news, and entertainment. These devices fall into a category somewhere between smartphones and full-blown computers. They are light on calculation, but high on easy content delivery. Devices such as the Sony Dash Personal Internet viewer (see Figure 7.30) are popular in kitchens and bedside tables where access to Internet radio stations, short videos, and quick information updates (like Facebook updates and current weather conditions) are needed. Originally, Internet appliances were marketed toward older computer users since these devices feature easy operation and a shallow learning curve. But the Apple iPad is propelling this category of devices into the hands of much younger users.

Kyodo via AP Images

Figure 7.29

The Remote Play feature of the PS Vita and the PS3 allows users to access PS3 features, like the PlayStation Store, directly from their Vita.

How can I use my home network to enhance photo sharing? Digital picture frames that display an array of changing digital photos have become quite popular with the rise in digital photography. Now digital picture frames such as the Kodak Pulse Digital Frame (see Figure 7.31) come with built-in wireless adapters for easy connection to home networks. Featuring a touch screen interface, this frame can access photos stored on your network or on an online photo-sharing site and display them. You can set up an e-mail address for the picture frame so that friends and family can e-mail pictures directly to the frame as soon as they are taken. Wouldn't it be nice to come home to new photos of your friend's trip to Cancun tonight?

How can I use my home network to enhance my home security? Monitoring cameras, both for indoor and outdoor use, are now available for the home and feature wireless connectivity. The cameras can connect to your network and be monitored by software like the Logitech Alert System. Security monitoring software allows you to view real-time images from the cameras at your home using portable devices such as an iPhone or Android phone (see Figure 7.32). The software can be configured to alert you via e-mail or text message when

ACTIVE HELP-DESK

Understanding Networking

In this Active Helpdesk call, you'll play the role of a helpdesk staffer, fielding calls about home networks—their advantages, their main components, and the most common types—as well as about wireless networks and how they are created.

Sony Electronics Inc.

Figure 7.30

Quick access to information and entertainment is the key feature of Internet appliances.

Eastman Kodak Company, KODAK PULSE Digital Frame / W1030S / 10 in.

Figure 7.31

Sending pictures directly to an electronic frame from your phone is possible when the frame is connected to your network.

the cameras detect movement, such as a vehicle entering your driveway. Some systems also allow you to receive alerts when there is a lack of movement. This can be useful for monitoring an aging relative or for monitoring the arrival of children coming home from school at a certain time.

As time goes on, many more types of entertainment devices and home gadgets will eventually be connected to your home network.

Configuring Software for Your Home Network

Once you install all the hardware for your network, you need to configure your operating system software for networking on your computers. In this section, you'll learn how to do just that using special Windows tools. Although configuration is different with Mac OS X, the setup is quick and easy. Linux is the most complex operating system to configure for a home network, though the difficulties are not insurmountable.

Windows Configuration

Is configuring software difficult? Windows makes configuring software relatively simple if you are using the same version of Windows on all of your computers. The Windows examples in this section assume you are using Windows 7 on all of your computers. In Windows 7, the process of setting up a network is fairly automated by various software wizards. As you learned in Chapter 4, a wizard is a utility program included

with software that you can use to help you accomplish a specific task. You can launch the Windows wizards from the Network and Sharing Center, which can be accessed via the Network and Internet group in the Control Panel. Before running any wizards, you should do the following:

1. Make sure there are network adapters on each node.

2. For any wired connections, plug all the cables into the router, nodes, and so on.

3. Make sure your broadband modem is connected to your router and that the modem is connected to the Internet.

4. Turn on your equipment in the following order (allowing the modem and the router about one minute each to power up and configure):
   a. Your broadband modem
   b. Your router
   c. All computers and peripherals (printers, scanners, and so on)

Other devices, such as televisions, Blu-ray players, and gaming consoles, can be added to the network after configuring the computers.

After you have completed these steps, open the Network and Sharing Center from the Control Panel (see Figure 7.33). If your computer has a wired connection to the network, you should automatically be connected to your home network. The network name should be the SSID name that you gave to your router. If you are connecting wirelessly, click on the Connect to a Network option. You will need

Courtesy of Logitech, Inc.

Figure 7.32

Logitech security products can help you monitor your home's security from your mobile devices.

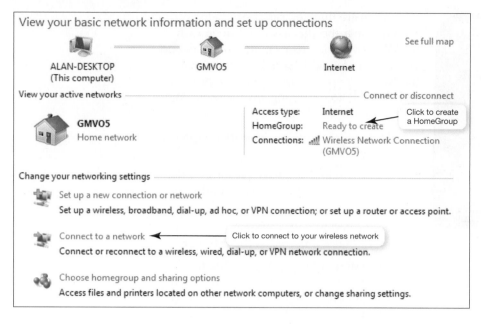

View your basic network information and set up connections

ALAN-DESKTOP (This computer) —— GMVO5 —— Internet

See full map

View your active networks ———————————— Connect or disconnect

GMVO5
Home network

Access type: Internet
HomeGroup: Ready to create ← Click to create a HomeGroup
Connections: ..ıll Wireless Network Connection (GMVO5)

Change your networking settings

Set up a new connection or network
Set up a wireless, broadband, dial-up, ad hoc, or VPN connection; or set up a router or access point.

Connect to a network ← Click to connect to your wireless network
Connect or reconnect to a wireless, wired, dial-up, or VPN network connection.

Choose homegroup and sharing options
Access files and printers located on other network computers, or change sharing settings.

Figure 7.33

The Windows Network and Sharing Center helps you configure your home network.

Figure 7.34

The Create a HomeGroup wizard (a) allows you to configure sharing options and (b) provides a password required for other computers to join the HomeGroup.

>The Create a HomeGroup settings can be accessed by clicking the Computer link on the Start menu, then clicking the **HomeGroup** icon, and then clicking the **View HomeGroup** settings link.

to enter your security passphrase to connect to your wireless network.

What if I don't have the same version of Windows on all my computers? Computers with various versions of Windows can coexist on the same network. Always set up the computers running the newest version of Windows first (Windows 7). Then consult the Microsoft Web site for guidance on how to proceed for configuring computers with previous versions of Windows on a Windows 7 network.

How do I differentiate the computers on my network? When you set up your Windows computer, you gave it a name. Each computer on a network needs a name that is different from the names of all other computers on the network so that the network can identify it. This unique name ensures that the network knows which computer is requesting services and data and can deliver data to the correct computer.

For ease of file and peripheral sharing, Windows 7 created a feature known as Home-

Group. If you have all Windows 7 computers on your network, you simply all join the same HomeGroup. After connecting your first Windows 7 computer to your network, you need to create a HomeGroup by clicking on the Ready to create link in the Network and Sharing Center (see Figure 7.33). The HomeGroup is a software device that makes it easier to allow computers on a Windows 7 network to share peripherals and information.

The first step in setting up a Home-Group (see Figure 7.34a) involves choosing sharing options for computers that belong to the HomeGroup. You can choose to share pictures, music, videos, documents, and printers with other Windows 7 computers that belong to the HomeGroup. Although these are global settings for every computer in the HomeGroup, you can change these settings on individual computers if you wish. In the second step of the HomeGroup setup, Windows generates a password (see Figure 7.34b). All other computers that subsequently are added to the network will need this password to join the HomeGroup. Once you have created the HomeGroup on the first computer, it will belong to that HomeGroup. You can then begin connecting other Windows 7 computers to the network and join them to the HomeGroup you created.

How do Macs connect wirelessly to networks? Generally, connecting Macs to a wireless network is a much easier process than connecting with Windows computers. You set up the security for a router on a Mac network just as was illustrated in the section on securing your wireless network. Therefore, logging your Mac onto the network will require knowing the SSID and its passphrase. When you boot up your Mac, the wireless card should be on by default. The network

a

Create a Homegroup

Share with other home computers running Windows 7

Your computer can share files and printers with other computers running Windows 7, and you can stream media to devices using a homegroup. The homegroup is protected with a password, and you'll always be able to choose what you share with the group.

Tell me more about homegroups

Select what you want to share:

☑ Pictures   ☐ Documents
☑ Music   ☑ Printers
☑ Videos

b

Create a Homegroup

Use this password to add other computers to your homegroup

Before you can access files and printers located on other computers, add those computers to your homegroup. You'll need the following password.

Write down this password:

4X25wF7Pa8

Print password and instructions

If you ever forget your homegroup password, you can view or change it by opening HomeGroup in Control Panel.

How can other computers join my homegroup?

login screen (see Figure 7.35) should appear with a list of available networks (that is, the ones the NIC in your Mac can detect). The locks next to the network names indicate a secure network, which will require a password. Enter the password for the network in the password box and click the Join button to connect to the network. For unsecure networks, the Join button can be clicked without entering anything in the password box.

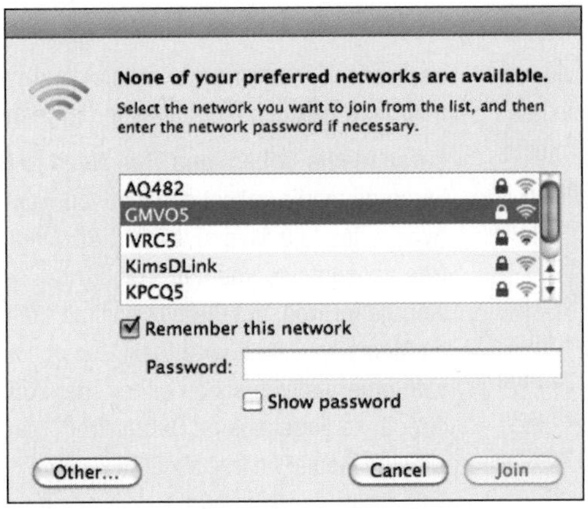

Why don't some networks appear as available? Networks with SSID broadcast turned off will not appear on the list of available networks. To join one of these secure networks, click the Other button on the available wireless networks dialog box. This will cause the Enter the name of the network dialog box to appear (see Figure 7.36). Then just enter the SSID name for your network in the Network Name box and the security passphrase in the Password box. Clicking the Join button will then connect you to the network. Checking the Remember this network check box will cause the computer to automatically connect to the network when it is available (that is, it becomes one of your preferred networks). You can have multiple preferred networks such as your home, school, and local coffee shop networks.

Assuming you installed and configured everything properly, your home network should now be up and running, allowing you to share files, Internet connections, and peripherals. You are now ready to configure other non-computer devices to connect them to your network.

Wireless Node Configuration and Testing

How do I hook up devices like a TiVo or gaming console to my network? For a wired connection, you would simply plug a cable into the device and your router. For wireless connections, there is usually a set of steps to follow in the setup menu for the device you are configuring. Assuming you set up a secure wireless network as described

Figure 7.35

The OS X available wireless networks dialog box.

in the security section of this chapter, you'll need to know the SSID name of your network and the security passphrase. Although each device's configuration steps will be slightly different, eventually, you will get to a screen where you need to input the SSID name and the passphrase. The Xbox 360 configuration screens are shown in Figure 7.38.

Once all your devices are connected to your network, you might want to check your Internet connection speed to see what kind of throughput you are achieving. You can check your speed on any device on your network that can access the Internet with a browser.

How can I test my Internet connection speed? Your ISP may have promised you certain speeds of downloading and uploading data. How can you tell if you are getting what was promised? There are numerous sites on the Internet, such as **www.speedtest.net** (see Figure 7.39) and **www.broadband.gov**, where you can test the speed of downloading files to your computer and uploading files to other computers. You can then see how your results compare to those of other users in your state and across the United States. Many factors can influence your Internet speeds, so be sure to run the test at several different times during the day over the course of a week before complaining to your ISP about not getting your promised speed.

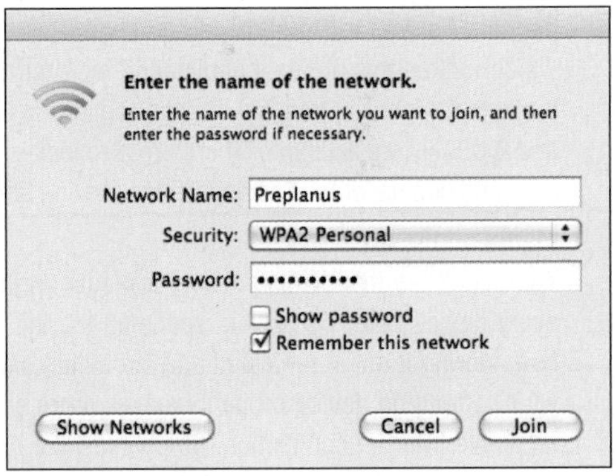

Troubleshooting Network Problems

What types of problems can I run into when installing wireless networks? The maximum range of wireless devices under the 802.11n standard is about 350 feet. But as you go farther away from your router, the throughput you achieve

Figure 7.36

The OS X Enter the name of the network dialog box.

TRENDS IN IT

Where Should You Store Your Files? The Cloud Is Calling!

You probably own a lot of electronic media such as songs, videos, e-books, and pictures. You also have other electronic files that you need to access periodically such as files you've created for school projects, your tax returns, and so on. You need to store your media where it is secure—backed up regularly and not accessible to unauthorized individuals. You also need to be able to access your media whenever you need it. So should you store your media on your home network? That might work if your network-attached storage is accessible via the Internet. The latest trend, however, is to store your files in the cloud (on the Internet). But there are a plethora of choices as to where to store your files. Deciding which option to use depends on how you want to access your files, if the files need to be shared, and how you use your files.

Files That Need Amending/Updating

If you use different computing devices such as a notebook, smartphone, and tablet, you may need to ensure that you have certain files with you at all times. Perhaps you are working on a term paper and you aren't sure what device you'll have with you the next time you have a brilliant idea to add to the paper. Having the current version of the file accessible on any device you use is critical in this instance, and means the file should probably be stored on each device. This ensures that you can work on the file even if your Internet access is interrupted or unavailable.

The most popular application for these types of files is Dropbox. Dropbox currently supports computers running the three most popular operating systems (Windows, OS X, and Linux) as well as Blackberrys, Android phones, iPhones, and iPads. After installing the Dropbox software on your devices, any files you store on your device in the Dropbox folder are automatically replicated to all your other devices via their Internet connection. Folders in Dropbox can be shared with other Dropbox users, which makes this an ideal application for sharing documents in group projects. Dropbox is free, but storage capacity is limited to between 2 GB and 8 GB for free accounts. Therefore, Dropbox is usually best for limited amounts of smaller files as opposed to sharing large media collections.

Media on the Go

You might like to view/listen to your media on the go. But storing it on every device takes up a lot of space on the individual devices. Therefore, storing it out in the cloud and streaming exactly what you want to your computing device probably makes more sense. But that requires an active Internet connection. Companies like Apple and Amazon with their iCloud and Cloud Drive offerings are trying to entice you to store all your media (and other files) on their servers. Both iCloud and Cloud Drive offer limited amounts of space for free, but you can pay a yearly fee for additional storage for your 100 GB collection of HD movies. However, both of these options are designed primarily for single users

as opposed to sharing of media. And with limited free storage, these might not be the best options for large media collections.

Large Media Collections That Need to Be Shared

For large media collections that you want to share with friends and relatives, sites like MediaFire and ADrive are popular choices. Both offer free accounts so you can test out the services. ADrive offers 50 GB of storage for free, but there is no limit to the amount of files you can store on MediaFire (even with their free account). You can easily share files with other individuals on either site. You can also post links to the files directly to Facebook or Twitter from MediaFire (Figure 7.37). However, with the MediaFire free account you can't upload files larger than 200 MB. This limit won't impact music or photos, but if you are planning on uploading HD movies, you'll need to opt for a pay account to enable uploading of files up to 10 GB per file.

The advantage of these sites is the large amount of free storage and the sharing abilities. However, the drawback to these sites is that they aren't designed for playing of streaming media (like iCloud and Cloud Drive are), so you need to download files to your device and store them locally before playing them.

No one solution is perfect for every file sharing situation, but the trend is definitely moving towards cloud storage as opposed to local network storage. You need to carefully examine the options available on each site to decide which one offers the features you need for the type of files you are storing and accessing. And make sure to carefully investigate file backup policies for each site, especially with free accounts. Some free accounts don't feature guaranteed backups of your media or the site might actually delete files in free accounts that haven't been accessed for a certain period of time. The pay accounts generally guarantee that the files are backed up on a regular basis. So don't ignore backup policies, because you want your files to be there when you need them!

www.mediafire.com (2011)

Figure 7.37

MediaFire offers unlimited storage and file sharing for free.

will decrease. Obstacles between wireless nodes also decrease throughput. Walls, floors, and large metal objects are the most common sources of interference with wireless signals. For example, placing a computer with a wireless network adapter

next to a refrigerator may prevent the signals from reaching the rest of the network. Similarly, a node that has four walls between it and the Internet connection will most likely have lower-than-maximum throughput.

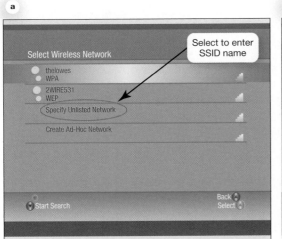

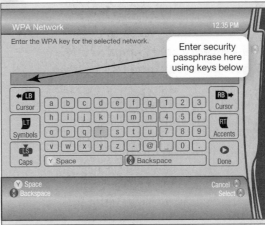

Select to enter
SSID name

Enter security
passphrase here
using keys below

Figure 7.38

Xbox 360 wireless
configuration screens.
(a) The Xbox will detect
available networks.
Select the Specify
Unlisted Network op-
tion to enter the SSID
name of your network.
(b) Enter the security
passphrase on the
appropriate security
screen.

What if a node on the network can't get adequate throughput?

Repositioning the node within the same
room (sometimes even just a few inches
from the original position) can often affect communication between nodes. If this
doesn't work, try moving the device closer
to the router or to other rooms in your
house. If these solutions don't work, you
should consider adding a wireless range
extender to your network.

A **wireless range extender** is a device that
amplifies your wireless signal to get it out to
parts of your home that are experiencing poor
connectivity. As shown Figure 7.40, Notebook
C on the back porch can't connect to the wireless network even though Computer B in the
den can connect to the network. By placing a
range extender in the den, where there is still
good connectivity to the wireless network,
the wireless signal is amplified and beamed
farther out to the back porch. This improves
the otherwise poor connectivity on the back
porch and allows Notebook C to make a good
connection to the network.

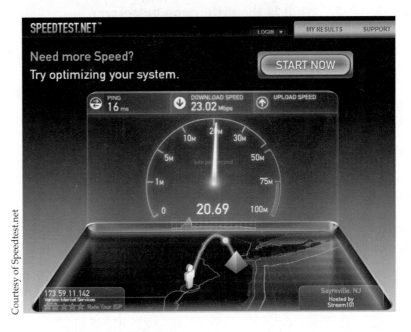

Courtesy of Speedtest.net

Hopefully, you'll now be able to connect
all your computing devices to your home
network and achieve the throughput you
need to move your data efficiently around
your home network.

Figure 7.39

Speed test showing a
download speed of 23.02
Mbps and upload of 20.69
Mbps, which is extremely
fast for a home Internet
connection.

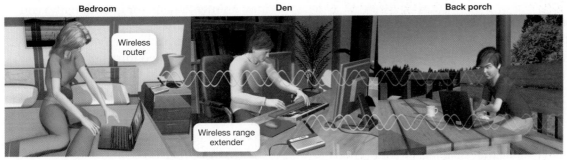

Computer A with
wireless network adapter

Computer B with
wireless range extender

Notebook C with
wireless network adapter

Figure 7.40

Because a wireless
range extender is in-
stalled in the den, Note-
book C on the back porch
can now connect to the
wireless network gen-
erated by the wireless
router in the bedroom.

1. What is a network, and what are the advantages/disadvantages of setting up one?

A computer network is simply two or more computers that are connected using software and hardware so they can communicate. Advantages of networks include allowing users to (1) share an Internet connection, (2) share peripheral devices, and (3) share files. A disadvantage is that the network must be administered.

2. What is the difference between a client/server network and a peer-to-peer network?

In peer-to-peer networks, each node connected to the network can communicate directly with every other node instead of having a separate device exercise central control over the network. P2P networks are the most common type of network installed in homes. Most networks that have 10 or more nodes are client/server networks. A client/server network contains two types of computers: a client computer on which users perform specific tasks and a server computer that provides resources to the clients and central control for the network.

3. What are the main components of every network?

To function, any network must contain four components: (1) transmission media (cables or radio waves) to connect and establish communication between nodes, (2) network adapters that allow the nodes on the network to communicate, (3) network navigation devices (such as routers and switches) that move data around the network, and (4) software that allows the network to run.

4. What are my options for connecting to the Internet?

Home users have many options for connecting to the Internet. A dial-up connection, in which you connect to the Internet using a standard phone line, was at one time the standard way to connect to the Internet. Today's broadband connections are faster and have made dial-up a legacy connection technology. Broadband connections include

cable, DSL, and fiber-optic cable. Satellite is a connection option for those who do not have access to faster broadband technologies. WiFi allows users to connect to the Internet wirelessly, but is not as fast as a wired connection.

5. Which type of network is most commonly found in the home?

Ethernet networks are the most common networks used in home networking. Most Ethernet networks use a combination of wired and wireless connections, depending upon the data throughput required. Wired connections usually achieve higher throughput than wireless connections.

6. What equipment and software do I need to build a network in my home?

All computing equipment that will connect to a network has to contain a network adapter. Network adapters allow computers to communicate (either wired or wirelessly) with network navigation devices such as routers and switches. Wired connections are usually made with Cat 6 twisted-pair cable. A router is needed to share an Internet connection as it transmits data between two networks (the home network and the Internet).

7. Why are wireless networks more vulnerable than wired networks, and what special precautions are required to ensure my wireless network is secure?

Wireless networks are even more susceptible to hacking than wired networks because the signals of most wireless networks extend beyond the walls of your home. Neighbors may unintentionally (or intentionally) connect to the Internet through your wireless connection, and hackers may try to access it. To prevent unwanted intrusions into your network, you should change the default password on your router to make it tougher for hackers to gain access, use a hard-to-guess SSID (network name), disable SSID broadcasting to make it harder for outsiders to detect your network, and enable security protocols such as WPA or WEP.

8. Besides computers, what other devices can I connect to a home network?

Connecting peripherals such as printers directly to a network allows them to be easily shared by all users on the network. Network-attached storage (NAS) devices allow for the storage and sharing of data files such as movies and music as well as providing a central place for file backups. Connecting digital entertainment devices (such as gaming consoles) provides the ability to stream movies and other entertainment directly from the Internet.

9. How do I configure the software on my computer and set up other devices to get my network up and running?

Windows 7 makes it easy to set up wired and wireless networks. Plug in the modem, router, and all cables, and then switch on the modem, router, and computers (in that order). Launch the Network and Sharing Center and select the appropriate links for setup. Make sure each computer has a distinct name and ensure that all computers are in the same HomeGroup. Devices such as gaming consoles each have their own setup procedures for connecting to wireless networks, but usually require the same information as needed for connecting a computer to a secured wireless network.

10. What problems might I encounter when setting up a wireless network?

You may not get the throughput you need through a wireless connection, and therefore you may need to consider a wired connection for certain devices. Distance from the router as well as walls, floors, and large metal objects between a device and the router can interfere with wireless connectivity. Wireless range extenders can amplify signals to improve connectivity in areas of poor signal strength.

 ## Companion Website

The Companion Website includes a variety of additional materials to help you review and learn more about the topics in this chapter. Go to: *www.pearsonhighered.com/techinaction*

chapter seven key terms

Word Bank

- Cat 6 cable
- client/server
- data transfer rate
- hacker(s)
- home network server
- LAN

- network adapter(s)
- network-ready
- peer-to-peer (P2P)
- piggybacking
- router
- switch

- throughput
- twisted-pair cable
- WAN
- wired
- wireless
- wireless range extender

Instructions: Fill in the blanks using the words from the Word Bank above.

Cindy needed to network three computers for herself and her roommates, Liu and Rosita. She decided that a(n) (1) _____ network was the right type to install in their dorm suite because a(n) (2) _____ network was too complex. Because they all liked to stream digital movies from the Internet, they needed a high (3) _____, but doubted they would achieve the promised (4) _____ in any network they installed. Although they knew using (5) _____ media would provide the fastest Ethernet networks, they decided to use (6) _____ media so that they could use their notebooks wherever they were in their suite. Therefore they needed to buy a(n) (7) _____ with wireless capability that would allow them to share the broadband Internet connection that Sharon already had through a local ISP. This device would also double as a(n) (8) _____, preventing the need to purchase a separate device. Fortunately, all their computers already had wireless (9) _____ installed, making it easy to connect the computers to the network. Cindy knew they would need to purchase some (10) _____, since the Xbox 360 they wanted to share only had a wired Ethernet adapter in it.

Cindy's roommate Rosita wanted to know if they could hook into the (11) _____, or small network, that was already deployed for the students in the dorm. This student network was already hooked into the college's (12) _____, or large network, which spanned all three of the college's campuses. She knew they would need to be careful when connecting to the network, because some students from the dorm had accidentally been illegally (13) _____ on a network from the cafe across the street. The connectivity for notebooks in the lounge at the end of the hall was very poor, so they needed to consider purchasing a(n) (14) _____ to extend the range of the wireless signal. As a final detail, Rosita suggested they get a(n) (15) _____ printer that would plug right into the router and allow them all to print whenever they needed to do so.

becoming
computer
literate

Your grandmother has moved into a new retirement community. She is sharing a large living space with three other residents. All four retirees have their own notebook computers. Your grandmother has asked you to advise her and her roommates on an appropriate network to install so that they can share an Internet connection, a laser printer, and movies that they want to stream from Netflix via the Internet. And your grandmother is an avid photographer and has thousands of digital photographs on her computer. She is very concerned about forgetting to back up the photographs after she takes new ones and wants her family to be able to access her photos via the Internet.

Instructions: Using the preceding scenario, draft a networking plan for your grandmother and her roommates using as many of the keywords from the chapter as you can. Be sure that your grandmother, who is unfamiliar with many networking terms, can understand your suggestions.

Instructions: Answer the multiple-choice and true–false questions below for more practice with key terms and concepts from this chapter.

Multiple Choice

1. Each device connected to a network is known as a
  a. peripheral.   b. network spoke.
  c. node.   d. computing unit.

2. Which of the following is a disadvantage of setting up a network?
  a. Peripherals are difficult to share.
  b. It is difficult to install Mac and Windows computers on the same network.
  c. Networks are too difficult for the average person to configure.
  d. Even peer-to-peer networks require some degree of network administration.

3. The most common type of network installed in the home is a
  a. peer-to-peer.
  b. client/server.
  c. peer/server.
  d. client-to-client.

4. A small network deployed in a home is referred to as a
  a. LAN.
  b. WAN.
  c. HAN.
  d. MAN.

5. The part of the network that establishes a communications channel between the nodes of the network is known as
  a. network operating software.
  b. transmission media.
  c. a network navigation device.
  d. a switch.

6. Throughput speed is always
  a. greater than bandwidth.
  b. the same as bandwidth.
  c. constant throughout a given transmission media.
  d. less than or equal to bandwidth.

7. The network navigation device that sends data packets to their intended node on a network is called a
  a. router.
  b. network interface card.
  c. switch.
  d. node facilitator.

8. The fastest broadband Internet service is usually
  a. fiber-optic.
  b. DSL.
  c. cable.
  d. satellite.

9. All of the following are methods to secure your wireless network except
  a. disable SSID broadcast.
  b. enable WPA.
  c. change your network name (SSID).
  d. disable WEP.

10. The device used to move data between two networks is called a
  a. gateway.
  b. switch.
  c. router.
  d. wireless range extender.

True–False

_____ 1. Actual data throughput is usually higher on wired networks than on wireless networks.

_____ 2. Network-ready devices contain Ethernet switches.

_____ 3. Home network servers are a specialized type of NAS device.

_____ 4. LANs cover a larger geographic area than WANs.

_____ 5. Gaming consoles are often connected to home wireless networks.

1. Dormitory Networking

Mikel, Dylan, Sanjay, and Harrison were sitting in the common room of their campus suite and complaining about their wireless network. They inherited the equipment from the last residents of the suite, and unfortunately their router uses the outdated 802.11g standard. They all have notebooks that have 802.11n network adapters, but their throughput is poor. Since they are often all surfing the Internet at the same time and trying to download movies, their network's performance has become unacceptable.

Since they all just sold last semester's books back to the bookstore for a total of $600, they decided this would be a good time to upgrade their network and peripherals. Dylan has an inkjet printer that gobbles up expensive cartridges, and Phil has a laser printer that just broke. The guys figure one good networked all-in-one printer should meet their needs since it would also provide them with photocopying capabilities. Mikel is concerned about backups for his computer. His external hard drive fell on the floor and no longer works reliably. He has a tremendous amount of schoolwork and photos on his computer that he is concerned about losing if his hard drive fails. Since the guys don't know much about networking, the four roommates have asked for your guidance. Consider the following, keeping in mind their $600 budget:

a. Research network-ready laser printers on sites such as **www.hp.com**, **www.epson.com**, and **www.brother.com**. What network-ready all-in-one printer would you recommend? Why?

b. Research 802.11n wireless routers at sites such as **www.netgear.com**, **www.linksys.com**, and **www.dlink.com**. What router do you think will meet the roommates' needs? Why?

c. How would you recommend addressing Mikel's backup concerns? Would you recommend an NAS device for the network, or do they have enough money left in their budget for a home network server? Research these devices and make an affordable recommendation. Check sites such as **www.tigerdirect.com** and **www.newegg.com** for competitive pricing.

2. Connecting Your Computer to Public Networks

You are working for a local coffee shop that offers free wireless access to customers. Your supervisor has asked you to create a flyer for patrons that warns them of the potential dangers of surfing the Internet in public places. Conduct research on the Internet about using public hotspots to access the Internet. Prepare a flyer that lists specific steps that customers can take to protect their data when surfing on publicly accessible networks.

3. Adding a Home Network Server for Backups to Your Network

You know that adding a home network server to your network would facilitate sharing of your digital media and would make backing up your computers easier. You need to consider the following questions when selecting an appropriate home network server:

a. What is the volume of shared media that you need to store? (In other words, how many music files, movies, and other media files do you have?)

b. What are the sizes of the hard drives of the computers on your network (for backup purposes)? What size hard drive would you need on a home network server to ensure you could back up all your computers as well as store your shared media?

c. Would you need to access files on the home network server when you are away from home or allow others (such as your cousins) to access them?

Research home network servers using sites such as **www.hp.com**, **www.acer.com**, and **www.lenovo.com**, or use the term "home server" in a search engine. Select a server that is appropriate for your home network. Prepare a summary of your findings and include the reasons for your selection.

1. Internet Access for a Small Business in a Remote Area

Your uncle owns a combination gas station/coffee shop/general store in a very small town in the Midwest. He currently is using dial-up Internet access to send e-mail and surf the Web. Some of his customers have indicated that they would love it if the store had broadband access. There is no local company that supplies broadband Internet service in the town where the business is located. Your uncle has asked you for ideas.

Investigate three satellite Internet service providers and prepare a summary of features and prices for your uncle. Make sure to find out what the download and upload speeds are for each provider. Also, ensure that the service agreement provides for your uncle using the Internet connection to provide access to his customers. Which service would you recommend to your uncle? Why?

2. Putting Computers to Work on Research Projects

Most computer CPUs use only a fraction of their computing power most of the time. Many medical research companies (such as those seeking cures for cancer and AIDS) could benefit from "borrowing" computer CPU time when computers are not being used or are being underutilized. Virtual supercomputers (which are really networks of computers) can be created using software installed on tens of thousands of computers. This type of computing is also known as *grid* or *distributed computing*. These virtual computing nets can be harnessed to solve complex problems when their owners are not using their computers. Assume that you are working for a business that has 100 computers and you would like to participate in a grid computing project. Investigate IBM's Worldwide Community Grid (**www.worldcommunitygrid.org**). Prepare a report for your boss that:

a. Describes the Worldwide Community Grid (WCG) and its objectives.
b. Lists current projects that the WCG is working on.
c. Describes the process for installing the WCG software on the company's computers.
d. Suggests a strategy for publicizing the company's participation in the WCG project that will encourage your employer's customers to participate.

3. Testing Your Internet Connection Speed

Visit **www.speedtest.net** and **www.broadband.gov** and test the speed of your Internet connection at your home and in the computer lab at your school. Try to repeat the test at two different times during the day.

a. What did you find out about download speeds at your home? Are you getting as much speed as was promised by your ISP? Would this speed be sufficient for a home-based business? What type of business packages does your ISP offer, and what speeds could you expect when paying for a business package?
b. How does the connection speed at your school compare to the speed at your home? Where do you think you should have a faster connection—at your school or at your home? Why might the connection speed at your school be slower than you think it should be?

Instructions: Some ideas are best understood by experimenting with them in our own minds. The following critical thinking questions are designed to demand your full attention but require only a comfortable chair—no technology.

1. Protecting Yourself on Public Wireless Networks

Many people use free public wireless networks to access the Internet. But many public networks don't have adequate security or may be under surveillance by hackers. To protect your sensitive data, there are certain activities you should not engage in on public networks. What types of activities should you avoid on a public network? What types of information should you only process on your secure home network?

2. Adding Devices to Your Network

We discussed adding devices other than computers and computer peripherals to your network in this chapter. Consider the following for your home network:

a. Do you currently stream or download movies from Netflix, Amazon Instant Video, or another service? If so, is your storage device sufficient, or do you need more capacity? If you don't currently download this type of entertainment, would your family do so if you had a device that was attached to your network? What type of device (DVR, home server, etc.) do you think would be most appropriate for the type of media that you enjoy? How much media would you need to download and view in a month to make purchasing equipment worthwhile?

b. Do you have a need for a home security system? Would internal and external cameras be appropriate for monitoring your home? Are there people in your house (babysitters, housekeepers, contractors, etc.) on a regular basis that might need monitoring? Would you monitor these people in real time or make recordings for later review?

3. Evaluating Your Network Storage Needs

You probably have media, such as videos, pictures, and music, that you access on a regular basis that you may already be sharing (or want to share) with family members. You could install an NAS device on your network to share the media, and perhaps you might even already have one. But this is usually only a good solution if the people you share media with are living in your household. For sharing media outside of the home, you could consider an NAS device that is accessible through the Internet or you could use an Internet-based media sharing solution. Consider the following:

a. What types of media do you need to share? With whom do you need to share them? Where are these people located? Do they all use your home network? If not, do they all have access to the Internet? How much space will the media you need to store occupy? Consider what you already have on hand plus what you might be acquiring in the future.

b. Investigate at least three different NAS devices (including home network servers) that feature the capacity you need. What is the cost of these devices? Can the devices be accessed over the Internet or do they require access to your network? What are the storage capacities of the devices?

c. Research at least three Internet-based media storing/sharing solutions such as Dropbox, MediaFire, Amazon Cloud Drive, MiMedia, Mediashare, and Wixi. What is the cost associated with each service? Are there individual file size limitations for storage? What is the total volume of media you can store? Is the media you store on the site easily sharable with others? Does the service allow storage of all the types of media you need to store?

d. Which solution would you implement? Be sure to justify your choice.

4. Preparing for a Career in Computer Networking

You've been told that preparing for a career as a network administrator, a person who installs and maintains networking equipment and software, might provide you with solid employment prospects after graduation. Research network administration careers on Web sites such as **www.bls.gov**, **www.careerbuilder.com**, and **www.salary.com**. Prepare a report that addresses the following:

a. What are the employment prospects for network administrators in the future? (The *Occupational Outlook Handbook* (**www.bls.gov/oco**) can provide you with projections.)

b. What types of salaries do entry-level positions command?

c. How much education do you need to prepare for this field?

d. What types of professional certifications are helpful in obtaining employment?

e. What are the typical duties of a network administrator?

f. Do you think you would pursue this type of job? What appeals to you about the position? What aspects of the job do you think you would not enjoy?

Providing Wireless Internet Access to the Needy

Problem

Wireless Internet access in the home is very desirable. However, not everyone is able to afford it, and this can put families, especially ones with school-aged children, at a severe disadvantage. Providing Internet access to the underprivileged is a way of closing the "digital divide" that exists between those who can afford Internet access and those who cannot.

Task

You are volunteering for a charity that wants to begin installing wireless networks in homes for needy families. The project is funded by charitable grants with the objective of providing basic broadband Internet access and simple networking capabilities in the home at no cost to the recipients. The assumption is that the families already have two notebook computers per family (provided through another charity) that have 802.11n wireless capabilities. You have volunteered to research potential network and Internet solutions.

Process

Break the class into three teams. Each team will be responsible for investigating one of the following issues:

1. **Internet service providers:** Research ISPs that serve the town where your school is located (don't forget to include satellite providers). Compare and contrast their lowest cost broadband access. Compare maximum upload and download speeds as well as costs. Be sure to consider the cost of the modems—whether they are purchased up front or rented on a monthly basis. Make sure to select what your group considers to be the best deal.
2. **Networking equipment and network-ready peripherals:** Each home needs to be provided with an 802.11n capable wireless router (to share the Internet access), a network-ready all-in-one printer, and a Blu-ray player capable of streaming digital video (for educational programs and movies). Research at least three different options for each of these devices. Since this is a grant and money is limited, be sure to consider price as well as functionality.
3. **Security:** The wireless networks need to be secured to keep hackers and piggybackers out. Work in conjunction with the group that is researching routers to determine the best type of router to purchase since it needs to support a strong wireless security protocol such as WPA. Make sure to consider what other types of protection are needed on the network, such as antivirus, anti-malware, and firewalls.

Present your findings to your class and come to a consensus about the solution you would propose for the charity. Provide your instructor with a report on your area suitable for presentation to the CEO of the charity.

Conclusion

Providing technology to underserved populations on a cost-effective basis will go a long way towards closing the digital divide and ensuring that disadvantaged youth have the Internet access they need to pursue their education and compete effectively in today's society.

Firing Employees for Expressing Views on Social Media Sites

In this exercise, you will research and then role-play a complicated ethical situation. The role you play may or may not match your own personal beliefs, but your research and use of logic will enable you to represent whichever view is assigned. An arbitrator will watch and comment on both sides of the arguments, and together the team will agree on an ethical solution.

Problem

The largest network, the Internet, provides the capability for vast social interaction. Social media sites such as Facebook, YouTube, and Twitter, as well as blogs and wikis, give everyone convenient ways to express their opinions. However, employers often are intolerant of employees who freely express negative opinions or expose inside information about their employers on social media sites. Given that most jurisdictions in the United States use the doctrine of employment at-will (that is, employees can be fired at any time for any reason, or even no reason), many employers are quick to discipline or terminate employees who express opinions with which the company disagrees. When such cases come to court, the courts often find in favor of the employers. It is clear that individuals must exercise extreme care when posting work-related content.

Research Areas to Consider

- Ellen Simonetti and Delta Airlines
- Fired for blogging about work
- Free speech
- Joyce Park or Michael Tunison

Process

1. Divide the class into teams.
2. Research the areas cited above and devise a scenario in which someone has complained about an employee blogging about a sensitive workplace issue such as cleanliness at a food manufacturing facility or employee romances.
3. Team members should write a summary that provides background information for their character—for example: employee, human resources manager, or arbitrator—and details their character's behaviors to set the stage for the role-playing event. Then, team members should create an outline to use during the role-playing event.
4. Team members should arrange a mutually convenient time to meet for the exchange, either using the collaboration feature of MyITLab, the discussion board feature of Blackboard, or meeting in person.
5. Team members should present their case to the class, or submit a PowerPoint presentation for review by the rest of the class, along with the summary and resolution they developed.

Conclusion

As technology becomes ever more prevalent and integrated into our lives, more and more ethical dilemmas will present themselves. Being able to understand and evaluate both sides of the argument, while responding in a personally or socially ethical manner, will be an important skill.

Under the Hood

IN FOCUS

SOME PEOPLE ARE DRAWN TO UNDERSTANDING things in detail, but many folks are happy just to have things work. If you use a computer, you may not have ever been tempted to "look under the hood." However, without understanding the hardware inside, you'll be faced with some real limitations. You'll have to pay a technician to fix or upgrade your computer. This won't be as efficient as fine-tuning it yourself, and you may find yourself buying a new computer sooner than necessary. If you're preparing for a career in information technology, understanding computer hardware will affect the speed and efficiency of the programs you design. And what about all those exciting advances you hear about? How do you evaluate the impact of a new type of memory or a new processor? A basic appreciation of how a computer system is built and designed is a good start.

We'll build on what you've learned about computer hardware in other chapters and go under the hood, looking at the components of your system unit in more detail. Let's begin by looking at the building blocks of computers: switches.

Switches

The **system unit** is the box that contains the central electronic components of the computer. But how, exactly, does the computer perform all of its tasks? How does it process the data you input? The CPU performs functions like adding, subtracting, moving data around the system, and so on using nothing but a large number of on/off switches. In fact, a computer system can be viewed as an enormous collection of on/off switches.

Electrical Switches

Computers work exclusively with numbers, not words. To process data into information, computers need to work in a language they understand. This language, called **binary language**, consists of just two numbers: 0 and 1. Everything a computer does, such as processing data or printing a report, is broken down into a series of 0s and 1s. **Electrical switches** are devices inside the computer that can be flipped between these two states: 1 and 0, signifying "on" and "off." Computers use 0s and 1s to process data because they are electronic, digital machines. They only understand two states of existence: on and off. Inside a computer these two possibilities, or states, are represented using the binary switches (or digits) 1 and 0.

You use various forms of switches every day. The on/off button on your DVD player is a mechanical switch: pushed in, it represents the value 1 (on), whereas

Figure 1

Water faucets can be used to represent binary switches.

popped out, it represents the value 0 (off). Another switch you use each day is a water faucet. As shown in Figure 1, shutting off the faucet so that no water flows could represent the value 0, whereas turning it on could represent the value 1.

Computers are built from a huge collection of electrical switches. The history of computers is really a story about creating smaller and faster sets of electrical switches so that more data can be stored and manipulated quickly.

Vacuum Tubes The earliest generation of electronic computers used devices called **vacuum tubes** as switches. Vacuum tubes act as computer switches by allowing or blocking the flow of electrical current. The problem with vacuum tubes is that they take up a lot of space, as you see in Figure 2. The first high-speed digital computer, the Electronic Numerical Integrator and Computer (ENIAC), was deployed in 1945. It used nearly 18,000 vacuum tubes as switches and filled approximately 1,500 square feet of floor space. That's about one-half the size of a standard high school basketball court! In addition to being large, the vacuum tubes produced a lot of heat and burned out frequently. Thus, vacuum tubes are impractical to use as switching devices in personal computers because of their size and reliability.

Since the introduction of ENIAC's vacuum tubes, two major revolutions have occurred in the design of switches, and consequently computers, to make them smaller and faster: the invention of the transistor and the fabrication of integrated circuits.

Figure 2

Computers can be constructed using vacuum tubes (see inset). The difference in size achieved by moving from tubes to transistors allowed computers to become desktop devices.

Transistors

Transistors are electrical switches that are built out of layers of a special type of material called a **semiconductor**, which is any material that can be controlled to either conduct electricity or act as an insulator (to prohibit electricity from passing through). Silicon, which is found in common sand, is the semiconductor material used to make transistors.

By itself, silicon does not conduct electricity particularly well, but if specific chemicals are added in a controlled way to the silicon, it begins to behave like a switch (see Figure 3). The silicon allows electrical current to flow easily when a certain voltage is applied; otherwise, it prevents electrical current from flowing, thus behaving as an on/off switch.

Figure 3

In "doping," a phosphorous atom is put in the place of a silicon atom. Because phosphorous has five electrons instead of four, the extra electron is free to move around.

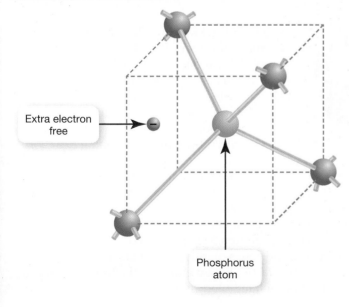

Extra electron free

Phosphorus atom

This kind of behavior is exactly what is needed to store digital information, the 0s (off) and 1s (on) in binary language.

Early transistors were built in separate units as small metal rods, with each rod acting as a single on/off switch. These first transistors were much smaller than vacuum tubes, produced little heat, and could quickly be switched from on to off, thereby allowing or blocking electrical current. They also were less expensive than vacuum tubes.

It wasn't long, however, before transistors reached their limits. Continuing advances in technology began to require more transistors than circuit boards could reasonably handle at the time. Something was needed to pack more transistor capacity into a smaller space. Thus, integrated circuits, the next technical revolution in switches, were developed.

Integrated Circuits Integrated circuits (or **chips**) are tiny regions of semiconductor material such as silicon that support a huge number of transistors (see Figure 4). Along with all the many transistors, other components critical to a circuit board (such as resistors, capacitors, and diodes) are also located on the integrated circuit. Most integrated circuits are no more than a quarter inch in size.

Because so many transistors can fit into such a small area, integrated circuits have enabled computer designers to create small yet powerful **microprocessors**, which are the chips that contain a CPU. The Intel 4004, the first complete microprocessor to be located on a single integrated circuit, was released in 1971, marking the beginning of the true miniaturization of computers. The Intel 4004 contained slightly more than 2,300 transistors. Today, more than 2 billion transistors can be manufactured in a space as tiny as the nail of your little finger!

This incredible feat has fueled an industry like no other. In 1951, the Univac I computer was the size of a large room. The processor memory unit itself, which cost more than $1 million to produce, was 14 feet long by 8 feet wide by 8.5 feet high and could perform about 1,905 operations per second. Thanks to advances in integrated circuits, the IBM PC released 30 years later took up just 1 cubic foot of space, cost $3,000, and performed 155,000 times more quickly. (For more information about computer history, see the Technology in Focus feature "The History of the PC" on page 38.)

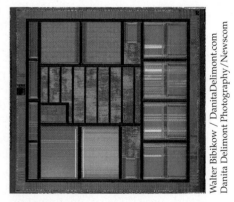

Figure 4

Integrated circuits use advanced fabrication techniques to fit millions of transistors into a quarter inch of silicon. This is an integrated circuit with areas marked out in black to show memory units, logic sections, and input/output blocks.

Computers use on/off switches to perform their functions. But how can these simple switches be organized so that they let you use a computer to pay your bills online or write an essay? How can a set of switches describe a number or a word, or give a computer the command to perform addition? Recall that to manipulate the on/off switches, the computer works in binary language, which uses only two digits, 0 and 1. To understand how a computer works, let's first look at the special numbering system called the *binary number system*.

The Binary Number System

A **number system** is an organized plan for representing a number. Although you may not realize it, you are already familiar with one number system. The **base 10 number system**, also known as **decimal notation**, is the system you use to represent all of the numeric values you use each day. It's called base 10 because it uses 10 digits, 0 through 9, to represent any value.

To represent a number in base 10, you break the number down into groups of ones, tens, hundreds, thousands, and so on. Each digit has a place value depending on where it appears in the number. For example, using base 10, in the whole number 6,954, there are 6 sets of thousands, 9 sets of hundreds, 5 sets of tens, and 4 sets of ones. Working from right to left, each place in a number represents an increasing power of 10, as shown here:

$$6,954 = 6 * (1,000) + 9 * (100) + 5 * (10) + 4 * (1)$$
$$= 6 * 10^3 + 9 * 10^2 + 5 * 10^1 + 4 * 10^0$$

Note that in this equation, the final number 1 is represented as 10^0 because any number raised to the zero power is equal to 1.

Anthropologists theorize that humans developed a base 10 number system because we have 10 fingers. However, computer systems, with their huge collections of on/off switches, are not well suited to thinking about numbers in groups of 10. Instead, computers describe a number in powers of 2 because each switch can be in one of two positions: on or off. This numbering system is referred to as the **binary number system**.

The binary number system is also referred to as the **base 2 number system**. Even with just two digits, the

Where Does Binary Show Up?

In this Sound Byte, you'll learn how to use tools to work with binary, decimal, and hexadecimal numbers. (These tools come with the Windows operating system.) You'll also learn where you might see binary and hexadecimal values when you use a computer.

binary number system can still represent all the values that a base 10 number system can (see Figure 5). Instead of breaking the number down into sets of ones, tens, hundreds, and thousands, as is done in base 10 notation, the binary number system describes a number as the sum of powers of 2. Binary numbers are used to represent every piece of data stored in a computer: all of the numbers, all of the letters, and all of the instructions that the computer uses to execute work.

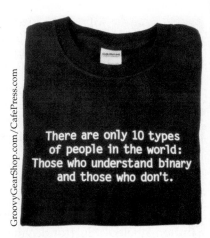

Figure 5

Computer humor—the value 2 is written as 10 in binary!

Representing Integers In the base 10 number system, a whole number is represented as the sum of ones, tens, hundreds, and thousands—that is, sums of powers of 10. The binary system works in the same way, but describes a value as the sum of groups of 1s, 2s, 4s, 8s, 16s, 32s, 64s, etc.—that is, powers of 2: 1, 2, 4, 8, 16, 32, 64, and so on.

Let's look at the number 67. In base 10, the number 67 would be six sets of 10s and seven sets of 1s, as follows:

$$\text{Base 10: } 67 = 6 * 10^1 + 7 * 10^0$$

One way to figure out how 67 is represented in base 2 is to find the largest possible power of 2 that could be in the number 67. Two to the eighth power is 256, and there are no groups of 256 in the number 67. Two to the seventh power is 128, but that is bigger than 67. Two to the sixth power is 64, and there is a group of 64 inside a group of 67.

67 has	1	group of	64	That leaves 3 and
3 has	0	groups of	32	
	0	groups of	16	
	0	groups of	8	
	0	groups of	4	
	1	group of	2	That leaves 1 and
1 has	1	group of	1	Now nothing is left

So, the binary number for 67 is written as 1000011 in base 2:

$$\text{Base 2: } 67 = 64 + 0 + 0 + 0 + 0 + 2 + 1$$
$$= (1 * 2^6) + (0 * 2^5) + (0 * 2^4) + (0 * 2^3) +$$
$$(0 * 2^2) + (1 * 2^1) + (1 * 2^0)$$
$$= (1000011) \text{ base 2}$$

SOUND BYTE Binary Numbers Interactive

This Sound Byte helps remove the mystery surrounding binary numbers. You'll learn about base conversion among decimal, binary, and hexadecimal systems interactively, using colors, sounds, and images.

It is easier to have a calculator do this for you! Some calculators have a button labeled DEC (for decimal) and another labeled BIN (for binary). Using Windows, you can access the Scientific Calculator that supports conversion between decimal (base 10) and binary (base 2) by choosing Start, All Programs, Accessories, and then clicking Calculator. From the View menu, select Programmer. You can enter your calculation in decimal and instantly see the binary representation in 64 bits, as shown in Figure 6.

Figure 6

The Windows Calculator in Programmer mode instantly converts from decimal values to binary.

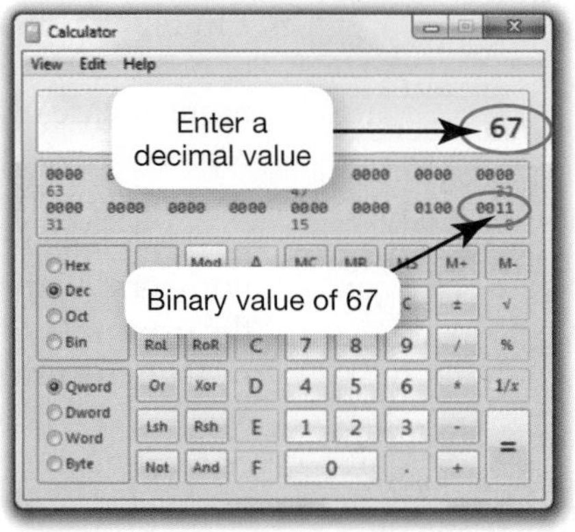

A large integer value becomes a very long string of 1s and 0s in binary! For convenience, programmers often use **hexadecimal notation** to make these expressions easier to use. Hexadecimal is a base 16 number system, meaning it uses 16 digits to represent numbers instead of the 10 digits used in base 10 or the 2 digits used in base 2. The 16 digits it uses are the 10 numeric digits, 0 to 9, plus six extra symbols: A, B, C, D, E, and F. Each of the letters A through F corresponds to a numeric value, so that A equals 10, B equals 11, and so on (see Figure 7). Therefore, the value 67 in decimal is 1000011 in binary or 43 in hexadecimal notation. It is much easier for computer scientists to use the two-digit 43 than the seven-digit string 1000011. The Windows Calculator in Programmer view also can perform conversions to hexadecimal notation. (You can watch a video showing you how to perform conversions between bases using the Windows Calculator in the Sound Byte titled "Where Does Binary Show Up?")

Representing Characters: ASCII We have just been converting integers from base 10, which *we* understand, to base 2 (binary state), which the computer understands. Similarly, we need a system that converts letters and other symbols that *we* understand to a binary state that the computer understands. To provide a consistent means for representing letters and other characters, certain codes dictate how to represent characters in binary format. Older mainframe computers use Extended Binary-Coded Decimal Interchange Code (EBCDIC, pronounced "Eb-sih-dik"). However, most of today's personal computers use the American National Standards Institute (ANSI, pronounced "An-see") standard code, called the **American Standard Code for Information Interchange** (**ASCII**, pronounced "As-key"), to represent each letter or character as an 8-bit (or 1-byte) binary code.

Each binary digit is called a **bit** for short. Eight binary digits (or bits) combine to create one **byte**. We have been converting base 10 numbers to a binary format. In such cases, the binary format has no standard length. For example, the binary format for the number 2 is two digits (10), whereas the binary format for the number 10 is four digits (1010). Although binary numbers can have more or fewer than 8 bits, each single alphabetic or special character is 1 byte (or 8 bits) of data and consists of a unique combination of a total of eight 0s and 1s.

The ASCII code represents the 26 uppercase letters and 26 lowercase letters used in the English language, along with many punctuation symbols and other special characters, using 8 bits. Figure 8 shows several examples of ASCII code representation of printable letters and characters.

Figure 7 | SAMPLE HEXADECIMAL VALUES

Decimal Number	Hexadecimal Value	Decimal Number	Hexadecimal Value
00	00	08	08
01	01	09	09
02	02	10	A
03	03	11	B
04	04	12	C
05	05	13	D
06	06	14	E
07	07	15	F

Figure 8 | ASCII STANDARD CODE FOR A SAMPLE OF LETTERS AND CHARACTERS

ASCII Code	Represents This Symbol	ASCII Code	Represents This Symbol
01000001	A	01100001	a
01000010	B	01100010	b
01000011	C	01100011	c
01011010	Z	00100011	#
00100001	!	00100100	$
00100010	"	00100101	%

Note: For the full ASCII table, see **www.asciitable.com**.

Representing Characters: Unicode Because it represents letters and characters using only 8 bits, the ASCII code can assign only 256 (or 2^8) different codes for unique characters and letters. Although this is enough to represent English and many other characters found in the world's languages, ASCII code cannot represent all languages and symbols, because some languages require more than 256 characters and letters. Thus, a new encoding scheme, called **Unicode**, was created. By using 16 bits instead of the 8 bits used in ASCII, Unicode can represent nearly 1,115,000 code points and currently assigns more than 96,000 unique character symbols (see Figure 9). The first 128 characters of Unicode are identical to ASCII, but because of its depth, Unicode is also able to represent the alphabets of all modern and historic languages and notational systems, including such languages and writing systems as Tibetan, Tagalog, Japanese, and Canadian Aboriginal syllabics. As we continue to become a more global society, it is anticipated that Unicode will replace ASCII as the standard character formatting code.

Representing Decimal Numbers The binary number system also can represent a decimal number. How can a string of 1s and 0s capture the information in a value such as 99.368? Because every computer must store such numbers in the same way, the Institute of Electrical and Electronics Engineers (IEEE) has established a standard called the *floating-point standard* that describes how numbers with fractional parts should be

represented in the binary number system. Using a 32-bit system, we can represent an incredibly wide range of numbers. The method dictated by the IEEE standard works the same for any number with a decimal point, such as the number –0.75. The first digit, or bit (the sign bit), is used to indicate whether the number is positive or negative. The next eight bits store the magnitude of the number, indicating whether the number is in the hundreds or millions, for example. The standard says to use the next 23 bits to store the value of the number.

Interpretation *All* data inside the computer is stored as bits. Positive and negative numbers can be stored using signed integer notation, with the first bit (the sign bit) indicating the sign and the rest of the bits indicating the value of the number. Decimal numbers are stored according to the IEEE floating-point standard, and letters and symbols are stored according to the ASCII code or Unicode. All of these different number systems and codes exist so that computers can store different types of information in their on/off switches. No matter what kind of data you input in a computer—a color, a musical note, or a street address—that data will be stored as a string of 1s and 0s. The important lesson is that the interpretation of 0s and 1s is what matters. The same binary pattern could represent a positive number, a negative number, a fraction, or a letter.

How does the computer know which interpretation to use for the 1s and 0s? When your brain processes language, it takes the sounds you hear and uses the rules of English, along with other clues, to build an interpretation of the sound as a word. If you are in New York City and hear someone shout, "Hey, Lori!" you expect someone is saying hello to a friend. If you are in London and hear the same sound—"Hey! Lorry!"—you jump out of the way because a truck is coming at you! You knew which interpretation to apply to the sound because you had some other information—that you were in England.

Likewise, the CPU is designed to understand a specific language or set of instructions. Certain instructions tell the CPU to expect a negative number next or to interpret the following bit pattern as a character. Because of this extra information, the CPU always knows which interpretation to use for a series of bits.

Figure 9

The written languages of the world require thousands of different characters, shown here. Unicode provides a system allowing digital representation of over 1,100,000 unique characters.

The CPU Machine Cycle

Any program you run on your computer is actually a long series of binary code describing a specific set of commands the CPU must perform. These commands may be coming from a user's actions or may be instructions fed from a program while it executes. Each CPU is somewhat different in the exact steps it follows to perform its tasks, but all CPUs must perform a series of similar general steps. These steps, illustrated in Figure 10, are referred to as a CPU **machine cycle** (or **processing cycle**).

1. **Fetch:** When any program begins to run, the 1s and 0s that make up the program's binary code must be "fetched" from their temporary storage location in random access memory (RAM) and moved to the CPU before they can be executed.

2. **Decode:** Once the program's binary code is in the CPU, it is decoded into the commands the CPU understands.

3. **Execute:** Next, the CPU actually performs the work described in the commands.

    Specialized hardware on the CPU performs addition, subtraction, multiplication, division, and other mathematical and logical operations at incredible speeds.

4. **Store:** The result is stored in one of the **registers**, special memory storage areas built into the CPU, which are the most expensive, fastest memory in your computer. The CPU is then ready to fetch the next set of bits encoding the next instruction.

No matter what program you are running, be it a Web browser or a word processing program, and no matter how many programs you are using at one time, the CPU performs these four steps over and over at incredibly high speeds. Shortly, we'll look at each stage in more detail so that you can understand the complexity of the CPU's design, how to compare different CPUs on the market, and what enhancements you can expect in CPU designs of the future. But first, let's examine a few of the CPU's other components that help it perform its tasks.

The System Clock

To move from one stage of the machine cycle to the next, the motherboard uses a built-in **system clock**. This internal clock is actually a special crystal that acts like a metronome, keeping a steady beat and thereby controlling when the CPU will move to the next stage of processing.

These steady beats or "ticks" of the system clock, known as the **clock cycle**, set the pace by which the computer moves from process to process. The pace, known as **clock speed**, is measured in hertz (Hz), a unit of measure that describes how many times something happens per second. Today's system clocks are measured in gigahertz (GHz), each of which represents 1 billion clock ticks per second. Therefore, in a 3 GHz system, there are 3 billion

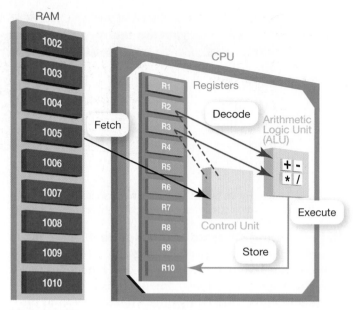

Figure 10

The CPU machine cycle.

clock ticks each second. Computers with older processors would sometimes need one or more cycles to process one instruction. Today, however, CPUs are designed to handle more instructions more efficiently, and are, therefore, capable of executing more than one instruction per cycle.

The Control Unit

The CPU, like any part of the computer system, is designed from a collection of switches. How can simple on/off switches "remember" the fetch-decode-execute-store sequence of the CPU machine cycle? How can they perform the work required in each of these stages?

The **control unit** of the CPU manages the switches inside the CPU. It is programmed by CPU designers to remember the sequence of processing stages for that CPU and how each switch in the CPU should be set (i.e., on or off) for each stage. With each beat of the system clock, the control unit moves each switch to the correct on or off setting and then performs the work of that stage.

Let's now look at each of the stages in the machine cycle in a bit more depth.

Stage 1: The Fetch Stage

The data and program instructions the CPU needs are stored in different areas in the computer system. Data and program instructions move between these areas as they are needed by the CPU for processing. Programs (such as Microsoft Word) are permanently stored on the hard drive because it offers nonvolatile storage, meaning the programs remain stored there even when you turn the power off. However, when you launch a program (that is, when you double-click an icon to execute the program), the program, or sometimes only the essential parts of a program, is transferred from the hard drive into RAM.

The program moves to RAM because the CPU can access the data and program instructions stored in RAM more than 1 million times faster than if they are left on the hard drive. In part, this is because RAM is much closer to the CPU than the hard drive is. Another reason for the delay in transmission of data and program instructions from the hard drive to the CPU is the relatively slow speed of mechanical hard drives. The read/write heads have to sweep over the spinning platters, which takes time. Even non-mechanical SSD hard drives have slower access speeds than RAM. RAM is a type of memory that gives very fast, direct access to data. As specific instructions from the program are needed, they are moved from RAM into registers (the special storage areas located on the CPU itself), where they wait to be executed.

The CPU's storage area is not big enough to hold everything it needs to process at the same time. If enough memory were located on the CPU chip itself, an entire program could be copied to the CPU from RAM before it was executed. This certainly would add to the computer's speed and efficiency, because there would be no delay while the CPU stopped processing operations to fetch instructions from RAM to the CPU. However, including so much memory on a CPU chip would make these chips extremely expensive. In addition, CPU design is so complex that only a limited amount of storage space is available on the CPU itself.

Cache Memory The CPU doesn't actually need to fetch every instruction from RAM each time it goes through a cycle. There is another layer of storage, called **cache memory**, that has even faster access than RAM. The word *cache* is derived from the French word *cacher*, which means "to hide." Cache memory consists of small blocks of memory located directly on and next to the CPU chip. These memory blocks are holding places for recently or frequently used instructions or data that the CPU needs the most. When these instructions or data are stored in cache memory, the CPU can retrieve them more quickly than would be the case if it had to access the instructions or data in RAM.

Taking data you think you'll be using soon and storing it nearby is a simple idea but a powerful one. This is a strategy that shows up in other places in your computer system. For example, when you are browsing Web pages, it takes longer to download images than text. Your browser software automatically stores images on your hard drive so that you don't have to wait to

download them again if you want to go back and view a page you've already visited. Although this cache of files is not related to the cache storage space designed into the CPU chip, the idea is the same.

Modern CPU designs include several types of cache memory. If the next instruction to be fetched is not already located in a CPU register, instead of looking directly to RAM to find it, the CPU first searches Level 1 cache. **Level 1 cache** is a block of memory that is built onto the CPU chip to store data or commands that have just been used.

If the command is not located in Level 1 cache, the CPU searches Level 2 cache. Depending on the design of the CPU, **Level 2 cache** is either located on the CPU chip but slightly farther away from the CPU than Level 1, or is on a separate chip next to the CPU and therefore takes somewhat longer to access. Level 2 cache contains more storage area than does Level 1 cache. For the Intel Core i7, for example, the Level 1 cache is 64 kilobytes (KB) and the Level 2 cache is 1 megabyte (MB).

Only if the CPU doesn't find the next instruction to be fetched in either Level 1 or Level 2 cache will it make the long journey to RAM to access it.

The current direction of processor design is toward increasingly large multilevel CPU cache structures. Therefore, some newer CPUs, such as Intel's Core i7 processors, have an additional third level of cache memory storage called **Level 3 cache**. On computers with Level 3 cache, the CPU checks this area for instructions and data after it looks in Level 1 and Level 2 cache, but before it makes the longer trip to RAM (see Figure 11). The Level 3 cache holds between 2 and 12 MB of data. With 12 MB of Level 3 cache, there is storage for some entire programs to be transferred to the CPU for execution.

As an end user of computer programs, you do nothing special to use cache memory. In fact, you are not even able to see that caching is being used—nothing special lights up on your system unit or keyboard. The advantage of having more cache memory is that you'll experience better performance because the CPU won't have to make the longer trip to RAM to get data and instructions as often. Unfortunately, because it is built into the CPU chip or motherboard, you can't upgrade cache; it is part of the original design of the CPU. Therefore, as with RAM, when buying a computer it's important, everything else being equal, to consider buying the one with the most cache memory.

Stage 2: The Decode Stage

The main goal of the decode stage is for the CPU's control unit to translate (or **decode**) the program's instructions into commands the CPU can understand. A CPU can understand only a tiny set of commands. The collection of commands a specific CPU can execute is called the **instruction set** for that system. Each CPU has its own unique instruction set. For example, the AMD Phenom II X6 six-core processor in a Gamer Mage system from iBuyPower has a different instruction set than does the Intel Core i5 used in a Dell Inspiron notebook. The control unit

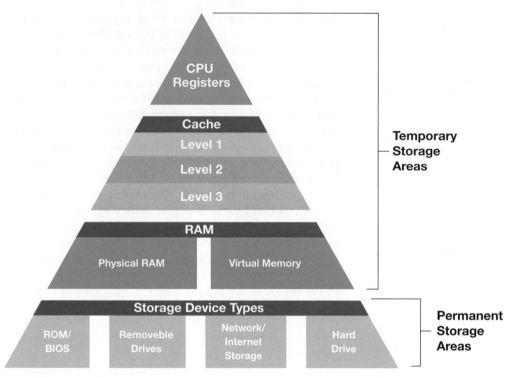

Figure 11

The CPU has multiple stages of internal memory, just a part of the overall hierarchy of memory storage.

interprets the code's bits according to the instruction set the CPU designers laid out for that particular CPU. Based on this process of translation, the control unit then knows how to set up all the switches on the CPU so that the proper operation will occur.

Because humans are the ones who write the initial instructions, all of the commands in an instruction set are written in a language called **assembly language**, which is easier for humans to work with than binary. Many CPUs have similar assembly commands in their instruction sets, including the commands listed here:

ADD	Add
SUB	Subtract
MUL	Multiply
DIV	Divide
MOVE	Move data to RAM
STORE	Move data to a CPU register
EQU	Check if equal

CPUs differ in the choice of additional assembly language commands selected for the instruction set. Each CPU design team works to develop an instruction set that is both powerful and speedy.

However, because the CPU knows and recognizes only patterns of 0s and 1s, it cannot understand assembly language directly, so these human-readable instructions are translated into long strings of binary code. The control unit uses these long strings of binary code called **machine language** to set up the hardware in the CPU for the rest of the operations it needs to perform. Machine language is a binary code for computer instructions, much like the ASCII code is a binary code for letters and characters. Similar to each letter or character having its own unique combination of 0s and 1s assigned to it, a CPU has a table of codes consisting of combinations of 0s and 1s for each of its commands. If the CPU sees a particular pattern of bits arrive, it knows the work it must do. Figure 12 shows a few commands in both assembly language and machine language.

Stage 3: The Execute Stage

The **arithmetic logic unit (ALU)** is the part of the CPU designed to perform mathematical operations such as addition, subtraction, multiplication, and division and to test the comparison of values such as *greater than, less than*, and *equal to*. For example, in calculating an average, the ALU is where the addition and division operations would take place. The ALU also performs logical OR, AND, and NOT operations. For example, in determining whether a student can graduate, the ALU would need to ascertain whether the student had taken all required courses AND obtained a passing grade in each of them. The ALU is specially designed to execute such calculations flawlessly and with incredible speed.

The ALU is fed data from the CPU's registers. The amount of data a CPU can process at a time is based in part on the amount of data each register can hold. The number of bits a computer can work with at a time is referred to as its **word size**. Therefore, a 64-bit processor can process more information faster than a 32-bit processor.

Stage 4: The Store Stage

In the final stage, the result produced by the ALU is stored back in the registers. The instruction itself will explain which register should be used to store the answer. Once the entire instruction has been completed, the next instruction will be fetched, and the fetch-decode-execute-store sequence will begin again.

Making CPUs Even Faster

Knowing how to build a CPU that can run faster than the competition can make a company rich. However, building a faster CPU is not easy. A new product launch must take into consideration the time it will take to design, manufacture, and test that processor. When the processor finally

Figure 12 | REPRESENTATIONS OF SAMPLE CPU COMMANDS

Human Language for Command	CPU Command in Assembly Language (Language Used by Programmers)	CPU Command in Machine Language (Language Used in the CPU's Instruction Set)
Add	ADD	1110 1010
Subtract	SUB	0001 0101
Multiply	MUL	1111 0000
Divide	DIV	0000 1111

hits the market, it must be faster than the competition if the manufacturer hopes to make a profit. To create a CPU that will be released 36 months from now, it must be built to perform at least twice as fast as anything currently available.

Gordon Moore, the cofounder of processor manufacturer Intel, predicted more than 40 years ago that the number of transistors on a processor would double every 18 months. Known as **Moore's Law**, this prediction has been remarkably accurate—but only with tremendous engineering ingenuity. The first 8086 chip had only 29,000 transistors and ran at 5 MHz. Advances in the number of transistors on processors through the 1970s, 1980s, and 1990s continued to align with Moore's prediction.

However, there was a time near the turn of the 21st century when skeptics questioned how much longer Moore's Law would hold true. These skeptics were proved wrong with the microprocessor's continued growth in power. Today's Intel i7 chip has 774 million transistors—more than 18 times the transistor count of the Pentium 4 from the year 2000. Moreover, Intel's Itanium 9300 flaunts a whopping 2.3 billion transistors! How much longer can Moore's prediction hold true? Only time will tell.

Processor manufacturers can increase CPU performance in many different ways. One approach is to use a technique called *pipelining* to boost performance. Another approach is to design the CPU's instruction set so that it contains specialized, faster instructions for handling multimedia and graphics. In addition, some CPUs, such as Intel's i7 980X or the AMD Phenom II X6 processors, now have six independent processing paths inside, with one CPU chip doing the work of six separate CPU units. Some heavy computational problems are attacked by large numbers of computers actually clustered together to work at the same time.

Pipelining

As an instruction is processed, the CPU runs sequentially through the four stages of processing: fetch, decode, execute, and store. **Pipelining** is a technique that allows the CPU to work on more than one instruction (or stage of processing) at a time, thereby boosting CPU performance.

For example, without pipelining, it may take four clock cycles to complete one instruction (one clock cycle for each of the four processing stages). However, with a four-stage pipeline, the computer can process four instructions at the same time. Like an automobile assembly line, instead of waiting for one car to go completely through each process of assembly, painting, and so on, you can have four cars going through the assembly line at the same time. When every component of the assembly line is done with its process, the cars all move on to the next stage.

Pipelined architectures allow several instructions to be processed at the same time. The ticks of the system clock (the clock cycle) indicate when all instructions move to the next process. The secret of pipelining is that the CPU is allowed to be fetching one instruction while it is simultaneously decoding another, executing a third, storing a fourth, and so on. Using pipelining, a four-stage processor can potentially run up to four times faster because some instruction is finishing every clock cycle rather than waiting four cycles for each instruction to finish. In Figure 13a, a nonpipelined instruction takes four clock cycles to be completed, whereas in Figure 13b, the four instructions have been completed in the same time using pipelining.

The number of stages in a pipeline depends entirely on design decisions. Earlier we analyzed a CPU that went through four stages in the execution of an instruction. The Intel Pentium 4 with hyper-threading featured a 31-stage pipeline, and the PowerPC G5 processor used a 10-stage pipeline. Thus, similar to an assembly line, in a 31-stage pipeline, as many as 31 different instructions can be processed at any given time, making the processing of information much faster. However, because so many aspects of the CPU design interact, you cannot predict performance based solely on the number of stages in a pipeline.

Does Your Computer Need More Power? Team It Up!

The history of computing shows us that processing power increases tremendously each year. One strategy in use now for continuing that trend is cluster computing. If one computer is powerful, then two are twice as powerful—if you can get them to work together. A *computing cluster* is a group of computers, connected by specialized clustering software, that works together to solve complex equations. Most clusters work on something called the *balancing principle*, whereby computational work is transferred from overloaded (busy) computers in the cluster to computers that have more computing resources available. Computing clusters, although not as fast as supercomputers (single computers with extremely high processing capabilities), can perform computations faster than one computer working alone and are used for complex calculations such as weather forecasting and graphics rendering. You can now rent time on computing clusters through services like PurePowua (**www.purepowua.com**), where you can upload and remotely control your job from your desktop as it runs on a cluster of computers.

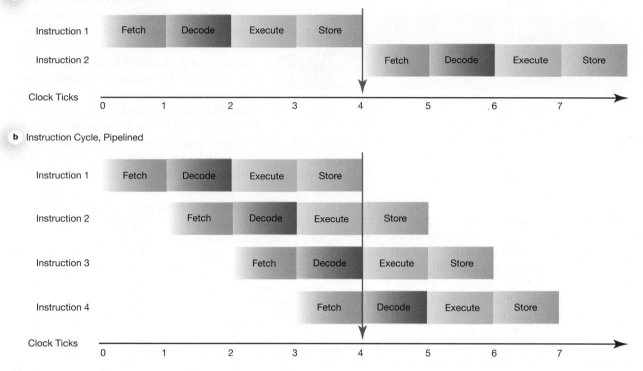

a Instruction Cycle, Non-Pipelined

Instruction 1 | Fetch | Decode | Execute | Store

Instruction 2 | Fetch | Decode | Execute | Store

Clock Ticks
0   1   2   3   4   5   6   7

b Instruction Cycle, Pipelined

Instruction 1 | Fetch | Decode | Execute | Store

Instruction 2 | Fetch | Decode | Execute | Store

Instruction 3 | Fetch | Decode | Execute | Store

Instruction 4 | Fetch | Decode | Execute | Store

Clock Ticks
0   1   2   3   4   5   6   7

Figure 13

Instead of (a) waiting for each instruction to complete, (b) pipelining allows the system to work on more than one set of instructions at one time.

There is a cost to pipelining a CPU as well. The CPU must be designed so that each stage (fetch, decode, execute, and store) is independent. This means that each stage must be able to run at the same time that the other three stages are running. This requires more transistors and a more complicated hardware design.

Specialized Multimedia Instructions

Each design team that develops a new CPU tries to imagine what users' greatest needs will be in four or five years. Currently, several processors on the market reflect this consideration by incorporating specialized multimedia instructions into the basic instruction set.

Hardware engineers have redesigned the chip so that the instruction set contains new commands that are customized to speed up the work needed for video and audio processing. For example, Intel has integrated into its processor designs Streaming Single Instruction Multiple Data (SIMD) Extensions, adding a special group of 157 commands to the basic instruction set. These multimedia-specific instructions work to accelerate video, speech, and image processing in the CPU.

Multiple Processing Efforts

Many high-end server systems employ a **quad processor design** that has four completely separate CPU chips on one motherboard. Often, these server systems can later be scaled so that they can accommodate four, six, or even twelve processors. The Cray Jaguar supercomputer has a total of 37,376 independent processors!

Meanwhile, Intel is promoting a technology called *multi-core processing* in its Core processor line of chips. Chips with dual-core processing capabilities have two separate parallel processing paths inside them, so they are almost as fast as two separate CPUs. It is not quite twice as fast because the system must do some extra work to decide which processor will work on which part of the problem and to recombine the results each CPU produces.

Dual-core processing is especially helpful because antivirus software and other security programs often run in the background as you use your system. A dual-core processor enables these multiple applications to execute much more quickly than with traditional CPUs. Six-core processors, like the Intel i7 Extreme Edition, are appearing in high-performance home-based systems now as well,

---

Today's Supercomputers: The Fastest of the Fast

Supercomputers are the biggest and most powerful type of computer. Scientists and engineers use these computers to solve complex problems or to perform massive computations. Some supercomputers are single computers with multiple processors, whereas others consist of multiple computers that work together.

The top spot on the June 2011 TOP500 List was won by the Japanese K computer. It operates at a peak of more than 8 petaflops (or 8 quadrillion operations per second). That's almost 90,000 times faster than the fastest personal computer. In fact, the K computer is faster than the next five supercomputer systems on the TOP500 List combined!

Check out the current crop of the world's fastest supercomputers at the TOP500 site (**www.top500.org**).

executing six separate processing paths. Multiprocessor systems are often used when intensive computational problems need to be solved in such areas as computer simulations, video production, and graphics processing.

Certain types of problems are well suited to a parallel-processing environment. In **parallel processing**, there is a large network of computers, with each computer working on a portion of the same problem simultaneously. To be a good candidate for parallel processing, a problem must be one that can be divided into a set of tasks that can be run simultaneously. So, for example, a problem where millions of faces are being compared with a target image for recognition is easily adapted to a parallel setting. The target face can be compared at the same time to many hundreds of faces. But if the next step of an algorithm can be started only after the results of the previous step have been computed, parallel processing will present no advantages.

A simple analogy of parallel processing is a laundromat. Instead of taking all day to do five loads of laundry with one machine, you can bring all your laundry to a laundromat, load it into five separate machines, and finish it all in approximately the same time it would have taken you to do just one load on a single machine. In real life, parallel processing is used in complex weather forecasting to run calculations over many different regions around the globe; in the airline industry to analyze customer information in an effort to forecast demand; and by the government in census data compilation.

Thus, what you can continue to expect from CPUs in the future is that they will continue to get smaller and faster and consume less power. This fits with the current demands of consumers for more powerful portable computing devices.

At the most basic level of binary 1s and 0s, computers are systems of switches that can accomplish impressive tasks. By understanding the hardware components that make up your computer system, you can use your system more effectively and make better buying decisions.

Multiple Choice

Instructions: Answer the multiple-choice questions below for more practice with key terms and concepts from this Technology in Focus feature.

1. Which is *not* a typical use of parallel processing systems?
   a. computer simulations
   b. word processing
   c. weather modeling
   d. graphics processing

2. What is another name for the base 10 number system?
   a. decimal notation
   b. binary number system
   c. hexadecimal notation
   d. integer system

3. Which encoding scheme can represent the alphabets of all modern and historic languages?
   a. base 2 number system
   b. Unicode
   c. ASCII
   d. scientific

4. Moore's Law is best described as
   a. an observation of the rate of increasing transistor density.
   b. a physical principle.
   c. a legal construct limiting performance.
   d. an advertising campaign by Intel.

5. To regulate the internal timing of a computer system, the motherboard uses
   a. a system clock.
   b. software simulation.
   c. RAM.
   d. a register.

6. Special areas of memory storage built into the CPU are known as
   a. switches.
   b. semiconductors.
   c. registers.
   d. integrated circuits.

7. Which is the correct set of steps in the machine cycle?
   a. execute, store, fetch, decode
   b. store, fetch, execute, decode
   c. decode, execute, fetch, store
   d. fetch, decode, execute, store

8. All data inside the computer is stored as
   a. bytes.
   b. bits.
   c. switches.
   d. cache memory.

9. Which statement about pipelining is *false*?
   a. Pipelining boosts CPU performance.
   b. Pipeline design is used in many modern CPUs.
   c. Pipelining requires a less complicated hardware design.
   d. Pipelining allows the computer to process multiple instructions simultaneously.

10. From fastest to slowest, which is the fastest sequence of accessing memory?
    a. RAM, Level 1 cache, Level 2 cache, Level 3 cache
    b. registers, Level 1 cache, Level 2 cache, RAM
    c. Level 1 cache, Level 2 cache, RAM, registers
    d. Level 2 cache, Level 1 cache, registers, RAM

chapter 8

digital lifestyle:
managing digital data and devices

Marilyn Nieves/
Vetta/Getty Images

A Digital Lifestyle

OBJECTIVE:

What are the changes that have brought us a digital lifestyle? *(p. 360)*

LockieCurrie/
iStockphoto.com

Digital Telephony

OBJECTIVES:

How do cell phone and smartphone components resemble a traditional computer? *(p. 362)*

Why would I use VoIP? *(p. 371)*

 Sound Byte: Smartphones Are Really Smart

Sound Byte: Connecting with Bluetooth

Active Helpdesk: Keeping Your Data on Hand

Palsur/
iStockphoto.com

Digital Media and Information

OBJECTIVES:

How is digital media different from analog? *(p. 373)*

How is digital media created and what changes has it brought? *(p. 375)*

How do I create and watch digital video? *(p. 383)*

Active Helpdesk: Using Portable Media Players

© ryccio/
iStockphoto.com

Digital Convergence

OBJECTIVE:

What new kinds of mobile devices are available? *(p. 390)*

Scan here for more info on How Cool Is This? ▶

how cool is *this?*

TiVo is not the only game in town. **PVR** (personal video recorder) software is now available, free of charge, for every style of operating system. Using a PVR, you can **record** standard or HD television broadcasts on your hard drive and then watch them when you have the time. **Free** programs like XBMC Media Center and MeediOS let you pause and rewind live TV shows and include features that allow you to automatically detect and **skip** commercials. You even have access to a TV **listings** guide and can schedule your PVR from any location using the Web.

grzym/Shutterstock.com

A Digital Lifestyle

Computers today are central to everyday life. Which part of your life isn't touched by some sort of computer or digital technology? Computer-like devices, such as smartphones and iPads, are everywhere. Much of your entertainment—playing games, watching movies and television, and downloading songs—is probably delivered digitally via the Internet.

Do you really understand how all this digital technology works? Do you know all of your options so you can enjoy the digital devices and digital media you purchase to the fullest extent? In this chapter, we explore the key aspects of your digital life—digital telephony, digital media, and digital convergence—and help you understand how the related technologies work so you can use them to your best advantage.

When did everything go "digital"? It used to be that everything was analog. Today, no matter what you're interested in—music, movies, television, radio, stock prices—digital information is the key. All forms of entertainment have migrated to the digital domain (see Figure 8.1). Phone systems and television signals are now digital streams of data. MP3 files encode digital forms of music, and digital cameras and video cameras are now commonplace. In Hollywood, feature films are being shot entirely with digital equipment, and many movie theaters use digital projection equipment. Satellite radio systems such as SiriusXM satellite radio and HD Radio are broadcast in digital formats.

What is special about digital? Any kind of information can be digitized (measured and converted to a stream of numeric values). Consider sound. It is carried to your ears by sound waves, which are actually patterns of pressure changes in the air. Images are our interpretation of the changing intensity of light waves around us. These sound and light waves are called **analog** waves or continuous waves. They illustrate the loudness of a sound or the brightness of the colors in an image at a given moment in time. They are continuous signals because you would never have to lift your pencil off the page to draw them; they are just long, continuous lines.

First-generation recording devices such as vinyl records and analog television broadcasts were designed to reproduce these sound and light waves. A needle in the groove of a vinyl record vibrates in the same pattern as the original sound wave. Analog television signals are actually waves that tell an analog TV how to display the same color and brightness as is seen in the production studio. However, it's difficult to describe a wave, even mathematically. The simplest sounds, such as that of middle C on a piano, have the simplest shapes, like the one shown in Figure 8.2a. However, something like the word *hello* generates a highly complex pattern, like the one shown in Figure 8.2b.

What advantages do digital formats have over analog ones? Digital formats describe signals as long strings of numbers. This digital representation gives us a simple way to describe sound and light waves exactly so that sounds and images can be reproduced perfectly each time. In addition, we already have easy ways to distribute digital information, such as streaming movies or attaching files to a Facebook message. Thus, digital information can be reproduced exactly and distributed easily. Both give it huge advantages over an analog format.

How can a sequence of numbers express complicated analog shapes? The answer is provided by something called *analog-to-digital conversion*. In analog-to-digital conversion, the incoming analog signal is measured many times each second. The strength of the signal at each

Figure 8.1 | ANALOG VERSUS DIGITAL ENTERTAINMENT

	Analog	Digital
Publishing	Magazines, books	Ebooks, ezines
Music	Vinyl record albums and cassette tapes	CDs and MP3 files
Photography	35-mm single-lens reflex (SLR) cameras Photos stored on film	Digital cameras, including digital SLRs Photos stored as digital files
Video	8-mm, VHS, and Hi8 camcorders Film stored on tapes	High-definition digital video (DV) cameras Film stored as digital files; distributed on DVD and Blu-ray Discs and streamed
Radio	AM/FM radio	HD Radio Sirius/XM satellite radio
Television	Conventional broadcast analog TV	High-definition digital television (HDTV)

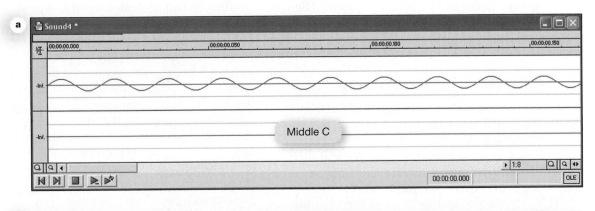

Middle C

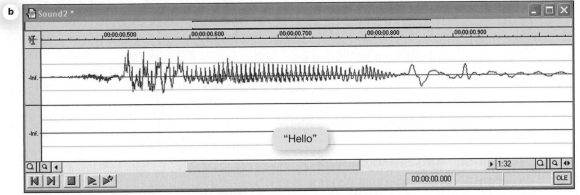

"Hello"

Figure 8.2

(a) This is an analog wave showing the simple, pure sound of a piano playing middle C. (b) This is the complex wave produced when a person says "Hello."

measurement is recorded as a simple number. The series of numbers produced by the analog-to-digital conversion process gives us the digital form of the wave. Figure 8.3 shows analog and digital versions of the same wave. In Figure 8.3a, you see the original, continuous analog wave. You could draw that wave without lifting your pencil from the page. In Figure 8.3b, the wave has been digitized and is no longer a single line; instead, it is represented as a series of points or numbers.

How has the change from analog to digital technologies affected our lifestyle? When the market for communication devices for entertainment media—like photographs, music, and video—switched over to a digital standard, we began to have products with new and useful capabilities. Small devices can now hold huge collections of a variety of types of information. We can interact with our information any time we like, in ways that, prior to the conversion to digital media, had been

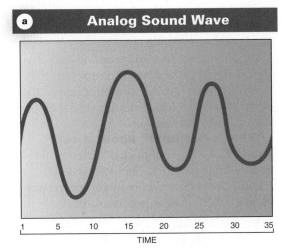

Analog Sound Wave

TIME

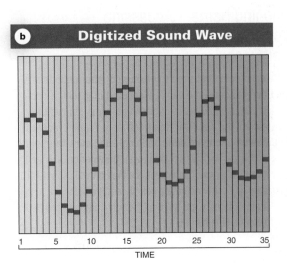

Digitized Sound Wave

TIME

Figure 8.3

(a) A simple analog wave. (b) A digitized version of the same wave.

too expensive or too difficult to learn. The implications of the shift to digital media are continually evolving.

Digital Telephony

Communication has changed radically in the digital age. Chapter 3 discussed the use of wikis, blogs, RSS feeds, and other Web-based tools for connecting people and their ideas. All of these software applications are dependent on digital information.

Hardware devices that support communication also have evolved because of digital technologies. **Telephony**, the use of equipment to provide voice communications over a distance, has shifted from an analog science to a digital one. In this section, we examine cell phones, smartphones, and Voice over Internet Protocol (VoIP) devices to see how they are changing to meet modern communication needs.

Cell Phones and Smartphones

What's the difference between a cell phone and a smartphone? The **cellular phone** (or **cell phone**) has evolved from a clunky, boxlike device to a compact, fully featured communication and information storage device. Cell phones offer all of the features available on a traditional telephone system, including automatic redial, call timers, and voice mail capabilities. Most cell phones also feature voice-activated dialing, which is important for hands-free operation. In addition, many cell phones offer Internet access, text messaging, personal information management (PIM) features, voice recording, GPS services, and digital image and video

capture. In fact, the category of inexpensive phones equipped with many of these abilities is now referred to as *feature phones*.

Smartphones extend the power of a cell phone. A smartphone requires a data plan from the cell phone provider. This is logical because a smartphone user is likely to spend a lot of time accessing the Internet to upload and download data. Most smartphones have larger screen areas, WiFi accessibility, and enough computing power to run versions of programs like Microsoft Excel or even video editing software.

Are cell phones and smartphones computers? Cell phones and smartphones have the same components as any computer: a processor (central processing unit, or CPU), memory, and input and output devices, as shown in Figure 8.4. Cell/smartphones also require their own operating system (OS) software and have their own application software. So modern cell phones and smartphones are computers.

How Cellular Works

How do cell phones use digital signals? When you speak into a cell phone, the sound enters the microphone as a sound wave. Because analog sound waves need to be digitized (that is, converted into a sequence of 1s and 0s that the cell phone's processor can understand), an **analog-to-digital converter chip** converts your voice's sound waves into digital signals. Next, the digital data must be compressed, or squeezed, into the smallest possible space so that it will transmit more quickly to another phone. The processor cannot perform the mathematical operations required at this stage quickly enough, so a specialized chip called the **digital signal processor** is included in the cell phone to handle the compression work. Finally, the digital data is transmitted as a radio wave through the cellular network to the destination phone.

When you receive an incoming call, the digital signal processor decompresses the incoming message. An amplifier boosts the signal to make it loud enough, and it is then passed on to the speaker.

What's "cellular" about a cell phone? A set of connected "cells" makes up a cellular network. Each cell is a geographic area centered on a **base transceiver station**, which is a large communications tower with antennas, amplifiers, receivers, and transmitters. When you place a call on a cell phone, a base station picks up the request for service. The station then passes the request to a central location called a **mobile switching center**. The reverse process occurs when you receive an incoming call. A telecommunications company builds its network by constructing a series of cells that overlap in an attempt to guarantee that its cell phone customers have coverage no matter where they are.

As you move during your phone call, the mobile switching center monitors the strength of the signal between your cell phone and the closest base station. When the signal is no longer strong enough between your cell phone and the base station, the mobile switching center orders the next base station to take charge of your call. When your cell phone "drops out," it may be because the distance between base stations was too great to provide an adequate signal.

Cell Phone Components

What does the processor inside a cell/smartphone do? Although the processor inside a cell/smartphone is obviously not as fast or as high-powered as a processor in a desktop computer, it is still responsible for a great number of tasks. The processor coordinates sending all of the data among the other electronic components inside the phone. It also runs the cell/smartphone's operating system, which provides a user interface so that you can change phone settings, store information, play games, and so on. Popular processors for cell/smartphones include the Qualcomm Snapdragon, the Apple A4, and the Marvell XScale processor. Some processors use dual-core processing technology, which is also used in some desktop processors.

When shopping for a new phone, be well prepared. Use published benchmarking results to compare performance. These benchmarks are often published on the *PC Magazine* Web site (**www.pcmag.com**) or at *Wired* (**www.wired.com**).

Is there a standard operating system for cell/smartphones? Each cell/smartphone manufacturer makes its own small changes to the operating system and designs its own user interface. So when moving between different cell/smartphones, you will likely see a different set of commands and icons.

There are a number of operating systems in the cell/smartphone market now. Many smartphones use the Windows Phone 7 operating system. Apple's iPhone uses iOS, a version of the OS X operating system that is used in Apple's personal computers. The HP Pre uses its own in-house-developed webOS. These operating systems are required to translate the user's commands into instructions for the processor.

There are several free operating systems that a manufacturer can use as a base for its cell/smartphone operating system. The most successful open source OS is the Android collection developed by Google. Other open source mobile operating systems include Meego, Symbian, and Openmoko. The advantage of an open source mobile OS is that you can leverage the creativity of many developers in creating great applications and new phone designs.

Figure 8.5 illustrates some of the different and creative user interfaces featured among cell/smartphone operating systems.

What does the memory chip inside a cell/smartphone do? The operating system and the information you save in your cell/smartphone, such as phone numbers and addresses, need to be stored in memory. The operating system is stored in read-only memory (ROM) because the phone would be useless without that key piece of software. As you learned earlier, two kinds of memory are used in computers: volatile memory, which requires power to

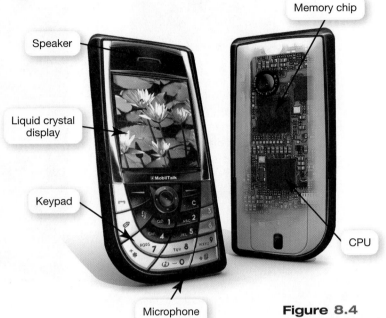

Figure 8.4

Inside your cell phone, you'll find a CPU, a memory chip, input devices such as a microphone and a keypad, and output devices such as a display screen and a speaker.

Figure 8.5

(a) iOS 5, (b) Windows Phone 7, and (c) Android are all cellular operating systems.

store data, and nonvolatile memory, which stores data even when the power is turned off. ROM is nonvolatile, or permanent, memory. This means that when you turn off your phone, the data that is stored in ROM, which includes the operating system, remains in memory.

Other phone data, such as ring tones, is stored in separate internal memory chips. Full-featured cell phones have as many as 200 MB of internal memory and support additional memory through micro SD flash cards that can store up to 64 GB, as shown in Figure 8.6. Micro SD cards are easy to install in a phone, while some models simply have external slots for an SD card. You can use that storage for contact data, ring tones, images, songs, videos, and even software applications such as language translators or video games. Not every smartphone allows memory upgrades in this way, however. For example, the iPhone series does not allow you to add any memory.

What input and output devices do cell/smartphones use? The primary input devices for a cell/smartphone are a microphone and a keypad. Some phones, such as the Samsung Impression (see Figure 8.7a), offer both a hidden keyboard and a touch-sensitive screen. The Apple iPhone provides a software-based keyboard (see Figure 8.7b) that supports more than 40 languages.

Cell phones often include a digital camera for capturing photos and video. These cameras are catching up to the quality level of standalone point-and-shoot cameras. For example, the Droid X2 offers a high-quality 8-megapixel (MP) camera with flash and video capture, and the Nokia N8 sports a 12 MP camera with Carl Zeiss lenses. Most cameras on cell/smartphones can record video as well as take still shots. Picture and video messaging is popular with many cell/smartphone users. They can transmit photos and video files via e-mail, post the files to Web sites such as Facebook, or send them directly to other phones.

Cell phone output devices include a speaker and a liquid crystal display (LCD). Higher-end models include full-color, high-resolution LCD screens. Newer on the market are OLED (organic light-emitting diode) displays, which allow very bright, sharp imaging and draw less power.

Figure 8.6

You can insert additional memory by installing a micro SD flash card in a smartphone.

Figure 8.7

(a) The Samsung Impression includes a touch screen and a built-in QWERTY keyboard. (b) The Apple iPhone has a touch keyboard that supports more than 40 languages and a range of character sets.

High-resolution displays are becoming increasingly popular because more people are using their cell/smartphones to send and receive the digital images included in multimedia text messages and e-mail, and even to watch TV (see Figure 8.8).

Cell/smartphone and cable providers are teaming up to deliver broadcast TV programs directly to cell/smartphones through services such as Verizon V CAST and Sprint TV. A developing standard named Mobile DTV allows cell/smartphones or other mobile devices like tablets to receive free broadcasts from television stations. Cable providers and vendors like Netflix also provide streaming video content to mobile devices. With all this video content, having a high-quality screen is becoming more and more important.

SOUND BYTE

Smartphones Are Really Smart

In this Sound Byte, you'll learn how to use a smartphone as a powerful tool to communicate, calculate, and organize your workload.

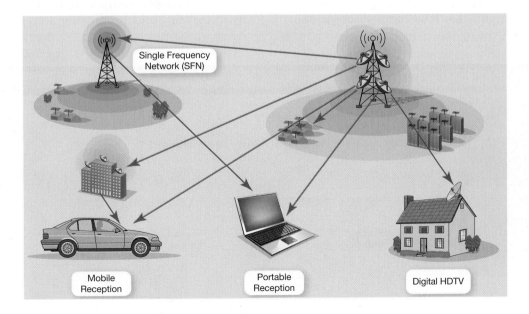

Figure 8.8

The Mobile DTV system allows local TV stations to broadcast live, digital content to mobile devices.

Figure 8.9

The Android Market is one of many online stores delivering software for mobile devices.

Figure 8.10

The Windows Sync Center makes it easy to arrange for synchronization of all your mobile devices.

>To launch Sync Center, click the **Start** button, select **Control Panel**, and double-click the **Sync Center** icon.

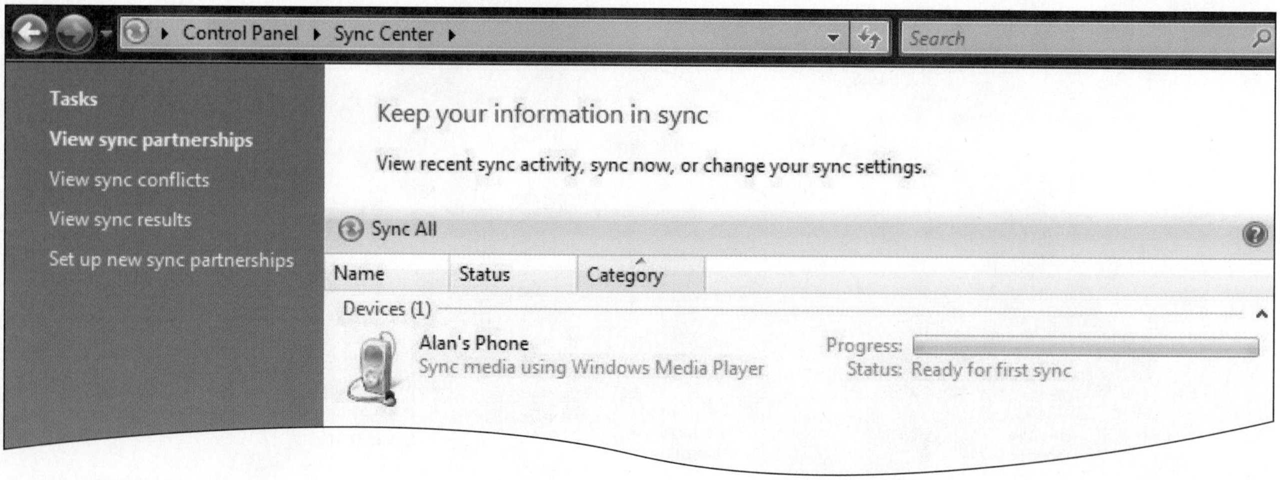

What cell/smartphone software is available? The operating system of most mobile devices comes with a standard collection of software such as a to-do list, contact manager, and calendar. Modified versions of application software such as Microsoft Word, Excel, Outlook, and PowerPoint are available for some high-end smartphones. A variety of games, tools, and reference applications are available from numerous software companies. A good source to locate software applications for your phone is GetJar (**www.getjar.com**). Many manufacturers have Web-based software stores, like iTunes for the Apple iPhone and the BlackBerry App World for RIM's BlackBerry devices. The Android developer community has held competitions to spur

the creation of new software applications for Android-based phones. Many software applications are available for Android through the Web and the Android Market (see Figure 8.9).

Synchronizing

How do I move information from my computer to my smartphone? There are two main ways to transfer information between your phone and computer—wired and wireless. Let's start by looking at wired solutions. The high-density micro SD cards available for phones have room for thousands of songs, videos, or data files. Some phones are designed with a flash card that can be easily removed and slipped directly into a flash card reader on the computer. Almost all phones are designed with a USB port. Some have a mini-USB connector, while other models require a special cable to connect the phone to a standard USB port. Once connected using a USB data cable, your phone will appear on your computer like an additional flash drive, and you can drag and drop files to it. You can also charge your phone through the USB cable.

You can coordinate the changes you make to your to-do lists, schedules, and other files on your phone with the files on your home or office computer. This process of updating your data so that the files on your cell/smartphone and computer are the same is called **synchronizing** or **syncing**. To synchronize your computer and the device, simply connect your phone via the appropriate USB cable.

Microsoft has recognized the vast increase in portable computing devices by integrating synchronization into the

Windows operating system. The Sync Center (see Figure 8.10), which is accessed from the Control Panel, allows you to set up automatic or manual synchronization. Make sure the device you are trying to set up synchronization parameters for is connected to your computer and then launch the Sync Center. Select the Set up new sync partnerships option to view available devices and configure their synchronization options.

How do I transfer information to and from my phone wirelessly? There are multiple technologies for handling wireless file transfer. **Bluetooth** technology uses radio waves to transmit data signals over short distances (approximately 30 feet for Bluetooth 1 and 60 feet for Bluetooth 2 and 3). Bluetooth 3 devices are the newest on the market and have a throughput about eight times faster than Bluetooth 2. Most cell/smartphones on the market today are Bluetooth-enabled, meaning they include a small Bluetooth chip that allows them to transfer data wirelessly to any other Bluetooth-enabled device. One benefit Bluetooth has over infrared, a wireless connection used in the past, is that a direct line of sight does not have to be present between two devices for them to communicate. You also can use Bluetooth

SOUND BYTE

Connecting with Bluetooth

In this Sound Byte, you'll learn what freedoms Bluetooth affords you, and how to use Bluetooth devices.

to synchronize your device with your computer. Bluetooth accessories such as earpieces, mice, keyboards, and even stereo headsets are available.

Another way to wirelessly transfer data to your phone is to use a WiFi 3G/4G connection through a cloud service. A number of Web services are now available to synchronize your e-mail, files, contacts, and calendars instantly and wirelessly. SugarSync, for example, will automatically wirelessly sync folders of data and the photos on your Android phone to your home computers (see Figure 8.11). These Web services

Figure 8.11

A cloud service allows you to keep the information on your phone instantly in sync with your other computing devices.

follow the model of "cloud computing," where Internet-based services and resources are distributed to users instead of being installed as an application on the user's computer. Apple's iOS 5 has integrated cloud support into several of the applications like Calendar, iTunes, PhotoStream, Contacts, and Mail.

There are other providers of wireless synchronization for mobile devices. Google Sync works with iPhones, Blackberry phones, Symbian, and Windows Mobile devices. All of your Google e-mail, calendar events, and contacts are automatically backed up online instantly on the Google servers. Even the Amazon Kindle uses wireless synchronization so that if you read a bit further in your e-book on your phone, when you get to your office, the Kindle software on your PC will have automatically updated to bookmark the new page you're on.

Text Messaging

What is SMS? Short message service (SMS)—often just called *text messaging*—is a technology that allows you to send short text messages (comprising up to 160 characters) over mobile networks. To send SMS messages from your cell/smartphone, you use the keypad or a pre-saved template and type your message. You can send SMS messages to other mobile devices or to any e-mail address. You also can use SMS to send short text messages from your home computer to mobile devices such as your friend's cell/smartphone.

How does SMS work? SMS uses the cell phone network to transmit messages. When you send an SMS message, an SMS calling center receives the message and delivers it to the appropriate mobile device using

something called *store-and-forward* technology. This technology allows users to send SMS messages to any other SMS device in the world.

Many SMS fans like text messaging because it allows the receivers to read messages when it is convenient for them and is quicker than e-mail. Companies now support texting in many ways, so for example, your bank may allow you to text commands to request account balances or details about your last transaction, and the bank will text the requested information back to you. As shown in the table in Figure 8.12, several companies provide useful services based on text messaging.

If you plan to do a lot of texting, check the phone's feature list in advance and look for a phone with a good text prediction algorithm. With such an algorithm, typing a single letter pulls up a list of popular words beginning with that letter, saving you typing time. For example, the T9 (Text on 9 keys) algorithm also "learns" from your usage patterns and displays the most-used word first.

Can I send and receive photos and videos using a cell/smartphone? SMS technology allows you to send only text messages. However, an extension of SMS called **multimedia message service (MMS)** allows you to send messages that include text, sound, images, and video clips to other phones or e-mail addresses. MMS messages actually arrive as a series of messages; you view the text, then the image, and then the sound, and so on. You can then choose to save just one part of the message (such as the image), all of it, or none of it. MMS users can subscribe to financial, sports, and weather services that will "push" information

Figure 8.12 | TEXT MESSAGING INFORMATION SERVICES

SMS Code	Service Name	Web site	Description
466453 (google)	Google SMS Search	**www.google.com/mobile/sms**	Obtains information such as addresses, phone numbers, driving directions, sports scores, and movie listings from the Google search engine.
44636 (4Info)	4INFO	**alerts.4info.com**	Similar to Google SMS, but also handles flight information and mobile coupons.
242 242 (cha cha)	ChaCha	**www.chacha.com**	Human "guides" provide answers to any question in conversational English.
3109043113	411 sms	**www.411sms.com**	Offers address and phone listings, turn-by-turn directions, movie showtimes, stock quotes, hot spot locations, dictionary definitions, horoscopes, and foreign language translations.

to them, sending it automatically to their phones in MMS format.

Mobile Internet

How do I get Internet service for my smartphone? Just as you have an Internet service provider (ISP) for Internet access for your desktop or notebook computer, you must have a **wireless Internet service provider** (or **wireless ISP**) to connect your smartphone to the Internet. Phone companies that provide phone calling plans (such as T-Mobile, Verizon, and AT&T) usually double as wireless ISPs. An Internet connectivity plan or text messaging plan is usually known as a **data plan**. Data charges are separate from phone calling charges and are provided at rates different from voice calls. Most carriers provide separate plans for different levels of texting usage and for various levels of data transfer to and from Internet sites. Before subscribing to a data plan, you should assess your needs: How often do you download new wallpaper, ring tones, or games? Do you use your smartphone's Internet access to download files from e-mails or from your company Web site? Begin by estimating how many kilobytes of data you transfer up and down from the Internet each month. Then select a plan that provides adequate service at a good price.

At what speed is digital information transferred to my smartphone? A smartphone connection is much slower than the Internet connection you have at your home. Although broadband speeds of 50 megabits per second (Mbps) are achievable at home using a cable or fiber-optic connection, your smartphone will connect at a much lower speed, depending on which technology you are using (see Figure 8.13).

Providers have introduced many smartphones based on two standards that support fast data transfer technologies:

411 for Answers

Most phone services charge as much as $2 for a 411 call for information on a phone listing or address. Now there is competition. The Bing 411 service is a free way to find out the address of, directions to, or phone number of a business or person. A call to 1-800-BING-411 gets you this information at no charge. If you say "text my phone," Bing 411 can text you the phone listing or even step-by-step driving directions.

If you are looking for a different kind of information, try the ChaCha service. You can either call (1-800-2chacha) or text (242 242) with any kind of question, and real human "guides" will find the answer and send it back to you. So, answers to questions like the following are just a free call or text away!

- How many calories are there in a slice of pizza?
- When is *American Idol* on tonight?
- Is there a way to get acrylic paint out of jeans?

| Figure 8.13 | CELLULAR CONNECTION SPEEDS |

Network	Availability	Speed (Mbps)
3G	300 major markets	0.6–2.3
WiFi	WiFi hot spots	4–5
4G	Major cities	5–12

Note: Speeds will vary depending on provider and location.

3G and 4G. 3G brought mobile device data transfer rates as high as 1.4 Mbps (or more, under ideal conditions). Uploading the video clip you just recorded at the park or downloading a large PDF file from your company intranet is quicker if you are in range of a WiFi signal. But 3G does have some advantages over WiFi. It is more reliable and less susceptible to interference. Moreover, you won't have to hunt for a WiFi hot spot, because 3G blankets most major urban areas with connectivity.

4G networks are now rolling out across the United States. The promise of 4G is incredible: mobile connection speeds of up to 100 Mbps! Currently, most providers

Figure 8.14

A MiFi device turns your 3G phone signal into a WiFi connection for you and four of your friends.

AP Images/PRNewsFoto/Verizon Wireless

cannot deliver true 4G speeds, but deliver speeds of 3 Mbps to 6 Mbps. These options are faster than 3G but do not meet the rate required to be true 4G, so they are referred to as "near 4G" networks. The expansion of 4G will usher in a new generation of mobile devices and applications that will continue to expand how we think of mobile computing.

Can I use my 3G signal to create a WiFi hotspot for my other devices?

There are devices available that will instantly create a mobile hot spot for you. MiFi (pronounced "my fi") devices, like the Verizon model shown in Figure 8.14, are often available free with a new account from major Internet providers like Verizon and Sprint. The MiFi can fit in a shirt pocket and run for up to four hours on a single charge. It connects to the Internet through the 3G wireless phone network and then distributes the WiFi signal over an area of 30 feet. These personal hot spots can then support up to five WiFi-enabled devices.

Another approach is **tethering**, which makes sure that as long as you have a 3G signal, your computer can access the Internet even when it tells you there are no available wireless networks. Several phones offer this capability. For example, an iPhone 4 can connect your notebook computer through wireless Bluetooth, and

Opera Mini

Figure 8.15

Microbrowser software like Opera lets you quickly switch between open browser windows.

then provide Internet access through the 3G network signal.

How do smartphones display content from the Internet?

On smartphones that have a limited amount of screen space, it is difficult to view Web pages without a great deal of horizontal scrolling. This is because most Web sites are designed for viewing on desktop monitors, which have much wider pixel widths than mobile screens. To enhance your Internet browsing experience on mobile devices, special microbrowser software runs on your phone. **Microbrowser** software provides a Web browser that is optimized to display Web content effectively on the smaller screen (see Figure 8.15). Popular versions of microbrowser software include Internet Explorer Mobile (included with the Windows Mobile OS), Safari on the iPhone, and Opera Mobile. Opera Mobile uses special small-screen rendering technology to reformat the Web images to fit on your smartphone screen, then zooms in with a simple tap. For the best Web experience, consider a phone that has a large screen, such as the HTC HD2, which boasts a 4.3-inch HD touch screen.

More and more Web sites are being created with content specifically designed for wireless devices. This specially designed content, which is text-based and contains no graphics, is written in a format called **Wireless Markup Language (WML)**. Content is designed so that it fits the smaller display screens of handheld mobile devices.

How convenient is e-mail on a cell/smartphone?

A popular feature of cell/smartphones with Internet access lets users check e-mail. BlackBerry handhelds were the first devices that were optimized to check e-mail. BlackBerry pioneered the "push" technology that delivers your e-mail automatically to your phone, so you do not have to deliberately ask for current mail to be delivered. Now many other systems also offer "push" technology. With Internet access, users can always send or receive e-mail through Web-based e-mail accounts like Gmail or Yahoo!

If receiving and sending e-mail while on the go is mission critical for you, check out smartphones with larger displays and integrated keyboards that make it easier to read and respond to messages.

Cell Phone/Smartphone Security

Can I get a virus on my cell/smartphone? Although viruses can already infect cell/smartphones, manufacturers and software engineers are bracing themselves for a tidal wave of viruses targeted to cell/smartphones. With half of users reporting that they send confidential e-mails using their phones and one third of users indicating that they access bank account or credit card information, cell/smartphones are the next most likely realm of attack by cybercriminals. The potential of cell/smartphone viruses ranges from the mildly annoying (certain features of your phone stop working) to the costly (your phone is used without your knowledge to make expensive calls).

Symantec, McAfee, and F-Secure are the leading companies currently providing antivirus software for mobile devices. Products are designed for specific cell/smartphone operating systems; for example, Symantec Mobile Security has versions for the Android, Windows Mobile, Blackberry, and Symbian OS. Often businesses will have their information technology department install and configure an antivirus solution like this for all the phones used in the organization.

Although viruses plaguing cell/smartphones have not yet reached the volume of viruses attacking PC operating systems, with the proliferation of mobile devices it is expected that such virus attacks will increase. If no antivirus program is available for your phone's operating system, the best precautions are common sense ones. Check the phone manufacturer's Web site frequently to see whether your cell/smartphone needs any software upgrades that could patch security holes. In addition, remember that you should not download ring tones, games, or other software from unfamiliar Web sites.

How do I keep my cell/smartphone number private? It seems that every time you fill out a Web form someone is asking for your phone number. If you are concerned about widely distributing your cell/smartphone number and potentially inviting lots of unwanted solicitation calls, you should consider using a virtual phone number. A virtual phone number is a phone number you create that can be assigned to ring on existing phone numbers. Companies such as Telusion (**www.tossabledigits.com**) will sell you a virtual number. Then, when you are filling out a registration form for some Web service, you can input your virtual phone number in the Web form instead of giving out your number. When you set up the virtual account, you can restrict the hours that you will receive calls from that number, and if you are receiving many unwanted calls, you can disable the virtual number without affecting your cell/smartphone service.

Voice over Internet Protocol

Digital telephone services cover more than just mobile phones. Cell phone service is still not 100 percent reliable, and dropped calls and poor reception are a problem in many areas. In addition, the call quality of landline phone service is often superior to cell/smartphone call quality. Landline phones can also be digital using a technology named VoIP (Voice over Internet Protocol). Often people who run home businesses maintain a landline to ensure high voice quality of calls. In many instances, landline phone plans can be cheaper than cell/smartphone plans, especially for international calls.

How is VoIP different from regular telephone service? Voice over Internet Protocol (VoIP) is a form of voice-based Internet communication that turns a standard Internet connection into a means to place phone calls, including long-distance calls. Traditional telephone communications use analog voice data and telephone connections. In contrast, VoIP uses technology similar to that used in e-mail to send your voice data digitally over the Internet.

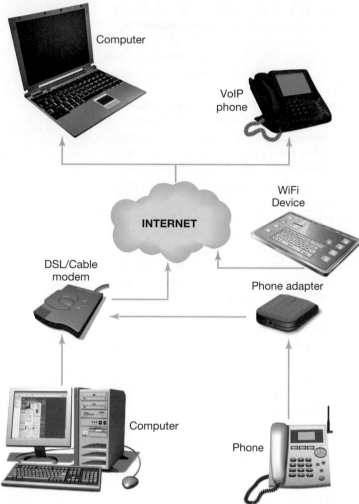

One limitation of VoIP used to be that when you made a call, you had to be at your computer. As VoIP moves out to mobile devices, however, it is possible to place VoIP calls from any WiFi hot spot. For example, there are Skype applications available for mobile devices, like the iPad and the Sony Vita. You can make free calls to other Skype users or make low-cost calls to non-Skype users.

What are the advantages and disadvantages of VoIP? For people who make many long-distance phone calls, the advantage of VoIP is it's free or low cost. Portability is another advantage because all you need is an Internet connection. With Internet accessibility so abundant, you can keep in touch with friends and family no matter where you are. As long as you are covered by a WiFi signal, you can plug in your headset or IP phone, sign on to your VoIP service, and make your call.

Although VoIP is affordable and convenient, it does have drawbacks. Some people regard sound quality and reliability issues as VoIP's primary disadvantages. Another drawback is the loss of service if power is interrupted. Although many traditional phones do not depend on electricity, your Internet connection and IP phone do. One serious drawback when VoIP service was first offered to the public was the inability for 911 calls to be traced back to the caller, unlike with a traditional phone. The FCC now requires all VoIP providers to provide traceable 911 services.

Another issue with VoIP is security. Security risks are similar to the risks associated with e-mail and include the problem of fraud. Spam or having a hacker break into a VoIP system to make unauthorized calls are serious but avoidable problems. In addition, encryption services that convert data into a form that is not easily understood by unauthorized people are being deployed to help protect the very nature of calls made over the Internet. Despite these concerns, VoIP continues to enjoy explosive growth, and the technology will continue to improve.

What new features come with having an Internet-based digital phone at home? Once you are using an Internet-based digital phone system, new features become possible. You can have your telephone messages automatically bundled up as e-mails and sent to your account. If you are watching television and a call comes in,

Figure 8.16

Depending on your VoIP service, you can hold conversations through a computer, a special VoIP telephone, or a regular telephone with an adapter.

What do I need to use VoIP? For the simplest and least costly VoIP service, you need speakers, a microphone, an Internet connection, and a VoIP provider (see Figure 8.16). Depending on the provider you choose, you also may need to install software or a special adapter.

Who are some VoIP providers? Skype is one very well-known provider. Creating a VoIP account with Skype (**www.skype.com**) is similar to creating an instant messaging (IM) account. Skype requires that both callers and receivers have the company's free software installed on their computers. With Skype you can change your online status, look at your contact list, and even integrate the service into your Facebook news feed. Other VoIP services, such as Vonage (**www.vonage.com**), are a bit more complicated to set up and are not free. Major ISPs, like Comcast or Verizon, also provide VoIP phone services as an option you can package with your Internet or cable television plan.

it can be displayed on the screen with caller ID information. Some learning management systems also use VoIP. For example if you are using MyITLab with this course, you can call your professor through VoIP without having their personal phone number.

Digital Media and Information

The entertainment industry has become an all-digital field. Today, books, movies, music, and photographs are created using digital recording devices, processed using digital software systems, and delivered over digital distribution channels. Let's explore what this means for you.

Digital Publishing

Are books dead? The publishing industry is in the process of migrating to digital materials. **Electronic text (etext)** is textual information stored as digital information so it can be stored, manipulated, and transmitted by electronic devices. With the increasing usage of etext, the market for printed materials is changing dramatically. In 2011, Amazon released a corporate report showing over the past year, for every 100 print books sold, it had sold 105 Kindle ebooks. Several authors, such as Stieg Larsson and James Patterson, have each sold over a million ebooks.

eReaders are devices that can display etext and have supporting tools, like note taking, bookmarks, and integrated dictionaries. They are selling at a brisk pace with a dizzying range of offerings in the market, including the Amazon Kindle, Barnes and Noble NOOK, and Sony eReader. Tablets are also helping to popularize the digitized ebook and the electronic versions of major magazines and newspapers. There is evidence that this is increasing all kinds of book buying, not just digital books. In 2011 Amazon had its greatest growth rate in sales, for all products combined, of the past ten years.

There are two popular technologies in representing digital text. Electronic ink (E ink) is a very crisp, sharp grayscale representation of text. The "page" is composed of millions of microcapsules with white and black particles in a clear fluid. Electronic signals can make each spot appear either white or black. E Ink devices reflect the light that shines on the page, like ordinary paper,

How Do You Find Your WiFi?

Detecting a nearby WiFi signal is important if you are looking for Internet connectivity while you are on the move. Some notebooks have a built-in WiFi scanner that displays a row of lights on the case whenever a WiFi signal is available. Keychain fobs that light up when they detect WiFi signals in the vicinity are also available.

If you are running Windows 7, the Connect to a Network dialog box (accessible from the Network and Sharing Center) shows the strength of all wireless networks within range of your computer.

At ThinkGeek (**www.thinkgeek.com**), you may find the most easy-to-use WiFi detector ever. The WiFi Detector t-shirt and the WiFi baseball cap have a logo that lights up to indicate the signal strength of a nearby WiFi network (see Figure 8.17). Find your WiFi and look . . . well, look geeky while doing so!

Figure 8.17

The WiFi Detector T-shirt and cap make a statement— a geeky statement.

Courtesy of ThinkGeek.com

and are not backlit. It is designed to mimic reading regular paper and is more comfortable for many people. E Ink gives great contrast and is much easier to read in direct sunlight. Examples of devices using E Ink include the Amazon Kindle and the Barnes and Noble NOOK.

Another option for presenting etext is high-resolution backlit monitors seen in readers like the iPad or the NOOK Color. These illuminate themselves instead of depending on room lighting conditions. The glass does reflect glare, though, which makes them hard to use in bright, direct sunlight. Some people experience more fatigue in reading from a backlit device than when using E Ink. Also note that electronic

Figure 8.18

The two main technologies for etext display are high-resolution backlit color screens, like on the iPad, and E Ink grayscale displays, like on the Amazon Kindle.

EMMANUEL DUNAND/AFP/Getty Images

ink readers have a battery life of a month or two on a charge while high-resolution color readers hold a single charge for 8–10 hours. Be sure to try both, shown in Figure 8.18, under a variety of conditions before you make a purchase decision.

Do I need a dedicated device just for reading etexts? No. There are software versions of the Kindle and the NOOK that are free downloads and run on either PC or Apple computers. Other texts that have no copyrights can be downloaded and read directly on a computer either as a PDF file or using software like the Microsoft Reader or the MobiPocket reader.

What features make eReaders popular? One big allure of digital publishing is distribution. Ease of access to digital books is very attractive. Even a 1,000-page book can be delivered directly to your eReader in under a minute. An incredible array of titles is available—over 950,000 books are available in just the Amazon Kindle store. In addition, there are millions of texts without copyright that are available for free. Most texts are available at a lower price than they would be in paper.

The basic features of ereading offer many advantages over paper books. Integrated

dictionaries pull up a definition just by highlighting a word. The Kindle, for example, can work with both English and German dictionaries, a help in reading foreign works. Note taking and marking highlights are supported so the text can be searched by your own notes or for specific terms. Notes you make on the book can be shared easily with others. URL links or links to a glossary can be live in the book. Bookmarks are immediately pushed through cloud technology so you can read on one device and pick up with the most current bookmark on another device.

What kinds of file formats are used in electronic publishing? Digital formats for publishing vary. Amazon uses a proprietary format (.azw extension), so books purchased for a Kindle are not transportable to a non-Kindle device. An open format also exists, ePub. Some eReaders support the ePub file format. There is an ePub reader plugin available for the browser Firefox and several standalone software ePub readers like Stanza or MobiPocket Reader.

There are a number of vendors associated with eReader devices. Amazon sells the Kindle device and it connects directly to the Amazon Kindle store. The Barnes and Noble NOOK device works with the

Figure 8.19

Ebooks and audio books can be borrowed freely at most public libraries.

Montgomery County Library

Barnes and Noble ebookstore. There are also many publishers selling ebooks online that can be read on any kind of device. Textbooks can be purchased in ebook format directly from the publisher; for example, the technology publisher O'Reilly has an online ebookstore. Another option is companies like CourseSmart, which offers a yearlong subscription to a digital text that then times out and disappears from your device.

Libraries are now including ebook and audiobook lending as part of their mission (Figure 8.19). Most libraries allow you to borrow up to ten ebooks at a time. There is never a late fee; the book just times out and disappears from your device when the borrowing period expires. Products like the Overdrive Media Console (**search.overdrive.com**) let you search to find which area library has the book you want. Log in to the library Web site and you can download a text any time of day or night. Libraries have a specific number of copies of each ebook title so you may be added to a waitlist if all the copies are checked out, just like with paper books.

Or you might be able to borrow an ebook from a friend. Lending of ebooks is now becoming a popular feature of eReader systems. The Barnes & Noble NOOK, for example, has a Lend Me feature on certain books. An eligible book can be loaned once for a period of 14 days.

Another source of free reading is Project Gutenberg. This repository site is a collection of over 36,000 free books in ePub, Kindle, and PDF formats. It contains books that are free in the United States because their copyright has expired. The catalog includes many classic titles like *War and Peace* by Leo Tolstoy or mystery novels by Agatha Christie.

Self-publishing is much easier in the age of digital texts. You can self-publish into the Amazon Kindle Store in a matter of minutes and earn a 70% royalty of sales. Companies like Smashwords (**www.smashwords.com**) take a Microsoft Word document from you, formatted to their specifications, and then make your book available through a number of vendors like the Apple iBooks store,

Barnes and Noble, and the Sony eReader store. Your book can also be distributed as an app to mobile marketplaces like the Android Market or the Apple App Store. Sites like Lulu.com include social marketing for your book so that you can promote it. They offer services from editors, designers, and marketers as well.

Digital Music

How is digital music created? All digital media, whether an image, a song, or a video, has the same basis—digitized information. Figure 8.20 shows the process of digitally recording a song:

1. Playing music creates analog waves.

2. A microphone feeds the sound waves into a chip called an *analog-to-digital converter (ADC)* inside the recording device.

3. The ADC digitizes the waves into a series of numbers.

4. This series of numbers can be recorded onto CDs and DVDs or sent electronically.

5. On the receiving end, a playback device such as a CD player or DVD player is fed that same series of numbers. Inside the playback device is a *digital-to-analog converter (DAC)*, a chip that converts the digital numbers to a continuous analog wave.

6. That analog wave tells the receiver how to move the speaker cones to reproduce

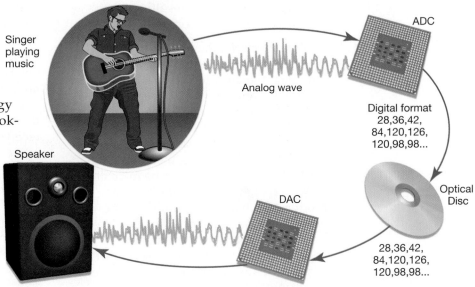

Figure 8.20

During the complete recording process, information changes from analog form to digital data and then back again to analog sound waves.

the original waves, resulting in the same sound as the original.

More precisely, the digital wave will be *close* to exact. How accurate it is, or how close the digitized wave is in shape to the original analog wave, depends on the sampling rate of the ADC. The **sampling rate** specifies the number of times the analog wave is measured each second. The higher the sampling rate, the more accurately the original wave can be re-created. However, higher sampling rates also produce much more data, and therefore result in bigger files. For example, sound waves on CDs are sampled at a rate of approximately 44,000 times a second. This produces a huge list of numbers for even a single minute of a song!

When sounds or image waves are digitized, it means that analog data is changed into digital data—from a wave into a series of numbers. The digital data is perfectly reproducible and can be distributed easily on CDs and DVDs or through the airwaves. The data also can be easily processed by a computer.

Are all music files MP3 files? The letters at the end of a file name (the file extension) indicate how the data in the file is organized. MP3 is the name of just one type of file format used to store digital music, but many others exist, such as AAC and WMA. If you buy a song from the iTunes Music Store, for example, you receive an .aac format file. There are also many video formats such as DivX, MPEG-4 (which usually has an .mp4 extension), WMV, and XviD. All file formats compete on sound and video quality and *compression*, which relates to how small the file can be and still provide high-quality playback. Be sure to check what kind of files your audio device understands before you store music on it.

How can I carry music files easily? Portable media players (PMPs) are small portable devices (such as iPods) that enable you to carry your digital audio files around with you. Many PMPs handle video and still images as well as music files.

Depending on the PMP, you can carry several hours of music or video—or

Figure 8.21 | SOME PORTABLE MEDIA PLAYERS AND THEIR CHARACTERISTICS

	Media Capacity	Built-in Flash Memory	Hard Drive Capacity	Connection to Computer	Other Features
Sansa Fuze Player	2,000 songs or 24 hours of video	2 GB to 8 GB	None, but 16 GB micro SD card supported	USB 2.0	FM radio, voice recorder, and available "radio" cards prefilled with 1,000 songs
Zune HD	As many as 16,000 songs or 20 hours of HD video	16 GB to 64 GB	None	USB 2.0 or wireless	Has HD radio, OLED screen, and multitouch navigation
Apple iPod touch	As many as 14,000 songs or 80 hours of video	8 GB to 64 GB	None	USB 2.0	Weighs only 4.05 ounces; flash memory enables skip-free playback
Apple iPod classic	As many as 40,000 songs or 200 hours of video	None	160 GB	USB 2.0	Has calendar feature that syncs with Outlook; can serve as a small, portable hard drive
Archos 7	As many as 2,000 songs or 24 hours of video	2 GB to 8 GB	None, but 32 GB SDHC card supported	USB 2.0	Includes 7" screen display, WiFi, and touch screen

possibly your entire music collection—in an incredibly small device. For example, an Apple iPod classic with a 160 GB hard drive is 4.1 inches by 2.4 inches (and only 0.41 inch thick), yet it can hold as many as 40,000 songs or 200 hours of video. The most compact players are slightly larger than a flash drive (although they hold less than 160 GB). Figure 8.21 shows several models of PMPs, all of which connect to computers via USB 2.0 ports.

Are PMP devices the only choice for portable media management? No, a number of electronic devices now incorporate the capability to carry electronic files and play music and video files. For example, netbooks, cell/smartphones, tablets, and mobile gaming systems also have support for playing both music and videos.

How do I know how much digital media a PMP can hold? The number of songs or hours of video a portable media player can hold depends on how much storage space it has. Most PMPs use built-in **flash memory**, a type of nonvolatile memory, to store files. Most PMPs that support video use a hard drive instead of flash memory and can store a much greater amount of music and video. Less expensive PMPs use flash memory ranging from 1 GB to 32 GB, whereas models that are more expensive use built-in hard drives, which provide as much as 160 GB of storage. Some of the PMPs that use flash memory allow you to add storage capacity by purchasing removable flash memory cards.

Another factor that determines how much music a player can hold is the quality of the MP3 music files. The size of an MP3 file depends on the digital sampling of the song. The same song could be sampled at 320 kbps or 64 kbps. The size of the song file will be five times larger if it is sampled at 320 kbps rather than the lower sampling rate of 64 kbps. The higher the sampling rate, the better quality the sound—but the larger the file size.

How do you control the size of an MP3 file? If you are *ripping*, or converting, a song from a CD into a digital MP3 file, you can select the sampling rate yourself. You decide by considering what quality sound you want, as well as how many songs you want to fit onto your

MP3 player. For example, if your player has 1 GB of storage and you have ripped songs at 192 kbps, you could fit about 694 minutes of music onto the player. The same 1 GB could store 2,083 minutes of music if it were sampled at 64 kbps. Whenever you are near your computer, you can connect your player and download a different set of songs, but you always are limited by the amount of storage your player has.

What if I want to access more music or video than the memory on my PMP allows? Some PMPs allow you to add memory by inserting removable flash memory cards. Flash memory cards are quiet and light, use tiny amounts of power, and slide into a special slot in the player. If you've ever played a video game on PlayStation or Xbox and saved your progress to a memory card, then you have used flash memory. Because flash memory is nonvolatile, when you store data on a flash memory card, you won't lose it when you turn off the player. In addition, flash memory can be erased and rewritten with new data. PMPs use a variety of different types of flash cards. Check your manual and then review the coverage of flash media in Chapter 2 for more details.

Another solution is to use a service that streams the music to you over WiFi or 3/4G networks. Companies like Rhapsody and Spotify charge a monthly subscription fee that entitles you to listen to any of the millions of tracks in their catalog. The music is not yours to own, however—if you stop your subscription you no longer have any access to the music. But because it is streamed to you, it also does not take up space on your device drive. Some streaming services offer options to allow some downloading; for example, your last 100 played songs may be actually stored on your device.

How do I transfer media files to my portable media player? All portable media players come with software that enables you to transfer audio and video files from your computer to the player. As noted earlier, players that hold thousands of songs and hours of video use internal hard drives to store the files. For example, devices such as Apple iPods can hold several gigabytes of data. To move large volumes of data

ACTIVE HELP-DESK · Using Portable Media Players

In this Active Helpdesk call, you'll play the role of a helpdesk staffer, fielding calls about portable media players, what they can carry, and how they store data.

between your computer and your PMP, you want a high-speed port. Most PMPs use a USB 2.0 port, which allows you to transfer two dozen MP3 files to the iPod in less than 10 seconds.

New services are appearing that will automatically push music to your mobile device. Apple's iOS 5 operating system supports iCloud technology. This means that as soon as you purchase a new song from iTunes, it is automatically pushed to all your registered iTunes devices—your Mac, your PC, your iPod touch, and your iPhone.

What if I want a lot of people to listen to my digital music? PMPs are great for individual listening, but to share music from a PMP, you have to connect it to an alternative device. Many audio receivers now come with a port or a dock so that you can connect a PMP device directly to them as another audio input source, like a Blu-ray player or a television. Most new cars are equipped with an auxiliary input to the speaker system to support connecting a PMP; others have a fully integrated software system that displays and runs the PMP playlists. Many Ford models use the Microsoft Sync system to allow you to navigate through your playlists with just voice commands. There are alarm clocks and home speaker docks that can mate, even wirelessly, with a PMP and broadcast brilliant sound.

How did the shift to digital music impact the music industry? The initial MP3 craze was fueled by sites such as MP3 .com, which originally stored its song files on a public server with the permission of the original artists or recording companies. Therefore, you were not infringing on a copyright by downloading songs from sites such as MP3.com (which still exists and now provides free music in streaming format).

Napster was a file exchange site created to correct some of the annoyances found by users of MP3.com. One such annoyance was the limited availability of popular music in MP3 format. With the MP3 sites, if you found a song you wanted to download, the link to the site on which the file was found often no longer worked. Napster differed from MP3.com because songs or locations of songs were not stored in a central public server, but instead were "borrowed" directly from other users' computers. This process of users transferring files between computers is referred to as **peer-to-peer (P2P) sharing**. Napster also provided a search engine dedicated to finding specific MP3 files. This direct search and sharing eliminated the inconvenience of searching links only to find them unavailable.

The problem with Napster was that it was so good at what it did. Napster's convenient and reliable mechanism to find and download popular songs in MP3 format became a huge success. The rapid acceptance and use of Napster—at one point, it had nearly 60 million users—led the music industry to sue the site for copyright infringement, and Napster was closed in June 2002. Napster has since reopened as a music site that sells music downloads and is sanctioned by the recording industry.

The reaction of the recording industry was to continue to enforce its absolute ownership over digital forms of its music. The industry even filed legal actions against individuals who had downloaded large amounts of music from Internet sites. This heavy-handed reaction to the new era of digital music ultimately backfired and left the music industry scrambling. Overall music sales have dropped significantly each year for the last decade. The recording industry is still trying to counter losing CD sales to digital forms of music. The approach they took early on did not allow them to adapt quickly enough to the new business models required by the shift to digital technologies.

So if I don't pay for a music download . . . is it illegal? Although you need to pay for most music you download, some artists post songs for free. Business models are still evolving as artists and recording companies try to meet audience needs while also protecting their own intellectual property rights. Several different approaches exist. One is to deliver something called *tethered downloads*, in which you pay for the music and own it, but are subject to restrictions on its use.

Another approach is to offer *DRM-free* music, which is music without any **digital rights management (DRM)**. DRM is a system of access control that allows only limited use of material that has been legally purchased. It may be the song can only run on certain devices or a movie can only be viewed a certain number of times. A DRM-free song can be placed on as many computers or players as you wish. These song files can be moved freely from system to system.

Why buy any music if peer-to-peer (P2P) sharing sites are still operating? When Napster was going through its legal turmoil, other P2P Web sites were quick to take advantage of a huge opportunity. Napster was "easy" to shut down because it used a central index server that queried other Napster computers for requested songs. Current P2P protocols (such as BearShare) differ from Napster in that they do not limit themselves to sharing only MP3 files. Video files are obtainable easily on P2P sites. More importantly, these sites don't have a central index server. Instead, they operate in a true P2P sharing environment in which computers connect directly to other computers. This makes them a prime source of unwanted viruses and spyware.

The argument these P2P networks make to defend their legality is that they do not run a central server like the original Napster, but only facilitate connections between users. Therefore, they have no control over what the users choose to trade. These legal nuances were not enough to keep the LimeWire service active, and it was shut down by court order in 2010. Note that not all P2P file sharing is illegal. For example, it is legal to trade photos or movies you have created with other folks over a P2P site.

People who oppose such file-sharing sites contend that the sites know their users are distributing files illegally and breaking copyright laws. Be aware that having illegal content on your computer, deliberately or by accident, is a criminal offense in many jurisdictions.

Will PMPs eliminate radio stations? Radio stations have always had certain advantages: early access to new music, and personalities and conversations that

add to the listening experience. However, the Internet allows artists to release new songs to their fans immediately (on sites such as Facebook) and without relying on radio airtime. This opens up new channels for artists to reach an audience and changes the amount of power radio stations have in the promotion of music. Many radio stations have increased listenership by making their stations available through Internet sites and by broadcasting in high-definition quality.

Can I create my own radio station? Another development that competes with radio (and television) is *podcasting*. In

BITS AND BYTES

Trick Out Your iTouch/iPhone

With more than 10 billion iTouch/iPhone apps downloaded, the App Store is a proven success. Some apps are games, some are just gimmicks, but many are great tools for a student. iFlipr is an app that connects you to 2.7 million flash cards. You can study for the MCAT exam or build and share your own custom flash card deck. iHomework organizes your teacher contact info, due dates for assignments, and research materials, and learning management systems like Blackboard have their own mobile apps. AudioNote lets your iPhone record audio in sync with handwritten notes you write down. Can't find the app you are dreaming of? The iPhone Developer University program is free and supports students and faculty in designing and coding mobile apps.

Chapter 3 you read that podcasting allows users to download audio and video content and then listen to those broadcasts on their PMPs whenever they want. Podcasting is paving the way for anyone to create a radio or television show at home and distribute it easily to an audience. Using free software such as Audacity (**audacity.sourceforge.net**) and a microphone, you can record voice-overs, sequence songs, and generate special effects for your recordings. Loyal fans can use podcasting software such as Juice (**juicereceiver.sourceforge.net**) or iTunes to find a podcast's latest episode and automatically transfer it to their portable media players. Plugging your iPod into a data port on your computer causes the iPod to search iTunes for new content from the podcasters you subscribe to and then automatically transfers the new files to your iPod. Podcasts are easy to subscribe to and download using iTunes (see Figure 8.22).

What if I want to publicize my band's music? Digital music has made

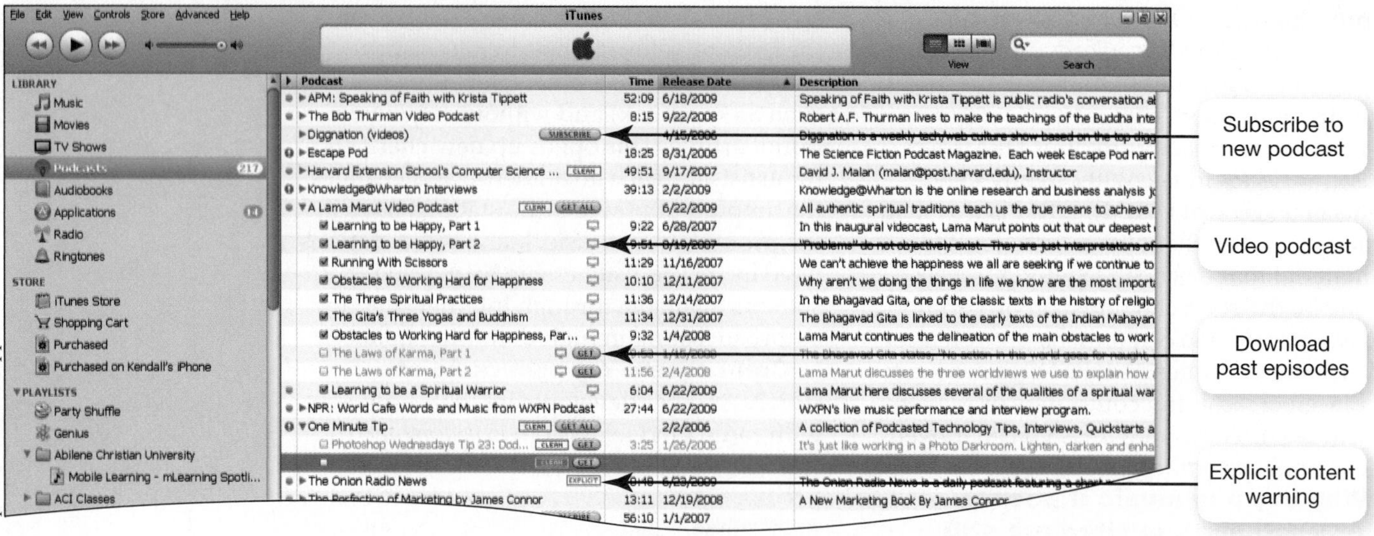

Figure 8.22

iTunes makes it easy to subscribe to and manage podcasts.

distributing your own recordings very simple. You can make your own creations available using apps like ReverbNation (**www.reverbnation.com**). You can quickly create a Web page for your band, post your songs, and start building a fan base through Facebook, for example. ReverbNation will send you reports detailing who is listening to your music and what they are saying about it. ReverbNation is also a way to connect with independent recording labels and to find places that want to book your band.

Digital Photography

What is "analog" photography? Before digital cameras hit the market, most people used some form of 35-mm single-lens reflex (SLR) camera. When you take a picture using a traditional SLR camera, a shutter opens, creating an aperture (a small window in the camera) that allows light to hit the 35-mm film inside. Chemicals coating the film react when exposed to light. Later, additional chemicals develop the image on the film, and the image is printed on special light-sensitive paper. A variety of lenses and processing techniques, special equipment, and filters are needed to create printed photos from traditional SLR cameras.

What is different about digital photography? Digital cameras do not use film. Instead, they capture images on electronic sensors called *charge-coupled device (CCD) arrays* and then convert those images to digital data, long series of numbers that represent the color and brightness of millions of points in the image. Unlike traditional cameras, digital cameras allow you to see

your images the instant you shoot them. Most camera models can now record digital video as well as digital photos.

How do I select a digital camera? With hundreds of models to choose from, where do you begin? The first question to answer is whether you want a compact "point-and-shoot" model camera or a more serious digital SLR. The larger digital SLR cameras allow you to switch among different lenses and offer features important to serious amateur and professional photographers (such as depth-of-field previewing). Although having such flexibility in moving up to a larger zoom lens is a great advantage, most of these cameras are also larger, heavier, and use more battery power than the tiny point-and-shoot models. Think about how you will be using your camera and decide which model will serve you best in the long run.

Next, you'll want to evaluate the quality of the camera on a number of levels. One great resource to use is Digital Photography Review (**www.dpreview.com**). The site's camera reviews evaluate a camera's construction as well as its features, image quality, ease of use, and value for the cost. In addition, the site provides comparisons to similar camera models by other manufacturers and feedback from owners of those models. Links are provided to several resellers, making it easy to compare prices as well.

Why not just use the camera on my cell/smartphone? Many cell/smartphones include a digital camera. These cameras often provide lower resolutions than stand-alone models and inferior lenses. Many features that photographers rely on are not often available in the cameras included on phones, such as different types of autofocus, image stabilization algorithms, and smile shutter, which waits to take a shot until your subject is smiling.

What determines the image quality of a digital camera? The overall image quality is determined by many factors: the quality of the lenses used, the file format and compression used, and the color management software. Another part of what determines the image quality of a digital camera is its **resolution**, or the number of data points it records for each image captured. A digital camera's resolution is measured in megapixels (MP). The prefix *mega* is short for millions. The word *pixel* is short for picture element, which is a single dot in a digital image. Point-and-shoot models typically offer resolutions from 10 MP to 15 MP. Professional digital SLR cameras, such as the Canon EOS-5D Mark II, can take photos at resolutions as high as 21.1 MP, but they sell for thousands of dollars.

If you're interested in making only 5" × 7" or 8" × 10" prints, a lower-resolution camera is fine. However, low-resolution images become grainy and pixelated when pushed to make larger-size prints. For example, if

flash card. The most common file types supported by digital cameras are raw uncompressed data (RAW) and Joint Photographic Experts Group (JPEG). Raw files have different formats and extensions depending on the manufacturer of a particular camera. The raw file records all of the original image information, so it is larger than a compressed JPEG file. JPEG files can be compressed just a bit, keeping most of the details, or compressed a great deal, losing some detail. Most cameras allow you to select from a few different JPEG compression levels.

Often cameras also support a very low-resolution storage option, enabling you to create files that you can easily attach to e-mail messages. This low-resolution setting typically provides images that are not useful for printing but are so small that they are easily e-mailed. Even people who have slow Internet connections are able to quickly download and view such images on-screen.

How do I move photos to my computer? Transferring photos to your computer allows you to store them and frees your flash card for reuse. Digital cameras have a built-in USB 2.0 port. Using a USB 2.0 cable, you can connect the camera to your computer and copy the converted images as

---

When you choose to compress your images, you will lose some of the detail, but in return, you'll be able to fit more images on your flash card.

---

you tried to print an 11" × 14" enlargement from a 2 MP image taken using your cell/smartphone's camera, the image would look grainy; you would see individual dots of color instead of a clear, sharp image. The 10 MP to 15 MP cameras on the market now have plenty of resolution to guarantee sharp, detailed images even with enlargements as big as 11" × 14".

What file formats are used for digital images? To fit more photos on the same size of flash memory card, digital cameras allow you to choose from several different file types in order to compress the image data into less memory space. When you choose to compress your images, you will lose some of the detail, but in return, you'll be able to fit more images on your

uncompressed files or in a compressed format as JPEG files. Another option is to transfer the flash card from your camera directly to the built-in memory card reader on your computer. Some camera models support wireless network connections so that you can transfer the images without the fuss of putting a cable in place. If your model doesn't, you can purchase a memory card with built-in WiFi: the Eye-Fi. Eye-Fi will wirelessly transfer your photos to Google Picasa, Facebook, or one of thirty other Web destinations. Eye-Fi Mobile X2 will upload images directly from your camera to your iPad or phone as well. It will also back up the photos and videos you take with your camera to your home computer. And when you are away from home, Eye-Fi comes with hot spot access so you can upload for free from any McDonald's, Starbucks, hotel, or airport.

Can I make my old photos digital? Obviously, not every document or image you have is in an electronic form. What about all the photographs you have already taken? What about an article from a magazine or a hand-drawn sketch? How can these be converted into digital format?

Digital scanners convert paper text and images into digital formats. Most scanners today are integrated into an all-in-one printer that supports printing, copying, and scanning with one unit. You can place any flat material on the glass surface of the scanner and convert it into a digital file. Most

.com) and Shutterfly (**www.shutterfly.com**), store your images and allow you to organize them into photo albums or to create hard-copy prints, mugs, T-shirts, or calendars.

Photo printers for home use are available in two technologies: inkjet and dye sublimation. The most popular and inexpensive ones are inkjet printers. As noted in Chapter 2, some inkjet printers are capable of printing high-quality color photos, although they vary in speed and quality. Some include a display window so that you can review the image as you stand at the printer, whereas others are portable, allowing you to print your photos wherever you are. Some printers even allow you to crop the image right

Photo printers for home use are available in two technologies: inkjet and dye sublimation.

scanner software allows you to store the converted images as TIFF files or in compressed form as JPEG files. Some scanners include hardware that allows you to scan film negatives or slides as well or even insert a stack of photos to be scanned in sequence.

Scanner quality is measured by its resolution, which is given in dots per inch (dpi). Most modern scanners can digitize a document at resolutions as high as 4,800 × 9,600 dpi, in either color or grayscale mode. The scanner software will also typically support optical character recognition (OCR). OCR software converts pages of handwritten or typed text into electronic files. You can then open and edit these converted documents with traditional word processing programs such as Microsoft Word.

How do I print a digital image? You can print a digital image using a professional service or your own printer. Most photo printing labs, including the film processing departments at stores such as Walmart and Target, offer digital printing services, as do many high-end online processing labs. The paper and ink used at processing labs are higher quality than what is available for home use and produce heavier, glossier prints that won't fade. You can send your digital photos directly to local merchants such as CVS and Walgreens for printing using Windows Live Photo Gallery. Online services, such as Flickr (**www.flickr**

at the printer without having to use special image editing software.

Unlike inkjet printers, which use an inkjet nozzle, dye-sublimation printers produce images using a heating element. The heating element passes over a ribbon of translucent film that has been dyed with bands of colors. Depending on the temperature of the element, dyes are vaporized from a solid into a gas. The gas vapors penetrate the photo paper before they cool and return to solid form, producing glossy, high-quality images. If you're interested in a printer to use for printing only photographs, a dye-sublimation printer is a good choice. However, some models print only specific photo sizes, such as 4" × 6" prints, so be sure the printer you buy will fit your long-term needs.

Do I need to print out my photos? You may decide not to print your photos at all. As noted earlier, online albums let you share your photos without having to print them. There are a number of digital scrapbooking sites that let you electronically design scrapbooks. Portable devices, such as tablets and cell/smartphones, also enable you to carry and display your photos. The iPad, for example, can be connected wirelessly to a TV and deliver slide shows of your photographs, complete with musical soundtracks you have selected. As we mentioned in Chapter 7, if you have networked your home, a television connected to your network (or to a network-enabled device like a PlayStation 3 or a networked Blu-ray player) can display all the photos and videos stored on your computer.

Digital Video

Where does digital video come from? Digital video comes from several sources, but now people often create their own digital videos. As a video creator, you may purchase dedicated digital camcorders to record digital video. Most cell/smartphones can record video, and digital cameras take video as well as digital still shots. Webcams also work as inexpensive devices for creating digital video.

There are many other sources of digital video available to you now. Television is broadcasting in digitally formatted signals. The Internet delivers a huge amount of digital video through Google Video, YouTube, communities like Vimeo (**www.vimeo.com**), and webcasting sites like Ustream (**www .ustream.tv**). Sites like Hulu (**www.hulu .com**) rebroadcast many current television shows as well as films and movie trailers. Many pay services are available to deliver digital video to you. These include on-demand streaming from cable providers, iTunes, Netflix's Instant Watch films, and Amazon's Instant Video download service.

How do I record my own digital video? Video equipment for home use stores information in a digital video (DV) format. This allows the cameras to be incredibly small and light. Such cameras don't require any tapes at all; they store hours of video on built-in hard drives or flash cards. Some models even record directly to DVD discs.

You can easily transfer video files to your computer and, using video editing software, edit the video at home, cutting out sections, resequencing segments, and adding titles. To do the same with analog videotape would require expensive and complex audio/video equipment available only in video production studios. You can save (or write) your final product on a CD or DVD and play it in your home DVD system or on your computer.

For true videophiles, cameras and burners are now available for high-definition video format.

What if I decide to add some special effects and a sound track? Video editing software presents a storyboard or timeline with which you can manipulate your video file, as shown in Figure 8.23. You can review your clips frame by frame or trim them at any point. You can order each segment on the timeline in whichever sequence you like and correct segments for color balance, brightness, or contrast.

In addition, you can add transitions to your video such as those you're used to seeing on TV—fades to black, dissolves, and so on. Just select the type of transition you want from the drop-down list and drag that icon into the timeline where you want the transition to occur.

Video editing software also lets you add titles, animations, and audio tracks to your video, including background music, sound effects, and additional narration. You can adjust the volume of each audio track to switch from one to the other or have both playing together. Finally, you can preview all of these effects in real time.

There is a lot to learn about digital video editing, and with the number of choices available, it is easy to be overwhelmed. Examine online tutorial resources such as Izzy Video podcasts (**www.izzyvideo.com**) to learn how to make the most impact with the editing and effects you apply to your raw video footage.

Figure 8.23

Adobe Premiere Elements allows you to build a movie from video clips and add sound tracks and special effects.

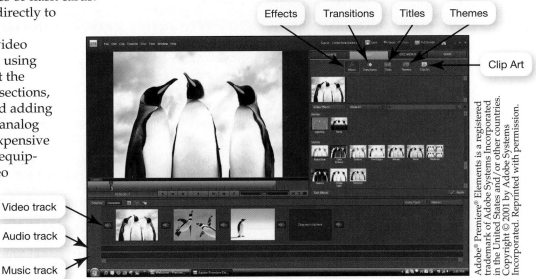

What kinds of files will I end up with? Once you're done editing your video file, you can save or export it in a variety of formats. Figure 8.24 shows some of the popular video file formats in use today, along with the file extensions they use.

Your choice of file format for your finished video will depend on what you want to do with your video. For example, the QuickTime streaming file format is a great choice if your file is really large and you plan to post it on the Web. The Microsoft AVI format is a good choice if you're sending your file to a wide range of users, because it's extremely popular and is commonly accepted as the standard video format for the Windows Media Player.

You also can try different compression choices to see which one does a better job of compressing your particular file. A **codec** (*co*mpression/*dec*ompression) is a rule, implemented in either software or hardware, that squeezes the same audio and video information into less space. Some information will be lost using compression, and there are several different codecs to choose from, each claiming better performance than its competitors. Commonly used codecs include MPEG-4, H.264, and DivX. There is no one codec that is always superior—a codec that works well for a simple interview may not do a good job compressing a live-action scene.

What if I want a DVD with a menuing system? If you want a DVD or Blu-ray with a menuing system, you can use special authoring software such as Pinnacle Studio HD or Adobe Encore. These DVD/Blu-ray software packages often include preset selections for producing video for specific mobile devices. These programs can also create final discs that have animated menu systems and easy navigation controls, allowing the viewer to move quickly from one movie or scene to another. Home DVD and Blu-ray players as well as gaming systems such as PlayStation and Xbox can read these discs.

What is the quickest way to get my video out to viewers? Because of the popularity of videos on the Web, products and services are now available that let you quickly upload your videos. Many mobile devices, such as smartphones and tablets, record HD video, and applications like Ustream allow you to broadcast live over the Web as you record. If you want to distribute your video through YouTube, there is a special Mobile Upload Profile that you can set up for your account. Once your unique e-mail address has been assigned, you can submit a video that you have on your phone to YouTube by e-mailing the file to the account address.

Of course, it is illegal for you to upload videos you do not own. You also cannot take

Figure 8.24 | TYPICAL FILE FORMATS FOR DIGITAL VIDEO

Format	File Extension	Notes
QuickTime	.qt .mov	You can download QuickTime player without charge from **www.apple.com/quicktime**. The pro version allows you to build your own QuickTime files.
Moving Picture Experts Group (MPEG)	.mpg .mpeg .mp4	MPEG-4 video standard adopted internationally in 2000; recognized by most video player software.
Windows Media Video	.wmv	Microsoft file format recognized by Windows Media Player (included with the Windows OS).
Microsoft Video for Windows	.avi	Microsoft file format recognized by Windows Media Player (included with the Windows OS).
RealMedia	.rm	Format from RealNetworks; popular for streaming video. You can download the player for free at **www.real.com**.
Adobe Flash Video	.flv	Adobe Flash video format, sometimes embedded in Shockwave files (*.swf).

Figure 8.25

Webcams are small enough to make them part of any activity.

a piece of a copyrighted video and post it publicly. The Ethics in IT section in this chapter presents several legal and ethical situations that are important for you to be aware of as a content creator in the digital age.

Webcasting, or broadcasting your video live to an audience, is another option that has become simpler. Inexpensive webcams (costing from $25 to $100) can be easily attached to your desktop or notebook computer. Many models of monitors have built-in webcams. Webcam models that are more expensive have motors that allow you to automatically rotate to track the sound, and some webcams are small enough that they can be mounted on your bike or helmet (see Figure 8.25). Services such as YouTube offer Quick Capture buttons, so with one click, your video can be recorded through your webcam and delivered to the Internet.

How can I distribute my video to the greatest number of viewers? Sites like **www.justin.tv** or **www.ustream.tv** let you quickly set up to webcast your video as it is captured to a live Internet audience. You can also display an interactive chat next to the video feed. Both the chat and the video are captured and archived for viewers who missed the live broadcast. iTunes offers free distribution of video podcasts, so you can build a following there for your video work.

There are also options for distributing your movie based on social media seeding. Distrify is an application that helps you to post your trailer on your Web site and allow viewers to immediately download the film, as well as add it to their Facebook page. This viral approach to marketing your own creation connects you directly with your audience and eliminates any cost of distribution.

Is all video digital now? The switch to digital video as a broadcasting medium has happened over the past few years. In June 2009, all television stations were required to make the move to digital signal broadcasting. You can go to **www.DTV.gov** to keep current on using conversion boxes to allow older television sets to operate with the new digital signal.

Movie production studios have also been moving toward digital video for many years. George Lucas, a great proponent of digital technology, filmed *Star Wars Episode II: Attack of the Clones* completely in digital format way back in 2002. It played in a special digital release at digital-ready theaters. The film *Slumdog Millionaire*, a 2009 film shot mainly in digital technologies, won the Academy Award for Cinematography. *Avatar*, currently the top-grossing film of all time, both was shot digitally and forced theaters to convert to digital projection

So you just returned from your trip to the Grand Canyon and all your friends are raving about the quality of the photographs you took. You decide to put the photographs out on Flickr so your friends can see them. You also think that maybe someone might see your photos and want to use them in a commercial publication such as a magazine. Because you own the copyright to your photos, you control how they can be used—and you want to protect your rights. You add a disclaimer to Flickr indicating that all rights are reserved on your photos. Anyone who wants to use them will need to contact you and request permission.

All of a sudden, you are bombarded by dozens of requests for permission to use your photographs for all sorts of purposes. A high school student in Illinois wants to feature one of your photos on her travel blog. A church in Georgia wants to use a photo for their newsletter to illustrate a story about a church member's trip to Arizona. An advertising agency in Seattle wants to modify your sunrise photo by inserting a family on a camping trip into the photo. You want to be ethical and protect your ownership rights as well (maybe the ad agency might even pay you!), but how are you going to manage all these photo permission requests?

Copyleft, a play on the word copyright, is designed for this situation. Copyleft is a term for various licensing plans that enable copyright holders to grant certain rights to the work while retaining other rights. The GNU General Public License is a popular copyleft license that is used for software. For other works, the Creative Commons, a nonprofit organization, has developed a range of licenses that can be used to control rights to works.

Creative Commons has various types of licenses available based on the rights you wish to grant. The company provides a simple form to assist you with selecting the proper license for your work. Creative Commons provides two licenses at **www.creativecommons.org/about/licenses** that could simplify your life. An *attribution license* permits others to copy, distribute, and display your copyrighted work, but only if they give you credit in the way you specify. Under this license, the high school student could use one of your photos as long as he or she gave you credit.

A *noncommercial license* allows anyone to copy, distribute, and display your work, but only for noncommercial purposes. The church in Georgia could use one of your photos under this license because it is not profiting from its use.

Both of these licenses can also be used to cover **derivative works**. A derivative work is based on the original work (one of your photos) but is modified in some way. The ad agency that wants to modify one of your photos is seeking permission to create a derivative work. If you had used an attribution license, the ad agency could use your work for a derivative purpose, but only if it attributed the original work to you as the author. If you had used a noncommercial license, the ad agency could not use your work to make a profit for itself.

The obvious advantage to using these Creative Commons licenses is that people won't constantly annoy you with permission requests to use your work. These licenses explain exactly how you are willing to have your work be used. Also, many advocates of copyleft policies feel that creativity is encouraged when people are free to modify other people's work instead of worrying about infringing on copyright.

Opponents of Creative Commons licenses often complain that these licenses have affected their livelihoods. If millions of images are out on Flickr with Creative Commons licenses that permit free commercial use, professional photographers might have a tougher time selling their work. Furthermore, Creative Commons licenses are irrevocable. If you make a mistake and select the wrong license for your work, or you later find out a work is valuable and you've already selected a license that allows commercial use, you're out of luck.

Many people find listings of Creative Commons licenses confusing. If there is a Creative Commons disclaimer at the bottom of a group of photos, does that mean all the photos are available under that license, or just some of them? What actually constitutes commercial use? Is displaying Google Adsense ads on your blog commercial use?

Each of us needs to carefully consider the value of our intellectual property and decide how best to conduct our digital livelihood. Understanding the meaning of copyright, and copyleft, is important both so that you respect the rights of others and so that you can simplify your life in granting permission rights to the works you create.

---

equipment to show the film. Moving to digital projection also allows a theater to show live concerts and sports events.

How is HD different from "plain" digital? HD stands for **high definition**. It is a standard of digital television signal that guarantees a specific level of resolution and a specific *aspect ratio*, which is the rectangular shape of the image. A 1080 HD TV displays 1,920 vertical lines and 1,080 horizontal lines of video on the screen, which is over six times as many pixels as standard definition. The aspect ratio used is 16:9, which makes the screen wider, giving it the same proportions as the rectangular shape

of a movie theater screen (see Figure 8.26). This allows televisions to play movies in the widescreen format that they were created for, instead of "letterboxing" the film with black bars on the top and the bottom of the screen.

What types of connectivity are provided on modern television sets? As video sources have increased, so have the number and types of connectors on a television. A typical HD set has at least three HDMI connectors, allowing game consoles, Blu-ray players, and cable boxes to be connected and produce the highest-quality output. HDMI is a single cable, with just one plug, that carries all of the video and all of the audio information. That means there is one connector, not three for different parts of the video signal and another two for the stereo sound signals!

Many sets have a built-in SD card reader. This allows users to display slide shows of photographs captured by their digital cameras. A PC VGA port is also included on most sets. This allows you to feed your computer's output video signal directly to the television so you can display an Internet browser or work on your files on the big screen. Sets are now incorporating a wireless network adapter so the set can stream video from the Internet without having a separate computer connected. Several manufacturers are offering TV sets that stream Internet content.

Samsung offers "smart television" models that have access to a Samsung app store and can download a YouTube app, Google Maps, Vimeo, or hundreds of others. Sony's Internet TV is a collaboration with Google. It allows a single search utility to check for content on the Internet, on your stored recorded programs, and on the TV guide listing, and contains a full browser and upgradeable operating system.

What advantages are there to watching digital video on my television? Because the signal can be stored into computer memory as it is delivered, a digital video television show can be paused, or can be rewound in real time. Other information services can be integrated with the broadcast; so if a telephone call came through during the show, a pop-up could appear identifying the caller. In the future, there will be more interactivity integrated so you can participate in live polls or chats on-screen as the show is broadcast.

Can I record the digital video that comes over my television? There are a variety of digital video recorders (DVRs) available to record the digital video from your television. These can record in either standard or HD quality and store the information on a hard drive. Useful features include being able to record two shows at once, being able to download movie

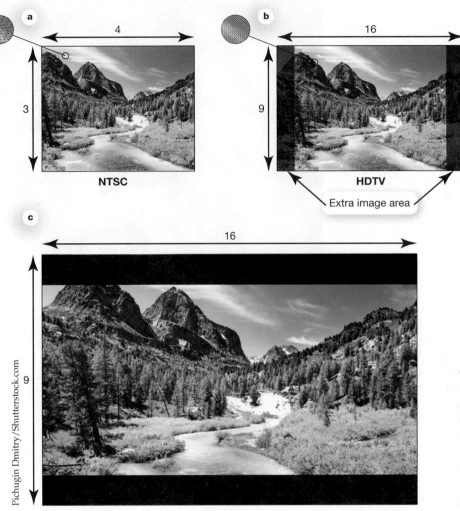

Pichugin Dmitry/Shutterstock.com

NTSC

HDTV

Extra image area

Letterbox

Figure 8.26

(a) Standard-definition television has a more "square" aspect ratio, while (b) high-definition television matches the 16:9 ratio used in the motion picture industry without resorting to (c) letterboxing.

purchases or rentals from the Internet directly to the DVR unit, and easily moving stored content to a mobile device like an iPad or a smartphone. Using a DVR, you can pause live TV or set up a schedule to capture every episode of a series, no matter when it airs. Models like TiVo even recommend new shows you might like based on what you have been watching. If you don't want to purchase a DVR or pay the monthly subscription fee for DVR service, you can install PVR (personal video recording) software on your computer, as we mentioned at the opening of the chapter. When connected to your cable signal, programs like BeyondTV (**www.snapstream.com**) turn your computer itself into a DVR.

How else can I get digital video to my TV? In addition to the broadcast content coming in to your TV, there are a number of streaming sources of digital video.

Figure 8.27

Slingbox can send your digital television content to your tablet, notebook, or phone, wherever you may be.

Cable providers offer a wide range of on-demand video services. Many older films, television episodes, and shows such as exercise classes are offered free of charge. Other premium content, like new-release movies, is offered for a fee. Just one click and you can instantly watch any offered movie for 24 hours, with full control—stopping, starting, and rewinding. Other providers, like Netflix, also offer streaming video content. While Netflix's original business model was to ship members discs physically in the mail, they now also offer Watch Instantly. Thousands of movies and TV series are available with just a click. You can view these shows on a television through any gaming console, a PC, an iPad, or a specialized device like the Roku digital video player.

Can I get digital video to watch on my portable device? Yes. Many DVR units, like TiVo, support software that allows you to transfer recorded shows to files on your PC and format them for viewing on a mobile device. There are also devices like Slingbox that take the video from your television and broadcast it to you over the Internet. With Slingbox, you can be in another room, or another country, and control and watch

your home television on your notebook or your smartphone (see Figure 8.27).

Digital Navigation

How has digitized information impacted navigation? Built and operated by the U.S. Department of Defense, the **global positioning system** (GPS) is a network of 21 satellites (plus 3 working spares) that constantly orbits the Earth. GPS devices use an antenna to pick up the signals from these satellites and use special software to transform those signals into latitude and longitude. Using the information obtained from the satellites, GPS devices determine the geographical location anywhere on the planet to within 3 feet (see Figure 8.28). The exact accuracy depends on such things as atmospheric conditions and interference from obstacles like mountains or buildings. Because they provide such detailed positioning information, GPS devices are now used as navigational aids for aircraft, recreational boats, and automobiles, and they even come in handheld models for hikers.

How do I get GPS in my car? Stand-alone GPS devices have dropped dramatically in price and size. Small, handheld units deliver turn-by-turn instructions and real-time traffic information. Several manufacturers, like Garmin and Magellan, make stand-alone GPS devices that can be mounted onto the windshield of your car.

GPS units are available with a wide range of features. Garmin, for example, offers numerous services on its line of GPS units. A Map mode displays your location and the current speed limit on a map that is updated in real time as you drive. When you enter a series of destinations into the unit, an optimal route is developed for you. A voice warns you of lane changes and approaching turns, giving you directions using the actual street name (such as "Turn right on Hancock Avenue"). Lane Assist flips into a 3D display mode and shows you how to navigate through lane changes in highway merges (see Figure 8.29). If you miss a turn, the unit automatically recalculates the required route and gives you directions to

get back on course. Flip to another screen, and it shows you how far you have to drive to the next gas station, restaurant, or hospital. Some models automatically mark the location of your car when you remove them from the vehicle, and can give you step-by-step directions back to your car.

In addition, most automotive companies now offer GPS systems as an installed

Figure 8.28

GPS computes your location anywhere on Earth from a system of orbiting satellites.

© Caryn Becker / Alamy

Figure 8.29

In addition to the driving applications shown, the Garmin nüvi series GPS devices are also able to provide Internet services.

option in their vehicles. Of course, GPS navigation can be added to any vehicle by using GPS on a mobile device like a smartphone.

Do GPS devices carry other information? Full-featured GPS models such as the Garmin nüvi 1490 series include MP3 players, audio book players, and the capability to display photos and connect to the Internet. Using Internet services such as MSN Direct, your GPS can keep you informed about the weather, traffic backups, local movie times, and even local gas prices.

How does GPS help me in an emergency? By the end of 2005, every cell/smartphone had to include a GPS chip. The Federal Communications Commission (FCC) mandated this to enable the complete rollout of the Enhanced 911 (E911) program. E911 automatically gives dispatchers precise location information for any 911 call. It also means your phone records may include this precise tracking information, which indicates where you are when you make a call.

Can I use the GPS chip on a family member's cell/smartphone? Cellular phone providers offer plans (for a monthly fee) that allow you to track where a phone is at any given time via a Web site.

For example, AT&T's service Family Maps allows parents to track all of the phones on their family plan in real time. Locations of all phones are displayed over the Web on a map, or the service will send an automatic text message alert with the phone's location at a specific time each day. So a parent could have a text or e-mail sent with their daughter's phone location each day at 3 P.M. to be sure she made it home from school. The person being tracked cannot turn off the service.

Digital Convergence

Once you are comfortable with digital communication and digital media, you'll want to be able to communicate and to access your music, books, and media all the time. Access to your digital assets is required in a modern business environment and is a great benefit in your personal life.

There is a wide range of devices that grant you mobile access to your digital resources. As more and more computing power is available in mobile processors, mobile devices have evolved to be able to do multiple tasks. **Digital convergence**, the

Figure 8.30

Tablets do not have hardware keyboards but can be paired wirelessly with a keyboard if desired.

© Pixellover RM 4/Alamy

Figure 8.31
The Asus Padphone lets you share the processor of the Phone with a tablet shell.

use of a single unifying device to handle media, Internet, entertainment, and telephony needs, is expressed in the range of devices now on the market.

Let's decide if you need more than one mobile device and which device is the right one for you.

What are the main categories of mobile devices? There are several major categories of mobile devices available now. Feature phones and smartphones were discussed earlier in this chapter. They have a wide set of abilities but are limited in computing power, display size, and keyboard size. **Netbooks** run a fully featured operating system but weigh in at 2 pounds or less. An **Internet tablet** is another type of very light, very portable device. Internet tablets do not offer full-size hardware keyboards but can be easily paired with a keyboard using Bluetooth (see Figure 8.30). The top-selling Apple iPad has a 9.7" multitouch screen and weighs in at only 1.5 pounds. The iPad runs a mobile OS named iOS and runs mobile touch versions of popular Apple productivity software Pages, Numbers, and Keynote. The iPad also supports video viewing, music, Internet browsing, and thousands of apps.

Netbooks and Internet tablets both carry files, music, and videos as well as provide specialized services. Then there is the full range of notebooks and tablet computers, and new blends of various features

are appearing in new devices all the time. For example, the Asus Padphone (see Figure 8.31) is a hybrid of a phone and a tablet "shell" that can be powered by the phone when a larger display is needed. Figure 8.32 lists the main features of several different mobile device categories.

What if I don't need a full notebook computer but do need Internet access? Lightweight Internet tablets have exploded in popularity. Manufacturers offer two versions of models, one with WiFi connectivity only and one with both WiFi and cellular connectivity (3G). Tablets have high-resolution multi-touch sensitive screens, integrated webcams, and GPS capabilities. There are models in a wide variety of sizes, with a range of operating systems and specifications (see Figure 8.33).

If a tablet is too expensive a solution, there are also netbooks and mobile gaming systems. Netbooks pack major computing power into a tiny package, and manufacturers try to extend battery life as long as possible. Screen sizes are typically between 8" and 10", and keyboards are less than full sized. Netbooks often come with a Windows operating system. Some users opt to install a flavor of Linux, however, because Linux requires fewer resources than Windows. Solid-state hard drives are a good choice for netbooks because they use less power and produce less heat. Many models include integrated webcams as well as Bluetooth, so

Figure 8.32 | MOBILE DEVICES: PRICE, SIZE, WEIGHT, AND CAPABILITIES

Device	Relative Price	Approximate Size	Approximate Weight	Standard Capabilities
Cell phone	$$ (Includes cost for the phone, a monthly plan, and Internet access)	5" × 2" × 0.5"	0.25 lb.	Voice, e-mail, some application software, and Internet connectivity
PMP	$$–$$$	4" × 2" × 0.5"	0.25 lb.	Storage of digital music, video, and other digital files; no Internet access
Smartphone	$$–$$$	4.5" × 2" × 0.75"	0.25 lb.	Camera, PIM capabilities, GPS, compass, application software, and access to the Internet
Internet tablet	$$$–$$$$	10" × 7" × 0.3"	0.5 lb.	Webcam, GPS, phone calls using VoIP, sharp resolution, and widescreen display
Netbook	$$$	10" × 7"	1–2 lbs.	8" and 10" screens and full-featured operating systems and applications; hardware keyboard.
Tablet PC	$$$$	10" × 8" × 1"	1–3 lbs.	PIM capabilities, access to application software, access to the Internet, and special handwriting- and speech-recognition capabilities
Notebook	$$$$–$$$$$	10" × 13" × 2"	5 to 8 lbs.	All the capabilities of a desktop computer plus portability

while netbooks are small and light, they still can serve many functions.

Mobile game systems have interesting combinations of features as well. The Sony Vita can play video games but also includes a Web browser, Skype, and an RSS reader. It uses Sony Memory Sticks to store data.

The screen is a 5″ OLED widescreen design with great clarity and brightness. With two cameras, a touch-sensitive screen, a rear touch pad, a gyroscope, an accelerometer, and dual analog control sticks, the Vita is a unique mobile offering.

Figure 8.33

iPad2 . . . Xoom . . . Galaxy? There are over 75 tablets on the market now. Finding the right digital device can be a challenge.

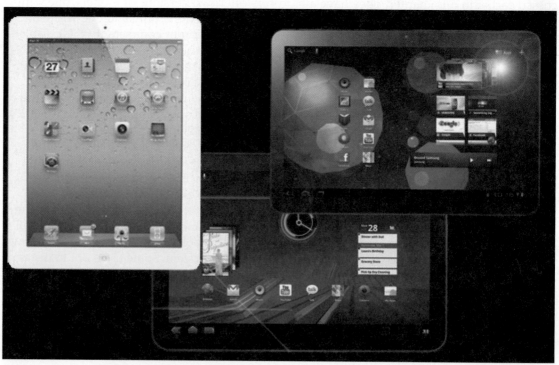

© oliver leedham/Alamy

Near Field Communication

Mobile devices have changed many aspects of our daily lives, and that trend will continue with the expansion of near field communication (NFC). NFC technology allows a device with an NFC chip to communicate with another NFC device with just a single touch. Data can be exchanged, or financial transactions can be processed just by bringing the devices within an inch of each other. This simple-sounding type of wireless communication has the potential to create a major shift in how we live.

Because NFC has such a short range (up to 1.5 inches) it is being used for secure credit card transactions. Both MasterCard and Visa are piloting programs that would allow cellular phones to "tap and go," meaning phone owners would no longer carry physical credit cards. Instead they could simply wave their phone near an NFC checkout device and have the transaction processed.

This seems similar to the Visa PayWave or MasterCard PayPass programs in place in some areas, where the credit card itself can simply be "waved" near a reader to process the transaction. But NFC acceptance would open the door to much, much more. Imagine waving your phone past an NFC reader at checkout and having it automatically transmit the proper loyalty card information, select and process any appropriate coupon offers, and pay all at once (see Figure 8.34). In countries like Japan, Spain, and Germany, NFC ticketing programs are already in place. The Deutsche Bahn rail system allows users to tap their phones to an NFC tag when they get on the train, and another on departing. The fare is automatically calculated and billed to their credit card monthly. The new "digital wallet" would be a single storage place for all of your financial needs.

But you also use your wallet to carry ID information. NFC can handle that as well. The swipe cards that verify your identity for entry into secure areas can be replaced using NFC to exchange stored virtual credentials. The same technology could replace doors protected with PIN numbers or anywhere a username/password verification is used. So opening a door or logging into a computer could all be managed with a tap of your NFC-enabled phone.

At the time of this writing, there are not many phones on the U.S. market with NFC chips, but all major carriers have announcements planned. Google has announced a mobile app known as Google Wallet that will collect your loyalty cards, gift cards, receipts, boarding passes, tickets, and keys within your phone.

So imagine a time, soon, when you are out to dinner with friends and need to split the bill. Your NFC phone is already linked to your PayPal account and you simply wave your phone next to your friend's phone to transfer him your share of the bill. Some are predicting the worldwide NFC market will grow to be worth $50 billion by 2014, making this a trend to watch.

YOSHIKAZU TSUNO / AFP / Getty Images / Newscom

Figure 8.34
NFC-equipped phones will shift how we handle financial transactions and identify ourselves.

1. What are the changes that have brought us a digital lifestyle?

The increased use of digital information has led to a period of greater creativity and control of our data. In a digital format, information is easy to carry, manipulate, and exchange. This has led to revolutionary changes in communication, entertainment media, and mobile computing.

2. How do cell phone and smartphone components resemble a traditional computer?

Like a traditional computer, a cell/smartphone has a central processor, memory, and an operating system. These components work in the same way as in a computer to process information and support communications, software applications, and other services.

3. Why would I use VoIP?

VoIP allows inexpensive communication using a computer or a WiFi-enabled phone. Because it is based on a digital format for information, it can support services like automatic delivery of phone messages to an e-mail account or texts to a mobile device.

4. How is digital media different from analog?

Digital media is based on a series of numeric data comprising number values that were measured from the original analog waveform. As a string of numbers, a digital photo or video file can be easily processed by modern computers.

5. How is digital media created and what changes has it brought?

Digital publishing is allowing a variety of new distribution methods into the industry. eReaders and online bookstores are bringing changes to the models of how to sell printed materials. Digital music is created by combining pure digital sounds with samples of analog sounds. It has meant changes for the recording industry, for performers, and for music listeners. It is now inexpensive to carry a music library, to create new songs, and to distribute them worldwide.

6. How do I create and watch digital video?

You can create digital video using any digital camera, webcam, or digital camcorder. Digital editing software allows you to add transitions, effects, and sound tracks. There are a great many sources of digital video, including free sources like YouTube and JustIn, as well as pay-per-view services like Amazon Video On Demand or cable providers' streaming video options.

7. What new kinds of mobile devices are available?

There is a wide array of mobile devices, and each has a unique set of tools and software collected together. Internet tablets, netbooks, and mobile gaming devices each have specific advantages. Digital convergence has brought us single devices that have the capabilities that used to require four or five separate tools. We now see products that allow us to interact with information in ways that had been too expensive or difficult before.

 Companion Website

The Companion Website includes a variety of additional materials to help you review and learn more about the topics in this chapter. Go to: *www.pearsonhighered.com/techinaction*

key terms  eight _{chapter}

key terms

eight buzzwords

Word Bank

- analog-to-digital converter
- Bluetooth
- cell phone
- digital convergence
- GPS
- Internet tablet
- microbrowser
- MMS
- netbook
- P2P
- PMP
- sampling rate
- smartphone
- SMS
- synchronize
- telephony
- VoIP
- webcam

Instructions: Fill in the blanks using the words from the Word Bank above.

Ananda knows that everything seems to be "digital" these days. In the past, she carried a traditional SLR camera but now she simply uses her (1) _____ to take photos. She can connect wirelessly to the computer to transfer the images because the phone supports (2) _____. Sometimes she doesn't bother to do that because she has already sent a(n) (3) _____ message to a friend with the image. Her old phone couldn't do that because it only supported (4) _____. If she upgraded to a(n) (5) _____, she could actually make many refinements and edits to the image without transferring it to the computer at all.

Nigel is a real fan of technology, and so he has selected a(n) (6) _____ instead of a cell/smartphone. He's always near a WiFi signal, so he doesn't need an actual phone. He doesn't even pay for traditional phone service at home, where he uses (7) _____ instead of a landline. He's fallen in love with his new device for many reasons. It can give him driving directions with its built-in (8) _____. The (9) _____ software displays full HTML Web pages right on the device. He used to have to sync his device each night, but now he uses wireless (10) _____ technology to synchronize instantly.

Niti can't quite decide what device will work best for his new life. He's moving to California and plans to be outside a lot, so he wants something very light. He thinks the two-pound (11) _____ might be ideal because he doesn't really need a full keyboard or a huge screen. When he's out biking, he has plans to wear his (12) _____ on his helmet and keep a video record of his excursion. He downloads free songs offered by bands that are just starting out from a(n) (13) _____ site. The songs have a much lower (14) _____ than he usually demands, but at least they don't take up much space on his hard drive. He's heard that electronics are merging with clothing more and more, so maybe soon (15) _____ will lead to a T-shirt that can take care of his mobile music needs!

Instructions: Write a report providing answers to the questions posed below, using as many of the key terms from the chapter as you can. Be sure the sentences are grammatically and technically correct.

You have a limited budget to spend on technology tools and toys in the years you will be a student. You are considering communication, entertainment media, and your need to be able to work and connect with your information when you are not at home. Which digital media services and products would you definitely invest in? How would you justify their value? What kinds of services and products would you use that are free or low cost? Has the migration to a digital lifestyle given you more freedom and creativity or just caused you more annoyance and expense?

Instructions: Answer the multiple-choice and true–false questions below for more practice with key terms and concepts from this chapter.

Multiple Choice

1. Which is *not* a factor that determines the quality of images taken with a digital camera?
   a. lens quality
   b. resolution
   c. file format
   d. eye-Fi

2. Cloud technology is important to mobile device owners because it
   a. allows you to carry video files.
   b. transmits weather and radar information.
   c. means you no longer need Internet access.
   d. allows instant synchronization of multiple devices.

3. The operating system of your cell/smartphone is stored in
   a. read-only memory.
   b. the display.
   c. the digital signal processor.
   d. random-access memory.

4. The quickest way to distribute your band's new song to a lot of listeners is to
   a. use an application to post it on Facebook.
   b. you cannot legally distribute music freely.
   c. e-mail the song to local radio stations.
   d. hand out CDs that you burned.

5. P2P is an acronym for
   a. packet-to-packet networking.
   b. peer-to-peer sharing.
   c. person-to-person texting.
   d. power-to-power delivery.

6. An analog signal is different from a digital signal because
   a. it is continuous.
   b. it has only specific discrete values.
   c. it is easier to duplicate.
   d. it is easier to transmit.

7. Flash memory is a type of
   a. nonvolatile memory.
   b. hard drive memory.
   c. SSD memory.
   d. volatile memory.

8. VoIP is phone service that
   a. works even when the electricity goes out.
   b. works over an Internet connection.
   c. requires no special setup for a secure connection.
   d. has extremely high quality and is very reliable.

9. Which of the following is *not* true about modern televisions?
   a. They incorporate wireless connectivity.
   b. They allow other services, like caller ID, to be integrated.
   c. You can purchase apps for them.
   d. They run word processing and spreadsheet software.

10. Which service allows you to use your cell/smartphone to send messages that contain images?
   a. MMS   b. ISP
   c. SMS   d. MiFi

True-False

_____ 1. Digital convergence means that all cellular networks will become 4G.

_____ 2. Digital music files must be converted to the MP3 format if they are transferred to a mobile device.

_____ 3. A codec is the algorithm that compresses and decompresses video files.

_____ 4. If your digital camera doesn't support wireless connectivity, you can use a memory card with built-in WiFi.

_____ 5. Some Internet-enabled devices use Skype instead of cell phone service for voice communications.

making the transition to... next semester

1. Choosing Mobile Devices to Fit Your Needs

As a student, which devices discussed in this chapter would have the most immediate impact on the work you do each day? Which would provide the best value (that is, the greatest increase in productivity and organization per dollar spent)? Consider the full range of devices, from cell/smartphones to notebook systems.

2. Ready . . . Set . . . Act!

As a student, you often give presentations or take on student teaching assignments. What would be the steps for creating a digital video recording of one of your presentations? What tools would you need to record? What kind of file would you end up producing? How would you distribute the video to a live Internet audience? How would you make a DVD of the performance?

3. Author, Author

As a new author of fantasy stories, you have written a collection of fiction shorts. You decide to publish them yourself. What options are there for you to use? How do they compare/contrast?

4. Choosing the Best Phone

Your friend wants to trim down the number of different devices that she carries. Visit the most popular cellular providers' Web sites and research options. Compare at least three different models of phones and list their price, music storage capacity, built-in memory, and expandability options.

a. Which of the three models you compared is the best value for your friend? Why?
b. What special features does the phone you chose have? What accessories would you recommend your friend buy to make the phone more useful?
c. Would you suggest buying a refurbished phone? Why or why not?

5. iTunes U

Download a free copy of iTunes software. In the iTunes Store, explore the iTunes U podcast directory, which contains free audio and video lectures published by major universities.

a. Look for the MIT Open Courseware collection. How many lectures are available?
b. If each lecture were 90 minutes on average and approximately 200 MB in size, how much storage would it take to save all of the video lectures in every course published by MIT?
c. Is there a mobile device that can store and play that much content? What devices could store the lectures from all of the courses in mathematics offered by MIT Open Courseware?

1. Corporate Mobile Communications Needs

Imagine your company is boosting its sales force and looking to the future of mobile technology. Your manager has asked you to research the following issues surrounding mobile communications for the company:

a. Do mobile communication devices present increased security risks? What would happen if you left a cell/smartphone at a meeting and a competitor picked it up? Are there ways to protect your data on mobile devices?

b. Can viruses attack cell/smartphones? Is there any special software on the market to protect mobile devices from viruses? How much would it cost to equip 20 devices with virus protection?

c. Is there a role for mobile communication devices even if employees don't leave the building? Which devices would be important for a company to consider for use within corporate offices? Are there software solutions that would work as well?

d. Should employees be allowed to use smartphones provided by the company for personal use even though files related to personal use might eat up potentially valuable memory and space? What restrictions should be put on personal use to protect the privacy of proprietary company information contained on the devices?

2. 5G and 4G Communications

The most recent generation of telecommunications (nicknamed "4G" for fourth generation) is currently allowing the speed of cellular network transmissions to hit 3–6 Mbps. In the near future, full 4G speeds of closer to 100Mbps will be available. But what is beyond that?

What is in place for the development of a 5G system? How do 4G and 5G compare to current broadband access over wired networks? What implications does that have for information access and e-commerce? What download speed would be ideal? Upload speed? How would it change how you communicate?

3. Subscription Versus Ownership

With the arrival of reliable, fast, networked digital information, businesses can track the location and status of all kinds of objects, such as cars and bicycles. This is introducing a new business model different from individual ownership—now using a car can become a "subscription" service.

What options are there for "subscribing" to a car instead of owning one? How about for a bicycle? Are there other businesses you can identify that would be able to take advantage of digital information and become subscription services instead of vendors of a physical product? What are the advantages to the consumer of subscription over ownership? What are the drawbacks?

4. Too Much Media?

Imagine you are a manager of 18 employees, all of whom work with constant Internet access. As a manager, what concerns might you have about their use of corporate bandwidth to download and view media files? Do you think it would benefit your business to block any MP3 file transfers? Should you put in place a block to prevent access to sites that store huge numbers of streaming videos? As a manager, are there concerns you might have if employees have digital cameras on their cell/smartphones? Would your answers be different in an academic setting?

5. Mobile Devices on the Highway

Mobile devices used in vehicles are becoming the norm in today's society. Consider the following:

a. Several car manufacturers provide Bluetooth option packages for their vehicles. What advantages are there to having Bluetooth connectivity in your car? Are there any disadvantages?

b. Examine the Microsoft Sync software package. List the features and services it provides. If you were a salesperson with a territory that you covered by car, how would Sync help you?

Instructions: Some ideas are best understood by experimenting with them in our own minds. The following critical thinking questions are designed to demand your full attention but require only a comfortable chair—no technology.

1. Digital Entertainment

Can you name a style of media that has not made the shift to digital? What advantages does digital photography offer? Digital video? What disadvantages come along with a digital format for entertainment media? Has the growth in digital media promoted an increased understanding between people or has it created more isolation?

2. The Ultimate Style

As mobile devices continue to evolve, they have become lighter and smaller, and we are beginning to see a convergence of computing and clothing.

a. What would the ultimate convergent mobile clothing be for you? Is there a limit in weight, size, or complexity?

b. Can you imagine uses for technology in fashion that would support better health? Better social relationships? A richer intellectual life?

3. Reinvent Yourself

The arrival of digital information has forced major shifts in several industries, such as publishing, music recording, and film. How has each industry reacted? Have they each found ways to reinvent the products and services they deliver to match the challenge of the Digital Age? What other industries have had to realign their business model because of digital information?

4. Too Much Information?

Consider the following questions:

a. Your rental car has a GPS installed. After you return it, the rental company uses the GPS data to determine whether you have driven the car at speeds above the speed limit. It then issues fines for violations of the rental contract. Does this lead to safer highways? Is it an infringement of your privacy?

b. Would you agree to insert a GPS-enabled tracking chip into your pet? Your child? What legislation do you think should be required regarding use of the tracking data from your phone records? Would you be willing to sell that information to marketing agencies? Should that data be available to the government if you were suspected of a crime?

5. Electronic Publishing

Explore the specifications of the Sony Portable Reader, the Barnes & Noble NOOK, the Amazon Kindle, and the Apple iPad. How would your study habits change if your textbooks were only delivered to you in electronic format on one of these devices? What unique advantages would there be? What disadvantages would there be? How would using such a device compare with just receiving the book as an electronic file, such as a PDF document, to your notebook computer?

eight team time

"...and one will rule them all."

Problem

Digital convergence posits the dream of one device that can do it all, for everyone. But there are so many different mobile devices saturating the market that many people are left in a state of confusion. Either they are buying too many devices and not using them, or they are paralyzed from buying anything because of the dilemma of too many choices.

Task

For each client scenario described below, the group will select the minimum set of devices that would support and enhance the client's life.

Process

1. Consider the following three clients:

   • A retired couple who now travel for pleasure a great deal. They want to be involved in their grandchildren's lives and will need support for their health , finances, and personal care as they age.
   • A young family with two children, two working parents, and a tight budget.
   • A couple in which each individual is a physician and they both adore technology.

2. Make two recommendations for your client in terms of digital technologies that will enhance their business or their lifestyle. Discuss the advantages and disadvantages of each technology. Consider value, reliability, computing needs, training needed, and communication needs, as well as expandability for the future.

3. As a group, prepare a final report that considers the costs, availability, and unique features of the recommendations you have made for each client.

4. Bring the research materials from the individual team meetings to class. Looking at the clients' needs, make final decisions as to which digital technologies are best suited for each client.

Conclusion

Digital information has allowed the development of a new style of living, both at home and at work. With so many digital solutions on the market today, recommending digital communication, media management, and mobility options needs to focus on converging to the minimum set of tools that will enhance life without adding complication to it.

When Everyone Has a Voice

In this exercise, you will research and then role-play a complicated ethical situation. The role you play might or might not match your own personal beliefs; in either case, your research and use of logic will enable you to represent the view assigned. An arbitrator will watch and comment on both sides of the arguments, and together the team will agree on an ethical solution.

Background

Much of the world's population is now equipped with Internet-ready camera phones. Sensors on these phones could measure for viruses or compute pollution indexes, while the cameras could be used to document a range of human behavior. This could create changes in political movements, art, and culture as everyone's experience is documented and shared.

Research Areas to Consider

- Evgeny Morozov RSA Animate

- Mobilebehavior.com

- Witness project

- Center for Embedded Network Sensing

Process

Divide the class into teams.

1. Research the sources cited above and devise a scenario in which mobile access could make an impact politically or environmentally, positively or negatively.

2. Team members should write a summary that provides background information for their character—for example, business owner, politician, reporter, and arbitrator—and details their character's behaviors to set the stage for the role-playing event. Then, team members should create an outline to use during the role-playing event.

3. Team members should arrange a mutually convenient time to meet for the exchange, either using the collaboration feature of MyITLab, the discussion board feature of Blackboard, or meeting in person.

4. Team members should present their case to the class, or submit a PowerPoint presentation for review by the rest of the class, along with the summary and resolution they developed.

Conclusion

As technology becomes ever more prevalent and integrated into our lives, more and more ethical dilemmas will present themselves. Being able to understand and evaluate both sides of the argument, while responding in a personally or socially ethical manner, will be an important skill.

securing your system

protecting your digital data and devices

karlkotasinc/
iStockphoto.com

Cybercrime

OBJECTIVE:

What is cybercrime and who perpetrates it? *(p. 406)*

© ImageState / Alamy

Viruses

OBJECTIVES:

From which types of viruses do I need to protect my computer? *(p. 409)*

What can I do to protect my computer from viruses? *(p. 411)*

 Active Helpdesk: Avoiding Computer Viruses

Sound Byte: Protecting Your Computer

Lauren Nicole /
Getty Images

Protecting Digital Assets from Hackers

OBJECTIVES:

How can hackers attack my computing devices, and what harm can they cause? *(p. 413)*

What is a firewall, and how does it keep my computer safe from hackers? *(p. 417)*

How do I create secure passwords and manage all of my passwords? *(p. 420)*

Scan here for more info on How Cool Is This? ▶

How can I surf the Internet anonymously and use biometric authentication devices to protect my data? *(p. 424)*

 Active Helpdesk: Understanding Firewalls

 Sound Byte: Installing a Personal Firewall

© D. Hurst / Alamy

Managing Online Annoyances

OBJECTIVE:

How do I manage online annoyances such as spyware and spam? *(p. 427)*

SVLuma /
Shutterstock.com

Protecting Yourself . . . from Yourself!

OBJECTIVES:

What data do I need to back up, and what are the best methods for doing so? *(p. 432)*

What is social engineering, and how do I avoid falling prey to phishing and hoaxes? *(p. 436)*

 Sound Byte: Managing Computer Security with Windows Tools

Adchariyaphoto /
Shutterstock.com

Protecting Your Physical Computing Assets

OBJECTIVE:

How do I protect my physical computing assets from environmental hazards, power surges, and theft? *(p. 440)*

 Sound Byte: Surge Protectors

how cool is *this?*

You have a lot of **information** in your **phone**. What happens if you lose your phone, damage it beyond repair, or want to **switch** phones? Transferring data can be very time consuming, or even impossible if you lose your phone. Apps like Snap Secure provide a solution by allowing you to **back up** the information and settings on your phone to a secure Web site at regular intervals (daily, weekly, etc.). Then if your phone is ever lost, stolen, or damaged, or if you are just upgrading to the latest model, you can easily **transfer** your information to a new or replacement phone. So install a backup app on your phone today and enjoy some peace of mind!

Talaj/iStockphoto.com

Cybercrime

The media is full of stories about malicious computer programs damaging computers, criminals stealing people's identities online, and attacks on corporate Web sites that have brought major corporations to a standstill. These are examples of cybercrime.

What is cybercrime? Cybercrime is any criminal action perpetrated primarily through the use of a computer. The existence of cybercrime means that computer users must take precautions to protect themselves. The FBI maintains a Web site (**www.fbi.gov/about-us/investigate/cyber/cyber**) specifically to inform the public about types of cybercrimes and methods of protecting yourself (see Figure 9.1).

Who perpetrates computer crimes? Cybercriminals are individuals who use computers, networks, and the Internet to perpetrate crime. Anyone with a computer and the wherewithal to arm him- or herself with the appropriate knowledge can be a cybercriminal.

What kinds of cybercrimes are conducted over the Internet? The Internet Crime Complaint Center (IC3) is a partnership between the Federal Bureau of Investigation (FBI) and the National White Collar Crime Center (NW3C). In 2010 (the latest data available at this book's publication), IC3 received almost 304,000 complaints related to Internet crime. The top four categories of complaints received were non-delivery of payments/merchandise, identity theft, auction fraud, and credit card fraud. Complaints not related to fraud still pertained to serious issues such as computer intrusions, extortion, blackmail, and child pornography. Much of the credit card fraud was perpetrated when credit card numbers were stolen by criminals tricking people into revealing sensitive information or by computer programs that gather credit card data.

What is the most financially damaging cybercrime plaguing individuals? Theft of personal data such as bank account numbers and credit/debit card numbers are of most concern to individuals because this information is usually used for fraudulent purposes that can cause individuals to lose a great deal of time and/or money. **Identity theft** occurs when a thief steals your name, address, Social Security number, birth date, bank account, and credit card information and runs up debts in your name. This can cause great distress as you're hounded by creditors trying to collect on the fraudulent debts. Many victims of identity theft spend months (or even years) trying to repair their credit and eliminate fraudulent debts.

What types of scams do identity thieves perpetrate? An identity thief could take out a mortgage on a home in your name and then quickly resell the house and abscond with the profits, leaving you owing a large sum of money on a house you never bought. Identity thieves might also pose as you to obtain medical services at hospitals. Then you may be denied coverage at a later date because the thief's treatment has exceeded the limit of covered services on your policy.

Perpetrators will often counterfeit your credit/debit cards so they can use them for fraudulent transactions. To keep you from detecting bogus charges in a timely manner, the thieves often request a change of address for your credit card bill or bank statement. By the time you realize that you aren't receiving your statements, the thieves have rung up large balances on your credit card or emptied your bank account. The thieves might also open new credit card

Figure 9.1

The FBI maintains a site dedicated to informing you about cybercrime.

Department of Justice

and bank accounts in your name. They then will write bad checks and not pay the credit card bills, which can ruin your credit rating.

Many people believe that the only way your identity can be stolen is by a computer. This is simply not true. The Federal Trade Commission (**www.ftc.gov**) has identified other methods thieves use to obtain others' personal information. These include (1) stealing purses and wallets, in which people often keep unnecessary valuable personal information such as their ATM PIN codes; (2) stealing mail or looking through trash for bank statements and credit card bills, which provide valuable personal information; and (3) posing as bank or credit card company representatives and tricking people into revealing sensitive information over the phone. And thieves are now installing skimming devices on ATM machines that record information, such as account numbers and passcodes, when people use their access cards at the ATMs.

Although foolproof protection methods don't exist, there are precautions that will help you minimize your risk, which we'll discuss later in this chapter.

With all the news coverage about identity theft and other cybercrimes, aren't people being more cautious? Unfortunately, most of us are not. Although most people are aware of spam, a recent survey by the Messaging Anti-Abuse Working Group (MAAWG) found that half of e-mail users in North America and Europe have opened spam. And the MAAWG discovered that 46 percent of people who opened spam did so intentionally—out of idle curiosity, to follow links to unsubscribe to unwanted e-mails (which only brings more spam), or because they are interested in the product being touted. Clearly, we are often our own worst enemies!

Are computer viruses a type of cybercrime? A computer **virus** is a computer program that attaches itself to another computer program (known as the host program) and attempts to spread to other computers when files are exchanged. Creating and disseminating computer viruses is one of the most widespread types of cybercrimes. Tens of thousands of new viruses or modified versions of old viruses are released each year. Some viruses cause only minor annoyances, while others cause destruction of data. Many viruses are now designed to gather sensitive information

such as credit card numbers. Viruses such as SpyEye Mobile Banking are used to trick users into downloading an infected file to their phones, which then is used to steal their online banking information. This illustrates how serious a threat a virus can pose to your digital security. You need to make sure your data is protected from viruses and other malicious software attacks.

Does cybercrime include the theft of computing devices? Although theft of computer equipment is not classified as a cybercrime (rather, it is considered larceny), the theft of tablets, cell phones, notebook computers, and other portable computing devices is on the rise. The resale value for used electronic equipment is high, which contributes to demand for stolen merchandise. The ease with which equipment can be sold online also fuels this problem.

In this chapter, we discuss serious threats to your digital security such as computer viruses and other activities of cybercriminals, less serious annoyances such as spyware and spam, and good security practices to keep yourself from undermining your digital security and exposing yourself to identity theft and other types of fraud. We also discuss methods for protecting your digital assets from attacks and unintentional damage.

Computer Threats: Computer Viruses

Computer viruses are threatening because they are engineered to evade detection. Viruses normally attempt to hide within the code of a host program to avoid detection. And viruses are not just limited to computers. Any computing device such as a smartphone, notebook, or tablet computer can be infected with a virus. Even your car, which now contains embedded computer systems, could catch a virus, especially if it connects to the Internet for software updates.

What do computer viruses do? A computer virus's main purpose is to replicate itself and copy its code into as many other host files as possible. This gives it a greater chance of being copied to another computer system to spread its infection. However, computer viruses require human interaction to spread. Although there might be a virus in a file on your computer, a virus cannot normally infect your computer until that file is opened or executed.

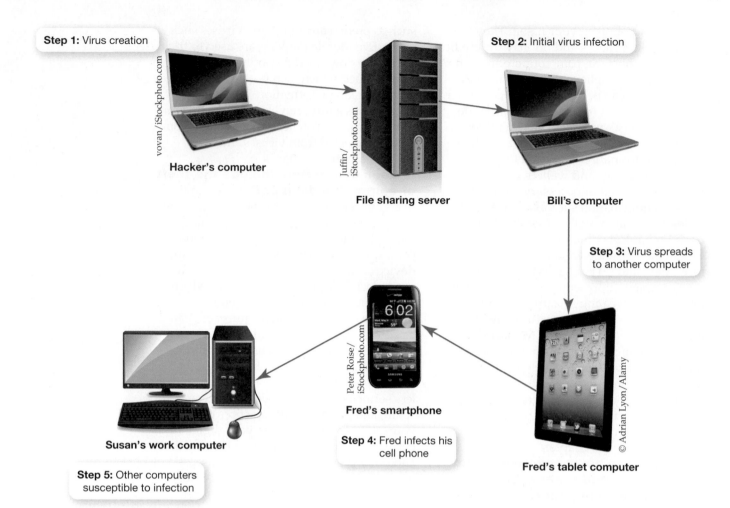

Step 1: Virus creation

Hacker's computer

vovan / iStockphoto.com

Juffin / iStockphoto.com

File sharing server

Step 2: Initial virus infection

Bill's computer

Step 3: Virus spreads to another computer

Susan's work computer

Step 5: Other computers susceptible to infection

Peter Roise / iStockphoto.com

Fred's smartphone

Step 4: Fred infects his cell phone

© Adrian Lyon / Alamy

Fred's tablet computer

Figure 9.2

Computer viruses are passed from one unsuspecting user to the next.

Although virus replication can slow down networks, it is not usually the main threat. The majority of viruses have secondary objectives or side effects, ranging from displaying annoying messages on the computer screen to destroying files or the contents of entire hard drives. Because computer viruses cause disruption to computer systems, including data destruction and information theft, virus creation and deployment is a form of cybercrime.

How does my computer catch a virus? If your computer is exposed to a file infected with a virus, the virus will try to copy itself and infect a file on your computer. If you never expose your computer to new files, then it will not become infected. However, this would be the equivalent of a human being living in a bubble to avoid catching viruses from other people—quite impractical.

Downloading infected audio and video files from peer-to-peer file sharing sites is a major source of virus infections. Shared

flash drives are also a common source of virus infection, as is e-mail, although many people have misconceptions about how e-mail infection occurs. Just opening an e-mail message will not usually infect your computer with a virus, although some new viruses are launched when viewed in the preview pane of your e-mail software. Downloading or running (executing) a file that is attached to the e-mail is a common way that your computer becomes infected. Thus, be extremely wary of e-mail attachments, especially if you don't know the sender. Figure 9.2 illustrates the steps by which computer viruses are often passed from one computer to the next:

1. An individual writes a virus program and attaches it to a music file of a popular music group's new hit song and posts it to a file sharing site.

2. Unsuspecting Bill downloads the "music file" and infects his computer when he listens to the song.

3. Bill sends his cousin Fred an e-mail with the infected "music file" and contaminates Fred's tablet computer.

4. Fred syncs his phone with his tablet and infects his phone as well when he plays the music file.

5. Fred e-mails the file from his phone to Susan, one of his colleagues at work. Everyone who copies files from Susan's infected computer at work, or whose computer is networked to Susan's computer, risks spreading the virus.

Types of Viruses

Although thousands of computer viruses and variants exist, they can be grouped into five broad categories based on their behavior and method of transmission.

Boot-Sector Viruses

What are boot-sector viruses? A **boot-sector virus** replicates itself into a hard drive's master boot record. The **master boot record** is a program that executes whenever a computer boots up, ensuring that the virus will be loaded into memory immediately, even before some virus protection programs can load. Boot-sector viruses are often transmitted by a flash drive left in a USB port. When the computer boots up with the flash drive connected, the computer tries to launch a master boot record from the flash drive, which is usually the trigger for the virus to infect the hard drive.

Logic Bombs and Time Bombs

What is a logic bomb? A **logic bomb** is a virus that is triggered when certain logical conditions are met—such as opening a file or starting a program a certain number of times. A **time bomb** is a virus that is triggered by the passage of time or on a certain date. For example, the Michelangelo virus was a famous time bomb that was set to trigger every year on March 6, Michelangelo's birthday. The BlackWorm virus (otherwise known as Kama Sutra, Mywife, or CME-24), another time bomb, spreads through e-mail attachments. Opening the attachment infects the computer, and on the third day of every month, the virus seeks out and deletes certain file types (such as executable or .EXE files) on Windows computers. The effects of logic bombs and time bombs range from the display of annoying messages on the screen to reformatting of the hard drive, which causes complete data loss.

CAPTCHA: Keeping Web Sites Safe from Bots

Automated programs called bots (or Web robots) are used to make tasks easier on the Internet. Search engines use bots in a technique called spidering to search and index Web pages. Unfortunately, bots can also be used for malicious or illegal purposes because these bots can perform some computing tasks much faster than humans. For example, bots can be used on ticket ordering sites to try to buy large blocks of high-demand concert tickets or to make repeated entries into contests in attempts to increase the chances of winning sweepstakes or prizes. Frequently, bots are used to post spam in the comments sections of blogs. Fortunately, Web site owners can easily deploy software known as a CAPTCHA program (see Figure 9.3) to prevent such bot activities.

CAPTCHA (Completely Automated Public Turing Test to Tell Computers and Humans Apart) programs generate distorted text and require that it be typed into a box. Because bots can't yet be programmed to read distorted text, which most people usually can, the CAPTCHA program is used to verify that a human is performing whatever task is being tested. The program helps Web site owners defend against all types of automated scams. If you want to try integrating a CAPTCHA program into your Web site (to protect your e-mail address), go to **www.google.com/recaptcha**, which offers free CAPTCHA tools to help you protect your data.

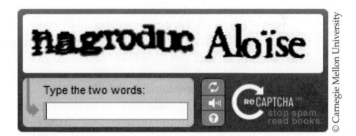

© Carnegie Mellon University

Figure 9.3
CAPTCHA programs like this one verify that a human, not a bot being used for malicious purposes, is performing the requested task.

Worms

What is a worm? Although often called a virus, a **worm** is subtly different. Viruses require human interaction to spread, whereas worms take advantage of file transport methods, such as e-mail or network connections, to spread on their own. A virus infects a host file and waits until that file is executed to replicate and infect a computer system. A worm, however, works independently of host file execution and is much more active in spreading itself. When the Conficker worm broke out, it quickly infected an estimated 9 million to 15 million individual computers. This worm spread through vulnerabilities in the Windows code and compromised computers by disabling certain software services and utility programs, such as Windows Update.

Script and Macro Viruses

What are script and macro viruses? Some viruses are hidden on Web sites in the form of scripts. A **script** is a series of commands—actually, a miniprogram—that is executed without your knowledge. Scripts are often used to perform useful, legitimate functions on Web sites, such as collecting name and address information from customers. However, some scripts are malicious. For example, say you receive an e-mail encouraging you to visit a Web site full of useful programs and information. When you click a link to display a video on the Web site you were directed to, a script runs that infects your computer with a virus without your knowledge.

A **macro virus** is a virus that attaches itself to a document that uses macros. A macro is a short series of commands that usually automates repetitive tasks. However, macro languages are now so sophisticated that viruses can be written with them. The Melissa virus became the first major macro virus to cause problems worldwide.

The Melissa virus was also the first practical example of an e-mail virus. **E-mail viruses** use the address book in the victim's e-mail system to distribute the virus. Anyone opening an infected document triggered the virus, which infected other Word documents on the victim's computer. Once triggered, the Melissa virus sent itself to the first 50 people in the address book on the infected computer. This helped ensure that Melissa became one of the most widely distributed viruses ever released.

Encryption Viruses

What are encryption viruses? When **encryption viruses** infect your computer, they run a program that searches for common types of data files, such as Microsoft Word and Excel files, and compresses them using a complex encryption key that renders your files unusable. You then receive a message that asks you to send money to an account if you want to receive the program to decrypt your files. The flaw with this type of virus, which keeps it from being widespread, is that law enforcement officials can trace the payments to an account and may possibly be able to catch the perpetrators. Still, we see these types of viruses from time to time.

Virus Classifications

How else are viruses classified? Viruses can also be classified by the methods they take to avoid detection by antivirus software:

- A **polymorphic virus** changes its own code or periodically rewrites itself to avoid detection. Most polymorphic viruses infect a particular type of file such as .EXE files, for example.

- A **multipartite virus** is designed to infect multiple file types in an effort to fool the antivirus software that is looking for it.

- **Stealth viruses** temporarily erase their code from the files where they reside and then hide in the active memory of the computer. This helps them avoid detection if only the hard drive is being searched for viruses. Fortunately, current antivirus software scans memory as well as the hard drive.

Given the creativity of virus programmers, you can be sure we'll see other types of viruses emerge in the future.

How can I tell if my computer is infected with a virus? Sometimes it can be difficult to definitely tell if your computer is infected with a virus. However, if your computer displays any of the following symptoms, it may be infected with a virus:

1. Existing program icons or files suddenly disappear. Viruses often delete specific file types or programs.

2. If you start your browser and it takes you to an unusual home page (i.e., one you didn't set) or it has new toolbars.

3. Odd messages, pop-ups, or images are displayed on the screen or strange music or sounds play.

ACTIVE HELP-DESK   Avoiding Computer Viruses

In this Active Helpdesk call, you'll play the role of a helpdesk staffer, fielding calls about different types of viruses and what users should do to protect their computer from them.

4. Data files become corrupt. However, files can become corrupt for reasons other than a virus infection.

5. Programs stop working properly, which could be caused by either a corrupted file or a virus.

6. Your system slows down or takes a long time to boot up.

Computer Safeguard: Antivirus Software and Software Updates

Certain viruses merely present minor annoyances, such as randomly sending an ambulance graphic across the bottom of the screen, as is the case with the Red Cross virus. Other viruses can significantly slow down a computer or network, or destroy key files or the contents of entire hard drives. The best defense against viruses is to install antivirus software. **Antivirus software** is specifically designed to detect viruses and protect your computer and files from harm. Symantec, Kaspersky, AVG, and McAfee are among the companies that offer highly rated antivirus software packages.

Although you can buy stand-alone antivirus software, antivirus protection is included in comprehensive Internet security packages such as Norton Internet Security, Kaspersky Internet Security, or McAfee Total Protection. These software packages will help protect you from other threats as well as from computer viruses.

Antivirus Software

How often do I need to run antivirus software? Although antivirus software is designed to detect suspicious activity on your computer at all times, you should run an active virus scan on your entire system at least once a week. By doing so, all files on your computer will be checked for undetected viruses. Most modern antivirus programs run scans in the background when your CPU is not being heavily utilized. But you can also configure the software to run scans automatically at specific times when you aren't normally using your system—for example, when

you are asleep (see Figure 9.4). Alternatively, if you suspect a problem, you can launch a scan and have it run immediately.

How does antivirus software work? Most antivirus software looks for virus signatures in files. A **virus signature** is a portion of the virus code that is unique to a particular computer virus. Antivirus software scans files for these signatures and thereby identifies infected files and the type of virus that is infecting them.

The antivirus software automatically scans files when they're opened or executed. If it detects a virus signature or suspicious activity, such as the launch of an unknown macro, it stops the execution of the file and virus and notifies you that it has detected a virus. It also places the virus in a secure area on your hard drive so that it won't spread infection to other files. This procedure is known as **quarantining**. Usually the antivirus software then gives you the choice of deleting or repairing the infected file. Unfortunately, antivirus programs can't always

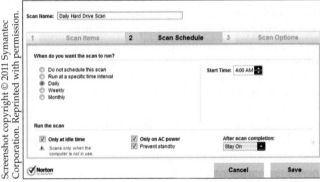

Figure 9.4

In Norton Internet Security, complete virus scans can be set up to run automatically. This computer will be scanned every day at 4 A.M.

fix infected files to make them usable again. You should keep backup copies of critical files so that you can restore them in case a virus damages them irreparably.

Most antivirus software will also attempt to prevent infection by inoculating key files on your computer. In **inoculation**, the antivirus software records key attributes about files on your computer, such as file size and date created, and keeps these statistics in a safe place on your hard drive. When scanning for viruses, the antivirus software compares the files to the attributes it previously recorded to help detect attempts by virus programs to modify your files.

Does antivirus software always stop viruses? Antivirus software catches known viruses effectively. Unfortunately, new viruses are written all the time. To combat unknown viruses, modern antivirus programs search for suspicious virus-like activities as well as virus signatures. However, virus authors know how antivirus software works. They take special measures to disguise their virus code and hide the effects of a virus until just the right moment. This helps ensure that the virus spreads faster and farther. Thus, your computer can be attacked by a virus that your antivirus software doesn't recognize. To minimize this risk, you should keep your antivirus software up to date.

My new computer came with antivirus software installed, so shouldn't I already be protected? Most new computers do come with antivirus software pre-installed. However, these are usually only trial versions of the software that only provide updates to the software for a limited period of time, usually 90 or 180 days. After that, you have to purchase a full version of the software to ensure that you are receiving current updates and remain protected from newly developed viruses. Most full versions of antivirus software provide updates for a year, after which you have to pay to renew your subscription to continue receiving updates.

How do I make sure my antivirus software is up to date? Most antivirus programs have an automatic update feature that downloads updates for virus signature files every time you go online (see Figure 9.5). Also, the antivirus software usually clearly shows the status of your update subscription so you can see how much time you have re-

maining until you need to purchase another version of your software.

What should I do if I think my computer is infected with a virus? Boot up your computer using the antivirus installation disc. (*Note:* If you download your antivirus software from the Internet, it is a good idea to copy your antivirus software to a DVD in case you have problems in the future.) This should prevent most virus programs from loading and will allow you to run the antivirus software directly from your disk drive. If the software does detect viruses, you may want to research them further to determine whether your antivirus software will eradicate them completely or whether you will need to take additional manual steps to eliminate the virus. Most antivirus company Web sites, such as the Symantec site (**www.symantec.com**), contain archives of information on viruses and provide step-by-step solutions for removing viruses.

Does my phone need protection from viruses? Since smartphones and other mobile devices are running operating systems and contain files, they are susceptible to infection by viruses. Cybercriminals are now hiding viruses in legitimate-looking apps for download to mobile devices. Many antivirus software companies now offer antivirus software specifically designed for mobile devices, like Trend Micro's Mobile Security for Android. You need to make sure you purchase the correct version of the software that is designed for the operating system on your mobile device.

Software Updates

Is there anything else I should do to protect my system? Many viruses exploit weaknesses in operating systems. Malicious Web sites can be set up to attack your computer by downloading harmful software onto your computer. According to research conducted by Google, this type of attack, known as a **drive-by download**, is common and affects almost 1 in 1,000 Web pages. To combat these threats, make sure your antivirus software and your operating system are up to date and contain the latest security patches. You can update your Windows operating system with an automatic update utility called Windows Update. When you enable automatic updates, your

Figure 9.5

Antivirus software, such as Norton Internet Security, provides for automatic updates to the software installed on the computer.

Screenshots copyright © 2011 Symantec Corporation. Reprinted with permission.

Click to check for updates

Time remaining on update subscription

computer searches for updates on the Microsoft Web site every time it connects to the Internet. Mac OS X has a similar utility for gathering updates.

Do updates only happen automatically? The default option in Windows 7 is to receive updates automatically. There are several other options you can choose from in Windows 7, as shown in Figure 9.6. The following options are noteworthy.

- Option 1: **Install updates automatically**. Selecting this option will automatically download and install updates at a time you have specified. *We strongly recommend that you select this option.*

- Option 2: **Check for updates but let me choose whether to download and install them**. This is only an appropriate choice if you have low bandwidth Internet access. Because downloads over dial-up can take a long time due to low bandwidth, you need to control when downloads will occur so they don't interrupt your workflow. But you need to be extra vigilant with this option because you may forget to install important updates.

- Option 3: **Give me recommended updates**. This option ensures you receive recommended (optional) updates as well as critical (necessary) updates.

- Option 4: **Microsoft Update**. This option ensures you receive updates for other Microsoft products besides Windows, such as Microsoft Office.

In the next section, we explore another major threat to your digital security—hackers.

Computer Threats: Hackers

Although there is a great deal of disagreement as to what a hacker actually is, especially among hackers themselves, a

SOUND BYTE

Protecting Your Computer

In this Sound Byte, you'll learn how to use a variety of tools to protect your computer, including antivirus software and Windows utilities.

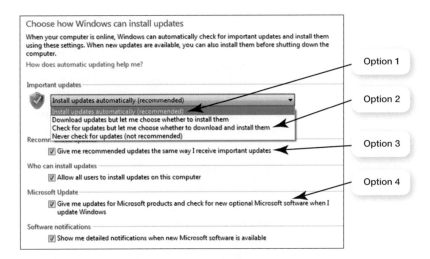

Figure 9.6

The Windows Update screen makes it easy for users to configure Windows to update itself.

>To enable automatic updates, click **Start**, select **Control Panel**, select **System and Security**, click the **Windows Update** link, and then click the **Change Settings** link.

hacker is most commonly defined as anyone who unlawfully breaks into a computer system—either an individual computer or a network (see Figure 9.7).

Are there different kinds of hackers? Some hackers are offended by being labeled as criminals and therefore attempt to classify different types of hackers. Hackers who break into systems for non-malicious reasons, not to steal or wreak havoc, or those under contract to test system security vulnerabilities are often referred to as **white-hat hackers** or ethical hackers. These individuals are usually security experts who are performing a needed service for a company by uncovering the vulnerabilities in computer systems. They believe in making security vulnerabilities known either to the company that owns the system or software or to the general public, often to embarrass a company into fixing a problem.

White-hat hackers look down on those hackers who use their knowledge to destroy information or for illegal gain. A term for these more villainous hackers is **black-hat hackers**. The terms *white hat* and *black hat* are references to old Western movies in which the heroes wore white hats and the outlaws wore black hats. There is even a class of hackers in between these two referred to as **gray-hat hackers**. Gray hats are a bit of a cross between black and white—they will

"Oh, we used to use a crystal ball, but hacking into your credit files is much more informative!"

www.CartoonStock.com

Figure 9.7

Hackers can find lots of personal information about you on the Internet.

often illegally break into systems merely to flaunt their expertise to the administrator of the system they penetrated or to attempt to sell their services in repairing security breaches. Regardless of the hackers' opinions, the laws in the United States and in many other countries consider any unauthorized access to computer systems a crime.

What Problems Can Hackers Cause?

Could a hacker steal my debit card or bank account number? If you perform financial transactions online, such as banking or buying goods and services, then you probably do so using a credit or debit card. Credit card and bank account information can thus reside on your hard drive and may be detectable by a hacker. Aside from your home computer, you have lots of personal data stored on various Web sites. Hackers often try to break into sites that they know contain credit card information. In April 2011, the PlayStation Network was breached by a hacker, forcing Sony to shut down the network until security flaws in the network could be researched and repaired. Sony announced that up to 100 million user accounts had potentially been exposed and that the hackers may have obtained individuals, names, passwords, birthdates, and credit card information.

Also, many sites require you to provide a login ID and password to gain access. Even if this data is not stored on your computer, a hacker may be able to capture it when you're online by using a packet analyzer (sniffer) or a keylogger (a program that captures all keystrokes made on a computer).

What's a packet analyzer? Data travels through the Internet in small pieces, each of which is called a **packet**. The packets are identified with an IP address, in part to help identify the computer to which they are being sent. Once the packets reach their destination, they are reassembled into cohesive messages. A **packet analyzer (sniffer)** is a computer program deployed by hackers that looks at (or sniffs) each packet as it travels on the Internet—not just those that are addressed to a particular computer, but all packets coming across a particular network, like the wireless network at your local coffee shop. Some packet sniffers are configured to capture all the packets into memory, whereas others capture only packets that contain specific content, such as credit card

numbers. Wireless networks can be particularly vulnerable to this type of exploitation because many people do not enable encryption of data when they set up their wireless networks (covered in Chapter 7).

A hacker might sit in a coffee shop connected to a wireless network and run a packet sniffer to capture data from other patrons who are using the wireless network. This makes it easy for hackers to intercept and read sensitive information transmitted without encryption, such as credit card numbers or the contents of e-mails.

What do hackers do with the information they "sniff"? Once a hacker has your debit/credit card information, he or she can either use it to purchase items illegally or sell the number to someone who will. If a hacker steals the login ID and password to an account where you have your bank card information stored (such as eBay or Amazon), he or she can also use your account to purchase items and have them shipped to him- or herself instead of to you. If hackers can gather enough information in conjunction with your bank card information, they may be able to commit identity theft.

Although this sounds scary, you can easily protect yourself from packet sniffing by installing a firewall (which we discuss later in this chapter) and using data encryption on a wireless network (which was covered in Chapter 7).

Trojan Horses and Rootkits

Besides stealing information, what other problems can hackers cause if they break into my computer? Hackers often use individuals' computers as a staging area for mischief. To commit widespread computer attacks, for example, hackers need to control many computers at the same time. To this end, hackers often use Trojan horses to install other programs on computers. A **Trojan horse** is a program that appears to be something useful or desirable, like a game or a screen saver, but while it runs does something malicious in the background without your knowledge. The term *Trojan horse* derives from Greek mythology and refers to the wooden horse that the Greeks used to sneak into the city of Troy and conquer it. Therefore, computer programs that contain a hidden, and usually dreadful, "surprise" are referred to as Trojan horses.

What damage can Trojan horses do? Often, the malicious activity perpetrated by a Trojan horse program is the installation of a backdoor program or a rootkit. **Backdoor programs** and **rootkits** are programs (or sets of programs) that allow hackers to gain access to your computer and take almost complete control of it without your knowledge. These programs are designed to subvert normal logon procedures to a computer and to hide their operations from normal detection methods. Using a backdoor program, hackers can access and delete all the files on your computer, send e-mail, run programs, and do just about anything else you can do with your computer. A computer that a hacker controls in this manner is referred to as a **zombie**. Zombies are often used to launch denial-of-service attacks on other computers.

Denial-of-Service Attacks

What are denial-of-service attacks? In a **denial-of-service (DoS) attack**, legitimate users are denied access to a computer system because a hacker is repeatedly making requests of that computer system through a computer he or she has taken over as a zombie. A computer can handle only a certain number of requests for information at one time. When it is flooded with requests in a denial-of-service attack, it shuts down and refuses to answer any requests for information, even if the requests are from a legitimate user. Thus, the computer is so busy responding to the bogus requests for information that authorized users can't gain access.

Couldn't a DoS attack be traced back to the computer that launched it? Launching a DoS attack on a computer system from a single computer is easy to trace. Therefore, most savvy hackers use a **distributed denial-of-service (DDoS) attack**, which launches DoS attacks from more than one zombie (sometimes thousands of zombies) at the same time. Figure 9.8 illustrates how a DDoS attack works. A hacker creates many zombies and coordinates them so that they begin sending bogus requests to the same computer at the same time. Administrators of the victim computer often have a great deal of difficulty stopping the attack because it comes

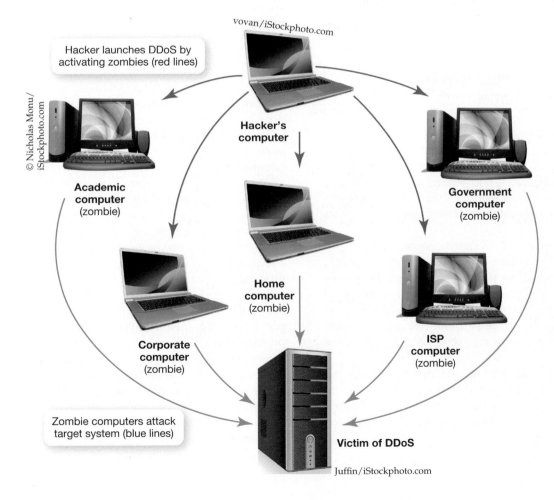

vovan/iStockphoto.com

Hacker launches DDoS by activating zombies (red lines)

© Nicholas Monu/ iStockphoto.com

Hacker's computer

Academic computer (zombie)

Government computer (zombie)

Corporate computer (zombie)

Home computer (zombie)

ISP computer (zombie)

Zombie computers attack target system (blue lines)

Victim of DDoS

Juffin/iStockphoto.com

Figure 9.8

Zombie computers are used to facilitate a distributed denial-of-service (DDoS) attack.

from so many computers. Often the attacks are coordinated automatically by botnets. A **botnet** is a large group of software programs (called *robots* or *bots*) that runs autonomously on zombie computers. Some botnets have been known to span 1.5 million computers.

DDoS attacks are a serious problem. The Web Hacking Incident Database report, issued by Trustwave, reported that DDoS attacks increased 22 percent in the second half of 2010 as compared to the first six months of that year. The mysterious online group Anonymous perpetrated attacks on Egyptian government sites in early 2011 in protest of the Egyptian government's restriction of access to certain Web sites such as Twitter. In December 2010, Anonymous launched DDoS attacks that shut down Mastercard.com and Visa.com as part of a protest against the persecution of the founder of Wikileaks (**www.wikileaks.ch**). Because many commercial Web sites receive revenue from users, either directly (such as via subscriptions to online games) or indirectly (such as when Web surfers click on advertisements), DDoS attacks can be financially distressing for the owners of the affected Web sites.

BITS AND BYTES

Are Your Photographs Helping Criminals Target You?

Smartphones today all contain GPS chips. The cameras in smartphones often use information gathered from the GPS chips to encode information onto photos in the form of geotags. **Geotags** are data attached to a photograph that indicate the latitude and longitude where you were standing when you took the photo. Geotagging photos is useful for applications that can take advantage of this information, but generally the geotags are just superfluous information. The problems arise when you share geotagged photos on the Web.

If you post a lot of photos, cybercriminals and cyberstalkers can use the information from the geotags on your photos to figure out the patterns of your movements. They may be able to ascertain when you are at work or that you are currently on vacation, which leads them to determine prime times for burglarizing your home. Some sites such as Facebook and Twitter have measures in place to limit the amount of geotagged information that can be seen in photos to prevent their users from unwittingly revealing personal information. However, many photo sharing sites do not have such protections in place.

The safest thing to do is not tag your photos with geotags in the first place. It is usually easy to disable location tracking on your smartphone. For instance, on the iPhone, you would go to the settings screen, select General, then Location Services, and choose Off. So stop geotagging your photos and make it tougher for the cybercriminals to figure out your movements.

How Hackers Gain Access

How exactly does a hacker gain access to a computer? Hackers can gain access to computers directly or indirectly. Direct access involves sitting down at a computer and installing hacking software. It is unlikely that such an attack would occur in your home. However, to deter unauthorized use, you may want to lock the room that your computer is in or remove key components, such as the power cord, when strangers such as repair personnel are in your house and may be unobserved for periods of time. You might also set up your computer so that it requires a password for a user to gain access to your desktop.

The most likely method a hacker will use to access a computer is to enter indirectly through its Internet connection. When connected to the Internet, your computer is potentially open to attack by hackers. Many people forget that their Internet connection is a two-way street. Not only can you access the Internet but also people on the Internet can access your computer.

Think of your computer as a house. Common sense tells you to lock your doors and windows to deter theft when you aren't home. Hooking your computer up to the Internet is like leaving the front door to your house wide open. Anyone passing by can access your computer and poke around for valuables. Your computer obviously doesn't have doors and windows like a house, but it does have logical ports.

What are logical ports? **Logical ports** are virtual—that is, not physical—communications gateways or paths that allow a computer to organize requests for information, such as Web page downloads or e-mail routing, from other networks or computers. Unlike physical ports (USB, FireWire, and so on), you can't see or touch a logical port; it is part of a computer's internal organization.

Logical ports are numbered and assigned to specific services. For instance, logical port 80 is designated for hypertext transfer protocol (HTTP), the main communications protocol for the World Wide Web. Thus, all requests for information from your browser to the Web flow through logical port 80. E-mail messages sent by simple mail transfer protocol (SMTP), the protocol used for sending e-mail on the Internet, are routed through logical port 25. Open logical ports, like open windows in a home, invite intruders, as illustrated in Figure 9.9. Unless you take precautions to restrict access to your logical ports, other people on the Internet may be able to access your computer through them.

Fortunately, you can thwart most hacking problems by installing a firewall.

Restricting Access to Your Digital Assets

Keeping hackers at bay is often just a matter of keeping them out. This can be achieved either by preventing them from accessing your computer (usually through your Internet connection), by protecting your digital information in such a way that it can't be accessed (with passwords, for example), or by hiding your activities from prying eyes. In the next section, we explore strategies for protecting access to your digital assets and keeping your Internet surfing activities from being seen by the wrong people.

Firewalls

A **firewall** is a software program or hardware device designed to protect computers from hackers. It's named after a housing construction feature that slows the spread of fires from house to house. Although installing either a software or a hardware firewall on your home network is probably sufficient, you should consider installing both for maximum protection. A firewall specifically designed for home networks is called a **personal firewall**. Personal firewalls are made to be easy to install. By using a personal firewall, you can close open logical ports to invaders and potentially make your computer invisible to other computers on the Internet.

Types of Firewalls

What software firewalls are there?
Most current operating systems include reliable firewalls. Security suites such as Norton Internet Security, McAfee Internet Security, and ZoneAlarm Internet Security Suite also include firewall software. Although the firewalls that come with Windows 7 and OS X will protect your computer, firewalls included in security suites often come with

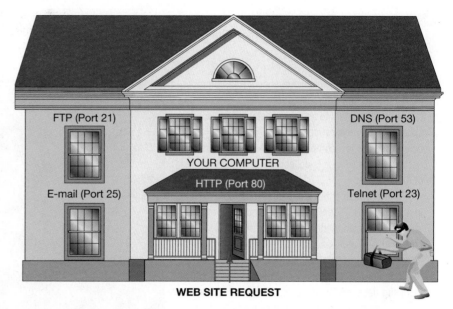

FTP (Port 21)   DNS (Port 53)

YOUR COMPUTER

E-mail (Port 25)   HTTP (Port 80)   Telnet (Port 23)

WEB SITE REQUEST

Figure 9.9
Open logical ports are an invitation to hackers.

additional features such as monitoring systems that alert you if your computer is under attack.

If you are using a security suite that includes a firewall, you should disable the firewall that came with your operating system. Many security suites will disable the Windows firewall for you to replace it with their own firewall. Two firewalls running at the same time can conflict with each other and can cause your computer to slow down or freeze up.

What are hardware firewalls? You can also buy and configure hardware firewall devices. Many routers sold for home networks include firewall protection. Just like software firewalls, the setup for hardware firewalls is designed for novices, and the default configuration on most routers keeps unused logical ports closed. Documentation accompanying routers can assist users with more experience in adjusting the settings to allow access to specific ports if needed.

ACTIVE HELP-DESK   Understanding Firewalls

In this Active Helpdesk call, you'll play the role of a helpdesk staffer, fielding calls about how hackers can attack networks and what harm they can cause, as well as what a firewall does to keep a computer safe from hackers.

On law enforcement television shows it is common-place now to see computer technicians working on suspects' computers to assist the detectives in solving crimes. It may look simple, but the science of computer forensics is a complex step-by-step process that ensures that evidence is collected within the confines of the law.

Forensic means that something is suitable for use in a court of law. There are many branches of forensic science. Forensic medicine involves the use of medical experts to express opinions on medical issues in court cases. Forensic pathologists provide evidence about the nature and manner of death in court cases involving deceased individuals. **Computer forensics** involves identifying, extracting, preserving, and documenting computer evidence. Whereas other forensic sciences usually use physical tools such as scalpels or medical lab tests to provide evidence, computer forensic professionals primarily rely on specialized software to collect their evidence. Computer forensics is performed by individuals known as computer forensic scientists.

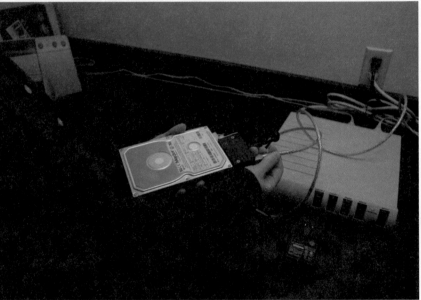

Mikael Karlsson / Alamy

Figure 9.10

Making exact copies of storage drives is the first thing computer forensics specialists do after police seize and secure computer equipment.

Phase 1: Obtaining and Securing Computer Devices

The first step in a computer forensics investigation is to seize the computer equipment that law enforcement officials believe contains pertinent evidence. Police are required to obtain a warrant to search an individual's home or a place of business. Warrants must be very specific and spell out exactly where detectives can search for evidence and what type of evidence they are seeking. If a warrant indicates that the police may search an individual's home for his laptop computer, they can't then confiscate a tablet computer they notice in his car. It is important to specify

How Firewalls Work

How do firewalls protect you from hackers? Firewalls are designed to restrict access to a network and its computers. Firewalls protect you in two major ways: by blocking access to logical ports and by keeping your computer's network address secure.

How do firewalls block access to your logical ports? To block access to logical ports, firewalls examine data packets that your computer sends and receives. Data packets contain information such as the address of the sending and receiving computers and the logical port the packet will use. Firewalls can be configured so that they filter out packets sent to specific logical ports. This process is referred to as **packet filtering**. Certain logical ports are very popular in hacker attacks. Firewalls are often configured to ignore requests that originate from the Internet asking for access to these ports. This process is referred to as **logical port blocking**. By using filtering and blocking, firewalls keep hackers from accessing your computer (Figure 9.11).

How do firewalls keep your network address secure? Every computer connected to the Internet has a unique address called an **Internet Protocol address** (**IP address**). Data is routed to the correct computer on the Internet based on the IP address. This is similar to how a letter finds its way to your mailbox. You have a unique postal address for your home. If a hacker finds out the IP address of your computer, he or she can locate it on the Internet and try to break into it. This is similar to how a conventional thief might target your home after

in the warrant all types of storage devices where potential evidence might be stored such as external hard drives, flash drives, and servers.

Once permission to collect the computers and devices containing possible evidence has been legally obtained, law enforcement officials must exercise great care when collecting the equipment. They need to ensure that no unauthorized persons are able to access or alter the computers or storage devices. The police must make sure the data and equipment are safe; if the equipment is connected to the Internet, the connection must be severed without data loss or damage. It is also important for law enforcement officials to understand that they may not want to power off equipment because potential evidence contained in RAM may be lost. After collecting and securing the devices, the computer forensic scientists take over the next phase of the investigation.

Phase 2: Cataloging and Analyzing the Data

It is critical to preserve the data exactly as it was found, or attorneys may argue that the computer evidence was subject to tampering or altering. Since just opening a file can alter it, the first task is to make a copy of all computer systems and storage devices collected (see Figure 9.10). The investigators only work from the copies to ensure that the original data always remains intact and preserved exactly as it was when it was collected.

After obtaining a copy to work from, the forensics professionals then attempt to find every file on the system, including deleted files. Files on a computer are not actually deleted, even if you empty the Recycle Bin, until the section of the hard disk they are stored on is overwritten with new data. Therefore, using special forensic software tools such as

SIFT, EnCase, and FTK, the forensic scientists catalog all files found on the system or storage medium and recover as much information from deleted files as they can. Files on a computer system also may be hidden, protected, or encrypted. Forensic software like FTK can readily detect hidden files and perform procedures to crack encrypted files or access protected files and reveal their contents.

The most important part of the process is documenting every step taken. Forensic scientists must clearly log every procedure performed because they may be required to provide proof in court that their investigations did not alter or damage information contained on the systems they examined. Detailed reports should list all files found, how the files were laid out on the system, which files were protected or encrypted, and the contents of each file. Finally, the computer forensic professionals are often called upon to present testimony in court during a trial.

Criminals are getting more sophisticated and are now employing anti-forensics techniques to try to foil computer forensic investigators. Although various techniques for hiding or encrypting data are popular, the most insidious anti-forensics techniques are programs that are designed to erase data if unauthorized persons (i.e., not the criminal) access a computer system, or the computer system detects forensics software in use. When computer forensic investigators detect these countermeasures, they must often use creative methods and custom-designed software programs to retrieve and preserve the data.

Computer forensics is an invaluable tool to law enforcement professionals in many criminal investigations, but only if the correct procedures are followed and the appropriate documentation is prepared.

finding out you collect antique cars by using your street address to locate your house.

Your IP address for your home network is assigned to your router by your ISP, but each device on your home network also has an IP address. Firewalls or routers use a process called **network address translation (NAT)** to assign internal IP addresses on a network. The internal IP addresses are used only on the internal network and therefore cannot be detected by hackers. For hackers to access your computer, they must know your computer's internal IP address. With a

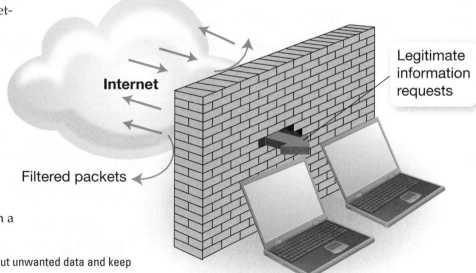

Figure 9.11

Firewalls use filtering and blocking to keep out unwanted data and keep your network safe.

NAT-capable router/firewall installed on your network, hackers are unable to access the internal IP address assigned to your computer, so your computer is safe. You can use NAT in your home by purchasing a hardware firewall with NAT capabilities. As noted earlier, many routers sold for home use are also configured as firewalls, and many feature NAT as well.

Knowing Your Computer Is Secure

How can I tell if my computer is at risk? For peace of mind you can visit several Web sites that offer free services that test your computer's vulnerability. One popular site is Gibson Research (**www.grc.com**). The company's ShieldsUP and LeakTest programs are free, easy to run, and can pinpoint security vulnerabilities in a system that is connected to the Internet. If you get a clean report from these programs, your system is probably not vulnerable to attack. Figure 9.12 shows the results screen from a ShieldsUP Common Ports probe test, which checks which logical ports in your computer are vulnerable. Ports reported as closed or in stealth mode are safe from attack. Ports reported as open are subject to exploitation by hackers. Installation of a hardware or software firewall should close any open ports.

What if I don't get a clean report from the testing program? If the testing program detects potential vulnerabilities and you don't have a firewall, you should install one as soon as possible. If the firewall is already configured and common ports (such as those shown in Figure 9.13) are identified as being vulnerable, consult your firewall documentation for instructions on how to close or restrict access to those ports.

Password Protection and Password Management

Passwords, used in conjunction with login IDs, are the major way we restrict access to computers, networks, and on-line accounts. You no doubt have many passwords that you need to remember to access your digital life. However, creating strong passwords—ones that are difficult for hackers to guess—is an essential piece of security that individuals sometimes overlook. Password cracking programs have become more sophisticated lately. In fact, some commonly available programs, such as John the Ripper, Hydra, and Cain and Abel, can test more than 1 million password combinations per second! Creating a secure password is therefore more important than ever.

Many people use extremely weak passwords. The Imperva Application Defense Center, a computer security research organization, conducted a review of 32 million passwords that were used at the Web site **www.rockyou.com**. More than 345,000 people were using "12345," "123456," or "123456789" as their password. And almost 62,000 people were using "password"!

Figure 9.12

ShieldsUP Common Ports test results.

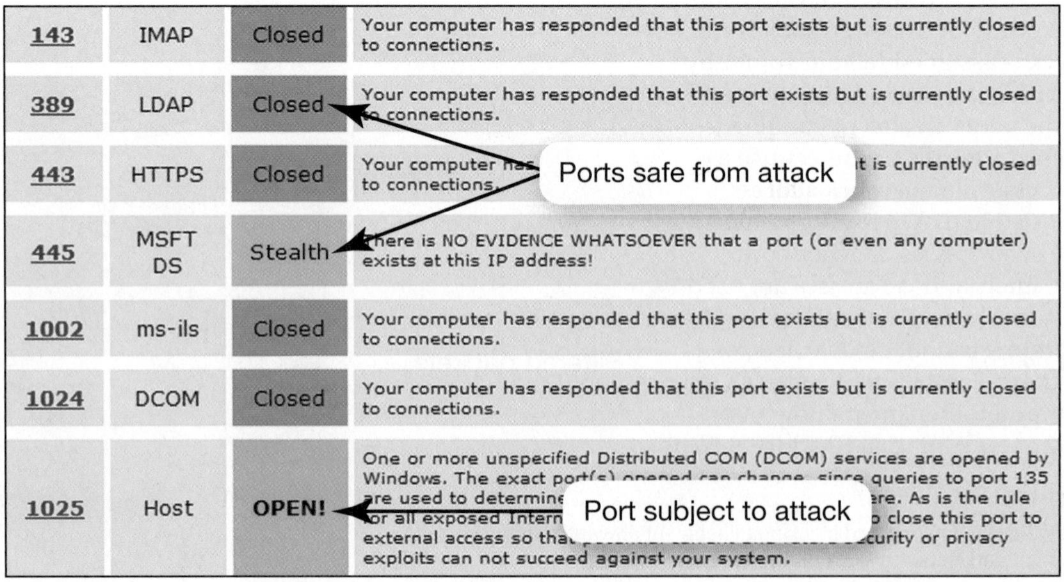

143	IMAP	Closed	Your computer has responded that this port exists but is currently closed to connections.
389	LDAP	Closed	Your computer has responded that this port exists but is currently closed to connections.
443	HTTPS	Closed	Your computer has responded that this port exists but is currently closed to connections.
445	MSFT DS	Stealth	There is NO EVIDENCE WHATSOEVER that a port (or even any computer) exists at this IP address!
1002	ms-ils	Closed	Your computer has responded that this port exists but is currently closed to connections.
1024	DCOM	Closed	Your computer has responded that this port exists but is currently closed to connections.
1025	Host	OPEN!	One or more unspecified Distributed COM (DCOM) services are opened by Windows. The exact port(s) opened can change, since queries to port 135 are used to determine ... As is the rule for all exposed Intern... close this port to external access so tha... curity or privacy exploits can not succeed against your system.

Ports safe from attack

Port subject to attack

Gibson Research Corporation

Passwords such as these are extremely easy for hackers to crack.

Web sites that need to be very secure, such as financial institutions, usually have very strong defenses to prevent hackers from cracking passwords. But sites that need less security, such as casual gaming sites or social networking sites, might have significantly less protection as evidenced by the break-in to the PlayStation Network in April 2011. Hackers will attack poorly defended sites for passwords because many people use the same password for every site on which they need to create one. So if a hacker can get your password from a poorly secured gaming site, they might still be able to access your bank account with the same password.

Creating Passwords

What constitutes a strong password? Strong passwords are difficult for someone to guess. They should not contain easily deduced components related to your life such as parts of your name, your pet's name, your street address, your telephone number, or the name of the Web site or institution for which you are creating the password (i.e., don't use Citibank for your online banking password). To create strong passwords, follow the basic guidelines shown here:

- Your password should contain at least 14 characters and include numbers, symbols, and upper- and lowercase letters.
- Your password should not be a single word or any words found in the dictionary.
- Your password should not be easily associated with you—such as your birth date, the name of your pet, or your nickname.
- Use a different password for each system or Web site you need to access. This prevents access to other accounts you maintain if one of your passwords is discovered.
- Never tell anyone your password or write it down in a place where others might see it.
- Change your password on a regular basis, such as every month, and change it sooner if you think someone may know it.

Figure 9.13 | COMMON LOGICAL PORTS

Port Number	Protocol Using the Port
21	FTP (File Transfer Protocol) control
23	Telnet (unencrypted text communications)
25	SMTP (Simple Mail Transfer Protocol)
53	DNS (domain name system)
80	HTTP (Hypertext Transfer Protocol)
443	HTTPS [HTTP with Transport Layer Security (TLS) encryption]

Figure 9.14 shows some possible passwords and explains why they are strong or weak candidates.

How can I check the strength of my passwords? You can use online password strength testers, such as The Password Meter (**www.passwordmeter.com**) or Microsoft's test (**www.microsoft.com/security/pc-security/password-checker.aspx**) to evaluate your passwords. The Password Meter (see Figure 9.15) provides guidelines for good passwords and shows you how integrating various elements, such as symbols, affects the strength score for your password.

You should make sure you change your passwords on a regular basis, such as monthly or quarterly. Your school or your employer probably requires you to change your password regularly. This is also a good idea for your personal passwords. You should also not use the same password for every account that you have. Because remembering constantly changing strong passwords for numerous accounts can be a challenge, you should use password-management tools, as described in the next section, to make the process easier to handle. If you have trouble thinking of secure passwords, there are many password generators

SOUND BYTE — **Installing a Personal Firewall**

Firewalls provide excellent protection against hackers on a home network. In this Sound Byte, you'll learn how to install and configure software firewalls to protect your computer.

Figure 9.14 | STRONG AND WEAK PASSWORD CANDIDATES

Strong Password	Reason
68v3tt3TiMMay516	Abbreviation for your favorite classic car (with 3s instead of Es), your favorite *South Park* character (using upper- and lowercase letters), and a random number
JcgE5397TbEp#	First initials of the title of the Black Eyed Peas song "Just Can't Get Enough" plus a random number and an abbreviation for the Black Eyed Peas ending with a hash symbol
DrP3pp3R167Water4ElePHANts	Your favorite beverage with a mix of alphanumeric characters and upper- and lowercase letters, your locker number at your gym, plus the title of a book that you like (with upper- and lowercase letters)
PhiLaPhiLLi3s#?Ham3Ls	Mix of numbers, symbols, and letters. Your favorite baseball team, a hash mark and question mark, and your favorite pitcher on the team. Letter Ls are all capitalized and the number 3 is used instead of the letter E

Weak Password	Reason
Sjones	Combination of first initial and last name
4wilsonkids	Even though this has an alphanumeric combination, it is too descriptive of a family
Johnson6634	Last name and last four digits of phone number are easily decoded
456OakSt	A street address is an easily decoded password

Figure 9.15

The Password Meter objectively evaluates your passwords.

available for free, such as Perfect Passwords (**www.grc.com/passwords.htm**) and the Bytes Interactive Password Generator (**www.goodpassword.com**).

How do I restrict access to my computer? Windows, OS X, and most other operating systems have built-in password (or passcode) protection for files as well as the entire desktop. After a certain period of idle time, your computer is automatically password locked and your password must be entered to gain access

to the computer. This provides excellent protection from casual snooping if you need to walk away from your computer for a period of time. If someone attempts to log on to your computer without your password, that person won't be able to gain access. It is an especially good idea to use passwords on notebook computers and tablets because this provides additional protection of your data if your computer is lost or stolen. Figure 9.16 shows the Set Passcode options on an iPad.

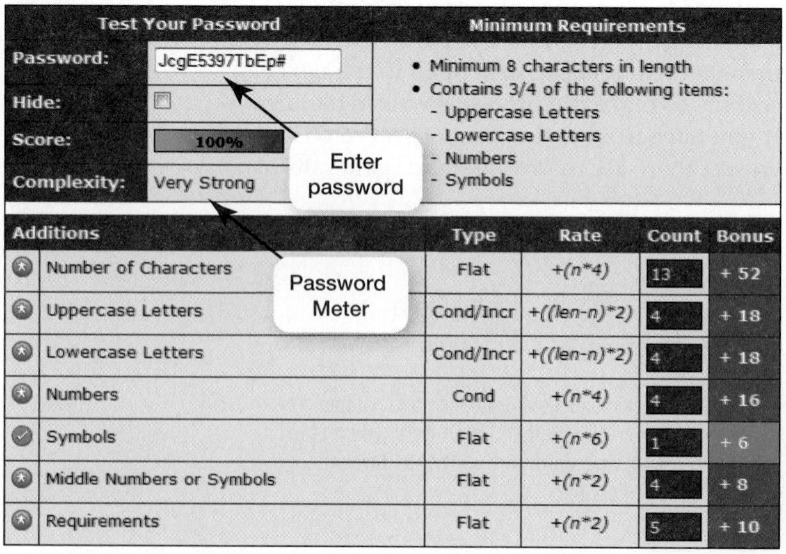

There are two types of users in Windows: administrators and standard users. Setting up a password on a standard user account prevents other standard users from being able to access that user's files. However, users with administrator privileges, like your parents, can still see your files if you are a standard user. So be aware that your files may not be safe from all prying eyes!

Managing Your Passwords

How can I remember all of my complex passwords? Good security practices suggest that you have different passwords for all the different Web sites that you access and that you change your passwords frequently. The problem with well-constructed passwords is that they can be hard to remember. Fortunately, password-management tools are now widely available. This takes the worry out of forgetting passwords because the password-management software does the remembering for you.

Where can I obtain password-management software? Most current Internet security suites and Web browsers make it easy to keep track of passwords by providing password-management tools. For example, to set up the password manager in Firefox, from the Tools menu, select Options, and then click the Security icon (the closed padlock) shown in Figure 9.17a. In the Passwords section, check *Remember passwords for sites* to have Firefox remember passwords when you log onto Web sites. Check *Use a master password*, which causes a dialog box to appear, and enter a well-designed, secure password. The next time you go to a Web site that requires a login, Firefox will display a dialog box prompting you to have Firefox remember the login name and password for this site. Then, when you return to the site and select a login option, enter the master password and the Firefox Password Manager will fill in the login and password information for you.

You also can see a list of sites maintained by the Firefox Password Manager by clicking the Show Passwords button, which displays the Saved Passwords dialog box (see Figure 9.17b). Passwords for each site are displayed after you click the Show Passwords button and enter the master password.

Even though you only need to remember the master password, you still need to make sure that it is a secure password (according to the rules we discussed earlier) and that you change it on a regular basis. Password managers are useful on the machine that you use on a regular basis. However, if you need to access your accounts from another computer, such as one at school, you will

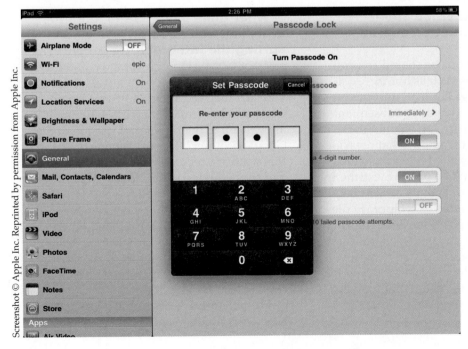

Screenshot © Apple Inc. Reprinted by permission from Apple Inc.

Figure 9.16

In the settings screen of your iPad, you can set a passcode that must be entered to gain access to your iPad.

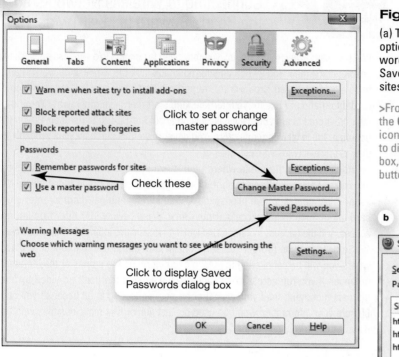

Figure 9.17

(a) The security tab in the Firefox browser options screen provides access to password-management tools. (b) The Firefox Saved Passwords dialog box displays all sites for which login information is saved.

>From the **Tools** menu, select **Options**. In the **Options** dialog box, click the security icon, click the **Saved Passwords** button to display the **Saved Passwords** dialog box, and then click the **Show Passwords** button.

still need to know the individual passwords for each site you wish to access.

So start using secure passwords and let your browser, on your main computer, relieve you of the problem of trying to remember them all.

Anonymous Web Surfing: Hiding from Prying Eyes

Should I be concerned about surfing the Internet on shared, public, or work computers? If you use shared computers in public places such as libraries, coffee shops, or college student unions, you should be concerned about a subsequent user of a computer spying on your surfing habits. You never know what nefarious tools have been installed by hackers on a public computer. When you browse the Internet, traces of your activity are left behind on that computer, often as temporary files. A wily hacker can glean sensitive information long after you have finished your latte and your surfing session. Many employers routinely review the Internet browsing history of employees to ensure that workers are spending their time on the Internet productively.

What tools can I use to keep my browsing activities private when surfing the Internet? The current versions of Google Chrome, Firefox, and Internet Explorer include privacy tools that help you surf the Web anonymously. Google Chrome's Incognito feature (see Figure 9.18) allows you to open a special version of the Google browser window. When surfing in this window, records of Web sites you visit and files you download do not appear in the Web browser's history files. Furthermore, any temporary files that were generated in that browsing session are deleted when you exit the Incognito window. The InPrivate Browsing feature of Internet Explorer and the Private Browsing feature of Firefox offer similar security features.

Portable privacy devices, such as the Iron-Key (**www.ironkey.com**), provide an even higher level of surfing privacy. Simply plug the device into an available USB port on the machine on which you will be working. All sensitive Internet files, such as cookies, Internet history, and browser caches, will be stored on the privacy device, not on the computer you are using. Privacy devices such as these often come preloaded with software designed to shield your IP address from prying eyes, making it difficult (if not impossible) for hackers to tell where you are surfing on the Internet. These privacy devices also have password-management tools that store all of your login information and encrypt it so it will be safe if your privacy device falls into someone else's hands.

Another free practical solution is to take the Linux OS with you on a flash drive and avoid using the public or work computer's operating system. The interfaces of many Linux builds, such as Ubuntu (see Figure 9.19), look almost exactly like Windows and are easy to use.

There are several advantages to using a Linux-based operating system on a public or work computer. First, your risk of picking up viruses and other malicious programs is significantly reduced because booting a computer from a flash drive completely eliminates any interaction with the computer's operating system. This, in turn, significantly reduces the chance that your flash drive will become infected by any malware running on the computer.

Next, virus and hacking attacks against Linux are far less likely than attacks against Windows. Because Windows has almost 90 percent of the operating system market, people who write malware tend to target Windows systems. Finally, when you run software from your own storage medium, such as a flash drive, you avoid reading and writing to the hard disk of the computer. This significantly enhances your privacy because you don't leave traces of your activity behind.

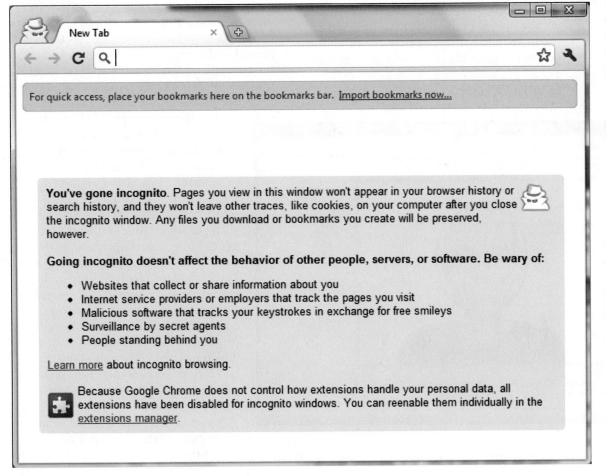

Figure 9.18

The Google Chrome Incognito feature (accessible from the wrench icon) allows you to surf without leaving a trail of your activities.

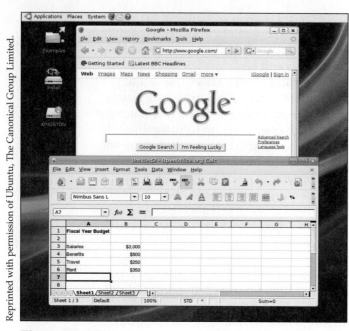

Figure 9.19

Ubuntu is a version of Linux that you can use to improve your security when using a public computer.

Pendrivelinux.com (**www.pendrivelinux .com**) is an excellent resource that offers many different versions of Linux for download and includes step-by-step instructions on how to install them on your flash drive. If you are a Mac user, there is an option for you, too. The gOS version of Linux provides a close approximation of OS X, so you can feel right at home.

Figure 9.20

Many Toshiba laptops offer face recognition software. Just stare into the webcam and you're logged on.

Do I need to take special precautions with my tablet devices? Tablets like the iPad run their own proprietary operating systems that differ from the operating systems deployed on laptop computers. Although tablet operating systems do contain security features, they may not be robust enough to satisfy business users who have a great deal of confidential information on their tablets, especially when the devices are connected to wireless networks. Third-party software developers are now offering many apps to enhance tablet security. Comprehensive suites like hidePad (**www.hidepad.com**) offer features such as government-grade encryption of data, enhanced e-mail security, and anonymous Web surfing. So look for security apps that are specifically designed for your tablet device if you often deal with sensitive data on your tablet, such as online banking.

Biometric Authentication Devices

Besides passwords, how else can I restrict the use of my computer? A **biometric authentication device** is a device that reads a unique personal characteristic such as a fingerprint or the iris pattern in your eye and converts its pattern to a digital code. When you use the device, your pattern is read and compared to the one stored on the computer. Only users having an exact fingerprint or iris pattern match are allowed to access the computer.

Because no two people have the same biometric characteristics (fingerprints and iris patterns are unique), these devices provide a high level of security. They also eliminate the human error that can occur in password protection. You might forget your password, but you won't forget to bring your fingerprint to the computer! Some notebooks, such as Lenovo, feature built-in fingerprint readers, and companies like SecuGen produce computer mice and keyboards that include built-in fingerprint readers. Other biometric devices, which include voice authentication and face pattern–recognition systems (see Figure 9.20), are now widely offered in notebook computers.

Make sure to utilize some (or all) of these methods to keep your activities from prying eyes and to restrict access to your digital information.

Managing Online Annoyances

Surfing the Web, sending and receiving e-mail, and chatting online have become a common part of most of our lives. Unfortunately, the Web has become fertile ground for people who want to advertise their products, track our Web browsing behaviors, or even con people into revealing personal information. In this section, we'll look at ways in which you can manage, if not avoid, these and other online headaches.

Malware, Adware, and Spyware

What is malware? **Malware** is software that has a malicious intent (hence the prefix *mal*). There are three primary forms of malware: adware, spyware, and viruses (which we have already discussed). Adware and spyware are not physically destructive like viruses and worms, which can destroy data. Known collectively as *grayware*, most are intrusive, annoying, or objectionable online programs that are downloaded to your computer when you install or use other online content such as a freeware program, game, or utility.

What is adware? **Adware** is software that displays sponsored advertisements in a section of your browser window or as a pop-up ad box. It is considered a legitimate, though sometimes annoying, means of generating revenue for those developers who do not charge for their software or information. Pop-up windows have been referred to as the billboards of the Internet because they appear and display advertisements or other promotional information when you install freeware programs or access certain Web sites. Fortunately, because Web browsers such as Firefox, Safari, and Internet Explorer have pop-up blockers built into their browsers, the occurrence of annoying pop-ups has been greatly reduced.

Some pop-ups, however, are legitimate and increase the functionality of the originating site. For example, your account balance may pop up on your bank's Web site. You can access the pop-up blocker settings in your browser (see Figure 9.21) and add Web sites for which you will allow pop-ups. Whenever a pop-up is blocked, the browser displays an information bar or plays a sound to alert you. If you feel the pop-up is legitimate, you can then choose to accept it.

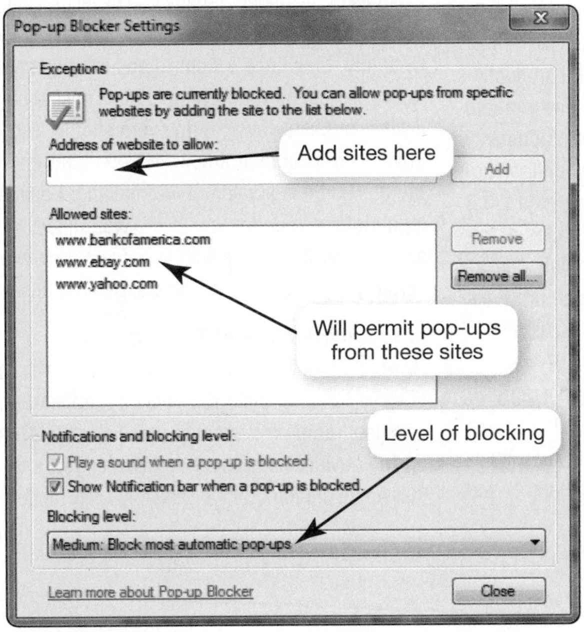

Figure 9.21

Internet Explorer's Pop-up Blocker Settings dialog box.

>Pop-up Blocker is found in the **Tools** menu on the Internet Explorer toolbar.

What is spyware? **Spyware** is an unwanted piggyback program that usually downloads with other software you want to install from the Internet. It runs in the background of your system. Without your knowledge, spyware transmits information about you, such as your Internet surfing habits, to the owner of the program so the information can be used for marketing purposes. Many spyware programs use tracking cookies, (small text files stored on your computer) to collect information, whereas others are disguised as benign programs that are really malicious programs, such as Trojan horses. One type of spyware program known as a **keystroke logger (keylogger)** monitors keystrokes with the intent of stealing passwords, login IDs, or credit card information.

Can I prevent spyware from spying on me? Many Internet security suites now include antispyware software. However, you can also obtain stand-alone spyware removal software and run it on your computer to delete unwanted spyware. Because there are so many variants of spyware, your

ETHICS IN IT

You Are Being Watched . . . But Are You Aware You're Being Watched?

Employee Monitoring in the Workplace

Think you aren't being closely watched by your employer? Think again! A recent survey of employers by the American Management Association and the ePolicy Institute revealed that, of the employers surveyed:

- 73 percent monitored e-mail messages
- 66 percent monitored Web surfing
- 48 percent monitored activities using video surveillance
- 45 percent monitored keystrokes and keyboard time
- 43 percent monitored computer files in some other fashion

There is a high probability that you are being monitored while you work and when you access the Internet via your employer's Internet connection.

The two most frequently cited reasons for employee monitoring are to prevent theft and to measure productivity. Monitoring for theft isn't new, because monitoring cameras have been around for years, and productivity monitoring has been a consistent process for assembly line workers for decades. However, the Internet has led to a new type of productivity drain that is of concern to employers. **Cyberloafing**, or cyberslacking, means doing anything with a computer, while you are being paid to do your job, that is not an approved function of your job. Examples of cyberloafing activities are playing games, reading personal e-mail, checking sports scores, watching videos, and buying personal-use products on e-commerce sites. Estimates of business productivity losses due to cyberloafing top $50 billion annually.

Like most other Americans, you probably feel you have a right to privacy in the workplace. Unfortunately, the laws in the United States don't support a worker's right to privacy. Laws such as the 1986 Electronic Communications Privacy Act (ECPA), which prohibits unauthorized monitoring of electronic communications, have been interpreted by the courts in favor of employers. The bottom line is that employers who pay for equipment and software have the legal right to monitor their usage.

But just because an action is legal doesn't mean it is ethical. It is difficult to argue that an employer doesn't have the right to take measures to prevent theft and detect low productivity. The ethical issue here is whether the people are adequately informed of monitoring policies. An ethical employer should inform employees of any monitoring. Employers have an ethical responsibility (and a legal one as well, depending on the jurisdiction) not to place monitoring devices in sensitive locations such as bathrooms and dressing areas. However, in many states, the employer does not need to inform the employees in advance that they are being monitored. Conscientious employers include monitoring disclosures in published employee policies to avoid confusion and conflict.

So, do your employers have an ethical right to monitor your activities? Certainly, they have a right to ensure they are getting a fair day's work from you, just as you have an ethical obligation to provide a fair effort for a fair wage. However, employers should also be willing to respect the privacy rights of their employees and treat them as professionals, unless there is some indication of wrongdoing. Because employers may have a legal right to monitor you in the workplace, you should work under the assumption that everything you do on your work computer is subject to scrutiny and behave accordingly. Do your online shopping at home!

Is Your iPhone or iPad Tracking You?

Have an iPhone or iPad? In April 2011 it was reported in the media that devices running Apple iOS version 4 appeared to be tracking their owner's geographic movements (see Figure 9.22) and storing them in a file on the device. It had been known for years that smartphone users (not just Apple customers) were having their movements tracked for the pur-

---

Internet security software may not detect all types that attempt to install themselves on your computer. Therefore, it is a good idea to install one or two additional stand-alone antispyware programs on your computer.

Because new spyware is created all the time, you should update and run your spyware removal software regularly. Windows comes with a program called Windows Defender, which scans your system for spyware and other potentially unwanted software. Malwarebytes Anti-Malware, Ad-Aware, and Spybot–Search & Destroy (all available from **www.download.com**) are other programs that are easy to install and update. Figure 9.23 shows an example of Ad-Aware in action. Antispyware software detects unwanted programs and allows you to delete the offending software easily.

Spam

How can I best avoid spam? Companies that send out **spam**—unwanted or junk e-mail—find your e-mail address either from a list they purchase or with software that looks for e-mail addresses on the Internet. Unsolicited instant messages are also a form of spam, called *spim*. If you've used your e-mail address to purchase anything online, open an online account, or participate in a social network such as Facebook, your e-mail address eventually will appear on one of the lists that spammers get.

One way to avoid spam in your primary account is to create a free Web-based e-mail address that you use only when you fill out forms or purchase items on the Web. For example, both Windows Live Mail and Yahoo! allow you to set up free

pose of serving up location-specific advertisements. But the fact that the phones were storing the information in local files had not been clear to owners of the equipment. In addition, when syncing devices with a computer or purchasing a new device, the tracking data is apparently transferred to the computer or new equipment. There is a disclaimer that gives Apple the right to accumulate this data contained in the 15,000-plus word iTunes terms and conditions contract, but many users were unaware of this provision, presumably because they did not read the entire iTunes contract prior to agreeing to it. Therefore, it does appear that Apple has a legal right to accumulate the data because consumers did agree to it when they installed iTunes.

Apple responded to these revelations by assuring customers that their phones weren't providing any person-specific tracking data to Apple. The phones keep track of WiFi hotspots and cell towers around your location (and up to 150 miles away) to allow your iOS device to precisely report its position when necessary. This data is reported to Apple in an encrypted form and on an anonymous basis (i.e., Apple doesn't know where you are right now). Apple did acknowledge that several software bugs were causing data to be stored for up to a year (instead of seven days) and that the data was inappropriately being backed up on a computer when devices were synced with it. Apple announced it would be quickly fixing these software bugs in a future software update.

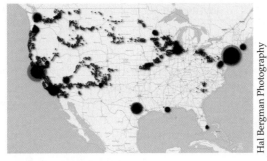

Figure 9.22

A misunderstanding about iPhone and iPad location services led people to believe their mobile devices were reporting to Apple their precise geographic location.

So did Apple do anything wrong? Although Apple did not appear to be behaving unethically, it gave the appearance of being inconsiderate of its customers' privacy rights when these issues came to light. Assuming customers always read a lengthy licensing agreement might not be the best strategy to inform customers their equipment is to some extent tracking their movements . . . for very valid functional reasons. Fortunately, despite what was originally reported, your iPhone or your iPad isn't really tracking your precise location and the bug fixes will ensure that only a limited amount of data (seven days' worth) is saved.

Companies do have an ethical obligation to ensure that you are informed about any type of monitoring so you can make informed choices about your behavior. Companies should take steps to ensure that their customers are aware of any monitoring and provide a procedure for discontinuing the monitoring if customers object to it. Location services can be turned off in iPhones, but are most customers aware that this can be done? What obligation does Apple have to its customers to inform them of their options? Behaving ethically means ensuring the majority of your customers understand what their devices are capable of doing and the options they have for modifying the device's behavior. This will help avoid embarrassing misunderstandings like the Apple iOS tracking flap. If customers had already understood that their phones weren't reporting their location to Apple, this would have been a nonissue.

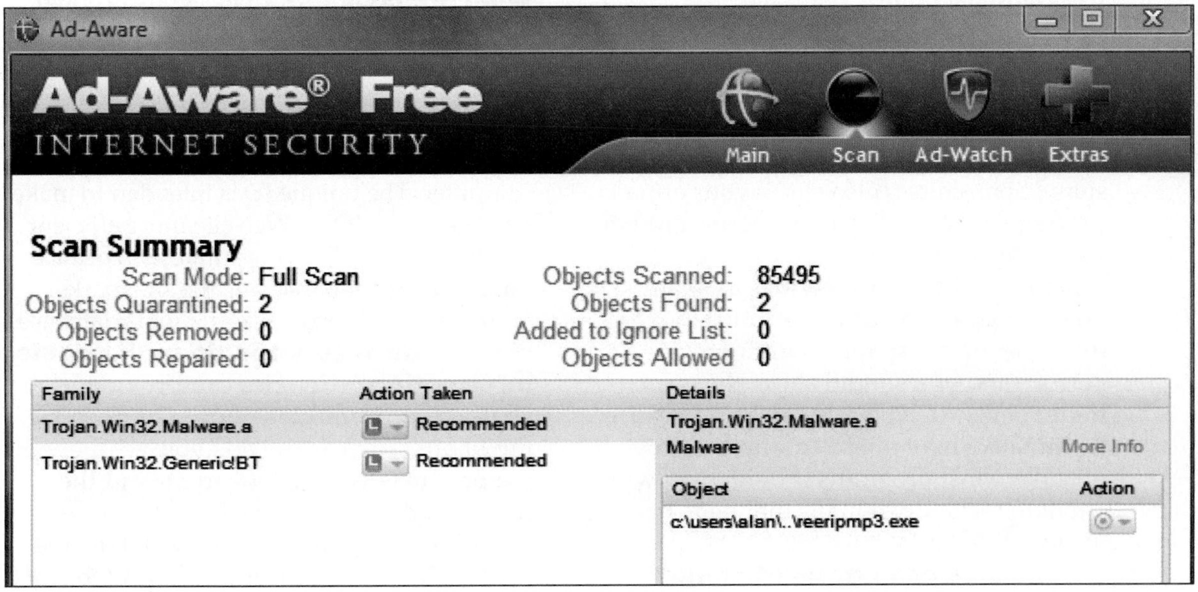

Figure 9.23

After performing a routine scan of a computer, Ad-Aware returns a log of problems found on the system.

Figure 9.24

In Yahoo! Mail, messages identified as spam are directed into a folder called "Spam" for review and deletion.

e-mail accounts. If your free Web-based e-mail account is saturated with spam, then you can abandon that account with little inconvenience. It's much less convenient to abandon your primary e-mail address.

Another way to avoid spam is to filter it. A spam filter is an option you can select in your e-mail account that places known or suspected spam messages into a folder other than your inbox. Most Web-based e-mail services, such as Windows Live Mail and Yahoo!, offer spam filters (see Figure 9.24). Files perceived to be spam are segregated in a special folder which is often named "Spam" or "Junk Mail". Microsoft Outlook also features a spam filter. Third-party programs that provide some control over spam include SPAMfighter and Cactus Spam Filter, both of which can be obtained at **www.download.com**.

How do spam filters work? Spam **filters** and filtering software can catch as much as 95 percent of spam by checking incoming e-mail subject headers and senders' addresses against databases of known spam. Spam filters also check your e-mail for frequently used spam patterns and keywords, such as "for free" and "over 21". E-mail that the filter identifies as spam does not go into your inbox but rather to a folder set up for spam. Spam filters aren't perfect, and you should check the spam folder before deleting its contents because legitimate e-mail might end up there by mistake. Most programs provide you with a tool to reclassify e-mails that have been misidentified as spam.

How else can I prevent spam? There are several additional ways you can prevent spam.

1. Before registering on a Web site, read its privacy policy to see how it uses your e-mail address. Don't give the site permission to pass on your e-mail address to third parties.

2. Don't reply to spam to remove yourself from the spam list. By replying, you are confirming that your e-mail address is active. Instead of stopping spam, you may receive more.

3. Subscribe to an e-mail forwarding service such as VersaForward (**www.versaforward.com**) or Sneakemail.com (**www.sneakemail.com**). These services screen your e-mail messages, forwarding only those messages you designate as being okay to accept.

Cookies

What are cookies? Cookies (also known as *tracking cookies*) are small text files that some Web sites automatically store on your computer's hard drive when you visit them. When you log on to a Web site that uses cookies, a cookie file assigns an ID number to your computer. The unique ID is intended to make your return visit to a Web site more efficient and better geared to your interests. The next time you log on to that site, the site marks your visit and keeps track of it in its database.

What do Web sites do with cookie information? Cookies can provide Web sites with information about your browsing habits, such as the ads you've opened, the products you've looked at, and the time and duration of your visits. Companies use this information to determine the traffic flowing through their Web site and the effectiveness of their marketing strategy and placement on Web sites. By tracking such information, cookies enable companies to identify different users' preferences.

Can companies get my personal information when I visit their sites? Cookies do not go through your hard drive in search of personal information such as passwords or financial data. The only personal information a cookie obtains is the information you supply when you fill out forms online.

Do privacy risks exist with cookies? Some sites sell the personal information their cookies collect to Web advertisers who are building huge databases of consumer preferences and habits, collecting personal and business information such as phone numbers, credit reports, and the like. The main concern is that advertisers will use this information indiscriminately, thus infiltrating your privacy. And you may feel your privacy is being violated by tracking cookies that monitor where you go on a Web site.

Should I delete cookies from my hard drive? Cookies pose no security threat since it is virtually impossible to hide a virus or malicious software program in a cookie. Since they take up little room on your hard drive, and offer you small conveniences on return visits to Web sites, there is no great reason to delete them. Deleting your cookie files could actually cause you the inconvenience of reentering data you have already entered into Web site forms. However, if you're uncomfortable with the accessibility of your personal information, you can periodically delete cookies or configure your browser to block certain types of cookies, as shown in Figure 9.25. Software such as

Cookie Pal (**www.kburra .com**) also can help you monitor cookies.

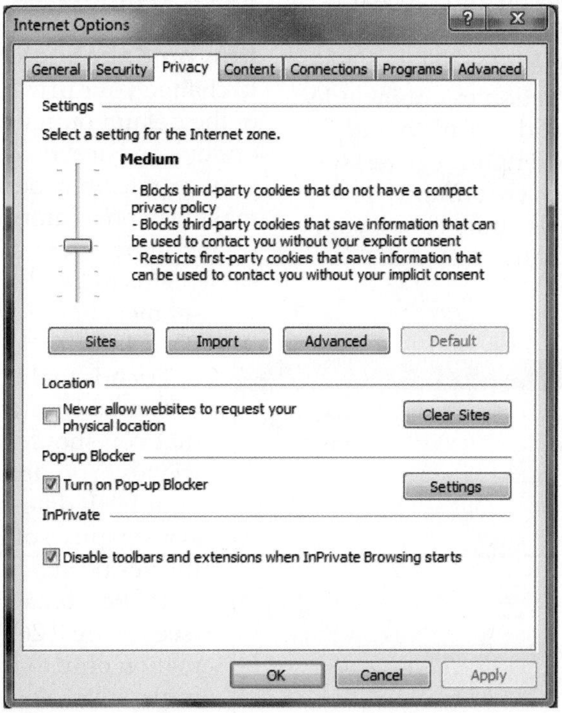

Protecting Yourself ... from Yourself!

People are often too trusting or just plain careless when it comes to protecting private information about themselves or their digital data. When was the last time you created a copy of your digital data, such as the thousands of photographs you have stored on your hard drive? The hard drive in your computer is likely to fail at some point, which may render all the data on it useless. What strategy do you have in place to protect your data from damage?

If you have a Facebook or Twitter account, you are probably constantly revealing information about your likes and dislikes, such as what movie you saw this weekend or the presents you received for your birthday. You might even be revealing information about where you live. Have you ever filled out an online form to enter a contest? Have you ever applied for a customer loyalty card at your local supermarket or electronics store? Think about how much information you voluntarily give up all the time in the course of running your digital life. Con artists and scammers take advantage of people's tendency to reveal information freely to compromise their privacy and commit theft.

In this section, we discuss ways to keep your data safe from damage, either accidental or intentional, and to keep unscrupulous individuals from tricking you into revealing sensitive information.

Figure 9.25

Tools are available, either through your browser (Internet Explorer is shown here) or as separate applications, to distinguish between cookies you want to keep and cookies you don't want on your system.

>On the Internet Explorer menu toolbar, click **Tools**, and then click **Internet Options**. The cookie settings are on the **Privacy** tab.

Protecting Your Personal Information

If a complete stranger walked up to you on the street and asked you for your address and phone number, would you give it to them? Of course you wouldn't! But many people are much less careful when it comes to sharing sensitive information online. And often people inadvertently share information that they really only intended to share with their friends. With cybercrimes like identify theft rampant, you need to take steps to protect your personal information.

What information should I never share on Web sites? Your Social Security number, phone number, date of birth, and street address are four key pieces of information that identity thieves need to steal an identity. This information should never be shared in a public area on any Web site.

Many sites, such as Facebook, ask for other potentially sensitive information when you sign up. This information might include your real name, e-mail address, birth date, zip code, and gender. After you register, social networking sites then encourage you to add profile details such as your school, your employer, your personal interests and hobbies, and who your friends are. Although it is fine to share this information with people you know, you need to be careful that your information isn't visible to everyone.

How can I tell who can see my information in a social network? Social networking sites, like Facebook, make privacy settings available in their account menus. If you have never changed your privacy settings in Facebook, you are probably sharing information more widely than you should. Since Facebook is designed to foster social interaction, the default privacy settings make it easy to search for people. Someone with nefarious intentions could glean quite a bit of information from your Facebook profile, including your contact information, which they might use to trick you into revealing other information that would lead to them stealing your identity.

How can I protect my information on Facebook? To begin, you need to change your privacy settings from some of the default options. Most critical privacy options on Facebook are now located in your profile. In general, it is a bad idea to make personal information available to the public, although this is a default setting for some items in Facebook. It's a good idea to set most of the options in your profile Basic Information section (Figure 9.26a) to Friends Only or to yourself because, presumably, these are personal details that you should wish to share only with friends. You definitely want to restrict your birth date to just yourself as this is a key piece of information identity thieves need.

In the Contact Information section (see Figure 9.26b), restricting this information only to friends or to yourself is imperative! You don't want scammers contacting you via e-mail or snail mail and trying to trick you into revealing sensitive information. So use discretion and keep your information as private as possible.

Backing Up Your Data

How might I damage the data on my computer? The data on your computer faces three major threats: unauthorized access, tampering, and destruction. As noted earlier, a hacker can gain access to your computer and steal or alter your data. However, a more likely scenario is that you will

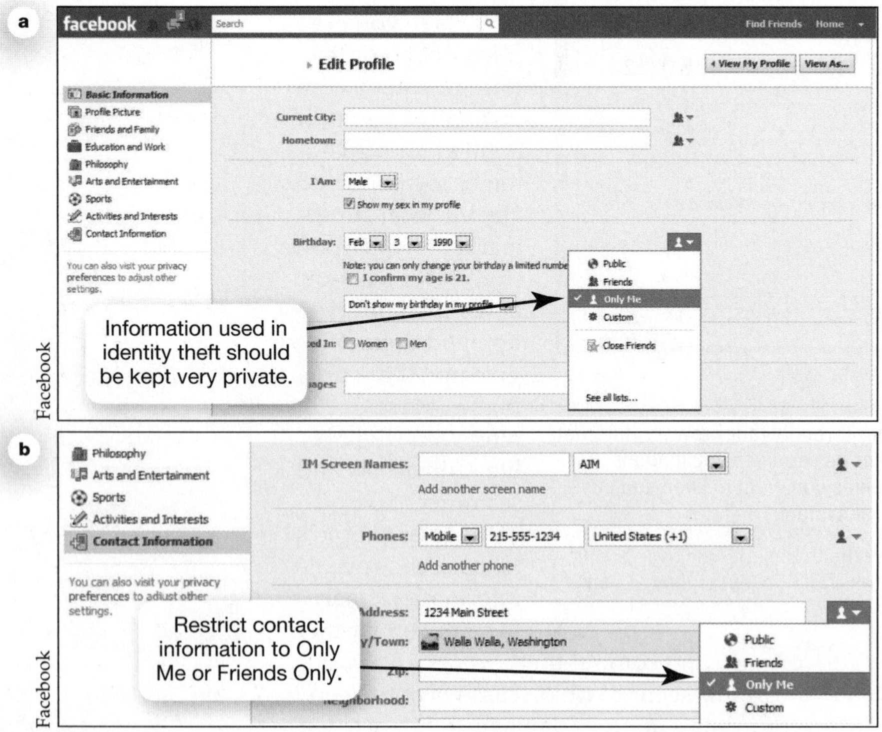

Figure 9.26

You should review the (a) Basic Information and (b) Contact Information privacy settings in Facebook to ensure you aren't sharing too much information.

lose your data unintentionally. You may accidentally delete files. You may drop your notebook on the ground, causing the hard drive to break, resulting in complete data loss. A virus from an e-mail attachment you opened may destroy your original file. Your house or dorm may catch fire and destroy your computer. Because many of these possibilities are beyond your control, you should have a strategy for backing up your files, which is especially important if you are running a small business. The backup strategy for small businesses is quite similar to the procedures recommended for individuals.

What exactly is meant by "backing up data"? **Backups** are copies of files that you can use to replace the originals if they are lost or damaged. To be truly secure, backups must be stored away from where your computer is located and should be stored in at least two different places. You wouldn't want a fire or a flood destroying the backups along with the original data. Removable storage media, such as external hard drives, Blu-ray Discs, and flash drives, have been popular choices for backing up files because they hold a lot of data and can be transported easily. Backing up files "in the cloud" is an excellent choice for a second backup location.

What types of files do I need to back up? Two types of files need backups—program files and data files.

A **program file** is used to install software and usually comes on DVDs or is downloaded from the Internet. If any programs came preinstalled in your computer, then you may have received a DVD that contains the original program. As long as you have the original media in a safe place, you shouldn't need to back up these files. If you have downloaded a program file from the Internet, however, you should make a copy of the program installation files on a removable storage device as a backup. If you didn't receive discs for installed programs with your computer, then see the next section for suggested strategies for backing up your entire computer.

A **data file** is a file you have created or purchased. Data files include such files as research papers, spreadsheets, music files, movies, contact lists, address books, e-mail archives, and your Favorites list from your browser.

Are there different ways to back up my files? Even with modest use, your files change. To back up the files that have changed, you can perform an incremental backup. To back up all files on your computer, you would perform an image backup.

An **incremental backup** (or **partial backup**) involves backing up only files that have changed or been created since the last backup was performed. Many of the key documents that you want to protect change only periodically: monthly banking statements, yearly tax returns, weekly employee payment records, or daily work documents. Using backup software that has an option for incremental backups will save a tremendous amount of time because backing up files that haven't changed is redundant.

An **image backup** (or **system backup**) means that all system, application, and data files are backed up, not just the files that changed. While incremental backups are more efficient, an image backup ensures you capture changes to application files, such as automatic software updates, that an incremental backup might not capture. The idea of imaging is to make an exact copy of the setup of your computer so that in the event of a total hard drive failure, you could copy the image to a new hard drive and have your computer configured exactly the way it was before the crash. This is a quick way to get up and running again.

How often should I back up my files? You should back up your data files frequently. How frequently depends on how much work you cannot afford to lose. You should always back up data files when you make changes to them, especially if those changes involve hours of work. It may not seem important to back up your term paper file when you finish it, but do you really want to do all that work again if your computer crashes before you have a chance to turn in your paper?

Because your program and operating system files don't change as often as your data files, you can perform image backups on a less frequent basis. Most backup software can be configured to do backups automatically so you don't forget to perform them. You might consider scheduling backups of your data files on a daily basis and an image backup of your entire system on a weekly basis.

To make backups easier, store all your data files in one folder on your hard drive.

For example, in Windows and most other operating systems, on your hard drive you will find a library (or folder) called Documents. You can create subfolders (such as History Homework, English Homework, and so on) within the Documents library. By storing all your data under one main library on your hard drive, you simply configure your backup software to back up that library and all subfolders beneath it.

Where do the backups of my files reside? This location is a decision that you need to make. You have three main choices:

1. **Online sites.** In essence, online storage is like using the Internet as an alternative to a portable storage device, such as an external hard drive or flash drive. The beauty of online storage is that your data is available anywhere you are; you do not need to be at your computer or have to lug around your external hard drive to access the information. More important, because the information is stored online, it is in a secure, remote location, so data is much less vulnerable to all the potential disasters, such as a flood, that could harm data stored in your computer or external hard drive. If you are taking advantage of one of these online storage services, selectivity is the key because of cost. Most services offer a certain amount of storage, say 5 GB, for free and then charge for additional storage. Although you might have hundreds of gigabytes of data sitting on your computer, perhaps you only need to store several gigabytes online so that they are always available.

    A convenient free storage option for Windows users is Windows Live SkyDrive (**skydrive.live.com**), which provides 25 GB of storage space. For non-Windows users or those needing even more storage space, check out ADrive (**www.adrive.com**) and its 50 GB of free storage. Fee-based plans at ADrive give users access to tools that allow them to schedule automatic backups of files and folders. However, image backups probably won't fit within the storage limits offered by free providers. For a fee, companies such as Carbonite (**www.carbonite.com**) and IBackup (**www.ibackup.com**) provide larger storage capacity.

    If you store a backup of your entire system on the Internet, then you won't need to buy an additional hard drive for backups. This method also takes the worry out of finding a safe place to keep your backups because they're always stored in an area far away from your computer: on the backup company's server. However, the yearly fees can be expensive, so a cheaper option may be to buy an external hard drive.

2. **Local drives.** External hard drives are popular options for performing backups of data files and for complete image backups. Affordable external drives are available with capacities of 4 TB or more. These drives are usually connected to a single computer and often come with their own backup software, although you could still use the backup software included with your operating system. Although convenient and inexpensive, using external hard drives for backups still presents the dilemma of keeping the hard drive in a safe location. You need to keep the hard drive connected to your computer to perform scheduled backups, but for ultimate safety the hard drive should be stored in a location separate from the computer in case of catastrophic events, such as a fire. And, your external hard drive still is subject to crashing, which could result in loss of your data. Therefore, using an external hard drive for backups is best done in conjunction with an online backup strategy for added safety.

3. **Network-attached storage devices and home servers.** Manufacturers such as Iomega, Western Digital, and Buffalo Technology now make network-attached storage (NAS) devices and servers designed for home networks. The NAS devices are essentially large

SOUND BYTE Managing Computer Security with Windows Tools

In this Sound Byte, you'll learn how to monitor and control your computer security using features built into the Windows operating system.

hard drives that are connected to a network of computers instead of one computer, and they can be used to back up multiple computers simultaneously. Home servers are not really servers like those found in client/server networks. Home servers act as high-capacity NAS devices for automatically backing up data and sharing files. Both NAS devices and home servers are easy to configure and are very useful if you have multiple computers within a single household that need backing up.

How do I perform a file backup? Windows 7 includes the Backup and Restore utility, which provides a quick and easy way to schedule file backups, restore files from backups, or perform image (system) backups. You can access Backup and Restore from the Control Panel. Before starting this utility, make sure your external hard drive or NAS device is connected to your computer or network and is powered on.

When you start the Backup and Restore utility for the first time, no backups will have ever been configured. Select the Set up backup option to launch the Set up backup dialog box (see Figure 9.27a) and display a list of available backup devices. Select a device and click Next to proceed. On the next screen, you have the option to let Windows choose what to back up or to choose for yourself what you want to back up. If you select the Let me choose option, the screen shown in Figure 9.27b displays. You can then click the appropriate check boxes to select the libraries you wish to back up. Click Next to proceed. On the following screen, you can review your settings and set up a schedule for the backups. When you click the Save settings and exit button, you are returned to the Back up or restore your files screen (see Figure 9.27c), which now shows the scheduled backup. You can also choose to restore backed-up files you have backed up from this screen.

From the Back up or restore your files screen, you also have two other options. If you click the Create a system image link, you will be walked through a series of steps to configure an image backup of your system. The Create a system repair disc link helps you create a DVD repair disc that can be used to boot your computer in case of

a serious Windows error. This disc is also used when you need to restore your computer from an image backup, so it is a good idea to create the repair disc before you begin using your computer heavily.

For Mac OS X users, backups are very easy to configure. The Time Machine feature in OS X detects when an external hard drive is connected to the computer or an NAS device is connected to your network. You are then asked if you want this to be your backup drive. If you answer yes, all of your files (including operating system files) are automatically backed up to the external drive or NAS device. You even have the option to go back in time and see what your computer looked like on a specific date. This is very handy for recovering a file that you wish you hadn't deleted.

No matter what backup strategy you choose, be sure to perform it on a regular basis, because nearly everyone needs to access backup files at one time or another.

Should I back up my files that are stored on my school's network? Most likely, if you're allowed to store files on your school's network, these files are backed up on a regular basis. You should check with your school's network administrators to determine how often they're backed up and how you would go about requesting

Figure 9.27

The Windows 7 Backup and Restore utility.
(a) Select your backup destination. (b) Choose locations to back up.
(c) Review your scheduled backups, restore files, and start wizards for system image and repair disc creation.

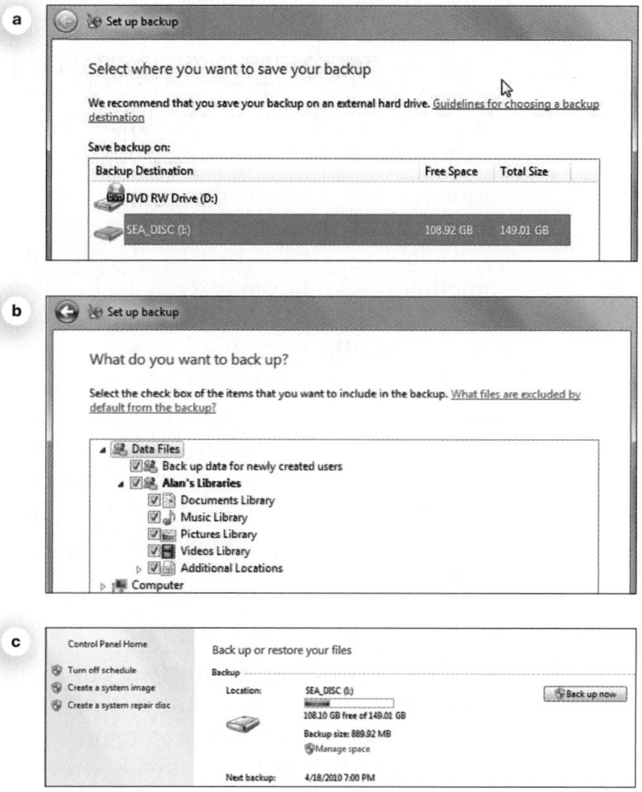

that files be restored from the backup media if they're damaged or deleted. But don't rely on these network backups to bail you out if your data files are lost or damaged. It may take days for the network administrators to get around to restoring your files. It is better to keep backups of your data files yourself, especially homework and project files, so that you can immediately restore them.

Social Engineering: Fooling the Unwary

What is social engineering? **Social engineering** is any technique that uses social skills to generate human interaction that entices individuals to reveal sensitive information. Social engineering often doesn't involve the use of a computer or face-to-face interaction. For example, telephone scams are a common form of social engineering because it is often easier to manipulate someone when you don't have to look at them.

How does social engineering work? Most social engineering schemes use a pretext to lure their victims. **Pretexting** involves creating a scenario that sounds legitimate enough that someone will trust you. For example, you might receive a phone call during which the caller says he is from your bank and that someone tried to use your account without authorization. The caller then tells you he needs to confirm a few personal details such as your birth date, Social Security number, bank account number, and whatever other information he can get out of you. The information he obtains can then be used to empty your bank account or commit some other form of fraud. Often pretexting is used to gain access to corporate computer networks. People will sometimes call random extensions in a large business, claiming to be from technical support. Eventually, the caller will find someone who has a problem and is happy that someone is willing to help. The scam artist will then elicit information such as logins and passwords from the victim as part of the process for "solving the problem." The most common form of pretexting in cyberspace is phishing.

Phishing and Pharming

How are phishing schemes conducted? **Phishing** (pronounced "fishing") lures Internet users to reveal personal information such as credit card numbers, Social Security numbers, or other sensitive information that could lead to identity theft. The scammers send e-mail messages that look like they are from a legitimate business such as an online bank. The e-mail states that the recipient needs to update or confirm his or her account information. When the recipient clicks the provided link, he or she goes to a Web site. The site looks like a legitimate site but is really a fraudulent copy the scammer has created. Once the e-mail recipient confirms his or her personal information, the scammers capture it and can begin using it.

Is pharming a type of phishing scam? Pharming is much more insidious than phishing. Phishing requires a positive action by the person being scammed, such as going to a Web site mentioned in an e-mail and typing in your bank account information. **Pharming** is when malicious code is planted on your computer, either by viruses or by visiting malicious Web sites, that alters your browser's ability to find Web addresses. Users are directed to bogus Web sites even when they enter the correct address of the real Web site or follow a bookmark that they previously had established for the Web site. So instead of ending up at your bank's Web site when you type in its address, you end up at a fake Web site that looks like your bank's site but is expressly set up for the purpose of gathering information.

How can I avoid being caught by phishing and pharming scams? You should never reply directly to any e-mail asking you for personal information. Never click on a link in an e-mail to go to a Web site. Instead, type the Web site address in the browser. Check with the company asking for the information and only give the information if you are certain it is needed.

Also, never give personal information over the Internet unless you know the site is secure. Look for the closed padlock, https, or a certification seal such as VeriSign to help reassure you that the site is secure. The latest versions of Firefox, Chrome, and Internet Explorer have phishing filters built in, so each time you access a Web site, the phishing filter checks for the site's legitimacy and warns you of possible Web forgeries. Finally, make sure you have Internet security software installed on your computer and that it is constantly being updated. Most Internet security packages can detect

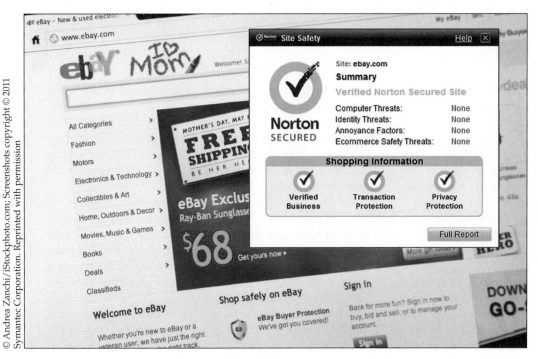

Figure 9.28

Not sure whether you are on the eBay Web site or a cleverly disguised phishing site? Norton Site Safety reassures you that all is well.

and prevent pharming attacks. The major Internet security packages—for example, McAfee and Norton (see Figure 9.28)—also offer phishing-protection tools. When you have the Norton Toolbar displayed in your browser, you are constantly informed about the legitimacy of the site you are visiting.

Another way to protect yourself is never to use your credit card number when you shop online. Although it sounds impossible, credit card providers such as Citibank are offering services such as virtual account numbers for their customers. Before purchasing a product online, you visit the credit card provider's site, where you are assigned a new virtual account number each time you visit. This number looks like a regular credit card number and is tied to your real credit card account. However, the virtual account number can be used only once. That means that if the number is stolen, it's

no good to thieves. They can't use the virtual account number, because you've already used it.

Scareware

What is scareware? Scareware is a type of malware that is downloaded onto your computer and tries to convince you that your computer is infected with a virus (see Figure 9.29) or other type of malware.

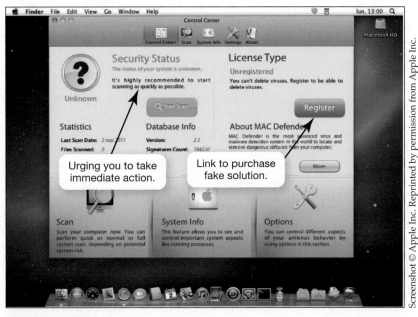

Figure 9.29

Preying on people's fears, scareware attempts to convince you that your computer is infected with a virus and to purchase a "solution."

Computers in Society: Spear Phishing: The Bane of Data Breaches

Most people have vast amounts of personal data residing in databases with the various companies with which they conduct business. Amazon.com has your credit card and address information. Your bank has your Social Security number, birth date, and financial records. Your local supermarket probably has a mailing address and e-mail address for you from when you joined their loyalty club to receive discounts on groceries. All of this data in various places puts you at risk when companies responsible for keeping your data confidential suffer a data breach.

A **data breach** occurs when sensitive or confidential information is copied, transmitted, or viewed by an individual who was never authorized to handle the data. Data breaches can be intentional or unintentional. Intentional data breaches occur when hackers break into digital systems to steal sensitive data. Unintentional data breaches occur when companies controlling data inadvertently allow it to be seen by unauthorized parties, usually due to some breakdown in security procedures or precautions.

In April 2011, Sony's PlayStation online network was breached and personal information, including names, e-mail addresses, and birth dates, for approximately 100 million user accounts was stolen. Sony officials promptly shut down the network and said they didn't see evidence that credit card data had been stolen but that they couldn't rule out the possibility. It was later revealed that credit card information was vulnerable.

In March 2011, Epsilon Marketing suffered a similar data breach. Epsilon conducts marketing programs for many major companies such as Barclays Bank of Delaware, Best Buy, Borders, Target, and TD Ameritrade. Epsilon mostly conducts e-mail correspondence campaigns on behalf of their clients, so they were mainly in possession of individuals' names and e-mail addresses. It was not in possession of customer financial data (such as credit card numbers).

Epsilon's clients and Sony sent correspondence to their customers to warn them of the data breaches and to be extra vigilant. Because even if financial data is not involved, data breaches pose serious risks to the individuals whose data has been compromised. The data thieves now have the basis with which to launch targeted social engineering attacks.

With regular phishing, cybercriminals just send out e-mails to a wide list of e-mail addresses, whether they have a relationship with the company or not; for example, a criminal might send out a general phishing e-mail claiming that a person's Citibank checking account had been breached. People who receive this e-mail that don't have any accounts at Citibank should immediately realize this is a phishing attack and ignore the instructions to divulge sensitive data.

But when cybercriminals obtain data on individuals that includes information about which companies those individuals have a relationship with, they can engage in much more targeted attacks known as **spear phishing**. Spear phishing e-mails are sent to people known to be customers of a company and have a much greater chance of successfully getting individuals to reveal sensitive data. If the criminals who breached Epsilon have a list of e-mail addresses of customers from Barclays Bank, for example, they can ensure that the spear phishing e-mails purport to come from Barclays and will include the customer's full name. This type of attack is much more likely to succeed in fooling people than just random e-mails sent out to thousands of people who might not have a relationship with the company mentioned in the phishing letter.

So how can you protect yourself after a data breach? You need to be extra suspicious of any e-mail correspondence from companies that were involved in the data breach. Companies usually never legitimately contact you by e-mail or phone asking you to reveal sensitive information or reactivate your online account by entering confidential information. Usually, these requests come via regular snail mail.

So if you receive any e-mails or phone calls from companies you deal with purporting to have problems with your accounts, your best course of action is to delete the e-mail or hang up the phone. Then contact the company that supposedly has the problem by a phone number that you look up yourself either in legitimate correspondence from the company (say the toll-free number on your credit card statement) or in the phone book. The representatives from your company can quickly tell if a real problem exists or if you were about to be the victim of a scam.

Pop-ups, banners, or other annoying types of messages will flash on your screen saying frightening things like "Your computer is infected with a virus . . . immediate removal is required." You are then directed to a Web site where you can buy fake removal or antivirus tools that provide little or no value. Panda Security estimates that scareware scams generate in excess of $34 million a month for cybercriminals. Some scareware even goes so far as to encrypt your files and then demand that you pay to have them unencrypted, which is essentially extortion.

Scareware is a social engineering technique because it uses people's fear of computer viruses to convince them to part with their cash. Scareware is often designed to be extremely difficult to remove from your computer and to interfere with the operation of legitimate security software like McAfee and Norton. Scareware is usually downloaded onto your computer from infected Web sites or Trojan horse files.

How do I protect myself against scareware? Most Internet security suites and antivirus and antimalware software packages now detect and prevent the installation of scareware. But make sure you never click on Web sites or pop-up boxes that say "Your computer might be infected, click here to scan your files" because these are often the starting points for installing malicious scareware files on your computer.

Hoaxes

What is a hoax? A **hoax** is an attempt to make someone believe something that is untrue. Hoaxes target a large audience and are generally perpetrated as practical jokes, instruments of social change (which poke fun at an established norm in an effort to change it), or merely ways to waste people's valuable time. Although there are hoax Web sites such as Pacific Northwest Tree Octopus (**www.zapatopi.net/treeoctopus**), most cyberspace hoaxes are perpetrated by e-mail.

Why do people concoct e-mail hoaxes? As opposed to garnering financial rewards, like in a phishing fraud, the motives of e-mail hoax creators can be more complex. Many people start an e-mail hoax just for the challenge of seeing if their "brainchild" can be spread globally. Other hoaxes start as innocent practical jokes between friends that take on lives of their own via the fast communication available on the Internet. Many hoaxes become so well known that they are accepted by society as true events even though they are false. Once this happens to a hoax, it becomes known as an **urban legend**. An example is the phony story about the man who woke up in a bathtub full of ice water and found that thieves had removed one of his kidneys. Hoaxes may be compared to acts of real-world vandalism like graffiti. Graffiti artists "make their mark" on the world, physically; hoaxers may consider they are making a similar mark when a bogus e-mail they have created becomes widespread.

Sometimes hoaxes are based on misinformation or are a way to vent frustration. An e-mail hoax that reappears every time there is a spike in gasoline prices is the Gas Boycott hoax. To boost the scheme's credibility, the e-mail touts it as having been invented by reputable businesspeople. The e-mail explains how boycotting certain gasoline companies will drive the price of gasoline down and urges recipients of the e-mail to join the fight. The originator of this hoax was probably frustrated by high gas prices and, armed with a poor understanding of economics, distributed this brainstorm. Unfortunately, this tactic can have no effect on gasoline prices because it only shifts demand for gasoline from certain oil companies to other sources. Because it does not reduce the overall demand for gasoline, the price of gas will not decline. Did you receive this e-mail and think it sounded like a plausible idea? How many people did you forward it to?

How can I tell if an e-mail is a hoax? Sometimes it is difficult to separate fact from fiction. Many hoax e-mails are well written and crafted in such a way that they sound very real. Before using the Forward button and sending an e-mail to all your friends, check it out at one of the many Web sites that keep track of and expose e-mail hoaxes. Check sites such as Snopes (**www.snopes.com**), Hoax-Slayer (**www.hoax-slayer.com**, shown in Figure 9.30), or TruthOrFiction.com (**www.truthorfiction.com**). These sites are searchable, so you can enter a few keywords from an e-mail you suspect may be a hoax and quickly find similar e-mails and explanations of whether they are true or false. Checking out e-mails before

Figure 9.30

Sites like Hoax-Slayer help you research potential hoaxes.

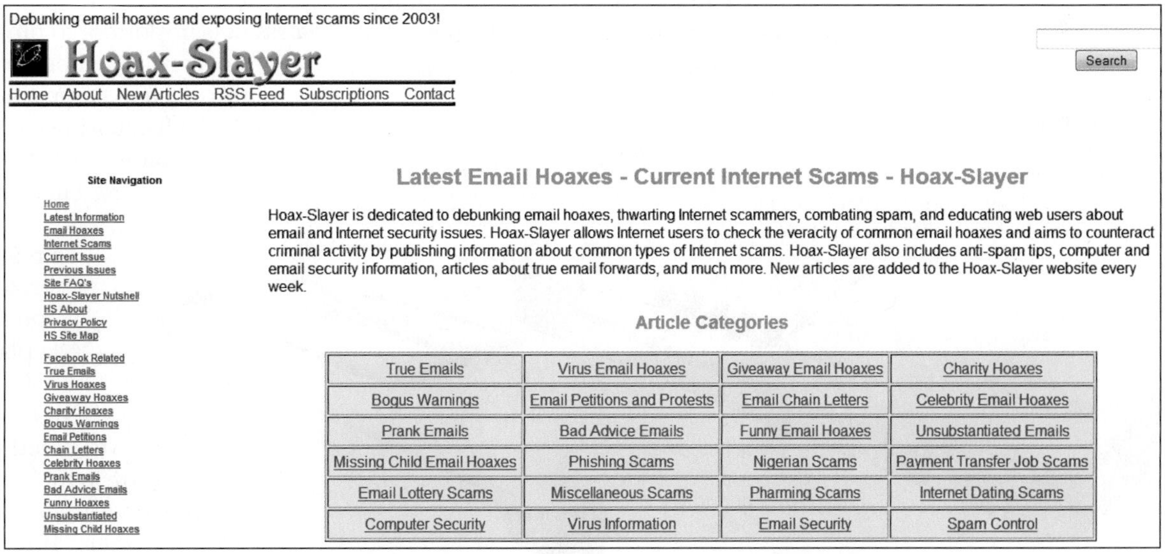

Debunking email hoaxes and exposing Internet scams since 2003!

Hoax-Slayer

Home   About   New Articles   RSS Feed   Subscriptions   Contact

Search

Site Navigation

Home
Latest Information
Email Hoaxes
Internet Scams
Current Issue
Previous Issues
Site FAQ's
Hoax-Slayer Nutshell
HS About
Privacy Policy
HS Site Map

Facebook Related
True Emails
Virus Hoaxes
Giveaway Hoaxes
Charity Hoaxes
Bogus Warnings
Email Petitions
Chain Letters
Celebrity Hoaxes
Prank Emails
Bad Advice Emails
Funny Hoaxes
Unsubstantiated
Missing Child Hoaxes

Latest Email Hoaxes - Current Internet Scams - Hoax-Slayer

Hoax-Slayer is dedicated to debunking email hoaxes, thwarting Internet scammers, combating spam, and educating web users about email and Internet security issues. Hoax-Slayer allows Internet users to check the veracity of common email hoaxes and aims to counteract criminal activity by publishing information about common types of Internet scams. Hoax-Slayer also includes anti-spam tips, computer and email security information, articles about true email forwards, and much more. New articles are added to the Hoax-Slayer website every week.

Article Categories

True Emails	Virus Email Hoaxes	Giveaway Email Hoaxes	Charity Hoaxes
Bogus Warnings	Email Petitions and Protests	Email Chain Letters	Celebrity Email Hoaxes
Prank Emails	Bad Advice Emails	Funny Email Hoaxes	Unsubstantiated Emails
Missing Child Email Hoaxes	Phishing Scams	Nigerian Scams	Payment Transfer Job Scams
Email Lottery Scams	Miscellaneous Scams	Pharming Scams	Internet Dating Scams
Computer Security	Virus Information	Email Security	Spam Control

Hoax-Slayer

forwarding them on to friends, family, and coworkers will save other people's time and help end the spread of these time wasters.

Protecting Your Physical Computing Assets

Your computer, tablet, or cell phone isn't useful to you if it is damaged. Therefore, it's essential to select and ensure a safe environment for it. This includes protecting it from environmental factors, power surges, power outages, and theft.

Environmental Factors

Why is the environment critical to the operation of my computer equipment? Computers are delicate devices and can be damaged by the adverse effects of abuse or a poor environment. Sudden movements, such as a fall, can damage your notebook computer or mobile device's internal components. You should make sure that your computer sits on a flat, level surface, and, if it is a notebook or a tablet, carry it in a protective case. If you do drop your device, have it professionally tested by a repair facility to check for any hidden damage.

Electronic components do not like excessive heat or excessive cold. Unfortunately, computers generate a lot of heat, which is why they have fans to cool their internal components. Make sure that you place your desktop computer where the fan's intake vents, usually found on the rear of the system unit, are unblocked so that air can flow inside. Chill mats that contain cooling fans and sit underneath notebook computers are useful accessories for dissipating heat.

And don't leave computing devices and phones in a car during especially hot or cold weather because components can be damaged by extreme temperatures.

Naturally, a fan drawing air into a computer also draws in dust and other particles, which can wreak havoc on your system. Therefore, keep the room in which your computer is located as clean as possible. Even in a clean room, the fan ducts can become packed with dust, so vacuum it periodically to keep a clear airflow into your computer. Finally, because food crumbs and liquid can damage keyboards and other computer components, consume food and beverages away from your computer.

Power Surges

What is a power surge? Power surges occur when electrical current is supplied in excess of normal voltage (120 volts in the United States). Old or faulty wiring, downed power lines, malfunctions at electric company substations, and lightning strikes can all cause power surges. A **surge protector** is a device that protects your computer against power surges (see Figure 9.31). To use a surge protector, you simply plug your electrical devices into the outlets of the surge protector, which in turn plugs into the wall.

How do surge protectors work? Surge protectors contain two components that are used to protect the equipment that is connected to them. Metal-oxide varistors (MOVs) bleed off excess current during minor surges and feed it to the ground wire, where it harmlessly dissipates. The MOVs can do this while still allowing normal current to pass through the devices plugged into the surge protector. Because the ground wire is critical to this process, it is important to plug the surge protector into a grounded power outlet.

During major surges that overwhelm the MOVs, a fuse inside the surge protector blows, which stops the flow of current to all devices plugged into the surge protector. After a major surge, the surge protector will no longer function and must be replaced.

Over time, the MOVs lose their ability to bleed off excess current, which is why you should replace your surge protectors every two to three years. Buy a surge protector

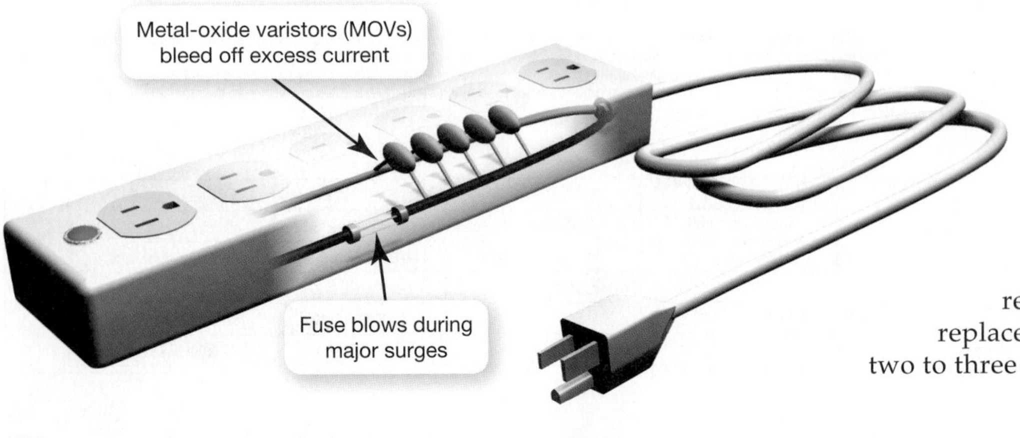

Figure 9.31

Anatomy of a surge protector.

Metal-oxide varistors (MOVs) bleed off excess current

Fuse blows during major surges

that includes indicator lights. Indicator lights illuminate when the surge protector is no longer functioning properly. Don't be fooled by old surge protectors—although they can still function as multiple-outlet power strips, they deliver power to your equipment without protecting it. A power surge could ruin your computer and other devices if you don't protect them. At $20 to $40, a quality surge protector is an excellent investment.

Besides my computer, what other devices need to be connected to a surge protector? All electronic devices in the home that have solid-state components, such as TVs, stereos, printers, and cell phones (when charging), should be connected to a surge protector. Printers and other computer peripherals all require protection. However, it can be inconvenient to use individual surge protectors on everything. A more practical method is to install a **whole-house surge protector** (see Figure 9.32). Whole-house surge protectors function like other surge protectors, but they protect *all* electrical devices in the house. Typically, you will need an electrician to install a whole-house surge protector, which will cost $300 to $400 (installed).

Is my equipment 100 percent safe when plugged into a surge protector? Surge protectors won't necessarily guard against all surges. Lightning strikes can generate such high voltages that they can overwhelm a surge protector. As tedious as it sounds, unplugging computers and peripherals during an electrical storm is the only way to achieve absolute protection.

How can I prevent my computers from losing power during a power outage? Computers can develop software glitches caused by a loss of power if not shut down properly. Mission-critical

Surge protector

Figure 9.32

A whole-house surge protector usually is installed at the breaker panel or near the electric meter.

computers and devices such as home servers or network storage devices often are protected by an **uninterruptible power supply (UPS)**, as shown in Figure 9.33, which is a device that contains surge protection equipment and a large battery. When power is interrupted, such as during a blackout, the UPS continues to send power to the attached computer from its battery. Depending on the battery capacity, you have between about 20 minutes and 3 hours to save your work and shut down your computer properly.

Deterring Theft

Because they are portable, notebooks, tablets, and cell phones are easy targets for thieves. You have four main security concerns with mobile devices: (1) keeping them from being stolen, (2) keeping data secure in case they are stolen, (3) finding the device if it is stolen, and (4) remotely recovering and wiping data off a stolen device.

Keep Them Safe: Alarms

What type of alarm can I install on my mobile device? Motion alarm software is a good inexpensive theft deterrent. Software such as LAlarm (www.lalarm.com) or Laptop Alarm (**www.syfer.nl**) is effective for notebooks. Apps such as SuperAlarm and Alarmomatic help secure your iPad or iPhone. Alarm software either detects motion, like your device being picked up, or sounds near your device and then sets off an ear-piercing alarm until you enter the disable code. Thieves normally prefer stealth and do not like

Figure 9.33

A UPS device should not be mistaken for a fat surge protector!

APC Media

it when attention is drawn to their activities, so alarms can be a very effective theft deterrent.

Keeping Mobile Device Data Secure

How can I secure the data on my mobile devices? Encrypting the data on your mobile device can make it extremely difficult, if not impossible, for thieves to obtain sensitive data from your stolen equipment. Encryption involves transforming your data using an algorithm that can only be unlocked by a secure code (or key). Encrypted data is impossible to read unless it is decrypted, which requires a secure password, hopefully known only to you.

Safe is an app that provides 256-bit encryption, which is very hard to crack, for data and images on your iPhone and iPad. If your password is not entered, no one can access the data and images on your iPhone or iPad. Control Data and Data Protection are similar apps for Android phones. ZoneAlarm DataLock and Safe-House are available for notebook computers to provide encryption for files or even entire hard drives.

Software Alerts and Data Wipes

How can my computer help me recover it when it is stolen? You've probably heard of LoJack, the theft-tracking device used in cars. Car owners install a LoJack transmitter somewhere in their vehicle. If the vehicle is stolen, police activate the transmitter and use its signal to locate the car. Similar systems now exist for computers. Tracking software such as Computrace LoJack for Laptops (**www.absolute.com**), PC PhoneHome, and Mac PhoneHome (**www.brigadoonsoftware.com**) enables your computer to alert authorities to the computer's location if it is stolen. A similar

tracking app for iPhones and iPads is iHound.

To enable your mobile device to help with its own recovery, you install the tracking software on your device. The software contacts a server at the software manufacturer's Web site each time the device connects to the Internet. If your device is stolen, you notify the software manufacturer. The software manufacturer instructs your device to transmit tracking information, such as an IP address, WiFi hotspot, or cell tower location, that will assist authorities in locating and retrieving the mobile device.

What if the thieves find the tracking software and delete it? The files and directories holding the software are not visible to thieves looking for such software, so they probably won't know the software is there. Furthermore, the tracking software is written in such a way that even if the thieves tried to reformat the hard drive, it would detect the reformat and hide the software code in a safe place in memory or on the hard drive. This works because some sectors of a hard drive are not rewritten during most reformattings. That way, it can reinstall itself after the reformatting is completed.

What if my device can't be recovered by the authorities? In the event that your laptop can't be recovered, software packages are available that provide for remote recovery and deletion of files. Computrace LoJack for Laptops has these features and allows you to lock your device to keep the thieves from accessing it or to remotely wipe its contents by deleting all your data from your notebook.

For all iOS devices, Apple offers the Find My iPhone app. Installing this app on your device and enabling it provides you with numerous tools that can assist you in recovering and protecting your mobile devices. Did you forget where you left your iPad? Just sign in with your Apple ID online to see a map showing the location of your iPad (see Figure 9.34). You can also remotely send a message to be displayed on your lost device, such as your phone number and a reward offer, so that someone who finds it will know what to do. And if you can't recover the device, you can remotely password lock it so no one can use it or, if necessary, wipe all the

SOUND BYTE Surge Protectors

In this Sound Byte, you'll learn about the major features of surge protectors and how they work. You'll also learn about the key factors you need to consider before buying a surge protector, and you'll see how easy it is to install one.

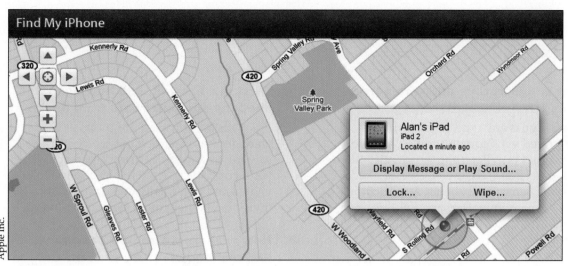

Figure 9.34

The Find My iPhone app can really help if your iPhone or iPad goes astray.

data off the device to completely protect your privacy.

How can I ensure that I've covered all aspects of protecting my digital devices? The checklist in Figure 9.35 is a guide to ensure you didn't miss any critical aspects of security. If you've addressed all of these issues, then you can feel reasonably confident that your Internet access will be secure and free from problems.

Taking a few precautions regarding your data security can provide huge benefits such as peace of mind and the avoidance of time spent correcting problems. So enjoy your computing experiences, but do so safely.

Figure 9.35 | COMPUTER SECURITY CHECKLIST

	Yes	No
Virus and Spyware Protection		
Is antivirus and antispyware software installed on all your devices?		
Is the antivirus and antispyware software configured to update itself automatically and regularly?		
Is the software set to scan your device on a regular basis (at least weekly) for viruses and spyware?		
Firewall		
Do all your computers and tablets have firewall software installed and activated before connecting to the Internet?		
Is your router also able to function as a hardware firewall?		
Have you tested your firewall security by using the free software available at **www.grc.com**?		
Wireless Security (see Chapter 7 for additional details)		
Have you changed the default password for your router?		
Have you changed the name (SSID) of your network and turned off SSID broadcasting?		
Have you enabled WPA or WEP encryption for your network?		
Software Updates		
Have you configured your operating systems (Windows, OS X, iOS) to install new software patches and updates automatically?		
Is other software installed on your device, such as Microsoft Office or productivity apps, configured for automatic updates?		
Is the Web browser you are using the latest version?		

1. What is cybercrime and who perpetrates it?

Cybercrime is any type of crime that is perpetrated via a computer or a Web site. Major types of cybercrime are identity theft, credit card fraud, computer viruses, illegally accessing computer systems, and auction fraud. Cybercriminals use computers, the Internet, and networks to commit their crimes.

2. From which types of viruses do I need to protect my computer?

A computer virus is a program that attaches itself to another program and attempts to spread to other computers when files are exchanged. Computer viruses can be grouped into five categories: (1) boot-sector viruses, (2) logic bombs and time bombs, (3) worms, (4) scripts and macros, and (5) encryption viruses. Once run, they perform their malicious duties in the background and are often invisible to the user.

3. What can I do to protect my computer from viruses?

The best defense against viruses is to install antivirus software. You should update the software on a regular basis and configure it to examine all e-mail attachments for viruses. You should periodically run a complete virus scan on your computer to ensure that no viruses have made it onto your hard drive.

4. How can hackers attack my computing devices, and what harm can they cause?

A hacker is defined as anyone who breaks into a computer system unlawfully. Hackers can use software to break into almost any computer connected to the Internet, unless proper precautions are taken. Once hackers gain access to a computer, they can potentially (1) steal personal or other important information, (2) damage and destroy data, or (3) use the computer to attack other computers.

5. What is a firewall, and how does it keep my computer safe from hackers?

Firewalls are software programs or hardware devices designed to keep computers safe from hackers. By using a personal firewall, you can close open logical ports to invaders and potentially make your computer invisible to other computers on the Internet.

6. How do I create secure passwords and manage all of my passwords?

Secure passwords contain a mixture of upper- and lowercase letters, numbers, and symbols, and are at least 14 characters long. Passwords should not contain words that are in the dictionary or easy-to-guess personal information, like your pet's name. Online password checkers can be used to evaluate the strength of your passwords. Utilities built into Web browsers and Internet security software can be used to manage your passwords and alleviate the need to remember numerous complex passwords.

7. How can I surf the Internet anonymously and use biometric authentication devices to protect my data?

The current versions of the popular browsers include tools, such as Chrome's Incognito feature, that hide your surfing activities by not recording Web sites that you visit, or files that you download, in your browser's history files. Biometric authentication devices use a physical attribute that is not easily duplicated to control access to data files or computing devices. Some notebooks today feature fingerprint readers and facial recognition software to control access.

8. How do I manage online annoyances such as spyware and spam?

The Web is filled with annoyances such as spam, pop-ups, cookies, spyware, and scams such as phishing that make surfing the Web frustrating and sometimes dangerous. Software tools help to prevent or reduce spam, adware, and spyware, while exercising caution can prevent serious harm caused by phishing, pharming, and other Internet scams and hoaxes.

9. What data do I need to back up, and what are the best methods for doing so?

Data files created by you, such as Word and Excel files, or purchased by you (such as music files) need to be backed up in case they are inadvertently deleted or damaged. Application software, such as Microsoft Office, may need to be reinstalled if files are damaged, so backups, such as the DVDs the application came on, must be maintained. Web sites such as ADrive and Windows Live SkyDrive are great for backing up individual files. External hard drives are popular choices for holding image backups of your entire system. Windows 7 and OS X contain solid backup tools that help automate backup tasks.

10. What is social engineering, and how do I avoid falling prey to phishing and hoaxes?

Social engineering schemes use human interaction, deception, and trickery to fool people into revealing sensitive information such as credit card numbers and passwords. Phishing schemes usually involve e-mails that direct the unwary to a Web site that appears to be legitimate, such as a bank site, but is specifically designed to capture personal information for committing fraud. To avoid phishing scams, you should never reply directly to any e-mail asking you for personal information, and never click on a link in an e-mail to go to a Web site. You can research topics you believe to be hoaxes at sites such as Snopes (**www.snopes.com**).

11. How do I protect my physical computing assets from environmental hazards, power surges, and theft?

Computing devices should be kept in clean environments free from dust and other particulates and should not be exposed to extreme temperatures (either hot or cold). You should protect all electronic devices from power surges by hooking them up through surge protectors, which will protect them from most electrical surges that could damage the devices. Mobile devices can be protected from theft by installing software that will (1) set off an alarm if the computer is moved; (2) help recover the computer, if stolen, by reporting the computer's whereabouts when it is connected to the Internet; or (3) allow you to wipe the contents of the digital device remotely.

Companion Website

The Companion Website includes a variety of additional materials to help you review and learn more about the topics in this chapter. Go to: *www.pearsonhighered.com/techinaction*

chapter nine

nine

key terms

Word Bank

- adware
- antivirus software
- botnet
- encryption
- firewall

- hacker(s)
- identity theft
- image backup(s)
- incremental backup(s)
- logical port(s)

- phishing
- social engineering
- spyware
- surge protector
- zombie(s)

Instructions: Fill in the blanks using the words from the Word Bank above.

Randy learned a lot about data security when a data breach occurred on an online gaming site on which he had personal information stored. He was the victim of various (1) _____ attacks including a phone call from a thief pretending to be from his bank. He received quite a few (2) _____ e-mails from (3) _____ that tried to get him to reveal his ATM password at sites that looked very similar to his online bank's real Web site. He wondered if this data breach had anything to do with the rash of pop-ups on his computer displaying various types of (4) _____ pushing useless products he had no interest in buying. When he installed new (5) _____ to check his computer for malware problems, the software informed him that his computer was infected with many types of (6) _____ that were recording information about where he was surfing on the Internet. He sure hoped none of these problems would lead to a hacker using his information to commit (7) _____ and clean out his bank account.

Randy figured he better ensure his network security was up to date. He checked his (8) _____ software that came with Windows 7 to ensure it was appropriately configured to close off his computer's (9) _____ to keep hackers at bay. Randy was cautious since his friend Stanley's computer was turned into a(n) (10) _____ by a hacker as part of a much larger (11) _____ that was used to launch a distributed denial of service attack on major Internet retailers.

Randy also wanted to ensure that he had copies of the data on his computer in case his defenses failed. Every day he performed a(n) (12) _____ on files that had changed since he last backed up his files. Weekly, his backup software was scheduled to execute a(n) (13) _____ , which made a complete backup of all of his data files and system files and stored them on an external hard drive. And since he didn't want his computer equipment damaged by fluctuations in electrical current he installed a(n) (14) _____ to help protect his valuable electronic gear. As a final measure he installed (15) _____ software on his phone to protect its data from prying eyes in case he ever lost it.

becoming computer literate

While attending college, you are working at a company that sells graphic t-shirts. Recently, several company employees were the victim of identity theft. Many of the affected employees seem to have fallen prey to phishing and scareware scams. A number of company computers were found to be infected with spyware. Your boss has asked you to help educate the company's employees about malware and social engineering scams.

Instructions: Using the preceding scenario, draft a memo for employees that educates them about malware and social engineering schemes and explains how they can protect themselves. Make sure to use as many of the keywords from the chapter as you can. Be sure that even employees who aren't computer literate can understand the report.

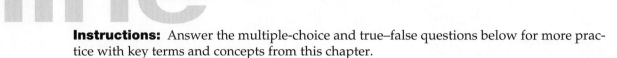

Instructions: Answer the multiple-choice and true–false questions below for more practice with key terms and concepts from this chapter.

Multiple Choice

1. When a hacker steals personal information with the intent of impersonating another individual to commit fraud, this is known as
   a. impersonation theft.
   b. scareware theft.
   c. identity theft.
   d. malware theft.

2. Viruses that activate on certain dates or with the passage of time are known as
   a. boot-sector viruses.
   b. script viruses.
   c. polymorphic viruses.
   d. time bombs.

3. Unlike a virus, _____ do not require human interaction to spread on their own.
   a. worms
   b. Trojan horses
   c. logic bombs
   d. macros

4. Antivirus software works by detecting virus code unique to a particular virus known as a
   a. virus footprint.
   b. virus signature.
   c. virus trace.
   d. virus pattern.

5. Which tool do hackers use to gain access to and take control of your computer?
   a. stealth viruses
   b. backdoor programs
   c. scareware
   d. phishing software

6. A computer that a hacker has gained control of in order to launch DoS attacks is known as a _____ computer.
   a. rootkit
   b. compromised
   c. zombie
   d. breached

7. Software designed to close logical ports in your computer is known as a(n)
   a. firewall.
   b. packet filter.
   c. antimalware blocker.
   d. network address translator.

8. Devices that use unique personal characteristics such as fingerprints or iris patterns to identify authorized computer users are called _____ devices.
   a. personal detection
   b. attribute authentication
   c. individual ID scanning
   d. biometric authentication

9. Programs that attempt to trick you into buying software by pretending your computer is infected with a virus fall into the class of malware known as
   a. virusware.
   b. scareware.
   c. spyware.
   d. adware.

10. A backup of only files that have changed since the last backup was executed is known as a(n)
   a. system backup.
   b. incremental backup.
   c. image backup.
   d. change backup.

True–False

_____ 1. Pretexting is an example of social engineering.

_____ 2. Sending e-mails to lure people into revealing personal information is a technique known as pharming.

_____ 3. Encrypting data is not an appropriate measure for protecting mobile devices such as phones.

_____ 4. Adware and spyware are both types of malware.

_____ 5. Password strength is primarily determined by the length of the password.

1. Backup Procedures

After reading this chapter, you know you should have a good backup strategy in place for your key data. Consider the following and prepare answers in an appropriate format as directed by your instructor.

a. How often do you back up critical data files such as homework files? What type of device do you use for backing up files? Where do you store the backups to ensure they won't be destroyed if a major disaster (such as a fire) destroys your computer? Do you use online sites for file backups?

b. List the applications (such as Microsoft Office) that are currently installed on your computer. Where is the media (DVDs) for your application software stored? For any software you purchased in an Internet download, have you burned a copy of the installation files to DVD/Blu-ray Disc in case you need to reinstall the software?

c. Have you ever made an image backup of your entire system? If so, what software do you use for image backups, and where are the image backups stored? If not, research image backup software on the Internet and find an appropriate package to use. Suppose you need to purchase an additional backup device to hold your image backup of your computer. Find one on the Internet that is appropriate. What is the total cost of the software and hardware you will need to implement your image backup strategy?

2. Protecting Your Computer for Free

There are many free options for protecting your computer from malware, and some are just as adequate as paid software options.

a. Research free antivirus and antimalware programs using sources such as *PC Magazine* (**www.pcmag.com**) and *PC World* (**www.pcworld.com**). What are the highest-rated free software packages available? Are versions available for your operating system? Do you have any of these tools installed on your computer already?

b. Many ISPs offer proprietary security software, including major brands such as Norton and McAfee, free to their subscribers. Research the ISP you use at home, or a local ISP if you don't have an ISP, and determine what free software they provide. Do you currently have security software provided by your ISP installed at home? Why or why not? When selecting an ISP, how important is it to you that they offer free security software?

3. Botnet Awareness

Botnets are serious computer infestations that affect large numbers of computers at one time. Still, many students are unaware of this threat even as botnets strike college campuses. Using the Internet, research botnets and prepare a short flyer for your fellow students that explains the threats posed by botnets and software that can be used to detect botnets.

4. Internet Security Suites

Full-featured Internet security suites offer comprehensive protection for your computer. But how do you know which suite meets your needs? Research the features of three Internet security suites such as Norton Internet Security, AVG Internet Security, Kaspersky Internet Security, Trend Micro Internet Security, or McAfee Internet Security. Prepare a document for your instructor comparing the features and prices of each security suite for a home with four computers. Explain which security suite you would choose for your home and why you would choose it.

1. File Backup Strategies

Your employer was recently the victim of a break-in, and all three dozen of its computers were stolen. Your company lost invaluable data because there was no comprehensive backup strategy in place for its computers. Your boss has asked you to prepare a report outlining a new file backup plan for the company. While preparing your report, consider the following:

a. How often should computer data be backed up? Should full backups or incremental backups be performed? Are image backups necessary?

b. Eighteen employees have notebook computers that they take off company premises. How will backups for notebooks be handled?

c. Research companies that provide online backup solutions for businesses. Which one provides the most cost-effective solution for backing up three dozen computers? Can backups be performed automatically as employees change data files?

2. Tracking Employees

Many corporations provide mobile devices, such as smartphones and tablet computers, to their employees who work outside the office. With apps such as Footprints (from Sollico Software) and GPS tracking (from LOCiMOBILE), it is easy for employers to track the whereabouts of their employees by tracking the location of their mobile devices. Consider the following:

a. How would you feel about your boss tracking your movements during the day? Should employers have to disclose to employees that they are being tracked? Should employers have the right to track employees to ensure they are not slacking off during work hours?

b. Should the tracking software have an option to allow employees to disable the tracking feature temporarily? Under what circumstances should it be permissible for an employee to turn off employer tracking?

c. Should employers be entitled to share employee tracking data with third parties such as law enforcement agencies? Why or why not? What threats are posed to the employee if the device containing their tracking data was lost or stolen?

3. Is Your Computer Vulnerable?

Visit Gibson Research (**www.grc.com**) and run the company's ShieldsUP and LeakTest programs on your personal computer.

a. Did your computer get a clean report? If not, what potential vulnerabilities did the testing programs detect? If ports were shown as being vulnerable, research what these ports do and explain what steps you will take to protect them. Make sure to include a screenshot of your reports with your assignment.

b. A properly configured firewall protects your computer from port vulnerabilities. Use the Internet to research firewall products and find three free firewall products. Which one appears to provide the best protection?

c. Besides adding a firewall to your system, what other measures should you take to protect your system from exploitation by hackers?

4. Computer Security Careers

Computer security professionals are among the highest-paid employees in information technology organizations. Using employment sites such as Monster.com, computerjobs.com, and dice.com, research computer security jobs available in the state where your school is located (try searching "computer security"). Select three entry-level computer security jobs from different employers and prepare a document comparing the following: What are the educational requirements for computer security jobs? What job skills are required? How much prior work experience are firms looking for? Are programming skills required? With cloud computing becoming more popular, how will that affect the outlook for computer security jobs?

Instructions: Some ideas are best understood by experimenting with them in our own minds. The following critical thinking questions are designed to demand your full attention but require only a comfortable chair—no technology.

1. Protecting Your Data from Data Breaches

You most likely have provided personal information to many Web sites and companies. Consider the following:

a. What information have you provided to companies that you wish you had never disclosed? What types of information have companies asked you for that you believe was totally unnecessary to maintain a relationship with them? List specific companies and examples of the extraneous information.

b. If customers' personal information is exposed in a data breach:

- How should customers be informed of the breach (e-mail, snail mail, phone call)? What reassurances should the company provide?
- If information was exposed that might lead to identity theft, should the company be responsible for compensating customers that are affected? Should the company be required to provide credit report monitoring to affected customers to help detect potential identity theft? For what period of time should the company accept responsibility for any identity theft that occurs?

2. Password Protection

You know from reading this chapter that secure passwords are essential to protecting your digital information. Consider the following:

a. How many online accounts do you have that have passwords? List them. Are the passwords for these accounts secure, based on the suggestions proposed in this chapter? Do you change your passwords on a regular basis?

b. How do you keep track of all of your passwords? Do you use password-management software? If so, what product are you using? How often do you change your master password? If you don't use password-management software, what methodology do you use for remembering and tracking your passwords?

3. Shouldn't Protection Be Included?

The Uniform Commercial Code, which governs business in every state except Louisiana, covers the implied warranty of merchantability. This warranty's basic premise is that a company selling goods guarantees that their products will do what they are designed to do (i.e., a car will transport you from place to place) and that there are no significant defects in the product. But computers are routinely sold with only trial versions of antimalware software.

a. Does the failure of OS manufacturers to include antimalware tools constitute a breach of the implied warranty of merchantability? Why or why not? Microsoft does have an antimalware product (Security Essentials), but it requires a separate download. Should Microsoft be required to include Security Essentials as part of the Windows product?

b. Computer hardware manufacturers don't make OS software, but they sell computers that would be unusable without an OS. What responsibility do they have in regard to providing antimalware protection to their customers?

4. Restricting Information to Keep You Safe

Many countries, such as China, have laws that control the content of the Internet and restrict their citizens' access to information. The United States, with the exception of specific areas such as cyberbullying and pornography, does not currently take steps to restrict its citizens' access to the Internet. Unfortunately, this freedom of information does carry some cost because some information on the Web can be potentially dangerous to the general public.

a. Do you think the U.S. government should censor information on the Web, such as instructions for making weapons, to protect the general public? Why or why not? If you think there should be some censorship, do you think such a law would violate the First Amendment right to free speech? Explain your answer.

b. Would you be willing to live with a lower level of information access to increase your sense of well-being? What topics do you feel would make you feel more secure if they were censored?

team time

Protecting Senior Citizens from Sharing Too Much Data

Problem

With the proliferation of e-commerce, electronic data capture, and electronic communication such as e-mail, individuals provide numerous companies with sensitive personal data. However, this only encourages hackers to attempt to breach computer systems, like they did to the PlayStation Network in April 2011, to steal sensitive information or to use social engineering techniques to fool the unwary. Senior citizens are one group that is often targeted by social engineering attacks because they are perceived to be less computer literate and more easily duped by social engineering tactics.

Task

The residents of a local retirement community, managed by your neighbor, have recently been the victim of phishing and phone pretexting attacks. In addition, recent examinations of residents' computers by a computer consultant determined that many computers were infected with spyware. Your neighbor has asked you to assist in educating the retirees about the dangers of disclosing too much information or revealing information to unauthorized parties.

Process

Break the class into three teams. Each team will be responsible for investigating one of the following issues:

1. **Phishing:** Research popular phishing scams and find examples of phishing e-mails sent to the unwary.

2. **Data breaches:** Research popular e-commerce sites or customer loyalty programs that senior citizens might use. Determine what types of data they collect and which pieces of data are not really needed to participate.

3. **Spyware and scareware:** Research typical examples of these types of malware and free solutions that can be used to protect computers from these threats.

Present your findings to the class and discuss methodologies for protecting individuals from cybercrime. Provide your instructor with a report of your findings and suggestions suitable for eventual presentation to the residents of the retirement community.

Conclusion

With the proliferation of electronic data, attempts by cybercrimals to collect sensitive information is inevitable. The best defense is educating individuals about the common types of scams and attacks and clearly explaining steps they can take to prevent themselves from falling prey to nefarious schemes.

Content Control: Censorship to Protect Children

In this exercise, you will research and then role-play a complicated ethical situation. The role you play may or may not match your own personal beliefs, but your research and use of logic will enable you to represent whichever view is assigned. An arbitrator will watch and comment on both sides of the arguments, and together the team will agree on an ethical solution.

Problem

Many parents use Web filtering software (also known as content-control software) to protect their children from objectionable content on the Internet. However, the software is also widely used in libraries, schools, and other public places where people other than parents are making decisions about what information to restrict. In 2000, the U.S. federal government began requiring libraries to use content filtering software as a condition to receiving federal funds under the provisions of the Children's Internet Protection Act (CIPA). Libraries that don't receive federal funds still do not have to install filtering software unless their state (like Virginia in 2007) passes laws requiring them to do so to receive state funding. Upon installation of the software, it is up to the library administrators to decide what content is restricted (as guided by the provisions of laws such as CIPA). Therefore, content restriction can vary widely from library to library.

Research Areas to Consider

- U.S. Supreme Court case *United States v. American Library Association* (2003)
- Content-filtering software and First Amendment rights
- Violating children's free speech rights
- Children's Internet Protection Act (CIPA)

Process

1. Divide the class into teams.
2. Research the areas cited above and devise a scenario in which parents have complained about their child not being able to access a certain Web site needed for school research.
3. Team members should write a summary that provides background information for their character—for example, parent, library administrator, and arbitrator—and details their character's behaviors to set the stage for the role-playing event. Then, team members should create an outline to use during the role-playing event.
4. Team members should arrange a mutually convenient time to meet for the exchange, using the chat room feature of MyITLab, the discussion board feature of Blackboard, or meeting in person.
5. Team members should present their case to the class or submit a PowerPoint presentation for review by the rest of the class, along with the summary and resolution they developed.

Conclusion

As technology becomes ever more prevalent and integrated into our lives, more and more ethical dilemmas will present themselves. Being able to understand and evaluate both sides of the argument, while responding in a personally or socially ethical manner, will be an important skill.

Careers in IT

It's hard to imagine an occupation in which computers are not used in some fashion. Even such previously low-tech industries as waste disposal and fast food use computers to manage inventories and order commodities. In this Technology in Focus feature, we explore various information technology (IT) career paths open to you.

Carol and Mike Werner/Alamy

Rewards of Working in Information Technology

There are many great reasons to work in the exciting, ever-changing field of information technology. In this section, we'll explore some reasons why IT fields are so attractive to graduates looking for entry-level positions.

IT Workers Are in Demand

If you want to investigate a career with computers, the first question you probably have is, "Will I be able to get a job?" After the dot-com bust in the early 2000s, many people thought the boom in computer-related jobs was over. However, current projections by the U.S. Department of Labor's Bureau of Labor Statistics report that computer-related jobs are among the

fastest-growing occupations through 2018 (see Figure 1). Recently, *Money* magazine and PayScale.com developed a list of the top 50 jobs in America based on job growth prospects, job satisfaction, and compensation for experienced workers. Software architects were number 1, and 14 of the top 50 jobs were IT careers. According to FINS Technology (**www.fins.com**), the average starting salary for IT jobs was increasing by 4.3 percent in 2011 from 2010 levels.

The number of students pursuing computer science degrees has been increasing over the past several years. The celebrity of IT icons such as Steve Jobs of Apple and Mark Zuckerberg of Facebook and the success of movies such as *The Social Network* are shining a positive spotlight on IT careers. The *New York Times* estimated that 11,000 computer science degrees would be awarded in the United States in 2011. This marks a reversal of a downward trend that had developed mainly because of the intense media discussion about the demise of Internet start-up companies in the early 2000s. Because of low enrollment since the "dot-com bust," shortages of computing professionals in the United States are projected over the next 5 to 10 years. In terms of job outlook, this is a perfect time to consider an IT career.

IT Jobs Pay Well

As you can see from Figure 1, median salaries in IT careers are robust. But what exactly affects your salary in an IT position? Your skill set and your experience level are obvious answers, but the size of an employer and its geographic location are also factors. Large companies tend to pay more, so if you're pursuing a high salary, set your sights on a large corporation. But remember that making a lot of money isn't everything—be sure to consider other quality-of-life issues such as job satisfaction. Of course, choosing a computer career isn't a guarantee you'll get a high-paying job. Just as in any other profession, you will need appropriate training and on-the-job experience to earn a high salary.

Figure 1 | HIGH-GROWTH IT TECHNOLOGY JOBS*

Occupation	Median Pay	Top Pay	10-Year Growth Rate	Total New Jobs
Computer software engineers	$94,180	$143,330	32%	295,000
Computer systems analyst	77,740	119,070	20	108,100
Computer support specialists	46,260	76,970	14	78,000
Network and computer systems administrators	69,160	108,090	23	78,900
Database administrators	73,490	115,660	20	24,400
Computer and information research scientists	100,660	153,120	24	7,000
Computer and information systems managers	115,780	166,400	17	49,500

*Excerpted from *Occupational Outlook Handbook*, 2010–2011 Edition, Bureau of Labor Statistics

So how much can you expect to start out earning? Although starting salaries for some IT positions (computer desktop support and helpdesk analysts) are in the modest range ($40,000 to $44,000), starting salaries for students with bachelor's degrees in information technology are fairly robust. But IT salaries vary widely, depending on experience level, the geographic location of the job, and the size of the employer.

To obtain the most accurate information, you should research salaries yourself in the geographic area where you expect to work. Job posting sites such as Monster.com can provide guidance, but Salary.com provides a free salary wizard to help you determine what IT professionals in your geographic area are making compared with national averages. You can add information such as your degree and the size of the company you are seeking to further fine-tune the figures. Figure 2 shows that for an entry-level programming position in Phoenix, Arizona, you could expect to earn a salary of between $43,285 and $70,048 at a company of 500 to 1,000 employees. Hundreds of IT job titles are listed, so you can tailor your search to the specific job in which you're interested.

IT Jobs Are Not Going "Offshore"

In the global economy in which we now operate, job outlook includes the risk of jobs being outsourced, possibly to other countries. **Outsourcing** is a process whereby a business hires a third-party firm to provide business services (such as customer-support call centers) that were previously handled by in-house employees. **Offshoring** occurs when the outsourcing firm is located (or uses employees) outside the United States. India was the first country to offer its workforce and infrastructure for offshoring, and countries such as China, Romania, and other former Eastern Bloc countries now vie for a piece of the action. The big lure of outsourcing and offshoring is cost savings: The outsourcing firm can do the work more cheaply than in-house employees can. Considering that the standard of living and salaries are much lower in many countries than they are in the United States, offshoring is an attractive option for many U.S. employers. It may also be faster to hire outside assistance if a business does not already employ workers with the required skill set.

However, outsourcing and offshoring do not always deliver the vast cost savings that chief executive officers

Figure 2

The salary wizard at Salary.com is easy to tailor to your location.

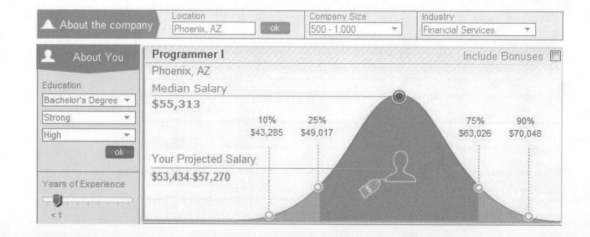

envision. TPI, a global sourcing advisory firm, conducted a survey that showed that the average cost savings from outsourcing was only 15 percent. Furthermore, other less-tangible factors can outweigh the cost savings from outsourcing. Some helpdesk jobs are being brought back to the United States because companies have experienced a backlash from consumers who have had difficulty understanding the employees with foreign accents who staff the support lines. Communications problems can arise between internal and external employees, for example, and cultural differences between the home country and the country doing the offshoring can result in software code that needs extensive rework by in-house employees to make it usable. Data also can be less secure in an external environment, or during the transfer between the company and an external vendor. A study by Deloitte Consulting found that 70 percent of survey participants had "negative experiences" with overseas outsourcing. And a survey in *CFO* magazine indicated that 22 percent of CFOs were planning to increase their outsourcing within the United States. Although outsourcing and offshoring won't be going away, companies are approaching these staffing alternatives with more caution and looking more to U.S. companies to provide resources.

So, many IT jobs are staying in the United States. According to *InformationWeek* magazine, most of the jobs in these three categories (see Figure 3) will stay put:

1. **Customer interaction:** Jobs that require direct input from customers or that involve systems with which customers interface daily.

2. **Enablers:** Jobs that involve getting key business projects accomplished, often requiring technical skills beyond the realm of IT, and good people skills.

3. **Infrastructure jobs:** Jobs that are fundamental to moving and storing the information that U.S.-based employees need to do their jobs.

Also, jobs that require specific knowledge of the U.S. marketplace and culture, such as social media managers, are also very likely to not be offshored.

Women Are in High Demand in IT Departments

Currently, women make up about 25 percent of the IT workforce (per the National Center for Women and Information Technology). This presents a huge opportunity for women who have IT skills, because many IT departments are actively seeking to diversify their workforces. In addition, although a salary gender gap (the difference between what men and women earn for performing the same job) exists in IT careers, it's smaller than in most other professions.

Choice of Working Location

In this case, location refers to the setting in which you work. IT jobs can be office-based, field-based, project-based, or home-based. Since not every situation is perfect for every individual, you can look for a job that suits your tastes and requirements. Figure 4 summarizes the major job types and their locations.

Constant Changes Avoid Boredom

In IT, the playing field is always changing. New software and hardware are constantly being developed. You will need to work hard to keep your skills up to date. You will spend a lot of time in training and self-study trying to learn new systems and techniques. Many individuals thrive in this type of environment because it keeps their jobs from becoming dull or routine.

You Work in Teams

When college and high school students are asked to describe their ideal jobs, the majority usually describe jobs that involve working in teams. Despite what many people think, IT professionals are not locked in lightless cubicles, basking in the glow of their monitors, and working on projects alone. Most IT jobs require constant interaction with other workers, usually in team settings. People skills are highly prized by IT departments. If you have good leadership and team-building skills, you will have the opportunity to exercise them in an IT job.

Figure 3 | JOBS THAT SHOULD REMAIN ONSHORE

Customer Interaction	Enablers	Infrastructure Jobs
Web application developers	Business process analysts	Network security
Web interface designers	Application developers (when customer interaction is critical)	Network installation technicians
Database and data warehouse designers/developers	Project managers (for systems with customers and business users who are located predominantly in the United States)	Network administrators (engineers)
Customer relationship management (CRM) analysts		Wireless infrastructure managers and technicians
Enterprise resource planning (ERP) implementation specialists		Disaster recovery planners and responders

Figure 4 | WHERE DO YOU WANT TO WORK?

Type of Job	Location and Hours	Special Considerations
Office-based	Report for work to the same location each day and interact with the same people on a regular basis. Requires regular hours of attendance (such as 9 A.M. to 5 P.M.).	May require working beyond "normal" working hours. May also require workers to be on call 24/7.
Field-based	Travel from place to place as needed and perform short-term jobs at each location.	Involve a great deal of travel and the ability to work independently.
Project-based	Work at client sites on specific projects for extended periods of time (weeks or months).	Can be especially attractive to individuals who like workplace situations that vary on a regular basis.
Home-based (telecommuting)	Work from home.	Involve very little day-to-day supervision and require an individual who is self-disciplined.

You Don't Need to Be a Mathematical Genius

Certain IT careers such as programming involve a fair bit of math. But even if you're not mathematically inclined, you can explore many other IT careers. IT employers also value such attributes as creativity, marketing, and artistic style, especially in jobs that involve working on the Internet or with social media.

IT Skills Are Portable

Most computing skills are portable from industry to industry. A networking job in the clothing manufacturing industry uses the same primary skill set as a networking job for a supermarket chain. Therefore, if something disastrous happens to the industry you're in, you should be able to switch to another industry without

having to learn an entire new skill set. Combining business courses with IT courses will also make you more marketable when changing jobs. For example, as an accounting major, if you minor in IT, employers may be more willing to hire you because working in accounting today means constantly interfacing with management information systems and manipulating data.

Challenges of IT Careers

Although there are many positive aspects of IT careers, there can be some challenges as well. The discussions that follow are not meant to discourage you from pursuing an IT career, but merely to make you aware of exactly what challenges you may face in an IT department.

Stress

Most IT jobs are hectic (see Figure 5). Whereas the average American works 42 hours a week, a survey by *InformationWeek* shows that the average IT staff person works 45 hours a week and is on call for another 24 hours. On-call time (hours an employee must be available to work in the event of a problem) has been increasing in recent years because more IT systems (such as e-commerce systems) require 24/7 availability. There are plenty of other high-stress jobs, such as air-traffic controller or physician, but IT jobs do tend to spawn more stressful situations and development

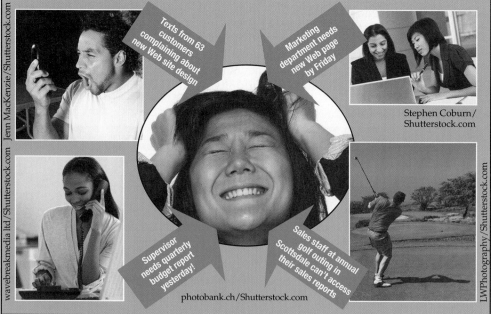

Texts from 63 customers complaining about new Web site design

Marketing department needs new Web page by Friday

Supervisor needs quarterly budget report yesterday!

Sales staff at annual golf outing in Scottsdale can't access their sales reports

Figure 5
Stress comes from multiple directions in IT jobs.

timelines since availability of information is so critical to businesses today.

I'm Just One of the "Guys"

A majority of IT jobs are filled by men, so some women view IT departments as *Dilbert*-like microcosms of antisocial geeks and don't feel they would fit in. Unfortunately, some mostly male IT departments do suffer from varying degrees of gender bias. Although some women may thrive on the challenge of enlightening these male enclaves and bringing them into the 21st century, others might find it difficult to work in such environments.

Not Another Training Course!

Although the constantly changing nature of IT can alleviate boredom, keeping up with the changes can also cause some stress. You will need to take training courses, do self-study, and perhaps take additional college courses such as graduate degrees to keep up with the vast shifts of technology. You need to accept that the concept of lifelong learning is much more important in IT careers than in some other fields.

What Realm of IT Should I Work In?

Figure 6 provides an organizational chart for a modern IT department that should help you understand the careers currently available and how they interrelate. The chief information officer (CIO) has overall responsibility for the development, implementation, and maintenance of information systems and infrastructure. Usually the CIO reports to the chief operating officer (COO).

The responsibilities below the CIO are generally grouped into two units: development and integration (responsible for the development of systems and Web sites) and technical services (responsible for the day-to-day operations of the company's information infrastructure and network, including all hardware and software deployed).

In large organizations, responsibilities are distinct and jobs are defined more narrowly. In medium-sized organizations, there can be overlap between position responsibilities. At a small shop, you might be the network administrator, database administrator, computer support technician, and social media manager all at the same time. Let's look at the typical jobs found in each department.

Working in Development and Integration

Two distinct paths exist in this division: Web development and systems development. Because everything involves the Web today, there is often a great deal of overlap between these paths.

Web Development

When most people think of Web development careers, they usually equate them with being a **webmaster**. However, today's webmasters usually are supervisors with responsibility for certain aspects of Web development. At smaller companies, they may also be responsible for tasks that the other individuals in a Web development group usually do:

- **Web content creators** generate the words and images that appear on the Web. Journalists, other writers, editors, and marketing personnel prepare an enormous amount of Web content, whereas **video producers**, **graphic designers**, and **animators** create Web-based multimedia. **Interface designers** work with graphic designers and animators to create a look and feel for the site and make it easy to navigate. Content creators have a thorough understanding of their own fields as well as HTML/XHTML, PHP, and JavaScript. They also need to be familiar with the capabilities and limitations of modern Web development tools so that they know what the Web publishers can accomplish.

- **Web programmers** build Web pages to deploy the materials that the content creators develop. They wield the software tools (such as Adobe Dreamweaver and Microsoft Expression) that develop the Web pages and create links to databases (using products such as Oracle and SQL Server) to keep information flowing between users and Web pages. They must possess a solid understanding of client- and server-side Web languages (HTML/XHTML, XML, Java, JavaScript, ASP, PHP, Silverlight, and PERL) and development environments such as the Microsoft .NET Framework.

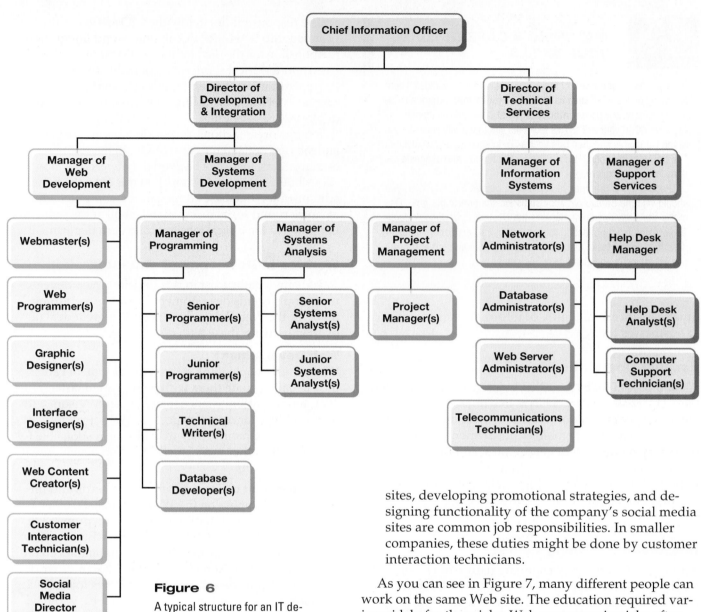

Figure 6

A typical structure for an IT department at a large corporation.

- **Customer interaction technicians** provide feedback to a Web site's customers. Major job responsibilities include answering e-mail, sending requested information, funneling questions to appropriate personnel (technical support, sales, and so on), and providing suggestions to Web publishers for site improvements. Extensive customer service training is essential to work effectively in this area.

- **Social media directors** are responsible for directing the strategy of the company on all social media sites where the company maintains a presence. Often supervising customer interaction technicians, these people make sure that customers have a quality experience while interacting with company employees and customers on sites such as Facebook, Twitter, and Yelp. Responding to comments left on

sites, developing promotional strategies, and designing functionality of the company's social media sites are common job responsibilities. In smaller companies, these duties might be done by customer interaction technicians.

As you can see in Figure 7, many different people can work on the same Web site. The education required varies widely for these jobs. Web programming jobs often require a four-year college degree in computer science, whereas graphic designers often are hired with two-year art degrees.

Systems Development

Ask most people what systems developers do and they will answer, "programming." However, programming is only one aspect of systems development. Because large projects involve many people, there are many job opportunities in systems development. An explanation of each key area follows.

- **Systems analysts** spend most of their time in the beginning stages of the system development life cycle (SDLC). They talk with end users to gather information about problems and existing information systems. They document systems and propose solutions to problems. Having good people skills is essential to success as a systems analyst. In ad-

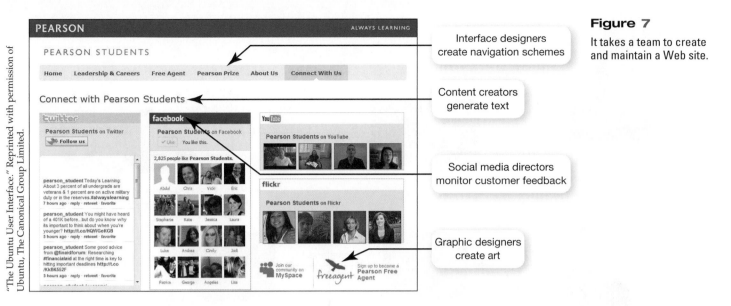

Figure 7

It takes a team to create and maintain a Web site.

Interface designers create navigation schemes

Content creators generate text

Social media directors monitor customer feedback

Graphic designers create art

dition, systems analysts work with programmers during the development phase to design appropriate programs to solve the problem at hand. Therefore, many organizations insist on hiring systems analysts who have both solid business backgrounds and previous programming experience (at least at a basic level). For entry-level jobs, a four-year degree is usually required. Many colleges and universities offer degrees in management information systems (MIS) that include a mixture of systems development, programming, and business courses.

- **Programmers** participate in the program development life cycle, attending meetings to document user needs and working closely with systems analysts during the design phase. Programmers need excellent written communication skills because they often generate detailed systems documentation for end-user training purposes. Because programming languages are mathematically based, it is essential for programmers to have strong math skills and an ability to think logically. Programmers should also be proficient at more than one programming language. A four-year degree is usually required for entry-level programming positions.

- **Project managers** usually have years of experience as programmers or systems analysts. This job is part of a career path upward from entry-level programming and systems analyst jobs. Project managers manage the overall systems development process: assigning staff, budgeting, reporting to management, coaching team members, and ensuring deadlines are met. Project managers need excellent time management skills because they are pulled in several directions at once. Many project managers obtain master's degrees to supplement their undergraduate degrees in computer science or MIS.

In addition to these key players, the following people are also involved in the systems development process:

- **Technical writers** generate systems documentation for end users and for programmers who may make modifications to the system in the future.

- **Network engineers** help the programmers and analysts design compatible systems, because many systems are required to run in certain environments (UNIX or Windows, for instance) and must work well in conjunction with other programs.

- **Database developers** design and build databases to support the software systems being developed.

Large development projects may have all of these team members on the project. Smaller projects may require an overlap of positions (such as a programmer also acting as a systems analyst). The majority of these jobs require four-year college degrees in computer science or management information systems. As shown in Figure 8, team members work together to build a system.

It is important to emphasize that all systems development careers are stressful. Deadlines are tight for development projects, especially if they involve getting a new product to market ahead of the competition. Nevertheless, if you enjoy challenges and can endure a fast-paced, dynamic environment, there should be plenty of opportunities for good systems developers in the decade ahead.

Working in Technical Services

Technical services jobs are vital to keeping IT systems running. The people in these jobs install and maintain the infrastructure behind the IT systems and work with end users to make sure they can interact with the systems effectively. These also are the *least likely* IT jobs to be outsourced because hands-on work with equipment and users is required on a regular basis. The two major categories of technical services careers are information systems and support services.

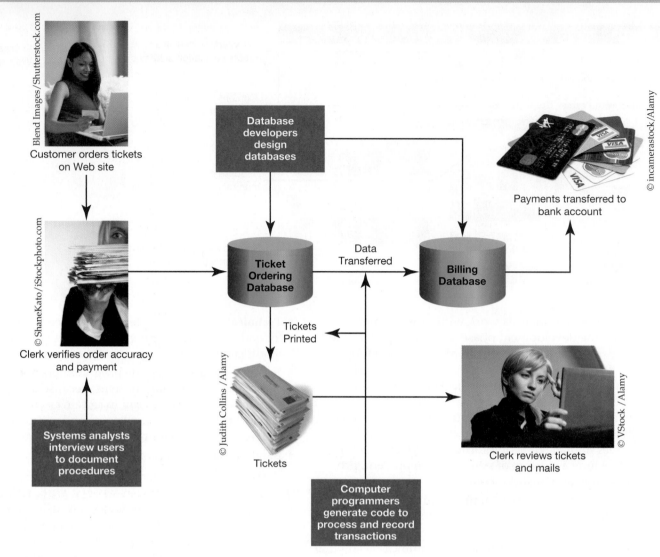

Customer orders tickets
on Web site

Clerk verifies order accuracy
and payment

Systems analysts
interview users
to document
procedures

Database
developers
design
databases

Ticket
Ordering
Database

Data
Transferred

Billing
Database

Payments transferred to
bank account

Tickets
Printed

Tickets

Computer
programmers
generate code to
process and record
transactions

Clerk reviews tickets
and mails

Figure 8

This is a flowchart of a ticket ordering system. Each member of the systems development team performs functions critical to the development process (as shown in the red boxes).

Information Systems

The information systems department keeps the networks and telecommunications up and running at all times. Within the department, you'll find a variety of positions.

- **Network administrators** (sometimes called *network engineers*) install and configure servers, design and plan networks, and test new networking equipment (see Figure 9). Network administrators are involved in every stage of network planning and deployment. They decide what equipment to buy and what type of media to use, and they determine the correct topology for the network. They also often develop policies regarding network usage, security measures, and hardware and software standards.

After the planning is complete, network administrators help install the network (either by supervising third-party contractors or by doing the work themselves). Typical installation tasks include configur-

ing and installing client computers and peripherals, running cable, and installing wireless media devices. Installing and configuring security devices and software are also critical jobs.

When equipment and cables break, network administrators must locate the source of the trouble and fix the problem. They also obtain and install updates to network software, and evaluate new equipment to determine whether the network should be upgraded. In addition, they monitor the network's performance to ensure that users' needs are met.

Because of the importance of the Internet to most organizations, network administrators ensure that the Internet connection is maintained at all times, which usually is a high priority on their to-do list. Finally, network administrators plan disaster recovery strategies (such as what to do if a fire destroys the server room).

Figure 9

At smaller companies, you may be fixing a user's computer in the morning, installing and configuring a new network operating system in the afternoon, and troubleshooting a wiring problem (shown here) in the evening.

- **Database administrators (DBAs)** install and configure database servers and ensure that the servers provide an adequate level of access to all users.
- **Web server administrators** install, configure, and maintain Web servers and ensure that the company maintains Internet connectivity at all times.
- **Telecommunications technicians** oversee the communications infrastructure, including training employees to use telecommunications equipment. They are often on call 24 hours a day.

Support Services

As a member of the support services team, you interface with users (external customers or employees) and troubleshoot their computer problems. These positions include the following:

- **Helpdesk analysts** staff the phones, respond to Internet live chat, or respond to e-mail and solve problems for customers or employees, either remotely or in person. Often helpdesk personnel are called upon to train users on the latest software and hardware.
- **Computer support technicians** go to a user's physical location and fix software and hardware problems. They also often have to chase down and repair faults in the network infrastructure.

As important as these people are, they often receive a great deal of abuse by angry users whose computers are not working. When working in support services, you need to be patient and not be overly sensitive to insults!

Technical services jobs often require two-year college degrees or training at trade schools or technical institutes. At smaller companies, job duties tend to overlap between the helpdesk and technician jobs. These jobs are in demand and require staffing in local markets, so they are staying onshore. You can't repair a computer's power supply if you are located in another country!

How Should I Prepare for a Job in IT?

A job in IT requires a robust skill set and formal training and preparation. Most employers today have an entry-level requirement of a college degree, a technical institute diploma, appropriate professional certifications, experience in the field, or a combination of these. How can you prepare for a job in IT?

1. **Get educated.** Two- and four-year colleges and universities normally offer three degrees to prepare students for IT careers: computer science, MIS, and information technology (although titles vary). Alternatives to colleges and universities are privately licensed technical (or trade) schools. Generally, these programs focus on building skill sets rapidly and qualifying for a job in a specific field. The main advantage of technical schools is that their programs usually take less time to complete than college degrees. However, to have a realistic chance of employment in IT fields other than networking or Web development, you should attend a degree-granting college or university.

2. **Investigate professional certifications.** Certifications attempt to provide a consistent method of measuring skill levels in specific areas of IT. Hundreds of IT certifications are available, most of which you get by passing a written exam. Software and hardware vendors (such as Microsoft and Cisco) and professional organizations (such as the Computing Technology Industry Association) often establish certification standards. Visit **www.microsoft.com**, **www.cisco.com**, **www.comptia.org**, and **www.sun.com** for more information on certifications.

    Employees with certifications generally earn more than employees who aren't certified. However, most employers don't view a certification as a substitute for a college degree or a trade school program. You should think of certifications as an extra edge beyond your formal education that will make you more attractive to employers. To ensure you're pursuing the right certifications, ask employers which certifications they respect, or explore online job sites to see which certifications are listed as desirable or required.

3. **Get experience.** In addition to education, employers want you to have experience, even for entry-level jobs. While you're still completing your education, consider getting an internship or part-time job in your field of study. Many colleges will help you find internships and allow you to earn credit toward your degree through internship programs.

4. **Do research.** Find out as much as you can about the company and the industry it is in before going on an interview. Start with the company's Web site and then expand your search to business and trade publications such as *Business Week* and *CIO* magazines.

How Do I Get Started on My IT Career?

Training for a career is not useful unless you can find a job at the end of your training. Here are some tips on getting a job.

1. **Find an internship.** Many employers recruit at schools, and most schools maintain a placement office to help students find jobs. Employees in the placement office can help you with résumé preparation and interviewing skills, and provide you with leads for internships and jobs.

   You should also develop a relationship with your instructors. Many college instructors still work in or previously worked in the IT industry. They can often provide you with valuable advice and industry contacts.

2. **Start networking.** Many jobs are never advertised but instead are filled by word of mouth. Seek out contacts in your field and discuss job prospects with them. Find out what skills you need, and ask them to recommend others in the industry with whom you can speak. Professional organizations such as the Association for Computing Machinery (ACM) offer one way to network. These organizations often have chapters on college campuses and offer reduced membership rates for students.

   The contacts you make there could lead to your next job. Local user groups that are made up of working professionals with similar interests (such as Microsoft programmers or Linux administrators) also are good sources of contacts. Figure 10 lists major professional organizations you should consider investigating.

   If you are a woman and are thinking about pursuing an IT career, there are many resources and groups that cater to female IT professionals and students. The oldest and best-known organization is the Association for Women in Computing, founded in 1978. Figure 11 provides a list of resources to investigate.

3. **Check corporate Web sites for jobs.** Many corporate Web sites list current job opportunities. For example, Google provides searchable job listings by geographic location. Check the sites of companies in which you are interested and then do a search on the sites for job openings or, if provided, click their Employment links.

4. **Visit online employment sites.** Most IT jobs are advertised online at sites such as Monster.com and Dice.com. Most of these sites allow you to store your résumé online, and Dice (see Figure 12) allows employers to browse résumés to find qualified employees.

   Other sites also offer career resources, including **www.computerjobs.com, www.techcareers.com, www.justtechjobs.com, www.linkedin.com, www.computerwork.com, www.careerbuilder.com,** and **www.gamasutra.com**. Begin looking at job postings on these sites early in your education, because these job postings detail the skill sets employers require. Focusing on coursework that will provide you with desirable skill sets will make you more marketable.

   The outlook for IT jobs should continue to be positive in the future. We wish you luck with your education and job search.

Figure 10 | PROFESSIONAL ORGANIZATIONS

Organization Name	Purpose	Web Site
Association for Computing Machinery (ACM)	Oldest scientific computing society. Maintains a strong focus on programming and systems development.	**www.acm.org**
Association for Information Systems (AIS)	Organization of professionals who work in academia and specialize in information systems.	**www.aisnet.org**
Association of Information Technology Professionals (AITP)	Heavy focus on IT education and development of seminars and learning materials.	**www.aitp.org**
Institute of Electrical and Electronics Engineers (IEEE)	Provides leadership and sets engineering standards for all types of network computing devices and protocols.	**www.ieee.org**
Information Systems Security Association (ISSA)	Not-for-profit, international organization of information security professionals and practitioners.	**www.issa.org**

Figure 11 | RESOURCES FOR WOMEN IN IT

Organization Name	Purpose	Web Site
Anita Borg Institute for Women and Technology	Organization whose aim is to "increase the impact of women on all aspects of technology."	**www.anitaborg.org**
Association for Women in Computing (AWC)	A not-for-profit organization dedicated to promoting the advancement of women in computing professions.	**www.awc-hq.org**
The Center for Women & Information Technology (CWIT)	Established at the University of Maryland, Baltimore County (UMBC), the organization is dedicated to providing global leadership in achieving women's full participation in all aspects of IT.	**www.umbc.edu/cwit**
Diversity/Careers in Engineering & Information Technology	An online magazine whose articles cover career issues focused on technical professionals who are members of minority groups, women, or people with disabilities.	**www.diversitycareers.com**
Women in Technology International (WITI)	A global trade association for tech-savvy, professional women.	**www.witi.com**

Figure 12

Employment sites such as Dice.com enable you to search for specific jobs within a defined geographic area.

The video gaming industry in the United States has surpassed the earning power of the Hollywood movie industry. In 2010, U.S. consumers bought over $18.5 billion worth of video games and accessories, whereas Hollywood took in just under $10.6 billion. Although some aspects of game development, such as scenery design and certain aspects of programming, are being sent offshore, the majority of game development requires a creative team whose members need to work in close proximity to each other. Therefore, it is anticipated that most game development jobs will stay in the United States. Consoles such as the Xbox 360 and the PlayStation 3 generate demand for large-scale games, but Xbox Live and PlayStation Network have also fueled demand for casual games. Also, the popularity of mobile devices such as smartphones and tablets is driving demand for lower-end, casual game applications. Casual games are games that can be played relatively quickly, often puzzle games. Demand for family-friendly games without violence, sex, and profanity is on the rise (see Figure 13). With all this demand, there are many opportunities for careers in game development.

Game development jobs usually are split along two paths: designers and programmers. Game designers tend to be artistic and are responsible for creating 2D and 3D art, game interfaces, video sequences, special effects, game levels, and scenarios. Game designers must master software packages such as Autodesk 3ds Max, Autodesk Maya, NewTek LightWave 3D, Adobe Photoshop, and Adobe Flash. Programmers are then responsible for coding the scenarios developed by these designers. Using languages and toolsets such as Objective-C, Unity, Apple Xcode, C, C++, Assembly, and Java, programmers build the game and ensure that it plays accurately.

Aside from programmers and designers, play testers and quality assurance professionals play the games with the intent of breaking them or discovering bugs within the game interfaces or worlds. **Play testing** is an essential part of the game development process because it assists designers in determining which aspects of the game are most intriguing to players and which parts of the game need to be repaired or enhanced.

No matter what job you may pursue in the realm of gaming, you will need to have a two- or four-year college degree. If you're interested in gaming, then look for a school with a solid animation or 3D art program or a computer game programming curriculum. Programming requires a strong background in mathematics and physics to enable you to realistically program environments that mimic the real world. Proficiency with mathematics (especially geometry) also helps with design careers. For more information on gaming careers, check out the International Game Developers Association site (**www.igda.org**) and Game Career Guide (**www.gamecareerguide.com**).

© Vinod Kurien / Alamy

Figure 13

Plants vs. Zombies, which has you grow plants to fend off encroaching zombie hordes, is an example of a popular casual game available for many different platforms.

Multiple Choice

Instructions: Answer the multiple-choice questions below for more practice with key terms and concepts from this Technology in Focus feature.

1. The individuals responsible for making a Web site easy to navigate are referred to as
   a. network engineers.
   b. graphic designers.
   c. Web programmers.
   d. interface designers.

2. What type of job involves a great deal of travel and the ability to work independently?
   a. field-based
   b. project-based
   c. office-based
   d. home-based

3. Which position is *not* typically a part of the information systems department?
   a. helpdesk analysts
   b. telecommunications technicians
   c. network administrators
   d. W eb server administrators

4. Outsourcing is thought to be an attractive option for many companies because of
   a. the emphasis on employee training.
   b. the cost savings that can be realized.
   c. increased data security.
   d. the opportunity to experience new cultures and ideas.

5. Which role best describes those employees who design solutions to problems?
   a. project managers
   b. network engineers
   c. systems analysts
   d. database developers

6. Which of the following statements about IT careers is *true*?
   a. IT employers typically prefer certification to experience.
   b. Women who have IT skills have limited opportunities.
   c. Most IT jobs are being moved offshore.
   d. IT jobs require frequent interaction with others.

7. Which task is *not* typically performed by a network administrator?
   a. developing network usage policies
   b. installing networks
   c. planning for disaster recovery
   d. Web site programming

8. Social media directors are the people who are responsible for
   a. orchestrating the company strategy in online venues.
   b. providing feedback to Web site customers.
   c. creating the look and feel of a Web site.
   d. deploying the materials prepared by content creators.

9. The oldest scientific computing organization is the
   a. Institute of Electrical and Electronics Engineers.
   b. Association for Computing Machinery.
   c. Information Systems Security Association.
   d. Association for Women in Computing.

10. Which position is part of the Web development department?
    a. systems analyst
    b. Web content creator
    c. programmer
    d. technical writer

behind the scenes:
software programming

Understanding Software Programming

OBJECTIVE:

Why do I need to understand how to create software? *(p. 470)*

The Life Cycle of an Information System

OBJECTIVE:

What is a system development life cycle, and what are the phases in the cycle? *(p. 470)*

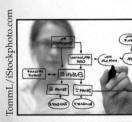

Life Cycle of a Program

OBJECTIVES:

What is the life cycle of a program? *(p. 474)*

What role does a problem statement play in programming? *(p. 474)*

How do programmers create algorithms and move from algorithm to code? *(p. 476)*

What steps are involved in completing the program? *(p. 482)*

 Active Helpdesk: Understanding Software Programming

 Sound Byte: Programming for End Users

 Sound Byte: Looping Around the IDE

Programming Languages: Many Languages for Many Projects

OBJECTIVES:

How do programmers select the right programming language for a specific task? *(p. 491)*

What are the most popular programming languages for different types of application development? *(p. 492)*

 Active Helpdesk: Selecting the Right Programming Language

 Sound Byte: 3D Programming the Easy Way

Scan here for more info on How Cool Is This? ▶

how cool is *this?*

Microsoft has a tool to make gaming programming simpler for all of us. The tool is called **XNA Game Studio**. This platform uses the C# programming language to develop video games for both Windows and the Xbox 360 game system. When the game is complete, the "developer" can distribute his or her creation to other players using the **Xbox Live** network. Windows Phone 7, the operating system for Windows-based mobile devices like the Microsoft Zune, now also supports XNA. So you can open up the Platformer Starter Kit and start creating your own 2D game in an afternoon!

Tour Microsoft's **App Hub** at **create.msdn.com/en-US/** to see the types of games players from all over the world have created.

Understanding Software Programming

Every day we face a wide array of tasks. Some tasks are complex and need a human touch; some require creative thought and high-level organization. However, some tasks are routine, such as alphabetizing a huge collection of invoices. Tasks that are repetitive, work with electronic information, and follow a series of clear steps are candidates for automation with computers.

Why would I ever need to create a program? Well-designed computer programs already exist for many tasks. For example, if you want to write a research paper, Microsoft Word allows you to do just that. The program has already been designed to translate the tasks you want to accomplish into computer instructions. To do your work, you need only be familiar with the interface of Word; you do not have to create a program yourself.

However, for users who cannot find an existing software product to accomplish a task, programming is mandatory. For example, imagine that a medical company comes up with a new smart bandage that is designed to transmit medical information about a wound directly to a diagnostic computer. No existing software product on the market is designed to accumulate and relay information in just this manner. Therefore, a team of software programmers will have to create smart-bandage software. (There is a lot of active research in the area of smart bandages in both academic and corporate settings.)

If I'm not going to be a programmer, why do I need to know some programming? Even if you'll never create a program of your own, knowing the basics of computer programming is still helpful. For example, most modern software applications enable you to customize and automate various features by using custom-built miniprograms called *macros*. By creating macros, you can ask the computer to execute a complicated sequence of steps with a single command. Understanding how to program macros enables you to add custom commands to Word or Excel, for example, and lets you automate frequently performed tasks, providing a huge boost to your productivity.

Understanding programming is therefore an important piece of getting the most out of your computer system. If you plan to use only existing, off-the-shelf software, having a basic knowledge of programming enables you to understand how application software is constructed and to add features that support your personal needs. If you plan to create custom applications from scratch, having a detailed knowledge of programming will be critical to the successful completion of your projects. In this chapter, we explore the stages of program development and survey the most popular programming languages.

The Life Cycle of an Information System

Generally speaking, a system is a collection of pieces working together to achieve a common goal. Your body, for example, is a system of muscles, organs, and other organized groups of cells working together. The college you attend is a system, too, in which administrators, faculty, students, and maintenance personnel work together. An **information system** includes data, people, procedures, hardware, and software. You interact with information systems all the time, whether you are at a grocery store, bank, or restaurant. In any of these instances, the parts of the system work together toward a similar goal. Because teams of individuals are required to develop such systems, they need to follow an organized process (set of steps) to ensure that development proceeds in an orderly fashion.

This set of steps is usually referred to as the system development life cycle (SDLC). Systems theory came long before programming: Everything is a part of something larger and something smaller. If you change one part of a system, other parts of the system also change. In this section, we provide you with an overview of systems development and show you how programming fits into the cycle.

System Development Life Cycle

Why do I need a process to develop a system? To create a modern software package, an entire team of people is needed, and a systematic approach is necessary. Those programs are generally far more complex than the ones you would write yourself, and they require many phases to make the product complete and marketable. They need to be available for multiple operating systems, work over networked environments, and be free of errors and well supported. Therefore, a process often referred to as the **system development life cycle (SDLC)** is used.

What steps constitute the SDLC? There are six steps in a common SDLC model, as shown in Figure 10.1. This system is sometimes referred to as a "waterfall" system because each step is dependent on the previous step being completed first. A brief synopsis of each step follows.

1. **Problem and Opportunity Identification:** Corporations are always attempting to break into new markets, develop new sources of customers, or launch new products. For example, when the founders of eBay developed the idea of an online auction community, they needed a system that could serve customers and allow them to interact with each other. At other times, systems development is driven by a company's desire to serve its existing customers more efficiently or to respond to problems with a current system. For example, when traditional brick-and-mortar businesses want to launch e-commerce sites, they need to develop systems for customers to purchase products.

   Whether solving an existing problem or exploiting an opportunity, corporations usually generate more ideas for systems than they have the time and money to implement. Large corporations typically form a development steering committee to evaluate systems development proposals. The committee reviews ideas and decides which projects to take forward based on available resources such as personnel and funding.

2. **Analysis:** In this phase, analysts explore in depth the problem to be solved and develop a program specification. The **program specification** is a clear statement of the goals and objectives of the project. It is also at this stage that the first feasibility assessment is performed. The feasibility assessment determines whether the project should go forward. You might have a great idea, but that doesn't mean that the company

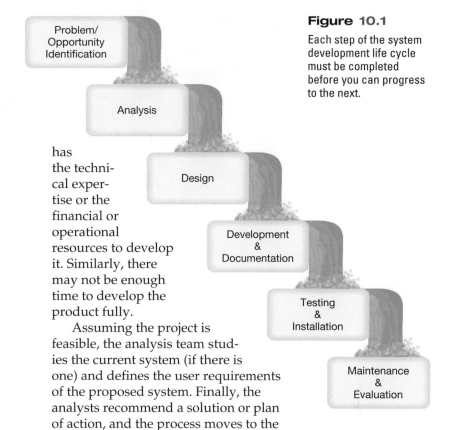

Figure 10.1

Each step of the system development life cycle must be completed before you can progress to the next.

has the technical expertise or the financial or operational resources to develop it. Similarly, there may not be enough time to develop the product fully.

Assuming the project is feasible, the analysis team studies the current system (if there is one) and defines the user requirements of the proposed system. Finally, the analysts recommend a solution or plan of action, and the process moves to the design phase.

3. **Design:** Before a house is built, blueprints are developed so that the workers have a plan to follow. The design phase of the SDLC has the same objective: generating a detailed plan for programmers to follow. The current and proposed systems are documented using flowcharts and data-flow diagrams. **Flowcharts** are visual diagrams of a process, including the decisions that need to be made along the way. **Data-flow diagrams** trace all data in an information system from the point at which data enters the system to its final resting place (storage or output). The data-flow diagram in Figure 10.2 shows the flow of concert ticket information.

The ultimate goal of the design phase with respect to system software development is to design a system that details the software, inputs and outputs, backups and controls, and processing requirements of the problem. It is also in this phase that the "make or buy" decision is made. Once the system plan is designed, a company evaluates existing software packages to determine whether it needs to develop a

Figure 10.2

Data-flow diagrams illustrate the way the data travels in a system.

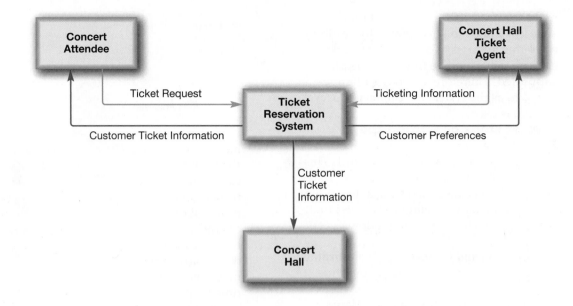

new piece of software or can buy something already on the market and adapt it to fit its needs. For instance, if it wants to start an online auction site to compete with eBay, it might not have to build its own system. Numerous online auction software packages are for sale. If the company cannot find an existing package that will work, then it would have to develop its own system. Alternatively, it could outsource (hire someone outside the corporation) to develop the program it needs.

4. **Development and Documentation:** It is during this phase that actual programming takes place. This phase is also the first part of the program development life cycle (PDLC), described in detail in the rest of the chapter.

5. **Testing and Installation:** The next step in the SDLC is testing the program to ensure it works properly and then installing the program so that it can be used.

6. **Maintenance and Evaluation:** Once the system is installed, its performance must be monitored to determine whether it is still meeting the needs of the end users. Bugs (errors) that were not detected in the testing phase but that the users discover subsequently must be corrected. Additional enhancements that users request are evaluated so that appropriate program modifications can be made.

The waterfall model is an idealized view of software development. Most developers follow some variation of it, however. For example, a design team may "spiral," so a group that is supporting the work of another group will work concurrently with that group on development. This contrasts with workflows in which the groups work independently, one after the other. Often there is a "backflow" up the waterfall, because even well-designed projects can require redesign and specification changes midstream.

Some people criticize the waterfall model for taking too long to provide actual working software to the client. This may contribute to **scope creep**, an ever-changing set of requests from the clients for additional features as they wait longer and longer to see a working prototype. Other developmental models are being used in the industry to address these issues (see the Bits and Bytes sidebar, "The More Minds the Better" to the left.)

The More Minds the Better

In each phase of software program creation, a style of interaction named joint application development (JAD) is useful in creating successful, flexible results. JAD is popular because it helps designers adapt to changes in program specifications quickly. In JAD, the customer is intimately involved in the project right from the beginning. Slow communication and lengthy feedback time make the traditional development process extremely time consuming. In JAD "workshops," there are no communication delays. Such workshops usually include end users, developers, subject experts, observers (such as senior managers), and a facilitator. The facilitator enforces the rules of the meeting to make sure all voices are heard and agreement is reached as quickly as possible. Also called accelerated design or facilitated team techniques, JAD's goal is to improve design quality by fostering clear communication. For more details, search using keywords like "JAD." "methodology," and "tutorial."

When Software Runs Amok

As in every profession, human beings make mistakes. In the field of software programming, mistakes can be costly. The Mariner 1 space probe launched in 1962 but diverted from its intended flight path just moments after launch. Within five minutes, Mission Control had to destroy the $18 million project. Cause? A programmer had incorrectly transcribed a handwritten formula into computer code, missing a single superscript bar. In 1996, Europe's newest unmanned rocket, the Ariane 5, had to be destroyed seconds after launch, along with its cargo of four scientific satellites. Cost: $500 million. The problem occurred when the guidance computer tried to convert rocket velocity from a 64-bit to a 16-bit value. Programmers had not properly coded for this and an overflow error resulted. When the guidance system shut down, control passed to the backup unit, which also failed because it was running the same algorithm.

When one switch in the AT&T network had a minor problem in 1990, system software fired off a message to the other 113 AT&T switching centers. This sparked a cascade of shutdowns, bringing down the entire network for nine hours. An estimated 75 million phone calls were missed and over 200,000 airline reservations were lost. A single line of code in a large software upgrade was in error and led to the shutdown.

The cost from software mistakes is not just monetary. In 1991, an Iraqi Scud missile destroyed an American Army barracks, killing 28 soldiers and injuring over 100. The Patriot defense system (Figure 10.3) had failed to intercept the missile because its software had made a rounding error and incorrectly computed the time, causing the system to ignore the incoming missile.

Could better software engineering practices have prevented these failures? Many different factors contributed to this set of accidents, including:

- Simple programming errors
- Inadequate safety engineering
- Poor human–computer interaction design
- Inadequate or inappropriate testing
- Too little focus on safety by the manufacturing organization
- Inadequate reporting structure at the company level

Who should be held responsible for producing defective software? Is it the corporate management that did not institute a defined software process? Is it the production managers, who forced tight schedules that demanded risky software engineering practices? What about the software engineers who wrote the defective code? What about users of the software? Can they be held responsible for accidents? What if they made changes to the system?

The organizations of engineers and software designers have tried to define ethical standards that will minimize the risk of negative impact from their work. The very first article of the code of ethics of the Institute of Electrical and Electronic Engineers (IEEE) states, "[We] accept responsibility in making engineering decisions consistent with the safety, health, and welfare of the public, and to disclose promptly factors that might endanger the public or the environment." ("IEEE Code of Ethics" by the Institute of Electrical and Electronic Engineers. Copyright © 2011 by IEEE. Reprinted by permission.) The Association for Computing Machinery (ACM) and the IEEE have established eight principles for ethical software engineering practices:

1. **Public:** Software engineers shall act consistently with the public interest.

2. **Client and Employer:** Software engineers shall act in a manner that is in the best interests of their client and employer consistent with the public interest.

3. **Product:** Software engineers shall ensure that their products and related modifications meet the highest professional standards possible.

4. **Judgment:** Software engineers shall maintain integrity and independence in their professional judgment.

5. **Management:** Software engineering managers and leaders shall subscribe to and promote an ethical approach to the management of software development and maintenance.

6. **Profession:** Software engineers shall advance the integrity and reputation of the profession consistent with the public interest.

7. **Colleagues:** Software engineers shall be fair to and supportive of their colleagues.

8. **Self:** Software engineers shall participate in lifelong learning regarding the practice of their profession and shall promote an ethical approach to the practice of the profession.

"Software Engineering Code of Ethics and Professional Practice" by IEEE-CS/ACM Joint Task Force on Software Engineering Ethics and Professional Practices. Copyright © 2011 by the Institute of Electrical and Electronic Engineers. Reprinted by permission

DoD photo by Tech. Sgt. James D. Mossman, U.S. Air Force

Figure 10.3

Software errors can cost millions, or cost lives as in the case of the failure of a missile defense system.

Can you think of other steps the software industry could take to make sure their work contributes positively to our society?

The Life Cycle of a Program

Programming often begins with nothing more than a problem or a request, such as "We can't get our budget reports out on time," or "Can you tell me how many transfer students have applied to our college?" When problems or requests such as these arise, someone realizes that computer programs could solve these problems more efficiently and reliably than the procedures currently in place. A proposal will be developed for a system to solve this problem and, as you recall from the earlier section, programming is part of the development stage for the overall project.

What is programming? Once a project has been deemed feasible and a plan is in place, the work of programming begins. **Programming** is the process of translating a task into a series of commands a computer will use to perform that task. It involves identifying which parts of a task a computer can perform, describing those tasks in a highly specific and complete manner, and, finally, translating this description into the language spoken by the computer's central processing unit (CPU).

How do programmers tackle a programming project? Just as an information system has a development life cycle, each programming project follows several stages from conception to final deployment. This process, described below, is sometimes referred to as the **program development life cycle (PDLC)**.

1. **Describing the Problem:** First, programmers must develop a complete description of the problem. The problem statement identifies the task to be automated and describes how the software program will behave.

2. **Making a Plan:** The problem statement is next translated into a set of specific, sequential steps that describe exactly what the computer program must do to complete the work. The steps are known as an **algorithm**. At this stage, the algorithm is written in natural, ordinary language (such as English).

3. **Coding:** The algorithm is then translated into programming code, a language that is friendlier to humans than the 1s and 0s that the CPU speaks but is still highly structured. By coding the algorithm, programmers must think in terms of the operations that a CPU can perform.

4. **Debugging:** The code then goes through a process of debugging in which the programmers repair any errors found in the code.

5. **Finishing the Project:** The software is tested by both the programming team and the people who will use the program. The results of the entire project are documented for the users and the development team. Finally, users are trained so that they can use the program efficiently.

Figure 10.4 illustrates the steps of a program life cycle.

Now that you have an overview of the process involved in developing a program, let's look at each step in more detail.

Describing the Problem: The Problem Statement

The **problem statement** is the starting point of programming work. It is a clear description of what tasks the computer program must accomplish and how the program will execute these tasks and respond to unusual situations. Programmers develop problem statements so that they can better understand the goals of their programming efforts.

What kind of problems can computer programs solve? Not every problem is well suited to a computerized solution. The strengths of computing machines are that they are fast and work

Figure 10.4

The stages followed by each programming project from conception to final deployment are collectively referred to as the program development life cycle.

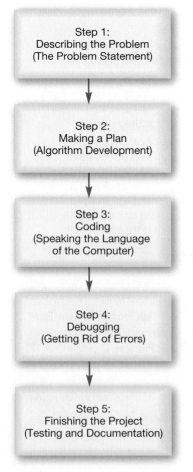

Step 1:
Describing the Problem
(The Problem Statement)

Step 2:
Making a Plan
(Algorithm Development)

Step 3:
Coding
(Speaking the Language of the Computer)

Step 4:
Debugging
(Getting Rid of Errors)

Step 5:
Finishing the Project
(Testing and Documentation)

ACTIVE HELP-DESK

Understanding Software Programming

In this Active Helpdesk call, you'll play the role of a helpdesk staffer, fielding calls about the life cycle of a program, the role a problem statement plays in programming, how programmers create algorithms and move from algorithm to code to the 1s and 0s a CPU can understand, and the steps involved in completing the program.

without error. Unlike humans, computers don't introduce mistakes because they're tired or stressed. Thus, as mentioned earlier, tasks that are repetitive, work with electronic information, and follow a series of clear steps are good candidates for computerization.

This might sound as if computers only help us with the dullest and most simplistic tasks. However, many sophisticated problems can be broken down into a series of easily computerized tasks. For example, pharmaceutical companies design drugs using complex computer programs that model molecules. Using simulation software to perform "dry" chemistry, chemists can quickly "create" new drugs and determine whether they will have the desired pharmacological effects. Scientists then select the most promising choices and begin to test those compounds in the "wet" laboratory.

Still, computers cannot yet act with intuition or be spontaneously creative. They can attack highly challenging problems such as making weather predictions or playing chess, but only in a manner that takes advantage of what computers do best—making fast, reliable computations.

How do programmers create problem statements? Most computer users understand what problems they want to computerize but not the details of the programming process. Therefore, the goal in creating a useful problem statement is to have programmers interact with users to describe three things relevant to creating a useful program: data, information, and method.

1. **Data** is the raw input that users have at the start of the job. It will be fed into the program.

2. **Information** is the result, or output, that the users require at the end of the job. The program produces this information from data.

3. **Method**, described precisely, is the process of how the program converts the inputs into the correct outputs.

For example, say you want to compute how much money you'll earn working at a parking garage. Your salary is $7.50 per hour for an eight-hour shift, but if you work more than eight hours a day, you will get time and a half, which is $11.25 per hour, for the overtime work. To determine how much money you make in any given day, you could multiply this in your mind, write it on a piece of paper, or use a calculator; alternatively, you could create a simple computer program to do the work for you. In this example, what are the three elements of the problem statement?

1. **Data (Input):** The data you have at the beginning of the problem, which is the number of hours you worked and the pay rate.

2. **Information (Output):** The information you need to have at the end of the problem, which is your total pay for the day.

3. **Method (Process):** The set of steps that will take you from your input to an output. In this case, the computer program would check if you worked more than eight hours. (That is important because it determines if you are paid overtime.) If you did not work overtime, then the output would be $7.50 multiplied by the total number of hours you worked ($60.00 for eight hours). If you did work overtime, then the program would calculate your pay as eight hours at $7.50 per hour for the regular part of your shift, plus an additional $11.25 multiplied by the number of overtime hours you worked. This processing thereby transforms your input into your desired output.

How do programmers handle bad inputs? In the problem statement, programmers also must describe what the program should do if the input data is invalid or just gibberish. (Users do make mistakes.) This part of the problem statement is referred to as **error handling**. The problem statement also includes a **testing plan** that lists specific input numbers the program would typically expect the user to enter. It then lists the precise output values that a perfect program would return for those input values. Later, in a testing process, programmers use the input and output data values from the testing plan to determine whether the program they created works in the way it should. We discuss the testing process later in this chapter.

Does the testing plan cover every possible use of the program? The testing plan cannot list every input that the program could ever encounter. Instead, programmers work with users to identify the categories of inputs that will be encountered, find a typical example of each input category, and specify what kind of output must be generated. In the preceding parking garage pay example, the error-handling process would describe what the program would do if you happened to enter "-8" (or any other nonsense character) for the number of hours you worked. The error handling would specify whether the program would return a negative value, prompt you to re-enter the input, or yell at you and shut down (well, maybe not exactly). We could expect three categories of inputs in the parking garage example. The user might enter:

- A negative number for hours worked that day
- A positive number equal to or less than eight
- A positive number greater than eight

The testing plan would describe how the error would be managed or how the output would be generated for each input category.

Is there a standard format for a problem statement? Most companies have their own format for documenting a problem statement. However, all problem statements include the same basic components: the data that is expected to be provided (inputs), the information that is expected to be produced (outputs), the rules for transforming the input into output (processing), an explanation of how the program will respond if users enter data that doesn't make sense (error handling), and a testing plan. Figure 10.5 shows a sample problem statement for our parking garage example.

Making a Plan: Algorithm Development

Once programmers understand exactly what the program must do and have created the final problem statement, they can begin developing a detailed algorithm, a set of specific, sequential steps that describe in natural language exactly what the computer program must do to complete its task. Let's look at some ways in which programmers design and test algorithms.

Do algorithms appear only in programming? Although the term *algorithm* may sound like it would fall only under the domain of computing, you design and execute algorithms in your daily

Figure 10.5 | COMPLETE PROBLEM STATEMENT FOR PARKING GARAGE EXAMPLE

Problem Statement			
Program Goal	Compute the total pay for a fixed number of hours worked at a parking garage.		
Input	Number of hours worked (a positive number)		
Output	Total pay earned (a positive number)		
Process	Total pay earned is computed as $7.50 per hour for the first eight hours worked each day. Any hours worked consecutively beyond the first eight are calculated at $11.25 per hour.		
Error Handling	The input (number of hours worked) must be a positive real number. If it is a negative number or other unacceptable character, the program will force the user to re-enter the information.		
Testing Plan	Input	Output	Notes
	8	8*7.50	Testing positive input
	3	3*7.50	Testing positive input
	12	8*7.50 + 4*11.25	Testing overtime input
	−6	Error message/ask user to re-enter value	Handling error

life. For example, say you are planning your morning. You know you need to (1) get gas for your car, (2) swing past the café and pick up a mocha latté, and (3) stop by the bookstore and buy a textbook before your 9 A.M. accounting lecture. You quickly think over the costs and decide it will take $150 to buy all three. In what order will you accomplish all these tasks? How do you decide? Should you try to minimize the distance you'll travel or the time you'll spend driving? What happens if you forget your credit card?

Figure 10.6 presents an algorithm you could develop to make decisions about how to accomplish these tasks. This algorithm lays out a specific plan that encapsulates all of the choices you need to make in the course of completing a particular task and shows the specific sequence in which these tasks will occur. At any point in the morning, you could gather your current data (your inputs)—"I have $20 and my Visa card, but the ATM machine is down"—and the algorithm would tell you unambiguously what your next step should be.

What are the limitations of algorithms? The deterministic nature of an algorithm enables us to describe it completely on a simple piece of paper. An algorithm is a series of steps that is completely known: At each point we know *exactly* what step to take next. However, not all problems can be described as a fixed sequence of predetermined steps; some involve random and unpredictable events. For example, although the program that computes your parking garage take-home pay each day works flawlessly, programs that predict stock prices are often wrong because many random events (inputs), such as a flood in India or a shipping delay in Texas, can change the outcomes (outputs).

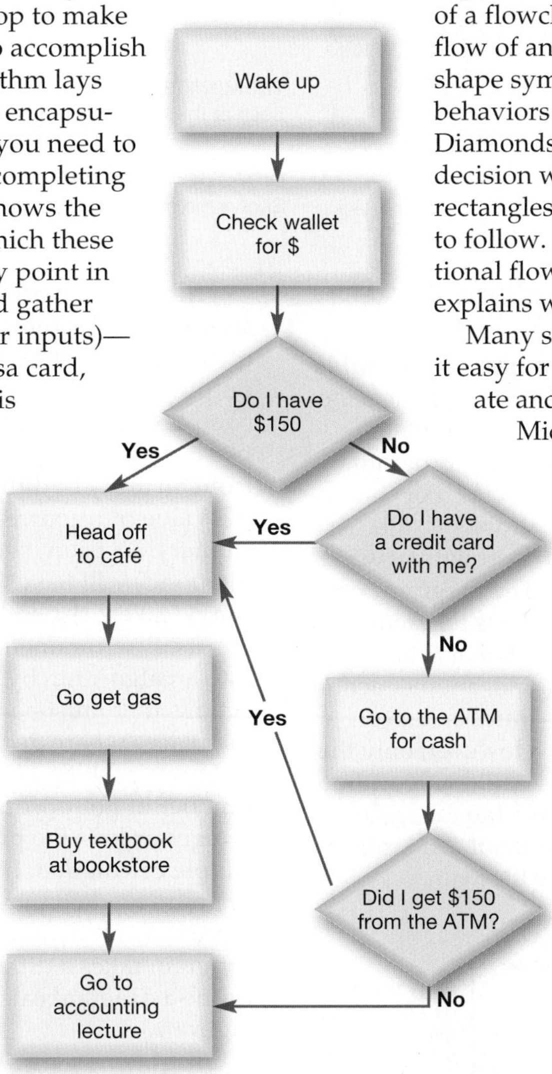

How do programmers represent an algorithm? Programmers have several visual tools at their disposal to help them document the decision points and flow of their algorithm.

Flowcharts provide a visual representation of the patterns the algorithm comprises. Figure 10.6 presents an example of a flowchart used to depict the flow of an algorithm. Specific shape symbols indicate program behaviors and decision types. Diamonds indicate that a yes/no decision will be performed, and rectangles indicate an instruction to follow. Figure 10.7 lists additional flowcharting symbols and explains what they indicate.

Many software packages make it easy for programmers to create and modify flowcharts. Microsoft Visio is one opular flowcharting program.

Pseudocode is a text-based approach to documenting an algorithm. In pseudocode, words describe the actions that the algorithm will take. Pseudocode is organized like an outline, with differing levels of indentation to indicate the flow of actions within the program. There is no standard set of vocabulary for pseudocode. Programmers use a combination of common words in their natural language and the special words that are commands in the programming language they are using.

Figure 10.6

An algorithm you might use to plan your morning would include several steps that encapsulate all of the decisions you might need to make and show the specific sequence in which these steps would occur.

Figure 10.7

Standard symbols used in flowcharts.

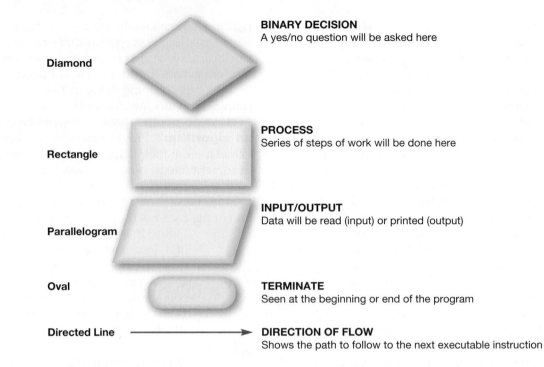

Diamond

BINARY DECISION
A yes/no question will be asked here

Rectangle

PROCESS
Series of steps of work will be done here

Parallelogram

INPUT/OUTPUT
Data will be read (input) or printed (output)

Oval

TERMINATE
Seen at the beginning or end of the program

Directed Line →

DIRECTION OF FLOW
Shows the path to follow to the next executable instruction

Developing the Algorithm: Decision Making and Design

How do programmers handle complex algorithms? When programmers develop an algorithm, they convert the problem statement into a list of steps the program will take. For simple problems, this list is straightforward: The program completes this action first, that action second, another action third, and so on. However, only the simplest algorithms execute the same series of actions every time they run.

Problems that are more complex involve choices and, therefore, cannot follow a sequential list of steps to generate the correct output. Instead, the list of steps created for complex problems includes **decision points**, places where the program must choose from an array of different actions based on the value of its current inputs. For example, a binary decision (shown in a flowchart as a diamond) will have two possible paths that can be taken, depending on the value of the inputs. Programmers convert a problem into an algorithm by listing the sequence of actions that must be taken and recognizing the places where decisions must be made.

In our parking garage example, if the number of hours you worked in a given day is eight or less, the program performs one simple calculation: It multiplies the number of hours worked by $7.50. If you worked more than eight hours in a day, then the program takes a different path and performs a different calculation, as shown in Figure 10.8.

What kinds of decision points are there? Two main types of decisions change the flow of an algorithm. One decision point that appears often in algorithms is like a "fork in the road" or a branch. Such decision points are called **binary decisions** because they can be answered in one of only two ways: *yes* (true) or *no* (false). For example, the answer to the question, "Did you work at most eight hours today?" (Is number of

Figure 10.8

Decision points force the program to travel down one branch of the algorithm or another.

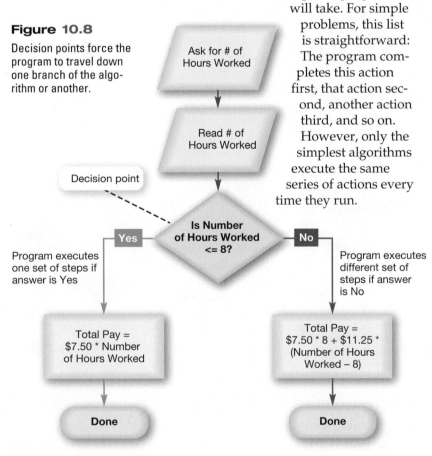

Ask for # of Hours Worked

Read # of Hours Worked

Decision point

Is Number of Hours Worked <= 8?

Yes — Program executes one set of steps if answer is Yes

No — Program executes different set of steps if answer is No

Total Pay = $7.50 * Number of Hours Worked

Total Pay = $7.50 * 8 + $11.25 * (Number of Hours Worked − 8)

Done

Done

hours worked <= 8 hours?), shown in Figure 10.8, is a binary decision because the answer can be only *yes* or *no*. The result of the decision determines which path the algorithm follows. If the answer is *yes*, the program follows one sequence of steps; if the answer is *no*, it follows a different path.

A second decision point that often appears in algorithms is a repeating loop. In a **loop**, a question is asked, and if the answer is *yes*, a set of actions is performed. Once the set of actions has finished, the question is asked again, creating a loop. As long as the answer to the question is *yes*, the algorithm continues to loop around and repeat the same set of actions. When the answer to the question is *no*, the algorithm breaks free of the looping and moves on to the first step that follows the loop.

In our parking garage example, the algorithm would require a loop if you wanted to compute the total pay you earned in a full week of work rather than in just a single day. For each day of the week, you would want to perform the same set of steps. Figure 10.9 shows how the idea of looping would be useful in this part of our parking garage program. On Monday, the program would set the Total Pay value to $0.00. It would then perform the following set of steps:

1. Read the number of hours worked that day.

2. Determine whether you qualified for overtime pay.

3. Compute the pay earned that day.

4. Add that day's pay to the total pay for the week.

On Tuesday, the algorithm would loop back, repeating the same sequence of steps it performed on Monday, adding the amount you earned on Tuesday to the Total Pay amount. The algorithm would continue to perform this loop for each day (seven times) until it hits Monday again. At that point, the decision "Are we still in the same week?" would become false. The program would stop, calculate the total pay for the entire week of work, and print the weekly paycheck. As you can see, there are three important features to look for in a loop:

1. A beginning point, or **initial value**. In our example, the Total Pay for the week starts at an initial value of $0.00.

2. A set of actions that will be performed. In our example, the algorithm computes the daily pay each time it passes through the loop.

3. A check to see whether the loop is completed, or a **test condition**. In our example, the algorithm should run the loop seven times, no more and no fewer.

Almost every higher-level programming language supports both making binary yes/no decisions and handling repeating loops. **Control structures** is the general term used for keywords in a programming language that allow the programmer to control (redirect) the flow of the program based on a decision.

How do programmers create algorithms for specific tasks? It's difficult for human beings to force their problem-solving skills into the highly structured, detailed algorithms that computing

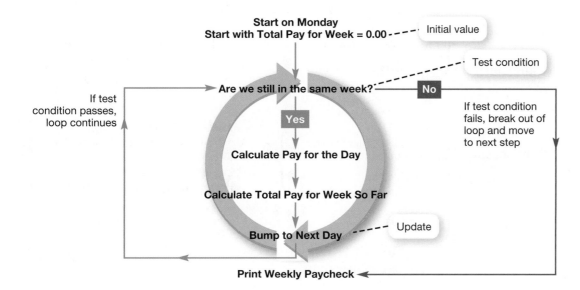

Start on Monday
Start with Total Pay for Week = 0.00 ----▸ Initial value

If test condition passes, loop continues

Are we still in the same week? ---- Test condition

No

Yes

If test condition fails, break out of loop and move to next step

Calculate Pay for the Day

Calculate Total Pay for Week So Far

Bump to Next Day ---- Update

Print Weekly Paycheck ◂

Figure 10.9

In this example of a loop, we stay in the loop until the test condition is no longer true. We then break free from the loop and move on to the next step in the algorithm, which is outside of the loop.

machines require. Therefore, several different methodologies have been developed to support programmers, including top-down design and object-oriented analysis.

Top-Down Design

What is top-down design? **Top-down design** is a systematic approach in which a problem is broken into a series of high-level tasks. In top-down design, programmers apply the same strategy repeatedly, breaking each task into successively more detailed subtasks. They continue until they have a sequence of steps that are close to the types of commands allowed by the programming language they will use for coding. Previous coding experience helps programmers know the appropriate level of detail to specify in an algorithm generated by top-down design.

How is top-down design used in programming? Let's consider our parking garage example again. Initially, top-down design would identify three high-level tasks: Get Input, Process Data, and Output Results (see Figure 10.10a).

Applying top-down design to the first operation, Get Input, we'd produce the more detailed sequence of steps shown in Figure 10.10b: Announce Program, Give Users Instructions, and Read the Input NumberHoursWorkedToday. When we try to refine each of these steps, we find that they are at the level of commands that most programming languages support (that is, they tell the computer to print and read statements). Therefore, the operation Get Input has been converted to an algorithm.

Next, we move to the second high-level task, Process Data, and break it into subtasks. In this case, we need to determine whether overtime hours were worked and compute the pay accordingly. We continue to apply top-down design on all tasks until we can no longer break tasks into subtasks, as shown in Figure 10.10c.

Object-Oriented Analysis

What is object-oriented analysis? A very different approach to generating an algorithm is object-oriented analysis. With **object-oriented analysis**, programmers first identify all of the categories of inputs that are part of the problem the program is trying to solve. These categories are called **classes**. For example, the classes in our parking garage example might include a Time-Card class and an Employee class.

Classes are further defined by information (data) and actions (methods or behaviors) associated with the class. For example, data for an Employee would include a Name, Address, and Social Security Number, whereas the methods for the Employee would be GoToWork(), LeaveWork(), and CollectPay(). Think of classes as the things around you in your world—books, accounts, shopping carts. The data of the class describes the class, so classes are often characterized as nouns, whereas methods are often characterized as verbs—the ways that the class acts and communicates with other classes. Figure 10.11 shows the data and methods the Employee class would contain.

In the object-oriented approach, programmers identify and define each class, as

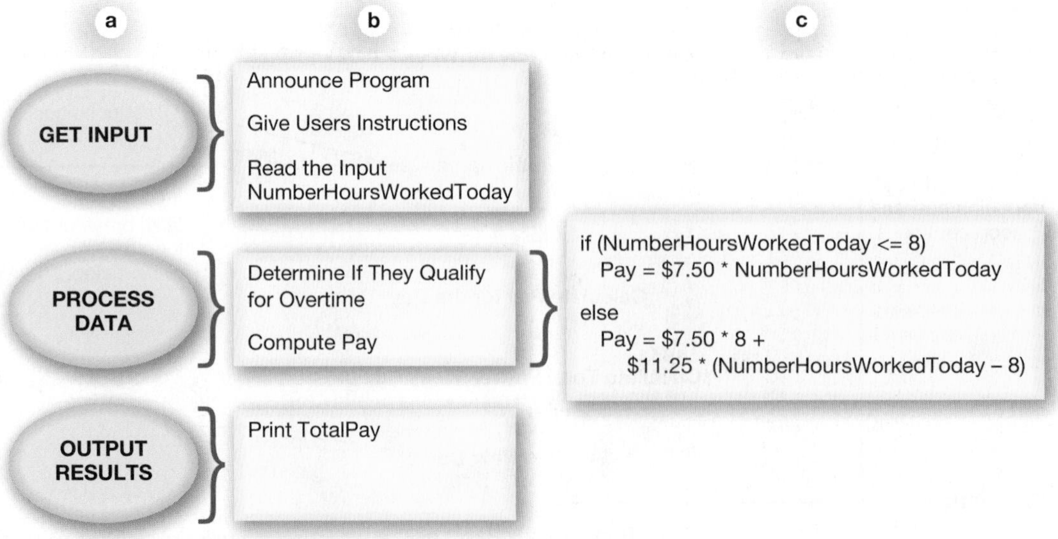

Figure 10.10

In this figure, (a) a top-down design is applied to the highest level of task in our parking garage example, (b) the tasks are further refined into subtasks, and (c) subtasks are refined into a sequence of instructions—an algorithm.

GET INPUT

- Announce Program
- Give Users Instructions
- Read the Input NumberHoursWorkedToday

PROCESS DATA

- Determine If They Qualify for Overtime
- Compute Pay

```
if (NumberHoursWorkedToday <= 8)
    Pay = $7.50 * NumberHoursWorkedToday
else
    Pay = $7.50 * 8 +
        $11.25 * (NumberHoursWorkedToday – 8)
```

OUTPUT RESULTS

- Print TotalPay

well as its data and methods. Programmers then determine how classes interact with each other. For example, when an Employee does GoToWork(), the Employee class must "talk" to the TimeCard class and punch in for the day, setting the StartTime on the TimeCard.

Programmers may need to create several different examples of a class. Each of these examples is an **object**. In Figure 10.11, John Doe, Jane Doe, and Bill McGillicutty are each Employee objects (specific examples of the Employee class). Each object from a given class is described by the same pieces of data and has the same methods; for example, John, Jane, and Bill are all Employees and can use the GoToWork, LeaveWork, and CollectPay methods. However, because they all have different pay grades (PayGrade 5, PayGrade 10, and PayGrade 4, respectively), and different Social Security numbers, they are all unique objects.

Why would a developer select the object-oriented approach over top-down design? Object-oriented analysis forces programmers to think in general terms about their problem, which tends to lead to more general and reusable solutions. An important aspect of object-oriented design is that it leads to **reusability**. Because object-oriented design generates a family of classes for each project, programmers can easily reuse existing classes from other projects, enabling them to produce new code quickly.

To take advantage of reuse, programmers must study the relationships between objects. Hierarchies of objects can be built quickly in object-oriented languages using the mechanism of inheritance. **Inheritance** means that a new class can automatically pick up all of the data and methods of an existing class, and then extend and customize those to fit its own specific needs.

The original class is called the **base class**, and the new, modified class is called the **derived class**, as illustrated in Figure 10.12. You can compare this with making cookies. For example, you have a basic recipe for sugar cookies (base class: sugar cookies). However, in your family, some people like chocolate-flavored sugar cookies (derived class: chocolate cookies),

and others like almond-flavored sugar cookies (derived class: almond cookies). All the cookies share the attributes of the basic sugar cookie. However, instead of creating two entirely new recipes—one for chocolate cookies and one for almond cookies—the two varieties inherit the basic sugar cookie (base class) recipe; the recipe is then customized to make the chocolate- and almond-flavored sugar cookies (derived classes).

With the object-oriented approach, the majority of design time is spent in identifying the classes required to solve the problem, modeling them as data and methods, and

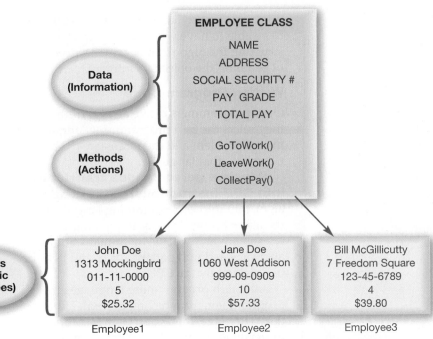

Figure 10.11

The Employee class includes the complete set of information (data) and actions (methods or behaviors) that describe an Employee.

Figure 10.12

In object-oriented programming (OOP), a single base class—for example, **Shape**—helps you quickly create many additional derived classes, such as **Polygon** and **Ellipse**.

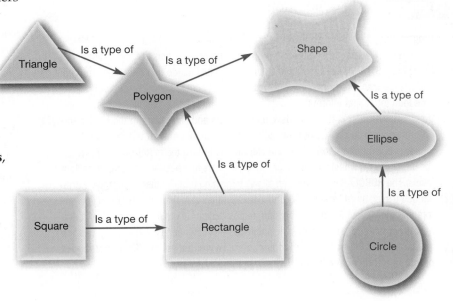

thinking about what relationships they need to be able to have with each other. Constructing the algorithm becomes a process of enabling the objects to interact.

Writing Program Code

Once programmers create an algorithm, they select the best programming language for the problem and then translate the algorithm into that language.

How is a person's idea translated into CPU instructions? Translating an algorithm into a programming language is the act of **coding**. Programming languages are somewhat readable by humans but then are translated into patterns of 1s and 0s to be understood by the CPU.

Although programming languages free programmers from having to think in binary language, the 1s and 0s that computers understand, they still force programmers to translate the ideas of the algorithm into a highly precise format. Programming languages are quite limited, allowing programmers to use only a few specific words while still demanding a consistent structure.

How exactly do programmers move from algorithm to code? Once programmers have an algorithm, in the form of either a flowchart or a series of pseudocode statements, they scan the algorithm and identify the key pieces of information it uses to make decisions. What steps are required for the calculation of new information? What is the exact

sequence of the steps? Are there points where decisions have to be made? What kinds of decisions are made? Are there places where the same steps are repeated several times? Once the programmer identifies the required information and the flow of how it will be changed by each step of the algorithm, he or she can begin converting the algorithm into computer code in a specific programming language.

What exactly is a programming language? A **programming language** is a kind of "code" for the set of instructions the CPU knows how to perform. Computer programming languages use special words and strict rules so programmers can control the CPU without having to know all of its hardware details.

What kinds of programming languages are there? Programming languages are classified into several major groupings, sometimes referred to as *generations*. With each generation in language development, programmers have been relieved of more of the burden of keeping track of what the hardware requires. The earliest languages—assembly language and machine languages—required the programmer to know a great deal about how the computer was constructed internally and how it stored data. Programming is becoming easier as languages continue to become more closely matched to how humans think about problems.

How have modern programming languages evolved? A **first-generation language (1GL)** is the actual **machine language** of a CPU, the sequence of bits (1s and 0s) that the CPU understands. A **second-generation language (2GL)** is also known as an **assembly language**. Assembly languages allow programmers to write their programs using a set of short, English-like commands that speak directly to the CPU and give the programmer direct control of hardware resources. A **third-generation language (3GL)** uses symbols and commands to help programmers tell the computer what to do. This makes 3GL languages easier for humans to read and remember. Most programming languages today, including BASIC, FORTRAN, COBOL, C/C++, and Java, are considered third generation.

Structured Query Language (SQL) is a database programming language that is an example of a **fourth-generation language (4GL)**.

Many other database query languages and report generators are also 4GLs. The following SQL command would check a huge table of data on the employees and build a new table showing all those employees who worked overtime:

```
SELECT Employee Name,
TotalHours FROM EMPLOYEES
WHERE "TotalHours" Total
More Than 8
```

But programmers must always work from algorithms, correct? Not if they are using a **fifth-generation language (5GL)**. Fifth-generation languages are considered the most "natural" of languages. In a 5GL, a problem is presented as a series of facts or constraints instead of as a specific algorithm. The system of facts can then be queried (asked) questions. PROLOG (PROgramming LOGic) is an example of a 5GL. A PROLOG program could be a list of family relationships and rules such as "Mike is Sally's brother. A brother and a sister have the same mother and father." Once a user has amassed a huge collection of facts and rules, she can ask for a list of all Mike's cousins, for example. PROLOG would find the answers by repeatedly applying the principles of logic, instead of by following a systematic algorithm that the programmer provided. Figure 10.13 shows small code samples of each generation of language.

Do programmers have to use a higher-level programming language to solve a problem with a computer? No, experienced programmers sometimes write a program directly in the CPU's assembly language. However, the main advantage of higher-level programming languages—C or Java, for example—is that they allow programmers to think in terms of the problem they are solving rather than worrying about the internal design and specific instructions available for a given CPU. In addition, higher-level programming languages have the capability to produce a program easily that will run on differently configured CPUs. For example, if programmers wrote directly in the assembly language for an Intel i7 CPU, then they would have to rewrite the program completely if they wanted it to run on a Sun workstation with the UltraSPARC CPU. Thus, higher-level programming languages offer **portability**—the capability to move a completed solution easily from one type of computer to another.

Coding: Speaking the Language of the Computer

What happens first when you write a program? All of the inputs a program receives and all of the outputs the program produces need to be stored in the computer's RAM while the program is running. Each input and each output item that the program manipulates, also known as a **variable**, needs to be announced early in the program so that memory space can be set aside. A **variable declaration** tells the operating system that the program needs to allocate storage space in

Figure 10.13 | SAMPLE CODE FOR DIFFERENT LANGUAGE GENERATIONS

Generation	Example	Sample Code
1GL	Machine	**Bits** describe the commands to the CPU. 1110 0101 1001 1111 0000 1011 1110 0110
2GL	Assembly	**Words** describe the commands to the CPU. ADD Register 3, Register 4, Register 5
3GL	FORTRAN, BASIC, C, Java	**Symbols** describe the commands to the CPU. Total Pay = Pay + Overtime Pay
4GL	SQL	**More powerful commands** allow complex work to be done in a single sentence. SELECT isbn, title, price, price*0.06 AS sales_tax FROM books WHERE price>100.00 ORDER BY title;
5GL	PROLOG	Programmers can build applications **without specifying an algorithm**. Find all the people who are Mike's cousins as: ?-cousin (Mike, family)

Programming languages are evolving constantly. New languages emerge every year, and existing languages change dramatically. Therefore, it would be extremely difficult and time consuming for programmers to learn every programming language. However, all languages have several common elements: rules of syntax, a set of keywords, a group of supported data types, and a set of allowed operators. By learning these four concepts, a programmer will be better equipped to approach any new language.

The transition from a well-designed algorithm to working code requires a clear understanding of the rules (syntax) of the programming language being used. **Syntax** is an agreed-upon set of rules defining how a language must be structured. The English language has a syntax that defines which symbols are words (for example, gorilla is a word but allirog is not) and what order words and symbols (such as semicolons and commas) must follow.

Likewise, all programming languages have a formal syntax that programmers must follow when creating code **statements**, which are sentences in a code. **Syntax errors** are violations of the strict, precise set of rules that defines the language. In a programming language, even misplacing a single comma or using a lowercase letter where a capital letter is required will generate a syntax error and make the program unusable.

Keywords are a set of words that have predefined meanings for a particular language. Keywords translate the flow of the algorithm into the structured code of the programming language. For example, when the algorithm indicates a decision point—a location where a binary decision must be made—the programmer translates that binary decision into the appropriate keyword or keywords from the language.

To illustrate further, in the programming language C++, the binary decision asking whether you worked enough hours to qualify for overtime pay would use the keywords **if else**. At this point in the code, the program can follow one of two paths: If you indicated through your input that you worked fewer than or equal to eight hours, it takes one path; if not (else), it follows another. Figure 10.14 shows the binary decision in the algorithm and the lines of C++ code for this decision using the if else keywords.

Loops are likewise translated from algorithm to code by using the appropriate keyword from the language. For example, in the programming language Visual Basic, programmers use the keywords **For** and **Next** to implement a loop. After the keyword For, an input or output item is given a starting value. Then the statements, or "sentences," in the body of the loop are executed. When the command Next is run, the program returns to the For statement and increments the value of the input or output item by 1. It then tests that the value is still inside the range given. If it is, the body of the loop is executed again. This continues until the value of the input or output item is outside the range listed. The loop is then ended, and the statement that follows the loop is run. If we think back to the parking garage example, the following lines of Visual Basic code loop to sum up the total pay for the entire week. In this statement, the starting value of the input item Day is 1, and the program loops through until Day equals 7. Then, when Day equals 8, we move out of the loop, to the line of code that comes after the loop:

```
For Day = 1 to 7
    Total Pay = Total Pay + Pay;
Next Day
```

Often, a quick overview of a language's keywords can reveal the unique focus of that language. For example, the language C++ includes the keywords public, private, and protected, which indicate that the language includes a mechanism for controlling security. Although people

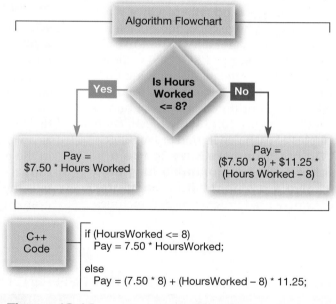

Figure 10.14

The binary decision in the algorithm has been converted into C++ code.

RAM. The following line of code is a variable declaration in the language Java:

```
int Day;
```

This variable's name is *Day*. The "int" that precedes the Day variable indicates that this variable will always be an integer (a whole number such as 15 or –4). This statement asks for enough RAM storage space to hold an integer. After the RAM space is found, it is reserved. As long as the program is running, these RAM cells will be saved for the Day variable, and no other program can use that memory until the program ends. From that point on, when the program encounters the symbol Day, it will access the memory it reserved as Day and find the integer stored there.

who are new to a language might not immediately understand how these keywords are used, examining the keywords of a language you are learning will often tell you what special features the language has and will help you ask important questions about it.

Each time programmers want to store data in their program, they must ask the operating system for storage space at a RAM location. **Data types** describe the kind of data that is being stored at the memory location. Each programming language has its own data types (although there is some degree of overlap among languages). For example, C++ includes data types that represent integers, real numbers, characters, and Boolean (true–false) values. These C++ data types show up in code statements as int for integer, float for real numbers, char for characters, and bool for Boolean values.

Because it takes more room to store a real number such as 18,743.23 than it does to store the integer 1, programmers use data types in their code to indicate to the operating system how much memory it needs to allocate. Programmers must be familiar with all of the data types available in the language so that they can assign the most appropriate data type for each input and output value, without wasting memory space.

Operators are the coding symbols that represent the fundamental actions of the language. Each programming language has its own set of operators. Many languages include common algebraic operators such as +, −, *, and / to represent the mathematical operations of addition, subtraction, multiplication, and division, respectively. Some lan-guages, however, introduce new symbols as operators. The language A Programmer's Language (APL) was designed to solve multidimensional mathematical problems. APL includes less familiar operators such as rho, sigma, and iota, each representing a complex mathematical opera-tion. Because it contains many specialized operators, APL requires pro-grammers to use a special keyboard (see Figure 10.15).

Programming languages sometimes include other unique operators. The C++ operator >>, for example, is used to tell the computer to read data from the keyboard or from a file. The C++ operator && is used to tell the computer to check whether two statements are both true. "Is your age greater than 20 AND less than 30?" is a question that requires the use of the && operator.

In the following C++ code, several operators are being used. The > operator checks whether the number of hours worked is greater than 0. The && operator checks that the number of hours worked is simulta-neously positive AND less than or equal to 8. If that happens, then the = operator sets the output Pay to equal the number of hours paid at $7.50 per hour:

```
if (Hours > 0 && Hours <= 8)
    Pay = Hours * 7.50;
```

Knowing operators such as these, as well as the other common elements described earlier, helps programmers learn new programming languages.

Figure 10.15

APL requires programmers to use an APL keyboard that includes the many specialized operators in the language.

The following line of C++ code asks that a decimal number (represented by the keyword *float*) be stored in RAM:

```
float TotalPay;
```

This line asks the operating system to find and reserve enough storage space for one real number. It then associates the symbol TotalPay with the address of the memory cell where that value will be stored.

Can programmers leave notes to themselves inside a program?
Programmers often insert a **comment** (or **remark**) into program code to explain the purpose of a section of code, to indicate the date they wrote the program, or to include other important information about

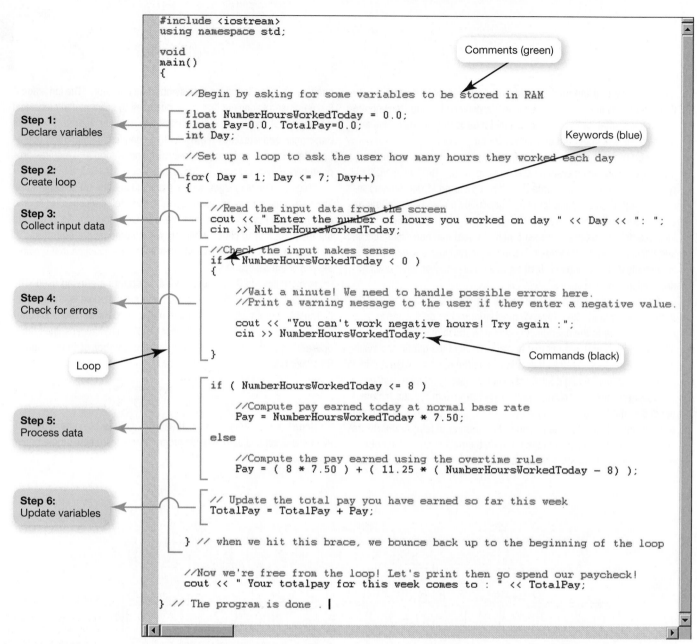

```cpp
#include <iostream>
using namespace std;

void
main()
{

    //Begin by asking for some variables to be stored in RAM

    float NumberHoursWorkedToday = 0.0;
    float Pay=0.0, TotalPay=0.0;
    int Day;

    //Set up a loop to ask the user how many hours they worked each day

    for( Day = 1; Day <= 7; Day++)
    {

        //Read the input data from the screen
        cout << " Enter the number of hours you worked on day " << Day << ": ";
        cin >> NumberHoursWorkedToday;

        //Check the input makes sense
        if ( NumberHoursWorkedToday < 0 )
        {

            //Wait a minute! We need to handle possible errors here.
            //Print a warning message to the user if they enter a negative value.

            cout << "You can't work negative hours! Try again :";
            cin >> NumberHoursWorkedToday;

        }

        if ( NumberHoursWorkedToday <= 8 )

            //Compute pay earned today at normal base rate
            Pay = NumberHoursWorkedToday * 7.50;

        else

            //Compute the pay earned using the overtime rule
            Pay = ( 8 * 7.50 ) + ( 11.25 * ( NumberHoursWorkedToday - 8) );

        // Update the total pay you have earned so far this week
        TotalPay = TotalPay + Pay;

    } // when we hit this brace, we bounce back up to the beginning of the loop


    //Now we're free from the loop! Let's print then go spend our paycheck!
    cout << " Your totalpay for this week comes to : " << TotalPay;

} // The program is done . |
```

Comments (green)

Keywords (blue)

Commands (black)

Step 1:
Declare variables

Step 2:
Create loop

Step 3:
Collect input data

Step 4:
Check for errors

Loop

Step 5:
Process data

Step 6:
Update variables

Figure 10.16

A complete C++ program that solves the parking garage pay problem.

the code so that fellow programmers can more easily understand and update it should the original programmer no longer be available. Comments are written into the code in plain English. The *compiler*, a program that translates codes into binary 1s and 0s, just ignores comments. Comments are intended to be read only by human programmers. Languages provide a special symbol or keyword to indicate the beginning of a comment. In C++, the symbol // at the beginning of a line indicates that the rest of the line is a comment. In Visual Basic, a single apostrophe or the keyword *REM*, short for *remark*, does the same thing.

What would completed code for a program look like? Figure 10.16 presents a completed C++ program for our parking garage example. We'll discuss later how you would actually enter this program on your system. This program, which is written in a top-down style, does not make use of objects. Each statement in the program is executed sequentially (that is, in order from the first statement to the last) unless the program encounters a keyword that changes the flow. In the figure, the program begins by declaring the variables needed to store the program's inputs and outputs in RAM (step 1). Next, the *for* keyword begins a looping pattern (step 2). All of the steps between the very first bracket ({) and the last one (}) will be repeated seven times to gather the total pay for each day of the week.

The next section (step 3) collects the input data from the user. The program then checks that the user entered a reasonable value (step 4). In this case, a positive number for hours worked must be entered. Next, the program processes the data (step 5). If the user worked eight or fewer hours, he or she is paid at the rate of $7.50, whereas hours exceeding eight are paid at $11.25.

The final statement (step 6) updates the value of the TotalPay variable. The last bracket indicates that the program has reached the end of a loop. The program will repeat the loop to collect and process the information for the next day. When the seventh day of data has been processed, the Day variable will be bumped up to the next value, 8. This causes the program to fail the test (Day <= 7?). At that point, the program exits the loop, prints the results, and quits.

Are there ways in which programmers can make their code more useful for the future? One aspect of converting an algorithm into good code is the programmer's ability to design general code that can adapt easily to new settings. Sections of code that will be used repeatedly, with only slight modification, can be packaged into reusable "containers" or components. Depending on the language, these reusable components are referred to as *functions*, *methods*, *procedures*, *subroutines*, *modules*, or *packages*.

In our program, we could create a function that implements the overtime pay rule. As it stands in Figure 10.16, the code works only in situations in which the hourly pay is exactly $7.50 and the bonus pay is exactly $11.25. However, if we rewrote this part of the processing rules as a function, we could have code that would work for any base pay rate and any overtime rate. If the base pay rate or overtime rate changed, the function would use whichever values it was given as input to compute the output pay variable. Such a function, as shown in Figure 10.17, may be reused in many settings without changing any of the code.

Compilation

How does a programmer move from code in a programming language to the 1s and 0s the CPU can understand? Compilation is the process by which code is converted into machine language—the language the CPU can understand. A **compiler** is a program that understands both the syntax of the programming language and the exact structure of the CPU and its machine language. It can "read" the **source code**, which comprises the instructions programmers have written in the higher-level language, and translate the source code directly into machine

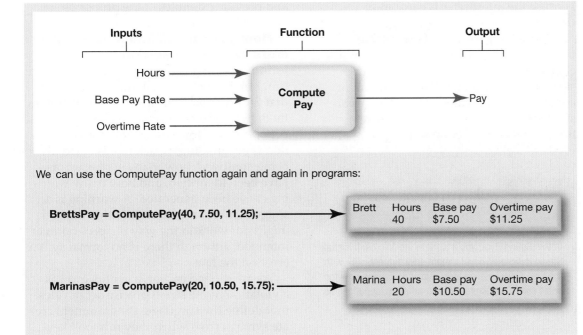

Figure 10.17

A function is a reusable component that can be used in different settings.

language—the binary patterns that will execute commands on the CPU. You can learn more about the details of the binary number system in the Technology in Focus section "Under the Hood" (see page 346).

Each programming language has its own compiler. It is a program that you purchase and install just like any other software on your system. Separate versions of the compiler are required if you want to compile code that will run on separate processor types. One version of a compiler would create finished programs for a Sun UltraSPARC processor, for example, and another version of the compiler would create programs for an Intel i7 CPU.

At this stage, programmers finally have produced an **executable program**, the binary sequence that instructs the CPU to run their code. Executable programs cannot be read by human eyes because they are pure binary codes. They are stored as *.exe or *.com files on Windows systems.

Does every programming language have a compiler? Some programming languages do not have a compiler, but use an interpreter instead. An **interpreter** translates the source code into an intermediate form, line by line. Each line is then executed as it is translated. The compilation process takes longer than the interpretation process because in compilation all of the lines of source code are translated into machine language before any lines are executed. However, the finished compiled program runs faster than an interpreted program because the interpreter is constantly translating and executing as it goes.

If producing the fastest executable program is important, programmers will choose a language that uses a compiler instead of an interpreter. For development environments in which many changes are still being made to the code, interpreters have an advantage because programmers

do not have to wait for the entire program to be recompiled each time they make a change. With interpreters, programmers can immediately see the results of their program changes as they are making them.

Coding Tools: Integrated Development Environments

Are there any tools that make the coding process easier? Modern programming is supported by a collection of tools that make the writing and testing of software easier. Compiler products feature an **integrated development environment (IDE)**, a developmental tool that helps programmers write, compile, and test their programs. As is the case with compilers, every language has its own specific IDE. Figure 10.18 shows the IDE for Microsoft Visual Studio using C++.

How does an IDE help programmers when they are typing the code? The IDE includes tools that support programmers at every step of the coding process. **Code editing** is the step in which a programmer physically types the code into the computer. An IDE includes an **editor**, a special tool that helps programmers as they enter the code, highlighting keywords and alerting them to typos. Modern IDE editors also automatically indent the code correctly, align sections of code appropriately, and apply color to code comments to remind programmers that these lines will not be executed as code. In addition, IDEs provide help files that document and provide examples of the proper use of keywords and operators.

How does the IDE help programmers after code editing is finished? Editing is complete when the entire program has been keyed into the editor. At that time, the programmer clicks a button in the IDE, and the compilation process begins. A pop-up window shows how the compilation is progressing, which line is currently being compiled, how many syntax errors have been identified, and how many warnings have been generated. A warning is a suggestion from the compiler that the code might not work in the way the programmer intended, although there is no formal syntax error on the line.

As mentioned earlier, a syntax error is a violation of the strict, precise set of rules that define the language. Programmers create syntax errors when they misspell key-

SOUND BYTE

Looping Around the IDE

In this Sound Byte, you'll work in the Microsoft Visual Studio integrated development environment (IDE) with the C++ programming language and examine how the basic control structures of programming languages do their work.

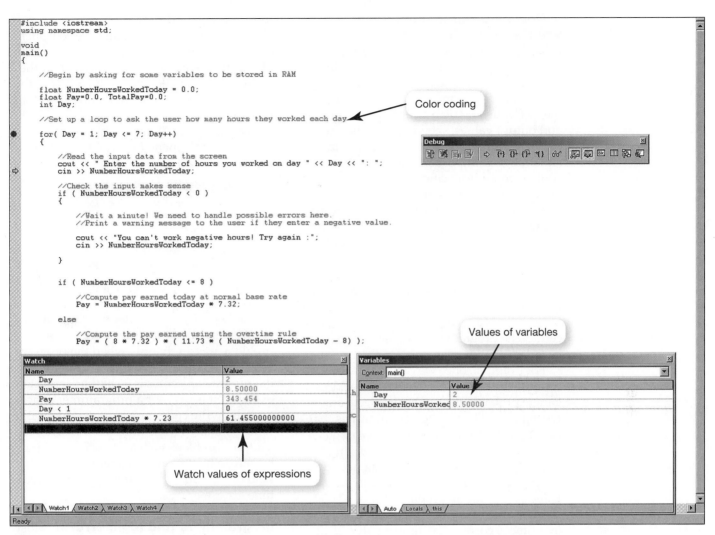

```
#include <iostream>
using namespace std;

void
main()
{

    //Begin by asking for some variables to be stored in RAM

    float NumberHoursWorkedToday = 0.0;
    float Pay=0.0, TotalPay=0.0;
    int Day;

    //Set up a loop to ask the user how many hours they worked each day

    for( Day = 1; Day <= 7; Day++)
    {
        //Read the input data from the screen
        cout << " Enter the number of hours you worked on day " << Day << ": ";
        cin >> NumberHoursWorkedToday;

        //Check the input makes sense
        if ( NumberHoursWorkedToday < 0 )
        {

            //Wait a minute! We need to handle possible errors here.
            //Print a warning message to the user if they enter a negative value.

            cout << "You can't work negative hours! Try again :";
            cin >> NumberHoursWorkedToday;

        }


        if ( NumberHoursWorkedToday <= 8 )

            //Compute pay earned today at normal base rate
            Pay = NumberHoursWorkedToday * 7.32;

        else

            //Compute the pay earned using the overtime rule
            Pay = ( 8 * 7.32 ) * ( 11.73 * ( NumberHoursWorkedToday - 8) );
```

Color coding

Values of variables

Watch

Name	Value
Day	2
NumberHoursWorkedToday	8.50000
Pay	343.454
Day < 1	0
NumberHoursWorkedToday * 7.23	61.455000000000

Watch1 / Watch2 / Watch3 / Watch4 /

Variables

Context: main()

Name	Value
Day	2
NumberHoursWorked	8.50000

Auto / Locals / this /

Ready

Watch values of expressions

Figure 10.18

The Visual Studio IDE for Microsoft Visual C++ helps the programmer when he or she is entering the code and when logical errors are found.

words (such as typing BEEGIN instead of BEGIN) or use an operator incorrectly (such as typing x = < y + 2 instead of x = y + 2). Once compilation is finished, the IDE presents all of the syntax errors in one list. The programmer can then click any item in the list to see a detailed explanation of the type of error. When the programmer double-clicks an item in the list, the editor jumps to the line of code that contains the error, enabling the programmer to repair syntax errors quickly.

Debugging: Getting Rid of Errors

Once the program has compiled without syntax errors, it has met all of the syntax rules of the language. However, this doesn't mean that the program behaves in a logical way or that it appropriately addresses the task the algorithm described. If program-

mers made errors in the strategy used in the algorithm or in how they translated the algorithm to code, problems will occur. The process of running the program over and over to find errors and to make sure the program behaves in the way it should is termed **debugging** (see Figure 10.19).

Figure 10.19

Debugging—the process of correcting errors in a program—combines logic with an understanding of the problem to be solved.

How do programmers know whether there is anything wrong with their program? At this point in the process, the testing plan that was documented as part of the problem statement becomes critically important to programmers. The testing plan clearly lists input and output values, showing how the users expect the program to behave in each input situation. It is important that the testing plan contain enough specific examples to test every part of the program.

In the parking garage problem, we want to make sure the program calculates the correct pay for a day when you worked eight or fewer hours and for a day when you worked more than eight hours. Each of these input values forces the program to make different decisions in its processing path (the sequence of steps that turns inputs into outputs). To be certain the program works as intended, programmers try every possible path.

For example, once we can successfully compile the example code for the parking garage problem, we can begin to use our testing plan. The testing plan indicates that an input of 3 for NumberHoursWorked Today must produce an output of Pay = 3 * $7.50 = $22.50. In testing, we run the program and make sure that an input value of 3 yields an output value of $22.50. To check that the processing path involving overtime is correct, we input a value of 12 hours. That input must produce Pay = 8 * $7.50 + (12 − 8) * $11.25 = $105.00.

A complete testing plan includes sample inputs that exercise all of the error handling required as well as all of the processing paths. Therefore, we would also want to check how the program behaves when NumberHoursWorkedToday is entered as −2.

If the testing plan reveals errors, why does the program compile? The compiler itself is a program. It cannot think through code or decide whether what the programmer wrote is logical. The compiler can only make sure that the specific rules of the language are followed, that all of the keywords are spelled correctly, and that the operators being used are meaningful to that language.

For example, if in the parking garage problem we happened to type the if statement as

```
if (NumberHoursWorkedToday > 88)
  //Use the Overtime Pay rule
```

instead of

```
if (NumberHoursWorkedToday > 8)
  //Use the Overtime Pay rule
```

the compiler would not see a problem. It doesn't seem strange to the compiler that you only get overtime after working 88 hours a day. These **logical errors** in the problem are caught only when the program executes. Another kind of error caught when the program executes is a **runtime error**. For example, it is easy for a programmer to accidentally write code for a loop that loops one time too many or one time too few. This can lead to a problem such as dividing a number by zero, a big "no-no" mathematically! That kind of forbidden operation generates a runtime error message.

Are there tools that help programmers find logic errors? Most IDEs include a tool called a **debugger** that helps programmers dissect a program as it runs. The debugger pauses the program while it is executing and allows the programmer to examine the values of all the variables. The programmer can then run the program in slow motion, moving it forward just one line at a time. Working through the program in this way lets the programmer see the exact sequence of steps being executed and the outcome of each calculation. He or she can then isolate the precise place in which a logical error occurs, correct the error, and recompile the program.

Finishing the Project: Testing and Documentation

Once debugging has detected all of the runtime errors in the code, it is time for users to test the program. This process is called *internal testing*. In internal testing, a group within the software company uses the program in every way it can imagine—including how it was intended to be used and in ways only

BITS AND BYTES

Many Languages on Display

At the 99 Bottles of Beer site **www.99-bottles-of-beer.net**, you can find a simple program that displays the lyrics to the song 99 Bottles of Beer on the Wall. If you have ever sat through round after round of this song on a long school bus trip, you know how repetitive it is. That means the code to write this song can take advantage of looping statements. This site presents the program in more than 1,400 different languages. Take a tour and see how much variety there is in programming!

new users may think up. The internal testing group makes sure the program behaves as described in the original testing plan. Any differences in how the program responds are reported back to the programming team, which makes the final revisions and updates to the code.

The next round of testing is external testing. In this testing round, people like the ones who eventually will purchase and use the software must work with it to determine whether it matches their original vision.

What other testing does the code undergo? Before its final commercial release, software is often provided free or at a reduced cost in a **beta version** to certain test sites or to interested users. By providing users with a beta version of software, programmers can collect information about the remaining errors in the code and make a final round of revisions before officially releasing the program. Often, popular software packages like Microsoft Windows and Microsoft Office are available for free beta download for months before the official public release.

What happens if problems are found after beta testing? The manufacturer will make changes before releasing the product to other manufacturers, for installation on new machines for example. That point in the release cycle is called **release to manufacturers** (or **RTM**). After the RTM is issued, the product is in **general availability** (or **GA**) and can be purchased by the public.

Users often uncover problems in a program even after its commercial release to the public. These problems are addressed with the publication of software updates or **service packs**. Users can download these software modules to repair errors identified in the program code. One famous example is the original Windows Vista operating system. It had a revision released as Service Pack 1 that, along with adding many bug fixes and security fixes, extended its compatibility so it would work with an additional 40,000 devices. To make sure you have the latest service pack for your Windows OS, visit the Windows Service Pack Center (**windows.microsoft.com/en-US/windows/downloads/service-packs**).

After testing, is the project finished? Once testing is completed, but before the product is officially released, the work of **documentation** is still ahead. At this point, technical writers create internal documentation for the program that describes the development and technical details, how the code works, and how the user interacts with the program. In addition, the technical publishing department produces all of the necessary user documentation that will be distributed to the program users. User training begins once the software is distributed. Software trainers take the software to the user community and teach others how to use it efficiently.

Programming Languages: Many Languages for Many Projects

In any programming endeavor, programmers want to create a solution that meets several competing objectives. They want the software to run quickly and reliably and to be simple to expand later when the demands on the system change. They also want it to be completed on time and for the minimum possible cost, and to use the smallest amount of system resources possible.

Because it will always be difficult to balance these conflicting goals, a wide variety of programming languages has been developed. Earlier in the chapter, you learned about the five main categories (generations) of programming languages. In this section, we discuss the specific programming languages that are members of these different generations. Although programming languages often share many common characteristics, each language has specific traits that allow it to be the best fit for certain types of projects. Sometimes a language builds a loyal following, and that pushes a programmer to apply the same language to every situation.

ACTIVE HELP-DESK

Selecting the Right Programming Language

In this Active Helpdesk call, you'll play the role of a helpdesk staffer, fielding calls about how programmers select the right programming language for a specific task and what the most popular Windows and Web applications are.

The ability to understand enough about each language to match it to the appropriate style of problem is an exceptionally powerful skill for programmers.

What languages are popular today? There are far too many languages for one person to become expert at them all, but understanding the range of languages and how they relate to one another is especially useful. One quick way to determine which languages are popular is to examine job postings for programmers. As of this writing, the languages most in demand include C/C++ and Java. In specific industries, certain languages tend to dominate the work. In the banking and insurance industries, for example, the programming language COBOL is still common, although most other industries rarely use it any more. The Tiobe Index uses a number of different techniques to get a feel for which languages are popular in the software industry at the moment (see Figure 10.20).

How do I know which language to study first? A good introductory programming course will emphasize many skills and techniques that will carry over from one language to another. You should find a course that emphasizes design, algorithm development, debugging techniques, and project management. All of these aspects of programming will help you in any language environment. **Pascal** is the only modern language that was specifically designed as a teaching language, but it is no longer taught frequently at the college level. Many colleges and universities have opted to have students begin with Java or C++.

How does anyone learn so many languages? Professional programmers can work in a great number of different languages. They become proficient at learning new languages because they have become familiar with the basic components, discussed in this chapter's Dig Deeper feature, that are common to all languages: syntax, keywords, operators, and data types. The Bits and Bytes piece "Many Languages on Display" earlier in this chapter directs you to a site that displays an old song in more than 1,400 different languages.

Selecting the Right Language

How do programmers know which language to select for a specific project? A programming team considers several factors before selecting the language it will use for a specific project.

- **Space available:** Not all languages produce code that takes up the same amount of space. Therefore, the target language should be well matched to the amount of space available for the final program. For example, if the program will be embedded in a chip for use in a cell phone, then it is important for the language to create space-efficient programs.

- **Speed required:** Although poorly written code executes inefficiently in any language, some languages can execute more quickly than others can. Some projects require a focus on speed rather

Position July 2011	Delta in Position	Programming Language	Status
1	=	Java	A
2	=	C	A
3	=	C++	A
4	↑	C#	A
5	↓	PHP	A
6	↑↑↑	Objective-C	A
7	↓	(Visual) Basic	A
8	↓	Python	A
9	↓	Perl	A
10	=	JavaScript	A
11	↑↑↑↑↑↑↑↑	Lua	A
12	=	Ruby	A
13	↑↑↑	Lisp	A
14	↓↓↓	Delphi/Object Pascal	A
15	↑↑↑↑↑↑↑↑↑	Transact-SQL	A−
16	↓	Pascal	A−
17	=	Assembly	B
18	↑↑↑↑	RPG (OS/400)	B
19	↑↑↑↑↑↑↑↑	Ada	B
20	↑↑↑↑↑↑↑↑↑	C shell	B

Figure 10.20

When attacking a problem, you can choose from many different programming languages. This chart of the Tiobe Index shows how popular certain languages are right now.

than size. These projects require a language that produces code that executes in the fastest possible time.

- **Organizational resources available:** Another consideration is the resources available in a manager's group or organization. Selecting a language that is easy to use and will be easy to maintain if there is a turnover in programmers is an important consideration. Managers also may factor in the existing pool of talent available for the project. Having to train five programmers to tackle a project in a new language would have significant disadvantages over allowing them to work in a familiar language.
- **Type of target application:** Certain languages are customized to support a specific environment (UNIX or Windows, for instance). Knowing which languages are most commonly used for which environments can be helpful.

Building Applications

What languages do programmers use if they want to build an application for Windows? Software programs that run under the Windows OS are extremely popular. These programs often have a number of common features—scroll bars, title bars, text boxes, buttons, and expanding or collapsing menus, to name a few. Several languages include customized controls that make it easy for programmers to include these features in their programs. The same is true for the OS X operating system. We'll look at tools that are helpful for building applications for each.

Can I just point and click to create a Windows application? In languages that support Windows programming, programmers can use the mouse to lay out on the screen where the scroll bars and buttons will be in the application. The code needed to explain this to the computer is then written automatically when the programmer says the layout is complete. This is referred to as **visual programming**, and it helps programmers produce a final application much more quickly.

Visual Basic

What if programmers want to have a model of their program before it's fully developed? Earlier in the chapter, you read about how information systems are developed through the system development life cycle (SDLC). Although the SDLC has been around for quite some time, it doesn't necessarily work for all environments and instances. Programmers often like to build a **prototype**, or small model, of their program at the beginning of a large project.

Although an entire project may not be finished for several months, it can be useful to have a simple shell or skeleton of what the final program will look like to help with design. Prototyping is a form of **rapid application development (RAD)**, an alternative to the waterfall approach of systems development described at the beginning of this chapter. Instead of developing detailed system documents before they produce the system, developers create a prototype first, then generate system documents as they use and remodel the product.

Prototypes for Windows applications are often coded in Microsoft **Visual Basic (VB)**, a powerful programming language used to build a wide range of Windows applications. One strength of VB is its simple, quick interface, which is easy for a programmer to learn and use. It has grown from its roots in the language BASIC (short for Beginner's All-purpose Symbolic Instruction Code) to become a sophisticated and full-featured object-oriented language. It is often used in the creation of graphical user interfaces for Windows.

Visual Basic 2010 is the current version of Visual Basic and is designed for building object-oriented applications for Windows,

> Programmers often like to build a prototype, or small model, of their program at the beginning of a large project.

Figure 10.21

The Toolbox in Visual Basic 2010 allows the programmer to drag and drop any of these items into a program.

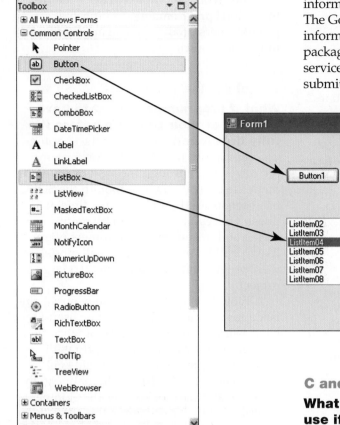

information or to check the spelling of a word. The Google Web service returns the requested information to your program in a standard package that you then decode. Before Web services, programs needed a human being to submit a search to Google and read over the results. Now the programs themselves can do this.

The power of .NET and Web services will continue to grow as more companies make some or all of their data available this way. The VB.NET programming tool has many supports for the Visual Basic programmer who is interested in using Web services.

C and C++

What languages do programmers use if the problem requires a lot of "number crunching"? A Windows application that demands raw processing power to execute difficult repetitive numerical calculations is most often a candidate for C/C++. For example, applications that simulate human cells and drug interactions have to solve elaborate mathematical equations many thousands of times each second, and are, therefore, excellent candidates for programming using C/C++. Several companies sell C/C++ compilers equipped with a design environment that makes Windows programming as visual as with VB.

Why was the C language developed? The predecessor of C++, **C**, was originally developed for system programmers. It was defined by Brian Kernighan and Dennis Ritchie of AT&T Bell Laboratories in 1978 as a language that would make accessing the operating system easier. It provides higher-level programming language features (such as *if* statements and *for* loops) but still allows programmers to manipulate the system memory and CPU registers directly. This mix of high- and low-level access makes C highly attractive to "power" programmers. Most modern operating systems (Windows 7, Mac OS X, and Linux) were written in C.

The **C++** language takes C to an object-oriented level. Bjarne Stroustrup, the

the Web, and mobile devices. Figure 10.21 shows how the interface of Visual Basic makes it easy to drag and drop entire programming components into an application. Visual Basic 2010 provides a multitude of features that are new or an improvement on the previous versions. These changes make development with Visual Basic easier and produce more efficient code than with any earlier version. Visual Basic 2010 and the .NET Framework are both part of Visual Studio 2010, which provides a complete set of developer tools.

How does the Microsoft .NET Framework help programmers? Too often, computer systems cannot exchange information—perhaps because they have different operating systems or use different rules for packaging data. The Microsoft .NET (pronounced "dot net") Framework is a software development environment designed to let Web sites "talk" to each other easily. The .NET Framework introduces Web services, which provide a standard way for software to interact. A **Web service** is a program that a Web site uses to make information available to other Web sites. For example, your Web site could use the Google Web service to search for

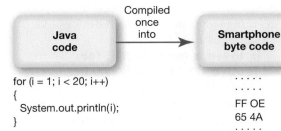

Compiled once into

Java code

for (i = 1; i < 20; i++)
{
   System.out.println(i);
}

Smartphone byte code

. . . . .
. . . . .
FF OE
65 4A
. . . . .
. . . . .

FF OE 65 4A

FF OE 65 4A

FF OE 65 4A

iMac

PC running Windows

Smartphone

Figure 10.22

Java programs can be compiled once and run on many different platforms.

developer of C++, used all of the same symbols and keywords as C, but he extended the language with additional keywords, better security, and more support for the reuse of existing code through object-oriented design.

Are C and C++ natural choices when I'm looking to learn my first language? Neither C nor C++ was intended as a teaching language. The notation and compactness of these languages make them relatively difficult to master. They are in demand in industry, however, because C/C++ can produce fast-running code that uses a small amount of memory. Programmers often choose to learn C/C++ because their basic components (operators, data types, and keywords) are common to many other languages.

Java and C#

What language do programmers use for applications that need to collect information from networked computers? Imagine that an insurance company with many locations wants a program that will run each night and will communicate with networked computers in many offices around the country, collecting policy changes and updates from that day's business and updating the company's main records. The team that writes this program would want to use a language that already provides support for network communications.

Java would be a good choice. James Gosling of Sun Microsystems introduced Java in the early 1990s. It quickly became popular because its object-oriented model enables Java programmers to benefit from its large set of existing classes. For

example, a Java programmer could begin to use the existing "network connection" class with little attention to the details of how that code itself was implemented. Classes exist for many graphical objects, such as windows and scroll bars, and for network objects such as connections to remote machines. Observing Java's success, Microsoft released a language named **C#** (pronounced "see sharp") that competes with Java.

Can a Java application work on any type of computer? An attractive feature of Java is that it is architecture neutral. This means that Java code needs to be compiled only once, after which it can run on many CPUs (see Figure 10.22). The Java program does not care which CPU, operating system, or user interface is running on the machine on which it lands. This is possible because the target computer runs a Java Virtual Machine (VM), software that can explain to the Java program how to function on any specific system. A Java VM installed with Microsoft Internet Explorer, for example, allows Internet Explorer to execute any **Java applet** (small Java-based program) it encounters on the Internet. Although Java code does not perform as fast as C++, the advantage of needing to compile only once

includes all of the keywords of C and then adds more keywords and features. It is often used together with a library called Cocoa. The Cocoa library, or framework, lets users program for the Mac OS X graphical user interface. The Cocoa Touch extension introduces a framework of methods that support gesture recognition for touch devices like the iPhone or iPad.

Is there a favorite IDE for Objective C? Many different IDE tools support Objective C, but OS X ships with a tool named Xcode (see Figure 10.23) that is often used to develop Objective C applications for OS X. The version 4 release of Xcode can be purchased and downloaded from the online Mac App Store.

Building Web Applications

What is the most basic language for developing Web applications? A document that will be presented on the Web must be written using special symbols called *tags*. Tags control how a Web browser will display the text, images, and other content tagged in the **Hypertext Markup Language (HTML)** or **eXtensible Hypertext Markup Language (XHTML)**. Although knowledge of HTML or XHTML is required to program for the Web, they are not in themselves programming languages. HTML and XHTML are just series of tags that modify the display of text. HTML was the original standard defining these tags. XHTML is a newer standard that corrects some of the inconsistencies found in HTML. To see more detail about HTML/XHTML tags, flip to the "HTML/XHTML" section in Chapter 13 (page 604). Many good HTML and XHTML tutorials are available on the Web at sites such as Learn the Net (**www.learnthenet.com**), Webmonkey (**www.webmonkey.com**), and the World Wide Web Consortium (**www.w3.org**). These sites include lists of the major tags that can be used to create HTML and XHTML documents.

Are there tools that help programmers write in HTML and XHTML? Several different programs are available to assist in the generation of HTML and XHTML. Adobe Dreamweaver and Microsoft Expression Web present Web page designers with an interface that is similar to a word processing program. Web designers can quickly insert text, images, and hyperlinks, as

before it can be distributed to any system is extremely important.

Objective C

What is the most popular language for writing Mac OS X applications? **Objective C** is the language most often used to program applications to run under Mac OS X. It is an object-oriented style of language, a superset of the C language so it

Figure 10.23

The Xcode IDE tool provides a supportive environment for developing OS X applications.

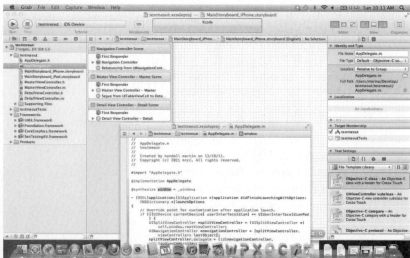

shown in Figure 10.24. The program automatically inserts the corresponding HTML or XHTML tags. For simple, static (nonchanging) Web pages, no programming is required.

Scripting Languages for the Web

Which programming languages do programmers use to make complex Web pages? To make their Web pages more visually appealing and interactive, programmers use scripting languages to add more power and flexibility to their HTML code. A **scripting language** is a simple programming language that is limited to performing a set of specialized tasks. Scripts allow decisions to be made and calculations to be performed. Several popular scripting languages work well with HTML, including JavaScript, VBScript, and PHP (Hypertext Preprocessor).

JavaScript is a scripting language that is often used to add interactivity to Web pages. JavaScript is not as fully featured as Java, but its syntax, keywords, data types, and operators are subsets of Java's. In addition, JavaScript has a set of classes that represent the objects often used on Web pages: buttons, check boxes, and drop-down lists.

The JavaScript button class, for example, describes a button with a name and a type—for example, whether it is a regular button or a Submit or Reset button. The language includes behaviors, such as click(), and can respond to user actions. For example, when a user moves his or her mouse over a button and clicks to select it, the button "knows" the user is there and jumps in and performs a special action (such as playing a sound).

Are there other scripting languages besides JavaScript? Programmers who are more familiar with Visual Basic than Java or C++ often use **VBScript**, a subset of Visual Basic, to introduce dynamic decision making into Web pages. **Dynamic decision making** means that the page can decide how to display itself based on the choices the reader makes. PHP, discussed in the following section, is another scripting language that has become extremely popular. It is a free, open source product that runs very efficiently on multiple platforms, including Windows, UNIX, and Linux.

ASP, JSP, and PHP

How are interactive Web pages built? To build Web sites with interactive capabilities, programmers use **Active Server Pages (ASP)**, **JavaServer Pages (JSP)**, or the scripting language **PHP (Hypertext Preprocessor)** to adapt the HTML or XHTML page to the user's selections. The user supplies information that is translated into a request by the main computer at the company that owns the Web site, often using a database query language such as SQL. Scripting code in ASP, JSP, or PHP controls the automatic writing of the custom HTML/XHTML page that is returned to the user's computer.

What does additional programming bring to a Web page? The most advanced Web pages interact with the user, collecting information and then customizing the content displayed based on the user's feedback. For example, as shown in Figure 10.25, the ABC online store's Web page will collect a customer bicycle inquiry for red bikes. It then asks ABC's main server for a list of red bicycles sold by the company. An ASP program running on the server creates a new HTML/XHTML page and delivers that to the user's browser, telling the customer what red bicycles (including details such as model and size) are currently sold by ABC.

Thus, ASP programs can have HTML/ XHTML code as their output. They use what the user has told them (via the list boxes, check boxes, and buttons on the page) to make decisions. Based on those results, the ASP program decides what HTML/XHTML to write. A small example of ASP writing

Figure 10.24
Adobe Dreamweaver is a popular tool for creating Web pages.

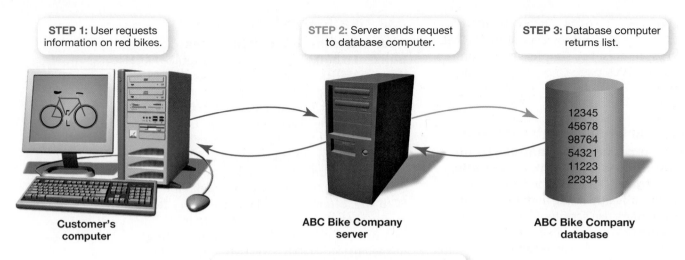

STEP 1: User requests information on red bikes.

STEP 2: Server sends request to database computer.

STEP 3: Database computer returns list.

Customer's computer

ABC Bike Company server

ABC Bike Company database

STEP 4: Server's ASP program writes HTML page.

Figure 10.25

An online store is an example of the client/server type of Internet application.

its own HTML/XHTML code is shown in Figure 10.26.

Flash and XML

What if a programmer wants to create a Web page that includes sophisticated animation? Many Web sites feature elaborate animations that interact with visitors. These sites include buttons and hyperlinks, along with animation effects. These components can be designed with **Adobe Flash**, a software product for developing Web-based multimedia. Flash includes

its own programming language, named **ActionScript**, which is similar to JavaScript in its keywords, operators, and classes.

Microsoft has a competing product named Silverlight that supports the development of rich multimedia and interactive Web applications. Other advances, like the collection of technologies referred to as **AJAX (Asynchronous JavaScript And XML)**, and the continued evolution of HTML5 allow the creation of Web applications that can update information on a page without requiring the user to do a

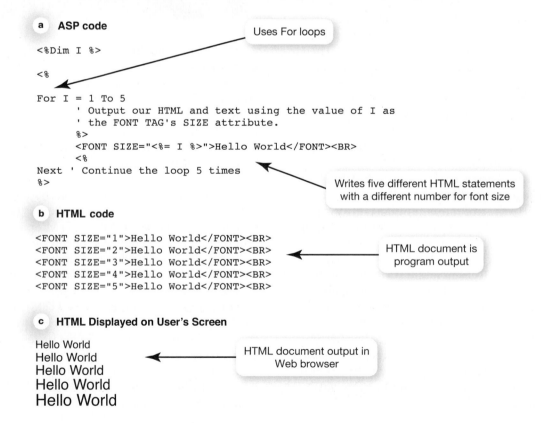

a   ASP code

Uses For loops

```
<%Dim I %>

<%

For I = 1 To 5
        ' Output our HTML and text using the value of I as
        ' the FONT TAG's SIZE attribute.
        %>
        <FONT SIZE="<%= I %>">Hello World</FONT><BR>
        <%
Next ' Continue the loop 5 times
%>
```

Writes five different HTML statements with a different number for font size

b   HTML code

```
<FONT SIZE="1">Hello World</FONT><BR>
<FONT SIZE="2">Hello World</FONT><BR>
<FONT SIZE="3">Hello World</FONT><BR>
<FONT SIZE="4">Hello World</FONT><BR>
<FONT SIZE="5">Hello World</FONT><BR>
```

HTML document is program output

Figure 10.26

An ASP program can (a) write HTML/XHTML code as its (b) output. This image illustrates how the HTML/XHTML page would (c) show up in a browser.

c   HTML Displayed on User's Screen

Hello World
Hello World
Hello World
Hello World
Hello World

HTML document output in Web browser

page refresh or leave the page. By using existing technologies to do more processing in the browser, users have a more responsive experience.

Is HTML/XHTML the only markup language for the Web? When Web sites communicate with humans, HTML/XHTML work well because the formatting they control is important. People respond immediately to the visual styling of textual information; its layout, color, size, and font design all help to transfer the message of the page to the reader. When computers want to communicate with each other, however, all of these qualities just get in the way. A third markup language, called **eXtensible Markup Language (XML)**, enables designers to define their own data-based tags, making it much easier for a Web site to transfer the key information on its page to another site.

Without XML, a Web site that wanted to look up current stock pricing information at another site would have to retrieve the HTML/XHTML page, sort through the formatting information, and try to recognize which text on the page identified the data needed. With XML, groups can agree on standard systems of tags that represent important data elements. For example, the XML tags required text missing. Must read: <stock> and </stock> might delimit key stock quote information. Mathematicians have created a standardized set of XML tags named MathML for their work, and biometrics groups continue to refine XML standards to describe and exchange data such as DNA and face scans. We discuss HTML/XHTML and XML in more detail in Chapter 13.

Figure 10.27 shows a table of popular programming tools with their features and the typical settings in which they are used.

Figure 10.27 | POPULAR PROGRAMMING TOOLS

Programming Language	Features	Typical Setting
C/C++ and C#	Can create compact code that executes quickly Provides high- and low-level access	Used in industrial applications such as banking and engineering
Objective C	Has a framework for writing iTouch/iPhone/iPad applications	Used to create applications for Mac OS X and Apple mobile devices
Flash ActionScript	Is similar in syntax to JavaScript but customized for the Flash animation environment	Used to control Flash animations
Microsoft Silverlight	Is a competitor to Adobe Flash, and supports rich multimedia capabilities	Used to deliver audio and video to Web pages
Java	Is architecture neutral Is object-oriented	Used to create applets that can be delivered over the Web
JavaScript	Is similar in syntax to Java Has classes that represent buttons, drop-down lists, and other Web page components	Creates code that lives on the client machine and supports interaction with Web pages
VBScript	Is similar in syntax to Visual Basic Has classes that represent buttons, drop-down lists, and other Web page components	Creates code that lives on the client machine and adds interaction to Web pages
Visual Basic	Is easy to learn and use Is object-oriented Has a drag-and-drop interface	Used in prototype development Used to design graphical user interfaces
Web Technologies		
ASP, JSP, PHP	Have a set of rules and standards that allow Web sites to create their own HTML code based on user actions	Control the automated writing of HTML pages
HTML/XHTML	Provide a set of tags that control the display of text on a Web page	Control layout and style of information presented on a Web page
XML	Enables users to define their own tags Facilitates exchange of information between Web sites	Used in the construction of Web services
AJAX	Uses a combination of existing technologies like JavaScript, CSS, and XML	Creates Web sites that can update without the user refreshing the page

Building Mobile Applications

How do programmers build applications for mobile devices? Special languages and supporting tools are helping speed the development of applications for mobile devices like smartphones and tablets. Programmers need to be able to take advantage of specific features like GPS capability, a compass, software keyboards, and touch-sensitive screens. In addition, the user interface has to take the smaller screen size into account.

What development tools are used for creating mobile apps for Apple's iOS platform? To start a complex project like an iPhone app requires a detailed prototype. Each of the many screens, all of the user interface elements, and all of the content needs to be organized and linked smoothly. Often programmers begin with a prototype, created quickly with drag-and-drop elements using products like MockApp or Interface Builder. MockApp (**www.mockapp.com**) is a template that uses PowerPoint or Keynote to construct

a working simulation of your application. Interface Builder is part of the Apple Xcode 4 development tool and requires a bit more expertise to use, but can also rapidly create a prototype.

When it is time to begin writing the code for an iOS app, most programmers turn to Objective C and use the Apple Xcode development toolset (see Figure 10.28).

Xcode lets the designer build the user interface (Interface Builder), code and debug the behavior of the application, and simulate it in a software version of the target device. After the program is running, performance can be profiled for speed, memory usage, and other possible problems.

Are there different tools for building apps for Android devices? Yes, the Android software development kit (SDK) is required to build apps targeting Android smartphones and tablets. There are many ways programmers work with the Android SDK including using well-known IDEs like Eclipse with special plug-ins for Android like the Android Development

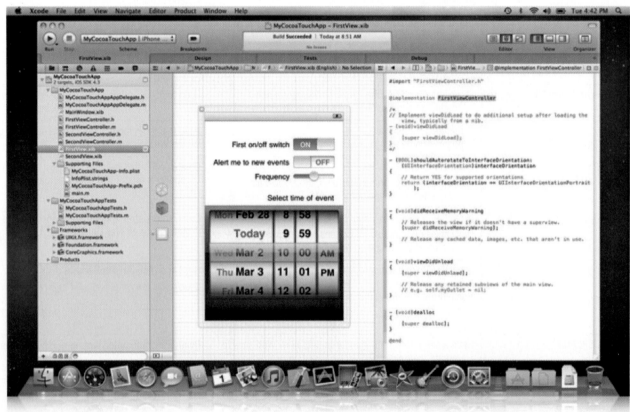

Screenshots © Apple Inc. Reprinted by permission from Apple Inc.

Figure 10.28

Xcode 4 integrates all the tools required to program iOS applications from scratch.

Tools (**developer.android.com/sdk/eclipse-adt.html**). Information on the latest version of the Android SDK, as well as tutorials, guides, and other resources, is available at the Android Developers page (**developer.android.com**).

I'm not a programmer, but can I make a simple app? Absolutely. If you have even a little programming experience, tools like Corona (**www.anscamobile.com/corona**) produce amazing games and apps quickly. Tens of millions of apps constructed using Corona have been downloaded, including the overnight sensation Bubble Ball by 14-year-old Robert Nay (**www.naygames.com**). Code can be deployed for an iOS device, Android device, or even the Barnes and Noble Nook Color. The advantage of Corona is that it supports a wide range of features like networking support to Facebook, easy animation, multimedia, and a physics engine, but requires only simple programming syntax.

If your goal is to make a mobile app that is very simple or even specific to one occasion, like a wedding, there are Web-based products that make that quick and easy. Magmito (**www.magmito.com**) supports developing a simple app with text and graphics and requires no programming knowledge.

Does an application need to be rewritten for every kind of mobile device? The programming environments like Corona and Magmito support publishing an application to several different types of devices. Although these can be great time savers for very simple applications, for programmers using specific features that make that device unique, or those who are concerned with extracting the ultimate performance, custom programming for each environment still is required.

The Next Great Language

What will be the next great language? It is never easy to predict which language will become the next "great" language. Software experts predict that as software projects continue to grow in size, the amount of time needed to compile a completed project will also grow. It is not uncommon for a large project to require 30 minutes or more to compile. Interpreted languages, however, have virtually no compile time because compilation occurs while the code is being edited. As projects get larger, the capability to be compiled instantaneously will become even more important. Thus, interpreted languages such as Python, Ruby, and Smalltalk could become more important in the coming years.

Will all languages someday converge into one? Certain characteristics of modern programming languages correspond well with how programmers actually think. These traits support good programming practices and are emerging as common features of most modern programming languages. The object-oriented paradigm is one example. Both Visual Basic and COBOL have moved toward supporting objects.

There will always be a variety of programming languages, however. Figure 10.29, in which the artist tries to give each language a "personality," illustrates that idea in lighthearted fashion.

Figure 10.29

There will always be a variety of languages, each with its own personality.

Emerging Technologies: Unite All Your Video Game Design Tools

Unity is a game development environment that supports home video game production by combining many tools into one package, giving you what you need to edit, test, and play your game idea quickly. It can generate real-time shadowing effects, for example, and has preprogrammed scripts integrated. After you've polished your production, Unity allows you to publish for Web, mobile, or console platforms. With over 500,000 developers using Unity, and over 60 million installs of the Unity browser plug-in, the potential of this tool is amazing.

You'll start with the built-in Unity editor so you can quickly assemble a 3D environment. Unity gives you access to its Asset Store right from the editor window. Art assets are supplied so you instantly have materials to create your own landscape. Tutorials and sample projects are there, as well as character models and textures. Grab a sound effect or some code to simulate a great explosion effect. If you create assets you'd like to distribute, you can also put those up for sale within the Asset Store.

Unity incorporates lighting control and shading, and the application of textures to develop rich terrains. Its built-in physics engine lets objects respond to gravity, friction, and collisions. One example is the "wheel collider," a module that simulates the traction of real car tires. Audio processing is included, with effects like echo, reverb, and a chorus filter, as are tools to make real-time networking available from your game.

Programming is handled through several flexible scripting languages—JavaScript, C#, and an implementation of Python named Boo.

There is a visual interface that lets you drag and drop objects to set variables, or you can choose to sync with an external IDE like Visual Studio. There is an integrated debugger so you can pause your game, check variable values, and quickly repair errors. When it is time to optimize the performance before your final release, you can use the built-in profiler. It reports statistics on where the processing time is being spent so you can fine tune gameplay.

Unity is available in a free downloadable version (**unity3d.com**) and in a pay version, Unity 3D Pro. The Pro version adds features but also can be licensed and used by companies. The free version of Unity can be used to create games that can be sold—there is no royalty or revenue sharing required. And there are modules to allow you to easily port your code to a number of target platforms: PC, iOS, Android, Web, as well as Xbox 360, PS3, and Wii.

You will also find an active community to support you as you learn. The Unify Community offers a Script Wiki (**www.unifycommunity.com/ wiki/**) to organize the many tutorials, tips, and programming resources that users have contributed. There is a dedicated IRC channel for live chatting with Unity users. If you need help distributing your finished game, you can join Union, a service that brings your game to new markets for you.

If you are interested in video game development, architectural visualizations, or just creating interactive animations, download Unity and realize the power of programming.

With over 500,000 developers using Unity, and over 60 million installs of the Unity browser plug-in, the potential of this tool is amazing.

Forcing a language to be so general that it can work for any task also forces it to include components that make it slower to compile, produce larger final executables, and require more memory to run. Having a variety of languages and mapping a problem to the best language creates the most efficient software solutions.

So what do I do if I want to learn languages that will be relevant in the future? No particular set of languages is best to learn, and there is no one best sequence in which to learn them. The Association for Computing Machinery (**www.acm .org**) encourages educators to teach a core set of mathematical and programming skills and concepts, but school and university departments are free to offer a variety of languages.

When you are selecting which programming languages to study, some geographical and industry-related considerations come into play. For example, in an area in which a large number of pharmaceutical companies exist, there may be a demand for Massachusetts General Hospital Utility Multi-Programming System (MUMPS). This language is often used to build clinical databases, an important task in the pharmaceutical industry. Review the advertisements for programmers in area newspapers and investigate resources such as ComputerJobs (**www .computerjobs.com**) to identify languages in demand in your area.

Whether or not you pursue a career in programming, having an understanding of how software is created will help you in many IT careers. Software is the set of instructions that allows us to make use of our hardware. Programming skills give you the power to understand, create, and customize a computer system.

1. Why do I need to understand how to create software?

Programming skills allow you to customize existing software products to accomplish tasks you need. Even if you are not planning to pursue programming as a career, a beginning-level knowledge of programming will let you create macros, customized mini-programs to speed up redundant tasks.

2. What is a system development life cycle, and what are the phases in the cycle?

An information system includes data, people, procedures, hardware, and software. Teams of individuals are required to develop systems. Those teams need to follow an organized process (or set of steps) to ensure that development proceeds in an orderly fashion. This set of steps is usually referred to as the system development life cycle (SDLC). There are six steps in the SDLC waterfall model discussed earlier in this chapter: (1) A problem or opportunity is identified. (2) The problem is analyzed, and a program specification document is created to outline the project objectives. (3) A detailed plan for programmers to follow is designed using flowcharts and data-flow diagrams. (4) Using this plan, the program is developed and documented. (5) The program is tested to ensure that it works properly and is installed so that it can be used. (6) Ongoing maintenance and evaluation ensure a working product.

3. What is the life cycle of a program?

Each programming project follows several stages from conception to final deployment. The problem statement identifies the task to be computerized and describes how the software program will behave. An algorithm is developed that specifies the sequence of steps that the program must take to complete the work. The algorithm is then translated into highly structured programming code. The code goes through the processes of debugging, in which the programmers find and repair any errors in the code; testing by the programming team; and further testing by the people who will use the program. The results of the entire project are documented for the users and the development team. Finally, users are trained so that they can use the program efficiently.

4. What role does a problem statement play in programming?

The problem statement is an explicit description of what tasks the computer program must accomplish and how the program will execute these tasks and respond to unusual situations. It describes the input data that users will have at the start of the job, the output that the program will produce, and the exact processing that converts these inputs to outputs. In addition, the problem statement identifies potential errors and plans to address these errors.

5. How do programmers create algorithms and move from algorithm to code?

For simple problems, programmers create an algorithm by converting a problem statement into a list of steps (or actions) the program will take. For more complex problems, programmers must identify where decision points occur in the list of steps. Some decisions are yes/no (binary), whereas others create a repeating action (loop). Algorithms are documented in the form of a flowchart or in pseudocode. Programmers use either top-down or object-oriented analysis to produce the algorithm.

Computer code uses special words and strict rules to enable programmers to control the CPU without having to know all of its hardware details. Programming languages are classified in several major groupings, sometimes referred to as *generations*, with the first generation being machine language—the binary code of 1s and 0s that the computer understands. Assembly language is the next generation; it uses short, English-like commands that speak directly to the CPU and give the programmer direct control of hardware resources. Each successive generation in language development has relieved programmers of some of the burden of keeping track of what the hardware requires and more closely matches how humans think about problems.

Compilation is the process by which code is converted into machine language, the language the CPU can understand. A compiler is a program that understands both the syntax of the programming language and the exact structure of the CPU and its machine language. It can translate the instructions written by programmers in the higher-level language into machine language, the binary patterns that will execute commands on the CPU. Each programming language has its own compiler. Separate versions are required to compile code that will run on each different type of processor.

6. What steps are involved in completing the program?

If programmers make errors in the algorithm or in translating the algorithm to code, problems will occur. Programmers debug the program by running it constantly to find errors and to make sure the program behaves in the way it should. Once debugging has detected all the code errors, users, both within the company and outside the company, test the program in every way they can imagine—both as it was intended to be used and in ways only new users may think up. Before its commercial release, software is often provided at a reduced cost or no cost in a beta version to certain test sites or to interested users for a last round of testing.

Once testing is complete, technical writers create internal documentation for the program and external documentation that will be provided to users of the program. User training, which begins once the software is distributed, teaches the user community how to use the software efficiently.

7. How do programmers select the right programming language for a specific task?

A programming team reviews several considerations before selecting the language. First, certain languages are best used with certain problems. Second, the target language should be well matched to the amount of space available for the final program. Third, some projects require the selection of a language that can produce code that executes in the fastest possible time. Finally, selecting a language with which the programmers are familiar is also helpful.

8. What are the most popular programming languages for different types of application development?

Visual Basic, C/C++, and Java are languages that enable programmers to include Windows control features such as scroll bars, title bars, text boxes, buttons, and expanding and collapsing menus. Objective C is a language used in programming applications to run under Mac OS X. Programmers use HTML/XHTML tags to structure for Web pages. For more complex Web development, scripting programs such as JavaScript and VBScript are popular. Web page animations are done with ASP, JSP, PHP, Flash, Silverlight and XML.

 Companion Website

The Companion Website includes a variety of additional materials to help you review and learn more about the topics in this chapter. Go to: *www.pearsonhighered.com/techinaction*

Word Bank

- algorithm
- beta version
- C/C++
- classes
- compiler
- debugger
- documentation
- HTML/XHTML
- inheritance
- interpreter
- JavaScript
- machine language
- object-oriented
- problem statement
- testing plan
- top-down
- Visual Basic

Instructions: Fill in the blanks using the words from the Word Bank above.

Cutting diamonds is not an exact science, but more of an art. Things don't always go well. At the Diamond Eye factory, we need to keep track of how many complete rings are made every hour and how many defective diamonds we have to reallocate. We begin by calling in the programming team to work with the cutters. Together, team members begin to build a software solution by creating a(n) (1) _____. All of the input and output information required is identified as well as the (2) _____, which lists specific examples of what outputs the program will produce for certain inputs. The team then begins to design the (3) _____ by listing all the tasks and subtasks required to complete the job. This approach is called (4) _____ design.

An alternative to this design method is the (5) _____ design model, which develops the program based on objects. Objects that have similar attributes and behaviors can be grouped into (6) _____. The benefit of using this type of design approach is that objects and classes can be reused easily in other programs. If necessary, new classes can be made by first "borrowing" the attributes of an existing class and then adding differentiating attributes. This concept is known as (7) _____.

To select the best language for this problem, the team considers the resources at Diamond Eye. Their small programming staff knows the visual programming language of (8) _____, but the most important factor for this application will be how fast it runs, so the language (9) _____ is selected. As the effort expands, the plan is to allow other offices to enter their data over the Web. Then there will be a round of hiring programmers who know (10) _____. For now, the program to track production and quality control has been written in programming language; the (11) _____ translates it to (12) _____, or the binary code that the CPU understands. After that step, the program is ready to be tested.

The (13)_____ helps identify errors in the program code. Then the programmers put together the necessary (14) _____ that explains the program and how to use it. However, because this is a program that is to be used internally, the program does not need to go through a test of the (15) _____ by a group of potential outside users.

becoming computer literate

Your new manager wants to design and deploy a tablet application to collect marketing information about potential customers. She wants to gather data and analyze it in one report, which can be shipped to the marketing department. So far management has not selected a final target device—it might be an Apple iPad or perhaps a Motorola Xoom.

Instructions: Write a memo to the manager describing what will have to be considered in the creation of this project. Write the memo using as many of the key terms from the chapter as you can. Consider what languages will need to be used, and what features will be critical to the application's success.

Instructions: Answer the multiple-choice and true–false questions below for more practice with key terms and concepts from this chapter.

Multiple Choice

1. In the SDLC, in which phase is the program specification developed?
a. problem and opportunity identification
b. analysis
c. design
d. development and documentation

2. The step of the SDLC in which we document the transfer of data from the point where it enters the system to its final storage or output is the
a. problem and opportunity phase.
b. analysis phase.
c. design phase.
d. development and document phase.

3. The life cycle of a program begins with describing a problem and making a plan. Then the PDLC requires
a. coding, debugging, and testing.
b. process, input, and output.
c. data, information, and method.
d. an algorithm.

4. What do companies provide to repair code errors for a program that has been released to the public?
a. beta versions
b. service packs
c. service agreements
d. maintenance programs

5. Which language is best for creating iOS-based mobile applications?
a. C/C++   b. Objective C
c. Java   d. ASP

6. A yes/no decision point in an algorithm is called a
a. loop.
b. binary decision.
c. test condition.
d. control structure.

7. In object-oriented analysis, classes are defined by their
a. objects and data.
b. data and methods.
c. operators and objects.
d. behaviors and keywords.

8. Which is NOT an advantage of Java?
a. Java is architecture neutral.
b. Java needs to compile only once prior to distribution.
c. Java supports network communications.
d. Java performs faster than C++.

9. Which is TRUE about XML?
a. XML supports the development of rich multimedia.
b. XML makes it possible to update Web pages without refreshing.
c. XML enables designers to define their own data-based tags.
d. XML has classes that represent drop-down lists and other Web elements.

10. Which of the following helps programmers write, compile, and test programs?
a. IDE   b. RAD
c. JAD   d. PDLC

True–False

_____ 1. When producing the fastest executable program is essential, programmers use a language with an interpreter.

_____ 2. Object-oriented design promotes a high level of reuse of existing code.

_____ 3. Comments that programmers insert to explain the purpose of the code are written with special binary symbols.

_____ 4. The SDLC and the PDLC are different because JAD and RAD are different.

_____ 5. Programmers often use ActionScript to code prototypes for Windows applications.

1. Learning to Program

Research the core programming sequence at the college you are attending.

a. What languages does the core sequence cover? Are there any introductory courses that use languages with less syntax, like Alice or Visual Logic?

b. How do the languages in the programming sequence reflect the popularity of the languages used in today's workplace?

c. How many sections of each of the classes are offered?

d. What can you infer about the percentage of students that stay in the programming track over time?

e. What does that result mean to the future of your community and your country?

2. Learn and Earn

Investigate summer internship positions for student programmers. Be sure to check into companies like Fog Creek, university programs like the University of Pennsylvania's SUNFEST, and sites like **www.onedayoneinternship.com.** What is the common set of requirements? What kinds of projects do interns produce? What internships are available in your local area?

3. A Ruby, a Perl, and a Python

Perl is an especially useful and convenient language to use for specific types of programming problems. Ruby and Python are also programming languages, each with its own specific advantages. Research Ruby, Perl, and Python, and identify the key features of these languages. Determine which programming situations call for using Ruby and which would be best suited for Perl or Python.

4. Interview Ready

There are many puzzles posted online that allegedly have been used by interviewers at tech companies like Google or Facebook in part of the interview process. (For a collection, look at the book *Algorithms for Interviews* by Adnan Aziz and Amit Parkash.) Here are a few sample questions that could come up in assessing your ability to create algorithms. Prepare solutions to each.

a. What method would you use to look up a word in a dictionary?

b. Imagine you have a closet full of shirts. It's very hard to find a shirt, so what can you do to organize your shirts for easy retrieval?

c. You have eight balls, all of the same size. Seven of them weigh the same, but one of them weighs slightly more. Can you find the ball that is heavier by using a balance and only two weighings?

5. Reuse, Reuse, Reuse

One key to being an efficient programmer is to reuse code. Programmers often use collections of prewritten code modules named application programming interfaces (APIs) to add functionality to their program with very little work. Research the set of APIs available from Google by visiting Google Code (**code.google.com**) and the Google Code Playground (**code.google.com/apis/ajax/playground/**).

1. Programming Is Not Just for Programmers

Macros are small programs that allow you to extend the capabilities of common applications like Microsoft Excel or Word. Think about the range of jobs at the place where you currently work.

a. How many individuals have a job in which repetitive tasks (entering data, formatting reports, etc.) or repetitive sequences of keystrokes are required to use the software they need?
b. How many individuals create macros, scripts, or shortcuts for doing their work in a faster, more automated fashion?
c. How many people actually program in a modern programming language?

2. Algorithm Design

Identify the most commonly performed task at your place of business. Think of a way to document it as an algorithm. Then study it to see if you can find a way to make it even more efficient. A small improvement to the most often performed task means big productivity gains. Review the Jolt Award winners at **drdobbs.com/joltawards/** to see examples of the kinds of efficiencies that have been introduced in the software field this year to boost productivity.

3. Choosing the Best Language

Using resources from the Web, determine which programming languages would be best to learn if you were going to program for the following industries:

a. Interactive learning games
b. Interactive architectural visualization for mobile devices and Web deployment
c. Database management
d. Robotics

4. Software Development . . . in PowerPoint?

The tool MockApp (**www.mockapp.com/download**) is a template for the presentation tools PowerPoint and Keynote. It provides an interface that allows you to drag and drop all of the visual components of an iPhone, iTouch, or iPad application onto a simulated screen. You can link button clicks and other interactions from one screen to the next and create a "working" simulation or prototype of a new iPhone, iTouch, or iPad application. Investigate this tool using either PowerPoint or Keynote. Design an iPhone application that would be either useful for you or successful in the marketplace.

5. Accessibility

Web designers and programmers can take specific steps to allow visually impaired users to access Web sites more easily. Examine the information on accessibility at Adobe's Accessibility Resource Center (**www.adobe.com/accessibility/**). What does accessibility mean in a software context? Explore the details of existing assistive technologies, such as screen readers. What are the legal requirements with which Web sites must comply in order to meet the needs of persons with disabilities? Why is maximizing accessibility important to everyone?

Instructions: Some ideas are best understood by experimenting with them in our own minds. The following critical thinking questions are designed to demand your full attention but require only a comfortable chair—no technology.

1. Using Data and Methods

Think about what classes would be important in modeling a band that is about to go on a national concert tour. The band already has a Web site, a presence on Twitter and Facebook, and a local following at area clubs. The band signed a new manager last year, and the members have all been with the group for a while now. They hope to get on bills with other independent-label bands. What data and methods would each class need? How would the classes be related to each other?

2. Class Hierarchy

A common test for deciding the structure of a class hierarchy is the "is a" versus "has a" test. For example, a motorcycle "has a" sidecar, so Sidecar would be a data field of a Motorcycle object. However, a motorcycle "is a" kind of vehicle, so Motorcycle would be a subclass of the base class Vehicle. Use the "is a" versus "has a" test to decide how a class structure could be created for computer peripherals. For example, consider that printers are a type of peripheral and there are laser printers, inkjet printers, 3D printers, color printers, black-and-white printers, and thermal printers. Work to separate the unique features into objects and to extract the most common features into higher-level classes.

3. First Programming Languages

By watching children learn language, we know that language acquisition is much easier at an early age. What if learning a programming language works the same way? What kinds of learning strategies would make a young child curious about programming? What kinds of games would illustrate developing algorithms?

4. Something for Nothing

The open source software movement depends on the participation of a number of people from all over the world. Some individuals donate time by writing code; others do testing or documentation. Projects are then made available free to users. Does the open source movement threaten or strengthen the software industry? Could it replace the existing business model for distributing software? Are there any benefits to working for free and giving your intellectual property away?

5. Gathering Insights

There are many different ways to decide which programming languages are the most popular today. The beta tool Google Insights lets you compare search patterns and usage across specific regions, categories, or time periods. How would Insights help you do the same thing? Where would you go to conduct a survey on which programming languages are popular? What individuals would you survey? How would you expect their answers to differ from one another?

Working Together for Change

Problem

You and your team have just been selected to write a software program that tells a vending machine how to make proper change from the bills or coins the customer inserts. The program needs to deliver the smallest possible amount of coins for each transaction.

Task

Divide the class into three teams: Algorithm Design, Coding, and Testing. The responsibilities of each team are outlined as follows.

Process

1. The Algorithm Design team must develop two documents. The first document should present the problem as a top-down design sequence of steps. The second document should use object-oriented analysis to identify the key objects in the problem. Each object needs to be represented as data and behaviors. Inheritance relationships between objects should be noted as well. You can use flowcharts to document your results.

   Consider using a product such as Microsoft Visio or the open source program Dia to create a visual representation of your objects and their relationships to each other.

2. The Coding team needs to decide which programming language would be most appropriate for the project. This program needs to be fast and take up only a small amount of memory. Use the Web to collect information about the language you select and be sure you have enough information to defend your selection.

   You may also consider using a product such as Visual Logic to try to develop the code for a prototype of the system. (The Web site **www.VisualLogic.org** offers a free demo version.) This language, based on Visual Basic, allows you to write code free from many constraints of syntax. Programs in Visual Logic look like flowcharts but actually execute!

3. The Testing team must create a testing plan for the program. What set of inputs would you test with to be sure the program is completely accurate? Develop a table listing combinations of inputs and correct outputs.

4. As a group, discuss how each team would communicate its results to the other teams. Once one team has completed its work, are the team members finished or do they need to interact with the other teams? How would the tools of a site such as SourceForge (**www.sourceforge.net**) help your development team across the life of the project?

Conclusion

Any modern programming project requires programming teams to produce an accurate and efficient solution to a problem. The interaction of the team members within the team as well as with the other teams is vital to successful programming.

Software That Kills

In this exercise, you will research and then role-play a complicated ethical situation. The role you play may or may not match your own personal beliefs, but your research and use of logic will enable you to represent whichever view is assigned. An arbitrator will watch and comment on both sides of the argument, and together the team will agree on an ethical solution.

Problem

The Therac-25 was a computerized radiation therapy machine. Between 1985 and 1987, six people were killed or badly harmed due to a software flaw in its programming. Although the therapeutic dose was expected to be about 200 rads, it was later estimated that one patient had received doses of radiation in the 15,000- to 20,000-rad range. (Doses of 1,000 rads can be fatal.) The error-prone software remained on the market for more than 18 months before the problem was recognized, acknowledged, and solved.

Does this situation indicate criminal conduct? Is this a situation that needs to be resolved in civil court, for monetary damages, but does not constitute a criminal act? Should this incident be seen as an example of the price society pays for using complex technology and no blame should be assigned?

Research Areas to Consider

- Therac-25 case resolution

- 2010 Toyota recalls for unanticipated acceleration

- Software errors in avionic software systems

- ACM Ethical Guidelines

Process

Divide the class into teams.

1. Research the areas cited above from the perspective of one of the following people: a software developer, the injured or noninjured patients, and the arbitrator.

2. Team members should write a summary that provides factual support for their character's position regarding the fair and ethical design of medical equipment and a policy for handling fair restitution for injured patients. Then, team members should create an outline to use during the role-playing event.

3. Team members should arrange a mutually convenient time to meet for the exchange, using the collaboration features of MyITLab, the discussion board feature of Blackboard, or meeting in person.

4. Team members should present their case to the class or submit a PowerPoint presentation for review by the rest of the class, along with the summary and resolution they developed.

Conclusion

As technology becomes ever more prevalent and integrated into our lives, more and more ethical dilemmas will present themselves. Being able to understand and evaluate both sides of the argument, while responding in a personally or socially ethical manner, will be an important skill.

chapter 11

behind the scenes:

databases and information systems

Database Basics

OBJECTIVES:

What is a database, and why is it beneficial to use databases? *(p. 516)*

What components make up a database? *(p. 518)*

What types of databases are there? *(p. 522)*

 Active Helpdesk: Understanding Database Management Systems

How Databases Operate

OBJECTIVES:

What do database management systems do? *(p. 524)*

How do relational databases organize and manipulate data? *(p. 532)*

 Active Helpdesk: Using Databases

 Sound Byte: Creating an Access 2010 Database

Sound Byte: Improving an Access 2010 Database

Database Warehousing and Storage

OBJECTIVE:

What are data warehouses and data marts, and how are they used? *(p. 537)*

Business Intelligence Systems and Data Mining

OBJECTIVES:

What is a business intelligence system, and what types of business intelligence systems are used by decision makers? *(p. 541)*

What is data mining, and how does it work? *(p. 547)*

 Active Helpdesk: Data Warehouses, Data Marts, and Information Systems

Scan here for more info on How Cool Is This? ▶

how cool is *this?*

how cool is *this?* Most useful sites on the Internet have databases integrated into them, or are actually databases themselves. One popular example is Twitter. But with the **millions** of Twitter users tweeting about all sorts of different things, how can you find Twitter users who generate tweets about subjects that fit your interests?

Justtweetit.com is a **database of Twitter** users that groups users by **logical topics of interest**. Are you an artist interested in following what other artists are tweeting about? Just click on the Artists link to find more than 550 active Twitter users who discuss art. What if you regularly tweet on a topic, such as fashion or video gaming, and want to have **more potential followers** find you? You can easily add yourself to the Justtweetit directory in the most appropriate of the hundreds of categories featured on the site. So start finding **more relevant tweets** today!

John Schwegel / Alamy

Life Without Databases

A **database** is a collection of related data that can be easily stored, sorted, organized, and queried. By creating an organized structure for data, we hope to make data more meaningful and therefore more useful. In other words, we are attempting to turn data into information. But why should you learn about databases?

Although you may never be called upon to construct a database, you probably use databases every day. For example, you might search a database in an attempt to extract relevant information. A key attribute of databases is that information can be filtered so that you only see the information you really want. Understanding how databases work and what you can do with a database will help you use them more effectively. Let's look at two examples.

Have you checked Facebook today? If so, you used a database even though you probably didn't realize it. When you load your Facebook page, you see a News Feed of items your friends have posted on their Facebook pages. Facebook is using your list of friends to comb through their databases to provide you with what it thinks is relevant information—in other words, what your friends are saying today—to display on your News Feed. But you might have a different idea of what is relevant. You might only be interested in updates from your friends that include photos. Or perhaps you want to see only items with links to other pages. You can select these options on your News Feed, and Facebook changes your feed to only include the items you want to see and filters out any items that don't match the criteria you specified.

Or perhaps you want your News Feed to show all the latest updates, not just what Facebook thinks is most important. Selecting the option Most Recent on your News Feed sorts all the items posted by your friends with the newest posts on top. Sorting and filtering are key attributes of most databases.

Suppose you enjoy playing collectible card games such as Magic: The Gathering (MTG) or Yu-Gi-Oh!. Collectible card games like MTG present players with a wide variety of cards, that have been issued over the years, that can be used in building decks to compete with other players. Remembering all the available cards when trying to design a deck can be daunting. But database applications such as Decked Builder allow you to easily search for available cards based on key card attributes such as the type of card (creature or sorcery), color, and rarity (see Figure 11.1).

Although you may not have realized it, apps like Decked Builder are really searchable databases.

Filtering and sorting information to enhance its usefulness to you and searching for relevant information are just three useful aspects of databases. In the rest of this chapter, you'll learn about the inner workings of databases and other ways they can be used to provide relevant information quickly and easily.

DECKED BUILDER by Tan Thor Jen. Copyright © Decked Studios. Reprinted by permission.

Figure 11.1

Decked Builder gives you the ability to search and filter information on Magic: The Gathering cards.

Should I use databases for managing all types of data?

Not every situation in which related data needs to be turned into organized information demands the complexity of a database. For simple tasks, lists are adequate. Often, word processing or spreadsheet software works for creating simple lists. A table you create in Microsoft Word can serve as a list, as can a spreadsheet you create in Microsoft Excel.

Figure 11.2 shows a simple "Books to Buy" list you might create in Excel before

	A	B	C	D
2	**Books To Buy**			
3				
4	**Class**	**Title**	**Author**	**Bought**
5	American Literature 1	Anthology of American Literature, Volume 1	McMichael et al.	
6	American Literature 1	Moby Dick	Melville	Yes
7	American Literature 1	The Last of the Mohicans	Cooper	Yes
8	English Composition 1	The Academic Writer's Handbook	Rosen	
9	English Composition 1	The Write Stuff: Thinking Through Essays	Sims	Yes
10	Intro to Business	Better Business	Solomon, Poatsy, Martin	Yes

Figure 11.2

A simple list created as a spreadsheet in Microsoft Excel is often sufficient to organize simple tasks.

beginning college. This list works well because it is simple and suited to just one purpose: to provide you with a list of the books you need to buy for a particular semester. If all the information that needed to be tracked were as simple as the information in Figure 11.2, there would be no need for databases.

When is a list not appropriate?
If complex information needs to be organized, or more than one person needs access to it, a list is not an efficient solution. For example, when you enrolled in college, you provided information about yourself to a number of people. This information included your name, your address, the classes you wished to take, and the meal plan you selected. Your school also tracks other information about you, such as your residence hall address. Consider the two lists shown in Figure 11.3. Figure 11.3a is a list the registrar's office might use to keep track of students, the classes they are taking, and the meal plan they selected. Figure 11.3b is a list the residence hall manager might use to track where students are housed.

What's the problem with having two lists? First, there is a great deal of duplicated data between the two lists in Figure 11.3. For example, each time Julio Garza registers for a class, his name

and address are entered. He needs to provide the same data to the residence hall manager when he receives his residence hall assignment. This **data redundancy**, though not a problem in the small lists in Figure 11.3, can be problematic when a college or university has 10,000 students. Imagine the time wasted by entering data multiple times, semester after semester. Imagine, too, the increased likelihood that someone will make a data entry mistake.

Second, each time the information in the list changes, multiple lists must be updated. If Mei Zhang moves, her data will need to be updated in all the lists that contain her address. It would be easy to overlook one or more lists or even one or more rows in the same list. This would lead to a state of **data inconsistency**. It would not be possible to tell easily which data was correct. In addition,

Figure 11.3

(a) A class registration list and (b) a list of residence hall assignments are two lists a college might create to keep track of student information.

a

Class Registration List - Spring Semester

SID #	Last Name	First Name	Home Address	City	State	Zip Code	Class Code	Class Name	# Of Credits	Meal Plan #
123456789	Finkel	Susan	645 Pine Street	Philadelphia	PA	19102-5674	CIS 110	Computer Literacy	3	1
123456789	Finkel	Susan	645 Pine Street	Philadelphia	PA	19102-5674	ENG 101	English Comp 1	3	1
123456789	Finkel	Susan	645 Pine Street	Philadelphia	PA	19102-5674	HIS 103	Western Civ 1	3	1
123456789	Finkel	Susan	645 Pine Street	Philadelphia	PA	19102-5674	CHE 140	Chemistry	4	1
123456789	Finkel	Susan	646 Pine Street	Philadelphia	PA	19102-5674	PSY 101	Intro to Psychology	3	1
789123456	Garza	Julio	421 West 3rd St	New Witten	SD	57584-1234	CIS 110	Computer Literacy	3	1
789123456	Garza	Julio	421 West 3rd St	New Witten	SD	57584-1234	SOC 101	Intro to Sociology	3	1
789123456	Garza	Julio	421 West 3rd St	New Witten	SD	57584-1234	PSY 101	Intro to Psych	3	1
678912345	O'Connor	Leanne	238 Grant Street	Beverly	MA	01915-4333				
567891234	Stinson	Arthur	345 Ryan Drive	Cedar Falls	IA	50613-3232	BIO 210	Anatomy & Physiology 1	3	3
567891234	Stinson	Arthur	345 Ryan Drive	Cedar Falls	IA	50613-3232	ENG 101	English Comp 1	3	3
567891234	Stinson	Arthur	345 Ryan Drive	Cedar Falls	IA	50613-3232	SOC 101	Intro to Sociology	3	3
456789123	Zhang	Mei	457 Blanchard St	Boston	MA	01901-3424	PSY 101	Intro to Psychology	3	2
456789123	Zhang	Mei	457 Blanchard St	Boston	MA	01901-3424	HIS 103	Western Civ 1	3	2
456789123	Zhang	Mei	457 Blanchard St	Boston	MA	01901-3424	ENG 102	English Comp 2	3	2

b

Residence Hall Assignment List - Fall

SID #	Last Name	First Name	Home Address	City	State	Zip Code	Residence Hall Name	Room Number
123456789	Finkel	Susan	645 Pine Street	Philadelphia	PA	19102-5674	Founder's Hall	303
789123456	Garza	Julio	421 West 3rd St	New Witten	SD	57584-1234	Bauer Hall	121
678912345	O'Connor	Leanne	238 Grant Street	Beverly	MA	01915-4333	Bauer Hall	214
567891234	Stinson	Arthur	345 Ryan Drive	Cedar Falls	IA	50613-3232	Berger Quad	317
456789123	Zhang	Mei	457 Blanchard St	Boston	MA	98107-4356	Mission	223

notice that Susan Finkel's last record in Figure 11.3a contains a different street address than that shown in her other records. It's impossible to tell which address is correct, again resulting in data inconsistency.

In addition, correct data can be entered into a list but in an inconsistent format. Look at students Julio Garza and Mei Zhang in Figure 11.3a. Both are registered for PSY 101, but two different course names appear: Intro to Psychology and Intro to Psych. Are these the same course? Which name is the correct one? Confusion arises when data is inconsistently entered. Establishing data consistency is difficult to do with a list.

Aside from data redundancy and inconsistency, are there any other problems with using lists instead of databases? What if someone accidentally entered Arthur Stinson's enrollment data twice in the list in Figure 11.3a? Any reports (such as student bills) that are generated based on this list will be inaccurate because of the duplicate data. For example, Arthur would be sent two separate bills for his classes, resulting in confusion and headaches.

In Figure 11.3a, each student has selected one of the college's meal plans, and this data must be entered into each row. What if someone enters a nonexistent meal plan in one of the rows pertaining to Susan Finkel? This is not only wrong, but also can be confusing to anyone viewing the list. With a list, anything can be entered in a row or column, even if that information is incorrect.

In addition, information can be organized in many ways. Consider the list of residence hall assignments in Figure 11.3b, which is organized alphabetically by last name. This works well for the accounting clerk, who needs to generate bills for student housing. However, for the residence manager who wants to see which residence hall rooms are still vacant, it would be more useful to have the data organized by residence hall and room number. Reorganizing multiple lists in this way can be labor intensive.

A final problem with lists is how to handle incomplete data. In Figure 11.3a, Leanne O'Connor has enrolled in the college but has not yet selected a meal plan or registered for courses. Her known information has been entered, but it's impossible to tell by looking at her record whether data relating to her course registrations and meal plans is available and just was not entered, or is truly missing.

Can't I just exercise caution and set rules for updating lists? Carefully following the rules when you update a list like the ones shown in Figure 11.3 can address many of the problems mentioned, but there is still room for error. Being careful does not avoid the most pressing problems of lists: (1) the inability of the data to be shared and (2) data redundancy. Even if you could surmount all of these problems, you cannot easily change a list to accommodate the disparate needs of many users.

How can I solve the problems associated with lists? For single topics, a list is sufficient. However, for any complex data that needs to be organized or shared, using a database is the most practical and efficient way to avoid the pitfalls associated with using lists.

Database Building Blocks

Almost any kind of data that needs organization and analysis can be put into a database. For example, eBay keeps track of the millions of items that users have for sale in a searchable database enabling you to find that used iPad you want to purchase. Media providers such as Netflix, which rents DVDs and streams video content to consumers, store subscribers' mailing addresses and payment information in a database. In this section, we explore the advantages of using databases as well as the terminology databases use to categorize data.

Advantages of Using Databases

How do databases make our lives easier? Without databases, you could not store and retrieve large quantities of information easily. Consider airline reservation systems. Thousands of people fly across the United States on any given day. Without a database, it would be extremely difficult to keep track of such a large number of airline reservations. In addition, although you can look up information fairly quickly in a list, even extremely large electronic databases can provide the information you request in seconds. Databases provide three main advantages: They enable information sharing, they promote data integrity, and they allow the flexible use of data.

How do databases make information sharing possible? Consider student records at a college. As noted earlier, without databases, financial aid, admissions, and student housing would all need their own student lists (files). The information in these lists might not match because each department would maintain its own records. If a change had to be made in a student's address, all three lists (the financial aid file, the admissions file, and the student housing file) would have to be changed.

As shown in Figure 11.4, with a database only one file is maintained, which reduces the possibility of errors when data is entered or updated. It also increases efficiency, because there are no files to reconcile with each other. A database therefore provides for data centralization. There is no need for multiple lists. Each department that needs to use student information accesses it from the same set of data.

How do databases promote data integrity? **Data integrity** means that the data contained in the database is accurate and reliable. **Data centralization** goes a long way toward ensuring data integrity. Instead of being in multiple lists that have to be maintained, your name and address information is maintained in only one place. If you move, your address must be changed only once.

How do databases provide flexibility? Another significant advantage of databases is that they are flexibly organized, enabling you to reorganize the information they contain in a variety of ways to suit the needs of the moment. Think back to the earlier example regarding lists. The registrar and housing manager need to see different information. With a list, you can organize information in only one way. If information is in a database, the registrar can easily view just the information she needs (such as the courses the student is taking). Likewise, the housing manager can easily view just the information he needs (such as the residence hall to which the student is assigned).

Data flexibility also makes information dissemination tasks easier. Suppose your school wants to send out a mailing about a new course to all business majors. Having the contact information of students available in a database makes it easy to merge the data, using an application such as Microsoft Word, and create personalized letters and address labels. Obviously, this would be much faster than generating these items manually, and the results should contain fewer errors. Thus, databases can manage larger amounts of data and process that data more efficiently.

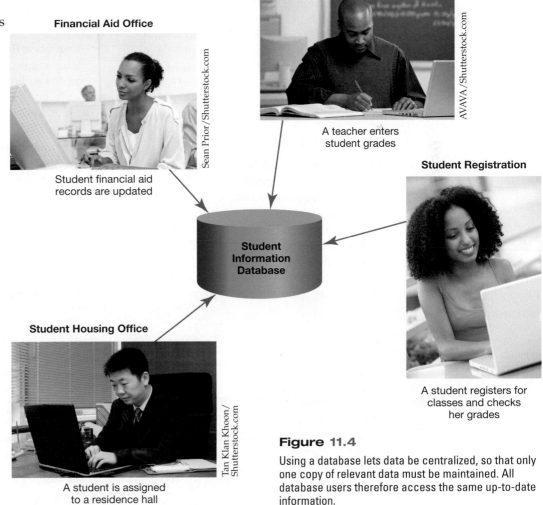

Financial Aid Office

Student financial aid records are updated

Sean Prior/Shutterstock.com

A teacher enters student grades

AVAVA/Shutterstock.com

Student Registration

A student registers for classes and checks her grades

Monkey Business Images/Shutterstock.com

Student Housing Office

A student is assigned to a residence hall

Tan Klan Khoon/Shutterstock.com

Student Information Database

Figure 11.4

Using a database lets data be centralized, so that only one copy of relevant data must be maintained. All database users therefore access the same up-to-date information.

Are there any disadvantages associated with databases? Databases are more complex to construct and administer than lists. They also can be time-consuming and expensive to set up. Great care must be exercised in the design of databases to ensure they will function as intended. Although average individuals can design small databases, it is helpful to have an experienced **database administrator** (or **database designer**), an individual trained in the design and building of databases, to assist with the construction of large databases.

Data privacy concerns also arise when using databases. Think about how much information you've provided to your school. The school probably has records of your Social Security number, birth date, address, and credit card information. These are things an identity thief would love to get their hands on. For this reason, many colleges and universities no longer use Social Security numbers as student identification (ID) numbers. Instead, they create a unique student ID number when you register, which helps protect your Social Security number from falling into the wrong hands. Despite the increased complexity of databases and the issues surrounding privacy, however, the advantages of databases far outweigh the administrative disadvantages.

Database Terminology

How is data stored in a database? Understanding how databases store information requires knowing the unique terminology developed to describe databases. As shown in Figure 11.5, databases have three main components: fields, records, and tables (or files).

Fields

What is a field? A database stores each category of information in a **field**. Fields are displayed in columns. The city where a student lives can be found in the City field in the student information table shown in Figure 11.5. Each field is identified by a **field name**, which is a way of describing the field. Zip Code is a field name in the database in Figure 11.5. In a database, fields have other characteristics to describe them, including field data types and field size.

What are data types? When fields are created in the database, the user assigns those fields a **data type** (or **field type**). The data type indicates what type of data can be stored in the field.

Common data types are listed with examples in Figure 11.6 and are described in the remainder of this section.

- A **text field** can hold any combination of alphanumeric data (letters or numbers), but is most often used to hold words. Although text fields can contain numbers (such as telephone numbers), they are stored as text and therefore cannot be used in calculations.

- A **numeric field** stores numbers. Unlike values in text fields, values in numeric fields can be used to perform calculations. For instance, the numbers stored in numeric fields can be used to calculate tuition owed.

- A **computational field** (or **calculated field**) is a numeric field that stores the contents of a calculation, which is generated with a formula in the numeric field. This is similar to a formula computation in a spreadsheet cell.

- A **date/time field** holds data such as birthdays and due dates.

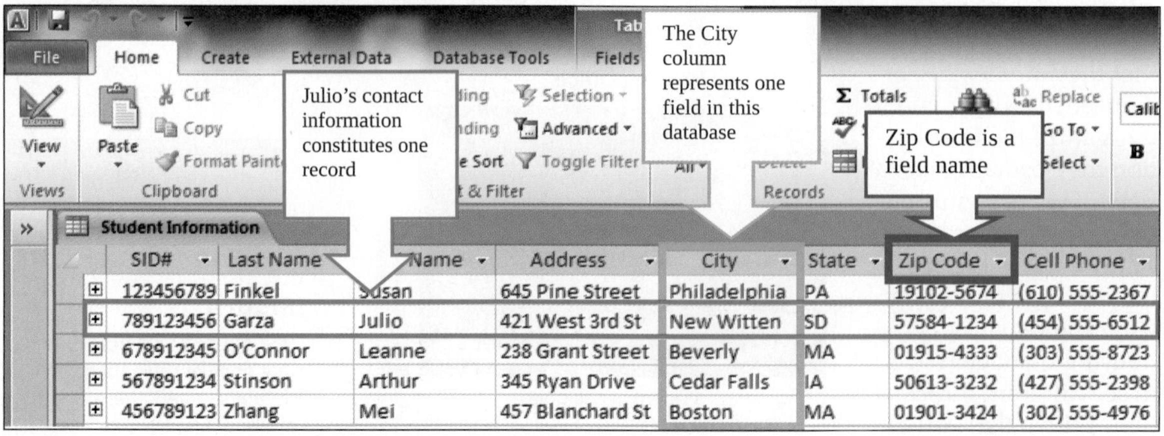

Figure 11.5

In a database, a category of information is stored in a field. A group of related fields is called a record, and a group of related records is called a table (or file).

Figure 11.6 | COMMON DATA TYPES AND SAMPLE DATA

Data Type	Used to Store	Examples
Text	Alphabetic or alphanumeric data	Cecilia PSY 101
Numeric	Numbers	512 1.789 $1,230
Calculated	Computational formulas	Credit hours × per-credit tuition charges
Date/Time	Dates and times in standard notation	2/21/2016; 10:48
Memo	Long blocks of text	Four score and seven years ago our fathers brought forth on this continent, a new nation, conceived in Liberty, and dedicated to the proposition that all men are created equal.
Object	Multimedia files or documents	MP3 file AVI file
Hyperlink	A hyperlink to a Web page	www.pearsonhighered.com/techinaction

- A **memo field** is like a text field but can hold long pieces of text. For example, a paragraph describing your high school achievements could be stored in a memo field.
- An **object field** holds items such as pictures, video clips, or documents.
- A **hyperlink field** stores hyperlinks to Web pages.

What is meant by field size? Field size defines the maximum number of characters or numbers that a field can hold. If a numeric field has a size of 5, it can hold a number as high as 99999. As a rule, you should tailor the field size to the length of the data it contains. If you define a field size of 50, space is reserved for 50 characters in that field, whether or not all 50 characters are used. Therefore, if you know that a character field will have a maximum of two characters, defining the field size as 50 wastes space and makes the files unnecessarily large. This can cause decreased database performance, especially in large databases.

Records and Tables

What are records and tables in databases? A group of related fields is called a **record**. For example, a student's name, address, and telephone number comprise a record. A group of related records is called a **table** (or **file**). A database file can contain multiple tables. Tables usually are organized by a common subject. Figure 11.5 shows a table that contains records representing contact information for students.

Primary Keys

Can fields have the same values in the same table? Yes, they can. It is possible that two students may live in the same town or have the same last name. However, to keep records distinct, each record must have one field that has a value unique to that record. This unique field is called a **primary key** or a **key field**. For example, as shown in Figure 11.7, in student records, the primary key is the student ID number (field name SID#). Establishing a primary

Figure 11.7

Unique student ID numbers make ideal primary keys, because even students with the same name won't have the same ID number.

SID#	Last Name	First Name	Address	City	State	Zip Code
123456789	Finkel	Susan	645 Pine Street	Philadelphia	PA	19102-5674
345678912	Garza	Julio	32 Owen Ave	Lansdowne	PA	19050-3423
789123456	Garza	Julio	421 West 3rd St	New Witten	SD	57584-1234
678912345	O'Connor	Leanne	238 Grant Street	Beverly	MA	01915-4333
567891234	Stinson	Arthur	345 Ryan Drive			50613-3232
456789123	Zhang	Mei	457 Blanchard St			01901-3424

Same name, different primary keys

Music Database Helps You Find New Music

You probably have hundreds of songs that you listen to regularly. Wouldn't it be great if you could receive music recommendations based on the common attributes of music you already enjoy, instead of random comments from your friends or less reliable data such as buying patterns? Many Internet radio offerings, such as Last.fm (accessible through Xbox Live, smartphones, and the Web) and Pandora are designed to work this way.

The Music Genome Project provides such recommendations by analyzing songs and categorizing them in a database according to almost 400 different attributes, such as "breathy female lead vocalist" or "club rap roots." Pandora Internet Radio (**pandora.com**) currently uses the Music Genome Project to provide music to listeners based on their music preferences.

With Pandora, you can create radio stations that play music based on facts you provide, called seeds. Seeds can be either song titles or the names of musical artists (see Figure 11.8). So, if you enjoy music from The Black Eyed Peas or like the song "Rolling in the Deep" (by Adele), you would enter these as seeds for a Pandora station. Pandora then would play music with attributes similar to the seeds you provided. You can't control which songs will play, because they are served up randomly, but they will likely be songs you will enjoy, even if you have never heard them before.

Figure 11.8

Bloomberg via Getty Images

A Pandora radio "station" can be set up based on a seed for your favorite musical group.

key and ensuring that it is unique makes it impossible to duplicate records.

What makes a good primary key? We already have many numbers that follow us through our lives that make excellent primary keys. In the past, Social Security numbers were often selected as primary keys in databases containing data about individuals. As mentioned previously, concerns about identity theft have led many businesses to abandon Social Security numbers as the primary means of identifying individuals. Driver's license numbers are unique within a particular state, as are the license plate numbers on cars. State government agencies often use these numbers to track individuals and their transactions.

Primary keys don't have to be numbers that already represent something. For example, when you place an order with Amazon.com, your transaction gets a unique order number. This number is the Amazon database's primary key. You refer to this number when checking your order status, returning merchandise, and so on. It is essential to have a unique number for each order because it would be difficult to keep track of it without one.

Database Types

Many different types of electronic databases have been used since the invention of the computer. The three major types of databases currently in use are relational, object-oriented, and multidimensional. Of these three, relational databases have the largest market share, but the market share of multidimensional databases is growing at a fast pace.

Relational Databases

What is a relational database? A **relational database** organizes data in table format by logically grouping similar data into a **relation** (a table that contains related data). As discussed earlier, each record in a database table is assigned a primary key to ensure that the record is unique. In relational databases, tables are logically linked to each other by including their primary keys in other tables with related information.

For example, at your college, a database about students would have a table with student contact information (name, address, and phone number) and another table with class registration information (class number and class name). These two tables would be linked by a common field such as a student ID number.

Who invented the relational database? E. F. Codd first significantly defined the relational model in 1970. Since then, much research and development has been done on the relational database model, and the model has proven to be extremely reliable for storing and manipulating data.

Object-Oriented Databases

What is an object-oriented database? An **object-oriented database** stores data in objects, rather than in tables. The models on which these databases are constructed evolved from the object-oriented programming paradigm, discussed in Chapter 10, which caught on in the programming community in the late 1980s. Objects contain not only data, but also methods for processing or manipulating that data. This allows object-oriented databases to store more types of data than relational databases and to access that data faster.

For example, a "student" object that contains data about the courses a student is taking might also store the instructions for generating a bill for the student based on his or her course load. Because object-oriented databases store the instructions for doing computations in the same place as they store the data, they can usually process requests for information faster than can relational databases (which would only store the student information).

Why would I use an object-oriented database? Whereas relational databases excel in the storage of **structured (analytical) data** (such as "Bill" or "345"), object-oriented databases are more adept at handling unstructured data. **Unstructured data** includes nontraditional data such as audio clips (including MP3 files), video clips, pictures, and extremely large documents. Data of this type is known as a **binary large object (BLOB)** because it is actually encoded in binary form.

Object-oriented databases are based on complex models for manipulating data. These models are much more complex than relational database models. Because businesses today need to store a greater variety of data, object-oriented databases are becoming more popular. Many relational database systems have been expanded to include object-oriented components. For a business to use its data in an object-oriented database, it needs to undergo a costly conversion process. However, once this initial cost is overcome, the faster access and reusability of the database objects can provide advantages for large businesses.

Object-oriented databases also need to use a query language to access and manage data. A **query language** is a specially designed computer language that is used to manipulate data in or extract data from a database. Many object-oriented databases use **Object Query Language (OQL)**, which is similar in many respects to **SQL (Structured Query Language)**, a standard language used to construct queries to extract data from databases.

ACTIVE HELP-DESK

Understanding Database Management Systems

In this Active Helpdesk call, you'll play the role of a helpdesk staffer, fielding calls about database management systems, what they do, and how people can use them.

Multidimensional Databases

What is a multidimensional database? A **multidimensional database** stores data in more than two dimensions. This distinguishes it from a relational database, which stores data in two-dimensional tables. Multidimensional databases organize data in a cube format. Each data cube has a *measure attribute*, which is the main type of data that the cube is tracking. Other elements of the cube are known as *feature attributes*, which all describe the measure attribute in some meaningful way. For example, sales of automobiles (measure attribute) could be categorized by various dimensions such as region, automobile color, automobile model, time period (such as current month), or salesperson—all feature attributes (see Figure 11.9). In addition, the database could be constructed to define different levels within a particular feature attribute (such as state and town within a region).

What are the advantages of multidimensional databases? The two main advantages of multidimensional databases are that they can easily be

Figure 11.9

Multidimensional databases describe data in at least three dimensions.

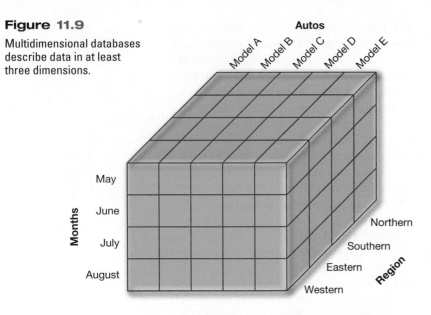

customized to provide information to a variety of users (based on their need), and they can process data much faster than pure relational databases can. The need for processing speed is especially critical when deploying a large database that will be accessed via the Internet. Therefore, large databases such as eBay that are accessed by many users needing to view data in different ways are usually designed as multidimensional databases. Oracle Corporation has slowly morphed its tried-and-true relational database into a multidimensional database in response to customer demand. This was primarily in response to customers who were using an Oracle database for applications deployed on the Web and needed better ways of storing and accessing image, audio, and video files. With multidimensional databases such as the current Oracle Database 11g, businesses do not have to abandon the proven relational database model, because multidimensional databases are based on proven relational database theory.

Database Management Systems: Basic Operations

Databases are created and managed using a **database management system (DBMS)**. A DBMS is specially designed application software (such as Oracle Database or Microsoft Access) that interacts with the user, other applications, and the database to capture and analyze data. The four main operations of a DBMS are

1. Creating databases and entering data
2. Viewing (or browsing) and sorting data
3. Querying (extracting) data
4. Outputting data

In the next sections, we look at each of these operations in detail.

Creating Databases and Entering Data

How do I create a database with a DBMS? To create a database with a DBMS, you must first define the data to be captured. Therefore, you must create a description of the data. This description is contained in the database's files and is referred to as the **data dictionary** or the **database schema**. The data dictionary defines the name, data type, and length of each field in the database. Describing the data helps to categorize and analyze it and sets parameters for entering valid data into the database (such as a 10-digit number in a phone number field).

How do I know what fields are needed in my database? Careful planning is required to identify each distinct piece of data you need to capture. Each field should describe a unique piece of data and should never combine two separate pieces of data.

For example, for student registration at a college, capturing the student's name, street address, city, state, and zip code is important. But should a student's name be placed in one field or two? Because first and last names are separate pieces of data, you would want to create a separate field for each. For instance, suppose you wish to send an e-mail message to students addressing all of them by their first names (such as "Dear Geri"). If Geri's first and last names are in the same field in the database, it will be difficult to extract just her first name for the salutation.

What does a data dictionary look like, and how do I create one? In Microsoft Access, the data dictionary is called the Field Properties box. Figure 11.10a shows the Field Properties box for a database table in Access. The first step in creating an entry in the data dictionary is to create a field name. Field names must be unique within a table. In the table in

Figure 11.10a, the field name StateAbbreviation is used to store the abbreviation for the state where the student lives.

Second, you must define a data type for each field. For the StateAbbreviation field, you use a text data type because state abbreviations are expressed using characters. Third, you should set a maximum field size (in this case, two characters) for the field. Data in the field can be shorter than the maximum but can never exceed it. Sometimes the field name may not be meaningful to the user of the database even though it makes sense to the designer. The Caption value in Microsoft Access allows you to display a name of your choice on forms and reports.

Finally, you can set a **default value** for a field. A default value is the value the database uses for the field unless the user enters another value. Though not appropriate for first names, because they vary widely, default values are useful for field data that is frequently the same. For example, setting a default value for a state field saves users from having to enter it for each student if most students live in one state.

You need to repeat these steps for each field in the table. When completed, the resulting Student Information table, shown in Figure 11.10b, is ready for data entry.

The attributes, such as data type and field size, shown in Figure 11.10a are **metadata**: data that describes other data. Metadata is an integral part of the data dictionary. You need to build the data dictionary for each table you will use in a database before you enter data into the database. This also has the benefit of forcing you to consider up front the data you need to capture and the metadata that describes it.

What happens if I forget to define a field in the data dictionary or if I want to add another one later? Databases are extremely flexible. You can add fields as needed, but this does not negate the need for proper planning and design of a database. You will need to populate (enter data into) any new fields that are added to your database. This could be difficult if you suddenly need to add a field for birth dates to a database that already

contains records for 10,000 individuals. If you plan to use this field to analyze the data, you need to have a plan for accumulating birth dates to ensure the completeness of the data.

Inputting Data

How do I get data into the database?
After you create a data dictionary for each table (or file) in the database and establish the fields you want the database to contain, you can begin creating individual records in the database. There's an old-fashioned way to get data into these records: you can key it directly into the database. However, today, a great deal of data already exists in some type of electronic format, such as word processing documents and spreadsheets. Fortunately, most databases can import data electronically from other application files, which can save an enormous amount of keying.

When importing data, most databases usually apply filters to the data to determine that it is in the correct format as defined by the data dictionary. Nonconforming data is flagged (either on-screen or in a report) so that you can modify the data to fit the database's format.

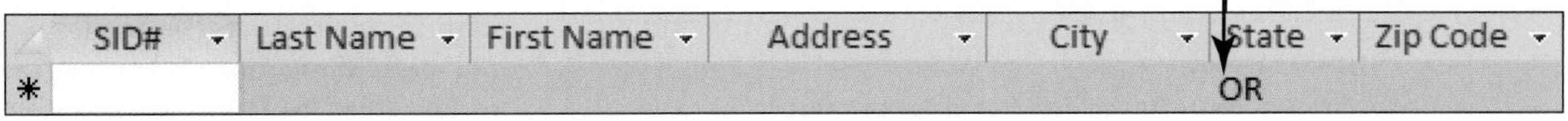

Figure 11.10

(a) The Field Properties box, shown for the Student Information table in an Access database, represents the database's data dictionary. (b) The Student Information table, ready for data input, results from setting up the data dictionary in Figure 11.10a.

a

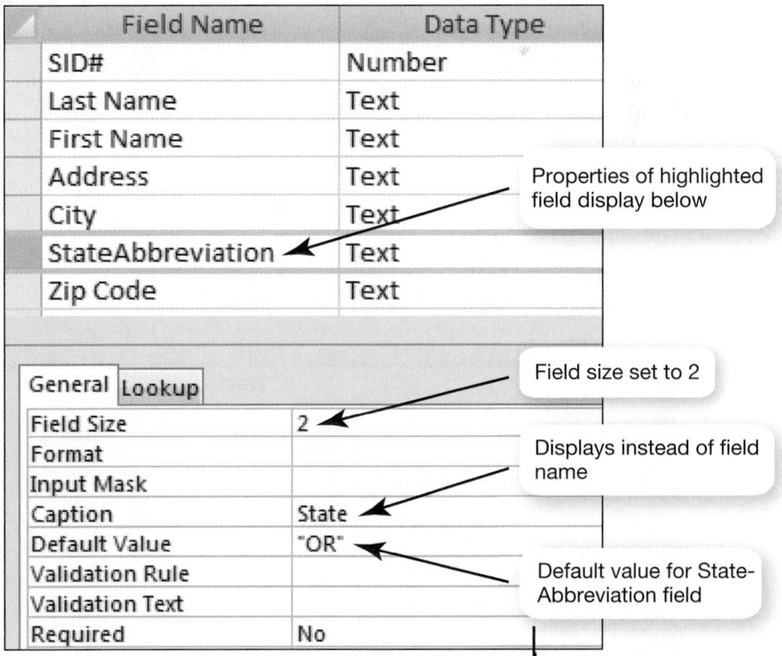

Field Name	Data Type
SID#	Number
Last Name	Text
First Name	Text
Address	Text
City	Text
StateAbbreviation	Text
Zip Code	Text

Properties of highlighted field display below

General	Lookup
Field Size	2
Format	
Input Mask	
Caption	State
Default Value	"OR"
Validation Rule	
Validation Text	
Required	No

Field size set to 2

Displays instead of field name

Default value for StateAbbreviation field

b

SID#	Last Name	First Name	Address	City	State	Zip Code
*					OR	

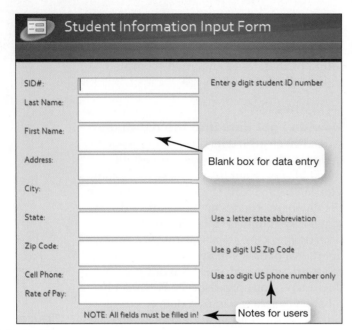

Student Information Input Form

SID#: [blank] — Enter 9 digit student ID number

Last Name: [blank]

First Name: [blank]

Address: [blank] — Blank box for data entry

City: [blank]

State: [blank] — Use 2 letter state abbreviation

Zip Code: [blank] — Use 9 digit US Zip Code

Cell Phone: [blank] — Use 10 digit US phone number only

Rate of Pay: [blank]

NOTE: All fields must be filled in! — Notes for users

Figure 11.11

The input form used for entering data into the Student Information table.

How can I make manual entry into a database more convenient? For small databases, or databases in which no electronic information is to be imported, you can create an input form to speed data entry. An **input form** provides a view of the data fields to be filled, with appropriate labels to assist database users in populating the database. Figure 11.11 shows an example of an input form for the Student Information table shown

Student Information	
Field Name	**Data Type**
SID#	Number
Last Name	Text
First Name	Text
Address	Text
City	Text
State	Text
Zip Code	Text
Cell Phone	Text
Rate of Pay	Currency

Error message displayed if invalid data is entered — Field Properties

Validation rule restricts entries

General	
Format	
Decimal Places	2
Input Mask	
Caption	
Default Value	
Validation Rule	>=7.25 And <=20
Validation Text	Enter pay rate at least $7.25 and <= $20
Required	No

Figure 11.12

A validation rule set to restrict rates of pay to a certain range.

in Figure 11.12. Each field has a label that indicates the data to be placed in the field. The data is represented by blank boxes. Notes have been added to the form to guide the users.

Data Validation

How can I ensure that only valid data is entered into the database? One feature of most DBMSs is the capability to perform data validation. **Validation** is the process of ensuring that data entered into the database is correct (or at least reasonable) and complete. When you registered for college, for example, the admissions clerk most likely asked you for your phone number. A phone number in the United States usually comprises 10 digits formatted in the following fashion: (610) 555-1234. A **validation rule** is set up in the student database to alert the user if a clearly wrong entry, such as "#^#-&*%-#@#&," "(Har) ryJ-ones," or "4567," is entered in the phone number field instead of a valid 10-digit phone number.

Validation rules are generally defined as part of the data dictionary. Violations of validation rules usually result in an error message being displayed on the screen so that the error can be addressed. Common types of validation checks include range, completeness, consistency, and alphabetic and numeric checks.

How does a range check work? A **range check** ensures that the data entered into the database falls within a certain range of numbers. For instance, rates of pay for student jobs usually fall within a certain range. Therefore, for a student pay rate field, you could set a **field constraint** (a property that must be satisfied for an entry to be accepted into the field) to restrict pay rates to a range you define.

Figure 11.12 shows how you set up a range check in a data dictionary (in the Field Properties box) for an Access database. A validation rule restricts the entries for the Rate of Pay field to amounts between $7.25 (minimum rate of pay) and $20.00 (the maximum rate of pay for students at the college). If users tried to enter a rate of pay less than $7.25 or greater than $20.00, they would be notified of an invalid range error, and the input would not be accepted.

What does a completeness check accomplish? If you have ever bought anything online, you have probably encountered error messages generated by completeness checks. In database systems, fields can be defined as "required," meaning data must be entered into them. A **completeness check**, such as the one shown in Figure 11.13, ensures that all fields defined as required have data entered into them. When a user submits this form, the database performs a completeness check and, in this case, notices that the required "First Name" field was left blank. An error message then displays to alert the user of the omission.

What is the function of a consistency check? A **consistency check** compares the values of data in two or more fields to see if these values are reasonable. For example, your birth date and the date you enrolled in school are often in a college's database. It is not possible for you to have enrolled in college before you were born. Further, most college students are at least 16 years old. Therefore, a consistency check on these fields might ensure that your birth date is at least 16 or more years before the date when you enrolled in college.

How are alphabetic and numeric checks used? You may want to restrict fields to only alphabetic or numerical data (such as for names and student ID numbers). An **alphabetic check** confirms that only textual characters (such as "Robin") are entered in a field. A **numeric check** confirms that only numbers are entered in the field. With these checks in place, "$J2.5n" would not be accepted as the price of a product or a first name. Figure 11.14 shows how you can set such checks and custom error messages in Access.

The field properties for the State field in Access is shown in Figure 11.14. The expression Like "??" tells Access to restrict entries for the State field to two alphabetic characters. Selecting "Yes" for the required attribute means that Access will not allow the field to be left blank. Error messages that display when validation checks fail can be customized by the user.

Viewing and Sorting Data

How can I view the data in a database? Displaying the tables on-screen and **browsing** through the data (viewing

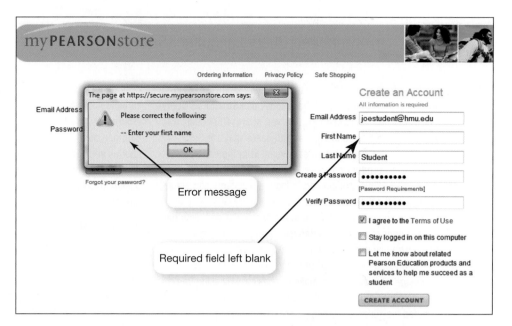

Figure 11.13

A database completeness check, like this one shown for myPearsonStore, ensures that all fields defined as required have data in them.

Field Name	Data Type	
SID#	Number	
Last Name	Text	
First Name	Text	
Address	Text	
City	Text	
State	Text	
Zip Code	Text	
Cell Phone	Text	
Rate of Pay	Currency	

Validation rule requires alpha characters

General	Lookup	
Field Size	2
Format	
Input Mask	
Caption	
Default Value	"OR"
Validation Rule	Like "??"
Validation Text	Please enter a valid two letter state abbreviation
Required	Yes
Allow Zero Length	Yes
Indexed	No

Error message for invalid entry

Field must contain data

Figure 11.14

An alphabetic check and a completeness check for the State field in an Access database.

To extract records from a database, you use a query language. Almost all relational and object-oriented databases today use Structured Query Language, or SQL. Oracle, Microsoft SQL Server, Microsoft Access, IBM DB2, and MySQL are examples of popular databases that use SQL.

When relational databases were first developed in the early 1970s, each DBMS software product contained its own query language. This meant that database administrators had to learn a new language whenever they worked with a different DBMS. The early query languages were mathematically based and often difficult to master. E. F. Codd, who has been called the father of relational databases, proposed a standardized query language when he worked at IBM in the mid-1970s.

The original language was called SEQUEL, short for *structured English query language*. The idea was to make queries easy by using English language–like sentence structure. Database software designers enthusiastically accepted the concept, developing a modified version of the original SEQUEL language, named SQL (pronounced "sequel"). Oracle first introduced SQL in a commercial database product in 1979. It has been the unofficial standard language for relational databases since then.

SQL uses relational algebra to extract data from databases. **Relational algebra** is the use of English-like expressions that have variables and operations, much like algebraic equations. Variables include table names, field names, or selection criteria for the data you wish to display.

Operations include directions such as *select* (which enables you to pick variable names), *from* (which tells the database which table to use), and *where* (which enables you to specify selection criteria). The two most common queries used to extract data using relational algebra are select queries and join queries.

A **select query** displays a subset of data from a table (or tables) based on the criteria you specify. A typical select query has the following format:

SELECT (Field Name 1, Field Name 2, ...)
FROM (Table Name)
WHERE (Selection Criteria)

The first line of the query contains variables for the field names you want to display. The FROM statement enables you to specify the table name from which the data will be retrieved. The last line (the WHERE statement) is used only when you wish to specify which records need to be displayed (such as all students with GPAs greater than 3.3). If you wish to display all the rows (records) in the table, then you do not use the WHERE statement. (See Figure 11.15.)

Suppose you want to create a cell phone list that includes all students from the Student Information table in Figure 11.15a. The SQL query you would send to the database would look like this:

a

	SID#	Last Name	First Name	Address	City	State	Zip Code	Cell Phone
⊞	123456789	Finkel	Susan	645 Pine Street	Philadelphia	PA	19102-5674	(610) 555-2367
⊞	789123456	Garza	Julio	421 West 3rd St	New Witten	SD	57584-1234	(454) 555-6512
⊞	678912345	O'Connor	Leanne	238 Grant Street	Beverly	MA	01915-4333	(303) 555-8723
⊞	567891234	Stinson	Arthur	345 Ryan Drive	Cedar Falls	IA	50613-3232	(427) 555-2398
⊞	456789123	Zhang	Mei	457 Blanchard St	Boston	MA	01901-3424	(302) 555-4976

Query applied to this table

SELECT (First Name, Last Name, Cell Phone)
FROM (Student Information Table)

Query applied to this table

SELECT (First Name, Last Name, Cell Phone)
FROM (Student Information Table)
WHERE (State = MA)

Produces this output

b

First Name	Last Name	Cell Phone
Susan	Finkel	(610) 555-2367
Mei	Zhang	(302) 555-4976
Arthur	Stinson	(427) 555-2398
Leanne	O'Connor	(303) 555-8723
Julio	Garza	(454) 555-6512

Produces this output

c

First Name	Last Name	Cell Phone
Leanne	O'Connor	(303) 555-8723
Mei	Zhang	(302) 555-4976

Figure 11.15

When the query on the left is applied to the (a) Student Information table, it restricts the output to (b) only a phone list. The query on the right, which uses a WHERE statement, further restricts the phone list to (c) only students from Massachusetts.

SELECT (First Name, Last Name, Cell Phone)
FROM (Student Information Table)

Figure 11.15b shows the output from this query.

What if you want a phone list that only shows students from Massachusetts? In that case, you would add a WHERE statement to the query as follows:

SELECT (First Name, Last Name, Cell Phone)
FROM (Student Information Table)
WHERE (State = MA)

This query restricts the output to students who live in Massachusetts, as shown in Figure 11.15c. Notice that the State field in the Student Information table can be used by the query (in this case, as a limiting criterion), but the contents of the State field are not required to be displayed in the query results. This explains why the output shown in Figure 11.15c doesn't show the State field.

When you want to extract data that is in two or more tables, you use a **join query**. The query actually links (or joins) the two tables using the common field in both tables and extracts the relevant data from each. The format for a simple join query for two tables is as follows:

SELECT (Field Name 1, Field Name 2)
FROM (Table 1 Name, Table 2 Name)
WHERE (Table 1 Name.Common Field Name = Table 2 Name.Common Field Name)
AND (Selection Criteria)

Notice how similar this is to a select query, although the FROM statement must now contain two table names. In a join query, the WHERE statement is split into two parts. In the first part (right after WHERE), the relation between the two tables is defined by identifying the common fields between the tables. The second part of the statement (after AND) is where the selection criteria are defined.

The AND means that both parts of the statement must be true for the query to produce results (i.e., the two related fields must exist and the selection criteria must be valid). Figure 11.16 illustrates using a join query for the Student Information and Roster Master tables to produce a class roster for students.

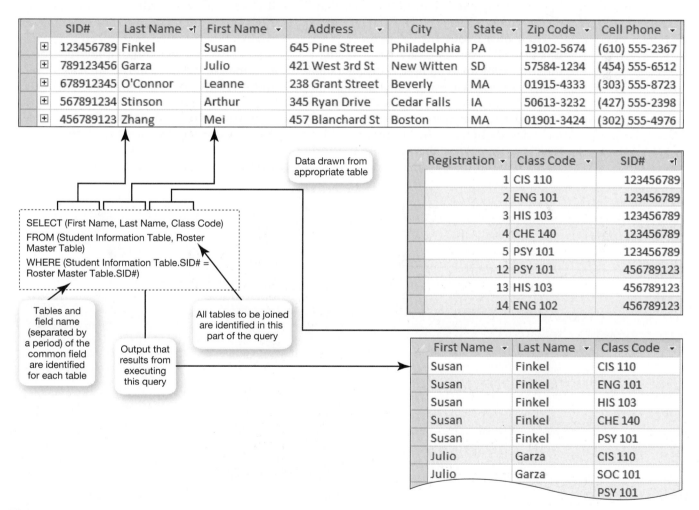

Figure 11.16

This join query will display a student roster for each student in the Student Information table. Notice that the WHERE statement creates the join by defining the common fields (in this case SID#) in each table.

records) is an option with most databases. In many instances you'll only want to view the data, not display the entire table. For example, if you want to register for an additional course for the current semester, the admissions clerk would browse the roster database to determine which courses you are already taking. However, browsing through a large database is time consuming unless the records are in an order that makes your task easy.

How can I reorder records in a database? You can easily **sort** a database into the order that you need. Sorting a database involves organizing it in a new fashion. Figure 11.17a shows an Access data table in which the records were input in no particular order. By highlighting a column (in this case Last Name) and then clicking the Sort Ascending button, the database displays the records in alphabetical order by last name, as shown in Figure 11.17b.

What if I want to find a particular piece of data in a database? Browsing records works for small databases, but if the amount of data you are managing is small, then you probably will just maintain it in a list anyway. To find data in a large database quickly and efficiently, you need to be able to request only the data you are seeking. Therefore, database management systems let you query the data to enable you to find what you're looking for.

Extracting or Querying Data

What is a query? A **query** is a question or inquiry. A **database query** is a question you ask the database so that it provides you with the records you wish to view. When you query a database, you instruct it to search for a particular piece of data, such as a student's grade point average (GPA). Queries also enable you to have the database select and display records that match certain criteria, such as all of the students who have GPAs of 3.3 or higher.

Is querying a database as simple as just asking the proper question? All modern DBMSs contain a query language that the software uses to retrieve

a

	SID#	Last Name	First Name	Address	City	State	Zip Code	Cell Phone
⊞	123456789	Finkel	Susan	645 Pine Street	Philadelphia	PA	19102-5674	(610) 555-2367
⊞	456789123	Zhang	Mei	457 Blanchard St	Boston	MA	01901-3424	(302) 555-4976
⊞	567891234	Stinson	Arthur	345 Ryan Drive	Cedar Falls	IA	50613-3232	(427) 555-2398
⊞	678912345	O'Connor	Leanne	238 Grant Street	Beverly	MA	01915-4333	(303) 555-8723
⊞	789123456	Garza	Julio	421 West 3rd St	New Witten	SD	57584-1234	(454) 555-6512

b

	SID#	Last Name	First Name	Address
⊞	123456789	Finkel	Susan	645 Pine Street
⊞	789123456	Garza	Julio	421 West 3rd St
⊞	678912345	O'Connor	Leanne	238 Grant Street
⊞	567891234	Stinson	Arthur	345 Ryan Drive
⊞	456789123	Zhang	Mei	457 Blanchard St

Figure 11.17

(a) Shown is an unsorted table. Notice that the Last Name column is selected (highlighted) for sorting. Selecting the sorting option "Ascending" produces the sorted output (b) with the records sorted in ascending alphabetical order by last name.

and display records. A query language consists of its own vocabulary and sentence structure, which you use to frame the requests. Query languages are similar to full-blown programming languages but are usually much easier to learn. The most popular query language today is Structured Query Language, or SQL.

Do I have to learn a query language to develop queries for my database? Modern database systems provide wizards (or other tools) to guide you through the process of creating queries. Figure 11.18 shows an example of an Access wizard being used to create a query. Highlighting an available field and then clicking the arrow button adds the field to the selected fields list. Selected fields display in the query. Highlighting a field on the selected fields list and clicking the back arrow removes the field from the list. The wizard speeds up the process of creating queries, and also removes the need to learn a query language.

The Query Wizard can be found on the Create tab, in the Queries group. Click Query Wizard and select Simple Query Wizard. When you use the Simple Query Wizard, you're actually using SQL commands without realizing it. The Simple Query Wizard takes the criteria you specify and creates the appropriate SQL commands behind the scenes.

However, you may want to create your own SQL queries in Access, modify existing queries at the SQL language level, or view the SQL code that the wizard created. To do so, open a query and select SQL View from the View drop-down box on the Home tab of the Ribbon. This displays the SQL code that makes up the query. Figure 11.19 shows the SQL code that the query in Figure 11.18 created.

Outputting Data

How do I get data out of a database? The most common form of

output for any database is a viewable (or printable) electronic report. Businesses routinely summarize the data within their databases and compile summary data reports. For instance, at the end of each semester your school generates a grade report for you that shows the classes you took and the grades you received.

Can I transfer data from a database to another software application? Database systems also can be used to **export** data to other applications. Exporting data involves putting it into an electronic file in a format that another application can understand. For example, the query shown in the wizard in Figure 11.18 may be used to generate a list of recipients for a form letter. In that case, the query output would be directed to a file that could be easily imported into Microsoft Word so that the data could be used in a mail merge process to generate letters.

Figure 11.18

(a) The Simple Query Wizard in Access displays all fields available in your table so that you can select the ones you need. (b) This information is displayed when you run the query defined in (a).

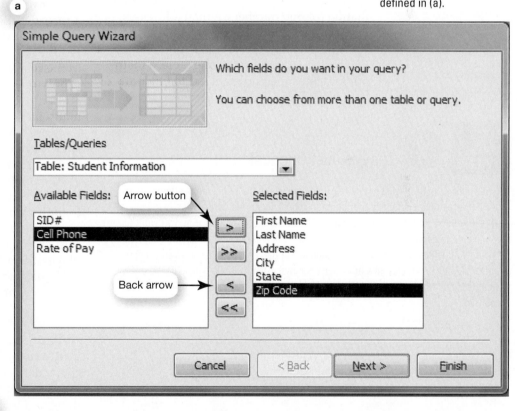

a

Simple Query Wizard

Which fields do you want in your query?

You can choose from more than one table or query.

Tables/Queries

Table: Student Information

Available Fields: Arrow button   Selected Fields:

SID#   First Name
Cell Phone   Last Name
Rate of Pay   Address
                                      City
         Back arrow   State
                                      Zip Code

Cancel   < Back   Next >   Finish

b

First Name	Last Name	Address	City	State	Zip Code
Susan	Finkel	645 Pine Street	Philadelphia	PA	19102-5674
Mei	Zhang	457 Blanchard St	Boston	MA	01901-3424
Arthur	Stinson	345 Ryan Drive	Cedar Falls	IA	50613-3232
Leanne	O'Connor	238 Grant Street	Beverly	MA	01915-4333
Julio	Garza	421 West 3rd St	New Witten	SD	57584-1234

```
SELECT [Student Information].[First Name], [Student Information].[Last Name], [Student
Information].[Address], [Student Information].[City], [Student Information].[State], [Student
Information].[Zip Code]
FROM [Student Information];
```

Figure 11.19

The SQL View window shows the SQL code that the wizard created for the query in Figure 11.18. Although it is a relatively simple SELECT statement, it is much easier to create with the wizard.

In the next section, we look at the operation of relational databases and explore how relationships are established among tables in these databases.

Relational Database Operations

As explained earlier, relational databases operate by organizing data into various tables based on logical groupings. For example, all student address and contact information (phone numbers, e-mail addresses, and so on) would be grouped into one table. Because not all of the data in a relational database is stored in the same table, a methodology must be implemented to link data between tables.

BITS AND BYTES

iTunes Smart Playlists— They're Just Queries!

Ever built a smart playlist in iTunes? If so, you've created a database query. iTunes is just a relational database that manages your media. A smart playlist (see Figure 11.20) allows you to define multiple criteria to create a playlist. Say you want all songs in the genre Rock, except for the artist P!nk and the album *Monkey Business*. When you define these criteria as "match all" in the smart playlist creation window, you will get a smart playlist that contains the music you want. You have built a query that tells iTunes exactly what music to extract from the database and include in your playlist.

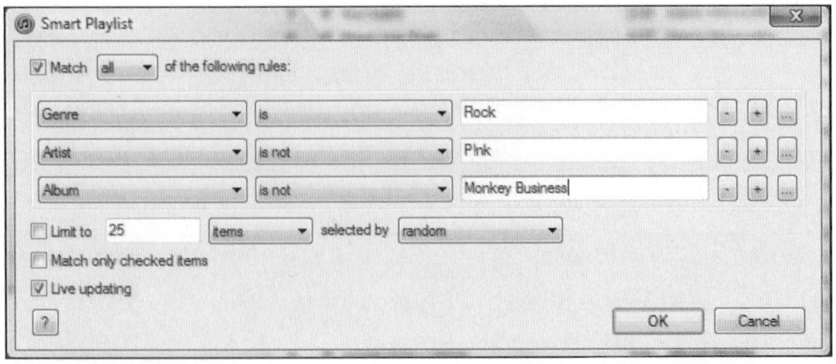

Screenshots © Apple Inc. Reprinted by permission from Apple Inc.

Figure 11.20

The iTunes Smart Playlist dialog box.

In relational databases, a link between tables that defines how the data is related is referred to as a **relationship**. To establish a relationship between two tables, both tables must have a common field (or column). Common fields contain the same data (such as student ID numbers), as shown in Figure 11.21. The fields do not have to have the same field name as long as they contain the same data.

Relationships in databases can take three forms: one-to-one, one-to-many, or many-to-many. A **one-to-one relationship** indicates that for each record in a table there is only one corresponding record in a related table. For example, a parking space can be occupied by only one car at a time, so a table that links assigned parking spaces to a table of faculty members (who are assigned parking spaces) would have a one-to-one relationship.

One-to-many relationships occur most frequently in relational databases. A **one-to-many relationship** is characterized by a record appearing only once in a table (such as the Student Information table in Figure 11.21) while appearing many times in the related Roster Master table. There is only one instance of a student ID in the Student Information table, but there can be many instances of the same student ID in the Roster Master table. Students can register for many classes, but each registration record can relate to only one student.

A **many-to-many relationship** is characterized by records in one table being related to multiple records in a second table and vice versa. For instance, a table of students could be related to a table of student employers. The employers could employ many students, and students could work for more than one employer.

Normalization of Data

How do I decide which tables I need and what data to put in them? You create database tables (or files) for two reasons: to hold unique data about a person or thing and to describe unique events or transactions. In databases, the goal is to reduce data redundancy by recording data only once. This process is called **normalization** of the data. Yet the tables must still work well enough together to enable you to retrieve the data when you need it. Tables should be grouped using logical data that can be identified uniquely.

Let's look at an example. In Figure 11.22, the Class Registration List—Spring Semester contains a great deal of data about individual students and their course registration. However, each table in a relational database should contain a related group of data on a single topic. There are two distinct topics in this list: student contact information and student registration information. Therefore, this list needs to be divided into two tables so that the distinct data (contact data and registration data) can be categorized appropriately. Data about each student is duplicated in this table. Normalizing the data eliminates this duplication.

The Student Information table in Figure 11.23 organizes all of the student contact information found in Figure 11.22 into a separate table. Notice that the information for each student needs to be shown only once, instead of multiple times (as in the list in Figure 11.22). The unique primary key for this table is the student's ID number. Student information might be needed in a variety of instances and by a variety of departments, but it needs to reside only in this one database table, which many departments of the school can share.

Student Information

	SID#	Last Name	First Name	Address	City
+	123456789	Finkel	Susan	645 Pine Street	Philadelphia
+	789123456	Garza	Julio	421 West 3rd St	New Witten
+	678912345	O'Connor	Leanne	238 Grant Street	Beverly
+	567891234	Stinson	Arthur	345 Ryan Drive	Cedar Falls
+	456789123	Zhang	Mei	457 Blanchard St	Boston

Common field in each table

Roster Master Table

Registration	Class Code	SID#
1	CIS 110	123456789
2	ENG 101	123456789
3	HIS 103	123456789
4	CHE 140	123456789
5	PSY 101	123456789
12	PSY 101	456789123
13	HIS 103	456789123
14	ENG 102	456789123

Figure 11.21

(a) The Student Information table and (b) the Roster Master table share the common field of student ID number. This allows a relationship to be established between the two tables.

Class Registration List - Spring Semester

SID #	Last Name	First Name	Home Address	City	State	Zip Code	Class Code	Class Name	# Of Credits
123456789	Finkel	Susan	645 Pine Street	Philadelphia	PA	19102-5674	CIS 110	Computer Literacy	3
123456789	Finkel	Susan	645 Pine Street	Philadelphia	PA	19102-5674	ENG 101	English Comp 1	3
123456789	Finkel	Susan	645 Pine Street	Philadelphia	PA	19102-5674	HIS 103	Western Civ 1	3
123456789	Finkel	Susan	645 Pine Street	Philadelphia	PA	19102-5674	CHE 140	Chemistry	4
123456789	Finkel	Susan	646 Pine Street	Philadelphia	PA	19102-5674	PSY 101	Intro to Psychology	3
789123456	Garza	Julio	421 West 3rd St	New Witten	SD	57584-1234	CIS 110	Computer Literacy	3
789123456	Garza	Julio	421 West 3rd St	New Witten	SD	57584-1234	SOC 101	Intro to Sociology	3
789123456	Garza	Julio	421 West 3rd St	New Witten	SD	57584-1234	PSY 101	Intro to Psych	3
678912345	O'Connor	Leanne	238 Grant Street	Beverly	MA	01915-4333			
567891234	Stinson	Arthur	345 Ryan Drive	Cedar Falls	IA	50613-3232	BIO 210	Anatomy & Physiology 1	3
567891234	Stinson	Arthur	345 Ryan Drive	Cedar Falls	IA	50613-3232	ENG 101	English Comp 1	3
567891234	Stinson	Arthur	345 Ryan Drive	Cedar Falls	IA	50613-3232	SOC 101	Intro to Sociology	3
456789123	Zhang	Mei	457 Blanchard St	Boston	MA	01901-3424	PSY 101	Intro to Psychology	3
456789123	Zhang	Mei	457 Blanchard St	Boston	MA	01901-3424	HIS 103	Western Civ 1	3
456789123	Zhang	Mei	457 Blanchard St	Boston	MA	01901-3424	ENG 102	English Comp 2	3

Figure 11.22

The column headings in yellow are related to student contact data, whereas the column headings in red relate to enrollment information. To construct an efficient database, these topics should be contained in separate tables.

Figure 11.23

Student contact data is grouped in the Student Information table and needs to be entered only once for each student. The primary key for each record is a unique student ID number.

SID#	Last Name	First Name	Address	City	State	Zip Code
123456789	Finkel	Susan	645 Pine Street	Philadelphia	PA	19102-5674
789123	[Primary Key] Julio		421 West 3rd St	New Witten	SD	57584-1234
678912		Leanne	238 Grant Street	Beverly	MA	01915-4333
567891234	Stinson	Arthur	345 Ryan Drive	Cedar Falls	IA	50613-3232
456789123	Zhang	Mei	457 Blanchard St	Boston	MA	01901-3424

Next, we could put the registration data found in Figure 11.22 for each student in a separate table, as shown in Figure 11.24. There is no need to repeat student name and address data in this table. Instead, each student can be identified by his or her student ID number. However, there are problems with this table. Each class name and class code has to be repeated for every student taking the course. Also,

SID#	Class Code	Class Name	Credits
123456789	CHE 140	Chemistry	4
123456789	CIS 110	Computer Literacy	3
123456789	ENG	English Comp 1	3
123456789	HIS	[SID# not unique] Western Civ 1	3
123456789	PSY 101	Intro to Psychology	3
456789123	ENG 102	English Comp 2	3
456789123	HIS 103	Western Civ 1	3
456789123	PSY 101	Intro to Psychology	3
567891234	BIO 210	Anatomy & Physiology 1	4
567891234	ENG 101	English Comp 1	3
567891234	SOC 101	Intro to Sociology	3
789123456	CIS 110	Computer Literacy	3

[Duplicate data]

Figure 11.24

Although it contains related data (registration information), this table still contains a great deal of duplicate data and no usable primary key.

Course Master Table

Class Code	Class Name	Credits
BIO 210	Anatomy & Physiology 1	4
CHE 140	Chemistry	4
CIS 110	Computer Literacy	3
ENG 101	English Comp 1	3
ENG 102	English Comp 2	3
HIS 103	Western Civ 1	3
PSY 101	Intro to Psychology	3
SOC 101	Intro to Sociology	3

Figure 11.25

Related information about courses (class code, class name, and the credits for the class) is grouped logically in one table. The unique class code is the primary key.

there is no unique field that can be used as a primary key for this table. SID# cannot be used because it will be entered on multiple records when a student enrolls in more than one course. This presents another opportunity to normalize the data further.

What can be done to fix the table in Figure 11.24? In Figure 11.24, we have identified more data that should be grouped logically into another separate table: class code and class name. Therefore, we should create another table for just this information. This enables us to avoid repeating class names and codes. Figure 11.25 shows the Course Master table. Note that the Class Code is unique for every course and acts as a primary key in this table.

To solve the other problems with the table in Figure 11.24, we need a way to identify uniquely each student registered for a specific course. This can be solved by creating a course registration code (number) that will be unique and assigned by the database as records are entered. Figure 11.26 shows the resulting Roster Master table. Only three fields are needed: the registration code number (the unique primary key), the class code, and the student's ID number. This approach greatly minimizes duplicate data.

How do I get the data in the tables to work together now that it is split up? The entire premise behind relational databases is that relationships

SOUND BYTE — Improving an Access 2010 Database

In this Sound Byte, you'll learn how to create input forms, queries, and reports to simplify maintenance of your CD and DVD database. You'll follow along step by step, using Microsoft Access wizards to create and modify queries to suit your needs.

are established among the tables to allow the data to be shared. As noted earlier, to establish a relationship between two tables, the tables must have a common field (column). This usually involves the primary keys of a table.

For instance, to track registrations by student in the Roster Master table in Figure 11.26, the student ID number is the logical piece of data to use. The student ID number is the primary key in the Student Information table in Figure 11.23; however, in the Roster Master table, the student ID number is called a **foreign key**—the primary key of another table that is included for purposes of establishing relationships with that other table. Figure 11.27 shows the relationships that exist among the Course Master, Roster Master, and Student Information tables. Join lines indicate established relationships between tables. Tables must contain fields with common data; this establishes relationships between them. Relationships among tables can be established whenever you need them if common data fields exist in the tables.

Because relationships are vital to the operation of the database, it is important to ensure that there are no inconsistencies in the data entered in the common fields of two tables. Each foreign key (SID# in the Roster Master table in Figure 11.26) entered into the table must be a valid primary key from the related table (SID# from the Student Information table in Figure 11.23).

For instance, if 392135684 is not a valid student ID number for any student listed in the Student Information table, then it should not be entered into the Roster Master table. Each entry in the Roster Master table must correspond to a student (linked by his or her SID#) in the Student Information table.

Roster Master Table		
Registration	Class Code	SID#
1	CIS 110	123456789
2	ENG 101	123456789
3	HIS 103	123456789
4	CHE 140	123456789
5	PSY 101	123456789
6	CIS 110	789123456
7	SOC 101	789123456
8	PSY 101	789123456
9	BIO 210	567891234
10	ENG 101	567891234
11	SOC 101	567891234
12	PSY 101	456789123
13	HIS 103	456789123
14	ENG 102	456789123

Figure 11.26

The Roster Master table shows only pertinent data related to a student's registration.

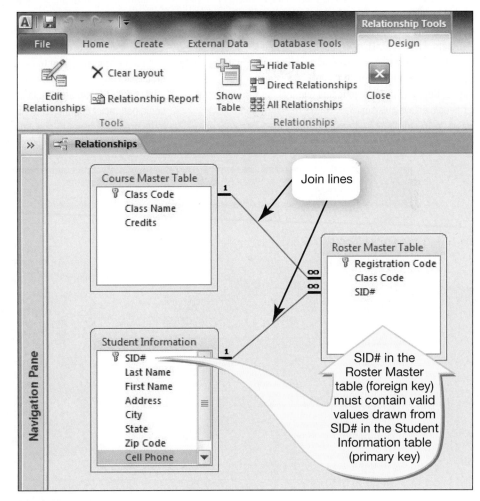

Figure 11.27

The Relationships screen in Microsoft Access visually represents the relationships established between tables.

Web 2.0 applications are mostly about enhancing communications and making it easy for users to create and disseminate their own content. So if you have a database that needs populating, why not seek help from the Web community to populate it, especially if it is designed as a resource for the masses.

The economy in the United States is largely a service-based economy. Businesses based in the United States tend to provide services to individuals or other businesses as the business climate has shifted away from manufacturing. Everyone needs haircuts and health care services, and many Americans love to eat out. But how do you find reliable service providers and good restaurants? Recommendations from friends and family are reliable, but what if no one in your circle of acquaintances knows of a good personal trainer or a great dentist? Why shouldn't the Internet be used to harness the power of millions of people's experiences to recommend reliable service providers? Two companies that have successfully plunged into this arena are Yelp and Angie's List.

Yelp (yelp.com) was conceived as the "yellow pages" for the 21st century. Yelp is free to use, and anyone can write a review of a business and post it to the site. The site has more than 15 million reviews of all types of businesses. Users can easily search the site, find service providers in their geographic area, and see what ratings (both good and bad) consumers gave them. Thinking about going to a Mexican restaurant in the San Jose area that you have never visited (see Figure 11.28)? A quick search on Yelp found more than 1500 restaurants that fit this broad criteria. Surely you'll be able to find one that fits your budget and that other people enjoyed visiting.

However, **Yelp.com** is not without its critics. Because Yelp allows anonymous posting, some people are afraid that businesses may try to up their ratings by posting their own positive reviews. And Yelp actively markets to businesses to pay for placement of ads on its site that some users may mistake for unsponsored reviews. (To avoid this kind of consumer misinterpretation, the Federal Communications Commission [FCC] now requires commercial Web sites to clearly identify reviews that are sponsored . . . but some consumers remain oblivious.) An alternative to Yelp that addresses these concerns is Angie's List.

Angie's List (**angieslist.com**) has the same basic premise as Yelp: to have individuals recommend businesses based on their experiences. However, whereas Yelp derives its revenue from advertising, Angie's List is a subscription service. Members pay a monthly fee to access the reviews on Angie's List. So what do you get for your fees that you don't get on Yelp? Angie's List does not permit anonymous reviews. This is a big benefit for business owners, because it makes it easier to contact dissatisfied customers and try to resolve issues. Angie's List also has a verification process with reviewers to ensure that businesses do not report on themselves. And businesses do not pay to advertise on Angie's List; they make the list only when they are reviewed by a consumer.

Both Yelp and Angie's List are searchable databases just like the other examples in this chapter. But whereas most companies usually populate databases with data that they generate or collect themselves, these Web sites rely on users to create their content. The databases still need to be well designed to capture this content, and there need to be processes in place to review the data entered for appropriateness. For instance, both Yelp and Angie's List would want to delete reviews that contained racist comments or hate speech. By harnessing the power of large groups of users to populate a database, the database owners can reap the rewards of saving time, effort, and money.

Figure 11.28

Yelp's database is populated with reviews created by users.

If this requirement is not applied to foreign keys, then a relationship cannot be enforced between tables.

How do I ensure that a foreign key field contains a valid primary key from the related table? To apply this restraint, when defining a relationship in a database, you have the option of enforcing referential integrity for that relationship. **Referential integrity** means that for each value in the foreign key of one table, there is a corresponding value in the primary key of the related table.

For instance, if you attempt to enter a record in the Roster Master table with an SID# of 156784522 and referential integrity is being enforced, the database checks to ensure that a record with SID# 156784522 exists in the Student Information table. If the corresponding record does not exist, then an error message displays. Establishing referential integrity between two tables helps prevent inconsistent data from being entered.

Who manages the data in a database? All of the data that is collected in databases needs to be stored and managed. Database administrators (DBAs) are the IT professionals responsible for designing, constructing, and maintaining databases. They review and manage data on an ongoing basis to ensure data is flowing smoothly into and out of the database. Figure 11.29 shows a view of the MySQL Enterprise Dashboard screen, a tool that is used primarily by DBAs when reviewing the performance of a database. Database administrators can monitor table usage and CPU utilization to help determine if database performance is acceptable.

In the next section, we explore how data is typically stored in large-scale business databases.

Data Storage

At the simplest level, data is stored in a single database on a database server, and you retrieve the data as needed. This works fine for small databases and simple enterprises where all of the data you are interested in is in a single database. Problems can arise, however, when the data you need is in multiple places. Large storage repositories called *data warehouses* and *data marts* help solve this problem.

Data Warehouses

What is a data warehouse? A data **warehouse** is a large-scale electronic repository of data that contains and organizes all the data related to an organization in one place. Individual databases contain a wealth of information, but each database's information usually pertains to one topic.

For instance, the order database at Amazon.com contains such information about book orders as the buyer's name, address, and payment information, and the book's name. However, the order database does not contain information on inventory levels of books, nor does it list suppliers from which out-of-stock books can be obtained. Data warehouses, therefore, consolidate information from disparate sources to present an enterprise-wide view of business operations.

Is data in a data warehouse organized the same way as in a normal database? Data in the data warehouse is organized by subject. Most databases focus on one specific operational aspect of business operations. For example, a large electronics retailer sells many types of electronics, such as televisions, computers, and mobile phones. Different departments in the retailer are responsible for each type of product and track the products they sell in different databases (one for television

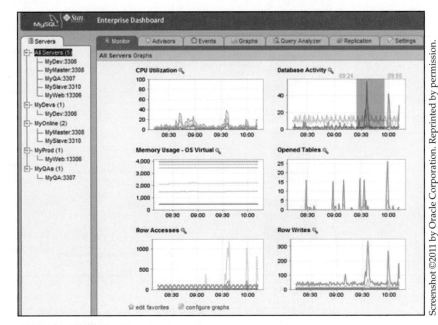

Screenshot ©2011 by Oracle Corporation. Reprinted by permission.

Figure 11.29

The Enterprise Dashboard in MySQL helps DBAs review database performance.

Emerging Technologies: Can Your Business Partner Deliver the Goods? Enhanced Databases Can Help You Decide!

You watch a weather forecast on television to gain information about the weather. The weather forecaster tells you that it will be sunny. When you get out of your car to go to class, rain is pouring down. Yes, you gathered relevant information. Too bad that it was inaccurate information!

Data and information stored in databases can be just as unhelpful as an inaccurate weather forecast if the information is incorrect or distorted. Although a poor weather report is probably nothing more to you than an inconvenience, accurate data in business is mission critical. Businesses rely on information in databases every day just to accomplish even routine tasks.

Developed to respond to business needs, **Alibaba.com** is one of the world's largest online business-to-business databases. Alibaba.com specializes in matching suppliers with buyers for all types of manufactured goods and raw materials. With the global nature of business, databases such as those maintained by Alibaba.com are essential tools that assist businesspeople in managing their global business. Figure 11.30 shows a search for short-sleeved women's cotton t-shirts in Vietnam. You could also use the terms "Vietnamese t-shirt manufacturers" in a search engine and you would probably find many leads. The information in the leads available online may be factually correct, but how do you determine how reliable these suppliers are?

There is a wealth of information online, provided by various sources, that you can use to evaluate potential suppliers before you contact them. However, it can be difficult for an individual to tell if the data has been altered or falsified. **Panjiva.com** is a Web site that also has a searchable database of over 1.5 million suppliers. However, the founders of Panjiva decided to make their database different. They gather data that indicates reliability of suppliers from sources such as government agencies, independent certification companies, nonprofit organizations, and customers.

Using the reliability information, Panjiva then creates ratings for companies (on a scale of 1 to 100) based on specific business performance criteria such as number of shipments to the U.S. market, their environmental record, and their capability to deliver shipments within promised time frames. Subscribers to Panjiva's database (companies such as The Home Depot) can then feel more comfortable about doing business with suppliers that Panjiva has rated for reliability.

Databases with enhanced information are the wave of the future in the business world. So, before you make that next crucial business decision, ask yourself how much you really know about your prospective business partner. If you don't know enough, then find a database that can make you feel more at ease.

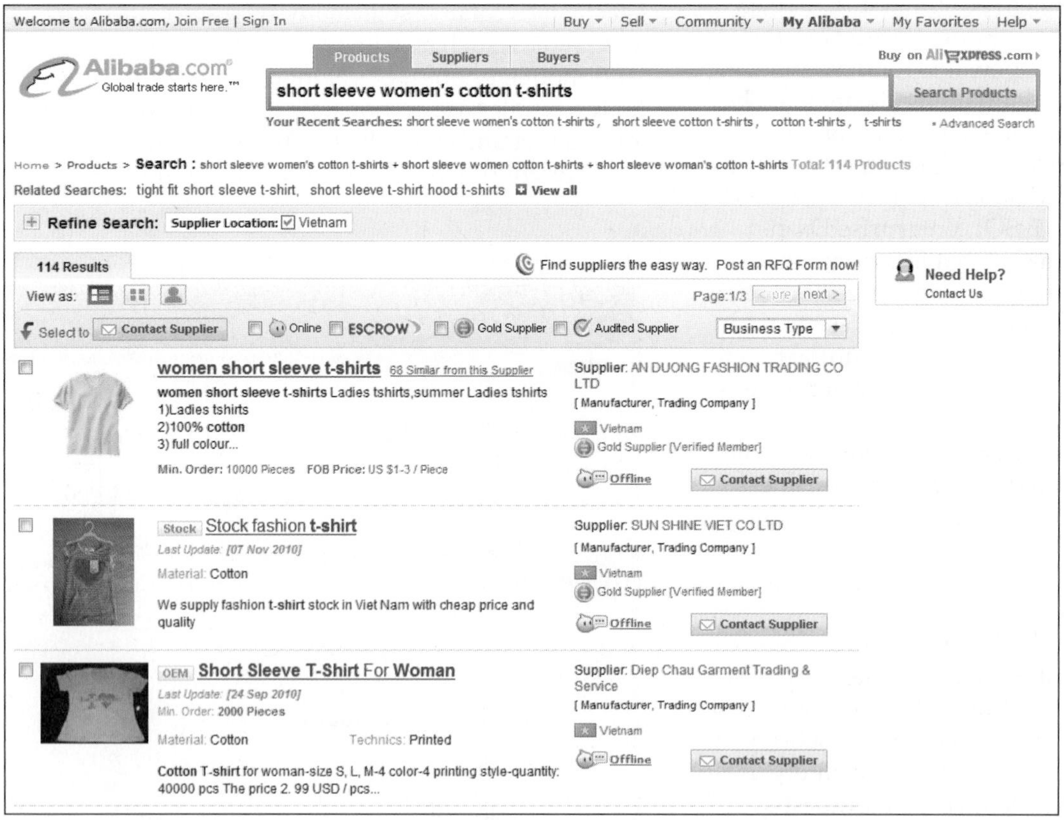

Figure 11.30

Using the database on **Alibaba.com**, a search for short-sleeved women's cotton t-shirts in Vietnam results in 114 links to vendors selling some type of women's t-shirt.

sales and one for mobile phone sales, for example), as shown in Figure 11.31.

These databases capture specific information about each type of electronics. The Television Sales database captures information about television features, installation costs, extended warranty details (and costs), and the cost of the television because this information is pertinent to determining the ultimate value of the television sale. The Mobile Phone Sales database captures information about the number of family members, calling and data plan features, and costs. But this database does not capture installation costs because they are not pertinent to mobile phones.

However, data on total electronic devices sold (and the resulting revenue generated) is critical to the management of the electronics retailer no matter what type of products are involved. Therefore, an electronics retailer's data warehouse would have a subject called Electronics Sales Subject (see Figure 11.31) that would contain information about *all* electronic devices sold throughout the company. The Electronics Sales Subject is a database that contains information from the other databases the company maintains. However, all data in the Electronics Sales Subject database is specifically related to electronics sales (as opposed to say appliances, which the retailer also carries).

From the Electronics Sales Subject database, it is easy for managers to produce comprehensive reports such as the Total Electronics Sales Report, as shown in Figure 11.31, which can contain information pertaining to all types of electronics sales.

Are data warehouses much larger than conventional databases? Data warehouses, unlike conventional databases, are vast repositories of information. The data contained within them is not operational in nature, but rather archival. Data warehouse data is **time-variant data**, meaning it doesn't all pertain to one period in time.

The warehouse contains current values, such as amounts due from customers, as well as historical data. If you want to examine the buying habits of a certain type of customer, then you need data about both current and prior purchases. Having time-variant data in the warehouse enables you to analyze the past, examine the present in

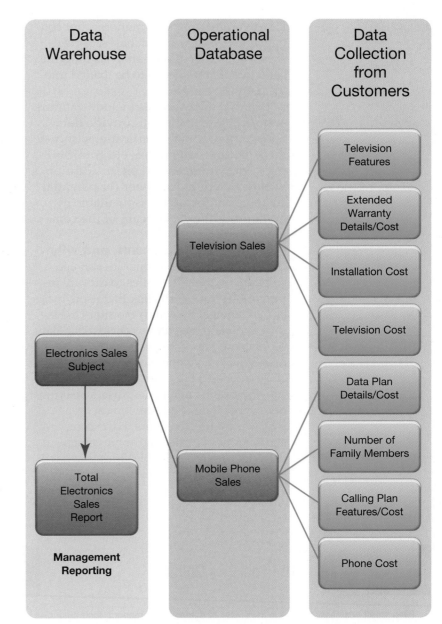

Figure 11.31

Data from individual databases is drawn together under appropriate subject headings in a data warehouse. Managers can then produce comprehensive reports that would be impossible to create from the individual databases.

light of historical data, and make projections about the future.

Populating Data Warehouses

How are data warehouses populated with data? Source data for data warehouses can come from three places:

- Internal sources (such as company databases)
- External sources (suppliers, vendors, and so on)
- Customers or visitors to a company's Web site

Internal data sources are obvious. Sales, billing, inventory, and customer databases all provide a wealth of information.

However, internal information is not contained exclusively in databases. Spreadsheets and other ad hoc analysis tools may contain data that needs to be loaded into the data warehouse.

External data sources include vendors and suppliers that often provide data regarding product specifications, shipment methods and dates, electronic billing information, and so on. In addition, a virtual wealth of customer (or potential customer) information is available by monitoring the clickstream of the company Web site.

What is a clickstream, and why is it important? Companies can use software on their Web sites to capture information about each click that users make as they navigate through the site. This information is referred to as **clickstream data**. Monitoring the clickstream helps managers assess the effectiveness of a Web site. Using clickstream data capture tools, a company can determine which pages users visit most often, how long users stay on each page, which sites directed users to the company site, and the user demographics. Such data can provide valuable clues to what a company needs to improve on its site to stimulate sales.

Data Staging

Does all source data fit into the warehouse? No two source databases are the same. Although two databases might contain similar information (such as customer names and addresses), the format of the data is most likely different in each database. Therefore, source data must be "staged" before entering the data warehouse. **Data staging** consists of three steps:

1. Extraction of the data from source databases
2. Transformation (reformatting) of the data
3. Storage of the data in the data warehouse

Many different software programs and procedures may have to be created to extract the data from varied sources and reformat it for storage in the data warehouse. The nature and complexity of the source data determine the complexity of the data staging process.

Once the data is stored in the data warehouse, how can it be extracted and used? Managers can query the data warehouse in much the same way you would query an Access database. However, because there is more data in the data warehouse, much more flexible tools are needed to perform such queries. Online analytical processing (OLAP) software provides standardized tools for viewing and manipulating data in a data warehouse. The key feature of OLAP tools is that they enable flexible views of the data, which the software user can easily change.

Data Marts

Is finding the right data in a huge data warehouse difficult? Looking for the data you need in a data warehouse can be daunting when there are terabytes of data. Therefore, small slices of the data warehouse, each called a **data mart**, are often created. Whereas data warehouses have an enterprise-wide depth, the information in data marts pertains to a single department.

For instance, if you work in the sales department, you need accurate sales-related information at your fingertips—and you do not want to wade through customer service data, accounts payable data, and product shipping data to get it. Therefore, a data mart that contains information relevant only to the sales department can be created to

---

CRM Tools Go Online

Even small businesses harness the power of databases to manage their customers. Customer relationship management (CRM) software contains sophisticated databases that are designed to manage and track all interactions with customers. Among other things, CRM software can 1) help salespeople manage their customer interactions, 2) provide communication paths for customers to solicit service and support, and 3) use analytical tools to identify the best prospects for marketing efforts based on customer interests and interactions with the company. Previously, CRM software was installed on salespeople's notebook computers or on servers at a company's home office. But with the widespread availability of wireless connections, many CRM products are now offered only online.

Zoho CRM is part of the online suite of free (and low-priced) tools offered by **www.zoho.com**. For a small business just getting started, Zoho CRM offers a free account for up to three users. Even though it is free, the software offers powerful features such as sales force automation (tracking customer leads and contacts), marketing automation (e-mail advertising campaigns), and customer support tracking and personal organization tools (calendars, to-do lists, call logging). And as the business grows, additional users can be added for a reasonable monthly fee. The database is stored totally online by Zoho, so it frees up a small business owner from the worries of database maintenance and backup.

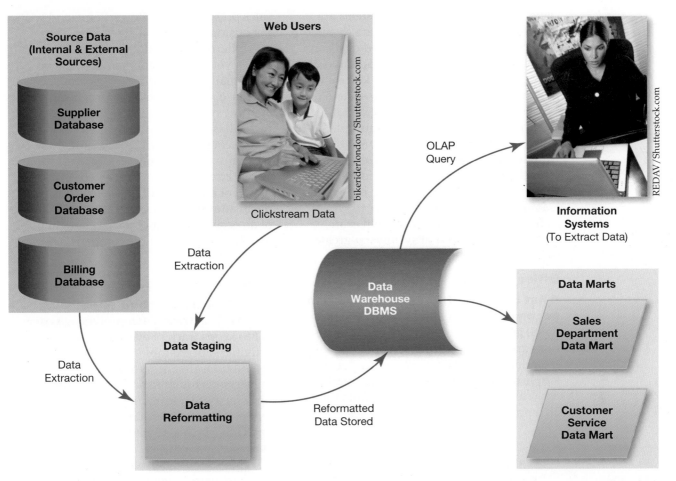

Source Data (Internal & External Sources)
- Supplier Database
- Customer Order Database
- Billing Database

Data Extraction

Web Users

bikeriderlondon/Shutterstock.com

Clickstream Data

Data Extraction

Data Staging

Data Reformatting

Reformatted Data Stored

Data Warehouse DBMS

OLAP Query

REDAV/Shutterstock.com

Information Systems (To Extract Data)

Data Marts
- Sales Department Data Mart
- Customer Service Data Mart

Figure 11.32

An overview of the data warehouse process.

make the task of finding this data easier. An overview of the data-warehousing process is illustrated in Figure 11.32. Data staging is vital because different data must be extracted and then reformatted to fit the data structure defined in the data warehouse's DBMS. Data can be extracted using powerful OLAP query tools, or it can be stored in specialized data marts for use by specific employee groups.

Now that you understand how databases are created and how data is stored in large-scale repositories, in the next section we'll explore the types of information systems that utilize databases to provide business intelligence to managers.

Managing Data: Information and Business Intelligence Systems

Making intelligent decisions about developing new products, creating marketing strategies, and buying raw materials requires timely, accurate information. An **information system** is a software-based solution used to gather and analyze information. A system that delivers up-to-the-minute sales data on shoes to the computer of Zappos' president is one example of an information system. Databases, data warehouses, and data marts are integral parts of information systems because they store the information that makes information systems functional.

All information systems perform similar functions, including acquiring data, processing that data into information, storing the data, and providing the user with a number of output options with which to make the information meaningful and useful (see Figure 11.33). Most information systems fall into one of five categories: (1) office support systems, (2) transaction-processing systems, (3) management information systems, (4) decision support systems, and (5) enterprise resource planning (ERP) systems. Each type of system almost always involves the use of one or more databases.

The latter three types of systems are often classified as business intelligence systems. **Business intelligence systems** are used to analyze and interpret data to enable managers to make informed decisions about how best to run a business. Data warehouses and data marts are key components of business intelligence systems because they enable access to wide ranges of information gathered from multiple sources. Increased access to information usually enables business intelligence systems to provide better information to managers in a timely fashion, which can lead to enhanced decision making.

In the following sections, we'll examine each of the five types of systems in greater detail.

Office Support Systems

What does an office support system accomplish? An **office support system (OSS)** is designed to improve communications and assist employees in accomplishing their daily tasks. Microsoft Office is an example of an OSS because it assists employees with routine tasks such as maintaining an employee phone list in Excel, designing a

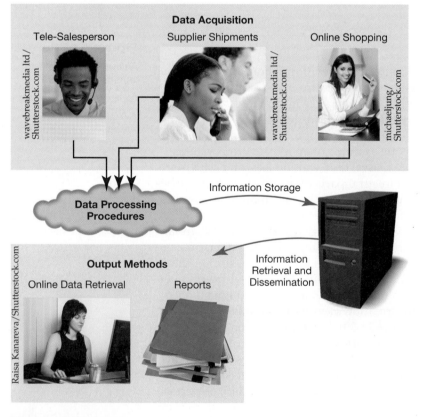

Figure 11.33

All information systems perform similar functions, including acquiring data, processing that data into information, storing the data, and providing the user with a number of output options with which to make the information meaningful and useful.

sales presentation in PowerPoint, and writing customer letters using Word.

Modern OSSs include software tools with which you are probably familiar, including e-mail, word processing, spreadsheet, database, and presentation programs. Office support systems have their roots in manual, paper-based systems that were developed before computers. After all, maintaining a company phone listing was necessary long before computers were invented. A paper listing of employee phone extensions typed by an administrative assistant is an example of an early OSS. A modern OSS might publish this directory on the company's intranet (its internal network).

Transaction-Processing Systems

What is a transaction-processing system? A **transaction-processing system (TPS)** keeps track of everyday business activities. For example, at your college, transactions that occur frequently include registering students for classes, accepting tuition payments, mailing advertisements, and printing course catalogs. Your college has TPSs in place to track these types of activities.

When computers were introduced to the business world, they often were first put to work hosting TPSs. Computers were much faster at processing large chunks of data than previous manual systems had been. Imagine having clerks type up tuition invoices for each student at a 10,000-student university. Obviously, a computer can print invoices much quicker from a database.

How do transactions enter a TPS? Transactions can be entered manually or electronically. When you order a sweater online, for example, you are providing data (such as your shipping address) that will reside in a TPS. When you purchase gasoline at a pay-at-the-pump terminal, the pump captures your credit card data and transmits it to a TPS, which automatically records a sale (gallons of gasoline and dollar value). Transactions are processed either in batches or in real time. Various departments in an organization then access the TPSs to extract the information they need to process additional transactions, as shown in Figure 11.34.

What is batch processing? **Batch processing** means that transaction data is accumulated until a certain point is reached, and then several transactions are processed all at once. Batch processing is appropriate for activities that are not time sensitive, such as developing a mailing list to mail out the new course catalogs that students have requested. The college could print a mailing label each time someone requests a catalog, but it is more efficient to batch the requests and process them all at once when the catalogs are ready to be addressed.

How does real-time processing work? For most activities, processing and recording transactions in a TPS occur in real time. **Real-time processing** means that the database is queried and updated while the transaction is taking place. For instance, when you register for classes online, if seats are still available for the classes you want, the database immediately records your registration in the class to ensure you have a seat. This **online transaction processing (OLTP)** ensures that the data in the TPS is as current as possible.

Management Information Systems

What is a management information system? A **management information system (MIS)** provides timely and accurate information that enables managers to make critical business decisions (i.e., they provide business intelligence). MISs were a direct outgrowth of TPSs. Managers quickly realized that the data contained in TPSs could be an extremely powerful tool only if the information could be organized and output in a useful form. Today's MISs are often built in as a feature of TPSs.

What does an MIS provide that a TPS does not? The original TPSs were usually designed to output detail reports. A **detail report** provides a list of the transactions that occurred during a certain time period. For example, during registration periods at your school, the registrar might receive a detail report that lists the students who registered for classes each day. Figure 11.35a shows an example of a detail report on daily enrollment.

Going beyond the detail reports provided by TPSs, MISs provide summary reports and exception reports. A **summary report** provides a consolidated picture of detailed data. These reports usually include some calculation (totals) or visual displays of information (such as charts and graphs). Figure 11.35b shows an example of a summary report displaying total daily credits enrolled by division.

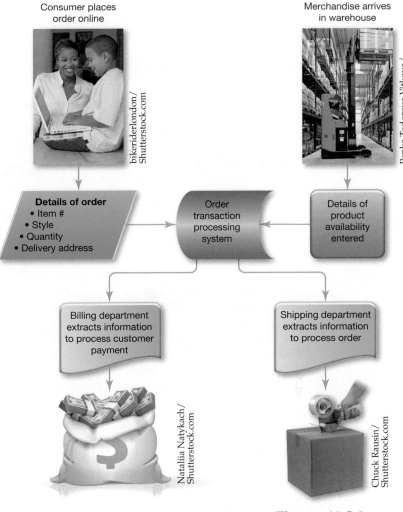

Figure 11.34

TPSs help capture and track critical business information needed for successful completion of business transactions such as selling merchandise over the Internet.

An **exception report** shows conditions that are unusual or that need attention by users of the system. The registrar at your college may get an exception report when all sections of a course are full, indicating that it may be time to schedule additional sections. Figure 11.35c shows an example of such an exception report.

Decision Support Systems

What is a decision support system? A **decision support system (DSS)** is another type of business intelligence system designed to help managers develop solutions for specific problems. A DSS for a marketing department might provide statistical information on customer attributes (such as income levels, buying patterns, and so on) that would assist managers in making decisions regarding advertising strategy. A DSS not only uses data from databases and data warehouses, but also enables users to add

a

Daily Enrollment Report

SID#	First Name	Last Name	Class Code	Class Name
123456789	Susan	Finkel		
			CHE 140	Chemistry
			CIS 110	Computer Lite
			ENG 101	English Comp
			HIS 103	Western Civ 1
			PSY 101	Intro to Psych
456789123	Mei	Zhang		
			ENG 102	English Comp
			HIS 103	Western Civ 1
			PSY 101	Intro to Psych

b

Daily Enrollment Summary

Division	Enrolled Credits
Computer Science	2
Humanities	3
Science and Engineering	2
Social Sciences	7
Total Credits	14

c

Course Sections Fully Enroll

Class Code	Class Name
CIS 110	Computer Literacy
ENG 102	English Comp 2
HIS 103	Western Civ 1

Figure 11.35

The three types of management information system reports are (a) detail report, (b) summary report, and (c) exception report.

their own insights and experiences and apply them to the solution.

What does a decision support system look like? Database management systems, while playing an integral part of a DSS, are supplemented by additional software systems in a DSS. In a DSS, the user interface provides the means of interaction between the user and the system. An effective user interface must be easy to learn. The other major components of a DSS are internal and external data sources, model management systems, and knowledge-based systems. As shown in Figure 11.36, all of these systems work together to provide the user of the DSS with a broad base of information on which to base decisions.

Internal and External Data Sources

What are internal and external data sources for decision support systems? Data can be fed into the DSS from a variety of sources. **Internal data sources** are maintained by the same company that operates the DSS. For example, internal TPSs can provide a wealth of statistical data about customers, ordering patterns, inventory

levels, and so on. An **external data source** is any source not owned by the company that owns the DSS, such as customer demographic data purchased from third parties, mailing lists, or statistics compiled by the federal government. Internal and external data sources provide a stream of data that is integrated into the DSS for analysis.

Model Management Systems

What function does a model management system perform? A **model management system** is software that assists in building management models in DSSs. A management model is an analysis tool that, through the use of internal and external data, provides a view of a particular business situation for the purposes of decision making. Models can be built to describe any business situation, such as the classroom space requirements for next semester or a listing of alternative sales outlet locations.

Internal models (such as a spreadsheet that shows current classroom use on a college campus) are developed inside an organization. External models (such as statistics about populations of students at two-year

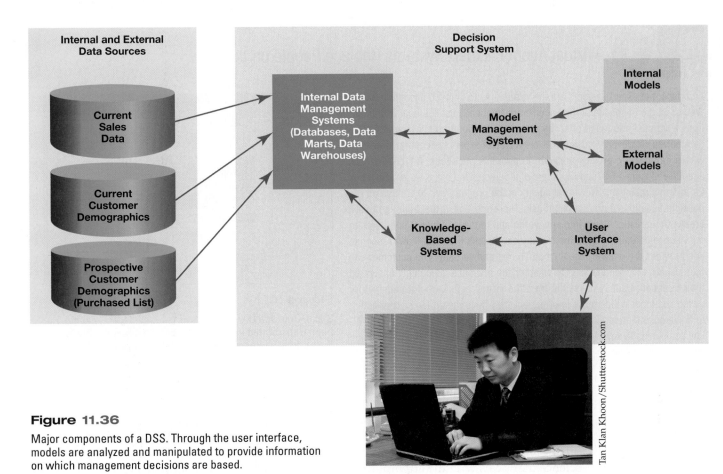

Internal and External Data Sources

Decision Support System

Figure 11.36

Major components of a DSS. Through the user interface, models are analyzed and manipulated to provide information on which management decisions are based.

colleges in the United States) are obtained from third parties. Model management systems typically contain financial and statistical analysis tools used to analyze the data provided by models or to create additional models.

Knowledge-Based Systems

What is a knowledge-based system, and how is it used in decision support systems? A knowledge-based system provides additional intelligence that supplements the user's own intellect and makes the DSS more effective. It can be an **expert system** that tries to replicate the decision-making processes of human experts to solve specific problems. For example, an expert system might be designed to take the place of a physician in a remote location such as a scientific base in Antarctica. A physician expert system would ask the patient about symptoms just as a live physician would, and the system would make a diagnosis based on the algorithms programmed into it.

Another type of knowledge-based system is a **natural language processing (NLP) system**. NLP systems enable users to communicate with computer systems using a natural spoken or written language instead of using a computer programming language. Individuals with disabilities who cannot use a keyboard benefit greatly from NLP systems because they can just speak to the computer and have it understand what they are saying without using specific computer commands. Using an NLP system can simplify the user interface, making it much more efficient and user friendly. The speech-recognition feature of Microsoft Windows is a type of NLP system. Great strides are being made in developing computers with NLP systems, such as the IBM computer Watson that competed on the game show *Jeopardy* in 2011 against two human opponents. Watson was able to correctly decipher the questions and provide correct responses to them the majority of the time. In fact, the computer easily beat the two human champions it was competing against.

Virtual Agents: Expert Systems Replace People on the Web

An offshoot of expert systems are the virtual agents that you encounter on the Web or on the telephone. Virtual agents are frequently used to deal with questions from customers and often try to appear as though they are real people themselves. However, virtual agents are a type of expert system that interfaces with a database to provide answers to people's questions. A typical virtual agent (see Figure 11.37) has a picture of a person (who has a name) and a box for entering questions. No virtual agent can be programmed to contain all the possible questions a human might ask. Therefore, the virtual agent software breaks the question down into key words and phrases, which it compares to a database containing question responses. It picks the most likely response and provides the answer, usually both in text and verbally. The customer can then usually give feedback as to whether the response adequately answered their question. Usually, if results from the virtual agent are not satisfactory or the customer needs more information, they have the option of connecting to a live customer service agent. Virtual agents, while not always perfect, allow companies to save money by answering common questions without using expensive human labor.

Figure 11.37

Spike, Gonzaga University's sports team mascot, has now been transformed into a virtual agent to direct people to the appropriate pages of the school's Web site.

Courtesy of Gonzaga University

All knowledge-based systems fall under the science of artificial intelligence. **Artificial intelligence (AI)** is the branch of computer science that deals with the attempt to create computers that think like humans. To date, no computers have been constructed that can replicate the thinking patterns of a human brain, because scientists still do not fully understand how humans store and integrate knowledge and experiences to form human intelligence.

How does a knowledge-based system help in the decision-making process? Databases and the models provided by model management systems tend to be extremely analytical and mathematical in nature. If we relied solely on databases and models to make decisions, then the answers would be derived with a "yes or no" mentality, allowing no room for human thought. Fortunately, human users are involved in these types of systems, providing an opportunity to inject human judgment and experience into the decision-making process.

The knowledge-based system also provides an opportunity to introduce experience into the mix. Knowledge-based systems support the concept of fuzzy logic. Normal logic is highly rigid: If "x" happens, then "y" will happen. **Fuzzy logic** enables the interjection of experiential learning into the equation by considering probabilities. Whereas

an algorithm in a database has to be specific, an algorithm in a knowledge-based system could state that if "x" happens, 70 percent of the time "y" will happen.

For instance, managers at Best Buy would find it extremely helpful if their DSSs informed them that 45 percent of customers who bought an iPad also bought a Smart Cover for it. This could suggest that designing a discount program for Smart Covers bought with iPads might spur sales. Fuzzy logic enables a system to be more flexible and to consider a wider range of possibilities than would conventional algorithmic thinking.

Enterprise Resource Planning Systems

What is an enterprise? An enterprise is any business entity, large or small. It could be the pizza shop on the corner or a Fortune 500 manufacturer of sports apparel. All businesses have data and information to manage, and large, complex organizations can benefit from managing that information with a central piece of software.

What does an enterprise resource planning system do? An **enterprise resource planning (ERP) system** is a broad-based software system that integrates multiple data sources and ties together the various processes of an enterprise to enable information to flow more smoothly. ERP systems use a common database to store and integrate information. This enables the information to be used across multiple areas of an enterprise.

For instance, human resource functions (such as the management of hiring, firing, promotions, and benefits) and accounting functions (such as payroll) are often the first processes integrated into an ERP system. Historically, human resource records and accounting records were kept in separate databases, but having the information reside in one database makes the management and paying of employees more streamlined. If manufacturing operations were then integrated into the ERP system, the data that was already in place regarding the employees and payroll could be easily used for determining the cost of running an assembly line (because the workers on the assembly line get paid) or for scheduling workers to run the assembly line. The objective of ERP systems is to accumulate all information relevant to running a business in a central location and make it readily available to whoever needs that information to make decisions.

Almost all Fortune 500 companies have implemented ERP systems, and many medium-sized companies are implementing them also. Although the corner pizza shop probably does not need an ERP system, it would be difficult to coordinate the activities of a multinational corporation without one.

Data Mining

Just because you have captured data in an organized fashion and have stored it in a format that seems to make sense doesn't mean that an analysis of the data will automatically reveal everything you need to know. Trends can sometimes be hard to spot if the data is not organized or analyzed in a particular way. To make data work harder, companies employ data-mining techniques.

Data mining is the process by which great amounts of data are analyzed and investigated. The objective is to spot significant patterns or trends within the data that would otherwise not be obvious. For instance, by mining student enrollment data, a school may discover that 35 percent of new engineering degree students are Latino.

Why do businesses mine their data? The main reason businesses mine data is to understand their customers better. If a company can better understand the types of customers who buy its products and can learn what motivates its customers to do so, it can market effectively by concentrating its efforts on the populations that are most likely to buy.

How do businesses mine their data? Data mining enables managers to sift through data in several ways. Each method produces different information that managers can then base their decisions on. Managers make their data meaningful through the following activities:

- **Classification:** To analyze data, managers need to classify it. Therefore, before mining, managers define data classes that they think will be helpful in spotting trends. They then apply these class definitions to all unclassified data to prepare it for analysis. For example, "good credit risk" and "bad credit risk" are two data classes that managers could establish to determine whether to grant car loans to applicants. Managers would then identify factors (such as credit history and yearly income) that they could use to classify applicants as good or bad risks.

- **Estimation:** When managers classify data, the record either fits the classification criteria or it doesn't. Estimation enables managers to assign a value to data based on some criterion. For example, assume a bank wants to send out credit card offers to people who are likely to be granted a credit card. The bank may run the customers' data through a program that assigns them a score based on where they live, their household income, and their average bank balance. This provides managers with an estimate of the most likely credit card prospects so that they can include them in the mailing.

- **Affinity grouping (or association rules):** When mining data, managers also can determine which data goes together. In other words, they can apply affinity

ACTIVE HELP-DESK

Data Warehouses, Data Marts, and Information Systems

In this Active Helpdesk call, you'll play the role of a helpdesk staffer, fielding calls about data warehouses, data marts, and information systems.

Data, Data Everywhere—But Is It Protected?

As databases have become commonplace, an ever-increasing amount of information about you and your habits has gone into various databases. Every time you purchase something with a credit card, there is a record of that transaction, and both the merchant from whom you purchased the item and the credit card company have information about your buying habits (see Figure 11.38).

Have you used a toll service that allows you to pay your tolls electronically by just driving through a lane without stopping? Toll records are routinely subpoenaed in court cases. Toll records were used in an Illinois court by a husband in a divorce case to prove his wife was rarely home and therefore unfit for custody of their son. All banking transactions are handled by computers (and hence databases) in the United States, and there is a high probability that your employer is electronically transferring your pay to your bank by direct deposit. If you engage in online banking and bill paying, yet another electronic trail of your financial life is being generated in databases.

Do you think you can avoid scrutiny by paying cash? Not if you are a member of a frequent shopper "club" (a popular promotion used by supermarkets and drug stores) and provide the checkout clerk with your personal information in exchange for coupons or a few dollars off your purchases. Remember, you never can be sure of how this data

might be used. In October 2004, a firefighter was arrested after his supermarket purchase records revealed he had purchased the same type of fire starters used in an arson case. After three months, the charges were dropped when another person pleaded guilty to committing the arson.

Because of the vast amount of electronic information processing that goes on today, you can't avoid having your personal information contained in databases. But do you actually know who has your data? You may have joined the frequent shopper club at CVS to get discounts and gave them your e-mail address and other contact information. But who did CVS give your e-mail address to?

Many consumers received a rude shock in March 2011 when they began receiving apologetic correspondence from companies alerting them that their e-mail addresses had potentially been exposed to misuse. Many companies (such as CVS) collect e-mail addresses so they can correspond with customers, but the e-mails don't come directly from those companies. Large marketing companies such as Epsilon are hired to manage customer e-mail programs for both large and small businesses. Unfortunately, Epsilon's database servers suffered an attack in March 2011 that exposed millions of individuals' e-mail

Lisa Quinones/Black Star/Newscom

Figure 11.38

Demonstrators are protesting the perceived erosion of individual privacy rights for United States citizens. Do you feel your privacy rights are threatened?

grouping or association rules to the data. For example, suppose analysis of a sales database indicates that two items are bought together 60 percent of the time. Based on this data, managers might decide that these items should be pictured on the same page of their Web site.

- **Clustering:** Clustering involves organizing data into similar subgroups, or clusters. It is different from classification in that there are no predefined classes. The data-mining software makes the decision about what to group, and it is up to managers to determine whether the clusters are meaningful. For example,

the data-mining software may identify clusters of customers with similar buying patterns. Further analysis of the clusters may reveal that certain socioeconomic groups have similar buying patterns.

- **Description and visualization:** Often, the purpose of data mining is merely to describe data so that managers can visualize it. Sometimes having a clear picture of what is going on with the data helps people to interpret it in new and different ways. For example, if large amounts of data revealed that right-handed women who live in rural environments

addresses. Inadvertently exposing information to inappropriate or unauthorized individuals is known as a *data breach*. Companies needed to warn their customers of potential spear phishing attacks that were likely to be launched against them.

Many phishing attacks are random. If a cyber-crook sends out 10,000 phishing e-mails claiming to be from Citibank, most of the people that receive them won't have a Citibank account and will ignore them. However, **spear phishing** attacks are more serious because they use e-mail addresses of customers that are known to have a relationship with a certain company. When you know you have e-mail addresses of customers that definitely have a relationship with a company, your phishing attacks are more likely to succeed . . . not unlike using a spear gun instead of a fish hook to hunt fish.

Although you might never be compromised as a result of this data breach, it does underscore the potential danger of having your information stolen by nefarious parties. What responsibility do companies to which you provide information have in safeguarding their data? Should they inform you that your data might be shared with other corporations and obtain your permission before sharing it? How should consumers be compensated (and by whom) if their data is misused?

What Can You Do?

Providing information and having it recorded in databases are part of our way of life now. Because refusing to give information out at all is bound to be impractical, you should ask the following questions related to data you are providing:

- **For what purpose is the data being gathered?** When the clerk at the electronics superstore asks for your zip code, ask why she wants it. (It is probably for some marketing purpose.)
- **Are the reasons for gathering the data legitimate or important to you?** When you purchase a movie on Blu-ray, is asking for your zip code really a legitimate request? However, to validate the warranty on a large-screen TV, you may need to give a clerk your address and zip code. Similarly, disclosing medical information to key people (such as your pharmacist) may be important to receiving good care and therefore is extremely important to you. If you don't see the advantage, then ask more questions or don't reveal the information.

- **How will the information gathered be protected once it has been obtained?** Ask about data protection policies before you give information. Most Web sites provide access to their data protection policies—readily available through clickable links or pop-up boxes—when they ask for information. If an organization doesn't have a data protection policy, then be wary of giving them sensitive information unless there is a compelling advantage to doing so (such as receiving good medical care). Data protection doesn't just refer to keeping data secure. It also means restricting access to the data to employees of the organization that need to use that data. A shipping clerk might need to see your address, for example, but doesn't need to see your credit card information.
- **Will the information collected be used for purposes other than the purpose for which it was originally collected?** This might be covered in a data protection policy. If it isn't, then ask about it. Will your information be sold to or shared with other companies? Will it be used for marketing other products to you?
- **Could the information asked for be used for identity theft?** Identity thieves usually need your Social Security number and your birth date to open credit card accounts in your name. Be especially wary when asked for this information, and make sure there is a legitimate need for this information. Most organizations and businesses are shying away from using Social Security numbers to track customers, because of the risk of identity theft. And do you really need an e-mail from someone on your birthday advertising a product? It really isn't worth exposing your birth date to potential misuse.
- **Are organizations that already have your data safeguarding it?** Don't just consider new requests for information. Think about organizations, such as banks, that already have your information and monitor their performance. Have they been in the news lately because of a major data breach? (Is your bank a customer of Epsilon, for instance?) You might want to consider switching institutions if yours has a poor record of data security.

Think carefully before providing information and be vigilant about monitoring your data when you can. It may make the difference between invasion of privacy and peace of mind.

never take philosophy courses, it would most likely spark a heated discussion about the reasons why. It would certainly provide plenty of opportunities for additional study on the part of psychologists, sociologists, and college administrators!

You may have noticed that products are frequently moved around in supermarkets. This is usually the result of data mining. With electronic scanning of bar codes, each customer's purchase is recorded in a database. By classifying the data and using cluster analysis, supermarket managers can determine which products people usually purchase with other products. The store then places these products close to each other so that shoppers can find them easily. For instance, if analysis shows that people often buy potato chips with soft drinks, it makes sense to place these items in the same aisle.

As the human race continues to accumulate data, the development of faster and bigger databases will be a necessity. You can expect to interact with more and more databases every year, even if you don't realize you are doing so. While you may never have to create a database, understanding how databases work will enable you to interact with them more effectively.

1. What is a database, and why is it beneficial to use databases?

Databases are electronic collections of related data that can be organized so that it is more easily accessed and manipulated. Properly designed databases cut down on data redundancy and duplicate data by ensuring relevant data is recorded in only one place. This also helps eliminate data inconsistency, which comes from having different data about the same transaction recorded in two different places. When databases are used, multiple users can share and access information at the same time. Databases are used any time complex information needs to be organized or more than one person needs to access it. In these cases, lists (which are used to keep track of simple information) are no longer efficient.

2. What components make up a database?

The three main components of a database are fields, records, and tables. A category of information in a database is stored in a field. Each field is identified by a field name, which is a way of describing the field. Fields are assigned a data type that indicates what type of data can be stored in the field. Common data types include text, numeric, computational, date, memo, object, and hyperlink. A group of related fields is a record. A group of related records is a table or file. To keep records distinct, each record must have one field that has a value unique to that record. This unique field is a primary key (or a key field).

3. What types of databases are there?

The three major types of databases currently in use are relational, object-oriented, and multidimensional. Relational databases are characterized by two-dimensional tables of data in which a common field is maintained in each of two tables and the information in the tables is linked by this field. Object-oriented databases store data in objects, not in tables. The objects also contain instructions about how the data is to be manipulated or processed. Multidimensional databases represent data in three-dimensional cubes to enable faster retrieval of information from the database.

4. What do database management systems do?

Database management systems (DBMSs) are specially designed applications (such as Oracle or Microsoft Access) that interact with the user, other applications, and the database itself to capture and analyze data. The main operations of a DBMS are creating databases, entering data, viewing (or browsing) data, sorting (or indexing) data, extracting (or querying) data, and outputting data. A query language is used to extract records from a database. Almost all relational databases today use structured query language, or SQL. However, most DBMSs include wizards that enable you to query the database without learning a query language. The most common form of output for any database is a printed report.

5. How do relational databases organize and manipulate data?

Relational databases operate by organizing data into various tables based on logical groupings. Because not all of the data in a relational database is stored in the same table, a methodology must be implemented to link data between tables. In relational databases, the links between tables that define how the data is related are referred to as relationships. To establish a relationship between two tables, both tables must have a common field (or column). Once linked, information can be drawn from multiple tables through the use of queries (for on-screen viewing of data) or report generators (used to produce printed reports).

6. What are data warehouses and data marts, and how are they used?

A data warehouse is a large-scale electronic repository of data that contains and organizes in one place all the relevant data related to an organization. Data warehouses often contain information from multiple databases. Because it can be difficult to find information in a large data warehouse, small slices of the data warehouse called *data marts* are often created. The information in data marts pertains to a single department within the organization, for example. Data warehouses and data marts consolidate information from a wide variety of sources to provide comprehensive pictures of operations or transactions within a business.

7. What is a business intelligence system, and what types of business intelligence systems are used by decision makers?

Business intelligence systems are used to analyze and interpret data to enable managers to make informed decisions about how best to run a business. An office support system (OSS) is designed to assist employees in accomplishing their day-to-day tasks and improve communications. A transaction-processing system (TPS) is used to keep track of everyday business activities. A management information system (MIS) provides timely and accurate information that enables managers to make critical business decisions. A decision support system (DSS) is designed to help managers develop solutions for specific problems. An enterprise resource planning (ERP) system is a large software system that gathers information from all parts of a business and integrates it to make it readily available for decision making. MIS, DSS, and ERP systems are all classified as business intelligence systems.

8. What is data mining, and how does it work?

Data mining is the process by which large amounts of data are analyzed to spot otherwise hidden trends. Through processes such as classification, estimation, affinity grouping, clustering, and description (visualization), data is organized so that it provides meaningful information that can be used by managers to identify business trends.

 Companion Website

The Companion Website includes a variety of additional materials to help you review and learn more about the topics in this chapter. Go to: *www.pearsonhighered.com/techinaction*

Word Bank

- business intelligence system
- computational field
- data dictionary
- data mining
- data warehouse
- decision support system
- expert system
- join query
- memo field
- metadata
- object field
- primary key
- record
- relational algebra
- select query
- table
- text field
- transaction-processing system (TPS)

Instructions: Fill in the blanks using the words from the Word Bank above.

Relational databases store data in two-dimensional (1) _____s. Properly constructed relational databases use a field called a(n) (2) _____ that contains values that uniquely identify each (3) _____. In a database, data such as "Julia" or "red" are normally stored in a(n) (4) _____. The result of a formula such as (credit hours × cost per credit) should be stored in a(n) (5) _____, whereas an MP3 file would appropriately be stored in a(n) (6) _____. Extremely lengthy textual data is best stored in a(n) (7) _____. Data used to describe other data (such as data type) is referred to as (8) _____ and is contained in the (9) _____ of a database.

Queries are used to extract data from a database. In relational databases, information is drawn from multiple tables using a(n) (10) _____. If you were performing a simple operation such as extracting data from a single table, you could use a(n) (11) _____.

Systems that record routine business activities (such as sales) are classified as (12) _____s. (13) _____s are used to analyze and interpret data to enable managers to make informed decisions about how best to run a business. When a company needs a data storage facility that contains and organizes all the data related to an organization, (14) _____s are used instead of individual databases. To spot significant patterns or trends within data that would otherwise not be obvious, managers often use a technique known as (15) _____.

becoming computer literate

Your best friend, Julio, has decided to launch a t-shirt business (along the lines of **Threadless.com**) to feature the artwork of students from a local art college. He has engaged a Web designer to design his Web site, but has asked you to advise him on the types of information he needs to record to enable him to make sound decisions about running the business. He knows t-shirts, but he realizes you are much more computer savvy.

Write a proposal that outlines what you intend to do for Julio. What kinds of databases should be created for this business? What kind of data must be captured to run the business efficiently? How should that information be organized? Julio will probably be away from his manufacturing facility quite frequently. Can the databases for the business be accessed online (say with a smartphone)? Julio has limited funding. Are there open source database alternatives that would work for the types of databases he will need?

Instructions: Answer the multiple-choice and true–false questions below for more practice with key terms and concepts from this chapter.

Multiple Choice

1. Two lists showing the same data about the same person is an example of
   a. data redundancy.
   b. data inconsistency.
   c. data disparity.
   d. data duplication errors.

2. Which of the following is NOT an advantage of using databases instead of lists?
   a. Data can be easily shared among users.
   b. Data entry errors can be minimized with databases.
   c. Data integrity can be ensured with a database.
   d. Databases are easier to build and maintain than lists.

3. In databases, tables are related using
   a. primary keys and foreign keys.
   b. boolean logic.
   c. data marts.
   d. database logic.

4. A field that has a unique entry for each record in a database table is called the
   a. logical key.
   b. master field.
   c. crucial field.
   d. primary key.

5. A primary key of one table that is also found in a related table is a
   a. linked key.
   b. foreign key.
   c. secondary key.
   d. subordinate key.

6. A(n) _____ database organizes data in two-dimensional tables.
   a. relational
   b. object-oriented
   c. rectangular
   d. multidimensional

7. Which of the following is one of the four main operations of a DBMS?
   a. querying data
   b. dissecting data
   c. structuring data
   d. consolidating data

8. Ensuring that a field must contain a number that is between two values is an example of a(n)
   a. alphabetic check.
   b. completeness check.
   c. range check.
   d. consistency check.

9. A system that is designed to help perform routine daily tasks is known as (a)n
   a. data mart.
   b. office support system.
   c. data warehouse.
   d. decision support system.

10. A system that tries to mimic human responses is an example of a(n)
   a. transaction-processing system.
   b. decision support system.
   c. expert system.
   d. knowledge-based system.

True–False

_____ 1. A query is used to extract information from a database.

_____ 2. Validation checks ensure that required fields in a database are filled in completely.

_____ 3. Normalization of data involves reducing data redundancy by recording data only once.

_____ 4. A transaction-processing system (TPS) is an example of a business intelligence system.

_____ 5. Data mining is often used to spot customer trends.

making the
transition to...
next semester **eleven** chapter

making the
transition to...
next semester

1. Understanding Database Design

Go to Bestbuy.com and look at the iPads (and other tablet computers) that are for sale. Best Buy uses a very sophisticated database to process transactions. But every good database starts with good design by creating a field for each unique piece of data. List as many fields as you can identify used to record information for a tablet computer for sale at Best Buy. Assign each field you identify a data type and suggest a reasonable field length.

2. Privacy Settings on Facebook

Facebook is a large database. It is important to protect personal information that is contained in a database, and with Facebook you are responsible for making decisions about sharing your information. The owners of Facebook are constantly tweaking the privacy settings on the site. If you have not checked your privacy settings lately, you may not be aware of the personal information that you are sharing with anyone who can access Facebook.

a. Log in to your Facebook account and access your privacy settings. Which information about you is accessible to everyone? Is any of your information only visible to your friends? What types of information is viewable by friends of your friends?

b. Did any of the privacy settings surprise you? Which privacy settings do you think you need to change? Why? If you don't think any changes to your settings are necessary, explain why you feel secure with your current privacy settings.

3. Designing Your Own Database

A group of students at your school wants to collect and refurbish used computer equipment and donate it to underprivileged individuals. To help this group, you want to create a database to facilitate the tracking of the donated equipment. Determine the following:

a. What fields do you need to capture information about the clients who are donating the computing equipment? What would be the primary key of the "client" table? Why would it be a good primary key?

b. What fields do you need in your database for identifying and categorizing the computer equipment? What would be a good primary key to use for the "computer inventory" table? Why would it be a good primary key?

c. Design a table that tracks the donation transactions. What fields from the other two tables would need to be included in the "donation transaction" table? Justify your answer.

4. Comparing Databases

Amazon.com and eCampus.com are two sites students frequently use to buy textbooks. On both sites you interact with a database to search for and purchase your textbooks. Visit both sites and search for several textbooks such as the ones you are using this semester. Compare your experiences on both sites. Consider the following (and make sure you fully explain each answer):

a. Which site is easier to use?

b. Which site offers better options for refining the results of your search (query) for a textbook?

c. What fields did you search on to find your textbooks? Would searching on another field have produced more accurate results?

d. What enhancements would you suggest to the owners of both sites to improve your shopping experience?

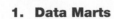
1. Data Marts

You are a summer intern in the information technology group of a regional chain of sporting goods stores. The company has been in business for 20 years and operates 40 locations in seven states. The 40 locations are organized into four regions (north, south, east, and west) of 10 stores each. Regional managers are responsible for inventory management, procurement of inventory, sales, and marketing for their particular region. The company has been processing all transactions electronically (with customers and suppliers), and it has captured all the data in a large data warehouse. Unfortunately, the regional managers are complaining that there is now so much information in the data warehouse that it has become somewhat difficult to sort through it and extract meaningful data. You have just been placed on the team that will be designing a new data strategy for the company.

a. Setting up data marts would probably help with the accessibility of information. What type of data marts would you suggest setting up for this company? Make sure you explain who will benefit from the data marts you suggest.

b. For the data marts you identified in the previous question, list the data that should be stored in each data mart and explain how the regional managers could make use of that information to manage their group of stores.

2. Recovering from a Data Breach

You have an internship in the marketing department of XYZ Drugs (a large retail pharmacy chain) that has an established buyer loyalty program. The buyer loyalty program provides customers with discounts when they present their loyalty card when making purchases. XYZ collects e-mail addresses when customers enroll in the program and have engaged a third-party marketing company (ABC Marketing) to routinely send out e-mails to customers advertising special deals.

Unfortunately, ABC has just informed XYZ that their servers suffered a major data breach and all of the names and e-mail addresses of XYZ's customers in ABC's database were illegally copied by unknown hackers. The head of XYZ's marketing department has put you on the team to determine how best to inform and reassure XYZ's customers of the possible consequences of the data breach. You are currently working on the draft e-mail to be sent to XYZ's customers. Consider the following:

a. What are the risks that XYZ's customers face from the data breach?

b. What steps should the customers take to mitigate the risks you just identified? You need to be tactful and careful in your suggestions to the customers because you want them to continue to trust XYZ with their personal information.

c. Your friends and family have been asking you about this data breach. Prepare a list of precautions that they can take with their personal data to avoid being victims of these types of data breaches (which may include not providing as much personal information to retailers). Try searching on the Internet for ideas using search terms such as "data breach protection" or "e-mail breach safeguards."

Instructions: Some ideas are best understood by experimenting with them in our own minds. The following critical thinking questions are designed to demand your full attention but require only a comfortable chair—no technology.

1. **Database Privacy Policies**

   Most likely you have provided quite a bit of personal information to various companies when you became their customer. Companies have an ethical responsibility to protect sensitive data obtained from customers. Consider the following:

   a. Think about a retailer (such as Costco or Sears) that you have done business with recently. What personal information did you provide to that retailer? What personal information should a company be precluded from disclosing to others? What information does the company have of yours that you don't care if they share with (or sell to) other companies?

   b. Most retailers have privacy policies that describe how your information will be used and safeguarded. Have you ever read a privacy policy from a retailer that you have done business with? If so, summarize the provisions of the policy. If not, review a privacy policy from a major online retailer and summarize its provisions. In your opinion, is the privacy policy you reviewed sufficient to protect your sensitive data?

2. **Social Security Database**

   The U.S. Social Security Administration (SSA) maintains a large database containing a great deal of information on the personal income of individuals. The information in this database could be easily sorted and categorized by attributes such as geographic location and age. This information would be of great value to marketing professionals for targeting marketing programs to consumers. Currently, the SSA is prohibited from selling this information to third parties. However, the SSA and other government agencies face increasing pressure to find ways to generate revenue or decrease expenses.

   a. Do you favor a change in the laws that would permit the SSA to sell names and addresses with household income information to third parties? Why or why not?

   b. Would it be acceptable for the SSA to sell income information to marketing firms if it did not include personal information, but only included income statistics for certain geographic areas? How is this better (or worse) than selling personal information?

   c. How would you feel about the SSA marketing financial products (such as investment opportunities and retirement plans) directly to consumers? Would this be a conflict of interest with the SSA's main mission, which is the collection of retirement taxes and the provision of old-age pensions?

3. **Information About You on Facebook**

   Most likely you have a Facebook page or some other social networking page (MySpace, LinkedIn, etc.). Facebook is a database, and information from your page is often shared with other databases when you permit it by participating in various games and other applications that require access to your personal data as a condition of participation. Think about the information that you have on your Facebook page (including photos and videos).

   a. What information is on your page that you wouldn't want your parents to know about? What information on your page might be of concern to a prospective employer? If you were considering transferring to another college or university, what things on your page might not impress the staff of the admissions office? What information might you consider removing from your Facebook page tonight?

   b. How many games and other applications do you estimate have access to your information? Check your privacy settings for your Facebook page and look in the Apps, Games and Web sites section to see how many apps you actually are using. Were you surprised at the difference in the actual number of apps and your estimate? What apps do you think you should disable to prevent them from accessing your information? Give reasons for the ones you will disable (don't trust them, don't use them, etc.).

eleven

Redesigning Facebook

Problem

Facebook is the most popular social media site and is also a database. But as with any product, there is always room for improvement. Facebook management has made decisions about what data they require from users who create Facebook accounts. They also have set up specific areas to display what management considers to be pertinent information on a user's main Facebook page. But perhaps you as a user would have designed Facebook differently.

Task

Your class has volunteered to work as a focus group for Facebook as part of a nationwide project to assess the usefulness of the information gathered by Facebook. Users often provide unique perspectives, and they should be consulted whenever possible during the design, implementation, and updates of Web sites. As heavy users of Facebook, management feels that student input is invaluable to ensuring currency and usability of its features.

Process

Divide the class into small groups.

1. Your group members should examine their individual Facebook accounts. If anyone in your group does not have a Facebook account, they should set one up. If you all have Facebook accounts, you might want to consider going through the process of setting up an account to reacquaint yourselves with the information that is required (or can be entered) when a Facebook account is first set up. Pay particular attention to the profile area of your account. What fields in the profile do you consider to be most useful? Which fields do you think are totally unnecessary and could be eliminated? What fields are missing from the profile that you think would be useful to you and your friends?

2. Investigate your account settings and application settings, paying particular attention to items that are displayed on the main page of your account. What changes would you make to these settings? Are options missing that you would find helpful to configuring your Facebook page?

3. Present your group's findings to the class. Compare your suggestions to those of other groups. Be sure to think about the needs of other groups of users (such as your parents or your grandparents), because they probably use Facebook in ways that you might not.

4. Prepare a list of recommendations for improvements to the current Facebook home page and settings pages. Clearly indicate how the proposed changes will benefit both users and the management of Facebook (retaining users, being able to better target advertising to users, and so on).

Conclusion

Facebook will most likely experience competition in the future from other social networking sites that will want to poach its huge base of users. To remain competitive, Facebook needs to consider the input of users like you to ensure that it delivers a cutting-edge product with features its customers want and need. Facebook's best chance of remaining on top of the social media heap is to be sensitive to the needs of its current users.

Private Information on Public Databases

In this exercise, you will research and then role-play a complicated ethical situation. The role you play might or might not match your own personal beliefs; in either case, your research and use of logic will enable you to represent the view assigned. An arbitrator will watch and comment on both sides of the arguments, and together the team will agree on an ethical solution.

Problem

As more tasks in our lives are conducted online, there is a tremendous amount of data that is accumulated about us in online databases. Unfortunately, much of this material is accessible in databases that are searchable by anyone with Internet access or to anyone willing to pay a small fee. Web sites such as **Spokeo.com** and **411.com** comb through publicly accessible databases such as social networking sites (Facebook or MySpace), online phone books, business sites where you have accounts (Yahoo! or MSN), and government (federal, state, and local) Web sites to compile information on individuals. There is probably a lot of information about you available on sites such as these that could expose you to risks such as identify theft.

Research Areas to Consider

- Electronic information privacy
- Electronic Privacy Information Center (**epic.org**)
- Protecting your online privacy
- Protecting yourself on Facebook
- Protecting yourself from data breaches

Process

1. Divide the class into teams.

2. Research the areas cited above and devise a scenario in which someone has complained about a Web site (such as **spokeo.com**) providing information that led to their identity being stolen.

3. Team members should write a summary that provides background information for their character—for example: victim of identity theft, Web site owner, or arbitrator—and details their character's behaviors to set the stage for the role-playing event. Then, team members should create an outline to use during the role-playing event.

4. Team members should arrange a mutually convenient time to meet for the exchange, either using the collaboration features of MyITLab, the discussion board feature of Blackboard, or meeting in person.

5. Team members should present their case to the class, or submit a PowerPoint presentation for review by the rest of the class, along with the summary and resolution they developed.

Conclusion

As technology becomes ever more prevalent and integrated into our lives, more and more ethical dilemmas will present themselves. Being able to understand and evaluate both sides of the argument, while responding in a personally or socially ethical manner, will be an important skill.

behind the scenes:

networking and security in the business world

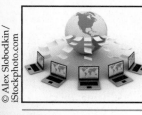

Basics of Client/Server Networks

OBJECTIVES:

What are the advantages of a business network? *(p. 562)*

How does a client/server network differ from a peer-to-peer network? *(p. 564)*

What are the different classifications of client/server networks? *(p. 565)*

What components are needed to construct a client/server network? *(p. 567)*

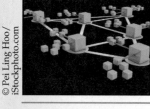

Servers and Network Topologies

OBJECTIVES:

What do the various types of servers do? *(p. 567)*

What are the various network topologies, and why is network topology important in planning a network? *(p. 571)*

Active Helpdesk: Using Servers

Sound Byte: Network Topology and Navigation Devices

Transmission Media

OBJECTIVE:

What types of transmission media are used in client/server networks? *(p. 576)*

Network Operating Systems and Network Adapters

OBJECTIVES:

What software needs to run on computers attached to a client/server network, and how does this software control network communications? *(p. 581)*

How do network adapters enable computers to participate in a client/server network? *(p. 582)*

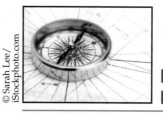

Network Navigation Devices

OBJECTIVE:

What devices assist in moving data around a client/server network? *(p. 584)*

 Sound Byte: What's My IP Address? (And Other Interesting Facts About Networks)

Network Security for Client/Server Networks

OBJECTIVE:

What measures are employed to keep large networks secure? *(p. 586)*

Sound Byte: A Day in the Life of a Network Technician

Scan here for more info on How Cool Is This? ▶

how cool is *this?*

Organizing a meeting with classmates to work on a **group project** can be **difficult**. Everyone's schedules rarely mesh to allow a face-to-face meeting, especially at commuter colleges. Facebook chat is useful, but wouldn't you rather be able to see the group members and share documents with them? You need OpenMeetings!

With **OpenMeetings**, you can quickly **establish a conference** on the Web using your webcam and microphone. You can also share documents via a whiteboard, let others in the meeting view your desktop, or record the meeting for those who can't attend. Best of all, OpenMeetings is a free, open source software module with no limitations on the number of users participating in a meeting.

The software has an intuitive interface that is easy to learn. It even has a module that allows it to be **integrated** into your **Facebook** page.

So stop **tearing your hair out** about getting your group together, and use OpenMeetings to **conduct your meetings online** in Facebook!

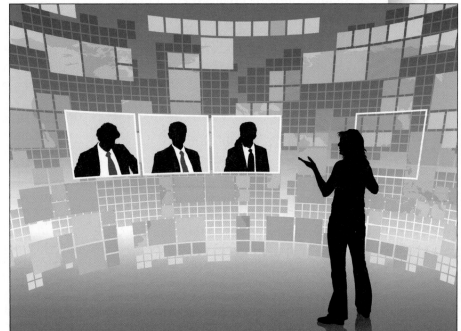

© Kamaga /iStockphoto.com

Networking Advantages

You learned about peer-to-peer networks in Chapter 7, and we'll expand your knowledge of networks in this chapter. Recall that a **network** is a group of two or more computers (or nodes) that are configured to share information and resources such as printers, files, and databases. But why do we network computers? Essentially, a network enables computers and other devices to communicate with each other. Home networks enable users to share an Internet connection, share peripherals, and share media. Businesses, such as your college or an insurance company, also gain advantages from deploying networks.

What advantages do businesses gain from networks? Large business networks provide advantages similar to those of home networks, and therefore have advantages over individual stand-alone computers:

- **Networks increase productivity.** Computers are powerful stand-alone resources. However, to increase productivity, people need to be able to share data and peripherals with coworkers and communicate with them efficiently.

Without a network, only one person at a time can access information because it resides on a single computer. Information sharing is therefore the largest benefit gained by installing a network.

- **Networks enable expensive resources to be shared.** Networks enable people to share peripherals such as printers, eliminating the need for duplicate devices. Without a network, the printer would have to be connected to one of your computers. Think about how often a printer sits idle. Compound that by having 25 students in a lab, all with their own printers. Having 25 printers sitting idle 95 percent of the time is a tremendous waste of money. Installing a network that enables one printer, working most of the time, to serve all 25 students saves money.

- **Networks facilitate knowledge sharing.** The databases you learned about in Chapter 11 become especially powerful when deployed on a network. Networked databases can serve the needs of many people at one time and increase the availability of data. Your college's databases are much more useful when all college employees can look up student records at the same time.

- **Networks enable software sharing.** Installing a new version of software on everyone's desktop in a college with 700 employees can be time consuming. However, if the computers are networked, all employees and students can access the same copy of a program from the server. Although the college must still purchase a software license for each user, with a network it can avoid having to install the program on every computer. This also saves space on individual computers, because the software doesn't reside on every computer.

- **Networks facilitate Internet connectivity.** Most college students and employees need to connect to the Internet to complete work. Providing each computer on a network with its own dedicated connection to the Internet is costly. Through a network, large groups of computers can share one Internet connection, reducing Internet connectivity expenses.

BITS AND BYTES

The Doctor Isn't In: Virtual Doctors

There is a shortage of physicians in the United States, especially in rural areas. Even if there are plenty of general practitioners in your area, is there an orthopedic surgeon or a neurologist available for a timely consult after your car accident? Computer networks are likely to provide solutions to these problems in the future in an emerging field known as telemedicine.

Initiatives such as Cisco's HealthPresence are helping patients get care locally regardless of where the doctors are located. Exam stations containing equipment and software can be installed in office parks, malls, or even mobile tractor-trailer facilities. The exam stations are often staffed with nurses or physicians' assistants who are in much greater supply than physicians. Patients visit the exam stations locally while the doctors can work remotely.

This telemedicine technology uses two-way video conferencing with high resolution cameras to enable the doctors and patients to see each other and converse. Medical equipment such as blood pressure cuffs, pulse meters, and ear, nose, and throat scopes are integrated with the video conferencing equipment so patient vital signs can be transmitted to the doctors. It's almost like being in the room with the doctor! Software deployed with the equipment is designed to facilitate the review and generation of electronic patient records.

So next time you need a doctor, maybe you won't have to wait for hours in a cold waiting room. A computer solution may be just what the doctor ordered!

- **Networks enable enhanced communication.** Social networking tools, e-mail, and instant messaging are extremely powerful applications when deployed on a network, especially one that is connected to the Internet. College students and professors can easily exchange information with each other and can share valuable data by transferring files to other users.

Are there disadvantages to using networks? Because business (or college) networks are often complex, additional personnel are usually required to maintain them. These people, called **network administrators**, have training in computer and peripheral maintenance and repair, networking design, and the installation of networking software.

Another disadvantage is that operating a network requires special equipment and software. However, most companies feel that the cost savings of peripheral sharing and the ability to give employees simultaneous access to information outweigh the costs associated with network administrators and equipment.

Client/Server Networks

Aside from the smallest networks, such as peer-to-peer networks, which are typically used in homes and small businesses, the majority of computer networks are based on the client/server model of computing. As you've learned, a **server** is a computer that both stores and shares resources on a network, whereas a **client** is a computer that requests those resources. A **client/server network** (also called a **server-based network**) contains servers as well as client computers. The inclusion of servers is what differentiates a client/server network from a typical peer-to-peer (P2P) network. Each node connected to a P2P network can communicate directly with every other node on the network instead of having a separate device exercise control over the network. Figure 12.1 illustrates the client/server relationship.

The main advantage of a client/server relationship is that it makes data flow more efficiently than in peer-to-peer networks. Servers can respond to requests from a large number of clients at the same time. In addition, servers can be configured to perform specific tasks, such as handling e-mail or database requests, efficiently.

Say you are hungry and go to a fast-food restaurant. In your role as the customer ordering food, you are the client making a request. The cook, in the role of the server, responds to the request and prepares the meal. Certainly, you could go to the restaurant and cook your own meal, but this hardly would be efficient. You would be floundering around in the kitchen with other customers as they try to cook their own meals. If the manager assigns specialized tasks to a fast-food cook (the server), many customers (clients) can be served efficiently at the same time. This is how servers work. One server can provide services efficiently to a large number of clients at one time.

Does my home network have a server? Peer-to-peer networks do not require servers to function efficiently, although some home networks now have specialized media servers for sharing media. In these networks, computers act as both clients and servers when appropriate.

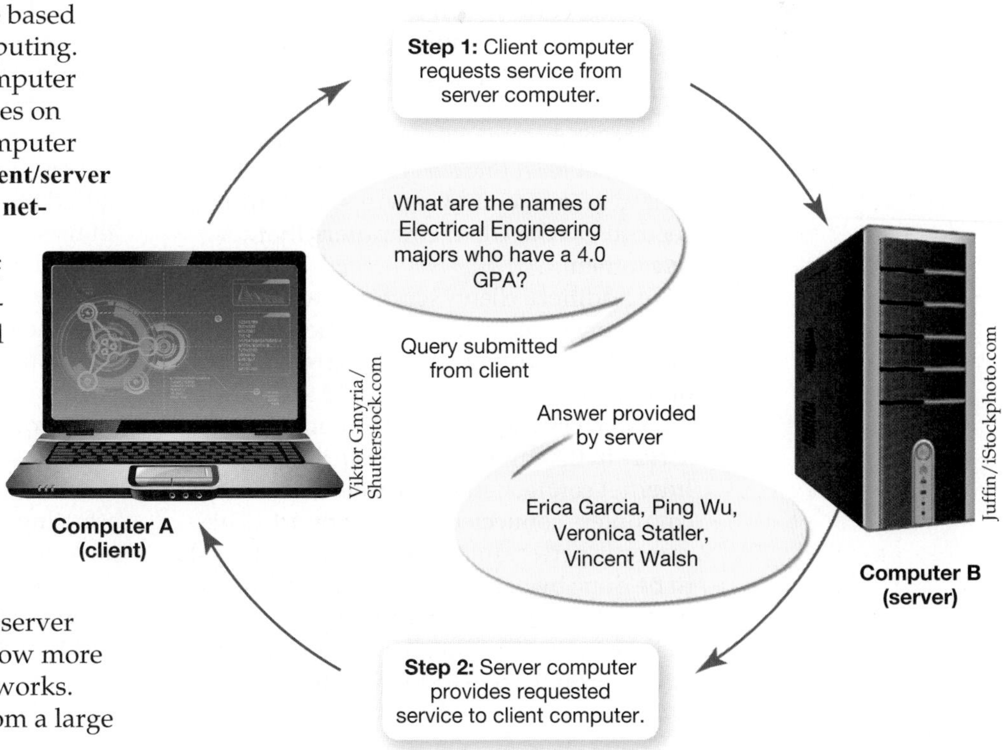

Viktor Gmyria/Shutterstock.com

Juffin/iStockphoto.com

Figure 12.1

Basic client/server interaction.

Step 1: Client computer requests service from server computer.

What are the names of Electrical Engineering majors who have a 4.0 GPA?

Query submitted from client

Answer provided by server

Erica Garcia, Ping Wu, Veronica Statler, Vincent Walsh

Computer A (client)

Computer B (server)

Step 2: Server computer provides requested service to client computer.

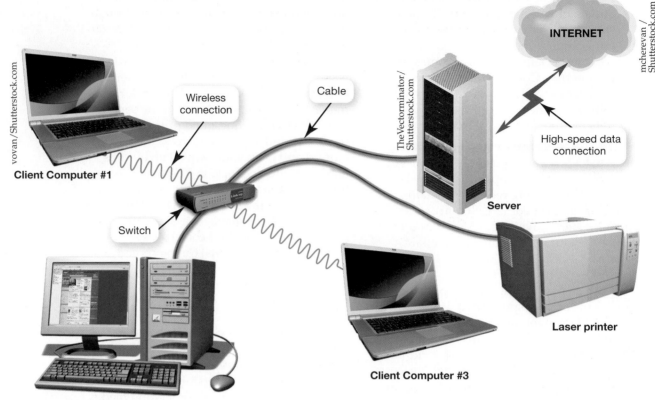

Client Computer #1

Wireless connection

Cable

INTERNET

High-speed data connection

Server

Switch

Laser printer

Client Computer #2

Client Computer #3

Figure 12.2

This small client/server network enables users to share a printer and an Internet connection.

When shouldn't a peer-to-peer network be used?

P2P networks become difficult to administer when they are expanded beyond 10 users. Each computer may require updating if there are changes to the network, which is not efficient with large numbers of computers. In addition, security can't be implemented centrally on a P2P network, but instead must be handled by each user. Client/server networks contain at least one server that provides shared resources and services, including security, to the client computers that request them.

In addition, client/server networks move data more efficiently than P2P networks, making them appropriate for large numbers of users. For example, Figure 12.2 shows a small client/server arrangement. The server in this figure provides printing and Internet connection services for all the client computers connected to the network. The server is performing tasks that would need to be done by each of the client computers in a P2P network. This frees resources on the clients for more efficiently performing processor-intensive tasks such as viewing a video or accessing a database.

Besides having a server, what makes a client/server network different from a peer-to-peer network?

The main difference is that in client/server networks, all clients connect to a server that performs tasks for them. Therefore, client/server networks are said to be **centralized**. Many tasks that individual users must handle on a P2P network can be handled centrally at the server. Peer-to-peer networks are **decentralized**. This means that users are responsible for creating their own data backups and for providing security for their computers.

For instance, data files are normally stored on a server. Therefore, backups for all users on a college's network can be performed by merely backing up all the files on the server. Security, too, can be exercised over the server instead of on each user's computer; this way, the server, not the individual user, coordinates data security.

Client/server networks also have increased scalability. **Scalability** means that more users can be added easily without affecting the performance of the other network nodes (computers or peripherals). Because servers handle the bulk of the printing, Internet access, and other tasks performed on the network, it is easy to accommodate more users by installing additional servers to help with the increased workload. Installing additional servers on a network is relatively simple and can usually be done without disrupting services for existing users.

Classifications of Client/Server Networks: LANs, WANs, MANs, and PANs

Networks are generally classified according to their size and the distance between the physical parts of the network. Four popular classifications are local area networks, wide area networks, metropolitan area networks, and personal area networks.

What are the basic classifications of client/server networks? A **local area network (LAN)** is a generally small group of computers and peripherals linked together over a relatively small geographic area. The computer lab at your school or the network serving the floor of the office building where you work is probably a LAN.

Wide area networks (WANs) comprise large numbers of users over a wider physical area or separate LANs that are miles apart.

Businesses often use WANs to connect two or more geographically distant locations. For example, a college might have a west and an east campus that are located in two different towns. The LAN at the west campus is connected to the LAN at the east campus, forming one WAN. WANs are connected either by dedicated telecommunications lines or by satellite links. Figure 12.3 shows an example of what part of a college's WAN might look like. Students on both campuses can share data and collaborate through the WAN.

Sometimes government organizations or civic groups establish WANs to link users in a specific geographic area, such as within a city or county. This special type of WAN is known as a **metropolitan area network (MAN)**. San Diego's Traffic Management Center (TMC) uses a MAN to analyze traffic patterns. You can check out the traffic maps they generate at **www.dot.ca.gov/sdtraffic**.

What sort of network connects devices such as smartphones and Bluetooth headsets? A **personal area network (PAN)** is a network used to connect computing devices that are in close proximity to each other. PANs may feature either wired or wireless connectivity. Bluetooth, a

Figure 12.3

A WAN comprises two or more LANs in different geographic locations connected by telecommunications media.

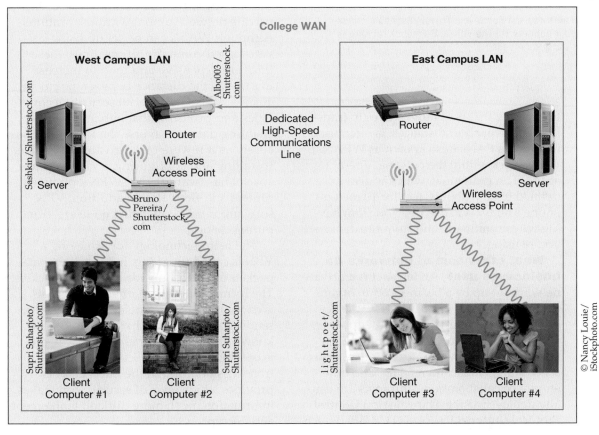

PAN Clothing: Organization and Power for Portable Gear

Now that people carry so many portable computing devices, clothing designers are starting to offer clothing that facilitates the storage, transportation, charging, and networking of their digital gadgets. The Scottevest (see Figure 12.4a) is one of a line of vests and jackets designed to hold iPods, smartphones, and even iPads. It also features a built-in PAN to help maintain connectivity of your devices. And because all the devices in your PAN need power, accessories such as the Voltaic Backpack (see Figure 12.4b) help recharge your digital devices using renewable energy sources. So don't forget to consider the perfect fashion accessory for your latest digital acquisition!

www.SCOTTEVEST.com

Voltaic Systems

Figure 12.4

(a) Shown here with an X-ray, the Scottevest Travel Vest has a convenient spot for all of your gadgets. (b) The Voltaic Backpack recharges your mobile devices using solar cells.

technology that uses radio waves to transmit data over short distances, is often used in wireless PANs (also known as WPANs). PANs work within the personal operating space of an individual, which is generally defined to be within 30 feet (or 10 meters) of one's body. WPANs free you from having wires running to and from the devices you're using.

What other sort of networks do businesses use? An **intranet** is a private network set up by a business or an organization that is used exclusively by a select group of employees, customers, suppliers, volunteers, or supporters. It can facilitate information sharing, database access, group scheduling, videoconferencing, and other employee collaborations. Intranets are usually deployed using Transmission Control Protocol/Internet Protocol (TCP/IP), which

is discussed in Chapter 13, and generally include links to the Internet. An intranet is not accessible by unauthorized individuals; a firewall protects it from unauthorized access through the Internet.

An area of an intranet that only certain corporations or individuals can access is called an **extranet**. The owner of an extranet decides who will be permitted to access it. For example, a company's customers and suppliers may be permitted to access information on the company's extranet. Extranets are useful for enabling **electronic data interchange (EDI)**, which allows the exchange of large amounts of business data (such as orders for merchandise) in a standardized electronic format. Walmart has an extranet that allows their employees, vendors, and contractors to easily share information. Other uses of extranets include providing access to catalogs and inventory databases and sharing information among partners or industry trade groups.

What security tools do intranets and extranets use? Because of security concerns, intranets and extranets often use virtual private networks to keep information secure. A **virtual private network (VPN)** uses the public Internet communications infrastructure to build a secure, private network among various locations. Although WANs can be set up using private leased communications lines, these lines are expensive and tend to increase in price as the distance between points increases. VPNs use special security technologies and protocols that enhance security, enabling data to traverse the Internet as securely as if it were on a private leased line. Installing and configuring a VPN requires special hardware such as VPN-optimized routers and firewalls. In addition, VPN software must be installed on users' computing devices.

The main technology for achieving a VPN is called **tunneling**. In tunneling, data packets are placed inside other data packets. The format of these external data packets is encrypted and is understood only by the sending and receiving hardware, which is known as a *tunnel interface*. The hardware is optimized to seek efficient routes of transmission through the Internet. This provides a high level of security and makes information much more difficult to intercept and decrypt.

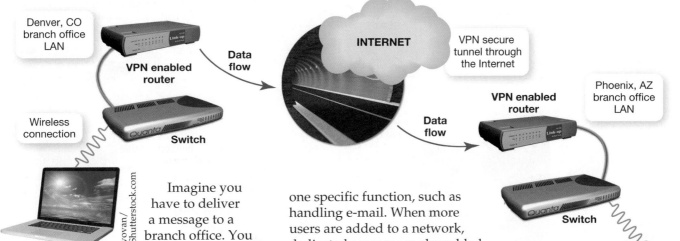

Imagine you have to deliver a message to a branch office. You could have one of your employees drive to the other office and deliver the message. But suppose he has to go through a bad neighborhood? The messenger could be waylaid by a carjacker. Using a VPN (as shown in Figure 12.5) is the equivalent of hiring a limousine and an armed guard to drive your employee through a private tunnel directly to the destination. Of course, a VPN avoids the enormous cost associated with the limo!

What are the key components of a client/server network? Client/server networks have many of the same components that P2P networks do, as well as some components specific to client/server networks. The key components of a client/server network are servers, network topologies (the layout of the components), transmission media, the network operating system, network adapters, and network navigation devices. Figure 12.6 shows the components of a simple client/server network. In the following sections, we will explore each component in more detail.

Servers

Servers are the workhorses of the client/server network. They interface with many different network users and assist them with a variety of tasks. The number and types of servers on a client/server network depend on the network's size and workload. Small networks (such as the one pictured in Figure 12.2) would have just one server to handle all server functions.

What types of servers are found on larger client/server networks? A **dedicated server** is a server used to fulfill one specific function, such as handling e-mail. When more users are added to a network, dedicated servers are also added to reduce the load on the main server. Once dedicated servers are deployed, the original server can become merely an authentication server or a file server.

What are authentication and file servers? An **authentication server** is a server that keeps track of who is logging on to the network and which services on the network are available to each user. Authentication servers also act as overseers for the network. They manage and coordinate the services provided by any other dedicated servers located on the network. A **file server** is a server that stores and manages files for network users. On the network at your workplace or school, you may be provided with space on a file server to store files you create.

What functions do dedicated servers handle? Any task that is repetitive or demands a lot of time from a computer's processor (CPU) is a good candidate to relegate to a dedicated server. Common types of dedicated servers are print servers, application servers, database servers, e-mail servers, communications servers, and Web servers. Servers are connected to a client/server network so that all client computers that need to use their services can access them, as shown in Figure 12.7.

Print Servers

How does a print server function? Printing is a function that takes a large quantity of CPU time and that most people do quite often. **Print servers** manage all client-requested printing jobs for all printers on a network, which helps client computers to complete more productive work by relieving them of printing duties.

Figure 12.5

Local area networks (LANs) in different cities can communicate securely over the Internet using VPN technology.

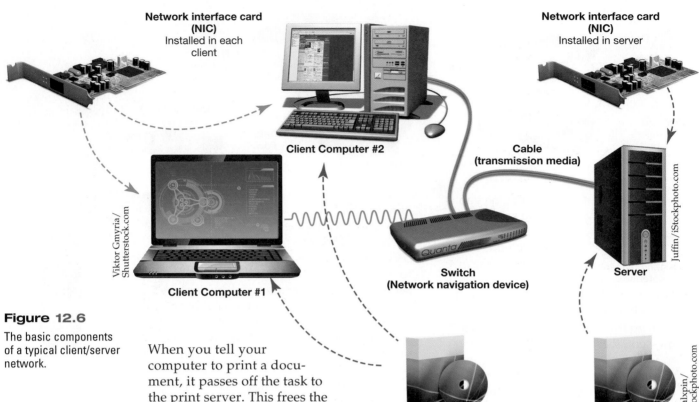

Network interface card (NIC)
Installed in each client

Client Computer #2

Network interface card (NIC)
Installed in server

Cable (transmission media)

Viktor Gmyria/Shutterstock.com

Client Computer #1

Switch (Network navigation device)

Server

Juffin /iStockphoto.com

Network operating software
Included in operating system software for client computers

Network operating software
Installed on server

© alxpin/iStockphoto.com

Figure 12.6

The basic components of a typical client/server network.

When you tell your computer to print a document, it passes off the task to the print server. This frees the CPU on your computer to do other jobs.

How does the printer know which documents to print? A **print queue** is a software holding area for print jobs. When the print server receives a printing request from a client computer, it puts the job into a print queue on the print server. Normally, each printer on a network has its own uniquely named print queue. Jobs receive a number when they enter the queue and go to the printer in the order in which they were received. Print queues thus function like the "take a number" machines at a supermarket deli. Thus, print servers organize print jobs into an orderly sequence to make printing more efficient on a shared printer. Another useful aspect of print servers is that network administrators can set them to prioritize print jobs. Different users and types of print jobs can be assigned different priorities so higher priority jobs will be printed first. For instance, in a company in which documents are printed on demand for clients, you would want these print jobs to take precedence over routine employee correspondence.

Application Servers

What function does an application server perform? In many networks, all users run the same application software on their computers. In a network of thousands of personal computers, installing application software on each computer is time consuming. An **application server** acts as a repository for application software.

When a client computer connects to the network and requests an application, the application server delivers the software to the client computer. Because the software does not reside on the client computer itself, this eases the task of installation and upgrading. The application needs to be installed or upgraded only on the application server, not on each network client.

Database Servers

What does a database server do? As its name implies, a **database server** provides client computers with access to information stored in databases. Often, many people need to access a database at the same time. For example, multiple college advisers can serve students at the same time because the advisers all have access to the student information database. This is made possible because the database resides on a database

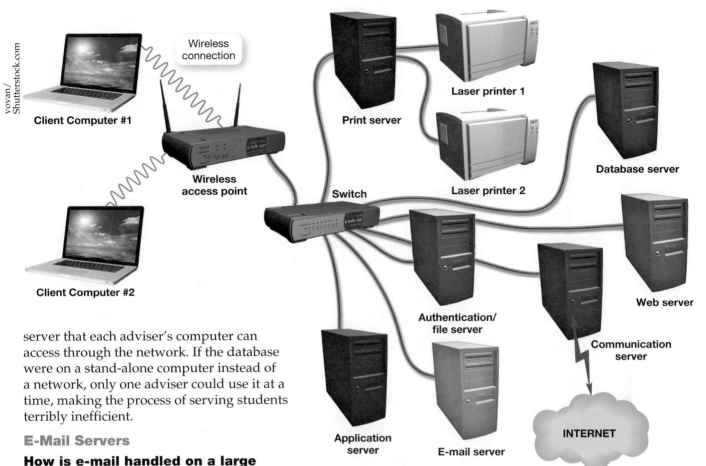

Client Computer #1

Wireless connection

Wireless access point

Client Computer #2

Print server

Laser printer 1

Laser printer 2

Switch

Database server

Authentication/ file server

Web server

Communication server

Application server

E-mail server

INTERNET

server that each adviser's computer can access through the network. If the database were on a stand-alone computer instead of a network, only one adviser could use it at a time, making the process of serving students terribly inefficient.

E-Mail Servers

How is e-mail handled on a large client/server network? The volume of e-mail on a large network could quickly overwhelm a server that was attempting to handle other functions as well. The sole function of an **e-mail server** is to process and deliver incoming and outgoing e-mail. On a network with an e-mail server, when you send an e-mail from your computer, it goes to the e-mail server, which then handles the routing and delivery of your message. The e-mail server functions much like a postal carrier, who picks up your mail and sees that it finds its way to the correct destination.

Communications Servers

What types of communications does a communications server handle? A **communications server** handles all communications between the network and other networks, including managing Internet connectivity. All requests for information from the Internet and all messages being sent through the Internet pass through the communications server. Because Internet traffic is substantial at most organizations, the communications server has a heavy workload.

The communications server often is the only device on the network connected to the Internet. E-mail servers, Web servers, and other devices needing to communicate with the Internet usually route all their traffic through the communications server. Providing a single point of contact with the outside world makes it easier to secure the network from hackers.

Web Servers and Cloud Servers

What function does a Web server perform? A **Web server** is used to host a Web site so it will be available through the Internet. Web servers run specialized software such as Apache HTTP Server (open

Figure 12.7

A typical large-scale client/server network with several dedicated servers installed.

ACTIVE HELP-DESK Using Servers

In this Active Helpdesk call, you'll play the role of a helpdesk staffer, fielding calls about various types of servers and client/server software.

Virtualization: Making Servers Work Harder

Servers have historically been deployed on client/server networks as dedicated machines that perform one specific task. But today there are good reasons why some businesses may consider having servers perform multiple tasks.

Computers produce a lot of heat and take up physical space. As a company grows, continually adding servers may exceed the available floor space and cooling capacity of a company's data center. And budgets may limit the ability to purchase additional dedicated servers when needed.

The concept of dedicated servers goes back to the days when servers had single-core processors. However, today's powerful multi-core processors allow computers to process data more quickly and efficiently than single-core machines. Sometimes just dedicating a computer to one task, such as an authentication server, might not come close to fully utilizing that server's computing potential.

Dedicated servers are mission critical when those servers handle processor-intensive operations. For instance, a major online retailer would have dedicated Web servers handling e-commerce traffic so that customers could purchase items quickly and efficiently. Motion picture companies, like Pixar, that are making movies featuring computer-generated images (CGI) need dedicated servers to process (render) the images. But small businesses don't necessarily require the computing power of a dedicated server for all of their computing needs. A company of 30 people would probably not generate a great deal of activity on an authentication server or an e-mail server. For all of these reasons, virtualization was born.

Virtualization involves using specialized software to make individual physical servers behave as though they are more than one physical device (see Figure 12.8). Each virtual server can operate as its own separate device and can even run its own operating system. Therefore, you could have a virtual e-mail server running Windows and a virtual Web server running Linux on the same physical server.

Creating virtual servers requires running specialized virtualization software on a physical server. The physical server then becomes known as the host. Virtual servers running on a host machine are known as **guest servers**. The computing power of the CPU is split between the guests running on the host. Therefore, it wouldn't be practical to run dozens of guest environments on one host because the computing power would become diluted. However, it is very possible to run two or three guest servers on one multi-processor physical server as long as the applications running on the virtual servers are not overly processor intensive. VMware, Microsoft Virtual Server, and XenServer are popular virtualization software packages.

Virtualization is a great way to provide backup servers at a low cost. Mission-critical servers, such as Web servers, need to be running and available to customers at all times. If a Web server for an e-commerce business fails, the company is unable to sell products until the server is repaired. With virtual servers, you could have a copy of your Web server running virtually on two separate physical machines (say server 1 and 2). If server 1 breaks, you could immediately have the virtual copy of your Web server on physical server 2 take over and the company could still be processing orders and conducting business.

While virtualization isn't the perfect solution for every business situation, it does offer intriguing possibilities and effective solutions for specific needs. Many companies today are actively exploring virtualization as a way to extend their computing resources and save money.

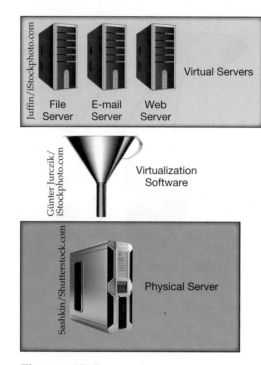

Figure 12.8

Virtualization software allows one physical server to appear to be multiple separate servers capable of handling three different processes.

source server software) and Microsoft Internet Information Services (IIS) that enable them to host Web pages. Not every large network has a Web server. Many colleges and businesses use a third-party Web hosting company to host their Web sites instead.

What is a cloud server? Servers no longer need to be physically located at a company's offices. **Cloud servers** are servers that are maintained by hosting companies, such as Rackspace Hosting, and that are connected to networks via the Internet. A company could choose to have any of the different types of servers discussed above hosted on cloud servers instead of maintaining them locally. Small businesses that don't have a large staff of computer professionals often choose to use cloud servers to save money.

Network Topologies

Just as buildings have different floor plans depending on their uses, networks have different blueprints denoting their layout. **Network topology** refers to the physical or logical arrangement of computers, transmission media (cable), and other network components. *Physical topology* refers to the layout of the "real" components of the network, whereas *logical topology* refers to the virtual connections among network nodes. Logical topologies usually are determined by network protocols instead of the physical layout of the network or the paths electrical signals follow on the network.

A **protocol** is a set of rules for exchanging communication. Although many people think that Ethernet is a type of network topology, it is actually a communications protocol. Therefore, an Ethernet network could be set up using almost any type of physical topology.

For example, assume that your class has to send a message to the class next door. You decide to arrange your class in a straight line from your classroom to the other classroom. Each student will whisper the message to the next student in the line until the message is eventually passed to a student in the other classroom. The arrangement of the students in a straight line is the physical topology. The passing of the message from student to student using spoken language is the logical topology. The use of English as the language is the protocol.

In this section, we will explore the most common network topologies (bus, ring, and star) and discuss when each topology is used. The type of network topology used is important because it can affect a network's performance and scalability. Knowing how the basic topologies work, and the strengths and weaknesses of each one, will help you understand why particular network topologies were chosen on the networks you use.

What does a bus topology look like?

In a **bus** (or **linear bus**) **topology**, all computers are connected in sequence on a single cable, as shown in Figure 12.9. This topology was deployed most often in peer-to-peer networks. It has largely become legacy technology due to the decreased cost of Ethernet networks, which use a star topology, and because a bus topology is not designed to easily support wireless connections. However, bus topologies are still found in some manufacturing facilities when connecting groups of computer-controlled machines.

Each computer on the bus network can communicate directly with every other computer on the network. **Data collisions**, which happen when two computers send data at the same time and the sets of data collide somewhere in the media, are a problem on all networks. When data collides, it is often lost or irreparably damaged. A limitation of bus networks is that data collisions can occur fairly easily because a bus network is essentially composed of one main communication medium (a single cable).

Because two signals transmitted at the same time on a bus network may cause a data collision, an **access method** has to be established to control which computer is allowed to use the transmission media at a certain time. Computers on a bus network behave like a group of people having a conversation. The computers "listen" to the network data traffic on the media. When no other computer is transmitting data (that is, when the "conversation" stops), the computer knows it is allowed to transmit data on the media. This means of taking turns "talking" prevents data collisions.

How does data get from point to point on a bus network?

The data is broadcast throughout the network via the media to all devices connected to the network. The data is broken into small segments, each called a **packet**. Each packet contains the address of the computer or peripheral device to which it is being sent. Each computer or device connected to the network listens for data that contains its address. When it "hears" data addressed to it, it takes the data off the media and processes it.

The devices (nodes) attached to a bus network do nothing to move data along the network. This makes a bus network a

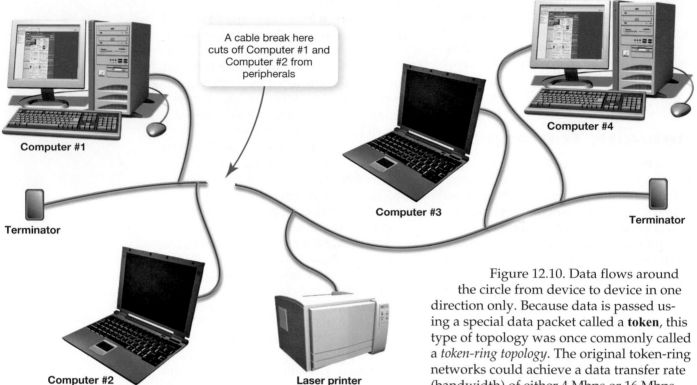

A cable break here cuts off Computer #1 and Computer #2 from peripherals

Computer #1

Terminator

Computer #2

Laser printer

Computer #3

Computer #4

Terminator

Figure 12.9

A linear bus topology.

passive topology. The data travels the entire length of the medium and is received by all network devices. The ends of the cable in a bus network are capped off by terminators (as shown in Figure 12.9). A **terminator** is a device that absorbs a signal so that it is not reflected back onto parts of the network that have already received it.

What are the advantages and disadvantages of bus networks? The simplicity and low cost of bus network topology were the major reasons it was deployed most often in P2P networks. The major disadvantage is that if there is a break in the cable, the bus network is effectively disrupted because some computers are cut off from others on the network. Only one computer can communicate at a time, so adding a large number of nodes to a bus network limits performance and causes delays in sending data. Because Ethernet networks don't suffer from these limitations, you rarely see bus topologies today.

Ring Topology

What does a ring topology look like? Not surprisingly, given its name, the computers and peripherals in a **ring** (or **loop**) **topology** are laid out in a configuration resembling a circle, as shown in

Figure 12.10. Data flows around the circle from device to device in one direction only. Because data is passed using a special data packet called a **token**, this type of topology was once commonly called a *token-ring topology*. The original token-ring networks could achieve a data transfer rate (bandwidth) of either 4 Mbps or 16 Mbps, but more recent token technologies can deliver speeds as high as 100 Mbps.

How does a token move data around a ring? A token is passed from computer to computer around the ring until it is grabbed by a computer that needs to transmit data. The computer "holds onto" the token until it has finished transmitting data. Only one computer on the ring can "hold" the token at a time, and usually only one token exists on each ring.

If a node has data to send, such as a document that needs to go to the printer, it waits for the token to be passed to it. The node then takes the token out of circulation and sends the data to its destination. When the receiving node receives a complete transmission of the data (in this example, when the document is received by the printer), it transmits an acknowledgment to the sending node. The sending node then generates a new token and starts it going around the ring again. This is called the **token method** and is the access method ring networks use to avoid data collisions.

A ring topology is an **active topology**, which means that nodes participate in moving data through the network. Each node on the network is responsible for retransmitting the token or the data to the next node on the ring. Large ring networks have the capability

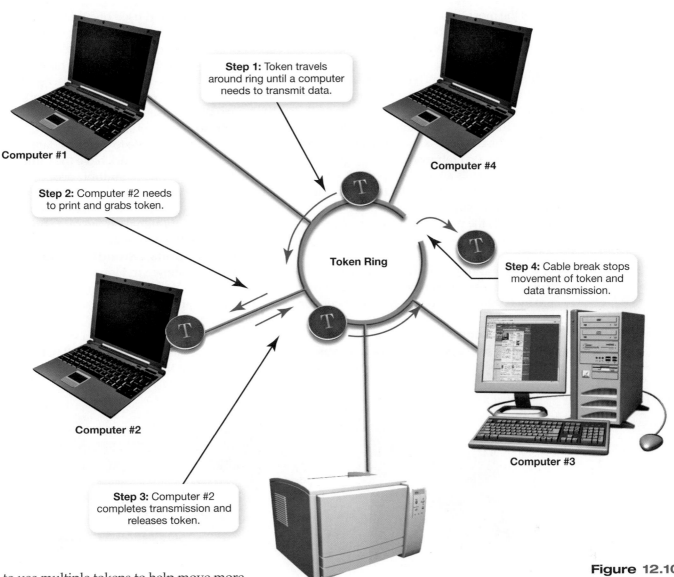

Step 1: Token travels around ring until a computer needs to transmit data.

Computer #1

Computer #4

Step 2: Computer #2 needs to print and grabs token.

Token Ring

Step 4: Cable break stops movement of token and data transmission.

Computer #2

Computer #3

Step 3: Computer #2 completes transmission and releases token.

Printer

Figure 12.10

A ring topology.

to use multiple tokens to help move more data faster.

What are the advantages and disadvantages of a ring topology? A ring topology provides a fairer allocation of network resources than does a bus topology. By using a token, a ring network enables all nodes on the network to have an equal chance to send data. One "chatty" node cannot monopolize the network bandwidth as easily as in a bus topology because it must pass the token on after sending a batch of data. In addition, a ring topology's performance will remain acceptable even with large numbers of users.

One disadvantage of a ring network is that if one computer fails, it can bring the entire network to a halt because that computer is unavailable to retransmit tokens and data. Another disadvantage is that problems in the ring can be hard for network administrators to find. It's easier to

expand a ring topology than a bus topology, but adding a node to a ring does cause the ring to cease to function while the node is being installed.

Star Topology

What is the layout for a star topology? A **star topology** is the most widely deployed client/server network layout today because it

SOUND BYTE

Network Topology and Navigation Devices

In this Sound Byte, you'll learn about common network topologies, the types of networks they are used with, and various network navigation devices.

offers the most flexibility for a low price. In a star topology, the nodes connect to a central communications device called a *switch* in a pattern resembling a star, as shown in Figure 12.11. The switch receives a signal from the sending node and retransmits it to the node on the network that needs to receive the signal. Each network node picks up only the transmissions addressed to it. Because the switch retransmits data signals, a star topology is an active topology. (We discuss switches in more detail later in this chapter.) The only drawback is that if the switch fails, the network no longer functions. However, it is relatively easy to replace a switch.

Many star networks use the Ethernet protocol. Networks using the Ethernet protocol are by far the most common type of network in use today.

How do computers on a star network avoid data collisions? Because most star networks are Ethernet networks,

they use the method used on all Ethernet networks to avoid data collisions: **CSMA/CD** (short for *carrier sense multiple access with collision detection*). With CSMA/CD, a node connected to the network uses carrier sense (that is, it "listens") to verify that no other nodes are currently transmitting data signals. If the node doesn't hear any other signals, it assumes that it is safe to transmit data. All devices on the network have the same right (that is, they have multiple access) to transmit data when they deem it safe. It is therefore possible for two devices to begin transmitting data signals at the same time. If this happens, the two signals collide.

What happens when the signals collide? As shown in Figure 12.12, when two nodes (#1 and #2) begin transmitting data signals at the same time, signals collide, and a node on the network (#3) detects the collision (Step 1). Node #3 then sends a special signal called a **jam signal** to all network nodes, alerting them that a collision has

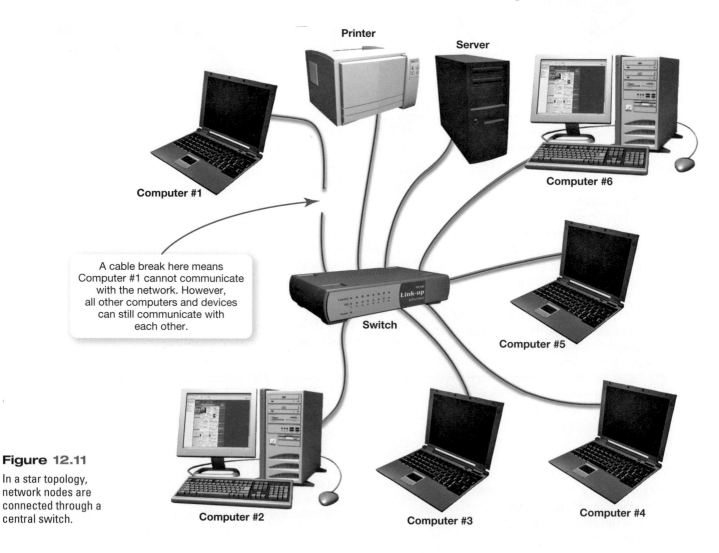

Printer

Server

Computer #1

Computer #6

A cable break here means Computer #1 cannot communicate with the network. However, all other computers and devices can still communicate with each other.

Switch

Computer #5

Computer #2

Computer #3

Computer #4

Figure 12.11

In a star topology, network nodes are connected through a central switch.

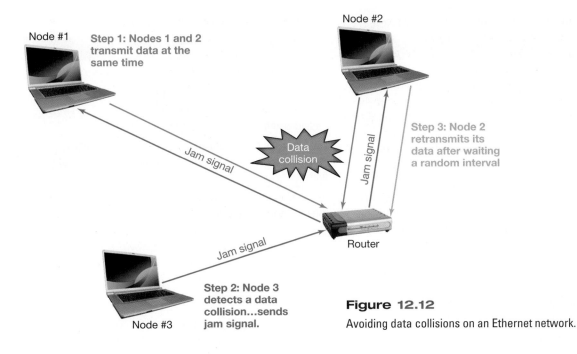

Node #1

Step 1: Nodes 1 and 2 transmit data at the same time

Node #2

Jam signal

Data collision

Jam signal

Jam signal

Step 3: Node 2 retransmits its data after waiting a random interval

Router

Step 2: Node 3 detects a data collision...sends jam signal.

Node #3

Figure 12.12

Avoiding data collisions on an Ethernet network.

occurred (Step 2). The original nodes #1 and #2 then stop transmitting and wait a random amount of time before retransmitting their data signals (Step 3). The wait times need to be random; otherwise, both nodes would start retransmitting at the same time and another collision would occur.

What are the advantages and disadvantages of a star topology? The main reason a star topology generally is considered to be superior to a ring topology is that if one computer on a star topology fails, it doesn't affect the rest of the network. This is extremely important in a large network in which having one disabled computer affect the operations of several hundred other computers would be unacceptable.

Another advantage is that it is easy to add nodes to star networks. Furthermore, performance remains acceptable even with large numbers of users. In addition, centralizing communications through a switch makes troubleshooting and repairs on star networks easier for network technicians. Technicians can usually pinpoint a communications problem just by examining the switch, as opposed to searching for a particular length of cable that broke in a ring network.

The disadvantage of star networks used to be cost. Because of the complexity of the

layout of star networks, they require more cable and used to be more expensive than bus or ring networks. Because the price of cable has fallen and wireless nodes are replacing many wired nodes on networks, this has ceased to be a barrier in most cases.

Comparing Topologies

Which topology is the best one? Figure 12.13 lists the advantages and disadvantages of bus, ring, and star topologies. Star topologies are the most common, mainly because large networks are constantly adding new users. The ability to add new users simply—by installing an additional switch—without affecting users already on the network is the deciding factor. The networks you'll encounter at school and in the workplace will almost certainly be laid out in a star topology. Bus topologies have become all but extinct now that most home networks utilize a star topology. Ring topologies are still popular in certain businesses where fair allocation of network access is a major requirement of the network.

Can topologies be combined within a single network? Because each topology has its own unique advantages, topologies are often combined to construct

Figure 12.13 | ADVANTAGES AND DISADVANTAGES OF BUS, RING, AND STAR TOPOLOGIES

Topology	Advantages	Disadvantages
Bus	It uses a minimal amount of cable. Installation is easy, reliable, and inexpensive.	Breaks in the cable can disable the network. Large numbers of users will greatly decrease performance because of high volumes of data traffic.
Ring	Allocates access to the network fairly. Performance remains acceptable even with large numbers of users.	Adding or removing nodes disables the network. Failure of one computer can bring down the entire network. Problems in data transmission can sometimes be difficult to find.
Star	Failure of one computer does not affect other computers on the network. Centralized design simplifies troubleshooting and repairs. High scalability: adding computers or groups of computers as needed is easy. Performance remains acceptable even with large numbers of users.	Requires more cable (and possibly higher installation costs) than a bus or ring topology. The switch is a single point of failure. If it fails, all computers connected to that switch are affected.

business networks. Combining multiple topologies into one network is known as constructing a **hybrid topology**. For instance, fair allocation of resources may be critical for reservation clerks at an airline (thereby requiring a ring network), but the airline's purchasing department may require a star topology. One disadvantage of hybrid topologies is that hardware changes must usually be made to switch a node from one topology to another.

Transmission Media

A variety of building materials are available for constructing a house; the ones chosen will depend on the needs of the builder. Similarly, when building a network, network engineers can use different types of media. **Transmission media**, whether for wired or wireless communications technology, comprise the physical system that data takes to flow between devices on the network. Without transmission media, network devices would be unable to communicate.

Why are wired connections used in business networks? Wired connections are popular in business networks because they generally provide higher throughput than wireless connections. Desktop computers still provide more computing power

for less money than notebooks, which makes desktop computers popular choices for business networks. Because desktops aren't often moved around, they are usually connected to a network with a wired connection.

Wired Transmission Media

What types of cable are commonly used for networks? Most home networks use twisted-pair cable as wired transmission media. For business networks, the three main cable types that are used today are twisted-pair, coaxial, and fiber-optic.

What are the important factors in choosing a cable type? Although each cable type is different, the same criteria always need to be considered when choosing a cable type:

- **Maximum run length:** Each type of cable has a maximum run length over which signals sent across it can be "heard" by devices connected to it. Therefore, when designing a network, network engineers must accurately measure the distances between devices to ensure that they select an appropriate cable.

- **Bandwidth:** As you learned in earlier chapters, bandwidth is the amount of data that can be transmitted across a transmission medium in a certain amount of time. Each cable is different and is rated by the maximum bandwidth it can support. Bandwidth is measured in bits per second, which represents how many bits of data can be transmitted along the cable each second.

- **Bend radius (flexibility):** When installing cable, it is often necessary to bend the cable around corners. The bend radius of the cable defines how many degrees a cable can be bent in a one-foot segment before it is damaged.

If many corners need to be navigated when installing a network, network engineers use cabling with a high bend radius.

- **Cable cost:** The cost per foot of different types and grades of cable varies widely. Cable selection may have to be made based on cost if adequate funds are not available for the optimal type of cabling.

- **Installation costs:** Twisted-pair and co-axial cable are easy and inexpensive to install. Fiber-optic cable requires special

Use Mobile Networking . . . to Fix Potholes?

Everyone has some sort of civic problem in their neighborhood. Maybe there is a park in your neighborhood that is cluttered with trash. Or a pothole by the mall that developed over the winter and still hasn't been fixed. Traditional methods for dealing with these problems, such as telephone or snail mail to alert the appropriate authorities, often don't result in speedy solutions. And what if you forgot exactly where that pothole was that you saw and you describe the location incorrectly? The street repair crew can't fix it if they can't find it. Now there is a solution available that makes use of mobile communication networks to speed problem resolutions along.

SeeClickFix (**www.seeclickfix.com**) is a Web site that is designed to allow citizens to report non-emergency problems to the appropriate

authorities, such as government agencies or utility companies. Using your mobile phone you can access SeeClickFix and create a problem ticket (see Figure 12.14). You write a description of the problem, attach appropriate pictures, and then either geo-tag the location or enter a street address of the problem. Local governments and utility companies sign up with SeeClickFix to monitor and resolve problems reported by citizens. If you are an official, you can acknowledge a problem to let people know it is being addressed or close an issue when it has been resolved. So stop complaining about problems and start reporting them!

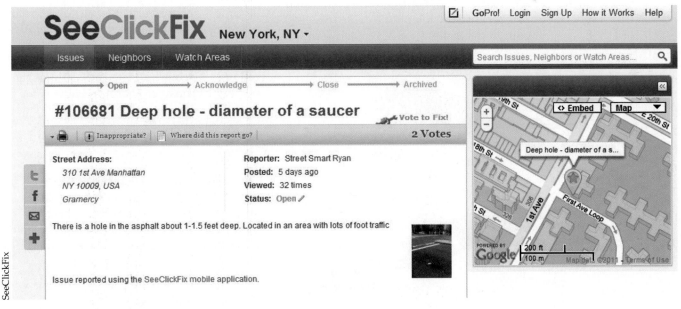

Figure 12.14

Reporting problems from your phone makes it easy to resolve neighborhood problems like potholes.

training and equipment to install, which increases the installation costs.

- **Susceptibility to interference:** Signals traveling down a cable are subject to two types of interference. Electromagnetic interference (EMI), which is caused when the cable is exposed to strong electromagnetic fields, can distort or degrade signals on the cable. Fluorescent lights and machinery with motors or transformers are the most common sources of EMI emissions. Cable signals also can be disrupted by radio frequency interference (RFI), which is usually caused by broadcast sources (television and radio signals) located near the network. Cable types are rated as to how well they resist interference.

- **Signal transmission methods:** Both coaxial cable and twisted-pair cable send electrical impulses down conductive material to transmit data signals. Fiber-optic cable transmits data signals as pulses of light.

In the sections that follow, we will discuss the characteristics of each of the three major types of cable. We will also discuss the use of wireless media as an alternative to cable.

Twisted-Pair Cable

What does twisted-pair cable look like? Twisted-pair cable should be familiar to you because the telephone cable (or wire) in your home is one type of twisted-pair cable. **Twisted-pair cable** consists of pairs of copper wires twisted around each other and covered by a protective sheath (jacket). The twists are important because they cause the magnetic fields that form around the copper wires to intermingle, which makes them less susceptible to outside interference. The twists also reduce the amount of crosstalk interference (the tendency of signals on one wire to interfere with signals on a wire next to it).

If the twisted-pair cable contains a layer of foil shielding to reduce interference, it is known as **shielded twisted-pair (STP) cable**. If it does not contain a layer of foil shielding, it is known as **unshielded twisted-pair (UTP) cable**. This type is more susceptible to interference. Figure 12.15 shows illustrations of both types of twisted-pair cable. Because of its lower price, UTP is more widely used, unless significant sources of interference must be overcome, such as in a production environment where machines create magnetic fields.

What types of UTP cable are available? There are different standard categories of UTP cable from which to choose. The two most common types of UTP cable used in business networks today are Category 6 (Cat 6) and Category 6a (Cat 6a). Cat 6 cable can handle a bandwidth of 1 gigabit per second (Gbps), whereas Cat 6a can handle a bandwidth of 10 Gbps.

Unless severe budget constraints are in place, network engineers usually install the highest-bandwidth cable possible because reinstalling cable later (which often requires tearing up walls and ceilings) can be very expensive. Therefore, new cable installed on business networks will usually be Cat 6a cable.

Coaxial Cable

What does coaxial cable look like? **Coaxial cable** should be familiar to you if you have cable television, because most cable television installers use coaxial cable. Coaxial cable (as shown in Figure 12.16) consists of four main components:

1. The core (usually copper) is in the very center and is used for transmitting the signal.

2. A solid layer of nonconductive insulating material (usually a hard, thick plastic) surrounds the core.

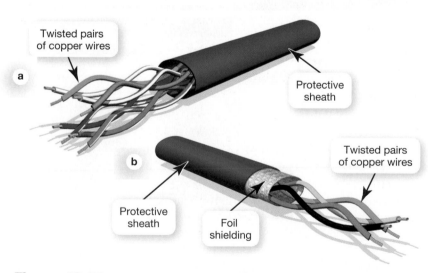

Figure 12.15

Anatomy of (a) unshielded twisted-pair (UTP) cable and (b) shielded twisted-pair (STP) cable.

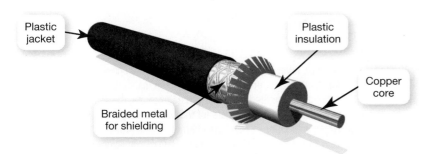

Plastic
jacket

Plastic
insulation

Copper
core

Braided metal
for shielding

Figure 12.16

Coaxial cable consists of
four main components: the
core, an insulated covering,
a braided metal shielding,
and a plastic jacket.

3. A layer of braided metal shielding covers the insulation to reduce interference with signals traveling in the core.

4. An external jacket of lightweight plastic covers the internal cable components to protect them from damage.Figure 12.16

Although coaxial cable used to be the most widely used cable in business networks, advances in twisted-pair cable shielding and transmission speeds, as well as twisted pair's lower cost, have reduced the popularity of coaxial cable. However, coaxial cable is still used in some manufacturing facilities where machinery creates heavy electrical interference.

Fiber-Optic Cable

What does fiber-optic cable look like? As shown in Figure 12.17, the core of **fiber-optic cable** is composed of a glass (or plastic) fiber (or a bundle of fibers) through which the data is transmitted. A protective layer of glass or plastic cladding is wrapped around the core to protect it. Finally, for additional protection, an outer jacket (sheath) is added, often made of a durable material such as Kevlar (the substance used to make bulletproof vests). Data transmissions can pass through fiber-optic cable in only one direction. Therefore, at least two cores are located in most fiber-optic cables to enable transmission of data in both directions.

How does fiber-optic cable differ from twisted-pair and coaxial cable? As we noted earlier, the main difference between fiber-optic cable and other types of cable is the method of signal transmission. Twisted-pair and coaxial cable use copper wire to conduct electrical impulses. In a fiber-optic cable, electrical data signals from network nodes are converted to light pulses before they are transmitted. Because EMI and RFI do not affect light waves,

fiber-optic cable is virtually immune to interference.

Wireless Media Options

What wireless media options are there? Although the word *wireless* implies "no wires," in businesses, **wireless media** are usually add-ons that extend or improve access to a wired network. In the corporate environment, wireless access is often provided to give employees a wider working area. For instance, if conference rooms offer wireless access, employees can bring their notebooks to meetings and gain access to the network during the meeting. However, when they go back to their offices, they may connect to the network through a wired connection. Accordingly, corporate networks are often a combination of wired and wireless media.

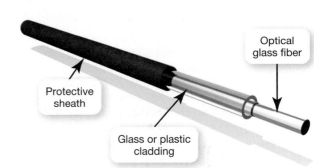

Protective
sheath

Optical
glass fiber

Glass or plastic
cladding

Figure 12.17

Fiber-optic cable is made up of a glass or plastic fiber (or a bundle of fibers), a glass or plastic cladding, and a protective sheath.

Comparing Transmission Media

Which medium is best for client/server networks? Network engineers specialize in the design and deployment of networks and are responsible for selecting network topology and media types. Their decision as to which transmission medium a network will use is based on the topology selected, the length of the cable runs needed, the amount of interference present, and the need for wireless connectivity. Coaxial cable has been

The OSI Model: Defining Protocol Standards

The Institute of Electrical and Electronics Engineers (IEEE) has taken the lead in establishing recognized worldwide networking protocols, including a standard of communications called the **Open Systems Interconnection (OSI)** reference model. The OSI model, which has been adopted as a standard throughout the computing world, provides the protocol guidelines for all modern networks. All modern network operating system (NOS) protocols are designed to interact in accordance with the standards set out in the OSI model.

The OSI model divides communications tasks into seven distinct processes called layers. Each layer of an OSI network has a specific function and knows how to communicate with the layers above and below it. Figure 12.18 shows the layers of the OSI model and their functions.

This layering approach makes communications more efficient because specialized pieces of the NOS perform specific tasks. The layering approach is akin to assembly-line manufacturing. Producing thousands of cars per day would be difficult if one person had to build a car on his or her own. However, by splitting up the work of assembling a car into specialized tasks (such as installing the engine or bolting on the bumpers) and assigning them to people who perform exceptionally well at certain tasks, greater efficiency is achieved. This is how the OSI layers work. By handling specialized tasks and communicating only with the layers above and below them, OSI layers make communications more efficient.

Let's look at how each OSI layer functions by following an e-mail you create and send to your friend:

- **Application layer:** Handles all interaction between the application software and the network. It translates the data from the application into a format that the presentation layer can understand. For example, when you send an e-mail, the application layer takes the e-mail message you created in Microsoft Outlook, translates it into a format your network can understand, and passes it to the presentation layer.

- **Presentation layer:** Reformats the data so that the session layer can understand it. It also handles data encryption (changing the data into a format that makes it harder to intercept and read the message) and compression, if required. In our e-mail example, the presentation layer notices that you selected an encryption option for the e-mail message and encrypts the data before sending it to the session layer.

- **Session layer:** Sets up a virtual (not physical) connection between the sending and receiving devices. It then manages the communication between the two. In our e-mail example, the session layer would set up the parameters for the communications session between your computer and the Internet service provider (ISP) where your friend has her e-mail account. The session layer then tracks the transmission of the e-mail until it is satisfied that all the data in the e-mail was received at your friend's ISP.

- **Transport layer:** Breaks up the data into packets and sequences them appropriately. It also handles acknowledgment of packets (that is, it determines whether the packets were received at their destination) and decides whether packets need to be sent again. In our e-mail example, the transport layer breaks up your e-mail message into packets and sends them to the network layer, making sure that all the packets reach their destination.

- **Network layer:** Determines where to send the packets on the network and identifies the best way to route them there. In our e-mail example, the network layer examines the address on the packets (the address of your friend's ISP) and determines how to route the packets so they get to the ISP and can ultimately get to the receiving computer.

- **Data link layer:** Responsible for assembling the data packets into frames (a type of data packet that holds more data), addressing the frames, and delivering them to the physical layer so they can be sent on their way. It is the equivalent of a postal worker who reads the address on a piece of mail and makes sure it is sent to the proper recipient. In our e-mail example, the data link layer assembles the e-mail data packets into frames, which are addressed with appropriate routing information that it receives from the network layer.

- **Physical layer:** Takes care of delivering the data. It converts the data into a signal and transmits it over the network so that it can reach its intended address. In our e-mail example, the physical layer sends the data over the Internet to its ultimate destination (your friend's ISP).

By following standardized protocols set forth by the OSI model, NOS software can communicate happily with the computers and peripherals attached to the network as well as with other networks.

Figure 12.18 | LAYERS OF THE OSI MODEL AND THEIR FUNCTIONS

Application layer	Handles all interfaces between the application software and the network
	Translates user information into a format the presentation layer can understand
Presentation layer	Reformats data so that the session layer can understand it
	Compresses and encrypts data
Session layer	Sets up a virtual (not physical) connection between the sending and receiving devices
	Manages communications sessions
Transport layer	Creates packets and handles packet acknowledgment
Network layer	Determines where to send the packets on the network
Data link layer	Assembles the data into frames, addresses them, and sends them to the physical layer for delivery
Physical layer	Transmits (delivers) data on the network so it can reach its intended address

Figure 12.19 | CHARACTERISTICS OF MAJOR CABLE TYPES

Cable Characteristics	Twisted-Pair (Cat 6)	Twisted-Pair (Cat 6a)	Fiber Optic
Maximum run length	328 feet (100 m)	328 feet (100 m)	Up to 62 miles (100 km)
Bandwidth	Up to 1 Gbps	Up to 10 Gbps	10 to 40 Gbps
Bend radius (flexibility)	No limit	No limit	30 degrees/foot
Cable cost	Extremely low	Low	High
Installation cost	Extremely low	Extremely low	Most expensive because of installation training required
Susceptibility to interference	High	High	None (not susceptible to EMI or RFI)

made largely obsolete by advances in twisted-pair cabling throughput and decreases in its cost.

Figure 12.19 compares the attributes of the major cable types. Most large networks have a mix of media. For example, fiber-optic cable may be appropriate for the portion of the network that traverses the factory floor, where interference from magnetic fields is significant. However, unshielded twisted-pair cable may work fine in the general office area. Wireless media may be required in conference rooms and other areas where employees are likely to connect their notebooks or where it is impractical or expensive to run cable.

Network Operating Systems

Merely using media to connect computers and peripherals does not create a client/server network. Special software known as a **network operating system (NOS)** needs to be installed on each client computer and server connected to the network to provide the services necessary for them to communicate. The NOS provides a set of common rules (a protocol) that controls communication among devices on the network. Modern operating systems, such as Windows 7 and Mac OS X, include NOS client software as part of the basic installation. However, the operating systems sold with stand-alone computers do not include the NOS server software needed to run a large network.

How does NOS software differ from operating system software? Operating system (OS) software is designed to facilitate communication between the software and hardware components of your computer. NOS software is specifically designed to provide server services, network communications, management of network peripherals, and storage. The major NOSs that include server software include Windows Server, Linux, UNIX, and SUSE Linux Enterprise Server.

To provide network communications, the client computer must run a small part of the NOS in addition to the OS. Windows 7 is an OS and is installed on home computers. As noted above, because it also has some NOS functionality, client computers (in a client/server network) that have Windows 7 installed as the OS do not need an additional NOS.

Do peer-to-peer networks need special NOS software? The software that P2P networks require is built into the Windows, Linux, and Macintosh operating systems. Therefore, if you have a simple P2P network, there is no need to purchase specialized NOS software. When a peer-to-peer network won't suffice, you can't use the networking software included in Windows and Mac OS X. Instead, you will need to purchase additional NOS software.

How does the NOS control network communications? Each NOS has its own proprietary communications language, file-management structure, and device-management structure. The NOS also sets and controls the protocols for all devices wishing to communicate on the network. Many different proprietary networking protocols exist, such as Microsoft NetBIOS Extended User Interface (NetBEUI) and the Apple File Protocol (AFP). These protocols were developed for a specific vendor's operating system. Proprietary protocols such as these do not work with another vendor's NOS.

However, because the Internet uses an open protocol (called TCP/IP) for communications, many corporate networks use TCP/IP as their standard networking protocol regardless of the manufacturer of their NOS. All modern NOSs support TCP/IP.

Can a network use two different NOSs? Many large corporate networks use several different NOSs at the same time. This is because different NOSs provide different features, some of which are more useful in certain situations than others are. For instance, although the employees of a corporation may be using a Microsoft Windows environment for their desktops and e-mail, the file servers and Web servers may be running a Linux NOS.

Because NOSs use different internal software languages to communicate, one NOS can't communicate directly with another. However, if both NOSs are using the same protocol (such as TCP/IP), they can pass information between the networks and it can be interpreted by the receiving network.

Network Adapters

As we noted in Chapter 7, client and server computers and peripherals need an interface to connect with and communicate on the network. **Network adapters** are devices that perform specific tasks to enable nodes to communicate on a network.

Network adapters are installed inside computers and peripherals. These adapters are referred to as network interface cards (NICs).

What do network adapters do? Network adapters perform three critical functions:

1. **They generate high-powered signals to enable network transmissions.** Digital signals generated inside the computer are fairly low powered and would not travel well on cable or wireless network media without network adapters. Network adapters convert the signals from inside the computer to higher-powered signals that have no trouble traversing the network media.

2. **They are responsible for breaking the data into packets and preparing the packets for transmission across the network.** They also are responsible for receiving incoming data packets and, in accordance with networking protocols, reconstructing them, as shown in Figure 12.20.

3. **They act as gatekeepers for information flowing to and from the client computer.** Much like a security guard in a gated community, a network adapter is responsible for permitting or denying access to the client computer (the community) and controlling the flow of data (visitors).

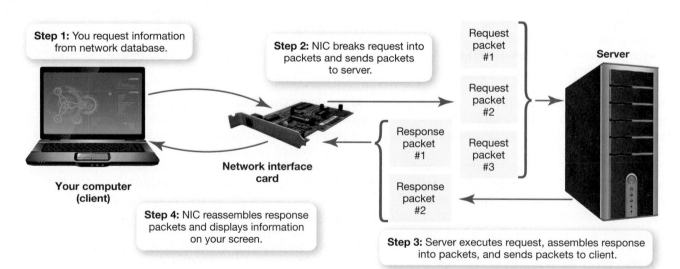

Step 1: You request information from network database.

Step 2: NIC breaks request into packets and sends packets to server.

Request packet #1

Request packet #2

Request packet #3

Response packet #1

Response packet #2

Server

Network interface card

Your computer (client)

Step 4: NIC reassembles response packets and displays information on your screen.

Step 3: Server executes request, assembles response into packets, and sends packets to client.

Figure 12.20

An NIC is responsible for breaking down data into packets, preparing packets for transmission, receiving incoming data packets, and reconstructing them.

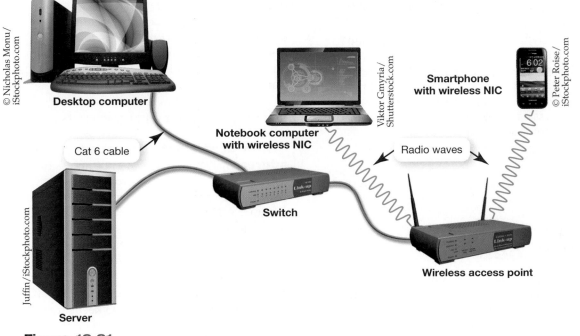

Desktop computer

Cat 6 cable

Notebook computer
with wireless NIC

Smartphone
with wireless NIC

Radio waves

Switch

Server

Wireless access point

© Nicholas Monu/
iStockphoto.com

Viktor Gmyria/
Shutterstock.com

© Peter Roise/
iStockphoto.com

Juffin/iStockphoto.com

Figure 12.21

This small corporate network has an added wireless access point.

You should note that there will not always be the same number of response packets as there are request packets. The number of packets depends on the volume of the data being sent. A simple response may have less data than a complex one.

Are there different types of network adapters? Although there are different types of network adapters, almost without exception, Ethernet (either wired or wireless) is the standard communications protocol used on most client/server networks. Therefore, the adapter cards that ship with computers today are Ethernet compliant. The majority of Ethernet adapters provide connection ports that accept RJ-45 (Ethernet) connector plugs for connection to twisted-pair cable. However, adapters that provide other types of connectors for direct connections to other types of network media are available.

Do wireless networks require network adapters? A computing device that connects to a network using wireless access needs to have a special network adapter card, called a **wireless network interface card (wireless NIC)**, installed in it. Notebook computers and other portable computing devices contain wireless NICs. To allow wireless connections, a network

must be fitted with devices called wireless access points. A **wireless access point (WAP)** gives wireless devices a sending and receiving connection point to the network.

Figure 12.21 shows an example of a typical corporate network with a wireless access point. The access point is connected to the wired network through a conventional cable. When a notebook, or other device with a wireless NIC, is powered on near a wireless access point, it establishes a connection with the access point using radio waves. Many devices can communicate with the network through a single wireless access point.

Do network adapters require software? Because the network adapter is responsible for communications between the client computer and the network, it needs to speak the same language as the network's special operating system software. Therefore, special communications software called a **device driver** is installed on all client computers in the client/server network. Device drivers enable the network adapter to communicate with the server's operating system and with the operating system of the computer in which the adapter is installed.

Network Navigation Devices

As mentioned earlier, data flows through the network in packets. Data packets are like postal letters. They don't get to their destinations without some help. In this section, we explore the various conventions and devices that help speed data packets on their way through the network.

MAC Addresses

How do data packets know where to go on the network? Each network adapter has a physical address similar to a serial number on an appliance. This is called a **media access control (MAC) address**, and it is made up of six two-position characters such as 01:40:87:44:79:A5. (Don't confuse this MAC with the Apple computers of the same name.) The first three sets of characters (in this case, 01:40:87) specify the manufacturer of the network adapter, whereas the second set of characters (in this case, 44:79:A5) makes up a unique address. Because all MAC addresses must be unique, there is an IEEE committee responsible for allocating blocks of numbers to network adapter manufacturers.

Are MAC addresses the same as IP addresses? MAC addresses and Internet Protocol (IP) addresses are not the same thing. A MAC address is used for identification purposes *internally* on a network, which is similar to giving people different names to differentiate them. An IP address is the address *external* entities use to communicate with your network and is similar to your home street address.

Think of it this way: The postal carrier delivers a package (data packet) to your dorm building based on its street address (IP address). The dorm's mail clerk delivers the package to your room because it has your name on it (MAC address) and not that of your neighbor. Both pieces of information are necessary to ensure that the package (or data) reaches its destination.

How does a data packet get a MAC address? Data packets are not necessarily sent alone. Sometimes groups of data packets are sent together in a package called a frame. A **frame** is a container that can hold multiple data packets. This is similar to placing several letters going to the same postal address in a big envelope. While the data packets are being assembled into frames, the NOS software assigns the appropriate MAC address to the frame. The NOS keeps track of all devices and their addresses on the network. Much like a letter that is entrusted to the postal service, the frame is delivered to the MAC address that the NOS assigned to the frame.

What delivers the frames to the correct device on the network? In a small bus network, frames just bounce along the wire until the correct client computer notices the frame is addressed to it and pulls the signal off the wire. This is inefficient in a larger network. Therefore, many types of devices have been developed to deliver data to its destination efficiently. These devices are designed to route signals and exchange data with other networks.

Are MAC addresses useful for anything besides identifying a particular network device? On networks with wireless capabilities, MAC addresses can be used to enhance network security. Most wireless routers and access points can be used to filter MAC addresses and eliminate addresses of unauthorized devices. Because each MAC address is unique, you can input a list of authorized MAC addresses into the router. If someone who is using an unauthorized network adapter attempts to connect to the network, he or she will be unable to make a connection. Although it would be impractical for a large organization, in which employees constantly are being hired and leaving,

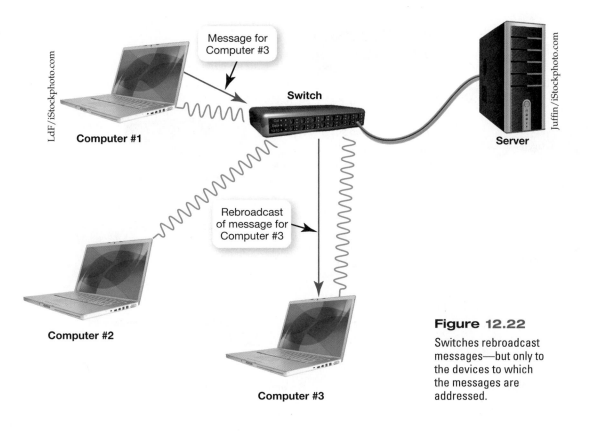

Message for
Computer #3

Switch

Server

Computer #1

Rebroadcast
of message for
Computer #3

Computer #2

Computer #3

Figure 12.22

Switches rebroadcast
messages—but only to
the devices to which
the messages are
addressed.

MAC address filtering is a useful security tool on home networks and small business networks.

Switches and Bridges

Which devices are used to route signals through a single network?

Switches and bridges are used to send data on a specific route through the network. A **switch** makes decisions, based on the MAC address of the data, as to where the data is to be sent and directs it to the appropriate network node. This improves network efficiency by helping to ensure that each node receives only the data intended for it.

Do all networks need a switch?

Switches are needed on Ethernet networks whether installed in the home or a business. Routers sold for home use have switches built into them. Figure 12.22 shows a switch being used to rebroadcast a message.

Are switches sufficient for moving data efficiently across all sizes of networks?

When a corporate network grows in size, performance can decline because many devices compete for transmission time on the network media. To solve this problem, a network can be broken into multiple segments known as collision domains. A **bridge** is a device that is used to send data between these different collision domains. A bridge sends data between collision domains, depending on where the recipient device is located, as indicated in Figure 12.23. Signals received by the bridge from collision domain A are forwarded to collision domain B only if the destination computer is located in that domain. Most home networks contain only one segment and therefore do not require bridges.

Routers

What device does a network use to move data to another network?

Whereas switches and bridges perform their functions within a single network, a **router** is designed to send information between two networks. To accomplish this, the router must look at higher-level network addresses (such as IP addresses), not MAC addresses. When the router

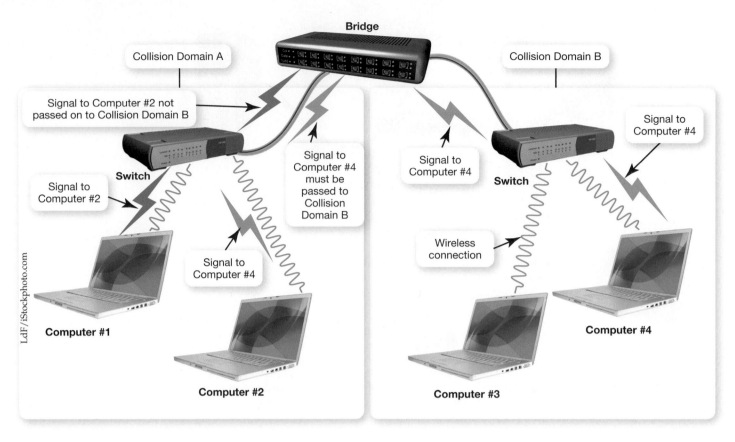

Figure 12.23

Bridges are devices used to send data between different network collision domains.

notices data with an address that does not belong to a device on the network from which it originated, it sends the data to another network to which it is attached or out onto the Internet.

Network Security for Client/Server Networks

A major advantage that client/server networks have over peer-to-peer networks is that they offer a higher level of security. With client/server networks, users can be required to enter a user ID and a password to gain access to the network. The security can be centrally administered by network administrators, freeing individual users of the responsibility of maintaining their own data security, as they must do on a peer-to-peer network.

In the following sections, we will explore the challenges network administrators face in keeping a client/server network secure.

What sources of security threats do all network administrators need to watch for? Threats can be classified into three main groups: human errors and mistakes, malicious human activity, and natural events and disasters.

- **Human errors and mistakes:** Everyone makes mistakes. For example, the clerk processing your tuition payment could accidentally post it to another student's account. A member of the computer support staff could mistakenly install an old database on top of the current one. Even physical accidents fall into this category; for example, someone could lose control of a car and drive it through the wall of the main data center.

- **Malicious human activity:** Malicious actions can be perpetrated by current employees, former employees, or third parties. For example, a disgruntled employee could introduce a virus to the network. Or a hacker could break into the student database server to steal credit card records.

- **Natural events and disasters:** Some events—such as broken water pipes, or disasters such as hurricanes and other acts of nature—are beyond human control. All can lead to the inadvertent destruction of data.

Who and what does a network need to be secure against? A network is vulnerable to unauthorized users and manipulation or misuse of the data contained on it. The person who sat next to you last semester in English class—and failed—may be interested in changing his or her grade to an A. Hackers may be interested in the financial and personal information (such as Social Security numbers and credit card numbers) stored in financial databases on a network. Thus, one of the network administrator's key functions is to keep network data secure.

Authentication

How do network administrators ensure that only authorized users access the network? Authentication is the process whereby users prove they have authorization to use a computer network. The type of authentication most people are familiar with consists of providing a user ID and password. For example, correctly entering the user ID and password on your college network proves to the network that you have authorized access. The access is authorized because the ID was generated by a network administrator when you became an authorized user of the network.

However, authentication can also be achieved through the use of biometric devices (discussed later in this chapter) and through possessed objects. A **possessed object** is any object that a user carries to identify himself and that grants him access to a computer system or computer facility. Examples include identification badges, magnetic key cards, and smart keys (similar to flash drives).

Can hackers use my account to log on to the network? If a hacker knows your user ID and password, he or she can log on and impersonate you. Impersonation can also happen if you fail to log out of a terminal on a network and someone comes along and uses your account. Sometimes network user IDs are easy to figure out because they have a certain pattern, such as

your last name and the first initial of your first name. If a hacker can deduce your user ID, he might use a software program that tries millions of combinations of letters and numbers as your password in an attempt to access your account. Attempting to access an account by repeatedly trying different passwords is known as a **brute force attack**. To prevent these attacks from succeeding, network administrators often configure accounts so that they will disable themselves after a set number of logon attempts using invalid passwords have been made. If a network account isn't set to disable itself after a small number of incorrect passwords is tried, a brute force attack may eventually succeed.

Access Privileges

How can I gain access to everything on a network? The simple answer is that you can't! When your account is set up on a network, certain access privileges are granted to indicate which systems you are allowed to use. For example, on your college network, your access privileges probably include the ability to access the Internet. You also might have access privileges to view your transcript and grades online. However, you definitely were not granted access to the grade reporting system, because this would enable you to change your grades. Likewise, you did not receive access to the financial systems; otherwise, you might be able to change your account, indicating that your bill was paid when it had not been.

How does restricting access privileges protect a network? Because network access accounts are centrally administered on the authentication server, it is easy for the network administrator to set up accounts for new users and grant them access only to the systems and software they need. The centralized nature of the creation of access accounts and the ability to restrict access to certain areas of the client/server network make it more secure than a peer-to-peer network. If you shouldn't go somewhere (such as into the files that record student grades), you can't get there on your school network!

Aside from improper access, how else do data theft and destruction occur? Data storage devices are becoming smaller even as their capacities are increasing. One problem that devices such as flash drives pose is theft of data or intellectual property. Because these devices are so portable and have such large memory capacity, it is easy for a disgruntled employee to walk out the front door with stacks of valuable documents tucked in his or her pocket. Industrial espionage has never been easier—and no spy cameras are needed!

Flash drives can also introduce viruses or other malicious programs to a network, either intentionally or unintentionally. Secure Network Technologies, a security consulting firm, decided to test a client's security procedures by leaving 20 flash drives at random locations around the client's office. By the end of the day, employees had picked up 15 of the flash drives and plugged them into computers on the company network. The flash drives contained a simple program to display images as well as a Trojan horse program. While the employees were viewing the images, the Trojan horse program enabled the consultants to access the company network and steal or compromise data. It isn't hard to imagine hackers leaving flash drives around your school that could act as "skeleton keys" to your school's network.

How should network administrators protect their networks from portable storage devices? First, educate employees about the dangers posed by portable media devices and other untrusted media. Second, create policies regulating the use of media in the workplace. Third, install security measures such as personal firewalls or antivirus software on all computers in the company. The firewalls should be able to prevent malicious programs from running, even if they are introduced to a computer via a flash drive. Last, lock down and monitor the use of USB devices. Although Microsoft networking software allows network administrators to shut off access to the USB ports on computers, this prevents employees from using flash drives and other USB devices for legitimate purposes.

Other software products, such as DeviceLock and Safend Data Protection Suite, can be deployed on a network to provide options such as detailed security policies. Such products can also monitor USB device connections and track which users have connected devices to the network (including devices other than flash drives).

Don't forget to inform the employees that their use of these devices is being monitored. That alone will be enough to scare many employees from connecting untrusted devices to the network.

Physical Protection Measures

Can any physical measures be taken to protect a network? Restricting physical access to servers and other sensitive equipment is critical to protecting a network. Where are the servers that power your college network? They are most likely behind locked doors to which only authorized personnel have access. Do you see any routers or switches lying about in computer labs? Of course you don't. These devices are securely tucked away in ceilings, walls, or closets, safe from anyone who might tamper with them in an attempt to sabotage the network or breach its security.

As shown in Figure 12.24, access to sensitive areas must be controlled. Many different devices can be used to control access. An **access card reader** is a relatively cheap device that reads information from a magnetic strip on the back of a credit card–like access card (such as your student ID card). The card reader, which can control the lock on a door, is programmed to admit only authorized personnel to the area. Card readers are easily programmed by adding authorized ID card numbers, employee numbers, and so on.

Biometric authentication devices are becoming more popular as prices of the

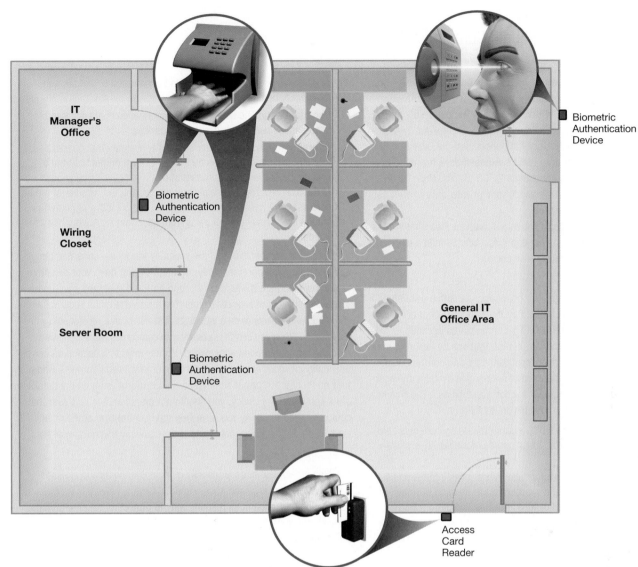

Figure 12.24

Access card readers can be used to limit access to semi-sensitive areas such as the IT office. Higher-security areas, such as the server room, may deserve the additional protection that biometric authentication devices offer.

devices fall. A **biometric authentication device** uses some unique characteristic of human biology to identify authorized users. Some devices read fingerprints or palm prints when you place your hand on a scanning pad. Other devices shine a beam of laser light into your eye and read the unique patterns of your retina to identify you. Facial recognition systems store unique characteristics of an individual's face for later comparison and identification. All of these devices are programmable. When an authorized individual uses a device for the first time, his or her fingerprints, face patterns,

or retinal patterns are scanned and stored in a database.

Financial institutions and retail stores are considering using such devices to attempt to eliminate the growing fraud problems of identity theft and counterfeiting of credit and debit cards. If fingerprint authorization were required at the supermarket to make a purchase, a thief who stole your wallet and attempted to use your credit card would be unsuccessful.

The biometric devices currently on the market don't always function as intended. Facial recognition and retinal scanning

The year 2011 might go down in history as the "Year of the Data Breach." One of the largest breaches ever to occur was the Sony PlayStation Network breach, which potentially exposed 100 million customers' data, including credit card numbers, to hackers. The Citigroup credit card data breach exposed financial data for over 360,000 customers. And the Epsilon data breach exposed data for millions of customers of that marketing company's 2,500 clients. None of these incidents makes you feel secure about your private data even if you weren't affected by these breaches.

Lots of companies have sensitive data about you. But what is their ethical responsibility to protect your data? And what should a company do for its customers when a data breach occurs?

Data Confidentiality

The objective for any company that possesses sensitive data should be information assurance. As defined by the National Security Agency (NSA), **information assurance** is "the set of measures intended to protect and defend information and information systems by ensuring their availability, integrity, authentication, confidentiality, and non-repudiation. This includes providing for restoration of information systems by incorporating protection, detection, and reaction capabilities." The five key attributes of secure information systems are as follows:

1. **Availability:** The extent to which a data-processing system is able to receive and process data. A high degree of availability is usually desirable.
2. **Integrity:** A quality that an information system has if the processing of information is logical and accurate and the data is protected against unauthorized modifications or destruction.
3. **Authentication:** Security measures designed to protect an information system against acceptance of a fraudulent transmission of data by establishing the validity of a data transmission or message, or the identity of the sender.
4. **Confidentiality:** The assurance that information is not disclosed to unauthorized persons, processes, or devices.
5. **Nonrepudiation:** A capability of security systems that guarantees that a message or data can be proven to have originated from a specific person and was processed by the recipient. The sender of the data receives a receipt for the data, and the receiver of the data gets proof of the sender's identity. The objective of nonrepudiation is to prevent either party from later denying having handled the data.

From your perspective, you are probably the most concerned about authentication and confidentiality. Companies that have your sensitive data shouldn't share it with unauthorized parties and should keep unauthorized people out of their databases. You are able to make decisions regarding confidentiality of data when you first establish a relationship with a company. When you create accounts with companies you should always read the terms and conditions, which usually include a section on confidentiality of information. Ethical companies disclose to you with whom they might share information. If you are uncomfortable about the details of its confidentiality policy, you should not create an account with that company. Unfortunately, you have very little control over authentication safeguards. That is the responsibility of the company that holds your data.

Authentication Failures

The data breaches that occur usually represent authentication failures— unauthorized people gained access to data. Clearly, when this happens a corporation has failed in its responsibility to protect its customers' data. No system is ever 100 percent safe against breaches, but most systems are adequately protected against all but the most determined hackers.

systems can sometimes be fooled by pictures or videos of an authorized user. Researchers have fooled biometric fingerprint readers by using fingers made out of modeling clay, using the fingers of cadavers, or having unauthorized persons breathe on the sensor, which makes the previous user's fingerprint visible. (Fingers leave an oily residue behind when they touch a surface.) Next-generation fingerprint readers will use specially designed algorithms that will detect moisture patterns on a person's fingers. Another approach may involve readers that detect an electrical current when a finger touches the reader, which is possible because the human body conducts electrical current. Future retinal readers may check whether a person blinks or his or her pupils contract when a bright light shines on them. Suffice it to say, these devices have a way to go before they are foolproof.

Firewalls

Are Internet connections on client/ server networks vulnerable to hackers? Just like a home network, any company's network that is connected to the Internet can attract hackers. For this reason, a well-defended business network, just like a well-defended home network, includes a firewall. Firewalls can be composed of software or hardware, and many sophisticated

But what ethical responsibilities does a company have to its customers after a data breach?

The first thing a company should do is admit the problem and inform its customers. The best way to protect yourself from misuse of your data is for you to know that your data has been compromised. The Federal Trade Commission (FTC) provides guidelines for companies that suffer a data breach. The FTC recommends the following course of action on its Web site:

1. Notify the appropriate law enforcement agencies.
2. Notify other affected businesses such as banks and credit card companies. These companies can then monitor the affected accounts for fraudulent activity.
3. Notify the individuals affected. You should explain what happened, what information was compromised, who to contact in your organization, and what the customers should do to protect themselves (which will vary based on the information compromised).

Citigroup did an admirable job by notifying its customers as soon as the extent of the breach was known. Sony was quick to disable its network after the breach occurred but was somewhat slow to notify customers of exactly what had happened. Epsilon informed its clients of the breach quickly so that each client could notify its affected customers. Some of Epsilon's clients notified their customers very quickly of the breach while some clients chose to do nothing. Forty-six states have enacted laws that require companies to notify you after personal information is breached . . . but companies don't always obey the laws.

How can you be aware of a data breach if the company that suffered it never tells you that your data was exposed? You should monitor Web sites such as the Privacy Rights Clearinghouse (**www.privacyrights .org/data-breach**) and Open Security Foundation's DataLossDB (**www.datalossdb.org**), which track data breaches; this might be the fastest way to find out your information has been compromised so you can take action. The FTC Web site on identity theft (**www.ftc.gov/bcp/ edu/microsites/idtheft/**) provides good guidelines to follow when your data has been exposed.

After notifying customers of a breach, the subsequent response by companies varies widely. Sony was very concerned about losing customers and welcomed back customers by giving them identity theft protection from security firm Debix, free games, and many in-game rewards such as currency and special items. Identity theft protection is one of the more common forms of compensation offered to customers after a data breach that involves financial data or Social Security numbers, but not every company offers it. And some companies merely stop at notifying customers and offer nothing in terms of compensation for the inconvenience.

Your best protection against data breaches is to provide as little information as possible to as few companies as possible. While this may cause some inconvenience, such as not having companies store your credit card information for subsequent purchases, it may save you a lot of aggravation down the road. You should also periodically monitor your credit reports for fraudulent activity, which could be the first sign of identity theft. By law in the United States, you are entitled to receive one free credit report every 12 months from each of the three major credit reporting bureaus. You can request the free credit reports at **www.annualcreditreport.com**. You should request one every 4 months from one of the agencies, which gives you the best free protection during the year. And be extra wary of spear phishing (targeted attempts at phishing) e-mails after a data breach. While companies may behave ethically after a data breach, your best protection is still your own vigilance!

firewalls include both. Routers are often equipped to act as hardware firewalls.

Does a firewall on a client/server network work the same way as a personal firewall installed on a home network does? Although a firewall on a business network may contain a few extra security options, making it even harder to breach than a personal firewall, the firewalls for business networks work on the same basic principles as a personal firewall. At a minimum, most firewalls work as packet screeners. **Packet screening** involves having an *external screening router* examining incoming data packets to ensure that they originated from or are authorized by valid users on the internal network. Unauthorized or suspect packets are discarded by the firewall before they reach the network.

Packet screening also can be configured for outgoing data to ensure that requests for information to the Internet are from legitimate users. This is done by an *internal screening router* and helps detect Trojan horse programs that may have been installed by hackers. As you learned in Chapter 9, Trojan horses masquerade as harmless programs but have a more sinister purpose. They often try to disguise where they are sending data from by using bogus IP addresses on the packets the programs send instead of using an authorized IP address belonging to the network.

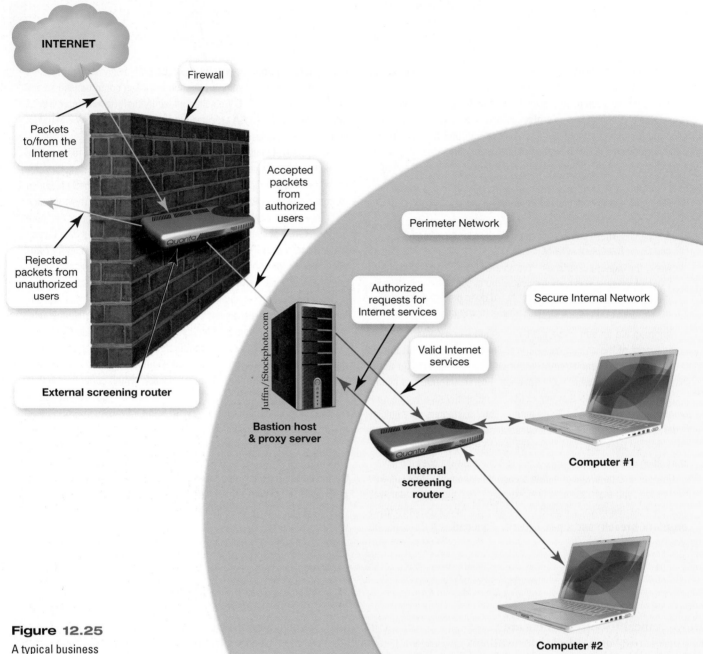

INTERNET

Firewall

Packets to/from the Internet

Accepted packets from authorized users

Perimeter Network

Rejected packets from unauthorized users

Secure Internal Network

External screening router

Authorized requests for Internet services

Valid Internet services

Juffin/iStockphoto.com

Bastion host & proxy server

Computer #1

Internal screening router

Computer #2

Figure 12.25

A typical business network firewall layout.

If packet screening is working, packets going into and out of the network are checked to ensure they are either from or addressed to a legitimate IP address on the network. If the addresses are not valid addresses on the network, the firewall discards them.

What other security measures does the firewall on a client/server network use? To increase security even fur-ther, most large networks add a **bastion host**, which is a heavily secured server located on a special perimeter network between the company's secure internal network and the firewall. A bastion host gets its name from the fortified towers (called *bastions*) located along the outer walls of medieval castles, which were specifically designed to defend the castles against attackers.

To external computers, the bastion host gives the appearance of being the internal network server. Hackers can waste a lot of time and energy attacking the bastion host. However, even if a hacker breaches the bastion host server, the internal network is not vulnerable because the bastion host is not on the internal network. Moreover, during the time the hackers spend trying to penetrate the bastion host, network administrators can detect and thwart their attacks.

Bastion hosts are a type of honey pot. A **honey pot** is a computer system that is set up to attract unauthorized users by appearing to be a key part of a network or a system that contains something of great value.

Bastion hosts are often configured as proxy servers. A **proxy server** acts as a go-between, connecting computers on the internal network with those on the external network (the Internet). All requests from the internal network for Internet services are directed through the proxy server. Similarly, all incoming requests from the Internet must pass through the proxy server. It is much easier for network administrators to maintain adequate security on one server than it is to ensure that security is maintained on hundreds or thousands of computers in a college network. Figure 12.25 shows a network secured by a firewall, a bastion host, and a screening router.

Now that you know a bit more about business network computing, you should be able to comfortably navigate the network at your college or your place of employment and understand why certain security measures have been taken to protect network data.

1. What are the advantages of a business network?

A network enables employees to communicate with each other more easily, even over large distances. Networks also enable resources, such as printers, to be shared, avoiding the cost of providing these resources to individual employees. Software can be deployed from a network server, thereby reducing the costs of installation on each user's computer. Finally, networks enable employees to share an Internet connection, avoiding the cost of providing each employee with a dedicated Internet connection.

2. How does a client/server network differ from a peer-to-peer network?

A client/server network requires at least one server to be attached to the network. The server coordinates functions such as file sharing and printing. In a peer-to-peer network, each node connected to the network can communicate directly with every other node on the network. In a client/server network, a separate device (the server) exercises control over the network. Data flows more efficiently in client/server networks than in peer-to-peer networks. In addition, client/server networks have increased scalability, meaning users can be added to the network easily.

3. What are the different classifications of client/server networks?

Local area networks (LANs) are small groups of computers (as few as two) and peripherals linked together over a small geographic area. A group of computers in rooms on one floor of a campus building is most likely a LAN. Wide area networks (WANs) comprise large numbers of users (or of separate LANs) that are miles apart and linked together. Colleges often use WANs to connect two or more campuses in separate towns. Sometimes government organizations or civic groups establish WANs to link users in a specific geographic area (such as within a city or county). These special WANs are known as metropolitan area networks (MANs). Personal area networks (PANs) are networks that connect personal use devices, such as phones and tablets, that are usually carried on your person.

4. What components are needed to construct a client/server network?

Client/server networks have many of the same components as peer-to-peer networks as well as some components specific to client/server networks, including servers, a network topology, transmission media, network operating system (NOS) software, network adapters, and network navigation devices.

5. What do the various types of servers do?

Dedicated servers are used on large networks to increase efficiency. Authentication servers control access to the network and ensure that only authorized users can log on. File servers provide storage and management of user files. Print servers manage and control all printing jobs initiated on a network. Application servers provide access to application software. Database servers store database files and provide access to users who need the information in the databases. E-mail servers control all incoming and outgoing e-mail traffic. Communications servers are used to control the flow of information from the internal network to outside networks. Web servers are used to host Web sites.

6. What are the various network topologies (layouts), and why is network topology important in planning a network?

In a bus topology, all nodes are connected to a single linear cable. Ring topologies are made up of nodes arranged roughly in a circle. The data flows from node to node in a specific order. In a star topology, nodes are connected to a central communication device (a switch) and branch out like points of a star. A hybrid topology blends two or more topologies in one network. Each topology has its own advantages and disadvantages. Topology selection depends on two main factors: (1) the network budget, and (2) the specific needs of network users (such as speed or fair allocation of resources).

7. What types of transmission media are used in client/server networks?

In addition to wireless media, three main cable types are used: twisted-pair cable, coaxial cable, and fiber-optic cable. Twisted-pair cable consists of pairs of wires twisted around each other to reduce interference. Coaxial cable is the same type of cable used by your cable TV company to run a signal into your house. Fiber-optic cable uses bundles of glass or plastic fiber to send signals using light waves. It provides the largest bandwidth but is expensive and difficult to install. Wireless media uses radio waves to send data between nodes on a network.

8. What software needs to run on computers attached to a client/server network, and how does this software control network communications?

Network operating system (NOS) software needs to be installed on each computer and server connected to a client/server network to provide the services necessary for the devices to communicate. The NOS provides a set of common rules (called a *protocol*) that controls communication between devices on the network.

9. How do network adapters enable computers to participate in a client/server network?

Without a network adapter, a computer could not communicate on a network. A network adapter provides three critical functions. First, it takes low-power data signals generated by the computer and converts them into higher-powered signals that can traverse network media easily. Second, it breaks the data generated by the computer into packets and packages them for transmission across the network media. Last, it acts as a gatekeeper to control the flow of data to and from the computer.

10. What devices assist in moving data around a client/server network?

Switches are devices that read the addresses of data packets and retransmit a signal to its destination instead of to every device connected to the switch. Bridges are devices used to send data between two different segments (collision domains) of the same network. Routers are used to route data between two different networks (such as between a college network and the Internet).

11. What measures are employed to keep large networks secure?

Access to most networks requires authentication procedures (such as having users enter a user ID and password) to ensure that only authorized users access the network. The system administrator defines access privileges for users so that they can access only specific files. Network equipment is physically secured behind locked doors, which are often protected by biometric authentication devices. Biometric devices, such as fingerprint and palm readers, use unique physical characteristics of individuals for identification purposes. Firewalls are employed to keep hackers from attacking networks through Internet connections. Packet screeners review traffic going to and from the network to ascertain whether the communication was generated by a legitimate user.

 Companion Website

The Companion Website includes a variety of additional materials to help you review and learn more about the topics in this chapter. Go to: *www.pearsonhighered.com/techinaction*

chapter

twelve

buzzwords

becoming
computer
literate

buzzwords

Word Bank

- authentication server
- bastion host
- bridge
- bus
- centralized
- client/server
- decentralized
- fiber-optic
- file server
- LAN
- packet screener
- router
- scalable
- star
- switch
- twisted-pair
- WAN
- wireless access point

Instructions: Fill in the blanks using the words from the Word Bank above.

Cheryl's company was quickly outgrowing its peer-to-peer network. Cheryl knew she would need to convert it to a(n) (1) _____ network next month. The current network was all in one building, was composed of 10 nodes, and was classified as a(n) (2) _____. The new network would need 35 nodes and would have to connect nodes in the existing building as well as the new manufacturing facility across town. This new network would be classified as a(n) (3) _____. The company was using proprietary manufacturing processes, so only authorized people would be permitted to access the network, necessitating the use of a(n) (4) _____. And since documents needed to be shared among employees and stored centrally, a(n) (5) _____ would also be a useful addition to the new network. The company anticipated hiring an additional 10 people per month for the next two years, so the network would need to be (6) _____.

Cheryl decided on an Ethernet network using the (7) _____ topology, since this was the most popular and easiest to implement. She knew she would need several network navigation devices including a(n) (8) _____ to move the data around the network and a(n) (9) _____ to send data between the network and the Internet. And as the network grew, she anticipated breaking into two different collision domains, necessitating a(n) (10) _____ to move data between them. Cheryl had a limited budget, so she knew she would need to install (11) _____ cable instead of the (12) _____ cable that would have given her much faster throughput.

For tight security, Cheryl planned to install a(n) (13) _____ to filter out unauthorized transmissions of data. And installing a(n) (14) _____ on the perimeter network would give the network an added layer of protection. With this type of network, security would be (15) _____, making it much more secure than the previous peer-to-peer network.

becoming computer literate

You've been hired as a summer intern for Floors-R-Us, a new small manufacturer of specialty wood flooring for the home construction industry. The company is in the process of planning its network. The initial staff consists of the company president, an office manager, and four office clerks who will work in cubicles in a typical office environment. There are also fifteen production workers and three production supervisors who will work on the factory floor. All employees will need access to the network. The production workers do not move more than 10 feet from their assigned work areas during their shift, but the production supervisors need to roam the entire factory floor and therefore need access to the network wherever they happen to be at the time.

Instructions: Draft a memo (with supporting diagrams, if necessary) that details how to deploy network connectivity in the office area and on the factory floor. Justify the network topology you select, explain your choice of transmission media, and indicate the device(s) needed to connect the computers in the factory and office networks together.

self-test

Instructions: Answer the multiple-choice and true–false questions below for more practice with key terms and concepts from this chapter.

Multiple Choice

1. Which of the following is an advantage of installing a client/server network in a business?
   a. centralization of network adapters
   b. decentralization of network security protection
   c. centralization of files and data
   d. decentralizaton of peripherals

2. Why are client/server networks often installed in businesses instead of peer-to-peer networks?
   a. Security is stronger on client/server networks.
   b. They eliminate the need for dedicated servers.
   c. They are less scalable than peer-to-peer networks.
   d. They are cheaper to install.

3. If a city deploys a network to assist in monitoring traffic flow, this network would be classified as a
   a. WAN.   b. MAN.
   c. PAN.   d. LAN.

4. Which of the following is necessary in every client/server network?
   a. packet screener
   b. bridge
   c. transmission media
   d. e-mail server

5. To ensure only authorized users can access a network, which server would a client/server network include?
   a. file
   b. authentication
   c. communications
   d. application

6. Which type of network topology is most scalable?
   a. star   b. ethernet
   c. ring   d. bus

7. Twisted-pair cable most likely would be used in a business network when
   a. cost is more important than speed.
   b. electrical or magnetic interference is present.
   c. very long cable runs are required.
   d. speed is more important than cost.

8. NOS software is needed
   a. on all computers in a client/server network.
   b. only on the servers in a client/server network.
   c. only if a communications server is deployed on a client/server network.
   d. only when configuring a network in a star topology.

9. On client/server networks, routers
   a. transfer data between two networks.
   b. route data between two collision domains on a single network.
   c. move data efficiently from node to node on the internal network.
   d. are necessary only in networks using the star topology.

10. Providing adequate security on a corporate network involves all of the following issues, except
    a. authentication.
    b. restricting access to servers.
    c. proprietary software lockout.
    d. limiting network access by requiring passwords.

True–False

_____ 1. Routers are used to route data between two or more network collision domains.

_____ 2. Two different types of network operating software can be deployed on the same network.

_____ 3. Fiber-optic cable is less susceptible to interference than twisted-pair cable.

_____ 4. Client/server networks are harder to administer than peer-to-peer networks.

_____ 5. An authentication server is used to host Web sites on a client/server network.

making the transition to... next semester

1. A Truly Wireless Campus

Most schools have wireless networks now, but these are mainly for the convenience of the students. School employees are often still tied down to desktop computers with wired connections. The primary reason for this is cost because desktop computers are cheaper than notebooks (for the same amount of computing power), and computers that stay in one place don't require as much maintenance and repair. Assuming your school can afford to begin transitioning to providing all employees with notebook computers (or other wireless computing devices), draft a plan that identifies the following:

a. Which two departments should be converted to wireless first?

b. What benefits will the employees in these departments gain from wireless connectivity?

c. How will wireless devices allow these employees to better serve or interact with the students?

d. What guidelines should the school establish for use of the computers when they are off campus?

e. What precautions should the school take to help recover the computers in the event they are lost or stolen?

2. Faster Networking for the Multimedia Department

Currently, the multimedia department at your school provides 20 Mac desktop computers in a wired Ethernet network for students to use to develop their multimedia projects. The lab uses one switch to connect all the computers, and the cabling is Cat 6 cable. The students are complaining about data transfers taking a long time on the network. Ten gigabit networks are used to provide extremely fast wired throughput. Research 10 gigabit network equipment. Write a proposal to explain how to convert the Mac network to a 10 gigabit network. Make sure to fully explain what equipment and cabling will be required and how much each component of the new network will cost.

3. Establishing a Business Network

You and three of your friends have a brilliant idea for a new line of clothing to be marketed to college students. All four of you attend colleges in different states. You want to set up a secure network for swapping your designs and other business ideas while you develop the business. Ultimately, you might establish a manufacturing facility/sales office in each town where you all currently go to college. Therefore, you will eventually need networks in your businesses in four varied geographic locations. Research ISPs that operate in multiple states and find one that you think can support your business networking needs. Consider using VPNs for increased security. How much will it cost you to establish connectivity in a secure environment for four point-to-point connections so that you and your business partners can communicate in the planning stages of your venture? When you establish the offices, how much will it cost to connect four networks (in different states) with twenty nodes at each network? What speed of data lines will you need to use between the offices?

1. Network Topology in the Workplace

You are interning at a small manufacturing company that is currently building a new manufacturing facility. All of the main manufacturing machines are computer-controlled and need to be connected to the client/server network in the administrative offices. Equal access for nodes on the factory floor is not an issue because the machinery will communicate infrequently with the network. The machinery generates a lot of electrical interference and wireless signals do not travel well on the factory floor due to the presence of metal beams. Consider the following:

a. What type of topology would you recommend for the factory network? Why?
b. What type of cabling would be appropriate to use in the factory portion of the network? Why?
c. What type of navigation device(s) would be required to enable the factory network to communicate with the administrative office network?

2. Transitioning to Cloud Hosting

The network administrator at the company for which you work has just quit. The company client/server network has an authentication server, a Web server, and a database server. The owner of the company has asked you to investigate whether it is feasible to use cloud servers to host all or part of the company network.

Investigate companies such as Rackspace Hosting (**www.rackspace.com**), GoGrid (**www.gogrid.com**), and NetDepot (**www.netdepot.com**) that offer cloud hosting services. Consider the following:

a. Do these companies offer turnkey services that will manage the entire network for the company? If turnkey services are not available, what servers can be hosted by these companies? What would be the monthly cost of hosting services?
b. Research cloud hosting. What concerns do businesses have about having their servers hosted in the cloud? What are the risks to the company and to its customers?
c. Do you think it is feasible to farm out the network hosting services and not hire a replacement for the local network administrator? What potential problems do you see arising with this scenario?

3. Authentication on a Client/Server Network

Authentication with logon IDs and passwords is only secure if the logon IDs are difficult to deduce and the passwords are secure. The company you work for establishes all logon IDs as the first initial of the given name and the full surname of the employees (i.e., John Smith would have the logon ID jsmith). Passwords can be as few as four letters or numbers and never have to be changed. You know from your coursework at school that these are inadequate security procedures. Research password security on the Internet and draft a memo for upper management that addresses the following:

a. Suggest a new scheme for creating logon IDs that would be difficult for a hacker to ascertain.
b. What length of passwords would you recommend? What combination of letters, numbers, and other symbols should they include?
c. How often would you recommend that employees be required to change their passwords? Would employees ever be allowed to repeat previous passwords?

Instructions: Some ideas are best understood by experimenting with them in our own minds. The following critical thinking questions are designed to demand your full attention but require only a comfortable chair—no technology.

1. Biometric Access on Campus

Biometric security devices are still expensive. But there are usually parts of any organization that need to be more secure than others, and you can often justify the cost of these devices for certain areas. Consider the following organizations and prepare a paper discussing in which areas of the business they could most benefit from installing biometric security devices:

a. Financial institution (bank)
b. Public university that conducts scientific research
c. Pharmaceutical company

2. Monitoring Computer Usage in the Workplace

Software tools for monitoring computer usage are readily available on the Internet, often for free (such as Best Free Keylogger). In most jurisdictions, it is legal for employers to install monitoring software on computer equipment they provide to employees. It is usually illegal for employees to install monitoring software on computers owned by their employers for purposes of monitoring computer usage of coworkers or bosses. Vernon Blake, a systems administrator in the Alabama Department of Transportation, installed monitoring software on his boss's computer without the boss's knowledge. He was fired even though he proved the boss was goofing off most of the time. Do you think this double standard is fair? What circumstances do you think would justify an employee monitoring other employers or their boss's computer usage? Whose approval should be sought before employees embarked on computer usage monitoring? Should whistleblowers have the right to conduct computer usage monitoring? Please fully explain your answers.

3. Acceptable-Use Internet Policies

Most schools have drafted acceptable-use policies for computers and Internet access to inform students and employees of the approved uses of college computing assets. Consider these areas of a potential college policy:

a. Should employees be allowed to use their computers and Internet access for personal tasks (such as checking non-college-related e-mail, accessing Facebook, or playing games)? If so, how much time per day is reasonable for employees to spend on personal tasks?
b. Should student computer and Internet usage be monitored to ensure compliance with the personal use policies? Should the college inform students that they are being monitored? What should the penalties be for violating these policies?
c. Many colleges block access to Web sites that enable students to participate in potentially illegal activities such as downloading music, gambling, or viewing pornography. Should colleges have the right to block students' access to these Web sites when they are on campus? Why or why not?

4. Wireless Network Layout

You are working for a local outlet of a national sandwich franchise (such as Subway). Now that most customers have portable devices with wireless access, they have come to expect connectivity while they eat. Management has asked you to survey customers to determine their needs. Draft a survey for your boss that helps determine the following:

a. Should Internet access be free? If access is not free, how much would customers pay?
b. What types of applications would the customers access while in the shop?
c. How important is WiFi access to their dining experience?

Protecting Yourself from Data Breaches

Problem

Individuals are constantly supplying personal data to companies that store it in networks. Data breaches are a continuing concern for both individuals and the companies that need to protect the privacy of their customers.

Task

Your campus bookstore recently suffered a major data breach and a number of students subsequently had their identities stolen. The vice president of academic affairs has asked your instructor to have your class prepare guidelines for students to guard against identity theft from data breaches.

Process

Divide the class into small teams.

1. Research major data breaches that have occurred recently. Determine what types of information were illegally accessed and determine how this information could be misused, such as identity theft, spear phishing, and so on. Prepare a suggested list of information that either should never be given out or should only be given out to trusted, reputable companies with no history of data breaches. Determine if anyone in your group has personal experience with identity theft, either through being a victim or by having family or friends who were victims of identity theft. Research ways to prevent identity theft and to resolve the problems associated with identity theft after it has occurred.

2. Meet as a class to discuss each group's findings. Do you feel most students are aware of the consequences of data breaches and identity theft? Would most students know what to do if their identities had been stolen? Try to obtain a consensus about which precautions are the most important ones to take to protect yourself.

3. Have each group prepare a multimedia presentation (PowerPoint, video, etc.) to educate the college community about data breaches and identity theft based on the results of the class discussion. Make sure that the presentations adequately explain any potentially unfamiliar concepts (such as what exactly is a data breach) to ensure all viewers of the media will be on an equal footing.

Conclusion

Having our personal data stored in more networks with more companies is a fact of life in the twenty-first century. But the best defense against misuse of your data is to understand the consequences of data breaches and the ways to protect yourself against cybercrimes such as identity theft.

Using Wireless Networks Without Permission

In this exercise, you will research and then role-play a complicated ethical situation. The role you play might or might not match your own personal beliefs; in either case, your research and use of logic will enable you to represent the view assigned. An arbitrator will watch and comment on both sides of the argument, and together the team will agree on an ethical solution.

Problem

Piggybacking occurs when people use a wireless network without the permission of the owner. Although piggybacking is illegal in many jurisdictions, it is often hard to detect. Piggybacking often happens inadvertently when people trying to connect to their own home network accidentally connect to their neighbor's wireless network. With the proliferation of wireless networks, many businesses have set up networks for their customers. However, because of the close proximity of many businesses to each other in areas such as shopping centers, the potential for inadvertent (or intentional) piggybacking of wireless networks exists. Also, sharing wireless connections between two entities (whether they be two households or two businesses) may violate the terms of service of the Internet service provider. And although wireless networks can be secured, it is often easier on the customers to leave them completely open, which can encourage piggybacking.

Research Areas to Consider

- Detecting wireless piggybacking
- Piggybacking laws (legality of piggybacking)
- Securing wireless networks

Process

Divide the class into teams.

1. Research the areas cited above and devise a scenario in which the owner of a coffee shop at a shopping center has accused the proprietor of the sandwich shop next door of encouraging the sandwich shop's patrons to piggyback on the coffee shop's wireless network.

2. Team members should write a summary that provides background information for their character—for example, coffee shop owner, sandwich shop owner, and shopping center manager (arbitrator)—and details their character's behaviors to set the stage for the role-playing event. Then, team members should create an outline to use during the role-playing event.

3. Team members should arrange a mutually convenient time to meet for the exchange, either using the collaboration feature of MyITLab, the discussion board feature of Blackboard, or meeting in person.

4. Team members should present their case to the class, or submit a PowerPoint presentation for review by the rest of the class, along with the summary and resolution they developed.

Conclusion

As technology becomes ever more prevalent and integrated into our lives, more and more ethical dilemmas will present themselves. Being able to understand and evaluate both sides of the argument, while responding in a personally or socially ethical manner, will be an important skill.

chapter 13
behind the scenes:
how the internet works

Management of the Internet

OBJECTIVE:
Who owns, manages, and pays for the Internet? *(p. 606)*

Internet Networking, Data Transmission, and Protocols

OBJECTIVES:
How do the Internet's networking components interact? *(p. 607)*

What data transmissions and protocols does the Internet use? *(p. 609)*

IP Addresses and Domain Names

OBJECTIVE:
Why are IP addresses and domain names important for Internet communications? *(p. 611)*

 Active Helpdesk: Understanding IP Addresses, Domain Names, and Protocols

HTTP, HTML, and Other Web Building Blocks

OBJECTIVE:
What are HTTP, HTML/XHTML, and XML used for? *(p. 617)*

 Sound Byte: Creating Web Pages with HTML

Communications over the Internet

OBJECTIVE:
How do e-mail, instant messaging, and Voice over Internet Protocol work, and how is information using these technologies kept secure? *(p. 623)*

Active Helpdesk: Keeping E-Mail Secure

Scan here for more info on How Cool Is This? ▶

how cool is *this?*

You probably have separate accounts for Facebook, YouTube, e-mail, and Twitter. You might even have a presence on Vimeo, Flickr, or Blogger or even have your own Web site. But how can someone, such as a college recruiter or a potential employer, quickly scan your entire **Web persona** from one place? Investigating someone's online **social life** can be time consuming.

About.me is a free Web site that allows you to create a page about yourself that can act as a portal to your online **presence**. You can set up your About.me page with a background photo that you supply that reflects your personality or interests. After that you can easily add links to all the social networking sites to which you belong and provide contact information such as an e-mail address. **Consolidating** all your information in one place makes it easy for someone to quickly review your online persona. It's a great place to showcase your online achievements and contributions for prospective employers.

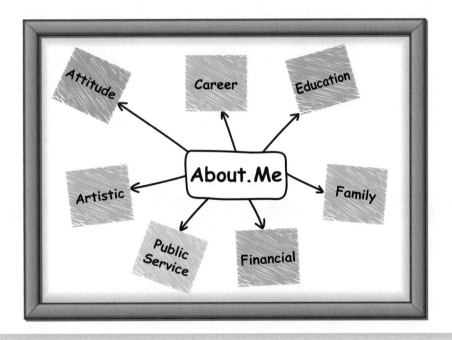

The Management of the Internet

The Internet is the largest network in the world. To keep a massive network like the Internet functioning at peak efficiency, it must be governed and regulated. However, no single entity is in charge of the Internet. In addition, new uses are created every day by a variety of individuals and companies.

Who owns the Internet? Even though the U.S. government funded the development of the technologies that spawned the Internet, no one really owns it. The particular local networks that constitute the Internet are all owned by different entities, including individuals, universities, government agencies, and private companies. Government entities such as the National Science Foundation (NSF) and the National Aeronautics and Space Administration (NASA), as well as many large, privately held companies, own pieces of the communications infrastructure (the high-speed data lines that transport data between networks) that makes the Internet work.

Does anyone manage the Internet? Because the individual networks that participate in the Internet are owned by several different entities, the Internet would cease to function without some sort of organization. Therefore, several nonprofit organizations and user groups, each with a specialized purpose, are responsible for its management. Figure 13.1 shows the major organizations that play a role in the governance and development of the Internet.

Many of the functions handled by these nonprofit groups were previously handled by U.S. government contractors because the Internet developed out of a defense project. However, because the Internet now serves the global community, not just the United States, assigning responsibilities to organizations with global membership is helping to speed the Internet's internationalization. Through close collaboration among the organizations listed in Figure 13.1 and a few others such as the Internet Network Information Center and the Internet Research Task Force, the Internet's vast collection of users and networks is managed.

Who pays for the Internet? You do! The National Science Foundation (NSF), which is a U.S. government–funded agency, still pays for a large portion of the Internet's infrastructure and funds research and development for new technologies. The primary source of NSF funding is your tax dollars. Originally, U.S. taxpayers footed the entire bill for the Internet, but as the Internet grew and organizations were formed to manage it, businesses, universities, and other countries began paying for Internet infrastructure and development. And, of course, the fees you pay to your ISP for Internet access also contribute to defraying the costs of the Internet.

Internet Networking

The Internet's response to our requests for information seems almost magical at times since so much information is now stored out

Figure 13.1 | MAJOR ORGANIZATIONS IN INTERNET GOVERNANCE AND DEVELOPMENT

Organization	Purpose	Web Address
Internet Society (ISOC)	Professional membership society comprising more than 100 organizations and more than 44,000 individual members in more than 180 countries. Provides leadership for the orderly growth and development of the Internet.	www.isoc.org
Internet Engineering Task Force (IETF)	A subgroup of ISOC made up of individuals and organizations that research new technologies for the Internet that will improve its capabilities or keep the infrastructure functioning smoothly.	www.ietf.org
Internet Architecture Board (IAB)	Technical advisory group to the ISOC and a committee of the IETF. Provides direction for the maintenance and development of the protocols that are used on the Internet.	www.iab.org
Internet Corporation for Assigned Names and Numbers (ICANN)	Organization responsible for management of the Internet's Domain Name System (DNS) and the allocation of IP addresses.	www.icann.org
World Wide Web Consortium (W3C)	Consortium of more than 300 member organizations that sets standards and develops protocols for the Web.	www.w3.org

in the "cloud." By simply entering a URL in your browser or going to a search engine and entering a search topic, you can summon up information that is stored on servers around the world. However, there is no magic involved, just a series of communication transactions that enable the Internet to function as a global network. In this section, we explore the various networks that make up the Internet, explain how to connect to them, and examine the workings of Internet data communications.

Connecting to the Internet

How are computers connected to the Internet? A "network of networks," the Internet is similar to the highway system in the United States. The top level of the highway system consists of interstate highways such as I-95, which runs up and down the East Coast; I-80, which runs from the Northeast to the West Coast; and I-5, which runs north and south along the West Coast. These are the fastest and largest roadways. Regional highways connect to the interstate highways, and local roads connect to the regional highways.

As shown in Figure 13.2, the main paths of the Internet, along which data travels the fastest, are known collectively as the **Internet backbone**. The 1s and 0s on the road represent data flow on the Internet. Analogous to the interstate highway system, the Internet backbone is a collection of large national and international networks, most of which are owned by commercial, educational, or government organizations (such as NASA). These backbone providers, which are required to connect to other backbone providers, have the fastest high-speed connections. At the time this was written, the large U.S. companies that provided backbone connectivity included Verizon, AT&T, Sprint, and Qwest.

How do the ISPs that form the Internet backbone communicate? Backbone ISPs initially connected with T lines. A **T line** carried digital data over twisted-pair wires. T-1 lines, which were the first to be used, transmit data at a throughput rate of 1.544 Mbps. T-3 lines, which were developed later, transmit data at 45 Mbps. Today, a backbone is typically a high-speed fiber-optic line, designated as an **optical carrier (OC) line**. OC lines come in a variety of speeds, as shown in Figure 13.3.

Figure 13.2

Just as regional and local highways connect to the interstate highways, local and regional ISPs connect to the Internet backbone.

The bandwidth of the connections between ISPs and end users depends on the amount of data traffic required. Whereas your home might connect to the Internet with DSL, cable, or even fiber-optic lines, the volume of Internet traffic at your college probably requires it to use an OC line to move data to the school's ISP. Large companies usually must connect to their ISPs using high-throughput OC lines.

How are the ISPs connected to each other? The points of connection between ISPs were once known as network access points (NAPs). Network access points were designed to move large amounts of data quickly between networks. They allowed the early Internet, which began as a government-funded

Figure 13.3	SPEED AND CONFIGURATION OF OC LINES
OC-1	0.052 Gbps
OC-3	0.155 Gbps
OC-12	0.622 Gbps
OC-24	1.244 Gbps
OC-48	2.488 Gbps
OC-96	4.976 Gbps
OC-192	9.953 Gbps
OC-768	39.813 Gbps

academic experiment, to grow into the modern Internet of many commercial companies working together—the Internet that we all know and use today. Now, private-sector companies make up the Internet system, and the data-exchange mechanism is known as an **Internet exchange point (IXP)**. A typical IXP is made up of one or more network switches to which ISPs connect. As you'll recall from Chapter 7, *switches* are devices that send data on a specific route through a network. By connecting directly to each other through IXPs, networks can reduce their costs and improve the speed and efficiency with which data is exchanged.

How do individuals connect to an ISP? Whether they dial up through a conventional modem or connect through high-speed access, individual Internet users enter an ISP through a **point of presence (POP)**, which is a bank of modems, servers, routers, and switches (see Figure 13.4) through which many users can connect to an ISP simultaneously. ISPs maintain multiple POPs throughout the geographic area they serve.

The Network Model of the Internet

What type of network model does the Internet use? The majority of Internet communications follows the **client/server model** of network communications, which we defined in earlier chapters as one in which client computers request services and other computers, known as servers, provide those services to the clients. In the case of the Internet, the clients are devices such as computers, tablets, and smartphones that use browsers (or other interfaces) to request services such as Web pages. Various types of servers from which clients can request services are deployed on the networks that make up the Internet:

- **Web server**: Computer that runs specialized operating systems, enabling it to host (provide Web space for) Web pages and other information and provide requested Web pages to clients.
- **Commerce server**: Computer that hosts software that enables users to purchase goods and services over the Web. These servers generally use special security protocols to protect sensitive information, such as credit card numbers, from being intercepted.
- **File server**: Computer that is deployed to provide remote storage space or to act as a storehouse for files that users can download. Google Docs and Flickr offer online storage services for productivity documents and pictures, respectively.

Do all Internet connections take place in a client/server mode? Certain services on the Internet operate in a peer-to-peer (P2P) mode, as depicted in Figure 13.5. For example, BitTorrent (**www.bittorrent.com**) is a popular file-sharing service through which Internet users can exchange files. BitTorrent and other file-sharing services require the user's computer to act as both a client and a server. When requesting files from another user, the

Figure 13.4

Home users connect to their ISPs through a single point of presence that can handle many simultaneous connections.

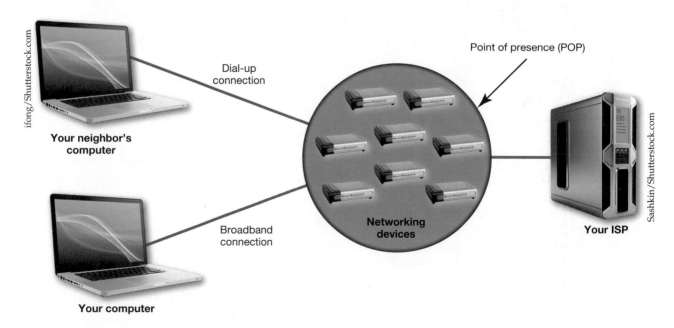

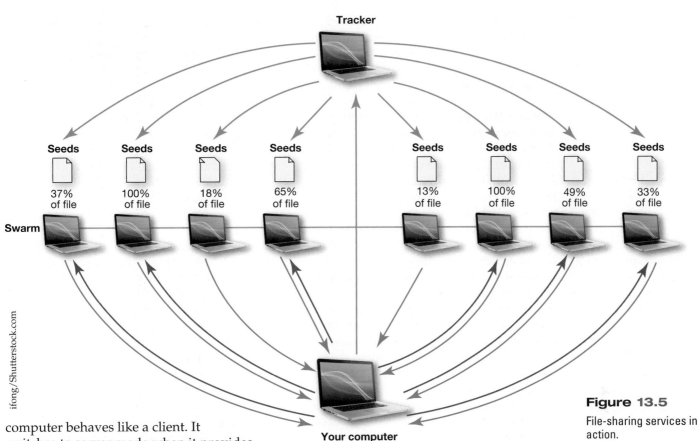

Tracker

Seeds 37% of file

Seeds 100% of file

Seeds 18% of file

Seeds 65% of file

Seeds 13% of file

Seeds 100% of file

Seeds 49% of file

Seeds 33% of file

Swarm

Your computer

ifong/Shutterstock.com

Figure 13.5

File-sharing services in action.

computer behaves like a client. It switches to server mode when it provides a file stored on its system to another computer. The following steps are illustrated in Figure 13.5:

1. Your computer, acting as a client, runs the BitTorrent software. Using this software, you request access to a particular file. Your computer transmits this request to a BitTorrent tracking server (tracker).

2. The BitTorrent tracker makes your computer aware of other users running BitTorrent software who have pieces of the file (called *seeds*).

3. Your computer determines that a group of users (called a *swarm*) has seeds for the file you need. Acting as a client, your computer requests the file from the computers in the swarm.

4. Computers in the swarm, acting as servers, then transmit pieces of the file to your computer. At the same time, the tracker might identify your computer as having a file another computer needs and assigns your computer to a swarm. Your computer would then act as a server when delivering that file to the computer that requested it.

Data Transmission and Protocols

Just like any other network, the Internet follows standard protocols to send information between computers. A **computer protocol** is a set of rules for exchanging electronic information. If the Internet is the information superhighway, then protocols are the rules of the road.

Why were Internet protocols developed? To accomplish the early goals of the Internet, protocols needed to be written and agreed upon by users. Each protocol had to be an **open system**, meaning its design would be made public for access by any interested party. This was in direct opposition to the **proprietary system** (private system) model that was the norm at the time.

As we mentioned in earlier chapters, when common communication protocols (rules) are followed, networks can communicate even if they have different topologies, transmission media, or operating systems. The idea of an open system protocol is that anyone can use it on his or her computer system and be able to communicate with any other computer using the same protocol. The biggest Internet tasks—communicating, collaborating, creating content, seeking information, and shopping—are all executed the same way on any system that is following accepted Internet protocols.

Were there problems developing an open system Internet protocol?

Agreeing on common standards was relatively easy. The tough part was developing a new method of communication because the technology available in the 1960s—circuit switching—was inefficient for computer communication. Circuit switching has been used since the early days of the telephone for establishing communication. In **circuit switching**, a dedicated connection is formed between two points (such as two people on telephones), and the connection remains active for the duration of the transmission. This method of communication is extremely important when communications must be received in the order in which they are sent, like telephone conversations.

When applied to computers, however, circuit switching is inefficient. Computers process communication in bursts. As a computer processor performs the operations necessary to complete a task, it transmits data in a group, or burst. The processor then begins working on its next task and ceases to communicate with output devices or other networks until it is ready to transmit data in the next burst. Circuit switching is inefficient for computers because the circuit either would have to remain open, and therefore unavailable to any other system, with long periods of inactivity or would have to be reestablished for each burst.

Packet Switching

If they don't use circuit switching, what do computers use to communicate?

Packet switching is the communications methodology that makes computer communication efficient. Packet switching doesn't require a dedicated communications circuit to be maintained. With packet switching, data is broken into smaller chunks called **packets** or **data packets.** The packets are sent over various routes at the same time. When the packets reach their destination, they are reassembled by the receiving computer. This technology resulted from one of the original goals of creating the Internet: If Internet nodes are disabled or destroyed, such as through an act of warfare or terrorism, the data can travel an alternate route to its destination.

What information does a packet contain?

Packet contents vary, depending on the protocol being followed. At a minimum, all packets must contain (1) an address to which the packet is being sent; (2) the address from where the packet originates; (3) reassembling instructions, if the original data was split between packets; and (4) the data that is being transmitted.

Sending a packet is like sending a letter. Assume you are sending a large amount of information in written format from your home in Philadelphia to your aunt in San Diego. The information is too large to fit in one small envelope, so you mail three different envelopes to your aunt. Each envelope includes your aunt's address, your return address, and the information being sent inside it. The pages of the letters in each envelope are numbered so that your aunt will know in which order to read them.

Each envelope may not find its way to San Diego by the same route. However, even if the letters are routed through different post offices, they will all eventually arrive in your aunt's mailbox. Your aunt will then reassemble the message in order and read it. The process of sending a message through the Internet works in much the same way. This process is illustrated in Figure 13.6, which traces an e-mail message sent from a computer in Philadelphia to a computer in San Diego.

Why do packets take different routes, and how do they decide which route to use?

The routers that connect ISPs with each other monitor traffic and decide on the most efficient route for packets to take to their destination. The router works in the same way as a police officer does while directing traffic. To ensure a smooth flow of traffic, police officers are deployed in areas of congestion, potentially directing drivers to alternate routes to their destinations.

TCP/IP

What protocol does the Internet use for transmitting data?

Although many protocols are available on the Internet, the main suite of protocols used is **TCP/IP**. The suite is named after the original two protocols that were developed for the Internet: the **Transmission Control Protocol (TCP)** and

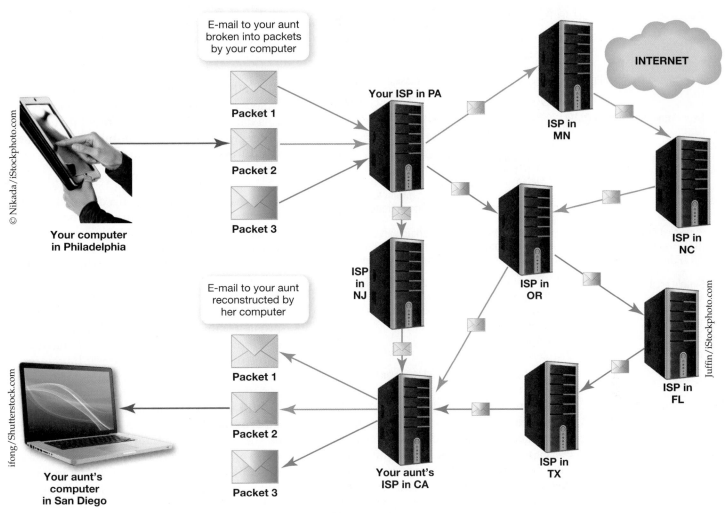

E-mail to your aunt broken into packets by your computer

Packet 1

Packet 2

Packet 3

Your computer in Philadelphia

Your ISP in PA

ISP in MN

INTERNET

ISP in NC

ISP in NJ

ISP in OR

ISP in FL

E-mail to your aunt reconstructed by her computer

Packet 1

Packet 2

Packet 3

Your aunt's computer in San Diego

Your aunt's ISP in CA

ISP in TX

© Nikada /iStockphoto.com

ifong/Shutterstock.com

Juffin /iStockphoto.com

Figure 13.6

Each packet can follow its own route to its final destination. Sequential numbering of packets ensures they are reassembled in the correct order at their destination.

the **Internet Protocol (IP)**. Although most people think that the TCP/IP suite consists of only two protocols, it actually comprises many interrelated protocols (covered later in this chapter), the most important of which are listed in Figure 13.7.

Which particular protocol actually sends the information? The Internet Protocol (IP) is responsible for sending the information from one computer to another. The IP is like a postal worker who takes a letter (a packet of information) that was mailed (created by the sending computer) and sends it on to another post office (router), which in turn routes it to the addressee (the receiving computer). The postal worker never knows whether the recipient actually receives the letter. The only thing the postal worker knows is that the letter was handed off to an appropriate post office that will assist in completing the delivery of the letter.

Internet Identity

Each computer, server, or device (such as a router) connected to the Internet is required to have a unique identification number. However, because humans are better at remembering and working with words than with numbers, the numeric IP addresses were given more "human," word-based addresses. Thus, domain names were born.

IP Addresses

What is an IP address? You will recall from Chapter 3 that an **IP address** is a unique identification number that defines each computer, service, or other device that connects to the Internet. IP addresses fulfill the same function as street addresses. For example, to send a letter to Rosa Juarez's house in Metamora, Illinois, you have to know her address. Rosa might live at 456 Walnut Street, which is not a unique address because many towns have a Walnut Street;

Figure 13.7 | TCP/IP PROTOCOL SUITE—MAIN PROTOCOLS

Internet Protocol (IP)	Sends data between computers on the Internet.
Transmission Control Protocol (TCP)	Prepares data for transmission and provides for error checking and resending of lost data.
User Datagram Protocol (UDP)	Prepares data for transmission; lacks resending capabilities.
File Transfer Protocol (FTP)	Enables files to be downloaded to a computer or uploaded to other computers.
Telnet	Enables user to log in to a remote computer and work on it as if sitting in front of it.
Hypertext Transfer Protocol (HTTP) and HTTP Secure (HTTPS)	Transfers Hypertext Markup Language (HTML) data from servers to browsers. HTTPS is an encrypted protocol for secure transmissions.
Simple Mail Transfer Protocol (SMTP)	Used for transmission of e-mail messages across the Internet.

but 456 Walnut Street, Metamora, IL 61548 *is* unique.

The numeric zip code is the unique postal identification for a specific geographic area. Zip codes are regulated by the U.S. Postal Service. Similarly, IP addresses must be registered with the **Internet Corporation for Assigned Names and Numbers (ICANN)** to ensure they are unique and have not been assigned to other users. The ICANN is responsible for allocating IP addresses to network administrators.

What's Your IP Address?

Curious as to what your IP address is? Just go to a Web site such as What Is My IP (**www.whatismyip.com**) or IP Chicken (**www.ipchicken.com**). Figure 13.8 displays the output from What Is My IP, which shows the IP address your PC is currently using.

Figure 13.8

Screenshot from WhatIsMyIP.com. Copyright © 2011 by WhatIsMyIP.com Reprinted with permission.

Some Web sites, such as WhatIsMyIP.com, determine your IP address for you.

What does an IP address look like? A typical IP address is expressed as follows:

$$197.169.73.63$$

An IP address expressed this way is called a **dotted decimal number** (also known as a **dotted quad**). However, recall that computers work with binary numbers. The same IP address in binary form is as follows:

$$11000101.10101001.01001001.00111111$$

Each of the 4 numbers in a dotted decimal number is referred to as an **octet**. This is because each number would have 8 positions when shown in binary form. Because 32 positions are available for IP address values (4 octets with 8 positions each), IP addresses are considered 32-bit numbers. A position is filled by either a 1 or a 0, resulting in 256 (2^8) possible values for each octet. Values start at 0 (not 1); therefore, each octet can have a value from 0 to 255. The entire 32-bit address can represent 4,294,967,296 values (or 2^{32}), which are quite a few Internet addresses!

Will we ever run out of IP addresses? When the original IP addressing scheme, **Internet Protocol version 4 (IPv4)**, was created in 1981, no one foresaw the explosive growth of the Internet in the 1990s. Four billion values for an address field seemed like enough to last forever. However, as the Internet grew, it quickly became apparent that we were going to run out of IP addresses.

Because the unique IP addressing system described earlier offers only a fixed number of IP addresses, a different addressing scheme known as **classless interdomain routing (CIDR)**, pronounced "cider," was developed. CIDR, or supernetting, allows a single IP address to represent several unique IP addresses by adding a **network prefix**, represented by a slash and a number, to the end of the last octet. The network prefix identifies how many of the possible 32 bits in a traditional IP address are to be used as the unique identifier, leaving the remaining bits to identify the specific host. For example, in the IP address 206.13.01.48/25, "/25" is the network prefix. It indicates that the first 25 bits are used as the unique network identifier; the remaining 7 bits identify the specific host site.

Are there other Internet addressing systems? Internet Protocol version 6 **(IPv6)** is an IP addressing scheme developed by the Internet Engineering Task Force (IETF) to make IP addresses longer, thereby providing more available IP addresses. IPv6 uses 8 groups of 16-bit numbers, referred to as **hexadecimal notation** (*hex* for short), which you learned about in the Technology in Focus piece titled "Under the Hood." An IPv6 address would have the following format:

XXXX:XXXX:XXXX:XXXX:XXXX:XXXX:XXXX:XXXX

Hex addressing provides a much larger field size, which will enable a much larger number of IP addresses (approximately 340 followed by 36 zeros). This should provide a virtually unlimited supply of IP addresses and will allow many different kinds of non-PC devices such as cell phones and home appliances to join the Internet more easily in the future. All modern operating systems can handle both IPv4 and IPv6 addresses. Although the majority of routing on the Internet still takes place using IPv4 addresses, the conversion to IPv6 addressing should accelerate now that we are finally running out of IPv4 addresses.

How does my computer get an IP address? You learned in Chapter 7 that IP addresses are assigned either statically or dynamically. **Static addressing** means that the IP address for a computer never changes and is most likely assigned manually by a network administrator or ISP. **Dynamic addressing**, in which your computer is assigned a temporary address from an available pool of IP addresses, is more common. A connection to an ISP could use either method. If your ISP uses static addressing, then you were assigned an IP address when you applied for your service and had to configure your computer manually to use that address. More often, though, an ISP assigns a computer a dynamic IP address, as shown in Figure 13.9.

How exactly are dynamic addresses assigned? Dynamic addressing is normally handled by the **Dynamic Host Configuration Protocol (DHCP)**, which belongs to the TCP/IP protocol suite. DHCP takes a pool of IP addresses and shares them with hosts on the network on an as-needed basis. ISPs don't need to maintain a pool of IP addresses for all of their subscribers because not everyone is logged on to the Internet at one time. Thus, when a user logs on to an ISP's server, the DHCP server assigns that user an IP address for the duration of the session. Similarly, when you log on to your computer at work in the morning, DHCP assigns an IP address to your computer. These temporary IP addresses may or may not be the same from session to session.

What are the benefits of dynamic addressing? Although having a static address would seem to be convenient,

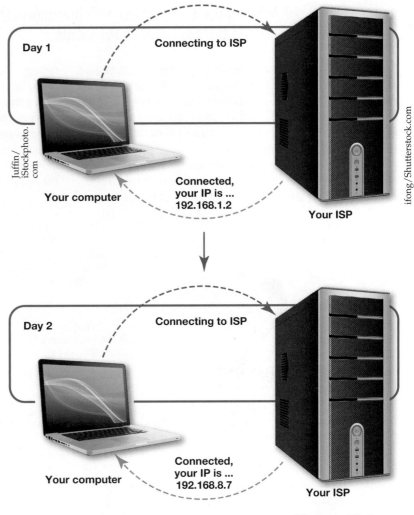

Figure 13.9

Dynamic IP addressing changes your IP address every time you connect to the Internet.

ACTIVE HELP-DESK

Understanding IP Addresses, Domain Names, and Protocols

In this Active Helpdesk call, you'll play the role of a helpdesk staffer, fielding calls about which data transmissions and protocols the Internet uses, and why IP addresses and domain names are important for Internet communications.

Making the Connection—Connection-Oriented Versus Connectionless Protocols

The Internet Protocol is responsible only for sending packets on their way. The packets are created by either the TCP or the **User Datagram Protocol (UDP)**. You don't decide whether to use TCP or UDP. The choice of protocol is made for you by the developers of the computer programs you are using or by the other protocols (such as those listed in Figure 13.7) that interact with your data packet.

As explained earlier, data transmission between computers is highly efficient if connections do not need to be established (as in circuit switching). However, there are benefits to maintaining a connection, such as

reduced data loss. The difference between TCP and UDP is that TCP is a connection-oriented protocol, whereas UDP is a connectionless protocol.

A **connection-oriented protocol** requires two computers to exchange control packets, thereby setting up the parameters of the data-exchange session, before sending packets that contain data. This process is referred to as **handshaking**. TCP uses a process called a **three-way handshake** to establish a connection, as shown in Figure 13.10a. Perhaps you need to report sales figures to your home office. You phone the sales manager and tell him or her that you are ready to report your

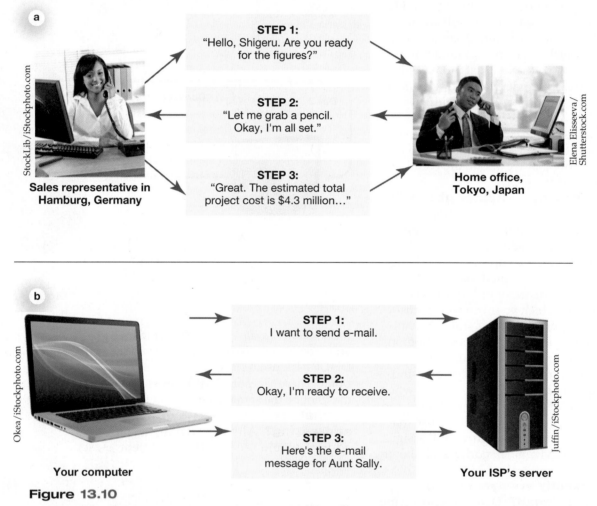

Figure 13.10

(a) Colleagues in Hamburg and Tokyo establish communication using a three-way handshake. (b) Here, two computers establish communication in the same way.

dynamic addressing provides a more se-cure environment by keeping hackers out of computer systems. Imagine how hard it would be for burglars to find your home if you changed your address every day!

Domain Names

I've been on the Internet, so why have I never seen IP addresses?

Computers are fantastic at relating to IP addresses and other numbers. However, humans remember names better than they

figures. The sales manager then prepares to receive the information by getting a pencil and a piece of paper. By confirming that he or she is ready and by your beginning to report the figures, a three-way (three-step) handshaking process is completed.

Your computer does the same thing when it sends an e-mail through your ISP, as shown in Figure 13.10b. It establishes a connection to the ISP and announces it has e-mail to send. The ISP server responds that it is ready to receive the e-mail. Your computer then acknowledges the ready state of the server and begins to transmit the e-mail.

A **connectionless protocol** does not require any type of connection to be established or maintained between two computers that are exchanging information. Just like a letter that is mailed, the data packets are sent without notifying the receiving computer or receiving any acknowledgment that the data was received. UDP is the Internet's connectionless protocol.

Besides establishing a connection, TCP provides for reliable data transfer. Reliable data transfer means that the application that uses TCP can rely on this protocol to deliver all the data packets to the receiver free from errors and in the correct order. TCP achieves reliable data transfer by using acknowledgments and providing for the retransmission of data, as shown in Figure 13.11.

Assume that two systems, X and Y, have established a connection. When Y receives a data packet that it can read from X, it sends back a **positive acknowledgment (ACK)**. If X does not receive an ACK in an appropriate period of time, it resends the packet. If the packet is unreadable (damaged in transit), then Y sends a **negative acknowledgment (NAK)** to X, indicating the packet was not received in understandable form. X then retransmits that packet. Acknowledgments ensure that the receiver has received a complete set of data packets. If a packet is unable to get through after being resent several times, the user is generally presented with an error message indicating the communications were unsuccessful.

You may wonder why you wouldn't always want to use a protocol that provides for reliable data transfer. On the Internet, speed is often more important than accuracy. For certain applications (such as e-mail), it's critically important that your message be delivered completely and accurately. For streaming multimedia, it's not always important to have every frame delivered accurately because most streaming media formats provide for correction of errors caused by data loss. It is, however, extremely important for streaming media to be delivered at a high rate of speed. Otherwise, playback quality can be affected. Therefore, a protocol such as TCP, which uses handshakes and acknowledgments, would probably not be appropriate for transmitting a movie trailer over the Internet whereas the Real-time Transport Protocol (RTP) would be better.

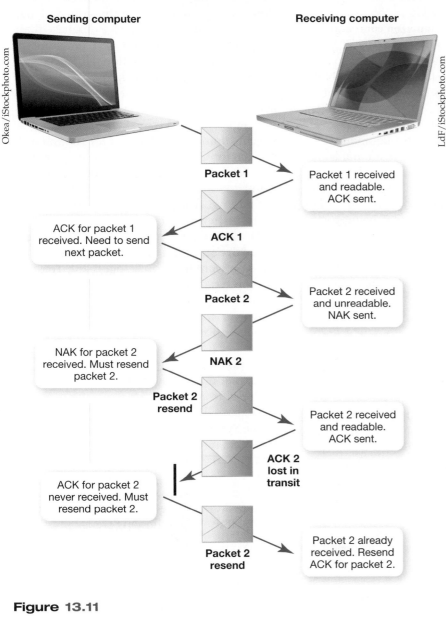

Sending computer   **Receiving computer**

Packet 1

Packet 1 received and readable. ACK sent.

ACK for packet 1 received. Need to send next packet.

ACK 1

Packet 2

Packet 2 received and unreadable. NAK sent.

NAK for packet 2 received. Must resend packet 2.

NAK 2

Packet 2 resend

Packet 2 received and readable. ACK sent.

ACK 2 lost in transit

ACK for packet 2 never received. Must resend packet 2.

Packet 2 resend

Packet 2 already received. Resend ACK for packet 2.

Figure 13.11

Packet acknowledgment in action.

remember strings of numbers. (Would you rather call your friend 4893257 or Jamar?) When the Web was being formed, a naming system was necessary so people could work with names instead of numbers. Hence, domain names were born.

As you learned in Chapter 3, a *domain name* is simply a name that takes the place of an IP address, making it easier for people to remember. For example, google.com is a domain name. The server where Google's main Web site is deployed has an IP address (such as 66.249.64.55), but it's much easier for you to remember to tell your browser to go to **www.google.com** than it is to recall the nine-digit IP address.

How are domains organized? Domains are organized by level. As you'll recall from Chapter 3, the portion of the domain name after the dot is the top-level domain (TLD). In the .com domain are popular sites such as Amazon (**www.amazon.com**) and Microsoft (**www.microsoft.com**). The TLDs are standardized pools (such as .com and .org) that have been established by ICANN. (Refer back to Figure 3.21 in Chapter 3 for a list of some of the TLDs that are currently approved and in use.) Within each top-level domain are many second-level domains. A **second-level domain** is a domain that is directly below a top-level domain. For example, in myawesomesite.com, myawesomesite is the second-level domain to the .com TLD. A second-level domain needs to be unique within its own TLD but not necessarily unique to all top-level domains. For example, myawesomesite.com and myawesomesite.org could be registered as separate domain names.

Who controls domain name registration? ICANN assigns companies or organizations to manage domain name registration. Because names can't be duplicated within a top-level domain, one company is assigned to oversee each TLD and maintain a listing of all registered domains. VeriSign is the current ICANN-accredited domain name registrar for the .com and .net domains. VeriSign provides a database that lists all the registered .com and .net domains and their contact information. However, for simplicity you can look up any .com or .net domain at the Network Solutions Web site (**www.networksolutions.com**) to see if it is registered and who owns it. Country-specific domains such as .au for Australia and .cn for China are controlled by groups in those countries. You can find a complete list of country-code top-level domains on the Internet Assigned Numbers Authority Web site (**www.iana.org**).

How does my computer know the IP address of another computer? Say you want to get to Google.com. To do so, you type the URL—"www.google.com"—into your browser's address box. However, the URL is not important to your computer; only the IP address of the computer hosting the Google site is. When you enter the URL in your browser, your computer must convert the URL to an IP address. To do this, your computer consults a database that is maintained on a **Domain Name System (DNS) server** that functions like a phone book for the Internet.

Your ISP's Web server has a default DNS server (one that is convenient to contact) that it goes to when it needs to translate a URL to an IP address (illustrated in Figure 13.12). It uses the following steps:

1. Your browser requests information from ABC.com.

2. Your ISP doesn't know the address of ABC.com, so it requests the address from its default DNS server.

3. The default DNS server doesn't know the IP address of ABC.com either, so it queries the root server of the .com domain.

4. The root server provides the default DNS server with the appropriate IP address of ABC.com.

5. The default DNS server stores the correct IP address for ABC.com for future

BITS AND BYTES

Guidelines for Choosing a Domain Name

A catchy, easily recognizable URL is the cornerstone of successful Web sites (think Zappos.com). Careful thought needs to go into choosing a domain name for your Web site before you invest the time and money in developing it. These guidelines should help.

- **Identify key words:** Think about the key words that describe the purpose of the Web site. Then try using them in different combinations until you find something suitable.

- **Use a unique name:** Don't make the name similar to the name of a site that is already successful. You don't want people going to their site by mistake.

- **Only use a .com domain:** If you are developing a commercial site, register it in the .com TLD. Most people assume Web sites all end in .com, so make sure that yours does.

- **Make the name short and easy to remember:** Thebestbookstoreintheknown universe.com may sound cool, but too many people will forget a word or mistype it. URLs need to be easily remembered. Bookuniverse.com would be better.

- **Use words everyone can spell:** Rhythm might describe a music site, but many people will misspell it. And don't use a word (such as aunt) that can be spelled differently (ant). Some people will choose the wrong one and not find your site.

- **Don't use hyphens or numbers:** This makes it hard to articulate the name of your site, and word of mouth is critical for a successful site. And people will always be typing the hyphens in the wrong place.

So keep these ideas in mind when you are picking a domain name for your latest and greatest million-dollar idea!

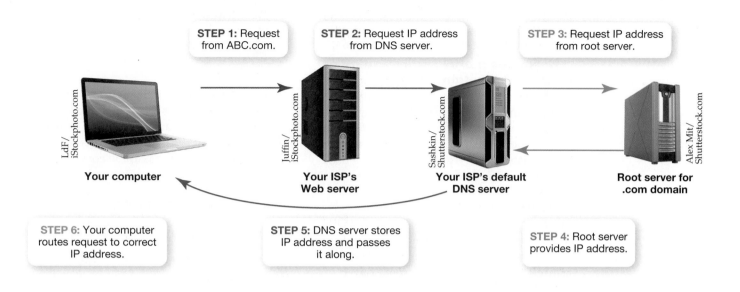

Your computer

Your ISP's Web server

Your ISP's default DNS server

Root server for .com domain

STEP 6: Your computer routes request to correct IP address.

STEP 5: DNS server stores IP address and passes it along.

STEP 4: Root server provides IP address.

LdF/ iStockphoto.com

Juffin/ iStockphoto.com

Sashkin/ Shutterstock.com

Alex Mit/ Shutterstock.com

Figure 13.12

DNS servers in action.

reference and returns it to your ISP's Web server.

6. Your computer then routes its request to ABC.com and stores the IP address in cache for later use.

7. Your ISP or network administrator defines the default DNS server. If the default DNS server does not have an entry for the domain name you requested, then it queries another DNS server.

8. If all else fails, your ISP's Web server will contact one of the 13 root DNS servers maintained throughout the Internet. Each **root DNS server** knows the location of all the DNS servers that contain the master listings for an entire top-level domain. Your default DNS server receives the information from the master DNS server (say, for the .com domain). It then stores that information in its cache for future use and communicates the appropriate IP address to your computer.

HTTP, HTML, and Other Web Building Blocks

Although most people think that the Internet and the Web are the same thing, the World Wide Web (WWW or the Web) is actually a grouping of protocols and software that resides on the Internet. The Web provides an engaging interface for exchanging graphics, video, animations, and other multimedia over the Internet. One other aspect that distinguishes the Web from the Internet is the Web's use of special languages such as HTML (Hypertext Markup Language) and protocols such as HTTP (Hypertext Transfer Protocol), which facilitate communication between computers using different system and application software.

Web Browser Security Protocols

Which Internet protocol does a browser use to send requests? The **Hypertext Transfer Protocol (HTTP)** was created especially for the transfer of hypertext documents across the Internet. **Hypertext** documents are documents in which text is linked to other documents or media (such as video clips, pictures, and so on). Clicking a

---

BITS AND BYTES

What Is an Internet Cache?

Your **Internet cache** is a section of your hard drive that stores information, such as IP addresses and frequently accessed Web pages, that you may need again. However, caching of domain name addresses also takes place in DNS servers. This helps speed up Internet access time because a DNS server doesn't have to query master DNS servers for TLDs constantly. However, caches have limited storage space, so entries are held in the cache only for a fixed period of time and then are deleted. The time component associated with cache retention is known as the time to live (TTL). Without caches, surfing the Internet would take a lot longer.

Beware—you can't always tell whether your browser is loading the current version of a page from the Web or a copy from your Internet cache. If a Web site contains time-sensitive information (such as a snow day alert on a college Web site), clicking the browser's Reload or Refresh button 🔄 will ensure that the most current copy of the page loads into your browser.

specific piece of text (called a *hyperlink*) that has been linked elsewhere takes you to the linked file.

How does a browser safeguard secure information? As you read in Chapter 3, some Web sites require extra layers of security to ensure that banking or purchasing transactions can be done safely and without personal and financial information being mishandled. Commerce servers use security protocols to protect sensitive information from interception by hackers.

Hypertext Transfer Protocol Secure (HTTPS) is actually a combination of HTTP and a network security protocol (usually SSL or TLS). HTTPS ensures data is sent securely over the Web. **Transport Layer Security (TLS)** and the **Secure Sockets Layer (SSL)** are two protocols that provide data integrity and security for transmissions over the Internet. Online shopping sites frequently use HTTPS to safeguard credit card information. Online banking sites and other Web sites that require user authentication beyond just a simple user ID and password also use HTTPS.

HTML/XHTML

How are Web pages formatted? Web pages are text documents that are formatted using HTML or XHTML. Style sheets (described in more detail later in this chapter) provide developers an easier way to update and revise Web pages. Although XHTML is the development environment of choice for Web developers today, many people still refer to Web site formatting as "HTML tagging."

HTML and XHTML are not programming languages; rather, they are Web languages. Web languages are sets of rules for marking up blocks of text so that a browser knows how to display them. Blocks of text in HTML/XHTML documents are surrounded by pairs of **HTML tags** (such as `<b>` and `</b>`, which indicate bolding). HTML tags surround and define HTML content. Each pair of tags and the text between them are collectively referred to as an **element**. The elements are interpreted by the browser, and appropriate effects are applied to the text. The following is an element from an HTML/XHTML document:

```
<i>This should be
italicized.</i>
```

The browser would display this element as:

*This should be
italicized.*

The first tag, `<i>`, tells the browser that the text following it should be italicized. The ending `</i>` tag indicates that the browser should cease applying italics to the text. Note that multiple tags can be combined in a single element such as the following:

```
<b><i>This should be bolded and
italicized.</i></b>
```

The browser would display this element as

**This should be bolded and
italicized.**

Tags for creating hyperlinks appear as follows:

```
<a href=www.pearsonhighered
.com>Pearson Higher Edu-
cation</a>
```

The code `<a href=www
.pearsonhighered.com>` defines the link's destination. The `<a>` tag is the anchor tag and creates a link to another resource on the Web (denoted by the `href` attribute), such as an HTML page, an image, or a sound. In this case, the link is to the **www
.pearsonhighered.com** Web page. The text between the open and close of the anchor tag, `Pearson Higher Education`, is the link label. The link label is the text, or image, that is displayed on the Web page as clickable text for the hyperlink.

Can you see the HTML/XHTML coding of a Web page? HTML/XHTML documents are merely text documents with tags applied to them. If you want to look at the HTML/XHTML coding behind your favorite Web page, just right-click anywhere on the page, select View Source from the shortcut menu, and the HTML/XHTML code for that page will be displayed, as shown in Figure 13.13. Alternatively, you can select View Source in Internet Explorer (or View Page Source in Firefox) from the browser menu. For more information on how to build Web pages, see the Sound Byte "Creating Web Pages with HTML."

XML

How is XML different from HTML/XHTML? As you learned in Chapter 10, the eXtensible Markup Language (XML)

```
Source of: http://www.pearsonhighered.com/educator/mylabmastering/index.page - Mozilla...
File  Edit  View  Help
<a class="ng_us_current" href="/educator/mylabmastering/index.page">Overview
<a href="/educator/mylabmastering/products/index.page">Products<span> </span
<a href="/educator/mylabmastering/proven-results/index.page">Proven Results<
<a href="/educator/mylabmastering/faculty-advisor-program/index.page">Facult
<a href="/educator/mylabmastering/training/index.page">Training Opportunitie
<a href="/educator/mylabmastering/workshops/index.page">Workshops<span> </sp
<a href="/educator/mylabmastering/contact-us/index.page">Contact Us<span> </
>

            </div>
            <div id="ng_us_header">
                        <div id="ng_us_headerTitleBar">
                        <strong>MyLab / Mastering</strong>
                        <h1>The moment you know.</h1>
            </div>
                        <p>Educators know it. Students know it.
            </div>
            <div id="ng_us_mainContent">

    <p><span class="ng_us_pdfTitle"> MyLab and Mastering</span>

    <br/>

    <a href="javascript:void(0);" title="The Moment You Know" cl
```

Figure 13.13
Viewing the source code of a Web site.

describes the content in terms of what data is being described rather than how it is to be displayed. Instead of being locked into standard tags and formats for data, users can build their own markup languages to accommodate particular data formats and needs.

For example, three pieces of typical information that need to be captured for an e-commerce transaction are a credit card number, a price, and a zip code. In HTML/XHTML, the paragraph tags (<p> and </p>) are used to define text and numeric elements. Almost any text or graphic can fall between these tags and be treated as a paragraph. Therefore, in our example, the HTML/XHTML code would appear as follows:

```
<p>1234567890123456</p>
(credit card number)
<p>12.95</p> (price)
<p>19422</p> (zip code)
```

The browser will interpret the data contained within the <p> and </p> tags as separate paragraphs. However, the paragraph tags tell us nothing about the data contained within them. Without the labels, which are not part of the HTML/XHTML code, we may not realize what data was contained within. In addition, tags don't provide any methodology for data validation. Credit card numbers are usually 16 numbers long, but

any length of data may be inserted between <p> and </p> tags. How would we know if the credit card number was a valid length? The answer lies in creating tags that are specific to the task at hand and that actually describe the data contained within them. Here's how our data might look in XML:

```
<credit_card_number>
1234567890123456</credit_
card_number>
<price>12.95</price>
<zip_code>19422</zip_code>
```

We have created the tags we need for data capture. Our XML specification provides a tag called "credit card number" that is used exclusively for credit card data.

How has XML influenced other Web page developments? XML has spawned quite a few custom packages for

SOUND BYTE
Creating Web Pages with HTML

Creating simple Web pages using Microsoft Word is relatively easy. In this Sound Byte, you'll learn the basics of Web page creation by setting up a Web site featuring a student résumé.

specific communities. For example, Mathematical Markup Language (MathML) is an XML-based markup language that is used to describe mathematical symbols and formulas so that they can be presented in a familiar way in Web documents. Wireless Markup Language (WML) uses XML to output Web resources on mobile devices; MusicXML is used to create and publish musical scores online; and GraphML is an XML-based format for creating graphs. These are just a few of the many examples that illustrate the goal of XML—information exchange standards that can be easily constructed and customized to serve a growing variety of online applications.

Common Gateway Interface

Can you use HTML/XHTML to make a Web page interactive? Because HTML/XHTML was originally designed to link text documents, HTML/XHTML by itself can't do all the amazing things we expect modern Web pages to do. As we mentioned earlier, HTML and XHTML are not programming languages; rather, they are sets of tags that determine how text is displayed and where elements are placed. Fortunately, the limitations of HTML/XHTML were recognized early, and the Common Gateway Interface (CGI) was developed.

Most browser requests merely result in a file such as the eBay home page (**www.ebay.com**) being displayed in your browser. Displaying a file is fine if you're just going to be reading text. However, to make a Web site interactive, you may need to run a program to perform a certain action (such as gathering a name and address and adding them to a database). The **Common Gateway Interface (CGI)** provides a methodology by which your browser can request that a program file be executed (run) instead of just being delivered to the browser. This enables functionality beyond the simple display of information.

CGI files can be created in almost any programming language, and the programs created are often referred to as **CGI scripts**. Common languages that are used to create CGI scripts are Perl, C, and C++. Because programming languages are extremely powerful, almost any task can be accomplished by writing a CGI script. You have probably encountered CGI scripts on Web pages without realizing it. Have you used a search engine to create a customized results page based on key words you entered? Have you filled out a form in which you asked to be added to a mailing list? Both of these tasks are commonly done using CGI scripts.

How are CGI programs executed? On most Web servers, a directory called **cgi-bin** is created by the network administrator who configures the Web server. All CGI scripts are placed into this directory. The Web server knows that all files in this directory are not just to be read and sent but also need to be run. Because this type of program runs on the Web server rather than inside your browser, it is referred to as a **server-side program**.

For instance, a button on bookuniverse.com's Web site may say "Click Here to Join Mailing List". Clicking the button (step 1 in Figure 13.14) may execute a script file, called "mailinglist.pl," from the cgi-bin directory on the Web server hosting the site (step 2). This file generates a form that is sent to your browser (step 3). The form includes fields for a name and e-mail address and a button

Figure 13.14

Information flow when a CGI program is run.

that says "Submit." After you fill in the fields and click the Submit button, the mailinglist.pl program sends the information back to the server (step 4). The server then records the information in a database.

Dynamic HTML

Can Web pages be made more interactive without accessing Web servers? Dynamic HTML (DHTML) is a combination of technologies—HTML/XHTML, cascading style sheets (explained later in this chapter), and JavaScript—that is used to create lively and interactive Web sites. Recall that the Web is based on a client/server network. Once a Web server processes a Web page and sends the page to the client computer that requested it, the receiving computer cannot get any new data from the server unless a new request is made. If interactivity is required on a Web page, this exchange of data between the client and server can make the interactivity inefficient and slow. DHTML technologies allow a Web page to change after it has been loaded. Change generally occurs in response to such user actions as clicking a mouse or mousing over objects on a page. DHTML brings special effects to otherwise static Web pages without requiring users to download and install plug-ins or other special software.

AJAX is the acronym for Asynchronous JavaScript and XML, a newer group of technologies that facilitates the creation of Web applications. These technologies can update information on the page without requiring the user to do a page refresh or leave the page. AJAX does not actually require the use of JavaScript or XML but can use a variety of Web programming techniques and languages. JavaScript and XML are frequently used by AJAX Web developers.

What is JavaScript? JavaScript is the most commonly used scripting language for creating DHTML effects. It was developed through the joint efforts of Netscape and Sun Microsystems, two software development companies. JavaScript is often confused with the Java programming language because of the similarity in their names. However, though they share some common elements, the two languages function quite differently.

Pure HTML/XHTML documents don't respond to user input. With JavaScript, though, HTML/XHTML documents can be made responsive to mouse clicks and typing. For example, JavaScript is often used to validate the information you input in a Web form, for example, to make sure you filled in all required fields.

When JavaScript code is embedded in an HTML/XHMTL document, it is downloaded to the browser with the HTML/XHTML page. All actions dictated by the embedded JavaScript commands are executed on the client computer. Without JavaScript and other scripting languages, Web pages would be lifeless.

How can you easily change the formatting of HTML/XHTML elements? In addition to the HTML/XHTML formatting tags described earlier, some tags describe areas of a Web page. This helps with layout. For example, the tag <h1> declares an area as a header. Similarly, <p> says, "This is a paragraph," and <table> says, "This is a table." In addition to tags defining certain areas as headers, paragraphs, or tables, Web developers needed additional tags to indicate how each header, paragraph, or table would be formatted and displayed. Although this system worked for a while, as more and more tags and attributes were created it became increasingly difficult to manage the differences between content and presentation layout.

To solve this problem, cascading style sheets were created. A **cascading style sheet (CSS)** is a list of statements (also known as *rules*) that defines in one single location how to display HTML/XHTML elements. Style rules enable a Web developer to define a style for each HTML/XHTML element and apply it to multiple elements on as many Web pages as needed. Essentially, a template is created upon which the formatting for many Web pages within a site will be based. Thus, when a global change is necessary, the developer only needs to change the style on the style sheet (template); all the elements in the Web document are then updated automatically (see Figure 13.15).

For example, a Web page has an <h1> heading tag, and all <h1> tags in the Web page are formatted with a white background and an orange border. Before CSS, if you wanted to change the border color from orange to yellow, you had to change the background color of every <h1> tag. With CSS, the change from orange to yellow only needs to happen once on the style sheet; all the `<h1>` tags on the Web pages then update to yellow without individual changes.

Where does the cascading come in? In Web documents, there are different layers of styles: external, embedded, and inline. Therefore, it's possible that different rules can be created for the same type of element. In other words, in an external style sheet, there might be a rule that defines the background color for all paragraphs as blue. Somewhere else, in an embedded style sheet, a rule for background color for paragraphs might be white; and in an inline style sheet, the background color might be light pink. Eventually, all these style sheets must be merged to form one style sheet for the document. This creates conflicts among rules. Therefore, rules are assigned weights so that when the rules are collected and merged, the rule or style with a higher weight overrides the rule or style with a lower weight. This hierarchy of competing styles creates a "cascade" of styles ranked according to their assigned weights.

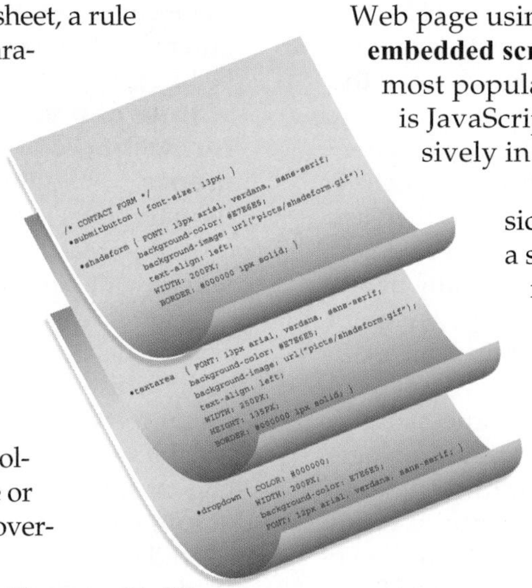

How are the individual components of a Web page organized? Just as cascading style sheets organize and combine the attributes of objects on a Web page, DHTML uses the **Document Object Model (DOM)** to organize the objects and page elements. The Document Object Model defines every item on a Web page—including graphics, tables, and headers—as an object. Then with DOM, similar to CSS, Web developers can easily change the look and feel of these objects.

Client-Side Applications

Aside from CGI scripts, are there other ways to make a Web site interactive? Sometimes running programs on the server is not optimal. Server-side program execution can require many communication sessions between the client and the server to achieve the goal. Often it is more efficient to run programs on your computer (the client). Therefore, client-side programs were created. A **client-side**

Figure 13.15

Cascading style sheets allow for the creation of formatting templates. Just as all the pages of this book have a similar look and feel, one style sheet can control the formatting of many Web pages.

program is a computer program that runs on the client computer and requires no interaction with a Web server. Client-side programs are fast and efficient because they run on your desktop and don't depend on data going back and forth to the Web server. Two main types of client-side methods exist. The first involves embedding programming language code directly within the HTML or XHTML code of a Web page using an **HTML/XHTML embedded scripting language**. The most popular embedded language is JavaScript, which is used extensively in dynamic HTML files.

The second type of client-side program is an **applet**, a small application that resides on a server. When requested, a compiled version of the program is downloaded to the client computer and run there. The Java language is the most common language used to create applets for use in browsers. The applets can be requested from the server when a Web page is loaded; they will run once they're downloaded to the client computer.

Although the user can experience some delay in functionality while waiting for the Java applet to download to the client, once the applet arrives, it can execute all its functions without further communication with the server. Games are often sent to your browser as applets. As an example, in Figure 13.16 your browser makes contact with a game on the game site ArcadePod.com (**www.arcadepod.com**) and makes your request to play a game (step 1). The Web server returns the Java applet (step 2) that contains all the code to run the game on your computer. Your computer executes the applet code, and the game runs on your computer (step 3).

Communications over the Internet

A new communications revolution was started when Internet use began to explode in the mid-1990s. The volume of Internet

Your computer

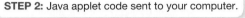

STEP 1: Request from browser for game.

STEP 2: Java applet code sent to your computer.

STEP 3: Computer executes Java applet code and game displays.

ArcadePod.com server

Figure 13.16

Deployment of a Java applet on a computer.

e-mail is growing exponentially every month. Unfortunately, it is estimated that 97 percent of it is spam. Texting and instant messaging are both popular methods of communication, and the popularity of Voice over Internet Protocol is also on the rise. In the following sections, we explore all of these communications media in more detail and show you how to keep your information exchanges efficient and secure.

E-Mail

Who invented e-mail? In 1971, Ray Tomlinson, a computer engineer who worked on the development of the ARPANET, the precursor to the Internet, for the U.S. government, created e-mail. E-mail grew from a simple program that Tomlinson wrote to enable computer users to leave text messages for each other on a single machine. The logical extension of this was sending text messages between machines on the Internet. Tomlinson created the convention of using the @ sign to distinguish between the mailbox name and the destination computer. E-mail became the most popular application on ARPANET; by 1973, it accounted for 75 percent of all data traffic.

How does e-mail travel the Internet? Just like other kinds of data that flow along the Internet, e-mail has its own protocol. The **Simple Mail Transfer Protocol (SMTP)** is responsible for sending e-mail along the Internet to its destination. SMTP is part of the Internet Protocol suite. As in most other Internet applications, e-mail is a client/server application. To send an e-mail message, you will need some form of e-mail software to compose the document as well as to include an attachment such as a spreadsheet or photograph. Popular client-based e-mail software (software that needs to be installed on your computer) includes Microsoft Outlook and Mozilla Thunderbird, as well as Web-based e-mail software such as Gmail, Yahoo!, and Hotmail.

As you read in Chapter 3, client-based software is installed on your computer, and all of its functions are supported and run from your computer. Web-based software is launched from a Web site; the programs and features are stored on the Web and are accessible anywhere you have access to an Internet connection. No matter which type of software you use, on the way to its destination your mail will pass through **e-mail servers**—specialized computers whose sole function is to store, process, and send e-mail.

Where are e-mail servers located? If your ISP provides you with an e-mail account, it runs an e-mail server that uses SMTP. For example, as shown in Figure 13.18, say you are sending an e-mail message to your friend Cheyenne. Cheyenne uses Verizon.net as her ISP. Therefore, your e-mail to her is addressed to Cheyenne@verizon.net.

When you send the e-mail message, your ISP's Web e-mail server receives it. The e-mail server reads the domain name (verizon.net) and communicates with a

Keeping track of where you have been on the Internet can be quite a challenge. Think about how many Web sites you visited today or when you were researching that paper for your history class last week. Can you remember all the sites you visited? Probably not—most of us don't have total recall.

Fortunately, tools built into browser software help us remember the sites we visit. For example, in Internet Explorer and Firefox, the history feature tracks all the sites visited over a period of time using the same browser on the same computer. If you have a Google account and use the Google Toolbar (an add-on for the Internet Explorer and Firefox browsers), the Google Web History feature tracks your entire browsing history regardless of what computer you may be using (as long as you are logged into your Google account and use the toolbar). But how private is your browsing history?

Most individuals in our society value privacy, which simply stated is the right to be left alone and unobserved to do as you please. But having your browsing habits recorded by the software you are using is tantamount to having someone looking over your shoulder and watching exactly what you are doing. Did you browse to a site today that you wouldn't want your parents, teacher, or boss to know about? If you haven't cleared the history file in your browser, anyone could easily call up the history in your browser and find out (see Figure 13.17)!

Google Web History is even more of a conundrum. Your entire browsing history is potentially contained in your Google file for all computers that you use (at home, school, and work). If you are browsing the Web at the local coffee shop and have not taken measures to secure your data transmissions on your notebook, any hacker could potentially intercept and gain access to your entire browsing history. This could reveal to a hacker places where you have financial resources (such as banks) and help direct them to Web sites where they can attempt to access your accounts. Many people would feel that their privacy was severely violated if their entire Web browsing history were seen by a stranger even if that person didn't use that information in a malicious way.

So where does convenience stop and privacy start? This is one of the thorny ethical dilemmas that we face in today's wired world. Having a browser history is extremely convenient when you can't remember the name of a cool site you visited last week. But having a list of all the sites you visited could be downright embarrassing if your boss looked through them and found out you were surfing the "jobs available" section of a competitor's Web site. Do you really want the next person to use the computer in the lab at school to know what you were shopping for on the Internet?

Although users can erase browser histories and Google Web History, this is not automatic and requires user intervention. The current versions of the popular browsers contain features called InPrivate Browsing (Internet Explorer), Incognito mode (Chrome), and Private Browsing (Firefox) that allow you to surf the Web without the browser retaining your history. But again, you must invoke these features to take advantage of them. Are you going to remember to do so every time you need to keep your browsing private? Fortunately, Firefox allows you to make Private Browsing the default for all your browsing sessions.

Should the makers of browser software and add-on tools be required to remind users periodically to purge their browsing history? Should the surfing tools that enhance privacy be automatically invoked by default so people won't forget to use them? Where does convenience end and privacy begin? What do you think?

History	Name	Location
Today	Basics : About Web History - Accounts Help	http://www.google.com/support/accounts/bin/answer.py?hl=en&answer=54068
Yesterday	google web history - Google Search	http://www.google.com/search?q=google+web+history&ie=utf-8&oe=utf-8&aq=
Last 7 days	IANA — .tv Domain Delegation Data	http://www.iana.org/domains/root/db/tv.html
June	/domains/root/db/#	http://www.iana.org/domains/root/db/#
May	IANA — Root Zone Database	http://www.iana.org/domains/root/db/
April	iana.org	http://iana.org/
March	IANA — Internet Assigned Numbers Authority	http://www.iana.org/
February	Top Level Domain Names / Country Codes	http://www.thrall.org/domains.htm
Older than 6 months	country domain names - Google Search	http://www.google.com/search?q=country+domain+names&ie=utf-8&oe=utf-8&
Tags	WHOIS Search for Domain Registration Informatio...	http://www.networksolutions.com/whois/index.jsp
All Bookmarks	who is - Google Search	http://www.google.com/search?q=who+is&ie=utf-8&oe=utf-8&aq=t&client=fire
	domainSearch.do	http://www.networksolutions.com/domainSearch.do
	Domain Name Search Results	http://www.networksolutions.com/domain-name-registration/domain-name-sear

Figure 13.17

Nothing embarrassing in this Firefox Web history. But what's lurking in your browser's history?

DNS server to determine the location of verizon.net. Once the address is located, the e-mail message is forwarded to verizon.net through the Internet and arrives at a mail server maintained by Cheyenne's ISP. The e-mail is then stored on Cheyenne's ISP's e-mail server. The next time Cheyenne logs on to her ISP and checks her mail, she will receive your message.

If e-mail was designed for text messages, why are we able to send files as attachments? SMTP was designed to handle text messages. When the need arose to send files by e-mail in the early 1970s, a program had to be created to convert binary files to text. The text that represented the file was appended to the end of the e-mail message. When the e-mail arrived at its destination, the recipient had to run another program to translate the text back into a binary file. The two most popular programs used for encoding and decoding binary files were uuencode and uudecode.

This was fine in the early days of the Internet when most users were computer scientists. However, when the Internet started to become popular in the early 1990s, it became apparent that a simpler methodology was needed for sending and receiving files. The **Multipurpose Internet Mail Extensions (MIME)** specification was introduced in 1991 to simplify attachments to e-mail messages. All e-mail client software now uses this protocol to attach files.

E-mail is still sent as text, but the e-mail client using the MIME protocol now handles the encoding and decoding for the users. For instance, when attaching a file, you click the attachment icon (usually a paperclip) and browse to the file you want to attach, which is located somewhere on a storage device. Your e-mail client transparently encodes and decodes the file for transmission and receipt.

BITS AND BYTES

Gmail Features You Should Know About

Many individuals use Gmail because it is free. But free doesn't necessary mean it isn't full featured. Gmail has some very useful features that can save you time, aggravation, and money. Here are a few to consider:

- **Drag-and-drop attachments:** You can drag files from your desktop or Windows Explorer and drop them onto the message you are creating to attach them instead of clicking the Attach button and searching for the file. However, this feature only works with the Chrome and Firefox browsers.

- **Attachment reminder:** How many times have you sent an e-mail and forgotten to attach the file you needed to send? When you send a Gmail message, if you used a phrase in the e-mail such as "I've attached" or "See attached" and you failed to attach a file, Gmail displays a gentle reminder in a pop-up box.

- **Make a phone call from within Gmail:** If you've installed the voice and video chat plug-in for Gmail, you can call any phone in the United States or Canada directly from Gmail . . . for free! Just click the Call Phone option in the Chat section of your Gmail screen to initiate the call.

- **Gmail Notifier:** This is a free application that, when installed, sends you alerts/pop-ups whenever you receive an e-mail message, thus eliminating the need to constantly check your inbox.

- **Offline Gmail:** You can store your old messages locally on your hard drive so you can access your mail and work on it even when you are offline.

For even more useful features, on your Gmail settings menu, click the Labs option to see the latest and greatest features deployed by Google.

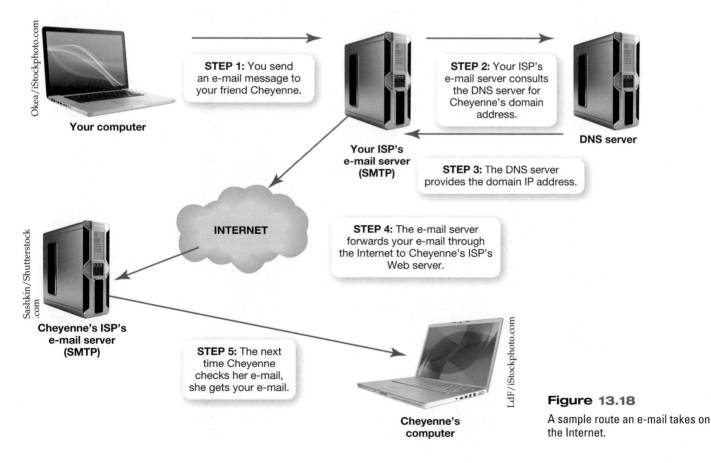

STEP 1: You send an e-mail message to your friend Cheyenne.

Your computer

STEP 2: Your ISP's e-mail server consults the DNS server for Cheyenne's domain address.

DNS server

Your ISP's e-mail server (SMTP)

STEP 3: The DNS server provides the domain IP address.

INTERNET

STEP 4: The e-mail server forwards your e-mail through the Internet to Cheyenne's ISP's Web server.

Cheyenne's ISP's e-mail server (SMTP)

STEP 5: The next time Cheyenne checks her e-mail, she gets your e-mail.

Cheyenne's computer

Figure 13.18

A sample route an e-mail takes on the Internet.

Keeping E-Mail Secure

In this Active Helpdesk call, you'll play the role of a helpdesk staffer, fielding calls about how e-mail works and how messages are kept secure.

E-Mail Security: Encryption and Specialized Software

If e-mail is sent in regular text, can other people read my mail? E-mail is highly susceptible to being read by unintended parties because it's sent in plain text. Additionally, copies of your e-mail messages may exist (temporarily or permanently) on numerous servers as the messages make their way through the Internet. To protect your sensitive e-mail messages, encryption practices are used.

How do you encrypt e-mail? **Encryption** refers to the process of coding your e-mail so that only the person with the key to the code, the intended recipient, can decode (or decipher) and read the message. Secret codes for messages can be traced almost to the dawn of written language. The military and government espionage agencies are big users of codes and ciphers. The trick is making the coding system easy enough to use that everyone who needs to communicate with you can do so.

There are two basic types of encryption: private key and public key. In **private-key encryption**, only the two parties involved

in sending the message have the code. This could be a simple shift code where letters of the alphabet are shifted to a new position (see Figure 13.19). For example, in a two-position right-shift code, the letter *a* becomes *c*, *b* becomes *d*, and so on. Alternatively, it could be a more complex substitution code (*a* = *h*, *b* = *r*, *c* = *g*, etc.). The main problem with private-key encryption is key security. If someone steals a copy of the code or is savvy about decoding, the code is broken.

In **public-key encryption**, two keys, known as a **key pair**, are created. You use one key for coding and the other for decoding. The key for coding is generally distributed as a **public key**. You can place this key on your Web site, for instance. Anyone wishing to send you a message can then download your public key and code the message using your public key.

When you receive the message, you use your **private key** to decode it. You are the only one who ever possesses the private key, and therefore it is highly secure. The keys are generated in such a way that they can work only with each other. The private key is generated first. The public key is then generated using a complex mathematical formula, often using values from the private key. The computations are so complex that they are considered unbreakable. Both keys are necessary to decode a message. If one key is lost, the other key cannot be used by itself.

What type of encryption is used on the Internet? Public-key encryption is the most commonly used encryption on the Internet. Tried-and-true public-key packages such as **Pretty Good Privacy (PGP)** are available for download at sites such as CNET Downloads (**download.cnet.com**), and you can usually use them free of charge (although there are now commercial versions of PGP). After obtaining the PGP software, you can generate key pairs to provide a private key for you and a public key for the rest of the world.

What does a key look like? A key is a binary number. Keys vary in length, depending on how secure they need to be. A 12-bit key has 12 positions and might look like this:

```
100110101101
```

Longer keys are more secure because they have more values that are possible. A 12-bit key provides 4,096 different

A = C	N = P
B = D	O = Q
C = E	P = R
D = F	Q = S
E = G	R = T
F = H	S = U
G = I	T = V
H = J	U = W
I = K	V = X
J = L	W = Y
K = M	X = Z
L = N	Y = A
M = O	Z = B

The word **C O M P U T E R** using the two-position code at the left now becomes:

E Q O R W V G T

This is difficult to interpret without the code key at the left.

Figure 13.19

Writing the word "COMPUTER" using a two-position right-shift encryption code.

possible values, whereas a 40-bit key allows for 1,099,511,627,776 possible values. The key and the message are run through a complex algorithm in the encryption program (such as PGP) that converts the message into unrecognizable code. Each key turns the message into a different code.

Is a private key really secure? Because of the complexity of the algorithms used to generate key pairs, it is impossible to deduce the private key from the public key. However, that doesn't mean your coded message can't be cracked. As you learned in Chapter 12, a brute force attack occurs when hackers try every possible key combination to decode a message. This type of attack can enable hackers to deduce the key and decode the message.

What is considered a safe key? In the early 1990s, 40-bit keys were thought to be totally resistant to brute force attacks and were the norm for encryption. However, in 1995, a French programmer used a unique algorithm of his own and 120 workstations simultaneously to attempt to break a 40-bit key. He succeeded in just eight days. After this, 128-bit keys became the standard. However, using supercomputers, researchers have had some success cracking 128-bit encryption. Therefore, strong encryption now calls for 256-bit keys. It is believed that even with the most powerful computers in use today, it would take hundreds of billions of years to crack a 256-bit key.

What is an easy way for me to try encrypted e-mail? Many e-mail services offer built-in encryption, and they mostly market toward businesses. However, Hushmail (**www.hushmail.com**) and Comodo SecureEmail (**www.comodo.com**) offer free versions of their secure e-mail to individuals. You can sign up on their Web sites and experiment with sending encrypted e-mail. And you don't need to abandon your current e-mail accounts—just use your secure account when you require secure communications.

Businesses often pay for encryption services that also provide other features such as confirmation of message delivery, message tracking, and overwriting of e-mail messages when they are deleted to ensure that copies don't exist. Companies such as Securus Systems (**www.safemessage.com**) and ZixCorp (**www.zixcorp.com**) provide these higher levels of service to businesses.

BITS AND BYTES

Random Numbers: We Wouldn't Have Encryption Without Them!

E-mail encryption, SSL encryption, and just about anything we do to achieve privacy on the Internet requires random numbers. Encryption is accomplished using random number sequences, which are sequences of numbers in which no patterns can be recognized. Even for an e-commerce transaction (say, buying a textbook from **www.BarnesandNoble.com**) that uses SSL encryption to encode your credit card number, as many as 368 bits of random data might be needed. Only 128 bits are needed for the encryption key, but other random data is needed to create authentication codes and to prevent replay attacks. Replay attacks occur when hackers attempt to copy packets traveling across the Internet and extract data (such as encryption codes) from them. The hackers then can replay (reuse) the data to gain access to networks or transactions.

So where do all these random numbers come from? Generating true random sequences is more difficult than it sounds. Most random number generators are really pseudo-random since they are all based on some sort of pattern to generate the numbers. However, in 1998, Mads Haahr of the School of Computer Science and Statistics at Trinity College in Dublin created the site RANDOM.org, which is dedicated to providing true random numbers for Web applications such as encryption algorithms. The numbers are generated based on atmospheric noise, which is truly random. The noise is gleaned from radios not tuned to a particular station, so they are broadcasting static. Anyone can access the Web site and download random numbers to be used for encryption or other vital services such as lottery drawings. For more information, check out their site at **www.random.org**.

Instant Messaging

What do you need to run instant messaging? As we explained in Chapter 3, instant messaging is the act of communicating over the Internet with one or more people in real time. It differs from e-mail in that conversations are able to happen at the same time rather than lagging by minutes or hours. Although you may not use instant messaging services beyond what is offered on Facebook, businesses today routinely use these services to keep employees in constant contact. Instant messaging requires the use of a client program that connects to an instant messaging service. AOL Instant Messenger (AIM), GoogleTalk, Yahoo! Messenger, Jabber, and Windows Live Messenger are the top five instant messaging services in use today. No matter which one you choose, you need to have the appropriate client software installed on your computing device. Instant messaging programs are often used on smartphones and tablets because it provides for real-time "conversations" with multiple individuals, including employees who may be at their desks and not using mobile devices.

Crowdsourcing: Harnessing the Power of Social Networks

Starting and running a small business involves a fair amount of risk, especially when running a merchandising business. Deciding what products to buy and resell to customers is tricky. Will your customers purchase the products you think are so wonderful? Will they buy them quickly enough so that you can free up your cash to purchase more inventory? What quantities should you stock? If you're an entrepreneur, you usually have to make these decisions yourself. Wouldn't it be better to let your customers tell you what to sell?

Many businesses harness the power of their customers (and potential customers) by using the Internet to take advantage of a new technique known as **crowdsourcing**. When you crowdsource, you take a task that an employee or a contractor usually performs and instead outsource that task to a large group of people, usually via the Internet. In this way, you can have many individuals work on a task to take advantage of aggregated brainpower. Or you can aggregate and analyze the results of feedback from the crowdsourcers to make informed business decisions. Two companies that exemplify the crowdsourcing model of customer-driven merchandise buying are Threadless (**www.threadless.com**) and ModCloth (**www.modcloth.com**).

Threadless is a t-shirt company, but what makes Threadless stand out from the hundreds of other t-shirt companies on the Web is that they invite artists and designers to submit designs for t-shirts as part of an ongoing contest. Threadless posts submitted designs on the site and then lets anyone who visits the site vote on the best designs. The designs with the most votes get made into shirts and offered for sale (see Figure 13.20), and the designers of shirts that get printed win a cash prize of $2,500.

Because potential customers have already indicated their interest in a particular design by voting on it, Threadless can be fairly confident that the designs they print will sell briskly.

ModCloth is a company founded in 2002 by two high-school students who were just 17 years old! They started selling only vintage clothing but then expanded to offer vintage-inspired designs by indie designers.

Threadlesstees.com

Figure 13.20

Threadless shirts such as Secrets of Mensa were voted on by customers before being offered for sale, a process known as crowdsourcing.

How does instant messaging work? The client software running on your device makes a connection with the chat server using your Internet connection, as shown in Figure 13.22. Once contact is established, you can log in to the server with your name and password. The client software provides the server with connection information (such as the IP address) for your device. The server then consults the list of contacts ("Buddies" or friends) that you have previously established in your account and checks to see if any of your contacts are online (step 1). If any are, the server sends a message back to your client providing the necessary connection information (the IP addresses) for your friends who are online (step 2). You can now click your friends' names to establish a chat session with them (step 3).

Because both your device and your friend's device have the connection information (the IP addresses) for each other,

Figure 13.21

Customers vote and comment on products that ModCloth is thinking about stocking.

When ordering clothing from designers, there is usually a minimum order quantity that often exceeds 100 pieces. Although the buyers for Mod-Cloth feel they have a good eye for what their customers like, it is still risky for a small business to order large quantities of items because they may take a long time to sell.

ModCloth started its Be the Buyer program to involve customers in the buying process. They post clothing they are considering buying on the ModCloth site, and then customers vote to either "Pick It" (stock the item) or "Skip It," as shown in Figure 13.21. Customers can post comments about the items, which range from humorous to construc-tive. ModCloth also provides links so that voters can easily share items with their friends on social networks like Facebook and Twitter. Constructive ideas from potential customers can be sent back to designers who might make suggested alterations to items before ModCloth orders them. When ModCloth orders a popular item, customers who indicated they liked it can be contacted via e-mail to stimulate sales.

So don't let all those customers who have friended you on your company's Facebook page sit idle. Put them to work helping you make your business more profitable!

the server isn't involved in the chat session. Chatting takes place directly between the two devices over the Internet.

Is sending an instant message secure? Most instant messaging services do not use a high level of encryption for their messages—if they bother to use encryption at all. In addition to viruses, worms, and hacking threats, instant messaging systems are vulnerable to eavesdropping, in which someone using a packet sniffer "listens in" on IM conversations. Although several measures are under way to increase the security of this method of real-time communication, major vulnerabilities still exist. And employers can install monitoring software to record instant message sessions. Therefore, it is not a good idea to send sensitive information using instant messaging because it is susceptible to interception and possible misuse by hackers. Also, your company may be monitoring and logging instant message sessions.

Voice over Internet Protocol (VoIP)

Is the Voice over Internet Protocol part of TCP/IP? As we covered in Chapter 8, Voice over Internet Protocol (VoIP) turns a standard Internet connection into a way to make free long-distance phone calls. VoIP is not part of the TCP/IP suite but is a collection of communication and transmission protocols that uses TCP/IP protocols to route phone calls across the Internet.

How does VoIP work? From a user's perspective, there is little difference between VoIP and traditional phone service (see Figure 13.23), although the technology behind the wires and devices is a bit different. As explained in Chapter 3, VoIP is a method of taking analog voice signals that normally travel telephone wires and turning them into digital data that can be transmitted over the Internet. Like e-mail, VoIP uses packet switching as the method of transferring data. Unlike circuit switching (the method used with traditional phone calls), when a VoIP call is made, the transmission lines are only used when the two computing devices are communicating, thus allowing the devices to accept and process other information. Because digital data is far more efficient than analog data with respect to size, transmission speed, and compression capabilities, VoIP's long-term advantage is that it will be able to handle more phone calls at the same time.

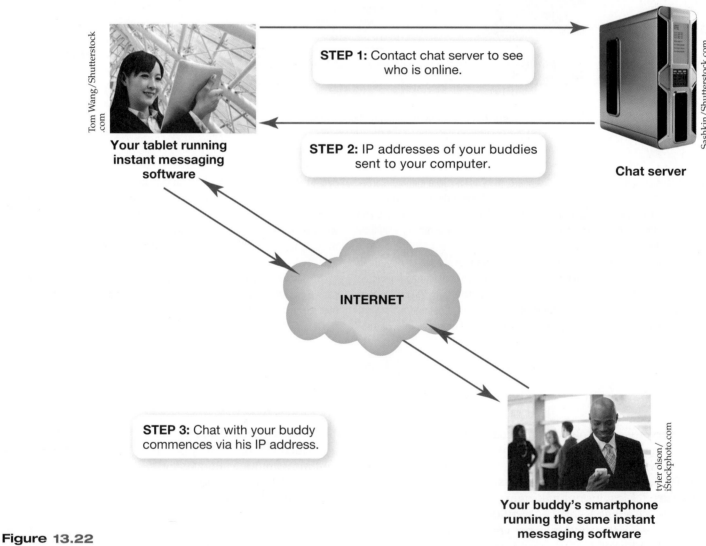

STEP 1: Contact chat server to see who is online.

Your tablet running instant messaging software

STEP 2: IP addresses of your buddies sent to your computer.

Chat server

INTERNET

STEP 3: Chat with your buddy commences via his IP address.

Your buddy's smartphone running the same instant messaging software

Figure 13.22

How an instant messaging program works.

Figure 13.23 | CONVENTIONAL AND VoIP CALLING COMPARED

Conventional Telephone Call	VoIP Telephone Call
1. Pick up the phone and wait for a dial tone to signal that you are connected to the local office of your telephone carrier.	1. Pick up the phone, which sends a signal to the computer or telephone adapter. The computer sends a dial tone, indicating that you have a connection to the Internet.
2. Dial the number of your friend's phone.	2. Dial the number of your friend's phone. The tones are converted into digital data.
3. The call is routed through the switch at your local carrier, passing through several switches along the way.	3. As long as the phone number is in a valid format, your VoIP company will translate the phone number into an IP address and then connects to the receiving device.
4. The phone at the other end rings, and your friend answers the call.	4. The signal "asks" the receiving device to ring, and your friend answers the call.
5. When the call is answered, a circuit is opened.	5. When your friend picks up the phone, each computer knows to expect packets of data from the other computer.
6. As you talk, the circuit remains open. No other data can be transmitted over the phone line during this time. A busy signal occurs if someone else tries to call.	6. As you talk, the packets of data are sent over the same Internet infrastructure as e-mail or a Web page. The digital data is translated into analog audio signals so that you and your friend can understand each other.
7. When you hang up, the circuit is closed, enabling another call to come in.	7. When you hang up, the session is terminated.

1. Who owns, manages, and pays for the Internet?

Management of the Internet is carried out by several nonprofit organizations and user groups such as the Internet Society (ISOC), the Internet Engineering Task Force (IETF), the Internet Architecture Board (IAB), the Internet Corporation for Assigned Names and Numbers (ICANN), and the World Wide Web Consortium (W3C). Each group has different responsibilities and tasks. Currently, the U.S. government (and subsequently the U.S. taxpayer) funds a majority of the Internet's costs.

2. How do the Internet's networking components interact?

Computing devices or networks connect to the Internet using Internet service providers (ISPs). These providers vary in size and work like the physical highway system. The largest paths, along which data travels the most efficiently and quickly, make up the Internet backbone. Homes and all but the largest businesses connect to the Internet through regional or local connections, which then connect to the Internet through the entities that make up the Internet backbone. The largest businesses, educational centers, and some government agencies such as NASA make up the Internet backbone.

3. What data transmissions and protocols does the Internet use?

Data is transmitted along the Internet using packet switching. Data is broken up into discrete units known as *packets*, which can take independent routes to the destination before being reassembled. Although many protocols are available on the Internet, the main suite of protocols used to move information over the Internet is TCP/IP. The suite is named after the original two protocols that were developed for the Internet: the Transmission Control Protocol (TCP) and the Internet Protocol (IP). Whereas TCP is responsible for preparing data for transmission, IP actually sends data between computers on the Internet.

4. Why are IP addresses and domain names important for Internet communications?

An IP address is a unique number assigned to all computers connected to the Internet. The IP address is necessary so that packets of data can be sent to a particular location (computer) on the Internet. A domain name is merely a name that stands for a certain IP address and makes it easier for people to remember it. For example, bookuni-verse.com is a domain name and is much easier to remember than the IP address 124.53.111.14. DNS servers act as the phone books of the Internet. They enable your computer to find out the IP address of a domain by looking up its corresponding domain name (which you typed into your browser).

5. What are HTTP, HTML/XHTML, and XML used for?

The Hypertext Transfer Protocol (HTTP) is the protocol used on the Internet to display Web pages in your browser. The Hypertext Markup Language (HTML) is a set of rules for marking up blocks of text so that a browser knows how to display them. Most Web pages are generated with at least some HTML code. Blocks of text in HTML documents are surrounded by a pair of tags (such as <b> and </b> to indicate bolding). These tags and the text between them are referred to as *elements*. By examining the elements, your browser determines how to display them on your computer screen. Because HTML was not designed for information exchange, eXtensible Markup Language (XML) was created. Instead of locking users into standard tags and formats for data, XML enables users to create their own markup languages to accommodate particular data formats and needs. XML is used extensively in e-commerce for exchanging data between corporations.

6. How do e-mail, instant messaging, and Voice over Internet Protocol work, and how is information using these technologies kept secure?

Simple Mail Transfer Protocol (SMTP) is the protocol responsible for sending e-mail over the Internet. As is true of most other Internet applications, e-mail is a client/server application. E-mail passes through e-mail servers whose functions are to store, process, and send e-mail to its ultimate destination. ISPs and portals such as Yahoo! maintain e-mail servers to provide e-mail functionality to their customers. Your ISP's e-mail server uses DNS servers to locate the IP addresses for the recipients of the e-mail you send. Encryption software, such as Pretty Good Privacy (PGP), is used to code messages so that they can be decoded only by the authorized recipients.

Companion Website

The Companion Website includes a variety of additional materials to help you review and learn more about the topics in this chapter. Go to: *www.pearsonhighered.com/techinaction*

key terms thirteen chapter

key terms

buzzwords

Word Bank

- AJAX
- applet
- circuit switching
- DNS server
- HTTP
- HTTPS
- ICANN
- Internet backbone
- IP addresses
- OC line
- packet switching
- PGP
- point of presence
- public-key encryption
- SMTP
- SSL
- TCP/IP

Instructions: Fill in the blanks using the words from the Word Bank above.

Jonathan has begun running an online auction business from his home. To provide the bandwidth his customers need, Jonathan had the phone company install a(n) (1) _____ instead of relying on a cable or DSL connection. To provide interactivity on his Web site, Jonathan is programming the Web pages with (2) _____ instead of using HTML. For customer data security, he is using the (3) _____ and (4) _____ protocols. He is currently developing another project with a partner in Japan. Because of the secrecy involved, Jonathan is encrypting his e-mail communications with the (5) _____ program that uses (6) _____. He knows that he needs the additional security because the (7) _____ protocol that handles Internet mail delivery does not provide for encryption.

Jonathan recently had to install some new servers to support his site, so he needed to apply to (8) _____, the organization that keeps track of assigning (9) _____, so he could have the appropriate means of identifying the new servers on the Internet. Fortunately, his ISP has a robust connection to the (10) _____, the main high-speed pipeline that transmits Internet traffic, so his customers experience good response time when surfing his site. Jonathan was worried last week when the (11) _____ to which his servers connect to his ISP went down for several hours and his customers couldn't access his site. But after replacing some faulty modems his ISP got everything back up and working. Given the vast amount of traffic on his Web site, Jonathan is glad that the modern Internet uses (12) _____ technology to transmit data packets. Certainly, the old (13) _____ technology that the phone company used to use for moving data would never serve his customers efficiently. Customers access Jonathan's site using the (14) _____ protocol through their browsers until they need to use a more secure protocol to make a purchase. But Jonathan knows that the main protocol for moving information on the Web is (15) _____ and that his business couldn't exist without it.

becoming computer literate

While attending college, you are working at a small manufacturer of bicycle messenger bags. The owner feels the employees don't know enough about how the Internet works and has charged your supervisor with preparing a presentation on Internet protocols and communications. Your supervisor has asked you to help draft the report that will be presented to the employees next month.

Instructions: Draft a report for your boss that details the main protocols in use on the Internet and how major communication mediums (such as e-mail and instant messaging) work. Make sure to explain how to keep such communications secure. Use as many of the key terms from the chapter as you can, and ensure that the report will be understandable by employees who may be less familiar with computers or the Internet than you are.

Instructions: Answer the multiple-choice and true–false questions below for more practice with key terms and concepts from this chapter.

Multiple Choice

1. Which is not a common protocol used on the Internet?
   a. TCP
   b. IP
   c. HTTP
   d. PGP

2. The large collection of national and international networks that comprises the highest-speed Internet connections is known as the
   a. TCP/IP pipeline.
   b. Internet backbone.
   c. HTTP conduit.
   d. XML gateway.

3. ISPs are connected to each other at
   a. Internet exchange points.
   b. points of presence.
   c. Internet intersections.
   d. DNS convergence points.

4. IP addresses that are assigned by an ISP from an available pool of IP addresses are
   a. called *static*.
   b. less secure.
   c. called *dynamic*.
   d. attractive to hackers.

5. The main suite of Internet protocols used to transmit data is called
   a. DNS.
   b. XML.
   c. HTTP.
   d. TCP/IP.

6. A(n) _____ takes the place of an IP address because it is easier for humans to recall than a long string of numbers.
   a. DNS
   b. CGI
   c. domain name
   d. HTML

7. _____ servers help other computers find IP addresses and URLs on the Internet.
   a. HTTP
   b. DNS
   c. CGI
   d. XML

8. _____ is a popular protocol for sharing files between computers.
   a. FTP
   b. HTTP
   c. DNS
   d. XHTML

9. The main use for DHTML is
   a. creating a secure connection between client and server.
   b. loading Web pages into a browser.
   c. encrypting e-mail messages.
   d. making Web pages interactive.

10. The protocol used to send e-mail over the Internet is
   a. HTTP.
   b. DHTML.
   c. DNS.
   d. SMTP.

True–False

_____ 1. The Internet is primarily managed by U.S. government agencies.

_____ 2. VoIP uses circuit switching technology.

_____ 3. All modern e-mail software uses encryption by default to ensure secure communication.

_____ 4. The type of encryption most commonly used on the Internet is public-key encryption.

_____ 5. Instant messages are generally not secure because most instant-messaging software does not provide for encryption of messages.

1. **Registering a Domain Name**

   A friend of yours wants to launch a company offering a line of t-shirts and other clothing for bicycling enthusiasts. She is having trouble coming up with a catchy domain name for the company.

   a. Think about words that could be used to describe clothing worn while bicycling. Compile a list of key words that someone might enter into a search engine if they were looking for a company that sells cool bicycling clothing.

   b. Try combining some key words (or parts of words) and develop at least five potential catchy, easy-to-spell domain names for the company.

   c. Check to see if the domain names you dreamed up are available in the .com domain (check on **www.networksolutions.com**). If none of the names are available, are any of the ones you created available for sale (check on **www.sedo.com** and **www.buydomains.com**)? If none of the ones you thought of are affordable, think up more until you find one that is available/affordable.

2. **Creating a Wiki Site: Issue 1**

   Your sociology instructor has asked your group to design a wiki site about preventing identity theft. The site will include textual and graphic information about identity theft as well as an interactive quiz. The wiki will be open for anyone to edit (just like Wikipedia), and it is hoped that other students will contribute to the site. The following issues need to be addressed:

   a. Which wiki hosting service will you use to host the site? Why do you think this is appropriate?

   b. What name would you choose for the site? What URL would you choose for the site?

   c. How would you publicize the site so that other students at your school can find it?

   d. Who will be responsible for monitoring and editing the site? What types of content would you remove from the site?

making the
transition to...
next semester

thirteen chapter

making the
transition to...
next semester

3. **Creating a Wiki Site: Issue 2**

You have been asked to assist your psychology professor in creating a wiki for her students. The wiki will be used by the students to develop an online study guide for the Introduction to Psychology class. Investigate the following two options and explain which option you will recommend and why:

a. Most schools provide course management software (CMS) such as Blackboard or Moodle to facilitate communication between faculty and students. Most CMS systems have the ability to host wikis. What CMS software does your school use? Is the wiki feature available? How much storage space is provided for wiki pages? Can the wiki be rolled over to the next semester so future classes can work on it?

b. Many sites host wikis free of charge, including PBworks (**www.pbworks.com**), Wikidot (**www.wikidot.com**), and Wikispaces (**www.wikispaces.com**). Investigate at least two free wiki services and compare their features. Include the following items and any other features that would be useful to your professor:

• Limitations on number of users that can participate in a single wiki

• Amount of disk storage space

• Restrictions on file uploads, including file size and number of files

• Membership restrictions (e.g., can the wiki be private or editable only by members?)

• Notification features (e.g., can members be notified of updates by e-mail or RSS feed?)

4. **Securing Your E-Mail Communications**

You have a brilliant idea for a new business and will begin developing it with several friends next semester. To help ensure no one steals your idea before you launch the business, you decide that encrypting your e-mail communications related to the business would be a good idea. Investigate the free secure e-mail products Hushmail (**www.hushmail.com**), S-Mail secure email (**www.s-mail.com**), and Comodo SecureEmail (**www.comodo.com**). Prepare a report for your friends that compares the features of these e-mail products and justifies the decision to use the e-mail package you chose.

1. Web Site Privacy Issues

Your employer, a distributor of aftermarket automotive accessories, recently discovered that an employee was using his Facebook account to post disparaging remarks about the company president. The employee was fired and has now lodged a wrongful discharge lawsuit against your employer. You don't feel comfortable with the way this employee was treated, and you are wondering if your employer's firing of the employee was legal. Investigate the following and prepare a narrative for your instructor:

a. Is the state in which you go to school an "employment-at-will" state? If so, generally an employee can be fired for almost any reason at any time as long as the firing does not violate another employment law (such as the Civil Rights Act). Should an employer have the right to fire a person for expressing an opinion about his or her boss or company on a social networking site? Why or why not?

b. Have employers been successful in terminating employees for making disparaging comments on social networking sites, wikis, and blogs? Research the case of Ellen Simonetti, whose firing over her blog posts is one of the most famous cases in this area. In your opinion, was Ms. Simonetti treated fairly? What kind of policy should an employer have to warn employees about the potential consequences of their actions on social networking sites?

c. If you were running a small business and you found out that one of your employees was disparaging you or the business on a public Web site, what would you do about it?

2. Creating an Online Presence for a Business

You work at a local coffee shop that offers live music on the weekends. Your boss has asked you to help the coffee shop enhance its Web presence to better connect with customers. The shop currently has a Web site but does not have pages on any social networking sites. Consider the following:

a. On which social networking sites would you create a page for the coffee shop? Why?

b. What types of information would you post on the social network pages for the coffee shop? What strategies would you use to make customers aware of the coffee shop's social networking sites?

c. What information would you solicit from customers who joined the coffee shop's social networking sites? How could you use crowdsourcing to help develop new products or services for the business?

3. "Googling" Yourself

At your company, someone was just fired because sensitive information related to a company product was associated with the person's name on the Internet. Discretion being the better part of valor, you decide to do a search for your name on the Web using a search engine such as Google (**www.google.com**) just to see what is out there. Prepare a report on what you found. Your report should answer the following questions:

a. Did you find any accurate information about yourself (such as your home page URL or résumé)? Did you find any erroneous information that you need to correct?

b. Did you find Web sites or information about other people with the same name as you? Could any of that information be damaging to your reputation if someone thought the other person was you? If so, provide examples.

c. Is there information that you found about yourself or others that you think should never be available on the Internet? Provide examples and an explanation of why you feel certain information should not be available.

d. Is there any information on social networking sites, such as Google+ or Facebook, that could be damaging to you if an employer or school administrator were to see it?

Instructions: Some ideas are best understood by experimenting with them in our own minds. The following critical thinking questions are designed to demand your full attention but require only a comfortable chair—no technology.

1. **Breaking Encryption**

   Encryption programs based on 256-bit encryption algorithms are currently considered unbreakable. Consider the following:

   a. Because of their secure nature, the U.S. government places restrictions on exports of these encryption products. The government is considering a requirement that all encryption products have a "backdoor" code that would allow government agencies (such as the FBI and CIA) to read encrypted messages. This became a heated topic of discussion after the terrorist attacks on September 11, 2001. Do you think this backdoor requirement should be implemented? Why or why not? What possible problems do you foresee if the backdoor code became known to people outside of sanctioned government agencies?

   b. Assuming you and a group of your friends develop a method for breaking 256-bit encryption, should you post that information on the Internet for anyone to use? Why or why not?

2. **Illegal File Sharing Among Students**

   The College Opportunity and Affordability Act, passed by Congress in 2008, almost included a provision requiring colleges to monitor and punish students who were illegally swapping or downloading copyrighted material such as music or movies.

   a. As a condition to receiving federal funding, should colleges be required to prevent students from illegally downloading or sharing material? Why or why not?

   b. What measures has your school taken to prevent the illegal downloading of media? Are these measures effective? What other actions would you recommend your school take?

3. **Encryption of E-Mail**

   a. Do you currently encrypt your personal e-mail? Why or why not? If you are sending business-related e-mail, do you think you should use encrypted e-mail? Explain your answers.

   b. Do you think your school should provide encrypted e-mail for student use? If a problem arises, such as a student accusing another student of sexual harassment, do you think the software used for encryption should have code that enables school administrators to break the encryption? Explain your answers.

   c. Should all U.S. government agencies be required to use encrypted e-mail? What agencies should be required to use encrypted e-mail? Are there agencies that would never need to use encrypted e-mail? Explain your answers.

Using Crowdsourcing in a Business

Problem

In today's fast-paced business environment, determining the right merchandise to sell is more critical than ever. Having a Web site that is designed to use crowdsourcing to either gather information about products you already carry, such as customer reviews on Amazon, or determine what merchandise you are going to stock (contests on Threadless) provides you with a competitive advantage. In this Team Time, you'll consider how best to take advantage of crowdsourcing in starting a new business venture.

Task

Your teacher has been contacted by the local chamber of commerce. There are three individuals who are starting new businesses who have requested help in designing their Web sites and their customer interaction programs. The businesses are a) a coffee shop that offers live music on nights and weekends; b) a clothing company for young, urban professionals; and c) a company that sells iPad, iPod, and iPhone accessories. You need to help these businesses choose an appropriate domain name for their company and suggest a crowdsourcing strategy for the business.

Process

Break the class into small teams of three or four students. Each team should select one of the businesses described above (or select their own business type). Multiple teams could work on the same type of business. Each team should prepare a report as follows:

1. Determine an appropriate domain name for the company's Web site. Make sure that the Web address you propose is available by using a Whois service such as **www .whois.net**. Make sure to consider the domain naming guidelines discussed in the Bits and Bytes in this chapter.

2. Decide on the general types of products that will be sold by the company. For each category of product, decide what product attributes you feel that customers will comment on when giving input on products to be sold on the site.

3. Decide if the company will solicit feedback from potential customers on all products to be sold or whether the company will offer a core selection of products without soliciting feedback from customers. Divide the products into two lists: core products and products subject to crowdsourcing.

4. Determine a social networking strategy for the company to promote its products on Facebook, Twitter, etc.. How will customers be driven to the company Web site to participate in the crowdsourcing for incentives, discount coupons, contests, and such?

5. Develop a PowerPoint presentation to summarize your findings and present your proposed solution to the class.

Conclusion

E-commerce Web sites are relatively cheap and easy to deploy using the vast array of tools available on the Internet today. But substantial risk exists when financing and stocking products to be sold. Gathering crowdsourcing feedback can help businesses minimize the risk of stocking unwanted products.

Privacy at School

In this exercise, you will research and then role-play a complicated ethical situation. The role you play may or may not match your own personal beliefs, but your research and use of logic will enable you to represent whichever view is assigned. An arbitrator will watch and comment on both sides of the arguments, and together the team will agree on an ethical solution.

Problem

Many Americans consider privacy to be a fundamental and unalienable right even though privacy is not specifically spelled out as a right in the U.S. Constitution or the Bill of Rights. Parents seem especially concerned about protecting their children's privacy rights. With the widespread use of technology, infringing on personal privacy rights has become easier, even if it is often done innocently or inadvertently.

School administrators are quickly learning that they need to craft policies that set appropriate boundaries and guidelines for monitoring students. Should school districts be allowed to monitor students? Should school districts be required to inform students and parents of any monitoring that takes place?

Research Areas to Consider

- Lower Merion school district in Pennsylvania uses webcams to monitor students in their homes.
- A school district in California uses RFID chips to take attendance.
- The Family Educational Rights and Privacy Act (FERPA)

Process

Divide the class into teams.

1. Research the areas cited above and devise a scenario in which a school district has been monitoring students without their knowledge and has potentially violated their privacy.

2. Team members should write a summary that provides background information for their character—for example: student or parent, school official, and arbitrator—and detail their character's behaviors to set the stage for the role-playing event. Then, team members should create an outline to use during the role-playing event.

3. Team members should arrange a mutually convenient time to meet for the exchange, either using the chat room feature of MyITLab, the discussion board feature of Blackboard, or meeting in person.

4. Team members should present their case to the class, or submit a PowerPoint presentation for review by the rest of the class, along with the summary and resolution they developed.

Conclusion

As technology becomes ever more prevalent and integrated into our lives, more and more ethical dilemmas will present themselves. Being able to understand and evaluate both sides of the argument, while responding in a personally or socially ethical manner, will be an important skill.

A

3D sound card An expansion card that enables a computer to produce sounds that are omnidirectional or three dimensional.

802.11 standard A wireless standard established in 1997 by the Institute of Electrical and Electronics Engineers; also known as WiFi (short for Wireless Fidelity), it enables wireless network devices to work seamlessly with other networks and devices.

access card reader A device that reads information from a magnetic strip on the back of a credit card–like access card (such as a student ID card); card readers are easily programmed by adding authorized ID card numbers, Social Security numbers, and so on.

access method A program or hardware mechanism that controls which computer is allowed to use the transmission media in a network at a certain time.

access time The time it takes a storage device to locate its stored data.

accounting software An application program that helps business owners manage their finances more efficiently by providing tools for tracking accounting transactions such as sales, accounts receivable, inventory purchases, and accounts payable.

ActionScript A programming language included in Flash; similar to JavaScript in its keywords, operators, and classes.

Active Server Pages (ASP) A scripting environment in which users combine HyperText Markup Language (HTML), scripts, and reusable Microsoft ActiveX server components to create dynamically generated Web pages.

active topology A network topology in which each node on the network is responsible for retransmitting the token, or the data, to other nodes.

Adobe Flash A software product for developing Web-based multimedia.

adware A program that downloads on your computer when you install a freeware program, game, or utility. Generally, adware enables sponsored advertisements to appear in a section of your browser window or as a pop-up ad box.

affective computing A type of computing that relates to emotion or deliberately tries to influence emotion.

aggregator A software program that goes out and grabs the latest update of Web material (usually podcasts) according to your specifications.

AJAX A collection of technologies that allows the creation of Web applications that can update information on a page without requiring the user to do a page refresh or leave the page.

algorithm A set of specific, sequential steps that describe in natural language exactly what a computer program must do to complete its task.

all-in-one computer A desktop system unit that houses the computer's processor, memory, and monitor in a single unit.

all-in-one printer See *multifunction printer*.

alphabetic check Confirms that only textual characters are entered in a database field.

analog Waves that illustrate the loudness of a sound or the brightness of the colors in an image at a given moment in time.

analog-to-digital converter chip Converts analog signals into digital signals.

antivirus software Software that is specifically designed to detect viruses and protect a computer and files from harm.

applet A small program designed to be run from within another application. Java applets are often run on your computer by your browser through the Java Virtual Machine (an application built into current browsers).

application programming interface (API) A block of code in the operating system that software applications need to interact with.

application server A server that acts as a repository for application software.

application software The set of programs on a computer that helps a user carry out tasks such as word processing, sending e-mail, balancing a budget, creating presentations, editing photos, taking an online course, and playing games.

artificial intelligence (AI) The science that attempts to produce computers that display the same type of reasoning and intelligence that humans do.

aspect ratio The width-to-height proportion of a monitor.

assembly language A language that enables programmers to write their programs using a set of short, English-like commands that speak directly to the central processing unit (CPU) and give the programmer very direct control of hardware resources.

audio editing software Programs that perform basic editing tasks on audio files such as cutting dead air space from the beginning or end of a song or cutting a portion from the middle.

augmented reality A combination of our normal sense of the objects around us with an overlay of information displayed.

authentication The process of identifying a computer user, based on a login or username and password. The computer system determines whether the computer user is authorized and what level of access is to be granted on the network.

authentication server A server that keeps track of who is logging on to the network and which services on the network are available to each user.

autonomy The freedom to work without constant direction and control.

B

backdoor program A program that enables a hacker to take complete control of a computer without the legitimate user's knowledge or permission.

backup A backup is a copy of computer files that you can use to replace the originals if they are lost or damaged.

Backup and Restore A Windows utility (found in the Control Panel) that allows the user to create a duplicate copy of all the data on a hard drive (or just the folders and files the user specifies) and copy it to another storage device, such as a DVD or external hard drive.

backward compatibility The accommodation of current devices being able to use previously issued software standards in addition to the current standards.

bandwidth (data transfer rate) The maximum speed at which data can be transmitted between two nodes on a network; usually measured in megabits per second (Mbps). See also *data transfer rate*.

base class The original object class from which other classes derive.

base transceiver station A large communications tower with antennas, amplifiers, and receivers/transmitters.

basic input/output system (BIOS) A program that manages the data between a computer's operating system and all the input and output devices attached to the computer; also responsible for loading the operating system (OS) from its permanent location on the hard drive to random access memory (RAM).

bastion host A heavily secured server located on a special perimeter network between a company's secure internal network and its firewall.

batch processing The process of accumulating transaction data until a certain point is reached, then processing those transactions all at once.

beta version A version of the software that is still under development. Many beta versions are available for a limited trial period, and are used to help the developers correct any errors before they launch the software on the market.

binary decision A decision point that can be answered in one of only two ways: *yes* (true) or *no* (false).

binary digit (bit) A digit that corresponds to the on and off states of a computer's switches. A bit contains a value of either 0 or 1.

binary language The language computers use to process data into information, consisting of only the values 0 and 1.

binary large object (BLOB) In databases, a type of object that holds extremely large chunks of data in binary form; this data is usually video clips, pictures, or audio clips.

biometric authentication device A device that uses some unique characteristic of human biology to identify authorized users.

bit depth The number of bits a video card uses to store data about each pixel on the monitor.

black-hat hacker A hacker who uses his knowledge to destroy information or for illegal gain.

bloatware The pre-installed software (often trial versions) on a new computer.

BLOB See *binary large object*.

blog See *Web log*.

Blu-ray disc A method of optical storage for digital data, developed for storing high-definition media. It has the largest storage capacity of all optical storage options.

Bluetooth A type of wireless technology that uses radio waves to transmit data over short distances (approximately 30 feet for Bluetooth 1 and 60 feet for Bluetooth 2). Often used to connect peripherals such as printers and keyboards to computers or headsets to cell phones.

bookmark A feature in some browsers that places a marker of a Web site's Uniform Resource Locator (URL) in an easily retrievable list. (Bookmarks are called Favorites in Microsoft Internet Explorer.)

Boolean operator A word used to refine logical searches. For Internet searches, the words AND, NOT, and OR describe the relationships between keywords in the search.

boot process The process for loading the operating system (OS) into random access memory (RAM) when the computer is turned on.

boot-sector virus A virus that replicates itself into the master boot record of a flash drive or hard drive.

botnet A large group of software applications (called *robots* or *bots*) that runs without user intervention on a large number of computers.

breadcrumb list A list that shows the hierarchy of previously viewed Web pages within the Web site that you are currently visiting. Shown at the top of some Web pages, it aids Web site navigation.

bridge A network device that is used to send data between two different local area networks (LANs) or two segments of the same LAN.

brightness A measure of the greatest amount of light showing when a monitor is displaying pure white; measured as candelas per square meter (cd/m2) or *nits*.

broadband A high-speed Internet connection such as cable, satellite, or digital subscriber line (DSL).

browser See *Web browser*.

browsing (1) The process of viewing database records. (2) The process of "surfing" the Web.

brute force attack An attack delivered by specialized hacking software that tries many combinations of letters, numbers, and pieces of a user ID in an attempt to discover a user password.

bus (linear bus) topology A system of networking connections in which all devices are connected to a central cable called the *bus* (or backbone).

business intelligence systems Used to analyze and interpret data to enable managers to make informed decisions about how best to run a business.

business-to-business (B2B) E-commerce transactions between businesses.

business-to-consumer (B2C) E-commerce transactions between businesses and consumers.

byte Eight binary digits (bits).

C

C The predecessor language of C++; developed originally for system programmers by Brian Kernighan and Dennis Ritchie of AT&T Bell Laboratories in 1978. It provides higher-level programming language features (such as if statements and for loops) but still allows programmers to manipulate the system memory and central processing unit (CPU) registers directly.

C# A programming language released by Microsoft to compete with Java. Pronounced *see sharp*.

C++ The successor language to C. Developed by Bjarne Stroustrup, C++ uses all of the same symbols and keywords as C but extends the language with additional keywords, better security, and more support for the reuse of existing code through object-oriented design.

cache memory Small blocks of memory, located directly on and next to the central processing unit (CPU) chip, that act as holding places for recently or frequently used instructions or data that the CPU accesses the most. When these instructions or data are stored in cache memory, the CPU can more quickly retrieve them than if it had to access the instructions or data from random access memory (RAM).

cascading style sheets (CSS) A list of statements (also known as rules) that define in one single location how HTML/XHTML elements are to be displayed.

Cat 6 cable A UTP cable type that provides more than 1 GB of throughput.

cellular phone (cell phone) A telephone that operates over a wireless network. Cell phones can also offer Internet access, text messaging, personal information management (PIM) features, and more.

central processing unit (CPU or processor) The part of the system unit of a computer that is responsible for data processing (the "brains" of the computer); it is the largest and most important chip in the computer. The CPU controls all the functions performed by the computer's other components and processes all the commands issued to it by software instructions.

centralized A type of network design in which users are not responsible for creating their own data backups or providing security for their computers; instead, those tasks are handled by a centralized server, software, and a system administrator.

CGI script A computer program that conforms to the Common Gateway Interface (CGI) specification, which provides a method for sending data between end users (browser users) and Web servers.

cgi-bin A directory where Common Gateway Interface (CGI) scripts are normally placed.

circuit switching A method of communication in which a dedicated connection is formed between two points (such as two people on telephones) and the connection remains active for the duration of the transmission.

class A collection of descriptive variables and active functions that together define a set of common properties. Actual examples of the class are known as *objects*.

classless interdomain routing (CIDR) Pronounced "cider," this is an addressing scheme that allows a single IP address to represent several unique IP addresses by adding a network prefix (a slash and a number) to the end of the last octet; also known as *supernetting*.

clickstream data Information captured about each click that users make as they navigate a Web site.

client A computer that requests information from a server in a client/server network (such as your computer when you are connected to the Internet).

client/server model A way of describing typical network functions. Client computers (such as your desktop PC) request services, and servers provide ("serve up") those services to the clients.

client/server network (server-based network) A type of network that uses servers to deliver services to computers that are requesting them (clients).

client-side program A computer program that runs on the client computer and requires no interaction with a Web server.

clock speed The steady and constant pace at which a computer goes through machine cycles, measured in hertz (Hz).

cloud server Servers that are maintained by hosting companies, such as Rackspace Hosting, and that are connected to networks via the Internet.

coaxial cable A single copper wire surrounded by layers of plastic insulation and sheathing; used mainly in cable television and cable Internet service.

code editing The step in which a programmer physically types the code into the computer.

codec A rule, implemented in either software or hardware, which squeezes a given amount of audio and video information into less space.

coding The process of translating an algorithm into a programming language.

cold boot The process of starting a computer from a powered-down or off state.

collaborative consumption Joining together as a group to use a specific product more efficiently.

command-driven interface Interface between user and computer in which the user enters commands to communicate with the computer system.

comment (remark) A plain English notation inserted into program code for documentation. The comment is not ever seen by the compiler.

commerce server A computer that hosts software that enables consumers to purchase goods and services over the Web. These servers generally use special security protocols to protect sensitive information (such as credit card numbers) from being intercepted.

Common Gateway Interface (CGI) Provides a methodology by which a browser can request that a program file be executed (or run) instead of just being delivered to the browser.

communications server A server that handles all communications between the network and other networks, including managing Internet connectivity.

compact disc (CD) A method of optical storage for digital data; originally developed for storing digital audio.

compilation The process by which code is converted into machine language, or the language the central processing unit (CPU) can understand.

compiler The program that understands both the syntax of the programming language and the exact structure of the central processing unit (CPU) and its machine language. It can "read" the source code and translate the source code directly into machine language.

completeness check A process that ensures that all database fields defined as "required" have data entered into them.

computational field (computed field) A numeric field in a database that is filled as the result of a computation.

computer A data-processing device that gathers, processes, outputs, and stores data and information.

computer forensics The application of computer systems and techniques to gather potential legal evidence; a law enforcement specialty used to fight high-tech crime.

computer literate Being familiar enough with computers that you understand their capabilities and limitations and know how to use them.

computer protocol A set of rules for accomplishing electronic information exchange. If the Internet is the information superhighway, then protocols are the driving rules.

computer-aided design (CAD) A 3D modeling program used to create automated designs, technical drawings, and model visualizations.

connectionless protocol A protocol that a host computer can use to send data over the network without establishing a direct connection with any specific recipient computer.

connection-oriented protocol A protocol that requires two computers to exchange control packets, which set up the parameters of the data exchange session, before sending packets that contain data.

connectivity port A port that enables the computer (or other device) to be connected to other devices or systems such as networks, modems, and the Internet.

consistency check The process of comparing the value of data in a database field against established parameters to determine whether the value is reasonable.

consumer-to-consumer (C2C) E-commerce transactions between consumers through online sites such as eBay.com.

contrast ratio A measure of the difference in light intensity between the brightest white and the darkest black colors that a monitor can produce. If the contrast ratio is too low, colors tend to fade when the brightness is adjusted to a high or low setting.

control structure The general term used for keywords in a programming language that allow the programmer to control, or redirect, the flow of the program based on a decision.

cookie A small text file that some Web sites automatically store on a client computer's hard drive when a user visits the site.

copyleft A simplified licensing scheme that enables copyright holders to grant certain rights to a work while retaining other rights.

core A complete processing section from a CPU, embedded into one physical chip.

course management software A program that provides traditional classroom tools,

such as calendars and grade books, over the Internet, as well as areas for students to exchange ideas and information in chat rooms, discussion forums, and e-mail.

CPU benchmarks Measurements used to compare performance between processors.

CPU usage graph Records your CPU usage for the past several seconds.

creative surplus A term used to describe the ability of the world's populace to volunteer and collaborate on large projects.

crisis mapping tool A tool that collects information from e-mails, text messages, blog posts, and Twitter tweets and maps them, making the information instantly publicly available.

crowdsourcing The process of taking a task that an employee or a contractor usually performs (such as product design) and instead outsourcing that task to a large group of people, usually via the Internet.

CSMA/CD A method of data collision detection in which a node connected to the network listens (that is, has carrier sense) to determine that no other nodes are currently transmitting data signals; short for Carrier Sense Multiple Access with Collision Detection.

custom installation The process of installing only those features of a software program that a user wants on the hard drive.

customer relationship management (CRM) software A business program used for storing sales and client contact information in one central database.

cybercrime Any criminal action perpetrated primarily through the use of a computer.

cybercriminal An individual who uses computers, networks, and the Internet to perpetrate crime.

cyberloafing Doing anything with a computer that is unrelated to a job (such as playing video games), while one is supposed to be working. Also called *cyberslacking*.

D

data Numbers, words, pictures, or sounds that represent facts, figures, or ideas.

data breach When sensitive or confidential information is copied, transmitted, or viewed by an individual who was never authorized to handle the data.

data centralization Having all data in one central location (usually a database). Data centralization helps ensure data integrity by requiring data to be updated only in one place if the data changes.

data collision When two computers send data at the same time and the sets of data collide somewhere in the media.

data dictionary (database schema) A file that defines the name, data type, and length of each field in the database.

data file File that contains stored data.

data inconsistency Any difference in data in lists caused when data exists in multiple lists and not all lists are updated when a piece of data changes.

data integrity The process of ensuring that data contained in a database is accurate and reliable.

data mart Small slices of a data warehouse.

data mining The process by which great amounts of data are analyzed and investigated. The objective is to spot significant patterns or trends within the data that would otherwise not be obvious.

data plan A connectivity plan or text messaging plan in which data charges are separate from cell phone calling charges and are provided at rates different from those for voice calls.

data redundancy When the same data exists in more than one place in a database.

data staging A three-step process: extracting data from source databases, transforming (reformatting) the data, and storing the data in a data warehouse.

data transfer rate (bandwidth) The maximum speed at which data can be transmitted between two nodes on a network; usually measured in megabits per second (Mbps).

data type (field type) An attribute of a data field that determines what type of data can be stored in the database field or memory location.

data warehouse A large-scale electronic repository of data that contains and organizes in one place all the data related to an organization.

database A collection of related data that can be easily stored, sorted, organized, and queried.

database administrator (database designer) An individual trained in the design, construction, and maintenance of databases.

database designer See *database administrator*.

database management system (DBMS) A type of specially designed application software (such as Oracle or Microsoft Access) that interacts with the user, other applications, and the database to capture and analyze data.

database query An inquiry the user poses to a database to extract a meaningful subset of data.

database server A server that provides client computers with access to information stored in a database.

database software An electronic filing system best used for larger and more complicated groups of data that require more than one table and the ability to group, sort, and retrieve data and generate reports.

data-flow diagram Diagram that traces all data in an information system from the point at which data enters the system to its final resting place (storage or output).

date field A field in a database that holds date data such as birthdays, due dates, and so on.

debugger A tool that helps programmers step through a program as it runs to locate errors.

debugging The process of repeatedly running a program to find errors and to make sure the program behaves in the way it should.

decentralized A type of network in which users are responsible for creating their own data backups and for providing security for their computers.

decision point A point at which a computer program must choose from a set of different actions based on the value of its current inputs.

decision support system (DSS) A system designed to help managers develop solutions for specific problems.

dedicated server A server used to fulfill one specific function (such as handling e-mail).

default value The value a database will use for a field unless the user enters another value.

denial-of-service (DoS) attack An attack that occurs when legitimate users are denied access to a computer system because a hacker is repeatedly making requests of that computer system that tie up its resources and deny legitimate users access.

derivative work Intellectual property that is based on an original work but is modified in some way.

derived class A class created based on a previously existing class (i.e., a base class). Derived classes inherit all of the member variables and methods of the base class from which they are derived.

desktop As its name implies, the computer's desktop puts at your fingertips all of the elements necessary for a productive work session and that are typically found on or near the top of a traditional desk, such as files and folders.

desktop computer A computer that is intended for use at a single location. A desktop computer consists of a case that houses the main components of the computer, plus peripheral devices.

desktop publishing (DTP) software Programs for incorporating and arranging graphics and text to produce creative documents.

detail report A report generated with data from a database that shows the individual transactions that occurred during a certain time period.

device driver Software that facilitates the communication between a device and the operating system.

Device Manager A feature in the Windows operating system that lets individuals view and change the properties of all hardware devices attached to the computer.

digital convergence The use of a single unifying device to handle media, Internet, entertainment, and telephony needs; is expressed in the range of devices now on the market.

digital divide The discrepancy between those who have access to the opportunities and knowledge computers and the Internet offer and those who do not.

digital rights management (DRM) A system of access control that allows only limited use of material that has been legally purchased.

digital signal processor A specialized chip that processes digital information and transmits signals very quickly.

digital subscriber line (DSL) A type of connection that uses telephone lines to connect to the Internet and that allows both phone and data transmissions to share the same line.

digital video (or versatile) disc (DVD) A method of optical storage for digital data that has greater storage capacity than compact discs.

digital video editing software A program for editing digital video.

digital video interface (DVI) Video interface technology that newer LCD monitors, as well as other multimedia devices such as televisions, DVD players, and projectors, use to connect to a PC.

directory A hierarchical structure that include files, folders, and drives used to create a more organized and efficient computer.

Disk Cleanup A Windows utility that removes unnecessary files from the hard drive.

disk defragmenter A utility that regroups related pieces of files on the hard drive, enabling faster retrieval of the data.

distributed denial of service (DDoS) attack An automated attack that is launched from more than one zombie computer at the same time.

Document Object Model (DOM) A means to organize objects and page elements in a Web page. DOM defines every item on a Web page, such as graphics, tables, and headers, as an object.

documentation A description of the development and technical details of a computer program, including how the code works and how the user interacts with the program.

domain name A part of a Uniform Resource Locator (URL). Domain names consist of two parts: the site's host and a suffix that indicates the type of organization. (Example: popsci.com)

Domain Name System (DNS) server A server that contains location information for domains on the Internet and functions like a phone book for the Internet.

dotted decimal number (dotted quad) One of the numbers in an Internet Protocol (IP) address.

drawing software (illustration software) Programs for creating or editing two-dimensional line-based drawings.

drive bay A special shelf inside a computer that is designed to hold storage devices.

drive-by download The use of malicious software to attack your computer by downloading harmful programs onto your computer, without your knowledge, while you are surfing a Web site.

dynamic addressing The process of assigning Internet Protocol (IP) addresses when users log on using their Internet service provider (ISP). The computer is assigned an address from an available pool of IP addresses.

dynamic decision making A mechanism that allows a Web page to decide how to display itself, based on the choices the reader makes as he or she looks at the page.

Dynamic Host Configuration Protocol (DHCP) The protocol that handles dynamic addressing. Part of the Transmission Control Protocol/Internet Protocol (TCP/IP) protocol suite, DHCP takes a pool of IP addresses and shares them with hosts on the network on an as-needed basis.

Dynamic HyperText Markup Language (DHTML or dynamic HTML) A combination of Web development technologies including HTML, cascading style sheets, and a scripting language that are used to add interactivity to a Web site after the Web site has been loaded onto the client computer.

E

e-commerce (electric commerce) The process of conducting business online for purposes ranging from fund-raising to advertising to selling products.

e-mail (electronic mail) Internet-based communication in which senders and recipients correspond.

e-mail client A software program that runs on a computer and is used to send and receive e-mail through the ISP's server.

e-mail server A server that processes and delivers incoming and outgoing e-mail.

e-mail virus A virus transmitted by e-mail that often uses the address book in the victim's e-mail system to distribute itself.

editor A tool that helps programmers as they enter code, highlighting keywords and alerting the programmers to typos.

electronic text (etext) Textual information stored as digital information so it can be stored, manipulated, and transmitted by electronic devices.

element The tags and the text between the tags in HyperText Markup Language (HTML).

embedded computer A specially designed computer chip that resides inside another device, such as a car. These self-contained computer devices have their own programming and typically neither receive input from users nor interact with other systems.

encryption The process of encoding data (ciphering) so that only the person with a corresponding decryption key (the intended recipient) can decode (or decipher) and read the message.

encryption virus A malicious program that searches for common data files and compresses them into a file using a complex encryption key, thereby rendering the files unusable.

enterprise resource planning (ERP) system Used to control many "back office" operations and processing functions such as billing, production, inventory management, and human resources management.

entertainment software Programs designed to provide users with entertainment. Computer games make up the vast majority of entertainment software.

ereader A device that can display etext and has supporting tools, like note taking, bookmarks, and integrated dictionaries.

ergonomics How a user sets up his or her computer and other equipment to minimize risk of injury or discomfort.

error handling In programming, the instructions that a program runs if the input data is incorrect or another error is encountered.

Error-Checking A Windows utility that checks for lost files and fragments as well as physical errors on a hard drive.

Ethernet network A network that uses the Ethernet protocol as the means (or standard) by which the nodes on the network communicate.

Ethernet port A port that is slightly larger than a standard phone jack and transfers data at speeds of up to 10,000 Mbps; used to connect a computer to a DSL or cable modem or a network.

event The result of an action, such as a keystroke, mouse click, or signal to the printer, in the respective device (keyboard, mouse, or printer) to which the operating system responds.

exception report A report that shows conditions that are unusual or that need attention by users of a system.

executable program The binary sequence (code) that instructs the central processing unit (CPU) to perform certain calculations.

expansion card (adapter card) A circuit board with specific functions that augment the computer's basic functions and provide connections to other devices; examples include the sound card and the video card.

expert system A system designed to replicate the decision-making processes of human experts to solve specific problems.

export The process of putting data into an electronic file in a format that another application can understand.

ExpressCard Notebooks are often equipped with an ExpressCard slot. The ExpressCard can add a solid state drive (SSD), eSATA and FireWire ports, and other capabilities to your system.

Extensible HyperText Markup Language (XHTML) A standard established by the World Wide Web Consortium (W3C) that combines elements from both Extensible Markup Language (XML) and HyperText Markup Language (HTML). XHTML has much more stringent rules than HTML does regarding tagging.

Extensible Markup Language (XML) A language that enables designers to define their own tags, making it much easier to transfer data between Web sites and Web servers.

extension (file type) In a file name, the three letters that follow the user-supplied file name after the dot (.); the extension identifies what kind of family of files the file belongs to, or which application should be used to read the file.

external data source Any source not owned by the company that owns a decision support system, such as customer demographic data purchased from third parties.

external hard drive An internal hard drive that is enclosed in a protective case to make it portable; the drive is connected to the computer with a data transfer cable and is often used to back up data.

external SATA (eSATA) A port that will connect to some external hard drive models.

extranet The portion of a company's intranet that is used to share business information with business partners such as vendors, suppliers, and customers.

F

Favorites A feature in Microsoft Internet Explorer that places a marker of a Web site's Uniform Resource Locator (URL) in an easily retrievable list in the browser's toolbar. (Called Bookmarks in some browsers.)

fiber-optic cable A cable that transmits data at close to the speed of light along glass or plastic fibers.

fiber-optic service (FiOS) Internet access that is enabled by transmitting data at the speed of light through glass or plastic fibers.

field A field where a category of information in a database is stored. Fields are displayed in columns.

field constraint Any property that must be satisfied for an entry to be accepted into the database field.

field name An identifying name assigned to each field in a database.

field size The maximum number of characters (or numbers) that a field in a database can contain.

fifth-generation language (5GL) A computer language that uses natural

language processing or expert systems to make the programming experience better matched to human thinking processes.

file A collection of related pieces of information stored together for easy reference; in database terminology, a file or *table* is a group of related records.

file allocation table (FAT) An index of all sector numbers that the hard drive stores in a table to keep track of which sectors hold which files.

file compression utility A program that takes out redundancies in a file to reduce the file size.

file management The process by which humans or computer software provide organizational structure to a computer's contents.

file name The first part of the label applied to a file; it is generally the name a user assigns to the file when saving it.

file path The exact location of a file, starting with the drive in which the file is located, and including all folders, subfolders (if any), the file name, and the extension. (Example: C:\Users\username\Documents\Illustrations\EBronte.jpg)

file server A computer deployed to provide remote storage space or to act as a repository for files that users can access.

File Transfer Protocol (FTP) A protocol used to upload and download files from one computer to another over the Internet.

financial planning software Programs for managing finances, such as Intuit's Quicken and Microsoft Money, which include electronic checkbook registers and automatic bill payment tools.

firewall A software program or hardware device designed to prevent unauthorized access to computers or networks.

FireWire 400 (IEEE 1394) An interface port that transfers data at 400 Mbps.

FireWire 800 One of the fastest ports available, moving data at 800 Mbps.

firmware System software that controls hardware devices.

first-generation language (1GL) The actual machine language of a central processing unit (CPU); the sequence of bits—1s and 0s—that the CPU understands.

flash drive A drive that plugs into a universal serial bus (USB) port on a computer and stores data digitally. Also called *USB drive*, *jump drive*, or *thumb drive*.

flash memory Portable, nonvolatile memory.

flash memory card A form of portable storage; this removable memory card is often used in digital cameras, portable media players, and personal digital assistants (PDAs).

flowchart A visual representation of the patterns an algorithm comprises.

folder A collection of files stored on a computer.

for Keyword in Visual Basic used with the Next keyword to implement a loop.

foreign key The primary key of another database table that is included for purposes of establishing relationships with another table.

fourth-generation language (4GL) A sophisticated level of programming language such as a report generator or database query language.

frame A container designed to hold multiple data packets.

freeware Any copyrighted software that can be used for free.

front side bus (FSB) See *local bus*.

full installation The process of installing all the files and programs from the distribution CD to the computer's hard drive.

fuzzy logic A type of logic that allows the interjection of experiential learning into an equation by considering probabilities.

G

gadget A mini-application that runs on the desktop, offering easy access to a frequently used tool such as weather or a calendar item.

gateway See *wireless router*.

general availability (GA) After the RTM is issued, the product is ready to be purchased by the public.

geotag Data attached to a photograph that indicate the latitude and longitude where you were standing when you took the photo.

gigabit Ethernet The most commonly used wired Ethernet standard deployed in devices designed for home networks which provides bandwidth of up to 1 Gbps.

gigabyte (GB) About a billion bytes.

gigahertz (GHz) One billion hertz.

Global Positioning System (GPS) A system of 21 satellites (plus 3 working spares), built and operated by the U.S. military, that constantly orbit the earth. They provide information to GPS-capable devices to pinpoint locations on the earth.

graphical user interface (GUI) Unlike the command- and menu-driven interfaces used in earlier software, GUIs display graphics and use the point-and-click technology of the mouse and cursor, making them much more user-friendly.

graphics double data rate 5 (GDDR5) A standard of video memory.

graphics processing unit (GPU) A specialized logic chip that is dedicated to quickly displaying and calculating visual data such as shadows, textures, and luminosity.

grey hat hackers A cross between black and white—they will often illegally break into systems merely to flaunt their expertise to the administrator of the system they penetrated or to attempt to sell their services in repairing security breaches.

guest server Virtual servers running on a host machine.

H

hacker Anyone who unlawfully breaks into a computer system (whether an individual computer or a network).

handshaking The process of two computers exchanging control packets that set up the parameters of a data exchange.

hard drive A device that holds all permanently stored programs and data; can be located inside the system unit or attached to the system unit via a USB port.

hardware Any part of the computer you can physically touch.

head crash Impact of read/write head against magnetic platter of the hard drive; often results in data loss.

hexadecimal notation A number system that uses 16 digits to represent numbers; also called a *base 16 number system.*

hibernate A power-management mode that saves the current state of the current system to the computer's hard drive.

high definition (HD) A standard of digital television signal that guarantees a specific level of resolution and a specific *aspect ratio,* which is the rectangular shape of the image.

high-definition multimedia interface (HDMI) A compact audio–video interface standard that carries both high-definition video and uncompressed digital audio.

hoax An e-mail message or Web site that contains information that is untrue, and is published with the purpose of deceiving others.

home area network (HAN) A network located in a home that is used to connect all of its digital devices.

home network server A device designed to store media, share media across the network, and back up files on computers connected to a home network.

home page The main or opening page of a Web site.

honey pot A computer system that is set up to attract unauthorized users by appearing to be a key part of a network or a system that contains something of great value.

host The portion of a domain name that identifies who maintains a given Web site. For example, *berkeley.edu* is the domain name for the University of California at Berkeley, which maintains that site.

HTML tag The bracketed information that surrounds elements of a Web page in order to convey information about them and define how their content is to be displayed.

HTML/XHTML embedded scripting language A client-side method of embedding programming language code directly within the HTML/XHTML code of a Web page.

hybrid topology A topology comprised of several topologies and combined into one network.

hyperlink A type of specially coded text that, when clicked, enables a user to jump from one location, or Web page, to another

within a Web site or to another Web site altogether.

hyperlink field A field in a database that stores hyperlinks to Web pages.

hypertext Text that is linked to other documents or media (such as video clips or pictures).

HyperText Markup Language (HTML) A set of rules for marking up blocks of text so that a Web browser knows how to display them. It uses a series of tags that defines the display of text on a Web page.

HyperText Transfer Protocol (HTTP) The protocol that allows files to be transferred from a Web server so that you can see them on your computer by using a browser.

HyperText Transfer Protocol Secure (or Over SSL) A protocol that will encrypt the information sent between your browser and the server.

hyperthreading A technology that permits quicker processing of information by enabling a new set of instructions to start executing before the previous set has finished.

I

icon A picture on a computer display that represents an object such as a software application or a file or folder.

identity theft The process by which someone uses personal information about someone else (such as the victim's name, address, and Social Security number) to assume the victim's identity for the purpose of defrauding others.

if else In the programming language C++, keywords for a binary decision within an algorithm.

image backup A copy of an entire computer system, created for restoration purposes.

image editing software (photo editing software) Programs for editing photographs and other images.

impact printer A printer that has tiny hammer-like keys that strike the paper through an inked ribbon, thus making a mark on the paper. The most common impact printer is the dot-matrix printer.

incremental backup A type of backup that only backs up files that have changed since the last time files were backed up.

information Data that has been organized or presented in a meaningful fashion.

information assurance The set of measures intended to protect and defend information and information systems by ensuring their availability, integrity, authentication, confidentiality, and nonrepudiation.

information system A system that includes data, people, procedures, hardware, and software and that is used to gather and analyze information.

information technology (IT) The set of techniques used in processing and retrieving information.

inheritance The ability of a new class of objects to pick up all of the data and methods of an existing class automatically and then extend and customize those to fit its own specific needs.

initial value A beginning point in a loop.

inkjet printer A nonimpact printer that sprays tiny drops of ink onto paper.

inoculation A process used by antivirus software; compares old and current qualities of files to detect viral activity.

input device A hardware device used to enter, or input, data (text, images, and sounds) and instructions (user responses and commands) into a computer. Some input devices are keyboards and mice.

input form A form that provides a view of the data fields to be filled in a database, with appropriate labels to assist database users in populating the database.

instant messaging (IM) A program that enables users to communicate online in real time with others who are also online.

integrated development environment (IDE) A development tool that helps programmers write, compile, and test their programs.

integrated help Documentation for a software product that is built directly into the software.

Internet A network of networks that is the largest network in the world, connecting millions of computers from more than one hundred countries.

Internet appliance A device used for easy access to the Internet, social networking sites, e-mail, video, news, and entertainment. These devices fall into a

category somewhere between smartphones and full-blown computers.

Internet backbone The main pathway of high-speed communications lines over which all Internet traffic flows.

Internet cache A section of your hard drive that stores information that you may need again for surfing (such as IP addresses and frequently accessed Web pages).

Internet Corporation for Assigned Names and Numbers (ICANN) The organization responsible for allocating IP addresses to organizations to ensure they are unique and have not been assigned to other users.

Internet exchange point A device that allows different Internet service providers to exchange information between networks.

Internet Protocol (IP) A protocol for sending data between computers on the Internet.

Internet Protocol address (IP address) The means by which all computers connected to the Internet identify each other. It consists of a unique set of four numbers separated by dots such as 123.45.178.91.

Internet Protocol version 4 (IPv4) The original IP addressing scheme.

Internet Protocol version 6 (IPv6) A proposed IP addressing scheme that makes IP addresses longer, thereby providing more available IP addresses. It uses eight groups of 16-bit numbers.

Internet service provider (ISP) Companies that specialize in providing Internet access. ISPs may be specialized providers, like Juno, or companies that provide other services in addition to Internet access (such as phone and cable television).

Internet tablet A very light, portable computing device without a keyboard.

interpreter A software program that translates source code into an intermediate form line by line. Each line is then executed as it is translated.

interrupt A signal that tells the operating system that it is in need of immediate attention.

interrupt handler A special numerical code that prioritizes requests from various devices. These requests then are placed in the interrupt table in the computer's primary memory.

intranet A private corporate network that is used exclusively by company employees to facilitate information sharing, database access, group scheduling, videoconferencing, and other employee and customer collaborations.

IP address See *Internet Protocol address*.

J

jam signal A special signal sent to all network nodes, alerting them that a data collision has occurred.

Java A platform-independent programming language that Sun Microsystems introduced in the early 1990s. It quickly became popular because its object-oriented model enables Java programmers to benefit from its set of existing classes.

Java applet A small Java-based program.

Java Server Pages (JSP) An extension of the Java servlet technology with dynamic scripting capability.

JavaScript A scripting language often used to add interactivity to Web pages. JavaScript is not as fully featured as Java, but its syntax, keywords, data types, and operators are a subset of Java's.

join query A database query that links (or joins) two database tables using a common field in both tables and extracts the relevant data from each.

K

kernel (supervisor program) The essential component of the operating system that is responsible for managing the processor and all other components of the computer system. Because it stays in random access memory (RAM) the entire time the computer is powered on, the kernel is called *memory resident*.

kernel memory The memory that the computer's operating system uses.

key pair A public and a private key used for coding and decoding encrypted data.

keyboard A hardware device used to enter typed data and commands into a computer.

keystroke logger A type of spyware program that monitors keystrokes with the intent of stealing passwords, login IDs, or credit card information.

keyword (1) A specific word a user wishes to query (or look for) in an Internet search. (2) A specific word that has a predefined meaning in a particular programming language.

kilobyte (KB) A unit of computer storage equal to approximately one thousand bytes.

knowledge-based system A support system that provides additional intelligence that supplements the user's own intellect and makes a decision support system (DSS) more effective.

L

laser printer A nonimpact printer known for quick and quiet production and high-quality printouts.

Last Known Good Configuration A Windows feature that starts the computer by using the registry information that was saved during the last shutdown.

latency The process that occurs after the read/write head of the hard drive locates the correct track, and then waits for the correct sector to spin to the read/write head.

legacy technology Comprises computing devices, software, or peripherals that use techniques, parts, and methods from an earlier time that are no longer popular.

library In Windows 7, a folder that is used to display files from different locations as if they were all saved in a single folder, regardless of where they are actually stored in the file hierarchy.

light-emitting diode (LED) display A newer, more energy efficient type of monitor. It may have better color accuracy and thinner panels than traditional LCD monitors.

Linux An open source operating system based on UNIX. Because of the stable nature of this operating system, it is often used on Web servers.

liquid crystal display (LCD) The technology used in flat-panel computer monitors.

live bookmark A bookmark that delivers updates to you as soon as they become available, using Really Simple Syndication (RSS).

local area network (LAN) A network in which the nodes are located within a small geographic area.

logic bomb A computer virus that runs when a certain set of conditions is met, such as when specific dates are reached on the computer's internal clock.

logical error A mistake in the design and planning of the algorithm itself rather than in the use of syntax in the coding.

logical port A virtual communications gateway or path that enables a computer to organize requests for information (such as Web page downloads and e-mail routing) from other networks or computers.

logical port blocking A condition in which a firewall is configured to ignore all incoming packets that request access to a certain port so that no unwanted requests will get through to the computer.

loop An algorithm that performs a repeating set of actions. A logical yes/no expression is evaluated. As long as the expression evaluates to TRUE (yes), the algorithm will perform the same set of actions and continue to loop around. When the answer to the question is FALSE (no), the algorithm breaks free of the looping structure and moves on to the next step.

M

Mac OS The first commercially available operating system to incorporate a graphical user interface (GUI) with user-friendly point-and-click technology.

machine language A set of instructions executed directly by the central processing unit (CPU).

macro A small program that groups a series of commands to run as a single command.

macro virus A virus that is distributed by hiding it inside a macro.

mainframe A large, expensive computer that supports hundreds or thousands of users simultaneously and executes many different programs at the same time.

malware Software that is intended to render a system temporarily or permanently useless or to penetrate a computer system completely for purposes of information gathering. Examples include spyware, viruses, worms, and Trojan horses.

management information system (MIS) A system that provides timely and accurate information that enables managers to make critical business decisions.

many-to-many relationship A database relationship in which one record in a database table (A) can have many related records in another table (B), and any record in table B can have many related records in table A.

mapping program Software that provides street maps and written directions to locations.

massively multiplayer online role-playing games (MMORPG) A gaming environment in which thousands of participants interact in a virtual game world by assuming roles of fictitious characters.

master boot record (MBR) A small program that runs whenever a computer boots up.

mastery The feeling of confidence and excitement from seeing your own skills progress.

media access control (MAC) address A physical address, similar to a serial number on an appliance, that is assigned to each network adapter; it is made up of six 2-digit characters such as 01:40:87:44:79:A5.

megabyte (MB) A unit of computer storage equal to approximately 1 million bytes.

memo field A text field in a database that is used to hold long pieces of text.

memory module (memory card) A small circuit board that holds a series of random access memory (RAM) chips.

menu A list of commands that displays on the screen.

menu-driven interface A user interface in which the user chooses a command from menus displayed on the screen.

metadata Data that describes other data.

metasearch engine A metasearch engine, such as Dogpile, searches other search engines rather than individual Web sites.

metropolitan area network (MAN) A wide area network (WAN) that links users in a specific geographic area (such as within a city or county).

microbrowser Software that makes it possible to access the Internet from a smartphone.

microphone (mic) A device that allows you to capture sound waves, such as those created by your voice, and transfer them to digital format on your computer.

Microsoft Disk Operating System (MS-DOS) A single-user, single-task operating system created by Microsoft. MS-DOS was the first widely installed operating system in personal computers.

mobile switching center A central location that receives cell phone requests for service from a base station.

model management system A type of software that assists in building management models in decision support systems (DSSs).

modem A communication device that works to translate digital data into an analog signal and back again.

modem card An expansion card that provides the computer with a connection to the Internet via conventional phone lines.

modem port A port that uses a traditional telephone signal to connect a computer to the Internet.

monitor (display screen) A common output device that displays text, graphics, and video as soft copies (copies that can be seen only on screen).

Moore's Law A prediction, named after Gordon Moore, the cofounder of Intel; states that the number of transistors on a CPU chip will double every two years.

motherboard A special circuit board in the system unit that contains the central processing unit (CPU), the memory (RAM) chips, and the slots available for expansion cards; all of the other boards (video cards, sound cards, and so on) connect to it to receive power and to communicate.

mouse A hardware device used to enter user responses and commands into a computer.

multidimensional database A database that stores data in multiple dimensions and is organized in a cube format.

multimedia Anything that involves one or more forms of media plus text.

multimedia message service (MMS) An extension of short message service (SMS) that enables messages that include text, sound, images, and video clips to be sent from a cell phone to other phones or e-mail addresses.

multimedia software Programs that include image, video, and audio editing software, animation software, and other specialty software required to produce computer games, animations, and movies.

multipartite virus Literally meaning "multipart" virus; a type of computer virus that attempts to infect both the boot sector and executable files at the same time.

multiplayer online game An online game in which play occurs among hundreds or thousands of other players over the Internet in a persistent or ever-on game environment. In some games, players can interact with other players through trading, chatting, or playing cooperative or combative mini-games.

Multiple Input Multiple Output (MIMO) A design in routers that provides for faster wireless data transmission by utilizing more than one antenna to transmit and receive data.

Multipurpose Internet Mail Extensions (MIME) A specification that was introduced in 1991 to simplify attachments to e-mail messages. All e-mail client software now uses this protocol for attaching files.

multitask The ability of an operating system to perform more than one process at a time.

multiuser operating system (network operating system) An operating system (OS) that enables more than one user to access the computer system at one time by efficiently juggling all the requests from multiple users.

N

natural language processing (NLP) system A system that enables users to communicate with computer systems using a natural spoken or written language as opposed to using computer programming languages.

negative acknowledgment (NAK) What computer Y sends to computer X if a packet is unreadable, indicating the packet was not received in understandable form.

netbook A computing device that runs a full-featured operating system but weighs two pounds or less.

network A group of two or more computers (or nodes) that are configured to share information and resources such as printers, files, and databases.

network adapter A device that enables the computer (or peripheral) to communicate with the network using a common data communication language, or protocol.

network address translation (NAT) A process that firewalls use to assign internal Internet Protocol (IP) addresses on a network.

network administration Involves tasks such as: (1) installing new computers and devices, (2) monitoring the network to ensure it is performing efficiently, (3) updating and installing new software on the network, and (4) configuring, or setting up, proper security for a network.

network administrator Someone who has training in computer and peripheral maintenance and repair, network design, and the installation of network software; installs new equipment, configures computers for users, repairs equipment, and assigns network access to users.

network architecture The design of a computer network; includes both physical and logical design.

network-attached storage (NAS) device A specialized computing device designed to store and manage network data.

network interface card (NIC) An expansion card that enables a computer to connect other computers or to a cable modem to facilitate a high-speed Internet connection.

network navigation device A device on a network such as a router, hub, and switch that moves data signals around the network.

network operating system (NOS) Software that handles requests for information, Internet access, and the use of peripherals for the rest of the network nodes.

network prefix The part of a network address under the CIDR IP addressing scheme. It consists of a slash and a number added to the end of the last octet in an IP address.

network topology The layout and structure of the network.

network-ready device A device (such as a printer or external hard drive) that can be attached directly to a network instead of needing to attach to a computer on the network.

Next In the Visual Basic programming language, the keyword used to implement a loop.

node A device connected to a network such as a computer, a peripheral (such as a printer), or a communications device (such as a modem).

nonimpact printer A printer that sprays ink or uses laser beams to make marks on the paper. The most common nonimpact printers are inkjet and laser printers.

nonvolatile storage Permanent storage, as in read-only memory (ROM).

normalization The process of recording data only once in a database to reduce data redundancy.

notebook computer A small, compact portable computer.

numeric check A data validation routine that confirms that only numbers are entered in a database field.

numeric field A field in a database that stores numbers.

O

object A variable in a program that is an example of a class. Each object in a specific class is constructed from similar data and methods.

object field A field in a database that holds objects such as pictures, video clips, or entire documents.

Object Query Language (OQL) A query language that is used to extract information from an object-oriented database.

Objective C The language most often used to program applications to run under Mac OS X.

object-oriented analysis An approach to software design that differs from the traditional "top-down" design. In object-oriented (OO) analysis, programmers first identify all of the classes (collections of data and methods) that are required to describe completely the problem the program is trying to solve.

object-oriented database A database that stores data in objects, not in tables.

octet Eight bits. For example, each of the four numbers in the dotted decimal notation of an Internet Protocol (IP) address is represented by an octet.

office support system (OSS) A system (such as Microsoft Office) designed to assist employees in accomplishing their day-to-day tasks and to improve communications.

offshore The process of sending jobs formerly performed in the U.S. to other countries.

one-to-many relationship A database relationship in which one record in a data table can have many related records in another data table.

one-to-one relationship A database relationship in which one record in a data table has only one related record in another data table.

online mapping service An alternative to more traditional mapping software programs; easily accessible with any Internet connection and updated more frequently than offline services. Examples include MapQuest, Yahoo! Maps, and Google Maps.

online transaction processing (OLTP) The immediate processing of user requests or transactions.

open source software Program code made publicly available for free; it can be copied, distributed, or changed without the stringent copyright protections of proprietary software products.

open system A system whose designs are public, enabling access by any interested party.

Open Systems Interconnection (OSI) Established by the Institute of Electrical and Electronics Engineers (IEE), a standard of communications adopted throughout the computing world that provides the protocol guidelines for all modern networks.

operating system (OS) The system software that controls the way in which a computer system functions, including the management of hardware, peripherals, and software.

operator Any of the coding symbols that represent the fundamental actions of a computer language.

optical drive A hardware device that uses lasers or light to read from, and maybe even write to, CDs, DVDs, or Blu-ray discs.

optical media Portable storage devices, such as CDs, DVDs, and Blu-ray discs, that use a laser to read and write data.

optical mouse A mouse that uses an internal sensor or laser to control the mouse's movement. The sensor sends signals to the computer, telling it where to move the pointer on the screen.

organic light-emitting diode (OLED) display A display that uses organic compounds to produce light when exposed to an electric current. Unlike LCDs, OLEDs do not require a backlight to function and therefore draw less power and have a much thinner display, sometimes as thin as 3 mm.

output device A device that sends processed data and information out of a computer in the form of text, pictures (graphics), sounds (audio), or video.

P

packet (data packet) A small segment of data that is bundled for sending over transmission media. Each packet contains the address of the computer or peripheral device to which it is being sent.

packet analyzer (sniffer) A computer hardware device or software program designed to detect and record digital information being transmitted over a network.

packet filtering A feature found in firewalls that filters out unwanted data packets sent to specific logical ports.

packet screening A process that involves examining incoming data packets to ensure they originated from, or are authorized by, valid users on the internal network.

packet switching A communications methodology in which data is broken into small chunks (called packets) and sent over various routes at the same time. When the packets reach their destination, they are reassembled by the receiving computer.

paging The process of swapping data or instructions that have been placed in the swap file for later use back into active random access memory (RAM). The contents of the hard drive's swap file then become less active data or instructions.

Pascal The only modern computer language that was specifically designed as a teaching language; it is seldom taught now at the college level.

passive topology When data merely travels the entire length of the communications medium and is received by all network devices.

path (subdirectory) The information after the slash indicates a particular file or path (or subdirectory) within the Web site.

path separator The backslash mark (\) used by Microsoft Windows and DOS in file names. Mac files use a colon (:), and UNIX and Linux use the forward slash (/) as the path separator.

peer-to-peer (P2P) network A network in which each node connected to the network can communicate directly with every other node on the network.

peer-to-peer (P2P) sharing The process of users transferring files between computers.

peripheral device A device such as a monitor, printer, or keyboard that connects to the system unit through a data port.

personal area network (PAN) A network used to connect wireless devices (such as Bluetooth-enabled devices) in close proximity to each other.

personal firewall A firewall specifically designed for home networks.

personal information manager (PIM) software Programs such as Microsoft Outlook or Lotus Organizer that strive to replace the various management tools found on a traditional desk such as a calendar, address book, notepad, and to-do lists.

pharming Planting malicious code on a computer that alters the browser's ability to find Web addresses and directs users to bogus Web sites.

phishing The process of sending e-mail messages to lure Internet users into

revealing personal information such as credit card or Social Security numbers or other sensitive information that could lead to identity theft.

PHP (Hypertext Preprocessor) A scripting language used to produce dynamic Web pages.

physical memory The amount of random access memory (RAM) that is installed in a computer.

piggybacking The process of connecting to a wireless network without the permission of the owner of the network.

pixel A single point that creates the images on a computer monitor. Pixels are illuminated by an electron beam that passes rapidly back and forth across the back of the screen so that the pixels appear to glow continuously.

platform The combination of a computer's operating system and processor. The two most common platform types are the PC and the Apple Macintosh.

platter A thin, round, metallic storage plate stacked onto the hard drive spindle.

plotter A large printer that uses a computer-controlled pen to produce oversize pictures that require precise continuous lines to be drawn, such as maps and architectural plans.

Plug and Play (PnP) The technology that enables the operating system, once it is booted up, to recognize automatically any new peripherals and configure them to work with the system.

plug-in (player) A small software program that "plugs in" to a Web browser to enable a specific function—for example, to view and hear certain multimedia files on the Web.

podcast A clip of audio or video content that is broadcast over the Internet using compressed audio or video files in formats such as MP3.

point of presence (POP) A bank of modems through which many users can connect to an Internet service provider (ISP) simultaneously.

polymorphic virus A virus that changes its virus signature (the binary pattern that makes the virus identifiable) every time it infects a new file. This makes it more difficult for antivirus programs to detect the virus.

port An interface through which external devices are connected to the computer.

portability The capability to move a completed solution easily from one type of computer to another.

portable media player (PMP) A small portable device (such as an iPod) that enables you to carry your MP3s or other media files around with you.

positive acknowledgment (ACK) What computer Y sends when it receives a data packet that it can read from computer X.

possessed object Any object that a user carries to identify him- or herself and that grants the user access to a computer system or computer facility.

power supply A power supply regulates the wall voltage to the voltages required by computer chips; it is housed inside the system unit.

power-on self-test (POST) The first job the basic input/output system (BIOS) performs, ensuring that essential peripheral devices are attached and operational. This process consists of a test on the video card and video memory, a BIOS identification process (during which the BIOS version, manufacturer, and data are displayed on the monitor), and a memory test to ensure memory chips are working properly.

preemptive multitasking When the operating system processes the task assigned a higher priority before processing a task that has been assigned a lower priority.

presentation software An application program for creating dynamic slide shows such as Microsoft PowerPoint or Apple Keynote.

pretexting The act of creating an invented scenario (the pretext) to convince someone to divulge information.

Pretty Good Privacy (PGP) A popular public-key encryption package.

primary key (key field) The unique field that each database record in a table must have.

print queue A software holding area for printing jobs.

print server A server that manages all client-requested printing jobs for all printers on the network.

printer A common output device that creates tangible or hard copies of text and graphics.

private key One-half of a pair of binary files that is needed to decrypt an encrypted message. The private key is kept only by the individual who created the key pair and is never distributed to anyone else. The private key is used to decrypt messages created with the corresponding public key.

private-key encryption A procedure in which only the two parties involved in sending a message have the code. This could be a simple shift code where letters of the alphabet are shifted to a new position.

problem statement A clear description of which tasks the computer program must accomplish and how the program will execute these tasks and respond to unusual situations. It is the starting point of programming work.

processing Manipulating or organizing data into information.

productivity software Programs that enable a user to perform various tasks generally required in home, school, and business. Examples include word processing, spreadsheet, presentation, personal information management (PIM), and database programs.

program A series of instructions to be followed by a computer to accomplish a task.

program development life cycle (PDLC) A number of stages, from conception to final deployment, which a programming project follows.

program file A file that is used in the running of software programs and does not store data.

program specification A clear statement of the goals and objectives of the project.

programming The process of translating a task into a series of commands a computer will use to perform that task.

programming language A kind of "code" for the set of instructions the central processing unit (CPU) knows how to perform.

project management software An application program, such as Microsoft Project, that helps project managers generate charts and tables used to manage aspects of a project.

projector A device that can project images from your computer onto a wall or viewing screen.

proprietary software Custom software application that is owned and controlled by the company that created it.

proprietary system A software product whose code is not generally available (is kept private) and that is generally developed and marketed by a single company.

protocol (1) A set of rules for exchanging data and communication. (2) The first part of the Uniform Resource Locator (URL) indicating the set of rules used to retrieve the specified document.

prototype A small model of a computer program, often built at the beginning of a large project.

proxy server Acts as a go-between for computers on the internal network and the external network (often the Internet).

pseudocode A text-based approach to documenting an algorithm.

public key One-half of a pair of binary files that is needed to decrypt an encrypted message. After creating the keys, the user distributes the public key to anyone he wishes to send him encrypted messages. A message encrypted with a public key can be unencrypted only using the corresponding private key.

public-key encryption A procedure in which the key for coding is generally distributed as a public key that may be placed on a Web site. Anyone wishing to send a message codes it using the public key. The recipient decodes the message with a private key.

purpose The understanding that you are working for something larger than yourself.

Q

QR (quick response) code A technology that lets any piece of print in the real world host a live link to online information and video content.

quarantining The placement (by antivirus software) of a computer virus in a secure area on the hard drive so that it won't spread infection to other files.

query The process of requesting information from a database.

query language A language used to retrieve and display records from a database. A query language consists of its own vocabulary and sentence structure, used to frame the requests.

QWERTY keyboard A keyboard that gets its name from the first six letters on the top-left row of alphabetic keys on the keyboard.

R

random access memory (RAM) The computer's temporary storage space or short-term memory. It is located in a set of chips on the system unit's motherboard, and its capacity is measured in megabytes or gigabytes.

range check A type of data validation used in databases to ensure that a value entered falls within a specified range (such as requiring a person's age to fall in a range of between 1 and 120).

rapid application development (RAD) A method of system development in which developers create a prototype first, generating system documents as they use and remodel the product.

read/write head The mechanism that retrieves (reads) and records (writes) the magnetic data to and from a data disk.

read-only memory (ROM) A set of memory chips, located on the motherboard, which stores data and instructions that cannot be changed or erased; it holds all the instructions the computer needs to start up.

real-time operating system (RTOS) A program with a specific purpose that must guarantee certain response times for particular computing tasks, or else the machine's application is useless. Real-time operating systems are found in many types of robotic equipment.

real-time processing The process of updating a database (or information system) immediately as changes are made.

Really Simple Syndication (RSS) technology An XML-based format that allows frequent updates of content on the World Wide Web.

record A collection of related fields in a database.

Recycle Bin A folder on a Windows desktop in which deleted files from the hard drive are held until permanently purged from the system.

redundant array of independent disks (RAID) A set of strategies for using more than one drive in a system.

referential integrity For each value in the foreign key of one table, there is a corresponding value in the primary key of the related table.

registry A portion of the hard drive containing all the different configurations (settings) used by the Windows operating system (OS) as well as by other applications.

relation A database table that contains related data.

relational algebra The use of English-like expressions that have variables and operations, much like algebraic equations.

relational database A database that logically groups similar data into relations (or tables).

relationship In relational databases, the link between tables that defines how the data are related.

release to manufacturers (RTM) The point in the software release cycle when changes are made after beta testing and the product re releases to other manufacturers.

resolution The clearness or sharpness of an image, which is controlled by the number of pixels displayed on the screen.

response time The measurement (in milliseconds) of the time it takes for a pixel to change color; the lower the response time, the smoother moving images will appear on the monitor.

reusability The ability to reuse existing classes of objects from other projects, enabling programmers to produce new code quickly.

ribbon An interface in the Microsoft Office suite that groups related commands into tabs for easy access.

ring (loop) topology A network configuration in which the computers and peripherals are laid out in a configuration resembling a circle. Data flows around the circle from device to device in one direction only.

root directory The top level of the filing structure in a computer system. In Windows computers, the root directory of the hard drive is represented as C:\.

root DNS server A group of servers maintained throughout the Internet to which ISP Web servers connect to locate the master listings for an entire top-level domain.

rootkit Programs that allow hackers to gain access to your computer and take almost complete control of it without your knowledge. These programs are designed to subvert normal logon procedures to a computer and to hide their operations from normal detection methods.

router A device that routes packets of data between two or more networks.

runtime error An error in the problem logic that is only caught when the program executes.

S

Safe mode A special diagnostic mode designed for troubleshooting errors that occur during the boot process.

sampling rate The number of times per second a signal is measured and converted to a digital value. Sampling rates are measured in kilobits per second.

satellite Internet A way to connect to the Internet using a small satellite dish, which is placed outside the home and is connected to a computer with coaxial cable. The satellite company then sends the data to a satellite orbiting the Earth. The satellite, in turn, sends the data back to the satellite dish and to the computer.

scalability The ability to easily add more users to a network without affecting the performance of the other network nodes (computers or peripherals).

scareware A type of malware that is downloaded onto your computer and tries to

convince you that your computer is infected with a virus or other type of malware.

scope creep In project management, an ever-changing set of requests from the clients for additional features as they wait longer and longer to see a working prototype.

script A list of commands (mini-programs or macros) that can be executed on a computer without user interaction.

scripting language A simple programming language that is limited to performing a specific set of specialized tasks.

scrollbar On the desktop, the bar that appears at the side or bottom of the window and controls which part of the information is displayed on the screen.

search engine A set of programs that searches the Web for specific words (or keywords) you wish to query (or look for) and then returns a list of the Web sites on which those keywords are found.

second-generation language (2GL) Also known as an assembly language. Second-generation languages deal directly with system hardware but provide acronyms that are easier for human programmers to work with.

second-level domain A domain that falls within top-level domains of the Internet. Each second-level domain needs to be unique within that particular domain but not necessarily unique to all top-level domains.

sector A section of a hard drive platter, wedge-shaped from the center of the platter to the edge.

Secure Sockets Layer (SSL) A protocol that provides for the encryption of data transmitted using the Internet. The current versions of all major Web browsers support SSL.

seek time The time it takes for the hard drive's read/write heads to move over the surface of the disk to the correct track.

select query A query that displays a subset of data from a table based on the criteria the user specifies.

Semantic Web (Web 3.0) An evolving extension of the World Wide Web in which information is defined in such a way to make it more easily readable by computers.

Serial Advanced Technology Attachment (Serial ATA) A type of hard drive that uses much thinner cables, and can transfer data more quickly than IDE drives.

server A computer that provides resources to other computers on a network.

server-side program A program that is run on a Web server as opposed to inside a Web browser.

service pack Software updates to problems in a program after its commercial release to the public. Users can download these software modules to repair errors identified in the program code.

service set identifier (SSID) A network name that wireless routers use to identify themselves.

shareware Software that enables users to "test" the software by running it for a limited time free of charge.

shielded twisted pair (STP) cable Twisted pair cable that contains a layer of foil shielding to reduce interference.

short message service (SMS) Technology that enables short text messages (up to 160 characters) to be sent over mobile networks.

Simple Mail Transfer Protocol (SMTP) A protocol for sending e-mail along the Internet to its destination.

simulation program Software, often used for training purposes, which allows the user to experience or control an event as if it is reality.

sleep mode A low-power mode for electronic devices such as computers that saves electric power consumption and saves the last-used settings. When the device is "woken up," work is resumed more quickly than when cold booting the computer.

smartphone A device that combines the functionality of a cell phone, a PMP, and a PDA into one unit. Smartphones have sophisticated operating systems, Web browsers, and the capability to run software applications.

social bookmark (tag) A keyword or term that Internet users assign to a Web resource such as a Web page, digital image, or video.

social engineering Any technique that uses social skills to generate human interaction for the purpose of enticing individuals to reveal sensitive information.

social networking A means by which people use the Internet to communicate and share information among their immediate friends, and meet and connect with others through common interests, experiences, and friends.

software The set of computer programs or instructions that tells the computer what to do and enables it to perform different tasks.

Software as a Service (SaaS) Software that is delivered on demand over the Internet.

software license An agreement between the user and the software developer that must be accepted before installing the software on a computer.

software piracy Violating a software license agreement by copying an application onto more computers than the license agreement permits.

software suite A collection of software programs that have been bundled together as a package.

solid state drive (SSD) A storage device that uses the same kind of memory that flash drives use, but can reach data in only a tenth of the time a flash drive requires.

sort (index) The process of organizing data in a database into a particular order.

sound card An expansion card that attaches to the motherboard inside the system unit and that enables the computer to produce sounds by providing a connection for the speakers and microphone.

source code The instructions programmers write in a higher-level language.

spam Unwanted or junk e-mail.

spam filter An option you can select in your e-mail account that places known or suspected spam messages into a folder other than your inbox.

speaker An output device for sound.

spear phishing Spear phishing is a targeted phishing attack that sends e-mails to people known to be customers of a company. Such attacks have a much greater chance of successfully getting individuals to reveal sensitive data.

spider A program used by search engines that constantly collects information on the Web, following links in Web sites and reading Web pages. Spiders get their name because they crawl over the Web using multiple "legs" to visit many sites simultaneously.

spooler A program that helps coordinate all print jobs being sent to the printer at the same time.

spreadsheet software An application program such as Microsoft Excel or Lotus 1-2-3 that enables a user to do calculations and numerical analyses easily.

spyware An unwanted piggyback program that downloads with the software you want to install from the Internet and then runs in the background of your system.

star topology An active topology (meaning that data is retransmitted) in which the nodes connect to a central communications device called a *switch*. The switch receives a signal from the sending node and retransmits it to the node that should receive it.

statement A sentence in programming code.

static addressing A means of assigning an Internet Protocol (IP) address that never changes and is most likely assigned manually by a network administrator.

stealth virus A virus that temporarily erases its code from the files where it resides and hides in the active memory of the computer.

streaming audio Technology that enables audio files to be fed to a browser continuously. This lets users avoid having to download an entire file before listening.

streaming video Technology that enables video files to be fed to a browser continuously. This lets users avoid having to download the entire file before viewing.

structured (analytical) data Data that can be identified and classified as discrete bits of information (such as a name or phone number). Unstructured data includes nontraditional data such as audio clips (including MP3 files), video clips, and pictures that must be viewed in their entirety rather than in discrete segments.

Structured Query Language (SQL) The most popular database query language today.

stylus A pen-shaped device used to tap or write on touch-sensitive screens.

subject directory A structured outline of Web sites organized by topics and subtopics.

summary report A report that summarizes data in some fashion (such as a total of the day's concession sales at an amusement park). Also known as a *summary data report*.

supercomputer A specially designed computer that can perform complex calculations extremely rapidly; used in situations in which complex models requiring intensive mathematical calculations are needed (such as weather forecasting or atomic energy research).

SuperFetch A memory-management technique used by Windows 7. Monitors the applications you use the most and preloads them into your system memory so that they'll be ready to go.

surge protector A device that protects computers and other electronic devices from power surges.

surround sound A type of audio processing that makes the listener experience sound as if it were coming from all directions.

surround-sound speakers Speaker systems set up in such a way that they surround an entire area (and the people in it) with sound.

S-video (super video) A type of technology used to transmit video signals; used on newer LCD monitors, as well as other multimedia devices such as televisions, DVD players, and projectors.

swap file (page file) A temporary storage area on the hard drive where the operating system "swaps out" or moves the data or instructions from random access memory (RAM) that have not recently been used. This process takes place when more RAM space is needed.

switch A device for transmitting data on a network. A switch makes decisions, based on the media access control (MAC) address of the data, as to where the data is to be sent.

syncing (or synchronizing) The process of updating data on portable devices (such as a cell phone or iPod) and computer so that they contain the same data.

syntax An agreed-upon set of rules defining how a programming language must be structured.

syntax error An error that violates the strict, precise set of rules that defines a programming language.

system development life cycle (SDLC) An organized process (or set of steps) for developing an information processing system.

system evaluation The process of looking at a computer's subsystems, what they do, and how they perform to determine whether the computer system has the right hardware components to do what the user ultimately wants it to do.

system file Any of the main files of an operating system.

system requirements The set of minimum storage, memory capacity, and processing standards recommended by the software manufacturer to ensure proper operation of a software application.

System Restore A utility in Windows that restores system settings to a specific previous date when everything was working properly.

system restore point In Windows, a snapshot of your entire system's settings used for restoring your system to a prior point in time.

system software The set of programs that enables a computer's hardware devices and application software to work together; it includes the operating system and utility programs.

system unit The metal or plastic case that holds all the physical parts of the computer together, including the computer's processor (its brains), its memory, and the many circuit boards that help the computer function.

T

T line A high-speed fiber-optic communications line that is designed to provide much higher throughput than conventional voice (telephone) and data (DSL or cable) lines.

table In database terminology, a group of related records. Also called a *file*.

tablet computer A mobile computer, such as the Apple iPad or Motorola XOOM,

integrated into a flat multitouch-sensitive screen. It uses an onscreen virtual keyboard, but separate keyboards can be connected via Bluetooth or wires.

tablet PC A notebook computer designed specifically to work with handwriting recognition technology.

Task Manager A Windows utility that shows programs currently running and permits you to exit nonresponsive programs when you click End Task.

Task Scheduler A Windows utility that enables you to schedule tasks to run automatically at predetermined times with no interaction necessary on your part.

taskbar In later versions of Windows operating systems, a feature that displays open and favorite applications for easy access.

tax preparation software An application program, such as Intuit's TurboTax or H&R Block's TaxCut, for preparing state and federal taxes. Each program offers a complete set of tax forms and instructions as well as expert advice on how to complete each form.

TCP/IP The main suite of protocols used on the Internet.

telephony The use of equipment to provide voice communications over a distance.

template A form included in many productivity applications that provides the basic structure for a particular kind of document, spreadsheet, or presentation.

terabyte 1,099,511,627,776 bytes or 2^{40} bytes.

terminator A device that absorbs a signal so that it is not reflected back onto parts of the network that have already received it.

test condition A check in software programming to see whether a loop is completed.

testing plan In the problem statement, a plan that lists specific input numbers that a software program would typically expect the user to enter. It then lists the precise output values that a perfect program would return for those input values.

tethering Approach which makes sure that as long as you have a 3G signal, your computer can access the Internet even when it tells you there are no available wireless networks. Several smartphones offer this capability.

text field A database field that can hold any combination of alphanumeric data (letters or numbers) and is most often used to hold text.

thermal printer A printer that works either by melting wax-based ink onto ordinary paper (in a process called *thermal wax transfer printing*) or by burning dots onto specially coated paper (in a process called *direct thermal printing*).

third-generation language (3GL, or high-level language) A computer language that uses symbols and commands to help programmers tell the computer what to do.

thrashing A condition of excessive paging in which the operating system becomes sluggish.

three-way handshake A process used by the Transmission Control Protocol (TCP) to establish a connection.

throughput The actual speed of data transfer that is achieved. It is usually less than the data transfer rate and is measured in megabits per second (Mbps).

time bomb A virus that is triggered by the passage of time or on a certain date.

time-variant data Data that doesn't all pertain to one period in time—for example, data in a data warehouse.

token A special packet containing data.

token method The access method that ring networks use to avoid data collisions.

toolbar A group of icons collected for easy access.

top-down design A systematic approach in which a programming problem is broken down into a series of high-level tasks.

top-level domain (TLD) The suffix, often of three letters, in the domain name (such as .com or .edu) that indicates the kind of organization the host is.

touch pad (track pad) A small, touch-sensitive screen at the base of a notebook keyboard that is used to direct the cursor.

touch screen A type of monitor (or display in a notebook or PDA) that accepts input from a user touching the screen.

track A concentric circle that serves as a storage area on a hard drive platter.

trackpoint device A small, joystick-like nub that enables you to move the cursor with the tip of your finger.

transaction processing system (TPS) A system used to keep track of everyday business activities (such as sales of products).

transceiver In a wireless network, a device that translates the electronic data that needs to be sent along the network into radio waves and then broadcasts these radio waves to other network nodes.

Transmission Control Protocol (TCP) A protocol that prepares data for transmission and provides for error checking and resending lost data.

transmission media The radio waves or cable that transport data on a network.

Transport Layer Security (TLS) A protocol that provides data integrity and security for transmissions over the Internet.

Trojan horse A computer program that appears to be something useful or desirable (such as a game or a screen saver), but at the same time does something malicious in the background without the user's knowledge.

tunneling The main technology for achieving a VPN (virtual private network). In tunneling, data packets are placed inside other data packets. The format of these external data packets is encrypted and is understood only by the sending and receiving hardware, which is known as a *tunnel interface*. The hardware is optimized to seek efficient routes of transmission through the Internet, making information much more difficult to intercept and decrypt.

twisted pair cable Cables made of copper wires that are twisted around each other and are surrounded by a plastic jacket (such as traditional home phone wire).

U

Uniform Resource Locator (URL) A Web site's unique address; an example is microsoft.com.

uninterruptible power supply (UPS) A device designed to power a computer from large batteries for a brief period during a loss of electrical power.

universal serial bus (USB) port A port that can connect a wide variety of peripheral devices to the computer, including keyboards, printers, mice, smartphones, PDAs, flash drives, and digital cameras.

UNIX An operating system originally conceived in 1969 by Ken Thompson and Dennis Ritchie of AT&T's Bell Labs. In 1974, the UNIX code was rewritten in the standard programming language C. Today there are various commercial versions of UNIX.

unshielded twisted pair (UTP) cable The most popular transmission media option for Ethernet networks. UTP cable is composed of four pairs of wires that are twisted around each other to reduce electrical interference.

unstructured data Nontraditional database data such as audio clips (including MP3 files), video clips, pictures, and extremely large documents. Data of this type is known as a *binary large object* (BLOB) because it is actually encoded in binary form.

urban legend A hoax that becomes so well known that it is accepted by society as true even though it is false. Also known as an *urban myth*.

User Datagram Protocol (UDP) A protocol that prepares data for transmission but that has no resending capabilities.

user interface Part of the operating system that enables individuals to interact with the computer.

utility program A small program that performs many of the general housekeeping tasks for the computer, such as system maintenance and file compression.

V

validation The process of ensuring that data entered into a database is correct (or at least reasonable) and complete.

validation rule A rule that is set up in a database to alert the user to possible wrong entries.

variable A name or symbol that stands for a value.

variable declaration A line of programming code that alerts the operating system that the program needs to allocate storage space in random access memory (RAM) for the variable.

VBScript A subset of Visual Basic; also used to introduce interactivity to Web pages.

vertical market software Software that is developed for and customized to a specific industry's needs (such as a wood inventory system for a sawmill) as opposed to software that is useful across a range of industries (such as word processing software).

video card (video adapter) An expansion card that is installed inside a system unit to translate binary data (the 1s and 0s the computer uses) into the images viewed on the monitor.

video graphics array (VGA) port A port to which a CRT monitor connects.

video log (vlog or video blog) A personal online journal that uses video as the primary content in addition to text, images, and audio.

video memory RAM that is included as part of a video card.

viewing angle Measured in degrees, this is the maximum angle at which a monitor can be viewed before the image quality degrades to unacceptable levels.

virtual memory The space on the hard drive where the operating system stores data if there isn't enough random access memory (RAM) to hold all of the programs you're currently trying to run.

virtual private network (VPN) A network that uses public communication pathways (usually the Internet) to provide branch offices or employees who are not at the office with secure access to the company network. VPNs maintain privacy by using secure data communication protocols.

virtualization Involves using specialized software to make individual physical servers behave as though they are more than one physical device. Each virtual server can operate as its own separate device and can even run its own operating system.

virus A computer program that attaches itself to another computer program (known as the host program) and attempts to spread itself to other computers when files are exchanged.

virus signature A portion of the virus code that is unique to a particular computer virus and makes it identifiable by antivirus software.

Visual Basic (VB) A programming language used to build a wide range of Windows applications quickly.

visual programming A technique for automatically writing code when the programmer says the layout is complete. It helps programmers produce a final application much more quickly.

VoIP (Voice over Internet Protocol) A technology that facilitates making telephone calls across the Internet instead of using conventional telephone lines.

volatile storage Temporary storage, such as in random access memory (RAM). When the power is off, the data in volatile storage is cleared out.

W

warm boot The process of restarting the system while it's powered on.

Web 2.0 Tools and Web-based services that emphasize online collaboration and sharing among users.

Web browser (browser) Software installed on a computer system that allows individuals to locate, view, and navigate the Web.

Web page authoring software Programs you can use to design interactive Web pages without knowing any HyperText Markup Language (HTML) code.

Web server A computer running a specialized operating system that enables it to host Web pages (and other information) and provide requested Web pages to clients.

Web service A program used by a Web site to make information available to other Web sites.

Web site A location on the Web.

Web-based application A program that is hosted on a Web site and does not require installation on the computer.

webcam A small camera that sits on top of a computer monitor (connected to the computer by a cable) or is built into a

notebook computer and is usually used to transfer live video.

webcast The broadcast of audio or video content over the Internet. Unlike a podcast, a webcast is not updated automatically.

white-hat hacker A hacker who breaks into systems just for the challenge of it (and who doesn't wish to steal or wreak havoc on the systems). Such hackers tout themselves as experts who are performing a needed service for society by helping companies realize the vulnerabilities that exist in their systems.

whole-house surge protector A surge protector that is installed on (or near) the breaker panel of a home and protects all electronic devices in the home from power surges.

wide area network (WAN) A network made up of local area networks (LANs) connected over long distances.

widget A mini-application developed for the Macintosh platform.

wiki A type of Web site that allows anyone visiting the site to change its content by adding, removing, or editing the content.

window In a graphical user interface, a rectangular box that contains programs displayed on the screen.

Windows An operating system by Microsoft that incorporates a user-friendly, graphical interface.

Windows 7 Microsoft operating system that builds upon the security and user interface upgrades that the Windows Vista release provided, and gives users with touch-screen monitors the ability to use touch commands to scroll, resize windows, pan, and zoom.

Windows Explorer The main tool for finding, viewing, and managing the contents of your computer by showing the location and contents of every drive, folder, and file.

wireless access point (WAP) A device similar to a switch in an Ethernet network. It takes the place of a wireless network adapter and helps relay data between network nodes.

Wireless Application Protocol (WAP) The standard that dictates how handheld devices will access information on the Internet.

wireless fidelity (WiFi) The 802.11 standard for wireless data transmissions established by the Institute of Electrical and Electronics Engineers (IEEE).

wireless Internet service provider (wireless ISP) An ISP that provides service to wireless devices such as PDA/smartphones.

Wireless Markup Language (WML) A format for writing content viewed on a cellular phone or personal digital assistant (PDA) that is text-based and contains no graphics.

wireless media Communications media that do not use cables but instead rely on radio waves to communicate.

wireless network interface card (wireless NIC) A card installed in a system that connects with wireless access points on the network.

wireless range extender A device that amplifies your wireless signal to get it out to parts of your home that are experiencing poor connectivity.

wizard A step-by-step guide that walks a user through the necessary steps to complete a complicated task.

word processing software Programs used to create and edit written documents such as papers, letters, and résumés.

World Wide Web (WWW or Web) The part of the Internet used the most. What distinguishes the Web from the rest of the Internet are (1) its use of common communication protocols (such as Transmission Control Protocol/ Internet Protocol, or TCP/IP) and special languages (such as the HyperText Markup Language, or HTML) that enable different computers to talk to each other and display information in compatible formats; and (2) its use of special links (called hyperlinks) that enable users to jump from one place to another in the Web.

worm A program that attempts to travel between systems through network connections to spread infections. Worms can run independently of host file execution and are active in spreading themselves.

z

zombie A computer that is controlled by a hacker who uses it to launch attacks on other computer systems.

Index